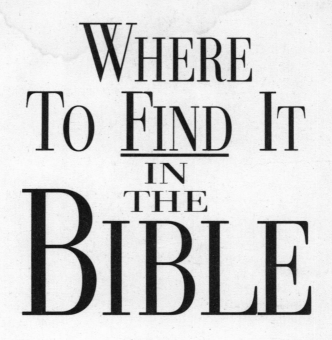

WHERE TO FIND IT IN THE BIBLE

WHERE TO FIND IT IN THE BIBLE

Ken Anderson

Illustrated by John Hayes

THOMAS NELSON
Since 1798

NASHVILLE   DALLAS   MEXICO CITY   RIO DE JANEIRO   BEIJING

Published in Nashville, TN, by Thomas Nelson. Thomas Nelson is a trademark of Thomas Nelson, Inc.

Thomas Nelson, Inc. titles may be purchased in bulk for educational, business, fund-raising, or sales promotional use. For information, please email SpecialMarkets@ThomasNelson.com.

Library of Congress Cataloging-in-Publication Data

Anderson, Ken, 1917–2006.
    Where to find it in the Bible / Ken Anderson.
        p.   cm.

    ISBN 13: 978-1-4185-0747-3
    1. Bible—Indexes.   I. Title.
BS432.A533   1996
220.3—dc20

95–59065
CIP

Printed in the United States of America
09 10 11 BPI   6 5

*Dedicated to
staff, associates and friends
in the ministry of InterComm.*

PREFACE

My lengthening ministry as a Christian writer and audiovisual producer has long involved constant dependence upon the Bible as a content resource. Concordances helped me locate specific words, verses, and passages.

But where do you look for Bible verses dealing with today's contemporary topics? How do you locate Scripture on topics such as credit cards, diet, race, networking, computers, women's rights, and politics?

I saw the need for a topical resource where, unlike a traditional concordance, the descriptive references used everyday speech rather than verbatim Scripture or fancy theological language. I developed a card file, elementary at first, then expanded.

"This should be in a book," a friend said one day. The end result is this combination of traditional and contemporary words, topics, and phrases with relevant Scripture references. You will find it equally useful for personal study of the Scriptures as well as for teaching and sermon preparation.

My wife and family teamed with me in the development of the final manuscript, making our "camaraderie" entry even more apt. The crew included two preteen grandsons who also diligently looked up verses to ensure the references are correct.

My God bless you as you use *Where to Find It in the Bible* to enrich your life and service.

Ken Anderson
Spring, 1996

Note: Unless otherwise specified, topics refer to content of all Bible versions. Specific references are designated as follows:

AB	Amplified Bible
Berk.	Berkeley Version
CEV	Contemporary English Version
GNB	Good News Bible
KJV	King James Version
LB	Living Bible
NASB	New American Standard Bible
NIV	New International Version
NKJV	New King James Version
NRSV	New Revised Standard Version
RSV	Revised Standard Version

ABANDONED

Mankind abandoned, Genesis 6:11–13.

Temporarily abandoned, Genesis 37:23–28.

The Lord promises not to abandon, Joshua 1:5 (LB).

Abandoned city, 1 Samuel 30:1–6; Lamentations 1:1.

Shunned by friends, Psalm 38:11.

Empty towns, Jeremiah 4:29 (CEV).

Abandoned Son of God, Matthew 27:46; John 16:32; Psalm 22:1.

Jews abandoned for Gentiles, Acts 18:6.

Abandoning ship, Acts 27:41–44.

Deserted apostle, 2 Timothy 4:16–17.

See Desolate, Forsaken, Loneliness.

ABASE

Egyptian abasement, Exodus 15:4.

Abased by angels, 2 Chronicles 32:21.

Self-inflicted abasement, Esther 7:1–10.

Pride abased, Psalm 101:5; Proverbs 15:25; 29:23; Isaiah 2:12.

Demeaned arrogance, Jeremiah 50:32; Malachi 4:1.

Royal abasement, Daniel 4:33.

Kings abased, Luke 1:52.

See Demean, Humility, Pride.

ABHOR

Abhorring laws, Leviticus 26:15 (NIV).

Idols rejected, Deuteronomy 7:25–26.

Attitude toward aliens, Deuteronomy 23:7.

Hatred of self, Job 42:6.

Evil despised, Romans 12:9.

See Hatred.

ABILITY

Lost skill, Genesis 4:9–12.

Building Tower of Babel, Genesis 11:1–6.

"Special ability," Genesis 47:6.

Talent, ability from God, Exodus 4:10–12; 6:30.

Not by strength alone, 1 Samuel 2:9.

Ability gives confidence, 1 Samuel 17:32–37.

Great ability, 1 Chronicles 26:6 (NKJV).

Jewish ability ridiculed, Nehemiah 4:1–10.

Skillful writer, Psalm 45:1.

Race not to swift, strong, Ecclesiastes 9:11.

Large, small shields, Jeremiah 46:3.

Strength, ability fail, Amos 2:14–16.

Ability of Jesus, Mark 6:2–6.

Discredited ability, John 5:31–38.

God given ability, Acts 6:8.

Confident of ability, 2 Corinthians 11:5–6.

See Skill, Talent.

ABNORMAL

Multiple fingers, toes, 2 Samuel 21:20.

Illicit relationship of sisters, Ezekiel 23:1–49.

See Disfigure, Handicap.

ABOLISH

Abolish idolatry, Isaiah 2:18.

Government politics concluded, 1 Corinthians 15:24.

Death destroyed, 1 Corinthians 15:26.

Old covenant, 2 Corinthians 3:13–15.

See Destruction.

ABOMINATION

Pagan sacrifices, Exodus 8:26.

Heathen lifestyle, Deuteronomy 18:9–12.

Abominable objects, practices, Deuteronomy 7:25; 18:12; 25:16; Proverbs 6:16–19; 12:22; 21:27; Luke 16:15.

Detested prayer, Proverbs 28:9.

People defiled, Jeremiah 3:1–3.

Beauty made abominable, Ezekiel 16:25 (NASB).

Certain judgment, Amos 1:3, 6, 9, 11, 13; 2:1, 4, 6.

Abomination of desolation, Daniel 9:27; 12:11; Matthew 24:15; Mark 13:14.

See Degradation, Depravity, Dissipation, Sacrilege.

ABORTION

Accidental abortion, Exodus 21:22–25.

Abortion desired, Job 3:11–16 (Berk., AB).

"Womb to tomb," Job 10:19 (CEV).

Fetus in God's care, Isaiah 44:2 (CEV).

Desiring abortion, Jeremiah 20:17 (CEV).

Fearfully, wonderfully made, Psalm 139:13–14 (Berk.).

Fetus development, Ecclesiastes 11:5 (NKJV, AB).

Abortive spiritual birth, 1 Corinthians 15:7 (Berk.).
See Infanticide, Pregnancy.

ABRASION

Civic disharmony, Exodus 5:15–21.
Avoiding difficulty, 1 Corinthians 10:32 (GNB).
Abrasive truth, Galatians 4:16.
Coping with divisive person, Titus 3:10.
Disruptive church methods, 3 John 9–10.
See Discontent, Friction, Hurt, Irritant, Malcontent.

ABSENCE

Missing, uncounted, Ecclesiastes 1:15.
Purposeful separation, John 14:28.
Feared reunion, 2 Corinthians 12:20–21.
Believers reunited, Philippians 1:25–26.
Remembering those absent, 1 Thessalonians 2:17.
See Lost.

ABSOLUTE

The Lord reigns forever, Psalm 9:7–8.
Changeless, ever-changing, Ecclesiastes 1:2–5.
Temporal transitions, eternal absolutes, Isaiah 40:7–8.
Sure deliverance, Daniel 3:16–18.
Changeless God, Malachi 3:6; Romans 11:29.
Believe the Gospel, Mark 1:14–15.
One gate to sheep pen, John 10:1–21.
No alternate way, John 14:6.
Divine decisions irrevocable, Romans 11:29.
Undying love, Ephesians 6:24.
Irrefutable truth, 1 Timothy 3:1 (AB).
Two things unchangeable, Hebrews 6:18.
Unshakable kingdom, Hebrews 12:28–29.
Changeless Christ, Hebrews 13:8.
Message unchanged, 1 John 2:24–25.
Past, present, future of Christ, Revelation 1:4.
See Certainty, Truth.

ABSOLUTION *See Forgiveness.*

ABSTINENCE

Abstinence prior to worship, Exodus 19:14–15; Leviticus 10:8.
Sexual abstinence, Numbers 30:3–12 (Berk.); 1 Thessalonians 4:3–4.
Marital continence, Exodus 19:15; 1 Corinthians 7:1–5.
Requirement for priests, Leviticus 10:9.
Clean, unclean animals for food, Leviticus 11:1–47.
Abstaining from fruit of grapes, Numbers 6:2–4.
Military sexual abstinence, 1 Samuel 21:1–5.
Covenant to avoid lust, Job 31:1.
Avoid temptation for wine, Proverbs 23:31.
Political leaders to abstain, Proverbs 31:4.
Abstaining from affection, Ecclesiastes 3:5.
Total abstinence, Jeremiah 35:5–8.
Daniel, the king's wine, Daniel 1:5, 8 (LB).
Nazarites forced to imbibe, Amos 2:12.
Example of John the Baptist, Luke 1:15.
Lifelong abstinence, Luke 7:33 (LB).
Abstain from idolatrous food, Acts 15:20.
Abstaining from meat, Romans 14:23; 1 Corinthians 8:1–13; 1 Timothy 4:3.
Abstinence from evil, 1 Thessalonians 5:22; 1 Peter 2:11.
Drinking wine, 1 Timothy 5:23.
See Alcohol, Beer, Drunkenness, Intemperance, Separation, Wine.

ABSURD

Sheer absurdity, 1 Corinthians 1:18 (AB).

ABUNDANCE

River with four sources, Genesis 2:10–14.
Egypt's grain abundance, Genesis 41:49.
Giving over abundance to the Lord, Exodus 36:2–7.
Ample harvest yearly, Leviticus 26:10; Amos 9:13; Revelation 22:2.
Responsibility in good times, Deuteronomy 28:47–48.
God-given prosperity, Deuteronomy 30:9; Isaiah 30:23.
Abundant blessing of nature, Deuteronomy 33:13–16.
Solomon's abundance, 1 Kings 10:14–29.
Making much of little, 2 Kings 4:1–7.

"Wonders without number," Job 5:9 (CEV).

Glory, majesty, Psalm 8:1.

God's abundant goodness, Psalm 31:19 (NRSV).

Abundant riches, Psalm 52:7.

Daily benefits, Psalm 68:19 (KJV).

Abundant rain, no crop, Proverbs 28:3.

More than needed, Ecclesiastes 5:11.

Abundant silver, chariots, Isaiah 2:7.

God's righteousness endures forever, Isaiah 51:8.

Expecting abundance from God, Hosea 12:6.

Plenty to eat, Joel 2:26.

Here today, gone tomorrow, Luke 12:13–21.

Multiple blessings, John 1:16.

Internal living water, John 7:38–39.

Full life Christ gives, John 10:10.

Blessing poured out, Romans 5:5; 2 Corinthians 1:5.

Abundant grace, Romans 5:17 (NASB, NRSV).

Overflowing with hope, Romans 15:13.

Assured wealth, 2 Corinthians 9:11.

Lavished wisdom, insight, Ephesians 1:7–8 (NASB).

Mercy, love, Ephesians 2:4–5 (GNB).

Abundant power, Ephesians 3:20.

Good, unproductive land, Hebrews 6:7–8.

All needed to live godly life, 2 Peter 1:3.

See Affluence, Contentment, Greed, Harvest, Plenty, Wealth.

ABUSE

Moral perversion, Genesis 19:5–9, 31–38.

Authority abused, Numbers 20:10–13.

Corrupted ordinances, 1 Samuel 2:12–17; 1 Corinthians 11:17–22.

Perverting truth, 2 Peter 2:10–22.

See Mistreatment, Torture.

ACADEMIC

Poor student's regret, Proverbs 5:12–13.

Seeing, hearing, not understanding, Mark 4:11–12.

Non-academic background, John 7:14–16.

Folly of intellectual pride, 1 Corinthians 3:18–20; 8:1–3.

Passing exam, 2 Corinthians 13:5–6.

See College, Education, Student, Teacher, Teaching.

ACCEPTANCE

Accepting circumstances, Genesis 43:14.

Symbol of acceptance, Exodus 28:38.

Acceptance of necessity, 1 Samuel 18:5.

Wishing for acceptance, 2 Samuel 24:23.

Prayer accepted by the Lord, Job 42:9.

Don't argue with creator, Isaiah 45:9 (CEV).

Israel accepted, Ezekiel 20:40.

Acceptable sacrifice, Ezekiel 43:27.

Sowing seeds various soils, Mark 4:3–20.

Doubt, then belief, Luke 1:28–38.

Accepting, rejecting, John 7:25–31.

Disciples acceptance of Saul, Acts 9:26.

Nations acceptable to God, Acts 10:34–35.

Few converts at Athens, Acts 17:34.

God's acceptance of those alien to Him, Romans 9:25.

Accepting one another, Romans 15:7.

Married, unmarried, 1 Corinthians 7:32–35.

Both fragrance, odor, 2 Corinthians 2:15–16.

Desiring acceptance, 2 Corinthians 5:9.

Making room in heart, 2 Corinthians 7:2 (CEV, GNB).

Right hand of fellowship, Galatians 2:9–10.

Good to be wanted, Galatians 4:18 (NASB).

Predestined acceptance, Ephesians 1:4–6.

Some accept, others reject, 1 Thessalonians 2:1–2.

Accepting oppressors, 1 Timothy 6:1.

See Camaraderie, Rapport, Receptive, Self-acceptance.

ACCESS

God's nearness in prayer, Deuteronomy 4:7.

Temple access closed, 2 Kings 16:18.

Importance of gates, Nehemiah 3:1–32.

Those who may ascend, Psalm 24:3–4.

Divinely opened gates, Isaiah 26:2.

Jesus as gate, John 10:9.

Access to God, Romans 5:2; Ephesians 2:18; 3:12.

Mediator between God and men, 1 Timothy 2:5.

Fearless, confident, bold, Hebrews 4:16 (AB).
See Authorization.

ACCIDENT

Accidental death, Numbers 35:22–25; Deuteronomy 19:4–7.
Infant crippled by nurse's error, 2 Samuel 4:4.
Irreverent accident, 2 Samuel 6:6–7.
Freak accident, 2 Kings 1:2–4.
Perilous activities, Ecclesiastes 10:9.
Divine punishment, Amos 2:13.
Fallen tower, Luke 13:4.
See Fortuity, Injury, Misfortune.

ACCLAIM

No prophet like Moses, Deuteronomy 34:10–12.
God's commendation, Job 1:8.
Glory to God alone, Psalms 115:1; 118:23.
Strong people's honor, Isaiah 25:3.
Divine request for glory, John 17:1–5.
Overt acclaim, Acts 10:25–26.
See Accolade, Applause, Citation, Honor, Praise.

ACCLAMATION

Jesus or Barabbas, Matthew 27:15–26.
See Plebiscite, Unanimity, Vote.

ACCOLADE

Honor unfitting fool, Proverbs 26:1.
Success, glory to God alone, 1 Corinthians 3:7.
Boasting about others, 2 Thessalonians 1:4.
See Acclaim.

ACCOMMODATIONS

Prophet's chamber, 2 Kings 4:8–10.
Small beds for tall people, Isaiah 28:20.
Accommodations for priests, Ezekiel 41:9–10.
See Guests, Hospitality, House.

ACCOMPANIMENT

Prophecy to sound of music, 2 Kings 3:15.
Offertory music, 2 Chronicles 29:28.
Reciting proverbs to musical accompaniment, Psalm 49:4.
See Music, Singing, Solo.

ACCOMPLICE

Accused of being accomplice, Acts 17:5–9.

ACCOMPLISHMENT

Creator's accomplishment, Genesis 1:10, 12, 18, 21, 25, 31.
Wonders performed by God's power, Exodus 34:10.
Wanting to share honors, Judges 12:1–3.
Work rewarded, Psalm 62:12.
Giving God glory, Psalm 118:23.
Delight in one's work, Ecclesiastes 2:10.
End better than beginning, Ecclesiastes 7:8.
God sees all, rewards good, Jeremiah 32:19.
Beyond belief, Habakkuk 1:5.
Vine, fruit, John 15:1–8.
Giving glory to the Lord, Romans 15:18–19.
Success belongs to God, 1 Corinthians 3:7.
Runner, prize, 1 Corinthians 9:24–27.
No one has what it takes, 2 Corinthians 2:16.
Let the Lord commend, 2 Corinthians 10:17–18.
Pride in good work, Galatians 6:4 (CEV, LB).
See Achievement, Performance, Success.

ACCORD *See Rapport, Unity.*

ACCOUNTABILITY

Family accountability, Joshua 7:1–26.
Age of accountability, 1 Samuel 3:7.
Personally accountable, 2 Samuel 12:1–15.
Able to understand, Nehemiah 8:2–3.
"Eternity in the heart," Ecclesiastes 3:11 (NIV).
Accountable at judgment, Ezekiel 18:20.
"Know right from wrong," Micah 3:1 (CEV).
Conversational accountability, Matthew 12:36.
Much received, greater accountability, Luke 12:48.
Financial accountability, Luke 19:15.
All accountable to God, Romans 14:12.
Responsibility for evil, James 1:13–15.
Time of judgment, 1 Peter 4:4–5.
Taking scriptures to heart, Revelation 1:3.
See Obligation, Responsibility.

ACCOUNTANT

Temple accounts, 2 Chronicles 34:14 (LB).

ACCREDITATION

Wisdom of Solomon, 1 Kings 4:29–34.

Provision for safe conduct, Nehemiah 2:7.

Prophet's certainty of divine voice, Jeremiah 32:1–12.

Status of John the Baptist and Christ, Luke 3:15–17.

Unaccepted in home community, Luke 4:23–24.

Jesus had no need for human credentials, John 5:31–40.

Genuineness of faith made known, 1 Thessalonians 1:1–10.

Approved by God rather than men, 1 Thessalonians 2:4–6.

New identity for slave, Philemon 17.

See Academic, Approval.

ACCUMULATE

Time to discard, Ecclesiastes 3:6.

See Affluence, Possessions.

ACCURACY

Splitting hair, Judges 20:16.

One lethal blow, 1 Samuel 26:7–8.

Lightning strikes mark, Job 36:32 (Berk.).

Weights, measures, Proverbs 20:10.

Flawless Word of God, Proverbs 30:5.

Plumb line measurement of righteousness, Isaiah 28:17.

Faulty bow, Hosea 7:16 (CEV).

Loss of right eye, Zechariah 11:17.

Accurate representation, Hebrews 1:3 (CEV).

See Inaccuracy.

ACCUSATION

Penalty for false accusation, Deuteronomy 19:16–19.

False accusation, 1 Samuel 13:14; Nehemiah 6:7; Job 2:5; 22:6; Jeremiah 37:13; Matthew 5:11; 27:12; Luke 6:7; 1 Peter 3:16.

Accusation, innocence, 1 Samuel 22:11–15.

Accusing the accuser, 1 Kings 18:16–18.

Satanic tirade, Job 1:6–12.

Assuming guilt, Job 6:29 (LB).

Crushing words, Job 19:2.

Ruthless witnesses, Psalm 35:11 (CEV).

Restoring what was not stolen, Psalm 69:4.

No reason for accusation, Proverbs 3:30.

Accusation against God, Jeremiah 4:10.

False charges, Daniel 6:5–24.

Satan the accuser, Zechariah 3:1–2.

Silence of Jesus, Matthew 26:57–67; 27:12–14.

Answering one, avoiding another, Matthew 27:11–14.

Jesus accused by family, Mark 3:20–21, 31–32.

Conflicting false accusations, Mark 14:56.

Accused by servant girl, Mark 14:66–69.

Given words for response, Luke 12:11–12.

Alleged blasphemy, John 5:18.

Moses as accuser, John 5:45.

Woman caught in adultery, John 8:3–11.

Trumped up charge, John 8:12–13 (LB).

Produce fruit, John 15:16 (LB).

Stephen's death, Acts 6:8 to 7:60.

Jealous backlash, Acts 16:16–24.

Unproved accusation, Acts 25:7.

Accuser guilty of same sin, Romans 2:1.

Need for two or three witnesses, 1 Timothy 5:19.

See Criticism, Demean, Gossip, Guilt, Innocence.

ACHIEVEMENT

No success outside God's will, Numbers 14:41–45.

Divine demands within reach, Deuteronomy 30:11.

No prophet like Moses, Deuteronomy 34:10–12.

Taking credit for God's blessing, Judges 7:2–3.

Report to mother-in-law, Ruth 3:16–17.

Son seeks to impress father, 1 Samuel 14:1–14.

Lavish display of wealth, Esther 1:4–8.

Display of talent, Psalm 45:1.

Skilled in one's work, Proverbs 22:29.

Emptiness of success, affluence, Ecclesiastes 2:4–11.

End exceeds beginning, Ecclesiastes 7:8.

Assurance of achievement, Isaiah 54:2–3.

Art of seduction, Jeremiah 2:33.

Something to boast about, Jeremiah 9:23–24.

God the creator and gods who perish, Jeremiah 10:11–12.

Ashamed of self-made idols, Jeremiah 10:14–15.

Riches gained unjustly, Jeremiah 17:11.

Skills of Daniel, friends, Daniel 1:20.

Giving God glory, Romans 15:17–19.

Divine commendation, 2 Corinthians 10:17–18.

Forgetting past, pressing toward future, Philippians 3:12–16.

Good purpose fulfilled, 2 Thessalonians 1:11.

Achieved forgiveness, Hebrews 1:3 (GNB).

See Accomplishment, Performance, Success, Victory.

ACKNOWLEDGMENT

Nebuchadnezzar's acknowledgment, Daniel 2:46–47.

Recognition of sovereign God, Daniel 4:34–37.

Wise use of names, Colossians 4:7–17.

See Admit, Awareness, Recognition.

ACOUSTICS

Acoustics across water from boat, Luke 5:1–3.

ACQUIESCENCE

Yielding to inevitable, 1 Samuel 24:1–22.

See Surrender.

ACQUITTAL

Longing for pardon, Job 7:21.

"Acquit me," Psalm 19:12–13 (CEV).

Given words to speak, Ephesians 6:19–20.

See Pardon.

ACRIMONY *See Attitude, Rancor.*

ACROPHOBIA

Men who fear height, Ecclesiastes 12:5.

Lofty place of temptation, Luke 4:5–8.

See Apprehension, Fear.

ACROSTIC

Hebrew language example, Psalm 119:1–176.

ACTION

"Tarried long enough," Deuteronomy 1:6 (Berk.).

"Take action," Ezra 10:4 (NRSV).

Defiled by one's actions, Psalm 106:39.

Time ripe for divine action, Psalm 119:126 (Berk.).

Path of righteous, way of wicked, Proverbs 4:18–19.

Hasty speech, Proverbs 29:20.

Words put into action, Isaiah 48:3.

Deeds, motives likened to eggs, Isaiah 59:4–5.

Time to act, Ezekiel 24:14.

Louder than words, Matthew 11:2–5.

Tree known by fruit, Matthew 12:33–35.

"Dressed for action," Luke 12:35 (NRSV).

Inner change validated, Luke 19:8–9.

Sowing and reaping, Galatians 6:7–10.

Committed speech, actions, Colossians 3:17.

Truth put into action, James 1:22–25.

Minds ready for action, 1 Peter 1:13 (GNB, NRSV).

See Conduct, Deeds, Performance.

ADAM

Name definition, Ecclesiastes 6:10 (AB).

ADAMANT

Refusal to be silenced, Mark 10:46–48.

See Determined, Dogmatic.

ADAPTABLE

"Everything suitable for its time," Ecclesiastes 3:11 (NRSV).

See Versatility.

ADDENDUM

Those only mentioned, Hebrews 11:32–40.

ADDICTION

Master and slave, 2 Peter 2:19.

See Alcohol, Drunkenness, Habits.

ADEQUATE

Labor, good food, Ecclesiastes 5:18–20.
God requires, God provides, Isaiah 2:3.
All-sufficient Lord, Isaiah 44:22–28.
God's everlasting righteousness, Isaiah 51:8.
Nothing too hard for God, Jeremiah 32:27.
See Plenty, Sufficient, Supply.

ADHESIVE

Tar replaced mortar, Genesis 11:3.

ADJURE See Oath.

AD LIB

Given right words, Isaiah 50:4 (CEV).
See Improvisation.

ADMINISTRATION

Father-in-law's advice, Exodus 18:15–27.
Unhappy with leadership, Numbers 16:1–4.
No prophet like Moses, Deuteronomy 34:10–12.
Commander of the Lord's army, Joshua 5:13–15.
Well-organized Israelites, Joshua 7:14.
Leader among trees, Judges 9:7–15.
Leadership by divine guidance, 2 Chronicles 31:20–21.
Once faithful city, Isaiah 1:21–23.
More than wealth makes a king, Jeremiah 22:14–15.
Family on throne forever, Jeremiah 33:17.
"Administration of the mystery," Ephesians 3:9 (NASB).
See Bureaucracy, Government, Leadership, Politics.

ADMIRATION See Appreciation, Love, Respect.

ADMIT

King Saul admitted David's righteousness, 1 Samuel 24:16–17.
Admitting many sins, Psalm 25:11.
Admission of God's superior power, Daniel 3:28–30.
See Acknowledgment, Confession.

ADMONITION

Brothers urged not to quarrel, Genesis 45:24.
Wounds of friend, Proverbs 27:6.
Honest rebuke, Proverbs 28:23.
Jesus scolding evil spirit, Mark 1:23–26.
Admonition at final parting, Acts 20:25–38.
Admonishing fellow laborers, Romans 15:14–16.
Sensitive correspondence, 1 Corinthians 4:14 (NIV).
Letters harsh, powerful, 2 Corinthians 10:10 (CEV).
Coaxing to admonish, Galatians 4:20 (AB).
Word to parents, Ephesians 6:4.
Admonition to followers, Colossians 3:16; 4:17.
Encourage weak, timid, 1 Thessalonians 4:18.
Warning, Titus 3:10.
See Prophecy, Sermon, Unction, Warning.

ADOLESCENCE

Ignorant generation, Judges 2:10.
Sacrifice of daughter, Judges 11:30–40.
Boy ministering in temple, 1 Samuel 2:18.
Juvenile kings, 2 Kings 21:1; 22:1.
Covenant to avoid lust, Job 31:1.
Child's service, Jeremiah 1:4–7.
Hard labor for boys, Lamentations 5:13.
Puberty described, Ezekiel 16:7–8.
God's message to children, Joel 1:1–3.
Holy Spirit, youth, Joel 2:28.
Boy with evil spirit, Mark 9:14–29.
Dying 12-year-old girl, Luke 8:41–56.
See Children, Juvenile Delinquency, Puberty.

ADOPTION

Adopted children, Genesis 15:3; 48:5; Exodus 2:10; Esther 2:7.
Selected as nation, Deuteronomy 14:1–2.
Becoming God's children, Psalm 27:10 (AB); John 1:12; Romans 8:15; 2 Corinthians 6:18; Galatians 4:3–7.
See Orphan.

ADORATION See Worship.

ADULATION

Avoiding insincerity, Job 31:21–22.
Deceptive lips, Psalm 12:2.
Nature, people praise the Lord, Psalm 148:1–14.
God's pure ego, Isaiah 42:8.
Herod as god, Acts 12:22.
See Accolade, Infatuation, Worship.

ADULT See Growth, Maturity.

ADULTERY

Foiled adulteress, Genesis 39:7–20.
Seventh commandment, Exodus 20:14.
Neighborhood relationship, Leviticus 20:10.
Defiled engagement, Deuteronomy 22:23–24 (GNB).
Cover of darkness, Job 24:15.
Repentant adulterer, Psalm 51:1–19.
Foolish adultery, Proverbs 6:32 (NRSV).
Folly of simpleton, Proverbs 7:6–23.
Profuse adultery, Jeremiah 3:6.
Adulterous wood, stone, Jeremiah 3:9.
Iniquity in heart, mind, Ezekiel 6:9; Matthew 5:27–28.
Wife's infidelity, Ezekiel 16:32.
"Worn out by adultery," Ezekiel 23:43 (NIV).
Instruction to marry adulterous woman, Hosea 1:2–3.
See Flirtation, Immorality, Lust, Passion.

ADVANCEMENT

Status advancement, Genesis 41:41–46 (LB).
Shepherd to king, 2 Samuel 7:8–12.
Big job, small man, Ephesians 3:8–9.
See Promotion.

ADVANTAGE

Taking advantage, Job 6:27.
Revenge for taking advantage, Proverbs 22:22–23.

ADVENT See Christmas.

ADVENTURE

Adventures to tell children, Exodus 10:1–2.
Wild donkey adventures, Job 39:5–12 (Berk.).
See Courage, Valor.

ADVERSARY

Israel's adversaries, Joshua 5:13.
Temple construction opposed, Ezra 4:5.
God as adversary, Job 22:21.
At peace with adversaries, Proverbs 16:7.
Incited mob, Acts 17:5–7.
Gospel enemies, 1 Corinthians 16:9.
See Antagonism, Demons, Enemy, Imprecation, Opponent, Satan, Soldier.

ADVERSITY

Penalty for wickedness, Leviticus 26:14–16; Deuteronomy 28:45–48; 32:24.
Judgment brings righteousness, Isaiah 26:9.
Frying pan to fire, Amos 5:19.
Persecution implements Gospel, Acts 8:3–4.
Always silver lining, Romans 8:28.
See total picture, Philippians 1:3–6.
Corrective chastening, Hebrews 12:5–11.
Vitalizing faith, 1 Peter 5:8.
See Accident, Misfortune, Problems, Suffering.

ADVERTISING

Ancient billboards, Deuteronomy 27:2–8.
Signboard, Mark 15:26 (LB).
See Billboard, Media, Publicity, Salesman.

ADVICE

Advice leads to tragedy, Genesis 37:14–20.
Father-in-law's advice, Exodus 18:13–27.
Good advice, Exodus 18:18–19 (GNB); 1 Kings 12:1–11.
Elder's advice, 1 Kings 12:1–11.
Search for advice, 1 Chronicles 13:1.
Good advice spurned, 2 Chronicles 10:1–19.
Self-advised, Nehemiah 5:7 (KJV).
Royal advisors, Esther 1:13.
Advisor needing advice, Job 4:3–6.
Open to advice, Job 6:24.
Voices of experience, Job 8:8–10.
Wicked advice, Psalm 1:1 (NRSV).
God's helpful advice, Proverbs 2:7 (CEV).
National guidance, Proverbs 11:14.
Fools spurn counsel, Proverbs 12:15.
Failed plans, Proverbs 15:22.
Accumulated advice gives wisdom, Proverbs 19:20.
Value of good advice, Proverbs 24:5–6.

Timely advice, Proverbs 25:11 (LB).
Seeking advice from idols, Isaiah 19:3 (CEV).
Avoid father's advice, Ezekiel 20:18.
Advice from Pilate's wife, Matthew 27:19.
Jesus rejected mother's advice, John 2:4 (GNB).
Paul's parting counsel, Acts 20:25–28.
See Counsel, Counseling.

ADVOCATE

People's welfare, Esther 10:3.
Advocate in Heaven, Job 16:19–21.
Those needing advocate, Proverbs 31:8–9.
Ineffective advocates, Jeremiah 15:1.
Holy Spirit our advocate, John 14:16 (NRSV).
Plea for Onesimus, Philemon 8–21.
Heaven's High Priest, Hebrews 8:1–2.
Role of Jesus, 1 Peter 3:22; 1 John 2:1–2.
See Mediator.

AESTHETICS

Pleasant odor, Genesis 8:21 (AB).
Temple fragrance, Exodus 30:34–38.
Aroma from altar, Leviticus 2:9; Numbers 15:7.
Aroma of food, Numbers 28:2.
Prophecy to sound of music, 2 Kings 3:15–16.
Fragrant burial, 2 Chronicles 16:14.

Matching colors, Luke 5:36.
Seaside residence, Acts 10:6.
See Ambrosia, Beauty, Emotion, Incense, Music, Sensitivity.

AFFECTATION

Egotist's parade, Esther 6:6–9.
Hypocrisy on display, Matthew 6:1–2, 16.
Empty sincerity, Mark 12:15–17.
Egotists, Mark 12:38–40.
God's love for David, Acts 13:22.
Exposed phoniness, 1 Corinthians 4:6–8.
False humility, Colossians 2:18.
Mark of false teachers, 2 Peter 2:18–19.
False claim of holy life, 1 John 1:8–10.
See Hypocrisy, Pretense, Sham.

AFFECTION

Frustrated grandfather, Genesis 31:28.
Turning to rejected brother, Judges 11:1–10.
Daughter-in-law's affection, Ruth 1:14–18.
Affection for child, Ruth 4:16 (GNB).
David, Jonathan, 1 Samuel 18:1–4; 19:1–6; 20:17, 41; 23:18; 2 Samuel 1:26.
Hug and kiss, 2 Samuel 15:5 (CEV).
Kiss of death, 2 Samuel 20:9–10.
"Kiss the Son," Psalm 2:12 (KJV, NIV).
Our Lord's enduring love, Psalm 136:1–26.
Superficial affection, Proverbs 20:6.

ADVERTISING

Embrace with propriety, Ecclesiastes 3:5.
"You are very dear," Isaiah 43:4 (CEV).
Everlasting love, Jeremiah 31:3.
False affection, Matthew 26:47–48.
Betrayal kiss, Mark 14:44–45.
Command to love, John 13:34; 15:12.
Love expressed through anguish, 2 Corinthians 2:4.
Loving too much, 2 Corinthians 12:15 (CEV).
Always in the heart, Philippians 1:7 (GNB).
Deep spiritual affection, 1 Thessalonians 2.7–12.
Paul's love for Onesimus, Philemon 12 (GNB).
Love each other deeply, 1 Peter 4:8.
Kiss of love, 1 Peter 5:14.
"Affection with love," 2 Peter 1:7 (NRSV).
Love in the truth, 3 John 1.
Love dearly, tenderly, Revelation 3:19.
See Camaraderie, Courtship, Emotion, Kiss, Love, Rapport, Romance.

AFFINITY

Twin grasping twin, Genesis 25:24–26.
David, Jonathan, 1 Samuel 18:1–4; 19:1–6; 20:17, 41; 23:18; 2 Samuel 1:26.
Believer's rapport, Psalm 119:63.
Two in agreement, Amos 3:3.
Commanded to love, John 13:34; 15:12.
Serving in unity, Acts 1:4; 2:44–47.
Perfect affinity, 1 Corinthians 1:10.
Sharing suffering, comfort, 2 Corinthians 1:7.
Bearing each other's burdens, Galatians 6:2.
Concern for followers, Colossians 2:1–5.
Daily exhortation, Hebrews 3:13.
Of one mind, 1 Peter 3:8.
Mutual affinity, 1 John 3:14; 4:7–13.
See Camaraderie, Companionship, Compatibility, Unity.

AFFIRMATION

Satan's "yea," Genesis 3:1 (KJV).
Vocal affirmation, Joshua 24:22.
Yes, no, James 5:12 (GNB).
See Acceptance, Agreement.

AFFLICTION

Divine concern, Exodus 3:7.
Receiving good, evil, Job 2:10; 5:17; Lamentations 3:22–39.
Longing for oblivion, Job 10:18–19.
Trouble since birth, Job 14:1.
Role of testing, Job 23:10; Psalm 66:10; Isaiah 48:10; 2 Corinthians 4:17; 1 Peter 1:7.
Desperate times, Psalm 60:3.
Scripture, suffering, Psalm 119:50, 67, 143.
Purposeful affliction, Psalm 119:75.
Affliction's furnace, Isaiah 48:10.
Place of disease, death, Jeremiah 16:1–13.
Glory in tribulation, Romans 5:3; 12:12.
Accepting affliction, 2 Corinthians 6:4–10; 7:4.
Sufficient grace, 2 Corinthians 12:9.
See Calamity, Disease, Illness, Persecution, Sickness, Trauma.

AFFLUENCE

Wealthy Abram, Genesis 13:2.
Wealth, power, envy, Genesis 26:12–18.
God-given ability to produce wealth, Deuteronomy 8:18.
Spiritual test, Deuteronomy 28:47–48.
Secure affluence, Judges 18:7.
Affluent in-law, Ruth 2:1.
Interested in making money, 1 Samuel 8:3 (GNB).
Divine simplicity, 2 Samuel 7:1–7.
Wisdom preferred to wealth, 1 Kings 3:1–15.
Temple, palace construction priorities, 1 Kings 6:38; 7:1.
Overwhelming royal affluence, 1 Kings 10:4–5.
Solomon's wealth, 1 Kings 10:23.
Space for treasures, 2 Chronicles 32:27.
Affluence lying in ruins, Job 3:13–15.
"Pant after their wealth," Job 5:5 (NRSV).
Riches vomited, Job 20:15.
Downfall of wicked wealth, Job 27:16–17.
Fall asleep rich, wake up poor, Job 27:19 (CEV).
Wealth, bribery, Job 36:18–19.
Divine wealth, thoughts, Psalm 10:3–6.
Lending money without interest, Psalm 15:5.
Eternal wealth, Psalm 19:8–11.
Trusting the Lord, Psalm 20:7.
Earth belongs to God, Psalm 24:1–2.
Never envy evil, Psalm 37:1 (LB).

Little with righteousness, wealth, evil, Psalm 37:16–17 (LB).

Short-lived prosperity, Psalm 37:35–36.

Transient wealth, Psalm 39:6.

Temporary affluence, Psalm 49:16–17.

Wealth gained hurting others, Psalm 52:7.

Envying the affluent, Psalm 73:3–28.

Greatest wealth, Psalm 119:14.

Obedience preferred to making money, Psalm 119:36.

Rich man's wealth, poor man's poverty, Proverbs 10:15 (Berk.).

Greatest wealth, Proverbs 10:22 (LB).

Worthless wealth at day of wrath, Proverbs 11:4.

Untrustworthy wealth, Proverbs 11:28.

Pretense of wealth, Proverbs 13:7.

Little with faith, much with turmoil, Proverbs 15:16.

Simple food in peace, quiet, Proverbs 17:1.

Character needed to handle wealth, Proverbs 19:10.

Rich, poor have common origin, Proverbs 22:2.

Negative aspects, Proverbs 23:1–8 (LB).

Evil resulting from wealth, Proverbs 29:16.

Emptiness of success, affluence, Ecclesiastes 2:4–11.

Unsatisfied with wealth, Ecclesiastes 4:8.

Hurt by wealth, Ecclesiastes 5:13 (NASB, NRSV).

God enables joy of affluence, Ecclesiastes 5:19 (NRSV).

Perils of national prosperity, Isaiah 2:7–8.

Ruined rich, Isaiah 5:17.

No desire for silver, gold, Isaiah 13:17.

Rejecting personal idols, Isaiah 31:7.

That which money cannot buy, Isaiah 55:1–2.

Potential harm of wealth, power, Jeremiah 5:27–28.

Wealth given away in judgment, Jeremiah 17:3.

Wealth, folly, greatness, Jeremiah 22:14–15.

Poor discover true wealth, Jeremiah 39:10; 40:11–12.

Boasting, trusting in wealth, Jeremiah 48:7; 49:4.

Wealth into hands of enemy, Lamentations 1:10.

Lost luster, Lamentations 4:1.

Worth weight in gold, Lamentations 4:2.

Repulsive jewelry, Ezekiel 7:20 (GNB).

Arrogant affluence, Ezekiel 16:49.

Swept away in judgment, Ezekiel 26:12–13.

Wealth confused with righteousness, Hosea 12:8.

Loss of summer house, Amos 3:15.

Houses destroyed, Amos 6:11.

Wealth from cheating, Micah 6:10 (LB).

Wealth incites violence, Micah 6:12.

Affluent at others' expense, Habakkuk 2:9 (CEV).

When judgment falls, Zephaniah 1:18.

Silver, gold, dust, dirt, Zechariah 9:3.

Humility in service, Matthew 11:7–15.

Gain world, lose soul, Matthew 16:26.

Wealth hinders salvation, Matthew 19:16–26.

Jesus accused of luxury, Matthew 26:6–13.

Deceitful wealth, Mark 4:19.

Rich young man, Mark 10:17–27.

Widow's small coins, Mark 12:41–44.

Affluence less blessing than poverty, Luke 6:20–25 (AB).

Own world, lose self, Luke 9:25.

Greed over possessions, Luke 12:13–15.

Hospitality of wealthy, Luke 14:12–14.

Rich man, Lazarus, Luke 16:19–31.

Spiritual perils of rich man, Luke 18:24.

Wealthy Creator, poor Savior, 2 Corinthians 8:9.

Nothing at birth, nothing at death, 1 Timothy 6:6–8.

Monetary wealth, wealth of good deeds, 1 Timothy 6:11–19.

Love of money, Hebrews 13:5.

High position in reality low, James 1:10.

Clothes do not always make the man, James 2:1–5.

Gold, silver corrode, James 5:1–3 (AB).

Judgment prelude, James 5:5–6 (GNB).

Sharing possessions, 1 John 3:17.

True wealth, Revelation 2:9.

Wealth temporal, spiritual, Revelation 3:15–18.

Weeping over lost affluence, Revelation 18:11–19.
See Possessions, Property, Wealth.

AFFRONT

Satanic defiance, Genesis 3:1–5; Job 1:6–12; 2:1–7.
Heathen gods affronted, Psalm 138:1.
God turns His back, Jeremiah 18:17.
Speaking out against the Lord, Exodus 17:7; Numbers 21:5.
Pseudo-sympathy, Job 2:11–13.
Challenging the Lord, Isaiah 5:18–25; 45:9–10.
Affronting prophets, Isaiah 30:10; Amos 2:12.
Opposition to rebuilding temple, Ezra 4:4–5.
Plot against city, Nehemiah 4:7–9.
Affronting one who affronts, Zechariah 3:1–2.
Flaunting Creator, Matthew 26:47–53.
Affronting enemy of truth, Acts 13:4–12.
Decisive resistance to opposition, Acts 18:6.
Archangel's reluctance to affront Satan, Jude 9.
See Defiance, Demean, Opposition.

AFRAID *See Apprehension, Fear.*

AFTERMATH

Shame, disgrace, Proverbs 18:3.
See Conclusion.

AFTERNOON

"Four o'clock," John 1:39 (LB).

AGE

Old Testament fathers, Genesis 11:10–26.
Assured longevity, Genesis 15:15.
Life's pilgrimage, Genesis 47:9.
Value established by age, Leviticus 27:1–8.
Marriage of young to old, Ruth 3:10.
Full life concluded, 1 Chronicles 29:28.
Aging caused by stress, Psalm 6:7.
Fear of old age, Psalm 71:9.
Assigned number of years, Psalm 90:10.
Prestigious gray hair, Proverbs 16:31.
Gamut of age, Isaiah 46:4.
King at sixty-two, Daniel 5:30–31.

Old, young received angelic announcements, Luke 1:5–38.
Both child, adult, Ephesians 5:1–3.
Discipline for the aged, Titus 2:2–3.
Respect for those older, 1 Peter 5:5.
See Birth, Birth Certificate, Old Age.

AGGRESSIVE

Demanding blessing, Genesis 32:26.
Commanded to avoid conflict, Deuteronomy 2:3–6, 19.
Eager for salvation, Mark 10:17.
Making most of opportunity, Ephesians 5:15–16; Colossians 4:5.
See Ambition, Energy, Initiative, Leadership.

AGILITY

Ambidextrous soldiers, 1 Chronicles 12:1–2.
Deer feet, 2 Samuel 22:34; 1 Chronicles 12:8; Song of Songs 2:17.
See Athletics, Skill.

AGITATE

Frustrating building of temple, Ezra 4:5.
Marks of evil character, Proverbs 6:16–19.
Inciting crowd to action, Matthew 27:20.
Jealous Jewish leaders, Acts 13:45–51.
See Abrasive, Irritation, Meddle, Mob Psychology.

AGNOSTIC

Claiming wisdom superior to God's, Psalm 73:6–11.
Agnostics revel in triumph, Psalm 74:4–10.
God made known through judgment, Ezekiel 11:7–12.
Seeing, hearing, not understanding, Mark 4:11–12.
Validity of Jesus questioned, John 8:12–30 (LB).
Doubt augmented by truth, John 8:45–47.
See Apostasy, Atheism, Cynical, Doubt, Irreligious. Skepticism, Unbelief.

AGONY

Anguish, misery, Job 6:2.
Rejecting light, Job 24:16 (GNB).
Rich man in Hades, Luke 16:23.
Spiritual trauma, 2 Corinthians 1:8–9.
Agonizing prayer, Colossians 4:12.

Wishing to die, Revelation 9:4–9.

Torment forever, Revelation 14:11; 20:10.

Suffering increases rejection, Revelation 16:10–11.

See Pain, Suffering, Torment, Torture, Trauma.

AGREEMENT

Treaty of agreement, Genesis 21:22–34.

Rebekah's consent, Genesis 24:57–58.

Wrong kind of unanimity, Exodus 16:2.

Congregation's agreement to law, Deuteronomy 27:14–26.

Those who broke faith with God, Deuteronomy 32:51.

Unison agreement, Joshua 24:22.

Penalty for broken agreement, Judges 2:1–5.

Removed sandal finalized agreement, Ruth 4:7.

Heart, soul, 1 Samuel 14:7.

Importance of treaty, 1 Kings 20:34.

Penalty for disobeying covenant, Jeremiah 11:1–5.

"Amen" of agreement, Jeremiah 28:5–6.

Husbands, wives wickedly agree, Jeremiah 44:16–19.

Agreement resulting from false oaths, Hosea 10:4.

Under contract to betray, Matthew 26:14–16.

Husband, wife in evil agreement, Acts 5:1–11.

Agreement with Holy Spirit, Acts 15:28 (GNB).

Practice, approval of heinous sins, Romans 1:32.

United mind, thought, 1 Corinthians 1:10.

Christian agreement, Philippians 4:2.

See Approval, Rapport, Unanimity.

AGREEMENT

Put it in writing, Nehemiah 9:38.

"Agree with God," Job 22:21 (NRSV).

Shake hands, Proverbs 6:1 (NKJV).

Prejudiced committee, Mark 15:1 (NKJV).

Healing by divine agreement, Luke 5:12–13.

See Contract.

AGRICULTURE

Productive land, Genesis 1:11–12.

Mankind's first vocation, Genesis 2:15; 3:23.

Laborious task, Genesis 3:17–19.

Ancient farmers, Genesis 4:2; 9:20; 1 Kings 19:19; 1 Chronicles 27:26; 2 Chronicles 26:10.

Lost farming skill, Genesis 4:9–12.

Livestock farmer, Genesis 4:20.

Seedtime, harvest, Genesis 8:22.

Man of the soil, Genesis 9:20.

Farming fortune, Genesis 13:2.

Limited fertility, Genesis 13:5–9.

Desiring best farmland, Genesis 13:10–11.

Abundant harvest, Genesis 26:12.

"Heaven's dew," Genesis 27:28 (NIV).

Farm animals identified, Genesis 30:37–43.

Discerning sheaves, Genesis 37:7.

Abundant Egyptian grain, Genesis 41:49.

Crop sharing, Genesis 47:23–24.

Unripened grain spared in plague, Exodus 9:32.

Sabbatical rest for land, Exodus 23:10–11.

Rainless sky, parched earth, Leviticus 26:19–20.

"Rain at right season," Deuteronomy 11:14–15 (CEV).

Stolen crops, Deuteronomy 28:33.

David's kindness to Jonathan's son, 2 Samuel 9:10.

Knowledge of plant life, 1 Kings 4:33.

Love for soil, 2 Chronicles 26:10.

"Pastureland," 2 Chronicles 31:19 (CEV).

Land cries out, Job 31:38–40.

Unable to manage wild ox, Job 39:9–13.

Rain for crops, pastures, Psalm 65:9–13 (v. 13, KJV).

Praise causes blessing, Psalm 67:5–6.

Rain on mown field, Psalm 72:6.

God the agriculturalist, Psalm 80:9.

Finest wheat, Psalm 81:16.

Promised harvest, Psalm 85:12.

Jubilant fields, Psalm 96:12 (Berk.).

Food for man, animals, Psalm 104:14.

Blessing on fields, herds, Psalm 107:37–38.

Earth entrusted to man, Psalm 115:16.

Spiritual bag of seed, Psalm 126:6 (CEV).

Grass housetops, Psalm 129:6–7.

Full barns, abundant flocks, Psalm 144:13.
Farming successfully, Proverbs 3:9–10.
Hoarded grain, Proverbs 11:26.
Good tilling, abundant harvest, Proverbs 12:11; 28:19.
Strong oxen produce good harvest, Proverbs 14:4.
First things first, Proverbs 24:27.
Good animal care, Proverbs 27:23–27.
Hard rain of little value, Proverbs 28:3.
Lady farmer, Proverbs 31:16.
Time to plant, uproot, Ecclesiastes 3:2.
Too concerned about weather, Ecclesiastes 11:4.
Foreigners rob fields, Isaiah 1:7.
Poor harvest, Isaiah 5:4–10.
Weeds replace vines, Isaiah 7:23.
Nile grain to Tyre, Isaiah 23:3.
Enriching fertilizer, Isaiah 25:10.
The Lord watches vineyard, Isaiah 27:2–3.
God guides farmer, Isaiah 28:24–26.
Promise of rain, Isaiah 30:23.
Spontaneous growth, Isaiah 37:30.
Barren land productive, Isaiah 41:18–20.
Meadow grass, thriving trees, Isaiah 44:4.
Desert to garden, Isaiah 51:3.
Flesh of pigs, rats, Isaiah 66:17.
Israel likened to harvest, Jeremiah 2:1–3.
Fertile land defiled, Jeremiah 2:7.
Corrupted vine, Jeremiah 2:21.
Beautiful land withheld, Jeremiah 3:19.
Break up unplowed ground, Jeremiah 4:3.
Ravaged vineyards, Jeremiah 5:10.
Refusing to glorify God for harvest, Jeremiah 5:24.
Harvest taken from disobedient farmer, Jeremiah 8:13.
Flowing with milk, honey, Jeremiah 11:5; 32:22.
Severe drought, Jeremiah 14:4–6.
Joy of restoration, Jeremiah 31:5–6.
Well-watered garden, Jeremiah 31:12.
Heifer, gadfly, Jeremiah 46:20.
Salt condemns land, Jeremiah 48:9.
Harvest celebrations terminated, Jeremiah 48:33 (CEV).
Land made desolate, Ezekiel 6:14.
Rural prosperity, Ezekiel 36:11 (KJV).
Good crops promised, Ezekiel 36:29–30.
Weeping for lost harvest, Joel 1:11.

Lifeless seeds, Joel 1:17.
Edenic land becomes desert, Joel 2:3.
Abundant rain, abundant harvest, Joel 2:23–24.
Swords to plowshares to swords, Joel 3:10 (LB); Micah 4:3 (LB).
Scant rainfall during growing season, Amos 4:7.
Despondent farmers, Amos 5:16.
Confused seasons, Amos 9:13.
Planting brings no harvest, Micah 6:15.
Though crops fail, trust the Lord, Habakkuk 3:17–18.
Salt pits, Zephaniah 2:9.
Harvest withheld, Haggai 1:10–11.
Promised harvest, Haggai 2:19.
Good seed, crops, Zechariah 8:12.
Prayer for rain, Zechariah 10:1.
Prophets turned farmers, Zechariah 13:1–5.
Parable of sower, Matthew 13:1–23; Luke 8:4–15.
Weeds, wheat, Matthew 13:24–30, 37–43.
Miracle of growth, Mark 4:26–29.
Fertile farm, Luke 12:16 (LB).
Fertilizing tree, Luke 13:8.
Day work only, John 9:4.
Vine, fruit, John 15:1–8.
Good crops, happy people, Acts 14:17.
Fruit of labor, 1 Corinthians 9:7.
Blessing on seed, harvest, 2 Corinthians 9:10.
Reap what is sown, Galatians 6:7–10.
Farmer's share of crop, 2 Timothy 2:6.
Land blessed by God, Hebrews 6:7–8.
Patient farmer, James 5:7.
Wages paid in grain, Revelation 6:6.
Harmless locusts, Revelation 9:3–4.
Harvest in final days, Revelation 14:14–20.
Twelve-month harvest, Revelation 22:2.
See Animals, Cattle, Farmer, Gleaners, Harvest, Nature, Vegetation, Seed, Soil, Weather.

AIDS *(References chosen are descriptive, not diagnostic.)*
Prevented infection spread, Numbers 5:1–4; 25:6–9.
Relevant statements, Deuteronomy 28:20, 22, 27, 34, 35, 37.
Sins of youth, Job 20:11–17 (KJV).

Young male prostitutes, Job 36:14.

Physical, social distress, Psalms 31:9–13; 38:5–11.

Loathsome disease, Psalm 38:7–11.

"Fatal disease," Psalm 41:8 (CEV).

Stalking pestilence of darkness, Psalm 91:6–8 (Berk.).

Sin-inflicted disease, Psalm 107:17.

Dreaded skin disease, Matthew 8:2–4.

Penalty for perversion, Romans 1:27 (AB).

See Deviate, Disease, Leprosy.

AIM *See Target.*

AIR

Letting in morning air, 1 Samuel 3:15.

High above sky, Romans 8:39 (LB).

See Wind.

AIR CONDITIONING

Cool private chamber, Judges 3:20 (NKJV).

Not bothered by scorching sun, Isaiah 49:10 (CEV).

AIRCRAFT

Cloud chariot, Psalm 104:3 (Berk.).

Those who fly, Isaiah 60:8.

Suggested prophecy of aircraft, Isaiah 60:8; 31:5; Ezekiel 1:19.

High in sky, Romans 8:39 (LB).

ALARM

Sudden attack, Judges 7:20–23.

Warning the wicked, Ezekiel 3:18.

Trumpeted warning, Ezekiel 33:3–6.

No need for alarm, Mark 13:7.

See Admonition, Warning.

ALCHEMY

Turned into gold, Job 23:10.

Stones into bread, Matthew 4:3.

Water into wine, John 2:1–11.

ALCOHOL

Noah's drunkenness, Genesis 9:18–27.

Lot, daughters, Genesis 19:30–38.

Sobriety in worship, Leviticus 10:8–10 (Note "wine or beer," GNB).

Sacrificial wine, Numbers 15:5–7.

Alcohol, pregnancy, Judges 13:2–5.

Alcoholic beverage other than wine, Judges 13:7.

Drinking for good spirits, Ruth 3:7.

Unlimited drinks, Esther 1:8.

Joy beyond wine's levity, Psalm 4:7.

False courage, Proverbs 20:1 (LB).

Wine, overeating, laziness, Proverbs 23:20–21.

Lingering over wine, Proverbs 23:30–33.

Medicinal wine, Proverbs 31:4–7; Mark 15:23; Luke 10:34; 1 Timothy 5:23.

Notorious bartenders, Isaiah 5:22.

AIR CONDITIONING

Wine drinking champions, Isaiah 5:22 (Berk.).

Eat, drink, make merry, Isaiah 22:13 (KJV).

Crying for wine, Isaiah 24:7–13.

Wine for sedation, Isaiah 24:11.

Festive wine, Isaiah 25:6.

Incapacitated by wine, Isaiah 28:1, 7.

Making poor decisions, Isaiah 28:7.

Drunk not with wine, Isaiah 51:21.

False sense of values, Isaiah 56:10–12.

Wine, divine judgment, Jeremiah 13:12–14.

Exemplary forefathers, Jeremiah 35:1–16.

False joy, Jeremiah 51:39.

Wine forbidden in temple, Ezekiel 44:21.

Alcoholism, immorality, Hosea 4:18 (CEV, LB).

Weeping drunkard, Joel 1:5.

Vow forcibly broken, Amos 2:12.

Exalting beer, wine, Micah 2:11 (LB).

Drinking women, Amos 4:1; Titus 2:3.

Abundant wine, beer predicted, Micah 2:11.

Excessive wine, Nahum 1:10.

Betrayed by wine, Habakkuk 2:5.

Intoxicating neighbors, Habakkuk 2:15.

Constant drinking, Haggai 1:6.

Avoiding fermentation, Matthew 9:17.

Storing wine, Matthew 9:17; Mark 2:22.

Changing water into wine, John 2:1–11.

Causing another to stumble, Romans 14:20–23.

Alcohol with food, 1 Corinthians 11:21 (AB).

Drunk from wine, filled with the Spirit, Ephesians 5:18.

Sobriety for elders, Titus 1:7.

Enslaved, 2 Peter 2:19.

Drunk with blood, Revelation 17:6.

See Abstinence, Beer, Drunkenness, Liquor, Wine.

ALCOHOLIC

Sad conduct, Proverbs 23:29–30 (GNB).

Delirium tremens, Proverbs 23:31–35 (GNB).

All-day drunk, Isaiah 5:11–12.

Crying for wine, Isaiah 24:11.

Excessive drinking, Isaiah 56:12 (CEV).

Excessive wine, Amos 6:6 (CEV).

See Drunkenness, Intemperance.

ALERT

"Ready when you are," 1 Kings 22:4 (GNB).

On constant alert, Nehemiah 4:11–23.

Be prepared, Jeremiah 1:17.

Ready to face enemy, Nahum 2:1.

Not found sleeping, Mark 13:35–37 (Note CEV).

Avoid spiritual peril, 1 Corinthians 16:13 (LB).

Making most of opportunity, Ephesians 5:15, 16.

Ready to serve, witness, Ephesians 6:15.

Ever watchful, Colossians 4:2 (GNB).

Minds ready for action, 1 Peter 1:13 (GNB).

"It escapes their notice," 2 Peter 3:5 (CEV).

Awake in time of judgment, Revelation 16:15.

See Awareness, Perception.

ALIEN

Alien, stranger, Genesis 23:4 (KJV).

Aliens barred from Passover, Exodus 12:43–45.

Foreigner's debt, Deuteronomy 15:3.

Alien wife's beauty treatment, Deuteronomy 21:10–13.

Attitude toward aliens, Deuteronomy 23:7.

Half Jewish, 1 Kings 7:13, 14 (LB).

Wearing foreign clothes, Zephaniah 1:8.

See Foreigner, Intruder, Race, Racism, Stranger, Xenophobia.

ALIENATION

Disrupted fellowship, Psalm 55:12–14.

See Divorce, Separation.

ALLEGATION *See Accusation.*

ALLEGORY

Understandable communication, Numbers 12:8.

Short story, apt application, 2 Samuel 12:1–4.

Lowly birth, royal beauty, Ezekiel 16:4–29.

Eagles, vine, Ezekiel 17:1–24.

See Literature, Parable, Short Story.

ALLIANCE

Defensive alliance, Joshua 9:1–2 (LB).

Allied against Israel, Joshua 11:1–5.

Egyptian alliance, 1 Kings 3:1 (GNB).

ALLOWANCE
King's allowance, Jeremiah 52:34.

ALLOY
Iron mixed with bronze, Jeremiah 15:12 (CEV).

ALMS See Philanthropy, Welfare.

ALOES
Planted by the Lord, Numbers 24:6.

ALONE See Abandoned, Privacy, Seclusion.

ALTAR
Altar of promise, Genesis 8:20–22.
Commemoration altars, Genesis 12:7; Exodus 24:4.
Altars in new locations, Genesis 13:18; 22:9; 26:25; 33:20; 35:7.
Offering with pleasing aroma, Numbers 15:14; Genesis 8:21.
Reconstructed altar, Judges 6:25–28.
King's first altar, 1 Samuel 14:35.
Prayer altar, 2 Samuel 24:25.
Altar of divine proof, 1 Kings 18:16–39.
Defiled altars, Hosea 8:11.
Useless altar fires, Malachi 1:10.
Sacrifice of one's self, Romans 12:1–2.
See Sacrifice.

ALTERNATIVE
Between two opinions, 1 Kings 18:21.
Better opinion, Isaiah 1:18.
Jesus or Barabbas, Matthew 27:15–26.
Gain world, lose soul, Mark 8:36.
Divine alternative, John 5:2–9.
No alternative to Jesus, John 6:66–69.
Judas' replacement, Acts 1:12–26.
See Choice, Escape, Free Will, Option, Rescue.

ALTITUDE See Acrophobia, Aircraft, Height.

ALTRUISTIC
Unselfish brothers, Genesis 33:1–11.
Returning good for evil, Genesis 50:15–21.
Providing for strangers, poor, Leviticus 23:22.
Providing another's need, Ruth 2:15–16.
Attitude toward enemy, 1 Samuel 24:1–22; 26:1–11.
Altruistic share of good fortune, 2 Kings 7:3–9.
Wise king's unselfish prayer, 2 Chronicles 1:7–12.
Leadership attitude, Nehemiah 5:14–18.
Altruism to enemies, Daniel 2:13–18.
Joseph's concern for Mary, Matthew 1:19.
Greatest in kingdom, Luke 9:46–48.
Outreach to poor, Acts 9:36–42.
Basic premise is love, 1 Corinthians 13:1–13.
Seeking others' good, 1 Corinthians 10:24; Philippians 1:26; 2:1–4.
Helping others, Philippians 4:2 (AB).
Prophets served future generations, 1 Peter 1:12 (GNB).
See Unselfishness.

ALZHEIMER'S
Forgotten prosperity, Lamentations 3:17.
Precious lingering memory, Ecclesiastes 12:6–7.
"Land of forgetfulness," Psalm 88:12 (NKJV).
See Geriatrics, Memory, Old Age, Senility.

AMATEUR
Father, inexperienced son, 1 Chronicles 22:5; 29:1.
Amateur theology, Acts 17:18 (Berk.).
Admitted amateur status, 2 Corinthians 11:6 (GNB).
See Athletics, Novice.

AMAZEMENT
Vindication by earthquake, Numbers 16:28–34.
Breathless queen, 1 Kings 10:4 (CEV).
"Faces aflame," Isaiah 13:8 (Berk.).
Ezekiel overwhelmed, Ezekiel 3:15.
Awesome acts of God, Joel 1:13–20.
Amazed audience, Matthew 7:28–29; 9:33; 13:54–58; Mark 1:22; 6:2.
Amazed at shallowness, Galatians 1:6 (Berk.).
See Awe, Emotion, Serendipity.

AMBASSADOR

God's representative, Exodus 7:1–2.

Messengers, envoys, Numbers 20:14; 21:21; 2 Samuel 5:11; 1 Kings 5:1; 20:2, 3; 2 Kings 14:8; 16:7; Ezekiel 17:13–15.

Sent from God, John 1:6–8.

Highest appointment, 2 Corinthians 5:20.

See Missionary.

AMBIDEXTROUS

Soldiers agile with either hand, 1 Chronicles 12:1–2.

Two-handed frustration, Ecclesiastes 4:6.

Ambidextrous evil, Micah 7:3.

Creative hands, Hebrews 1:10 (GNB).

See Athletics, Skill.

AMBIENT *See Aura.*

AMBIGUOUS

Confused languages, Genesis 11:1–8.

Ambiguous statements, Numbers 23:27 (KJV); 2 Kings 5:25 (KJV); 1 Chronicles 26:18 (KJV).

Avoiding ambiguity, Habakkuk 2:2.

Comprehension of Jesus' followers, Luke 9:44–45.

Accused of babbling, Acts 17:18.

Trumpet's uncertain sound, 1 Corinthians 14:8.

Ambiguous gospel, Galatians 1:6–7.

See Vague.

AMBITION

Ambition of secular society, Genesis 11:1–4.

Campaigning for office, 2 Samuel 15:1–4.

Full obedience desired, Psalm 119:1–5.

Determination to fulfill destiny, Psalm 132:1–5.

"Make hay while sun shines," Proverbs 10:5 (LB).

Man's plans, God's purposes, Proverbs 16:1; 19:21.

Desire to exceed neighbor, Ecclesiastes 4:4.

Search for schemes, Ecclesiastes 7:29.

Seeking great things in rebellion against God, Jeremiah 45:4–5.

Indulgent mother, Matthew 20:21.

Desire for prominence, Luke 22:24.

Continual lust for more, Ephesians 4:19 (GNB, NEB).

Making most of opportunity, Ephesians 5:15–16; Colossians 4:5.

Ready to serve, witness, Ephesians 6:15.

Paul's supreme desire, Philippians 3:7–11.

Motivated to Christian lifestyle, 1 Thessalonians 4:11–12.

Goal for goodness, 2 Thessalonians 1:11 (LB).

Desire to be overseer, 1 Timothy 3:1.

Dangerous motivation toward wealth, 1 Timothy 6:9–10.

Uncertain tomorrows, James 4:13–16.

See Initiative, Motivation.

AMBIVALENCE

Mistaking love for hatred, Deuteronomy 1:27.

Saul, David, 1 Samuel 16:21–22; 18:28–29.

Hatred toward loved one, 2 Samuel 13:12–19.

Accusation against David, 2 Samuel 19:6.

Mixed motivations, Esther 7:7.

Wound, heal, Job 5:18 (CEV).

Complaint, praise, Psalm 22:1–11, 22–31.

Beloved but wicked, Jeremiah 11:15.

Accusing, praising the Lord, Jeremiah 20:7, 11–13.

Judgment, mercy, Daniel 6:16 (CEV).

Swords to plowshares to swords, Joel 3:10 (LB); Micah 4:3 (LB).

Negative attitude toward blessing, Jonah 4:1–11.

Divine love, hatred, Malachi 1:2–3.

Alleged concern for Jesus, Luke 13:31.

Friends, enemies, Romans 11:28 (GNB).

Praise, profane, James 3:9–12.

See Affection, Hatred, Hypocrisy, Love.

AMBROSIA

Food in presence of enemies, Psalm 23:5.

Satisfying fare, Psalm 103:5.

Deceptive delicacies, Proverbs 23:3.

See Aesthetics, Delicacy, Gourmet.

AMBUSH

Deceptive maneuver, Joshua 8:3–17.

Citizen's ambush, Judges 9:25.

Deceitful murder, 2 Samuel 3:27.

Rear attack, 2 Samuel 5:22–25.
Enemies on trail, Psalm 56:6 (LB).
Traps for men, Jeremiah 5:26.
Fearing public places, Jeremiah 6:25.
Led into false security, Jeremiah 41:4–7.
See Deceit, Devious.

AMEN

Unison agreement, Deuteronomy 27:15;
Nehemiah 5:13.
Fulfillment in Christ, 2 Corinthians 1:20.
"Come, Lord Jesus," Revelation 22:20–21.

AMENDS See Restitution.

AMENITIES

Amenities to visitors, Genesis 18:3–5.
Nature's blessings, Deuteronomy 33:13–16.
See Courtesy, Hospitality.

AMNESTY

No qualification for amnesty, Genesis
18:16–33.
Death penalty waived, 1 Samuel 11:13;
2 Samuel 19:16–23.
Revenge left to God's timing, 1 Samuel
26:1–11.
Amnesty by public choice, Matthew 27:16–
26; Mark 15:7–15; Luke 23:18; John
18:40.
Divine amnesty, Romans 6:23; Ephesians
2:1–9.
See Forgiveness, Pardon, Parole.

AMPUTATION

Cut off arm, 1 Samuel 2:31 (KJV).
See Surgery.

AMUSEMENT

Inappropriate laughter, Genesis 18:10–15.
Wicked revelry, Exodus 32:6.
Samson's performance, Judges 16:25.
Hand to hand matches, 2 Samuel 2:14.
Dancing children, Job 21:11–12.
Meaningless amusement, Ecclesiastes
2:1–2.
Spiritual need ignored, Isaiah 5:12.
Strumming harps, Amos 6:5.
Worship of fishing, Habakkuk 1:16.
Children playing, Zechariah 8:5.

Refusing to be amused, Matthew 11:16.
See Hedonism, Humor, Laughter, Playboy, Pleasure, Relaxation.

ANALOGY

Fool's likeness, Proverbs 26:1–11.
Illustration in heavens, Isaiah 55:9.
Baskets of figs, Jeremiah 24:1–10.
Jesus' use of figures of speech, Mark 8:14–
21.
Human body likened to temple, John 2:18–
22.
See Simile.

ANALYSIS

Asking God to search, guide, Psalm 139:23–
24.
See Introspection, Inventory, Rationalize, Self-examination.

ANARCHY

Following personal whim, Deuteronomy
12:8–9.
Contempt for temple, government, Deuteronomy 17:12; Ezra 7:26.
Positive anarchy of ants, Proverbs 6:6–8.
Many rulers during rebellion, Proverbs
28:2.
Brother against brother, Isaiah 19:2.
Egypt's future distress, Isaiah 19:12.
People turning against each other, Isaiah
3:5–7; Zechariah 8:10.
Destructive shepherds, Jeremiah 12:10.
Every man on his own, Jeremiah 23:36.
No God, no king, Hosea 10:3.
Distorted sense of right, Amos 3:10.
Family disloyalty, Micah 7:2, 6.
Fish have no ruler, Habakkuk 1:14.
Slaves against masters, Zechariah 2:9.
Men attacking each other, Zechariah 14:13.
See Civil Disobedience, Disobedience, Mob Psychology, Rebellion.

ANATOMY

"Fenced with bones, sinews," Job 10:11
(KJV).
Fallen shoulder blade, Job 31:22 (NRSV).
Talking bones, Psalms 35:10 (Berk.).
Body function, Ecclesiastes 12:1–5 (AB).
See Physique.

ANCESTORS

Recorded ancestry, Genesis 10:1–32.
Nations' ancestor, Genesis 17:4 (Berk.).
Suffering penalty of ancestor's sin, Exodus 20:5–7.
Honored great-grandfather, Numbers 17:3 (AB).
Promise to ancestors, Judges 1:2–3.
Lineage of David, Ruth 4:13–17.
Prophet's lineage resumé, Ezra 7:1–6.
Confessing ancestors' sins, Nehemiah 9:2.
Ancestral sins, Psalm 79:8.
Chip off old rock, Isaiah 51:1 (CEV).
Don't imitate ancestors, Zechariah 1:1–6.
Genealogy of Jesus, Matthew 1:1–17; Luke 3:29–32.
Hypocrisy toward ancestors, Matthew 23:29–32.
God the original ancestor, Luke 3:38 (CEV).
Father Abraham, Romans 4:17.
Endless genealogies, 1 Timothy 1:4; Titus 3:9.
"Message to our ancestors," Hebrews 1:1 (CEV).
"Famous ancestor," Hebrews 7:4 (CEV).
Melchizedek's ancestry, Hebrews 7:6.
"Men of old," Hebrews 11:2 (NASB).
From aged loins, Hebrews 11:11–12.
Spiritual ancestors, Hebrews 13:7.
See Forefathers, Heritage, History, Influence, Parents.

ANCHOR

Anchored love, Psalm 91:14 (Berk.).
Anchor against storm, Acts 27:29.
Anchors abandoned, Acts 27:40 (CEV).
Firmly-anchored faith, Colossians 2:5.
Soul's anchor, Hebrews 6:19.
See Confidence, Maritime.

ANCIENT

"Ancient of days," Daniel 7:9, 22.
Lauded ancients, Hebrews 11:4–40.
See Antiquity.

ANECDOTE

Illustrative anecdote, Judges 9:8–15.

ANESTHETIC

Anesthesia first used, Genesis 2:21.
Satanic anesthesia, Ephesians 5:14.

ANGELS

Abraham's heavenly visitors, Genesis 18:1–10.
Amenities to angels, Genesis 19:1–4.
Angels spoken of as men, Genesis 19:1–13.
Angelic authority, Genesis 22:11–12.
Guidance by assigned angel, Genesis 24:7.
Personal angel, Genesis 24:40; Genesis 48:16 (Berk.); Acts 12:11, 15.
Give heed to angels, Exodus 23:20–23.
Donkey, angel, Numbers 22:23–28.
Commander of the Lord's army, Joshua 5:13–15.
Angelic guidance, Judges 2:1–5 (LB).
Angel's secret name, Judges 13:16–18.
Mistaking angel for God Himself, Judges 13:21–23.
Alluding to angels, 2 Kings 6:16.
Association with Satan, Job 1:6; 2:1.
Anonymous spirit, Job 4:15–16.
Angels mistrusted, Job 15:15 (CEV).
Innumerable host, Job 25:3 (GNB).
"One of a thousand angels," Job 33:23 (CEV).
Give praise to God, Psalm 29:1.
Deliverance for those in need, Psalm 34:7.
Bread of angels, Psalm 78:25.
Role of guardian angels, Psalm 91:9–12; Exodus 23:20.
Angels obedient to the Lord, Psalm 103:20.
"Servants of fire," Psalm 104:4 (LB).
Soldiers destroyed by angel, Isaiah 37:36.
Angel subdued lions, Daniel 6:22.
Gabriel, Daniel, Daniel 9:20–21.
Strengthening angel, Daniel 10:15–19.
National guardian, Daniel 12:1 (LB).
Angels, dreams, visions, Zechariah 1:7–17.
Ministry of angel to prophet, Zechariah 1:8–21 (Note continuing chapters).
Guiding angel, Zechariah 3:1 (AB).
Encouraging angel, Zechariah 3:6 (CEV).
"Catch you in their arms," Matthew 4:6 (CEV).
Ministry following temptation, Matthew 4:11.
Agent of judgment, Matthew 13:41–42.

Children's angels, Matthew 18:10.
"Bright as lightning," Matthew 28:3 (NIV).
Angelic protection, Mark 1:12–13.
Angel described as "a young man," Mark 16:5–7 (LB).
Angelic birth announcements, Luke 1:5–38.
Frightened by angel, Luke 1:11–12.
Gabriel's two assignments, Luke 1:11–38.
Firstborn's name given by angel, Luke 1:13.
Rejoicing angels, Luke 15:10.
Angelic intervention, Acts 5:17–20; 12:4–11.
Human face resembled angel, Acts 6:15.
Guided by angel, Acts 8:26.
Angel seen in vision, Acts 10:3–4.
Ministering angels, Acts 12:8–10; 27:21–25.
Possible reference to angels, 1 Corinthians 4:15.
Demons masquerade as angels, 2 Corinthians 11:14–15.
New Testament apocrypha, 1 Timothy 1:3–4 (LB).
Christ superior to angels, Hebrews 1:4–8.
Status of angels, Hebrews 1:5–14.
Unaware encounter with angels, Hebrews 13:2.
Angels' curiosity, 1 Peter 1:12.
Chained angels, Jude 6.
Mighty deliverance, Jude 14–15 (GNB).
Message delivered by angel, Revelation 1:1.
Assigned to God, Revelation 3:5.
Angel choir, Revelation 5:11–12.
Illuminating presence, Revelation 18:1.
Do not worship angels, Revelation 19:10; 22:9.
One angel versus Satan, Revelation 20:1–3.
See Archangel, Demons, Guardian.

ANGER

Murder incited by anger, Genesis 4:3–8.
Anger subsided, Genesis 27:44.
God's anger, Exodus 4:14; Numbers 11:1; 12:9; Deuteronomy 9:20; Joshua 7:1; Judges 2:14; 2 Samuel 24:1; 1 Kings 14:15; 15:29–30; 16:2, 26, 33; 22:53; 2 Kings 13:3; 17:11; 22:13; 23:19; 1 Chronicles 13:10; 2 Chronicles 28:25;

Psalms 2:12; 7:11 (LB); Hosea 12:14; John 3:36; Romans 1:18; 2:8; Ephesians 5:6.
Red-faced anger, Exodus 11:8.
Wrath waxes hot, Exodus 32:10 (KJV).
Fierce anger, Numbers 25:4.
Things done in rage, Deuteronomy 19:4–7.
God's hot anger, Judges 2:14 (NKJV).
Dangerous hot temper, Judges 18:25; Proverbs 22:24–25.
Angered by divine remedy, 2 Kings 5:1–12.
Memory dimmed by anger, Esther 2:1.
Flashing eyes, Job 15:12.
Overflowing anger, Job 40:11 (NRSV).
Anger without sin, Psalm 4:4 (Berk.).
Short temper, Psalms 30:5; 37:8 (Berk.).
Foam at the mouth, Psalm 59:7 (Berk.).
Debilitating anger, Proverbs 14:17; Ecclesiastes 7:9.
Gentle words, quiet anger, Proverbs 15:1; 17:27.
Controlled anger, Proverbs 16:32.
Hot-tempered man, Proverbs 19:19.
Pacified by bribery, Proverbs 21:14.
Lacking self-control, Proverbs 25:28.
Fool, wise man, Proverbs 29:11.
Anger stirs dissension, Proverbs 29:22.
Anger incited, Proverbs 30:33.
Enraged by hunger, Isaiah 8:21.
God like angry soldier, Isaiah 42:13.
Postponed anger, Isaiah 48:9 (Berk.).
Cup of God's wrath, Jeremiah 25:19–29.
"Heat of my spirit," Ezekiel 3:14 (NKJV).
Anger full force, Ezekiel 5:13 (GNB).
Anger eliminated, Hosea 14:4 (CEV, LB); Colossians 3:8; Titus 1:7.
Continual anger, Amos 1:11.
Unjustified anger, Jonah 4:4, 9.
Once angry, now furious, Zechariah 1:15 (CEV).
Concern becomes anger, Zechariah 8:2 (LB).
Anger as murder, Matthew 5:21–22.
"Jesus was angry," Mark 3:5 (CEV).
Furious opposition, Luke 6:11.
Resentment to spiritual truth, Acts 5:30–33.
"Ground their teeth," Acts 7:54 (NRSV).
Anger at sunset, Ephesians 4:26.
Futility of anger, James 1:19–20 (CEV).
See Disgust, Hatred, Reaction, Temper.

ANGST

What ails you? Genesis 21:17 (NKJV).
Nation in mourning, Numbers 14:39.
Royal lament, 1 Chronicles 21:17.
Remorse for disobedience, Matthew 27:3–5.
See Attitude, Melancholy.

ANGUISH

Cry of bitterness, Genesis 27:34.
"Pining away," Psalm 6:2 (CEV).
Debilitating anguish, Psalm 31:10.
Heart-smitten, Psalm 102:4 (KJV).
No song for heavy heart, Proverbs 25:20.
Inner torment, Lamentations 1:20.
Joy turns to sorrow, Lamentations 5:15.
Cup of suffering, Matthew 26:39, 42 (GNB).
Gethsemane prayer, Mark 14:35–36.
Gnashing teeth, Acts 7:54.
Futile wish to die, Revelation 9:4–6.
Refusal to repent, Revelation 16:10–11.
See Anxiety, Pain, Persecution, Stress, Suffering, Torment, Torture.

ANIMAL

Created animals wild, domestic, Genesis 1:24–25.
Man, animals vegetarian, Genesis 1:29–30.
Serpent's intelligence, Genesis 3:1.
Respect for humans, Genesis 9:2.
Experimental animal breeding, Genesis 30:37–39.
Markings on goats, Genesis 31:8–9 (KJV).
Liability for treacherous animal, Exodus 21:28–32.
Sex with animals forbidden, Exodus 22:19; Leviticus 18:23; 20:15; Deuteronomy 27:21.
Kindness to animals, Exodus 23:5.
Animals require day of rest, Exodus 23:12.
Cross-breeding forbidden, Leviticus 19:19.
Distinction animal, human, Leviticus 24:21.
Badger's skin, Numbers 4:10 (NKJV).
Livestock drinking water, Numbers 20:19.
Donkey crushes man's foot, Numbers 22:25.
Talking donkey, Numbers 22:28–30.
Unicorn, Numbers 24:8 (KJV).
Working ox rewarded, Deuteronomy 25:4.

Cohabiting with animals forbidden, Deuteronomy 27:21.
Cruelty to foxes, Judges 15:4–5.
Cruelty to horses, 2 Samuel 8:4.
Killed by lions, 2 Kings 17:26.
Royal apes, baboons, 2 Chronicles 9:21.
Fox's strength, Nehemiah 4:3.
Learning from animals, Job 12:7.
Consistent cattle breeding, Job 21:10.
Gestation for mountain goats, Job 39:1–2 (Berk.).
Untamed wild ox, Job 39:9–12.
Horse sense, Job 39:19–25.
Possible hippopotamus reference, Job 40:15 (Berk.).
Crocodile on hook, Job 41:1 (Berk.).
Mortal dominion, Psalm 8:6–8.
"Wild dog region," Psalm 44:19 (Berk.).
Lacking understanding, Psalm 49:20.
Divine ownership, Psalm 50:9–12.
"Pastures clothed with flocks," Psalm 65:13 (NKJV).
Animal intelligence, Psalm 73:22 (GNB).
Mountains rich with game, Psalm 76:4.
Wild boars, Psalm 80:13 (GNB).
Nocturnal animals, Psalm 104:20–23 (LB).
Playful whales, Psalm 104:26 (LB).
Proper care, Proverbs 12:10.
Beast of burden, Proverbs 14:4.
Men seen as animals, Ecclesiastes 3:18–19.
Distinction between man, animal, Ecclesiastes 3:21.
Live dog, dead lion, Ecclesiastes 9:4 (GNB).
Animals wiser than people, Isaiah 1:3.
Harmonious nature, Isaiah 11:6–9; 65:25.
Lion's courage, Isaiah 31:4.
Lions, wolves, leopards, Jeremiah 5:6.
"Haunt of jackals," Jeremiah 9:11 (KJV, NIV).
Hungry wild animals, Jeremiah 14:4–6.
Death by disease, Jeremiah 16:4.
Jackals, ostriches, Lamentations 4:3.
Destructive animals hinder life, travel, Ezekiel 14:12–16.
Ferocious lions, Ezekiel 19:1–9.
Lion superior to crocodile, Ezekiel 32:2 (CEV).
Animals desire clean food, water, Ezekiel 34:19.
Leadership among sheep, Ezekiel 34:20–21.

Lions fierce, docile, Daniel 6:21–24.
Prophetic goat's swift speed, Daniel 8:5.
Bear robbed of cubs, Hosea 13:8.
Wild animal relationship to God, Joel 2:22.
Sea serpent, Amos 9:3.
Sackcloth on animals, Jonah 3:8.
Lion's secure habitat, Nahum 2:11.
Four beautiful horses, Zechariah 6:2–3.
Donkey served Jesus, Matthew 21:1–7; Mark 11:1–7.
One lost sheep, Luke 15:1–7.
Animals, plants, Romans 8:22 (LB).
Animals share harvest, 1 Corinthians 9:9.
Men, animals different flesh, 1 Corinthians 15:39.
Trained animals, James 3:7.
See Animal Rights, Carnivorous, Donkey, Dragon, Horse.

ANIMAL RIGHTS

Overworked donkey, Exodus 23:5.
Mistreated donkey, Numbers 22:27.
Hamstrung horses, 2 Samuel 8:4; 1 Chronicles 18:4.
Righteous man, animal rights, Proverbs 12:10.
Kindness to birds, Deuteronomy 22:6.
Rescued ox, Luke 14:5.
See Animal.

ANIMISM

Nature worship forbidden, Deuteronomy 4:15–20; 17:2–7.
Golden rats, 1 Samuel 6:4–5, 11.
Learning from nature, Job 12:7–8.
Homage to sun, moon, Job 31:26–28.
Worship trees, garden, Isaiah 1:29.
Worshiping wood, stone, Jeremiah 2:27.
Adulterous wood, stone, Jeremiah 3:9.
Sun worship, Ezekiel 8:16.
Star worship, Zephaniah 1:5.
God's message in nature, Romans 1:20.
See Heathen, Idolatry, New Age, Pagan.

ANIMOSITY

Unanimous complaint, Exodus 16:2.
Jealous wife, 1 Samuel 1:3–7.
Wealth, prestige, resentment, Esther 5:10–14.
At odds with one's Maker, Isaiah 45:9.
See Covet, Hatred, Jealousy.

ANKLE

Sprained ankle avoided, 2 Samuel 22:37.

ANNIHILATE

Men, animals, birds destroyed, Zephaniah 1:3; Genesis 7:4.
See Catastrophe, Destruction.

ANIMAL RIGHTS

ANNIVERSARY

Looking back many years, Deuteronomy 2:7.

Recording historic date, Nehemiah 6:15.

Important date recorded, Ezekiel 24:2.

Date to remember, Haggai 2:18.

See Birthday, Celebration, Commemorate.

ANNOUNCEMENT

Coming plague announced, Exodus 9:5 (LB).

Single trumpet, double trumpet, Numbers 10:1–4.

Trumpet message, 1 Samuel 13:1–3.

Royal announcement, Ezra 1:2–4.

History's premier announcement, Isaiah 9:6–7.

Advance notice, Isaiah 40:3.

Proclaiming year of Lord, Isaiah 61:1–3.

Royal decree of disobedience, Daniel 3:4–7.

Announcement preaching, Matthew 3:1–3.

"Shouting in the desert," Mark 1:3 (GNB).

Angelic announcements, Luke 1:15–38.

See Proclamation.

ANNOY

Disturbing privacy of others, Proverbs 25:17.

See Offend.

ANNUL

Earth governments annulled, 1 Corinthians 15:24 (Berk.).

Annulled legalism, Ephesians 2:15 (AB).

ANOINTING

Anointed objects, Exodus 29:36; 30:26; 40:10; Leviticus 8:11; Numbers 7:1.

Personal anointing, Leviticus 8:30; 1 Samuel 10:1; 16:13; 1 Kings 1:39; 19:16; 2 Kings 9:3; 11:12; 23:30.

Different person, 1 Samuel 10:6.

David's respect for King Saul, 1 Samuel 24:1–7; 26:7–11.

Anointing oil of joy, Psalm 45:7.

Refuse evil anointing, Psalm 141:5 (NRSV).

Messianic anointing, Isaiah 61:1; Daniel 9:24; Luke 4:18; Acts 4:27; 10:38.

Hand of the Lord, Ezekiel 1:3.

Anointed to serve, Zechariah 4:14.

Healing anointment, Mark 6:13; Luke 10:34; James 5:14.

Sending out the Twelve, Luke 9:1–6.

Sanctifying truth, John 17:17.

Anointing abides, teaches, 1 John 2:27 (CEV).

See Commitment, Consecration, Holy Spirit, Ordination.

ANONYMITY

Anonymous grave, Deuteronomy 34:6.

God knows all men, Psalm 139:1–16.

Forgotten men, Ecclesiastes 1:11.

Anonymous assailant, Matthew 26:51–52; Mark 14:47; Luke 22:49–51; John 18:10–11.

Anonymity prevented, Mark 7:24.

Jesus and the crowd, Luke 4:30.

Ignored by others, known to God, 2 Corinthians 6:9 (LB).

Anonymous faith heroes, Hebrews 11:35–39.

Unknown name, Revelation 19:12.

See Humility, Secrecy, Stranger, Unknown.

ANSWER

Nonverbal response, Judges 6:36–40; 1 Kings 18:37–38.

Mother's answered prayer, 1 Samuel 1:10–28.

"Time for the Lord to act," Psalm 119:126 (CEV).

Answers to unasked questions, Isaiah 65:1 (CEV).

Answer delayed ten days, Jeremiah 42:7.

Daniel looked to God for answers, Daniel 2:14–28.

Assured answer, Luke 7:18–22.

One question answered with another, Luke 20:1–8.

Patiently awaiting answers, Hebrews 6:13–14.

See Nonverbal Communication, Question, Response.

ANTAGONISM

Wealth, prestige, resentment, Esther 5:10–14.

"All who want me dead," Psalm 40:14 (CEV).

"I hurl my shoe," Psalm 108:9 (NRSV)

Demon multitude, Luke 8:26–31.
Bad characters incited, Acts 17:5–7.
See Adversary, Demons, Enemy, Opposition, Satan.

ANTAGONIST

"Worthless bums," Acts 17:5 (CEV).

ANTHEM *See Choir, Hymn, Music.*

ANTICHRIST

"Horrible thing," Daniel 12:11 (LB).
Many will claim to be Christ, Matthew 24:4–5.
Man of sin, 2 Thessalonians 2:1–11.
World deceivers, 2 John 7–11.
See Millennium, Second Coming, Tribulation.

ANTICIPATION

Spiritual preparation, future victory, Joshua 3:5.
Preparing to receive promised water, 2 Kings 3:15–17.
"Brace yourself," Job 38:3 (NIV).
Heaven anticipated, Psalm 61:4.
Longing fulfilled, Proverbs 13:12, 19.
Watchmen on walls, Isaiah 62:6.
Anticipating disaster, Ezekiel 30:2–3.
Anticipating much from God, Hosea 12:6 (LB).
Behind devastation, ahead anticipation, Joel 2:3.
Watching in hope, Micah 7:7.
Anticipating the unbelievable, Zechariah 8:6 (LB).
Aged Simeon saw promised Savior, Luke 2:25–32.
Anticipant prayer, John 17:20.
Eager longing, Romans 8:18 (GNB).
Looking forward in trust, Romans 8:24 (LB).
God's preparation for those who love Him, 1 Corinthians 2:9–10.
Anticipated salvation of Jew, Gentile, Galatians 3:6–9.
No turning back, Hebrews 11:13–16, 24–26.
Asking, believing, James 1:5–7.
Eternal inheritance, 1 Peter 1:3–4.
See Aspiration, Expectation, Hope, Horizon.

ANTIPHONAL

Antiphonal chorus, Isaiah 6:3 (LB).
See Music.

ANTIQUITY

Creator predates creation, Psalm 90:1–2.

ANTI-SEMITISM

Persecuted Jews, Nehemiah 1:1–3.
"Decrepit Jews," Nehemiah 4:2 (Berk.).
Plot to destroy Jews, Esther 3:1–6.
Enemies of Israel, Jeremiah 30:16–17.
Mixing human blood with sacrifices, Luke 13:1.
Jews ordered out of Rome, Acts 18:1–2.
See Islam, Israel, Prejudice, Racism.

ANTITHESIS *See Contrast.*

ANXIETY

What ails you? Genesis 21:17 (NKJV).
Insurmountable opposition, Exodus 14:5–14.
Anxiety episode, Deuteronomy 28:66–67.
Rest in divine protection, Deuteronomy 33:12.
Command to courage, Joshua 1:9.
"The Lord calms our fears," Judges 6:24 (CEV).
Counselor of distressed, discontented, 1 Samuel 22:2.
Lifted from deep waters, 2 Samuel 22:17.
Desire for peace, security, 2 Kings 20:19.
Curdled like cheese, Job 10:10.
Terrified by the Lord, Job 23:16.
Internal tension, Job 30:27.
Total trust all circumstances, Psalm 3:1–8.
"Give heed to my sighing," Psalm 5:1 (NRSV).
Wrestling with anxiety, Psalm 13:2, 5.
Ever present Lord, Psalm 14:4–5.
Light overcomes darkness, Psalm 18:28.
"Restful water," Psalm 23:3 (Berk.).
Refuge from destroying storms, Psalm 57:1 (NRSV).
Shaky fence, sagging wall, Psalm 62:3 (CEV).
Day of anxiety, Psalm 86:7 (Berk.).
Heart pierced within, Psalm 109:22 (NRSV).
Distress, anguish, Psalm 116:3 (NRSV).
God knows my anxieties, Psalm 139:23 (NKJV).

Heavyhearted, Proverbs 12:25.
"Make a wreck of me," Isaiah 38:12 (CEV).
Dangerous anxiety, Luke 21:34 (NIV).
Beyond endurance, 2 Corinthians 1:8.
Total trust, 1 Peter 5:7 (AB).

APATHY

Complacent women, Isaiah 32:9.
Those who pass by, Lamentations 1:12.
Heart of flesh, stone, Ezekiel 11:19.
Refusing to see, hear, Ezekiel 12:1–2.
Zion's complacency, Amos 6:1.
Neither seek nor ask, Zephaniah 1:6.
Carefree people, Zephaniah 2:15.
Hearts like flint, Zechariah 7:11–12.
Rejected invitation, Matthew 22:1–14.
Caring neither for God or man, Luke 18:1–5.
See Backsliding, Carnality, Unconcerned, Worldliness.

APHORISM

Origin of saying, 1 Samuel 10:11–12.
Deeds reveal person, 1 Samuel 24:13.
Lily among thorns, Song of Solomon 2:2.
"Freedom," play on words, Jeremiah 34:17.
See Figure of Speech.

APOCRYPHA

New Testament apocrypha, 1 Timothy 1:3 (LB).

APOLOGETICS

Challenge to prove divinity, John 10:22–39.
Prove all things, 1 Thessalonians 5:21.
See Doctrine, Theology.

APOSTASY

Apostasy examples, Exodus 32:1; Deuteronomy 13:12–13; Judges 2:17; Nehemiah 9:26; Ezekiel 36:20; Acts 7:39; 2 Timothy 4:10; Hebrews 6:6; 1 John 2:19.
No God, no priest, no law, 2 Chronicles 15:3.
National resistance to law, Psalm 2:1–3.
Increasing apostasy, Isaiah 1:5 (Berk.).
Truth that perished, Jeremiah 7:28.
Shepherds lose senses, Jeremiah 10:21 (LB).
Ministration of evil prophets, Jeremiah 23:10–14.

Apostate Israel, Hosea 1:9–10 (LB).
Fruit identifies trees, Matthew 12:33–35.
Weeds in wheat, Matthew 13:24–30.
Rejected faith, Matthew 24:10.
Resurrection teaching opposed, Acts 4:1–4.
Resorting to history as defense, Acts 7:1–60.
Senseless human arguments, Colossians 2:8 (CEV).
Holding onto faith, 1 Timothy 1:19; Hebrews 3:12; 2 Peter 3:17.
Warnings against apostasy, 2 Timothy 4:4; Hebrews 3:12; 2 Peter 3:17.
Believers' desertion, 2 Timothy 1:15.
Turning away from God, Hebrews 3:12.
Unpardonable sin, Hebrews 6:4–6.
Those who go away, 1 John 2:18–19.
Blessing without belief, Jude 5.
Pretense of spiritually dead church, Revelation 3:1.
See Liberalism, Modernism, Syncretism, Unbelief.

APOSTLE

Names of twelve apostles, Matthew 10:2–4.
Apostles selected from disciples, Luke 6:13.
Special messenger, 1 Corinthians 1:1 (AB).

APOTHECARY *See Pharmacy.*

APPARENT *See Visibility.*

APPEARANCE

Handsome physique, Genesis 39:6–7.
Angel's description, Judges 13:6.
Outward appearance, 1 Samuel 16:7; 2 Corinthians 5:12.
Boy's appearance, 1 Samuel 16:12.
Neglecting personal appearance, 2 Samuel 19:24.
Happy heart, cheerful face, Proverbs 15:13.
Dress up, look your best, Ecclesiastes 9:8 (CEV).
Prophetic description of Jesus, Isaiah 53:2.
Varied facial appearance, Ezekiel 1:10.
No wash, shave, combed hair, Daniel 10:3 (LB).
Comb hair, wash face, Matthew 6:17 (CEV).
Whitewashed tombs, Matthew 23:27; John 7:24.
See Countenance.

APPEASE

Grumbling people, Exodus 16:2–18.
Sacrifice for sin, Micah 6:7.
Refusing to appease, Galatians 1:9–10.
See Satisfaction.

APPETITE

Human, animal vegetarians, Genesis 1:29–30; 2:16.
Angels with appetites, Genesis 19:1–3.
Taste for game, Genesis 25:27–28.
Esau's foolish hunger, Genesis 25:29–34.
Craving for meat, Numbers 11:4–5.
Hungry as lion, Numbers 23:24.
Physical, spiritual appetites, Deuteronomy 8:10–14.
Food as lust, Deuteronomy 12:15, 20 (KJV).
Appetite loss, 1 Samuel 1:7; 20:34; 28:23; Psalm 102:4; 107:18; Job 3:24.
Sufficient food, no complaint, Job 6:5.
Sorrow numbs appetite, Psalms 42:3; 102:9.
Sin causes appetite loss, Psalm 107:17–18.
Disciplined appetite, Proverbs 23:2.
Excessive food, drink, Proverbs 23:20.
Lazy man's appetite, Proverbs 26:15.
Bitter tastes sweet, Proverbs 27:7.
Unappeased appetites, Ecclesiastes 6:7; Isaiah 9:20.
Dream of food, Isaiah 29:8.
Hungry dogs, Isaiah 56:11.
King's lost appetite, Daniel 6:18.
Appetite for righteousness, Matthew 5:6.
Four thousand hungry people, Mark 8:1–9.
Too much concern for food, Luke 12:22, 29.
Hunger-induced trance, Acts 10:10.
Tension numbed appetite, Acts 27:33–36.
Appetite for lust, Ephesians 4:19.
Spiritual milk desired, 1 Peter 2:2–3.
Sweet mouth, sour stomach, Revelation 10:9–10.
See Cooking, Famine, Food, Gourmet, Hunger.

APPETIZING See Gourmet.

APPLAUSE

Long live the King! 2 Kings 11:12.
Scornful applause, Job 34:37; Lamentations 2:15.

Nature applauds, Psalm 98:8; Isaiah 55:12.
Rejoicing in malice, Ezekiel 25:6–7 (See LB).
Nineveh fate applauded, Nahum 3:19.
See Accolade, Praise.

APPLICATION

"How to use wisdom," Psalm 105:22 (CEV).

APPOINTMENT

Job qualification, Genesis 41:37–40.
Night emergency, Exodus 12:31–32.
Commission with encouragement, Deuteronomy 3:28.
Appointment with death, Deuteronomy 32:48–50.
Excuse for avoiding appointment, Nehemiah 6:1–3 (CEV).
Request to see king, Daniel 2:16.
Chosen to build temple, Zechariah 6:9–15.
Appointment requested, Acts 20:17 (GNB, LB).
Christ's appointment, Hebrews 5:5.
See Position.

APPRAISAL

Counting the cost, Luke 14:28–30.
"Spiritually appraised," 1 Corinthians 2:14 (NASB).
Honest personal appraisal, James 1:22–24.
See Assessment, Evaluation, Survey.

APPRECIATION

Forgotten favor, Genesis 40:14, 23.
Unappreciated donkey, Numbers 22:21–30.
Mutual appreciation, Ruth 2:8–13.
Grateful foreigner, Ruth 2:10.
Vicarious appreciation, 2 Samuel 9:1; 10:2.
Showing no appreciation, Psalm 78:9–18.
National appreciation lacking, Psalm 106:1–43.
Gratitude for great forgiveness, Luke 7:39–50.
No thanks for service rendered, Luke 17:7–10.
Ten healed of leprosy, Luke 17:12–18.
Appreciate clergy, teachers, 1 Thessalonians 5:12–13 (CEV).
See Gratitude, Thanksgiving.

APPREHENSION

Anxious thoughts, Psalm 139:23.
Unnecessary fear, 1 Kings 1:50–53.
Fearing responsibility, 1 Chronicles 13:12.
No fear of bad news, Psalm 112:7.
Unnecessary fears, Isaiah 8:12–14.
Needless worry, Matthew 6:25–27.
Holy fear as motivation, Hebrews 11:7.
Reverent fear, 1 Peter 1:17.
See Fear, Indecision, Uncertainty.

APPRENTICE

Joshua under Moses, Exodus 17:10; Numbers 27:18–23.
Moses given perfume formula, Exodus 30:22–25.
Divinely acquired skills, Exodus 31:1–5.
Father assists son, 1 Chronicles 22:5; 29:1.
Paul discipling Timothy, 2 Timothy 2:1–2.
See Novice, Skill, Teaching.

APPROPRIATE

Role in Kingdom, Esther 4:14.
Proper time, procedure, Ecclesiastes 8:5–6.
Doing what she could, Mark 14:8.
See Tact, Timing.

APPROVAL

People responded with one voice, Exodus 24:3.
Sandal removed, Ruth 4:7.
Authorized travel, Nehemiah 2:1–8.
Approved by strong people, Isaiah 25:3.
"The Lord's approval," Lamentations 3:37 (CEV).
God's approval of His Son, Matthew 3:17.
Pharisees' empty sincerity, Mark 12:15–17.
Approved by God, 1 Corinthians 4:5.
Approval of men or God? Galatians 1:10.
Paul's approval of followers, Colossians 4:7–17.
Approval by faith, Hebrews 11:2 (NASB, NRSV).

APPROXIMATE

"Around the middle of March," Ezekiel 29:17 (LB).

APTITUDE

God requires, provides, Isaiah 2:3.
Victory more than ability, Isaiah 25:11.
Candidates chosen for government service, Daniel 1:3–5.
See Ability, Intelligence, Skill, Talent.

AQUATIC

Water plants, Job 8:11–12.

ARAB

"Wild donkey of a man," Genesis 16:12 (NIV).
Arab nation almost lost, Genesis 21:14–20.
Ishmael's skill with weapons, Genesis 21:20 (NRSV).
Jewish domination, Genesis 24:60.
Ishmael's descendants, Genesis 25:13–16.
Arab ancestors took Joseph to Egypt, Genesis 37:24–28.
Arabian merchants, 2 Chronicles 9:14.
Generous Arabs, 2 Chronicles 17:11.
Arabs opposing God, 2 Chronicles 26:7; Nehemiah 2:19; 4:7.
Jeremiah's adversary, Nehemiah 2:19.
Arab enemies, Nehemiah 6:1.
Desert tribes, Psalm 72:9–10.
Desert nomad, Jeremiah 3:2 (GNB).
Israel, Egypt, Ezekiel 29:16 (LB).
Sins of Damascus, Amos 1:3.
Arab converts, Acts 2:11.
See Islam, Jihad.

ARBITRATION

Property dispute, Genesis 26:19–22.
Divine surveillance, Genesis 31:48–50.
Mediation between two mothers, 1 Kings 3:16–28.
Wishing for arbitration, Job 9:33.
Call for arbitration, Isaiah 5:3 (Berk.).
Deliverance beyond mortal strength, Romans 7:15–25.
See Negotiations.

ARBOR

Abraham's tree planting, Genesis 21:33.
Choosing king from among trees, Judges 9:7–20.
See Trees.

ARCHANGEL

Voice of resurrection, 1 Thessalonians 4:16.
Archangel versus Satan, Jude 9.
See Angels.

ARCHAEOLOGY

Ruins rebuilt, Isaiah 58:12; 61:4.

ARCHERY

Boy archer, Genesis 21:20.
Death of Saul, 1 Samuel 31:3 (KJV).
Lamenting the bow, 2 Samuel 1:17–18.
Sibling archers, 1 Chronicles 8:40.
King's assassination, 2 Chronicles 35:23.
"Words like deadly arrows," Psalm 64:3 (NIV).
Divine marksman, Psalm 64:7.
"Arrow that flies by day," Psalm 91:5.
Warrior's prowess, Psalm 127:4.
"Sharp arrow," Proverbs 25:18.
"Wounds at random," Proverbs 26:10 (NIV).
"Deadly arrows," Proverbs 26:18.
"Flaming arrows," Ephesians 6:16 (NRSV).
See Accuracy, Athletics.

ARCHITECTURE

Creation's dome, Genesis 1:7–8 (GNB).
Tower of Babel, Genesis 11:1–6.
Curse on rebuilding, Joshua 6:26.
Altar site, 2 Samuel 24:18–25.
Solomon's temple procedures, 1 Kings 5:12–18.
Longer time constructing palace than temple, 1 Kings 6:37–38; 7:1.
Temple plans, 1 Chronicles 22:5; 28:11–21.
Huge, beautiful, 2 Chronicles 2:9 (LB).
Cities, castles, towers, 2 Chronicles 27:4 (KJV).
Rebuilding Jerusalem wall, Nehemiah 6:1.
Master builder, Psalm 127:1.
New temple measurements, Ezekiel 40:5–49.
Future temple, Haggai 2:9.
Impressive structure not permanent, Mark 13:1–2.
Complimented architect, Hebrews 3:3 (LB).
Divine architect, Hebrews 11:10.
Builder honored more than building, Hebrews 3:3.
See Building, Carpenter, Construction, Design, Plan, Ruins.

AREA

Chosen area, Genesis 13:10–13.
Jerusalem's width, length, Zechariah 2:1–2.
See Length.

ARGUMENT

Strife among brothers, 2 Samuel 2:27–28.
Argument with God, Job 3:2–3.
Always last word, Job 16:3.
Tactful approach, Job 16:4, 6.
Winning argument, Job 32:1.
Make tumult, Psalm 2:1 (Berk.).
Cause made valid, Psalm 37:6.
Gentle words subdue anger, Proverbs 15:1.
Good counsel against argument, Proverbs 17:14.
Loving quarrels, Proverbs 17:19.
Silence elevates fool, Proverbs 17:28.
Avoiding strife brings honor, Proverbs 20:3.
Evidence turns against accuser, Proverbs 25:8.
Gentle tongue, Proverbs 25:15.
Meddling in quarrel, Proverbs 26:17.
"Present your case," Isaiah 41:21 (Berk.).
Disputing mercy, justice, Ezekiel 33:10–20.
Wisdom, tact, Daniel 2:14.
Agree with adversary, Matthew 5:25 (KJV).
Entangling words, Matthew 22:15 (Berk.).
Daring to dispute God, Romans 9:20.
Avoid dispute, Romans 14:1.
"You keep arguing," 1 Corinthians 1:11 (CEV).
Trivial disagreements, 1 Corinthians 6:2.
Paul's logic, Galatians 2:14–17.
Promoting controversies, 1 Timothy 1:3–4.
Vain argument, 1 Timothy 1:6 (AB).
Petty controversy, 2 Timothy 2:14 (AB).
Terminology, 2 Timothy 2:14, 23.
"Morbid craving for controversy," 1 Timothy 6:4 (NRSV).
"Stupid, senseless arguments," 2 Timothy 2:23 (CEV).
Gentleness in disputes, 2 Timothy 2:23–26.
Heads up all situations, 2 Timothy 4:5.
Useless topics, Titus 3:9.
See Debate, Quarrel.

ARID

Iron skies, bronze soil, Leviticus 26:18–20.
Land produces sparingly, Isaiah 5:10.
Water provided, Isaiah 41:17–19 (CEV).
Desert journey, Jeremiah 2:2.
Rain withheld, Amos 4:7–8.
Dry topsoil, Mark 4:5–6.
See Desert, Drought, Weather.

ARISE

"Up, follow," Genesis 44:4 (KJV).

ARK

Ark called boat, Genesis 6:14 (CEV).
Measurement in feet, Genesis 6:14–15 (LB).
Interior description, Genesis 6:14 (AB).

ARM

Powerful divine arm, Exodus 6:6.
Everlasting arms, Deuteronomy 33:27 (CEV).
An arm like God's, Job 40:9.
Holy arm, Psalm 98:1 (CEV).
Revealed arm, Isaiah 53:1.
Symbolic broken arm, Ezekiel 30:21–22.

ARMAGEDDON

Fate of world governments, Psalm 2:7–9.
Coming decisive battle, Daniel 11:36–45.
Judgment Valley, Decision Valley, Joel 3:12–14 (CEV).
See Antichrist, Rapture, Second Coming.

ARMAMENT

Iron chariots, Judges 1:19; 4:3.
Futility of war, 2 Samuel 1:27.
Primitive artillery, 2 Chronicles 26:15.
The Lord's armament, Psalm 35:2.
See Army, Military, Pacifism, Soldier, War, Weapons.

ARMY

Conscription age, Numbers 26:2–4.
Army strategy, Joshua 8:6–7.
Army at full strength, Judges 9:29; Ezekiel 37:10.
Army of chosen men, 2 Samuel 6:1.
Nations' armies face divine wrath, Isaiah 34:2.
Warrior with hands tied, Jeremiah 14:9 (CEV).
Vast army, Revelation 9:16.
See Armament, Cavalry, Disarmed, Draft Dodgers, Mercenaries, Military, Soldiers.

AROMA

Anointing oil formula, Exodus 30:22–25.
Altar incense, Leviticus 4:7.
Aroma pleasant to the Lord, Numbers 15:14.
Aromatic bed, 2 Chronicles 16:14.
Rejected aroma of feasts, Amos 5:21 (KJV).

Stench, fragrance, 2 Corinthians 2:16.
Fragrant stewardship, Philippians 4:18.
See Fragrance, Stench.

AROUSED

Aroused by faith, Hebrews 11:24 (AB).

ARREST

Sabbath breaking arrest, Numbers 15:32–34.
City of refuge, Numbers 35:6–15.
Apprehended by speech manner, Judges 12:5–6.
Imprisoned for tax evasion, 2 Kings 17:4.
House arrest, Jeremiah 37:15; Ezekiel 3:24–25 (LB); Acts 28:16.
Refusal to arrest Jesus, John 7:45–46 (LB).
House entry, Acts 8:3.
Posting bond, Acts 17:9.
Angel to arrest, chain Satan, Revelation 20:1–3.
See Indictment, Jail, Prison.

ARROGANCE

Arrogant gods, Exodus 18:11.
Arrogant before the Lord, 1 Samuel 2:3.
Presumed ease facing enemy, Deuteronomy 1:41–45.
Flattering lips, boastful tongue, Psalm 12:3–4.
Strutting arrogance, Psalm 12:8.
Presuming God does not hear, Psalm 59:7–8.
Arrogance brought low, Isaiah 2:17–18.
Haughty, ruthless, Isaiah 13:11.
Arrogance, insolence, Isaiah 16:6 (Berk.).
Those who do not blush, Jeremiah 6:15.
Boast only about the Lord, Jeremiah 9:23–24.
Pride, arrogance, Jeremiah 48:29.
Arrogant affluence, Ezekiel 16:49.
Israel's arrogance, Hosea 5:5.
Proud, arrogant strut, Zephaniah 3:11 (CEV).
Ironical evaluation of weak Christians, 1 Corinthians 4:8–18.
Evil queen refuses to admit sin, Revelation 18:7–8.
See Pride, Rebellion, Self-image, Vanity.

ARROWS

Signal arrows, 1 Samuel 20:20.
Victory arrow, 2 Kings 13:15–19.
"Arrows of lightning," 2 Samuel 22:15 (LB);
 Psalm 18:14 (LB).
Flaming arrows, Psalm 7:13.
Divine arrows, Psalms 18:14; 45:5; 77:17;
 144:6.
See Archery.

ARSON

Method for burning fields, Judges 14:4–5.
See Fire.

ART

Celestial artistry, Psalm 19:1.
Artwork destroyed, Psalm 74:6.
Engraved hearts, altars, Jeremiah 17:1.
Jerusalem sketch, Ezekiel 4:1.
Wall murals, Ezekiel 8:7–12; 23:14.
See Artist, Sculptor, Talent.

ARTESIAN

Water without rain, 2 Kings 3:16–17.
Water pouring from well, Jeremiah 6:7.
See Water.

ARTHRITIS

Searing pain, Psalm 38:7.
Dry bones, Proverbs 17:22.

ARTIFICIAL

Cheap glaze, Proverbs 26:23 (GNB).
Ego displayed by teachers of law, Mark
 12:38–40.
False humility, Colossians 2:18.
See Insincerity, Sham.

ARTIST

Separating light, darkness, Genesis 1:4, 17–
 18.
Talents provided by Holy Spirit, Exodus
 31:1–5.
Chisel at work, Deuteronomy 10:1.
Man of skill, Proverbs 22:29.
Idols fashioned from firewood, Isaiah
 44:15–17.
Temple decor, Ezekiel 41:17–20.
See Art, Skill, Talent.

ASCENSION

Elijah, whirlwind, 2 Kings 2:11.
Christ's ascension foretold, Psalm 68:18.
Ascension event, Mark 16:19; Acts 1:9.
Ascension impact, Hebrews 4:14; 9:24;
 1 Peter 3:22.
See Flight, Height, Upward.

ASCETICISM

Ascetic diet, Matthew 3:4.
Negative asceticism, Colossians 2:22–23;
 1 Timothy 4:1–5.
Practice of celibacy, 1 Corinthians 7:7–9;
 Revelation 14:4.
See Abstinence.

ASHAMED

Ashamed to mention Lord's name, Amos
 6:10.
Hiding light, Matthew 5:15.
Judas' guilt, Matthew 27:3.
Ashamed to identify, Luke 22:53–62.
See Humiliation, Repentance.

ASININE *See Stupidity.*

ASKING

Invitation to ask, 1 Kings 3:5.
Asking for spring rains, Zechariah 10:1.
Ask, seek, knock, Matthew 7:8; Luke 11:9.
Asking in faith, Matthew 21:22.
Assured answers, John 14:13–14; 15:7.
Asking for wisdom, James 1:5.
Confident asking, 1 John 5:14.
See Faith, Intercession, Prayer.

ASPHALT

Babel building material, Genesis 11:3 (NKJV).
Perilous asphalt pits, Genesis 14:10 (NKJV).

ASPIRATION

Aspiring spiritual perfection, Psalm
 119:1–5.
Aspiring to be greatest in kingdom, Luke
 9:46–48.
See Ambition, Determination, Vision.

ASSASSINATION

Murder for pay, Deuteronomy 27:25.
Death of king, Judges 3:21.

Death of King Saul's killer, 2 Samuel 1:1–16.

Brother avenged, 2 Samuel 3:27.

Recruited to turn against king, 2 Kings 9:14–24.

King destroyed by associates, 2 Kings 12:19–20.

Slain at temple worship, 2 Kings 19:37.

Assassinated governor, Jeremiah 41:2.

See Murder.

ASSEMBLY *See Congregation, Worship, Rally.*

ASSERTIVE

Conditions for answered prayer, Exodus 32:31–32.

Approach to God, Psalm 51:1–7.

Repetitious prayer, Luke 11:5–13.

See Greed, Selfishness.

ASSESSMENT

Presumed ease of facing enemy, Deuteronomy 1:41–42.

Sunbelt's ridicule, Nehemiah 4:1–10.

Character assessment, Job 6:29–30 (GNB).

Varied assessments, 2 Corinthians 6:8–10.

Believer's resources, Ephesians 1:18–23.

Good land, unproductive land, Hebrews 6:7–8.

See Evaluation, Inventory.

ASSETS

Creditor takes all, Psalm 109:11.

Lavish assets, no assets, Mark 8:36.

ASSIGNMENT

King's business, 1 Samuel 21:2 (NKJV).

Assignment for everyone, Nehemiah 3:1–32.

Trustworthy messenger, Proverbs 25:13.

Chosen to build temple, Zechariah 6:9–15.

Extended ministry, Acts 18:11.

ASSISTANCE

Neighborly assistance, Ezra 1:6.

God's presence in trouble, Psalm 14:4–5.

Forsaken Savior, Psalm 22:1.

Worthless help, Psalm 108:12.

Holy Spirit's assistance, John 14:26 (NASB, NKJV, CEV).

See Teamwork.

ASSISTANT

Those in authority, those assisting, Numbers 18:1–7 (LB).

God's assistants, 2 Corinthians 6:4 (Berk.).

Church helpers, 1 Timothy 3:8–13 (GNB).

Ministry assistant, 2 Timothy 1:16–18.

See Companionship, Servant.

ASSOCIATION

Rejected son's bad companions, Judges 11:1–3.

Satan's association with angels, Job 1:6; 2:1.

Separated from evil, Psalm 1:2.

Worthless people, Psalm 26:4 (GNB, NRSV).

Good and bad association, Proverbs 15:20.

Two in agreement, Amos 3:3.

Guilt by association, Matthew 9:9–13.

Jesus calling associates, Mark 3:13.

United to follow Jesus, Luke 8:1–3.

Bad company, good character, 1 Corinthians 15:33 (NASB).

Believers, unbelievers, 2 Corinthians 6:14.

Avoid sharing others' sins, 1 Timothy 5:22.

See Assistant, Camaraderie, Cooperation, Fellowship, Teamwork.

ASSURANCE

Promise to Abram, Genesis 12:2–3; 15:1; 17:1.

Entering Egypt reassured, Genesis 46:1–4.

God's nearness, Deuteronomy 4:7.

Righteous assurance, Joshua 22:31.

Assurance of good, evil, Joshua 23:15.

"Covenant love," Psalm 21:7 (Berk.).

Refuge, strength, Psalm 46:1–3.

"God is for me!" Psalm 56:9.

Confidence in God, not men, Isaiah 36:4–10.

No fear of danger, Isaiah 43:1–2.

Desert passage, Isaiah 43:19.

End assured from beginning, Isaiah 46:10–11.

God knows best, Isaiah 48:17–18.

Walking in dark, Isaiah 50:10.

Heaven, earth temporal, salvation eternal, Isaiah 51:6.

God fulfills promises, Jeremiah 29:10–11.

Nothing too hard for God, Jeremiah 32:27.

Daily love, faithfulness, Lamentations 3:22–24.

Assurance in fiery furnace, Daniel 3:16–17.

God's presence assured, Haggai 1:13.

Believe the Gospel, Mark 1:14–15.

Help assured, John 6:37.

Twofold assurance, John 13:20; 14:12 (Berk.).

Ever present Lord, Acts 2:25–28.

Assured protection, Acts 18:9–11.

Certain of erroneous belief, Acts 19:35–36.

Standing at end struggle, Ephesians 6:13.

Work begun, completed, Philippians 1:6.

Standing firm, Philippians 1:27–30.

Need fulfilled, Colossians 1:15–23.

Full comprehension, Colossians 2:2.

In-depth conviction, 1 Thessalonians 1:5.

Eternal encouragement, 2 Thessalonians 2:16–17.

Absolute confidence, 2 Timothy 1:12.

Faithful Lord, 2 Timothy 2:13.

Coming to High Priest with confidence, Hebrews 4:14–16.

God cannot lie, Hebrews 6:18–20.

Eternal guarantee, Hebrews 7:22.

Full assurance, Hebrews 10:9–23.

Perfect Savior, perfect salvation, Hebrews 10:11–14.

Certain faith, Hebrews 11:1 (NASB, NRSV).

Obedience toward unknown objective, Hebrews 11:8.

Assurance of promises fulfilled, Hebrews 11:13.

Internal assurance, 1 John 3:24.

Shielded from evil, 1 John 5:18.

The God who keeps, provides, Jude 24–25.

See Confidence.

ASTOUNDED *See Awe, Amazement, Serendipity, Surprise.*

ASTRAL PROJECTION

Transported by the Spirit, Ezekiel 8:3; Acts 8:39.

Instantaneous boat passage, John 6:21.

Visit to third heaven, 1 Corinthians 12:2–4.

ASTROLOGY

Sun, moon, stars not worshiped, Deuteronomy 4:19; 17:2–3.

Warning against false predictions, Deuteronomy 18:10–12; Jeremiah 27:9.

Worship of stars, 2 Kings 21:3, 5; Zephaniah 1:5.

Zodiac constellations designed by God, Job 9:9.

Homage to sun, moon, Job 31:26–28.

"Laws of the heavens," Job 38:33 (NIV).

Astrology decried, described, Isaiah 47:10–15 (GNB, NRSV).

Exhumed star-worshipers' bones, Jeremiah 8:1–2.

Signs in the sky, Jeremiah 10:2 (See LB).

Silent stars, Daniel 2:1–4; 4:7; 5:7–9.

Wise astrologers, Matthew 2:1 (LB).

"Spirits of the universe," Colossians 2:8 (NRSV).

See Constellations, Cult.

ASTRONAUT

Elijah and whirlwind, 2 Kings 2:11.

Exploring sky, sea, Psalm 107:23–26.

Skyward ascent, Amos 9:2.

Nest among stars, Obadiah 4.

See Aircraft, Flight, Space.

ASTRONOMY

Creation of sky, Genesis 1:8, 14–17.

Sun, moon preside, Genesis 1:16–18 (LB).

Creation's vastness, Genesis 2:1.

Bethlehem star, Numbers 24:17; Matthew 2:1–8.

Sun, moon, stars not worshiped, Deuteronomy 4:19.

Strength of rising sun, Judges 5:31.

Lord of heavens, 1 Samuel 1:3 (LB).

Celestial and earthly temples, 1 Kings 8:12–13 (GNB).

Dark stars, Job 3:9.

Sealed star light, Job 9:7.

Southern Cross area, Job 9:9 (GNB, NIV).

Moon clouds, Job 26:9 (CEV).

Invisible sun, Job 37:21.

Creation's scope, Job 38:4–13, 31–33.

Great heavens, small man, Psalm 8:1–4 (LB).

Sky proclaims God's glory, Psalm 19:1–6.

Created heavens, Psalm 33:6.

Sun rising, setting, Psalm 50:1.

Greatness in sky, Psalm 57:11 (GNB).

Ancient skies, Psalm 68:32–33.

Ageless sun, moon, Psalm 72:5, 17.

Day, night, sun, moon, Psalm 74:16–18, 22 (NRSV).

New Moon, Psalm 81:3.

Stars give praise, Psalm 89:5 (GNB).

Enduring sun, moon, Psalm 89:36–37.

Moon designates seasons, Psalm 104:19.

Space cannot contain God's love, Psalm 108:4–5.

Work of creation, Psalm 136:5–9.

Stars numbered, named, Psalm 147:4; Isaiah 40:26.

Earth, sky show God's wisdom, Proverbs 3:19–20.

Wisdom preceded creation, Proverbs 8:24–31.

Sun, moon, stars darkened, Isaiah 13:10.

Disgraced moon, shamed sun, Isaiah 24:23 (NKJV).

Bright moon, brighter sun, Isaiah 30:26.

Sky, stars removed, Isaiah 34:4.

Sun's shadow reversed, Isaiah 38:7–8.

Heavens, hand of God, Isaiah 40:12.

Creator's care for creation, Isaiah 42:5–7 (CEV).

Creator of stars, Isaiah 45:12 (CEV).

Sun, moon not needed, Isaiah 60:19.

God of all nature, Jeremiah 31:35.

Space depth, breadth, Jeremiah 31:37.

Wise men, Matthew 2:1–2 (GNB).

Failed sunlight, Luke 23:45 (NRSV).

Variety among stars, 1 Corinthians 15:41.

Christ the Creator, Colossians 1:15–17.

Morning star as gift, Revelation 2:28.

Falling stars, Revelation 6:13; 9:1.

Star named wormwood, Revelation 8:11 (CEV).

Celestial garments, Revelation 12:1, 4.

Hailstones from sky, Revelation 16:21.

Flight of earth, sky, Revelation 20:11.

No sun, moon, Revelation 21:23–24.

Bright morning star, Revelation 22:16.

See Heaven, Morning Star, Sky, Space, Space/ Time, Star, Sun.

ASTUTE

Proper time, procedure, Ecclesiastes 8:5–6.

Wisdom of Gamaliel, Acts 5:30–40.

Eyes of heart, Ephesians 1:18–19.

Discerning good, evil, Hebrews 5:11–14.

See Tact, Wisdom.

ASYLUM

No hiding place, Leviticus 26:25.

Cities of refuge, Numbers 35:6; Deuteronomy 4:41–43; 19:1–14; Joshua 20:1–9; 1 Chronicles 6:67.

Rahab's shelter, Joshua 2:17–21.

David's retreat from Saul, 1 Samuel 27:1–12.

See Hiding Place, Protection.

ATHEISM

No God in Israel, 2 Kings 1:3.

Atheistic defiance, 2 Kings 18:17–25.

No God, no priest, no law, 2 Chronicles 15:3.

No room for God, Psalm 10:4 (LB, "God is dead").

Fool's voice, Psalms 14:1 (See LB, AB); 53:1.

Universal God consciousness, Ecclesiastes 3:11.

Living under other lords, Isaiah 26:13.

Judgment makes God known, Ezekiel 11:7–12.

Doubt augmented by truth, John 8:45–47.

Atheistic denial, 1 John 2:22.

See Agnostic, Irreligious, Skepticism, Unbelief.

ATHLETICS

Ishmael, the archer, Genesis 21:20.

Wrestling with God, Genesis 32:22–30.

Athletic physique, Genesis 39:6–7.

"Able-bodied men," Deuteronomy 3:18 (NIV).

Tall, strong, Deuteronomy 9:2.

Dehydration, Judges 15:17–19.

Hairbreadth accuracy, Judges 20:16.

A head taller, 1 Samuel 9:2.

Stature of King Saul, 1 Samuel 10:23–24.

Mighty, brave men, 1 Samuel 14:52.

Limited stamina, 1 Samuel 30:9–10.

Strength, agility from God, 2 Samuel 22:33–37.

Feet like deer, 2 Samuel 22:34.

Bend bronze bow, 2 Samuel 22:35.

Ambidextrous agility, 1 Chronicles 12:1–2 (LB).

Swift runner, Job 9:25.

Vigorous stride shortened, Job 18:7 (CEV).

God as pugilist, Psalm 3:7.

Wood-chopping fame, Psalm 74:5 (KJV).

Strong as bull, Psalm 92:10.

Physical strength of limited value, Psalm 147:10–11.

Swimming breast stroke, Isaiah 25:11.

Feet barely touch ground, Isaiah 41:3 (CEV).

Men against horses, Jeremiah 12:5.

Strong oarsmen, Ezekiel 27:26.

Crooked bow misses target, Hosea 7:16 (LB).

Defeated archer, Amos 2:15.

Disciple's foot race, John 20:4.

Runner, prize, 1 Corinthians 9:24–27.

Avoid aimless effort, 1 Corinthians 9:26.

Hindrance to good race, Galatians 5:7.

Physical training, godliness, 1 Timothy 4:7–8 (AB).

Playing according to rules, 2 Timothy 2:5.

Finishing race, 2 Timothy 4:7.

Running with perseverance, Hebrews 12:1–2.

See Boxing, Competition, Physical, Referee, Running, Sportsman, Sprinter.

ATONEMENT

Substitutionary sacrifice, Genesis 22:1–13.

Animal typology, Leviticus 4:15–21.

Payment for sin, Isaiah 40:1–2.

Sin Bearer, Isaiah 53:4–12.

Cleansing fountain, Zechariah 13:1.

Atoning blood, Matthew 26:28.

Not understanding atonement, Mark 9:30–32.

Mixed blood, Luke 13:1.

Lamb of God, John 1:29.

Redeemer's death, resurrection, Acts 17:2–3; 1 Corinthians 15:3–5.

Divine propitiation, Romans 3:24–26.

Justifying redemption, Romans 5:1–12.

Redemption details, Ephesians 2:1–18.

Christ's blood—power, meaning, Hebrews 7:23–28.

Our heavenly advocate, 1 John 2:1–2.

See Cross, Redeemer.

ATROCITY See Carnage, Violence.

ATTACK

Ready for enemy, Nehemiah 4:16–18.

Neighborhood watch, Proverbs 27:10.

Dangerous roads, Jeremiah 6:25.

See Adversary, Enemy, Opposition.

ATTAINMENT

No success outside God's will, Numbers 14:41–45.

Attainment assured, Numbers 21:34.

Son seeks to impress father, 1 Samuel 14:1–14.

Humble man's ambition, Proverbs 30:7–8.

Completion better than beginning, Ecclesiastes 7:8 (CEV).

Riches gained unjustly, Jeremiah 17:11.

Authority over demons, Luke 10:17–20.

More than conquerors, Romans 8:28–39.

Good purpose fulfilled, 2 Thessalonians 1:11.

See Ambition, Goal.

ATTENDANCE

Fearing worship attendance, Numbers 17:12–13.

Vast assembly, 1 Kings 8:65.

Multitudes at worship, Psalm 42:4.

Constant attendance, Luke 2:36–37; 24:53.

Customary Sabbath observance, Luke 4:16.

Large crowd, Luke 8:19–21.

ATTENTION

"Be quiet," 1 Samuel 15:16 (NKJV).

"Take note!" Job 1:12 (Berk.).

"Pay attention," Job 20:2 (NRSV).

"Be smart, listen," Job 34:16 (CEV).

"Observe!" Job 36:22 (Berk.).

"Open ear," Psalm 40:6 (NRSV).

"No one paid attention," Proverbs 1:24 (NASB).

"Be attentive," Proverbs 4:20 (NRSV).

Failing to listen, Proverbs 18:13.

Listen up, Isaiah 28:14.

Be silent, listen, Isaiah 41:1 (CEV).

Close attention, Ezekiel 40:4.

Careful listening, Luke 8:18.

Getting rebel's attention, Acts 9:1–5.

See Heed, Preaching, Response, Students, Teaching.

ATTESTATION

Self witness, Joshua 24:22.

Names wisely used, Colossians 4:7–17.

Message verifies itself, 1 Thessalonians 1:8–10.

Trustworthy saying, 1 Timothy 4:9–10.

Signs, wonders, miracles, Hebrews 2:4.

See Witness.

ATTITUDE

Negative attitude, Genesis 4:3–7.

Good attitude displayed, Genesis 13:8–9.

Humble submission, Genesis 16:9 (AB).

Positive worship attitude, Leviticus 22:29.

Contagious bad attitude, Deuteronomy 20:8 (LB).

Bitter attitude toward life, Ruth 1:20–21.

Servant attitude, Ruth 2:13.

Food, drink, good spirits, Ruth 3:7.

Open to rebuke, 2 Samuel 16:5–12.

Childlike attitude, 1 Kings 3:7.

Boastful attitude, 1 Kings 12:13–14.

Pagan king's altered attitude, Ezra 1:1–4, 7–8; 5:8—6:12; 7:13–26.

Leadership attitude, Nehemiah 5:14–18.

Optimistic attitude toward trouble, Job 1:21–22.

Willing to listen, Job 6:24 (GNB).

Joyful spirit from the Lord, Job 8:21.

Prosperous men's attitude toward poor, Job 12:5 (Berk.).

"Faultfinder," Job 40:2 (Berk.).

Debilitating sorrow, Psalm 31:10.

"Cheer up!" Psalm 31:24 (LB).

Without guile, Psalm 32:2 (KJV).

New, right spirit, Psalm 51:10 (RSV).

Serve with gladness, Psalm 100:1–2.

Rejoicing attitude, Psalm 118:24.

Positive attitude toward problems, Psalm 119:71; Proverbs 14:10.

Restricted attitude, Psalm 137:4.

God's attitude to proud, humble, Psalm 138:6.

Happy heart, cheerful face, Proverbs 15:13, 30; 17:22.

Gloomy, cheerful, Proverbs 15:15 (LB).

Pride brings destruction, Proverbs 16:18.

Will to live, Proverbs 18:14.

Hot temper, Proverbs 19:19.

Enjoying another's failure, Proverbs 24:17–18.

Hatred of life, Ecclesiastes 2:17.

Sorrow sublimates laughter, Ecclesiastes 7:3–4.

Patience versus pride, Ecclesiastes 7:8.

Positive lifestyle, Ecclesiastes 8:15.

Attitude control over anxiety, Ecclesiastes 11:10.

Evaluating desolate circumstances, Jeremiah 33:10–11.

Pride, arrogance, Jeremiah 48:29.

Bitterness, anger, Ezekiel 3:14.

Sour grapes, Jonah 4:1–11.

Fair-minded attitude, Matthew 1:19 (Berk.).

Attitude toward those disliked, Matthew 5:38–48.

Effect of attitudes, understanding, Matthew 13:14–15.

Nature of Kingdom of Heaven, Matthew 19:14.

Changed attitude of demon possessed man, Mark 5:2–10, 18.

"Salt" of good spiritual attitude, Mark 9:50.

True humility, Luke 7:6–7.

"Sad and gloomy," Luke 24:17 (CEV).

Violent rebuke, Acts 7:51–58.

"Nobler attitude," Acts 17:11 (Berk.).

Cruel attitude, Romans 12:14 (AB).

Weak, strong evaluated, Romans 14:1–8.

More harm than good, 1 Corinthians 11:17–32.

Refresh other's spirit, 1 Corinthians 16:18.

Radiant face, 2 Corinthians 3:18.

Servant attitude, 2 Corinthians 4:5.

Making room in heart, 2 Corinthians 7:2.

New awareness, 2 Corinthians 7:10–13.

Grieving Holy Spirit, Ephesians 4:30.

Attitude toward opposition, Philippians 1:15–18.

"Keep being glad," Philippians 1:18 (CEV).

Truly Christian attitude, Philippians 2:5–8 (LB).

No complaining, arguing, Philippians 2:14.

Gentleness always, Philippians 4:5.

Attitude decides lifestyle, Philippians 4:8–9.

Enmity against God, Colossians 1:21.

Keys to positive attitude, 1 Thessalonians 5:16–18.

Attitude toward wealth, 1 Timothy 6:17–19.

"Not quarrelsome but kindly," 2 Timothy 2:24 (NRSV).

Attitude toward deserters, 2 Timothy 4:16.

Response to discipline, Hebrews 12:5–11.

Persecution, suffering, James 1:2–6.

Negative thoughts, 1 Peter 2:1.

Gentleness, reverence, 1 Peter 3:15 (CEV).

Attitude toward suffering, 1 Peter 4:12–16.

See Disposition, Frame-of-Reference, Response.

ATTORNEY See Lawyer, Litigation.

(MAIN) ATTRACTION

"Main attraction," John 3:29 (LB).

ATTRIBUTES

Heart realities, Proverbs 27:19.

Creator determines attributes, 1 Corinthians 4:7.

Mature Christian life, 2 Peter 1:5–9.

See Character, Gifts, Personality.

AUDACITY

Misunderstanding goodwill, 2 Samuel 10:1–4.

Fool's audacity, Psalm 14:1.

Deliberate falsehoods, Jeremiah 8:8.

See Discourtesy, Impertinence, Rudeness.

AUDIENCE

Witnessing history, Joshua 24:31.

Ears test words, Job 34:3.

Let earth hear, Isaiah 34:1.

Some listen, some refuse, Ezekiel 3:27.

Mountain audience, Ezekiel 6:1–7.

Unannounced meeting, Matthew 5:1–2.

Amazed audience, Matthew 7:28 (AB, LB); 9:33; 13:54–58.

Overflow audience, Matthew 13:1–2.

Story for arriving audience, Luke 8:4–15.

Mother, brothers held back by crowd, Luke 8:19–21.

Packed audience, Luke 11:29 (KJV).

Thronged thousands, Luke 12:1 (KJV).

Tax collectors, sinners, Luke 15:1.

Crowd curiosity, John 6:1–2.

Relatives, friends, Acts 10:24–27.

Eager listeners, Acts 17:11–12.

Gentile audiences replaced Jewish, Acts 18:4–6.

Jews wanted miracles, Greeks wisdom, 1 Corinthians 1:22–24.

Welcoming message, 1 Thessalonians 1:6.

See Congregation, Mob Psychology, Students.

AUDIOVISUAL

Burning bush, Exodus 3:1–6.

Egyptian magic, divine visuals, Exodus 4:1–9.

Hearing, seeing, Job 42:5.

Concise illustration, Jeremiah 13:3–9 (AB).

Extensive use of parables, Mark 4:34.

Seeing, hearing, Luke 10:24.

Illustrative coin, Luke 20:24.

Finger visual, John 8:6.

Crucifixion portrayed, Galatians 3:1 (LB).

See Visual.

AURA

Radiating prior experience, Exodus 34:29; Psalm 34:5; Ecclesiastes 8:1; Acts 6:15.

Glory filled tabernacle, Exodus 40:34.

Earth covered with glory, Numbers 14:21; Habakkuk 3:3.

Path of righteous, Proverbs 4:18.

Reflected glory, Daniel 12:3; 2 Corinthians 3:18.

Yuletide ambience, Luke 2:9.

Flashing light from heaven, Acts 22:6.

No need for sunlight, Revelation 22:5.

See Illumination, Light, Aurora Borealis, Spectacular.

AURORA BOREALIS

Northern glow, Job 37:22 (Berk.).

AUTHENTICITY

Pagan wise men discredited, Daniel 2:1–11.

Seeking authentic Messiah, Matthew 11:1–5.

Expecting sign from heaven, Mark 8:11–12.

Jesus authenticated, John 1:22–28; 10:41.

Purpose of miracles, John 2:11; 10:25, 37–38.

Truth-centered living, John 3:21.

Questioned validity of Jesus, John 8:12–30; 10:24–30.

Jesus, Pilate, John 19:19–22.

Authenticating miracles, Acts 2:22.

Authentic Scripture, 1 Corinthians 14:37–38.

Mutual authenticity, 2 Corinthians 10:7.

See Genuine, Honesty, Truth.

AUTHOR

"Beautiful sayings," Genesis 49:21 (Berk.).
Poetic Moses, Exodus 15:1–18.
God's finger, Deuteronomy 9:9–10.
Aged musician, Deuteronomy 31:14–30; 32:1–43.
Holy Spirit authorship, 2 Samuel 23:2.
Prolific penman, 1 Kings 4:32.
Celebration songs, Psalm 21:13 (LB).
Skillful writer, Psalm 45:1.
Speedy, many thoughts, Psalm 45:1 (LB).
Unwritten concepts, Psalm 106:2 (Berk.).
Author's identity, Ecclesiastes 1:12.
Thesaurus needed, Ecclesiastes 12:10.
Diamond-pointed pen, Jeremiah 17:1 (KJV).
Writing book, Jeremiah 30:2.
Dangerous writing—truth, Jeremiah 36:4–32.
Discarded scroll, Jeremiah 51:63.
Writing kit, Ezekiel 9:2, 11.
Many aspirant writers, Luke 1:1–4 (GNB).
Author recalls previous writing, Acts 1:1–2.
Effective writer, poor speaker, 2 Corinthians 10:10 (NRSV).
Scripture's Author, 2 Peter 1:20–21.
Author commends author, 2 Peter 3:15–16.
Reluctant author, 2 John 12.
Angelic resource, Revelation 1:1–3.
"Write promptly," Revelation 1:11 (AB).
See Communication, Fiction, Literature, Writing.

AUTHORITY

Creator's command, Genesis 1:3, 6, 9, 14–15, 20, 24, 26.
Moon, sun preside, Genesis 1:16–18 (LB, KJV).
Human authority over creation, Genesis 1:26–29.
The eternal "I am," Exodus 3:13–14.
Sovereign authority, Exodus 6:1–8, 28–29.
Moses, man with authority, Exodus 7:1–2.
Final authority, Deuteronomy 1:17.
God-given authority, Deuteronomy 2:25.
Speaking with divine authority, Leviticus 23:1–2, 9–10, 23–24.
Those in authority, those assisting, Numbers 18:1–7 (LB).
Authority of father, husband, Numbers 30:3–16.
Broadened authority, Deuteronomy 1:9–13.
Prolonged authority, 1 Samuel 13:1.

Spear as authority symbol, 1 Samuel 26:7.
Power over citizens, foreigners, 2 Samuel 22:44–46.
King's flaunting attitude, 1 Kings 12:1–14.
Prophet authenticated, 1 Kings 18:10–24.
God's saving name, Psalm 54:1.
Wealth as authority symbol, Proverbs 22:7.
Fools given authority, Ecclesiastes 10:6.
God speaks, acts, Isaiah 44:24–28.
Jeremiah's reluctance to proclaim, Jeremiah 1:1–10, 17–18.
Demons dispelled, Matthew 8:16 (LB).
Authority of teachers, masters, Matthew 10:24.
Contrasting authority, Matthew 12:22–32.
Jesus spoke with authority, Luke 4:31–37 (LB).
Finger of God, Luke 11:20; Acts 3:11–16.
Satanic authority, Luke 12:5 (NRSV).
Jesus' obedience to authority, John 12:50.
Protective authority, John 17:11.
Jesus accused of disrespect, John 18:19–24.
Authority challenged, John 19:8–11.
Rules to obey, Acts 16:4 (GNB).
Scripture as authority, Acts 18:28.
Demons unmoved by lack of authority, Acts 19:13–16.
Insulting high rank, Acts. 23:4–5.
Truth declared with power, Romans 1:4.
Relationship of men, women, 1 Corinthians 11:2–16.
Holy Spirit's witness, 1 Corinthians 12:3.
Ultimate world authority, 1 Corinthians 15:24.
Spiritual weapons, 2 Corinthians 10:1–5.
Severe, constructive authority, 2 Corinthians 13:10 (Berk.).
Authority vindicated, Galatians 6:17 (AB).
Wives, husbands, Ephesians 5:22–23.
Savior, King, Colossians 1:15–20.
Christ, Head over all, Colossians 2:9–10.
Overthrowing man of sin, 2 Thessalonians 2:8.
Desire to be overseer, 1 Timothy 3:1.
God does not lie, Titus 1:2.
Leadership with authority, Titus 2:15.
Superior to angels, Hebrews 1:3–4.
Submission to authority, 1 Peter 2:13–17.
Ministering in Lord's name, 3 John 7.
Wrong church authority, 3 John 9–10.

Authority over evil, Jude 9.
Earth's sovereign, Revelation 1:5.
Satanic authority. Revelation 13:2.
Temporary authority, Revelation 13:5.
Ten kings' one-hour reign, Revelation 17:12.
Given authority, Revelation 20:4.
See Dictator, Leadership, Politics, Royalty, Scripture.

AUTHORIZATION
Jerusalem travel documents, Nehemiah 2:1–8.
Authorized promise, Psalm 105:8 (Berk.).

AUTOBIOGRAPHY
Nehemiah's autobiography, Nehemiah 1:1 (LB).
Jeremiah's introduction, Jeremiah 1:1 (CEV).

AUTOGRAPH
"Here is my signature," Job 31:35 (NASB, NRSV).
Paul's signature, Colossians 4:18; 2 Thessalonians 3:17.
See Graphology.

AUTOMOBILE
Presumed automobile prophesy, Nahum 2:4.

AUTUMN
Designated seasons, Genesis 1:14; Psalm 104:19.
Harvest time, Genesis 8:22; Deuteronomy 24:19; Ruth 1:22; 2 Samuel 21:9.
Home at harvest time, Ruth 1:22.
Temple completion, 1 Kings 6:37–38 (Note: Ziv is May, Bul is November).
Temple foundation completed, 1 Kings 8:2 (Note: Ethanim is October).
September tour, Ezra 3:1 (LB).
September project completion, Nehemiah 6:15 (LB).
Mid-September, Nehemiah 8:1 (LB).
No time for sleeping, Proverbs 10:5.
Autumn crocus, Isaiah 35:1 (AB).
Bird migration, Jeremiah 8:7.
"October," Jeremiah 41:1 (LB).
Early October, Haggai 2:1 (LB).
Late November, Zechariah 7:1 (LB).
See Seasons.

AVANT-GARDE *See Original, Unprecedented.*

AVARICE *See Greed.*

AVENGE
Not do unto others, Proverbs 24:29.
Love to those who cause grief, 2 Corinthians 2:5–11.
Leave revenge to God, 2 Thessalonians 1:6–7.
See Revenge.

AVOID *See Ignore.*

AWAKENING
Awakened people, 1 Kings 18:39.
Awakening key, 2 Chronicles 7:14.
Awakening tears, Ezra 10:1.
Woman's awakening witness, John 4:39.
Day of Pentecost, Acts 2:37–41.
Two communities awaken, Acts 9:35.
Antioch awakening, Acts 11:19–21.
Corinth awakening, Acts 18:8.
Ephesians awakening, Acts 19:17–20.
"Keep awake," Revelation 2:2 (AB).
See Evangelism, Revival.

AWARENESS
Edenic nakedness, Genesis 3:8–11.
Joseph aware of brothers, Genesis 42:7.
Future potential awareness, Genesis 48:17–20.
Aware of God's mercy, Exodus 4:29–31.
Guilt by daylight, Exodus 22:2–3.
Awareness responsibility, Leviticus 5:1.
Donkey's awareness, Numbers 22:25.
Aware of God's blessing, Deuteronomy 4:32–34.
Young boy's awareness, 1 Samuel 3:3–18.
Aware of another's loyalty, 1 Samuel 24:1–22.
Meaningless work, wealth, Ecclesiastes 4:8.
Something to boast about, Jeremiah 9:23–24.
Lord's powerful presence, Ezekiel 3:22 (GNB).
Knowing who is Lord, Ezekiel 6:10, 14; 7:4, 9, 27; 12:16, 20; 13:9, 23.
Aware of sinful past, Jonah 3:10.
Recognizing Son of God, Mark 15:39.
Seeing, understanding, Luke 10:23–24.
Not understanding, Luke 18:31–34.
Identity immediately recognized, John 1:29–31.
New awareness, 2 Corinthians 7:10–13.

Comprehending faith, Ephesians 3:14–19.
Aware of false prophets, 1 John 4:1–6.
See Discovery, Frame-of-Reference, Intellectual, Sensitivity.

AWE

Standing on holy ground, Exodus 3:1–6.
Queen overwhelmed, 1 Kings 10:5.
In awe of God, Job 25:2; Isaiah 6:1–8; Ezekiel 38:20.
Awesome Lord, Psalm 47:2 (NKJV).
King, priests, prophets, Jeremiah 4:9 (NKJV).
"Gasp at the sight," Jeremiah 49:17 (LB).
Ezekiel overwhelmed, Ezekiel 3:15.
Awed by vision, Daniel 10:7–8.
Talking to God, Daniel 10:15–21.
Silent earth, Habakkuk 2:20.
Reverence to the Lord, Zechariah 2:13.
Amazed audience, Matthew 7:28–29; 9:33; 13:54–58.
Amazed disciples, Matthew 8:27.

Overwhelmed with wonder, Mark 9:15.
Terrorized awe, Luke 2:9 (AB).
Awe-stricken Pilate, John 19:8.
Contemplating Christ's glory, Ephesians 1:18–23.
See Amazement, Reverence, Wonder, Worship.

AWKWARD See Bungler, Inexperience, Novice.

AWOL

Frightened soldiers, 1 Samuel 13:7–8.
See Deserter.

AXE

Spears, battle-axe, Psalm 35:3 (NASB).

AXIOM

Origin of saying, 1 Samuel 10:11–12.
Jews wanted miracles, Greeks wisdom, 1 Corinthians 1:22–24.
Welcoming message, 1 Thessalonians 1:6.
See Aphorism, Figure of Speech.

B

BABEL

Babel's heights, Jeremiah 51:53.

BABY See Infant.

BACHELOR

No record of Joshua's family, Joshua 1:1.
Promises to eunuchs, Isaiah 56:3–5.
"Gift of staying single," Matthew 19:11 (CEV).
Marriage renounced, Matthew 19:12.
Bachelor's marriage counsel, 1 Corinthians 7:1–40.
Did Paul consider marriage, 1 Corinthians 9:5 (CEV).
144,000 apparent bachelors, Revelation 14:1–5.
See Eunuch, Marriage, Single.

BACKBITING

Continual backbiting, Psalm 50:20.
Tongue like storm, Proverbs 25:23.

BACKGROUND

"Quarry from which you were mined," Isaiah 51:1 (LB).

Sorceress' sons, Isaiah 57:3.
Humble background, Amos 7:14–15.
Prophet from Galilee, John 7:41–52.
Military background, Acts 10:25–26.
Resume Old Testament events, Acts 13:16–41.
See Ancestors, Family, Heritage.

BACKSLAPPING

Flattered king, 2 Samuel 14:5–17.
Partiality to none, Job 32:21.
Deceptive flattery, Psalm 12:2.
Rebuke exceeds flattery, Proverbs 28:23; 29:5.
Tongue tip hypocrisy, Luke 20:20–26; Acts 12:19–23.
See Applause, Approval, Commendation, Exaggeration, Insincerity.

BACKSLIDING

Causes of backsliding, Exodus 17:7; Deuteronomy 8:11–14; Psalm 106:14; Proverbs 16:18; Mark 4:18–19; 1 Timothy 6:10; 2 Peter 1:9.

Good leader needed, Exodus 32:1–6.

Wayward community, Deuteronomy 13:12–18.

Egypt forbidden, Deuteronomy 17:16.

Journey never retaken, Deuteronomy 28:68.

Wayward people, Joshua 22:18.

Backsliding prone, Judges 2:18–19; Hosea 11:7.

National backsliding, Judges 10:16.

Told to seek pagan gods, Ruth 1:15.

Unrestrained backsliding, 1 Samuel 3:13.

Futile restoration effort, 1 Samuel 4:1–11.

Restoration, 1 Samuel 15:24–25.

Failure into success, 1 Kings 8:33–34.

Old age, spiritual decline, 1 Kings 11:4.

Turning away, 1 Kings 11:9.

Secret disobedience, 2 Kings 17:9.

Backslidden king, 2 Chronicles 12:1.

"Make me faithful again," Psalm 51:10 (CEV).

Rampant backsliding, Psalm 53:3 (Berk.).

David's perilous experience, Psalm 73:2.

Stubborn, rebellious, Psalm 78:8.

Blessings quickly forgotten, Psalm 106:13.

Once astray, then obedient, Psalm 119:67.

Choosing evil, Psalm 125:5.

Rewards for conduct, Proverbs 14:14.

Massive backsliding, Isaiah 1:1–4.

Grieving Holy Spirit, Isaiah 63:10.

Divinely hardened hearts, Isaiah 63:17.

Ignoring delivering God, Jeremiah 2:5–8, 27 (See LB).

Backslider's rebuke, Jeremiah 2:19.

Backslider's dilemma, Jeremiah 3:1.

Call to backsliders, Jeremiah 3:14 (NKJV).

Waywardness cure, Jeremiah 3:22.

Leaders, people backslide, Jeremiah 5:3–5.

Perpetual backsliding, Jeremiah 8:5 (RSV).

Ineffective leadership, backsliding people, Jeremiah 15:1.

Spiritual conspiracy, Jeremiah 17:13.

Repentant backslider, Jeremiah 31:19.

Wishing return to Egypt, Jeremiah 42:1–22; 43:1–7.

Inevitable judgment awaits disobedience, Jeremiah 44:15–28.

Impudent Israel, Ezekiel 2:4.

Righteous man becomes unrighteous, Ezekiel 3:20–21; 18:24–28.

Deeds of darkness, Ezekiel 8:12.

When good people sin, Ezekiel 18:24 (CEV).

Backslider's fate, Ezekiel 18:26.

Actions betray speech, Ezekiel 33:31.

Time of refinement, Daniel 11:35.

Israel forgot God, Hosea 8:14.

Certain judgment, Hosea 9:7.

Blessing lost to idols, Hosea 9:10.

Dangerous material blessings, Hosea 13:6.

Sin, boasting, Amos 4:4–5.

Overt backsliding, Jonah 1:1–3.

Hearts like flint, Zechariah 7:11–12.

Unsavory salt, hidden lights, Matthew 5:13–16.

Serving two masters, Matthew 6:24.

Miracles, hard hearts, Matthew 11:20.

Love grown cold, Matthew 24:12.

Unfulfilled promise, Mark 14:27–31, 66–72.

Looking back, Luke 9:62; Galatians 4:9.

Backsliding disciples, John 6:66.

Shame items, Romans 6:21.

Fallen restored, Romans 11:23.

Missing mark, 1 Corinthians 4:1–21.

Wayward believers, 1 Corinthians 5:9–12.

Wasted grace, 2 Corinthians 6:1 (GNB).

Astonishing Galatians, Galatians 1:6–9.

Led astray, Galatians 2:13.

Weak, miserable, Galatians 4:9.

Counselling backsliders, Galatians 6:1 (CEV, LB).

Ignorant, obstinate, Ephesians 4:18 (Berk.).

Shipwrecked faith, 1 Timothy 1:18–20.

Money causes backsliding, 1 Timothy 6:20 (CEV).

Deserters, 2 Timothy 1:15; 4:10.

Wandering from truth, 2 Timothy 2:17–18.

Worldliness, 2 Timothy 4:9–10.

Warning against backsliding, Hebrews 2:1 (AB).

Hearts astray, Hebrews 3:10, 12.

Fallen from truth, Hebrews 6:4–6 (AB).

Danger continuing sin, Hebrews 10:26–27.

Backslider restored, James 5:19–20.

Avoid former error, 1 Peter 1:14.

Straying like sheep, 1 Peter 2:25 (CEV).

Backs turned, 2 Peter 2:20–22.

Lost stability, 2 Peter 3:17 (NRSV).

Straying from body, 1 John 2:18–19.

Full reward lost, 2 John 8.

Ephesians backsliding, Revelation 2:4–5.

Permanently listed in Book of Life, Revelation 3:2–5.

Neither cold nor hot, Revelation 3:15–16.
See Apostasy, Carnality.

BAD NEWS

Bad report penalized, Numbers 14:36–37.
God's prophet proclaimed truth, 1 Kings 14:1–18.
Good news, bad news, Jeremiah 42:6.
Repeated bad news, Jeremiah 51:31–32.

BAGPIPES

Babylonian bagpipes, Daniel 3:5, 10, 15.

BAIL

Posting bond, Acts 17:9.

BAKING

Fast food, Genesis 18:6.
Bible bakers, Genesis 40:1; Jeremiah 37:21; Hosea 7:4.
Sabbath baking for Sabbath, Exodus 16:23.
Oven baked offering, Leviticus 2:4.
Ten bakers, one oven, Leviticus 26:26.
Bread loaf vitality, Judges 7:13–15.
Hot coals for baking, 1 Kings 19:6.
Raisin cakes, Isaiah 16:7.
Bakers' street, Jeremiah 37:21 (Berk.).
Unclean fuel, defiled food, Ezekiel 4:12–15.
Spiritual yeast, Matthew 13:33.
See Bread, Cooking, Recipe.

BALANCE

Idol kept erect, Isaiah 40:20.
Those who stumble easily, Jeremiah 12:5.
Balanced life, Luke 2:52.
Varied gifts, 1 Corinthians 12:27–30.
Self-controlled, 1 Peter 1:13.

BALDNESS

Bald as vultures, Micah 1:16.

BALLAD

Ballad of good grapes, Isaiah 5:1–8.

BALM

Balm in Gilead, Jeremiah 8:22; 46:11.
Pain therapy, Jeremiah 51:8.

BANDIT

Bandits crucified, Matthew 27:38, 44 (GNB).
Jesus treated like a bandit, Mark 14:48 (NRSV).
See Thief.

BANISHMENT

"Uproot," 2 Chronicles 7:20.
See Oblivion.

BANKER

Generous loan policy, Deuteronomy 15:7–8.
Mortgaging land, Nehemiah 5:3.
Rich versus poor, Proverbs 22:7.
Commercial centers, Ezekiel 27:12–23.
Currency values, Ezekiel 45:12.
Storing treasures, Matthew 6:19–20.
Temple money changers, Matthew 21:12; Mark 11:15; John 2:15.
See Currency, Money, Mortgage, Treasure, Wages.

BANKRUPTCY

Powerless, helpless, Job 6:13.
Total loss, Psalm 109:11.
Deceitful man's loss, Jeremiah 17:11.
Remembered treasures, Lamentations 1:7.
Prosperity forgotten, Lamentations 3:17.
Debtors take over, Habakkuk 2:7.
Fortunes restored, Zephaniah 2:7.
Insolvency, Matthew 18:21–25.
See Failure.

BANNED See Censure, Forbidden.

BANNER See Flag.

BANQUET

Egyptian birthday, Genesis 40:20.
Eating, rejoicing, Deuteronomy 27:7.
Pagan banquet, Judges 9:27.
Banquet for enemies, 2 Kings 6:18–23.
Week-long banquet, Esther 1:5.
Family festivity, Job 1:4–5, 13.
Richest food, Psalm 63:5.
Breakfast banquet, Ecclesiastes 10:16–17.
"Feasts are made for laughter," Ecclesiastes 10:19 (NRSV).

Banquet hall love banner, Song of Songs 2:4.

One thousand guests, Daniel 5:1.

Plenty to eat, Joel 2:2–6.

Feeding the 5,000, Matthew 14:13–21; Mark 6:30–44; Luke 9:10–17; John 6:1–13.

Birthday banquet, Mark 6:21.

Banquet for Jesus, Luke 5:27–35.

Honored seating, Luke 14:7–11.

Cana wedding, John 2:1–11.

Love feast, John 13:1–2.

Heaven's wedding supper, Revelation 19:9.

See Feast, Festivity, Food, Gourmet.

BAPTISM

Unworthy of baptism, Matthew 3:7–8.

Baptism of suffering, Matthew 20:20–24 (KJV).

Believer's baptism, Matthew 28:19; Mark 16:16; Acts 2:38; 10:48; Galatians 3:27; Colossians 2:12.

"John the baptizer," Mark 1:4 (NRSV).

Jesus' baptism, Mark 1:9.

Baptism as witness, Luke 3:3 (LB).

Water, spirit, John 3:5.

Abundant water, John 3:23.

Jesus, disciples, John 4:1–2.

Simultaneous conversion, baptism, Acts 8:36–37.

Red Sea baptism, 1 Corinthians 10:1–2 (CEV).

Baptized for dead, 1 Corinthians 15:29.

Symbolic Ark, 1 Peter 3:20–22 (GNB).

Water, blood, 1 John 5:6 (GNB).

BARBECUE

Meat roasted over fire, Exodus 12:8–9.

BARBER

Baldness benefit, Leviticus 13:40.

Haircut honors dead, Deuteronomy 14:1–2.

Samson's uncut hair, Judges 13:4–5.

Wait until beards grow, 1 Chronicles 19:5.

Head shaved, Job 1:20.

More trouble than hair, Psalm 40:12.

Anointed hair, beard, Psalm 133:2.

Divine barbering, Isaiah 7:20 (LB).

Remorseful hair cut, Jeremiah 7:29.

Heads shaved, beards cut, Jeremiah 48:37.

Sharp sword shaver, Ezekiel 5:1.

Hair trimmed, Ezekiel 44:20.

Head shaved for mourning, Micah 1:16.

Hairs of head numbered, Luke 12:7.

Apostolic haircut, Acts 18:18.

See Coiffure, Hair.

BARGAIN *See Cost.*

BARGAINING

Bargaining for a city, Genesis 18:20–33.

Bargain birthright, Genesis 25:27–34.

Life for life, Joshua 2:14.

Best price, Proverbs 20:14.

Greatest bargain, Isaiah 55:1–2.

BARBECUE

Bad exchange, Jeremiah 2:11.
Sadistic bargaining, Matthew 14:7–10.
Judas' infamy, Matthew 26:14–16.

BARREN

Childlessness, Genesis 16:1–4; 29:31–34;
30:1–24; 1 Samuel 1:1–20; Luke 1:5–25.
Household infertility, Genesis 20:17–18.
Samson's birth, Judges 13:1–8.
Motherhood, barren woman, Psalm 113:9.
Miscarriage, Hosea 9:14.
Rejoicing although barren, Galatians 4:27
(NRSV).
See Childless, Fruitless, Infertility.

BARRIER

River, sea, Psalm 114:3–5.
Sins become roadblock, Isaiah 59:2 (CEV).
Very large stone, Mark 16:4.

BARTENDER

Mixing drinks, Isaiah 5:22.
See Alcohol.

BARTER

Bartering animals, land, people, Genesis
47:13–21.
Valuables bartered for food, Lamentations
1:11.
Cash, produce, Ezra 3:7.
Bad exchange, Jeremiah 2:11.
Commercial centers, Ezekiel 27:12–23.
Prostitute's payment, Hosea 2:5.
Barley for wife, Hosea 3:2.
See Merchandise.

BASEMENT

Light hidden in cellar, Luke 11:33 (NASB,
NRSV).

BASHFUL

Tongue sticks to roof of mouth, Job 29:10.
Both timid, bold, 2 Corinthians 10:1.
Witness unashamed, 2 Timothy 1:8–9.
See Reticent, Sly, Timidity.

BASICS

Milk, honey, Exodus 3:17.
Food, water, Job 22:7–8.

Day of small things, Zechariah 4:10.
See Foundation.

BASTARD See Illegitimacy.

BATH

Washing traveler's feet, Genesis 18:4; 19:2.
Egyptian princess' bath, Exodus 2:5.
Ceremonial cleansing, Leviticus 14:8;
2 Kings 5:10–14.
Bathed but unclean, Numbers 19:7.
Prostitutes, chariots, 1 Kings 22:38.
Soda, soap, Jeremiah 2:22.
See Cleanliness, Cleansing, Soap, Washing.

BATTLE See War.

BEACH

"Ocean boundaries," Job 38:8 (CEV).
Waterfront audience, Matthew 13:2.
Fisherman's catch, Matthew 13:48.
Broiling fish, John 21:9.
Kneeling in sand, Acts 21:5.
Seaside miracle, Acts 28:1–6.
See Ocean.

BEARD See Whiskers.

BEAST

Beauty, beast, 1 Samuel 25:3.
See Animals.

BEAUTICIAN

Alien wife's beauty treatment, Deuteronomy 21:10–14.
Palace procedure, Esther 2:2–13.

BEAUTY

Beauty in creation, Genesis 2:9; Psalm 19:1;
Ecclesiastes 3:11.
Feminine beauty admired, Genesis 6:1–2
(Berk.).
Wife's beauty, Genesis 12:11; 1 Samuel
25:3.
Beautiful Rebekah, Genesis 24:16.
Face, figure, Genesis 29:17 (Berk.).
Means to personal safety, Deuteronomy
21:10–14.
Beauty, brains, 1 Samuel 25:3.
Tempting beauty, 2 Samuel 11:2.

B

Loveliest wives, 1 Kings 20:3 (NKJV).
Most beautiful women, Esther 1:11; 2:1–4.
Beauty treatment, Esther 2:8–12.
Beautiful daughters, Job 42:15.
Feminine beauty, Psalm 45:11.
Beauty skin deep, Proverbs 11:22; 31:30.
Bald women of Zion, Isaiah 3:16–17.
Jerusalem allegory, Ezekiel 16:4–14.
Squandered beauty, Ezekiel 16:15, 25 (ASB).
Nature's beauty, Hosea 14:5–6; Matthew 6:28–29.
Beautiful young women, Zechariah 9:17.
Mountain of Transfiguration, Matthew 17:1–8.
"Beautiful before God," Acts 7:20 (NRSV).
God's gift, 1 Corinthians 4:7.
Radiant face of Moses, 2 Corinthians 3:7–8.
Flowers wither, 1 Peter 1:24
Inner beauty, 1 Peter 3:3–4.
Earth, heaven, 1 Corinthians 15:40 (GNB).
Patience full bloom, James 1:4 (LB).
See Beast, Lady.

BEAUTY CONTEST

All time beauty, 1 Kings 1:3 (LB).

BED

Earth, stone, Genesis 28:11.
Frogs in bed, Exodus 8:3.
King-sized bed, Deuteronomy 3:11.
Gold, silver, Esther 1:6.
Bedtime meditation, Psalm 4:4 (LB).
Fragrant bed, Proverbs 7:17.
Mortgaged bed, Proverbs 22:27.
Beds inlaid with ivory, Amos 6:4.
Family size, Luke 11:7.
See Dreams, Sleep.

BEDLAM See Turmoil.

BEER

Fermented drink not wine, Numbers 6:3; Deuteronomy 29:6; Judges 13:7.
Bitter beer, Isaiah 24:9.
See Alcohol.

BEES

"Like a swarm of bees," Deuteronomy 1:44 (NIV); Psalm 118:12.
Beehive in lion's carcass, Judges 14:8.

Whistling for bees, Isaiah 7:18.
See Insects.

BEGGING

Children begging, Psalm 37:25; 109:10.
Handicap induced begging, Mark 10:46–52; John 9:1–12.
Beggar, rich man, Luke 16:19–31.
"Beggar's bag," Mark 6:8 (GNB).
Surprised beggar, Acts 3:1–8.
See Poverty.

BEGINNER See Inexperience, Novice.

BEGINNING

God at outset, Genesis 1:1.
New calendar, Exodus 12:2.
Beginning to end, Deuteronomy 31:24.
"Spring of the day," 1 Samuel 9:26 (KJV).
Initial foundations, Psalm 102:25.
Beginning of wisdom, knowledge, Psalm 111:10; Proverbs 1:7; 9:10.
Before earth's creation, Proverbs 8:23.
Beyond comprehension, Ecclesiastes 3:11.
End contained in beginning, Isaiah 46:10.
New day dawning, Isaiah 60:1 (CEV).
Beginning of sorrows, Matthew 24:8; Mark 13:8.
Eternal Word, John 1:1.
Alpha, omega, Revelation 21:6.

BEGUILE

Beguiling city, Nahum 3:4 (LB).
See Seduction, Temptation.

BEHAVIOR

Wise behavior, 1 Samuel 18:14 (NKJV).
Path of righteous, way of wicked, Proverbs 4:18–19.
"Human inclinations," 1 Corinthians 3:3 (NRSV).
Exemplary behavior, 1 Corinthians 13:1–13; Philippians 1:9–10; 2 Thessalonians 3:7–10; 1 Timothy 3:2; Titus 2:11–15.
Observing legalism, Colossians 2:16.
Resurrection lifestyle, Colossians 3:1–17.
Tactful conversation with others, Colossians 4:6.
Blameless behavior, 1 Thessalonians 2:10 (NASB, NKJV).

Excellent behavior, 1 Peter 2:12 (CEV).
Mature Christian attributes, 2 Peter 1:5–9.
See Character, Conduct, Frame-of-Reference.

BEHEADED

John the Baptist, Matthew 14:10; Mark 6:16, 27; Luke 9:9.
Beheaded martyrs, Revelation 20:4.
See Capital Punishment.

BELIEVER

Idols in heart, Ezekiel 14:1–11.
Weak believers, Matthew 6:30; 8:26; 14:31; 16:8; John 12:42.
Believers' potentials, Mark 9:23; 11:24; Luke 17:6; John 14:12.
Resurrection belief, John 2:22.
First believers, John 2:23.
Miracle-motivated believer, John 4:53; Acts 9:36–42.
Believers' rationale, John 7:31.
"Out of the believer's heart," John 7:38 (NRSV).
Response to Christ's message, John 8:30; 10:42.
Secret believers, John 12:42–43 (LB).
Jesus prayed for believers, John 17:6–26.
God-fearing Jews, Acts 2:5.
Jailer's belief, Acts 16:25–35.
Sincere believers, Acts 17:10–12.
Sins confessed by new believers, Acts 19:17–20.
Holy Spirit's temple, 1 Corinthians 3:16–17.
Hopeless yet believing, Romans 4:18.
Confident believer, 2 Timothy 1:12.
Faith pleases God, Hebrews 11:6.
Clean in society of deceit, Revelation 3:4, 10.
All tribes, nations, Revelation 7:9–10.
See Congregation, Convert, Discipleship, Followers.

BELITTLE

Wounds considered scratches, Jeremiah 8:11.
See Incidental.

BELLS

Garment bells, Exodus 28:33; 39:25.
Bells on horses, Zechariah 14:20.

BELOVED

Sacrificing daughter, Judges 11:30–40.
Dawn of love, Ruth 3:1–18.
Beloved, barren, 1 Samuel 1:2–11.
Mutual love between friends, 1 Samuel 20:17.
Esteemed of the Lord, Isaiah 66:2.
The Lord's signet ring, Haggai 2:23.
Apple of His eye, Zechariah 2:8.
Earth marriage, Heaven relationships, Mark 12:18–27.
Mother's gentle spirit, 1 Thessalonians 2:7–8.
See Bride, Romance.

BENEDICTION

First divine blessing, Genesis 1:22–28.
Melchizedek's blessing, Genesis 14:18–20.
Blessing given Rebekah, Genesis 24:60.
Father's blessing, Genesis 49:26.
Blessing people, Leviticus 9:22; Joshua 22:6; 2 Samuel 6:18.
Priestly blessing, Numbers 6:24–26.
Assigned to pronounce benedictions, Deuteronomy 10:8.
Lengthy benediction, Deuteronomy 33:1–29.
Blessing, warning as death approaches, Joshua 23:14–16.
Mother-in-law's benediction, Ruth 1:8–9.
Blessing populace, 2 Samuel 6:18.
Psalm of benediction, Psalm 67:1–7.
Prayer of Jesus, John 17:1–5.
Paul, Ephesians elders, Acts 20:17–38.
Brief benedictions, Romans 15:33; Galatians 6:18; 2 Thessalonians 3:18.
Apostolic benediction, 2 Corinthians 13:14.
Call to world evangelization, Romans 16:25–27.
Trinitarian benediction, 2 Corinthians 13:14.
King eternal benediction, 1 Timothy 1:17.
Grace, mercy, peace, 2 John 3.
God keeps, provides, Jude 24–25.
Prophecy prelude, Revelation 1:4–6.
Outcry of praise, Revelation 7:11–12.
Faith proclamation, Revelation 15:3–4.
Wedding of the Lamb, Revelation 19:6–8.

Concluding benediction, Revelation 22:21.
See Blessing, Commitment, Prayer.

BENEFACTOR

Divine benefactor, Deuteronomy 7:6–26; Acts 14:15–18; Philippians 4:19.
Synagogue's Gentile benefactor, Luke 7:4–5.
Unrecognized benefactor, John 1:10.
Lady benefactor, Romans 16:2 (NRSV).
See Stewardship.

BENEFICIARY

Others provide benefits, Joshua 14:13.
Beneficiaries by command, Joshua 17:4.
Divine goodness, Isaiah 57:13; Romans 4:13; Colossians 1:12.
Exercising a will, Hebrews 9:16–17.
See Heir, Inheritance, Legacy.

BENEVOLENCE

Kindness to handicapped, 2 Samuel 9:1–13.
Concern for needy, Job 29:16; Proverbs 21:13.
Those deserving benevolence, Proverbs 3:27.
Generosity rewarded, Proverbs 11:25; 22:9; Matthew 25:34–40.
Opportune benevolence, Proverbs 18:16.
Lending to the Lord, Proverbs 19:17.
Pretense benevolence, Proverbs 25:14.
Concern for enemy, Proverbs 25:21.
Benevolence, personal needs, Proverbs 28:27.
Hypocrite's benevolence, Mark 14:3–8.
Caring for poor, Proverbs 29:7; Romans 12:13; Galatians 2:10; Ephesians 4:28.
Benevolent woman, Proverbs 31:20.
Care of others, Isaiah 58:10.
Private benevolence, Matthew 6:2–4.
Benevolent Heavenly Father, Matthew 7:1–11.
Sharing with others, Luke 3:11; 1 John 3:17.
Stewardship principles, Luke 6:38.
Good Samaritan, Luke 10:30–37.
First things first, Luke 10:38–42.
Hospitality that cannot be returned, Luke 14:12–14.
Woman who helped poor, Acts 9:36–42.

Recognized kindness, Acts 10:4.
Reaching out to others, Acts 11:27–30.
More blessed to give than to receive, Acts 20:35.
Sharing blessings, Romans 15:26–27.
Macedonian generosity, 2 Corinthians 8:1–5.
See Generosity, Philanthropy, Transmutation, Welfare.

BEREAVEMENT

Grief for wife, Genesis 23:1–4.
Jacob's sorrow, Genesis 37:32–35; 42:38.
Overt mourning, Exodus 12:29–30.
Mourner's shaved head, Deuteronomy 14:1–2.
Seventy-day bereavement, Genesis 50:3.
One-month bereavement, Numbers 20:29; Deuteronomy 34:8.
Weeping, fasting, 2 Samuel 1:12.
Torn clothes, sackcloth, 2 Samuel 3:31.
United in sorrow, Ruth 1:1–9.
Organized mourning, Amos 5:16–17.
Mourning music, Matthew 9:23.
Sorrowing mother, Luke 7:12.
Jesus wept, John 11:35.
Loving sorrow, Acts 9:39.
Truth comforts, 1 Corinthians 15:12–20; 1 Thessalonians 4:13–18.
Tears wiped away, Revelation 21:3–4.
See Death, Grief, Sorrow.

BESETTING SIN

"Everything that slows us down," Hebrews 12:1 (CEV).

BEST

"Pick of the heap," Hebrews 7:4 (AB).

BETRAYAL

Captive's information about enemy, Judges 8:13–14.
Deceitful Delilah, Judges 16:15–19.
Disloyal priest, Judges 18:4–26.
Turning against friends, Job 17:5.
Close friend deceived, Psalms 41:9; 55:12–14.
Betrayed by friends, Psalm 55:20; Lamentations 1:19.
Parable of two eagles, Ezekiel 17:2–10.

Family dishonor, Micah 7:6; Matthew 10:21.

Jesus betrayed, Matthew 26:14–16, 47–50; Mark 14:43–46; Luke 22:3–6; Zechariah 11:12–13.

Peter's denial, Matthew 26:31–35, 69–75.

Implicated by bread morsel, John 13:21–27.

See Deceit, Deceived, Deception.

BETROTHAL

Laborious betrothal, Genesis 29:18–20.

Betrothed's army exemption, Deuteronomy 20:7.

Deceitful betrothal, 1 Samuel 18:17.

Fiance's death, Joel 1:8 (LB).

Virgin's betrothal, Luke 1:26–38.

See Engagement.

BEWILDERED

Walking in darkness, Psalm 82:5.

Spirit of dizziness, Isaiah 19:14.

Foolish Galatians, Galatians 4:1–5.

See Confusion.

BIAS

Negative, positive, Numbers 13:17–33.

Favoring one against another, 1 Corinthians 4:6.

See Fanaticism, Opinion.

BIBLE

Not by bread alone, Deuteronomy 8:3; Job 23:12; Jeremiah 15:16; Matthew 4:4.

Joy, light, Psalms 19:8; 119:105, 130; Proverbs 6:23; 2 Peter 1:19.

Sweeter than honey, Psalms 19:10; 119:103.

Eternal book, Psalm 119:89; Isaiah 40:8; Matthew 5:18; 24:35; 1 Peter 1:25.

"The book of the Lord," Isaiah 34:16 (NKJV).

Beloved Bible, Psalm 119:47, 72, 97, 140.

Rain, snow, Isaiah 55:10–11.

Bible as joy, delight, Jeremiah 15:16.

Fire, hammer, Jeremiah 5:14; 23:29.

Commissioning Bible authors, Jeremiah 36:1–3; Ezekiel 1:2–3; 2 Peter 1:21.

Edible scroll, Ezekiel 3:1.

"People need every word," Matthew 4:4 (CEV).

Cleansing water, Ephesians 5:26.

Spirit's sword, Ephesians 6:17.

Important reading, Colossians 4:16.

Inspired Bible, 2 Timothy 3:16.

Dynamic Bible, Hebrews 4:12.

Milk, solid food, Hebrews 5:12; 1 Peter 2:2.

Divine mirror, James 1:23–25.

See Inspiration, Memorization, Scripture.

BIBLE STUDY *See Study.*

BIG *See Large.*

BIGOTRY

Abrasive nationalism, Esther 3:8–9.

Bigoted religious leaders, Matthew 21:15.

Well-intentioned bigotry, Mark 9:38.

Pharisee attitude, John 8:33–38.

Name-calling, John 8:48–49.

Spiritual blindness, John 9:39–41.

Presumed justification, Philippians 3:3–6.

Ignorant bigotry, 1 Timothy 1:13.

See Prejudice, Racism, Xenophobia.

BILLBOARD

Stone billboards, Deuteronomy 27:2–8.

Calvary's sign board, Mark 15:26 (LB).

See Advertising, Media.

BIOGRAPHY

Thumbnail biographies, Genesis 25:12–18; Judges 10:1–5.

Limited biography, 2 Kings 15:13–15.

Beginning to end, 1 Chronicles 29:29–30.

Satan's brief biography, Isaiah 14:12–15.

Biographies of Christ, Luke 1:1–4 (LB).

Life of Jesus, John 21:25; 1 Timothy 3:16.

See Literature.

BIOLOGY

Church body parts, 1 Corinthians 12:12–21.

See Animals, Birds, Body, Flesh, Nature, Trees.

BIRDS

Rugged, genteel, Genesis 8:6–11 (GNB).

Types of birds: Genesis 8:8; Leviticus 11:13–19; Numbers 11:31–32; Deuteronomy 14:12–18; Job 28:7; 30:29; 38:41; 39:13, 27; Psalms 84:3; 102:6; Song of Songs 2:12; Isaiah 14:23; 34:15; Jeremiah 8:7; Matthew 10:29–31; 23:37; 26:34.

E

Birds subservient to humans, Genesis 9:2.
Vultures repulsed, Genesis 15:11 (GNB).
On eagle's wings, Exodus 19:4; 2 Samuel
1:23; Proverbs 23:5; Isaiah 40:30–31.
Inedible birds, Leviticus 11:13–19; Deuter-
onomy 14:12–18.
Birds of prey, Isaiah 34:15.
Not endangering species, Deuteronomy
22:6–7.
Fledglings flight, Deuteronomy 32:11.
Learn from birds, Job 12:7.
Southern flight, Job 39:26.
Creator, ornithologist, Psalm 50:11.
Nesting sites, Psalms 84:3; 104:16–17; Isa-
iah 34:13–15; Matthew 8:20.
Way of an eagle, Proverbs 30:18–19.
Tale-bearing birds, Ecclesiastes 10:20.
Distressed thrush, dove, Isaiah 38:14.
Honoring the Lord, Isaiah 43:20.
Bird migration, Jeremiah 8:7.
Surrogate mother, Jeremiah 17:11.
Jackals, ostriches, Lamentations 4:3.
Women flying like birds, Zechariah 5:9.
Value of sparrow, soul, Matthew 10:29–31.
Incriminating rooster, Matthew 26:34, 74–
75; Mark 14:29–31, 66–72.
Vultures, Luke 17:37.
Speaking eagle, Revelation 8:3.
See Dove, Eagle, Flight, Nature, Vulture.

BIRTH

With the Lord's help, Genesis 4:1 (NASB,
NRSV).
Births known in advance, Genesis 16:11;
18:10; Judges 13:3; 1 Kings 13:2; 2 Kings
4:16; Isaiah 9:6.
Rachel's death, Genesis 35:16–20.
Stillborn infant, Job 3:16; Psalm 58:8.
Birth of mountains, Psalm 90:2.
Rue the day "a boy is born," Job 3:3 (NIV).
Animals born in secret, Job 39:1.
Evil infant, Psalm 7:14 (CEV).
Secure infant, Psalm 22:9.
Stillborn child, Psalm 58:8 (Berk.).
Mountains given birth, Psalm 90:2 (Berk.).
Regretted birth, Ecclesiastes 7:1.
Wonders of human gestation, Ecclesiastes
11:5.
Time of birth, Isaiah 13:8; 26:17–18.
Birth pangs, Isaiah 21:3.

No strength for delivery, Isaiah 37:3.
Labor pains, Isaiah 42:14 (Berk.).
Men with labor pains, Jeremiah 30:6.
Anticipating, giving birth, Jeremiah 31:8.
Improper postnatal care, Ezekiel 16:4–5.
Dramatic events, Luke 1:57–66.
Born at wrong time, 1 Corinthians 15:8
(CEV).
See Abortion, Childbirth, Gestation, Miscarriage,
Pregnancy.

BIRTH CERTIFICATE

Two prostitutes, stolen child, 1 Kings 3:16–
28.
Lost family records, Nehemiah 7:64.
Divine registration, Psalm 87:6.
Command to increase population, Jere-
miah 29:4–6.

BIRTH CONTROL

Physical procedure, Genesis 38:8–10.
Population growth, Exodus 1:7.
Doors shut to womb, Job 3:10 (KJV).
Children a heritage, Psalm 127:3–5.
Mandate for large families, Jeremiah
29:4–6.
Nursing, pregnancy, Hosea 1:8.
Husband's option, John 1:13.
See Conception, Contraception.

BIRTHDAY

Old Testament fathers, Genesis 11:10–26.
Birthday parties, Genesis 40:20; Matthew
14:6–11.
Remembering family birthdays, Genesis
43:33.
120th birthday, Deuteronomy 31:2 (KJV).
Family birthday celebrations, Job 1:4–5 (LB,
AB).
Day of birth regretted, Job 3:1–26; Jere-
miah 15:10; 20:14–18.
Birthdays all too often, Job 9:25–26.
Number of birthdays determined, Job 14:5.
Time flies, Job 16:22.
God's numberless years, Job 36:26.
Brevity of life, Psalm 39:4–5.
Counting the days, Psalm 90:12 (LB).
Morbid birthday gift, Matthew 14:6–12.
Age misunderstood, John 8:57.
See Age, Old Age, Time.

BIRTHRIGHT

Birthright sale, Genesis 25:29–34; Hebrews 12:16–17.
Ranked by time of birth, Genesis 43:33.
Firstborn's rights, Deuteronomy 21:15–16; 2 Chronicles 21:3.
See Citizenship.

BISHOP

Requirements for overseer, 1 Timothy 3:1–7; Titus 1:7.
See Clergy, Leadership.

BITE See Teeth.

BITTERNESS

Bitter fruit, Deuteronomy 32:32.
Bitterness of soul, Job 3:20; Proverbs 14:10.
Forsaking the Lord, Jeremiah 2:19.
Punished conscience, Jeremiah 4:18.
Gall of bitterness, Lamentations 3:15.
Filled with bitterness, Acts 8:23.
"Cursing and bitterness," Romans 3:14 (NIV, NKJV).
Bitterness overcome, Ephesians 4:31.
Bitter roots, Hebrews 12:15.
Bitterness harbored in heart, James 3:14.
See Animosity, Hatred, Jealousy.

BLACK

Black is beautiful, Song of Songs 1:5 (NRSV).
Skin, hair, Song of Songs 1:5–6; 5:11 (KJV).
Black man and the cross, Mark 15:21 (Note: Cyrene, North African city).
See Prejudice, Racial.

BLACKMAIL

Joseph's initial attitude to brothers, Genesis 42:1–34.
Love exploited, Judges 16:4–21.
Conniving against Daniel, Daniel 6:3–24.
Misused relationship, Matthew 26:47–50; Mark 14:43–46; Luke 22:47–48; John 18:1–4.

BLACKOUT

Egyptian darkness, Exodus 10:21–33.
Majestic Sinai, Deuteronomy 4:11.
Crucifixion darkness, Matthew 27:45.
Eternal blackout, Jude 6.
See Oblivion.

BLACKSMITH

Dangerous blacksmiths, 1 Samuel 13:19.
Philistine restrictions, 1 Samuel 13:19–21.
Blacksmith at work, Isaiah 44:12.
Source of blacksmith's skill, Isaiah 54:16.
Four blacksmiths, Zechariah 1:20 (LB).
See Iron, Skill.

BLAME

Passing blame to others, Genesis 3:8–13.
Accepting blame, Genesis 42:21–22; 43:8–9.
Avoid blaming God, Job 1:22.
Self-inflicted disaster, Jeremiah 44:7.
Pardon for nation's guilt, Joel 3:21.
Blamed for storm at sea, Jonah 1:10–12.
Guilt of Judas, Matthew 27:3.
Looking for something to criticize, Mark 3:2.
Blaming women, 1 Timothy 2:14.
Seeing light, walking in darkness, 2 Peter 2:21.
See Conscience, Guilt, Responsibility.

BLAMELESS

Blameless conduct, Psalm 119:1 (RSV).
See Innocence.

BLASPHEMY

Pharaoh dared defy God, Exodus 5:2.
Misusing God's name, Exodus 20:7; Deuteronomy 5:11; Leviticus 19:12; Matthew 5:34–36; James 5:12.
Blasphemy examples, Leviticus 24:11; 2 Chronicles 32:16; Isaiah 37:17, 23.
Angry cursing, Leviticus 24:10–14.
Praising God, making idol, Judges 17:1–5.
Putting blame on God, 2 Kings 6:33.
Insulting God, 2 Chronicles 32:17; Nehemiah 9:26.
Idol in temple, 2 Chronicles 33:7 (LB).
"Sneering at God," Psalm 1:1 (CEV).
Presuming God does not hear, Psalm 59:7–8.
Blasphemous vanity, Psalm 73:9–11.
Habitual cursing, Psalm 109:17–18.
Challenging God, Isaiah 5:18–19.
Ultimate defamation, Isaiah 44:7.
God does not yield glory to another, Isaiah 48:11.

Accusing the Lord of deception, Jeremiah 4:10.

Defiled identity, Ezekiel 20:39 (LB).

Conspiracy against the Lord, Ezekiel 35:13.

Beast's blasphemy, Daniel 7:25.

Self-declared deity, Daniel 11:36–37; 2 Thessalonians 2:4.

Vulgar signs, Malachi 1:13 (CEV).

Laughing at truth spoken by Jesus, Matthew 9:23–24.

Jesus accused of satanic power, Matthew 9:32–34; 12:24; Luke 11:15.

Unpardonable sin, Matthew 12:22–32; Mark 3:28–30 (AB, LB).

Making fun of Jesus, Matthew 27:41 (CEV).

Jesus called deceiver, Matthew 27:62–63.

Alleged blasphemy, John 5:18.

Jesus accused of demon possession, John 10:19–21.

Accepting praise belonging only to God, Acts 12:22–23.

Antichrist's exaltation, 2 Thessalonians 2:4.

Learning not to blaspheme, 1 Timothy 1:20.

Blaspheming name of Jesus, James 2:7.

Bold, arrogant, 2 Peter 2:10.

Endeavoring to make God a liar, 1 John 1:8–10.

Blasphemous heads, Revelation 13:1.

Utterances of the Beast, Revelation 13:5.

Those who refuse to repent, Revelation 16:10–11.

BLEMISH

Scourge of rape, Genesis 34:1–24.

Blemished meat, Exodus 22:31.

Infected skin, Leviticus 13:1–3.

Unblemished priests, Leviticus 21:17–24.

Eye gouged out, 1 Samuel 11:1–2.

BLAME

Unblemished restoration, Nehemiah 6:1.
Habitual cursing, Psalm 109:17–18.
Silver to dross, wine to water, Isaiah 1:22.
Mutilated lamb, Amos 3:12.
Loss of arm, eye, Zechariah 11:17.
See Disfigure, Handicap, Injury.

BLESSING

Blessing, protection for Ishmael, Genesis 21:9–21.
Material blessing, Genesis 24:35;26:12; 48:15–16; Exodus 23:25; Deuteronomy 29:5; 1 Kings 3:13; Proverbs 10:22; Isaiah 30:23; Joel 2:26; Zechariah 10:1.
Parental blessing, Genesis 27:21–40; 28:1; 2 Samuel 13:25.
Benefiting from another, Genesis 39:5.
Famine numbs memory of blessings, Genesis 41:31.
"Bless the lads," Genesis 48:16 (KJV).
Performing wonders, Exodus 34:10.
Curse becomes blessing, Deuteronomy 23:5.
Forgotten blessings, Psalm 106:7–8.
Blessing others, Joshua 14:13; Psalm 129:8.
Leadership blessing, Joshua 22:6; 1 Kings 8:14.
Blessing of pregnancy, 1 Samuel 2:20.
Household blessing, 2 Samuel 7:29.
Requirements for blessing, 1 Kings 8:56–61.
Promise, warning, 1 Kings 9:1–9.
Abundant blessing, Nehemiah 9:25; Psalm 133:3.
Righteousness brings blessing, Psalm 18:20–21.
Blessing, righteousness, Psalm 24:5.
"Enriched," Psalm 32:10 (Berk.).
"Many and many," Psalm 40:5 (LB).
Abundant blessings, Psalm 68:9.
Honey from the rock, Psalm 81:16.
Divine wonders, Psalm 88:10–12.
Blessing of faithfulness, Proverbs 28:20.
Blessing held in abeyance, Isaiah 1:19–20.
Forsaken source of blessing, Jeremiah 2:13.
Obedience to covenant, Jeremiah 11:1–5.
Lesser blessing forgotten, Jeremiah 16:14–15.
Blessings leading to backsliding, Hosea 13:6.
Blessings surmount problems, Zechariah 9:12 (LB).
Cursed blessings, Malachi 2:2.

Good stewardship blessing, Malachi 3:8–10.
Source of blessing, Matthew 5:11–12 (Note verses 3–10).
First things first, then blessing, Matthew 6:33.
Touching Jesus, Mark 5:24–30.
Prophet, widow, Luke 4:23–26.
Discipleship blessing, Luke 18:29–30.
Touch of the Master's hand, John 2:1–11.
Desire for material blessing, Acts 1:6.
Temporal blessings, Acts 14:17.
Put right, Romans 3:20–21 (GNB); 5:1 (GNB).
Blessing by default, Romans 11:11–12.
Not one blessing missed, 1 Corinthians 1:7.
A blessing to others, 2 Corinthians 7:13–16.
Those who refresh, 1 Corinthians 16:18.
Illness brings blessing, Galatians 4:13–14.
"Every blessing in heaven," Ephesians 1:3 (LB).
Blessing to many, Philippians 1:25–26.
Every good gift, James 1:16–17.
Abundant grace, peace, 1 Peter 1:2; Jude 2.
Scripture finale, Revelation 22:21.
See Abundance, Affluence, Anointing, Goodness, Provision.

BLIGHT See Mildew.

BLINDNESS (Physical)

Instant blindness, Genesis 19:11; 2 Kings 6:18; Acts 9:8.
Blinded slave set free, Exodus 21:26.
Kindness to unsighted, Leviticus 19:14; Deuteronomy 27:18.
No blind clergy, Leviticus 21:16–23.
Possible example of cataracts, 1 Samuel 4:14–15.
Partial blindness as disgrace, 1 Samuel 11:2–11.
Healing blind, deaf, dumb, Isaiah 35:5–6.
Healed of blindness, Matthew 9:27–31; 12:22; 20:30–34; 21:14; Mark 8:22–25; 10:46–52; Luke 7:21–22; John 9:1–12.
Last healing prior to Crucifixion, Matthew 20:29–34.
Blind man's active faith, Mark 10:46–52 (CEV).
Convert's blindness, Acts 9:8.
Blindness, sorcerer, Acts 13:6–12.
See Eyes, Sight.

BLINDNESS *(Spiritual)*

Eyes that cannot see, Deuteronomy 29:4.

Leading the blind, Isaiah 42:16.

Spiritual blindness, Isaiah 59:10; Matthew 6:23; 15:14; Ephesians 4:18; 1 John 2:11.

Becoming as blind men, Zephaniah 1:17.

Darkness within, Matthew 6:23; Ephesians 4:18; 2 Peter 1:5–9.

Look, never see, Matthew 13:14 (CEV).

Blind leading blind, Matthew 15:14.

Blind worship, Matthew 23:19.

Seeing, hearing, not understanding, Luke 10:24.

Messianic blindness, John 7:25–36.

Questioning validity of Jesus, John 8:12–30.

Pagans certain of error, Acts 19:35–36.

Look, never see, Acts 28:26 (CEV).

Covenant blindness, 2 Corinthians 3:14.

Blinded by Satan, 2 Corinthians 4:1–6.

Blinded by hatred, 1 John 2:11.

See Carnality, Prejudice.

BLISS

Ignorance is bliss, Ecclesiastes 1:18.

BLOOD

Food containing blood, Genesis 9:4; 1 Samuel 14:31–33.

Blood sprinkling, Exodus 12:7; 24:8; Leviticus 4:6; Numbers 19:4; Hebrews 11:28; 12:24; 1 Peter 1:2.

Identified by blood, Exodus 12:13.

Blood atonement, Exodus 30:10; Leviticus 17:11; John 6:56; 19:34; Acts 20:28; Romans 5:9; Hebrews 9:7, 14, 21–22; 1 Peter 1:18–19; 1 John 1:7; Revelation 1:5; 5:9.

Mixing human blood with sacrifices, Luke 13:1.

Nectar of judgment, Revelation 16:5–6.

See Altar, Life, Redemption, Sacrifice.

BLOODSHED

Brutal human sacrifice, Deuteronomy 18:9–12.

Innocent blood, 1 Kings 2:31; Isaiah 59:7.

City saturated with blood, 2 Kings 21:16.

Foot wash in enemy blood, Psalm 58:10.

Righteous victims, Lamentations 4:13; Joel 3:19.

Sacrificial bloodshed, Hebrews 9:22.

See Carnage.

BLOSSOM

Aaron's rod, Numbers 17:5, 8.

Fruitful nation, Isaiah 27:6.

Living desert, Isaiah 35:1–2.

Fig tree, Habakkuk 3:17.

See Flowers, Fragrance, Garden.

BLUEPRINT

Temple blueprint, 1 Chronicles 28:11, 19 (LB).

The Lord plans in advance, Isaiah 25:1.

Prenatal plan for Jeremiah, Jeremiah 1:4–5.

Drawing plan for battle, Ezekiel 4:1–3.

See Construction.

BLUNDER

Blaming God for personal blunder, Proverbs 19:3.

BLUSH

Embarrassed Ezra, Ezra 9:6.

Blushing moon, Isaiah 24:23 (Berk.).

Not knowing how to blush, Jeremiah 6:15; 8:12.

"Do not blush," 2 Timothy 1:8 (AB).

See Embarrassment, Shame.

BOASTING

Goliath's macho, 1 Samuel 17:44.

Windy mouth, Job 8:2.

Hedonistic boasting, Psalm 10:3.

Boasting about God, Psalm 44:8.

Talk is cheap, Proverbs 20:6 (GNB).

Clouds without rain, Proverbs 25:14.

Future plans, Proverbs 27:1.

Satan's taunts, Isaiah 14:12–15; Ezekiel 28:12–19.

Only reason to boast, Jeremiah 9:23–24.

"Talks-Big-Does-Nothing," Jeremiah 46:17 (CEV).

False claims, Jeremiah 48:14–20 (GNB).

Claiming to make Nile river, Ezekiel 29:9.

Boasting of hypocrisy, Amos 4:4–5 (LB).

"We did it on our own," Amos 6:13 (CEV).

Unable to live up to boasting, Matthew 26:31–35, 69–75; Mark 14:27–31, 66–72; John 13:37–38; 18:15–18, 25–27.

Truth disbelieved, John 5:31–38.

Proud sorcerer, Acts 8:9–10.
Self-confidence, 2 Corinthians 3:4 (GNB).
"Boast about us," 2 Corinthians 5:12 (NRSV).
Self-praise, commendation from the Lord, 2 Corinthians 10:13–18.
Spiritual pride, Romans 2:17–21.
See Bragging, Vanity.

BOAT

Ark called boat, Genesis 6:14 (CEV).
Apparent ferryboat, 2 Samuel 19:18.
Speedboat, Job 9:26.
Conveyance for audience, John 6:22–23.
Use of lifeboat, Acts 27:30.

BODY

Corruption after death, Genesis 3:19; Job 19:25–26; 21:23–26; Ecclesiastes 3:20; John 11:39; Acts 13:36.
Death's nearness, 1 Samuel 20:3; Psalm 103:14; Isaiah 2:22.
Demons use physical bodies, Matthew 8:31.
Human body enslaved, serving, Romans 6:19 (CEV).
Holy Spirit's temple, 1 Corinthians 3:16–17.
Resurrection bodies, 1 Corinthians 15:35–44.
Only a tent, 2 Corinthians 5:4 (AB).
See Athletics, Physique.

BODYGUARD

Trained men, Genesis 14:14.
Without bodyguard, 1 Samuel 21:1.
"Godliness and integrity," Psalm 25:21 (LB).
Shielded by God's power, 1 Peter 1:5.
See Protection.

BODY LANGUAGE See Nonverbal Communication.

BODY OF CHRIST

Many invited, few chosen, Matthew 22:1–14.
Spiritual family, Luke 8:19–21.
Relationships in Christ, John 19:26–27.
Jews, centurion, Acts 10:22, 28, 34–35.
Peter, Gentiles, Acts 11:1–3; 18:6.
Message to Gentiles, Acts 15:13–21.
New Testament church, Acts 16:15.

Paul's scope of prayer, Romans 1:8–10; 1 Corinthians 1:4–9; Ephesians 1:11–23; Philippians 1:3–6; Colossians 1:3–14.
Body member function, Romans 12:4–8; 1 Corinthians 12:12–27.
Preference to others, Romans 12:10.
Mutual belief, 2 Corinthians 10:7.
Result of promise, Galatians 4:21–31.
The Church a mystery, Ephesians 1:9–10; 3:2–3.
Members of God's family, Ephesians 2:19–22.
Servant to the church, Colossians 1:24–26.
Christian community as family, 1 Timothy 5:1–2.
Long promise fulfilled, Titus 1:1–3.
Slave, brother, Philemon 8–21.
Relationship in Christ, Hebrews 2:11–13.
Divine nature, 2 Peter 1:4.
God's children, 1 John 3:1–3.
Love one another, 1 John 4:7–11.
Seven churches, Revelation 1:20.
See Church, Congregation.

BOILS

Judgment of boils, Exodus 9:9.
Priestly inspection of boils, Leviticus 13:18.
Poultice application, 2 Kings 20:7; Isaiah 38:21.
Tested by boils, Job 2:7.

BOISTEROUS

Boisterous woman of folly, Proverbs 9:13 (NASB).
See Loud.

BOLDNESS

Challenge to boldness, Deuteronomy 31:6; Joshua 1:6; 10:25; 2 Samuel 10:12; 1 Chronicles 28:20.
Fearless preacher, 1 Kings 18:16–18.
Fearing wrong things, Isaiah 8:12–14.
God-given boldness, Jeremiah 1:17–19; Daniel 6:4–10.
Under death threat, Jeremiah 26:12–16.
Proclaiming with boldness, Ezekiel 33:21–33.
Daring Daniel, Daniel 6:10.
Bold request, Mark 15:43.
Boldness of ordinary men, Acts 4:13.

Endowed boldness, Acts 4:31.

Bold preaching, Acts 14:3; 19:8; 28:31.

Moses, Isaiah, Romans 10:19, 20 (GNB).

Approaching God boldly, Ephesians 3:12; Hebrews 4:16; 10:19.

Standing firm, Philippians 1:17–30.

Not embarrassed by Paul's chains, 2 Timothy 1:16–18.

Bold leadership, Titus 2:15.

Boldness in Christ, 1 John 5:14 (NRSV).

See Bravery, Courage, Fearless, Valor.

BOND

Posting bond, Acts 17:9.

BONDAGE

Right to be set free, Leviticus 25:47–55.

Sold into bondage, Judges 4:2.

Evil bondage, Proverbs 5:22; John 8:34; Acts 8:23; Romans 6:16; 7:23.

Sold to creditors, Isaiah 50:1.

Restoration of Israel prophesied, Jeremiah 30:8–17.

Free men ruled by slaves, Lamentations 5:8.

Bound by infirmity, Luke 13:12 (KJV).

Those enslaved think they are free, John 8:31–36.

Chains increased ministry, Philippians 1:12–14.

Escape from bondage, 2 Timothy 2:26.

Bondage defined, 2 Peter 2:19.

Satan bound, Revelation 20:1–3.

See Prison, Slavery.

BONES

Desecrated bones, 2 Kings 23:13–14; Psalm 53:5; Jeremiah 8:1; Ezekiel 6:5.

Talking bones, Psalm 35:10 (Berk.).

Bones of unborn child, Ecclesiastes 11:5 (KJV).

Broken arms, Ezekiel 30:20–26.

Valley of dry bones, Ezekiel 37:1–14.

BOOK OF LIFE

Divine registry, Psalm 87:6.

Book of Life, Philippians 4:3.

Name recorded, Revelation 3:5; 20:15; 21:27.

Book opened, Revelation 20:12.

BONES

YES JAY... IT'S TRUE, I WAS VERY CLOSE TO FEMUR

BOOKS

Immutable book, Proverbs 30:5–6; Revelation 22:19.
Dialogue immortalized, Job 19:23.
Endless book supply, Ecclesiastes 12:12.
Book thrown into river, Jeremiah 51:63 (GNB).
Scroll of remembrance, Malachi 3:16–18.
Source of joy, Luke 10:20.
Public book burning, Acts 19:19.
Volumes of judgment, Revelation 20:12.
See Author, Literature, Writing.

BOOMERANG

Bad deeds boomerang, Obadiah 15 (LB).

BOREDOM

Boring life, Ecclesiastes 2:1–11 (CEV).
See Monotony.

BORN AGAIN See Conversion, Regeneration, Salvation.

BORROWING

Slain giant's sword, 1 Samuel 17:50–51 (LB).
Borrowed property, Exodus 22:14; 2 Kings 6:5.
Lend to those in need, Deuteronomy 15:8; Psalms 37:26; 112:5; Matthew 5:42; Luke 6:35.
Borrowing, not repaying, Psalm 37:21.
Power of loaned money, Proverbs 22:7.
See Debt, Mortgage.

BOTANY

Solomon's botanical knowledge, 1 Kings 4:33.
See Agriculture, Horticulture, Trees.

BOTHER See Disruption, Dissension, Meddle.

BOTTOM LINE

"Punch line" conclusion to stewardship appeal, 2 Corinthians 9:15.

BOUNDARY See Landmark.

BOUNTIFUL

Bountiful nature, Deuteronomy 33:13–16.
Given true contentment, Proverbs 30:7–9.
Eternal righteousness, Isaiah 51:8.

No enemy plunder, Isaiah 62:8–9.
Eating to satisfaction, Joel 2:26.
God's grace lavished, Ephesians 1:7–8.
Good land, unproductive land, Hebrews 6:7–8.
See Abundance, Affluence, Plenty, Wealth.

BOW AND ARROW See Archery.

BOXING

Hand-to-hand fighting, 2 Samuel 2:14.
"Fist of the mighty," Job 5:15 (CEV).
Divine pugilism, Psalm 3:7.
Avenging fist, Ezekiel 25:12–13, 16 (LB).
Boxing technique, 1 Corinthians 9:26 (NASB, NRSV).
See Athletics.

BRACELET

Betrothal gift, Genesis 24:22.
Worldliness object, Isaiah 3:19.
Bracelets worn by men, Ezekiel 16:11.
See Jewelry.

BRAGGING

Windy speech, Job 3:4 (LB).
Big mouths, Judges 9:38.
Proper time for boasting, 1 Samuel 2:1–3.
Affront to the Lord, Psalm 10:3.
Nothing to brag about, Psalm 49:6–9; 1 Corinthians 1:29; 2 Corinthians 4:6, 7; Ephesians 2:8–10.
Self-proclaimed greatness, Psalm 75:5 (CEV).
Dishonest stewardship, Proverbs 25:14.
Boast about the Lord, Jeremiah 9:23–24.
Only a loud noise, Jeremiah 46:17 (See CEV).
Don't blow your own horn, Matthew 6:2 (CEV).
Insincere loyalty, Matthew 26:31–35, 69–75.
"Stop bragging," 1 Corinthians 3:21 (CEV).
Bragging at its worst, James 3:14 (LB).
Evil boasting, James 4:16.
See Boasting, Pride, Vanity.

BRAIN

Right, left hemispheres, Ecclesiastes 10:2.
Computer capability, 1 Corinthians 2:16; Ephesians 3:18; Philippians 2:5.
See Frame-of-Reference, Intelligence, Mentality, Mind, Thinking, Thought.

BRAND

"Brand mark of Jesus," Galatians 6:17 (NRSV).

BRAVERY

Brave Joshua, Numbers 14:6–9.
Bold Gideon, Judges 7:7–23.
Boy versus giant, 1 Samuel 17:1–51.
Nehemiah's boldness, Nehemiah 6:10–13.
Brave woman, Esther 4:13–16.
Imputed bravery, Proverbs 28:1; Ephesians 3:12; Hebrews 4:16.
Unwavering courage, Daniel 6:10.
Facing adversaries, Philippians 1:27–28.
Challenge to be brave, Hebrews 4:16 (GNB).
See Boldness, Courage, Valor.

BRAWN

Mighty Samson, Judges 14:6; 16:3–30.
Hand-slain bear, lion, 1 Samuel 17:32–37.
Youth's glory, Proverbs 20:29.
Race not to swift, strong, Ecclesiastes 9:11.
See Athletics, Physical, Physique, Strength.

BREAD

Royal bread, Genesis 14:18.
Scarcity of bread, Genesis 47:12–13 (KJV).
Donkey bread-bearer, 1 Samuel 16:20.
Day-old bread, 1 Samuel 21:6.
Abundant supply, 1 Samuel 25:18.
Bread delivered by air, 1 Kings 17:6.
New grain bread, 2 Kings 4:42.
Bread dough stewardship, Nehemiah 10:37 (NKJV).
"Bread of tears," Psalm 80:5.
Ashes as bread, Psalm 102:9 (Berk.).
Sustaining bread, Psalm 104:15.
Half-baked loaf, Hosea 7:8 (GNB).
Daily bread, Matthew 6:11.
Sacramental bread, Matthew 26:26; Mark 14:22; 1 Corinthians 11:23–26.
"Bread of the Presence," Luke 6:4 (NRSV).
See Baking, Food.

BREAKFAST

Morning feast, Ecclesiastes 10:16–17.
Seaside breakfast, John 21:11–15 (Note verse 15 Berk.).

BREAK-IN

City wall penetrated, 2 Kings 25:4.

BREATH

Creative breath, Genesis 2:7; Psalm 33:6.
Omnipotent breath, 2 Samuel 22:16; Job 4:9; Psalm 18:15; Isaiah 30:33.
"Blazing breath of God," Job 15:30 (CEV).
Bad breath, Job 17:1 (KJV).
Husband's breath offends wife, Job 19:17.
Breath for dry bones, Ezekiel 37:5.
Life-giving breath, Acts 17:25.
Breath of judgment, 2 Thessalonians 2:8.
See Life.

BREEDING

Breeding superior animals, Genesis 30:29–43.
"Prize calves," Matthew 22:4 (CEV).

BREVITY

Six-word obituary, Numbers 20:1.
"A short time," Numbers 26:1 (Berk.).
Momentary joy, Job 10:20.
Life "like a fleeting shadow," Job 14:2 (NIV).
Shortest short story, Ecclesiastes 9:13–15.
Learning put into few words, Ecclesiastes 12:13 (CEV).
Short chapter, Jeremiah 45:1–5.
Single chapter books, Obadiah 1–21; Philemon 1–21; 2 John 1–13; 3 John 1–14; Jude 1–25.
Two-word command, Mark 2:14.
Blind man's request, Mark 10:46–52.
Verse with two words, John 11:35.
Brief sermon, Acts 17:22–31.
Profound truth briefly presented, Ephesians 3:1–3.
Ten kings' one-hour reign, Revelation 17:12.

BRIBERY

Bribery distorts truth, Exodus 23:8.
God cannot be bribed, Deuteronomy 10:17 (CEV).
Blinded by bribes, Deuteronomy 16:19.
Asking special favor, Judges 1:13–15.
Bribed to deceive, Judges 16:5.
Sons accept bribes, 1 Samuel 8:3.
International bribery, 1 Kings 15:19.

Bribing invader, 2 Kings 15:19–20.
Anti-Semitic bribery, Esther 3:8–9.
Riches, bribes, Job 36:18–19.
Seeking favor with gifts, Psalm 45:12 (Berk.).
Bribes to be hated, Proverbs 15:27.
"Works like magic," Proverbs 17:8 (GNB).
Thwarting justice, Proverbs 17:23; Amos 5:12.
Use of gift, Proverbs 18:16.
Pacifying bribe, Proverbs 21:14.
Bribes corrupt character, Ecclesiastes 7:7.
Refusing bribery, Isaiah 33:15–16.
God accepts no incentive, Isaiah 45:13.
Daniel's integrity, Daniel 5:17.
Skilled in evil, Micah 7:3.
Jesus betrayed, Matthew 26:14–16, 47–50; Mark 14:10–11; Luke 22:3–6; Zechariah 11:12–13.
Resurrection perjury, Matthew 28:11–15.
Bribe offered for spiritual secret, Acts 8:9–24.
Attempting to induce bribery, Acts 24:26.

BRIDE

Search for bride, Genesis 24:1–66; Esther 2:17.
Engagement, marriage, Deuteronomy 20:7
Blessing of good wife, Proverbs 18:22.
Prophetic bride, Isaiah 62:5.
Adulterous brides, Hosea 4:13 (LB).
Bride of Christ, 2 Corinthians 11:2; Revelation 19:7; 22:17.
Remarriage, Romans 7:2–3; 1 Timothy 5:14.
See Marriage, Wedding, Wife.

BRIDEGROOM

Extended honeymoon, Deuteronomy 24:5.
Bridegroom's festivity, Judges 14:10.
Colorful entrance, Psalm 19:4–5.
Christ as bridegroom, Matthew 9:15; 25:1–10; John 3:29.
See Husband, Marriage, Wedding.

BRIDGE

Bridge across Jordan, 2 Kings 2:13–14.

BRIERS See Thorns.

BRILLIANCE

"God shines forth," Psalm 50:2 (RSV).
"Brightness of God's own glory," Hebrews 1:3 (CEV).
Illuminating splendor, Revelation 18:1.

BRIMSTONE

Brimstone upon Sodom, Genesis 19:24; Luke 17:29.
Threatened brimstone, Job 18:15; Psalm 11:6.

BROAD-MINDED See Openness.

BROIL

Meat broiled, not cooked, Exodus 12:9.

BROKENHEARTED

Heartbroken from scorn, Psalm 69:20.

BROTHER

Relationship to stepsister, Genesis 20:12.
Jacob, Esau, Genesis 25:21–26; 27:1–46; 33:1–20.
Restored rapport, Genesis 27:1–45; 33:1–15.
Sibling jealousy, Genesis 37:1–36.
Joseph and brothers, Genesis 37–45.
Avoid quarrelling, Genesis 45:24.
Brother born of evil woman, Judges 11:1–10.
Conflict avoided, 2 Chronicles 11:23.
Israel, Judah, Jeremiah 3:11.
Strife before birth, Hosea 12:3.
Brothers called to serve, Mark 1:16–19.
Family jealousy, Luke 15:11–32.
One brother tells another, John 1:41.
Jesus rejected by brothers, John 7:5.
Prenatal differences, Romans 9:11–13.
See Children, Family.

BROTHERHOOD

One common father, Malachi 2:10.
Becoming brother of Jesus, Matthew 12:50.
Supreme brotherhood identity, John 13:34.
Brotherhood of believers, Acts 9:17; 21:20; Romans 16:23–24.
Mutual acceptance, Romans 15:7.
Loved by the Lord, 2 Thessalonians 2:13.
Servant becomes brother, Philemon 16.

Christ our brother, Hebrews 2:17–18 (GNB).
Brother love, hatred, 1 John 2:9–11.
See Body of Christ, Church, Congregation.

BRUISE

Blue wound, Proverbs 20:30 (KJV).

BRUTALITY

Slaves mistreated, Exodus 21:20–21.
Distress makes people like animals, Deuteronomy 28:53–57.
Cutting off thumbs, toes, Judges 1:7.
No mercy shown, 2 Chronicles 36:17 (CEV).
See Cruelty, Sadistic, Torture.

BUDGET

Advance budget estimate, Luke 14:28–30.
Unanticipated need, no funds, John 6:5–7.

BUFFET

"Eat what you want," Isaiah 55:1 (CEV).

BUILDING

Threshing floor altar site, 2 Samuel 24:18–25.
Larger building needed, 2 Kings 6:1–2.
Temple building fund, 2 Kings 12:9–14.
Tears of joy at temple foundation, Ezra 3:10–13.
Worthless wood from vines, Ezekiel 15:1–5.
Delay building temple, Haggai 1:2–3.
Temporary temple, Matthew 24:1–2.
Estimate cost before construction, Luke 14:28–30.
Ark built in faith, Hebrews 11:7.
See Architecture, Construction, Design, Foundation, Plan.

BULLHEADED

Defiant sin, Numbers 15:30–31.
King who desecrated temple, 2 Chronicles 26:16–21.
Fool airs opinion, Proverbs 18:2.
See Stubborn.

BUNGLER

"One bungler destroys much good," Ecclesiastes 9:18 (NRSV).

BUOYANT

Floating ax head, 2 Kings 6:5–7 (GNB).
Rock sinks in river, Jeremiah 51:63.

BURDEN

Big load, one animal, Exodus 4:20.
Burdens lifted daily, Psalm 68:19.
Burden for wayward, Psalm 119:136.
Jeremiah's anguish, Jeremiah 4:19.
Fountain of tears, Jeremiah 9:1.
The Lord's burden, Jeremiah 23:33 (Berk.).
Specified time for bearing burden, Ezekiel 4:4–7.
Burdened people, Ezekiel 9:4.
Heart of flesh, stone, Ezekiel 11:19.
Mourning over message, Daniel 10:1–3.
Burden lightened, Matthew 11:28–30.
Burdened for city, Acts 17:16.
Sacrificial burden for Israel's salvation, Romans 9:1–4.
Burdened unto death, 2 Corinthians 1:8–9 (GNB).
Concern for followers, Colossians 1:28–29; 2:1–5; 1 Thessalonians 3:1–5.
See Concern, Empathy.

BUREAUCRACY

Politicians eyeing each other, Ecclesiastes 5:8–9.
See Administration, Government, Politics.

BURIAL

Choice place for burial, Genesis 23:6–9, 19.
Burial promise to father, Genesis 47:28–31.
Remains returned to homeland, Genesis 50:5 (LB).
Remains of Joseph, Genesis 50:26; Exodus 13:19; 14:11.
Untouched graves, Numbers 19:16.
Disgrace of no burial, Deuteronomy 28:26; Psalm 79:2; Ecclesiastes 6:3; Jeremiah 7:33.
Buried by God, Deuteronomy 34:5–6.
Cave burial, Joshua 10:26–27 (CEV).
Proper burial, Joshua 24:32.
Burial sites, Judges 16:31; 1 Samuel 25:1; 31:13; 2 Kings 21:18; 1 Chronicles 10:11–12; 2 Chronicles 33:20; Jeremiah 26:23; Matthew 27:7, 57–59; Luke 23:50–53.

Significance of burial, 2 Samuel 2:4–6.
Stolen bones, 2 Samuel 21:11–14.
Shared tomb, 1 Kings 13:30–31.
Garden grave site, 2 Kings 21:26.
Grave left undisturbed, 2 Kings 23:16–18.
Fragrant tomb, 2 Chronicles 16:14.
King denied royal burial, 2 Chronicles 28:27.
Palace internment, 2 Chronicles 33:20.
Buried alive, Psalm 55:15.
Trampled body, Isaiah 14:19.
No one to bury dead, Jeremiah 9:22; 14:16.
Ignominious burial, Jeremiah 41:9.
Satanic opposition, Jude 9.
See Cremation, Death, Exhume, Funeral, Grave, Tomb, Tombstone.

BURNING See Fire.

BUSINESS

Taking unfair advantage, Leviticus 25:17.
Unfinished business, Deuteronomy 20:5–9.
Business integrity, Deuteronomy 25:13; Proverbs 11:1; 20:14; 21:6.
King's business, 1 Samuel 21:2, 8 (NKJV).
Import, export business, 1 Kings 10:28–29.
Sabbath merchandising, Nehemiah 10:31; 13:15–18.
Business is bad, Psalm 37:7, 16, 35–40.
Pointless business, Psalm 39:6; Ecclesiastes 2:20.
"Crooked deals," Psalm 101:3 (LB, Berk.).
Justice in business, Psalm 112:5.
Careful discretion, Proverbs 6:1–5 (LB).
Tiny business experts, Proverbs 6:6.
Lazy, diligent, Proverbs 10:4; 13:4.
Dishonest weights, measures, Proverbs 11:1; 20:10, 23; Ezekiel 45:9–10; Hosea 12:7.
Dishonest purchase, Proverbs 20:14.
Skilled businesswomen, Proverbs 31:16; Acts 16:13–15.
"Busyness" begets dreams, Ecclesiastes 5:3 (KJV).
Industrial insomnia, Ecclesiastes 5:12.
Earth's business, Ecclesiastes 8:16 (NRSV).
Tyre businessmen, Isaiah 23:7–8.
Refusing bribes, malpractice, Isaiah 33:15–16.

Cheating customers, Isaiah 59:6 (LB).
Evil men prosper, Jeremiah 12:1–3 (LB).
Neither debtor nor creditor, Jeremiah 15:10 (LB).
Open on Sabbath day, Jeremiah 17:21–27 (LB).
Silver used as payment, Jeremiah 32:25.
Judgment on buyer, seller, Ezekiel 7:12.
Prosperity lost in judgment, Ezekiel 27:1–36.
Cheating in business, Amos 8:5–6.
Many merchants, Nahum 3:16.
Economic collapse, Zephaniah 1:11 (LB).
No wages, no business activity, Zechariah 8:10.
Correct procedure paying taxes, Mark 12:17.
Business greed, Luke 12:16–20.
Shrewd business, Luke 16:1–8.
Market, trade, John 2:16 (NRSV).
Profit determined by integrity, Acts 19:23–41.
Fair dealing, Romans 12:17 (Berk.).
Weeping businessmen, Revelation 18:11–15 (AB).
See Commerce, Merchandise.

BUSY

Overworked, 2 Corinthians 6:5 (GNB).

BUSYBODY

Strategy of Jesus with accusers, Matthew 21:25–27.
Looking for small point to criticize, Mark 3:1–6.
Jesus, Pharisees, Luke 14:1–6.
Disciples of darkness, John 8:13–59.
Blind man, Pharisees, John 9:13–34.
Arguing doctrine, Acts 15:1–3.
Controversial teachings, 1 Timothy 1:3–4.
Pointless quarrelling over words, 2 Timothy 2:14.
See Gossip, Opposition.

BUTCHER

Sheep on way to butcher, Romans 8:36 (CEV).
See Slaughter.

BUTTER See Milk.

—————————————————— **C** ——————————————————

CABINET

Solomon's cabinet, 1 Kings 4:1–6 (LB).
See Government, Leadership, Politics.

CALAMITY

Calamity avalanche, Job 1:13–19.
Day of calamity, Psalm 18:18.
Judgment brings righteousness, Isaiah 26:9.
God creates calamity, Isaiah 45:7 (NKJV).
Successive bad news, Jeremiah 51:31–32.
Street calamity, Lamentations 2:21.
Frying pan into fire, Amos 5:19.
Plundered city, Nahum 2:8–10; 3:3–4.
Persecution assists spread of Gospel, Acts 8:3–4.
Fear causes people to glorify God, Revelation 11:13.
Most severe earthquake, Revelation 16:18.
See Disaster, Trauma.

CALENDAR

Creation of days, Genesis 1:5.
Specific days, dates, Genesis 1:3–31; 2:1–3; 7:11; Exodus 16:1; Numbers 1:1; 9:1; 2 Kings 25:1–3, 8–9; Ezra 3:6; Ezekiel 29:1.
Spring activity, 1 Kings 6:1 (LB).
First month of year, Exodus 12:1–2.
Twelve months, 1 Chronicles 27:1–15.
Job finished, Nehemiah 6:15.
Month, day recorded, Esther 8:9; 9:1.
Wipe birthday from calendar, Job 3:3–6.
Lunar designations, Psalm 104:19.
Time for everything, Ecclesiastes 3:1–8.
Dates measured by reign of kings, Jeremiah 1:2–3; Daniel 1:1; Haggai 1:1; Zechariah 1:1 (Note dates more generalized: Isaiah 1:1; Micah 1:1).
Months of year:
 January—*Tebeth,* Esther 2:16.
 February—*Shebat,* Zechariah 1:7.
 March—*Adar,* Esther 3:7.
 April—*Abib,* Exodus 13:4.
 May—*Ziv,* 1 Kings 6:1.
 June—*Sivan,* Esther 8:9.
 July—*Tammuz,* Jeremiah 39:2; Zechariah 8:19.
 August—*Ab,* Numbers 33:38; Zechariah 7:3.
 September—*Elul,* Nehemiah 6:15.
 October—*Ethanim,* 1 Kings 8:2.
 November—*Bul,* 1 Kings 6:38.
 December—*Chisleu,* Ezra 10:9.
Recognizing specific date, Ezekiel 1:1.
Date related to earthquake, Amos 1:1.
Unknown date, Matthew 24:36; Mark 13:32.
See Date, Year.

CALL

Call to ministry, Genesis 12:1; Exodus 3:2–10; Numbers 27:18–23; Deuteronomy 31:23; Joshua 1:1–9; 4:1–16; Judges 6:11–14; 1 Kings 16:19; Isaiah 6:8–10; Acts 26:16.
Child's call, 1 Samuel 3:4–10 (AB).
God's chosen ministers, Psalm 65:4.
Rejecting God's call, Psalm 81:11; Isaiah 65:12; Jeremiah 7:13; Jonah 1:1–2.
Called before birth, Isaiah 49:1; Jeremiah 1:4–10 (LB).
Selecting priests, Levites, Isaiah 66:21.
Those not called, Jeremiah 23:21.
Specific call, Ezekiel 1:3.
Shepherd called to preach, Amos 7:14–15 (CEV).
Donkey chosen to serve, Matt 21:2–3.
Calling of disciples, Mark 1:16–20; 2:13–17.
Macedonian vision, Acts 16:9–10.
Jesus' kindness, Romans 1:5 (CEV).
Relation between call, ability, Romans 11:29.
Apostolic credentials, Galatians 1:1, 15–17.
"Upward call," Philippians 3:14 (NASB, NKJV).
Christ Himself ordained for service, Hebrews 5:4–6.
Chosen of the Lord, 1 Timothy 1:12 (LB).
Saved, called, 2 Timothy 1:9.
"Confirm your call," 2 Peter 1:10 (NRSV).
See Ministry, Vision.

CALLOUSED

Stubborn Pharaoh, Exodus 5:1–9.
Stiff neck, hard heart, 2 Chronicles 36:11–13; Nehemiah 9:17; Proverbs 29:1.

Hardness of heart, Psalms 78:32; 95:8; Proverbs 28:14; Jeremiah 5:3; Zechariah 7:12.

Refusing to weep, Isaiah 22:12–13.

Calloused women, Isaiah 32:9.

No awe of God, Jeremiah 2:19.

Those who pass by, Lamentations 1:12.

Hard hearts witness miracles, Matthew 11:20.

"Heartless," Matthew 19:8 (CEV).

Cares of this world, Matthew 22:1–6.

Caring neither for God or man, Luke 18:1–5.

Calloused to another's mistreatment, Acts 18:17.

People not seeking God, Romans 10:20–21 (CEV).

See Hardness, Indifference.

CALM

Keeping calm, Ecclesiastes 10:4.

Four winds restrained, Revelation 7:1.

See Patience, Restraint.

CALORIES

Going without dessert, Daniel 10:3 (LB).

CAMARADERIE

Wrong kind of camaraderie, Exodus 23:2; Numbers 11:4–10.

Kindred spirits, Numbers 11:16–17.

United behind new leader, Joshua 1:16–18.

In-law camaraderie, Ruth 1:16–19.

Unity, heart and soul, 1 Samuel 14:7.

Working diligently together, Nehemiah 4:6.

Abandoned by friend in time of trouble, Job 6:14–17.

Sharing with deserving friends, Proverbs 3:27–28.

Enduring camaraderie, Proverbs 17:17.

Two better than one, Ecclesiastes 4:8–12.

Lover, beloved, Song of Songs 2:3–6.

Weeping, rejoicing together, Isaiah 66:10.

Walking in agreement, Amos 3:3.

Divine camaraderie, Zechariah 1:3.

Mutual justice, mercy, compassion, Zechariah 7:8–10.

The Lord's own family, Mark 3:32–35.

At peace with each other, Mark 9:50.

Three-month guest, Luke 1:56.

Like teacher, like student, Luke 6:40.

United followers, Luke 8:1–3.

Sharing common goal, Luke 10:1–2.

Measure of friendship, Luke 11:5–8.

"My friend," Romans 2:1–2 (GNB).

Gentle motherly spirit, 1 Thessalonians 2:7–8.

No place for arguments, 2 Timothy 2:24–26.

See Brotherhood, Fellowship, Support, Unanimity.

CAMOUFLAGE

Isaac deceived by Jacob, Genesis 27:1–46.

Judah deceived by daughter-in-law, Genesis 38:13–19.

Camouflaged language, Genesis 42:23.

Disguising true identity, Joshua 9:3–6.

Shadows, men, Judges 9:34–37.

Pretended insanity, 1 Samuel 21:12–15.

False piety, Isaiah 58:1–2 (LB).

King Herod, Magi, Matthew 2:7–8, 12.

See Scheme.

CAMPAIGNING

Winning people's favor, 2 Samuel 15:1–6.

See Politics.

CAMPFIRE

No Sabbath fire, Exodus 35:3.

Honor bonfire, 2 Chronicles 16:14 (CEV).

Twigs set ablaze, Isaiah 64:1–2.

CAMPING

Tent meeting equipment, Numbers 4:31–32.

Camping outside residence, Nehemiah 8:13–17.

Lakeside teaching site, Mark 4:1.

See Tent.

CANCEL

Circumcision invalidated, Romans 2:25.

CANCER

Apparent malignancy, 2 Chronicles 21:18–19; Jeremiah 15:18.

CANDID

Honest rebuke, Proverbs 28:23.

Speaking candidly with God, Jeremiah 15:15–18.

Candid attitude to danger, Luke 13:31–32.
Wisdom of Gamaliel, Acts 5:34–40.
"Speaking in human terms," Romans 3:5 (NASB).
Frankness, sincerity, 1 Corinthians 1:12 (GNB).
Willing to be accepted as fool, 2 Corinthians 11:16–19.
See Relaxation.

CANDIDATES

Candidates to replace queen, Esther 2:1–4.
Replacement for Judas, Acts 1:21–26.
See Politics.

CANDLES

"Candle of the wicked," Job 21:17 (KJV).
Candle snuffers, 2 Kings 25:14 (KJV); Jeremiah 52:18 (LB).
See Lamps.

CANDY See Diabetes, Sweetness.

CANNIBALISM

Eating offspring, Deuteronomy 28:53; 2 Kings 6:28–29; Isaiah 9:20; Jeremiah 19:9; Lamentations 2:20; 4:10.
Eating one's own flesh, Isaiah 49:26.
Mothers eat children, Lamentations 4:10.
Fathers, children eating each other, Ezekiel 5:10.
Butchered nation, Micah 3:1–3.
Flesh of evil woman, Revelation 17:16.
Eating flesh of kings, Revelation 19:18.
See Heathen.

CANON

Many writers, Luke 1:1–4.

CAPABILITY

Jewish capability, Exodus 1:6–10.
Special gifts from God, Exodus 31:1–5.
Capability ridiculed, Nehemiah 4:1–3.
Incapable fools, Ecclesiastes 10:6.
What God requires, He provides, Isaiah 2:3.
Success requires more than capability, Isaiah 25:11.
Choice of candidates for government service, Daniel 1:3–5.
Evil capability, Micah 2:1.

Source of capability, Ephesians 6:10–18.
Qualifications of Christ as Savior, King, Colossians 1:15–20.
Prepared to succeed as believer, Hebrews 13:20–21.
See Ability, Talent.

CAPITAL PUNISHMENT

Divine institution, Genesis 9:6; James 1:15 (LB).
Premeditated murder, Exodus 21:14.
Death to kidnappers, Exodus 21:16.
Death to idolaters, Exodus 22:20; Deuteronomy 13:6–10.
Sabbath-breaker, Exodus 35:2; Numbers 15:32–36.
Divine execution, Leviticus 10:1–2.
Death to false prophets, Deuteronomy 13:1–10.
Crime deterrent, Deuteronomy 17:12; Ecclesiastes 8:11.
Death to juvenile delinquent, Deuteronomy 21:18–21.
Achan's execution, Joshua 7:25–26.
Trampled by horses, 2 Kings 9:30–33.
Death for treason, 2 Chronicles 23:12–15.
Hanged on self-constructed gallows, Esther 7:10.
Criminals eradicated, Psalm 101:8 (Berk.).
Royal threat, Daniel 2:8 (Berk.).
Roman government option, John 18:28–32.
Ananias, Sapphira, Acts 5:1–10.
See Beheaded, Execution, Stoning.

CAPRICIOUS

Changed plan, 2 Corinthians 1:17 (AB).
See Instability.

CAPTAIN

Divine captain, 2 Chronicles 13:12 (KJV).

CAPTIVE

Lot taken captive, Genesis 14:11–12.
Death to captives, Numbers 31:15–18; Deuteronomy 20:16–20.
Leaders, subjects put to death, Joshua 10:16–27.
Samson's captivity, Judges 16:5–30.
Captives unharmed, 1 Samuel 30:1–2.

Captives put to work, 2 Samuel 12:29–31; 1 Chronicles 20:1–3.

Brutality, indecency, Lamentations 5:11–13.

See Prison.

CARAVAN

Caravan taking boy Joseph to Egypt, Genesis 37:25–28.

Beersheba to Egypt, Genesis 46:6.

Queen of Sheba's caravan, 1 Kings 10:1–2.

Forty camel loads, 2 Kings 8:9.

Journey to Jerusalem, Ezra 8:31.

See Journey, Transportation.

CAREER

Woodcutters, water carriers, Joshua 9:26–27.

King David's long reign, 2 Samuel 5:4.

Experiencing God's blessing, Psalms 90:17; 138:8.

Enjoyment of work, Ecclesiastes 3:22.

Abundant opportunities, Matthew 9:37–38.

Advice to unmarried women, 1 Corinthians 7:25–26.

Ultimate career—life of love, Ephesians 5:1–2.

See Call, Ministry, Vocation.

CARELESS

Carelessness in duty, 1 Samuel 26:7–16; 2 Chronicles 24:5.

Lazy man's house, Ecclesiastes 10:18.

Lax in the Lord's work, Jeremiah 48:10.

Careless construction, Matthew 7:26.

Careless investment, Matthew 25:14–25.

See Neglect, Reckless.

CARESSING See Petting.

CARING

Providing for strangers, poor, Leviticus 23:22.

Caring tears, Nehemiah 1:4.

Preventive care for children, Job 1:4–5.

Concern for human weakness, Psalm 41:1.

Sharing with those deserving, Proverbs 3:27–28.

Looking after one's house, Ecclesiastes 10:18.

Neither sorrow, joy, Jeremiah 16:5–9.

Jeremiah's broken heart, Jeremiah 23:9.

Heart of flesh, stone, Ezekiel 11:19.

Caring friends facilitate healing, Mark 2:1–5; Luke 5:17–20.

Sincere care for poor, Luke 11:37–41.

Sharing with others, Luke 12:48.

Pharisee attitude to Sabbath kindness, Luke 13:10–17.

False concern for safety of Jesus, Luke 13:31.

Reaching out for those in need, Luke 14:12–14.

Hospitality toward unbeliever, Luke 15:1–2.

Father's loving heart, Luke 15:20.

Reluctance expressing concern, Romans 9:1–2.

Friend's misfortune, 2 Timothy 1:16–17.

See Compassion, Empathy, Involvement.

CARNAGE

Massive battle toll, 2 Samuel 10:18.

"Valley of Slaughter," Jeremiah 7:32 (NIV, NKJV).

Third of mankind destroyed, Revelation 9:18.

See Bloodshed, Destruction, War.

CARNALITY

Reluctant to leave sinful city, Genesis 19:15–16.

Motherhood by incest, Genesis 19:30–38.

Avoiding sorcery, Numbers 24:1–2.

People quick to disobey, Judges 2:10–13; 3:7, 12; 4:1.

Wanton woman, Judges 19:1–3.

Unable to be near ark of God, 1 Samuel 5:10–11.

Trivial sin, 1 Kings 16:31.

Doing right but not wholeheartedly, 2 Chronicles 25:2.

Evil boasting, Psalm 52:1.

Craving evil, Proverbs 21:10.

Adulterous preference, Ezekiel 16:32.

Testing God's patience, Isaiah 7:13.

Merriment instead of weeping, Isaiah 22:12–13.

Listeners who hear nothing, Isaiah 42:20.

Blatant carnality, Jeremiah 23:14.

"A nuisance to the Lord," Jeremiah 23:33 (CEV).

Carnal worshipers, Jeremiah 26:2–9.

Reasoning of backslidden people, Ezekiel 33:21–33.

Incapable of purity, Hosea 8:5.

Hostility in house of God, Hosea 9:8.

Sins doubled, Hosea 10:9 (CEV).

Feeding on wind, Hosea 12:1.

Abundant blessing can turn to backsliding, Hosea 13:6.

Continued sinning, certain judgment, Amos 1:3, 6, 9, 11, 13; 2:1, 4, 6.

Neither seeking the Lord or asking about Him, Zephaniah 1:6.

Defiled offerings, defiled people, Haggai 2:13–14.

Preferring demons to deliverance, Matthew 8:28–34.

Witnessing miracles with hard hearts, Matthew 11:20.

Grounds for divorce, Matthew 19:8.

Mind-set, Mark 8:33 (NRSV).

Marriage on earth, relationship in Heaven, Mark 12:18–27.

Afraid to profess faith, John 12:42–43.

Pleasures causing spiritual death, Romans 6:21.

Sinful passions aroused by law, Romans 7:5.

Struggle between flesh, spirit, Romans 7:15–18.

Put to death by Spirit, Romans 8:13–14.

Grace offered those who reject, Romans 10:21.

"You are still fleshly," 1 Corinthians 3:3 (NASB).

Assuming spiritual success, 1 Corinthians 4:1–21.

Immoral pride, 1 Corinthians 5:1–2.

"Do anything we want," 1 Corinthians 6:12 (CEV).

Danger of testing God, 1 Corinthians 10:14–22.

Living by world's standards, 2 Corinthians 10:2.

Gross sins, unrepentant, 2 Corinthians 12:21.

From spiritual to carnal, Galatians 3:2–3.

Reaping what is sown, Galatians 6:7–10.

"Stupid, godless people," Ephesians 4:17 (CEV).

Anger and the devil, Ephesians 4:26–27.

Enmity against God, Colossians 1:21.

Unintentional sin, Hebrews 9:7.

Sin clings closely, Hebrews 12:1 (NRSV).

Evil desire causes sin, James 1:13–15.

Bitter envy, selfish ambition, James 3:13–16.

Submit to God, resist the devil, James 4:7.

Gentile enjoyment, 1 Peter 4:3 (AB).

Evil desires, 2 Peter 1:4.

Dangerous corrupt desire, 2 Peter 2:4–10.

Those who carouse, 2 Peter 2:13–16.

Kept from will of God, 1 John 2:15–17.

Danger of losing full reward, 2 John 8.

Physical pollution, Jude 8.

Corrupted clothing, Jude 23 (GNB).

Losing first love, Revelation 2:4.

Those with little strength, Revelation 3:8.

Neither hot nor cold, Revelation 3:15.

Refusing to repent, Revelation 9:20–21.

See Backsliding, Flesh, Hedonism, Immorality, Lust, Materialism, Orgy.

CARNIVOROUS

Man, animals originally vegetarian, Genesis 1:29–30 (See 2:9).

Lions, wolves, leopards, Jeremiah 5:6.

Feast for animals following great battle, Ezekiel 39:1–20.

Locusts who attack only people, Revelation 9:3–6.

Women's hair, lions' teeth, Revelation 9:8.

See Animals.

CAROUSING

Waiting for Moses, Exodus 32:1–6.

From one sin to another, Jeremiah 9:3.

End to noisy songs, Ezekiel 26:13.

Doing what pagans do, 1 Peter 4:3.

See Hedonism.

CARPENTER

Carpenters build palace, 2 Samuel 5:11.

Lazy man's carpentry, Ecclesiastes 1:18.

Selecting wood to make idol, Isaiah 40:20.

Only a carpenter's Son, Mark 6:1–3.

Builder's honor exceeds building, Hebrews 3:3.

See Construction, Skills.

CARVING

Graven images forbidden, Exodus 20:4 (KJV).

Carving wood, stones, Exodus 31:1–5.

Cedar carvings, 1 Kings 6:18.

Destroyed paneling, Psalm 74:6.

See Sculpture.

CASH

Services paid in cash, Deuteronomy 2:6.

CASTRATION See Eunuch.

CASUAL

Casual speech, Ruth 2:5; 4:1 (LB).
See Candid.

CATACLYSM

Calamity, woe, disaster, Ezekiel 7:26 (LB).
Sky, mountains, islands, Revelation 6:14.
See Catastrophe, Disaster.

CATARACTS

Eli likely endured cataracts, 1 Samuel 4:14–15.

CATASTROPHE

God's promise to Noah, Genesis 9:8–16.
Gentle flowing waters, mighty flood, Isaiah 8:6–7.
Judgment brings righteousness, Isaiah 26:9.
Sudden overthrow, Lamentations 4:6.
Judgment avalanche, Ezekiel 14:21.
Persecution enhances spread of Gospel, Acts 8:3–4.
Destruction on earth, in sky, Revelation 6:12–14.
Fallen Babylon, Revelation 14:8.
Greatest earthquake of all time, Revelation 16:18–20.
See Disaster.

CATERING

Food, drink provided in desert, 2 Samuel 16:1–4.

CATTLE

Creation of livestock, Genesis 1:25.
First record veal for food, Genesis 18:7.
Cows, bulls as gifts, Genesis 32:13–15.
Israel's livestock preserved, Exodus 9:1–7.
Golden calves, Exodus 32:1–4; Deuteronomy 9:15–16; 1 Kings 12:28; 2 Kings 10:28–29; 17:16; 2 Chronicles 11:13–16; Psalm 106:19.
Red heifer, Numbers 19:1–3.
Blessing for calves, Deuteronomy 7:13.
Good milk yield, Deuteronomy 32:14 (GNB).
Cows as draft animals, 1 Samuel 6:7.
Consistent breeding, Job 21:10 (NKJV).
Grass-fed cattle, Psalm 104:14.
Cow hates reproof, Proverbs 12:1 (Berk.).
Gadfly from north, Jeremiah 46:20.
Fat, lean cattle, Ezekiel 34:20 (NKJV).
Beth Aven calf-idol, Hosea 10:5.
Hungry cattle, Joel 1:18 (CEV).
See Cheese, Milk.

CAUSE

Creation's first cause, Genesis 1:1.
Pure from impure, Job 14:4.
Righteousness by Scripture memorization, Psalm 119:11.
Cause, effect, Proverbs 3:9–10; Isaiah 51:15–16.
Creative source, Proverbs 30:4.
No effect without cause, Amos 3:3–8.
Good, bad fruit, Matthew 12:33.
Out of heart, Matthew 15:10–20; Mark 7:20–23.
Good things stored in heart, Luke 6:45.
See Frame-of-Reference, Motivation.

CAUTION

Caution before evil deed, Exodus 2:11–12, 14.
Take care, Deuteronomy 5:1 (Berk.).
Estimate before expenditure, Luke 14:28–30.
Parable of shrewd management, Luke 16:1–8.
Avoid being slothful, Romans 12:11 (KJV).
Diligent work for Christian employer, 1 Timothy 6:2.
Church business, Titus 1:5.
Dead men make no sales, James 1:10–11.
Evil business, Revelation 18:3 (GNB).
Lost export business, Revelation 18:11–19.
See Bargaining, Barter, Commerce, Merchandise.

CAVALRY

Vast cavalry, Revelation 9:15–16.
See Horse, Military.

CAVE

Cave residence, Genesis 19:30 (NRSV).
Burial site, Joshua 10:26–27 (CEV).

CELEBRATION

Feast on day of weaning, Genesis 21:8.
Celebrate Passover, Exodus 12:24 (CEV).
Victory song, Exodus 15:1–18.
Three festivals honoring God, Exodus 23:14–17.
Use of trumpets, Numbers 10:10.
Reviewing many years of blessing, Deuteronomy 2:7.
"Big celebration," Deuteronomy 14:26 (CEV).
Jamboree, 2 Samuel 6:5.
Temple dedication, 1 Kings 8:62–66.
Seven-day celebration, 2 Chronicles 7:8.
Time to rejoice, not weep, Nehemiah 8:9–10.
"I feel like celebrating," Psalm 13:5 (CEV).
Town, country praising the Lord, Isaiah 42:11.
Celebrate freedom, Isaiah 48:20 (CEV).
Celebrate, shout, Zephaniah 3:14 (CEV).
Banquet for Jesus, Luke 5:27–35.
Rejoicing in heaven when sinner repents, Luke 15:3–10 (Note v. 9 CEV).
Prodigal's return, Luke 15:22–24 (NRSV).
Dinner honoring Jesus, John 12:2.
Celebrating death of two witnesses, Revelation 11:7–11.
See Commemorate, Festivity.

CELEBRITY

No prophet like Moses, Deuteronomy 34:10–12.

Famous Joshua, Joshua 6:27.
Solomon's fame, 1 Kings 4:29–34; 10:1.
David's fame, 1 Chronicles 14:17.
Seeking audience with ruler, Proverbs 29:26.
The Lord should be celebrity, Isaiah 26:8.
Celebrity status of Jesus, Matthew 8:1; John 7:1–10; 12:9–13.
Humility in greatness, Matthew 23:12.
Distinguished guest, Luke 14:8.
Respect of Cornelius for Peter, Acts 10:25–26.
Few big names, 1 Corinthians 1:26 (LB).
See Fame.

CELIBACY

Relationship of Joseph, Mary, Matthew 1:25.
Remarriage after divorce, Matthew 19:8–12.
Renouncing marriage for spiritual service, Matthew 19:10–12.
Some celibate, some married, 1 Corinthians 7:8, 27.
Pauline advice, 1 Corinthians 7:27.
Cultist celibacy, 1 Timothy 4:3.
Celibacy as virtue, Revelation 14:4.
See Eunuch, Marriage, Single.

CEMETERY See Burial.

CENSURE

Temple rebuilding halted, Ezra 4:12–24.
Refusal to obey king's edict, Esther 1:10–20.

CELEBRITY

He who helped others becomes discouraged, Job 4:3–5.

Insulting censure, Job 20:3 (NRSV).

Wounds of friend, Proverbs 27:6.

Futile effort to suppress truth, Jeremiah 38:1–6.

Looking for something to criticize, Mark 3:2.

Christian method of rebuke, 2 Thessalonians 3:14–15.

See Criticism, Opposition, Rejection.

CENSUS

Census in Israel, Numbers 1:2; 26:2.

Harmful census, 2 Samuel 24:1 (LB).

Men of military age, 2 Samuel 24:2.

Census by satanic impetus, 1 Chronicles 21:1.

Enumeration of exiles, Ezra 2:3–64.

Divine registration, Psalm 87:5–6.

God's command to increase population, Jeremiah 29:4–6.

Taking census at birth of Jesus, Luke 2:1–5 (See NRSV "enrollment").

See Statistics.

CENTENARIAN

Abraham's old age, Genesis 17:17 (Berk.).

Young at one hundred, Isaiah 65:20.

See Geriatrics, Old Age.

CENTURION

Centurion's servant, Matthew 8:5–13.

Convinced centurions, Matthew 27:54; Mark 15:39, 44.

God-fearing centurion, Acts 10:1–33.

Unwise centurion, Acts 27:11.

See Military, Soldier.

CEREMONY

Circumcision at advanced age, Genesis 17:10–27.

Seven-day ordination, Exodus 29:35.

Woman's purification, Numbers 5:11–31.

Royalty confirmation, 1 Samuel 11:12–15.

Improvised ceremony for new king, 2 Kings 9:11–13.

Religious works involved in idolatry, Isaiah 46:1.

Washing hands before eating, Matthew 15:1–9.

King Agrippa's pomp, Acts 25:23.

See Protocol.

CERTAINTY

Equal certainty good things, bad, Joshua 23:15.

Time for everything, Ecclesiastes 3:1–8.

Certainty of God's plans, purposes, Isaiah 14:24.

Promise of judgment fulfilled, Lamentations 2:17.

Divine love, faithfulness day-by-day, Lamentations 3:22–24.

"It will happen," Habakkuk 2:3 (CEV).

Believe Good News, Mark 1:14–15.

Certainty of disciples, John 17:6–7.

Divine decisions irrevocable, Romans 11:29.

Confident now of future fulfillment, Hebrews 11:13.

No lie comes from truth, 1 John 2:20–21.

See Assurance.

CERTIFICATION *See Credentials, Documentation, Sponsorship, Validity.*

CHAFF

Wind-swept chaff, Job 21:18; Psalm 1:4; Isaiah 17:13.

Burned straw, Isaiah 5:24.

Chaff from threshing floor, Hosea 13:3; Matthew 3:12.

CHAINS *See Fetters.*

CHALLENGE

Challenge to possess land, Deuteronomy 1:21.

March on with strong soul, Judges 5:21.

Smallest, weakest, Judges 6:14–16.

Come up, fight, 1 Samuel 14:8–12.

Giant challenge, 1 Samuel 17:4–10.

Overcoming obstacles with God's help, 2 Samuel 22:30.

Confidence to face challenge, Psalm 18:29.

Challenging God, Isaiah 5:18–19.

Challenging enemy, Isaiah 8:9–10.

Life or death, Daniel 2:1–10.

Challenge to work for divine cause, Haggai 2:4.

Becoming fishers of men, Matthew 4:19.

Abundant fishing follows challenge, Luke 5:1–11.
See Threat.

CHAMPAGNE

Foaming wine with dregs, Psalm 75:8.

CHANCE

Death by measurement, 2 Samuel 8:2.
Death of king by random arrow, 2 Chronicles 18:33–34.
Coin toss decision, Nehemiah 10:34 (LB).
"Time and chance," Ecclesiastes 9:11.
Guidance omens, Ezekiel 21:21.
Casting lots to determine guilt, Jonah 1:7.
Chosen by lot, Luke 1:9.
Casting lots to determine God's will, Acts 1:23–26.
See Fortuity, Happenstance.

CHANGE

God's command to Abram, Genesis 12:1–9.
Internal, external change, Genesis 35:2.
Time for change, Deuteronomy 1:6.
Tear down, build, Ecclesiastes 3:3.
Don't imitate ancestors, Zechariah 1:1–6.
Comparing old, new, Luke 5:36–39.
Paul feared Corinthian reunion, 2 Corinthians 12:20–21.

CHAOS

Warriors stumbling over each other, Jeremiah 46:12.
Community despair, Ezekiel 7:27.
See Anarchy, Destruction, Peril, War.

CHAPLAIN

Chaplain's role in battle, Deuteronomy 20:1–4.

CHARACTER

Blameless man, Genesis 6:9.
Father's actions influence son, Genesis 9:18–27.
Angel's description of unborn Ishmael, Genesis 16:11–12.
Prenatal description, Genesis 25:21–34.
Father's predictions, Genesis 49:1–28.
Exemplary prophet, 1 Samuel 12:3.
Deeds reveal person, 1 Samuel 24:13.

Kindness to enemy, 2 Samuel 9:1–8.
Refusing water which endangered others, 2 Samuel 23:15–17.
God's commendation of Job, Job 1:8.
Pure cannot come from impure, Job 14:4.
The Lord judges integrity, Psalm 7:8.
Characteristics of holy life, Psalm 15:1–5.
"True to myself," Psalm 26:1 (CEV).
Description of in-depth character, Psalm 51:6.
Good character, Psalm 106:3 (LB).
Marks of evil character, Proverbs 6:16–19.
Good, evil influence, Proverbs 11:16.
Lacking character with wealth, Proverbs 19:10.
Childhood evidence, Proverbs 20:11.
The Lord knows inmost being, Proverbs 20:27.
Disguising true self by false speech, Proverbs 26:24–26.
Face reflects inner person, Proverbs 27:19.
Sometimes better poor than rich, Proverbs 28:6.
Wife of noble character, Proverbs 31:10–31.
Youth building character, Ecclesiastes 11:9.
Eloquent description of noble person, Isaiah 32:8.
Bribes refused, Isaiah 33:15–16.
"A lady forever," Isaiah 47:7 (NKJV).
Evil deeds, motives likened to eggs, Isaiah 59:4–5.
Some juice left in grapes, Isaiah 65:8.
Search for one honest person, Jeremiah 5:1.
Act of shame, Jeremiah 13:26.
Heart, mind determine character, Jeremiah 17:10.
Description of righteous man, Ezekiel 18:5–9.
Practice deceit, Hosea 7:11.
Mark of man who pleases the Lord, Micah 6:8.
Fasting in secret, Matthew 6:16–18.
Trees, people, Matthew 7:20 (LB).
Seasoned with salt, Mark 9:50.
Revealing thoughts of heart, Luke 2:34–35.
Balanced life of Jesus, Luke 2:52.
Good fruit, bad fruit, Luke 6:43–45.
Those of good character welcomed truth, Luke 8:15.

Clean outside, dirty inside, Luke 11:37–41.

Jesus knew what was in men, John 2:24–25.

Heart motivation, Acts 13:22.

Noble character of Bereans, Acts 17:11.

Character within, Romans 2:28–29.

"Proven character," Romans 5:4 (NASB).

Man's dual nature, Romans 7:21–25.

Character determined before birth, Romans 9:11–13.

Always doing what is right, Romans 12:17.

Overcome evil with good, Romans 12:21.

Bad company, good character, 1 Corinthians 15:33.

Standing firm in faith, 1 Corinthians 16:13–14.

Fruit of Spirit, Galatians 5:22–23.

Ultimate career, life of love, Ephesians 5:1–2.
See Conduct, Exemplary, Lifestyle.

CHARACTER ASSASSINATION

Stripped of one's honor, Job 19:9.
See Demean, Gossip, Slander.

CHARACTERISTIC

Variety in nature, Proverbs 30:18–19.

CHARIOT

Vehicle of distinction, Genesis 41:42–43.

Travel by chariot, Genesis 46:29; 2 Kings 9:16; Acts 8:26–30.

Battle chariots, Exodus 14:7; Joshua 11:4.

Iron chariots, Joshua 17:16; Judges 1:19; 4:13.

Three thousand strong, 1 Samuel 13:5.

Charioteers defeated, 2 Samuel 10:18.

Community of chariots, 1 Kings 9:19.

Escape vehicle, 1 Kings 12:18.

Replacement order, 1 Kings 20:25.

Death vehicle, 1 Kings 22:35.

Chariot of fire, 2 Kings 2:11.

Faith in chariots, Psalm 20:7; Isaiah 31:1.

Chariots of God, Psalm 68:17; Isaiah 66:15; Habakkuk 3:8.

Clouds as chariots, Psalm 104:3.

Similarity to modern traffic, Nahum 2:4.

Chariots put to flames, Nahum 2:13.
See Transportation.

CHARISMATIC

No signs for rejected people, Psalms 74:9; 77:14.

Dreams, visions, Word of God, Jeremiah 23:25–32.

Speaking in new tongues, Mark 16:17.

Laying on of hands, Acts 19:1–7.

Role of tongues, 1 Corinthians 12:27–31; 14:1, 5.

Believers, unbelievers, 1 Corinthians 14:22 (GNB).
See Gift, Glossolalia, Holy Spirit, Tongues.

CHARITY

Giving to poor, lending to the Lord, Proverbs 19:17.

Concern for poor, Proverbs 28:27.

Those who cannot help themselves, Proverbs 31:8–9.

Open arms to poor, Proverbs 31:20.

Real meaning of fasting, Isaiah 58:3–7.

Care of those in need, Acts 4:32–35.

Woman who helped poor, Acts 9:36–42.

Devout centurion, Acts 10:2.

Kindness to poor recognized by the Lord, Acts 10:4.

Reaching out to help others, Acts 11:27–30.

Looking after needs of poor, Romans 15:26–27.

Remembering the poor, Galatians 2:10.
See Benevolence, Welfare.

CHARM

No protective "charm," Jeremiah 7:4 (LB).

CHASTITY

Proof of chastity, Deuteronomy 22:13–21.

Geriatric chastity, 1 Kings 1:1–4.

Those who looked after king's harem, Esther 2:14.

Covenant of personal purity, Job 31:1.

Purity by determination, Proverbs 2:10–22; Colossians 3:5.

Lust in heart, Proverbs 6:24–25; Matthew 5:28.

Puberty described, Ezekiel 16:5–9.

Pregnant virgin, Matthew 1:25 (LB).

Avoid evil associates, 1 Corinthians 5:11.

Temple of Holy Spirit, 1 Corinthians 6:13–19.

No hint of immorality, Ephesians 5:3–4.
Challenge to purity, 1 Timothy 5:22.
See Morality, Purity.

CHATTER

Thoughtless words, Job 38:2 (Berk.).
Godless chatter, 2 Timothy 2:16.
See Loquacious, Trivia.

CHAUVINISM

Two girls per man, Judges 5:30.
Avoiding woman as cause of death, Judges
    9:52–55.
Honoring husband, Psalm 45:10–11.
See Husband, Women's Rights.

CHEAP

People sold for next to nothing, Psalm 44:12
    (NKJV).
Poor people valued at shoe price, Amos 2:6.

CHEATING

Dishonest scales, Deuteronomy 25:13;
    Proverbs 11:1; Hosea 12:7; Micah 6:11.
Divine hatred for cheating, Proverbs 11:1
    (LB).
Deceptive purchasing, Proverbs 20:14.
"You enjoy cheating," Hosea 12:7 (CEV).
Children sold for illicit use, Joel 3:3.
Cheating in business, Amos 8:5–6 (See CEV).
Skin people alive, Micah 3:2 (CEV).
Wealth from cheating, Micah 6:10 (LB).
Can dishonesty be acquitted? Micah 6:11.
Marriage cheating, Malachi 3:5 (CEV).
Cheating the Lord, Malachi 3:8–9.
Expensive gain, Matthew 16:26.
Agreement to cheat, Acts 5:2 (CEV).
"We have cheated no one," 2 Corinthians
    7:2 (NKJV).
Failing to pay workman's wages, James 5:4.
See Dishonesty, Unscrupulous.

CHEEK

Striking, 1 Kings 22:24; Job 16:10.
Turning cheek, Lamentations 3:30; Mat-
    thew 5:39; Luke 6:29.
See Forbearance, Patience.

CHEER

Cheer that shook ground, 1 Samuel 4:5.
Singing to heavy heart, Proverbs 25:20.
Cheering convalescent, Isaiah 39:1.
See Compassion, Encouragement, Pity.

CHEESE

Bread, cheese, 1 Samuel 17:17–18.
Cheese from cow's milk, 2 Samuel 17:27–
    29.
Anxiety like curdled cheese, Job 10:10.

CHEMICALS

Chemicals cause unproductive land, Deu-
    teronomy 29:23.
See Ecology.

CHERISH See Affection, Love.

CHEWING See Teeth.

CHILD See Children.

CHILD ABUSE

Abused boy Joseph, Genesis 37:12–36.
Threatened torture, 1 Kings 3:16–27.
Wartime slaughter, Isaiah 13:16.
Children slaughtered, Ezekiel 9:6; Matthew
    2:13–18.
Boys traded for prostitutes, Joel 3:3.
See Juvenile Delinquent.

CHILDBIRTH

Birth pangs, Genesis 3:16.
Rapid delivery, Exodus 1:15–18 (LB).
Husband's death brings death to wife,
    1 Samuel 4:19–20.
Secure delivery, Psalm 22:9.
Delivery pain, Isaiah 26:17.
Bearing firstborn, Jeremiah 4:31.
Men suffering childbirth pains, Jeremiah
    30:6.
Courage wavers, Jeremiah 49:22.
Joy of childbirth, John 16:21.
Childbirth in heaven, Revelation 12:1–6.
See Birth, Pregnancy.

CHILDHOOD

Helpless infants, Numbers 11:12.
Child's calling, 1 Samuel 3:1–10.

Wild donkey's colt, Job 11:12.
Childhood training, Deuteronomy 6:4–9;
 Proverbs 22:6.
Childhood memories, Proverbs 4:3–4.
Discipline in childhood, Proverbs 22:15.
Street children, Zechariah 8:5.
Childhood same as slavery, Galatians 4:1.
Childhood guardians, Galatians 4:2.
Fickle childhood, Ephesians 4:14.
Remnant childhood, Hebrews 5:12–13.

CHILDISH

Corrective discipline, Proverbs 22:15.
Senseless children, Jeremiah 4:22.
Spiritual infants, 1 Corinthians 3:1–2.
Marks of immaturity, 1 Corinthians 13:11.
Limited rights of immature, Galatians 4:1–3.
Acting like infants, Ephesians 4:14; He-
 brews 5:12.
See Immaturity.

CHILDLESS

Barrenness of Abram, Sarai, Genesis 11:30;
 15:2; 16:1–5.
Infertility in household of Abimelech, Gen-
 esis 20:17–18.
Lifetime infertility, 2 Samuel 6:23.
No son to carry name, 2 Samuel 18:18.
Eunuch's name preserved, Isaiah 56:3–5.
Given son in declining years, Luke 1:5–25.
See Barren, Impotence.

CHILDLIKE

Childlike attitude, 1 Kings 3:7.
Spirit of weaned child, Psalm 131:2.
Childlike faith, Mark 10:15; Luke 18:16.
Adults toward evil, children toward God,
 1 Corinthians 14:20.
Adults like newborns, 1 Peter 2:2.
See Discipleship, Trust.

CHILDREN

Spoken of as "seed," Genesis 12:7; 22:18
 (KJV).
Parental favorites, Genesis 25:28 (KJV).
Adoptions, Genesis 15:3; 48:5; Exodus 2:10;
 Esther 2:7.
Births predicted in advance, Genesis 16:11;
 18:10; Judges 13:3; 1 Kings 13:2; 2 Kings
 4:16; Isaiah 9:6; Luke 1:13.

Abraham's relationship to stepsister, Gene-
 sis 20:12, 16.
Children born in old age, Genesis 21:1–7.
Weaning of Isaac, Genesis 21:8.
Fetal competitors, Genesis 25:22.
Personality differences, Genesis 25:27 (KJV).
Grieved parents, Genesis 26:34–35.
Gift from God, Genesis 48:8–9.
"Bless the lads," Genesis 48:16 (NKJV).
Adventures to tell children, Exodus 10:1–2.
Children learn by asking questions, Exodus
 12:26–27.
Father's sin charged to children, Exodus
 20:5–6; 34:6–7; Numbers 14:18.
"Little ones," Deuteronomy 29:11 (NKJV);
 Joshua 1:14 (NRSV).
Favorite son, Deuteronomy 33:24–25 (GNB).
Sacrificed children, Leviticus 20:1–5.
Surrogate spiritual children, Numbers
 3:11–13.
Death to enemy women, children, Num-
 bers 31:7–18.
Teaching children, Deuteronomy 4:9;
 31:13; Proverbs 22:6; Isaiah 28:9.
Divine promises to children, Deuteronomy
 5:16; Psalm 27:10; Proverbs 8:32; Mark
 10:14; Acts 2:39.
Truth impressed upon children, Deuteron-
 omy 6:7 (Berk.).
Threat to firstborn, Joshua 6:26.
No sons, only daughters, Joshua 17:3.
Affection to child, Ruth 4:16 (GNB).
Good works performed by children, 1 Sam-
 uel 2:18; 2 Kings 5:2–3; 2 Chronicles
 24:1–2; John 6:9.
Prophetic message to child, 1 Samuel 3:1–14.
Children who need conversion, 1 Samuel 3:7.
Son's influence over father, 1 Samuel 19:1–6.
David's many children, 2 Samuel 5:13–15.
God's promise to David, 2 Samuel 7:12.
Parental influence, 1 Kings 9:4; 22:52;
 2 Chronicles 17:3; 22:3; Jeremiah 9:14;
 Matthew 14:8; 2 Timothy 1:5.
Children offered in pagan sacrifices,
 2 Kings 3:26–27; 16:1–3; Ezekiel 16:20.
Little girl's influence, 2 Kings 5:1–3.
Good children, evil fathers, 2 Kings 12:2;
 18:3; 22:2; 2 Chronicles 34:3.
Twelve-year-old king, 2 Kings 21:1.
Eight-year-old king, 2 Kings 22:1 (CEV).

Josiah, child king, 2 Chronicles 34:1.

Fate of father, fate of sons, Esther 9:12–14.

Grim future, Job 27:14.

"Pet bird for little girls," Job 41:5 (CEV).

Children give praise to God, Psalm 8:2.

God looks after fatherless, Psalm 10:14.

Beautiful daughter, Psalm 45:10–11.

Tell next generation, Psalm 48:13.

Child given confidence in the Lord, Psalm 71:5–6, 17–18.

Lineage of faith, Psalm 78:1–8.

Future generations, Psalm 102:18.

Father's compassion for children, Psalm 103:13–14.

Barren woman becomes happy mother, Psalm 113:9.

Young man's way to purity, Psalm 119:9.

Children the Lord's special blessing, Psalm 127:3–5.

Healthy children, Psalm 128:3 (LB).

Sadistic killing of children, Psalm 137:9.

Prayer for sons, daughters, Psalm 144:12 (CEV).

Child's receptive mind, Proverbs 4:3–4 (NASB).

Sons wise, shameful, Proverbs 10:5.

Sparing rod, Proverbs 13:24.

Insecure children, Proverbs 14:26.

Children proud of parents, Proverbs 17:6; Zechariah 10:7.

Hurt of foolish son, Proverbs 17:25.

Children rob parents, Proverbs 19:26; 28:24.

Character begins with childhood, Proverbs 20:11.

Properly training child, Proverbs 22:6.

Folly yields to discipline, Proverbs 22:15; 23:13–14.

Children bring joy to parents, Proverbs 23:22–25.

Wise son fortifies father, Proverbs 27:11.

Scolding, spanking, Proverbs 29:15 (LB).

Discipline rewarded, Proverbs 29:17.

Those who dishonor parents, Proverbs 30:11.

Wise child, foolish king, Ecclesiastes 4:13 (KJV).

Having one hundred children, Ecclesiastes 6:3.

Government in children's hands, Isaiah 3:4.

Spiritual teaching, Isaiah 54:13 (KJV).

Children of evil parents, Isaiah 57:3.

Those yet unborn, Jeremiah 1:4–5; Hebrews 7:1, 10.

Like father, like children, Jeremiah 16:10–13 (LB).

Better not to have had children, Jeremiah 22:30.

Father's command regarding wine, Jeremiah 35:1–14.

Protecting orphans, widows, Jeremiah 49:11.

Children dying in mothers' arms, Lamentations 2:12.

Children without food, drink, Lamentations 4:4.

Cannibalistic mothers, Lamentations 4:10.

Children sacrificed to idols, Ezekiel 16:20; 23:37.

When to disobey parents, Ezekiel 20:18–21.

Unblemished children, Daniel 1:4.

Unable to have children, Hosea 9:11.

Lost value of children, Joel 3:3 (LB).

Disciplining those much loved, Amos 3:2.

No descendants of Nineveh, Nahum 1:14.

Children playing in streets, Zechariah 8:5.

Gospel turns children against parents, Matthew 10:32–36.

Jesus recognized childhood comprehension, Matthew 11:25.

Desiring prestigious sons, Matthew 20:20–28.

Transcending human relationships, Matthew 22:41–46.

Jesus saw greatness in children, Matthew 18:1–6; Mark 9:42.

Failing to see importance of children, Matthew 19:13–15; Mark 10:13–16; Luke 18:15–17.

Children praise the Lord, Matthew 21:16.

Jesus' compassion for sick girl, Mark 5:21–42.

Child's value, example, Mark 9:36–37.

"Little followers," Mark 9:42 (CEV).

Joy, delight to parents, Luke 1:14–15.

Obedience of child Jesus, Luke 2:41–52.

Balanced life of Jesus, Luke 2:52.

Concern for only child, Luke 9:38.

Blessing babies, Luke 18:15–17.

Parents support children, not children parents, 2 Corinthians 12:14.

Imitating parents, Ephesians 5:1 (LB).

Disciplining children, Ephesians 6:4; 1 Timothy 3:4.

Children's encouragement, instruction, Colossians 3:20–21.

Grandmother's faith passed on to grandson, 2 Timothy 1:5.

Bible influence from infancy, 2 Timothy 3:15.

Exemplary children, Titus 1:6 (AB).

The Lord takes His children's hands, Hebrews 8:9.

God's law in mind, heart, Hebrews 8:10.

Importance of discipline, Hebrews 12:5–11.

Children of good parents, 2 John 4.

Christian children, 3 John 4.

See Childhood, Daughter, Family, Infant, Nepotism, Names, Offspring, PKs, Progeny, Son.

CHILD SUPPORT

Avoiding child support, 1 Timothy 5:8.

CHIROPODIST

Foot problems, 2 Chronicles 16:12.

Beautiful feet, Isaiah 52:7.

CHIVALRY

Moses' gallantry, Exodus 2:15–19.

See Courtesy, Women's Rights.

CHOICE

Choice of place to live, Genesis 13:10–13.

Choosing the Lord, Genesis 28:21; Ruth 1:16; 1 Kings 18:39; 2 Kings 5:17; Psalms 16:2; 31:14; 63:1; 73:25; 118:28; 140:6.

Willing to contribute, Exodus 35:20–29.

Limited freedom, Numbers 36:6.

The Lord's choice, Deuteronomy 7:6; Psalm 4:3; 1 Corinthians 1:26; Ephesians 1:4; James 2:5; 1 Peter 2:10.

Blessing, curse, Deuteronomy 11:26–28 (CEV).

Choice rewarded, Deuteronomy 30:1–20.

Family's choice, serve God, Joshua 24:15.

Loving choice, Ruth 1:16.

Israel's wrong choice, 1 Samuel 12:18–19 (GNB).

Man's choice versus God's, 1 Samuel 16:1–13.

Three choices, 2 Samuel 24:11–17.

Second best, 1 Kings 2:13–25.

Given choice, 1 Kings 3:5.

Discerning choice, 1 Kings 3:9.

Choosing between two options, 1 Kings 18:21.

God's will, freedom of choice, Ezra 7:18.

Choose heart's direction, Job 11:13 (NRSV).

Choosing to follow truth, Psalm 119:30 (Berk.).

Evil by choice, Proverbs 1:29; Isaiah 65:12; 66:3.

Man's choice, God's guidance, Proverbs 16:9.

Better option than scarlet sin, Isaiah 1:18.

Gentle waters, flood waters, Isaiah 8:6–7.

Choice contrary to God's will, Isaiah 66:3.

Way of life, way of death, Jeremiah 21:8.

Valley of decision, Joel 3:14.

Choose good, not evil, Amos 5:15 (CEV).

Barabbas or Christ, Matthew 27:15–26; Mark 15:6–15; Luke 23:18–19, 25; John 18:38–40; Acts 3:14.

Choosing to be clean, Mark 1:41 (NRSV).

Choice to receive, believe, John 1:12.

Wind chooses, John 3:8 (NRSV).

Ultimate choice, John 3:36.

Jesus' choice of sacrifice, John 10:17–18.

Most meaningful choice, John 15:16.

Freedom of choice removed, Romans 9:14–24 (LB).

Discipline preference, 1 Corinthians 4:21.

"Hard choice to make," Philippians 1:23 (CEV).

Good deed by choice, Philemon 12 (GNB).

God's choice, 1 Thessalonians 1:4 (CEV).

Moses' choice, Hebrews 11:24–25.

See Decision, Predestination, Selection, Volition.

CHOIR

In charge of temple music, 1 Chronicles 6:31–46; 9:33.

Choir, orchestra, 1 Chronicles 15:16; 25:6–7; Ecclesiastes 2:7–8 (LB).

Military music, 2 Chronicles 20:21.

Singers appointed, Nehemiah 7:1.

Singing "loudly and clearly," Nehemiah 12:40–41 (LB).

Payment to choir members, Nehemiah 12:47.

Unpaid choir, Nehemiah 13:10 (LB).

Singing trees, Psalm 96:12.

Antiphonal rendition, Isaiah 6:3 (LB).

Choir of angels, Revelation 5:11–12.
See Hymn, Music.

CHOIR DIRECTOR

Able director, Nehemiah 12:40–42.

CHRIST

Angelic Christ, Genesis 48:16 (AB).
Type of sin-bearing, Numbers 21:6–9.
Names of Christ, Numbers 24:17; Joshua
5:15; Psalm 2:2; Song of Songs 2:1; Isaiah
9:6; 11:1; 53:3; Haggai 2:7; Zechariah 3:8;
Matthew 11:19; John 1:1; 6:48; 10:7; Acts
10:36; Romans 10:12; Hebrews 13:20;
3 John 7; Revelation 5:5–6, 8; 19:13.
Ezekiel's vision of the Lord, Ezekiel 1:26–28.
Abraham's "seed," Galatians 3:16.
"The Christ," Hebrews 6:1 (NASB).
Beginning, End, Revelation 22:13.
See Jesus, Messiah, Preexistence, Redeemer.

CHRISTIAN

Faithful people, Psalm 16:3 (GNB).
Biblical names for Christians, Matthew
5:13; John 10:27; 15:14–15; 1 Corinthi-
ans 12:18, 25; Ephesians 5:1; 2 Timothy
2:4; 1 Peter 2:11, 16; 3:7; 1 John 2:1.
First designation of Christians, Acts 11:26.
"God's loved ones," Romans 1:7 (Berk.).
"God's people," 2 Corinthians 1:1 (GNB).
"Religion" used as synonym, Titus 1:1–2
(GNB).
Suffering as a Christian, 1 Peter 4:16.
"Royal race," Revelation 1:6 (AB).
See Believer, Body of Christ, Discipleship.

CHRISTMAS

Initial prophecy of Christ's birth, Genesis
3:15.
Bethlehem's alternate name, Genesis 35:19.
Star of Bethlehem, Numbers 24:17.
One came, saved, was forgotten, Ecclesias-
tes 9:14–15.
Virgin Birth prophesied, Isaiah 7:14 (NRSV).
Messiah prophesied, Isaiah 9:1–7.
Similarity to Christmas tree, Jeremiah
10:3–5.
Bethlehem prophecy, Micah 5:2.
Christmas rumors, Matthew 2:3 (LB).

CHRISTMAS

Time between birth, Magi, Matthew 2:16.

Hard-hearted generosity, Matthew 7:11 (LB).

Yuletide ambience, Luke 2:9.

See Magi, Nativity.

CHURCH

Family of God, Deuteronomy 14:2.

Church dinners, Deuteronomy 14:22–26 (CEV).

Generation away from potential extinction, Judges 2:10.

Place of blessing, Psalm 84:4.

Prophet's vision, Isaiah 11:10 (KJV).

Place of refuge, Isaiah 37:1.

Search for wisdom, Isaiah 37:14.

Church for all nations, Micah 4:2.

Christ's frequent attendance, Matthew 12:9; Mark 1:21.

Divinely instituted church, Matthew 16:18.

Recognition by Jesus, Matthew 18:17.

Many invited to wedding banquet, few chosen, Matthew 22:1–14.

Daily attendance, Luke 2:36–37; 24:52–53.

Childhood pattern, Luke 4:16.

Varied congregational membership, Luke 18:10.

Prayer of Jesus for His own, John 17:20–23.

Kingdom not of this world, John 18:36.

New relationships in Christ, John 19:26–27.

Message to Gentiles, Acts 15:13–21; 18:6.

Strong churches winning converts, Acts 16:5.

Special greeting to house church, Romans 16:5.

Boasting about church, 1 Corinthians 5:6 (AB).

Church a "mystery," Ephesians 1:9–10; 3:2–3.

Spiritual commonwealth, Philippians 3:20 (Berk.).

God's household, Ephesians 2:19–20; 1 Timothy 3:15.

Truth pillar, 1 Timothy 3:15 (AB).

Promised from time's beginning, Titus 1:1–3.

Admonition to attend worship, Hebrews 10:25.

Living stones, 1 Peter 2:5.

No churches in heaven, Revelation 21:22.

See Attendance, Congregation, Synagogue.

CHURCH AND STATE

Illustrate role of religion in politics, Jeremiah 37; 38.

Government, religious leaders crucified Jesus, Mark 8:31 (CEV).

See Citizenship, Government.

CHURCH GROWTH

Rapid church growth, Acts 4:4; 21:20.

Church planting, Acts 14:27.

See Evangelism.

CHURCH LEADER See Clergy, Elder.

CINNAMON

Fragrant cinnamon, Exodus 30:23; Proverbs 7:17.

Garden variety, Song of Songs 4:14.

Cargoes of cinnamon, spice, Revelation 18:13.

CIRCUMCISION

Circumcision covenant, Genesis 17:1–27.

Requirement for Old Testament marriage, Genesis 34:1–24.

Punishment for neglect, Exodus 4:24–25.

Circumcision knives, Joshua 5:3.

Wilderness delay, Joshua 5:7.

Vulgar dowry request, 1 Samuel 18:25.

Circumcision's meaning, Jeremiah 4:4; Romans 2:28–29.

Uncircumcised hearts, Jeremiah 9:25–26; Acts 7:51.

Performed on eighth day, Luke 1:59 (NRSV).

Date of circumcision, Acts 7:8; Genesis 17:12.

Subject of legalism, Acts 15:1; Galatians 5:2.

Spiritual, not literal, Romans 2:29 (NRSV).

Titus' exemption, Galatians 2:3.

Spiritual circumcision, Colossians 2:11 (LB).

See Legalism.

CIRCUMSTANCES

Childless Abram promised offspring, Genesis 15:1–6.

Circumstances test covenant of promise, Genesis 22:1–18; 13:16; 15:5.

Accepting circumstances, Genesis 43:14.

Evil turned to good, Genesis 50:19–21.

Circumstances gave Moses doubts, Exodus 5:22–23.

Doubting God's goodness in circumstances, Judges 6:11–13.

Romance caused by famine, Ruth 1:1.

Lost donkeys, new king, 1 Samuel 9:1–10:1.

Circumstances from the Lord, Psalm 16:5.

Circumstances change way, direction, Psalm 32:9.

"No matter what happens," Psalm 34:1 (LB).

Waters up to neck, Psalm 69:1.

God has made each day for His purpose, Psalm 118:24.

The Lord does as He pleases, Psalm 135:6.

Accept good, bad, Ecclesiastes 7:14.

"Evil times," Ecclesiastes 9:12.

Prosperity, disaster in God's control, Isaiah 45:7.

Do not question Potter, Isaiah 45:9.

Success whatever circumstances, Jeremiah 17:7–8.

Obedience in all circumstances, Jeremiah 32:6–7; 42:6.

Thanking God in adverse circumstances, Jeremiah 33:10–11.

Though crops fail, trust the Lord, Habakkuk 3:17–18.

Circumstances should not hinder confidence, Luke 8:22–25.

Reversed circumstances, Luke 16:19–26.

Human, divine circumstances, John 11:21–22, 32.

Divine power supersedes circumstances, John 11:38–44.

Unpleasant circumstances glorify God, Acts 16:16–40.

Imprisonment made Rome ministry possible, Romans 1:13.

All circumstances good, Romans 8:28.

Nothing separates us from God's love, Romans 8:37–39.

New convert accepts circumstances, 1 Corinthians 7:24, 30 (LB).

Illness caused Paul to preach Gospel, Galatians 4:13–14.

Adverse circumstances bring blessing, Philippians 1:12–14.

Thankful in all circumstances, 1 Thessalonians 5:18.

Reason for circumstances, Philemon 15–16.

Circumstances not necessarily reality, Hebrews 11:11–12.

See Fortuity, Happenstance.

CIRCUS

Tamed animals, James 3:7.

CISTERN

Personal cisterns, 2 Kings 18:31.

Water for livestock, 2 Chronicles 26:10.

Cisterns dug in disobedience, Jeremiah 2:13.

See Wells.

CITATION

Honor not fitting fool, Proverbs 26:1.

Reward for good mother, Proverbs 31:31.

Jesus cited John the Baptist, Matthew 11:11–14.

Let the Lord commend, 2 Corinthians 10:17–18.

See Commendation, Honor.

CITIZEN

Contented citizens, 1 Kings 4:20.

CITIZENSHIP

Civil disobedience, Exodus 1:15–21.

Duty of citizens to new leadership, Joshua 1:16–17.

Citizen responsibility, 1 Samuel 12:13–15.

Obedience to civil law, Ezra 7:26; Ecclesiastes 8:2.

Rights of citizens, Nehemiah 5:4–13.

Noncomplaining, Psalm 144:14 (NKJV).

Upright citizens, Proverbs 11:11.

Obeying law, Proverbs 28:7 (AB).

Search for one honest person in city, Jeremiah 5:1.

Israel travelers in their own country, Jeremiah 14:8.

Exiles subjected themselves to government, Jeremiah 29:4–7.

Lowered standards of civil obedience, Ezekiel 5:7.

Civil disobedience, Daniel 3:1–30.

Daniel's prayer for himself, nation, Daniel 9:1–19.

Paying taxes, Matthew 17:27; 22:21; Luke 20:21–25.

Good words for centurion, Luke 7:4–5.

Valued Roman citizenship, Acts 16:35–39.

Protection for Roman citizen, Acts 22:24–29.

Submission to government authority, Romans 13:1; Titus 3:1; 1 Peter 2:13–14.

Aliens, exiles, 1 Peter 2:11 (RSV).

Aspects of good citizenship, Romans 13:7.

Praying for those in authority, 1 Timothy 2:1–4.

Christian citizenship, Titus 3:1; 1 Peter 2:13–17.

Citizens of New Jerusalem, Revelation 21:27.

See Alien, Church and State, Xenophobia.

CITY

Cities of refuge, Exodus 21:13; Numbers 35:6; Deuteronomy 4:41–42; 19:1–7; Joshua 20:2; 1 Chronicles 6:67.

Babylon lies deserted, Isaiah 13:19–22.

Description of destroyed Jerusalem, Lamentations 1:1.

City without food, Lamentations 1:11.

Demeaned cities, Ezekiel 25:5 (AB).

City's spiritual name, Ezekiel 48:35.

Nineveh, large city, Jonah 3:3.

New Jerusalem, Revelation 21:2, 15–27.

See Community, Neighborhood, Street, Urban.

CIVIL DISOBEDIENCE

Obeying God first, Daniel 3:1–30.

See Anarchy, Mob Psychology.

CIVILITY

Joseph's example, Genesis 47:1–10.

Christ's teaching, Luke 14:8–10.

Example of civility, Philippians 2:19–23.

Civility practiced, 3 John 1–6.

CIVIL WAR

Civil war in Israel, 2 Chronicles 11:1 (LB).

CLAIM

Claiming long term promise, Joshua 14:6–15.

Small claims court, 1 Corinthians 6:2 (NASB).

CLAMOR See Noise, Shouting.

CLANDESTINE See Stealth, Wiles.

CLAPPING

Prophet's emphasis, Ezekiel 21:14.

See Applause.

CLARITY

Understandable communication, Numbers 12:8.

Inscribing Law of God clearly on stones, Deuteronomy 27:8.

Written with iron tool, Jeremiah 17:1–2.

Trampled grass, muddied water, Ezekiel 34:18–19.

Message written with clarity, Habakkuk 2:2.

Speaking without figures of speech, John 16:29–30.

Speaking effectively, Acts 14:1.

Clarifying scripture, Acts 18:26 (Berk.).

Spiritual truth in human terms, Romans 6:19.

Clear call to action, 1 Corinthians 14:8.

Importance of being understood, 1 Corinthians 14:13–19.

Understandable message, 2 Corinthians 1:13–14 (See AB).

Clarity of Gospel message, Galatians 1:8.

Disagreement clarified, Philippians 3:15 (CEV).

Taught clearly, Hebrews 9:8.

Faint outline, Hebrews 10:1 (GNB).

Some things better spoken than written, 2 John 12; 3 John 13–14.

See Communication, Eloquence, Speech.

CLASS

Poverty no excuse for mistreatment, Exodus 23:6.

Known by pedigree, Numbers 1:18.

Classless day of judgment, Isaiah 24:2.

Simple people brought to Christ, 1 Corinthians 1:26–31.

No class distinction in Christ, Ephesians 6:9.

Paul could have boasted of class status, Philippians 3:2–11.

Wrong of discrimination, James 2:1–4.

See Prejudice, Racism.

CLAY

Brick-making, 2 Samuel 12:31.

Earth like clay seal, Job 38:14.

Potter, clay, Isaiah 29:16; 41:25; 45:9; 64:8; Jeremiah 18:6; Romans 9:21.

CLEANLINESS

Washing traveler's feet, Genesis 18:4; 19:2; 43:24.

Clean clothes, Genesis 35:2; Exodus 19:14.

Cleanliness next to godliness, Exodus 40:32.

Pronounced clean, Leviticus 13:6.

Shower, shave, Numbers 8:7.

Feminine daintiness, Ruth 3:3.

Worship preparation, 2 Samuel 12:20.

Washing prostitutes, chariots, 1 Kings 22:38.

Snow water, Job 9:30 (KJV).

Strength from clean hands, Job 17:9.

Priestly requirement, Isaiah 52:11.

Soda, soap, Jeremiah 2:22.

Laundry soap, Malachi 3:2.

"Wash your face," Matthew 6:17 (NIV).

Outward purity, Matthew 23:26.

Hands, utensils washing ceremony, Mark 7:1–4.

Washed with pure water, Hebrews 10:22.

See Purity, Sanitation.

CLEANSING

Clean hearts, bodies, clothing, Genesis 35:2.

Bathed but unclean, Numbers 19:7.

Spiritual cleansing, Psalm 51:2.

Whiter than snow, Psalm 51:7.

Prayer for inner peace, righteousness, Psalm 139:23–24.

Come, let us reason, Isaiah 1:18.

Soda, soap, Jeremiah 2:22.

Beyond cleansing, Jeremiah 6:29.

Profaned name sanctified, Ezekiel 36:23.

Clean hearts, changed lives, Ezekiel 36:25–27.

Fountain washes away sin, Zechariah 13:1.

Refined gold, silver, Malachi 3:2–4.

Sprinkle before eating, Mark 7:4 (LB).

Congregational cleansing, 1 Corinthians 5:1–13.

Sanctifying work of Spirit, 1 Peter 1:1–2.

Rid of evil traits, 1 Peter 2:1.

See Bath, Detergent, Holiness, Purity.

CLERGY

Born of clergy stock, Exodus 2:1–2 (AB).

Seven-day ordination, Exodus 29:35.

No marriage to divorcees, prostitutes, Leviticus 21:7.

Holiness by occupation, Leviticus 21:8.

High quality lives for clergymen, Leviticus 21:17–23.

Speaking by divine authority, Leviticus 23:1–2, 9–10, 23–24.

Military exemption, Numbers 1:47–49 (GNB).

Wishing all could be prophets, Numbers 11:29.

Stoning leaders, Numbers 14:1–11.

Contesting clergy, Numbers 16:3–7.

Responsibility for sin, Numbers 18:1 (Berk.).

Food for priests, Numbers 18:11–13.

Priests owned no property, Numbers 18:20.

Speaking what the Lord commands, Numbers 23:11–12.

Concerned pastor's compassionate prayer, Deuteronomy 9:25–29.

Clergy's twofold responsibility, Deuteronomy 10:8–9.

Do not neglect Levites, Deuteronomy 12:19.

Clergy decision not court of law, Deuteronomy 17:8–9.

New clergy's earnestness, Deuteronomy 18:6–7.

Detecting false prophet, Deuteronomy 18:21–22.

People without spiritual guidance, Judges 2:18–19.

Unique calling, circumstances, Judges 17:7–13.

Hired priest, Judges 18:4 (See 5–26).

Priests who worshiped idols, Judges 18:30–31.

Evil sons as priests, 1 Samuel 2:12–17, 22–25.

Grief for ark greater than death of sons, 1 Samuel 4:16–18.

Priest who served as judge, 1 Samuel 7:15–16.

Paying prophet's services, 1 Samuel 9:6–8.

Looking back across exemplary life, 1 Samuel 12:3.

Layman posing as prophet, 1 Samuel 13:8–14.

Lost influence, 1 Samuel 15:11.

Prophet's village, 1 Samuel 20:1 (CEV).

Refusal to turn against clergy, 1 Samuel 22:16–17.

Unqualified for priesthood, 1 Kings 12:31.

Anyone could be priest, 1 Kings 13:33.

Prophet named troublemaker, 1 Kings 18:16–18.

One remaining prophet, 1 Kings 18:22.

Priest, king, 2 Kings 11:15–18.

Priest's role in government, 2 Kings 12:1–2 (GNB).

Priest consulted prophetess, 2 Kings 22:14.

No God, no priest in Israel, 2 Chronicles 15:3.

Trustworthy priests, 2 Chronicles 20:20.

Priests in short supply, 2 Chronicles 29:34.

Book of Law lost in temple, 2 Chronicles 34:14–15.

Encourage priests, 2 Chronicles 35:2.

Mocking preacher, 2 Chronicles 36:16.

Priests tax-free, Ezra 7:24.

Clergy wives, Ezra 9:1–2.

Priests married to unbelievers, Ezra 10:18–44.

Clergy, manual labor, Nehemiah 3:1–2.

Ezra standing above people, Nehemiah 8:5.

People pleased with priests, Nehemiah 12:44.

Priests support themselves, Nehemiah 13:10–11.

Priest's office defiled, Nehemiah 13:29.

Great company proclaims God's Word, Psalm 68:11.

Shepherd angry at sheep, Psalm 74:1.

Clergy as flaming fire, Psalm 104:4.

Do not touch God's anointed, Psalm 105:15.

Jesus a priest forever, Psalm 110:4.

Righteous people, priests, Psalm 132:9, 16.

Evening ministry, Psalm 134:1.

Ministry accompanied by praise, Psalm 135:1–2.

Preacher in politics, Ecclesiastes 1:12 (NKJV).

Professional prophet, Isaiah 3:2 (AB).

Isaiah answered God's call, Isaiah 6:8.

Blinded prophets, seers, Isaiah 29:10.

People request pleasant sermons, Isaiah 30:10.

Listeners hear nothing, Isaiah 42:20.

Instructed tongue, Isaiah 50:4.

The Lord puts words in mouth, Isaiah 51:16.

Touch no unclean thing, Isaiah 52:11.

Selecting priests, Levites, Isaiah 66:21.

Fear, reluctance proclaiming message, Jeremiah 1:6–10.

Rebellious priests, Jeremiah 2:8.

Shepherds after God's own heart, Jeremiah 3:15.

Prophets called windbags, Jeremiah 5:13 (LB).

Corrupt clergy, congregation, Jeremiah 5:30–31; 6:13 (LB).

Priests rule by their own authority, Jeremiah 5:31.

Depraved clergy, Jeremiah 8:10.

Shepherds do not seek the Lord, Jeremiah 10:21.

Serving rebellious people, Jeremiah 15:19–21 (LB).

Must influence, not be influenced, Jeremiah 15:19 (LB).

Strong preaching ridiculed, Jeremiah 17:15 (LB).

No shunning responsibility, Jeremiah 17:16 (LB).

Jeremiah attacked with words, Jeremiah 18:18.

Wicked priests persecuted Jeremiah, Jeremiah 20:1–2.

Bold prophet sustained, Jeremiah 20:7–11.

Malicious shepherds, Jeremiah 23:1–4.

Ministration of evil prophets, Jeremiah 23:10–14.

Madman's simulation, Jeremiah 29:26.

Jeremiah persecuted prophesying truth, Jeremiah 37—38.

Shepherds led sheep astray, Jeremiah 50:6 (See also Micah 3:5–7).

Dying in search for food, Lamentations 1:19.

King, priest forsaken, Lamentations 2:6.

Prophets with no vision, Lamentations 2:9, 14 (CEV).

Jeremiah's compassion, Lamentations 3:40–51.

Priests, elders without honor, Lamentations 4:16.

Courage to minister under any circumstances, Ezekiel 2:6–7.

Visionless prophets, Ezekiel 13:3.

Women preachers, Ezekiel 13:17 (CEV).

Preachers save only themselves, Ezekiel 14:12–13, 19–20 (GNB).

Watchman's responsibility, Ezekiel 33:1–9.

Ridiculed prophet, Ezekiel 33:30–33 (LB).

Self-centered shepherds, Ezekiel 34:2.

Shepherd seeks scattered sheep, Ezekiel 34:12.

Priests' two functions, Ezekiel 40:44–46.

Accommodations for priests, Ezekiel 41:9–10; 42:13.

Temple garments worn by priests, Ezekiel 42:14; 44:19.

Priests' hairstyle, Ezekiel 44:20.

Restrictions on priests' marriages, Ezekiel 44:22.

Proclaiming difference between holy, common, Ezekiel 44:23.

Priests served as judges, Ezekiel 44:24.

Priests own no property, Ezekiel 44:28.

Priests given best food, Ezekiel 44:29–31.

Levites' land not to be sold, Ezekiel 48:13–14.

Finger pointed at prophet, Hosea 4:4 (LB).

Reprobate priests, Hosea 4:17.

Priests commit shameful crimes, Hosea 6:9.

Degraded clergy, Hosea 9:7.

Role of prophet in people's deliverance, Hosea 12:13.

Priests mourn wayward people, Joel 1:9, 13.

Prophets told to "shut up," Amos 2:12 (LB).

Conveying revelation of the Lord, Amos 3:7.

False prophets, Micah 2:6, 11.

Filled with the Spirit, Micah 3:8.

Services performed for money, Micah 3:11.

Sleeping shepherds, Nahum 3:18.

Arrogant prophets, profane priests, Zephaniah 3:4 (GNB).

Sent by the Lord, Zechariah 2:11.

Satanic opposition, Zechariah 3:1–2.

Shepherds desert flock, Zechariah 11:17.

Silent prophets, Zechariah 13:1–5.

Prophets ashamed of message, Zechariah 13:4–6.

Priests defiled altar, Malachi 1:6–14.

Messenger of the Lord, Malachi 2:7.

People without shepherd, Matthew 9:36.

Blind leaders of blind, Matthew 15:14.

Not practicing what they preached, Matthew 23:1–3.

Messenger's simple attire, Mark 1:6.

Pretense performance, Mark 12:38–40.

Love of money, Luke 16:14.

Jesus proclaimed depths of truth, John 6:60–69.

Truly caring for sheep, John 10:11–13.

Tend lambs, shepherd sheep, John 21:15–18 (NASB).

"Captain of the temple," Acts 4:1 (NASB).

Requisite for bold proclamation, Acts 4:31–32.

Clergymen's conversion, Acts 6:7.

Message rejected, Acts 7:1–60.

Misunderstanding from healing, Acts 14:8–18.

Successful preaching, Acts 14:21.

Short sermons, long sermons, Acts 16:19–32; 20:7.

Self-supported ministry, Acts 18:1–5; 20:32–35.

Asleep during sermon, Acts 20:7–12.

Personal evaluation of ministry, Acts 20:17–38.

Impugning High Priest, Acts 23:2–4.

Praying preacher, Romans 1:9–10.

Priestly duty to proclaim Gospel, Romans 15:16.

Concluding area ministry, Romans 15:23–24.

Message simplicity, 1 Corinthians 2:1–5.

Ministers merely servants, 1 Corinthians 3:4–9.

Recognition of apostle, 1 Corinthians 9:1–6.

Payment for spiritual service, 1 Corinthians 9:9–14.

Servant attitude preaching Gospel, 1 Corinthians 9:19–23.

Paul followed Christ's example, 1 Corinthians 11:1.

Women's ministry, 1 Corinthians 11:5.

Gift of prophecy, 1 Corinthians 14:1–5.

Good church organization, 1 Corinthians 14:33–40.

Message motivated, 1 Corinthians 16:13–14.

Making profit from Word of God, 2 Corinthians 2:17.

Made able for ministry, 2 Corinthians 3:6.

Ambassadors in the world, 2 Corinthians 5:18–21.

Marks of disciple, 2 Corinthians 6:3–13.

Rapport between ministers, 2 Corinthians 8:16–18.

Famed ministry, 2 Corinthians 8:18 (NASB, NRSV).

Ministry with spiritual weapons, 2 Corinthians 10:1–5.

"Eminent apostles," 2 Corinthians 12:11 (NASB, NRSV).

Mark of an apostle, 2 Corinthians 12:12.

Apostle's credentials, Galatians 1:1.

Trying to please others, Galatians 1:10.

Face-to-face encounter, Galatians 2:11–21.

Poor health in ministry, Galatians 4:13–14.

Paul's great compassion, Galatians 4:19–20.

Penalty for misleading others, Galatians 5:10.

Special messenger, Ephesians 1:1 (AB).

Less than least, Ephesians 3:8–9.

Worthy of calling, Ephesians 4:1.

Speaking truth in love, Ephesians 4:15.

Praying for preachers, teachers, Ephesians 6:19–20; Colossians 4:3–4.

Great love for followers, Philippians 1:3–11; Colossians 1:28–29; 2:1–5.

Envy, rivalry among preachers, Philippians 1:15.

"Upward call," Philippians 3:14 (NASB, NKJV).

Servant to the church, Colossians 1:24–29.

Ministry duties, Colossians 4:17 (AB).

Motivated preaching, teaching, 1 Thessalonians 2:1–6.

Ministering with gentleness, 1 Thessalonians 2:7.

Love, fellowship in ministry, 1 Thessalonians 2:7–9.

Followers are joy, crown, 1 Thessalonians 2:17–20.

Praising God for ministry success, 1 Thessalonians 3:8–10.

Be thoughtful of leaders, 1 Thessalonians 5:12–13 (CEV).

Purpose, means of spiritual success, 2 Thessalonians 1:11–12.

Employment to support one's ministry, 2 Thessalonians 3:6–10.

Thankful for ministry privilege, 1 Timothy 1:12–14.

Message Paul was called to proclaim, 1 Timothy 2:5–7.

Devoted to preaching, teaching, 1 Timothy 4:13–14.

Christian worker's remuneration, 1 Timothy 5:17–18 (AB, GNB).

Sinful lives, 1 Timothy 5:24 (LB).

Good deeds unseen, 1 Timothy 5:25 (LB).

Pride in false doctrine, 1 Timothy 6:3–5.

Herald, apostle, teacher, 2 Timothy 1:11.

God's plan for Gospel perpetuation, 2 Timothy 2:1–4.

Ministry mandate, 2 Timothy 4:1–5.

Ministry credentials, Titus 1:1–3.

Christian leadership example, Titus 3:1–2.

High priest like other men, Hebrews 5:1–3.

Jesus as clergyman, Hebrews 7:23–28.

Ultimate High Priest's sanctuary service, Hebrews 8:1–6.

Pastor as leader, example, Hebrews 13:7.

Those who keep watch, Hebrews 13:17.

Searching prophets, 1 Peter 1:10–12.

Ministry of holiness, 1 Peter 1:15–16.

Speaking, serving to God's glory, 1 Peter 4:11.

Shepherds of God's flock, 1 Peter 5:1–4.

Aging worker's continuing zeal, 2 Peter 1:13–14.

Proclaiming angel, Revelation 14:6–7.

See Congregation, Denomination, Pastor, PKs, Preaching, Shepherd.

CLEVER

Protection for baby Moses, Exodus 2:4–9.

"Sharp as a tack," Psalm 52:2 (LB).

"Cleverness of the clever," 1 Corinthians 1:19 (NASB).

CLIMATE

Seasons after Flood, Genesis 8:22.
Lord of time, seasons, Psalm 74:16–17.
One who governs wind, wave, Proverbs 30:4.
Rain, rivers, Ecclesiastes 1:7.
See Meteorologist, Weather.

CLIMBING *See Upward.*

CLOSED

Closed doors reopened, 2 Chronicles 29:3, 7.

CLOSENESS

Kept at distance, Numbers 24:17.
The Lord's nearness in prayer, Deuteronomy 4:7.
Nearness of God's Word, Deuteronomy 30:14.
Two inseparable women, Ruth 1:14–18.
Ever-present Good Shepherd, Psalm 23:1–4.
Scripture declares the Lord's nearness, Psalm 119:151.
Coming close to God, James 4:8.
See Affinity, Camaraderie, Fellowship, Intimacy.

CLOTH

Cloth makers' shops, Isaiah 36:2 (CEV).
See Linen.

CLOTHING

Skin garments, Genesis 3:21.
Deceitful apparel, Genesis 27:2–29.
Durable clothing, Deuteronomy 8:4; 29:5.
Women not to wear men's clothing, Deuteronomy 22:5.
Mixed materials, Deuteronomy 22:11.
Costly clothing, 2 Samuel 1:24; 1 Peter 3:3–4.
Blue, white clothing, Esther 8:15.
Royal garments, Psalm 45:14–15.
Sackcloth, Isaiah 3:24.
Clothed with righteousness, faithfulness, Isaiah 11:5.
Seductive clothing, Ezekiel 13:17–18.

Clothes make the man, Daniel 5:29.
Nature's clothing, Matthew 6:28–29.
Proper garment repair, Matthew 9:16.
Clothing in kings' palaces, on prophet in desert, Matthew 11:7–9.
Rich man, poor man, Luke 16:19–31.
Teachers in flowing robes, Luke 20:46–47; 21:1–4.
Royal robes, Acts 12:21.
Fine clothing compared to personal qualities, 1 Peter 3:3–4.
Those wearing clean robes, Revelation 22:14.
See Seamstress, Wardrobe.

CLOUDS

God appears in cloud, Exodus 19:9; 24:15; 34:5; Numbers 11:25.
Guiding cloud, Exodus 13:21.
Time of murmuring, Exodus 16:8–10.
Cloud function, Job 26:8.
Storage for rain, Job 37:16; Ecclesiastes 1:7.
Forgiveness like cloud, Isaiah 44:22.
Cloudy day, Ezekiel 30:3 (KJV).
Clouds as divine dust, Nahum 1:3.
Cloud of transfiguration, Matthew 17:5.
Second Coming cloud, Revelation 1:7.
Celestial cloud setting, Revelation 14:14.
See Weather.

COAL *See Fuel, Ore.*

COAX

Coaxing to persuade, Galatians 4:20 (AB).

COBRA *See Snakes.*

COERCION

Edenic coercion, Genesis 3:1–7.
Coerced by woman's wiles, Judges 14:11–19; 16:15–21.
Divine coercion, Ezekiel 38:4.
See Temptation, Wiles.

COGNATION

Bible-centered mentality, Psalm 1:2.
Glory of kings, Proverbs 25:2.
See Concentration, Meditation, Thought.

COIFFURE

Pulling out hair, Nehemiah 13:25.
Bald women, Isaiah 3:17, 24.
Haircut in response to vow, Acts 18:18.
Hair cutting instruction, 1 Corinthians 11:14–15.
Hairstyles, jewelry, 1 Timothy 2:9–10 (CEV).
See Barber, Hair.

COIN TOSS

Decision by coin toss, Nehemiah 10:34 (LB).
See Chance.

COLD

Persistent winter, Genesis 8:22.
No old-age warmth, 1 Kings 1:1–4.
Driving winds, Job 37:9.
God's icy breath, Job 37:10 (NRSV).
Icy blast, Psalm 147:17.
Warm fire, John 18:18.
Rain, cold, Acts 28:2.
Shivering cold, 1 Corinthians 4:11 (AB).
See Freeze, Snow, Winter.

COLLABORATION

Wrong kind of unanimity, Numbers 11:4–10.
Collaboration between in-laws, Ruth 3:1–18.
Working diligently together, Nehemiah 4:6.
As iron sharpens iron, Proverbs 27:17.
Two in agreement, Amos 3:3.
United behind common goal, Luke 10:1–2.
See Cooperation.

COLLATERAL

Guarantee to father, Genesis 42:37.
Loan collateral, Deuteronomy 24:10–13.

COLLECTOR See Hobby.

COLLEGE

Three-year training program, Daniel 1:3–5.

COLOR

Spectrum in sky, Genesis 9:13–16.
Sky blue, Exodus 24:10.
Blue, purple, scarlet, Exodus 25:3–5; 26:1, 31, 36; 38:18.
Blue cord, Exodus 28:28.

Reminder of divine commandments, Numbers 15:38–40.
Red heifer, Numbers 19:2.
Absence of color, Job 10:20–22.
Whiter than snow, Psalm 51:7.
Darkened skies, Joel 3:14–15.
Darkness of perdition, Matthew 8:12; 22:13; 25:30; 2 Peter 2:4.

COMBAT See Military.

COMEDY See Humor.

COMFORT

Noah as comforter, Genesis 5:29.
Respite from heat, Genesis 18:1.
Springs, palm trees, Exodus 15:27.
Rainy weather, Ezra 10:13.
Avoiding sun, Nehemiah 7:3.
Search for shade, Job 7:2 (CEV).
Miserable comforters, Job 16:2.
Comfort rather than criticism, Job 16:4–5.
In trouble, God ever-present, Psalm 14:4–5.
Comfort from the Lord, Psalm 86:17; Isaiah 12:1; 51:3; 66:13; 2 Corinthians 1:3.
"Cool of the day," Song of Songs 4:6 (NASB).
Gladness, joy overcome sorrow, sighing, Isaiah 35:10.
Lambs, shepherd, Isaiah 40:11.
Sure comfort, Isaiah 51:12.
Balm in Gilead, Jeremiah 8:22.
Mourning forbidden in time of judgment, Jeremiah 16:5–7.
Padding for comfort in deliverance, Jeremiah 38:11–13.
No one to comfort, Lamentations 1:2.
Faithfulness, compassion new each morning, Lamentations 3:22–23.
Shade provided for Jonah, Jonah 4:6.
Cushion for Jesus, Mark 4:38.
Comforting Savior, Luke 7:13; John 14:1; 16:33.
Sharing comfort through experience, 2 Corinthians 1:3–5.
Secret of deliverance, 2 Corinthians 4:7–18.
Death of Christians, 1 Thessalonians 4:13–18.
Eternal encouragement, 2 Thessalonians 2:16–17.

Divine comfort, 2 Thessalonians 3:16.

Christ's temptation helps those tempted, Hebrews 2:18.

Eternal comfort, Revelation 7:16.

Tears forever wiped away, Revelation 7:17.

See Relief.

COMMAND

Creator's command, Genesis 1:3 (CEV).

"Up, follow," Genesis 44:4 (KJV).

Do not alter God's commands, Deuteronomy 4:2.

Chain of command, Numbers 18:1–7 (LB); Colossians 4:1.

Request instead of command, Philemon 8–9.

See Leadership, Mandate.

COMMEMORATE

Three festivals honoring God, Exodus 23:14–17.

Purpose of Sabbath, Exodus 31:16.

Captured city named after conqueror, Numbers 32:42.

Strange name, Joshua 5:3 (LB).

Commemorative music, Isaiah 12:5–6.

See Honor.

COMMENDATION

High compliments for David, 1 Samuel 29:6–9.

Divine estimation, 2 Samuel 7:8–9 (GNB).

Some good in Judah, 2 Chronicles 12:12.

Self-commendation, Nehemiah 5:19.

Commended for speaking truth, Job 42:8.

Accepting praise, Proverbs 27:21.

Industrious woman, Proverbs 31:10–31.

Strong people's honor, Isaiah 25:3.

"God thinks highly of you," Daniel 10:11 (CEV).

Evaluation of John the Baptist, Matthew 11:11–14.

God's commendation of His Son, Mark 1:10–11.

Avoiding commendation, John 7:1–13.

Commended by others, 2 Corinthians 5:12 (NRSV).

Let the Lord commend, 2 Corinthians 10:17–18.

Paul's commendation of Timothy, Philippians 2:19–23.

"Whatever is commendable," Philippians 4:8 (NRSV).

Wise use of followers' names, Colossians 4:7–17.

See Compliment, Honor.

COMMERCE

Supply cities, Exodus 1:11 (NKJV).

Need for roads, Deuteronomy 19:3.

Import, export, 1 Kings 10:28–29.

Local, national, international, 2 Chronicles 9:21; Proverbs 31:14–18; Revelation 18:10–24.

Willing to sell, Proverbs 11:26.

Nile grain brought to Tyre, Isaiah 23:3.

Waterfront prosperity, Jeremiah 51:13.

Control of trade routes, Ezekiel 26:2 (LB).

Tyre property taken away, Ezekiel 27:1–36.

Using temple for business purposes, Mark 11:15–17; Luke 19:45–46; John 2:14–17.

Converts' limited profits, Acts 19:23–28.

Luxury no longer for sale, Revelation 18:11–13.

See Barter, Business, Merchandise, Salesmen, Trade.

COMMISSION

Moses laid hands on Joshua, Deuteronomy 34:9.

Great Commission, Matthew 28:16–20.

Commission to preach, teach, Luke 4:14–21.

Barnabas, Saul commissioned, Acts 13:2–3.

Paul's commission to minister, Acts 23:11.

Entrusted with secret things of God, 1 Corinthians 4:1–2.

"Send them on their mission," 3 John 6 (CEV).

See Calling, Dedication.

COMMITMENT

Aroma of good sacrifice, Genesis 8:20–21; Leviticus 23:18; 2 Corinthians 2:15; Ephesians 5:1–2.

Abraham's commitment tested, Genesis 22:1–14.

Lifetime servant, Exodus 21:2–6.

Verbal commitment, Exodus 24:7.

Anointing objects, Exodus 40:9–10.

Dedicating residence to the Lord, Leviticus 27:14.

Those who do not follow wholeheartedly, Numbers 32:11.

"Be careful," Deuteronomy 5:1 (Berk.).

Preparation for future blessing, Joshua 3:5.

Call for total faithfulness, Joshua 24:14.

Commitment under pressure, Judges 10:6–16.

Prenatal commitment, 1 Samuel 1:11–12.

Mother's reward for committing son, 1 Samuel 2:18–21.

Report to idols, 1 Samuel 31:9 (GNB).

Wealth given to the Lord, 2 Samuel 8:9–12.

Solomon's partial commitment, 1 Kings 3:3; 22:43.

Total commitment, 1 Kings 20:4.

Personal treasures to temple, 1 Chronicles 29:3–4.

"I am your servant," Nehemiah 1:6 (CEV).

Committed workers, Nehemiah 4:6.

Working from morning to night, Nehemiah 4:21.

Total commitment to project, Nehemiah 5:14–16.

Self-righteous, Job 32:1.

Set apart, Psalm 4:3.

Committing to the Lord, Psalm 31:5.

"Resign yourself," Psalm 37:7 (Berk.).

Keeping vow to God, Psalm 65:1.

Fulfill vow to God, Ecclesiastes 5:4–5.

Commitment of two loves, Song of Song 6:3; 8:6.

Answering call of God, Isaiah 6:8.

Stand firm or not at all, Isaiah 7:9.

Meaningless oaths, Isaiah 48:1–2.

Coming to the Lord with clean vessel, Isaiah 66:20.

Vow to Queen of Heaven, Jeremiah 44:24–30.

Someone to stand in gap, Ezekiel 22:30.

Disciples left occupation to follow Jesus, Matthew 4:20–22.

Counting cost, Matthew 8:19–20.

Losing life to save it, Mark 8:35 (AB).

Lose life, find again, Matthew 10:39.

Calling of Simon, Andrew, James, John, Mark 1:16–20.

Daily action, Luke 9:23 (LB).

No looking back, Luke 9:62.

Commitment at crucifixion, Luke 23:46.

Willingness to face persecution, Acts 21:10–14.

Once slaves to sin, now righteousness, Romans 6:18.

Living sacrifice, Romans 12:1–2 (NASB).

Hard worker, Romans 16:6, 12 (NASB).

In race one wins; serving God all win, 1 Corinthians 9:24–27.

Daily death of true commitment to Christ, 1 Corinthians 15:30–31.

Holy Spirit in life commitment, 2 Corinthians 3:7–8.

Marks of disciple in service, 2 Corinthians 6:3–13.

Beyond highest hope, 2 Corinthians 8:5 (LB).

Crucified with Christ, Galatians 2:20.

Habitual commitment, Galatians 5:16 (AB).

In union with the Lord, Ephesians 6:10 (GNB).

Loving Christ with undying love, Ephesians 6:24.

Poured out like drink offering, Philippians 2:17; 2 Timothy 4:6.

Filled with knowledge of God's will, Colossians 1:9–12.

Eternal commitment, 2 Timothy 1:12.

True disciple described, 2 Timothy 2:1–4.

Paul endured everything to help others, 2 Timothy 2:10.

Supreme commitment of Christ as Redeemer, Hebrews 10:5–7.

Pleasing God, Hebrews 11:5; 1 Peter 4:19 (AB).

Commitment in suffering, 1 Peter 4:19.

See Dedication, Discipleship.

COMMITTEE

Value of many advisers, Proverbs 11:14; 12:15; 15:22.

Consultation, Mark 15:1 (KJV).

COMMONPLACE

Silver, gold commonplace, 2 Chronicles 1:15.

Writing with ordinary pen, Isaiah 8:1.

Ordinary people, Jeremiah 26:23 (GNB, Romans 12:15 CEV; 2 Corinthians 3:7).

Ignored message, Ezekiel 3:4–7.
See Ordinary, Value.

COMMON SENSE

"Use common sense," Proverbs 3:21 (CEV).
Common sense vanished, Jeremiah 49:7
(CEV).

COMMONWEALTH

"Commonwealth of Israel," Ephesians 2:12
(NASB, NRSV).
The church a commonwealth, Philippians
3:20 (Berk.).

COMMUNICATION

God's rainbow, Genesis 9:12–17.
Those who spoke one common language,
Genesis 11:1, 5–9.
God spoke to Abram in deep sleep, Genesis
15:12–15.
Pretending not to understand, Genesis
42:23.
Faltering lips, Exodus 6:12–30.
Divine use of visions, dreams, Numbers
12:4–6.
Understandable communication, face to
face, Numbers 12:8.
Place for words, Deuteronomy 27:2–3.
Inscribing Law of God on stones, Deuteron-
omy 27:8.
Putting instructions in writing, Deuteron-
omy 31:9.
Foot to neck, Joshua 10:24.
Identification by manner of speech, Judges
12:5–6.
Communication with the dead, 1 Samuel
28:8–20.
Report to idols, 1 Samuel 31:9 (GNB).
Making sure someone listens, 2 Samuel
20:17.
Speaking to inanimate object, 1 Kings 13:2.
Message from thistle to cedar tree, 2 Kings
14:9.
Communication methods, 2 Chronicles
30:1–10; Esther 1:22.
Encouraging communication during crisis,
2 Chronicles 32:6–7.
The Lord's attentive ear, Nehemiah 1:11.
Petition of protest, king's response, Ezra
4:12–22.

Language barrier, Nehemiah 13:23–37.
Seven-day silence, Job 2:13.
Communication disbelieved, Job 12:4.
Testing words, Job 12:11.
Asking God to withdraw, Job 13:20–21.
Tip of tongue, Job 33:2.
Testing speech, Job 34:3.
Communication with God, Psalm 18:25.
God speaks through nature, His Word,
Psalm 19:1–14.
"Open ear," Psalm 40:6 (NRSV).
Twisting words, Psalm 56:5.
Communicating with God, Psalm 99:6.
Message conveyed by fool, Proverbs 26:6.
Iron sharpens iron, Proverbs 27:17.
"Not able to tell it," Ecclesiastes 1:8 (NASB).
Secret thoughts expressed, Ecclesiastes
10:20.
Finding right words, Ecclesiastes 12:10.
Earth permeated with divine knowledge,
Isaiah 11:9.
Call for decision, Isaiah 16:3.
News conveyed by chariot, Isaiah 21:9.
Too young to understand, Isaiah 28:9.
"Senseless sound," Isaiah 28:13 (Compare
CEV, NIV, NKJV).
Farmer illustrates over-communication, Isa-
iah 28:24.
Speaking in language understood, Isaiah
36:11.
Mouth like sharpened sword, Isaiah 49:2.
Instructed tongue, Isaiah 50:4.
Boldness of speech given by God, Jeremiah
1:6–10.
Those of strange language, Jeremiah 5:15.
Smoke signal, Jeremiah 6:1 (LB).
Letter to exiles in Babylon, Jeremiah 29:4–
23.
Divine invitation to communicate, Jere-
miah 33:3.
Danger of writing truth, Jeremiah 36:4–32.
Be eager to listen, Ezekiel 3:4–9.
Young Hebrews taught Babylonian commu-
nication, Daniel 1:3–5.
Writing on wall, Daniel 5:5.
Message not understood, Daniel 12:4 (LB).
Message written with clarity, Habakkuk
2:2.
Gigantic flying scroll, Zechariah 5:1–2.
Lips that preserve knowledge, Malachi 2:7.

Celestial announcement, Matthew 2:1–2.

Communication by dreams, Matthew 2:12, 19–20.

Effect of attitudes on understanding, Matthew 13:14–15.

Word of mouth, Mark 1:28.

Simple truth not understood, Mark 9:10 (NIV).

Mute's written communication, Luke 1:63.

Spectacular communication from heaven, Luke 2:8–14.

Jesus knew when He had been touched, Luke 8:43–48.

Unable to understand Crucifixion, Luke 9:44–45.

When great truth sounds like nonsense, Luke 24:9–11.

Slow to understand, Luke 24:15–31.

Symbolism misunderstood, John 2:19–21.

No one spoke as Jesus spoke, John 7:45–46.

Rapport with communicator, John 8:47.

Some heard thunder, others angel's voice, John 12:28–29.

Jesus accused of riddles, John 16:25–30 (LB).

Multilingual information, John 19:20.

Sufficient communication conveys message, John 20:30–31.

Day of Pentecost, Acts 2:1–12.

Speaking plainly, Acts 2:29 (Berk.).

Not understanding what one reads, Acts 8:27–35.

Speaking effectively, Acts 14:1.

Gathering together for report, Acts 14:27.

Teaching with reasoning, Acts 17:1–3.

Quoting poets of Athens, Acts 17:28.

Encouraged in vision, Acts 18:9–10.

Falling asleep during long sermon, Acts 20:7–12.

Effect of speaking in people's language, Acts 22:2.

Seeing light, not understanding voice, Acts 22:9.

Use of eyes for impact, Acts 23:1.

Message communicated in nature, Romans 1:18–20.

Entrusted with conveying God's Word, Romans 3:1–2.

Truth communicated in human terms, Romans 6:19.

Words beyond normal vocabulary, Romans 8:16, 26–27.

Prayer for acceptable ministry, Romans 15:31–32.

Conversation enriched in Christ, 1 Corinthians 1:5–6.

Tongues without content, 1 Corinthians 14:6.

Clear call to action, 1 Corinthians 14:8.

Importance of being understood, 1 Corinthians 14:13–19; 2 Corinthians 1:13–14.

Tact with unbelievers, 2 Corinthians 2:15–16.

Earning right to be heard, 2 Corinthians 4:1–2.

Lifestyle communicated by example, 2 Corinthians 6:4–10.

Hearts opening to each other, 2 Corinthians 6:11–13.

Writing more effective than speaking, 2 Corinthians 10:10.

Information without eloquence, 2 Corinthians 11:6.

"You have me puzzled," Galatians 4:20 (CEV).

Profound truth briefly presented, Ephesians 3:1–3.

Paul's insistence to followers, Ephesians 4:17.

Fathers should not exasperate children, Ephesians 6:4.

Keeping in touch, Ephesians 6:21–22.

Good news between believers, Philippians 2:19.

Invisible made visible, Colossians 1:15.

Fullness of deity in Christ, Colossians 2:9.

Prayer supports successful communication, Colossians 4:3–4.

Wise use of names, Colossians 4:7–17.

Communication with followers, Colossians 4:8.

Onesimus introduced, Colossians 4:9; Philemon 10–11.

Gospel communicated with words, power, 1 Thessalonians 1:4–5.

Importance of welcoming message, 1 Thessalonians 1:6.

Communicating with gentle spirit, 1 Thessalonians 2:7.

Responsibility of those who hear, 1 Thessalonians 2:13.

Teaching by means of speech, writing, 2 Thessalonians 2:15; 1 Timothy 3:14–15.

Quarreling over words, 2 Timothy 2:14.

Convincing message, 2 Timothy 4:2 (NRSV).

Responsibility to proclaim message, Titus 1:1–3.

Make teaching attractive, Titus 2:10.

Superior communication, Hebrews 1:1–4; 3:5–8.

Faith gives credibility, Hebrews 4:2.

Scripture's penetrating impact, Hebrews 4:12.

"Hard to explain," Hebrews 5:11 (CEV).

Short letter, Hebrews 13:22.

Responsibility proclaiming God's message, 1 Peter 4:11.

Divine purpose in giving Scriptures, 2 Peter 1:20–21.

Purpose of Peter's letters to friends, 2 Peter 3:1.

Writing difficult to understand, 2 Peter 3:15–16.

World's viewpoint, 1 John 4:5.

In person rather than correspondence, 2 John 12; 3 John 13–14.

Those who take Scriptures to heart, Revelation 1:3.

Cry of doom, Revelation 8:13.

God in direct fellowship with men, Revelation 21:3–5.

See Conversation, Message, Nonverbal Communication, Preaching, Tangible, Teaching, Witness.

COMMUNION

Aliens barred from Passover, Exodus 12:43–45.

Talking to God, 2 Chronicles 6:4 (LB).

Thirst for living God, Psalm 42:1–2.

Deep calls to deep, Psalm 42:7.

Highest motive life can know, Psalm 27:4.

The Lord listens to those who listen, Zechariah 7:13.

The Lord's table, Matthew 26:17–30; Mark 14:12–26; Luke 22:7–38; 1 Corinthians 11:23–30.

"Feast of thin bread," Matthew 26:17 (CEV); Luke 22:1 (CEV).

You near to God, He near to you, James 4:8.

Believing without seeing, 1 Peter 1:8–9.

See Prayer, Worship.

COMMUNISM

Believers under pagan leaders, Genesis 39:2–4, 20–23.

Godless king, nation, Daniel 11:36–39.

Christian kind of sharing, Acts 2:44.

See Socialism.

COMMUNITY

Building first city, Genesis 4:17.

Small town spared disaster of large city, Genesis 19:15–22.

Prevent spreading infection, Leviticus 13:45–46.

Holy community, Numbers 16:3.

Community welfare storehouse, Deuteronomy 14:28–29 (CEV).

Well-situated city, poor water, 2 Kings 2:19–22.

"Your town is strong," 2 Kings 10:2 (CEV).

Priest, king, 2 Kings 11:15–18.

Community degradation, Isaiah 1:21, 26.

Community in turmoil, Isaiah 22:2.

Town, country praising the Lord, Isaiah 42:11.

Depravity of entire city, Jeremiah 5:1.

Community gods, Jeremiah 11:13.

When God establishes good community, Jeremiah 30:20.

Least, greatest, Jeremiah 42:1–3.

Total destruction of community, Jeremiah 51:20–23.

Time of despair for entire community, Ezekiel 7:27.

Judgment on evil community, Zephaniah 3:1.

Salt, light in world, Matthew 5:13–16.

Nazareth's low reputation, John 1:46.

Early Christian and community, Acts 2:46–47.

Message-saturated community, Acts 5:28.

Christians keeping in touch, Ephesians 6:21–22.

Future community where all know the Lord, Hebrews 8:11.

Example to unbelievers, 1 Peter 2:12.

Residence for demons, evil spirits, Revelation 18:2.

City of total integrity, Revelation 21:27.

See City, Neighborhood, Urban.

COMPANIONSHIP

Companions in danger, 1 Samuel 22:23.

"We enjoyed being together," Psalm 55:14 (CEV).

Spiritual companions, Psalm 119:63.

Walking in good company, Proverbs 2:20; 13:20.

Avoid evil companions, Proverbs 24:1.

Two better than one, Ecclesiastes 4:9.

Disciples two-by-two, Luke 10:1; Acts 13:2.

Wife traveling with husband, 1 Corinthians 9:5.

Prison companion, Colossians 4:10.

Disobedient companions, 2 Thessalonians 3:14.

Desire for companionship, 2 Timothy 4:9–10.

See Brotherhood, Camaraderie, Fellowship, Friendship.

COMPARISON

Comparing sun, moon, stars, Genesis 1:16.

Comparing weakness, strength, Deuteronomy 9:1.

Saul's thousands, David's ten thousands, 1 Samuel 18:7; 21:11; 29:5.

Incomparable God, Psalm 86:8; Jeremiah 10:6.

Beyond comparison, Psalm 89:6; Isaiah 46:5.

Comparing two unfaithful nations, Jeremiah 3:11.

Jerusalem's sin compared to Sodom's, Ezekiel 16:51 (CEV).

Wiser than Daniel, Ezekiel 28:3.

Moses, Jesus, John 1:17.

Sufferings, glory, Romans 8:18.

Stewardship comparison, 2 Corinthians 8:8.

Christ's "weakness," ours, 2 Corinthians 13:4.

COMPASS

Eastern defense, Genesis 3:24.

Points of compass, Genesis 13:14; Acts 27:12.

Searching all directions for God, Job 23:8–9 (GNB).

Creator of north, south, Psalm 89:12.

Expanse from east to west, Psalm 103:12.

Wind direction, Ecclesiastes 1:6.

Unknown way to town, Ecclesiastes 10:15.

Falling tree, Ecclesiastes 11:3.

Travellers from north, west, Isaiah 49:12.

Terror from the north, Jeremiah 1:11–16.

Weather from the north, Ezekiel 1:4.

Disaster all directions, Ezekiel 7:2–3 (LB).

Idol to the north, Ezekiel 8:5 (LB).

House facing east, Ezekiel 11:1.

Multidirectional goat horns, Daniel 8:8 (CEV).

North to east, Amos 8:12.

Pathway for lightning, Matthew 24:27.

Three gates each direction, Revelation 21:13.

See Direction, Navigation.

COMPASSION

Compassion for baby Moses, Exodus 2:5–6.

Divine concern for suffering people, Exodus 3:7.

Leader's compassionate prayer, Deuteronomy 9:25–29.

Compassion to enemy, 2 Samuel 9:1–13; Proverbs 24:17–18.

Compassion to prisoners, 2 Chronicles 28:15.

Pity fallen Jerusalem, 2 Chronicles 30:14–15.

Lack of compassion, Job 12:5.

Caring for weak, Psalm 41:1.

Continuous compassion, Psalm 78:38.

God's abounding compassion, Psalms 86:15; 119:156.

Penalty for lack of compassion, Proverbs 21:13 (LB).

No compassion for evil, Isaiah 9:17.

Divine compassion never decreases, Isaiah 54:10.

Pointless compassion, Jeremiah 7:16.

Jeremiah's compassion, Jeremiah 9:1.

Judgment precedes compassion, Jeremiah 12:14–17; Lamentations 3:32.

Crying out to those who reject, Jeremiah 22:29.

Loved with everlasting love, Jeremiah 31:3.

The Lord shows no pity in judgment, Lamentations 2:2.

Compassion new every morning, Lamentations 3:22–26.

Ezekiel feared Israel's destruction, Ezekiel 11:13.

Heart of flesh, of stone, Ezekiel 11:19.

Divine compassion for lost, Ezekiel 18:23, 32.

New heart, new spirit, Ezekiel 36:26.

Daniel's compassion for condemned wise men, Daniel 2:10–13, 24.

Demonstrated compassion, Hosea 11:4.

Joseph's compassion for pregnant Mary, Matthew 1:19.

Compassion of Jesus, Matthew 9:36; 23:37; Luke 13:34; 19:41–44.

"Filled with pity," Mark 1:41 (GNB).

Good Samaritan, Luke 10:30–37.

Full measure of compassion, Luke 14:1–14.

Compassionate preaching, Acts 20:30–31.

Consideration shown to Paul, the prisoner, Acts 27:3.

Kind islanders, Acts 28:2.

Paul's compassion for Israel, Romans 9:1–4; 10:1.

Divine compassion to disobedient, Romans 10:21.

Strong looking after weak, Romans 15:1.

Love expressed through anguish, 2 Corinthians 2:4.

Paul's compassion for Galatians, Galatians 4:19–20.

"Gently lead," Galatians 6:1–2 (CEV).

Carrying each other's burdens, Galatians 6:2.

Concern for those ill, Philippians 2:26–27.

Tears of compassion, Philippians 3:18 (CEV).

Struggle over converts, Colossians 2:1.

Wide compassion, 1 Thessalonians 3:1–5.

Compassion for slave, Philemon 8–21.

See Concern, Empathy, Mercy, Sympathy.

COMPATIBILITY

Compatible brothers, Psalm 133:1.

Two walk together, Amos 3:3.

Shared suffering, comfort, 2 Corinthians 1:7.

Adapting to others, Ephesians 5:22 (AB).

Avoid disruptive conduct, Philippians 2:14–16.

"Try to get along," 1 Thessalonians 5:13 (CEV).

See Camaraderie.

COMPENSATION

Compensation for intentional injury, Exodus 21:18–19.

God accepts no price or reward, Isaiah 45:13.

Stone rejected by builders, Matthew 21:42.

See Honorarium, Salary, Stipend.

COMPETENCE

Competent man needed, Genesis 47:6 (NKJV).

Jewish competence ridiculed, Nehemiah 4:1–3.

Race not to swift, strong, Ecclesiastes 9:11.

When God sends, He guides, Isaiah 2:3.

Least, greatest, Jeremiah 42:1–3.

Qualifications for following Jesus, Luke 9:23–26.

Competence comes from God, 2 Corinthians 3:4–5.

God provides competence, Hebrews 13:20–21.

See Ability, Skill, Talent.

COMPETITION

Fetal competitors, Genesis 25:22.

Competing for father's love, Genesis 37:1–4; Luke 15:25–31.

Unable to compete, Exodus 9:11.

One on one, 1 Samuel 17:8–10.

David, Saul, 1 Samuel 18:6–16.

Evil world versus God, Psalm 2:1–4.

Joyful competition, Psalm 19:5 (Berk.).

At peace with one's enemies, Proverbs 16:7.

Gloating over enemy failure, Proverbs 24:17–18.

Keeping up with the Joneses, Ecclesiastes 4:4.

"The Lord tolerates no rivals," Nahum 1:2 (GNB).

Strong man, stronger man, Luke 11:21–22.

Jesus evaded accusation of competition, John 4:1–3.

Coming in second, Acts 1:23–26.

Competitive Christians, Romans 13:13; 15:20 (LB); Galatians 5:26.

Run to win, 1 Corinthians 9:24–27.

Competition purposely avoided, 2 Corinthians 10:16 (LB).

Ministry to Jews, to Gentiles, Galatians 2:8.

"Competing against one another," Galatians 5:26 (NRSV).

See Athletics, Covet, Envy, Jealousy.

COMPILATION

Biographies of Christ, Luke 1:1–4 (LB).

COMPLACENCY

Thinking it easy to face enemy, Deuteronomy 1:41–45.

Wicked complacency, prosperity, Job 21:7–18.

"Complacency of fools," Proverbs 1:32 (NRSV).

Who cares? Isaiah 57:1.

Complacent nation, Jeremiah 49:31.

Those who pass by, Lamentations 1:12.

Relegating judgment to distant future, Ezekiel 12:26–28.

Sodom's pride, laziness, Ezekiel 16:49 (LB).

Abundant blessing can turn to backsliding, Hosea 13:6.

Warning the complacent, Amos 6:1–4.

Jonah asleep during storm, Jonah 1:5–6.

Complacent evil doers, Zephaniah 1:12 (CEV).

God's displeasure with complacency, Zechariah 1:14–15.

Sleepy disciples, Matthew 26:36–46.

Sin of complacency, James 4:17.

Blind confidence, Revelation 18:7.

See Attitude, Careless, Carnality, Powerless, Undependable.

COMPLAIN

Complaining to God, Exodus 5:22–23; Numbers 11:10–15; Psalm 142:1–2.

Remembering Egypt instead of trusting God, Exodus 16:2–3.

Rejected advice of elders, 1 Kings 12:1–11.

Animal complaints, Job 6:5 (LB).

Bitterness against God, Job 23:2.

"Faultfinder," Job 40:2 (Berk.).

"Quit complaining," Psalm 39:1 (LB).

Still alive, shouldn't complain, Lamentations 3:39 (CEV).

Sour grapes, Ezekiel 18:2.

Howl like jackal, moan like owl, Micah 1:8.

Martha's discontent with Mary, Luke 10:38–42.

"Do not grumble," John 6:43 (NASB).

Talking back to God, Romans 9:20–21.

Do everything without complaint, Philippians 2:14–15.

Forgive complaints, Colossians 3:12 (NASB, NRSV).

See Discontent, Friction.

COMPLETION

Creation task well done, Genesis 1:31.

Frustrated project, Genesis 11:1–9.

Rebuilt temple, 2 Chronicles 6:10–11; Zechariah 4:9.

Finished plans, 2 Chronicles 8:16.

Jerusalem wall dedicated, Nehemiah 12:27–43.

Termination of testing, Job 23:10.

Finished work of Jesus, John 19:30 (CEV).

Good work begun, completed, Philippians 1:3–6.

Finish the work, 2 Corinthians 8:11.

Life's work completed, 2 Timothy 4:6–8.

Divine plan completed, Revelation 21:9.

Culmination of Bible's message, Revelation 22:20–21.

See Accomplishment, Ending, Finale.

COMPLEXITY

Beyond comprehension, Ecclesiastes 8:16–17.

National guilt, Matthew 27:25.

Adam's sin, Romans 5:12.

COMPLICITY

Aiding thief, Psalm 50:18.
Guilt shared between man, wife, Acts 5:1–2.
National guilt, Matthew 27:25.
Adam's sin, Romans 5:21.

COMPLIMENT

High compliments, 1 Samuel 29:6–9.
Public relations approach, 1 Kings 1:42.
Some good in Judah, 2 Chronicles 12:12.
Avoiding partiality, flattery, Job 32:21–22.
Flattering lips speak deception, Psalm 12:2.
Praise, glory belong to God, Psalm 115:1; 1 Corinthians 3:7.
Word of encouragement, Proverbs 12:25 (LB).
Timely word, Proverbs 15:23.
Honor not fitting fools, Proverbs 26:1, 8.
Folly of flattery, Proverbs 28:23.
Noble person eloquently described, Isaiah 32:8.
Talented people encouraging each other, Isaiah 41:7.
Jesus' evaluation of John the Baptist, Matthew 11:11–14.
Duty of true servant, Luke 17:7–10.
Complimented, encouraged followers, Acts 20:1–2; Romans 1:8; 2 Corinthians 1:13–14; Philippians 1:3–6; Colossians 2:5; 1 Thessalonians 1:3; 2 Thessalonians 1:3–4; 2 Timothy 1:3–5.
"Good things to say," Romans 16:1 (CEV).
Complimenting friends, Romans 16:3–16.
Paul's compliment to those who followed teachings, 1 Corinthians 11:2.
Expression of confidence, 2 Corinthians 7:4 (LB).
Paul's commendation of Timothy, Philippians 2:19–23.
Wise use names of followers, Colossians 4:7–17.
No search for praise, 1 Thessalonians 2:6 (GNB).
Boasting about perseverance, faith of others, 2 Thessalonians 1:4.
Compliments precede request, Philemon 1–7.
Complimented for skills, Hebrews 3:3 (LB).

One author commended another, 2 Peter 3:15–16.
Strength, weakness at Ephesus, Revelation 2:1–6.
Commendation before reproof, Revelation 2:2–6, 13–16, 19–20.
One worthy of praise, Revelation 5:13–14.
See Commendation, Encouragement, Praise.

COMPOSURE

Divine composure, Genesis 2:2; Mark 4:39.
Song of composure, Deuteronomy 31:19–22 (LB).
Facing enemy, Nehemiah 4:1–23; 8:2–3.
Lack of composure, Daniel 6:18–20.
Facing violent death, Acts 7:59–60.
Keeping courage, Acts 27:21–26.
See Maturity, Peace, Tranquility, Repose.

COMPREHENSION

Eyes see, ears hear, Deuteronomy 29:2–4.
Those able to understand, Nehemiah 8:2–3.
Outer fringe of comprehension, Job 26:14 (GNB).
Full of words about subject, Job 32:17–22.
Learning what cannot be seen, Job 34:32.
God-given ability to understand, Psalm 119:125.
Unable to comprehend reality, Ecclesiastes 8:16–17.
Too young to understand, Isaiah 28:9.
Refusal, inability to read, Isaiah 29:11–12.
Delayed comprehension, Jeremiah 30:24.
Childhood comprehension, Matthew 11:25.
Effect of attitudes on comprehension, Matthew 13:14–15.
Hearing, not understanding, Mark 4:10–13 (LB).
Thoroughness of Jesus with disciples, Mark 4:34.
Too frightened to comprehend Resurrection, Mark 16:1–8.
Simeon understood Savior's dual mission, Luke 2:28–32.
Joseph, Mary did not understand Son's conduct, Luke 2:41–50.
Use of parables to illustrate truth, Luke 8:9.
Unable to understand coming Crucifixion, Luke 9:44–45.

Seeing, hearing, not understanding, Luke 10:24.

Unable to accept identity of Jesus, John 10:24–30.

Holy Spirit's guidance, John 16:12–14.

Lack of understanding what one reads, Acts 8:27–35.

Full comprehension, Acts 10:34 (Berk.).

Seeing light, not understanding voice, Acts 22:9; 9:1–7.

Easily understood, Romans 6:19 (LB).

What God has prepared exceeds human perception, 1 Corinthians 2:9–10.

Folly of intellectual pride, 1 Corinthians 3:18–20.

Enough sense to understand, 1 Corinthians 10:15 (CEV).

Understanding Scripture, 2 Corinthians 3:15–16 (CEV).

Eyes of heart, Ephesians 1:18–19.

Slow to learn, Hebrews 5:11.

That which is not understood, Jude 10.

See Clarity, Communication, Frame of Reference, Hearing, Simplicity, Understanding.

COMPROMISE

Unacceptable compromise, Exodus 8:25–28.

Desire to be like unbelievers, 1 Samuel 8:1–22.

Calling disobedience compromise, 1 Samuel 15:9–15 (LB).

Abner's compromise with David, 2 Samuel 3:6–21.

Compromised commitment of King Solomon, 1 Kings 3:3.

Heathen worship for Solomon's wives, 1 Kings 11:8.

Incomplete faithfulness to God, 1 Kings 22:43.

Failing to be completely obedient, 2 Kings 14:1–4; 15:1–4, 34–35.

Secretly disobeying the Lord, 2 Kings 17:9.

Worshiping the Lord, other gods, 2 Kings 17:33.

Assisting evil, 2 Chronicles 19:2.

Doing right, not wholeheartedly, 2 Chronicles 25:2.

Day as night, night as day, Job 17:12 (LB).

Calling evil good, good evil, Isaiah 5:20.

Those who do not want to hear truth, Isaiah 30:10–11.

Hezekiah intimidated, Isaiah 36:4–10.

Desire to be like others, Ezekiel 20:32–38.

No one can serve two masters, Matthew 6:24.

Marriage between unbelievers, believers, 1 Corinthians 7:16.

Refusal to compromise, 1 Thessalonians 2:3–4.

No hospitality to false teachers, 2 John 10–11.

Jezebel's influence in Thyatira church, Revelation 2:20.

See Cult, Syncretism, Worldliness.

COMPULSION

Compulsion to preach hard message, Jeremiah 20:7–11.

Witness by compulsion, Acts 4:20.

COMPUTER

Beyond digital analysis, 1 Corinthians 2:9; Ephesians 3:17–19.

COMRADE

"True comrade," Philippians 4:3 (NASB).

Fellowship comrade, Philemon 17 (AB).

CONCEIT

Goliath's macho, 1 Samuel 17:42–44.

Haughtiness despised, 2 Samuel 22:28.

Sanballat's taunts, Nehemiah 4:1–3.

Enemy's loss of self-confidence, Nehemiah 6:16.

God's attitude toward conceit, Job 37:24 (Berk.).

Conceited affluence, Psalm 49:5–6; Proverbs 25:14.

Limitless conceit, Psalm 73:7.

Wise in one's own eyes, Proverbs 3:7; 26:5–16.

Impaired by conceit, Proverbs 14:6 (GNB).

Worse than a fool, Proverbs 26:12 (LB).

Proud, conceited, put down, Isaiah 2:12 (CEV).

Conceited women, Isaiah 3:16.

Empty boasting, Isaiah 16:6.

Boast only about the Lord, Jeremiah 9:23–24.

No time for conceit, Romans 11:20 (NASB).

Avoid conceit, Romans 12:16.

Conceited false doctrine, 1 Timothy 6:3–5 (AB, CEV).

"Swollen with conceit," 2 Timothy 3:4 (NRSV).

Evil queen refused to admit sin, Revelation 18:7–8.

See Ego, Pride, Vanity.

CONCENTRATION

Distraction among soldiers, Deuteronomy 20:5–9.

Single-minded concentration, Nehemiah 5:16.

Listening carefully, Job 13:17.

Bible-centered mentality, Psalm 1:2.

Concentrating on the Lord, Psalms 25:15; 141:8.

Eyes fixed on commandments, Psalm 119:6 (NASB).

Eyes straight ahead, Proverbs 4:25.

Glory of kings, Proverbs 25:2.

Concentrated thought, action, Jeremiah 32:39.

Intent on message, Ezekiel 2:6–9; 3:1–11.

"Listen closely," Micah 1:2 (AB).

"Single purpose," Acts 1:14 (CEV).

Paying attention to Scripture, Hebrews 2:1–3.

Fix thoughts on Jesus, Hebrews 3:1.

Concentrated study, 1 Peter 1:10–11.

"It escapes their notice," 2 Peter 3:5 (NASB).

See Cogitation, Thought.

CONCEPT

Precepts in depth, Isaiah 28:13 (KJV).

God's "foolish" ideas, 1 Corinthians 1:21 (LB).

CONCEPTION

Season for conception, Genesis 18:10 (AB, Berk., NKJV).

Closed wombs, Genesis 20:17–18.

Apparent allusion to semen, Job 10:10 (Compare GNB, NIV).

See Abortion, Childbirth, Impotence, Pregnancy.

CONCERN

Concern for family welfare, Exodus 4:18.

How are you? Exodus 18:7 (KJV).

Father's concern for children, Job 1:4–5.

Too concerned to sleep, Psalm 132:4–5.

Who cares? Jeremiah 15:5.

Heart of flesh, of stone, Ezekiel 11:19.

Concern for human need, Mark 8:1–2.

Love expressed through anguish, 2 Corinthians 2:4.

Christians keeping in touch, Ephesians 6:21–22.

One who cares, Philippians 2:20 (CEV, NRSV).

Revived concern, Philippians 4:10 (NASB, NRSV).

Concern for others' spiritual needs, Colossians 1:9.

See Burden, Empathy, Rapport, Sympathy.

CONCERT

Village concert, Judges 5:11 (LB).

CONCILIATORY

Abram's attitude toward Lot, Genesis 13:8–9.

Peace offer prior to battle, Deuteronomy 20:10.

Attempted conciliation, 1 Corinthians 4:13 (NASB).

See Tact.

CONCISE

Six-word obituary, Numbers 20:1.

Shortest short story, Ecclesiastes 9:13–15.

Two-word command, Mark 2:14.

Concise resume God's plan through ages, Romans 1:1–6.

See Brevity.

CONCLUSION

"An end of praying," 2 Chronicles 7:1 (KJV).

Job's happy ending, Job 42:10–17.

Last words of David, 2 Samuel 23:1–7; Psalm 72:20.

Solomon's testimony summation, Ecclesiastes 12:13–14.

Ezekiel's prophecy of "the end," Ezekiel 7:2.

Last statement of great prophet, Ezekiel 48:35.

Prayer of Jesus, John 17:1–5.
Paul's "punch line" to stewardship appeal, 2 Corinthians 9:15.
Bible's conclusion, Revelation 22:20–21.
See Ending, Finale.

CONCUBINE
Preferred treatment for concubines, Esther 2:8–14.

CONCUR
Agreement voiced by congregation, Deuteronomy 27:14–26.
Saul's admission of David's righteousness, 1 Samuel 24:16–17.
Two in agreement, Amos 3:3.
See Agreement, Unanimity.

CONDEMNATION
Self-condemnation, 2 Samuel 24:10; Job 9:20; 42:6.
Pause in condemnation, Job 21:1–3.
Wounds of friend, Proverbs 27:6.
No condemnation, Isaiah 50:9; Romans 8:1.
Second judgment on evil king, Jeremiah 36:27–32.
Continued sinning, certain judgment, Amos 1:3, 6, 9, 11, 13; 2:1, 4, 6.
Looking for something to criticize, Mark 3:2.
Redeemer also Judge, John 5:22–24.
Earth stands condemned, Romans 9:28.
Falling into hands of living God, Hebrews 10:31.
See Gossip, Judgment.

CONDESCEND
Lower myself, honor you, 2 Corinthians 11:7 (CEV).
Prerequisite to salvation, Hebrews 2:17–18.
See Humility, Submission.

CONDITION
Divine ultimatum, Exodus 15:26.
Spiritual preparation for future victory, Joshua 3:5.
Conditions for God's blessing, judgment, 2 Chronicles 7:11–22.
God's blessing dependent upon obedience, Jeremiah 11:1–5.

God's great invitation, Jeremiah 33:3.
For God's return to us, we return to Him, Zechariah 1:3.
Conditions of relationship with the Lord, 2 Timothy 2:11–13.
See Blessing.

CONDITIONAL
Forgiveness based on "perhaps," Acts 8:22 (NIV).

CONDOLENCE
David's sympathy, 2 Samuel 10:2; 1 Chronicles 19:1–4.
Job's friends, Job 2:11.
Mary, Jesus, John 11:23–35.

CONDUCT
Promised answered prayer, Exodus 33:17.
Lifestyle, example, Deuteronomy 4:5–9.
Wisely perfect, Psalm 101:2 (KJV).
Defiled by actions, Psalm 106:39.
Path of righteous, way of wicked, Proverbs 4:18–19.
Pride, evil behavior, perverse speech, Proverbs 8:13.
Conduct evaluated, Proverbs 14:8.
Actions louder than words, Proverbs 20:11.
Guilt, innocence, Proverbs 21:8.
Conduct, conversation linked together, Proverbs 22:11.
Evil deeds, motives likened to eggs, Isaiah 59:4–5.
Heart, mind determine conduct, Jeremiah 17:10.
Reward for good, evil conduct, Jeremiah 22:3–5.
Practice what you preach, Ezekiel 33:31; Luke 3:7–8; Romans 2:21 (GNB).
Exploiting poor, Amos 5:11.
False prophets recognized by fruit, Matthew 7:15–20.
Actions speak louder than words, Matthew 11:18–19.
Tree known by fruit, Matthew 12:33–35; Luke 6:43–45.
Apostles' specific guidelines, Luke 6:12–49.
Reward for good works, Romans 2:5–11.
Pleasures which cause spiritual death, Romans 6:21.

"I do not understand my own actions," Romans 7:15 (NRSV).

True measure of spirituality, Romans 14:17–18.

Responsibility to others, 1 Corinthians 8:9–13.

Augmenting witness, 1 Corinthians 10:30–33 (LB).

Doing all for God's glory, 1 Corinthians 10:31.

Worship more harm than good, 1 Corinthians 11:17–32.

Exemplary conduct, 2 Corinthians 4:2 (AB).

Importance of conduct, 2 Corinthians 5:10.

Pleasing God, people, 2 Corinthians 8:21.

Worldly standards, 2 Corinthians 10:2.

Reap what you sow, Galatians 6:7–10.

Worthy of calling, Ephesians 4:1.

New lifestyle in Christ, Ephesians 4:22–24.

Right, wrong attitude, disposition, Ephesians 4:31–32.

Sensible, intelligent, Ephesians 5:15 (AB).

Slaves, masters, Ephesians 6:5–9.

No need to be ashamed, Philippians 1:20 (LB).

Judged by legalism observance, Colossians 2:16.

Lifestyle risen with Christ, Colossians 3:1–17.

Earning right to be heard, 1 Thessalonians 4:11, 12.

Captive to will of Satan, 2 Timothy 2:25–26.

Proper teaching for all ages, Titus 2:1–10.

Self-condemnation those causing difficulty, Titus 3:10–11.

God's law in mind, heart, Hebrews 8:10.

Instruction for living Christian life, Hebrews 13:1–9.

Faith without works, James 2:14–18.

True faith demonstrated, James 3:13.

Those who sow in peace, James 3:18.

Witness by conduct, 1 Peter 2:12 (NRSV).

"Eager to do what is good," 1 Peter 3:13 (NRSV).

Attributes of mature Christian life, 2 Peter 1:5–9.

Doing what is right, 1 John 2:29.

Warn against false teaching, wrong conduct, Jude 3–4.

See Frame-of-Reference, Lifestyle, Performance, Walk.

CONFERENCE

Dates for assembly, Exodus 12:16; Numbers 28:18, 26; 29:7.

Community assembled for information, Exodus 35:1.

Vast assembly, 1 Kings 8:65.

Seeking leadership consensus, then unanimity, 1 Chronicles 13:1–4.

"A serious meeting," Ezra 10:9 (CEV).

Day after day reading Scriptures, Nehemiah 8:17–18.

Futile attempt to hold retreat, Luke 9:10–11.

Gathering church members for ministry report, Acts 14:27–28.

Ministry summary, Acts 21:19.

Countryside retreat, John 3:22.

Good organization in church, 1 Corinthians 14:33–40.

CONFESSION

Pharaoh's insincerity, Exodus 9:27–30.

Son's confession to mother, Judges 17:1–5 (LB).

"Throwing himself down," Ezra 10:1 (NRSV).

Nehemiah's prayer, Nehemiah 1:4–7.

Confessing ancestors' sins, Nehemiah 9:2.

Immediate confession, Psalm 32:6 (LB).

Confession, restoration, Psalm 50:1–23.

Folly of concealing sin, Proverbs 28:13.

Confessing to priest, Ecclesiastes 5:6 (GNB).

Private confession, Matthew 18:15–17.

Judas' remorse, suicide, Matthew 27:3–5.

Confess to each other, James 5:16.

Our Advocate with Heavenly Father, 1 John 2:1–2.

See Conscience, Guilt, Remorse.

CONFIDENCE

God's assurance to Abram, Genesis 15:1.

Trusting God against unsurmountable opposition, Exodus 14:5–14.

Confident in face of danger, Numbers 14:8–9.

Determined, confident, Joshua 1:7, 9, 18 (GNB).

March on with strong soul, Judges 5:21.

Not by strength alone, 1 Samuel 2:9.

Confident ability, 1 Samuel 17:32–37.

Lack of confidence facing danger, 1 Samuel 27:1.

Sinful dependence on number of fighting men, 1 Chronicles 21:17.

Giving confidence during crisis, 2 Chronicles 32:6–7.

Sure of God's plan, purpose, Job 42:2.

Facing opposition with confidence, Psalm 3:6.

The Lord our sure refuge, Psalm 9:9–10.

God's unfailing love, Psalm 13:5–6.

Confidence to face challenge, Psalm 18:29.

Confidence in chariots or the Lord? Psalm 20:7.

Sure faith, Psalm 27:1.

All in God's hands, Psalm 31:15.

Confidence in midst of trouble, Psalm 34:19.

Be still, wait, Psalm 37:7.

Wrongly placed confidence, Psalms 44:6; 49:6–7; 146–3; Jeremiah 17:5; 48:7; Ezekiel 33:13.

Steadfast inner spirit, Psalms 51:10; 57:7.

God's love, strength, Psalm 62:11–12.

No fear day, night, Psalm 91:4–6.

Sure the Lord is God, Psalm 100:3.

Steady heart, no fear, Psalm 112:8 (NRSV).

Fear of man, Psalm 118:6–9.

Confident of God's help, Psalm 119:81 (LB).

Trusting God like small child, Psalm 131:2.

The God who answers prayer, Psalm 138:1–3.

Prayer for instruction, confidence, Psalm 143:10.

Certainty of God's promises, Psalm 145:13.

Gossip betrays confidence, Proverbs 20:19.

Trustworthy messenger, Proverbs 25:13.

Fear of man a snare, Proverbs 29:25.

Strength, dignity, Proverbs 31:25.

Pointless confidence in men, Isaiah 2:22.

In time of danger, Isaiah 7:4; Luke 7:1–10.

Danger of fearing wrong things, Isaiah 8:12–14.

Kept in perfect peace, Isaiah 26:3.

Tested stone in Zion, Isaiah 28:16.

Confidence in the Lord rather than men, Isaiah 36:4–10.

Dramatic use of silence, Isaiah 36:13–21.

Do not question Potter, Isaiah 45:9.

Confident in one's own wickedness, Isaiah 47:10.

All in God's hands, Isaiah 49:4.

Certainty of answered prayer, Isaiah 49:8.

Walking with confidence in the dark, Isaiah 50:10.

Fear, reluctance proclaiming message, Jeremiah 1:6–10.

Confidence in difficult times, Jeremiah 1:17.

Erroneous confidence, Jeremiah 7:8.

Those who trust the Lord, Jeremiah 17:7–8.

The Lord like mighty warrior, Jeremiah 20:11.

Nothing too hard for the Lord, Jeremiah 32:17.

Thanking God in adverse circumstances, Jeremiah 33:10–11.

Safest place in trouble, persecution, Jeremiah 42:1–22; Ezekiel 34:25.

Uplifted banner, Jeremiah 50:2.

Mercies new each morning, Lamentations 3:22–26; Zephaniah 3:5.

Confidence facing fiery furnace, Daniel 3:16–18.

Mountains crumble but God's ways eternal, Habakkuk 3:6.

Believe in Good News, Mark 1:14–15.

Disciples lacked faith, Mark 4:36–41.

No need to fear in Jesus' presence, John 6:20.

Antidote for troubled hearts, John 14:1.

Pagans certain of erroneous belief, Acts 19:35–36.

Going with confidence into difficult places, Acts 20:22–24.

Sure of destiny, Acts 27:23–24.

Hope when no basis for hope, Romans 4:18–22.

Nothing can separate us from God's love, Romans 8:37–39.

Confident of the Lord's blessing, Romans 15:29.

Confidence comes from God, 2 Corinthians 3:4–5.

Confidence in unseen, 2 Corinthians 4:18.

Living by faith, not by sight, 2 Corinthians 5:1–7.

Admitted lack of confidence, 2 Corinthians 10:1–2.

God can do more than we ask, imagine, Ephesians 3:20–21.

Standing at end of struggle, Ephesians 6:13.

Firm whatever circumstances, Philippians 1:27–30.

Prayer brings peace, Philippians 4:6–7.

Absolute confidence in Whom we believe, 2 Timothy 1:7, 12.

Approach high priest with confidence, Hebrews 4:14–16.

Confidence rewarded, Hebrews 10:35.

Obedience toward unknown objective, Hebrews 11:8.

Faith to believe what has not been received, Hebrews 11:13.

Kingdom that cannot be shaken, Hebrews 12:28–29.

Not alarmed, Hebrews 13:6 (AB).

Believing wisdom will be granted, James 1:5–7.

Abundant grace, peace, 1 Peter 1:2.

God of all grace, 1 Peter 5:10.

Absolute confidence of salvation, 1 John 3:13.

No fear in love, 1 John 4:18.

See Assurance, Certainty, Faith, Guidance, Promise, Trust.

CONFIDENTIAL

Intimate talks, Psalm 55:14 (GNB).

Betrayed by gossip, Proverbs 11:13.

Careful with words, Ecclesiastes 12:10.

Whispers to be proclaimed, Matthew 10:27.

Evil cannot be kept confidential, Luke 12:2–3.

See Secrecy, Secret.

CONFIRMATION

"Confirm your call," 2 Peter 1:10 (NRSV).

CONFISCATION

Confiscated property, Lamentations 5:2.

CONFLICT

David fought the Lord's battles, 1 Samuel 25:28.

Futility of strife among brothers, 2 Samuel 2:27–28.

Struggle between strong, weak, 2 Samuel 3:1.

At peace with enemies, Proverbs 16:7.

Provocation by fool, Proverbs 27:3.

Noise of battle, destruction, Jeremiah 50:22.

Love your enemy, Matthew 5:43–48.

Family conflict, Matthew 10:34–39.

Satan divided against himself, Matthew 12:22–32.

No peace on earth, Mark 13:6–8.

Clash of personalities, Acts 15:36–41.

Stress between evil, good, Romans 7:14–20.

Those who purposely cause trouble, Romans 16:17.

Lawsuits among believers, 1 Corinthians 6:1–8.

Purpose of conflict, 1 Corinthians 11:19 (Berk.).

Purpose of trouble, 2 Corinthians 4:17–18.

Peter, Paul face-to-face, Galatians 2:11–21.

Handling conflict with firmness, love, 1 Timothy 1:3–7.

See Abrasion, Argument, Discord, Dispute, Jealousy, Opposition, Strife.

CONFORMITY

Following wrong of others, Exodus 23:2; Deuteronomy 12:29–30.

Desiring pagan political structure, 1 Samuel 8:1–22.

Conforming to pagan ways, 2 Kings 17:13–15.

Conformity to Christ, Romans 8:29.

Conformed, transformed, Romans 12:1–2.

See Influence, Syncretism.

CONFRONTATION

Satan's confrontation with Jesus, Luke 4:1–13.

Critics of Jesus, Luke 20:1–8.

CONFUSION

Wandering Israelites, Exodus 14:1–4.

Confusing shadows, Judges 9:34–37.

Lamp of the Lord, 2 Samuel 22:29.

Confused about God, Job 10:2–12.

Day as night, night as day, Job 17:12 (LB).

"Make a tumult," Psalm 2:1 (Berk.).

Walking about in darkness, Psalm 82:5.

"At their wits' end," Psalm 107:27 (Berk.).

Let the Lord direct, Proverbs 20:24 (LB).

"Nothing makes sense," Ecclesiastes 1:2 (CEV).

A fool does not know way to town, Ecclesiastes 10:15.

Spirit of dizziness, Isaiah 19:14.

"My head spins," Isaiah 21:4 (CEV).

Sick drunk, Isaiah 28:7.

Walking in dark, Isaiah 50:10.

Blind without guidance, Isaiah 59:9–10.

Warriors stumbling over each other, Jeremiah 46:12.

Government disarray, Ezekiel 7:26–27.

Confused between monotheism, idolatry, Daniel 3:28–30; 4:18.

From one peril to another, Amos 5:19.

Herod's lack of perception, Luke 9:7–9.

Confused Pharisees, John 9:13–16.

"Terribly upset," Acts 15:24 (CEV).

Conflicting accusations, Acts 21:33–34.

Avoiding confusion in worship, 1 Corinthians 14:29–33, 40.

See Distraction.

CONGENIAL

In-depth congeniality, Nehemiah 8:10–12.

Brief congeniality, Job 20:5.

Abundant laughter, joy, Psalm 126:2; Philippians 1:26.

Medicinal attitude, Proverbs 17:22.

Time to laugh, Ecclesiastes 3:4.

Fools' laughter, Ecclesiastes 7:6.

Wells of salvation, Isaiah 12:3.

Gladness, joy, Isaiah 35:10.

Christian lifestyle, 1 Corinthians 10:31; 1 Peter 1:8–9.

See Attitude, Lifestyle, Optimism.

CONGESTION

City population in one tower, Judges 9:51 (GNB).

City, country, Isaiah 5:8 (KJV).

Congested Jerusalem, Zechariah 2:4 (LB).

CONGRATULATE

Congratulate the dead, Ecclesiastes 4:2 (Berk.).

Whatever success, glory belongs to God, 1 Corinthians 3:7.

See Acclaim, Commendation, Praise.

CONGREGATION

Passover forbidden to aliens, Exodus 12:43–45.

Wrong kind of unanimity, Exodus 16:1–2.

People responded with one voice, Exodus 24:1–7.

Those who serve, give, Exodus 35:10–35; 36:4–7.

Fire must not go out, Leviticus 6:12.

Gathering together, Leviticus 8:1–4; Numbers 1:17–18; 8:9; Joshua 18:1; Judges 20:1.

Leading disgruntled congregation, Numbers 11:4–15.

Every member a prophet, Numbers 11:26–30.

Holy community, Numbers 16:3.

One man brings guilt on all, Numbers 16:22.

Rebels in congregation, Numbers 20:10.

Loaning money within congregation, Deuteronomy 23:19–20.

Congregation in agreement, Deuteronomy 27:14–26.

Uniting behind new leader, Joshua 1:16–18.

Unanimous voice, Joshua 22:16.

Weakness of people without guidance, Judges 2:18–19.

David's army of chosen men, 2 Samuel 6:1.

Owning share of king, 2 Samuel 19:43.

David's mighty men, 2 Samuel 23:8–39.

Those who will not listen, 2 Kings 17:14.

Least, greatest in society, 2 Kings 23:2.

All worship, 2 Chronicles 29:28.

Group confession, Nehemiah 1:6.

Faithful to God's house, Nehemiah 10:39.

Multitude as one, Nehemiah 8:1.

Faithful people, Psalm 16:3 (GNB).

Love of worship, Psalm 26:8.

Strengthened by the Lord, Psalm 28:8 (NRSV).

Congregational dissension, Psalm 55:12–14.

Shepherd's anger, Psalm 74:1.

Leading flock, Psalm 77:20.

In-depth obedience within congregation, Psalm 103:17–21.

All people join in praise, Psalm 106:48.

Fulfilling vows to the Lord, Psalm 116:14, 18–19.

People, priests clothed with righteousness, Psalm 132:9, 16.

Not wanting to hear truth, Isaiah 30:10–11.

Satisfied with deceitful priests, Jeremiah 5:30–31 (LB).

Best leadership ineffective with backsliders, Jeremiah 15:1.

Preaching rejected, Jeremiah 26:7–9.

"Amen" of agreement, Jeremiah 28:5–6 (NIV).

Pastor facing rebellious people, Ezekiel 2:4–9; 3:1–11.

Those who disbelieved message, Ezekiel 20:49.

Innocent congregation, guilty priests, Hosea 4:4 (CEV).

Calling congregation to pray, Joel 1:14; 2:16.

Prominent member, Amos 7:13 (CEV).

Those who dislike strong preaching, Amos 7:16.

"Listen, all of you," Micah 1:2 (CEV).

Refusing to listen, Zechariah 1:4.

Church authority, Matthew 18:17 (CEV).

Sheep without shepherd, Mark 6:34.

People at peace with each other, Mark 9:50.

Tax collectors, sinners, Luke 15:1.

Jesus proclaimed depths of spiritual truth, John 6:60–69.

Prayer of Jesus for His own, John 17:20–23.

Message welcomed, Acts 2:41 (Berk.).

Dissension, jealousy in church, Acts 6:1.

Attentive audience, Acts 8:6.

Winning large number of people, Acts 14:21.

Gathering church members for ministry report, Acts 14:27–28.

Many teachers, Acts 15:35.

Growing New Testament church, Acts 16:5.

Paul's house church, Acts 28:30–31.

Paul's consistent prayer for other Christians, Romans 1:8–10; 1 Corinthians 1:4–9; Ephesians 1:11–23; Philippians 1:3–6; Colossians 1:3–14.

Function of body members, Romans 12:4–8.

Honor others above yourself, Romans 12:10.

Harmony with others, Romans 12:16–18.

Serving the Lord in unity, Romans 15:5–6.

Special greeting to house church, Romans 16:5.

Keep eye on offenders, Romans 16:17 (NRSV).

Need for unity among believers, 1 Corinthians 1:10–17.

Serving together in effective cooperation, 1 Corinthians 3:1–16.

Discipline within congregation, 1 Corinthians 5:1–13.

Wrong attitudes in worship, 1 Corinthians 11:17–32.

Purpose of conflict, 1 Corinthians 11:19 (Berk.).

Gifts, service in congregation, 1 Corinthians 12:4–11.

One body, many parts, 1 Corinthians 12:12–30.

Forgiveness in congregation, 2 Corinthians 2:5–11.

Building up believers, 2 Corinthians 12:19 (NRSV).

Fearing disunity, abrasion, 2 Corinthians 12:20.

Need for stability in congregation, Galatians 1:6–9.

Wasted effort in preaching, Galatians 4:11.

Carrying each other's burdens, Galatians 6:2, 5.

Relationships within fold, Galatians 6:10.

"Listening to the message," Ephesians 1:13 (NASB).

Members of God's family, Ephesians 2:19–22.

"Dwelling place for God," Ephesians 2:22 (NRSV).

Serving God in unity, Ephesians 4:3.

Varied talents in body of Christ, Ephesians 4:11–13.

Imitators of God expressing love to others, Ephesians 5:1–2.

Conduct, activity in worship, Ephesians 5:19–21.

Praying for those who minister, Ephesians 6:19–20.

United for singular purpose, Philippians 1:27–28 (LB).

Like-minded people serving in love, Philippians 2:1–2.

Faithful without pastoral supervision, Philippians 2:12–13.

Instruction on church unity, Philippians 4:1–9.

Concern for pastor, Philippians 4:10–19; Colossians 4:3–4.

Relentless effort on followers' behalf, Colossians 1:28–29.

Christ-centered life, Colossians 3:1–17.

Careful conduct toward unbelievers, Colossians 4:5.

Welcoming message, 1 Thessalonians 2:13.

Followers are joy, crown, 1 Thessalonians 2:17–19.

Overflowing love, 1 Thessalonians 3:12.

Church officers, 1 Thessalonians 5:12 (LB).

Thanking God for others, 2 Thessalonians 1:3.

Growing, persevering Christians, 2 Thessalonians 1:4.

Avoid making enemies of wrongdoers, 2 Thessalonians 3:14–15.

Praying together without dispute, 1 Timothy 2:8.

God's household, 1 Timothy 3:15.

Public scripture reading, 1 Timothy 4:13.

Christian community a family, 1 Timothy 5:1–2.

Convert's public testimony, 1 Timothy 6:12.

Unbelieving church members, 2 Timothy 3:5 (LB).

Needs of new congregation, Titus 1:5–9.

Proper teaching for all ages, Titus 2:1–10.

Singing God's praises in congregation, Hebrews 2:12.

Encouraging one another, Hebrews 3:13.

Confident of growth in followers, Hebrews 6:9.

Example to each other, Hebrews 10:24–25.

Brotherly love, Hebrews 13:1.

"Obey your leaders," Hebrews 13:17 (NRSV).

Hospitality to all, James 2:1–4.

Cause of discord, James 4:1–2.

Do not grumble against each other, James 5:9.

Love one another deeply, 1 Peter 1:22; 1 John 4:7–11.

Living stones built of Loving Stone, 1 Peter 2:4–8.

Judgment begins with family of God, 1 Peter 4:17.

"Lesser rank," 1 Peter 5:5 (AB).

Message for all ages, 1 John 2:12–14.

Disruption in congregation, 3 John 9–10.

Disruptive people infiltrate believers, Jude 3–4.

Holy Spirit speaks to churches, Revelation 2:29.

Measure temple, count worshipers, Revelation 11:1.

Song for exclusive congregation, Revelation 14:1–3.

No churches in heaven, Revelation 21:22.

Ministry of Holy Spirit, church in evangelism, Revelation 22:17.

See Body of Christ, Church, Discipline, Fellowship, Missionary, Parishioner, Preaching, Sanctuary, Soul-Winning, Unity, Witness.

CON MAN

Victim of con man, Psalm 109:11 (KJV).

Speech disguises malicious heart, Proverbs 26:24–26.

CONNIVANCE

Premeditated murder, Exodus 21:14.

Compromising leadership, Exodus 32:1–2.

Augmenting evil, Psalm 50:18; Proverbs 24:24; 28:4; Romans 1:32.

Prophets who see nothing, Ezekiel 13:1–3.

Spineless Pilate, Matthew 27:17–26.

Deceitful resurrection claim, Matthew 27:62–66; 28:11–15.

Stephen's death, Acts 8:1.

Paul's shadowed past, Acts 22:19–20.

See Deceit, Deception.

CONQUEST

Go possess the land, Deuteronomy 1:21.

Spare trees, Deuteronomy 20:19–20.

Land to be conquered, Joshua 13:1–33.

Overcoming obstacles with God's help, 2 Samuel 22:30.

Laying land completely waste, 2 Kings 3:19.

Divide, conquer, Psalm 55:9 (LB).

Stark, bloody vengeance, Psalm 58:10.

Lands of other nations, Psalm 111:6.

Glory of conquest, Psalm 149:6–9; Ezekiel 39:21–22.

Temper control, Proverbs 16:32.

Victory requires more than ability, Isaiah 25:11.

Gleeful plundering, Ezekiel 36:5.

Aid to pagan conqueror, Daniel 1:1–2.

Ultimate conquest, Obadiah 19–21.

Man of sin overthrown, 2 Thessalonians 2:8.

See Victory.

CONSCIENCE

Birth of conscience, Genesis 3:6–11.

Guilty conscience, Genesis 42:1–23; Ezra 9:6.

Much heart searching, Judges 5:16.

Soothing music, 1 Samuel 16:14–23.

David's clear conscience, 1 Samuel 20:1; 24:1–7.

Convicting parable, 2 Samuel 12:1–10.

Things known in heart, 1 Kings 2:44.

Sin considered trivial, 1 Kings 16:31.

Tears of contrition, confession, Ezra 10:1.

Clear conscience, Job 27:6; 1 Corinthians 4:4; 1 John 3:19–20.

Role of Scripture, Psalm 19:7–11.

Agony of guilt, Psalm 38:4.

Indelible awareness of sin, guilt, Psalm 51:3.

Not always dependable, Proverbs 16:25.

Taste of stolen food, Proverbs 20:17.

Inmost being, Proverbs 20:27 (LB).

Self-justification, Proverbs 21:2.

Conscience music, Proverbs 29:6.

Eternity in men's hearts, Ecclesiastes 3:11.

Encumbered with guilt, Isaiah 1:4.

CON MAN

Countenance betrays conscience, Isaiah 3:9.

Conscience distresses heart, Jeremiah 4:18.

Not knowing how to blush, Jeremiah 6:15.

God tests heart, mind, Jeremiah 11:20.

Conscience caused insomnia, Daniel 6:18.

Wealth numbs conscience, Hosea 12:8.

Hoard plunder, insensitive to right, Amos 3:10.

"Know right from wrong," Micah 3:1 (CEV).

Remorse of Judas, Matthew 27:3–5.

Realization of sin, Luke 5:8.

Eye affects conscience, Luke 11:34 (AB).

Responsive conscience, Acts 2:37.

Hues of conscience, Acts 23:1; 1 Corinthians 8:7; 1 Timothy 3:9; 4:2; Hebrews 10:22.

Conscience toward God, men, Acts 24:16.

No scriptural guidance, Romans 2:14–15.

Lingering shame, Romans 6:21.

Conscience at ease, Romans 7:9 (LB).

Conscience in conflict, Romans 7:15–25.

Conscience ruled by Holy Spirit, Romans 9:1 (GNB).

Variety in conscience, Romans 14:1–23; 1 Corinthians 8:7–13; Titus 1:15.

Role of grief in repentance, 1 Corinthians 5:1–2.

Trustworthy conscience, 2 Corinthians 1:12.

New awareness in heart, 2 Corinthians 7:10–13.

Lost sensitivity, Ephesians 4:19 (NIV, NRSV).

Do not grieve Holy Spirit, Ephesians 4:30.

Cannot buy clear conscience, Hebrews 9:9.

Value of good conscience, Hebrews 9:14.

Made clean, Hebrews 10:22 (GNB).

Conscience disobeyed, James 4:17 (GNB).

Seeing light, walking in darkness, 2 Peter 2:21.

Those who refuse to repent, Revelation 16:10–11.

See Conviction, Guilt, Repentance, Mercy.

CONSCIENTIOUS

Abram's attitude toward Lot, Genesis 13:5–9.

Conscientious pagan maiden, Exodus 2:5–10.

Boaz, Ruth, Ruth 2:5–10; 3:7–18.

David's conscientious example, 2 Samuel 9:1–13.

Sympathy toward father's loneliness, 2 Samuel 14:1–24.

Conscientious king, 1 Kings 20:32–34.

Conscientious leadership, Nehemiah 5:8–19.

Mordecai, Esther, Esther 2:7.

Nebuchadnezzar's conduct in conquest, Jeremiah 39:1–14.

Joseph's initial attitude toward Mary, Matthew 1:18–19.

Good Samaritan, Luke 10:30–36.

See Compassion, Kindness.

CONSCIENTIOUS OBJECTOR

Avoiding war, Numbers 32:6.

CONSCIOUSNESS

Injured man half dead, Luke 10:30.

CONSCRIPTION

Conscription age, Numbers 26:2–4.

Taking care of business, Deuteronomy 20:5–9.

Mighty, brave men, 1 Samuel 14:52.

Forced labor, 1 Kings 9:15.

United enemy, 2 Kings 3:21.

Chosen for temple service, Luke 1:8–9.

CONSECRATION

Set apart, Exodus 32:29.

Dedicating new house, Deuteronomy 20:5.

Willing consecration, Judges 5:2.

Threshing floor site for altar, 2 Samuel 24:18–25.

Call to consecration, 1 Chronicles 29:5.

National commitment, 2 Kings 23:3; 2 Chronicles 15:15.

Volunteer service, 2 Chronicles 17:16.

Motive for consecration, Nehemiah 4:6.

Give heart to God, Psalm 40:7–8.

Heart, body consecration, Proverbs 23:26.

Coming with clean vessel, Isaiah 66:20.

Take cross, follow, Matthew 16:24; Mark 8:34; Luke 9:23.

Dual responsibility, Acts 6:1–4.

Consecration altar, Romans 12:1–2.

Dying daily, 1 Corinthians 15:31.

Consecration complete, 2 Corinthians 7:1 (AB).

To God, each other, 2 Corinthians 8:5.

Abandoning all for Christ, Philippians 3:8.

See Commitment, Dedication, Responsibility, Volition.

CONSENSUS

Unanimous complaint, Exodus 16:2; Numbers 11:4–6.

Public agreement, 1 Kings 18:24 (GNB).

Seeking national consensus, 1 Chronicles 13:1–4.

See Unanimity.

CONSENT

Mutual consent, Acts 5:1–2 (NRSV).

See Agreement, Approval, Decision.

CONSEQUENCES

Warning against disobedience, Genesis 2:17; Proverbs 13:15; Ezekiel 18:13; Romans 2:9.

Consequences of righteousness, Genesis 7:1; Psalm 18:24.

Consequences of father's obedience, Genesis 22:15–18.

Result of good deed, Exodus 2:15–22.

Reward for doing right, Deuteronomy 6:18–19.

Spoils of war, Joshua 7:11–12.

Enriching kindness, Ruth 2:5–12.

Humility delays disaster, 1 Kings 21:29.

Aftermath to spiritism, 1 Chronicles 10:13.

Unanswered prayer, Psalm 66:18; Isaiah 59:2.

Guidance follows commitment, Proverbs 3:5–6.

Pursuit of evil, Proverbs 11:19.

Certain judgment, Proverbs 11:21.

Misfortune, prosperity, Proverbs 13:21.

Justice delayed, Ecclesiastes 8:11.

Reward for tithing, Malachi 3:10; Luke 6:38.

Beatitudes, Matthew 5:3–12.

Result of believing, Acts 16:31.

Consequence of Adam's sin, Romans 5:12; 6:23.

Diversified labor, 1 Corinthians 3:8.

No escape ignoring salvation, Hebrews 2:3.

Faith rewarded, Hebrews 11:6.

See Doubt, Judgment, Obedient, Results.

CONSERVATION

Saving trees in conquered city, Deuteronomy 20:19.

No wasted food, John 6:12.

See Ecology.

CONSERVATIVE

Wise incline to right, Ecclesiastes 10:2.

CONSIDERATION

Returning neighbor's lost property, Deuteronomy 22:1–3.

Padding for Jeremiah's comfort, Jeremiah 38:11–13.

Joseph wanted to spare Mary public disgrace, Matthew 1:19.

First things first, Luke 10:38–42.

Consideration shown Paul, prisoner, Acts 27:3.

Tactful conversation with others, Colossians 4:6.

Tact in times of duress, James 1:19–20.

See Thoughtful.

CONSISTENT

Continuing altar fire, Leviticus 6:12.

Abstaining from wine, grapes, Numbers 6:2–4.

Follow all of God's commands, Deuteronomy 8:1.

Consistently evil, Judges 13:1.

Consistent relationship with God, 2 Chronicles 15:2 (LB).

"Steady love," Psalm 33:18 (LB).

Undivided heart, Psalm 86:11.

Our Lord's enduring love, Psalm 136:1–26.

Message proclaimed "again and again," Jeremiah 25:3–4 (NIV).

Loved with everlasting love, Jeremiah 31:3.

The Lord's love, faithfulness day by day, Lamentations 3:22–24.

Undivided heart, Ezekiel 11:19.

Good trees, good fruit, Matthew 7:18 (LB).

Take up cross daily, Luke 9:23 (See LB).

Divine consistency, Philippians 1:6.

Present, absent, Philippians 1:27–28.

Consistent life, 1 Thessalonians 4:11–12; James 3:13.
Persevere in life, doctrine, 1 Timothy 4:16.
"Hold to the standard," 2 Timothy 1:13 (NRSV).
Consistent goodness, James 3:13 (LB).
See Balance, Dependability.

CONSOLATION

Our rock, our song, Psalm 40:1–3.
Refuge, strength in trouble, Psalm 46:1–3.
Help through the night, Psalm 63:1–8.
Sheep of His pasture, Psalm 100:1–5.
Steadfast heart, Psalm 108:1–5.
Help in sorrow, Psalm 116:1–6, 15.
No song for heavy heart, Proverbs 25:20.
See Comfort, Empathy.

CONSPIRACY

Conspiracy of Joseph's brothers, Genesis 37:12–18.
Guards unwilling to follow king's evil command, 1 Samuel 22:16–17.
Conspiracy of Absalom, 2 Samuel 15:1–12.
Murderous officials, 2 Kings 12:19–21; 14:19; Daniel 6:1–5.
Plot to kill Paul, Acts 23:12–22.
See Deceit, Treachery.

CONSTANT

Pledge of lifelong loyalty, Ruth 1:15–17; 1 Samuel 20:42.
Earth remains constant, Ecclesiastes 1:4.
Mercies new each morning, Lamentations 3:22–26.
One never changes, Hebrews 1:10–12; 13:8.
See Absolute, Consistent, Dependability.

CONSTELLATIONS

Constellations known by Creator, Job 38:31; Isaiah 13:10; Amos 5:8.
See Astrology, Astronomy.

CONSTRUCTION

Man who built cities, Genesis 10:11–12.
Specific materials, Genesis 11:3.
Using natural stones, Exodus 20:25.
Cooperative congregation, Exodus 36:3–7.
Sky-high walls, Deuteronomy 9:1.

Organization for building temple, 1 Kings 5:12–18.
Quiet temple construction, 1 Kings 6:7.
Funding temple repair, 2 Kings 12:4–12 (CEV).
Preliminary preparations for temple, 1 Chronicles 22:2–5 (GNB).
Nails in abundance, 1 Chronicles 22:3.
Cities, castles, towers, 2 Chronicles 27:4 (KJV).
With praise to God, Ezra 3:10.
Delegated responsibility, Nehemiah 3:1–32.
Nehemiah's skill rebuilding wall, Nehemiah 6:1.
House the Lord built, Psalm 127:1.
Grass on housetops, Psalm 129:6–7.
Carpentry of lazy man, Ecclesiastes 10:18.
Replacement materials, Isaiah 9:10.
Building palace, Jeremiah 22:14.
No building programs, Jeremiah 51:26.
Using poor mortar, Ezekiel 13:10–14 (NKJV).
"Beauty to perfection," Ezekiel 27:4 (NIV).
New temple in Jerusalem, Ezekiel 40–43.
Support design, Ezekiel 41:6; 42:6.
Professional technique, Amos 7:7.
Mortar, brickwork, Nahum 3:14.
Paneled houses, Haggai 1:3.
Chosen to build temple, Zechariah 6:9–15.
Impressive construction, impending ruins, Mark 13:1–2.
Determining cost before expenditure, Luke 14:28–30.
Jesus, Cornerstone, Acts 4:11 (NKJV, AB).
See Architecture, Carpenter, Design, Prefabrication.

CONSULTATION

Advice for king, 1 Chronicles 13:1.
Consulting idols, Isaiah 19:3.
In private session, Galatians 2:2 (GNB).
See Advice.

CONSUMMATE See Perfection.

CONTACT See Touch.

CONTAGIOUS

Deathly plague, Ezekiel 6:11–12 (Note also Exodus 7–11).
See Disease, Epidemic, Plague.

CONTAMINATION

Mildew in house, Leviticus 14:33–47.
Unwashed hands, Leviticus 15:11.
Avoiding contamination, Numbers 5:1–4.
Touch of death, Numbers 19:13.
Caution against contamination, Isaiah 52:11.
See Unclean.

CONTEMPLATE

Contemplation day, night, Psalm 1:2.
"Think this over," Psalm 107:43 (Berk.).
Contemplating the Lord's work, Psalm 111:2.
Thought precedes action, Proverbs 29:20.
See Meditation.

CONTEMPORARY

Daily manifestation, Psalm 19:1 (Berk.).
Contemporary compassion, Lamentations 3:22–23.
Examples from daily life, Galatians 3:15.
See Now, Today.

CONTEMPT

Burning with anger, 1 Samuel 17:28.
Opposition to rebuilding walls, Nehemiah 2:19; 4:3.
World versus God, Psalm 2:1–4.
Defiance of a fool, Psalms 14:1; 53:1.
Scorn for acts of humility, Psalm 69:10–12.
Prayer for good attitude, Psalm 119:22.
False witness against Jesus, Mark 14:53–59.
Contempt for miracle, John 9:13–34.
No cause for contempt, Romans 14:3, 10 (NASB).
See Hatred.

CONTEMPT OF COURT

Demeaned judge, Deuteronomy 17:12.

CONTENTMENT

Tent or palace, 2 Samuel 7:1–7.
Food-induced contentment, 1 Kings 4:20 (GNB).
Everyone very happy, 1 Chronicles 12:40 (CEV).
"Restful water," Psalm 23:3 (Berk.).

Contented with little, Psalm 37:16–17.
Believer's contentment, Psalm 84:10–12.
"Wonderful to be grateful," Psalm 92:1 (CEV).
Desires satisfied, strength renewed, Psalm 103:5 (See 37:4).
Satisfaction only from the Lord, Psalm 107:8–9.
"Oh, the bliss," Psalm 112:1 (Berk.).
Rejoicing in day the Lord has made, Psalm 118:24.
No citizen complaints, Psalm 144:14 (KJV).
Contentment aids good health, Proverbs 14:30 (CEV).
Little with contentment, Proverbs 15:16.
Do not envy sinners, Proverbs 23:17; 24:19–20.
Happiness from honesty, Proverbs 30:7–9.
Joy in working, Proverbs 31:13 (NASB).
Accomplishment better than wealth, Ecclesiastes 2:10.
Special gift of God, Ecclesiastes 3:12–13.
Contented life of toil, Ecclesiastes 5:18–20.
Enjoying life, Ecclesiastes 8:15.
Live within income, Luke 3:14.
Secret of contentment, Philippians 4:11–13.
Godliness with contentment, 1 Timothy 6:6–8; Hebrews 13:5.
Do not grumble against each other, James 5:9.
See Peace, Rest, Satisfaction, Tranquility.

CONTEST

Beauty contest, Esther 2:1–4.

CONTEXTUALIZATION

Pagan worship elements, Deuteronomy 12:1–4.
Message adaption to Greek mentality, John 1:1–14. ("Word" translated from Greek "logos," basic concept in Greek philosophy.)
Divine witness in natural revelation, Acts 14:8–19.
Relating Gospel message through Old Testament, Acts 17:1–3; Philippians 3:3–11.
Witnessing to intellectuals, Acts 17:16–34.
Contextual mode to other cultures, circumstances, 1 Corinthians 9:19–22.
See Tact, Witness.

CONTINENCE

David, palace women, 2 Samuel 20:3.
Overcoming lust, Romans 13:14.
Husband, wife, 1 Corinthians 7:5 (LB).
See Abstinence, Eunuch, Morality, Restraint.

CONTINUITY

Endless disasters, Deuteronomy 32:32 (GNB).
Moses to Joshua, Joshua 1:5.
Continuing loyalty, Joshua 1:16–17.
Broken continuity of faith, Judges 2:10.
Joyful leadership transfer, 1 Kings 1:47–48.
Generation to generation, Psalms 48:12–13; 78:4–8.
One generation tells next, Psalm 145:4; Isaiah 59:21.
Pentecostal blessing, Acts 11:15.
Continuity of example, 1 Corinthians 11:1.
God's plan for Gospel perpetuation, 2 Timothy 2:1–4.
One who never changes, Hebrews 1:10–12.

CONTRACEPTION

Onan's procedure, Genesis 38:8–10.
See Birth Control.

CONTRACT

Treaty between Abraham, Abimelech, Genesis 21:22–34.
Grave site under contract, Genesis 23:20.
Nonverbal contract, Genesis 24:2–4.
Conditional sales, Leviticus 25:29–31.
Daughter's contract altered by father, Numbers 30:3–5, 10–15.
God's covenant through many generations, Deuteronomy 5:2–3.
Those who broke faith with God, Deuteronomy 32:51.
Fate of favorite daughter, only child, Judges 11:29–39.
Conditional terms, Ruth 4:1–10.
Symbol of transaction, Ruth 4:7.
Purchase order, 1 Kings 5:8–11.
Importance of treaty, 1 Kings 20:34.
Contractual statement, Proverbs 3:5–6.
Servants bound by contract, Isaiah 21:16.
Penalty for disobeying covenant, Jeremiah 11:1–5.

Ownership documents, Jeremiah 32:10–14, 16.
Legal conflicts from false oaths, Hosea 10:4.
Meeting God's terms, Jonah 3:9 (AB).
Betrayal contract, Matthew 26:14–16.
Human covenant, Galatians 3:15.
See Agreement, Guarantee, Mortgage.

CONTRADICTION

Saying one thing, meaning another, Exodus 14:5–8; Psalms 55:12–23; 78:34–37; Proverbs 26:18–26; Isaiah 29:13–16.
Worship without true reverence, Amos 5:21–24.
Insincere piety, Matthew 23:1–39; Mark 12:38–40; Luke 6:46; 11:39–52.
Practice what you preach, Romans 2:21–25.
Avoid contradiction, 1 Timothy 6:20 (NRSV).
Beyond contradiction, Hebrews 7:7 (AB).
See Hypocrisy, Sham.

CONTRAST

Light separated from darkness, Genesis 1:4–5.
Reversal of fortunes, Numbers 33:3–4.
Palace, ark, 2 Samuel 7:1–2.
"What a different story," Psalm 1:4 (LB).
Red Sea as desert, Psalm 106:9.
Path of righteous, way of wicked, Proverbs 4:18–19.
Positives, negatives, Ecclesiastes 3:1–8.
Gentle flowing waters, mighty flood waters, Isaiah 8:6–7.
Contrast between temporal, spiritual, Isaiah 40:7–8.
Light shining in darkness, Isaiah 60:1–2.
Fate of good, evil, Isaiah 65:13–14.
Faithless Israel, unfaithful Judah, Jeremiah 3:11.
Contrast mercy, blessing, Lamentations 3:22–26.
Prophet an exception to those warned, Micah 3:7–8.
Pagan nations and those who follow the Lord, Micah 4:5.
Mary's reaction compared to shepherds, Luke 2:19–20.
Contrast in family members' love, Luke 15:11–32.

Law of Moses, message of Christ, John 1:17.

Crippled man, beautiful gate, Acts 3:2.

Man's evil, God's righteousness, Romans 3:5–8.

Holy God, lost sinners, Romans 5:8.

Man's guilt, God's grace, Romans 5:17.

Life, death, Romans 8:2.

Gloom today, glory tomorrow, Romans 8:18.

Sad but joyful, poor but rich, 2 Corinthians 6:9 (LB).

Freedom versus slavery, Galatians 5:1.

Flesh versus Spirit, Galatians 5:18–23.

Deceit, truth, Ephesians 4:14–15.

Darkness, light, Ephesians 5:8–14.

That which is truly high, truly low, James 1:9–10.

Cain, Abel, 1 John 3:12 (GNB).

Women's hair, lions' teeth, Revelation 9:8.

See Variety.

CONTRIBUTION

Asking for much, 2 Kings 4:3.

Temple collection box, 2 Kings 12:9–14 (GNB).

"Small amount of silver," Nehemiah 10:32 (CEV).

Moses, Christ, John 1:17.

Serving without pay, 1 Corinthians 9:7.

Giving from continuity of desire, 2 Corinthians 9:10–11.

No help from pagans, 3 John 7.

See Participation, Philanthropy, Stewardship.

CONTRITE

Unworthy of being in king's presence, 2 Samuel 19:24–28.

Broken hearts, crushed spirit, Psalms 34:18; 51:17.

Reverence before the Lord, Isaiah 66:2.

Repentant grief, Joel 2:13; 1 Corinthians 5:1–2; 2 Corinthians 7:10.

Contrite Judas, Matthew 27:3.

See Repentance.

CONTROL

God in control, Jeremiah 34:1–3; 36:1–3; 44:29–30.

Controlled by Christ's love, 2 Corinthians 5:14 (GNB).

Desire to be church officer, 1 Timothy 3:1.

Controlled tongue, body, James 3:2 (LB).

Man enslaved to whatever masters him, 2 Peter 2:19.

Holy Spirit's control, Revelation 21:10 (GNB).

CONTROVERSY

Discontent with leadership, Numbers 14:1–4.

Two factions, 1 Kings 16:21–22.

Strife caused by pride, hatred, Proverbs 10:12; 13:10.

Evidence turns against accuser, Proverbs 25:8.

Promoting controversy, 1 Timothy 1:4.

"Morbid craving for controversy," 1 Timothy 6:4 (NRSV).

Foolish questions, Titus 3:9.

See Abrasion, Argument, Dispute, Mob Psychology.

CONVALESCENCE

Good sleep, Psalm 3:5.

Sustained on sickbed, Psalm 41:3.

Restored to health, Isaiah 38:16.

Illness, near death, Philippians 2:25–30.

See Health, Medicine, Physician, Therapy.

CONVERSATION

Speaking neither good, evil, Genesis 31:24.

Spiritual matters, Deuteronomy 6:4–7.

Prophetic error, Deuteronomy 18:21–22.

Samson, Philistine woman, Judges 14:7.

Casual speech, Ruth 2:5; 4:1 (LB).

Talking to God, 2 Chronicles 6:4 (LB).

Left with nothing to say, Nehemiah 5:8.

Windy conversation, Job 8:2.

Accused of not speaking sensibly, Job 18:2.

Resolving not to sin with one's mouth, Psalm 17:3.

Keeping tongue from speaking wrong, Psalm 39:1.

Words known before spoken, Psalm 139:4.

Serpent tongues, Psalm 140:3.

How to avoid gossip, Psalm 141:3.

Speech of righteous, wicked, Proverbs 10:11.

Worth listening to, Proverbs 10:20 (LB).

Good, evil tongue, Proverbs 10:31–32.

Fruit of lips, Proverbs 12:14.

Words aptly spoken, Proverbs 15:23; 25:11; Ecclesiastes 5:2.

Silence elevates fool, Proverbs 17:28.

Fool's opinions, Proverbs 18:2.

Know your subject, Proverbs 20:15 (GNB).

Gossip talks too much, Proverbs 20:19.

Guarding tongue, Proverbs 21:23.

Conduct, conversation linked together, Proverbs 22:11.

Disguising true self by false speech, Proverbs 26:24–26.

"Foul mouthed," Isaiah 6:5 (LB).

Discussing God's goodness, Jeremiah 16:14–15 (LB).

Saying yes, no, Matthew 5:37.

Words condemn, acquit, Matthew 12:37.

Not what goes into mouth, what comes out, Matthew 15:10–20.

"Talk is cheap," Mark 2:9 (LB).

Use of gracious words, Luke 4:22.

Speaking quietly, Luke 10:23 (LB).

Talking about latest ideas, Acts 17:21.

Conversation enriched in Christ, 1 Corinthians 1:5–6.

Foolish talk, coarse joking, Ephesians 5:4.

Discussion topic, Ephesians 5:19–20.

Giving correct information, Colossians 4:6 (LB).

Exemplary speech, 1 Timothy 4:12.

Speaking to varied age groups, 1 Timothy 5:1–2.

Avoid godless chatter, 2 Timothy 2:16.

Seriousness, sound speech, Titus 2:7–8 (GNB).

Quick to listen, slow to speak, James 1:19.

Deceitful, unruly tongue, James 1:26.

Guard tongue well, James 3:3–6.

Insulting language, 1 Peter 2:1 (GNB).

Speaking, serving to glory of God, 1 Peter 4:11.

Empty, boastful words, 2 Peter 2:18.

More effective spoken than written, 2 John 12; 3 John 13–14 (GNB).

Pride, blasphemy, Revelation 13:5.

See Communication, Gossip, Silence, Speech, Tact.

CONVERSATIONAL CONTROL

Strategic speech control, James 3:2–5.

CONVERSION

Egyptian conversions, Exodus 14:30–31.

Child's need for conversion experience, 1 Samuel 3:7.

Saul changed by Holy Spirit, 1 Samuel 10:6–10.

Conversion motivated by fear, Esther 8:17.

Conversion experience, Psalm 18:16–19.

Blameless before the Lord, Psalm 26:1, 11.

Song of transformation, Psalm 40:1–4.

Depth of mercy, forgiveness, Psalm 51:1–2.

Spiritual heritage, Psalm 61:5.

"Transplanted," Psalm 92:13 (Berk.).

Purging fire, Isaiah 6:6–7.

Walking in the Way, Isaiah 35:8.

Light has come, Isaiah 60:1.

Disgraced youth's repentance, Jeremiah 31:19.

Repentance in tears, Jeremiah 50:4–5.

Former prisoner at king's table, Jeremiah 52:33.

Heart of stone, of flesh, Ezekiel 11:19.

Giving heart to idols, Ezekiel 14:4 (GNB).

Turning from wicked past, Ezekiel 16:59–63.

New heart, spirit, Ezekiel 36:26.

Pagan king's conversion, Daniel 4:34.

Purified, made spotless, Daniel 12:10.

All who call will be saved, Joel 2:32.

Remembering date of decision, Haggai 2:18.

National conversions, Zechariah 2:11.

New garments, Zechariah 3:1–7.

Joshua's salvation, Zechariah 3:1–7; 6:9–15.

Old Testament conversion, Malachi 2:6.

Mark of conversion, Luke 3:7–14 (LB).

Celebrating call to follow Jesus, Luke 5:27–32.

Conversion can bring family division, Luke 12:49–53.

Need for repentance, Luke 13:3–5.

Being born again, John 3:1–8 (See "born anew" NRSV).

Personal experience, John 4:42.

Responding to Jesus, John 8:30.

Healed of blindness, John 9:1–7.

Instant conversion, John 9:35–38.

Turning to light before darkness comes, John 12:35–36.

Key to conversion, John 20:30–31.

Salvation in no other name, Acts 4:12.

Converted sorcerer, Acts 8:9–13.

Simultaneous conversion, baptism, Acts 8:35–36.

Saul's conversion, Acts 9:1–19; 7:58; 8:1–3; 9:20–21.

Roman leader influenced by sorcerer, Acts 13:6–12.

Jailer converted, Acts 16:25–34.

Synagogue ruler's conversion, Acts 18:8.

Scrolls destroyed by converted sorcerers, Acts 19:19.

Process of time, Acts 26:28.

"Back from death," Romans 6:13 (LB).

Spiritual life follows natural life, 1 Corinthians 15:45–49.

New creation in Christ, 2 Corinthians 5:17.

Self-examination, 2 Corinthians 13:5.

Set apart from birth, Galatians 1:15–17.

Darkness to light, Ephesians 5:8–10.

Those who have died with Christ, Colossians 2:20–23.

Risen with Christ, Colossians 3:1–17.

Blasphemer becomes Gospel minister, 1 Timothy 1:12–14.

God's grace to worst of sinners, 1 Timothy 1:15–16.

Faith gives message credibility, Hebrews 4:2.

Birth through word of truth, James 1:18.

Living hope, 1 Peter 1:3–5.

Becoming chosen people, 1 Peter 2:9.

Reaction of former associates, 1 Peter 4:3–4 (GNB).

Walking in light, 1 John 1:5–7.

Doing what is right, 1 John 2:29.

Purifying privilege, 1 John 3:1–3.

Confidence in conversion, 1 John 3:24.

Wearing clean robes, Revelation 22:14.

See Convert, Decision, Repentance, Salvation.

CONVERT

Attitude toward foreigners, 1 Kings 8:41–43.

Lambs, shepherd, Isaiah 40:11.

Way of backslider, of convert, Ezekiel 33:17–20.

Burning stick snatched from fire, Zechariah 3:2.

One lost sheep, Matthew 18:12–14.

First believers, John 2:23.

Those who believed, John 10:42.

Secret believers, John 12:42–43.

Immature new convert, Acts 8:13–24.

Centurion Cornelius, Acts 10:1–33.

Do not hinder new converts, Acts 15:19.

Reconnaissance ministry, Acts 15:36.

Prominent women converts, Acts 17:4.

Few converts in Athens, Acts 17:34.

Asia's first convert, Romans 16:5.

Christ's testimony confirmed in converts, 1 Corinthians 1:4–6.

Simple people converted, 1 Corinthians 1:26–31.

One plants, one waters, God gives growth, 1 Corinthians 3:6–9.

Spiritual father, 1 Corinthians 4:15.

Seal of apostleship, 1 Corinthians 9:1–2.

Convert as written witness, 2 Corinthians 3:1–3.

Boasting about converts, 2 Corinthians 10:8.

Convert follow-up, 2 Corinthians 13:5–10; 1 Thessalonians 3:1–5.

Recorded in Book of Life, Philippians 4:3.

Paul struggled over converts, Colossians 2:1.

Trophy, joy, 1 Thessalonians 2:20 (LB).

True son in faith, 1 Timothy 1:2.

Convert's testimony to congregation, 1 Timothy 6:12.

Prison convert, Philemon 10.

New converts persecuted, Hebrews 10:32–33.

Redeemed from all nations, Revelation 7:9–17.

See Believer, Conversion, Secret.

CONVICTION

Much heart searching, Judges 5:16.

Isaiah's conviction of sin, Isaiah 6:5.

Understanding brings terror, Isaiah 28:19.

Knowing what is right, Isaiah 51:7.

Power of holy words, Jeremiah 23:9.

Message believed by messenger, Ezekiel 3:10–11 (LB).

Reaction to prophet's message, Ezekiel 21:7.

Wealth numbs conscience, Hosea 12:8.

Multitudes in valley of decision, Joel 3:14.

Pharisees knew Jesus was talking about them, Matthew 21:33–46.

Tears of conviction, Matthew 26:75 (CEV).

Ridden with remorse, Matthew 27:3–5.

Impact of spiritual power, Mark 5:17.

Herod disturbed but enjoying truth, Mark 6:20 (GNB).

Revealing thoughts of heart, Luke 2:34–35.

Realization of sin in Jesus' presence, Luke 5:8.

Drawn to Christ by Heavenly Father, John 6:44.

Impact of Jesus' teaching, John 7:44–46.

Day of Pentecost, Acts 2:37–38.

Tolerating convictions of others, Romans 14:1–8.

Speaking with conviction, 2 Corinthians 4:13.

Awareness in hearts of Corinthians, 2 Corinthians 7:10–13.

Hold truth firmly, Hebrews 2:1 (GNB).

Do not harden heart, Hebrews 3:7–8, 15.

God searches mind, heart, Revelation 2:23.
See Conscience, Duress, Guilt.

CONVINCING

Vindication by earthquake, Numbers 16:28–34.

Mouth like sharpened sword, Isaiah 49:2.

Preaching with authority, Luke 4:32.

Difficulty convincing others, Romans 9:1–2.

Convincing message, 2 Timothy 4:2 (NRSV).
See Persuasion.

CONVOCATION

Sacred assembly, Exodus 12:16; Leviticus 23:3; Numbers 28:18, 26.

Disciples assembled, Luke 9:1.

COOKING

Man in kitchen, Genesis 19:3.

Implements for making food, Exodus 8:3; Leviticus 2:5, 7; 1 Samuel 2:13–14;

1 Kings 17:12; Isaiah 47:2; Ezekiel 4:3; Amos 6:6.

Broiled meat, Exodus 12:8.

Cooked manna, Exodus 16:5 (CEV).

How not to cook young goat, Exodus 23:19.

Food with pleasant aroma, Numbers 28:2.

Chef Gideon, Judges 6:19.

Ancient dishwashing, 2 Kings 21:13.

Boiled water, Isaiah 64:2.

Each pot sacred, Zechariah 14:20–21.

Sickbed to kitchen, Matthew 8:14–15 (CEV).
See Baking, Food, Gourmet, Meals, Menu.

COOL

Cool private chamber, Judges 3:20 (NKJV).

"Cool in spirit," Proverbs 17:27 (NRSV).

"Cool of the day," Song of Songs 4:6 (NASB).

Keep cool, 2 Timothy 4:5 (AB).

COOPERATION

Willing to serve, contribute, Exodus 35:10–35; 36:4–7.

Ox, donkey cannot plow together, Deuteronomy 22:10.

Cooperation for survival, Joshua 9:1–2 (LB); 10:1–5; 11:1–5.

Nation united, Joshua 10:29–42.

"No help at all," Judges 5:15 (CEV).

Cooperation refused, Ezra 4:1–3.

Hearty cooperation, Nehemiah 4:6.

Living together in unity, Psalm 133:1–3.

Iron sharpens iron, Proverbs 27:17.

Advantage in cooperation, Ecclesiastes 4:9–12.

No one to help, Isaiah 63:5.

Two in agreement, Amos 3:3.

Mutual faith required for healing, Mark 6:4–6.

The Lord's cooperation, Mark 16:20 (Berk.).

Those for, against, Luke 11:23.

Laying on hands, Acts 13:1–3.

United mind, thought, 1 Corinthians 1:10.

Total function Body of Christ, 1 Corinthians 12:14–20.

Harmonious ministry to Jews, Gentiles, Galatians 2:8.

Philippians shared ministry expense, Philippians 4:15–19.

"Uncontentious," Titus 3:2 (NASB).
See Camaraderie, Rapport, Unanimity.

CORDIALITY

Warm salutation, 1 Samuel 25:6.
False cordiality, Psalm 28:3.
Troubled by angel's cordial greeting, Luke 1:28–31.
Many greetings to friends, Romans 16:3–16.

CORNERSTONE

Christ's rejection, Psalm 118:22.
Cornerstone in Zion, Isaiah 28:16.
Christ, the Cornerstone, 1 Peter 2:6–8.

CORONATION

Queen's coronation, Esther 2:17.
Simulated coronation, John 12:12–19.
Coronation mockery, John 19:1–3.
Christ's ultimate coronation, Revelation 17:14; 19:16.

CORPSE

Choice place for burial, Genesis 23:6.
Slaughtered male citizens, Genesis 34:27.
Eyes closed in death, Genesis 46:4.
Embracing corpse, Genesis 50:1.
Cause of defilement, Leviticus 22:4; Numbers 9:10; 19:13.
Respect for death, Numbers 19:16.
Covering corpse, 2 Samuel 20:12.
Mother's concern, 2 Samuel 21:10 (LB).
Body fed to dogs, 2 Kings 9:34–37.
Angelic slaughter, 2 Kings 19:35; Isaiah 37:36.
Obliterated army, 2 Chronicles 20:24.
Food for birds, Psalm 79:2; Jeremiah 16:4; 34:20.
Thrown into cistern, Jeremiah 41:9.
"Refuse in the streets," Isaiah 5:25 (NIV, See Jeremiah 9:22).
Respected, desecrated, Isaiah 14:18–19.
Unburied bodies, Isaiah 34:3; Jeremiah 16:4.
Death valley, Jeremiah 31:40.
Laid before idols, Ezekiel 6:5.
Abundant corpses, Nahum 3:3.
Corpse-like appearance, Mark 9:26.
Sabbath propriety, John 19:31.
Bodies lying in street, Revelation 11:8.

Refused burial, Revelation 11:9.
See Burial, Death, Funeral.

CORPULENCE *See Obesity.*

CORRECTION

Refusing father's correction, 1 Samuel 2:22–25.
Willing for correction, Job 6:24.
Rebuked by righteous man, Psalm 141:5.
Reprove, receive insults, Proverbs 9:7 (NASB).
Willing to be disciplined, corrected, Proverbs 10:17; 12:1; 25:12.
Value of open rebuke, Proverbs 27:5.
Friend's counsel, Proverbs 27:9.
Those who refuse counsel, Proverbs 29:1.
Sins paid back, Isaiah 65:6.
The Lord guides, corrects, Jeremiah 10:23–24.
Problem of legalism, Acts 15:1–11.
Instruction in effective witness, Acts 18:24–26.
Productive correction, 2 Corinthians 7:8–9.
Helping someone who has sinned, Galatians 6:1.
Take correction patiently, Hebrews 12:7 (CEV).
See Criticism.

CORRESPONDENCE

Seeking guidance from correspondence, 2 Kings 19:14–19.
Letters to, from kings, Ezra 4:7–22; 5:8–17; 7:11–26.
Tactical correspondence, Nehemiah 6:1–19.
Important information, Esther 9:20–22.
Good news from distant land, Proverbs 25:25.
Letters to convalescent, Isaiah 39:1.
Jeremiah's letter to exiles, Jeremiah 29:1–23.
Important letter to friend, Luke 1:1 (LB).
Writing difficult letter, 2 Corinthians 2:4 (LB).
Letters of recommendation, 2 Corinthians 3:1.
More easily written than spoken, 2 Corinthians 10:10; 13:10.

Circular letter, Colossians 4:16.

Identified by handwriting, 2 Thessalonians 3:17.

Teaching by correspondence, 1 Timothy 3:14–15.

Letter on slave's behalf, Philemon 1–25.

Short letter, Hebrews 13:22.

Purpose of letters to friends, 2 Peter 3:1.

Better spoken than written, 3 John 13–14 (GNB).

Necessary correspondence, Jude 3 (NRSV).

CORROSION

Oil protection against rust, Isaiah 21:5.

Deteriorating material investment, Matthew 6:19–20.

CORRUPTION

Vanishing faithful, Psalm 12:1 (LB).

Corrupt from birth, Psalm 58:3.

Deceptive wages, Proverbs 11:18.

Moral rot in government, Proverbs 28:2 (LB).

Silver to dross, wine to water, Isaiah 1:22.

Ravages of wickedness, Isaiah 9:18.

Corruption among priests, Jeremiah 5:31; Ezekiel 22:26; Matthew 27:20.

Defiled with blood, Lamentations 4:14.

Despising those who tell truth, Amos 5:10.

Shameless evil, Zephaniah 3:5 (CEV).

Bad corrupts good, Matthew 13:24–30.

Roman official wanted bribe, Acts 24:26.

Gaining benefit misusing others, James 5:4–5.

Surviving in evil surroundings, 2 Peter 2:4–9.

Sin committed in broad daylight, 2 Peter 2:13–23.

Suggested social disease, Jude 7–8.
See Bribery, Deceit, Dishonesty.

COSMETICS

Aroma of romance, Ruth 3:3.

Body lotions, 2 Samuel 12:20 (NIV).

Eye makeup, 2 Kings 9:30; Ezekiel 23:40.

Extensive beauty treatment, Esther 2:9, 12.

Perfumed clothing, Psalm 45:8.

Jewelry, cosmetics snatched away, Isaiah 3:18–24.

Makeup in poor taste, Jeremiah 4:30.

Anointing Jesus, Matthew 26:6–13; Mark 14:3–9.

Expensive perfume on Jesus' feet, John 12:1–8.
See Fragrance, Myrrh, Perfume.

COSMIC

Cosmic powers, Ephesians 6:12 (Berk., GNB).
See New Age.

COST

Cheap stewardship refused, 2 Samuel 24:21–24.

Stingy man's food, Proverbs 23:6–8.

High cost discipleship, Luke 14:26–27.

Need for counting cost, Luke 14:28–30.

Cost of spiritual blindness, Luke 19:41–44.

High cost resurrection relevance, Philippians 3:10.
See Finance, Sacrifice, Stewardship.

COSTUME

Clothed with righteousness, faithfulness, Isaiah 11:5.

Cloud robe, rainbow hat, Revelation 10:1.

Beautiful jewels adorning evil woman, Revelation 17:4.
See Clothing, Wardrobe.

COUNSEL

Family counsel, Genesis 49:1–2.

Aged father's counsel, 1 Kings 2:1–9.

Kings consulted Solomon, 1 Kings 4:34.

Little girl's influence, 2 Kings 5:1–3.

Self-advised, Nehemiah 5:7.

He who counseled others becomes discouraged, Job 4:3–5.

Miserable comforters, Job 16:2.

God's Word undergirds good counsel, Psalm 37:30–31.

Righteous man's rebuke, Psalm 141:5.

Refusing counsel, Proverbs 1:29–31.

Wise listen to good counsel, Proverbs 9:9; 20:18.

Good, bad sources for advice, Proverbs 12:5.

Taking advice, Proverbs 13:10.

Multitude of counselors, Proverbs 15:22.

Refreshing counsel, Proverbs 18:4 (GNB).

Advice, instruction, Proverbs 19:20.
Making plans, waging war, Proverbs 20:18.
Advice from friend, Proverbs 27:9.
Those who refuse counsel, Proverbs 29:1.
Paul's counsel, sad parting, Acts 20:25–38.
Eager for proper counsel, 1 Thessalonians 3:1–5.
Gently instruct backslider, 2 Timothy 2:23–26.
See Advice, Counseling.

COUNSELING

Moses seated as judge, Exodus 18:13–24.
Counselors needed, Deuteronomy 1:12–13.
Priest served as judge, 1 Samuel 7:15–17.
Counseling distressed, discontented, 1 Samuel 22:2.
Advice as from God, 2 Samuel 16:23.
Guidance in king's court, 1 Chronicles 27:32–33.
Consulting oneself, Nehemiah 5:7.
Supreme choice of Counselor, Isaiah 9:6.
"Spirit of counsel," Isaiah 11:2 (Berk.).
Instructed tongue, Isaiah 50:4.
Helping wayward believer, Ezekiel 3:20–21.
No message from counselor, Ezekiel 7:26.
Promised Counselor, John 14:16–17.
Counselor shares from experience, 2 Corinthians 1:3–4.
Gentle like mother, 1 Thessalonians 2:7.
Gentle counsel, Hebrews 5:2.
Restoring backslider, James 5:19–20.
See Counsel, Guidance.

COUNTENANCE

Variety of facial expressions, Genesis 4:5; 31:2 (KJV); Judges 13:6; 1 Samuel 16:12; Nehemiah 2:2–3; Proverbs 15:13; 25:23; Matthew 17:2; 2 Corinthians 3:7, 18.
Facial scowl, Genesis 4:6 (GNB).
Countenance reveals feelings, Nehemiah 2:1–3; Job 15:12.
Encouraging facial expression, Job 29:24.
Divine countenance, Psalms 4:6; 44:3.
Faces made radiant, Psalm 34:5.
"Face-healer," Psalm 42:11 (Berk.).
God's shining face, Psalm 80:3, 7.
Haughty eyes, Proverbs 21:4.
Face reflects heart, Proverbs 27:19.
Sad face, Ecclesiastes 7:3; Ezekiel 27:35.

Wisdom brightens countenance, Ecclesiastes 8:1 (NASB).
Countenance betrays conscience, Isaiah 3:9.
Face set like flint, Isaiah 50:7.
Making faces, Isaiah 57:4 (LB).
Variation of facial appearance, Ezekiel 1:10.
Gloomy countenance, Daniel 1:10 (Berk.).
Master of intrigue, Daniel 8:23.
Holier-than-thou pretense, Matthew 6:16.
Face of an angel, Acts 6:15.
Result of close walk with God, 2 Corinthians 3:7–18.
See Attitude, Face.

COUNTERFEIT

Friends, brothers not trustworthy, Jeremiah 9:4–8.
Counterfeit Christs in later days, Matthew 24:4–5, 24.
Ego displayed by teachers of Law, Mark 12:38–40.
Ultimate identification of hypocrite, Luke 13:23–27.
Disciples disbelieved Saul's conversion, Acts 9:26–27.
Counterfeit Christian leaders, 2 Corinthians 11:13–15.
Genuine ministry not counterfeit, 2 Corinthians 13:6 (Berk.).
False humility, Colossians 2:18.
Counterfeit intellectualism, 1 Timothy 6:20.
Deceitful claim of holy life, 1 John 1:8–10.
Feigning life when spiritually dead, Revelation 3:1.
See Deceit, Disguise, False.

COUNTRY *See Kingdom, Nations.*

COUP

Frustrated coup effort, 1 Kings 1:5–53.

COUP DE GRACE

Saul's suicide, 1 Samuel 31:4–6 (See 2 Samuel 1:1–16).
Strange death of Absalom, 2 Samuel 18:9–15.
See Suicide.

COURAGE

Fear submits to assurance, Exodus 14:13–14.

Courage at God's command, Joshua 1:9.

Lost courage, Joshua 5:1.

Courageous old age, Joshua 14:10–12.

People risked lives, Judges 5:18.

March on with strong soul, Judges 5:21.

Facing big opposition, Judges 7:7–23; 1 Samuel 17:32, 50.

Courageous youth, 1 Samuel 14:6–45.

Prophet's lost courage, 1 Kings 19:1–4.

Facing danger to assist David, 1 Chronicles 9:15–19.

"Don't give up," 2 Chronicles 15:7 (CEV).

Strength, courage, 2 Chronicles 32:6–7 (KJV).

Laughing at fear, Job 39:22.

Facing ten thousand, Psalm 3:6.

Moving ahead in spite of circumstances, Psalm 44:18.

Steady hearts, no fear, Psalm 112:8 (NRSV).

Witness to those in authority, Psalm 119:46.

Bold stouthearted, Psalm 138:3.

Alcoholic courage, Proverbs 20:1 (LB).

Courage in troubled times, Proverbs 24:10.

Mighty lion, Proverbs 30:30.

Fearing wrong things, Isaiah 8:12–14.

Sufficiency of our God, Isaiah 41:10 (CEV).

Face set like flint, Isaiah 50:7.

"Put on your strength," Isaiah 52:1 (Berk.).

Weary but winning, Isaiah 57:10.

Be courageous or a fool, Jeremiah 1:17 (LB).

Courage to face adverse circumstances, Ezekiel 2:6–7.

"Hard like a diamond," Ezekiel 3:9 (CEV).

Witness in king's court, Daniel 3:8–18.

Courage to expose king's sin, Daniel 5:18–28 (CEV).

Faith before loyalty to king, Daniel 6:5–11.

Failed courage, Amos 2:14–16.

Bravest soldier loses courage, Zephaniah 1:14 (GNB).

Attempted walk on water, Matthew 14:22–31.

Prayer augments courage, Luke 18:1.

Reward of standing firm, Luke 21:19.

Fear of authority, John 19:38.

Courageously preaching Christ, Acts 3:12–26.

Endeavoring to silence Peter, John, Acts 4:16–20.

Ministry under persecution, Acts 5:37–42; 8:1.

Confidence in difficult places, Acts 20:22–24.

Willing for suffering, death, Acts 21:13.

Paul arrested, asked witness opportunity, Acts 21:37—22:21.

Win over evil, Romans 12:21 (GNB).

Stand firm, not shaken, 1 Corinthians 15:58 (CEV).

Strength in subdued approach, 2 Corinthians 10:1.

Do not lose heart, Ephesians 3:13 (NRSV).

Never give up, Ephesians 6:18 (GNB).

Prayer not to be ashamed, Philippians 1:20.

Standing firm whatever circumstances, Philippians 1:27–30.

Without fear, Philippians 1:28 (AB).

Boldly facing opposition, 1 Thessalonians 2:1–2.

Power, love replace timidity, 2 Timothy 1:7.

Not embarrassed by Paul's chains, 2 Timothy 1:16–18.

Blood of Christ gives courage, Hebrews 10:19 (CEV).

"Stand up straight," Hebrews 12:12 (CEV).

Faithful to point of death, Revelation 2:13.

Holding on to faith, Revelation 2:25.

See Boldness, Hero, Martyr.

COURT

Moses seated as judge, Exodus 18:13–24.

Responsibility to witness, Leviticus 5:1.

Fairness in trials, Deuteronomy 1:15–17.

Securing verdict, Deuteronomy 17:9.

Court venue, Deuteronomy 21:19; 25:7; Judges 4:5.

Circuit court, 1 Samuel 7:15–16.

"Judges are wolves," Zephaniah 3:3 (CEV).

Theological dispute secular courtroom, Acts 18:12–17.

God's Word valid in secular court, Romans 3:4 (CEV).

Small claims court, 1 Corinthians 6:2 (NASB).

See Justice, Lawyer, Verdict.

COURTESY

Sister in strange country, Genesis 12:10–13.

Returning neighbor's lost property, Deuteronomy 22:1–3.

Courtesy to stranger, Ruth 2:14–18.

Gentleness of Boaz to Ruth, Ruth 3:7–15.

Wasted compliments, Proverbs 23:8.

One of ten grateful for healing, Luke 17:11–19.

Courteous conversation, Colossians 4:6.

"Courtesy to everyone," Titus 3:2 (NRSV).

Respect for everyone, 1 Peter 2:17.

See Hospitality, Human Relations, Tact.

COURTSHIP

Noticing opposite sex, Genesis 6:1–2 (Berk.).

Arranged marriages, Genesis 21:21; 24:1–67.

Asking for guidance sign, Genesis 24:14.

Angelic assistance, Genesis 24:40.

Seven-year wait, Genesis 29:18–20.

Rape, romance, Genesis 34:1–3.

Moses, Zipporah, Exodus 2:16–22.

Samson, Philistine woman, Judges 14:1–7.

Kidnapped brides, Judges 21:23.

Women's initiative, Ruth 3:1–18.

Bargaining hearts, 1 Samuel 18:17.

Times of restraint, Ecclesiastes 3:5.

No romantic serenades, Psalm 78:63 (Berk., NIV).

Stealing heart, Song of Songs 4:9.

Males easily find wild donkey, Jeremiah 2:24.

Evil woman's courtship, Hosea 2:11–16 (LB).

See Marriage, Romance.

COUSIN

Marriage of cousins, 2 Chronicles 11:18 (LB).

COVENANT

Everlasting covenant, Genesis 8:20–22.

God's promise to Abram, Genesis 13:14–17; 15:1–25. (Note: Some see "dust of the earth" as Jewish or earthly family and "the stars" as future church or heavenly family.)

Keeping covenant between people, Joshua 9:16–21.

"Covenant love," Psalm 21:7 (Berk.).

Divine covenant with believers, Psalm 145:13, 18.

Freedom for slaves, Jeremiah 34:8–21.

Neither good, evil father to son, Ezekiel 18:3–20.

Ratified covenant, Luke 22:20 (AB).

See Agreement, Contract.

COVET

Tenth commandment, Exodus 20:17.

Servant's greed, 2 Kings 5:20–27.

Evil heart's desire, Psalm 10:3; Proverbs 1:19.

Coveting another's wealth, Psalm 49:16–20.

Coveting good fortune of wicked, Psalm 73:2–5, 12.

Longings of wicked, Psalm 112:10.

Antidote for covetousness, Psalm 119:36.

Unsatisfied craving, Proverbs 13:4.

Perilous envy, Proverbs 14:30.

Covetousness compared to stewardship, Proverbs 21:25–26.

Envying sinners, Proverbs 23:17; 24:19–20.

Never satisfied, Ecclesiastes 5:10–11.

Greedy dogs, Isaiah 56:11.

Greedy for gain, Jeremiah 6:13.

Covet definition, Luke 12:15 (AB).

Clergy not coveting laity prosperity, Acts 20:32–35.

Evil desire, Romans 13:9 (AB).

See Greed, Jealousy, Self-interest, Selfishness.

COWARD

Cowardly brothers, Genesis 42:21–28.

Frightened by falling leaf, Leviticus 26:36.

Feeling small like grasshoppers, Numbers 13:33.

Infectious cowardice, Deuteronomy 20:8.

Melting because of fear, Joshua 2:24.

Thousand flee one enemy, Joshua 23:10; Isaiah 30:17.

Timid soldiers, 1 Samuel 23:1–5.

Dubious loyalty, 1 Chronicles 12:19.

Effort to incite cowardice, Nehemiah 6:10–13 (CEV).

Turning away from battle, Psalm 78:9.

Bold front, Proverbs 21:29.

Fleeing from nothing, Proverbs 28:1.

Fear of man, Proverbs 29:25; Galatians 2:12.

Captured without fight, Isaiah 22:3.

"Afraid-of-Everything," Jeremiah 20:3 (CEV).

Egypt's plight, Jeremiah 46:17–24.

Brave warriors flee naked, Amos 2:16.

Cowardly Pharisees, Matthew 21:45–46.

Peter's denial, frightened disciples, Matthew 26:31–35, 69–75.

Coming to Jesus at night, John 3:2.

Those who dare not witness, John 7:12–13; 12:42–43.

Pharisees unable to face rebuke, John 8:1–11.

Accused of weakness, 2 Corinthians 10:10–11 (CEV).

Cowardly Christians, 2 Timothy 4:16.

See Fear, Weakness.

CRAFT

God saw His work was good, Genesis 1:10, 12, 18, 25.

Need for skillful handwork, Exodus 28:8.

Bestowed ability, Exodus 31:1–4.

Display of good talent, Psalm 45:1.

Skilled at work, Proverbs 22:29.

Woman's skilled hands, Proverbs 31:22, 24–25.

Skillful detail, technique, Isaiah 44:12–13.

Men have talent, God is sovereign, Jeremiah 10:8–10.

Ashamed of idols he made, Jeremiah 10:14–15.

Potter's wheel, Jeremiah 18:1–12.

Poor craftsmanship, Ezekiel 13:10–14.

See Ability, Skill, Talent.

CRAFTY

Satan as crafty serpent, Genesis 3:1.

Mother's camouflage, Genesis 27:11–16.

Deception at Gilgal, Joshua 9:3–6.

Very crafty, 1 Samuel 23:22.

Crafty tongue, Job 15:5.

King Herod, Magi, Matthew 2:7–8, 13.

Plot against Jesus, Matthew 26:4; Mark 14:1.

Jesus, crafty Pharisees, Luke 20:41–47.

Deceitful scheming, Ephesians 4:14.

See Deceit, Deception.

CRAVING

Continual lust for more, Ephesians 4:19.

See Hedonism, Lust.

CREATION

Creator's command, Genesis 1:3 (CEV).

"One day," Genesis 1:5 (NASB).

Plurality in human creation, Genesis 1:26.

Creation, gift to mankind, Genesis 1:28–31.

Successful completion, Genesis 2:1 (LB).

Learning about creation, Deuteronomy 4:32.

Ancient mountains, Deuteronomy 33:15.

Gratitude for creation, Nehemiah 9:6.

Fallen creation, Job 25:5 (Berk.).

Space/time, Job 26:7–14.

Creator's perspective, Job 38:4–11.

Creation's greatness, human smallness, Psalm 8:3–4.

Daily manifestation, Psalm 19:1 (Berk.).

Sky proclaims God's glory, Psalm 19:1–6.

Creation by divine command, Psalm 33:6.

Creation illustrates divine love, Psalm 36:5–6; 136:5–9.

Act of divine strength, Psalm 66:6.

Ancient skies, Psalm 68:32–33.

Greatest of all works, Psalm 86:8 (Berk., KJV).

North, south created, Psalm 89:12.

Birth of mountains, Psalm 90:2 (Berk.).

Creative design, Psalm 104:24 (Berk.).

Fearfully, wonderfully made, Psalm 139:14.

Nature, people praise Creator, Psalm 148:1–4.

Each star known by name, Psalm 147:4.

Earth, sky show God's wisdom, Proverbs 3:19–20; 8:24–31; Jeremiah 10:12.

Power unleashed in nature, Proverbs 30:4.

Heavens, hand of God, Isaiah 40:12.

God's purpose creating earth, Isaiah 45:18.

New heaven, new earth, Isaiah 65:17.

Idols cannot create, Jeremiah 10:11.

Divine resources demonstrated, Jeremiah 32:17–21.

God who made, sustains universe, Jeremiah 51:15–16.

Claiming creation of Nile river, Ezekiel 29:9 (CEV).

Christ as Creator, John 1:1–4, 10; Colossians 1:15–17.
Creator continuing work, John 5:17.
Ultimate purpose of creation, human life, Romans 8:18–23.
Men, animals different flesh, 1 Corinthians 15:39.
Creator, sustainer all things, Hebrews 1:3, 10–12.
Universe formed at God's command, Hebrews 11:3.
Successive ages, Hebrews 11:3 (AB).
Earth formed out of water, 2 Peter 3:5.
Breath of life, Revelation 13:15 (GNB).

CREATIVITY

Adam's creativity, Genesis 2:19.
Creator's power, authority, Job 9:1–10.
Good talent displayed, Psalm 45:1.
Producing, enjoying, Psalm 49:3–4.
Skilled in one's work, Proverbs 22:29.
Artist is mortal, Isaiah 44:11.
Ashamed of idols he had made, Jeremiah 10:14–15.
Builder, work, Hebrews 3:3.
See Ability, Inspiration, Skill.

CREATOR

Praising Creator, Nehemiah 9:6.
Creator's power, authority, Job 9:1–10.
"Outskirts of His ways," Job 26:14 (NRSV).
Creation proclaims God's righteousness, Psalm 50:6.
Creator knows creation, Psalm 50:11.
Ruler over all nature, Psalm 89:8–13.
Eternal God predates creation, Psalm 90:1–2.
Creator's work, Psalm 95:1–5.
Difference between Creator, idols, Psalm 96:5.
Nature praises Creator, Psalm 96:11–12.
Eternal God, temporal creation, Psalm 102:25–27.
Poem to God of nature, Psalm 104:1–26.
Creator's command, Psalm 104:7–9 (LB).
Skillful Creator, Psalm 136:5 (NASB).
Creator urged not to abandon creation, Psalm 138:8.
Creator's hands, Psalm 143:5.
Each star known by name, Psalm 147:4.

Savior, Creator, Proverbs 30:4.
Remembering Creator, Isaiah 17:7–8.
Creator's wisdom, greatness, Isaiah 40:12–28.
Creator cares for His creation, Isaiah 42:5–7.
Created light, darkness, Isaiah 45:7 (KJV).
God's purpose creating earth, Isaiah 45:18.
Fearsome Creator, Isaiah 64:3 (CEV).
Heavenly throne, earthly footstool, Isaiah 66:1.
Earth, sky reflect God's wisdom, Jeremiah 10:12.
Omnipresent Creator, Jeremiah 23:23–24.
Creator's ownership, Jeremiah 27:5.
Sovereign power, Jeremiah 32:17.
Earth, man, Zechariah 12:1.
Christ as Creator, John 1:1–4, 10; Colossians 1:15–17; Hebrews 1:3, 10–12.
Author of life itself, Acts 3:15.
One who fills universe, Ephesians 4:10.
Jesus Christ, Word of life, 1 John 1:1–4; John 1:1–3.
Unique name for Jesus, Revelation 3:14.
See Creation, God, Christ.

CREDENTIALS

Jesus had no need for credentials, John 5:31–40.
Credentials to visiting instructors, Acts 15:22–31.
Qualifications of Savior, King, Colossians 1:15–20.
Ministry credentials, Titus 1:1–3.
Elder's credentials, Titus 1:5–9.
See Documentation.

CREDIBILITY

Moses feared lack of credibility, Exodus 4:1.
Seeing is believing, 1 Kings 10:6–9.
Some good in Judah, 2 Chronicles 12:12.
Credibility of God's plans, purposes, Isaiah 14:24.
The Lord's message revealed, Isaiah 53:1.
Message believed by messenger, Ezekiel 3:10–11 (LB).
Despising those who tell truth, Amos 5:10.
Isaiah validated ministry of Jesus, Matthew 12:15–21.
Believe Good News, Mark 1:14–15.

Preaching with credibility, Luke 4:32.

Refusal to believe resurrection truth, Luke 24:11–12.

Disciples' initial mistrust of Paul, Acts 9:26.

Faith gives message credibility, Hebrews 4:2.

No lie comes from truth, 1 John 2:20–21.

Testimony of man, testimony of God, 1 John 5:9.

See Dependability, Honesty, Integrity, Reputation.

CREDIT

Loans to poor, Exodus 22:25–27.

Credit encouraged, Deuteronomy 15:8; Matthew 5:42.

No interest charge to locals, Deuteronomy 23:19–20.

Security for loan, debt, Deuteronomy 24:6; Job 24:3.

Cruel creditor's demands, 2 Kings 4:1.

Lender rules borrower, Proverbs 22:7.

Charging high interest, Proverbs 28:8.

Shrewd settlement, Luke 16:1–8.

Obligation to pay debts, Romans 13:8.

See Borrowing, Creditors, Debt, Finances, Foreclosure, Mortgage.

CREDITORS *See Credit, Debt.*

CREED

New Testament creeds, confessions, John 1:1–14; 2 Corinthians 4:1–6; 5:18–19; Philippians 2:5–11; Colossians 1:15–20; Hebrews 1:1–3.

Pagans certain of erroneous belief, Acts 19:35–36.

Futility of no resurrection message, 1 Corinthians 15:13–19.

Concise gospel thesis, 1 Timothy 4:9–10.

See Doctrine.

CREMATION

Drama of Abraham, Isaac, Genesis 22:2.

Form of judgment, Leviticus 20:14; 21:9.

Sudden massive cremation, Numbers 16:35.

Penalty for sacrilege, Joshua 7:15.

Stoned to death, then burned, Joshua 7:25.

Daughter's fiery death, Judges 11:30–40.

Saul, his sons, 1 Samuel 31:11–13.

Burning human skeletons, 1 Kings 13:1–2.

Bones exhumed, burned, 2 Kings 23:16; 2 Chronicles 34:5.

Children burned, 2 Chronicles 28:3.

Burned royal bones, Amos 2:1.

Kinsman's duty, Amos 6:9–10.

Surrendered to flames, 1 Corinthians 13:3.

CRIME

Rising crime rate. Genesis 6:11 (LB).

Stabbing death, 2 Samuel 3:27; 4:6; 20:10.

Conspiracy against leadership, 2 Samuel 15:10; 1 Kings 16:15–20; Esther 2:21.

Roadside ambush, 2 Kings 12:21.

Criminals in pagan temple, 2 Kings 19:37.

Planning perfect crime, Psalm 64:6.

History's greatest crime, Matthew 27:35; Mark 15:20; Luke 23:33; John 19:18.

Wages of crime, Acts 1:18 (Berk.).

See Capital Punishment, Murder, Robbery, Stealing, Thieves.

CRIMINAL

Habitual criminal, Psalm 69:27.

Boastful criminals, Psalm 94:4 (GNB).

Criminal motivated by hunger, Proverbs 28:21.

Habitual criminal, Ecclesiastes 8:12.

Pardon for nation's blood guilt, Joel 3:21.

Cheating, polluting, Amos 8:5–6.

Night criminals, Micah 2:1–2.

Notorious Barabbas, Matthew 27:16.

See Crime.

CRIPPLED *See Handicap.*

CRISIS

Power of God's name, Exodus 6:1–8.

Bad advice, Job 2:9–10.

Sure refuge, Psalm 46:1–11.

Value of crisis, Proverbs 20:30.

Crisis tests strength, Proverbs 24:10.

Go to neighbor for help, Proverbs 27:10.

Silver, gold no value when judgment falls, Zephaniah 1:18.

See Calamity, Trauma.

CRITICISM

Rule to follow when criticizing, Numbers 23:8.

Father's criticism refused, 1 Samuel 2:22–25.

Open to criticism, Job 6:24–25; Proverbs 15:32.

Ashamed critic, Job 11:3 (Berk.).

Response to criticism, Job 16:1–5.

Job accused of not speaking sensibly, Job 18:2.

Verbal persecution, Job 19:2.

Admitting personal error, Job 19:4.

Zophar upset by criticism, Job 20:2–3.

Tantalizing critics, Job 21:3.

Thick skin, Job 34:7.

Faultfinder versus Almighty, Job 40:2 (NRSV).

Criticizing family members, Psalm 50:20.

Razor sharp tongue, Psalm 52:2–4.

Avoiding leader's criticism, Psalm 105:15.

Above criticism, Psalm 119:165 (NKJV, AB).

Tongues of serpents, Psalm 140:3.

Acceptable rebuke, Psalm 141:5.

Unable to take criticism, Proverbs 9:8.

Willing to be disciplined, Proverbs 10:17.

Silent when others err, Proverbs 11:12.

Cutting remarks, Proverbs 12:18 (LB).

Healing tongue, deceitful tongue, Proverbs 15:4.

Word power, Proverbs 18:21.

Faithful wounds of friend, Proverbs 27:6.

Friend's valued counsel, Proverbs 27:9.

Rebuke better than flattery, Proverbs 28:23.

Refusing criticism, Proverbs 29:1.

Secret words of disdain, Ecclesiastes 7:21–22.

Waiting for friend to fail, Jeremiah 20:10 (CEV).

Dislike for strong preaching, Amos 7:16.

Satan's role as accuser, Zechariah 3:1–2.

Untruthful criticism, Matthew 5:11.

Criticize, be criticized, Matthew 7:1 (LB).

Judging, criticizing others, Matthew 7:1–5.

Slander spoken against Jesus, Matthew 11:18–19.

Jesus criticized for picking grain on Sabbath, Matthew 12:1–8.

Jesus criticized for casting out demons, Matthew 12:22–32.

Response of Jesus to critics, Matthew 21:23–27; Mark 14:53–62.

Jesus criticized on cross, Matthew 27:39–44.

Jesus criticized for healing, Mark 2:6–12.

Looking for something to criticize, Mark 3:1–6.

Jesus' family thought Him deranged, Mark 3:20–21 (Note v. 31).

Jesus confounded critics, Mark 11:29–33.

Trying to catch Jesus in His own words, Mark 12:13–17.

Rejoice when criticized for faith, Luke 6:22–23.

Wrong of criticizing others, Luke 6:37; Romans 2:1.

Speck in brother's eye, plank in your own, Luke 6:41–42.

Folly of unfounded criticism, Luke 8:49–56.

Jesus watched by Pharisees, Luke 14:1.

Critics confronted, Luke 20:1–8.

Harassing Jesus, John 5:16 (LB).

Judging mere appearances, John 7:24.

Dissension, jealousy in the church, Acts 6:1.

Criticizing others, Romans 2:1.

God the only judge, Romans 8:33.

Proper attitude to weak, Romans 14:1.

Judging others, Romans 14:13.

Help weak rather than criticize, Romans 15:1.

Coping with criticism, 1 Corinthians 4:3–4 (AB).

Criticizing another's conduct, 1 Corinthians 10:27–33.

Judging one's self, 1 Corinthians 11:28–32.

Overlooking criticism, 2 Corinthians 6:9 (LB).

Positive, productive criticism, 2 Corinthians 7:8–13.

Letters harsh, powerful, 2 Corinthians 10:10 (CEV).

Trying to please others, Galatians 1:10.

Fathers should not exasperate children, Ephesians 6:4.

Paul's attitude toward opponents, Philippians 1:15–18.

Judged by food, drink, Colossians 2:16.

Conversation full of grace, Colossians 4:6.

Criticizing pastor, 1 Timothy 5:19 (LB).

Living above criticism, Titus 2:8.

Remember your past before criticizing others, Titus 3:1–3.

Merely men, Hebrews 5:1 (LB).

Slow to criticize, James 3:1 (LB).

"Don't say cruel things," James 4:11 (CEV).

Slander no one, James 4:11–12.

Do not grumble against each other, James 5:9.

Judgment begins with God's family, 1 Peter 4:17.

Commendation before reproof, Revelation 2:2–6, 13–16, 19–20.

See Slander.

CROCODILE

"Leviathan" thought to be crocodile, Job 41:1–16.

CROSS

A worm, not a man, Psalm 22:6 (Berk.).

Crucifixion agony, ignominy, Isaiah 53:1–12 (CEV).

Redeemer, King, Isaiah 63:1.

Prophecy of Judas, thirty pieces of silver, Zechariah 11:12–13.

Crucifixion prophecy, Zechariah 12:10–11.

Disciples could not understand, Mark 9:30–32; Luke 9:44–45.

Jesus foretold death, resurrection, Mark 10:32–34.

Vineyard parable, Mark 12:1–12.

Weight of sin, not cross, killed Jesus, Mark 15:33–37, 44.

Jesus could not die until time had come, Luke 4:28–30.

Jesus willingly lay down His life, John 10:17–18.

Prior to Cross, Jesus saw resurrected Lazarus, John 12:1–10; 11:1–44.

Jews had no right to crucify, John 18:28–32.

God's perfect timing in Christ, Romans 5:6.

Setting free from power of sin, Romans 8:1–4.

Jesus took penalty for all, Hebrews 2:9.

First covenant validated with blood, Hebrews 9:18–22.

Willing to suffer with Christ, Hebrews 13:11–14.

Vision of resurrected Christ, Revelation 1:17–18.

See Atonement, Crucifixion, Redemption.

CROSS-CULTURAL

Earth divided, people scattered, Genesis 10:5; 11:1–9.

Abraham, Lot, Sodom, Gomorrah, Genesis 18:20–33; 19:1–29.

Clash of moral viewpoints, Genesis 39:1–23.

Joseph's relevance to Pharaoh, Genesis 41:1–40.

Solomon, Queen of Sheba, 1 Kings 10:1–13.

Bible is cross-cultural, Isaiah 55:5; Micah 4:3–4; Romans 10:12–13.

Value of heathen culture, Jeremiah 10:1–5.

Jesus and cross-cultural communication, John 4:4–26.

Philip, Ethiopian eunuch, Acts 8:26–40.

Peter's lesson in cultural prejudice, Acts 10:9–23; 11:1–14.

Paul, Athenians, Acts 17:16–27.

Cultural dissipation of revealed truth, Romans 1:21–32.

See Alien, Contextualization, Prejudice, Racism, Xenophobia.

CROSS-EXAMINATION

Cross-examined by the Lord, Psalm 26:2 (LB).

Evidence questioned, Proverbs 18:17.

See Question.

CROWDS

Very great gathering, Genesis 50:9 (NKJV).

God can single out individual, Deuteronomy 29:21.

Vast assembly, 1 Kings 8:65.

Myriads of people, Psalm 3:6 (Berk.).

Multitudes making decisions, Joel 3:14.

Crowd forced Jesus into boat, Matthew 13:1–2; Mark 4:1.

Entire town gathered, Mark 1:33.

Overflow crowd, Mark 2:1–5.

Avoiding undisciplined crowd, Mark 3:9–10 (NKJV).

Triumphal entry Jesus into Jerusalem, Mark 11:1–10.

Potential Passover mob violence, Mark 14:1–2.

Crowd stirred up against Jesus, Mark 15:11–15; 11:8–10.

Crucifixion of Jesus, Mark 15:21–32.

Entry through roof, Luke 5:17–26.

Thronging thousands, Luke 12:1.

Jesus' enemies feared public opinion, Luke 22:3–6.

Curious to see miracles performed, John 6:2, 26–27.

Drawn to main attraction, John 3:29 (LB).

Influence of many, Acts 4:21.

Entire city in uproar, Acts 19:23–41.

City aroused by troublemakers, Acts 21:30.

See Audience, Mob, Mob Psychology.

CROWNS

Priestly headpiece, Leviticus 8:9.

Crowns of vanquished kings, 2 Samuel 1:5–10; 12:29–31 (See LB).

Crown, covenant, 2 Kings 11:12.

Crowned with glory, honor, Psalm 8:5.

Crowned with love, compassion, Psalm 103:3–4.

Crown of thorns, Matthew 27:29; Mark 15:17; John 19:2.

Believer's crown, 1 Corinthians 9:25; 2 Timothy 4:8; Revelation 3:11.

Victory wreath, Philippians 4:1 (AB).

Crown of life, James 1:12; Revelation 2:10.

Crown of glory, 1 Peter 5:4.

Crowns laid before the Lord, Revelation 4:10.

See Reward.

CRUCIFIXION

Ignored by holy God, Psalm 22:1–4 (LB).

Dying Savior, Isaiah 53:1–12.

Parable of owner's son, Matthew 21:33–42.

Crucifixion foretold, Matthew 26:2; Mark 8:31; 9:31; 10:32–33.

Seven sayings on the cross, Matthew 27:46; Luke 23:34, 43, 46; John 19:26–28, 30.

Jesus could not die until time had come, Luke 4:28–30.

Predicted crucifixion, resurrection, John 2:19–21.

Symbolic serpent, John 3:14.

Jesus avoided early death, John 7:1.

Before crucifixion, Jesus saw resurrected Lazarus, John 12:1–10; 11:1–44.

Messiah crucified, John 12:32–34 (LB).

Jews had no right to crucify, John 18:28–32.

Act of ignorance, Acts 3:15–17.

"Reverent submission," Hebrews 5:7 (NRSV).

Vision of resurrected Christ, Revelation 1:17–18.

See Atonement, Cross, Redemption, Resurrection.

CRUELTY

Brotherly brutality, Genesis 37:19–24.

Male infants destroyed, Exodus 1:22.

Animal mistreatment, Numbers 22:27–28; Judges 15:4–5; 2 Samuel 8:4; 1 Chronicles 18:4.

Body mutilation, Judges 1:6; 1 Samuel 11:2; 2 Kings 25:7.

People burned to death, Judges 9:49.

Prophet's ignominy, Jeremiah 38:6.

Into fiery furnace, Daniel 3:12–27.

Mental cruelty, Matthew 5:11; Acts 9:16.

Killing prisoners to prevent escape, Acts 27:42–43.

Bodily harm, Romans 8:17; 2 Corinthians 4:11; 1 Peter 2:20.

See Brutality, Persecution, Sadistic.

CULT

Wayward community, Deuteronomy 13:12–18.

Penalty for false message, Deuteronomy 18:20 (GNB).

Detecting false prophet, Deuteronomy 18:21–22.

Twisting truth, Jeremiah 7:8 (LB).

Wrong Scripture interpretation, Jeremiah 8:8.

Dreams versus truth, Jeremiah 23:25–32 (CEV).

Prophecy of imagination, Ezekiel 13:1–23.

Cults prevented, Micah 5:12.

Making new laws, Matthew 23:2 (LB).

Hindering others from entering kingdom, Matthew 23:13–15.

Many claiming to be Christ, Matthew 24:4–5, 11, 24; Mark 13:22–23.

Those who fast while others do not, Mark 2:18–20.

Only one gate to sheep pen, John 10:1–21.

Avoid wrong teaching, Romans 16:17.

Futility of no resurrection message, 1 Corinthians 15:13–19.

"Twist God's message," 2 Corinthians 4:2 (CEV).

"Phonies," 2 Corinthians 11:12–13 (LB).

Strong warning, Galatians 1:8–9 (LB).

False disciples dilute Gospel, Galatians 2:4–5.

Impact of error, Galatians 2:13.

Bewitched Galatians, Galatians 3:1 (CEV).

Alienated from truth, Galatians 4:17.

People's trickery, Ephesians 4:14 (NRSV).

Danger of deceptive philosophy, Colossians 2:8.

Teachings which cause controversy, 1 Timothy 1:3–4 (NASB, NRSV).

"Empty talk," 1 Timothy 1:6 (CEV).

"Fooled by evil spirits," 1 Timothy 4:1 (CEV).

Demon theology, 1 Timothy 4:1–4.

"Hypocrisy of liars," 1 Timothy 4:2 (NRSV).

Proud of false doctrine, 1 Timothy 6:3–5.

Godless chatter, opposing ideas, 1 Timothy 6:20–21.

Wandering from truth, 2 Timothy 2:17–18 (NRSV).

Those deceived who deceive others, 2 Timothy 3:13.

Rejecting sound doctrine, 2 Timothy 4:3–4.

Ministering for dishonest gain, Titus 1:10–16.

Careful of strange teachings, Hebrews 13:9.

Cleverly invented stories, 2 Peter 1:16.

False teachers, destructive heresies, 2 Peter 2:1–3 (AB, GNB).

False message, 2 Peter 2:19 (AB).

Falling away from truth, 2 Peter 3:17.

Walking in darkness, 1 John 1:5–7.

Leading believers astray, 1 John 2:26.

Counterfeit anointing, 1 John 2:27.

Test of spirits, false prophets, 1 John 4:1.

Avoid false gods, 1 John 5:21 (GNB).

Many deceivers, 2 John 7.

"Anyone who goes too far," 2 John 9 (NASB).

Those of another teaching unwelcome, 2 John 10–11.

Warn against false teaching, Jude 3–4 (AB).

Discerning those who are false, Revelation 2:2.

Finality of Scripture record, Revelation 22:18–19.

See Error, Heresy, New Age, Syncretism.

CULTURE

"Manner of life," Judges 18:7 (LB).

Culture affected by intermarriage, Nehemiah 13:23–26.

Influence of nation upon nation, Jeremiah 10:2.

Language, literature, Daniel 1:3–4.

Noble character of Bereans, Acts 17:11.

Ministry to all cultures, Romans 1:14–17.

Wisdom, foolishness, 1 Corinthians 1:18–21.

Adapting to culture, 1 Corinthians 9:19–23.

See Cross-Cultural.

CUNNING

Cunning craftsmen, 1 Chronicles 22:15 (KJV).

Machines made by cunning inventors, 2 Chronicles 26:15 (KJV).

See Craft, Skill.

CURDS See Food.

CURIOSITY

Father's nudity, Genesis 9:22–23.

Plight of Lot's wife, Genesis 19:17, 26.

Baby Moses, Pharaoh's daughter, Exodus 2:5–6.

Moses, burning bush, Exodus 3:1–3.

Death for looking into ark, 1 Samuel 6:19.

Endless curiosity, Ecclesiastes 1:8.

Investigate scheme of things, Ecclesiastes 7:25.

Roadside curiosity, Jeremiah 48:19.

Those who pass by, Lamentations 1:12.

"You stood there and watched," Obadiah 11 (CEV).

Waiting to see spectacle of judgment, Jonah 4:5.

Large crowds witness miracles, Matthew 4:23–25; 8:1, 18; 19:2; Luke 14:25; John 6:1–2.

Asking to see miracle, Matthew 12:38.

Things people go to see, Luke 7:24–26.

Compassionless curiosity, Luke 10:32.

Curiosity led to blessing, Luke 18:35–43.

Drawn to main attraction, John 3:29 (LB).

Needing signs, wonders to believe, John 4:48.

Motivated by curiosity, John 6:2; 12:9.

Mind your own business, John 21:21–22.

Staring at those God uses, Acts 3:12.

Intellectual curiosity, Acts 17:21 (NRSV).

Following crowd in confusion, Acts 19:32.

Curiosity of angels, 1 Peter 1:12.

Suffering as meddler, 1 Peter 4:15.

See Investigation.

CURRENCY

Gold as legal tender, Genesis 13:2; 1 Chronicles 21:25.

First use of money, Genesis 17:12–13, 23, 27.

Silver as legal tender, Genesis 20:16.

Cash paid for services, Deuteronomy 2:6.

Silver not precious metal, 1 Kings 10:21, 27.

Purchasing field with silver, Jeremiah 32:25.

Value, designation of currency, Ezekiel 45:12.

Time of economic collapse, Zephaniah 1:11.

Coin from fish's mouth, Matthew 17:27.

Small coin, Mark 12:41–43; Luke 21:1–2.

Legal currency, Mark 12:16; Luke 20:24.

See Finances, Money.

CURSE

Penalty for disobedience, Deuteronomy 28:15–68.

Mother's predicament, Judges 17:1–5.

Venereal disease, 2 Samuel 3:29 (GNB).

Punishment for curses, 1 Kings 2:8–9.

Cursing expertise, Job 3:8 (LB).

Exiles instructed to use curse, Jeremiah 29:21–23.

Blessing becomes curse, Malachi 2:2 (CEV).

Old Testament conclusion, Malachi 4:6.

See Blasphemy, Imprecation, Judgment.

CUSTOM

Accepting another's custom, Romans 14:1–8.

See Culture, Tradition.

CUSTOMARY

"As always, as usual," Mark 10:1 (LB).

CYBERNETICS

Negative cybernetics, Exodus 16:2.

United as one, Judges 20:11.

Many with single objective, 1 Chronicles 12:38; Nehemiah 4:16–17.

Complex human body, Psalm 139:14.

Cybernetics of combined spiritual effort, Matthew 18:19.

Body functioning, 1 Corinthians 12:12–26.

Unified in evil purpose, Revelation 17:13.

See Body of Christ, Unity.

CYNICAL

Calamity hungered for Job, Job 18:12.

Youth chides wisdom of age, Job 32:6–9.

Fool's likenesses, Proverbs 26:1–11.

Common destiny, Ecclesiastes 9:1–2.

Cynical tongues silenced, Luke 20:20–26.

See Sarcasm.

D

DAIRY

Curds, milk, Genesis 18:8; Deuteronomy 32:14.

Herds of cows, Genesis 32:15.

Animal plague, Exodus 9:2–3.

Large herds, Numbers 32:1.

Division of pasture lands, Joshua 14:3–4.

Milk as beverage, Judges 4:19.

Inexperienced cows, 1 Samuel 6:7.

Dairy product in desert, 2 Samuel 17:29.

Milk to butter, Proverbs 30:33.

Small herd, abundant milk, Isaiah 7:21–22.

Beautiful heifer, gadfly, Jeremiah 46:20.

See Cheese, Milk.

DAM

Miraculously stopping river flow, Joshua 3:15–16.

DAMNATION See Demons, Hell, Judgment Lost, Satan.

DANCING

Tambourines, dancing, Exodus 15:19–21.
Backslidden dancers, Exodus 32:19.
Dance of death, Judges 11:30–39; Matthew 14:6–12.
Celebration dancing, 1 Samuel 18:6–7.
Dancing before the Lord, 2 Samuel 6:14–16.
Infant dancers, Job 21:11.
Sorrow gives way to dancing, Psalm 30:11.
Dance of praise, Psalms 149:3; 150:4.
Time to dance, Ecclesiastes 3:4.
Israel dancing, Jeremiah 31:4.
Dancing curtailed, Lamentations 5:15.
Music without dancing, Matthew 11:17.
See Music.

DANGER

Holding hands, Genesis 19:16.
Jacob reassured, Genesis 46:1–4.
Safety in dangerous area, Numbers 24:21 (GNB).
Lives at risk, Judges 5:18.
Companions in danger, 1 Samuel 22:23.
Overlooking danger, Esther 4:9–16.
Wicked bend their bows, Psalm 11:2.
Facing danger with confidence, Psalm 27:3.
In grave danger, Psalm 73:2.
Do not fear, Isaiah 8:12–14.
Thousands flee, Isaiah 30:17.
Safely through danger, Isaiah 43:2.
Fear of public places, Jeremiah 6:25.
Snorting enemy horses, Jeremiah 8:16.
Unsuspected danger, Jeremiah 11:18–19.
Good news, bad news, Jeremiah 34:1–7.
Loud noise, Jeremiah 46:17.
Watchman's responsibility, Ezekiel 33:1–9.
Assured safety, Ezekiel 34:25.
Returning from battle, Micah 2:8 (GNB).
River gates open, Nahum 2:6.
Neighbor versus neighbor, Zechariah 8:10.
Jesus facing danger, Luke 13:31–33; John 7:1.
Avoiding unnecessary danger, John 11:53–54.
Angelic protection, Acts 27:21–25.
Risked their necks, Romans 16:4 (NASB, NKJV, NRSV).
See Peril, Persecution.

DAREDEVIL

Careless about danger, Proverbs 22:3.

DARING

Daring Daniel, Daniel 6:10.

DARKNESS

Total darkness, Genesis 1:2–4.
No travel after sunset, Genesis 28:11.
The Lord our lamp, 2 Samuel 22:29.
No God, no priest, no law, 2 Chronicles 15:3.
Time of day for evil, Job 24:14–17.
Dark, slippery path, Psalm 35:6; Jeremiah 23:12.
Walking in darkness, Psalm 82:5; Proverbs 2:13–15; 1 John 1:6.
"Regions dark and deep," Psalm 88:6 (NRSV).
God sees through darkness, Psalm 139:12.
Deep darkness, Proverbs 4:19.
Deepest darkness illuminated, Isaiah 9:2.
Darkness as light, Isaiah 42:16.
Creator of darkness, light, Isaiah 45:7.
Land of darkness, Isaiah 45:19.
Light in darkness, Isaiah 50:10.
Vain search for light, Isaiah 59:9.
Covenant with day, night, Jeremiah 33:20–21.
Evil covered by darkness, Ezekiel 8:12
Prophetic sunset, Micah 3:6 (CEV).
Eternal darkness, Matthew 8:12; 22:13; 25:30.
Fear at night, Luke 2:8–14.
Light, darkness in conflict, John 1:5; Romans 13:12–13.
Jesus, Nicodemus, John 3:2; 19:39.
Loving darkness, avoiding light, John 3:19–20.
Night walking, John 11:9–10.
Plight of Judas, John 13:27–30.
Spiritual darkness, Acts 13:8–11.
Cover of darkness, Acts 17:10.
Darkness to light, Acts 26:18.
Night navigation, Acts 27:27–29.
Deeds of darkness, Romans 13:12.
No hiding place, 1 Corinthians 4:5.
Stars light up sky, Philippians 2:15 (GNB).
"Domain of darkness," Colossians 1:13 (NASB).

Not of the darkness, 1 Thessalonians 5:4.
"Dark shadows," James 1:17 (CEV).
See Night.

DATA See Statistics.

DATE

Recognizing specific date, Ezekiel 1:1.
Recorded date, Ezekiel 24:1–2.
Date of prison release, Jeremiah 52:31 (NKJV, LB, NIV).
Date to remember, Haggai 2:18.
Future date unknown, Matthew 24:36; 25:13; Mark 13:32.
See Calendar.

DATELINE

Day/night ocean boundary, Job 26:10.

DAUGHTER

Daughter's rights, Exodus 21:7–10.
Marriage to both mother, daughter forbidden, Leviticus 20:14.
Father's authority, Numbers 30:3–5.
Given in marriage, Judges 1:12–13; 1 Samuel 17:25; 18:20–21.
Daughter's request, Judges 1:13–15.
Daughter sacrificed, Judges 11:29–40.
Father decides daughter's relationship, Judges 15:1–2.
Exploiting daughter's love, 1 Samuel 18:20–29.
Beautiful daughters, Job 42:15.
Father's attitude toward daughter, 1 Corinthians 7:36–38 (NASB).
See Children, Daughter-in-Law, Family, Virgin.

DAUGHTER-IN-LAW

Cause of parental grief, Genesis 26:34–35.
Ruth, Naomi, Ruth 1:8–18.
Valued more than seven sons, Ruth 4:13–15.
See Bride, Marriage.

DAWN

Meeting God at dawn, 1 Samuel 1:19 (NKJV).
Cloudless dawn, 2 Samuel 23:4.
Morning's eyelids, Job 3:9 (Berk., NRSV).
Show dawn its place, Job 38:12 (Berk.).

Night concludes, day begins, Romans 13:12.
See Morning.

DAY

Sacred day, Numbers 29:1, 7, 12, 35.
Long working hours, Nehemiah 4:21.
Day, night, Job 38:19.
Praise throughout day, Psalm 92:2.
Sunrise, sunset, Ecclesiastes 1:5; Psalm 113:3.
Pleasant sunshine, Ecclesiastes 11:7.
Dark days, Ecclesiastes 11:8.
Day passes quickly, Jeremiah 6:4–5.
God's covenant with day, night, Jeremiah 33:20–21.
Specific day, Ezekiel 1:1.
Twelve-hour day, John 11:9 (GNB).
See Last Days.

DAYBREAK See Dawn, Sunrise.

DAYDREAMING

Hard work, fantasy, Proverbs 28:19.
Daydreaming leads to senseless talk, Ecclesiastes 5:7 (CEV).
Dozing, day dreaming, Isaiah 56:10 (CEV).

DEACON See Elder.

DEAD See Death.

DEAD SEA

Waters purified, Ezekiel 47:8 (LB).

DEAFNESS

Kindness to the deaf, Leviticus 19:14.
Aged hearing impairment, 2 Samuel 19:35; Ecclesiastes 12:4.
Dull ears, Isaiah 6:10.
Deafness healed, Isaiah 35:5–6.
Refusing to hear, Jeremiah 6:10.
Turning deaf ear, Jeremiah 18:18; Ezekiel 12:2; Zechariah 7:11; 2 Timothy 4:4.
Signing, Luke 1:62.
Hearing without understanding, Luke 10:24.
Spiritually deaf, Acts 28:26 (CEV).
See Hearing, Perception.

DEATH

Return to earth, Genesis 3:19.

Promised pleasant death, Genesis 15:15.

"Give up the ghost," Job 11:20 (KJV); 13:19 (KJV).

"Breathed his last," Genesis 25:17 (NKJV).

Closing dead man's eyes, Genesis 46:4.

"Yielded up the ghost," Genesis 49:33 (KJV).

Embracing corpse, Genesis 50:1.

Egyptian embalming, Genesis 50:2–3.

Natural death, Numbers 19:16 (GNB).

Death preferred, Numbers 20:3; 1 Kings 19:4.

Impending death announcement, Deuteronomy 31:14 (LB).

Way of all earth, Joshua 23:14 (CEV, LB).

Fatal shock, 1 Samuel 4:12–18.

Consciousness after death, 1 Samuel 28:12–19 (LB).

"The mighty have fallen," 2 Samuel 1:19 (NIV).

Death by measurement, 2 Samuel 8:2.

Reaction to son's death, 2 Samuel 12:16–23.

Joy turned to sadness, 2 Samuel 19:2 (LB).

Last words of David, 2 Samuel 23:1–7.

King's death in battle, 1 Kings 22:34–37; 2 Chronicles 18:33–34.

Put house in order, 2 Kings 20:1.

Time expired, 1 Chronicles 17:11 (KJV).

King denied royal grave, 2 Chronicles 28:27.

Eager for death, Job 3:21–22 (See CEV).

Righteous youth spared death, Job 4:7 (CEV).

Sudden death, Job 4:20 (GNB).

Death at old age, Job 5:26 (See KJV).

Anxious to die, Job 6:11 (LB).

Dust to dust, Job 10:9 (LB).

Deepest night, shadow, Job 10:22.

Short, sorrowful life, Job 14:1 (CEV).

Wasting away, Job 14:10 (KJV).

Journey of no return, Job 16:22.

Awaiting grave, Job 17:1.

Name forgotten, Job 18:17 (See LB).

Death status, attitudes, Job 21:23–25.

"Land of death," Job 26:6 (CEV).

Unmourned dead, Job 27:15.

Dying at home, Job 29:18 (CEV).

Presuming "God is dead," Psalm 10:4 (LB).

"Sleep of death," Psalm 13:3 (KJV).

Darkest valley, Psalm 23:4 (See NRSV).

Guidance until death, Psalm 48:14 (Berk.).

Death seen as shepherd, Psalm 49:14 (CEV, LB, NASB, NRSV).

Light of life gone, Psalm 49:19.

Death to pompous, Psalm 49:20 (LB).

Death's terrors, Psalm 55:4.

Deathbed repentance, Psalm 66:13–14.

Terminal sleep, Psalm 76:5.

Early death, Psalm 78:63–64 (LB).

"Regions dark and deep," Psalm 88:6.

Always near death, Psalm 88:15 (Berk.).

Fleeting life span, Psalm 89:47–48.

Life ends like a sigh, Psalm 90:9 (NRSV).

"Land of silence," Psalm 94:17 (NRSV).

Death in mid-life, Psalm 102:23–24 (LB, Berk.).

Righteous man remembered, Psalm 112:6.

Staring death face-to-face, Psalm 116:3 (LB).

Believer's death, Psalm 116:15.

Death terminates leadership, Psalm 146:3–4.

Forgotten dead, Ecclesiastes 2:16.

Humans, animals, Ecclesiastes 3:21.

Happiness after death, Ecclesiastes 4:2 (Berk.).

Nakedness of birth, death, Ecclesiastes 5:15.

Death inevitable, Ecclesiastes 7:1–2.

A time to die, Ecclesiastes 7:17.

No power over day of death, Ecclesiastes 8:8.

Forgotten after death, Ecclesiastes 9:5.

Sobered look at life, death, Ecclesiastes 11:8 (GNB).

Weak, frail, dying, Isaiah 2:22 (AB).

Covenant with death, Isaiah 28:15.

Preparing to die, Isaiah 38:1 (CEV, NRSV).

Death during best years, Isaiah 38:9 (CEV).

Death cannot praise God, Isaiah 38:18.

Peace in death, Isaiah 57:2 (CEV).

Ignominy of death, Jeremiah 8:1–2.

No one to bury dead, Jeremiah 14:16.

Numerous widows, Jeremiah 15:8.

Mourning forbidden, Jeremiah 16:5–7.

Peaceful, honorable death, Jeremiah 34:4–5.

Inequity in life, death, Ezekiel 13:19.

Death of wife, Ezekiel 24:15–27.

"Down to the pit," Ezekiel 26:20 (AB).

"World of the dead," Ezekiel 32:23 (CEV, GNB).

Promised resurrection, Daniel 12:13 (LB).

Life, death, Jonah 2:6 (LB).

Death never satisfied, Habakkuk 2:5.

Joshua after death, Zechariah 3:1–10; 6:11 (NKJV).

"Dark land of death," Matthew 4:16 (GNB).

Physical, spiritual death, Matthew 8:21–22.

Earth relationships differ in Heaven, Matthew 22:23–30.

Creator's power over death, Mark 5:38–42.

Life's final moment, Mark 15:37–39.

No need for tears, Luke 7:11–13.

Alive to God, Luke 20:38.

Spiritual commitment of Jesus, Luke 23:46.

Mortals resurrected, John 5:28–29.

True immortality, John 8:51.

Death's purpose, John 11:4 (LB).

Falling asleep, John 11:11–15; Acts 7:60.

Post-resurrection, pre-resurrection fellowship, John 12:1–10 (See 11:1–44).

Threat to kill resurrected Lazarus, John 12:10.

Better option, John 16:5–7.

Life's work concluded, John 17:4.

Aware of imminent death, John 18:1.

Sin caused Jesus' death, John 19:28–30, 33.

Vulgar death of Judas, Acts 1:18.

Messianic implications, David and Jesus, Acts 2:29–35.

Martyr's death, Acts 7:54–56.

Falling asleep, John 11:11–14; Acts 7:60.

Death is king, Romans 5:17 (Berk.).

Doomed enemy, 1 Corinthians 15:26.

Death swallowed in victory, 1 Corinthians 15:53; Isaiah 25:8 (KJV).

Eden serpent's harmless sting, 1 Corinthians 15:55.

Earthly, eternal, 2 Corinthians 5:1.

To die brings gain, Philippians 1:21–24 (AB).

Death annulled, 2 Timothy 1:10 (AB).

Apostle's anticipation, 2 Timothy 4:6–8.

Probate will, Hebrews 9:16–17.

His death, our life, 1 Thessalonians 5:10.

Rich man like wildflower, James 1:10–11.

Joy in afterlife, James 5:11 (LB).

Withered grass, flowers, 1 Peter 1:24–25.

Death predicted, 2 Peter 1:13–14 (NRSV).

Death desired in vain, Revelation 9:4–6.

Happy experience, Revelation 14:13 (GNB).

Blood of dead man, Revelation 16:3.

See Burial, Grave, Immortality, Terminal, Tomb.

DEATHBED

Last words, 1 Kings 2:1–4.

Temporary piety when dying, Psalm 78:34.

Thief on cross, Matthew 27:38, 44; Mark 15:27; Luke 23:32–33, 39–43.

DEATH PENALTY *See Capital Punishment.*

DEBASE

World versus God, Psalm 2:1–3.

Silver to dross, wine to water, Isaiah 1:22.

Defiled with blood, Lamentations 4:14.

See Corruption, Defile, Demean, Vulgar.

DEBATE

"Present your case," Isaiah 41:21 (NIV).

Wise put to shame, Jeremiah 8:9.

Debating rank in kingdom, Luke 9:46–48.

Concise, brief debate, Luke 20:1–8.

Light versus darkness, John 8:13–59.

Apollos, Jewish leaders, Acts 18:27–28.

Brilliant debaters, 1 Corinthians 1:20 (LB).

See Argument.

DEBAUCHERY

Cities given to debauchery, Genesis 18:16–33.

Sexual relations with animals, Leviticus 20:15–16.

Devoted to destruction, Leviticus 27:29.

Defiance against God, Psalm 2:1–3.

Corrupt from birth, Psalm 58:3.

Self-imposed debauchery, Psalm 106:39.

Silver to dross, wine to water, Isaiah 1:22.

Sin parade, Isaiah 3:16 (AB).

Ravages of wickedness, Isaiah 9:18.

Sick drunk, Isaiah 28:7.

Corrupted vine, Jeremiah 2:21.

Running after foreign gods, Jeremiah 2:25.

From one sin to another, Jeremiah 9:3.

Adulterous sisters, Ezekiel 23:1–49.

Adultery exhaustion, Ezekiel 23:43.

In-depth debauchery, Hosea 4:2; 8:11.

Sow the wind, Hosea 8:7.

Hate good, love evil, Micah 3:2 (NKJV).
Pre-rapture conditions, Matthew 24:37–38.
Continual lust, Ephesians 4:19.
Drunken debauchery, Ephesians 5:18 (AB).
"Inhuman, implacable," 2 Timothy 3:3 (NRSV).
Sin in broad daylight, 2 Peter 2:13–22.
Unrepentant debauchery, Jude 7 (AB); Revelation 9:21 (AB).
See Carnality, Decadent, Drunkenness, Immorality, Lust, Promiscuity.

DEBILITY

Leadership debilitated, Joshua 1:9.
Melted by fear, Joshua 2:24.
Strength debilitated by sin, Psalm 31:10 (LB).
Poetic description of old age, Ecclesiastes 12:1–7.
Drained of power, Isaiah 37:27.
Waste away, Isaiah 64:7.
See Handicap

DEBT

Refusing to become indebted, Genesis 14:22–24.
Debt to relatives, others, Deuteronomy 15:1–3.
"Paid in full," Deuteronomy 15:2 (LB).
Miraculous repayment, 2 Kings 4:1–7.
Mortgaged property, Nehemiah 5:3.
Children taken for debts, Job 24:9.
Sold to creditors, Isaiah 50:1 (LB).
Creditors seize all, Psalm 109:11.
Bed taken for debt, Proverbs 22:27.
Debt mercifully canceled, Matthew 18:23–27.
Love the only debt, Romans 13:8 (CEV).
Pay what is owed, Romans 13:7–8.
Debt owed by slave, Philemon 18–19.
See Credit, Finances, Mortgage.

DECADENT

Prone to idolatry, Exodus 32:19–26.
Rebels' destiny, Numbers 14:35.
Defiant sin, Numbers 15:30–31.
Blatant decadence, Numbers 25:6–9.
Lack of discernment, Deuteronomy 32:28.
Homosexual activity, Judges 19:22.

Immorality in place of worship, 1 Samuel 2:22–25.
Spiritual decline, 1 Samuel 3:1.
Cannibalism, 2 Kings 6:24–29.
Desecrated temple, 2 Chronicles 26:16–21.
Guilty man's plea, Esther 7:7.
Lamp of the wicked, Job 18:5–6.
Boasting of evil, Psalm 52:1–4.
Total decadence, Psalm 53:3.
Corrupt from birth, Psalm 58:3.
Like idol, like follower, Psalm 135:15–18.
Deep darkness, Proverbs 4:19.
Playing with fire, Proverbs 6:27–28.
Once faithful city, Isaiah 1:21–23.
Haughty women, Isaiah 3:16.
Every mouth vile, Isaiah 9:17.
Powerless, cumbersome idols, Isaiah 46:1–2.
Sinful barriers, Isaiah 59:1–2.
Evil's end result, Isaiah 59:7–8.
Skilled in seduction, Jeremiah 2:33.
Utterly defiled, Jeremiah 3:1–3.
God's law falsified, Jeremiah 8:8.
Forgetting how to blush, Jeremiah 8:12.
Deceitful heart, Jeremiah 17:9.
Lifetime evil, Jeremiah 32:30.
Unredeemable paganism, Jeremiah 51:9.
Self-deceived prophets, Ezekiel 13:1–3.
Hindered worship, Hosea 5:4.
Iniquity by design, Micah 2:1.
Drunk with blood of saints, Revelation 17:6.
See Carnality, Debauchery, Hedonism, Irreligious, Irreverence.

DECAY

Foul odor of disobedience, Exodus 16:19–20, 22–24.
Worms in dead bodies, Isaiah 66:24.
Old Testament object lesson, Jeremiah 13:1–11.
See Putrid, Stench.

DECEIT

Like father, like son, Genesis 20:1–16; 26:7–11.
Deceitful birthright, Genesis 27:1–46.
Jacob deceived about Rachel, Genesis 29:14–30.
Sibling jealousy, Genesis 37:1–36.

Protection through deceit, Exodus 1:15–21.

Secret message for doomed king, Judges 3:19–21.

Confusing with shadows, Judges 9:34–37.

Samson, wife's riddle, Judges 14:11–19.

Exploiting daughter's love, 1 Samuel 18:20–29.

Deceitful report, 1 Samuel 27:10–11.

Deceitful rapport, 2 Samuel 3:27.

David's plot against Uriah, 2 Samuel 11:14–17.

Amnon, Tamar, 2 Samuel 13:1–14.

Kiss of death, 2 Samuel 20:9–10.

Ill-fated nuptial request, 1 Kings 2:13–25.

Schemer eager for others' wealth, Job 5:5 (NASB).

Whitewashed lies, Job 13:4 (NRSV).

Parents of trouble, vicious lies, Job 15:35 (CEV, NRSV).

Day as night, night as day, Job 17:12 (LB).

Not one truthful word, Psalm 5:9 (LB).

"Lips free of deceit," Psalm 17:1 (NRSV).

Without deceit, Psalm 32:2 (Berk.).

"Plots against good people," Psalm 37:12 (CEV).

Motives different from speech, Psalm 55:21; Proverbs 26:24–26.

"Cunningly conceived plot," Psalm 64:6 (NRSV).

Deceitful to God, Psalm 73:27 (Berk.).

Forbidden deceit, Psalm 101:7.

All men liars, Psalm 116:11.

Winking eyes, Proverbs 6:13 (Berk.).

Stolen sweetness, Proverbs 9:17.

Deceptive wages, Proverbs 11:18.

Deceitful pretense, Proverbs 12:9.

Hurtful deceit, Proverbs 26:28.

Deceitful sympathy, Isaiah 39:1–5.

Absent truth, Isaiah 59:15.

Calling good deceitful, Jeremiah 4:10.

Clinging to deceit, Jeremiah 8:5.

Cordial lips, deceitful heart, Jeremiah 9:8; 12:6.

Deceitful heart, Jeremiah 17:9 (CEV).

Temporary freedom for slaves, Jeremiah 34:8–22.

Deceitful kings, Daniel 11:27.

Truth despised, Amos 5:10.

Dishonest scales, weights, Micah 6:11.

Deceitful tongues, Micah 6:12; Romans 3:13.

Herod, Magi, Matthew 2:7–8, 13.

Deceitful Judas, Matthew 26:47–48; Mark 14:10–11, 43–46.

Resurrection believed deceitful, Matthew 27:62–66; 28:11–15.

"Don't let anyone fool you," Mark 13:5 (CEV).

Pretended honesty, Luke 20:20.

Discerned duplicity, Luke 20:23.

Ananias, Sapphira, Acts. 5:1–11.

Deceit against Paul, Acts 23:12–22.

Exposed by trickery, 2 Corinthians 12:16.

Deceitful leadership, Ephesians 4:14 (NRSV).

"Lusts of deceit," Ephesians 4:22 (NASB).

Satan's evil tricks, Ephesians 6:10–11 (GNB).

"Plausible argument," Colossians 2:4 (NRSV).

"Fooled by evil spirits," 1 Timothy 4:1 (CEV).

Deceiving those who deceive, 2 Timothy 3:13.

Deceitful preaching, teaching, Titus 1:10–16.

Benefit gained by deceit, James 5:4–5.

Invented stories, 2 Peter 1:16.

Heretical teaching, 2 Peter 2:1–2.

Self-deceit, Jude 17–18.

Pretense of spiritual life, Revelation 3:1.

See Deceived, Deception, Devious, False, Falsehood, Folly, Lie.

DECEIVED

Deceived hearts, Deuteronomy 11:16 (KJV).

Friend deceives friend, Jeremiah 9:5.

Deceived by the Lord, Ezekiel 14:9 (GNB).

"They will fool many people," Matthew 24:5 (CEV).

Deceived by truth, John 7:45–47.

See Deceit.

DECEPTION

Satan's reasoning, Genesis 3:1–5.

Wife poses as sister, Genesis 12:10–20; 20:2; 26:7.

Sibling impersonation, Genesis 27:6–23.

Hiding father's gods, Genesis 31:31–35.

Circumcision ploy, Genesis 34:13–31.

Joseph deceiving brothers, Genesis 42–44.

Murderous deceit, Judges 3:12–21.

Samson, Delilah, Judges 16:4–20.

Pretended madness, 1 Samuel 21:10–15.

Incest by deception, 2 Samuel 13:1–14.
Attempted deception, Nehemiah 6:1–14.
Deceptive wages, Proverbs 11:18.
Hurt by deception, Proverbs 26:28.
Deliberate deception, Isaiah 5:20.
Friends, brothers untrustworthy, Jeremiah 9:4–8.
Self-deception, Jeremiah 37:9 (LB).
Believing lie, Jeremiah 43:1–7.
Truth despised, Amos 5:10.
Herod's Nativity ploy, Matthew 2:7–12.
Awkward Pharisee, Matthew 22:15–22.
Contemplated deception, Mark 14:1.
Ananias, Sapphira, Acts 5:1–9.
Accused of deception, 2 Corinthians 12:16 (LB).
See Deceit, Lie.

DECISION

Harmed by wrong decision, Genesis 16:1–6.
Freedom of decision, Genesis 24:54–58.
Garment for decision making, Exodus 28:15, 29.
God changed His mind, Exodus 32:14.
Good, bad decisions, Deuteronomy 30:15.
Personal decision of divine guidance, 1 Samuel 14:36–41.
Two options, 1 Kings 18:19–21.
Decision conditioned by God's will, Ezra 7:18.
Coin toss, Nehemiah 10:34 (LB).
Throwing dice, Joshua 14:1–2 (LB).
Time for decision, Joshua 24:15.
No change of mind, Psalm 110:4.
Choosing truth, Psalm 119:30.
Oath to follow Scripture, Psalm 119:106.
"Inspired decisions," Proverbs 16:10 (NRSV).
Decision without facts, Proverbs 18:13 (LB).
Flip coin, Proverbs 18:18 (LB).
Correct choice, Proverbs 21:2.
Decision requested, Isaiah 16:3.
Divine decision changed, Jeremiah 26:19.
"I won't change my mind," Amos 1:3 (CEV).
Date of decision, Haggai 2:18.
Immediate decision, Matthew 4:20–22.
Jesus, Barabbas, Matthew 27:15–26.
Urged to action, Mark 1:15 (LB).
Prayer precedes decision, Luke 6:12–16.
Prepared for persecution, Luke 21:12–15.

Decision to turn back, John 6:66–71.
Reaching out to God, Acts 17:27.
King not persuaded, Acts 26:28.
Mind made up, 2 Corinthians 2:1 (NKJV).
"Determine what is best," Philippians 1:9–10 (NRSV).
Challenge to decide, Hebrews 3:7–14.
Determined resistance, 1 Peter 5:8–9.
See Choice, Determination.

DECODE

Let earth hear, Isaiah 34:1.
Misunderstood message, John 12:29.
See Communication.

DECORATION

Decorated garden, Esther 1:6.

DECREE

Temple stop work order, Ezra 4:17–23; 6:1–5; 7:12–26.
Sanballat's opposition, Nehemiah 6:5–6.
Queen versus king, Esther 1:10–22.
Political pressure, Daniel 6:1–28.
Call for census taking, Luke 2:1–7.
Ecclesiastical decisions, Acts 16:1–5.
See Announcement.

DEDICATION

Set apart, Exodus 32:29.
Anointed objects, Exodus 40:9–10.
Sanctuary elements, Numbers 7:1.
Dedicatory speech, 1 Kings 8:14–21.
Temple dedication, 1 Kings 8:22–53, 62–66; Ezra 6:15–16.
Decisive dedication, Romans 12:1 (AB).
Dying daily, 1 Corinthians 15:31.
Following God's will, Colossians 1:9–12.
See Commitment, Consecration.

DEEDS

Documented ownership, Jeremiah 32:14.
Faith title deed, Hebrews 11:1 (AB).
See Contract.

DEEPER LIFE

Continual communion, Psalm 1:1–3.
Fully committed life, Psalm 34:4–7.
Undivided heart, Psalm 86:11.
Deep foundation, Luke 6:46–49.

Taught by Holy Spirit, 1 Corinthians 2:10.
In-depth commitment, Ephesians 3:14–21.
Deeper lifestyle, Philippians 4:8.
Knowing God's will, Colossians 1:9–12.
See Commitment, Discipleship.

DEFAMATION

Ark of Covenant in heathen temple, 1 Samuel 5:1–5.
Stripped of honor, Job 19:9.
Temple defamation, Daniel 5:1–4.
See Desecration.

DEFAULT

Edenic bliss defaulted, Genesis 3:22–24.
Default by disobedience, Numbers 14:21–45; 20:9–12; Deuteronomy 32:48–52.
Eternal wealth forfeited, Matthew 19:16–22.
Price of disobedience, Hebrews 4:6.
See Failure.

DEFEAT

Pharaoh's army wiped out, Exodus 14:28.
Vanquished king, 1 Samuel 31:1–6; 2 Samuel 1:1–12.
Failure into success, 1 Kings 8:33–34.
Defeat caused by sin, 2 Kings 17:7; 18:11–12.
Utter defeat, 2 Kings 13:7.
Loathing life, Job 10:1.
Hopeless future, Job 17:11.
Shamed by defeat, Psalm 25:2.
Broken hearts, spirits, Psalm 34:18 (Berk.).
No help from God, Psalm 44:9.
Enemy bones scattered, Psalm 53:5.
Food for jackals, Psalm 63:10.
Desolation of defeat, Isaiah 1:7.
Satan's defeat, Isaiah 14:12–17.
Death of mighty army, Isaiah 18:6 (LB).
No resistance to capture, Isaiah 22:3.
"Silent ruin," Isaiah 23:7 (LB).
Desolate city, Isaiah 27:10.
Defeated time after time, Jeremiah 4:20 (CEV).
Predestined defeat, Jeremiah 34:1–5.
Certain defeat, Jeremiah 37:1–10; 38:14–28.
Defeat aftermath, Jeremiah 39:1–7.
Battlefield bedlam, Jeremiah 46:12.

Augmented defeat, Jeremiah 46:15.
Hiss of fleeing serpent, Jeremiah 46:22.
Continual bad news, Jeremiah 51:31–32.
Giving up to enemy, Lamentations 1:5.
Cause of defeat, Lamentations 4:12–13.
Broken bow symbol, Hosea 1:5.
Ninety percent loss, Amos 5:3.
Irreparable ruin, Micah 2:10.
Ninevah's fate applauded, Nahum 3:19.
"Never give up," 2 Corinthians 4:16 (CEV); Ephesians 6:18 (GNB).
See Destruction, Submission, Vanquished.

DEFECTION

Frightened soldiers, 1 Samuel 13:7, 8.
See AWOL.

DEFECTIVE

Animals with no defects, Exodus 12:5.
Unqualified for priesthood, Leviticus 21:17–23.
Disgraced by blindness, 1 Samuel 11:2–11.
Multiple fingers, toes, 2 Samuel 21:20.
No-defect church, Ephesians 5:25–27.
Lamb of God, 1 Peter 1:19.
See Handicap, Maim.

DEFENSE

Weapons-makers eliminated, 1 Samuel 13:19.
Self-defense, 2 Samuel 2:22–23.
Defending, working, Nehemiah 4:21.
Unwalled villages, Ezekiel 38:10–12.
Lime from royal bones, Amos 2:1 (CEV).
Undefended gates, Nahum 3:13.
"Laugh at fortresses," Habakkuk 1:10 (CEV).
City without walls, Zechariah 2:3–5.
Defenseless by choice, Mark 15:1–15.
Jesus avoided danger, John 7:1, 30.
Divine Savior, human defense, John 8:59.
Paul's defender, Acts 23:16–22.
Paul before Felix, Acts 24:1–21.
Shield of faith, Ephesians 6:16.
See Protection.

DEFENSELESS

Defenseless by choice, Mark 15:1–15.

DEFENSIVE

Defending personal intelligence, Job 13:2.
Upset by criticism, Job 20:2–3.
Avoid being defensive, Luke 21:14.
Jesus defensive, John 7:1.

DEFIANT

Pharaoh defied God, Exodus 5:2.
Openly defy moral standard, Numbers 25:6–9.
Fool's defiance, Psalm 14:1.
Heathen gods defied, Psalm 138:1.
Inevitable result of defiance, Jeremiah 44:15–28.
See Affront, Anarchy, Opposition.

DEFILE

Self-defilement, Psalm 106:39.
Guilty fingers, lying lips, Isaiah 59:3.
Broken jar, Jeremiah 48:38.
Pagans enter sanctuary, Lamentations 1:10.
Blood defilement, Lamentations 4:14.
Internal evil, Mark 7:23.
Cleansed from defilement, 2 Corinthians 7:1 (NASB, NRSV).
Corrupting tongue, James 3:6.
Antidote to uncleanness, 1 John 3:1–3.
Temple court defiled, Revelation 11:1–2.
See Corruption, Debauchery, Depravity, Desecration.

DEFINITION

Heathen definition of God, Daniel 5:11.
Terse, conclusive, John 1:30–31.

DEGENERATE

Corrupt from birth, Psalm 58:3.
Silver to dross, wine to water, Isaiah 1:22.
Blood defilement, Lamentations 4:14.
Refusing to repent, Revelation 16:10–11.
See Debauchery.

DEGRADATION

People out of control, Exodus 32:25.
Desecrated ark, 1 Samuel 5:1–2.
Blaming God, 2 Kings 6:33.
Death of princess, 2 Kings 9:30–37.
Community degradation, restoration, Isaiah 1:21, 26.
Art of seduction, Jeremiah 2:33.

Disease, death, Jeremiah 16:1–13.
Sick drunk, Jeremiah 25:27.
Defiled with blood, Lamentations 4:14.
Lying in own blood, Ezekiel 16:6.
Sodom's women, Ezekiel 16:49.
Continual defilement, Ezekiel 20:31.
Promiscuous sisters, Ezekiel 23:1–49.
Treasures in pagan temple, Daniel 1:2.
Alcohol, nudity, Habakkuk 2:15.
Dog returns to vomit, 2 Peter 2:22.
See Carnality, Debauchery, Defile.

DEITY

"Fullness of Deity," Colossians 2:9 (NASB, NRSV).
See Christ, God, Trinity.

DELAY

Dangerous procrastination, Genesis 19:12–16.
Enemy progress delayed, Exodus 14:24–25.
Waiting patiently, Psalm 130:5–6.
"Tarried long enough," Deuteronomy 1:6 (Berk.).
Time to move on, Deuteronomy 2:3.
King's diary, Esther 6:1–2.
No more delay, Isaiah 13:22.
Noon schedule delayed, Jeremiah 6:4–5.
Delayed by disobedience, Jeremiah 8:20.
Temple procrastinators, Haggai 1:3–4.
Lazarus' resurrection delayed, John 11:6–44.
Delayed response, Acts 24:25.
Uncertain schedule, 1 Timothy 3:14–15.
Abraham's patience, Hebrews 6:13–15.
Second Coming as scheduled, Hebrews 10:37.
See Hindrance, Procrastination.

DELEGATE

Delegating work, Exodus 18:17–27; Nehemiah 3:1–32.
The Lord delegates responsibility, Deuteronomy 1:9–18.
Delegating aid to widows, Acts 6:1–4.
See Organization, Responsibility.

DELIBERATION

Eyes intent on the Lord, Psalm 25:15.
Deliberate attention, Proverbs 4:25.

Glory of kings, Proverbs 25:2.
Fear, obey God, Ecclesiastes 12:13–14.
Deliberate iniquity, Micah 2:1.
See Concentration.

DELICACY

Taste of manna, Exodus 16:31; Psalm 78:25.
Sugar cane, Exodus 30:23.
Fruits, flavors, Song of Songs 4:13–14.
Imported sweets, Jeremiah 6:20.
Barter items, Ezekiel 29:19.
Tree of life, Revelation 2:7.
Hidden manna, Revelation 2:17.
See Gourmet.

DELIGHT *See Happiness, Joy.*

DELINQUENCY

Juvenile delinquent executed, Deuteronomy 21:18–21.
Sons of sorceress, Isaiah 57:3.
Unfaithful sons, Jeremiah 3:19.
Father's evil influence, Jeremiah 16:10–12.
God loves delinquents, Hosea 11:1–4.
Multiple delinquency, Amos 2:1, 6 (AB).
Prodigal son, Luke 15:11–32.
See Reprobate.

DELIRIUM TREMENS

Drunkard's fantasies, Proverbs 23:31–35.

DELIVERANCE

Lot's rescue, Genesis 14:12–16.
Joseph's predicted deliverance, Genesis 50:24–25.
Lamp of the Lord, 2 Samuel 22:29.
Help from God, not man, Psalm 60:11–12.
Power of God's name, Psalm 118:8–12.
Promised deliverance, Isaiah 37:33–34.
Israel's assurance in Egypt, Jeremiah 46:27.
Too little, too late, Amos 3:12.
Certain revelation, Habakkuk 2:3.
Deliverance decried, Matthew 8:28–29.
Many demons, Mark 5:15.
Thwarted murder, Luke 4:28–30.
Rebuked demon, Luke 4:33–36.
Angelic deliverance, Acts 5:17–20; 12:4–11.
Harmless snake bite, Acts 28:1–6.
Only Christ delivers from sin, Romans 7:24–25; Hebrews 7:23–28.

Prostitute's deliverance, Hebrews 11:31.
Delivered from continual sin, 1 John 3:4–6.
Celebrating oppressors' death, Revelation 11:7–11.
See Escape, Exorcism, Redemption, Rescue.

DELUSION

Delusion in Eden, Genesis 3:1–6.
Religious but deluded, Matthew 3:7–10; 23:1–7.
Mortality delusion, Luke 12:16–21; James 4:13–14.
Wisdom surmounts delusion, Acts 5:34–40.
Potential delusion of faith, 1 Corinthians 15:19 (AB).
See Carnal, Deception.

DEMEAN

Joseph demeaned by brothers, Genesis 37:19.
Strong man demeaned, Judges 16:23–30.
Demeaned servant, 2 Kings 8:13.
"Feeble Jews," Nehemiah 4:1–2 (NIV, NKJV).
Stripped of honor, Job 19:9.
"Laugh at the evil doer," Psalm 52:6 (NRSV).
Heart breaking insults, Psalm 69:20 (NRSV).
Making fun of others, Psalm 70:3.
Wounds of friend, Proverbs 27:6.
Princes demeaned by slaves, Ecclesiastes 10:7.
"A thing of the past," Lamentations 1:6 (GNB).
Shake heads, sneer, Lamentations 2:15 (CEV).
Learning from insults, Lamentations 3:30 (CEV).
Treated like garbage, Lamentations 3:45 (CEV).
Jesus demeaned, Mark 10:34 (CEV); 15:16–20, 29–30.
Making game demeaning Jesus, Mark 14:65 (GNB).
Vulgar demeaning, John 9:34 (LB).
Demeaned Christians, Galatians 3:1 (AB).
"Look down on you," Titus 2:15 (NRSV).
See Defamation, Gossip, Insult, Slander.

DEMOCRACY

"We, the people," Nehemiah 10:28, 34 (GNB).

DEMOGRAPHICS *See Census, Population, Statistics.*

DEMONS

Informed by divination, Genesis 30:27.

Protected by blessing, Numbers 22:12.

God's use of demons, 1 Samuel 16:15.

"Evil spirit from God," 1 Samuel 16:16 (NIV, NKJV).

Exorcism, Acts 19:11–13.

Demon use of bodies, Matthew 8:28–33; Mark 5:1–5.

Jesus accused of demonism, Matthew 9:32–34; 12:22–32; John 8:48–52.

Depraved spirits, Matthew 10:1 (Berk.).

Authority over evil, Matthew 10:1–8; Romans 8:37–39; Colossians 2:15; Jude 9.

Shrieking demons, Mark 3:11 (LB).

Satan versus Satan, Mark 3:20–26.

Name of demon, Mark 5:8–9 (GNB).

Demon rebuked, Mark 9:25.

Demons recognized Jesus, Luke 4:33–36, 41.

Mary Magdalene's seven demons, Luke 8:2.

Multiple demon possession, Luke 8:30.

Demon confronted Jesus, Luke 9:37–43.

Mute demon, Luke 11:14.

Crippled by demon, Luke 13:10–16.

Controlled by Satan, Luke 22:3; John 13:27; 1 Timothy 5:15.

Jesus accused of demon possession, John 10:19–21.

Tormented by demons, delivered, Acts 5:16.

Contending sorcerer, Acts 13:6–8.

Reverence to demons, Acts 17:22 (AB).

Demons cause physical harm, Acts 19:13–16.

Pagan idols, 1 Corinthians 10:20.

False angels, 2 Corinthians 11:14–15.

Enslaved by demons, Galatians 4:8–9 (NRSV).

"Cosmic powers," Ephesians 6:12 (NRSV).

Satanic cause of anger, Ephesians 4:26–27.

Armor of God, Ephesians 6:10–18.

Cosmic powers, Ephesians 6:12 (Berk.).

Rescue from darkness, Colossians 1:13–14.

Hindered by Satan, 1 Thessalonians 2:18.

Possessed by Satan, 1 Timothy 1:18–20.

Demon theology, 1 Timothy 4:1–4 (See CEV).

Deceived widows, 1 Timothy 5:11–15.

Satan's trap, 2 Timothy 2:25–26.

Resisting Satan, James 4:7; 1 Peter 5:8–9.

Testing false spirits, 1 John 4:1–6.

Angels versus demons, Revelation 12:7–9.

Global control, 1 John 5:19; Revelation 16:13–14.

Demon residence, Revelation 18:2.

See Evil, Exorcism, Satan.

DEN

Shelter from oppressor, Judges 6:2.

Animal dens, Job 37:8.

Den of robbers, Jeremiah 7:11.

Lions' den, Daniel 6:6–24.

DENIAL

Denying Christ, Matthew 10:33; Mark 8:38; 2 Timothy 2:12.

Peter's denial, Matthew 26:34, 69–70, 73–74.

See Ashamed, Rejection, Self-denial.

DENOMINATION

"Rules taught by men," Isaiah 29:13 (NIV).

Division among people, John 7:40–43.

Exclusive interpretation, Acts 15:1.

Credentialed ministry, Acts 15:22–31.

Courtroom dispute, Acts 18:12–17.

Differing views, Romans 14:1–8; 1 Corinthians 1:10–17.

Harmonious ministry, Jews, Gentiles, Galatians 2:8.

Spiritual envy, Philippians 1:15–19.

False doctrine prevented, 1 Timothy 1:3–5.

Common faith, Titus 1:4.

See Clergy, Doctrine, Syncretism, Theology.

DENTISTRY

Tooth loss compensation, Exodus 21:27.

"Fangs of the wicked," Job 29:17 (NIV, NKJV).

Broken teeth, Psalm 3:7.

Bad tooth, Proverbs 25:19; Lamentations 3:16.

"Grinders cease," Ecclesiastes 12:3 (NKJV).

Children's teeth, Jeremiah 31:29; Ezekiel 18:2.

Clean teeth, Amos 4:6 (AB).

See Teeth.

DEN

DEPARTURE

Scattered departure, Genesis 11:8.

Change of direction, Genesis 13:5–13.

Romantic venture, Genesis 24:10.

Three-day journey, Genesis 30:36.

Flight from Egypt, Exodus 14:1–28; Psalm 105:23–38.

River crossing, Joshua 3:1–17.

Departure into battle, Judges 1:1–3.

Homeward journey, Ruth 1:3–7; Luke 15:13, 17–20.

Wrong motives, 1 Samuel 15:17–19.

Travel in two directions, Jonah 1:1–3; 3:1–3.

Time to depart, Micah 2:10.

Advance notice, John 7:33; 13:33; 14:28; 17:11.

Greatest journey, 2 Timothy 4:6–8.

See Itinerary, Journey, Travel.

DEPENDABILITY

Weights, measures, Deuteronomy 25:13–16.

Not one promise failed, Joshua 21:45.

Divine promises, Joshua 23:14–15; 2 Chronicles 6:4, 14–15; Hebrews 6:18.

False dependence, 1 Chronicles 21:17.

The Lord's enduring love, Psalm 136:1–26.

Confidence betrayed, Proverbs 11:13.

Springs that fail, Jeremiah 15:18.

Dependable faithfulness, 1 Corinthians 4:2.

Dependable lifestyle, Ephesians 5:15–16.

Spiritual dependability, Ephesians 6:5–8; Colossians 3:23–24.

Unsupervised dependability, Philippians 2:12–13.

See Faithfulness, Honesty, Integrity.

DEPRAVITY

Knowing good, evil, Genesis 3:22.

Pre-deluge depravity, Genesis 6:5, 12.

Lifelong depravity, Genesis 8:21.

Mercy withheld, Genesis 18:16–33.

"Shriek of sins," Genesis 18:20 (AB).

Modified murder, Genesis 37:19–27.

Depraved silver, gold, Deuteronomy 7:25–26.

Becoming like animals, Deuteronomy 28:53–57.

Quick to disobey, Judges 2:10–13, 19; 3:7, 12; 4:1.

Broken altars, slain prophets, 1 Kings 19:10.

Parental depravity, 2 Kings 3:1–3.

Desecrated street corners, 2 Chronicles 28:24.

Persistent depravity, Nehemiah 9:28.

Self-condemnation, Job 9:2–3, 20.

"Accounted wicked," Job 9:29 (NASB).

Purity cannot come from impurity, Job 14:4; 15:14–16.

Attacking God, Job 15:13 (CEV).

Man, nature, Job 25:4–6.

World against God, Psalm 2:1–3.

"Pregnant with evil," Psalm 7:14.

Vanished faithful, Psalm 12:1.

Proud depravity, Psalm 12:8; 52:1–4.

Divine view, Psalm 14:2–3.

Conceived in sin, Psalms 51:5; 58:3.

Human nature, Psalm 53:2–3.

Depraved at birth, Psalm 58:3.

Devoid of kindness, Psalm 109:16.

Universal depravity, Psalm 130:3; Proverbs 20:9; Ecclesiastes 7:20; 9:3; Isaiah 9:17; 53:6; Romans 3:23; 5:12–14; 1 Corinthians 15:22; Galatians 3:22; 1 John 5:19.

"Warped minds," Proverbs 12:8 (NIV).

Fool's mockery, Proverbs 14:9.

Childhood folly, Proverbs 22:15.

Hidden sin, Proverbs 28:13; Isaiah 29:15.

Divine plans, mortal schemes, Ecclesiastes 7:29.

National guilt, Isaiah 1:4; Micah 7:2.

Faithful city now depraved, Isaiah 1:21.

Calling good evil, evil good, Isaiah 5:20.

Holiness of God, Isaiah 6:1–5.

Ravaged by debauchery, Isaiah 9:18.

Confident in evil, Isaiah 47:10.

Hindered prayer, Isaiah 59:1–2.

Status of depravity, Isaiah 59:14.

Filthy rags, Isaiah 64:6.

"Give lessons to a prostitute," Jeremiah 2:33 (CEV).

Claiming innocence, Jeremiah 2:34–35.

Profuse wickedness, Jeremiah 3:5; Micah 7:2–4; Matthew 12:34–35.

Debauchery comparisons, Jeremiah 3:11.

Search for one honest person, Jeremiah 5:1.

Depraved prophets, priests, Jeremiah 8:10.

Leopard's spots, Jeremiah 13:23.

Deceitful heart, Jeremiah 17:9.

Inevitable judgment, Jeremiah 44:15–28.

False shepherds, Jeremiah 50:6.

Jerusalem depravity, Ezekiel 16:44–52.

Death sentence, Ezekiel 18:4.

Depravity enumerated, Ezekiel 18:10–13, 14–17.

Adulterous sisters, Ezekiel 23:1–49.

Worn out by adultery, Ezekiel 23:43.

Relished wickedness, Hosea 4:8.

Three or four sins, Amos 1:3, 6, 9, 11, 13; 2:1, 4, 6.

Ignorant of doing right, Amos 3:10.

Hate good, love evil, Micah 3:2; Amos 5:15.

Depraved heart, Matthew 15:19.

Sinners, Pharisees, Matthew 21:31–32.

Resurrection foes, Matthew 27:62–66; 28:11–15.

Source of uncleanness, Mark 7:15–23.

Love of darkness, John 3:19–21.

Father of sin, John 8:44.

Truth disbelieved, John 8:45–47.

Spiritual blindness, sight, John 9:39–41.

Rejecting evidence, John 12:37–38.

Common universal sin, John 16:9 (LB).

Intellectual idolatry, Acts 17:16–34.

Depravity described, Romans 1:28–32.

Self-condemnation, Romans 2:1.

Spiritual hardness, Romans 2:5.

Sin's sinfulness, Romans 7:13.

Natural man, 1 Corinthians 2:14.

Sinful nature, Galatians 5:19–21.

No God, no hope, Ephesians 2:12.

Intellectual debauchery, Colossians 1:21.

Deception, wickedness, 2 Thessalonians 2:10 (NASB, NRSV).

"Corrupt minds," 1 Timothy 6:5 (Japanese *kusatta*, "rotten minds").

Last days' conduct, 2 Timothy 3:1–5.

Pre-conversion, Titus 3:3.

Rampant outgrowth, James 1:21 (AB).

Breaking law, James 2:10.

Depraved malignancy, 1 Peter 2:1 (AB).

Rejecting appointed destiny, 1 Peter 2:8.

Slaves of depravity, 2 Peter 2:13–22.

"Love not the world," 1 John 2:15–17 (KJV).

Denying Christ, 1 John 2:22–23.

Evil exhibit, Jude 7 (AB).

Refusing to repent, Revelation 9:20–21.

Mark of the Beast, Revelation 13:16–18; 14:9–10.

Sins recorded in Heaven, Revelation 18:4–5.

Continuing debauchery, Revelation 22:11.

See Blasphemy, Carnality, Debase, Decadent, Disobedient.

DEPRESSION

Deep waters, 2 Samuel 22:17.

Broken hearts, spirits, Psalm 34:18; Proverbs 17:22.

Desperate times, Psalm 60:3.

Walking in darkness, Isaiah 9:2.

No joy, Jeremiah 48:33.

Hopeless hope, Romans 4:18–22.

God comforts the depressed, 2 Corinthians 7:6 (NASB).

See Anxiety, Stress.

DERANGED

"Crazy man," 1 Samuel 18:10 (CEV).

DESCENDANTS

No descendants, Nahum 1:14.

DESCRIPTION

Wilderness description, Deuteronomy 8:15.

Angel's description, Judges 13:6.

Concise life of Christ, 1 Timothy 3:16.

New Jerusalem, Revelation 21:15–17.

DESECRATION

Improper entry into holy place, Leviticus 16:2.

King Saul's body, 1 Samuel 31:8–10.

Ark of the Lord, 2 Samuel 6:6–11.

Temple murder, 2 Kings 19:37.

Temple fire, 2 Kings 25:8–9.

Challenging God, Isaiah 5:18–19.

Fasting in mockery, Isaiah 58:4–5.

Trample Sabbath, Isaiah 58:13 (Berk.).

Pigs, rats, Isaiah 66:17.

Ruined Babylon, Jeremiah 51:37.

Pagans desecrate sanctuary, Lamentations 1:10.

Sacred articles in pagan temple, Daniel 1:1–2.

Temple goblets misused, Daniel 5:1–4.

Priests defile altar, Malachi 1:6–14.

Laughing at Jesus, Matthew 9:23–24.

Accusation against Jesus, Matthew 12:1–13.

Commercialized temple, Matthew 21:12–13.

Sacrificial blood desecrated, Luke 13:1.

See Defamation, Defile, Iconoclastic, Irreverence, Sacrilege.

DESERT

Desert sacrifices, Exodus 5:3.

Sinai desert, Exodus 19:2.

Desert landmark, Exodus 23:31.

Scapegoat, Leviticus 16:22.

Desert of Zin, Numbers 20:1.

Wilderness description, Deuteronomy 8:15.

Desert of Maon, 1 Samuel 23:24.

Wasteland, 2 Samuel 2:24.

Wild donkey habitat, Job 39:5–6.

"Scorching desert," Psalm 107:103–104 (CEV).

Desert water, Isaiah 43:20 (CEV).

"Empty of human life," Job 38:26 (NRSV).

Desert to become garden, Isaiah 51:3.

Remembered wilderness, Jeremiah 2:2–6.

Desert windstorm, Jeremiah 4:11–12 (CEV).

Travellers' desert retreat, Jeremiah 9:2.

Desert dwellers, Obadiah 19 (CEV).

Wasteland forever, Zephaniah 2:9.

John's desert habitat, Luke 1:80.

Desert road, Acts 8:26.

See Arid, Terrain.

DESERTER

Twenty-two thousand cowards, Judges 7:3.

Terrified by Goliath, 1 Samuel 17:24.

Fearful David, 2 Samuel 15:14.

Deserting battlefield, Psalm 78:9; Jeremiah 41:11–14.

Refusing battle call, Ezekiel 7:14.

Gethsemane desertion, Matthew 26:56.

Quickly deserting truth, Galatians 1:6.

Deserter Demas, 2 Timothy 4:9–10.

See AWOL, Backsliding, Coward.

DESIGN

Species distinction, Genesis 1:24–25.

Gold cup designs, Esther 1:7.

Snowflake design, Job 38:22.
Design of eye, ear, Psalm 94:9.
Divine advance planning, Isaiah 25:1.
Earth's design, Isaiah 45:18.
Beauty to perfection, Ezekiel 27:4.
Temple plan, Ezekiel 40:5–49.
See Blueprint, Plan, Purpose.

DESIRE

Selfish desire, Numbers 11:4; Mark 10:35–37.
Divinely-implanted desires, Psalms 37:4 (CEV), 145:16; 2 Corinthians 8:16.
Desires known to Lord, Psalm 38:9.
Desired obedience, Psalm 119:1–5.
Evil desire, Proverbs 21:10; Habakkuk 2:4–5; Mark 4:19; 1 Corinthians 10:6.
Fulfilled desires, Psalm 73:25; Proverbs 13:12.
Spiritual desire, Isaiah 26:9; Luke 6:21; 1 Peter 2:2.
Jesus said, "I want to," Mark 1:41 (CEV).
Fulfilling Satan's desires, John 8:44.
Carnal gratification, Ephesians 2:3.
Impure desires, Ephesians 4:19; James 1:13–15.
Paul's supreme desire, Philippians 3:7–11.
Unfulfilled desire, James 4:2.
Love of the world, 1 John 2:15–16.
See Lust, Self-interest, Selfishness.

DESOLATE

Fate of godless, Job 15:34.
Desolated by terror, Psalm 73:19.
Day of the Lord, Isaiah 13:9.
Overnight desolation, Isaiah 15:1.
Haunt of jackals, Jeremiah 9:11.
Made desolate by salt, Jeremiah 48:9.
Object of horror, Jeremiah 49:17.
Desolate city, Lamentations 1:1.
Retribution, Ezekiel 25:12–14; Joel 3:19.
Stark terror, Nahum 2:10.
See Abandoned, Desert, Forsaken.

DESPAIR

Driven to suicide, 1 Samuel 31:4; 2 Samuel 17:23; 1 Kings 16:18; Acts 1:18.
Desiring death, Numbers 11:10–15; 1 Kings 19:3–5; Job 3:21; 7:15; Jeremiah 8:3; Jonah 4:3; Revelation 9:6.

Without hope, Job 7:6; Lamentations 3:18.
Hopeless future, Job 17:11.
Troubles outnumber hair count, Psalm 40:11–12.
Hope versus despair, Psalm 42:5; Jeremiah 31:15–17.
Darkness everywhere, Isaiah 59:9.
Despairing harvest, Jeremiah 8:20.
Anxiety, despair, Ezekiel 12:19.
Withered joy, Joel 1:12.
Bravest soldiers despair, Zephaniah 1:14 (GNB).
Despair at sea, Acts 27:20.
Desiring death, Revelation 9:6.
Unrepentant agony, Revelation 16:10–11.
See Anxiety, Despondency, Disappointment, Grief, Tension, Trauma.

DESPERATION

Desperate times, 2 Kings 6:24–31.
Plea for mercy, Esther 7:7.
Face to wall, Isaiah 38:2.
Resorting to cannibalism, Lamentations 2:20.
See Despondency, Panic.

DESPISE See Hatred.

DESPONDENCY

Great sorrow, Genesis 37:34–35; 2 Samuel 18:32–33.
Despondent patriarch, Numbers 11:10–15; 17:12–13.
Despondency described, Deuteronomy 28:65–67.
Leader's lament, Joshua 7:7; 1 Kings 19:3–4.
Despondent over circumstances, Job 3:1–26; 10:1; 17:13–16; Jeremiah 18:12; 48:33.
"Crushed in spirit," Psalm 34:18 (NRSV); Proverbs 17:22 (CEV).
Hating life, Job 10:1; Jeremiah 15:10.
Questioning God, Psalm 77:7–9.
Glimmer of hope, Proverbs 13:12.
Spiritual loneliness, 2 Corinthians 7:5–7.
See Anxiety, Despair, Discouragement, Pessimism.

DESPOT

Egyptian despotism, Exodus 1:8–14; 5:8–9.
Son worse than father, 1 Kings 12:1–11.
Oppressed people, Ecclesiastes 4:1–3; Isaiah 5:7.
Despots serve God, Jeremiah 25:11–14.
See Dictator, Totalitarian.

DESSERT

Going without dessert, Daniel 10:3 (LB).

DESTINY

Destined for greatness, Genesis 18:16–19.
Sympathy, destiny, Exodus 2:5–6.
Children destined for war, Job 27:15.
Time for everything, Ecclesiastes 3:1–8.
Pre-planned destiny, Isaiah 25:1; 46:8–11; 49:1; Jeremiah 1:5; Ephesians 1:4; 1 Peter 2:8.
"Who controls human events?" Isaiah 41:4 (CEV).
Jerusalem's destiny, Jeremiah 31:38–40.
Savior's dual mission, Luke 2:28–32.
Destined crucifixion, John 7:30.
Jesus knew His destiny, John 13:1.
Confident of destiny, Acts 27:23–25.
Revealed destiny, Romans 8:18–23.
See Chance, Fate, Fortuity, Predestination.

DESTRUCTION

Canaanite devastation, Numbers 21:3.
No survivors, Deuteronomy 2:34; 3:6; Joshua 6:21; 8:24–29.
Destructive cities, nations, 2 Chronicles 15:6.
"Rebuild ruins," Job 3:14 (NRSV).
Divine destruction, Isaiah 34:2.
Total destruction, Jeremiah 25:9.
Earth's destruction, Zephaniah 1:2–3 (GNB).
Destroyed beyond remedy, Micah 2:10.
Flaming destruction, Malachi 4:1.
Babylon destroyed, Revelation 18:21.
See Judgment.

DETAIL

Intricate temple details, Ezekiel 40—42.
Details avoided, Hebrews 9:5.
See Design, Plan.

DETERGENT

Futile washing method, Job 9:30–31.
Soda, soap, Jeremiah 2:22.
See Cleansing, Soap.

DETERIORATE See Death, Decay, Rust.

DETERMINATION

Relentless determination, Numbers 23:24.
Strong soul, Judges 5:21.
"Don't give up," 2 Chronicles 15:7 (CEV).
Consistent determination, Psalm 44:18.
Wholehearted determination, Psalm 119:10.
Standing firm, Isaiah 7:9.
Face like flint, Isaiah 50:7.
Divine determination, Jeremiah 23:20.
Heart, action, Jeremiah 32:38–39.
Determined to obey, Colossians 1:9–12.
See Diligence, Resolute.

DETERMINISM

Permitted accidents, Exodus 21:12–13.
Divine determinism, Job 42:2; Psalm 135:6; Isaiah 43:13; 46:8–11; Lamentations 2:17; Daniel 2:19–23.
Determined actions, Psalm 139:1–16.
Determined events, Ecclesiastes 3:1–8.
Divine plan, purpose, Isaiah 14:24.
Mortal inability to determine, Jeremiah 10:23.
Determined destiny, Jeremiah 15:2–3.
Future determinations, Ezekiel 12:26–27.
God's acts, purposes, Daniel 2:19–23.
Endowed determinism, Colossians 1:9–12.
See Destiny, Fortuity, Predestination.

DETEST See Hatred.

DEVELOPMENT

Samuel's development, 1 Samuel 2:26; 3:19–21.
Time to enlarge, Isaiah 54:2.
National development, Isaiah 66:8.
Spiritual development, Jeremiah 17:7–8.
Development of boy Jesus, Luke 2:52.
Enlarged harvest, 2 Corinthians 9:10.
Developing faith, 2 Thessalonians 1:3.
See Growth, Maturity, Progress.

DEVIATE

Origin of sodomy, Genesis 19:5.
Forbidden male relationship, Leviticus 20:13.
Homosexual example, Judges 19:22–24.
Male prostitutes, 1 Kings 14:24.
Temple, shrine deviates, 1 Kings 15:12; Job 36:14.
Adultery with wood, stone, Jeremiah 3:9.
Sexual deviation described, Romans 1:26–27 (CEV).
Body pollution, Jude 8 (GNB).
See Homosexual, Lesbian, Sodomy.

DEVIL See Satan.

DEVIOUS

Devious temple builders, Ezra 4:1–4.
Sanballat's devious scheme, Nehemiah 6:1–9.
Devious plans thwarted, Job 5:12.
Devious weights, scales, Micah 6:11.
See Disruption, Hindrance, Manipulate.

DEVOTIONS

Morning devotions, 1 Samuel 1:19; 2 Chronicles 29:20; Job 1:5; Psalms 5:3; 57:8; 119:147; Mark 1:35; Luke 4:42; John 8:2.
God's word in the morning, Ezekiel 12:8.
Closet prayer, Matthew 6:5–6.
Devotional priority, Matthew 10:37–39.
Undistracted devotion, 1 Corinthians 7:35 (NASB, NKJV).
See Intercession, Meditation, Prayer, Quiet Time.

DEVOUT

Devout men, Genesis 5:24; 6:8–9; 2 Chronicles 31:20; Job 1:1; Luke 2:25–35.
Predicted future devoutness, Genesis 18:17–19.
Idols rejected, Genesis 35:2–3.
Devout expectant father, Judges 13:8.
Doing right, being faithful, 2 Chronicles 31:20.
Blameless, upright, Job 1:1.
Boldness in prayer, Daniel 6:10.
Righteous, devout, Luke 2:25–35.
Devout woman, Luke 2:36–37.
Devout appraisal, John 1:47.

Devout centurion, Acts 10:1–2.
Exemplary congregation, Acts 11:22–24.
See Commitment, Consecration, Discipleship, Holiness, Separation, Spirituality.

DEXTERITY

Gifted dexterity, Exodus 31:1–5.
Impaired dexterity, Judges 1:6.
Heartfelt dexterity, Nehemiah 4:6.
Futile dexterity, Isaiah 25:11.
Skilled seduction, Jeremiah 2:33.
Broken arms, Ezekiel 30:21–22.
See Ability, Agility, Athletics.

DIABETES

Going without dessert, Daniel 10:3 (LB).
Imported cane sugar despised, Jeremiah 6:20 (AB).
"Deceptive food," Proverbs 23:3 (NKJV).
"Too much honey is bad," Proverbs 25:27 (GNB).
"Bitter food tastes sweet," Proverbs 27:7 (GNB).

DIAGNOSIS

Leprosy diagnosed, Leviticus 13:18–23 (NRSV).
Asking prophet about son's illness, 1 Kings 14:1–14.
Hezekiah's terminal illness, Isaiah 38:1.
Great Physician, Mark 2:17.
See Health, Medicine, Therapy.

DIAMOND

Diamond pen point, Jeremiah 17:1 (GNB).

DIARY

King's diary, Esther 6:1–2.
Need for diary, Job 19:23–24.
Tear-stained page, Psalm 56:8.

DICHOTOMY

Conflicting human nature, Romans 7:18–25 (CEV, NRSV).

DICTATION

Voice of the Lord, Jeremiah 32:1–12.
Jeremiah's dictation, Jeremiah 36:4, 15–16.
Dictated Bible, 2 Peter 1:21.
See Secretary.

DICTATOR

Wandering leaders of earth, Job 12:14–15.
Weakness of one-man government, Proverbs 11:14.
Unjust government, Isaiah 10:1–2.
Oppressed people, Isaiah 26:13.
Have no fear, Romans 13:3–4 (GNB).
See Despot, Totalitarian.

DIET

Meat diet, Genesis 43:16.
Bread without yeast, Exodus 12:15.
Bread, meat, Exodus 16:1–12.
Edible, inedible insects, Leviticus 11:20–23.
Grape abstinence, Numbers 6:2–4.
Greedy for meat, Numbers 11:31–34 (CEV).
No more manna, Joshua 5:12.
Pregnancy diet, Judges 13:1–5.
Refreshing breakfast, Judges 19:5–8.
Forbidden to taste, 1 Samuel 14:24–28.
Simple, happy diet, Proverbs 15:17; 17:1.
Watching calories, Proverbs 23:1–2, 20–21.
Regular meal times, Ecclesiastes 10:17.
Pigs, rats, Isaiah 66:17.
Royal diet refused, Daniel 1:8–16.
Red meat, Amos 6:4.
John the Baptist's diet, Matthew 3:4.
Pigs' diet, Luke 15:16.
Special dinner guest, Luke 24:29–30.
Vegetarian, nonvegetarian, Romans 14:2; Daniel 1:12.
No better, no worse, 1 Corinthians 8:8.
Stomach god, Philippians 3:19.
Legalistic diet, 1 Timothy 4:3; Hebrews 13:9.
See Food, Gluttony, Gourmet, Health, Vegetarian.

DIFFICULTY

"Rivers of difficulty," Isaiah 43:2 (LB).
Grateful for problems, Jeremiah 33:10–11.
Means of ministry, Acts 28:17–28.
See Antagonist, Enemy, Hindrance, Obstacles.

DIGESTION

Happy meals, Deuteronomy 27:7; Acts 14:17.
Enforced indigestion, 1 Samuel 14:24.
Digestive disease, 2 Chronicles 21:15.
Love aids digestion, Proverbs 15:17.
Stingy man's food, Proverbs 23:6–8.
Regular meal regular hours, Ecclesiastes 10:17.
Undigestible food, Jonah 2:10.
Attitude and food, Acts 14:17.
Wine aids digestion, 1 Timothy 5:23.
See Appetite, Diet, Food, Health.

DIGNITY

Royal bearing, Judges 8:18.
Respected dignity, Job 29:7–10.
Dignified captive, Daniel 2:46.
Dignified older men, Titus 2:2 (NASB).
See Maturity.

DILEMMA

Blind man in dark, Deuteronomy 28:29.
Walking in darkness, Psalm 82:5.
Wit's end, Psalm 107:27.
Joseph's dilemma with Mary, Matthew 1:18–19.
Pilate's dilemma, Matthew 27:19–22.
Light, darkness, John 12:35.
See Confusion, Obstacles.

DILIGENCE

Ruth in field of Boaz, Ruth 2:5–7.
Diligent people, Nehemiah 4:6; Ecclesiastes 9:10; Ephesians 5:15–16; Colossians 4:5.
Useless diligence, Psalm 127:2 (GNB).
Ant's example, Proverbs 6:6–8; 30:25.
Satisfaction from diligence, Proverbs 13:4.
Result of hard work, Proverbs 22:29 (LB).
Fantasy, diligence, Proverbs 28:19.
Diligent woman, Proverbs 31:14–15.
Sleeping when the Lord returns, Mark 13:35–37.
Working hard, Romans 12:11 (GNB, KJV).
Diligent discipleship, Ephesians 6:5–8 (NRSV); Colossians 2:23–24.
Diligent slaves, 1 Timothy 6:1–2.
"Do your job well," 2 Timothy 4:5 (CEV).
Personal diligence, Titus 3:14.
Work precedes rest, Hebrews 4:11.
Examples of diligence, Hebrews 12:1–3.
See Determination, Energy, Industrious, Motivation.

DIMENSIONS

Immeasurable dimension, Job 11:7–9.
Divine dimensions, Psalm 36:5–6.
Depth of purpose, Proverbs 20:5.
Given eternal viewpoint, Jeremiah 33:3.
Measuring temple area, Ezekiel 40:5–49.
Measuring width, length of Jerusalem, Zechariah 2:1–2.
God's unsearchable riches, Romans 11:33–36.
Dimensions of spiritual understanding, 1 Corinthians 2:9–10.
Dimensions of Christian experience, Ephesians 3:16–19.
City's identical length, width, Revelation 21:16 (NRSV).
See Area.

DIOGENES

Search for one righteous man, Psalm 53:2 (LB).

DIPLOMACY

Christian diplomacy, Philemon 1–25.
Enemy negotiations, Nehemiah 6:1–12.

DIRECTION

Points of compass, Genesis 13:14; Acts 27:12.
Travel directions, Deuteronomy 1:2.
Change of direction, Deuteronomy 2:3.
Asking directions, 1 Samuel 9:11–14.
Altar facing all directions, 2 Chronicles 4:1–4.
North, South, East, West, Job 2:2 (KJV).
Fool does not know way to town, Ecclesiastes 10:15.
North to east, Amos 8:12.
In obedience toward unknown objective, Hebrews 11:8.
See Compass, Guidance.

DIRECTIVE

Ultimate demands for obeying law, Joshua 1:18.
Pagan king persuaded to permit temple rebuilding, Ezra chapters 4—8.
Keep eyes on the Lord, Psalm 25:15.
See Decree, Guidance, Instruction.

DIRGE

Dirge to a king, 2 Samuel 1:17–27.
King's lament, 2 Samuel 3:33–34.
See Anguish.

DIRT See Dust.

DIRTY See Unclean.

DISAGREEMENT

Peace before battle, Deuteronomy 20:10.
Futile disagreement, 2 Samuel 2:27–28.
Disagreeing prophets, 1 Kings 22:6–25.
Preventing disagreement, Proverbs 17:14, 19.
Words of restraint, Proverbs 17:27.
Potential value of disagreement, Proverbs 27:17.
Disagreement quickly settled, Matthew 5:25.
Settled out of court, Luke 12:58.
Doctrinal disagreement, Acts 15:2, 3; 1 Corinthians 11:16; Galatians 2:11–21.
Settling disputes between Christians, 1 Corinthians 6:1–7.
Tolerant to others, 1 Corinthians 6:20 (LB).
Disagreement clarified, Philippians 3:15.
Settling disagreements, Philippians 4:3; 2 Timothy 2:23–26.
"Petty controversy," 2 Timothy 2:14 (AB).
See Argument, Conflict, Debate, Dispute, Opinion.

DISAPPOINTMENT

Prepared circumstances, Deuteronomy 8:16.
Unharvested vineyard, Deuteronomy 28:39: Micah 6:15.
More victorious in death than life, Judges 16:30.
Facing disappointment without complaining, Job 1:22.
Disappointed with life, Job 10:1 (Berk.).
Hope a dying gasp, Job 11:20.
Mourning unanswered prayer, Psalm 35:13–14.
No fear of bad news, Psalm 112:7–8.
Agony of waiting, joy of fulfillment, Proverbs 13:12.
Disappointed parents, Proverbs 17:25.
Handling disappointment, Proverbs 19:23.
Awakening to find dream untrue, Isaiah 29:8.
Lost harvest, Isaiah 17:10–11.

Frustrated hopes, Jeremiah 14:19.

Jonah's Nineveh disappointment, Jonah 4:1–3.

Houses unoccupied, Zephaniah 1:13.

Expecting much, receiving little, Haggai 1:9.

"Deep groan," Mark 8:11–12 (GNB).

Purpose of suffering, Romans 5:3.

Made sad by those who should cause joy, 2 Corinthians 2:3 (LB).

Rejoicing although prayer not answered, 2 Corinthians 12:7–10.

Surprised, astonished, Galatians 1:6 (AB).

Disappointment widened influence, Philippians 1:12–14.

Sharing troubles, Philippians 4:14.

Attitude toward deserting friends, 2 Timothy 4:16.

Reason for circumstances, Philemon 15–16.

Made perfect through suffering, Hebrews 2:10.

Confident now of promises fulfilled, Hebrews 11:13.

All tears wiped away, Revelation 21:4.

See Discouragement, Trauma.

DISARMAMENT

No weapons in Israel, 1 Samuel 13:19–22.

Coming world peace, Psalm 46:9; Isaiah 2:4; 11:6–9.

Break the bow, Jeremiah 49:35; Hosea 1:5–7.

Forbidden to prepare for battle, Jeremiah 51:3.

Weapons for fuel, Ezekiel 39:10.

Armament abolished, Hosea 1:5–7.

Tools of war destroyed, Micah 4:3.

World peace impossible without Christ, Matthew 24:6–8.

See Armament, Peace, War.

DISARMED

Strong man disarmed, Luke 11:21–22.

See Soldier.

DISARRAY *See Confusion.*

DISASTER

God's promise to Noah, Genesis 9:8–16.

Small town spared large city's disaster, Genesis 19:15–22.

Death caused by shock, 1 Samuel 4:12–18.

Predicted disasters, 2 Samuel 3:29 (LB).

Disaster aid, Job 30:24 (NRSV).

Facing disaster with confidence, Psalm 57:1.

Unanticipated disaster, Ecclesiastes 9:12 (NRSV).

Gentle waters, flood waters, Isaiah 8:6–7.

One night's destruction, Isaiah 15:1.

Judgment brings righteousness, Isaiah 26:9.

Slaughter on battlefield, Isaiah 37:36.

Leaders, priests, prophets lose heart, Jeremiah 4:9.

Disobedience brings disaster, Jeremiah 4:18.

Disaster in all directions, Ezekiel 7:2–3 (LB).

Great disaster, Ezekiel 7:5.

Fourth of earth destroyed, Revelation 6:7–8.

Disaster upon all earth, Revelation 8:6–13.

Greatest all-time earthquake, Revelation 16:18–20.

Hailstones from sky, Revelation 16:21.

One-hour conflagration, Revelation 18:17–19.

See Cataclysm, Defeat, Destruction.

DISCARD

Time to discard, Ecclesiastes 3:6.

Valuable objects discarded, Isaiah 2:20.

See Rejection, Unworthy, Valueless, Worthless.

DISCERNMENT

Pharaoh's motivation discerned, Exodus 9:27–30.

Discerning clean, unclean, Leviticus 10:10.

Falsehood discerned, Deuteronomy 18:21–22.

Lack of discernment, Deuteronomy 32:28.

Importance of discerning, Job 12:11; 34:1–3.

Difference between mind, heart, Job 38:36.

"Discerning minds," Psalm 90:12 (Berk.).

Asking God for discernment, Psalm 119:125.

Persistent search for discernment, Proverbs 2:1–6.

Man of understanding, Proverbs 11:12.

Discerning eyes, Proverbs 20:8; Matthew 6:22–23.

Man's ways may seem right, Proverbs 21:2.

Fear, obey God, Ecclesiastes 12:13–14.

Diet, discernment, Isaiah 7:15.

Discernment of evil, Isaiah 8:12.

Discerning false prophets, dreams, oracles, Jeremiah 23:25–30.

Undivided heart, Ezekiel 11:19.

Teaching discernment holy, common, Ezekiel 44:23.

Discerning queen, Daniel 5:10–11.

Walking in ways of the Lord, Hosea 14:9.

Unknown thoughts of the Lord, Micah 4:12.

Shrewd, innocent, Matthew 10:16.

Lack of discernment, Matthew 12:1–8.

Discerning weather, not signs of times, Matthew 16:1–4.

Not understanding words of Jesus, Mark 15:29–30; 14:58.

Centurion at Cross, Mark 15:39.

Simeon discerned Savior's mission, Luke 2:28–32.

Discerning others' thoughts, Luke 6:8.

Herod's lack of discernment, Luke 9:7–9.

Discerning what others never knew, Luke 10:23, 24.

Deity discerned, John 1:47–49 (LB).

Divine discernment, John 2:24–25 (GNB).

Attitude gives discernment, John 7:17.

Motivations discerned from appearances, John 7:24.

Wisdom of Gamaliel, Acts 5:30–40.

Not discerning what one reads, Acts 8:27–35.

Evaluating weak, strong, Romans 14:1–8.

Folly of intellectual pride, 1 Corinthians 3:18–20.

Discerning others, 2 Corinthians 5:16.

Eyes of heart, Ephesians 1:18–19.

Lost sensitivity, Ephesians 4:19 (NIV, NRSV).

Knowledge, insight, Philippians 1:9.

Proper understanding of the law, 1 Timothy 1:8–11.

Discerning good from evil, Hebrews 5:14.

Doctrinal discernment, 2 Peter 3:15–16.

False spirits discerned, 1 John 4:1–6; Revelation 2:2.

Mind with wisdom, Revelation 17:9.

See Comprehension, Perception, Understanding, Wisdom.

DISCIPLESHIP

Servant for life, Exodus 21:2–6.

Battle-experienced soldiers given preference, Numbers 31:27–31.

Material security versus God's will, Numbers 32:14–27.

Old Testament discipleship, Deuteronomy 5:1.

Taking care of business, Deuteronomy 20:5–9.

Eagle training young to fly, Deuteronomy 32:11.

Moses as disciple, Joshua 22:2 (LB).

Care required in loving God, Joshua 23:11.

Disqualified to build temple, 1 Chronicles 22:7–8.

Characteristics of holy life, Psalm 15:1–5.

Key to walking with God, Psalm 18:25–26.

Trusting servant, Psalm 86:2 (NRSV).

Weeping in determination, Psalm 126:5–6.

Those who seek find, Proverbs 8:17.

Old Testament discipleship, Isaiah 8:16.

Definition meaning of fasting, Isaiah 58:3–7.

Sincere search for God, Jeremiah 29:10–14.

Lax in doing the Lord's work, Jeremiah 48:10.

Someone to stand in gap, Ezekiel 22:30.

Those who obey the Lord, Joel 2:11.

Those who hunger, thirst for righteousness, Matthew 5:6.

Salt, light in the world, Matthew 5:13–16.

Counting cost, Matthew 8:19–20.

Following Jesus, Matthew 9:9.

Marks of disciple, Matthew 10:24–25; 16:25; Luke 14:23–26; John 8:31; 13:35; 14:15; 15:8.

Loving God above all, Matthew 10:37–39.

Jesus makes burden light, Matthew 11:28–30.

Jesus evaluated His mother, Matthew 12:46–50.

Mark of disciple, Matthew 16:24.

Forsaking all follow Christ, Matthew 19:28–30; Mark 10:28–31; Luke 18:28–30.

Attitude of servant, Matthew 23:8–12.

Calling Simon, Andrew, James, John, Mark 1:16–20.

Discipleship denied, Mark 5:18–19 (NIV).

Wishing easy discipleship, Mark 8:31–38.

First must be last, Mark 9:35.

Disciples promoted to apostles, Luke 6:12–15.

Family loyalty, cost of discipleship, Luke 14:26, 27.

True servant's duty, Luke 17:7–10.

Follow light, avoid darkness, John 8:12.

Death of wheat kernel, John 12:24–26.

Role of hardship, Acts 14:21, 22.

Itinerary of Paul, Barnabas, Acts 15:36.

Discipling new converts, Acts 18;23.

Confidence in difficult places, Acts 20:22–24.

First a servant, then a ministry, Romans 1:1.

Hindrance, Romans 7:23 (LB).

Devotion to one another, Romans 12:10.

Disciple's mother, Romans 16:13 (GNB).

Testimony confirmed in convert, 1 Corinthians 1:4–6.

Depth of disciple's thought, 1 Corinthians 2:6–16.

"Our first duty," 1 Corinthians 4:2 (CEV).

Discipling example, 1 Corinthians 4:15–16.

Marriage, discipleship, 1 Corinthians 7:32–35.

Servant attitude in preaching Gospel, 1 Corinthians 9:19–23.

One winner per race, all win serving God, 1 Corinthians 9:24–27.

Follow Christ's example, 1 Corinthians 11:1.

Dying daily, 1 Corinthians 15:31.

Loving those who cause grief, 2 Corinthians 2:5–11.

Marks of disciple, 2 Corinthians 6:3–13.

Sharing leader's concerns, 2 Corinthians 8:16.

Pledged to truth, 2 Corinthians 13:8.

Crucified with Christ, Galatians 2:20.

Serve one another in love, Galatians 5:13.

Live for Christ, gain in death, Philippians 1:21.

Consider others better, Philippians 2:3–4.

Forgetting past, pressing forward, Philippians 3:12–16.

Filled with knowledge of God's will, Colossians 1:9–12.

Life centered in Christ, Colossians 3:1–17.

Diligent discipleship, Colossians 3:23–24.

Properly motivated, 1 Thessalonians 1:3.

True son in the faith, 1 Timothy 1:2.

Danger of financial priorities, 1 Timothy 6:10.

True disciple description, 2 Timothy 2:1–4.

Persecution inevitable, 2 Timothy 3:12.

Servant and apostle, Titus 1:1.

Toward maturity, Hebrews 6:1.

Faithfully running race, Hebrews 12:1–2.

Strangers in the world, 1 Peter 1:1–2, 17.

Spiritual building materials, 1 Peter 2:4–5.

Becoming chosen people, 1 Peter 2:9.

Walking in Christ's steps, 1 Peter 2:21–25.

"Eager to do what is good," 1 Peter 3:13 (NRSV).

Resisting Satan, 1 Peter 5:8–9.

Taking Scriptures to heart, Revelation 1:3.

Partial holiness insufficient, Revelation 2:1–6, 13–15, 18, 20.

Holding on to faith, Revelation 2:25.

Clean in society of deceit, Revelation 3:4, 10.

See Commitment, Dedication, Followers.

DISCIPLINE

Poor leadership causes laxity, Exodus 32:25.

Purpose for moral, physical cleanliness, Leviticus 20:26.

Group participation destroying blasphemer, Leviticus 24:14–16.

Lacking spiritual discipline, Deuteronomy 12:8–9.

Care required in loving God, Joshua 23:11.

Whipping with thorns, briers, Judges 8:16.

Honey refused, 1 Samuel 14:24–26.

Undisciplined son, 1 Kings 1:5–6.

Regulation of worship music, 1 Chronicles 6:31–32.

Discipline of the Lord, judgment of men, 1 Chronicles 21:13.

Degrees of punishment, Ezra 7:26.

Less punishment than deserved, Ezra 9:13.

Laws, regulations, Nehemiah 9:13.

Wild ox must be tamed, Job 39:9–12.

Keep cool head, Psalm 6:1 (Berk.).

Evil resisted, Psalm 18:23.

Bit, bridle, Psalm 32:8–9.

Discipline does not alter God's love, Psalm 89:32–33.

Blessing of divine discipline, Psalm 94:12–13.

Discipline and clean living, Psalm 119:7 (LB).

Accepting discipline, Proverbs 3:11 (AB).

Discipline of good father, Proverbs 3:11–12.

Those who hate discipline, Proverbs 5:12–13.

Willingness to be disciplined, corrected, Proverbs 10:17.

Positive value, Proverbs 12:1.

"Wise child loves discipline," Proverbs 13:1 (NRSV).

Discipline of children, Proverbs 13:24; 19:18.

Value of punishment, Proverbs 22:15 (LB, GNB).

Folly in child's heart, Proverbs 22:15; 23:13–14; 29:15.

Eating too much honey, Proverbs 25:16.

Discipline for horse, donkey, fool, Proverbs 26:3.

Scolding, spanking children, Proverbs 29:15 (LB).

Discipline rewarded, Proverbs 29:17.

Compelled to discipline, Isaiah 1:5–6 (LB).

Sins paid back, Isaiah 65:6.

Resisted discipline, Jeremiah 5:3.

Discipline with justice, Jeremiah 30:11.

Discipline with love, Jeremiah 31:20 (LB).

Those who resist discipline, Jeremiah 32:33.

Youth benefits from discipline, Lamentations 3:27 (LB).

Rod of discipline, Ezekiel 21:13.

Torn but healed by the Lord, Hosea 6:1.

Discipline for those most loved, Amos 3:2.

Those who refuse correction, Zephaniah 3:2.

Attitude of students to teachers, Matthew 10:24.

Jesus disciplined demons, Mark 1:33–34.

Discipline for doubting angel, Luke 1:18–20.

Mother reprimanded boy Jesus, Luke 2:41–50.

Barren branches, John 15:2.

Struggle against sin, Romans 6:12–13.

Both kind, stern, Romans 11:22.

Keep eye on troublemakers, Romans 16:17 (NRSV).

Whip or smile, 1 Corinthians 4:21 (AB).

Incest not disciplined in Corinth, 1 Corinthians 5:1–2.

Satan's disciplines, 1 Corinthians 5:5.

Deal strongly, 1 Corinthians 5:12 (LB).

Expelled church member, 1 Corinthians 5:13 (AB).

Engaged couples, 1 Corinthians 7:36.

Exercising Christian liberty, 1 Corinthians 8:9.

Runner, prize, 1 Corinthians 9:24–27.

Painfulness of good correction, 2 Corinthians 7:8–9.

Law as preliminary disciplinarian, Galatians 3:23–25 (NRSV).

Helping someone who has sinned, Galatians 6:1.

Discipline of children, Ephesians 6:4.

Good discipline, stability, Colossians 2:5 (NASB).

Invalid self-abasement, Colossians 2:18 (NRSV).

Avoid antagonizing those who do wrong, 2 Thessalonians 3:14–15.

Preventing teaching of false doctrine, 1 Timothy 1:3–5.

Satan as teacher, 1 Timothy 1:18–20.

Public discipline, 1 Timothy 5:20.

Disciplined for maturity, 1 Timothy 4:13; 2 Timothy 1:7.

Disciplined good soldier, 2 Timothy 2:1–4.

Athlete's discipline, 2 Timothy 2:5.

Gently applied discipline, 2 Timothy 2:23–26 (NRSV).

Elder's disciplined family, Titus 1:6.

Discontinued discipline, Titus 3:10.

Jesus and discipline, Hebrews 5:8–9.

Correct, discipline, punish scourge, Hebrews 12:6 (AB).

Taking correction patiently, Hebrews 12:7 (CEV, NRSV).

Discipline, prayer, 1 Peter 4:7 (NRSV).

See Commitment, Growth, Maturity, Reproof, Undisciplined.

DISCONTENT

Unhappy with present leadership, Numbers 14:1–4.

People united in discontent, Joshua 9:18–19.

Beloved but barren, 1 Samuel 1:2–11.

Complaining to the Lord, Job 10:1; 23:2; Psalms 55:2; 77:3; 142:2.

Never satisfied, Proverbs 27:20; 30:15–16.

Chasing the wind, Ecclesiastes 1:17–18.

Discontent with government, Ecclesiastes 4:13–16.

Those who complain accept instruction, Isaiah 29:24.

At odds with one's Maker, Isaiah 45:9.

Discontented with living space, Isaiah 49:20.

Eunuch's plight, Isaiah 56:3–5.

Daughters taught to wail, Jeremiah 9:20.

Desire for more, Luke 3:14.

Prodigal and brother, Luke 15:11–31.
See Complain, Insincerity, Insurrection, Mob Psychology, Opposition.

DISCORD

Mourning music, Job 30:31.
Accusation without basis, Proverbs 3:30.
Hot-tempered man, Proverbs 15:18.
An honor to avoid strife, Proverbs 20:3.
Settle discord quickly, Matthew 5:25.
Mob incited against Paul, Silas, Acts 17:5–7.
Purposely causing discord, Romans 16:17.
Paul, Peter in discord, Galatians 2:11.
Teachings which cause controversy, 1 Timothy 1:3–4.
Argumentive terminology, 2 Timothy 2:14.
See Abrasive, Argument, Dispute, Unrest.

DISCOUNT

Discounting bill, Luke 16:1–8.

DISCOURAGEMENT

Disrupted communication, Exodus 6:12.
Down and out, Joshua 7:10.
Once full, now empty, Ruth 1:21.
Discouraged with righteous effort, Psalm 73:13.
"Whenever I feel low," Psalm 142:3 (CEV).
Fainthearted, Psalm 143:4–7.
Poverty's debilitating effects, Proverbs 10:15.
Discouraged by illness, Isaiah 38:9–12.
"My life has turned sour," Isaiah 38:15 (CEV).
"Pine away," Jeremiah 31:12 (Berk.).
Joy, gladness gone, Jeremiah 48:33.
No one to restore spirit, Lamentations 1:16.
Vision comes to nothing, Ezekiel 12:22–25.
Exercising hope without basis, Romans 4:18–22.
Certain victory in Christ, 1 Corinthians 15:57–58.
God encourages, 2 Corinthians 7:6 (GNB).
Dynamic of Cross, 2 Corinthians 13:4.
Do not lose heart, Ephesians 3:13 (NRSV).
See Complain, Despondency, Pessimism.

DISCOURTESY

Surly, mean, 1 Samuel 25:3.
Act of kindness misinterpreted, 2 Samuel 10:1–4.
Youth discourtesy to age, Isaiah 3:5.

Rejecting wedding invitation, Matthew 22:1–14.
Enemy who took bread, John 13:18.
See Rudeness.

DISCOVERY

Great discoveries possible, Jeremiah 33:3.
Disciples' discovery of Jesus, John 1:41–45.
Incredible discoveries awaiting, 1 Corinthians 2:9.
Understanding divine dimensions, Ephesians 3:16–19.
See Awareness, Vision.

DISCREDIT

"Do not nullify," Galatians 2:21 (NRSV).
See Demean, Disdain.

DISCRETION

"Discreet and wise," Genesis 41:39 (KJV).
Clean, unclean meat, Leviticus 11:1–47.
Discretion in physical relationships, Leviticus 18:1–30 (chapter 20).
Foolish sins, Numbers 12:11.
Search for wisdom, insight, Proverbs 2:1–6.
Lack of discretion, Proverbs 7:6–23.
Making wise choices, Proverbs 8:6–11.
Speaking what is fitting, Proverbs 10:32.
Guided by integrity, Proverbs 11:3, 6.
Judgment, understanding, Proverbs 11:12.
Conduct in king's presence, Proverbs 25:6–7.
Discretion in neighborly visits, Proverbs 25:17.
Discreet speech, thought, Ecclesiastes 5:2.
Learned discretion, Isaiah 28:26 (KJV).
Indiscreet daughters of Babylon, Isaiah 47:1–3.
Aware of false prophets, 1 John 4:1–6.
See Perception, Tact, Wisdom.

DISCRIMINATION

Man, woman as plurality, Genesis 1:26–27.
God's plan for women's rights, Genesis 3:16.
Generic name for man, woman, Genesis 5:2.
Egyptian discrimination against Hebrews, Genesis 43:32.
Same rules for all, Numbers 15:15.
Census involved men twenty or older, Numbers 26:2.

Daughters with no brother, Numbers 27:1–11.

Samson desired Philistine wife, Judges 14:1–2.

Abundant reward for kind act, 1 Samuel 30:11–18.

Daughters assist rebuilding wall, Nehemiah 3:12.

Pledge to avoid intermarriage, Nehemiah 10:30.

Wealth, prestige couldn't numb resentment, Esther 5:10–14.

Faith of Canaanite woman, Matthew 15:21–28.

Treatment given Gentiles, Matthew 20:25.

Mutual hatred Samaritans, Jews, Luke 9:51–56.

Deliverance from discrimination, Acts 10:24–28.

One in Christ, Galatians 3:28.

Slave, owner have same Master, Ephesians 6:9.

Wrong of discrimination, James 2:1–4.

Darkness of hatred, 1 John 2:9–11.

See Racism, Women's Rights, Xenophobia.

DISCUSSION

Value of discussion, Proverbs 15:22.

Moses, Elijah, Jesus, Luke 9:30–31 (GNB).

Profuse discussion in Athens, Acts 17:21.

See Debate, Reason.

DISDAIN

Veteran soldier disdained boy's abilities, 1 Samuel 17:42.

Worth less than dogs, Job 30:1.

Disdained acts of humility, Psalm 69:10–11.

Enemy's disdain, Psalm 74:10.

Sticking out tongue, Isaiah 57:4 (LB).

Scarecrow in melon patch, Jeremiah 10:5.

Object of horror, Jeremiah 49:17.

See Demean, Dislike.

DISEASE

Wasting diseases, Leviticus 26:15, 16.

Divine immunity, Exodus 15:26; Deuteronomy 7:15.

Skin infection, Leviticus 13:9–17; Deuteronomy 28:27.

Leprosy, Exodus 4:6–7; Deuteronomy 24:8; 2 Kings 5:1–14; 2 Chronicles 26:19–21.

Affliction resulting from sin, Psalm 107:17; Isaiah 3:16–17.

Sin as disease, Romans 5:12 (LB).

"He is a weakling," 2 Corinthians 10:10 (CEV).

Suggestion of social disease, Jude 6–7; Leviticus 15; 22:4–5.

See Aids, Epidemic, Health, Medicine.

DISEMBOWEL

Morbid judgment, Zephaniah 1:17.

See Brutality, Carnage, Desecrate, Torture.

DISFIGURE

Cutting off thumbs, big toes, Judges 1:6–7.

Gouging out eyes, Judges 16:18–21; 1 Samuel 11:1–2.

Mutilated corpses, 2 Samuel 4:12.

Self-inflicted wounds, 1 Kings 18:28; Mark 5:5.

Noses, ears cut off, Ezekiel 23:25.

See Torment, Torture.

DISGRACE

Causing contempt, 2 Samuel 12:14; Nehemiah 5:9; Ezekiel 36:20; Romans 2:23, 24.

Becoming byword, Job 17:6.

Scattered enemy bones, Psalm 53:5.

Causing disgrace to others, Psalm 69:6–8.

Fall of Moab, Jeremiah 48:16–39.

Disgracing the Lord, Ezekiel 6:9 (CEV).

Evil in broad daylight, 2 Peter 2:13–23.

Disgrace of getting caught, Jeremiah 2:26.

Prophet in public disgrace, Jeremiah 20:1–2.

Disgraced disobedience, Daniel 9:7 (CEV).

See Demean, Shame.

DISGUISE

Daughter-in-law's disguise, Genesis 38:13–19.

Disguising true identity, Joshua 9:3–6.

David feigns madness, 1 Samuel 21:12–14.

Seance disguise, 1 Samuel 28:8.

Queen in disguise, 1 Kings 14:1–18.

Prophet in disguise, 1 Kings 20:38.

Royal disguise, 1 Kings 22:30; 2 Chronicles 35:20–24.

Wolves as sheep, Matthew 7:15.

See Camouflage.

DISGUST

"Don't eat disgusting animals," Deuteronomy 14:3 (CEV).

Detesting display of emotion, 2 Samuel 6:14–16.

Thrown shoe, Psalm 108:9 (NRSV).

"Seen it all," Ecclesiastes 1:2 (CEV).

Disgusted with unbelief, Acts 18:5, 6.

See Anger, Disappointment.

DISHARMONY

Enemy disharmony, Psalm 55:9 (LB).

Disharmony in communities, families, Matthew 12:25.

Meetings do more harm than good, 1 Corinthians 11:17–18.

Those who dilute Gospel message, Galatians 1:6–9.

See Abrasion, Complain, Strife, Unrest.

DISHONESTY

Inaccurate weights, Leviticus 19:35–36; Proverbs 11:1; Hosea 12:7; Micah 6:11.

"Crooked deals," Psalm 101:3 (LB).

Dishonest report for personal gain, 2 Samuel 1:2–16.

Neighborhood dishonesty, Psalm 12:2.

Practicing deceit, Psalm 101:7.

Lying tongue, Proverbs 12:19–22; 13:5.

Fortune made by dishonesty, Proverbs 21:6.

Extortion, bribe, Ecclesiastes 7:7.

Stolen eggs like unjust riches, Jeremiah 17:11.

Despising those who tell truth, Amos 5:10.

Dishonest price, Amos 8:5–6.

"You crooks," Micah 2:10 (CEV).

Wealth by extortion, Habakkuk 2:6.

King Herod, Magi, Matthew 2:7–8, 13.

"You cheat people," Luke 11:42 (CEV).

"Crooked judge," Luke 18:6 (CEV).

Ananias, Sapphira, Acts 5:1–11.

Rule of integrity, Romans 12:17.

Truth, deceit, Ephesians 4:14–15.

Taking advantage of others, James 5:4–5.

See Deceit, Falseness, Perjury, Unscrupulous.

DISHWASHING

Necessary ceremony, Mark 7:1–4.

DISLIKE

Dislike among family members, Genesis 4:2–9; 27:1–46; 37:1–11; Luke 15:11- 32.

Becoming stench, 2 Samuel 10:6.

DISHWASHING

Saul's dislike for David, 1 Samuel 18:8; 16:21.

Attitude toward those disliked, Matthew 5:38–47.

Quarrelsome Christians, 1 Corinthians 1:10–17; 3:3; 2 Corinthians 12:20; Philippians 4:2.

See Abrasion, Friction, Jealousy.

DISLOYALTY

Disloyal to Moses, Exodus 32:23.

Broken disloyalty to God, Deuteronomy 32:51.

Proper disloyalty, 1 Samuel 22:16–17.

Servants disloyal to masters, 1 Samuel 25:10.

Philistine commander feared David's loyalty, 1 Samuel 9:1–11.

Disloyal government officials, 2 Kings 12:19–20.

Disloyalty in battle, Jeremiah 41:11–14.

Obeying alien laws, Ezekiel 5:7–9.

See Estrangement, Traitors.

DISOBEDIENCE

First act of disobedience, Genesis 3:1–11.

Plight of Lot's wife, Genesis 19:17, 26.

Foul odor of disobedience, Exodus 16:19–24.

Unauthorized fire for worship, Leviticus 10:1.

Penalty for national disobedience, Numbers 14:22–24.

Complaint about Moses' leadership, Numbers 16:12–14.

Disobeying instructions, Numbers 20:1–12.

Severe penalty for disobedience, Numbers 20:8–12 (AB).

Curse upon disobedience, Deuteronomy 11:26–28.

Obedience, disobedience, Deuteronomy 28:1–68.

Disobedience of faithful, 1 Samuel 12:15–20.

Disobeying command to do evil, 1 Samuel 12:16–17.

Better fall into God's hands than men's, 2 Samuel 24:10–14.

Incomplete faithfulness to God, 1 Kings 22:43.

"We have broken faith," Ezra 10:2 (NRSV).

Disobedience flaunting God's mercy, judgment, Psalm 8:32.

Judgment withheld against disobedience, Psalm 78:38.

Detestable disobedience, Isaiah 1:7 (AB).

"Trying God's patience," Isaiah 7:13 (CEV).

Spiritual vagabonds, Jeremiah 2:31.

Sorrow of disobedience, Jeremiah 3:21.

Obedience, disobedience, Jeremiah 7:22–26.

Birds compared to people, Jeremiah 8:7.

Disobedience negates God's blessing, Jeremiah 11:14; 18:17.

Judgment upon disobedient people, Jeremiah 15:1–2; 44:1–14.

Trust in man, Jeremiah 17:5, 13.

Obedience cited as lesson, Jeremiah 35:1–16.

Disobedience negates past righteousness, Ezekiel 18:24.

When to disobey parents, Ezekiel 20:18–19.

Disobedient Israel, Ezekiel 20:21.

Civil disobedience, Daniel 3:1–30.

God's love for errant child, Hosea 11:1–4.

Disobedience causes downfall, Hosea 14:1.

Three sins, even four, Amos 1:3, 6, 9, 11, 13; 2:1, 4, 6.

Denied materialistic possessions, Amos 6:11.

Disobedience to God's call, Jonah 1:3.

Rebellious disobedience, Zephaniah 3:2.

Disobedient forefathers, Zechariah 1:4–6.

Salt loses flavor, lights are hidden, Matthew 5:13–16.

Seeming disobedience of boy Jesus, Luke 2:41–51.

Wrath of God, Ephesians 5:6.

Disobeying gospel, 2 Thessalonians 1:8.

Avoid association with disobedient, 2 Thessalonians 3:14–15.

Unable to hold true to faith, 1 Timothy 1:18–20.

Disobedience by neglect, Hebrews 2:2–3.

Sure judgment upon false teaching, 2 Peter 2:1–10.

See Apostasy, Backsliding, Obedience, Rebellion.

DISORGANIZATION

Condemned to disorganization, Deuteronomy 28:20.

Too many shepherds, Jeremiah 12:10.

Warriors stumbling over each other, Jeremiah 46:12.

Forgetting necessities, Mark 8:14.

See Confusion.

DISPENSATIONAL

Specific dispensations, Daniel 7:1–14 (AB).

See Prophesy, Second Coming.

DISPLAY

Boasting of religious zeal, 2 Kings 10:16.

Palace treasures, 2 Kings 20:12–15.

Display of wealth, Esther 1:4; Isaiah 39:2.

Status symbols, Esther 5:11.

Displayed acts of charity, Matthew 6:1–4.

Overt fasting, Matthew 6:16.

Public performance, Matthew 23:5.

Ego displayed by law teachers, Mark 12:38–40.

Pomp, honor, Luke 20:46; Acts 25:35.

See Ego, Exhibitionism, Pride.

DISPOSABLE

Disposable cooking utensil, Leviticus 6:28.

DISPOSITION

Danger of bad disposition, Judges 18:25.

Good food, good disposition, Ecclesiastes 5:18–20.

Right, wrong attitudes, disposition, Ephesians 4:31–32.

Kind to everyone, 2 Timothy 2:24.

Disposition pleasing God, James 1:19–20.

See Attitude, Frame-of-Reference.

DISPUTE

Abram's attitude toward Lot, Genesis 13:8–9.

Disputes solved by clergy, Deuteronomy 17:8–9.

Futility of strife, 2 Samuel 2:27–28.

Evidence turns against accuser, Proverbs 25:8.

Settle misunderstandings quickly, Matthew 5:25.

Theological dispute in secular courtroom, Acts 18:12–17.

Daring to dispute God, Romans 9:20.

Paul, Peter in dispute, Galatians 2:11.

Teachings which cause controversy, 1 Timothy 1:3–4.

Dispute over words, 2 Timothy 2:14, 23.

Rules for teacher handling dispute, 2 Timothy 2:23–26.

See Abrasion, Argument.

DISQUALIFIED

Disqualified to build temple, 1 Chronicles 22:7–8.

DISRESPECT

Disrespect toward judge, Deuteronomy 17:12.

Elisha's bald head, 2 Kings 2:23–24.

Disrespect for age, Job 30:1; Lamentations 5:12.

Disrespect for parents, Proverbs 30:17.

Youth disrespects age, Isaiah 3:5.

Idols replace delivering God, Jeremiah 2:5–8.

Jehoiakim burned scroll dictated by Jeremiah, Jeremiah 36:1–26.

Disrespect for temple, Ezekiel 25:3 (LB).

Jesus accused of disrespect, John 18:19–24.

See Demean, Disdain, Ridicule, Scoff, Scorn, Taunt.

DISRUPTION

Disruption thwarted, 1 Samuel 7:9–11.

Blind man rebuked for calling Jesus, Matthew 20:29–34.

Disrupt those who are wrong, 2 Corinthians 11:12 (LB).

Wrong kind of authority in congregation, 3 John 9–10.

See Hindrance, Opposition.

DISSATISFACTION

Fruits of bitterness, Deuteronomy 32:32.

Meaningless accomplishment, Ecclesiastes 2:11.

Deluded heart, Isaiah 40:20.

Those never satisfied, Haggai 1:5–6.

Those who purposely caused trouble, Romans 16:17.
See Attitude, Complain, Unrest.

DISSENSION

Jealous brother, sister, Numbers 12:1–9.
Causes for dissension, Proverbs 30:21–23.
Mockery of fasting, Isaiah 58:4–5.
For Jesus or against Him, Luke 11:23.
Doctrinal debate, Acts 15:1–2.
Leadership personality clash, Acts 15:36–41.
"A veritable plague," Acts 24:5 (Berk.).
Troublemakers, Romans 16:17.
Controversial teaching, 1 Timothy 1:3–4.
See Conflict, Quarrel, Strife, Unrest.

DISSIPATION

End of dissolute life, 2 Kings 9:30–37.
Corrupt from birth, Psalm 58:3.
Irreligious entertainment, Isaiah 5:12.
From one sin to another, Jeremiah 9:3.
Continual lust for more, Ephesians 4:19.
Excessive dissipation, 1 Peter 4:3.
See Carnality, Immorality.

DISTANCE RUNNING

Running long race, Jeremiah 12:5.

DISTINCTION

Respect at city gate, Job 29:7–10.
Honor not fitting fool, Proverbs 26:1.
Role of humility in greatness, Matthew 23:12.
Respect of Cornelius for Peter, Acts 10:25–26.
See Attainment, Leadership, Respect, Success.

DISTINGUISHED

Distinguished in God's sight, Luke 1:15 (AB).

DISTORTION

Bribery distorts truth, Exodus 23:8.
Negative, positive viewpoints, Numbers 13:17–33.
Charming, deceitful speech, Proverbs 26:24–26.
Calling evil good, good evil, Isaiah 5:20.
Falsifying the law, Jeremiah 8:8.

Believing lie, Jeremiah 43:1–7.
See Apostasy, Deceit, Hypocrisy, Falsehood.

DISTRACTION

Sexual distraction, Deuteronomy 17:17.
Distracted soldiers, Deuteronomy 20:5–9.
Household distractions, Luke 10:39.
"Undistracted devotion," 1 Corinthians 7:35 (NASB, NKJV).
See Confusion, Disruption.

DISTRAUGHT

"I am pining away," Psalm 6:2 (NASB).
See Distress, Guilt.

DISTRESS

"David was miserable," 1 Chronicles 21:13 (CEV).
Inevitable distress, Job 5:7; 14:1.
Companion of night creatures, Job 30:29.
Desperate times, Psalm 60:3.
Distress, restoration, Psalm 71:20.
Overcome by trouble, Psalm 116:3.
Limited strength, Proverbs 24:10 (NASB).
Distress day, night, Ecclesiastes 2:23.
When God refuses to hear, answer, Jeremiah 11:14.
Distressed shepherds, leaders, Jeremiah 25:36.
King's distress, Daniel 6:13–18.
"Terribly upset," Acts 15:24 (CEV).
Appetite lost during distress, Acts 27:33–36.
"Many a pang," 1 Timothy 6:10 (NASB).
Distress of those unrepentant, Revelation 16:10–11.
See Agony, Persecution, Suffering.

DISTURB

Progress purposely disturbed, Ezra 4:1–5; Nehemiah 4:8.
Job's disturbing "friends," Job 2:11–13.
Disturbing the prophets, Isaiah 30:6–11; Amos 2:12.
Satanic disturbance, Zechariah 3:1–2; 1 Peter 5:8.
Blind man's disturbance, Mark 10:46–48.
Silencing disturber, Acts 13:1–13.
Unprincipled loungers, Acts 17:5 (Berk.).
Enough is enough, Acts 18:5–8.

Open door in spite of opposition, 1 Corinthians 16:5–9.

"Those who unsettle," Galatians 5:12 (NRSV).

Trouble from layman, 2 Timothy 4:14–15.

See Conflict, Irritation, Opposition.

DISUNITY

"Not united by faith," Hebrews 4:2 (NASB, NRSV).

See Discontent, Discord.

DIVERSION

Temporal excitement, 1 Corinthians 7:31 (LB).

See Entertainment.

DIVERSITY

Variety in nature, Proverbs 30:18–19.

Diverse gifts, service, Romans 12:6; 1 Corinthians 12:4–11.

No two alike, 1 Corinthians 4:7.

Diversity in all creation, 1 Corinthians 15:39–46.

God intends diversity to produce unity, Ephesians 4:11–13.

The Lord invites diversity in prayer, Ephesians 6:18.

See Variety, Original.

DIVIDE

Divided loyalties of married people, 1 Corinthians 7:32–35.

See Separation.

DIVINATION

Information by divination, Genesis 44:15.

Remunerated fortune tellers, Numbers 22:7.

Practice of sorcery, divination, Deuteronomy 18:14.

Seeking guidance for sacred object, 1 Samuel 6:2.

False oracles, prophets, Jeremiah 23:33–40.

False encouragement, Jeremiah 27:9; Zechariah 10:2.

Certain guidance, Ezekiel 13:22–23.

Seeking omen at road fork, Ezekiel 21:18–23.

Slave girl fortune teller, Acts 16:16–18.

See Fortune-Telling, Spiritism.

DIVINITY *See Christ, God, Trinity.*

DIVISION

Divided enemies, Psalm 55:9 (LB).

Satan divided against himself, Matthew 12:22–32.

Division concerning Jesus, Luke 12:51; John 7:12–43; 9:16; 10:19.

Those who would alienate from truth, Galatians 4:17.

Following personal desires, Jude 17–18.

See Abrasion, Dispute, Disruption, Factions, Jealousy.

DIVISIVE *See Factions.*

DIVORCE

Earliest conditions of divorce, Exodus 21:10–11; Ezra 10:1–16.

Divorce, remarriage, Deuteronomy 24:1–4.

Rejected young wife, Isaiah 54:6 (CEV).

Exception in divorce, Jeremiah 3:1 (LB).

Wife leaves husband, Jeremiah 3:20 (KJV).

Wife returns to husband, Hosea 2:7 (CEV).

Divorce displeases God, Malachi 2:13–16 (LB).

Quiet divorce, Matthew 1:19.

Cause, procedure, Matthew 5:31–32; 19:7–8.

Jesus on divorce, Matthew 19:3–9; Mark 10:11–12.

Conditions prior to return of Christ, Matthew 24:37–38.

Conflicting views, Mark 10:2–10 (LB).

Plain talk about divorce, Romans 7:1–3; 1 Corinthians 7:10–11.

Hurt to children, 1 Corinthians 7:14 (LB).

People without love, 2 Timothy 3:3.

See Estrangement, Love, Loyalty, Marriage.

DOCTOR *See Physician.*

DOCTRINE

Refreshing doctrine, Deuteronomy 32:2 (KJV).

To whom taught, Isaiah 28:9 (KJV).

Practice of error, Isaiah 32:6.

Shepherds lead sheep astray, Jeremiah 50:6.

Knowing old, new, Matthew 13:52 (LB).

Doctrine of Pharisees, Matthew 16:12.

Response of Jesus to critics, Matthew 21:23–27; Mark 11:29–33.

New doctrine, Mark 1:27 (KJV).

Manmade rules, Mark 7:7 (GNB).

Sabbath doctrine of Pharisees, Luke 6:1–11.

Argument over ceremonial washing, John 3:25.

Disagreement as to ministry of Jesus, John 7:42–43.

Debate over doctrinal issues, Acts 15:1–2.

Certain of erroneous belief, Acts 19:35–36.

One day more sacred than another, Romans 14:5.

Doctrinal disagreement, 1 Corinthians 1:10–17.

Message of wisdom to mature Christians, 1 Corinthians 2:6.

Following teachings of good men, 1 Corinthians 3:4.

Danger of overconfidence in theology, 1 Corinthians 10:12.

Disagreeing with doctrine, practice, 1 Corinthians 11:16.

Wrong attitudes toward Lord's Supper, 1 Corinthians 11:20–22.

We only know in part, 1 Corinthians 13:12.

Love greatest biblical truth, 1 Corinthians 13:13. (Note: Faith speaks of doctrine, hope of prophecy, but love of lifestyle.)

Deeds as good as doctrine, 2 Corinthians 9:13 (LB).

Preaching false doctrine, 2 Corinthians 11:4–15.

Pledged only to truth, 2 Corinthians 13:8.

Doctrinal weakness, Galatians 1:6–9.

False disciples would dilute gospel, Galatians 2:4–5.

Paul, Peter face-to-face, Galatians 2:11.

Bewitched Galatians, Galatians 3:1.

Persuaded by every kind of teaching, Ephesians 4:14.

Envy among those who preach Christ, Philippians 1:15.

Paul wanted followers to know truth, Colossians 2:2–4.

Dead to principles of world, Colossians 2:20–23.

Teachings cause controversy, 1 Timothy 1:3–4.

Deep truths, 1 Timothy 3:9.

Theology of demons, 1 Timothy 4:1–4.

Proud of false doctrine, 1 Timothy 6:3–5.

Godless chatter, opposing ideas, 1 Timothy 6:20–21.

Holy Spirit, sound doctrine, 2 Timothy 1:13–14.

Pointless dispute over words, 2 Timothy 2:14.

Wander from truth, 2 Timothy 2:17–18.

Avoid foolish arguments, 2 Timothy 2:23.

Rejecting sound doctrine, 2 Timothy 4:3–4.

Faith held in common, Titus 1:4.

Student of sound doctrine, Titus 1:9.

Proper teaching all ages, Titus 2:1–10.

Avoid foolish arguments about law, Titus 3:9.

Teaching, learning doctrinal truths, Hebrews 6:1–3 (LB).

Beware strange teachings, Hebrews 13:9.

Doctrine difficult for some to understand, 2 Peter 3:15–16.

Bad teaching among good people, Revelation 2:13–15.

See Denominations, Heresy, Scripture, Syncretism, Theology.

DOCUMENT

Documented opposition to rebuilding temple, Ezra 4:12–16 (See 6:1–5).

Authorization for travel, Nehemiah 2:1–8.

Written survey description, Joshua 18:8.

Documents of ownership, Jeremiah 32:1.

Persecution documents, Acts 9:1–2.

Documented credentials to visiting instructors, Acts 15:22–31.

Letters of introduction, 1 Corinthians 16:3.

See Contract, Credentials.

DOCUMENTATION

David documented ability to face Goliath, 1 Samuel 17:32–37.

Permission to rebuild temple, Ezra 5:8–17; 6:1–12.

Authorization for travel, Nehemiah 2:1–8.

Loss of family records, Nehemiah 7:64.

Willingness to admit wrongdoing, Job 6:24.

Prayer answers documented, Psalm 99:6.

Put it in writing, Daniel 6:6–9.

Jesus' ministry documented, Matthew 11:4–5.

Official documentation, Luke 1:1–4.

Knowledge of Old Testament history, Acts 7:1–60.

Old Testament documentation of gospel, Acts 13:16–41.

See Authenticity, Validity.

DOG

No dogs barking, Exodus 11:7.

Symbol of contempt, 1 Samuel 17:43; 24:14; 2 Samuel 3:8; 2 Kings 8:13; Proverbs 26:11; Isaiah 56:10.

Canine scavengers, 1 Kings 14:11; 21:19; 22:38.

Man's underrated friend, Job 30:1.

Pack of evil dogs, Psalm 22:16 (LB).

Prowling at night, Psalm 59:6, 14.

Do not grasp ears, Proverbs 26:17.

Live dogs, dead lions, Ecclesiastes 9:4.

Children's bread given to dogs, Matthew 15:26.

Medicinal tongues, Luke 16:21.

Human "dogs," Philippians 3:2; Revelation 22:15.

See Animals.

DOGMATIC

Ineptness of king's viewpoint, 1 Kings 12:1–15.

Fool airs own opinion, Proverbs 18:2.

Pagans certain of erroneous belief, Acts 19:35, 36.

See Headstrong, Opinion, Prejudice.

DOLPHIN

Dolphin, porpoise, Exodus 35:23 (AB).

DOME

Dome above earth, Genesis 1:6 (NRSV).

Creator's design, Genesis 1:7–8 (GNB).

DOMESTICATE

Wild ox, Job 39:9–12.

Wild animals domesticated, Isaiah 11:6–7.

See Tame.

DOMINATION

Hurt by domination, Ecclesiastes 8:9.

See Influence.

DONATION

Jewelry given to God, Exodus 35:22.

Ample donations, Exodus 36:5.

Varied gifts, Numbers 7:3.

Personal treasures, 1 Chronicles 29:3, 4.

Freely receive, freely give, Matthew 10:8.

More blessed to give, Acts 20:35.

Some pay, others receive, 2 Corinthians 11:7–8.

See Contribution, Stewardship.

DONKEY

Role of donkey in Isaac's near sacrifice, Genesis 22:3.

Talking donkey, Numbers 22:26–34.

Incompatible ox, donkey, Deuteronomy 22:10.

Riding white donkeys, Judges 5:10.

Thirty in a row, Judges 10:3.

Lost donkeys, 1 Samuel 9:3–4.

Divine privilege, Matthew 21:1–2.

See Animals, Horse.

DONOR *See Benevolence, Stewardship, Tithe.*

DOOM

As good as dead, Numbers 17:12–13.

Pagan altar forecast, 1 Kings 12:32—13:1–3.

"I am doomed," Isaiah 6:5 (CEV).

"Eternal doom," John 3:18 (LB).

See Condemnation, Destiny.

DOOR

Door secured, Genesis 19:10.

Doorway reminders, Deuteronomy 11:20–21.

Golden door, 1 Kings 7:50.

Out and away, 2 Kings 9:3.

Repaired temple doors, 2 Chronicles 29:3.

Ancient doors, Psalm 24:7–9.

Door of hope, Hosea 2:15.

Christ the door, John 10:7–9 (KJV).

Door of opportunity, 1 Corinthians 16:8–9.

See Gate.

DOUBT

Doubt overcome by faith, Genesis 15:1–6.
Disobedience, doubt, Genesis 16:1–16.
God's guidance questioned, Exodus 5:22–23.
Doubting divine authority, Exodus 6:12.
Fear, doubt, Deuteronomy 1:21 (LB).
Doubting in difficult times, Judges 6:11–13.
Questioning God's ways, Job 9:24 (AB); 10:3 (NIV); 13:3 (AB).
Doubters proved wrong, Psalm 4:6 (LB).
Doubting antidote, Psalm 46:10.
Effort to instill doubt, Isaiah 36:1–20.
Divine integrity questioned, Jeremiah 20:7–8.
Doubt hinders spiritual sight, Matthew 6:23.
Doubt rebuked, Matthew 14:31.
Doubt faces evidence, Matthew 28:17 (GNB).
Deliverance from doubt, Mark 9:23–24 (GNB).
Doubters rebuked, Mark 16:14.
Angelic announcements doubted, Luke 1:18, 34.
Doubt augmented by hearing truth, John 8:45–47.
Continuing to doubt sure evidence, John 12:37–38.
No shadow of doubt, Acts 2:36 (Berk.).
Doubt does not alter truth, Romans 3:3.
Beyond doubt, Romans 8:38 (AB).
"Sheer absurdity," 1 Corinthians 1:18 (AB).
Implications of doubting resurrection, 1 Corinthians 15:12–19.
Message death smell, 2 Corinthians 2:16.
Sinful, unbelieving hearts, Hebrews 3:12.
Faith sure antidote for doubt, Hebrews 11:1–3.
Lost stability, 2 Peter 3:17 (NRSV).
Helping those who doubt, Jude 22–23.
See Carnality, Unbelief, Hedonism.

DOVE

Messenger dove, Genesis 8:8–11.
Sacrificial doves, Genesis 15:9.
Doves used in purification, Leviticus 12:6, 8; 14:22; Numbers 6:10.
Mourning dove, Isaiah 38:14.
Slave girls moan like doves, Nahum 2:7.
Doves as symbols, Matthew 3:16; Luke 3:22; John 1:32.
See Birds.

DOWNCAST

God consoles the downcast, 2 Corinthians 7:6 (NRSV).

DOWNHEARTED

Joy, gladness gone, Jeremiah 48:33.

DOWN PAYMENT

Function of Holy Spirit, Ephesians 1:14 (AB).

DOWRY

Dowry paid in service, Genesis 29:18.
Dowry paid by Hosea, Hosea 3:2.

DRAFT DODGER

Those who sit at home, Numbers 32:6.
See AWOL, Soldier.

DRAGON

Depiction of dragon, Job 41:19–21.

DRAMA

Joseph, brothers in Egypt, Genesis 42–45.
Crossing Red Sea, Exodus 14:21–28.
Samson's finale, Judges 16:23–30.
David, Goliath, 1 Samuel 17:1–51.
Crucifixion drama, Matthew 27:15–54.
Midnight prayer, Acts 16:16–34.
Dramatic storm, shipwreck, Acts 27:13–44.
Silence in heaven, Revelation 8:1.
Sounding forth cry of doom, Revelation 8:13.
See Excitement, Emotion, Theater.

DREAD

Unnecessary fear, 1 Kings 1:50–53.
Needless worry, Matthew 6:25–27.
See Fear, Panic, Worry.

DREAMS

Thick, dreadful darkness, Genesis 15:12.
Seeking God's will, Genesis 28:11–22.

Revealing future, Genesis 37:5–10.

Divine utilization of visions, dreams, Numbers 12:4–6.

Dreams as vehicles of evil, Deuteronomy 13:1–5; Zechariah 10:2.

Perilous bread loaf, Judges 7:13.

Symbol of unreality, Job 20:8.

Warning in dreams, Job 33:14–17.

Cause of dreams, Ecclesiastes 5:3.

Dreaming of food, awakening hungry, Isaiah 29:8.

Prophetic dreams of delusion, Jeremiah 23:25–29.

Pleasant sleep, Jeremiah 31:26.

Interpreting visions, dreams, Daniel 1:17 (Chapters 2, 3, 4).

Dreamless sleep, Micah 3:6.

Instructional dream, Matthew 1:20–21.

Macedonian vision, Acts 16:9–10.

Assured in a vision, Acts 18:9–11.

See Nightmare, Vision.

DRINK

Bad drinking water, 2 Kings 2:19–22 (GNB).

See Thirst.

DRONE

Those who do nothing, Isaiah 30:7.

See Lazy.

DROUGHT

Famine conditions, Genesis 12:10; 26:1; Ruth 1:1; 2 Kings 4:38; Jeremiah 14:16; Nehemiah 5:3.

Rain falling as dust, Deuteronomy 28:24.

Cause of drought, 2 Samuel 21:1–9.

No dew, rain, 1 Kings 17:1.

Drought, abundance, Psalm 107:33–35.

Land mourns, wastes away, Isaiah 33:9.

Water provided, Isaiah 41:17–19 (CEV).

Long-term drought, Jeremiah 12:4.

Land made barren, Jeremiah 14:3–6.

Parching east wind, Hosea 13:15.

Drought broken, Joel 2:22–24.

Scattered showers during growing season, Amos 4:7–8.

See Arid.

DROWNING

Danger of deep water, Psalm 69:1–3.

DRUGS

Jesus refused drugs, Matthew 27:34 (CEV); Mark 15:23 (LB).

DRUNKENNESS

Godly woman thought drunk, 1 Samuel 1:9–17.

Royal drinking party, 1 Kings 20:16.

Unlimited consumption, Esther 1:8.

"Drinking spree," Esther 3:15 (LB).

Drunkard's song, Psalm 69:12 (Berk.).

Led astray by alcohol, Proverbs 20:1.

Bloodshot eyes, Proverbs 23:29–31.

Drunken spree, Isaiah 5:11; Romans 13:13.

Sick drunk, Isaiah 28:1–8; Jeremiah 25:27.

"Can't walk straight," Isaiah 51:17 (CEV).

Pseudo drunkenness, Isaiah 29:9–10.

Drunken watchmen, Isaiah 56:10–12.

Drunkenness fostered by the Lord, Jeremiah 13:12–14.

Dead drunk, Jeremiah 51:57.

"Wine flowed freely," Daniel 5:1 (LB).

Drunkard's foolishness, Hosea 7:5 (LB).

Sobering drunkard, Joel 1:5 (CEV).

Too much wine, Nahum 1:10.

Drunken nudity, Habakkuk 2:15.

Drunk wedding guests, John 2:10 (NRSV).

Morning sobriety, Acts 2:15 (AB).

Spiritual drunken stupor, 1 Corinthians 15:34 (AB).

See Alcohol, Delirium Tremens, Liquor, Wine.

DULL *See Imperceptive.*

DUMBFOUNDED *See Awe, Serendipity, Surprise.*

DUNG

Dung used for baking, Ezekiel 4:15.

DUPLICITY

Feigned madness, 1 Samuel 21:13.

Pretense of mourning, 2 Samuel 14:2.

Alleged religious loyalty, 2 Kings 10:18–19.

Friends, brothers not trusted, Jeremiah 9:4–8.
King Herod, Magi, Matthew 2:7–8, 13.
Satan's use of Scripture, Matthew 4:1–11.
Pretended piety, Luke 20:20–23.
Camouflaged objective, Acts 23:15.
See Hypocrisy, Sham.

DURABILITY

Durable feet, clothing, Deuteronomy 8:4.
See Dedication, Determination, Endurance, Energy, Tenacity, Virility.

DURESS

Desperate times, Psalm 60:3.
Jeremiah's anguish, Jeremiah 4:19.
No food during times of duress, Acts 27:33–36.
See Anxiety, Conscience, Guilt, Stress.

DUTY

Collecting daily manna, Exodus 16:4.
Carelessness in duty, 1 Samuel 26:7–16.
Half stand guard, other half work, Nehemiah 4:21.
Daily vows, Psalm 61:8.
Entrusted with secret things of God, 1 Corinthians 4:1–2.
Aim for perfection, 2 Corinthians 13:11.
See Assignment, Responsibility.

DYNAMIC

Muted dynamics, 2 Corinthians 10:1.
See Influence, Leadership, Personality.

DYSENTERY

Violent illness, 2 Chronicles 21:12–15.
Severe stomach pains, Job 20:14.
Healing for fever, dysentery, Acts 28:8.

E

EAGERNESS

David's eagerness to confront Goliath, 1 Samuel 17:48.
Full of words, about to burst, Job 32:17–22.
Eager horses straining for action, Zechariah 6:7.
Young man eager for truth, Mark 10:17.
Early to temple, Luke 21:38.
Eager for ministry, John 4:40.
Disciple who outran Peter, John 20:4.
Eagerness to be baptized, Acts 8:36–37.
Open, receptive, Acts 10:33; 17:19.
See Enthusiasm, Zeal.

EAGLE

Symbolic strong wings, Exodus 19:4.
Forbidden food, Leviticus 11:13; Deuteronomy 14:12.
Swift flight, 2 Samuel 1:23; Proverbs 23:5.
Sky hunter, Job 9:26.
Longevity, Psalm 103:5.
Renewed strength, Isaiah 40:30–31.
See Birds.

EAR

Abandoned earrings, Genesis 35:4.
Pierced ear, Exodus 21:5–6.

Act of consecration, Exodus 29:20; Leviticus 8:23.
Ears tingle, 1 Samuel 3:11 (NRSV).
See Deafness, Earrings, Hearing, Noise.

EARNESTNESS *See Commitment, Determination, Serious, Zeal.*

EARNINGS

Prostitute's unacceptable offering, Deuteronomy 23:18.
Debtor's earning power, Deuteronomy 24:6.
Giving fee rather than receiving, Ezekiel 16:32–34.
No wages, no business, Zechariah 8:10.
Woman who helped support Jesus, Luke 8:3.
Wages an obligation, not gift, Romans 4:4.
See Honorarium, Salary, Stipend, Wages.

EARRINGS

Earrings, foreign gods, Genesis 35:4.
From earrings to idol, Exodus 32:1–4.
Earrings offered to the Lord, Exodus 35:22; Numbers 31:50.

Large collection of earrings, Judges 8:22–27.

Wise man's rebuke likened to earring, Proverbs 25:12.

Decked with jewels, Hosea 2:13 (AB).
See Jewelry.

EARTH

Primordial planet, Genesis 1:2–7.

As long as earth endures, Genesis 8:22.

Earth divided into continents, Genesis 10:25.

Sacred responsibilities for earth itself, Leviticus 25:1–7.

Mineral wealth, Deuteronomy 8:9.

Ancient concept of foundations, 1 Samuel 2:8; Job 9:6.

Dust of humility, Nehemiah 9:1.

Earth as object in space, Job 26:7.

Earth's wealth belongs to God, Psalms 24:1; 50:9–12; 95:4–5.

Passing humanity, enduring earth, Ecclesiastes 1:4.

Earth's shape known since antiquity, Isaiah 40:22.

Creator cares for His creation, Isaiah 42:5–7.

Design, purpose, Isaiah 45:18.

Earth's destruction, Isaiah 51:6; 2 Peter 3:10–13; Revelation 20:11; 21:1.

Gold, silver belong to God, Haggai 2:8.
See Creation, Ecology, Nature, Natural Resources.

EARTHQUAKE

Trembling mountain, Exodus 19:17–18.

Judgment by earthquake, Numbers 16:28–34.

Mountains shaken, Judges 5:5; 1 Kings 19:11–12.

Army in panic, 1 Samuel 14:15.

Shaken earth, 2 Samuel 22:8; Haggai 2:21.

Earthquake description, Isaiah 24:19–20.

Between cross, empty tomb, Matthew 27:51; 28:2.

Spiritual earthquake, Acts 4:31.

Prison doors opened, Acts 16:25–31.

Great earthquake, Revelation 6:10–17.

Greatest earthquake, Revelation 16:18–20.
See Catastrophe, Flood, Storm.

EASE

At ease in time of crisis, Numbers 32:6.

Selfish ease, Nehemiah 9:35.

Faith without works, James 2:14; 4:17.
See Indifference, Luxury.

EAST

East of Eden, Genesis 3:24 (GNB).
See Compass.

EASTER

Prophecy of Christ riding on donkey, Zechariah 9:9.

Judas and thirty pieces of silver, Zechariah 11:12–13.

Prophecy of the cross, Zechariah 12:10–11.

First recorded Easter observance, Acts 12:3.

Easter experienced personally, Ephesians 1:15–21.
See Cross, Crucifixion, Passover, Resurrection.

EATING

Overeating, Numbers 11:18–20 (LB).
See Banquet, Feast, Food, Gluttony, Gourmet.

ECLECTIC

Proper seeking for truth, Proverbs 23:23.

Receptive to truth, Acts 10:33; 13:42; 17:11.

Improper research, 1 Corinthians 1:20.

Comparing spiritual with spiritual, 1 Corinthians 2:13 (NKJV).

Unwise comparison, 2 Corinthians 10:12.
See Comparison, Intellectual, Secular.

ECLIPSE

Daytime darkness, Job 5:14; Amos 8:9.

One cannot look at sun, Job 37:21.

Sun, moon darkened, Isaiah 13:10; Joel 2:10; Matthew 24:29.

Covered heavens, Ezekiel 32:7.
See Astronomy, Moon, Sun.

ECOLOGY

Human role, Genesis 1:29; Deuteronomy 20:19–20; Psalm 115:16.

Scarce land, Genesis 13:5–7.

Induced pollution, Exodus 7:19–21.

Water purified, Exodus 15:25; 2 Kings 2:19–22.

Avoid pollution, Numbers 35:33–36.

Protection of birds, Deuteronomy 22:6.

Chemicals make land unproductive, Deuteronomy 29:23.

Forest clearance, Joshua 17:15–18.

Ruined land, 2 Kings 3:19.

Good to the land, Job 31:38 (CEV).

Changing land, human wickedness, Psalm 107:33–35.

Water pollution, Proverbs 25:26.

Rotting forest, fields, Isaiah 10:18 (CEV).

Foul-smelling canals, Isaiah 19:6.

People defile earth, Isaiah 24:5.

Altered wetlands, Isaiah 35:7 (CEV).

Dying earth, Isaiah 51:6.

New heaven, new earth, Isaiah 65:17.

Fertile land defiled, Jeremiah 2:7; 16:18.

Parched land, wildlife gone, Jeremiah 12:4.

Barren island, Ezekiel 26:14.

Dead Sea water purified, Ezekiel 47:8 (LB).

Merchants desecrate land, Nahum 3:16.

Sacred trash cans, Zechariah 14:20 (LB).

Earth subjected to Christ, Hebrews 2:7–8.

Spark ignites forest fire, James 3:5.

Harmless locusts, Revelation 9:3–4.

See Conservation, Earth, Erosion, Nature, Pollution, Wetlands.

ECONOMICS

Make ends meet, Philippians 4:11 (Berk.).

ECONOMY

Good time and bad, Genesis 41:35, 36; Ecclesiastes 7:14.

Failure of money, Genesis 47:15 (KJV).

Mortgaging to buy food, Nehemiah 5:3–5.

First things first, Proverbs 24:27.

Woman with economic skills, Proverbs 31:10–31.

God's great bargain, Isaiah 55:1, 2.

No wages, no opportunities, Zechariah 8:10.

Treasures on earth or in heaven, Matthew 6:19–21.

Human equations and divine power, John 6:1–13.

Spiritual economics, Acts 3:6.

See Business, Finances, Money, Prosperity.

ECSTASY

Shouting, weeping, Ezra 3:10–13.

Visions of God, Ezekiel 1:1.

Drunk on wine, filled with Spirit, Ephesians 5:18.

See Emotion, Euphoric, Happiness, Joy, Passion.

EDIBLE

Edible scroll, Ezekiel 3:1–3 (LB).

See Food.

EDIFICATION

Mutual spiritual growth, Romans 14:19; 15:2; 1 Corinthians 14:3, 26.

Knowledge versus love, 1 Corinthians 8:1.

Strengthening others, 2 Corinthians 12:19.

Body of Christ built up, Ephesians 4:10–13.

See Maturity, Worship.

EDIFICE

Humble sanctuary, 2 Samuel 7:1–13.

EDUCATION

Forbidden knowledge, Genesis 2:16–17.

Learning about creation, Deuteronomy 4:32.

Wisdom exceeds material gain, 1 Kings 3:5–15; 4:29–34.

Nationwide education for all, 2 Chronicles 17:7–9.

Teaching with parables, Psalm 78:1–8.

Stated learning objectives, Proverbs 1:1–6.

Spiritual education, Proverbs 15:33 (GNB).

Wisdom, understanding greater than money, Proverbs 16:16.

Squandered education opportunities, Proverbs 17:16 (CEV, LB).

Properly training child, Proverbs 22:6.

Knowledge gives strength, Proverbs 24:5–6.

Finding wisdom like eating honey, Proverbs 24:13–14.

Vast knowledge, Ecclesiastes 1:16 (AB).

Education causing grief, Ecclesiastes 1:18.

Knowledge better than wealth, Ecclesiastes 7:12.

Wearisome study, Ecclesiastes 12:12.

Ultimate knowledge, Ecclesiastes 12:13.

Sealed scroll, Isaiah 29:11–12.

EDIBLE SCROLL

HIGH FIBER DIET

Greatest treasure, Isaiah 33:6.

Misled by incorrect knowledge, Isaiah 47:10.

Eager to learn, Isaiah 50:4 (CEV).

Three-year training program, Daniel 1:3–5.

Worldwide education, Habakkuk 2:14.

Teaching truth, Malachi 2:6.

Attitude of students to teachers, Matthew 10:24.

Perception of adults compared to children, Matthew 11:25.

Hearing, not understanding, Matthew 13:14–15.

Old, new perspective, Matthew 13:52 (LB).

Student, teacher, Luke 6:40.

Mouth speaks what heart contains, Luke 6:43–45.

Truth understood by children, Luke 10:21.

Knowledge beyond classroom, John 7:14–16.

Holy Spirit as teacher, John 14:26.

Simple men confound scholars, Acts 4:13.

Egyptian wisdom, Acts 7:22.

Interest of intelligent man, Acts 13:6–7.

Intellectual pride, Acts 17:16–34.

Erudite man, Acts 22:3.

Educated, ignorant, Romans 1:14 (GNB).

Wisdom, foolishness, 1 Corinthians 1:18–21.

Message of wisdom to mature Christians, 1 Corinthians 2:6.

Folly of intellectual pride, 1 Corinthians 3:18–20; 8:1–3.

Faith is ultimate intelligence, 1 Corinthians 3:18–23.

"Knowledge causes arrogance," 1 Corinthians 8:1 (NASB).

Information without eloquence, 2 Corinthians 11:6.

"Learned to have faith," Galatians 3:25 (CEV).

Spirit of wisdom, revelation, Ephesians 1:17.

Learn what pleases the Lord, Ephesians 5:10.

Home school, Ephesians 6:4.

Both knowledge, insight, Philippians 1:9.

Godless chatter, false knowledge, 1 Timothy 6:20–21.

Unable to acknowledge truth, 2 Timothy 3:7.

Sure antidote for doubt, Hebrews 11:1–3.

Lacking wisdom, ask God, James 1:5–6.

See Instruction, Students, Learning, School, Teacher, Teaching.

EFFEMINATE

Men become like women, Isaiah 19:16; Jeremiah 50:37; 51:30.

Women soldiers, Nahum 3:13.

See Deviate.

EFFORT

Effort required in loving God, Joshua 23:11.

"Grasping for the wind," Ecclesiastes 2:17 (NKJV).

Sow wheat, reap thorns, Jeremiah 12:13.

Be not slothful, Romans 12:11 (KJV).

Lifeblood extended, Philippians 2:17 (LB).

Effort for the Lord, Colossians 3:23–24.

See Initiative, Motivation, Performance.

EGO

God only rightful ego display, Genesis 1:1; Isaiah 42:8.

"Make name for ourselves," Genesis 11:4 (AB).

Captured city named after captor, Numbers 32:42.

Fame, honor decreed by God, Deuteronomy 26:19.

Appealing to king's ego, Ezra 4:14.

Evaluating faithfulness, Nehemiah 5:19.

Ego flaunts wealth, prestige, Esther 5:11.

Contempt for unfortunate, Job 12:5.

Glory belongs only to the Lord, Psalm 115:1.

Sluggard's ego, Proverbs 26:16.

Proud of ability, Isaiah 5:21.

Artist only mortal, Isaiah 44:11.

Pharaoh a loud noise, Jeremiah 46:17.

Self-deification of self, Ezekiel 16:23–25.

Ego versus faith, Daniel 3:8–20.

Religion of sham, Matthew 23:5–7.

Asking for prestige, not earning it, Mark 10:11–40.

Ego displayed by teachers of law, Mark 12:38–40.

"Claiming to be somebody," Acts 5:36.

Sorcerer's ego, Acts 8:9–10.

Price paid for flagrant ego, Acts 12:19–23.

Falsely evaluating one's self, 2 Corinthians 10:12.

Exalting self, 2 Corinthians 11:17.

Egotistical preaching, Philippians 1:15 (LB).

Paul's wise use names of followers, Colossians 4:7–17.

One worthy of praise, Revelation 5:13–14.

Evil queen refused to admit sin, Revelation 18:7–8.

See Conceit, Humility, Pride, Self-image, Status, Vanity.

ELDER

Civic leaders, Exodus 3:16; 4:29; 19:7; Joshua 23:2.

Seventy elders, Exodus 24:1.

Initial appointment of elders, Deuteronomy 1:9–15.

Matrimonial concern of elders, Judges 21:16.

Town council, Ruth 4:2.

Elders, nobles, 1 Kings 21:8.

Wife of elder, Proverbs 31:23.

Elders' traditions, Matthew 15:2.

Chief priests, elders, Matthew 21:23; Mark 15:1.

Associates of high priest, Matthew 26:57.

Gifts to elders, Acts 11:30.

Elders consulted, Acts 15:2.

Chosen for church duty, Acts 14:23; 16:4; 20:28–32.

Honored good work, 1 Timothy 5:17–19.

High standard, Titus 1:5–9; 1 Peter 5:1–5.

Healing ministry, James 5:14–15.

See Clergy, Leadership.

ELECTION

Selection of leader, Numbers 27:16.

Elect of the Lord, Deuteronomy 7:6; John 15:16; Ephesians 1:4; 1 Peter 1:2.

Divinely elected king, Deuteronomy 33:5 (LB).

Selection by lot, Nehemiah 11:1.

Choosing best leader, Deuteronomy 17:14–15; Hosea 8:4.

Trees seek a king, Judges 9:7–15.

Put out of office, Isaiah 22:19.

See Government, Leadership, Politics.

ELEMENTARY

Repetition without progress, Hebrews 6:1–3 (LB).

ELEPHANT

Animal thought to be elephant, Job 40:15–24 (Note AB).

ELEVENTH HOUR

Battle won at gate, Isaiah 28:6.

ELIXIR

Restored youth, Ruth 4:15 (LB).

ELOQUENCE

Moses lacked eloquence, Exodus 4:10.

Eloquent threats, 2 Kings 18:13–37; 19:5–7.

The Lord's voice—powerful, majestic, Psalm 29:4.

Smooth tongue, warlike heart, Psalm 55:21.

Eloquent thoughts, Psalm 92:5.

Depth, freshness, Proverbs 18:4 (GNB).

Words aptly spoken, Proverbs 25:11.

"Eloquent orator," Isaiah 3:3 (KJV).

Eloquent description of noble person, Isaiah 32:8.

Mouth like sharpened sword, Isaiah 49:2.

Instructed tongue, Isaiah 50:4.

Endowed eloquence, Jeremiah 1:6–10.

Wood destroyed by fire, Jeremiah 5:14.

Guided speech in difficult times, Matthew 10:19–20.

Gracious speech, Luke 4:22.

Eloquence of Jesus, Luke 19:48; John 7:46.

"Unfettered eloquence," Acts 4:13 (AB).

Spiritual truth in human terms, Romans 6:19.

Unnecessary eloquence, 1 Corinthians 2:1.

Eloquence avoided, 1 Corinthians 2:4 (AB).

Love the most eloquent of all, 1 Corinthians 13:1–13.

Eloquent preaching, 1 Corinthians 14:6–12.

Lacking eloquence, 2 Corinthians 10:10.

Information without eloquence, 2 Corinthians 11:6.

Fine-sounding arguments, Colossians 2:4.

Communication with prayer support, Colossians 4:3–4.

Eloquence in witness, 1 Thessalonians 1:8.

Eloquent accolades of faithfulness, Hebrews 11:32–40.

Bible's eloquent conclusion, Revelation 22:1–21.

See Communications, Preaching, Speech.

EMASCULATION See Eunuch.

EMBALMING

Egyptian embalming, Genesis 50:1–3, 26.

Spices, perfumes, Mark 16:1 (LB); John 19:40; 2 Chronicles 16:14.

See Burial, Corpse, Death.

EMBARRASSMENT

Fear of being killed by woman, Judges 9:54.

Embarrassing sons, 1 Samuel 8:1–3.

Simpleton's taunt, Psalm 39:8 (Berk.).

God embarrassed, Malachi 1:7 (CEV).

Joseph avoided embarrassing Mary, Matthew 1:19–25 (CEV).

Made to look foolish, Matthew 22:34 (CEV).

Embarrassed disciples, Mark 9:34–35.

Jesus embarrassed opponents, Luke 13:10–17.

Coming to Jesus at night, John 3:1–2.

Paul prayed not to be ashamed, Philippians 1:20.

Gazingstock, Hebrews 10:33 (AB).

See Disgrace, Humiliation, Shy.

EMBRACE

"Hug and kiss," 2 Samuel 15:5 (CEV).

Father, prodigal, Luke 15:20.

EMBROIDERY

Embroidered sash, Exodus 28:39.

Tabernacle finery, Exodus 35:35.

Skilled craftsman, Exodus 38:23.

Specialized products, Ezekiel 27:16.

EMERGENCY

"Hurry up," Genesis 19:14 (GNB).
Reaction to emergency, Genesis 19:14–17.
Neighbor's assistance, Proverbs 27:10.
See Crisis.

EMINENT

"Most eminent apostles," 2 Corinthians 12:11 (NASB, NRSV).

EMOTION

Hagar's love for Ishmael, Genesis 21:14–16.
Death of wife, Genesis 23:1–2 (LB).
Isaac meeting Rebekah, Genesis 24:62–67.
Bitter emotion, Genesis 27:34; Joshua 7:6.
Fears of Joseph, Genesis 42:24; 43:29–30.
Estranged brothers, Genesis 45:1–15.
Joseph's eagerness to meet father, Genesis 46:29.
Stirred hearts, Exodus 35:21 (NKJV).
Clever wiles of Samson's wife, Judges 14:11–19.
Joshua's lament, Joshua 7:6.
Citywide outcry, 1 Samuel 4:13–14.
"Terribly upset," 1 Samuel 8:6 (LB).
Profuse tears of gratitude, 1 Samuel 20:41.
Emotional confession, 1 Samuel 24:16–17.
Emotionally exhausted, 1 Samuel 30:1–4.
Loss of friends, 2 Samuel 1:11–12, 26; 3:33–37; 18:19–33.
Returning ark to Jerusalem, 2 Samuel 6:5.
Weeping, mourning, 2 Samuel 19:1–4.
Divine grief, 1 Chronicles 21:14–15.
Emotional joy building temple, Ezra 3:10–13.
Physical act of disdain, Ezra 9:3.
Tears of contrition, Ezra 10:1.
Emotional response to Scriptures, Nehemiah 8:9.
Emotion for others not remembered, Job 30:25.
Emotional worship, Job 37:1.
Creation of emotions, Job 38:36.
Broken heart, spirit, Psalm 34:18.
Sweetness of God's promises, Psalm 119:103.
Songs of Zion silenced, Psalm 137:1–4.
Uplifting emotions, Proverbs 4:23.
Hotheaded fool, Proverbs 14:16–17.

Zeal without knowledge, Proverbs 19:2; Romans 10:1–2.
Beware hot-tempered man, Proverbs 22:24–25.
Lacking self-control, Proverbs 25:28.
Angry man causes dissension, Proverbs 29:22.
Weeping, laughter, Ecclesiastes 3:4.
Showing restraint, Ecclesiastes 3:5.
Death silences emotion, Ecclesiastes 9:5–6.
Unquenched love, Song of Songs 8:7.
Moon, sun emote, Isaiah 24:23.
Drunk but not from wine, Isaiah 29:9; 51:21.
Make loud noises, Jeremiah 3:23 (CEV).
Anguish of guilt, Jeremiah 4:18–19.
"Fountain of tears," Jeremiah 9:1.
Skilled in wailing, Jeremiah 9:17–20.
Jeremiah tried to suppress feelings, Jeremiah 20:9.
Power of holy words, Jeremiah 23:9.
Weeping, wailing as judgment comes, Jeremiah 25:34.
Tears of joy, Jeremiah 31:9.
Joy, gladness gone, Jeremiah 48:33.
Tears of repentance, Jeremiah 50:4.
No one to comfort, Lamentations 1:16.
Heated spirit, Ezekiel 3:14 (KJV).
Ezekiel overwhelmed, Ezekiel 3:15.
Knocking knees of frightened king, Daniel 5:6.
Emotional overload, Daniel 8:27.
Daniel overwhelmed by vision, Daniel 10:7–8.
Preaching with compassion, Joel 2:17.
Weeping wailing, Micah 1:8.
Noisy crying, mourning, Zephaniah 1:10–11 (CEV).
Celebrate, shout, Zephaniah 3:14 (CEV).
Concern becomes anger, Zechariah 8:2 (LB).
Loss of children under Herod, Matthew 2:18.
Weeping, misunderstanding, Matthew 17:22–23.
Very upset, Matthew 26:22 (GNB).
Crushing sorrow, Matthew 26:38 (GNB).
Evil emotions, Matthew 26:65.
Mixed emotions, Matthew 28:8.
Gethsemane emotion, Mark 14:33.

Crowd stirred up against Jesus, Mark 15:11–15; 11:8–10.

Frightened shepherds, Luke 2:8–10.

Mary's emotions compared to shepherds', Luke 2:19, 20.

Effect of music upon emotions, Luke 7:31–32.

Joy of Jesus, Luke 10:21.

Speaking quietly, Luke 10:23 (LB).

Concern of Jesus for Jerusalem, Luke 13:34; 19:41–44.

Heaven's emotion when sinner repents, Luke 15:3–10.

Clouded reality, Luke 24:41.

Sustaining joy of disciples, Luke 24:50–53.

Emotion from within, John 7:38–39.

Tears of Jesus, John 11:35.

Too excited to open door, Acts 12:12–16.

Emotional teaching, Acts 20:31 (GNB).

Sorrow of parting, Acts 20:36–38.

Empathy in sorrow, Acts 21:13.

"Too deep for words," Romans 8:26 (NASB, NRSV).

Deep spiritual concern, Romans 9:1 (LB).

Keep your spiritual fervor, Romans 12:11.

Characteristic of God, 2 Corinthians 1:3–4.

Moved to tears, 2 Corinthians 2:4 (GNB).

Running over with joy, 2 Corinthians 7:4 (GNB).

Spiritual sorrow, 2 Corinthians 7:10–11.

Fervent prayer, 2 Corinthians 9:14 (LB).

Anger without sin, Ephesians 4:26.

Drunk on wine, filled with Spirit, Ephesians 5:18.

Affection Jesus gives, Philippians 1:8.

Paul's tears, Philippians 3:18.

Rejoice in the Lord, Philippians 4:4.

Convicting power of Holy Spirit, 1 Thessalonians 1:4–5.

Remembering tears, anticipating joy, 2 Timothy 1:3–4.

Cries of Jesus to His Father, Hebrews 5:7.

Call to repentant emotions, James 4:9.

Happy singing, James 5:13.

Lamenting lost wealth, Revelation 18:11–19.

See Excitement, Fear, Joy, Mob Psychology, Sorrow.

EMPATHY

Remembering from experience, Exodus 23:9.

Shared misery, Job 2:13.

Male pangs as of childbirth, Jeremiah 30:6.

Faith of friends, a man's healing, Mark 2:1–5.

Empathy for others, 2 Corinthians 1:3–4; 11:29 (GNB).

Sharing another's difficulty, Philippians 4:14.

Paul's concern for followers, Colossians 2:1–5.

High priest's weaknesses, Hebrews 5:2.

Remembered tears of others, 2 Timothy 1:3–4.

Experiencing what is taught to others, 2 Timothy 2:6.

Empathy with prisoners, Hebrews 13:3.

See Concern, Involvement, Rapport, Sharing.

EMPHASIS

Emphasizing divine guidance, Joshua 1:8; 23:6.

Improper emphasis, 2 Kings 13:14–19.

Jeremiah's emphasized message, Jeremiah 25:3–4.

Use of hand gestures, Acts 13:16.

"Punch line" conclusion, 2 Corinthians 9:15.

Set free for freedom, Galatians 5:1.

Emphasis on folly of legalism, Galatians 5:12.

Paul's emphasis to followers, Ephesians 4:17.

"Insist on these things," Titus 3:8 (NRSV).

"The main point," Hebrews 8:1 (NKJV, NRSV).

Importance of repetition, 2 Peter 1:12–15.

Emphasis to former command, 1 John 2:7–8.

See Reinforcement, Repetition.

EMPLOYEE

Faithful employee, Proverbs 25:13 (LB).

Employees diligent for Christian employer, 1 Timothy 6:2.

Trustworthy employees, Titus 2:9–10.

Wages withheld, James 5:4.

See Employment, Labor, Servant, Wages, Work.

EMPLOYMENT

Women employed, Genesis 29:9.

Fair wages commanded, Leviticus 19:13.

Hiring those who need employment, Deuteronomy 24:14–15.

Room, board, clothes, spending money, Judges 17:7–13.

Sabbath duty shifts, 2 Kings 11:4–8.

Thousands working on government project, 2 Chronicles 2:2.

Amos, the shepherd, Amos 1:1.

Concern of centurion for servant, Matthew 8:5–13.

Workers earn their pay, Matthew 10:10; Luke 10:7; 1 Timothy 5:18.

Women with means helped support Jesus, Luke 8:3.

Association of tent makers, Acts 18:1–3.

Evangelist supporting himself, 1 Corinthians 9:6–7.

Slaves, masters, Ephesians 6:5–9.

Consistent worker, Ephesians 6:6–7 (LB).

Relationship of slaves to masters, Colossians 3:22–25; 4:1.

Paul as model in daily conduct, employment, 2 Thessalonians 3:6–10.

Employees diligent for Christian employer, 1 Timothy 6:2.

Trustworthy employees, Titus 2:9–10.

Withheld wages, James 5:4.

See Employee, Labor, Management, Wages, Servant, Work.

EMPTINESS

"Months of emptiness," Job 7:3 (NRSV).

Life's emptiness, Job 14:1–2 (GNB).

Emptiness rewards emptiness, Job 15:31 (NRSV).

Meaningless life, Ecclesiastes 1:2; 2:1.

Emptiness of mere toil, Ecclesiastes 4:7–8.

Unsatisfied dreams, Isaiah 29:7–8.

Plight of wicked, righteous fulfillment, Isaiah 65:13–14.

Earth, sky under judgment, Jeremiah 4:23–26.

Stalks with no grain, Hosea 8:7.

Unrequited emptiness, Micah 6:14.

Continual lust for more, Ephesians 4:19.

Empty prayers, James 4:3.

Realized emptiness, James 4:10 (LB).

Springs without water, 2 Peter 2:17.

Those who partake but do not possess, Jude 12–13.

See Lost, Unfulfilled.

EMULATION

Like father, like children, Numbers 32:14.

More depraved than those from whom depravity learned, Ezekiel 16:44–52.

Desire to emulate others, Ezekiel 20:32–38.

Examples to one another, Hebrews 10:24.

Christ the perfect example, 1 Peter 2:21–25.

See Example, Influence, Model.

ENCOUNTER

Jesus versus Satan, Luke 4:1–13.

Jesus, John the Baptist, John 1:29–34.

Need for personal encounter, Colossians 2:1.

ENCOURAGEMENT

No need to fear, Genesis 26:24; 2 Kings 6:16; Isaiah 41:10; 43:1.

Encouraging leadership, Exodus 14:13.

Strength of rising sun, Judges 5:31.

Miserable encouragement, Job 16:2–3.

Encourage rather than criticize, Job 16:4–5.

Encourage those who deserve, Proverbs 3:27.

Nourishment of kind words, Proverbs 10:21; 12:25 (LB); 15:23; 16:24.

Hope deferred, longing fulfilled, Proverbs 13:12.

Good news, cheerful looks, Proverbs 15:30.

Encouragement refused, Proverbs 25:20.

Mutual encouragement, Isaiah 41:7.

Divine encouragement, Isaiah 41:13; Matthew 9:2; 14:27; 17:7; Acts 23:11.

Gift of encouragement, Isaiah 50:4.

Challenge to work for divine cause, Haggai 2:4.

Surest therapy for anxious hearts, John 16:33.

Paul took time to encourage, Acts 20:1–2.

Encouragement in time of storm, Acts 27:22.

Strong help weak, Romans 15:1.

Skill of giving compliments, Romans 16:3–16; 1 Corinthians 11:2; 2 Corinthians 7:4–7.

Encouraging others, 1 Corinthians 16:18.

"God, the Encourager," 2 Corinthians 7:6 (Berk.).

Truthful hyperbole, 2 Corinthians 7:14.

Encouraged by new convert, Galatians 1:23–24.

Mutual encouragement, Philippians 2:1–2 (LB).

Wise use of names of followers, Colossians 4:7–17.

Encouraging believers, 1 Thessalonians 2:11–12.

Paul encouraged by conduct of Thessalonians, 1 Thessalonians 3:6–10.

Boasting about perseverance, faith of others, 2 Thessalonians 1:4.

Strengthened by the Lord, 2 Thessalonians 2:16–17.

Not embarrassed by friend's misfortune, 2 Timothy 1:16–17.

Encouraging one another daily, Hebrews 3:13.

Encouraging others, Hebrews 10:24.

Remember those in prison, Hebrews 13:3.

See Compliments, Sharing.

ENDEARMENT *See Beloved.*

ENDING

David's last words, 2 Samuel 23:1–7.

God pronounces "the end," Ezekiel 7:2.

Prophetic finale, Ezekiel 48:35.

Completed wrath of God, Revelation 15:1.

See Conclusion, Finale.

ENDORSEMENT

God's commendation of Job, Job 1:8.

Endorsement of Jesus, Matthew 3:17.

Evaluation of John the Baptist, Matthew 11:11–14.

See Accreditation, Approval.

ENDURANCE

Stressed endurance, Jeremiah 12:5.

Endowed endurance, Habakkuk 3:19.

Enduring endurance, Matthew 10:22; Ephesians 6:13.

"Endurance builds character," Romans 5:4 (CEV. Japanese *nerareta*, "kneaded," as with bread dough).

Love endures all, 1 Corinthians 13:8–13.

Not weary in doing good, Galatians 6:9.

"Endure everything with patience," Colossians 1:11 (NRSV).

Inspired by hope, 1 Thessalonians 1:3.

Unflinching endurance, 2 Thessalonians 1:4 (AB).

Enduring hardness, Hebrew 12:7.

Learning to endure, James 1:2–4, 12.

Job's endurance, James 5:11; Revelation 13:10 (GNB).

Patient endurance, Revelation 3:10 (AB).

See Dedication, Determination, Energy, Permanence, Survival, Tenacity, Virility.

ENEMY

Protected from superior enemy, Exodus 14:15–31.

Kindness to enemy, Exodus 23:4–5; 2 Samuel 9:1–8 (See Proverbs 25:21–22).

Harass, attack, Numbers 25:17 (NKJV).

Exaggerating size of enemy, Deuteronomy 1:28.

No fear of great enemy, Deuteronomy 9:1–3; Psalm 27:3.

Enemies in all directions, 1 Samuel 12:11.

Prayer for guidance confronting enemy, 2 Samuel 5:17–19.

David, defeated Moabites, 2 Samuel 8:2.

Enemy conquered through blindness, 2 Kings 6:8–23.

Arm of flesh, 2 Chronicles 32:8.

Enemies, bandits, Ezra 8:31.

Enemy's loss of self-confidence, Nehemiah 6:16.

Rejoicing in trouble of others, Job 31:29.

Facing opposition with confidence, Psalm 3:6; 4:8.

Anguished assault, Psalm 7:1–2.

David became leader to strangers, Psalm 18:43–45.

Like evil dogs, Psalm 22:16 (LB).

Let the Lord face your enemy, Psalm 35:1–7.

Returning good for evil, Psalm 35:11–16 (GNB).

"Vicious enemies," Psalm 41:5 (CEV).

"Ruthless men," Psalm 54:3 (LB).

Enemy falls into pit he designed, Psalm 57:6.

"Summit conference," Psalm 83:5 (LB).

"Show him how it feels!" Psalm 109:6 (LB).

Those who hate peace, Psalm 120:6–7.

Do not rejoice in enemy's failure, Proverbs 24:17–18.

Turning back battle at gate, Isaiah 28:6.

Thousand fear one adversary, Isaiah 30:17.

Egyptians were but men, Isaiah 31:3.

Dependence upon God's promises, Isaiah 37:1–38.

Angel destroys enemy soldiers, Isaiah 37:36.

Persecutors put to shame, Jeremiah 17:18.

Only loud noise, Jeremiah 46:17.

Babylon's defeat, Jeremiah 50:46.

Giving up to enemy, Lamentations 1:5.

Plundering with glee, Ezekiel 36:5.

Nine out of ten lost in battle, Amos 5:3.

Gates wide open to enemy, Nahum 3:13.

Love your enemy, Matthew 5:43–48.

Enemy can kill body, not soul, Matthew 10:28.

Silence of Jesus before accusers, Matthew 26:57–67.

Basics of Golden Rule, Luke 6:27–36.

Jesus avoided enemies, John 7:1.

Hated by the world, John 15:18–21.

Forgiving spirit of martyr, Acts 7:60.

Mob incited against Paul, Silas, Acts 17:5–7.

Christian attitude to enemies, Romans 5:10; 12:14, 20.

Wishing to get rid of Christians, Galatians 1:13 (LB).

Revenge in God's hands, 2 Thessalonians 1:6–7.

See Adversary, Espionage, Opposition.

ENERGY

Creator's need for rest, Genesis 2:2.

Old man's spirit, Genesis 45:27.

"Gird up his loins," 1 Kings 18:46 (KJV).

Energizing food, 1 Kings 19:7–8.

Weeping until exhausted, 1 Samuel 30:4.

Too exhausted to cross ravine, 1 Samuel 30:10, 21.

Wasted energy, Job 39:13 (NRSV).

Exerting strength for the Lord, Psalm 29:1 (KJV).

Worn out, Ecclesiastes 3:9 (Berk.).

Energy in full use, Ecclesiastes 9:10.

Working with dull axe, Ecclesiastes 10:10.

Feet of deer, Habakkuk 3:19.

Creator's energy, John 5:17.

Holy Spirit, resurrection, Romans 8:11; Ephesians 1:18–21.

Vigor, strength, Colossians 1:11 (AB).

Energy for spiritual labor, Colossians 1:29.

Working hard for the Lord, Colossians 3:23–24.

Energizing faith, 1 Thessalonians 1:3 (AB).

See Tenacity, Tireless, Virility, Weariness.

ENGAGEMENT

Bride for Isaac, Genesis 24:1–58; 25:19–20.

Bridal consent to marriage, Genesis 24:58.

Engagement for marriage, Deuteronomy 20:7.

Fate of virgin, Deuteronomy 22:23–27.

Ruth proposed to Boaz, Ruth 3:9 (GNB).

Commitment of two loves, Song of Songs 6:3.

Death of fiance, Joel 1:8 (GNB).

Like the Lord's signet ring, Haggai 2:23.

Decision to marry, 1 Corinthians 7:36.

See Betrothal, Marriage, Morality, Romance.

ENJOYMENT *See Pleasure.*

ENLISTMENT *See Recruitment.*

ENMITY

Enmities, Galatians 5:20 (NASB, NRSV).

ENTERTAINMENT

Heterosexual activity for homosexual, Judges 19:22–25.

Fighting to death for entertainment, 2 Samuel 2:12–16.

Joy of victory, Psalm 126:2.

Hired musicians, Ecclesiastes 2:8.

Nonspiritual entertainment, Isaiah 5:12.

Forgotten prostitute, Isaiah 23:16.

Wild parties, Romans 13:13 (LB).

Lovers of pleasure, 2 Timothy 3:4.

See Revelry, Socializing, Television.

ENTHUSIASM

Stirred hearts, willing spirits, Exodus 35:21 (NKJV).

Those lacking enthusiasm, Numbers 32:11.

Enthusiastic workers, Nehemiah 4:6.

Full of enthusiasm, Job 32:17–22.

"Make my eyes sparkle," Psalm 13:3 (CEV).

Enthusiastic "amen," Jeremiah 28:5–6.

Shouting message John 1:15 (CEV).

Retained spiritual enthusiasm, Romans 12:11.

Immature enthusiasm, 1 Timothy 3:6.

ENTICEMENT

Agents of enticement, Exodus 22:16; 2 Chronicles 18:20; Proverbs 1:10; James 1:14.

Prostitute's procedure, Proverbs 7:6–26.

ENVIRONMENT

Choice of environment, Genesis 13:10–13.

Parental environment, Proverbs 6:20–23.

Sons of sorceress, Isaiah 57:3.

"No place to raise a family," Jeremiah 16:2 (CEV).

Evil influence of fathers, Jeremiah 16:10–12.

Mouths speak what hearts contain, Luke 6:43–45.

Marred creation liberated, Romans 8:20–21.

Earth under judgment, Romans 9:28.

Childhood environment, 2 Timothy 3:14–15.

Surviving in evil surroundings, 2 Peter 2:4–9.

See Background, Culture, Family, Heritage, Home, Parents.

ENVY

Examples of envy, Genesis 4:5; 37:5, 11; Numbers 11:28, 29; 12:2; 1 Samuel 18:6–9; Esther 5:13; Psalm 73:3; Mark 15:10; Acts 13:45.

Envy caused by wealth, Genesis 26:12–14.

Sibling envy, Genesis 37:11.

Never envy evil, Psalm 37:1 (LB); Proverbs 24:19–20.

Someone enviable, Psalm 41:1 (AB).

Envying evil affluence, Psalm 73:2–28.

Physical result of envy, Proverbs 14:30.

Neighborhood envy, Ecclesiastes 4:4.

Envying another's success, Daniel 6:4.

Proper envy, Luke 10:23 (AB).

Religious envy, Acts 13:45.

Israel's envy of Gentiles, Romans 11:13–14.

Purification of love, 1 Corinthians 13:4.

Avoid being cause of envy, Galatians 5:26.

Envy as cause of murder, 1 John 3:12.

See Covet, Jealousy.

EPIDEMIC

Outbreak of tumors, 1 Samuel 5:9.

Fatal epidemic, 2 Samuel 24:15 (Berk.).

Nationwide epidemic, Ezekiel 14:19 (LB).

See Contagious, Disease, Plague.

EPILEPSY

Epileptic son, Matthew 17:14–18.

EPITAPH *See Funeral, Tombstone.*

EPOCH

"Time and epochs," 1 Thessalonians 5:1 (NASB).

EQUALITY

Apparel worn by opposite sex, Deuteronomy 22:5.

Jealous wife, 1 Samuel 1:3–7.

Prosperity of wicked, Jeremiah 12:1.

See Fairness.

EQUAL RIGHTS

God's plan for women's rights, Genesis 3:16.

Generic name for man, woman, Genesis 5:2.

Women employed, Genesis 29:9.

Census of men only, Numbers 26:2.

Spoils for conqueror, Judges 5:30.

Fear of being killed by woman, Judges 9:54.

Daughters rebuilding wall, Nehemiah 3:12.

Without partiality, Job 34:18–19.

One upright man, no upright women, Ecclesiastes 7:28.

Dominant wives, Amos 4:1.

Woman's role in marriage, 1 Corinthians 7:4.

Role of women, 1 Corinthians 11:2–16.

Rapport of wives, husbands, Ephesians 5:22–33.
See Prejudice, Racism, Women, Women's Rights.

EQUANIMITY *See Calm, Patience, Quiet.*

EQUIPMENT
Dull ax, Ecclesiastes 10:10.

EQUITY
Evil prosperity, Jeremiah 12:1.
Receiving what one deserves, Zechariah 1:6.
Justice, equity, Proverbs 2:9 (NASB, NRSV).
Sun rises on evil, good, Matthew 5:44–45.
Equal vineyard workers' pay, Matthew 20:1–16.
No divine favoritism, Acts 10:34–35; Romans 10:12.
Eternal inheritance, 1 Peter 1:3–4.
See Fairness, Partiality.

EROSION
Mountains, soil, stones, Job 14:18–19.
Gullies formed by rain, Job 38:25 (Berk.).

EROTIC
Mixing religion with immorality, Numbers 25:1–2.
Continual lust for more, Ephesians 4:19.
See Hedonism, Immorality, Lust, Masturbation.

ERROR
Creator's grief, Genesis 6:5–8.
Deceived hearts, Deuteronomy 11:16 (KJV).
Youth points out mistakes of age, Job 32:6–12.
Way of wicked, Proverbs 4:19.
Willing to correct error, Proverbs 10:17.
Misled by error, Isaiah 47:10.
Believing lie, Jeremiah 43:1–7.
Priests who gave false teaching, Malachi 2:7–9.
Light becomes darkness, Luke 11:35.
Men love darkness rather than light, John 3:19–21.
Not accepting truth, John 5:41–47.
Poisoning the mind, Acts 14:2.
Pagans certain of error, Acts 19:35–36.
"Self-condemned," Galatians 2:11 (NRSV).

Impact of error, Galatians 2:13.
Empty words, Ephesians 5:6.
False humility, Colossians 2:18.
Teachings cause controversy, 1 Timothy 1:3–4.
False teaching like gangrene, 2 Timothy 2:17 (NRSV).
Ignorant, misguided, Hebrews 5:2 (NASB).
Detecting presence of false prophets, 1 John 4:1–3.
See Mistake, Wrong.

ERUDITE *See Education, Intelligence, Wisdom.*

ESCAPE
Deliverance from great flood, Genesis 7:7–8.
City of destruction, Genesis 19:15–30.
Escape from mad king, 1 Samuel 19:9–18.
"Rock of escape," 1 Samuel 23:28 (LB).
Escape on camels, 1 Samuel 30:17.
Saved from death, Esther 2:21–23; 5:14.
No place to escape, Job 34:21; Jeremiah 25:35; 48:44; Matthew 23:33; 1 Thessalonians 5:2–3; Hebrews 2:2–3.
Take flight, Psalm 55:6.
Cooperative waterways, Psalm 114:3–5 (LB).
Get away from it all, Jeremiah 9:2.
Egypt as place of refuge, Jeremiah 41:16–18.
Safest place during trouble, persecution, Jeremiah 42:1–22.
Attempted, aborted escape, Jonah 1:3, 17.
Jesus sought no escape from cross, John 12:27.
Escape from prison, Acts 5:18–20.
Safety of darkness, Acts 17:10.
Deliverance from drowning, Acts 27:30–34.
See Pardon, Refuge.

ESPIONAGE
Treasures surveyed for subsequent thievery, Isaiah 39:1–6.
Method of false teachers, 2 Peter 2:1.
See Enemy.

ESSENTIALS
Food and clothing, 1 Timothy 6:8.

ESTATE

Divided estate, Genesis 13:7–18.
Selfish estate, Deuteronomy 8:13–14.
Husband did not provide for family, 2 Kings 4:1–7.
Spiritual, material estates, Matthew 6:19–21.
Greedy estate owner, Luke 12:16–20.
See Inheritance.

ESTEEM

Respect for those older, Job 32:4.
Loving esteem, Song of Songs 5:10–16.
Esteemed for strength, Isaiah 25:3.
Cornelius' esteem for Peter, Acts 10:25–26.
See Appreciation, Respect.

ESTIMATION

Monetary value, Leviticus 27:25 (KJV).
Underestimating enemy, Deuteronomy 1:41–44.
Boy's underestimated abilities, 1 Samuel 17:42.
Low estimation of servant, 2 Kings 8:13.
See Evaluation.

ESTRANGEMENT

Estrangement among twelve tribes, Judges 21:1–6.
Estrangement of King Saul, Samuel, 1 Samuel 15:34–35.
Estranged from birth, Psalm 58:3.
Straying from faith, Jeremiah 2:5.
Israel's spiritual estrangement, Ezekiel 14:5.
Lip service, Matthew 15:8.
See Disloyalty, Divorce.

ETERNAL

Habitation of God, Isaiah 57:15; Micah 5:2.
One who never changes, Hebrews 1:10–12.
Imperishable seed, 1 Peter 1:23.
Past, present, future of Jesus, Revelation 1:4–8; 11:17; 22:13.
See Unchangeable.

ETERNAL LIFE

Life forever, Psalms 21:4; 121:8.
Old Testament concept, Daniel 12:2.

Impossible to earn, Matthew 19:16–21; John 14:6.
All this and heaven, too, Luke 18:29–30.
Key to eternal life, John 3:16; 5:24–25; 12:25.
Bread of Heaven, John 6:50–58.
Eternal purpose of Scripture, John 20:30–31.
See Conversion, Salvation.

ETERNITY

No time in eternity, Job 24:1 (NRSV).
God predates His creation, Psalms 90:1–2; 102:25–27.
"Surely there is a hereafter," Proverbs 23:18 (NKJV).
Eternity in human hearts, Ecclesiastes 3:11.
Eternal God, Isaiah 44:6; 57:15.
"Time comes to an end," Luke 21:24 (CEV).
Eternal preparation, 1 Corinthians 2:9–10.
Eternity awareness, 2 Corinthians 5:1–10.
Excluded from God's presence, 2 Thessalonians 1:9.
God's plan from beginning of time, 2 Timothy 1:8–10.
Church promised from beginning of time, Titus 1:1–3.
God's eternal existence, Revelation 1:8.
Eternity of eternities, Revelation 1:18 (AB).
See Infinite.

EULOGY

David's lament for King Saul, Jonathan, 2 Samuel 1:17–27.
Death of Abner, 2 Samuel 3:33.
High praise at funerals, Job 21:32 (CEV).

EUNUCH

Eunuch's duties, Acts 8:27.
Eunuch by accident, Deuteronomy 23:1.
Like a dry tree, Isaiah 56:3.
By birth or by choice, Matthew 19:12.
Ethiopian eunuch, Acts 8:27–39 (CEV).
Incisive approach to legalism, Galatians 5:12 (NEB, NIV, GNB).
See Celibacy.

EUPHEMISM

Death likened to sleep, Deuteronomy 31:16 (KJV); Daniel 12:2; Mark 5:39; John 11:11;

Acts 13:36; 1 Corinthians 15:6; 1 Thessalonians 4:13.
Sacrifice thank offerings, Psalm 107:22.
Fragrant sacrifice, Ephesians 5:2.
Euphonious speech, Colossians 4:6.
See Tact.

EUPHORIC

Desires satisfied, strength renewed, Psalm 103:5.
Labor, good food, Ecclesiastes 5:18–20.
See Ecstasy, Happiness, Pleasure.

EUROPE

Israel, northern Europe, Ezekiel 38:15–19; 39:1–5.

EUTHANASIA

Seeking death, Revelation 9:6.
See Despair, Coup de Grace.

EVADE See Escape.

EVALUATION

Tribes of Israel evaluated, Deuteronomy 33:1–29.
Goliath's inaccurate evaluation, 1 Samuel 17:42–44.
God's evaluation of Job, Job 1:8.
Job asked for honest scales, Job 31:6.
Making correct evaluation, Job 34:1–3.
Difference between mind, heart, Job 38:36.
"Think this over," Psalm 107:43 (Berk.).
Sanballat's ridicule of Jewish capability, Nehemiah 4:1–10.
Jesus' evaluation of John the Baptist, Matthew 11:11–14.
Winning converts to error, Matthew 23:15.
Weak, strong, Romans 14:1–8.
Test the quality, 1 Corinthians 3:13 (NASB).
Believer's status evaluated, Ephesians 1:18–23.
Church at Ephesus evaluated, Revelation 2:1–6.
See Appraisal, Assessment, Estimation, Survey.

EVANGELISM

Tent for inquirers, Exodus 33:7.
Tip of tongue, 2 Samuel 23:2.
Benediction for missions, Psalm 67:1–2.

Those who proclaim God's word, Psalm 68:11.
International evangelism, Psalms 96:3, 10; 105:1; Isaiah 12:4–5; 45:22; 66:19.
"Tell the world," Psalm 9:11 (LB).
Sow in tears, reap with joy, Psalm 126:5–6.
Alert during harvest, Proverbs 10:5.
Wise win souls, Proverbs 11:30.
Eternity in human hearts, Ecclesiastes 3:11.
Nighttime evangelism, Isaiah 21:11–12.
Shout the message, Isaiah 40:9; 58:1.
Beautiful feet of evangels, Isaiah 52:7.
Effective evangelism guaranteed, Isaiah 55:10–11.
Announcing Savior's coming, Isaiah 62:11.
Deaf ear to message, Jeremiah 5:12–13.
Evangelism unnecessary, Jeremiah 31:34; Hebrews 8:10–11.
Failure to evangelize, Ezekiel 3:18–19.
Some will listen, some refuse, Ezekiel 3:27.
Silenced evangelism, Ezekiel 7:26.
Repentance identified, Ezekiel 9:3–11.
Shepherds ignore lost sheep, Ezekiel 34:1–31.
Coming revival in Israel, Ezekiel 39:28–29.
Courageous Daniel, Daniel 5:18–26.
"Sound a warning," Hosea 8:1 (CEV).
Famine for word of the Lord, Amos 8:11–12.
Ninevites heeded Jonah's warning, Jonah 3:3–6.
Inviting others to come, Zechariah 8:20–22.
Old Testament evangelism, Malachi 2:6.
"How to bring in people," Matthew 4:19 (CEV).
Unfinished task, Matthew 10:23.
Parable of sower, Matthew 13:1–23; Luke 8:4–15.
Worth of one lost sheep, Matthew 18:12–14; Luke 15:1–7.
Some refuse, others accept, Matthew 22:1–10.
Great commission, Matthew 28:16–20; Mark 16:15.
Sowing seed on various kinds of soil, Mark 4:3–20.
Fishers of men, Luke 5:1–11 ("Catching people," NRSV).
Itinerant evangelism, Luke 8:1.

Praying for harvesters rather than harvest, Luke 10:1–2.

Streets and alleys, Luke 14:16–24.

Gospel preaching, Luke 20:1.

Harvest time is now, John 4:35–38.

Lifting up Jesus, John 12:32.

Motivating follower of Christ, Acts 1:6–8.

Message saturation, Acts 5:28.

Resisting the Holy Spirit, Acts 7:51.

Fruit of effective witness, Acts 11:20–21.

Tactful witness, Acts 17:21–28 (CEV).

Few converts at Athens, Acts 17:34.

Divine guidance in evangelism, Acts 18:20–21.

Zealous ministry of Apollos, Acts 18:24–28.

All Jews, Greeks heard message, Acts 19:10.

Places Paul needed to visit, Acts 19:21.

House evangelism, Acts 28:30–31.

Delayed harvest, Romans 1:13.

Evangelizing civilized, uncivilized, Romans 1:14–15 (CEV).

Reaching first-time hearers, Romans 10:14–15.

Jealousy in evangelism, Romans 11:14 (NRSV).

Priestly duty to proclaim Gospel, Romans 15:16.

Benediction centered on world evangelism, Romans 16:25–27.

One plants, another waters, God gives growth, 1 Corinthians 3:6–9.

Sensitive to other cultures, 1 Corinthians 9:19–23.

Gospel message in brief, 1 Corinthians 15:1–5.

Faithful whatever the difficulties, 1 Corinthians 15:57–58.

"Tremendous opportunities," 2 Corinthians 2:12 (LB).

"Tricking people into believing," 2 Corinthians 4:2 (LB).

More and more reached, 2 Corinthians 4:15.

Ministry with spiritual weapons, 2 Corinthians 10:1–5.

Evangelistic shoes, Ephesians 6:15 (CEV).

Rapid spread of Gospel, Colossians 1:6.

Church and its outreach, Colossians 1:24–27.

Converts are joy, crown, 1 Thessalonians 2:17–20.

Rapidly spreading message, 2 Thessalonians 3:1.

Why Paul became an evangelist, 1 Timothy 2:1–7.

Evangelism not needed, Hebrews 8:11.

Prison evangelism, Hebrews 13:3.

Turning sinner from error, James 5:20.

The Lord wants all to be saved, 2 Peter 3:9.

Helping doubters, Jude 22–23.

Open door, Revelation 3:8.

All tribes, nations, Revelation 7:9–17.

Proclaiming angel, Revelation 14:6–7.

Combined ministry Holy Spirit, church, Revelation 22:17.

See Contextualization, Outreach, Preaching, Soul-Winning, Street Evangelism, Witness.

EVANGELIST

Prophesied ministry of John the Baptist, Luke 1:11–17.

Itinerant ministry, Luke 8:1; 9:6.

Healing, evangelism, Acts 14:8–18.

Evangelist with four daughters, Acts 21:8–9.

"A real pest," Acts 24:5 (CEV).

Evangelist's role, 1 Corinthians 3:4–9.

Material payment to evangelists, 1 Corinthians 9:9–14; 2 Corinthians 2:17; 1 Timothy 5:17–18.

Specific calling, Ephesians 4:11.

Evangelist's prayer request, Ephesians 6:19–20; Colossians 4:3–4.

Evangelist's past experience, 1 Timothy 1:12–14.

Called to evangelize, 1 Timothy 2:5–7.

Evangelist, apostle, teacher, 2 Timothy 1:11.

Second-generation evangelist, 2 Timothy 4:1–5.

Called to ministry of holiness, 1 Peter 1:15–16.

See Evangelism, Herald, Ministry, Service, Vocation.

EVAPORATION

Rain, rivers, Ecclesiastes 1:7.

Ocean evaporation falls on earth, Amos 5:8.

See Weather.

EVERLASTING See Eternity.

EVICTION

Thrown out of the land, Leviticus 20:22 (LB).

Jesus evicted, Luke 4:28–30.

See Rejection.

EVIDENCE

Dove provided evidence for Noah, Genesis 8:10–11.

Trumped up evidence, Genesis 37:29–33.

Drama between Tamar and Judah, Genesis 38:11–26.

Circumstantial evidence against Joseph, Genesis 39:6–20.

Guilt of murder exposed, Exodus 2:11–14.

Ninth commandment, Exodus 20:16.

Responsibility for giving evidence, Leviticus 5:1.

Need for adequate witnesses, Deuteronomy 17:6; 19:15.

Giving false testimony, Deuteronomy 19:16, 21.

Proof of chastity, Deuteronomy 22:1–21.

David's plea for evidence of guilt, 1 Samuel 20:1.

One man's head, 1 Samuel 20:20–22.

Seeing is believing, 1 Kings 10:1–13.

Presenting evidence, 1 Kings 18:7–15.

Living evidence, 2 Kings 8:5.

Evidence turns against accuser, Proverbs 25:8.

Do not betray confidence, Proverbs 25:9.

Confirmed evidence, Matthew 18:16.

Attempt to prevent resurrection of Jesus, Matthew 27:62–66; 28:11–15.

Unable to believe certain evidence, Luke 24:36–43.

Jesus' attitude toward human testimony, John 5:34.

Marks of cross as identity, John 20:20–29.

Case against Paul, Acts 23:23–30.

Always get facts, Romans 14:1.

Incriminating evidence, Revelation 18:24.

See Certainty, Pragmatic, Proof, Validity.

EVIL

Evil made attractive, Genesis 3:6.

Pre-deluge depravity, Genesis 6:5.

No curse on those blessed, Numbers 22:12.

Evil aids God's plans, Judges 14:1–4; Jeremiah 25:11–14; Revelation 17:17.

Source of demons, 1 Samuel 16:15; 18:10.

Death of infamous hero, 1 Samuel 17:51.

Evil sanctioned, 1 Kings 22:23.

God's command to destroy, 2 Kings 9:6–7.

Ultimate result of evil, Job 20:4–11.

The old path, Job 22:15.

Peril to evil doers, Psalms 5:10 (Berk.); 7:15–16 (Berk.).

Sinful nature inherited, Psalm 51:5.

Wicked as wax, Psalm 68:2.

Man's wrath praises God, Psalm 76:10 (KJV).

Evil versus evil, Psalm 140:11 (NRSV).

Evil categorized, Proverbs 6:16–19 (LB).

When evil prospers, Ecclesiastes 8:12.

"Hatred of evil," Proverbs 8:13 (NKJV, NRSV).

Kingdom of idols, Isaiah 10:10.

Evil Assyrians led by hook in nose, Isaiah 37:29.

Those who trust in wickedness, Isaiah 47:10–11.

Source of evil, Isaiah 54:16–17.

Backsliders, Isaiah 63:17.

Clinging to deceit, Jeremiah 8:5.

Wicked prosperity, Jeremiah 12:1–3.

Evil outweighs good, Ezekiel 33:12 (CEV).

Hosea commanded to marry evil woman, Hosea 1:2–3.

Curse concludes Old Testament, Malachi 4:6 (Compare Revelation 22:21).

Evil influence over good, Matthew 13:24–30.

Evil effort avoided by Jesus, Luke 4:28–30.

Satan entered Judas, Luke 22:3.

Devil apostle, John 6:70–71.

Approving wrong done by others, Acts 8:1.

Good law reveals evil sin, Romans 7:13–14.

Those handed over to Satan, 1 Timothy 1:18–20.

Love good, hate evil, Hebrews 1:9.

God tempts no one, James 1:13–14.

Work of devil, 1 John 3:7–8.

Test false spirits, 1 John 4:1–6.

Inevitable defeat of Satan, Revelation 12:1–9.

Demons powerless against angel Michael, Revelation 12:7–9.

Mark of beast, Revelation 13:16–18; 14:9–10.

Sins piled up to heaven, Revelation 18:4–5.

Evil queen refuses to admit sin, Revelation 18:7–8.

One angel binds Satan, Revelation 20:1–3.
See Carnality, Depravity, Devious, Sin,

EVOLUTION

Distinction of species, Genesis 1:24–25; 1 Corinthians 15:39.

Human, animal similarity, Ecclesiastes 3:18–19 (NRSV).

Creator's statement, Isaiah 45:11–12 (LB).

Need for designer, Hebrews 3:4.

Alternative to evolution, Hebrews 11:1–3.

Earth formed out of water, 2 Peter 3:5 (NRSV).
See Creation, Design, Nature.

EXAGGERATION

Sky-high city walls, Deuteronomy 9:1.

I've seen it all, Job 13:1 (Berk.).

Exaggerated involvement, Proverbs 6:1–5.

Commitment exaggerated, Matthew 8:19–20.

Exaggeration of truth, Acts 21:17–24.

"Not to exaggerate," 2 Corinthians 2:5 (NASB).
See Hyperbole.

EXALTED

Calvary to Heaven, Mark 15:33–37; 16:19.
See Achievement, Citation, Promotion, Height.

EXAMINATION

Hard questions, correct answers, 1 Kings 10:1–3.

Self-examination, Lamentations 3:40; Matthew 7:5; 1 Corinthians 11:28; 2 Corinthians 13:5.

Daniel, friends passed oral exam, Daniel 1:18–20.
See Scrutiny, Testing.

EXAMPLE

Abraham's good example, Genesis 21:22.

Laughingstock, Exodus 32:25.

Avoid bad example, Deuteronomy 18:9.

Righteous king's ignored example, 2 Chronicles 27:2.

Parents poor example, 2 Chronicles 30:7.

Like father, like son, 2 Kings 15:34.

"Quit complaining," Psalm 39:1 (LB).

Preparation for witnessing, Psalm 51:10–13.

Fearing poor personal example, Psalm 69:6.

Exemplary ant, Proverbs 6:6–8.

Giving heed to instruction, Proverbs 16:20.

Righteous father's example, Proverbs 20:7.

Children affect parents' reputation, Proverbs 27:11.

Exemplary Rechabites, Jeremiah 35:1–16.

Avoid father's example, Ezekiel 20:18 (LB).

Belshazzar rejected father's example, Daniel 5:18–24.

Learning from bad example, Zechariah 1:4–6.

Example of persecuted prophets, Matthew 5:11–12.

Example, exhortation, Matthew 16:21–25.

Practice what you preach, Matthew 23:1–3.

Example of lamp, displayed, not hidden, Mark 4:21–22.

Jesus taught by His example, Luke 11:1–4; 1 Peter 2:21–25.

Exemplary queen, Luke 11:29–31.

Living example from within, Luke 11:33–36.

Warned by bad example, Luke 17:32.

Paul showed confidence in difficult places, Acts 20:22–24.

Truly Christian lifestyle, Romans 12:9–21 (Note verse 17).

Example for converts, 1 Corinthians 4:15–16.

Liberty in eating, drinking, 1 Corinthians 8:7–13.

Example to others, 1 Corinthians 10:32–33.

Paul followed example of Christ, 1 Corinthians 11:1.

Wrong attitudes in worship, 1 Corinthians 11:17–32.

Good example through God's grace, 2 Corinthians 1:12.

Deserving right to be heard, 2 Corinthians 4:1–2.

Lifestyle demonstrated by example, 2 Corinthians 6:4–10.

Supreme example of the Lord Jesus, 2 Corinthians 8:7–9.

Sharing concerns of leader, 2 Corinthians 8:16.

Right, wrong example, Ephesians 4:31–32.

Loving example, Ephesians 5:1–2.

Imprisonment helped others witness boldly, Philippians 1:12–14.

Witness by example, Philippians 1:28–29 (CEV).

Total commitment, example of Jesus, Philippians 2:5–11.

Worthy example to others, Philippians 3:17.

Imitators of Paul, 1 Thessalonians 1:6.

Exemplary believers, 1 Thessalonians 1:7.

Example in daily conduct, employment, 2 Thessalonians 3:6–10.

Grace to worst of sinners, 1 Timothy 1:15–16.

Young Christians set example, 1 Timothy 4:12.

Good, bad examples, 1 Timothy 5:24–25.

Paul's example to Timothy, 2 Timothy 3:10–11.

Elder's family must be exemplary, Titus 1:6.

Example set by good teacher, Titus 2:6–7.

Those who show initiative, Hebrews 6:11–12.

Service in sanctuary of ultimate High Priest, Hebrews 8:1–6.

Mutual examples, Hebrews 10:24–25.

Example of living by faith, Hebrews 12:1–3.

Living in good relationships, Hebrews 12:14–15.

Exemplary leadership, Hebrews 13:7.

Witness of good life, 1 Peter 2:12.

"In His steps," 1 Peter 2:21 (NIV).

Convincing example, 1 Peter 4:4 (NRSV).

Taught by example to show love, 1 John 4:7–11.

See Emulation, Model, Reputation.

EXAMS

All answers correct, 1 Kings 10:1–3.

Cramming for exams, Ecclesiastes 12:12 (See GNB).

Daniel passed exam, Daniel 1:9.

EXASPERATION

Moses exasperated with grumbling people, Exodus 17:4.

"At their wits end," Psalm 107:27 (NKJV, NRSV).

Trying God's patience, Isaiah 7:13.

See Disgust, Impatience.

EXCELLENCE

Attainable excellence, Deuteronomy 30:11.

Divine perfection, Deuteronomy 32:4; Psalm 18:30.

Leadership under divine guidance, 2 Chronicles 31:20–21.

Man of excellent character, Job 1:1–8.

Creator's excellence, Genesis 1:31; Psalm 8:1; Isaiah 12:5.

Excellence in counsel, wisdom, Isaiah 28:29.

Youthful excellence, Daniel 1:3–4.

Emulate divine perfection, Matthew 5:48.

Spiritual excellence, 2 Corinthians 8:7.

See Exemplary, Model, Perfection, Performance, Quality, Skill.

EXCEPTION

Making an exception, John 2:1–4, 11 (LB).

Exceptional Pharisee, John 3:1.

EXCERPT

Sermon excerpt, Mark 1:7 (LB).

See Brevity.

EXCITEMENT

Romantic meeting, Genesis 24:62–67.

"A tremendous day," Joshua 4:14 (LB).

Causing ears to tingle, 1 Samuel 3:11.

Harvesters see ark of God, 1 Samuel 6:13.

Returning ark to Jerusalem, 2 Samuel 6:5.

Exciting life, Proverbs 14:14 (LB).

Happy, excited, Matthew 5:12 (CEV).

Too excited to open door, Acts 12:12–16.

See Emotion.

EXCLUSIVE

Select few travelled with Jesus, Mark 5:37.

Exclusive spiritual source, 2 Timothy 2:1 (AB).

Song for exclusive congregation, Revelation 14:1–3.

See Restriction.

EXCOMMUNICATION

Excommunicated blind man, John 9:34 (CEV).

EXCUSES

Blaming another, Genesis 3:12.

Claim of inadequacy, Exodus 3:11; 4:10; Judges 6:15; Jeremiah 1:7.

Excused idolatry, Exodus 32:24.

Blaming employer, Matthew 25:24–25.

First things first, Luke 9:59–62.

Excuses for not attending banquet, Luke 14:16–24.

See Blame.

EXECUTION

Royal executioner, Daniel 2:14; Mark 6:27.

No right to crucify, John 18:28–32.

See Capital Punishment.

EXEGESIS

Words without knowledge, Job 38:2.

Emmaus exegesis, Luke 24:32, 45 (AB).

Philip and eunuch, Acts 8:27–35.

See Preaching, Teaching.

EXEMPLARY

Exemplary prophet, 1 Samuel 12:3.

Finest man on earth, Job 1:1–8; 2:3 (LB).

Search for one righteous man, Psalm 53:2 (LB).

Exemplary youth, Daniel 1:4 (See CEV).

Exemplary discipleship, 2 Corinthians 8–9.

Like no one else, Philippians 2:19–20.

Setting example for others, Philippians 3:17.

See Character, Frame-of-Reference, Reputation.

EXECUTION

EXERCISE

Running to bring bad news, 2 Samuel 18:24–33.

Impetus for keeping in shape, 1 Corinthians 6:19–20.

Foot racing, Jeremiah 12:5; 1 Corinthians 9:24–26.

Physical training and godliness, 1 Timothy 4:8.

See Athletics, Physical.

EXHAUSTION

Long hours, hard work, Exodus 18:14–18 (LB).

Exhausted beyond tears, 1 Samuel 30:4.

Exhausted soldiers, 1 Samuel 30:9–10.

"Completely worn out," Psalm 31:9 (GNB).

See Rest, Weariness.

EXHIBITIONISM

Attitude toward father's privacy, Genesis 9:20–27.

David did not conduct himself as king, 2 Samuel 6:17–23.

Gross exhibitionism, 2 Samuel 12:11 (CEV).

Sexual display, 2 Samuel 16:21–23.

Palace treasures, 2 Kings 20:12–15.

Display of wealth, Esther 1:4, 10–12.

"Holy array," Psalm 29:2 (NASB).

Asking God to go public, Psalm 109:27 (LB).

Early morning religiosity, Proverbs 27:14.

Fool demonstrates lack of wisdom, Ecclesiastes 10:3.

Stripped and barefoot, Isaiah 20:2–4.

Display of possessions, Isaiah 39:2–4.

Programmed exhibitionism, Ezekiel 12:3–14 (CEV).

Rend heart, not clothing, Joel 2:13.

Humiliating impropriety, Nahum 3:5.

Acts of charity not made public, Matthew 6:1–4.

Street corner piety, Matthew 6:5 (Berk.).

Discreet fasting, Matthew 6:16–18 (KJV).

"Showoffs," Matthew 15:7 (CEV).

Ego displayed by law teachers, Mark 12:38–40.

Proud Pharisee, humble publican, Luke 18:9–14.

Exhibition prayers, Luke 20:46–47; 21:1–4.

Exhibitionism avoided, John 7:1–10.

"A big show," Acts 25:23 (CEV).

Apostles on exhibition, 1 Corinthians 4:9.

Do not serve God to please men, Colossians 3:23–24.

See Display, Ego, Nudity, Pride, Vanity.

EXHILARATION

Joy beyond levity of wine, Psalm 4:7.

See Ecstasy.

EXHORTATION *See Admonition.*

EXHUME

Bones exhumed, 2 Chronicles 34:5, Jeremiah 8:1–3.

See Burial, Corpse.

EXISTENCE

Before all others, John 1:1 (LB).

EXORCISM

Musical exorcism, 1 Samuel 16:23.

Saul expelled mediums, spiritualists, 1 Samuel 28:3.

Demons forced out, Mark 1:34 (CEV).

Jesus rebuked demon, Luke 4:33–36, 41.

Submissive demons, Luke 10:17–20.

Cured by casting out of demon, Luke 13:10–13.

Miracles in ministry of Paul, Acts 19:11–12.

Modified use of name of Jesus, Acts 19:13.

Vain effort to cast out evil spirits, Acts 19:13–16.

See Deliverance, Demons, Iconoclastic, Sorcery.

EXOTIC

Exotic becomes commonplace, 2 Chronicles 1:15.

EXPANSION

Need for larger building, 2 Kings 6:1–2.

Time to enlarge, Isaiah 54:2.

Build, extend, Micah 7:11.

See Growth, Vision.

EXPECTATION

Dubious expectations, 2 Corinthians 12:20.

Believing wisdom will be granted, James 1:5–7.

Eternal inheritance, 1 Peter 1:3, 4.

See Anticipation, Confidence.

EXPEDIENT

Such a time as this, Esther 4:13–17.
Asking God to hasten, Psalm 70:1.
Right time for everything, Ecclesiastes 3:1–8.
Urgent need to evangelize, Isaiah 21:11–12.
Divine time, mortal time, John 7:6.
Judas told to act quickly, John 13:27.
Instant baptism, Acts 16:33.
Now is the day of salvation, 2 Corinthians 6:2.
Meaning of "today" in God's reckoning, Hebrews 4:7.
See Urgency.

EXPEDITE

"What needs to be done," Isaiah 38:1 (CEV).
See Hurry.

EXPENSES

Unlimited expense account, Ezra 7:20.
No need for expense money, Mark 6:8–11.
Some to pay, others receive, 2 Corinthians 11:7–8.
See Honorarium.

EXPERIENCE

Recalling past experience, Exodus 23:9.
Learning from experience, Deuteronomy 4:3, 32–35.
Parents to share experience with children, Deuteronomy 11:1–7.
Seeing with your own eyes, Deuteronomy 29:2–4.
Good, bad experiences, Deuteronomy 30:1–3.
Young eagle trained to fly, Deuteronomy 32:11.
Consulting old men, 1 Kings 12:6 (KJV).
Years of experience, Job 12:12; 32:7–8; Psalm 37:25.
Witnessing of personal experience, Psalm 51:10–13.
Path of righteous, way of wicked, Proverbs 4:18–19.
Experienced in wisdom, Ecclesiastes 1:16.
Facing problems while young, Lamentations 3:27.
Belshazzar rejected father's experience, Daniel 5:18–24.

Experiencing God's kingdom within, Luke 17:20, 21.
Lesson from experience, Acts 5:11 (AB).
Shared experience encourages others, Acts 14:19–22.
Power of personal testimony, Acts 21:37—22:21; 26:1–18.
Beyond human perception, experience, 1 Corinthians 2:9–10.
Troubles prepare us to help others, 2 Corinthians 1:3–4.
Deep meanings in Israel's experiences, 2 Corinthians 10:1–13.
Learning by experience, Hebrews 5:8 (LB).
Experiencing reality of Christ, 1 John 1:1–4.
See Maturity, Suffering, Testing.

EXPERTISE

Sanballat's ridicule of Jewish capability, Nehemiah 4:1–10.
Proper time, procedure, Ecclesiastes 8:5–6.
Legality expert, Luke 10:25–37.
Qualifications of Savior, King, Colossians 1:15–20.
Erroneous claims to expertise, 1 Timothy 1:3–7.
"Do your job well," 2 Timothy 4:5 (CEV).
Expertise in iniquity, 2 Peter 2:14.
See Ability, Skill, Talent.

EXPLANATION

No reason given, 1 Kings 11:22 (LB).

EXPLOITATION

David refused water that cost lives of his men, 2 Samuel 23:15–17.
Exploiting poor, Amos 5:11.
Exploiting limited by converts' transformation, Acts 19:23–28.
Paul exploited no one, 2 Corinthians 7:2.
See Greed, Misuse.

EXPLOITS See Boldness, Bravery, Courage, Valor.

EXPLORATION

Searching for treasure, Job 28:1–4, 9–11.

EXPLOSION

Blast of God, Job 4:9.

EXPOSITION

Speaking language understood, Isaiah 36:11.
Exposition of parables, Matthew 13:36–43; Mark 4:34; Luke 8:11–15.
Meaning of fig tree, Matthew 24:32–34.
Informal theology lesson, Luke 24:27.
Proof from the scriptures, Acts 18:28.
See Clarity, Exegesis, Teaching.

EXPRESSION See Attitude, Countenance, Emotion, Excitement.

EXTEMPORANEOUS

Moses' need for words, Exodus 4:10–12.
Given words to speak, Ephesians 6:19–20.
See Ad Lib.

EXTINGUISH

Put out tempter's fire, Ephesians 6:16 (GNB).

EXTORTION

Wealth from extortion, Psalm 62:10 (See NRSV).
Usurping rights of poor, Isaiah 10:2.
Extortionists exterminated, Isaiah 16:4.
Unjust earnings at others' expense, Ezekiel 22:12.
Mistreatment of poor, Amos 5:11.
Greed, self-indulgence, Matthew 23:25.

Making fair collections, Luke 3:13.
See Cheating, Dishonesty.

EXTRAVAGANCE

Silver stewardship, Numbers 7:13; 10:2.
Wasted luxury, Mark 14:3–9.
God's extravagant grace, Ephesians 1:7–8.
See Affluence, Greed, Luxury.

EXTREMITY

Extremity of God's patience, Genesis 6:1–6.
Horizon to horizon, Psalm 103:12.
Highest height, deepest depth, Isaiah 7:10–11.
Anyone who goes too far, 2 John 9.
See Patience, Ultimatum.

EYES

Closing eyes of corpse, Genesis 46:4.
Eyes have seen, Deuteronomy 29:2–3.
Possible cataracts, 1 Samuel 4:14–15.
Flashing eyes, Job 15:12.
"Ogle at a girl," Job 31:1 (Berk.).
"Make my eyes sparkle," Psalm 13:3 (CEV).
Winking eyes, Proverbs 6:13 (Berk.).
Unable to weep, Lamentations 2:11 (LB).
Bodies full of eyes, Ezekiel 10:12.
Abominations of eyes, Ezekiel 20:7 (KJV).
Blessing implements, Luke 10:23.
Eye-to-eye with sorcerer, Acts 13:9–11.
Paul possibly poor eyesight, Galatians 6:11.
See Blindness, Sight.

F

FABLES

Controversial myths, 1 Timothy 1:4.
Old wives' tales, 1 Timothy 4:7.
Substitute for truth, 2 Timothy 4:4.
Jewish myths, Titus 1:14.
Cleverly invented stories, 2 Peter 1:16.
See Deceit.

FABRIC See Clothing, Linen, Textiles.

FABRICATION

Friends and brothers fabricate, Jeremiah 9:4–8.
Fabricating king, Matthew 2:7, 8, 13.

Fabricated stories, 2 Peter 2:3.
See Deceit, Dishonesty, Lie.

FACADE

Ego display by teachers of law, Mark 12:38–40.
False humility, Colossians 2:18.
Making the false claim of a holy life, 1 John 1:8–10.
See Pretense.

FACE

"Faces of lions," 1 Chronicles 12:8.
Saving face, Psalm 43:5 (Berk.); Acts 16:35–40.

Loss of face, 2 Chronicles 32:21; Psalm 109:29.

Transfigured, Exodus 34:29–35; Matthew 17:2; Mark 9:2.

Countenance betrays conscience, Isaiah 3:9.

Variation of facial appearance, Ezekiel 1:10.

Four faces, Ezekiel 10:21.

Simulated expression of fasting, Matthew 6:16.

See Countenance.

FACETIOUS

Paul chided Corinthians, 2 Corinthians 11:16–21.

See Sarcasm.

FACIAL EXPRESSION See Countenance.

FACILITY

Need for larger building, 2 Kings 6:1–2.

See Provisions.

FACTIONS

Stronger, weaker, 2 Samuel 3:1.

Reputation as troublemaker, 2 Samuel 20:1.

Building program factions, Ezra 4:3–5.

Message caused factions, Luke 12:51; John 7:12, 43; 10:19–21.

Those who purposely cause trouble, Romans 16:17.

Personality clashes, doctrinal factions, 1 Corinthians 1:10–17; 3:4–9.

See Argument, Disharmony, Disruption, Orthodoxy.

FACTS

Facts before decisions, Proverbs 18:13 (LB).

"Present your case," Isaiah 41:21.

Knowledge of Old Testament facts, Acts 7:1–60.

Unable to get facts, Acts 21:34 (Berk.).

Always get the facts, Romans 14:1.

See Opinion, Prejudice, Truth.

FAILURE

When God terminates a project, Genesis 11:1–9.

Vineyards with little harvest, Deuteronomy 28:38–42.

Turning failure into success, 1 Kings 8:33–34.

Contempt for unfortunate, Job 12:5.

Admitted failure, Job 17:11.

Success doomed to failure, Job 24:22 (CEV).

Debilitating effects of poverty, Proverbs 10:15.

Gloating over enemy's failure, Proverbs 24:17–18.

"Keep me from failure," Jeremiah 17:18 (CEV).

Enemies rejoice, Lamentations 1:21.

Ridicule of once-exalted city, Lamentations 2:15.

Failed visions, Ezekiel 12:22–25.

Failure of Nebuchadnezzar's wise men, Daniel 2:1–11.

Architectural failure, Matthew 7:27.

Failure at healing, Matthew 17:16.

Fishermen's failure, Luke 5:1–11.

Death to failing guards, Acts 12:18–19.

Faith versus failure, Romans 4:18–22.

Failed life, 1 Corinthians 3:15; Hebrews 4:6.

Fear of failure, Galatians 2:1–2.

Successful failure, 1 Thessalonians 2:1–2.

See Defeat, Disappointment.

FAINT

Fainting wounded, Lamentations 2:12.

Total weakness, Ezekiel 7:17.

Exhausted, ill, Daniel 8:27.

See Illness, Weakness, Weariness.

FAINT HEARTED

"Encourage the faint hearted," 1 Thessalonians 5:14 (NRSV).

FAIRNESS

Avoid partiality, Deuteronomy 1:17.

Joseph's fairness in Egypt, Genesis 47:13–26.

Mutual fairness, Leviticus 25:17.

"More than fair," Ezra 9:15 (CEV).

Fair punishment, Nehemiah 9:33 (CEV).

Consistent fairness, Job 32:21–22.

"The Lord loves fairness," Psalm 37:27–28 (Berk.).

Divine fairness, Psalm 103:10.

Prosperity of wicked, Jeremiah 12:1–3.

Suffering for just and unjust, Jeremiah 49:12.

Disputing fairness of God's ways, Ezekiel 33:10–20.

Parable of fairness in vineyard, Matthew 20:1–16.

"God treats everyone alike," Romans 3:22 (CEV).

No favoritism with God, Colossians 3:25.

"God is always fair," Hebrews 6:10 (CEV).

See Equity, Justice, Partiality.

FAITH

God as first priority, Genesis 1:1.

Doubt overcome by faith, Genesis 15:1–6.

Continuity of family faith, Deuteronomy 4:9–10.

Stand still, see what God will do, 1 Samuel 12:16.

Sure of Divine goodness, 2 Samuel 22:31.

Concern about army more than faith, 2 Samuel 24:10.

Opening eyes to God's provision, 2 Kings 6:16–17.

Failure to give proper emphasis, 2 Kings 13:14–19.

Faith and works, 1 Chronicles 19:13.

Those who seek, those who forsake, 2 Chronicles 15:2.

Evil counsel to people of faith, 2 Chronicles 32:10–15.

No need for King's protection, Ezra 8:21–23.

Unwavering faith, Job 1:22; 2:10; 13:15.

Advocate in heaven, Job 16:19.

Classic faith statement, Job 19:25–26.

Sure faith, Psalm 27:1.

Proof positive, Psalm 34:8 (LB).

Let God fulfill His purpose, Psalm 57:2.

Lineage of faith, Psalm 78:5–8.

God blesses small, great alike, Psalm 115:13.

God's eternal faithfulness, Psalm 117:2.

Faith better than trusting man, Psalm 118:5–9.

Faith present, future, Psalm 131:3.

Certainty of God's promises, Psalm 145:13.

Faith greater than physical strength, Psalm 147:10–11.

Faith formula, Proverbs 3:5–6.

Humility, faith key to success, Proverbs 22:4.

Promised security, Proverbs 29:25; Nahum 1:7.

Stand firm or not at all, Isaiah 7:9.

Poised faith, Isaiah 26:3.

Faith under fire, Daniel 3:16–17.

Humble faith, Daniel 9:18.

Faith in stolen idol, Hosea 10:5.

Righteous live by faith, Habakkuk 2:4.

Faith in God the greatest strength, Zechariah 12:5.

Faith touches God's willingness, Matthew 8:2–4.

Faith makes things happen, Matthew 8:13 (CEV).

Confidence in Jesus' power, Matthew 9:18–25.

Peter's faltering faith, Matthew 14:22–31.

Faith supersedes racist tradition, Matthew 15:21–28.

Too stubborn for faith, Matthew 17:17 (CEV).

Faith removes mountains, Matthew 17:20; 21:21–22; Mark 4:30–32.

Supportive faith, Mark 2:1–5.

Disciples lacked faith, Mark 4:36–41.

Faith of others required for healing, Mark 6:4–6.

Faith's unlimited potential, Mark 9:23–24 (LB).

Insufficient faith, Mark 9:24 (GNB).

Childhood faith, Mark 10:13–16.

Active faith of blind Bartimaeus, Mark 10:46–52.

Certainty of answered prayer, Mark 11:24.

Centurion's faith, Luke 7:1–10.

Small faith in a great God, Luke 11:20; 17:5–6.

Frailty of human faith, Luke 22:31–38.

Taking Jesus at His word, John 4:50.

Trusting Moses, John 5:45 (NKJV).

Faith at time of death, John 11:25–26.

"Great faith," Acts 6:5 (CEV).

Resurrection the central message, Acts 17:2–3.

Living by faith, Romans 1:17; Galatians 3:11; Hebrews 10:38.

Faith of Abraham, Romans 4:1–3.

Never doubt, question, Romans 4:20 (CEV).

Justified by faith, Romans 5:1–2 (AB).

Confident of the unseen, Romans 8:24–25; 2 Corinthians 4:18.

Conflicting faith, works, Romans 9:30–33; Galatians 3:2–5; James 2:17.

Faith given, not generated, Romans 10:17.

Measured faith, Romans 12:3 (Berk.).

Faith as standard of conduct, Romans 14:23; Hebrews 11:6.

Joy, peace in believing, Romans 15:13.

Faith is ultimate intelligence, 1 Corinthians 3:18–23.

Living by faith, not sight, 2 Corinthians 5:1–7.

Self-examination, 2 Corinthians 13:5.

Abraham, the church, Galatians 3:6–9.

Love validates faith, Galatians 5:6.

Faith as shield, Ephesians 6:16.

Spiritual need fulfilled in Christ, Colossians 1:15–23.

Salvation, living, Colossians 2:6 (LB).

Faith put into practice, 1 Thessalonians 1:3 (GNB).

Faith, love together, 1 Thessalonians 5:8.

Faith continuity in persecution, 2 Thessalonians 1:4.

Shipwrecked faith, 1 Timothy 1:19.

Mystic secret, 1 Timothy 3:9, 16 (AB).

Fight the good fight, 1 Timothy 6:12.

Unwavering faith, 2 Timothy 1:12.

"More faith," Titus 1:1 (CEV).

"Common faith," Titus 1:4 (NASB, NKJV).

Jesus seen by faith, Hebrews 2:9.

Failure to combine hearing, believing, Hebrews 4:1–3.

Faith gives credibility, Hebrews 4:2.

Abandoned faith, Hebrews 6:6 (GNB).

Assurance, confirmation, title deed, Hebrews 11:1 (AB).

Old Testament faith chapter, Hebrews 11:1–40 (Japanese Bible: **Faith,** "Believe and look up").

Sustaining faith, Hebrews 11:13.

Faith beyond doubt, James 1:6.

Persevering faith, 1 Peter 1:5.

Believing without seeing, 1 Peter 1:8–9.

Overcoming faith, 1 John 5:4.

See Believer, Commitment, Confidence, Trust.

FAITHFULNESS

God's faithfulness, Deuteronomy 7:7–9; 1 Corinthians 1:9.

Faithful reading of the law, Joshua 8:35.

Trustworthy promises, 1 Kings 8:56.

Reward to the faithful, 2 Samuel 22:26–27.

Faithful to God's house, Nehemiah 10:39.

Undivided heart, Psalm 86:11.

Proclaiming divine faithfulness, Psalm 89:1.

Trustworthy messenger, Proverbs 25:13.

"Faithfulness is dead," Jeremiah 7:28 (GNB).

Beaten for being faithful, Jeremiah 20:1–2.

Faithful message brings threat of death, Jeremiah 26:1–16.

Imprisoned for faithfulness, Jeremiah 37:1–21.

Faithfulness new each morning, Lamentations 3:23.

Faithful in all circumstances, Daniel 3:17–18 (CEV).

Rewarded faithfulness, Matthew 10:32–33.

Faithful when Christ returns, Mark 13:35–37; 1 Timothy 6:11–16.

Courage, faithfulness, Acts 23:1–5.

"Our first duty," 1 Corinthians 4:2 (CEV).

"You never disappoint," 2 Corinthians 1:7 (CEV).

Faithful without pastoral supervision, Philippians 2:12–13.

Faithful unto death, Philippians 2:25–30; Revelation 2:13.

"I do my share," Colossians 1:24 (NASB).

Partial faithfulness insufficient, Revelation 2:1–6, 13–15.

Holding on to the faith, Revelation 2:25.

Beheaded for faithfulness, Revelation 20:4.

See Commitment, Discipleship, Martyr, Reward.

FAKE

Fake silver, Isaiah 1:22 (CEV).

See False.

FALL

Adam's fall, Genesis 3:6–7.

Image of God, image of man, Genesis 5:1–3.

Sin of first parent, Isaiah 43:27.

Entry of sin into world, Romans 5:12.

Death came by Adam, 1 Corinthians 15:21.
Guilt of first woman, 1 Timothy 2:14.
See Carnality, Debauchery, Disobedience, Sin.

FALSE

False body, 1 Samuel 19:12–17.
Bold front, Proverbs 21:29.
False friends, brothers, Jeremiah 9:4–8; Galatians 2:3–4.
Despising truth, Amos 5:10.
False humility, Colossians 2:18.
False teachers, prophets, 2 Peter 2:1; 1 John 4:1.
Counterfeit anointing, 1 John 2:27.
Detecting false prophets, 1 John 4:1–3.
Feigning life, spiritually dead, Revelation 3:1.
See Counterfeit, Deceit, Imitation.

FALSEHOOD

Primordial falsehood, Genesis 3:4–5.
Abram's falsehood concerning his wife, Genesis 12:10–13.
Open honesty, Leviticus 19:11–12.
Rahab's falsehood to protect spies, Joshua 2:1–6.
David's falsehood to protect his life, 1 Samuel 20:5–7.
Misrepresenting motives, Ezra 4:11–16.
Test of integrity, Job 31:5–6.
Inborn deceitfulness, Psalms 10:7; 52:2–8.
Flattering lips, Psalm 12:2.
Guarded tongue, Psalm 34:13.
Mouth given to deceit, Psalm 50:19.
Smooth as butter, Psalm 55:21.
Deceit disallowed, Psalm 101:7.
Deceitful hand, mouth, Psalm 144:8.
Lying lips, Proverbs 12:22.
Bread of deceit, Proverbs 20:17.
Believing a lie, Jeremiah 43:1–7.
Deliberate falsehood, Ezekiel 14:9 (LB).
See Deceit, Lie, Situation Ethics.

FAME

Heroes of old, Genesis 6:4.
"Make ourselves famous," Genesis 11:4 (Berk.).
Bestowed fame, Genesis 12:2 (LB); 1 Samuel 2:7.
Men of renown, Numbers 16:2 (NKJV).

Greatness of Moses, Deuteronomy 34:10–12.
Famous Joshua, Joshua 6:27.
Legitimate fame, Ruth 4:14.
Little known royal family, 1 Samuel 14:49.
Famous David, 2 Samuel 7:9; 8:13.
Worldwide acclaim, 1 Kings 4:31; 10:1.
Local celebrities, 1 Chronicles 12:30.
David's fame, 1 Chronicles 14:17.
Given great name by the Lord, 1 Chronicles 17:21.
Byword to all, Job 17:6.
Divine fame, Psalm 111:4 (CEV).
Dreaded armies, Jeremiah 6:24 (See LB).
Vanished fame, Lamentations 4:7–8.
Worldwide fame, Zephaniah 3:20 (See CEV).
Fame of Jesus, Matthew 4:24; 9:31; Luke 5:15.
Fame of Jesus because of miracles, Mark 1:35–45.
First last, last first, Mark 10:31.
Predicted future fame, Luke 1:15 (AB).
Avoiding limelight, John 7:4 (Berk.).
Respect of Cornelius for Peter, Acts 10:25–26.
Famed ministry, 2 Corinthians 8:18 (NASB, NRSV).
See Celebrity, Image, Notoriety, Self-image.

FAMILIARITY

The Lord knew Moses face-to-face, Deuteronomy 34:10.
Familiarity breeds contempt, Mark 6:4; John 4:44.
Becoming too familiar, 1 Timothy 6:2.
See Rapport.

FAMILY

Musical father, Genesis 4:21.
Dead son replaced, Genesis 4:25.
Large families encouraged, Genesis 9:1, 7 (CEV).
Family unity, Genesis 13:8.
Promise to childless Abram, Genesis 15:1–6.
Son of disobedience, Genesis 16:1–16 (Note 15:1–6).
Children born at advanced age, Genesis 16:16; 17:1–21; 21:1–7.
Family forecast, Genesis 18:17–19.

Preserving family line through incest, Genesis 19:30–38.

Abraham, Isaac, Genesis 22:1–14.

Parents unhappy with daughters-in-law, Genesis 26:34–35.

Bond between relatives, Genesis 29:1–14.

Strife, intrigue, rapport, Genesis 31:17–55.

Father as spiritual leader, Genesis 35:1–5.

Keeping family together, Genesis 45:10.

Family conference, Genesis 49:1–2.

Checking on family welfare, Exodus 4:18.

Servant's family, Exodus 21:1–11.

Identified by family name, Exodus 33:11; Numbers 11:28; 13:16; 14:6, 30; Joshua 1:1; 2:1; Judges 2:8; 1 Kings 16:34.

Visual reminders, Numbers 15:37–41.

Family clans, Numbers 26:1–48.

Family name preserved, Numbers 27:1–11; Deuteronomy 25:5–10.

Continuity of faith, Deuteronomy 4:9–10; Psalm 145:4–7; Isaiah 59:21; Joel 1:3.

Respect within family, Deuteronomy 5:16; Ephesians 6:2.

Family influence, Deuteronomy 6:4–9; 11:16–21.

Rejecting wrong family influence, Deuteronomy 13:6–10.

Adopted into God's family, Deuteronomy 14:1–2; Isaiah 63:16; Hosea 11:1; John 1:12; Romans 8:15; 2 Corinthians 6:18; Galatians 4:4–6.

Family name protected, Deuteronomy 25:5–10.

Prolific family, Judges 12:8–9.

Formerly childless mother, 1 Samuel 1:5, 20; 2:21.

Three deaths in one family, 1 Samuel 4:12–20.

Sons replace father as Judges, 1 Samuel 8:1.

King Saul's little known children, 1 Samuel 14:49.

Kidnapped families repatriated, 1 Samuel 30:1–25.

Futility of family strife, 2 Samuel 2:27–28.

Strong family ties, 2 Samuel 16:5–8.

Adonijah's bid to dethrone David, 1 Kings 1:1–27.

Heathen worship for Solomon's wives, 1 Kings 11:8.

Famous family, 1 Chronicles 12:30.

Together in worship, 2 Chronicles 20:13; Nehemiah 12:43; Matthew 21:15.

Daughters assist rebuilding wall, Nehemiah 3:12.

Concern for family, Job 1:4–5.

Intimate friendship with God, Job 29:4.

Ostrich's family, Job 39:13–17.

Slander against relatives, Psalm 50:20.

Warning to highborn, Psalm 62:9.

Stranger to one's family, Psalm 69:8.

Continuity of faith, Psalm 78:4–7.

Secure offspring, Psalm 89:4.

God's faithfulness through generations, Psalms 100:5; 103:17–18; 119:90.

Righteous father blesses family, Psalm 112:1–3.

Children a blessing from the Lord, Psalms 127:3–5; 128:3–6.

Children of young parents, Psalm 127:4.

Healthy children, Psalm 128:3 (LB).

Family unity, Psalm 133:1–3.

Prayer for sons, daughters, Psalm 144:12 (CEV).

Family discord, Proverbs 6:19 (NRSV).

Troublemakers, Proverbs 11:29.

Greedy family members, Proverbs 15:27 (NRSV).

Domestic peace, quiet, Proverbs 17:1.

Family integrity, Proverbs 20:7 (NRSV).

Family wisdom, Proverbs 24:3 (AB).

No family to look after, Ecclesiastes 4:8 (NASB).

One hundred children, Ecclesiastes 6:3.

Desire for family name, Isaiah 4:1.

God-given children, Isaiah 8:18.

Obstinate children, Isaiah 30:1–5.

Endless name, Isaiah 56:5 (Berk.).

Smallest family powerful, Isaiah 60:22 (CEV).

Enemies within family, Jeremiah 12:6; Micah 7:6.

Children worse than parents, Jeremiah 16:10–12.

Disgrace of childlessness, Jeremiah 22:30.

Family responsibility for sin, Ezekiel 18:4–20.

Immoral parents, Hosea 1:2 (LB).

Purpose of families, Joel 1:3.

Chosen families, Amos 3:2.

Gospel divides households, Matthew 10:32–36; Luke 12:49–53.

Communities, families, Matthew 12:25.

Jesus' family, Matthew 12:46–56; 22:41–46.

Earthly relationships in heaven, Matthew 22:23–30; Mark 12:18–25.

Family of Jesus thought Him deranged, Mark 3:20–21.

Jesus evaluated earthly relationships, Mark 3:31–35.

Leaving all to follow Jesus, Mark 10:28–31.

Rebellion within family, Mark 13:12.

Obedience of the child Jesus to His parents, Luke 2:41–52.

Genealogy of Jesus, Luke 3:23–37.

Context of one's spiritual family, Luke 8:19–21.

Family rejection of discipleship, Luke 14:26–27.

Jesus rejected by His own people, John 1:11.

Unbelieving brothers of Jesus, John 7:5.

Satan as spiritual father, John 8:44.

Grief-stricken family, John 11:17–44.

Devout family, Acts 10:1–2, 7, 22.

Families united in faith, Acts 16:13–15, 25–34.

Spiritual family, Romans 12:10 (AB).

Paul's relatives, Romans 16:21.

Family finances, 2 Corinthians 12:14–15.

Family rapport, Ephesians 6:1–4; Colossians 3:18–21.

Welfare begins at home, 1 Timothy 5:3–8.

Disobedience to parents, 2 Timothy 3:2.

Influence of Scriptures since childhood, 2 Timothy 3:14, 15.

Family of elder must be exemplary, Titus 1:6.

Melchizedek had neither father nor mother, Hebrews 7:1–3.

Moses rejected Pharaoh's daughter, Hebrews 11:23, 24.

Esau sold his birthright, Hebrews 12:16, 17.

God's grace among those of all ages, 1 John 2:12–14.

Becoming children of God, 1 John 3:1–3.

Loving families, 1 John 4:21 (NRSV).

Children walking in truth, 2 John 4.

Joy of Christian children, 3 John 4.

See Ancestors, Children, Daughter, Daughter-in-Law, Home, Parents, Son.

FAMILY ALTAR

Family worshiping together, Joshua 24:15.

Bring message home, Luke 8:39.

Devout family, Acts 10:2.

FAMILY TREE

Ancestral records, 1 Chronicles 9:1 (LB).

See Genealogy.

FAMINE

Motivated by famine, Genesis 12:10; 26:1; Ruth 1:1.

Famine predicted in dream, Genesis 41:27.

Scarcity of food, Leviticus 26:26; 1 Kings 17:7–16; 2 Kings 25:3.

Cannibalism, Deuteronomy 28:53; 2 Kings 6:28; Jeremiah 14:1–6.

Cause of famine, 2 Samuel 21:1.

Inflation due to famine, 2 Kings 6:25.

People in search of bread, Lamentations 1:11.

Children dying in mothers' arms, Lamentations 2:12.

Bread secured at risk of death, Lamentations 5:9.

Harvest failure, Hosea 9:2; Joel 1:11.

Intense famine, Joel 1:17–18.

Famine causes spiritual rejection, Amos 4:6.

Faith in time of famine, Habakkuk 3:17–18.

Famines in last days, Matthew 24:7.

Roman famine, Acts 11:28.

Famine as judgment, Revelation 18:8.

See Drought, Hunger, Thirst.

FAN

Spectators, Hebrews 12:1 (LB).

FANATIC

Prophets of Baal, 1 Kings 18:28.

Fanatic emotion, Ezra 10:1.

Zeal without knowledge, Proverbs 19:2; Romans 10:2.

Fanatic neighbor, Proverbs 27:14.

Family of Jesus thought Him deranged, Mark 3:20–21.

Mob fanaticism, John 19:15; Acts 21:36; 22:23.

Negative fanaticism, Acts 7:51–60.

Paul as fanatic Jew, Acts 9:1–5; Galatians 1:13–14.

See Zeal.

FANFARE

Stewardship fanfare, Matthew 6:2.

FANTASY

Hard work and fantasy, Proverbs 28:19.

FAREWELL *See Parting.*

FARMER

Mankind's first occupation, Genesis 2:15; 3:23.

Famous farmers, Genesis 4:2; 9:20; 1 Kings 19:19; 1 Chronicles 27:26.

Seedtime, harvest, Genesis 8:22.

Farmer Noah, Genesis 9:20.

Prosperous farmer, Genesis 26:12–15.

Meat to eat, Genesis 9:3.

Farmers' holiday, Leviticus 25:1–4.

Much livestock, Deuteronomy 3:19.

Sheep shearing celebration, 2 Samuel 13:23–29 (NRSV).

Farmer's ministry call, 1 Kings 19:19–21.

Royal sheep farmer, 2 Kings 3:4.

Absentee farmer, 2 Kings 8:1–6.

Clergy return to farms, Nehemiah 13:10.

Love for the soil, 2 Chronicles 26:10.

Successful farming, Proverbs 3:9–10.

Successful cattle raising, Job 21:10.

Broken-down fences, Psalms 62:3 (GNB); 80:12 (Berk.).

Livestock struck by lightning, Psalm 78:48.

Lazy farmer, Proverbs 20:4 (NRSV).

Produce sales, Proverbs 27:26.

Fruitful, fantasy farming, Proverbs 28:19.
Overly concerned about weather, Ecclesiastes 11:4.
Farmers taught by God, Isaiah 28:24–29.
"More crops than you need," Isaiah 30:23 (CEV).
Commuting farmers, Jeremiah 31:24.
Fat, lean cattle, Ezekiel 34:20 (KJV).
Lamenting farmers, Amos 5:16.
Livelihood from land, Zechariah 13:5.
"Prize calves," Matthew 22:4 (CEV).
"You are God's field," 1 Corinthians 3:9.
Planting illustration, 1 Corinthians 15:36 (AB).
Hard work rewarded, 2 Timothy 2:6 (LB).
Patient with weather, James 5:7.
See Agriculture, Breeding, Harvest, Seed, Soil.

FASHION

When silver was out of style, 1 Kings 10:21.
Discussing latest intellectual subjects, Acts 17:21.
Head covering and hair style, 1 Corinthians 11:13–16.
See Clothing, Wardrobe, Style.

FAST FOOD

Abraham's fast food, Genesis 18:6–8.

FASTING

Moses fasted forty days, Deuteronomy 9:11–18.
In time of sorrow, 1 Samuel 31:13; 1 Chronicles 10:12; 2 Samuel 3:35.
During national crisis, 2 Samuel 1:12.
Fasting for people's sins, Ezra 10:6.
In need of courage, Esther 4:16.
Humbled by fasting, Psalm 35:13.
Scorn for acts of humility, Psalm 69:10–11.
Weakness from fasting, Psalm 109:24.
Real meaning of fasting, Isaiah 58:3–7.
Egypt's desolation, Ezekiel 29:11–13.
Distraught king, Daniel 6:18 (KJV).
Prayer and fasting, Daniel 9:3.
Fasting for repentance, Joel 1:13–14.
Animals and men fast together, Jonah 3:7.
Insincere fasting, Zechariah 7:1–6.
Joyful fasting, Zechariah 8:19.
Example of Jesus, Matthew 4:1–2.
Pretense of fasting, Matthew 6:16 (CEV).

Disciples did not fast, Matthew 9:14–15.
Some fast, others do not, Mark 2:18–20.
Four thousand people fasting three days, Mark 8:1–3.
Jesus in desert, Luke 4:1–2.
Time to eat, to fast, Luke 5:33–35.
Worship and fasting, Acts 13:2–3.
Fasting with evil intent, Acts 23:12–13.
Anxiety, lost appetite, Acts 27:33–36 (AB).
Little value in itself, 1 Corinthians 8:8.
See Denial, Discipline.

FATALISM

All in God's hands, Psalm 31:15.
See Chance, Fortuity, Predestination.

FATE

Death by random arrow, 2 Chronicles 18:33, 34.
If I perish, I perish, Esther 4:16.
All days pre-ordained, Psalm 139:16.
Time for everything, Ecclesiastes 3:1–8.
Things planned long ago, Isaiah 25:1.
Individual fate, Jeremiah 15:2.
Filled with knowledge of God's will, Colossians 1:9–12.
See Chance, Fortuity, Predestination.

FATHER

Musical father, Genesis 4:21.
Forefathers of all mankind, Genesis 9:18–19.
Exemplary fathers, Genesis 17:18; 35:1–5; 2 Samuel 12:15–16; 1 Chronicles 29:19.
Father's love to God and son, Genesis 22:1–14.
Father's finances, Genesis 31:1.
Father's sorrow and joy, Genesis 45:25–28.
Children suffer father's sin, Exodus 20:5–7; 34:6–7; Numbers 14:18.
No male survivors, Numbers 27:1–11.
Father's authority over daughter, Numbers 30:3–5.
Father prays for guidance, Judges 13:8.
Attitude toward affections of daughters, Judges 15:1–2.
Salaried father, Judges 17:7–13.
Father's famous son, 1 Samuel 1:1–20.
Father's immoral sons, 1 Samuel 2:22–23.

Eli's grief for ark and sons, 1 Samuel 4:16–18.

Son's influence over father, 1 Samuel 19:1–6.

Father, son together in death, 2 Samuel 1:23.

Rivalry between father, son, 2 Samuel 15:1–37.

David's rebellious son, 2 Samuel 18:5.

Father would have died for son, 2 Samuel 18:32–33.

Famous father's more famous son, 1 Kings 1:47–48.

Aged father's counsel to son, 1 Kings 2:1–9.

Son succeeded Solomon, 1 Kings 11:41–43.

Like father, like son, 2 Kings 15:34.

Sacrifice of son, 2 Kings 16:3.

Idolatrous father sacrificed sons, 2 Chronicles 28:3.

Killed by his own sons, 2 Chronicles 32:21.

Repentance of unrepentant son, 2 Chronicles 33:1–13.

Attention to Scriptures, Nehemiah 8:13.

Fate of father, fate of sons, Esther 9:12–14.

Job's concern over family festivity, Job 1:4–5.

Compassionate father, Psalm 103:13–14 (Berk.).

Discipline of good father, Proverbs 3:11–12; 4:1–10.

Leaving inheritance to children, Proverbs 13:22.

Rebel's father, Proverbs 17:21 (LB).

Influence of good father, Proverbs 20:7 (GNB, LB).

Like father, like children, Jeremiah 16:10–13.

Fathers unable to help children, Jeremiah 47:3.

Neither good nor evil transmitted to son, Ezekiel 18:3–20 (GNB).

Father's poor example, Ezekiel 20:18 (LB).

Refusal to learn from father's experience, Daniel 5:18–24.

Father, son to share prostitute, Amos 2:7.

God's total approval of His Son, Matthew 3:17.

Concern for only child, Luke 9:38.

Compassion for lost son, Luke 15:11–32.

Both kind, stern, Romans 11:22.

Father imitated by children, Ephesians 5:1 (LB).

Father inspires children, 1 Thessalonians 2:11–12.

Timothy, spiritual son, 1 Timothy 1:2, 18; 2 Timothy 1:2; 2:1.

Faithful training, Hebrews 12:10 (LB).

See Family, Parents.

FATHER-IN-LAW

Helpful father-in-law, Exodus 18:14–24.

FAULT

None without fault, Proverbs 20:9; 2 Corinthians 7:8–12; Galatians 6:5 (LB).

Faultfinders, Mark 3:2.

Only God can judge, Romans 8:33.

Avoid enmity with those at fault, 2 Thessalonians 3:14–15.

Love overlooks faults, 1 Peter 4:8.

Compliments precede faults, Revelation 2:2–6, 13–16, 19–20.

Faults made known, Revelation 3:19 (AB).

See Error, Mistake, Weakness.

FAULTFINDING

Faultfinder contends with God, Job 40:2 (NRSV).

See Complain, Criticism, Gossip, Slander.

FAULTLESS

Covered with God's love, Ephesians 1:4 (LB).

Living above blame, Philippians 2:14–16 (LB).

FAVOR

"A big favor," 1 Samuel 23:21 (CEV).

Royal favor, Proverbs 16:15; 19:12.

FAVORITISM

Preference one person for another, Genesis 27:6–17; 29:30, 34; 37:3, 4; 43:34; Deuteronomy 21:15–17; 1 Samuel 1:4–5.

Jealousy of younger brother, Genesis 37:1–36.

Israel's love for Joseph, Genesis 37:3.

Favored son, Deuteronomy 33:24.

Favored daughter, only child, Judges 11:29–39.

Favoritism in romance, Ruth 2:14–15.

Favoritism to no one, Job 32:21–22; 34:18–19.

"God has no favorites," Job 33:6 (CEV).

God's favorite, Isaiah 44:2 (CEV).

Evil seemingly favored, Jeremiah 12:1.

Israel loved best of all, Jeremiah 31:20 (CEV).

Good favor used to glorify God, Daniel 1:9–10.

Jerusalem, apple of God's eye, Zechariah 2:8.

Sun rises on all men, Matthew 5:43–48.

No racial boundaries, Acts 10:34–35; Romans 10:12.

Favoring one against another, 1 Corinthians 4:6.

No favoritism with God, Ephesians 6:9; Colossians 3:25.

Avoid partiality, 1 Timothy 5:21.

See Nepotism, Partiality, Preference.

FEAR

"Terror of God," Genesis 35:5.

Frightened by falling leaf, Leviticus 26:36.

Guilt-motivated fear of worship, Numbers 17:12–13.

No fear of man, Deuteronomy 1:17.

Fear, doubt, Deuteronomy 1:21 (LB).

Needless fear, Deuteronomy 9:1–3.

Contagious fear, Deuteronomy 20:8 (LB).

Ten thousand cowards, Deuteronomy 32:30.

Scared to death, Joshua 2:24; 6:1 (LB).

"Heart melted," Joshua 5:1 (NKJV).

Not sure of God's protection, 1 Samuel 27:1–2.

Fear of another's popularity, 2 Samuel 15:13–14.

Unnecessary fear, 1 Kings 1:50–53.

Fearful of opposition, 1 Kings 19:1–5.

Turning to the Lord in fear, 2 Chronicles 20:2–12, 29.

Fear tactics, Ezra 4:4.

Hair stands up, Job 4:15 (Berk.).

Surrounded by terror, Job 15:24.

Fear of another's circumstances, Job 33:6–7.

Reverent fear, Psalm 19:9 (AB); Romans 11:20 (AB).

Fear of future, Psalm 55:4–8.

Fear of man, Psalm 118:6–9; Proverbs 29:25; Isaiah 51:12.

Imagined fears, Proverbs 28:1.

Hearts like trees in storm, Isaiah 7:2–4 (LB).

One who lights deepest darkness, Isaiah 9:2.

Thousand flee one enemy, Isaiah 30:17.

"Shake and shudder," Isaiah 32:11 (CEV).

Strength for the fearful, Isaiah 35:3–4; 38:1–6.

Sufficiency of our Lord, Isaiah 41:10.

Nothing to fear, Isaiah 51:12.

Fear of speaking to older people, Jeremiah 1:6–7.

Boldness to proclaim God's message, Jeremiah 1:8–10.

Frightened by enemy horses, Jeremiah 8:16.

False turning to God, Jeremiah 21:1–14.

Courage and cowardice, Jeremiah 26:13–15, 20–24.

Weak knees, limp hands, Ezekiel 7:17; 21:7; Hebrews 12:12.

Knocking knees of frightened king, Daniel 5:6.

Confident though sitting in darkness, Micah 7:8.

Futility of worry, Matthew 6:25–27.

Fear no one, Matthew 10:26–28 (CEV).

Needless fear, Matthew 14:30; 17:6; Mark 4:35–41; 5:33; John 6:20.

Fearful at empty tomb, Mark 16:1–8.

Frightened by an angel, Luke 1:11–12.

Fear at night, Luke 2:8–14 (See NKJV).

Circumstances and confidence of faith, Luke 8:22–25.

"Don't be afraid of people," Luke 12:4 (CEV).

Parents of man born blind, John 9:18–23.

Afraid to confess Christ, John 12:42.

Standing firm in all circumstances, Philippians 1:27–30.

Peace available at all times, 2 Thessalonians 3:16.

Motivated by holy fear, Hebrews 11:7.

"Hair stand on end," James 2:19 (AB).

Reverent fear of God, 1 Peter 1:17; Revelation 11:13.

Fear to avoid, 1 Peter 3:14.

See Apprehension, Terrorism, Threat, Worry.

FEARLESS

No fear of enemy on all sides, Psalms 3:6; 27:3.
Fearless day, night, Psalm 91:5.
No fear of man, Psalm 118:6.
Peaceful sleep, Proverbs 3:24.
Confidence in the Lord, Isaiah 12:2.
Not one moment's fear, Philippians 1:28 (AB).
See Boldness, Courage.

FEASIBLE *See Tangible, Pragmatic.*

FEAST

Historic wedding feasts, Genesis 29:22; Judges 19:20; Esther 2:18; John 2:1–11.
Food, revelry, Exodus 32:6; Judges 9:27; 1 Samuel 25:36.
Eating, rejoicing, Deuteronomy 27:7; Song of Songs 2:4.
Banquet for thousands, Daniel 5:1.
Eating to complete satisfaction, Joel 2:26.
Guests at banquet, Luke 14:8–24.
See Banquet, Celebration, Festival, Marriage, Meals.

FEATURES

Radiant face of Moses, Exodus 34:30; 2 Corinthians 3:7–8.
Wisdom alters facial features, Ecclesiastes 8:1.
Variation of facial appearance, Ezekiel 1:10.
Jesus at transfiguration, Matthew 17:2.
Features like lightning, Matthew 28:3.
Evidence of having been with Jesus, Acts 4:13.
Influence of persecution, Acts 6:15.
Personal features forgotten, James 1:23–25.
See Countenance.

FEEBLE

"This feeble bunch," Nehemiah 4:2 (CEV).

FEELINGS

Hurt feelings, Jeremiah 4:19 (Berk.); 2 Corinthians 7:8 (CEV).

FEET

No blisters, Deuteronomy 8:4 (Berk.).
Taking care of one's feet, 2 Samuel 19:24.
Trampled by hungry mob, 2 Kings 7:17–20.
Foot disease, 2 Chronicles 16:12.
Feet restrained from evil, Psalm 119:101 (NKJV).
Beautiful feet, Song of Songs 7:1; Isaiah 52:7.
Boots worn in battle, Isaiah 9:5.
Feet strengthened for conquest, Micah 4:13.
At feet of Jesus, Matthew 15:30; Mark 5:22–23; Luke 7:37–38; 10:39; John 11:32; Revelation 1:17.
Impotent feet, Acts 14:8 (KJV).
See Foot Washing, Running, Walk.

FELLOWSHIP

Divine promise of fellowship, Leviticus 26:1–13.
Food, fellowship, Deuteronomy 14:23 (See CEV); 15:20.
Fellowship offerings, 1 Samuel 11:15.
Becoming one in spirit, 1 Samuel 18:1–4.
Friendship centered in the Lord, 1 Samuel 20:42.
Companions in danger, 1 Samuel 22:23.
Painful silence, Job 2:13.
Undependable friends, Job 6:15–17.
Cowardly fellowship, Job 6:21 (AB).
Godless fellowship, Job 15:34.
World's greatest fellowship, Psalm 16:3 (GNB).
Glorifying God together, Psalm 34:3.
Disrupted fellowship, Psalm 55:12–21 (LB, GNB).
Rich spiritual feast, Psalm 63:5 (NRSV).
Kindred hearts, Psalm 119:63.
Live together in unity, Psalm 133:1–3 (RSV).
Worthwhile conversation, Proverbs 20:5.
Avoid evil fellowship, Proverbs 24:1.
Two better than one, Ecclesiastes 4:9–12.
Shelter from wind, Isaiah 32:2.
Messiah left alone, Isaiah 63:5.
Agreement requisite to fellowship, Amos 3:3.

Neighbors enjoy fellowship, Zechariah 3:10.

Stewardship, fellowship, Matthew 5:23–24.

Jesus fellowshipped with "sinners," Mark 2:15–17.

Fellowship, witness, Mark 5:18–20.

People at peace, Mark 9:50.

Fellowship singing, Mark 14:26.

Varying styles of ministry, Luke 9:1–62.

The Lord who is always at hand, Acts 2:25–28.

Experiencing fellowship, Acts 2:42; 1 Corinthians 1:9; Philippians 2:1; 1 John 1:3–7.

Sharing Scripture insights, Acts 18:24–26.

Fellowship of leader, followers, Acts 20:36–38.

One-week visit, Acts 21:3–4.

Fellowship of prayer, Romans 1:8–10; Ephesians 1:11–23; Philippians 1:3–6; Colossians 1:3–14.

Mutual encouragement, Romans 1:11–12.

Honor others above yourself, Romans 12:10.

Fellowship of joy and sorrow, Romans 12:15.

Fellowship of unbelievers, Romans 13:13 (LB).

Those weak in faith, Romans 14:1.

Accepting one another, Romans 15:7.

Enjoyable company, Romans 15:24.

Refreshed together, Romans 15:32 (LB).

Greetings to friends, Romans 16:3–16.

Believers in agreement, 1 Corinthians 1:10–17.

Men, women in ministry, 1 Corinthians 11:11.

Imbalance in food, fellowship, 1 Corinthians 11:20–22.

Different gifts, service, 1 Corinthians 12:4–11.

Fellowship in worship, 1 Corinthians 14:26.

Greet with holy kiss, 1 Corinthians 16:20.

Sharing both suffering, comfort, 2 Corinthians 1:7.

Fellowship of bad feelings, 2 Corinthians 2:2 (CEV).

Need for ministry fellowship, 2 Corinthians 2:12–13.

Freedom in Spirit, 2 Corinthians 3:17.

Hearts open wide, 2 Corinthians 6:11–13.

Make place in hearts, 2 Corinthians 7:2 (CEV).

Paul's visit with Peter, Galatians 1:18.

Right hand of fellowship, Galatians 2:9–10.

Do good to all, especially believers, Galatians 6:10.

Members of God's family, Ephesians 2:19–22.

Imitators of God expressing love to others, Ephesians 5:1–2.

Keeping in touch, Ephesians 6:21–22.

Channel of much blessing, Philippians 1:25–26.

Like-minded people, Philippians 2:1–2.

Unity in the church, Philippians 4:1–9.

Sharing each other's troubles, Philippians 4:14.

Greetings from Rome to Philippi, Philippians 4:21–23.

Thanking God for fellowship, Colossians 1:3–6.

Concern for development of followers, Colossians 2:1–5.

"Welded together in love," Colossians 2:2 (Berk.).

"Put up with each other," Colossians 3:13 (CEV).

Prison fellowship, Colossians 4:10; 2 Timothy 1:16–18.

Fellowship in ministry, 1 Thessalonians 2:7–9.

Remembered fellowship, 1 Thessalonians 2:17–20; 3:1–5.

Overflowing love, 1 Thessalonians 3:12.

Brotherly love, 1 Thessalonians 4:9.

Encouraging each other, 1 Thessalonians 5:11.

Thanking God for others, 2 Thessalonians 1:3 (AB).

Avoid inept Christians, 2 Thessalonians 3:6.

Timothy, spiritual son, 1 Timothy 1:2, 18; 2 Timothy 1:2; 2:1.

Harmonious prayer fellowship, 1 Timothy 2:8.

"Like fresh air," 2 Timothy 1:16 (AB).

Not embarrassed by friend's misfortune, 2 Timothy 1:16–17.

Avoid foolish arguments, 2 Timothy 2:23.

Slave who became brother, Philemon 16.

Use of guest room, Philemon 22.

Need for mutual encouragement, Hebrews 3:13.

Example in fellowship with each other, Hebrews 10:24–25 (CEV).

Living in good relationships, Hebrews 12:14–15.

Love each other as brothers, Hebrews 13:1.

Avoid discrimination in fellowship, James 2:1–4.

Confessing sins one to another, James 5:16.

"Genuine mutual love," 1 Peter 1:22 (NRSV).

Built of Living Stone, 1 Peter 2:4–8.

Kiss, greeting, 1 Peter 5:14.

Ministry-based fellowship, 1 John 1:1–3.

Darkness of hatred, 1 John 2:9–11.

Love one another, 1 John 4:7–11.

Love in truth, 3 John 1.

Conversation better than correspondence, 3 John 13–14.

Brothers, companions, Revelation 1:9.

Fellowship with the Lord Himself, Revelation 3:20.

When God comes to live with men, Revelation 21:1–4.

See Companionship, Camaraderie, Rapport, Unanimity.

FEMALE See Mother, Mother-in-Law, Sister, Women, Women's Rights.

FEMINIST

Generic name for both sexes, Genesis 5:2.

Women at historic events, Matthew 28:8; Mark 15:47; Luke 2:36–38; John 20:1; Acts 16:13–14.

See Marriage, Mother, Women's Rights.

FENCE See Farmer.

FERMENTATION

Bread without yeast, Genesis 19:3.

Vented wineskin, Job 32:19 (Berk.).

Using new skins, Matthew 9:17.

Fermentation of wine, Mark 2:22.

See Alcohol, Leaven.

FEROCITY

"Faces of lions," 1 Chronicles 12:8.

Women's hair, lion's teeth, Revelation 9:8.

FERRY See Boat.

FERTILITY (Earth)

Blood poured onto ground, Deuteronomy 12:23–24.

Straw, manure, Isaiah 25:10.

"Fat valley," Isaiah 28:4 (KJV).

Barren land made fertile, Isaiah 41:18–20.

Meadow grass, thriving trees, Isaiah 44:4.

Fertile country, Jeremiah 2:7 (NKJV).

Human bones fertilize soil, Jeremiah 8:1–3 (NRSV).

Desert becomes garden, Ezekiel 36:35.

See Agriculture.

FERTILITY (Human)

Creator's command, Genesis 1:28; 9:7.

Pregnancy at advanced age, Genesis 16:16; 17:1–21; 21:1–5.

Wombs closed, opened, Genesis 20:17–18.

Pregnancy in answer to prayer, Genesis 25:21.

Old Testament morality, Genesis 30:1–24.

Beyond age of childbearing, Ruth 1:11.

Prayer for fertility, Ruth 4:11–12 (LB).

Fruitful, barren wives, 1 Samuel 1:2–8, 20; 2:21.

Childless Hannah, 1 Samuel 1:5, 20; 2:21.

Blessing of producing children, Psalm 127:5.

Fertility gods, Jeremiah 2:20 (GNB).

See Childless, Pregnancy.

FERVENT

"Fervent love," 1 Peter 4:8 (NASB).

FESTIVAL

"Festival of Shelters," 1 Kings 8:65 (CEV).

"Festival of Booths," John 7:2 (NASB, NRSV).

See Feast, Holiday.

FESTIVITY

Calamity at family gathering, Job 1:18–19.

Time to rejoice, not weep, Nehemiah 8:9–10.

Celebrating wall rebuilding, Nehemiah 8:16–18.

Godless entertainment, Isaiah 5:12.

Revelry of Tyre and Sidon, Isaiah 23:6–12.
Banquet for Jesus, Luke 5:27–35.
See Banquet, Celebration, Holiday.

FETISH

Burdensome images, Isaiah 46:1.
Magic charms, Ezekiel 13:18.
See Magic.

FETTERS

Great strength tested, Judges 16:21–30.
Shackles, hook in nose, 2 Chronicles 33:11;
Psalm 149:6–9.
Young king humiliated, 2 Chronicles
36:5–6.
Prophet in chains, Jeremiah 40:1–5.
Chained between two soldiers, Acts 12:1–
19.
Extra chains for prize prisoner, Acts 21:33.
See Bondage, Prison.

FETUS

Desiring prenatal death, Job 3:11.
Destiny of unborn, Psalm 139:15–16.
Divine call to unborn, Isaiah 49:1.
God's prenatal plan for Jeremiah, Jeremiah
1:4–5; 20:17.
See Abortion, Pregnancy.

FEVER

Debilitating fever, Leviticus 26:14–16.
Smitten with fever, Deuteronomy 28:22.
Burning fever, Job 30:30.
Hunger-induced fever, Lamentations 5:10
(NRSV).
Ailing mother-in-law, Matthew 8:14.
Fever and dysentery, Acts 28:8.
See Sickness.

FIANCÉE

Pregnant fiancée, Luke 2:5 (LB).

FICKLE

Love like morning mist, Hosea 6:4.
Pretended weddings, funerals, Luke 7:32
(LB).
Fickle Galatians, Galatians 1:6–9.
"Wanting to have ears tickled," 2 Timothy
4:3 (CEV).
See Insincerity.

FICTION

Shortest short story, Ecclesiastes 9:14–15
(Note "surprise" ending).
Fables, myths, 1 Timothy 1:4 (AB).
"Godless fiction," 1 Timothy 4:7 (AB); 2 Tim-
othy 4:4 (AB).
Cleverly invented stories, 2 Peter 1:16; 2:3.
See Literature, Parable.

FIDELITY

Joseph's integrity, Genesis 39:6.
Honest expense accounts, 2 Kings 12:13–
15.
Faithful workmen, 2 Chronicles 34:12.
Responsible warehousing, Nehemiah 13:13.
Search for one honest person, Jeremiah
5:1.
Free from corruption, negligence, Daniel
6:4.
Fidelity requirement, 1 Corinthians 4:2.
See Character, Dependability, Integrity.

FIFTH COLUMN

Disruption among believers, Jude 3–4.
See Disturb, Opposition.

FIGHT *See Boxing, Conflict, Wrestling.*

FIGS

Leaves for garments, Genesis 3:7.
Symbol of abundance, Numbers 13:23;
Deuteronomy 8:7–9.
Figs commercialized, Nehemiah 13:15.
Medicinal figs, 2 Kings 20:7; Isaiah 38:21.
See Fruit.

FIGURE OF SPEECH

Blood cries out, Genesis 4:10.
Earth's nausea, Leviticus 18:25.
Furnace of persecution, Deuteronomy
4:20; Jeremiah 11:4.
Intoxicated arrows, Deuteronomy 32:42.
Stones with ears, Joshua 24:27; Psalm
77:16.
Divine arrows, Job 6:4.
Foam on water, Job 24:18.
Heart led by eyes, Job 31:7.
Animated bronze, iron, Job 40:18.
Pregnant with evil, Psalm 7:14.
Clothed pastures, Psalm 65:13 (NKJV).

Broken heart, Psalm 69:20.

Tongues rule earth, Psalm 73:9.

Tablet of heart, Proverbs 3:3.

Lamp of the Lord, Proverbs 20:27.

Secrets between hands, Matthew 6:3.

Misunderstood figure-of-speech, Matthew 16:5-12.

Temple of Christ's body, John 2:19-21.

Jesus spoke figuratively, John 16:25-30 (NRSV).

"Speaking plainly," John 16:29 (NRSV).

"Turn on the light," 1 Corinthians 4:5 (LB).

Holy Spirit's temple, 1 Corinthians 6:19.

Body communication, 1 Corinthians 12:15-16.

Eyes of heart, Ephesians 1:18.

"Home in your hearts," Ephesians 3:17 (GNB).

Shipwrecked faith, 1 Timothy 1:19.

Great rock, 2 Timothy 2:19 (LB).

Lion's mouth, 2 Timothy 4:17.

Mobility of heart, Philemon 12 (GNB).

Harvest of righteousness, James 3:18.

Clothe with humility, 1 Peter 5:5.

Springs without water, 2 Peter 2:17.

See Literature, Metaphor.

FILTH

Soda, soap, Jeremiah 2:22.

New garments for Joshua, Zechariah 3:1-7.

See Putrid, Stench, Unclean.

FILTHY LUCRE *See Bribery, Materialism.*

FINALE

Last words of David, 2 Samuel 23:1-7; Psalm 72:20.

Last verse of Psalms, Psalm 150:6.

Ezekiel's prophecy of "the end," Ezekiel 7:2.

Last statement of great prophet, Ezekiel 48:35.

Fulfillment of times, Ephesians 1:9-10.

Christ suffered once for all, Hebrews 9:24-28.

End is near, 1 Peter 4:7.

The last hour, 1 John 2:18.

Conclusion of Bible, Revelation 22:20-21; Malachi 4:6.

See Completion, Conclusion, Ending, Finish, Termination.

FINANCE

Monetary values, Leviticus 27:25.

Temple collection box, 2 Kings 12:9-14 (GNB).

Interest-bearing loan, Psalm 15:5 (AB).

Avoid unwise financial ties, Proverbs 6:1-5 (LB).

Neither debtor nor creditor, Jeremiah 15:10 (LB).

Treasures on earth or in heaven, Matthew 6:19-21.

Advance cost estimation, Luke 14:28-30.

Human equations, divine power, John 6:1-13.

Importance of paying debts, Romans 13:8.

Sharing ministry expense, Philippians 4:15-19.

Paul worked to provide income, 1 Thessalonians 2:9; 2 Thessalonians 3:6-10.

Endured poverty glorifies God, Hebrews 11:37-38.

Avoid pagan financing, 3 John 7.

See Cost, Investment, Money, Stewardship.

FINDING

Finders not keepers, Leviticus 6:3.

Things past finding out, Job 9:10 (NKJV).

Seek, find, Matthew 7:7-8; Luke 11:9-10.

Finding treasure, Matthew 13:44-45.

Lost sheep found, Luke 15:4-7.

Finding lost coin, Luke 15:8-9.

FINISH *See Finale.*

FIRE

Sodom aflame, Genesis 19:28.

Purified by fire, Ezekiel 22:20-22; Zechariah 13:9; Malachi 3:2; 1 Corinthians 3:13; 1 Peter 1:7.

Death by fire, Judges 9:49.

Angel ascending in flame of fire, Judges 13:20.

Fiery foxes, Judges 15:4-5.

Flaming identification, 2 Kings 1:9-17.

"Blazing breath of God," Job 15:30 (CEV).

"Go up in flames," Isaiah 5:24 (CEV).
Excrement used as fuel, Ezekiel 4:9–15.
Satan's fiery arrows, Ephesians 6:16.
Lake of fire, Revelation 19:19–21.
See Fuel, Kindling.

FIRST CLASS

First-class soldier, 2 Timothy 2:3 (AB).

FISH

Clean, unclean, Deuteronomy 14:9–10 (LB).
Tax-paying fish, Matthew 17:27.
Fish scale blindness, Acts 9:18 (GNB).

FISHERMAN

Water teeming with fish, Genesis 1:20–21.
Idols like fish, Exodus 20:4.
Abundant seas, Deuteronomy 33:19
Lake property, Deuteronomy 33:23 (NRSV).
Song to fish by, Isaiah 42:10.
Dried up waters, Isaiah 50:2 (NKJV).
Fishermen as agents of judgment, Jeremiah 16:16–18.
Fisherman's paradise, Ezekiel 47:9–10.
Men caught like fish, Habakkuk 1:14–15.
Fisherman's pagan worship, Habakkuk 1:16 (LB).
Fishers of men, Matthew 4:19; Mark 1:17; Luke 5:1–11.
Miraculous catch, John 21:1–12.
Fishermen called boys, John 21:5 (LB).
See Sportsman.

FIST

"Two fists full," Ecclesiastes 4:6 (NASB).

FITNESS

Hindrance to worship, Leviticus 21:16–23.
Death of healthy person, Job 5:26.
Candidates for government service, Daniel 1:3–5.
Qualifications for following Jesus, Luke 9:23–26.

FLAG

Tribal and family banners, Numbers 2:2; 10:14–25.
Raise the flag, Psalm 20:5.
Enemy flags, Psalm 74:4.
Banner of love, Song of Songs 2:4.

Divine banner summons earth's nations, Isaiah 5:26.
Messiah likened to banner, Isaiah 11:10–12.
Frightened by military flags, Isaiah 31:9.
Flag of proclamation, Jeremiah 50:2.
Summons to action, Jeremiah 51:12.

FLASHBACK

Herod and John the Baptist, Mark 6:14–29.

FLATTERY

Sincere sibling flattery, Genesis 33:10.
King likened to angel, 2 Samuel 14:17.
Flattering lips, Psalm 12:2–3.
Evil flattery, Psalms 36:1–4; 78:36; Proverbs 2:16; Romans 16:18.
Self-flattery, Psalm 36:2.
Adulteress' lips drip honey, Proverbs 5:3.
False flattery, Proverbs 24:24.
Rebuke better than flattery, Proverbs 28:23.
Flattering one's neighbor, Proverbs 29:5.
Dishonest flattery, Matthew 22:16; Luke 20:21.
Empty sincerity of Pharisees, Mark 12:15–17.
Glory belongs to God alone, 1 Corinthians 3:7.
Complimenting those previously rebuked, 2 Corinthians 7:14.
Flattery avoided in fund raising, 1 Thessalonians 2:5–6.
See Exaggeration, Obsequity, Sham.

FLAVOR

Food with good flavor, Genesis 27:4–31.
Sweet water, Exodus 15:25.
Gourmet manna, Exodus 16:31.
Unable to detect flavors, 2 Samuel 19:35.
Tasteless egg white, Job 6:6.
Avoid craving delicacies, Proverbs 23:3.
Hunger improves flavor, Proverbs 27:7.
Bitter flavor, Matthew 27:34.
Sweet in mouth, sour in stomach, Revelation 10:9–11.
See Delicacy, Food, Gourmet, Taste.

FLEDGLING

Protected fledglings, Deuteronomy 32:11.

FLEECE

Gideon's procedure, Judges 6:36–40.
See Guidance.

FLESH

Men from dust, Genesis 2:7.
Flesh from dust, Psalm 103:14.
Put out offending eye, Matthew 5:29.
Self-crucified, Romans 6:6.
Flesh, spirit, Romans 7:15–18.
Put on Christ, Romans 13:14.
"You are still fleshly," 1 Corinthians 3:3 (NASB).
Subduing the flesh, Galatians 5:16; Colossians 3:5.
Continual lust for more, Ephesians 4:19.
Fleshly desire, James 1:13–15.
See Carnality, Lust, Worldliness.

FLIES

"Whistle for flies," Isaiah 7:18.

FLIGHT

Flying serpent, Isaiah 30:6 (Berk.).
"Wind in their wings," Zechariah 5:9.
See Aircraft, Astronaut.

FLIGHTY *See Unstable.*

FLIRTATION

Noticing opposite sex, Genesis 6:1–2 (Berk.).
Ogled eyes, Genesis 39:7 (Berk.).
Lustful look, Job 31:1 (See Berk.).
Haughty women of Zion, Isaiah 3:16–17.
Learned flirtation, Jeremiah 2:33.
Adulterous look, Hosea 2:2.
See Adultery, Promiscuity, Prostitute, Seduction, Temptation, Temptress.

FLOATING *See Buoyant.*

FLOCK *See Sheep, Shepherd.*

FLOGGING *See Whipping.*

FLOOD

Noah's escape, Genesis 7:1–24.
"Roaring floods," Genesis 7:17 (LB).
Evil men destroyed, Job 22:16.
Flood waters restrained, Job 28:11 (KJV, Note NKJV).
Never another flood, Psalm 104:9.
Divine promise, Isaiah 54:9.
Rising waters, Jeremiah 47:2.
Flood authenticated by Jesus, Matthew 24:36–39.
Apostolic validation, 1 Peter 3:18–22; 2 Peter 2:4–5.

FLOOD

THEY ALL LAUGHED AT NOAH'S FLOOD ROBE.

Water spewed from serpent's mouth, Revelation 12:15–16.
See Judgment.

FLOWERS

Blossoming staff, Numbers 17:8.
Joyful blossoms, Isaiah 35:1 (AB).
Lilies of the field, Matthew 6:28–29.
Wildflowers, Luke 12:27 (CEV).
See Garden, Horticulture.

FLUENT

Tip of tongue, Job 33:2.
Fluent deception, Psalm 12:1–2.
Mouth like sharpened sword, Isaiah 49:2.
See Eloquence, Speech.

FOG

Fog vapor, Genesis 2:6 (AB).

FOG INDEX

Seemingly "foggy" translation, 1 Chronicles 26:18 (KJV).

FOLLOWERS

Choosing mighty and brave, 1 Samuel 14:52.
Army of chosen men, 2 Samuel 6:1; 23:8–39.
Cost of following Jesus, Mark 8:34 (NRSV).
Follow light to avoid darkness, John 8:12.
Sheep and shepherd, John 10:27; 12:26.
Concern for follower, 2 Timothy 1:3.
In His steps, 1 Peter 2:21.
See Discipleship, Example, Leadership.

FOLLOW-UP

Convert follow-up, Acts 15:36.
Shepherding new converts, Acts 16:36–40.
Teaching new converts, Acts 18:23.
Third visit, 2 Corinthians 13:1.
Concern for followers, 2 Corinthians 13:5–10.
Follow-up liaison, 1 Thessalonians 3:1–5.
Congregational follow-up, Titus 1:5–9.
See Convert, Discipleship, Instruction, Teaching, Reinforcement.

FOLLY

National folly, Psalm 9:15.
Folly of overconfidence, Psalm 49:13.
"Adorned with folly," Proverbs 14:18 (NRSV).
Folly of fools, wisdom of discerning, Proverbs 15:14.
Foolish repetition, Proverbs 26:11.
Folly of not listening, Isaiah 48:17–18.
Hatching unlaid eggs, Jeremiah 17:11.
See Foolish, Stubborn.

FOMENT *See Controversy, Devious, Jealousy, Scheme.*

FOOD

Let land produce, Genesis 1:11–12.
Vegetarian man, animals, Genesis 1:29–30.
Meat as food, Genesis 9:3.
Stolen supply, Genesis 14:11.
Food and hospitality, Genesis 18:1–8.
Food eaten by angels, Genesis 19:1–4; Judges 13:16.
Taste for wild game, Genesis 25:27–28; 27:2–4.
Lentil soup, Genesis 25:34.
Last request, Genesis 27:1–4.
Tasty food, Genesis 27:7.
Spices, myrrh, pistachio, almonds, Genesis 43:11.
Basic food, Exodus 3:17.
Forbidden food, Leviticus 11:13–40.
Edible, inedible insects, Leviticus 11:20–23.
"Miserable food," Numbers 21:5 (Berk.).
All you can eat, Deuteronomy 12:15–20 (KJV).
Craving for meat, Deuteronomy 12:20.
Vitality of bread, Judges 7:13–15.
Comforted by food, Judges 19:5 (NKJV).
Sampling food offered for sacrifice, 1 Samuel 2:13–14.
Soldiers denied nourishment, 1 Samuel 14:24–30.
Food containing blood, 1 Samuel 14:31–33.
Energizing food, 1 Kings 19:7.
Unpalatable food, 2 Kings 4:40.
Eating unplanted crop, 2 Kings 19:29.
Salt improves flavor, Job 6:6.
Loathsome food, Job 6:7 (Berk.).
Worm's feast, Job 24:20.
Blessing better than food, Psalm 63:5.

Manna, bread of angels, Psalm 78:25.

Hunger inspires hard work, Proverbs 16:26.

Avoid over-eating, Proverbs 23:1–3.

Wisdom like eating honey, Proverbs 24:13–14.

Too lazy to eat, Proverbs 26:15.

Nutritious food, Ecclesiastes 10:17.

Curds, honey, Isaiah 7:15.

Lion eating straw, Isaiah 11:7.

Harvest, food's first stage, Isaiah 28:28.

Eating ashes, Isaiah 44:20.

Abominable food, Isaiah 66:17.

Bread secured at risk of death, Lamentations 5:9.

Food defiled by unclean fuel, Ezekiel 4:12–15.

Priests given best food, Ezekiel 44:28–31.

Failure of harvest, Hosea 9:2.

Plenty to eat, Joel 2:26.

Forbidden food denied, Zechariah 9:7.

Cooking pots in the Lord's house, Zechariah 14:20–21.

Food of John the Baptist, Matthew 3:4.

Food supplied to those who trust, Matthew 6:31.

Sabbath corn picking, Matthew 12:1–8; Mark 2:23–27.

Feeding five thousand, Matthew 14:13–21; Mark 6:30–44; 8:1–9.

Mealtime prayer, Mark 14:22.

Jesus needed food, Luke 4:1–2.

Banquet celebrating commitment, Luke 5:27–32.

Feasting not fasting, Luke 5:33 (LB).

Food for dead girl, Luke 8:55.

Too concerned for food, Luke 12:29.

Spiritual food, John 4:34.

High food cost, John 6:5–7.

Leftovers, John 6:12 (Berk.).

Food desired above spiritual results, John 6:26–40.

Dinner honoring Jesus, John 12:2.

Love feast, John 13:1–2.

Bread implicated Judas, John 13:21–27.

Trance caused by hunger, Acts 10:10.

No food unclean, Romans 14:14.

Eating an act of faith, Romans 14:23.

Limited spiritual diet, 1 Corinthians 3:1–2.

Offered to idols, 1 Corinthians 8:5–13 (LB).

Unmuzzled ox, 1 Corinthians 9:9–14.

Physical hunger, spiritual sustenance, 1 Corinthians 11:34.

Stomach as god, Philippians 3:19.

Sweet in mouth, sour to stomach, Revelation 10:9–10.

Wedding supper in heaven, Revelation 19:9.

See Diet, Famine, Feast, Gourmet, Hunger, Kosher, Meals, Taste.

FOOL

Egyptian fools, Exodus 10:2 (LB, NRSV).

Fool's perception, 1 Samuel 26:21; Proverbs 12:15.

Blind atheism, Psalms 14:1; 53:1.

Gullibility, Proverbs 14:15.

Repetitive folly, Proverbs 26:11.

Fool's wisdom, Proverbs 26:12.

Courageous or fool, Jeremiah 1:17 (LB).

End result for materialist, Luke 12:16–21.

Fools for Christ's sake, 1 Corinthians 4:10.

Pauline sarcasm, 2 Corinthians 11:16–29.

See Rebellion, Stubborn.

FOOLISH

Foolishly blaming God, Job 1:22 (KJV).

Wild donkey's colt, Job 11:12.

No wise man, Job 17:10.

Foolish woman, Proverbs 9:13–16.

Careless about danger, Proverbs 22:3.

Parables to a fool, Proverbs 26:1–12.

Foolish drunkard, Hosea 7:5 (LB).

Tolerate another's foolishness, 2 Corinthians 11:1 (GNB).

Our own foolish past, Titus 3:3.

See Ignorance.

FOOT WASHING

Courtesy to guests, Genesis 18:4.

Washing one's own feet, Genesis 19:2; 43:24.

Matrimonial duty, 1 Samuel 25:40–41.

Act of love, Luke 7:44; John 13:5; 1 Timothy 5:10.

See Sacrament.

FORBEARANCE

Divine wrath delayed, Isaiah 48:9.

Tolerance toward bad reports, 1 Corinthians 11:18–19.

Golden Rule demonstration, 2 Corinthians 2:5–11.

Humble, gentle, patient, Ephesians 4:2.

Forgive as the Lord forgave, Colossians 3:13.

See Forgiveness, Golden Rule, Pardon, Patience.

FORBIDDEN

Forbidden fruit, Genesis 2:17.

Sweetness of stolen things, Proverbs 9:17.

Forbidden mountain, Hebrews 12:18–21.

See Restriction.

FOREBODING

Prayer in foreboding danger, Nehemiah 4:7–9.

Judgment at hand, Ezekiel 7:2–12.

Impending persecutions, Mark 13:9.

Wolves among sheep, Acts 20:28–31.

Satan's relentless pursuit, 1 Peter 5:8.

See Danger, Peril.

FORECAST See Prediction.

FORECLOSURE

"Merciful creditor," Ezekiel 18:7 (LB).

Charge no interest, Exodus 22:25.

Protecting debtor's earning power, Deuteronomy 24:6.

See Mortgage, Debt.

FOREFATHER

Mankind's three forefathers, Genesis 9:18–19.

Ancient traditions, Matthew 15:2.

Genealogy of Jesus, Luke 3:23–37.

See Ancestors.

FOREIGNER

Forbidden marriage between foreigners, Genesis 24:2.

Foreword to Golden Rule, Exodus 22:21; 23:9.

Passage denied to foreigners, Numbers 20:14–21.

Foreigner's debt, Deuteronomy 15:3.

Aliens succeed above locals, Deuteronomy 28:43–44.

Foreigners seeking help, 2 Samuel 22:45–46.

Influx of immigrants, 2 Chronicles 15:9.

Census of aliens, 2 Chronicles 2:17–18.

Secret nationality, Esther 2:20.

Centurion named Cornelius, Acts 10:1–33.

See Alien, Xenophobia.

FOREKNOWLEDGE

Foreknowledge of son's future, Genesis 49:1–27.

Destiny set for rebellious people, Numbers 14:35.

Moses foretold death site, Deuteronomy 32:48–50.

Informed prophet, 1 Kings 14:1–5.

Prophet knew decreed fate, 2 Kings 6:31–32.

Words of prophet fulfilled, 2 Kings 7:17–20.

Chosen to build temple, 1 Chronicles 28:2–10.

God's plans remain firm, Job 42:2.

"A tale that is told," Psalm 90:9 (AB).

The Lord does what pleases Him, Psalm 135:6.

One who knows all our ways, Psalm 139:1–16.

Righteous path, wicked way, Proverbs 4:18–19.

Steps directed by the Lord, Proverbs 20:24.

Unknown tomorrow, Proverbs 27:1.

Meaningless future, Ecclesiastes 2:15–16.

Roundelay of life, Ecclesiastes 6:10.

No one knows, Ecclesiastes 10:14.

Reluctant to test the Lord, Isaiah 7:10–12.

Divine plan, purpose, Isaiah 14:24.

Foretold, planned, brought to pass, Isaiah 37:26.

Nation's future foretold, Isaiah 42:9; 44:7; Daniel 2:28–29.

Crucifixion foretold, Matthew 26:2; Mark 8:31; 9:31; 10:32–33.

One who knows future, Isaiah 45:1–13; Acts 15:17–18.

Future in God's hands, Isaiah 46:8–11.

Called before birth, Isaiah 49:1; Jeremiah 1:5.

Distant future, Ezekiel 12:26–27.

Divine plan foretold, Amos 3:7.

Future needs known to God, Matthew 6:8.

Sacred secret, Matthew 24:36; Mark 13:26–33; 1 Thessalonians 5:1–2.

Father's prophecy of son, Luke 1:67–79.

Isaiah's prophecy confirmed, Luke 4:17–22.

Advance Passover preparation, Luke 22:7–13.

Gospel foretold, Galatians 3:6–9.

See Predestination, Prophecy.

FOREMOST *See Importance.*

FORERUNNER

Running ahead of chariot, 2 Samuel 15:1.

John the Baptist, Malachi 3:1; Mark 1:2–8; Luke 3:1–20.

Jesus has made advance preparations, Hebrews 6:19–20.

See Preparation.

FORESTRY

All kinds of trees, Genesis 2:9.

Living among trees, Genesis 13:18; 14:13; 18:1.

Landmark tree, Genesis 21:33.

Protected trees, Deuteronomy 20:19–20 (See LB).

Clearing new land, Joshua 17:14–18.

Trees seek king, Judges 9:7–15.

Finest trees felled, 2 Kings 19:23.

Forest ranger, Nehemiah 2:8.

"Native green tree," Psalm 37:35 (Berk.).

Forest fame, Psalm 74:5.

Tree lies where it falls, Ecclesiastes 11:3.

Cut down thickets, Isaiah 10:34.

Trees flaunt woodcutters, Isaiah 14:8.

Reforestation, Isaiah 44:14.

Lumber for idols, Jeremiah 10:2–5.

Garden of Gethsemane, John 18:1.

Spark ignites forest, James 3:5.

See Ecology, Trees.

FORETHOUGHT

Wise ant, Proverbs 6:6–8.

Danger foreseen, Proverbs 23:3.

FOREWORD

World history foreword, Genesis 1:1–2.

Foreword to Proverbs, Proverbs 1:1–6.

FORGERY

Forged signature, 1 Kings 21:1–16.

Alleged letters, 2 Thessalonians 2:2 (AB).

See Counterfeit.

FORGIVENESS

Filial forgiveness, Genesis 45:14–15.

Evil act forgiven, Genesis 50:15–21.

Forgiving spirit, Exodus 23:4–5; Proverbs 24:17; 25:21–22.

Parable convinces need to forgive, 2 Samuel 14:1–21.

Forgiving prayer, Job 42:7–10.

Forgiven sins honor God, Psalm 25:11.

God's forgiveness and punishment, Psalm 99:8.

Forgiven, forgotten, Psalm 103:12.

None deserves forgiveness, Psalm 130:3–4 (NRSV).

Depth of mercy and grace, Psalm 145:8–9.

Love's power, Proverbs 10:12.

Controlled anger, Proverbs 19:11.

God's reason for forgiving, Isaiah 43:25 (CEV).

Forgiveness like cloud swept away, Isaiah 44:22–23.

God's love to faithless Israel, Jeremiah 3:12–13.

God's total forgiveness, Jeremiah 50:20.

Anger forever gone, Hosea 14:4 (CEV, LB).

Forgiving Lord, Joel 2:12–13.

Given a second chance, Jonah 1:1–3; 3:1–3.

Forgiving grace, mercy of God, Micah 7:18.

Stewardship, forgiveness, Matthew 5:23–24.

Forgiving, forgiven, Matthew 6:14–15.

Principles of forgiveness, Matthew 18:21–22; Mark 11:25; Luke 6:37; 17:3–4; 2 Corinthians 2:7–10; James 5:15–16.

Forgiven, not forgiving, Matthew 18:23–35.

Judging, being judged, Luke 6:37.

Gratitude for great forgiveness, Luke 7:39–50.

Full measure of forgiveness, Luke 17:3–4.

Martyr's forgiving spirit, Acts 7:60.

Truly forgiven, Romans 4:8.

God's forgiven enemies, Romans 5:10.

Forgiving member of congregation, 2 Corinthians 2:5–11.

Forgive complaints, Colossians 3:12 (NASB, NRSV).

Forgiveness, patience, Colossians 3:13.

Sins of ignorance, 1 Timothy 1:12–14.

Paul's attitude toward deserters, 2 Timothy 4:16.

Record cleared, Hebrews 1:3 (LB).

Mercy of salvation, Hebrews 10:17.

Love and forgiveness, 1 Peter 4:8.

Our advocate with Heavenly Father, 1 John 2:1, 2.

See Discipleship, Fellowship, Love, Rapport.

FORGOTTEN

Perished memory, Job 18:17.

Forgiven and forgotten sin, Psalm 103:12.

Divine blessings forgotten, Psalm 106:7–8, 21.

People and events forgotten, Ecclesiastes 1:11.

Wise and fools soon forgotten, Ecclesiastes 2:16.

Former things not brought to mind, Isaiah 65:17.

Covenant ark forgotten, Jeremiah 3:16.

Forgotten Sabbath, Lamentations 2:6.

Divine memory, Luke 12:6.

See Alzheimer's, Memory.

FORMALITY

Unaware of the Lord's presence, Genesis 28:16.

More than religious performance, Psalms 51:16–17; 69:30–31.

Formality in worship, Ecclesiastes 5:1; Hosea 6:6; Micah 6:6–7.

Meaningless formality, Isaiah 1:13; 29:13.

Priest's formal garments, Ezekiel 42:14.

Mere formalism, Amos 5:21–23.

Clothing of kings and prophets, Matthew 11:7–9.

Washing hands before eating, Matthew 15:1–2.

"Listen, sir," Luke 19:8 (GNB).

Formality without reality, Matthew 23:23; Galatians 4:9–11; Colossians 2:20; 2 Timothy 3:1–5.

Performance of religion, Romans 2:17–29.

Paul's prior formalism, Philippians 3:4–7.

See Liturgy, Worship.

FORMIDABLE

City walls to sky, Deuteronomy 9:1.

One plus God equals majority, 1 Samuel 14:6–14.

FORMULA

Formula for success, Joshua 1:8.

FORNICATION See Immorality.

FORSAKEN

Forsaken at Calvary, Psalm 22:1; Matthew 27:46.

Brothers forsake, Psalm 69:8 (LB).

Has God forsaken? Psalm 77:8; Isaiah 49:14.

Briefly abandoned, Isaiah 54:7.

Forsaken in sorrow, Lamentations 1:16.

See Abandoned, Forsaken.

FORTRESS

"Laugh at fortresses," Habakkuk 1:10 (CEV).

See Protection, Shelter.

FORTUITY

"Nurse" for baby Moses, Exodus 2:1–10.

No chance accident, Exodus 21:12–13.

Death by measurement, 2 Samuel 8:2.

Random arrow, 2 Chronicles 18:33–34.

Time for everything, Ecclesiastes 3:1–8.

God's perfect timing, Isaiah 49:8.

Purposeful circumstance, Philemon 15–16.

See Chance, Happenstance, Purpose.

FORTUNES

Reversal of fortunes, Esther 5:9—7:10.

Poor discovered true wealth, Jeremiah 39:10; 40:11–12.

See Blessing.

FORTUNE-TELLING

Follow God, not dreamers, Deuteronomy 13:1–5 (CEV).

"Silly lies," Zechariah 10:2 (LB).

Pretended belief in divination, Genesis 44:5.

Divination outlawed, Deuteronomy 18:9–13.

Future cannot be known, Ecclesiastes 7:14.

"Chirp and mutter," Isaiah 8:19–20 (GNB).

Fortune-tellers made fools, Isaiah 44:25 (GNB).
Tools of fortune-teller, Isaiah 65:11.
Royal fortune-tellers, Daniel 2:1–4.
King's dream interpreted, Daniel 2:24–49.
Fortune teller's conversion, Acts 16:16–19.
See Divination, Sorcery.

FORTY

Duration of flood, Genesis 7:17.
Spying in Canaan, Numbers 13:25.
Years of wandering, Numbers 32:13.
Arrogant giant, 1 Samuel 17:4–16.
Reign of David, Solomon, 1 Kings 2:11; 11:42.
Probation for Ninevah, Jonah 3:4.
Temptation of Jesus, Luke 4:1–2.
Ministry after resurrection, Acts 1:3.

FOSSILS

Waters that covered earth, Psalm 104:7–9.

FOSTER PARENTS

Queen's foster father, Esther 2:7.

FOUNDATION

Weak as spider's web, Job 8:14.
Building on rock or sand, Matthew 7:24–27.
Laying good foundation, 1 Corinthians 3:10.
See Building.

FOUNDER

Building first city, Genesis 4:17.
Father of history, Genesis 12:1–3; 17:5.
Author of our faith, Hebrews 12:2.

FOUNTAIN

Evil fountain, Jeremiah 6:7 (LB).
Water pollution, Proverbs 25:26.
Forsaken springs of living water, Jeremiah 2:13.
Temple fountain, Joel 3:18; Zechariah 13:1.
"Fountain of truth," John 3:33 (LB).
Fountain of hope, Romans 15:13 (Berk.).
"Springs of living water," Revelation 7:17.
See Water.

FOXHOLE

"Foxhole" promises, Psalm 66:13–14.

FRACTIONS

Loss by thirds, Revelation 8:12.

FRACTURE

Symbolic broken arm, Ezekiel 30:21–22.

FRAGILE

Fragile as spider's web, Job 8:14.

FRAGRANCE

Aroma of good sacrifice, Genesis 8:20–21; Leviticus 23:18; 2 Corinthians 2:15; Ephesians 5:1–2.
Fragrance for worship, not personal enjoyment, Exodus 30:34–38.
No fragrance permitted in sin offering, Leviticus 5:11.
David's use of lotion, 2 Samuel 12:20.
Multiple spices, Song of Songs 3:6.
Fragrant terrain, Song of Songs 4:6; 8:14.
Fragrant garments, Song of Songs 4:11.
Stench instead of fragrance, Isaiah 3:24.
Sweet fragrance rejected, Jeremiah 6:20 (LB).
Expensive perfume on Jesus' feet, John 12:1–8 (NKJV).
Modern commerce in luxuries, Revelation 18:11–13.
See Cosmetics, Perfume.

FRAIL *See Powerless, Inept, Weakness, Vulnerability.*

FRAME-OF-REFERENCE

Wisest man's frame-of-reference, 1 Kings 4:29.
Distant knowledge sources, Job 36:3.
Bible-centered mentality, Psalm 1:2.
Pleasant boundary lines, Psalm 16:6.
Developing spiritual frame-of-reference, Psalms 19:14; 139:23–24.
Limited frame-of-reference, Psalm 94:11 (LB).
Visual discipline, Psalm 101:3.
Idol maker's frame-of-reference, Psalm 115:4–8.

Warped minds, men of wisdom, Proverbs 12:8.

Motivated by frame-of-reference, Proverbs 23:7 (KJV).

Thought control, Ecclesiastes 11:10.

Learning to think clean, Isaiah 1:16–20 (AB).

Pagan king's frame-of-reference, Isaiah 37:10.

Perspective of God, man, Isaiah 55:8–9.

Inability to understand, explain, Jeremiah 9:12.

Enhanced frame-of-reference, Jeremiah 33:3.

Knowing who is the Lord, Ezekiel 6:10, 14; 7:4, 9, 27; 2:16, 20; 13:9, 23; 14:11.

Intelligent views, Daniel 1:4 (Berk.).

People without understanding, Hosea 4:14.

Child's frame-of-reference, Joel 1:1–3; 2 Timothy 3:15.

Exterior, interior revelations, Psalm 19:1–12; Amos 4:13.

Living the good life, Micah 6:8.

Sins of the heart, Matthew 5:27–28.

Causing bad conduct, Matthew 12:35; 15:18–19 (NKJV); Mark 7:15–23; Luke 2:34–35.

Unable to understand, Matthew 16:5–12.

Thoughts of the heart, Luke 2:34–35.

Good from good, evil from evil, Luke 6:45.

Limited frame-of-reference, Luke 9:44–45; 18:31–34.

Empty minds in darkness, Romans 1:21 (GNB).

Sin and rebellion as frame-of-reference, Romans 1:21–32.

Preferring darkness to light, John 3:19–21.

Contrasting thought patterns, Romans 8:5–11.

Renewed frame-of-reference, Romans 12:2.

Disciple's frame-of-reference, 1 Corinthians 2:6–16; Ephesians 3:16–19.

Conscience defiled by weakness, 1 Corinthians 8:7.

Spirit of wisdom, revelation, Ephesians 1:17.

Futility thinking, Ephesians 4:17–19.

Knowledge of God's will, Colossians 1:9–14; 2:2–3.

Alienated frame-of-reference, Colossians 1:21 (CEV).

Sublime frame-of-reference, Colossians 2:2–3.

Taken captive by wrong thinking, Colossians 2:8.

Enriching one's frame-of-reference, Colossians 3:1–2.

Internal frame-of-reference, Colossians 3:16 (AB).

Christ-centered frame-of-reference, Hebrews 3:1.

Implanted frame-of-reference, Hebrews 8:10.

Eternal frame-of-reference, Hebrews 10:34.

Mentality of success, 1 Peter 1:15.

Cleansed frame-of-reference, 1 Peter 2:1.

Virtues added to grace, 2 Peter 1:5–9.

Worldly frame-of-reference, 1 John 4:5.

See Conduct, Lifestyle, Mind.

FRANKINCENSE

Use in holy oil, Exodus 30:34–38.

Meal offerings, show bread, Leviticus 2:1–2, 15; 24:7.

Excluded from some offerings, Leviticus 5:11.

Imported product, Isaiah 60:6.

See Fragrance, Myrrh, Perfume.

FRANKNESS *See Candor, Honesty.*

FRAUD

Do not defraud neighbor, Leviticus 19:13.

Despising the truthful, Amos 5:10.

No acquittal of fraud, Micah 6:11.

Conversion considered a fraud, Acts 9:26–27.

Believers in litigation, 1 Corinthians 6:3–8.

Fraudulent gain, James 5:4–5.

False teachers, 2 Peter 2:1.

See Deceit, Dishonesty, Heterodoxy.

FREE *See Gratis.*

FREEDOM

Freedom of choice, Genesis 13:10–13.

"Rid of bondage," Exodus 6:6 (KJV).

Slavery preferred, Deuteronomy 15:16–17.

King imprisoned, set free, 2 Kings 24:15; 25:27–29.

Freedom of worship, 2 Chronicles 11:16
(LB).

Freed slaves, Job 3:19.

Wild donkey set free, Job 39:5–6.

Youthful freedom, Ecclesiastes 11:9.

Yoke removed, Isaiah 9:4; 10:27; 14:25.

Celebrate freedom, Isaiah 48:20 (CEV).

Proclaiming freedom, Isaiah 61:1.

Slaves set free, enslaved again, Jeremiah
34:8–22.

Prophet captured, given freedom, Jeremiah 40:1–4.

Slaves rule free men, Lamentations 5:8.

Truth sets free, John 8:31–32, 36.

Freedom from legalism, Acts 10:24–28; Romans 7:1–6.

Clean, unclean, Acts 11:4–10.

No license to sin, Romans 6:1.

Freedom from sin's mastery, Romans 6:14.

Deliverance through Christ alone, Romans
7:24–25.

No longer slaves, Romans 8:15 (LB).

Unmuzzled ox, 1 Corinthians 9:9–14.

Freedom in the Spirit, 2 Corinthians 3:17.

Childhood a time of "slavery," Galatians 4:1.

"Christ has set us free," Galatians 5:1 (CEV).

Called to be free, Galatians 5:13 (CEV).

Filled with knowledge of God's will, Colossians 1:9–12.

Rescued from darkness, Colossians 1:13–
14.

Freedom under authority, 1 Peter 2:13–17.

Christian liberty, 1 Peter 2:16.

See Conversion, Liberty.

FREELOADING

Some pay, others only receive, 2 Corinthians 11:7–8.

FREEWILL

Freewill offerings, Leviticus 22:21–23;
23:38; Numbers 15:3; Deuteronomy
12:6, 17; 16:10; 2 Chronicles 31:14; Ezra
1:4; 3:5; 7:16; 8:28.

Valley of decision, Joel 3:14.

Good deed by choice, Philemon 14 (GNB).

See Choice, Decision, Opportunity.

FREEZE

Hot days, cold nights, Genesis 31:40.

Icy breath of God, Job 37:10.

Destructive sleet, Psalm 78:47 (LB, KJV).

Heavy snow, Psalm 147:16.

See Cold, Winter.

FRICTION

Friction over building program, Ezra 4:3–5.

Purposely causing friction, Romans 16:17.

See Abrasion, Conflict, Opposition, Troublemaker.

FRIEND

David, Jonathan, 1 Samuel 18:1–4; 19:1–6;
20:17, 41; 23:18; 2 Samuel 1:26.

False friends, 2 Samuel 16:16–23.

Adversarial friends, Job 2:11–13.

Friend in need, Job 6:14.

Evil friends, Psalm 50:18.

Loss of close friends, Psalms 55:12–14;
88:8.

Closer than nearest kin, Proverbs 18:24
(NRSV).

Wounds of friend, Proverbs 27:6.

Friend's counsel, Proverbs 27:10.

God's friend, Isaiah 41:8 (CEV).

Slandering friends, Jeremiah 9:4–5.

Anticipating friend's failure, Jeremiah
20:10.

Betrayed by friends, Lamentations 1:2, 19.

"Hired friends," Hosea 8:10 (LB).

Best friend untrustworthy, Micah 7:5 (CEV).

Friends of paralytic man, Mark 2:1–12;
Luke 5:17–26.

Letter to friend, Luke 1:1 (LB).

Definition of friend, John 15:12–17.

"My friend," Romans 2:1–3 (GNB).

Friendly to many, Romans 16:1–2.

Conduct of true friend, 2 Timothy 1:16–
18.

*See Camaraderie, Companionship, Fellowship,
Friendship.*

FRIENDLESS

No one to comfort, Lamentations 1:2.

See Abandoned, Rejection.

FRIENDSHIP

Harmful friendship, Deuteronomy 13:6–9.

One in spirit, 1 Samuel 18:1–4.

Loyalty between father, close friend, 1 Samuel 19:1–2.

Friendship at cutting edge, 1 Samuel 20:1–4.

Spiritually-centered friendship, 1 Samuel 20:42.

Marks of true friendship, 2 Samuel 1:23; John 15:13–15.

False friends, 2 Samuel 16:16–23.

Governments on friendly terms, 1 Kings 5:1.

Ministry friendship, 2 Kings 2:2.

Friends became adversaries, Job 2:11–13.

Friend in need, Job 6:14.

Undependable friends, Job 6:15–17.

Misused friendship, Job 6:27 (GNB).

Rejected friendship, Job 17:5.

Alienating friendship, Job 19:13–22.

Friendship betrayal, Psalms 41:9; 55:12–14 (LB).

Lost friendship, Psalm 88:8.

Choosing friends wisely, Psalm 119:63 (CEV).

Good, bad, Proverbs 13:20.

Forgiveness enhances friendship, Proverbs 17:9 (CEV).

Friends in times of need, Proverbs 17:17 (See GNB).

Purchased friendship, Proverbs 19:4.

Friendship overdone, Proverbs 25:17.

Wounds of friend, Proverbs 27:6.

Two better than one, Ecclesiastes 4:9–12 (See CEV).

Shelter from wind, Isaiah 32:2.

No help from wrong friends, Jeremiah 2:37.

Friends, brothers not trusted, Jeremiah 9:4–5.

Waiting for friend to fail, Jeremiah 20:10.

Betrayed by friends, Lamentations 1:2, 19.

Friends of paralytic man, Mark 2:1–12; Luke 5:17–26.

"Salt of friendship," Mark 9:50 (GNB).

Friendship of Herod, Pilot, Luke 23:12.

True meaning of friend, John 15:12–17.

Barnabas, Saul, Acts 9:26–27.

Friends of Paul, the prisoner, Acts 27:3.

Greetings to friends, Romans 16:3–16.

Consistent friendship, 2 Corinthians 4:8–9 (GNB).

Conduct of true friend, 2 Timothy 1:16–18.

Friend forsakes, 2 Timothy 4:10–17.

Timothy released from prison, Hebrews 13:23.

Worldly friends, James 4:4.

See Camaraderie, Fellowship.

FRIVOLOUS

Beautiful but dumb, Proverbs 11:22.

Explored frivolity, Ecclesiastes 2:3 (Berk.).

See Flirtation.

FRONT

"At the front in everything," 2 Corinthians 8:7 (AB).

FROTH

Foam on water, Job 24:18.

FRUGALITY

Food supply gathered, Genesis 41:35–36.

Use money carefully, Ezra 7:17 (CEV).

Careful frugality, Proverbs 13:11.

Choice food and oil, Proverbs 21:20.

Frugal with time, Proverbs 31:27.

No food wasted, Matthew 14:20; 15:37.

Unnecessary frugality, Mark 14:4–5.

Counsel of Jesus, John 6:12.

See Miser, Stingy.

FRUIT

Good grapes among bad, Isaiah 65:8 (LB).

Creation of fruits, Genesis 1:11–12.

Fruitful staff, Numbers 17:8.

Care of fruit trees, Deuteronomy 20:19, 20.

Apple of God's eye, Deuteronomy 32:10; Psalm 17:8.

"Summer fruit," 2 Samuel 16:2 (KJV).

Eating wild fruit, Isaiah 37:30.

Beautiful tree destroyed, Jeremiah 11:16.

Tree growth and trust in the Lord, Jeremiah 17:7–8.

Tree known by fruit, Matthew 12:33–35.

Grafted branches, Romans 11:24.

Good and unproductive land, Hebrews 6:7–8.

Unripe fruit, Revelation 6:13 (AB).

Bloody grapes, Revelation 14:20.
Monthly harvest, Revelation 22:2 (AB).
See Harvest.

FRUITFUL

Faithfully bearing fruit, Psalm 1:3 (LB).

FRUITLESS

Fruitless lives, Job 15:34–35 (LB).
Those who do nothing, Isaiah 30:7.
Harvest past, summer ended, no salvation, Jeremiah 8:20.
Stalks with no grain, Hosea 8:7.
See Reward.

FRUSTRATION

Frustrated with life, Job 6:11.
"Months of emptiness," Job 7:3 (NRSV).
Plans torn apart, Job 17:11 (CEV).
Two-handed frustration, Ecclesiastes 4:6 (KJV).
See Confusion, Disappointment, Emptiness, Futility.

FRYING PAN

Use of frying pan, Leviticus 2:7.
Frying pan to fire, Amos 5:19.

FUEL

Olive oil for lamps, Leviticus 24:1–4 (LB).
Ark transport chopped up for fuel, 1 Samuel 6:14.
Green, dry, Psalm 58:9.
Fuel from twigs, Isaiah 27:11.
Scarcity of fuel, Lamentations 5:4.
Human excrement used for fuel, Ezekiel 4:12–15.
Vines burn poorly, Ezekiel 15:3–4 (LB).
See Fire.

FUGITIVE

Fugitive of Moses, Exodus 2:11–15.
Sheltering a slave, Deuteronomy 23:15–16.
David's flight from Saul, 1 Samuel 21:10–11.
Flight from revenge murder, 2 Samuel 13:30–38.
Fugitive slaves, 1 Kings 2:39–40.

Holy family's escape to Egypt, Matthew 2:13–15.
Return of fugitive, Philemon 1–25.
See Refuge, Refugee.

FULFILLMENT

"Rich fulfillment," Psalm 66:12 (NKJV).
Fulfillment from the Lord, Psalms 84:11; 107:8–9.
Desires satisfied, strength renewed, Psalm 103:5.
Agony of waiting, joy of fulfillment, Proverbs 13:12.
Futile search for fulfillment, Ecclesiastes 1:16–18.
Emptiness of success, affluence, Ecclesiastes 2:4–11.
Eating, drinking, Ecclesiastes 2:24–26.
Work provides fulfillment, Ecclesiastes 3:13.
Labor, good food, Ecclesiastes 5:18–20.
Fulfilled life, Ecclesiastes 11:8.
Reward for obedience, Isaiah 48:17–18.
Wicked plight, righteous fulfillment, Isaiah 65:13–14.
Ancient paths, good way, Jeremiah 6:16.
Unsatisfied sword, Jeremiah 46:10.
Promise of fulfillment, Jeremiah 50:19.
Eating to complete satisfaction, Joel 2:26.
Fulfilled promise, Luke 2:25–32.
Those who hunger, Luke 6:21.
Satisfied by miracle food, Luke 9:17.
Fulfilled from within, John 7:37–39.
Christ gives fulfillment, John 10:10; 15:11.
Continual fulfillment, Acts 14:17.
Hope fulfilled by Holy Spirit, Romans 15:13.
Fulfilled by lavished grace, Ephesians 1:7–8.
"Fullness of deity," Colossians 2:9 (NASB, NRSV).
Oil of joy, Hebrews 1:9.
Disciplined fulfillment, Hebrews 12:11.
Inexpressible joy, 1 Peter 1:8–9.
Peace in Christ, 1 Peter 5:14.
Joy of good reputation, 3 John 3–4.
Totality of Son of God, Revelation 22:13.
Invitation to the thirsty, Revelation 22:17.
See Contentment, Maturity, Satisfaction.

FUMIGATION

Temple purification, Nehemiah 13:9.

FUN

Living for fun, James 5:5 (LB).
"Wild parties," 2 Peter 2:13 (CEV).
See Amusement, Hedonism.

FUNCTION

How things function, Ecclesiastes 7:25.
Threshing grain, grinding flour, Isaiah 28:28.
Function of salt, light, Matthew 5:13–16.
Gifts in Body of Christ, 1 Corinthians 12:27–30.
Proper function of the law, 1 Timothy 1:8–11.
See Work (Physical).

FUND-RAISING

Goal over subscribed, Exodus 36:6–7.
Temple fund-raising, 2 Kings 12:4–5.
Generous man's popularity, Proverbs 19:6 (NASB).
Financial misuse of temple, Mark 11:15–17.
Apostolic view of funding, Acts 20:32–35.
Dependence upon God for material support, 1 Corinthians 9:7–18.
Divine example for Christian giving, 2 Corinthians 8:9.
Making appeal, 2 Corinthians 9:1–2, 6–7.
Pledge collected, 2 Corinthians 9:5.
Avoid flattery, 1 Thessalonians 2:5.
Pagan funds excluded, 3 John 7.
Paul's efforts, Romans 15:28 (GNB).
See Contribution, Offering, Stewardship.

FUNERAL

Burial site, Genesis 23:1–20; 25:8–10; 50:4–9; 1 Samuel 31:11–13; 2 Samuel 2:4–6.
Funeral procession, Genesis 50:7–9.
Solemn funeral service, Genesis 50:10 (LB).
Pagan hairstyle, Deuteronomy 14:1 (LB).
Embalming in Egypt, Genesis 50:2–3.
National mourning, 1 Samuel 25:1.
Significance of burial, 2 Samuel 2:4–6.

Delegation sent to express condolence, 2 Samuel 10:1–2.
Respect for the dead, 2 Samuel 21:13–14.
Body of evil woman, 2 Kings 9:34–37.
Funeral of wicked man, Job 21:31–33 (GNB).
Sobering experience, Ecclesiastes 7:2 (CEV).
Grave cannot praise God, Isaiah 38:18.
No mourning for king, Jeremiah 22:18–19 (CEV).
Peaceful and honorable death, Jeremiah 34:4–5.
Funeral dirge, Ezekiel 19:1–14.
Funeral music, Matthew 9:23–24.
No funeral for Jesus, Matthew 27:57–60; Mark 15:42–47; Luke 23:50–55; John 19:38–42.
Grief at burial of Stephen, Acts 8:2.
Funeral instructions, Hebrews 11:22 (RSV).
See Burial, Death, Epitaph, Grave, Tomb.

FUNGUS See Mildew.

FURLOUGH See Missionary.

FURNITURE

Gold lampstand, Exodus 25:31.
Home furnishings, Proverbs 24:3–4.
See Home, Table.

FUTILITY

"Ranting and raving," 1 Kings 18:29 (GNB).
Wishing for day not to exist, Job 3:6.
Love futility, Psalm 4:2 (Berk.).
Chasing wind, Ecclesiastes 2:11; Hosea 12:1.
Emptiness of mere toil, Ecclesiastes 4:7–8.
Lifetime futility, Ecclesiastes 7:15 (NASB).
Gods and cooking fires, Isaiah 44:14–20.
Futility of removing stain, Jeremiah 2:22.
Feeding on the wind, Hosea 12:1 (NRSV).
Shriveled seeds, Joel 1:17.
Too little, too late, Amos 3:12.
Possibility, futility, Luke 18:27.
Futility of no resurrection message, 1 Corinthians 15:13–19.
See Emptiness, Hopeless.

FUTURE

Promise to Abraham, Genesis 13:14–17; 15:1–21. (Note: some "dust of the earth" as Jewish or earthly family, "the stars" as the future church or heavenly family.)

Predicted deliverance, Genesis 50:24–25.

God's promise to David, 2 Samuel 7:12.

Invincible plan, Job 42:2.

Future assured, Psalms 2:7–9; 25:14.

All in God's hands, Psalm 31:15.

Future hope, Psalm 37:37.

Hope for the future, Psalm 42:5.

Fear of future, Psalm 55:4–5.

Children not yet born, Psalms 78:6; 102:18; Isaiah 49:1.

Future of evil, Psalm 92:6–7.

Bright path of righteous, Proverbs 4:18.

Future in God's hands, Proverbs 20:24.

Boast about future, Proverbs 27:1.

Enjoy present, accept future, Ecclesiastes 3:22.

God plans future, Isaiah 14:24; Jeremiah 29:11–13.

Morning is coming, Isaiah 21:11–12.

New future assured, Isaiah 43:19; Habakkuk 2:3.

Future in God's hands, Isaiah 46:8–11; 1 Corinthians 2:9–10.

Tools of fortune-teller, Isaiah 65:11.

Good news, bad news, Jeremiah 34:1–7.

Desperate king consulted prophet, Jeremiah 38:14–28.

Book of future, Daniel 10:20 (LB).

Prophecy hidden from prophet, Daniel 12:8–9, 13.

Future growth assured, Micah 7:11.

City with no future, Nahum 1:14.

Death, resurrection foretold, Matthew 16:21; 20:17–19.

Angel prophesied John the Baptist's future, Luke 1:11–17.

Confidence in unseen future, 2 Corinthians 4:18.

Foreseen future, Galatians 3:8.

Fulfillment of future, Ephesians 1:9–10.

Citizenship in Heaven, Philippians 3:20–21.

Son in body of ancestor, Hebrews 7:9–10.

Uncertain future, James 4:13–16.

Imperishable future inheritance, 1 Peter 1:3–4.

Unlimited future blessing, 1 John 3:1–3.

Sure word of prophecy, Revelation 22:10.

See Promise, Prophecy, Tomorrow.

G

GAMBLING

"Throwing dice before the Lord," Joshua 14:1–2 (LB).

Make a bet, Judges 14:12 (CEV).

Gambling for Christ's robe, John 19:23–24.

See Coin Toss, Lots, Stock Market.

GAME

Dangerous game, Hosea 12:1 (LB).

Making a game of tormenting Jesus, Mark 14:64–65 (GNB).

GANGS

Street gangs, Proverbs 1:10–16 (LB).

Prostitute son's gang, Judges 11:1–3 (RSV).

GARDEN

Let the land produce, Genesis 1:11–12.

Earth as fruitful garden, Genesis 1:29.

God's garden, Genesis 2:8.

Dressing the garden, Genesis 2:15 (KJV).

Planned pollination, Deuteronomy 22:9.

Vegetable garden, 1 Kings 21:2.

Garden slug, Psalm 58:8.

Fruits, vegetables, Psalm 104:14 (Berk.).

Gardens, orchards, Ecclesiastes 2:5.

Romantic garden, Song of Songs 5:1.

Wastelands become like Eden, Isaiah 51:3.

Becoming well-watered garden, Isaiah 58:11; Jeremiah 31:12.

Exceeding garden of God, Ezekiel 31:8–18.

Flowers wither, seeds perish, 1 Peter 1:23–25.

See Agriculture, Fruit, Horticulture, Vegetable.

GARDENER

Adam as Eden's gardener, Genesis 2:15 (LB).

Consecrated gardeners encounter impurity, Isaiah 66:17.

Gardens to be planted, Jeremiah 29:5.

GARDENER

God as gardener, John 15:1 (CEV, NIV).
Jesus mistaken as gardener, John 20:15.
See Farmer, Fruit, Vineyard.

GARMENT

Garments of salvation, Isaiah 61:10.
Not dressed for wedding, Matthew 22:11.
A building as a garment, 2 Corinthians 5:2–3.
White clothes, Revelation 3:18.
Robes washed white, Revelation 7:14.
Garments for quick departure, Revelation 16:15.
Bright, clean linen, Revelation 19:8.
See Clothing, Style, Wardrobe.

GATE

Place of meeting, Genesis 19:1; 23:10; 34:20; Psalm 69:12.
City gates, Deuteronomy 3:5; Joshua 6:26; 1 Samuel 23:7; 2 Samuel 18:24.
Four thousand gatekeepers, 1 Chronicles 23:5.
Gatekeepers at their posts, 2 Chronicles 35:15.
Wooden gate, Nehemiah 1:3.
Brass gate, Isaiah 45:2.

Iron gate, Acts 12:10.
Sabbath gate, Ezekiel 46:1.
See Door.

GEMS

Imported gems, 1 Kings 10:1–2.
Gems in royal crown, 1 Chronicles 20:2.
Temple gems, 1 Chronicles 29:2.
Pagan gems, Daniel 11:38.
Spiritual gems, temporal straw, 1 Corinthians 3:11–15.
See Jewelry.

GENDER

Male, female, Genesis 1:27.
Confused physical description, Job 21:23–24 (KJV, NIV).
"Brother men," Acts 13:38 (Berk.).
Gospel transcends gender, Galatians 3:28.

GENEALOGY

Common ancestors, Genesis 9:19 (CEV).
Loss of family records, Nehemiah 7:64.
Genealogy of Jesus, Matthew 1:1–17.
Davidic lineage of Christ, Romans 1:3.
Endless genealogies, 1 Timothy 1:4.
See Ancestors, Heritage.

GENERATION

Faith lost in one generation, Judges 2:10.

GENERATION GAP

Youth, elders, 2 Chronicles 10:6–11.
Parents, children, Ephesians 6:1–4.

GENEROSITY

Generous giving with willing heart, Exodus 25:2.
Consistent generosity, Psalm 37:26.
Deserved generosity, Proverbs 3:27–28.
Giving to poor is lending to the Lord, Proverbs 19:17.
Blessing for generous man, Proverbs 22:9.
Generous to all, Matthew 5:42.
Secret acts of charity, Matthew 6:1–4.
Generous payment in vineyard, Matthew 20:1–16.
"Generous hearts," Acts 2:46 (NRSV).
Generosity of poor, 2 Corinthians 8:2–5 (GNB).
Grace of giving, 2 Corinthians 8:7.
Generosity rewarded, 2 Corinthians 9:6–11.
Holy Spirit's fruit, Galatians 5:22 (NRSV).
God's generous grace, Ephesians 1:7–8.
Extreme poverty induces generosity, 2 Corinthians 8:2 (NRSV).
See Giving, Philanthropy, Stewardship.

GENETICS

Like father, like son, Genesis 5:1–3.
Genetic animal experiment, Genesis 30:37–39.
Seeds, animals, Leviticus 19:19.
Productive cattle, Job 21:10 (KJV).

GENITALS

"Private parts," Deuteronomy 25:11.

GENOCIDE

Destructive flood, Genesis 7:23 (AB).
Arab race's precarious inception, Genesis 21:9–21.
Threatened population reduction, Deuteronomy 28:62.
Urban genocide, Joshua 6:21.
National genocide, 1 Samuel 15:3.

Scarcity of people, Isaiah 13:12.
Community destruction, Jeremiah 51:20–23.
"End of the Philistines," Amos 1:8 (CEV).
Endangered earth, Romans 9:28–29.
One-fourth of earth destroyed, Revelation 6:8.
See Scorched Earth, Terrorism, War.

GENTILE

All nations included, Genesis 22:17–18.
Gentile who loved God, Job 1:1–3.
Jewish rapport, Zechariah 8:23.
Devout Gentiles, Malachi 1:11 (LB).
Gentile believers, Matthew 8:11 (LB); Romans 9:25–26.
Gentile ministry predicted, Luke 2:32.
Gentile Cornelius, Acts 10:1–33.
Gentile conversions, Acts 11:1; 13:48; 15:7.
Gentile serendipity, Romans 10:20.
See Alien, Foreigner, Islam, Xenophobia.

GENTLENESS

Gentle attitude, Genesis 33:1–11.
Gentle Moses, Numbers 12:3 (Berk.).
"Like gentle rain," Deuteronomy 32:2 (CEV).
Gentleness of Boaz to Ruth, Ruth 3:7–15.
Made great by gentleness, 2 Samuel 22:36 (LB).
Gentle shepherd, Isaiah 40:11; Matthew 11:20; 2 Corinthians 10:1.
"Blessed are the gentle," Matthew 5:5 (Berk.).
Lambs among wolves, Luke 10:3.
Jesus with little children, Luke 18:15–17.
Gentle reproof, Galatians 6:1.
Like mother of little children, 1 Thessalonians 2:7.
Life-style of disciple, 2 Timothy 2:24; Titus 3:1–2.
"Gentleness born of wisdom," James 3:13 (NRSV).
Heaven's wisdom, James 3:17.
See Kindness, Meekness.

GENUFLECT

Deep bow, Genesis 18:2–3.
Bowing in respect, Genesis 23:7, 12; 33:6–7.
Dream sheaves genuflect, Genesis 37:7.
"They bowed down," Genesis 43:26 (CEV).

Genuflect to father-in-law, Exodus 18:7.
Bowing down before king, 1 Samuel 24:8.
Response to genuflection, 2 Samuel 15:5.
Bowing before the Lord, Nehemiah 8:3–6.
Faces to the ground, Isaiah 49:23.
Obeisance in new creation, Isaiah 66:23.
King bowing before captive, Daniel 2:46.
Worship of Christ child, Matthew 2:11.
Kneeling for mercy, Matthew 18:26.
Falling at Jesus' feet, Luke 8:41.
Command not to worship angels, Revelation 19:10.
See Awe, Courtesy, Formality.

GENUINE

Genuine and false foundations, Matthew 7:24–27.
Authentic Messiah, Matthew 11:1–5.
Genuine wisdom, Acts 5:33–39.
Genuine friendship, Acts 9:26–27.
Seal of genuineness, 2 Corinthians 1:21–22.
Marks of Jesus, Galatians 6:17 (See Berk.).
Validity of faith, 1 Thessalonians 1:8–10.
True son in faith, 1 Timothy 1:2.
Nongenuine profession, 1 John 2:4–6.
See Authenticity, Validity.

GEOGRAPHY

Origin of continents, Genesis 10:25.
Nations unborn, Genesis 25:23.
Geographical guidance, 2 Samuel 2:1.
Lord of hills, valleys, 1 Kings 20:28.
Joyful river, Psalm 46:4.
Higher rock, Psalms 61:1–2; 62:2, 6–7.
Farthest seas, Psalm 65:5
Sun-drenched earth, Psalm 113:3.
Sustaining hills, Psalm 121:1.
Wisdom predates geography, Proverbs 8:24–31.
Inhabited earth, Proverbs 8:31 (NKJV).
Durable earth, Ecclesiastes 1:4.
Role of Damascus, Isaiah 7:7–9 (LB).
Geographical dust, Isaiah 40:15–17.
Commercial centers, Ezekiel 27:12–23.
Beloved mountains, Ezekiel 36:1–12.
Oceanic mountains, Jonah 2:6 (LB).
Mountains tremble, crumble, Habakkuk 3:6.
Geographical giant, Revelation 10:2.

Altered marine geography, Revelation 21:1.
See Earth, Mountains, Nature, Ocean.

GEOLOGY

Earth's surface, Genesis 1:9–10; Psalms 18:15; 24:1–2; 104:5–13.
Mineral wealth, Genesis 2:11–12; Job 28:5–6, 9–11.
Listening stones, Joshua 24:27 (LB).
Geothermal heat, Job 28:5–6.
Time to scatter, gather stones, Ecclesiastes 3:5.
Advent majesty, Micah 1:3–4.
Mountains crumble, truth endures, Habakkuk 3:6.
Rivers, streams alter earth, Habakkuk 3:9 (CEV).
Living stones, 1 Peter 2:4–8.
See Minerals, Mountains, Rock.

GEOMETRY

Shortest distance, straight line, Psalm 107:7.
Geometric Christian experience, Ephesians 3:16–19.
Perfect square, Revelation 21:16 (GNB).
See Mathematics.

GERIATRICS

Old man's confident faith, Romans 4:18–22.
Age of man before flood, Genesis 6:3.
Old Testament fathers, Genesis 11:10–26.
Bearing children at advanced age, Genesis 16:16; 17:1–21; 21:1–7.
"Full of years," Genesis 25:8.
Life as pilgrimage, Genesis 47:9.
Geriatric debility, 2 Samuel 19:35; Lamentations 3:4.
Keeping warm in old age, 1 Kings 1:1–4.
Old man and revenge, 1 Kings 2:5–9.
Solomon's wayward old age, 1 Kings 11:4–6.
Death of healthy, vigorous person, Job 5:26.
Endless life not desired, Job 7:16.
Geriatric wisdom, Job 12:12.
Life's end, Job 16:22.
Wicked live to ripe old age, Job 21:7.

Geriatric reminiscence, Job 29:4–6; Psalm 37:25.

Youth defers to age, Job 32:4–9.

Job's longevity, Job 42:16–17.

Short life, Psalm 39:4–6.

Faith in old age, Psalm 71:9, 17–18.

Satisfying long life, Psalm 91:16

Fruitful old age, Psalm 92:14–15.

Lifelong commitment Psalm 119:111–112.

Years added to life, Proverbs 10:27.

Splendor of gray hair, Proverbs 16:31.

Youth, old age, Proverbs 20:29.

Care of aged parents, Proverbs 23:22–25.

Sustained to old age, Isaiah 46:4 (CEV).

Geriatric yoke, Isaiah 47:6.

Good old days, Ecclesiastes 7:10.

Enjoy life but with reservation, Ecclesiastes 11:8.

God's wrath upon all ages, Jeremiah 6:11.

King at sixty-two, Daniel 5:30.

Gray hair unnoticed, Hosea 7:9.

Young prophesy, old dream dreams, Joel 2:28.

Ripe old age, Zechariah 8:4.

Aged Simeon saw promised Savior, Luke 2:25–32.

Ministry of elderly widow, Luke 2:36–38.

Old age forecast, John 21:18.

Abraham's confident faith, Romans 4:18–22.

Old age, young spirit, 2 Corinthians 4:16.

How to rebuke older man, 1 Timothy 5:1.

Geriatric life-style, Titus 2:2–3.

Paul as an old man, Philemon 9.

Abraham as good as dead, Hebrews 11:12.

Geriatric discipleship, 2 Peter 1:13–14.

See Birthday, Life, Longevity, Old Age.

GERMANE *See Relevant.*

GERMANY

Some believe Gomer an ancient tribe in area of Germany, Ezekiel 38:6.

GERMS

Multiple diseases, Deuteronomy 28:61.

See Disease, Health, Sanitation.

GESTATION

Gestation for mountain goats, Job 39:1–2.

Prenatal destiny, Psalm 139:15–16; Jeremiah 1:4–5.

Gestation vitality, Luke 1:39–44.

See Pregnancy.

GESTURE

Shake out lap, Nehemiah 5:13 (KJV, NIV).

Eyes, feet, fingers, Proverbs 6:13.

Prophet's hand clap, Ezekiel 21:14.

Clap hands, stomp feet, Ezekiel 25:6.

Dipping into dish, Matthew 26:23 (GNB).

Use of hand gestures, Acts 13:16.

See Nonverbal Communication.

GETHSEMANE

Prayers of Jesus, Hebrews 5:7.

GHOST

Fear of ghost, Mark 6:49 (GNB).

GHOST TOWN

Palace empty as ghost town, Jeremiah 22:6 (CEV).

Fate of Tyre, Ezekiel 26:18–19 (CEV).

GIANT

Giant's perspective, Numbers 13:33.

Giant king's bed, Deuteronomy 3:11 (LB).

Remnant giants, Joshua 13:12 (NKJV).

Goliath, 1 Samuel 17:4–6.

Six-fingered giant, 2 Samuel 21:16, 20.

Giants like Goliath, 1 Chronicles 20:5–8.

Great monster, Ezekiel 29:3.

Giant angel, Revelation 10:1–3.

See Physique.

GIDDY

Beautiful but dumb, Proverbs 11:22.

GIFT

Betrothal gifts, Genesis 24:53.

Gifts for Joseph in Egypt, Genesis 43:11–15.

Gifts for estranged brothers, Genesis 45:21–23.

Gift of spring water, Judges 1:13–15.

Town given as gift, 1 Samuel 27:5–6.

Gift from plunder, 1 Samuel 30:26.

Royal gift, 1 Kings 10:10; 2 Chronicles 9:12.

Gifts celebrate prosperity, Job 42:10–11.

Seeking favor with gifts, Psalm 45:12 (Berk.).

Divine promise, Psalm 84:11.

Secret gift, Proverbs 21:14.

Gift for departing visitor, Jeremiah 40:5.

Parting gifts, Micah 1:14 (CEV).

Gifts of Magi, Matthew 2:11.

Gift of rest, Matthew 11:28.

Water given as gift, Revelation 21:6 (NRSV).

See Honorarium, Skill, Talent.

GIFTS (Spiritual)

Given a new spirit, Ezekiel 11:19.

Gift of tongues, Acts 2:1–4.

Gift not purchased, Acts 8:20 (AB).

Free gift of salvation, Romans 5:16–18; 6:23; 12:6–8.

Spiritual gifts, 1 Corinthians 12:1–31; Ephesians 4:11–13; Hebrews 2:4; 13:20–21.

Tongues, prophecy, 1 Corinthians 14:22 (LB).

"Rich variety," Ephesians 3:10 (NRSV).

Gift fanned into flame, 2 Timothy 1:6.

See Capability, Skill, Talent.

GIGANTIC See Immensity.

GIRLS

Girls as loot, Judges 5:30 (LB).

Plight of young girls, Lamentations 3:51 (LB).

GIVING

Giving from the heart, Exodus 25:2; 35:5.

Generosity provides abundance, Deuteronomy 15:1–6 (LB).

Freewill offering, Deuteronomy 16:10.

Wholehearted giving, 1 Chronicles 29:9.

According to ability, Ezra 2:69.

Challenge to tithe, Malachi 3:10.

Giving to glorify God, Matthew 6:1–4.

Widow's mite, Mark 12:42; Luke 21:2.

First day giving, 1 Corinthians 16:2.

Giving in sparse times, 2 Corinthians 8:2–7.

Sowing and reaping, 2 Corinthians 9:6–7.

See Benevolence, Philanthropy, Stewardship, Tithe.

GLADNESS

Oil of gladness, Hebrews 1:9 (NASB, NRSV).

See Happiness, Joy, Fulfillment.

GLASS

"Gold and glass," Job 28:17 (NRSV).

GLEANERS

Gleaning strangers, poor, Leviticus 19:9–10; 23:22; Deuteronomy 24:19–20.

Gleaning seeds of romance, Ruth 2:2, 8, 23.

Grapes left for gleaners, Jeremiah 49:9.

See Benevolence, Harvest, Poor.

GLOATING

Gloating over wealth, Job 31:25 (NASB).

GLOOM

Birthday gloom, Job 3:4–9.

Joy and gladness gone, Jeremiah 48:33.

See Pessimism, Sadness.

GLORIFY

Nature, people praise the Lord, Psalm 148:1–14.

Lights shining, Matthew 5:16.

Fruit of unity, Romans 15:5–6.

Gratitude for redemption, 1 Corinthians 6:19–20.

See Praise.

GLORY

Shekinah glory, Ezekiel 9:3 (AB).

Abundant glory, Psalm 8:1 (LB).

Mount of transfiguration, Matthew 17:1–8.

Resurrection, exaltation, Ephesians 1:18–23.

See Aura, Awe.

GLOSSOLALIA See Tongues.

GLUTTONY

Manna, maggots, Exodus 16:18–27.

Enforced gluttony, Numbers 11:18–20, 31–34.

Craving for meat, Deuteronomy 12:20.

Knife to throat, Proverbs 23:1–3.

Sure road to poverty, Proverbs 23:21.

Too much honey, Proverbs 25:16.

Overstuffed fool, Proverbs 30:21–22.

Full stomach hinders sleep, Ecclesiastes 5:12 (NASB).

Best meats, finest wine, Isaiah 25:6.

Stuffed with food, Isaiah 28:1 (CEV).

Canine gluttony, Isaiah 56:11.

Symbolic gluttony, Jeremiah 51:34.

Affluent gluttony, Amos 6:4–7.

Eat, drink, be merry, Luke 12:19–20.

Sacrilegious eating, 1 Corinthians 11:20–22.

Physical hunger, spiritual supply, 1 Corinthians 11:34.

Immoral gluttony, Ephesians 4:19.

Stomach as god, Philippians 3:19.

See Food, Undisciplined.

GOAL

Desire for full obedience, Psalm 119:1–5.

Eyes on goal, Proverbs 4:25–27.

Man's plans, God's purposes, Proverbs 19:21.

Goal oriented, Isaiah 32:8; Jeremiah 32:38–39.

Enlarged goals, Isaiah 54:2–3.

Self-centered goals, Jeremiah 45:4–5.

"Aim in life," 2 Timothy 3:10 (NRSV).

See Ambition, Objective.

GOATS

Markings on rams, Genesis 31:10 (KJV).

GOD

God seen by humans, Genesis 12:7; 16:13–14; 17:1; 18:1; 26:2; 35:9; Exodus 3:16; 1 Kings 3:5; 9:2; 2 Chronicles 1:7; 3:1; Isaiah 6:1–9.

God defined, Exodus 3:13–14.

Two of God's names, Exodus 6:3 (KJV).

Angel mistaken for God, Judges 13:21–23.

God destroys enemies, 1 Samuel 15:1–10.

Limiting God, 1 Kings 20:28.

God's attributes, actions, Nehemiah 9:6–37.

God accused of wrong, Job 7:2–3 (CEV).

Questioning God, Job 9:24 (AB).

Unfathomable God, Job 11:7.

Enmity with God, Job 22:21 (GNB).

God thought ignoring wrong, Job 24:12 (AB).

Declaring God's greatness, Job 36:22–26.

Age of God, Job 36:26.

God of creation, Job 38—39.

Presuming "God is dead," Psalm 10:4 (LB).

God's anger, love, Psalm 30:5.

Awesome God, Psalm 47:2.

"Friend of mine," Psalm 54:4 (LB).

God's name, Psalm 68:4 (NKJV).

The Lord awakens, Psalm 78:65.

Divine love, happiness, Psalm 80:3 (LB).

"God of gods," Psalm 84:7 (NRSV).

Hidden God, Psalm 89:46.

Creator greater than creation, Psalm 108:4–5.

God consciousness in human hearts, Ecclesiastes 3:11.

Omniscient God, Isaiah 40:13–14.

First, last, only, Isaiah 44:6.

Incomparable God, Isaiah 46:5.

God never forgets, Isaiah 49:15.

God's thoughts above man's thoughts, Isaiah 55:8–9.

Unprecedented God, Isaiah 64:4.

Accusing God, Jeremiah 4:10.

Near, far, Jeremiah 23:23.

God's visible glory, Ezekiel 43:1–5.

God identified among "holy gods," Daniel 5:11.

God visualized, Daniel 7:9.

God's thoughts, Amos 4:13 (CEV).

Forgiving God, Micah 7:18–19.

Misconception about God, Zephaniah 1:12.

"Abba, Father," Mark 14:36; Romans 8:15; Galatians 4:6 (Note: Spanish Bible translates word **Pepito** as "Daddy.")

God incarnate in Christ, John 10:30; 14:9–14.

See God through Jesus, John 12:44–46.

All-encompassing goodness, Romans 4:16.

Kind and stern, Romans 11:22.

Mediator between God and men, 1 Timothy 2:5.

Majestic God, Hebrews 8:1.

God's great love, 1 John 3:1–3.

See Creator, Christ, Omnipotence, Trinity.

GODS AND GODDESSES

"All of you are gods," Psalm 82:6 (CEV).

God of gods, Psalm 136:2.

Queen of Heaven, Jeremiah 7:18.

God identified among "holy gods," Daniel 5:11.

Goddess Artemis, Acts 19:24, 28, 35.

Nonexistent gods, Galatians 4:8 (AB).

See Heathen, Idolatry, Pagan.

GOLD

First record of gold, Genesis 2:11–12.

Ornaments, Genesis 24:22; Exodus 3:22; 11:2.

Solomon's annual take, 1 Kings 10:14–17. (Note: 666 talents equal to 25 tons!)

Two hundred tons, 1 Chronicles 29:6 (CEV).

Royal splendors, 2 Chronicles 9:17–24.

Finest gold, Job 23:10 (AB).

More precious than gold, Psalm 19:10; 119:127.

Apples of gold, Proverbs 25:11.

See Jewelry, Money, Treasure, Value.

GOLDEN RULE

First statement of Golden Rule, Leviticus 19:18.

Negative reciprocation, Leviticus 24:19–20.

Memories of Egypt, Deuteronomy 10:19; 24:17–18.

Returning lost property, Deuteronomy 22:1–3.

Bad example of others, Deuteronomy 25:17–18.

Golden rule exemplified, 2 Kings 6:8–23.

Evil for good, Psalm 35:12.

Golden Rule reversed, Psalm 109:5; Proverbs 21:13; 24:29; Matthew 18:21–35; Galatians 5:15.

Old Testament negative, Proverbs 24:29.

Golden Rule Old Testament version, Obadiah 15.

Mercy to those who show mercy, Matthew 5:7.

Criticizing, criticized, Matthew 7:1–2 (CEV, LB).

Golden Rule defined, Matthew 7:12 (See CEV).

Seeking mercy, mistreating another, Matthew 18:23–35.

Golden Rule basics, Luke 6:27–36.

Golden Rule in action, Luke 6:38 (CEV); 2 Corinthians 2:5–11; 1 Thessalonians 5:15.

Altruistic motives, 1 Corinthians 10:24.

Returning good for evil, 1 Thessalonians 2:14–16.

Inverted Golden Rule, 2 Thessalonians 1:6 (AB).

Golden Rule stated negatively, Revelation 18:6.

See Conduct, Life-style, Reciprocation.

GOOD

Good, bad, Deuteronomy 30:1–3.

Claim of good works, Nehemiah 5:19.

Evil outweighs good, Ezekiel 33:12 (CEV).

See Altruistic, Virtue.

GOODNESS

Degrees of evil, 2 Kings 17:1–2.

"God is good," Psalm 73:1 (NRSV).

Residual goodness, Isaiah 65:8.

Goodness of God, Matthew 7:7–11.

Goodness always appropriate, Mark 3:1–6.

Only God is good, Mark 10:17–18.

God's goodness leads to repentance, Romans 2:4 (NKJV).

Legalistic view of goodness, Colossians 2:16.

Consistent goodness, James 3:13 (LB).

See Benevolence, Kindness, Love.

GOOD OLD DAYS

Looking back, Psalm 77:5 (LB).

Good life remembered, Lamentations 1:7 (CEV).

See Reminiscence.

GOOD WORKS

Trying to do right, Psalm 26:9–11 (LB).

Good works insufficient for salvation, Matthew 19:16–26; Romans 10:5 (LB).

Scope of good works, Matthew 25:35–36.

Good works rewarded, Matthew 26:6–13.

Conduct toward enemies, Luke 6:35.

Roman built synagogue, Luke 7:1–4 (See LB).

Patriotic, religious good works, Luke 7:4–5.

"Lovely fruit," John 15:16 (LB).

Rewarded good works, Romans 2:5–11.

Faith in action, 1 Thessalonians 1:3; James 2:17–18.

Rich in good deeds, 1 Timothy 6:18.

Sin of not doing good, James 4:17.

See Conduct, Stewardship.

GOSPEL

Gospel in one chapter, Isaiah 53:1–12.
Unique parable, Ecclesiastes 9:14–15.
Enigmatic message, Luke 9:44–45.
Lifting up Jesus, John 12:32.
Post-resurrection message, Acts 4:2.
Power of gospel over evil, Acts 8:9–13.
"The Way," Acts 22:4; 24:22.
Promised good news, Romans 1:2 (GNB).
Gospel seen as foolishness, 1 Corinthians 1:18.
Gospel message in brief, 1 Corinthians 15:1–5.
Old Testament gospel, Galatians 3:6–9.
Gospel's inherent power, 1 Thessalonians 1:5 (AB).
"Wonderful treasure," 2 Timothy 1:14 (CEV).
Heeding the gospel, Hebrews 2:1–3.
Eternal life given, 1 John 5:11–12.
See Scripture.

GOSSAMER

"Gossamer thread," Job 8:14 (Berk., NRSV).

GOSSIP

Speak neither good nor evil, Genesis 31:24.
Circumstantial evidence, Genesis 39:6–20.
False, malicious reports, Exodus 23:1 (CEV).
Gossip condemned, Leviticus 19:16.
Basic rule for gossips, Numbers 23:8.
Need for adequate witnesses, Deuteronomy 17:6; 19:15; 1 Timothy 5:19.
Giving false testimony, Deuteronomy 19:16–21.
Intimidation for pay, Nehemiah 6:12–13.
Secret report, Job 4:12.
Protection from gossip, Job 5:21.
Subject for gossip, Job 17:6; 30:9.
Avoid private gossip, Job 19:4.
Scorn consumed like water, Job 34:7.
Pray for those who hurt you, Job 42:10.
Only God knows how many foes, Psalm 3:1–2.
Dishonest words, Psalm 5:9.
Neighborhood lies, Psalm 12:2.
Gossiper unfit for worship, Psalm 15:1–3 (GNB).
"Don't spread gossip," Psalm 15:3 (CEV).
Divine vindication, Psalm 17:2.

Committed not to gossip, Psalm 17:3; Proverbs 4:24.
Scorn, lies, Psalm 31:11–13 (LB).
"Contentious tongues," Psalm 31:20 (NRSV).
Gossip hinders happiness, Psalm 34:12–13.
Amused by another's stumbling, Psalm 35:15 (NRSV).
Muzzled mouth, Psalm 39:1 (See Berk.).
Exaggerated gossip, Psalm 41:7–8 (GNB).
Always ready to gossip, Psalm 50:19 (NRSV).
Gossip against brother, Psalm 50:20.
Razor-sharp tongue, Psalm 52:2–4 (Berk.).
Gossip against innocent person, Psalm 59:4.
Gossip as sin, Psalm 59:12.
Lying mouths silenced, Psalm 63:11.
Malicious gossip, Psalm 64:3 (LB).
"Stumble over their own tongue," Psalm 64:8 (NKJV).
Hatred without reason, Psalm 69:4.
Gossip in high places, Psalm 69:12 (CEV).
Heartbreaking insults, Psalm 69:20 (NRSV).
Gossip about misfortune, Psalm 69:26 (Berk.).
Taunted by others, Psalm 89:50 (NRSV).
Neighborhood gossip, Psalm 101:5; Proverbs 11:9; 1 Timothy 5:13.
Lying tongues, Psalm 109:1–3.
Target for gossip, Psalm 109:25, 29, 31.
Scriptural protection against gossip, Psalm 119:69–70, 78.
Prayer when hurt by gossip, Psalms 120:1–2; 123:3–4; Lamentations 3:55–66.
Vindication from gossip, Psalm 135:14.
Gossip like snake's fangs, Psalm 140:3.
Avoiding gossip, Psalm 141:3; Luke 6:37; Ephesians 4:29.
Corrupt mouth, Proverbs 6:12–14; Micah 6:12.
Pride, behavior, gossip, Proverbs 8:13.
Speech of righteous, of wicked, Proverbs 10:11.
Fool's gossip, Proverbs 10:18.
Gossip betrays confidence, Proverbs 11:13; 20:19; 25:9.
Habitual talebearer, Proverbs 11:13 (Berk.).
Lying lips, truthful speech, Proverbs 12:22.
Healing tongue, deceitful tongue, Proverbs 15:4.

Gossip alienates friendship, Proverbs 16:28 (CEV); 17:9.

Sin of listening to gossip, Proverbs 17:4.

"Choice morsels" for gossip, Proverbs 18:8 (LB); 26:22.

Loquacious gossip, Proverbs 20:19 (LB).

Keeping another's confidence, Proverbs 25:9.

Gossip's potential harm, Proverbs 25:18 (LB); Galatians 5:15.

Silence combats gossip, Proverbs 26:20; Amos 5:13.

Choice morsels, whispered gossip, Proverbs 26:22 (AB).

Hatred-motivated gossip, Proverbs 26:28.

Bread of idleness, Proverbs 31:27 (AB).

Gossip has wings, Ecclesiastes 10:20.

Power of words, Isaiah 29:20–21.

Confidence overcomes gossip, Isaiah 51:7.

Deceitful tongue, Jeremiah 9:3.

"Practiced tongues," Jeremiah 9:5, 8 (LB).

Attacked by words, whispers, Lamentations 3:62 (CEV).

Bloody tales, Ezekiel 22:9.

Gossip set to music, Micah 2:4.

Gloating enemies, Habakkuk 2:5 (GNB).

Plotting people's ruin, Habakkuk 2:10.

Punishment for those who mock, Zephaniah 2:9–10.

Satan the accuser, Zechariah 3:1–2.

Joseph wanted to protect Mary from gossip, Matthew 1:19.

Rejoice when victimized by gossip, Matthew 5:11–12.

Superficial judgment, John 7:24 (Berk.).

Judging, criticizing, Matthew 7:1–5; Romans 14:13; 1 Corinthians 10:27–29.

Gossip attacks against Jesus, Matthew 9:10–12; 11:18–19; Mark 14:53–59; John 7:12.

Words condemn or acquit, Matthew 12:37.

Gossip denotes unclean heart, Matthew 15:10–20.

Avoid going public, Matthew 18:15–17.

Silence of Jesus, Matthew 27:12–14.

Searching for gossip subjects, Mark 3:1–6.

Rejoice when criticized for faith, Luke 6:22–23.

Inaccurate gossip, John 7:24; 8:3–11.

Productive "gossip," Romans 1:8 (LB).

Gossip among vilest of sins, Romans 1:29–30 (GNB).

No excuse for gossip, Romans 2:1 (GNB).

Deceitful tongues, Romans 3:13.

Response to hurtful gossip, Romans 12:14.

Attitude toward weakness, Romans 14:1.

Love prevents gossip, 1 Corinthians 13:6.

Spiritual solution to gossip, Galatians 6:1–5.

Words kindly spoken, Philippians 4:8 (Berk.).

Conversation full of grace, Colossians 4:6.

Positive "gossip," Colossians 4:7; 1 Thessalonians 3:6.

Minding one's own business, 1 Thessalonians 4:11.

Root cause of gossip, 2 Thessalonians 3:11 (AB).

Gossip-free deacons, 1 Timothy 3:8 (NKJV).

"Malicious gossips," 1 Timothy 3:11 (NASB).

House to house gossiping, 1 Timothy 5:13 (CEV).

Godless chatter, 1 Timothy 6:20; 2 Timothy 2:16.

Talk spreads like gangrene, 2 Timothy 2:17 (NASB, NRSV).

Older women to avoid gossip, Titus 2:3 (CEV).

Living above criticism, Titus 2:8.

Slander no one, Titus 3:2; James 4:11–12 (CEV).

Fear of man, Hebrews 13:6.

Deceitful, unruly tongue, James 1:26 (AB).

Guard tongue well, James 3:3–6.

Decline retribution, 1 Peter 3:9.

Shaming those who gossip, 1 Peter 3:16.

Insulted because of name of Christ, 1 Peter 4:14.

Pride leads to gossip, 3 John 9–10.

Those who do not lie, Revelation 14:5.

See Character Assassination, Slander, Tongue.

GOURMET

Tasty food, Genesis 27:4, 7, 9.

Boiled meat, Exodus 12:8.

Delectable manna, Exodus 16:31.

Forbidden specialty, Exodus 23:19.

Holy food, Numbers 18:8–13.

Aromatic food, Numbers 28:2.

Best cut of meat, 1 Samuel 9:23–24 (LB); Amos 6:4.

"Fit for a king," 2 Samuel 13:27 (GNB).

Best spices, 2 Chronicles 9:9.

Loathe dainty food, Job 33:20 (NRSV).

"Delicious food," Psalm 23:5 (LB).

River of delights, Psalm 36:8.

Gourmet soul food, Psalm 63:5.

"Bread of angels," Psalm 78:25.

Evil delicacies, Psalm 141:4.

Deceptive delicacies, Proverbs 23:3.

Gourmet to garbage, Lamentations 4:5.

Gourmet food for priests, Ezekiel 44:28–31.

Gourmet food avoided, Daniel 1:8–16; 10:2–3.

Choice lamb, Amos 6:4.

Gourmet figs, Micah 7:1.

Sweet food turns stomach sour, Revelation 10:10.

See Banquet, Delicacy, Feast, Food, Refrigeration, Sweetness, Taste.

GOVERNMENT

Government for the people, Genesis 41:25–57.

Scriptural attitude toward government, Matthew 22:18–21; Acts 5:29; Romans 13:1–7; 1 Timothy 2:1–3.

Fairness in time of famine, Genesis 47:13–26.

Civil disobedience, Exodus 1:15–21.

Change of leadership, Exodus 2:23–25.

Strain of increased population, Deuteronomy 1:9–13.

Respecting church, state, Deuteronomy 17:12.

Senseless nation, Deuteronomy 32:28.

Gideon's insistence on theocracy, Judges 8:22–23.

Five mayors, 1 Samuel 6:16 (LB).

Sons replaced father, 1 Samuel 8:1 (LB).

Monarchy replaces theocracy, 1 Samuel 8:1–22.

God's preference, man's choice, 1 Samuel 10:17–19.

Good government procedure, 1 Samuel 12:13–25.

Respect for disliked leader, 1 Samuel 24:1–11; 26:9–10.

Immorality in politics, 2 Samuel 3:6–11.

Government departments, 2 Samuel 8:15–18; 20:23–26; 1 Kings 4:1–7.

Fairness to all, 2 Samuel 8:15.

Servants of the people, 2 Samuel 19:43.

Solomon's prayer for wisdom, discernment, 1 Kings 3:1–15.

Solomon's cabinet, 1 Kings 4:1–7.

Solomon's good, large reign, 1 Kings 4:20–21.

Servant leader, people serving, 1 Kings 12:7.

King's leprosy, 2 Kings 15:5.

High officials, 2 Kings 19:2 (CEV).

Disgusting government acts, 2 Kings 21:11 (CEV).

David's good leadership, 1 Chronicles 18:14.

Good government, corrupt citizens, 2 Chronicles 27:2.

Obey God and government, Ezra 7:26.

Government travel authorization, Nehemiah 2:1–8.

Citizen's rights, Nehemiah 5:5.

Royal "drinking spree," Esther 3:15 (LB).

Government for the people, Esther 10:3.

Fate of world governments, Psalm 2:7–9.

God over nations, Psalm 9:7–8.

Nations dig pit, fall in, Psalm 9:15.

Causing kings to fear, Psalm 76:12 (NRSV).

Divine council, Psalm 82:1 (NRSV).

Corrupt government, Psalm 94:20 (Berk.).

Righteous government and citizens, Proverbs 14:34.

Justice makes strong government, Proverbs 16:12 (GNB).

"False speech," Proverbs 17:7 (NRSV).

Government secured by love, Proverbs 20:28.

Peril of poor advice, Proverbs 25:5 (GNB).

Nations cease to exist, Proverbs 27:24 (GNB).

Stable government, "moral rot," Proverbs 28:2 (LB).

Detestable prayers of lawbreakers, Proverbs 28:9.

Hiding from evil government, Proverbs 28:28.

Good, bad government, Proverbs 29:2.

Sobriety, good government, Proverbs 31:4–7.

City government, Proverbs 31:23.

Discontent with government, Ecclesiastes 4:13–16.

Evils of bureaucracy, Ecclesiastes 5:8–9.

Misused tax revenues, Ecclesiastes 10:19 (AB).

Government controlled by children, Isaiah 3:4.

Unjust laws, oppressive decrees, Isaiah 10:1–4.

Community in turmoil, Isaiah 22:2.

National righteousness, Isaiah 26:2 (CEV); Jeremiah 7:28.

Exemplary government, Isaiah 32:1–4.

All governments displease God, Isaiah 34:2.

Delicate Babylon, Isaiah 47:1 (CEV).

Lost confidence in government, Jeremiah 4:9.

Government for good of people, Jeremiah 29:4–7.

Local government, Jeremiah 30:20.

King, priest forsaken, Lamentations 2:6.

Misguided by evil government, Ezekiel 11:1–4.

Wicked government officials, Ezekiel 22:27.

World's most powerful king, Ezekiel 26:7 (CEV).

Government-sponsored education, Daniel 1:3–20.

High position in pagan government, Daniel 2:48–49.

One thousand government officials, Daniel 5:1 (CEV).

King at sixty-two, Daniel 5:30–31.

Distinguished government position, Daniel 6:3.

God's guidance refused, Hosea 8:4.

King given, taken away, Hosea 13:11.

Continued sinning, certain judgment, Amos 1:3, 6, 9, 11, 13.

"See that justice is done," Micah 6:8 (CEV).

Ineffective government, Habakkuk 1:4 (CEV).

Leaderless people, Habakkuk 1:14.

Church, state, Haggai 1:1 (CEV).

Evil government leadership, Malachi 3:5.

Government taxes, Matthew 22:15–22; Luke 20:21–25.

"Rulers lord it over them," Mark 10:42 (NRSV).

Census at time of Jesus' birth, Luke 2:1–5.

Embarrassed government officials, Acts 16:35–40.

Government action refused, Acts 18:12–17.

Pagan official rebuked religious dispute, Acts 19:35–41.

Government bribes, Acts 24:26.

Government leaders serve divine purposes, Romans 9:17–18.

Submission to authorities, Romans 13:1–7; Titus 3:1; Hebrews 13:17; 1 Peter 2:13–17.

City director of public works, Romans 16:23.

Privileged citizenship, Ephesians 2:19–20.

Spiritual citizenship, Philippians 3:20.

Praying for government, 1 Timothy 2:1–4.

World government, Revelation 13:7.

Demons in world politics, Revelation 16:13–14.

One-hour reign of ten kings, Revelation 17:12.

See Bureaucracy, Cabinet, Leadership, Politics.

GRACE

Old Testament definition, Exodus 34:6–7.

Divine grace demonstrated, Nehemiah 9:17.

Repetition of forgiving grace, Psalm 78:38.

Present grace, future glory, Psalm 84:11 (AB).

Undeserved grace, Psalm 103:9–10.

Extended grace, Psalm 145:8–9.

The Lord's hand remains upraised, Isaiah 5:25; 9:21; 10:4.

"Grace upon grace," John 1:16 (NRSV).

Undeserving sinners, Romans 1:5 (LB).

"Abundance of grace," Romans 5:17 (NASB, NRSV).

Grace received in vain, 2 Corinthians 6:1 (See GNB).

Lavished grace, Ephesians 1:7–8 (NASB, NRSV).

GRACE BEFORE MEALS

Prayer before eating, 1 Samuel 9:13.

Jesus offered table grace, Matthew 14:19; 15:36; 1 Corinthians 11:24.

Feeding five thousand, John 6:11.

Apostolic blessing, Acts 27:35.

Thankful for food, 1 Corinthians 10:30 (NASB, NKJV, NRSV).
See Gratitude, Prayer.

GRAFT See Bribery, Bureaucracy, Corruption, Deceit, Dishonesty.

GRAMMAR
Capitalized pronouns, Matthew 2:11 (Berk.).
Jesus spoke of Himself in third person, Luke 18:31–33.
Modern grammar, John 14:23 (Compare CEV).

GRANDCHILDREN
Thousands of grandchildren, Genesis 24:60.
Joy of seeing grandchildren, Genesis 48:11.
Birth of grandson, Ruth 4:13–16.
Grandchildren, great-grandchildren, Job 42:16.
No grandchildren, Psalm 109:9.
Inheritance for grandchildren, Proverbs 13:22.
Blessing of grandchildren, Proverbs 17:6.
No descendants in Nineveh, Nahum 1:14.
See Children, Family, Grandparents.

GRANDPARENTS
Prolific lineage, Genesis 24:60.
Frustrated grandfather, Genesis 31:22–29.
Grateful grandfather, Genesis 48:11.
Honored great-grandfather, Numbers 17:3 (AB).
Birth of grandson, Ruth 4:13–16.
Grandmother mentioned by name, 1 Kings 15:10.
Confessing sins of ancestors, Nehemiah 9:2.
Grandfather's longevity, Job 42:16–17.
Living to see children's children, Psalm 128:5–6.
Message from generation to generation, Psalm 145:4–7; Joel 1:3.
Grandfather's legacy, Proverbs 13:22.
Proud grandfathers, Proverbs 17:6 (GNB).
Obeying parents, grandparents, Jeremiah 35:1–16.
Grandfather's lineage, Zephaniah 1:1.
Forefathers gone, Zechariah 1:5.
Grandmother's healing, Matthew 8:14–15.

Tales grandmothers told, 1 Timothy 4:7 (AB).
Grandmother's transmitted faith, 2 Timothy 1:5.
Grandmother's influence, Titus 2:3–5.
See Forefathers, Geriatrics, Old Age, Longevity.

GRAPES See Vineyard.

GRAPHOLOGY
Authentic handwriting, 2 Thessalonians 3:17 (LB).

GRASS
Preferred grass, Genesis 13:1–11.
Green pastures, Psalm 23:2.
Death and morning grass, Psalm 90:5–6.
Life likened to grass, Psalm 103:15–16; Isaiah 37:27; 40:7–7; 51:12; 1 Peter 1:24.
Grass provided by God, Psalm 104:14.
Sparse mountain pasture, Jeremiah 50:6.
Trampled grass, Ezekiel 34:18.
See Shepherd, Vegetarian.

GRATIS
Gratis abundance, Isaiah 55:1–2.
Serving without pay, 1 Corinthians 9:7.
Free drinking water, Revelation 21:6.

GRATITUDE
Joseph's kindness forgotten, Genesis 40:1–23; 41:9.
Thanksgiving offering, Leviticus 7:12.
Idolatrous gratitude, Judges 17:1–5.
Gratitude visibly expressed, Ruth 2:10.
Life-giving expression of gratitude, 1 Samuel 14:45.
Tears of gratitude, 1 Samuel 20:41.
Seeking recipient of thanks, 2 Samuel 9:1.
Reciprocation of kindness, 2 Samuel 10:2; 2 Kings 4:13.
Song of praise, 2 Samuel 22:1–51.
Gratitude for God's faithfulness and goodness, 1 Kings 8:14–21.
Grateful morning and evening, 1 Chronicles 23:30.
Value of sacrifice and offering, Psalm 50:23.
Joy of gratitude, Psalm 92:1 (CEV).
Grateful for God's enduring love, Psalm 106:1.
Say "thank you" to God, Psalm 107:1 (LB).

Thanksgiving leads to witnessing, Psalm 107:1–3.

Hymn of gratitude, Psalm 136:1–26.

Grateful in adverse circumstances, Jeremiah 33:10–11.

Daniel's gratitude for wisdom, Daniel 2:19–23.

Tears of gratitude, Luke 7:36–50.

Gratitude for great forgiveness, Luke 7:39–50.

No need to express gratitude, Luke 17:9.

Ten percent gratitude, Luke 17:12–19.

Jesus gave thanks, John 6:11.

Joyful gratitude, Colossians 1:11, 12.

Overflowing gratitude, Colossians 2:6–7.

Grateful for success in ministry, 1 Thessalonians 3:8–10.

Correct and required gratitude, 2 Thessalonians 1:3 (LB).

Gratitude for privilege of ministry, 1 Timothy 1:12–14.

See Praise, Thanksgiving.

GRATUITY

Royal gratuities refused, Daniel 5:17.
See Honorarium.

GRAVE

Desecrated graves, Jeremiah 9:5, 8.

Not to be touched, Numbers 19:16–18.

Preferred to earthly home, Job 17:13.

Wishing burial near parents' grave, 2 Samuel 19:37.

Respect for dead bodies, 2 Samuel 21:13–14.

Zero activity in grave, Ecclesiastes 9:10.

Rock-hewn graves, Isaiah 22:16.

Ignominious burial, Jeremiah 22:19.

Grave robbed of victory, 1 Corinthians 15:55.

See Burial, Tomb.

GRAVITY

Earth forces, Psalm 104:5 (LB).

Law of gravity, Proverbs 26:27.

GRAZING *See Grass.*

GREATNESS

Greatness of Moses, Deuteronomy 34:10–12.

Conditional greatness, 2 Kings 5:1.

Great by divine instigation, 2 Chronicles 1:1.

Assured greatness in heaven, Matthew 5:19.

Jesus not recognized in hometown, Matthew 13:55–58.

Role of humility in greatness, Matthew 20:26; 23:11–12.

Greatness of Jesus, John 21:25.

Contemplating Christ's greatness, Ephesians 1:18–23.

Qualifications of Christ's greatness, Colossians 1:15–20.

See Attainment, Fame, Prestige.

GREED

Greed for land, Genesis 13:5–7; Deuteronomy 2:5.

Dispute over water rights, Genesis 26:19–22.

Manna supply forbid greed, Exodus 16:16–18.

"They grew fat on plunder," Judges 5:7 (NRSV).

Interested only in money, 1 Samuel 8:3 (GNB).

Payment sought for master's ministry, 2 Kings 5:20–27.

Greed causing harm of others, Psalm 52:7.

Greedy prayer, Psalm 106:14–15.

No thought of kindness, Psalm 109:16.

Greed hurts family, Proverbs 15:27.

Three things never satisfied, Proverbs 30:15–16.

Money never satisfies, Ecclesiastes 5:10.

"Greedy dogs," Isaiah 56:11 (Berk.).

Dishonest gain, Jeremiah 17:11; 22:17.

Prospering from another's failure, Ezekiel 26:1–3.

Selfish shepherds, Ezekiel 34:2.

Greed for plunder, Amos 3:10.

Grape pickers leave a few grapes, Obadiah 5.

Wealth by extortion, Habakkuk 2:6, 9 (CEV).

Greedy as wolves, Zephaniah 3:3.

"What will we get?" Matthew 19:27 (CEV).

Thirty silver coins, Matthew 26:14–16, 47–50.

Folly of material greed, Luke 12:13–21.

Christianity for personal advantage, Romans 16:17–18.

Greedy lust, Ephesians 4:19.

Greed for money, 1 Timothy 6:9–10.

Unsatisfied greed, James 4:1–2.

Corrosion of gold and silver, James 5:1–3.
See Affluence, Lust, Money, Selfishness.

GREETING

Father, son greeting, Exodus 18:7.
Spiritual warmth, Ruth 2:4.
Hearty, healthful greeting, 1 Samuel 25:6.
Angelic greeting, Luke 1:28–31.
Apostle's greeting, Romans 16:3–16; 1 Corinthians 1:1–3; Philippians 4:21–23.
Friends greeted by name, 3 John 14.
See Salutation.

GRIEF

Father's grief, Genesis 37:33–35.
Time of mourning concluded, Genesis 50:4.
Shaving head of mourner, Deuteronomy 14:1–2.
Grief for ark greater than for sons, 1 Samuel 4:16–18.
Death of grieving widow, 1 Samuel 4:19–20.
Personal grief put aside, 2 Samuel 19:1–8.
Unmanly grief, Job 6:2 (AB).
Eyes grown dim, Job 17:7.
Eyes weakened by sorrow, Psalm 6:7.
No song for heavy heart, Proverbs 25:20.
Grieving the Holy Spirit, Isaiah 63:10; Ephesians 4:30.
Professional grief, Jeremiah 9:17–20.
Grief-stricken city, Lamentations 1:4.
Grief of Jesus, Luke 19:41–44.
Grief of others remembered, 2 Timothy 1:3–4.
Refusal to repent, Revelation 16:10–11.
See Mourning, Sorrow, Tears.

GROAN

Jesus groaned, Mark 7:34 (GNB); 8:12 (CEV).

GROCERIES

Grocery shopping, John 4:8.
Meat market products, 1 Corinthians 10:25 (NASB, NKJV, NRSV).

GROUND RULES See Restriction.

GROWTH

Growth in spirit and character, 1 Samuel 2:26.
National growth, 2 Samuel 24:3 (See LB).

From strength to strength, Psalm 84:7.
Sure road to maturity, Proverbs 9:1–6.
Enlarge your plans, Isaiah 54:2–3; Micah 7:11.
Guidance, correction, Jeremiah 10:23–24.
Trust produces growth, Jeremiah 17:7–8.
Shriveled seeds, Joel 1:17.
Tiny seed becomes great tree, Matthew 13:31–32.
Seed time to harvest, Mark 4:26–29.
Parable of mustard seed, Mark 4:30–32.
Balanced life of Jesus, Luke 2:52.
Early church growth, Acts 9:31.
Growth through suffering, Romans 5:3–4 (Japanese: "kneaded character").
Learn what pleases the Lord, Ephesians 5:10.
Certain spiritual growth, Philippians 1:6.
Growth formula, Philippians 3:12–16.
Growing in God's will, Colossians 1:9–12.
Salvation, growing, Colossians 2:6–7.
Strong hearts, 1 Thessalonians 3:13.
Increasing love, 1 Thessalonians 4:10.
Growing faith, love, 2 Thessalonians 1:3.
Diligent quest for spiritual growth, 1 Timothy 4:13.
Disciplined growth, 2 Timothy 1:7.
Growth in spiritual perception, Hebrews 5:11–14.
Confident of followers' growth, Hebrews 6:9.
Growth through testing, James 1:2–4.
Initiative to rid evil traits, 1 Peter 2:1.
Spiritual milk promotes growth, 1 Peter 2:2–3.
Additions to faith, 2 Peter 1:5–9.
Growing in grace, 2 Peter 3:18.
Good health, spiritual growth, 3 John 2.
Growing faith, Jude 20.
See Discipleship, Maturity.

GRUDGE

Do not seek revenge, Leviticus 19:18; Proverbs 20:22; 24:29.
Golden Rule exempted, Proverbs 24:29.
Repaying evil for evil, Romans 12:17; 1 Peter 3:9.
Avoid grudges, Colossians 3:13 (LB).
See Retribution.

GRUESOME See Sadistic, Torture.

GRUMBLING

"Do not grumble," John 6:43 (NASB).
See Attitude, Complain.

GUARANTEE

God's promise to Noah, Genesis 9:8–16.
Son's guarantee to father, Genesis 42:37.
Guarantee well-being, Psalm 119:122 (NRSV).
Eternal life guaranteed, 1 John 5:11–12.
See Assurance, Covenant, Pledge, Promise.

GUARDIAN

Household guardians, Genesis 14:14.
Guardian of the people, Esther 10:3.
Shielded by God's power, 1 Peter 1:5.
See Advocate.

GUERRILLA

David's guerrilla force, 1 Samuel 27:6–11.

GUESTS

Formal greeting, Genesis 18:2.
Courtesy to departing guests, Genesis 18:16.
Mistreatment of guests, 2 Samuel 10:1–5.
Variety of guests, 1 Kings 1:41, 49; Proverbs 9:18; 25:17; Matthew 22:11; Luke 7:39–50; Acts 18:1–3; 1 Corinthians 10:27; Hebrews 13:2.
King Solomon's royal guest, 1 Kings 10:1–13.
Room for prophet, 2 Kings 4:8–10.
Departure of unwelcome guests, Psalm 105:38.
Infrequent visits, Proverbs 25:17.
One thousand banquet guests, Daniel 5:1.
Hospitality for apostles, Matthew 10:9–15.
Invited guest, John 2:2.
Coming to stay awhile, 1 Corinthians 16:5–6.
Christian attitude to guests, 2 Corinthians 7:13–15.
See Hospitality, Visitor, Welcome.

GUIDANCE

Creation of light, Genesis 1:3, 14–19.
Obedient to guidance, Genesis 12:1–14.
Moral guidance, Genesis 20:1–18.

Seeking specific guidance, Genesis 24:11–17.
Angelic guidance, Genesis 24:40.
Seeking God's will by divination, Genesis 30:27.
Reassuring guidance, Genesis 46:1–4.
Doubting divine guidance, Exodus 5:22–23.
Guidance against insurmountable opposition, Exodus 14:5–14.
Strange test of guidance, Exodus 16:2–5.
Guardian angel, Exodus 23:20.
Guided by ark of covenant, Numbers 10:29–33.
Laity guidance, Numbers 12:1–2.
Confidence in face of danger, Numbers 14:8–9.
Guidance in choice of leader, Deuteronomy 17:14–15.
Continuity guidance, Joshua 1:6–9.
Specific orders, Joshua 8:8.
Gideon's fleece, Judges 6:36–40.
Scriptural guidance from God Himself, 1 Samuel 3:21.
Personal decision, divine guidance, 1 Samuel 14:36–41.
Asking the Lord for guidance, 2 Samuel 2:1–4; 5:12, 17–19.
Guidance in life of David, 2 Samuel 7:1–16.
Assurance of divine guidance, 2 Samuel 7:18–29.
Lamp of the Lord, 2 Samuel 22:29.
Strength, guidance, 2 Samuel 22:33.
Work of spirit within man, Job 32:8.
God guides in different ways, Job 33:14.
Guiding angel, Job 33:23–25.
Guidance in midst of enemies, Psalm 4:8.
Guided by Scripture, Psalms 19:7–11; 119:18, 24, 105.
Author and finisher of our salvation, Psalm 25:4–5.
Confidential guidance, Psalm 25:14.
"Lead me in a smooth path," Psalm 27:11 (NKJV).
Implanted heart guidance, Psalms 37:3–5; 20:4–5.
Success delights the Lord, Psalm 37:23–24.
Divine plans for us, Psalm 40:5.
Divine guidance, Psalm 73:24; Proverbs 21:1.
Prayer for undivided heart, Psalm 86:11.

Light promised upright, Psalm 97:11.

Prayer for guidance in Bible study, Psalm 119:18.

Guided by lamp of Scripture, Psalm 119:105.

Asking God for discernment, Psalm 119:125.

The Lord fulfills His purposes, Psalm 138:8.

Prayer for inner peace, righteousness, Psalm 139:23–24.

Prayer for guidance, Psalm 143:10.

Classic request for guidance, Proverbs 3:5–6 (CEV, NRSV).

Bright path of righteous, Proverbs 4:18.

Those who seek, find, Proverbs 8:17.

Guided by good teaching, Proverbs 9:9.

Choice, guidance, Proverbs 16:9.

Divine wisdom and human motives, Proverbs 19:21.

Steps directed by the Lord, Proverbs 20:24.

Guiding watercourse, Proverbs 21:1.

Letting God teach His ways, Isaiah 2:3.

Stop trusting in man, Isaiah 2:22.

Perfect faithfulness of God, Isaiah 25:1.

Guidance for farmer, Isaiah 28:24–26.

Prayer brings prompt guidance, Isaiah 30:19–21.

The Lord our King, Isaiah 33:22.

Way of holiness, Isaiah 35:8.

Doors opened permanently, Isaiah 45:1–5.

End known from beginning, Isaiah 46:10–11.

God knows what is best, Isaiah 48:17–18.

Certain supply of guidance, Isaiah 49:10; 58:11.

Walking with confidence, Isaiah 50:10.

Stumbling without guidance, Isaiah 59:10.

Ask for ancient paths, good way, Jeremiah 6:16.

Evil guidance, Ezekiel 20:24–25 (NIV, NKJV).

Sovereign guidance, Jeremiah 10:23; Hosea 14:9.

Road signs, guideposts, Jeremiah 31:21.

Follow your nose, Ezekiel 21:16 (KJV).

Seeking omen at fork in road, Ezekiel 21:18–23.

Guidance of Holy Spirit, Ezekiel 36:26–27.

Enforced guidance, Ezekiel 38:4.

No divine guidance, Hosea 3:4 (CEV).

Key to divine guidance, Hosea 12:6.

Prophet conveys revelation of the Lord, Amos 3:7.

Famine for words of the Lord, Amos 8:11–12.

Taught the way of the Lord, Micah 4:2.

Ignorant of God's thoughts, Micah 4:12.

Broken staff, Zechariah 11:10.

Holy family guided to Egypt, Matthew 2:12–21.

Led into temptation, Matthew 4:1.

Guidance to twelve apostles, Matthew 10:5–42; 11:1.

Two-word command, Mark 2:14.

Holy Spirit guided Jesus, Luke 4:1–2.

Night's prayer before decision, Luke 6:12–16.

Follow light, avoid darkness, John 8:12.

Shepherd, sheep, John 10:1–6.

Walking in light, John 12:35–36.

Finding the way, John 14:1–14.

Promised guidance, John 14:16–17.

Instruction for apostles, Acts 1:1–2.

Asking for guidance but depending on earthly procedure to obtain result, Acts 1:24–26.

Guided by angel, Acts 8:26.

Ananias guided to Saul, Acts 9:10–17.

Guidance from Holy Spirit, Acts 13:1–3.

Preaching hindered by Holy Spirit, Acts 16:6–7.

Macedonian vision, Acts 16:9–10.

Assured of guidance in a vision, Acts 18:9–11.

God's will for ministry appointments, Acts 18:20–21.

The Lord Himself commissioned Paul to minister, Acts 23:11.

Guidance in prayer, Romans 8:26–27.

All things work for good, Romans 8:28.

Concluding ministry in area, Romans 15:23–24.

The Lord opens door, 2 Corinthians 2:12.

Guided by revelation, Galatians 2:2.

The law as a guide to Christ, Galatians 3:24.

Guided by illness, Galatians 4:13–14.

God works out everything in His will, Ephesians 1:11–12.

Foolishness of missing God's will, Ephesians 5:17.

Promise to know God's will, Colossians 1:9–14.

Father guides children, 1 Thessalonians 2:11–12.

Communication in person and by writing, 1 Timothy 3:14–15.

Ministering spirits, Hebrews 1:14.

Ignorant, misguided, Hebrews 5:2 (NASB).

Led by God's hand, Hebrews 8:9.

Faith obedience, Hebrews 11:7–12.

Going in obedience toward unknown objective, Hebrews 11:8.

If you lack wisdom, ask God, James 1:5–6.

Horses and ships, James 3:3–4.

Eyes of the Lord on the righteous, 1 Peter 3:12.

Divine purpose in giving Scriptures, 2 Peter 1:2–4.

Light totally apart from darkness, 1 John 1:5–7.

Living by truth, 1 John 1:9–10.

Springs of living water, Revelation 7:16–17. *See Direction.*

GUILE

Scheme to hinder Nehemiah, Nehemiah 6:1–9.

Hurt of being deceitful, Proverbs 26:28.

Friends and brothers not trusted, Jeremiah 9:4–8.

Skilled in doing evil, Micah 7:3.

Wealthy by extortion, Habakkuk 2:6.

King Herod and the Magi, Matthew 2:7–8, 13.

"Guileless in what is evil," Romans 16:19 (NRSV).

See Deceit, Devious.

GUILT

Passing blame to others, Genesis 3:8–13, 17–19.

Cain's denial of guilt, Genesis 4:8–10.

Guilt less than murder, Genesis 37:19–27.

Circumstantial evidence, Genesis 39:6–20.

False accusation, Genesis 39:11–20.

Fabricated guilt, Genesis 44:1–34.

Murder exposed, Exodus 2:11–14.

Old Testament scapegoat, Leviticus 16:20–22.

One brings guilt upon all, Numbers 16:22.

Clergy responsibility, Numbers 18:1.

Guilt of leadership, Numbers 20:12.

Insufficient murder witness, Numbers 35:30; Deuteronomy 17:6; 19:15.

False witness, Deuteronomy 19:16–19.

Innocent not to share with guilty, Deuteronomy 24:16.

Accidental death, Numbers 35:22–25; Deuteronomy 19:4–7.

Sacrifice for unsolved guilt, Deuteronomy 21:1–9.

Guilty before God, man, 1 Samuel 2:22–25.

Plea for evidence of guilt, 1 Samuel 20:1.

Accused of murder for abetting suicide, 2 Samuel 1:1–16.

Parable of guilt, 2 Samuel 12:1–7.

Claim of righteousness, innocence, 2 Samuel 22:21–25.

Conscience-stricken, 2 Samuel 24:10–17.

Executing fathers, sparing sons, 2 Kings 14:5–6.

"Do not cover their guilt," Nehemiah 4:5 (NRSV).

Agonizing guilt, Psalm 38:4; Proverbs 28:17.

Awareness of sin, guilt, Psalm 51:3.

Guilt added to guilt, Psalm 69:27 (NRSV).

God's forgiveness, Psalm 130:3–4.

Stealing food, Proverbs 6:30–31.

Evil attitude toward guilt, Proverbs 17:15.

Those who accuse guilty, Proverbs 24:24–25.

Abundant guilt, Isaiah 1:4.

Guilt atoned by fire, Isaiah 6:6–7.

Past guilt, Isaiah 43:18.

Not expecting to be caught, Isaiah 47:7 (CEV).

Indelible guilt stain, Jeremiah 2:22.

Disgrace of getting caught, Jeremiah 2:26.

Innocence proclaimed, guilt obvious, Jeremiah 2:34–35.

Sincere disgrace realizing sinfulness, Jeremiah 3:24–25.

Total forgiveness, Jeremiah 50:20.

Ezekiel bearing sin of people, Ezekiel 4:4–6.

Degrees of sin in God's sight, Ezekiel 16:48–52.

Parents and children responsible for sin, Ezekiel 18:4–20.

Innocent congregation, guilty priests, Hosea 4:4 (CEV).

Blamed for prostitution, Hosea 4:13–14 (See CEV).

Nation's bloodguilt pardoned, Joel 3:21.

Casting lots to determine guilt, Jonah 1:7.

Admitting guilt, Jonah 1:10–12.

Pondering choice of sacrifice for sin, Micah 6:7.

Guilt cannot be overlooked, Micah 6:11.

Guilt must be punished, Nahum 1:3.

Unpardonable sin, Matthew 12:31–32.

Hypocrisy akin to murder, Matthew 23:29–32.

Accomplice to murder, Matthew 26:14–16; 27:3.

Delayed realization, Mark 14:66–72.

Guilty of much, of less, Luke 7:36–50.

Indictment of Pharisees, Luke 11:45–54.

Hidden guilt, John 3:20.

Truth versus guilt, John 7:45–46.

Universal guilt, John 8:6–11.

Morsel of bread to implicate guilt, John 13:21–27.

"Not guilty," John 19:6 (LB).

Sin of ignorance, Acts 3:17; 1 Timothy 1:12–14.

Approving wrong done by others, Acts 8:1.

Guilt by snake bite, Acts 28:1–6.

Guilt of self-righteousness, Romans 2:1–16.

No accounting of past sins, Romans 4:8 (GNB).

Blame for evil placed on women, 1 Timothy 2:14.

Those who turn backs, 2 Peter 2:20–22.

Guilty of all, 1 Samuel 15:23; James 2:10.

Deserved punishment for wilful sin, Hebrews 10:28–31.

See Conscience, Court, Verdict.

GUITAR

Heaven's guitars, Revelation 5:8 (AB).

GULF STREAM

Paths in sea, Isaiah 43:16.

GULLIBLE

Believing anything, Proverbs 14:15.

Gullible to error, Galatians 1:6; 3:1–5.

Do not be fooled, Colossians 2:4 (GNB).

Wind-tossed, James 1:6.

See Fool, Naive.

GYPSY *See Nomad.*

GUITAR

H

HABIT

Serving God habitually, Genesis 24:40 (AB).
Habitual sin, Psalm 92:9 (Berk.).
Cursing habitually, Psalm 109:17–19.
Habitual disobedience, Jeremiah 2:5 (AB).
Habitual evil, Jeremiah 13:23; 22:21; Micah 2:1; Ephesians 2:2 (AB).
Habitual idolatry, Hosea 4:12 (AB).
Habitual joy, confidence, Romans 5:4–5 (AB).
Habitual hospitality, Romans 12:13 (LB).
Habitually spiritual, Galatians 5:16 (AB); 2 Peter 1:5–8.
Enslaved by what masters you, 2 Peter 2:19.
Habitual sin, 1 John 3:9 (AB).

HAIL

Hailstorm in Heaven, Revelation 11:19 (AB).

HAIR

"Baldness between your eyes," Deuteronomy 14:1 (KJV).
Uncombed hair, Daniel 10:3 (LB).
Old, gray, 1 Samuel 12:2.
Strength in uncut hair, Judges 16:17.
Rapport with gray-haired, aged, Job 15:10.
Enumerated hair, Psalm 40:11–12; Matthew 10:30; Luke 12:7.
Crown of splendor, Proverbs 16:31; 20:29 (See GNB).
Haughty women become bald, Isaiah 3:16–17 (See 4:4).
Hair cut in mourning, Jeremiah 7:29.
Priests with well-groomed hair, Ezekiel 44:20.
Coming gray hair, Hosea 7:9.
Hair cut in response to vow, Acts 18:18.
Disgraceful long hair, 1 Corinthians 11:14–15.
"Fancy hairdos," 1 Timothy 2:9 (CEV).
"Hair stand on end," James 2:19 (AB).
See Barber, Coiffure.

HALF-BREED

"Mob of half-breeds," Zechariah 9:6 (CEV).

HALITOSIS See Breath.

HALL OF FAME

"Wise men's hall of fame," Proverbs 15:31–32 (LB).

HALLOWED See Sacred.

HALLOWEEN

Graveyard spirits, Isaiah 65:4 (LB).

HALLUCINATION See Trance.

HANDICAP

Respect the handicapped, Leviticus 19:14; Deuteronomy 27:18.
Hindrance to worship, Leviticus 21:16–23.
Cutting off thumbs, big toes, Judges 1:7.
Kindness to crippled son, 2 Samuel 9:1–13.
Ankle sprain avoided, 2 Samuel 22:37.
Handicapped by leprosy, 2 Kings 5:1.
Feeble hands, Job 4:3.
Helping blind, lame, Job 29:15.
Misusing the unfortunate, Psalm 10:8–10 (Berk.).
Help the handicapped, Proverbs 31:8 (GNB).
Lame plunder, Isaiah 33:23.
Blind see, deaf hear, Isaiah 35:5.
Spiritually blind and deaf, Isaiah 42:18–20.
Dull weapons, Jeremiah 21:4 (AB).
Stricken mute, Luke 1:11–22.
Deaf signing, Luke 1:62.
Mute demon, Luke 11:14.
Body crippled by demon, Luke 13:10–13.
Purpose of blindness, John 9:1–12.
Vanity antidote, 2 Corinthians 11:30; 12:7–10.
Thorn in flesh, 2 Corinthians 12:7.
Illness a blessing, Galatians 4:13–14.
Apparent poor eyesight, Galatians 6:11.
Handicapped by chains, Ephesians 6:19–20.
Handicap enhanced ministry, Philippians 1:12–14.
Crutch support, Hebrews 11:21.
Level path for lame, Hebrews 12:13.
See Blindness, Lame.

HANDS

Holding hands in time of danger, Genesis 19:16.

Prestigious right hand, Genesis 48:14.

Conquering right hand, Exodus 15:6.

Hands of Moses supported in battle, Exodus 17:11–12.

Sacramental hand, Leviticus 1:4.

Laying on of hands, Numbers 27:18; Deuteronomy 34:9; Matthew 19:15; Acts 6:6; 1 Timothy 4:14; 2 Timothy 1:6.

Left-handed, Judges 3:15.

Right-handed murder, Judges 5:26.

Seven hundred left-handed soldiers, Judges 20:16.

Helping hand, 2 Kings 10:15.

Right-hand source, Psalm 16:8.

Uplifted hands, Psalms 28:2; 63:4.

The Lord's right hand, Psalms 48:10; 118:16.

Hands gesture praise, Psalms 134:2; 141:2.

Prayer posture, Psalm 143:6; Lamentations 2:19; 1 Timothy 2:8.

Shake hands, Proverbs 6:1 (NKJV).

Right hand in oath, Isaiah 62:8.

Hand of judgment, Daniel 5:5–6.

Secrets between hands, Matthew 6:3.

Healing hands, Matthew 9:25; Mark 6:5; 7:32; Luke 4:40; 13;13; Acts 3:7; 9:41; 28:8.

HAIR

SAMSON HAS A BAD HAIR DAY.

Hayes

Hands washed of guilt, Deuteronomy 21:6; Psalm 26:6–7; Matthew 27:24.
Speaking with signing, Luke 1:62.
Too hasty with hands, 1 Timothy 5:22.
See Ambidextrous, Touch.

HANDSOME

Handsome young man, 1 Samuel 9:2 (NKJV).
Boy David, 1 Samuel 16:12.
Handsome Absalom, 2 Samuel 14:25 (GNB).
Most handsome man, Psalm 45:2 (NRSV).
Outstanding among ten thousand, Song of Songs 5:10.
Handsome princes, Lamentations 4:7.
Attractive young men, Zechariah 9:17.
See Physique, Virility.

HANDWRITING

Using large letters, Galatians 6:11.
Identified by handwriting, 2 Thessalonians 3:17.
Personal handwriting, Colossians 4:18.
See Autograph, Graphology, Signature.

HAPPENSTANCE

No mere happenstance, Genesis 45:4–7.
Random arrow, 2 Chronicles 18:33–34.
See Chance, Fortuity.

HAPPINESS

Happy eating, Deuteronomy 27:7.
Everyone very happy, 1 Chronicles 12:40 (CEV).
Strength in happiness, Nehemiah 8:10.
Reading Scriptures daily, Nehemiah 8:17–18.
Heart's desire, Psalm 37:4.
Oil of joy, Psalm 45:7; Hebrews 1:9.
Promised happiness, Psalm 97:11.
Key to happiness, Psalm 100:3 (LB).
Desires satisfied, strength renewed, Psalm 103:5.
Delight in Bible study, Psalm 119:24.
Enjoying fruit of labor, Psalm 128:2.
Evasive happiness, Ecclesiastes 1:16–18; 6:8 (AB).
Crown of happiness, Isaiah 35:10 (CEV); 51:11 (CEV).
Forgotten happiness, Lamentations 3:17 (RSV, GNB).

"Make everyone happy," Luke 2:10 (CEV).
Banquet for Jesus, Luke 5:27–35.
Living water from within, John 7:37–39.
Joy complete, John 15:11.
Sharing comfort through experience, 2 Corinthians 1:3–5.
Theology should bring happiness, 2 Corinthians 1:24 (GNB).
Rejoice in the Lord, Philippians 4:4.
"Oil of gladness," Hebrews 1:9 (NASB, NRSV).
Joy of problems, testing, James 1:2–4.
Inexpressible happiness, 1 Peter 1:8–9.
Joy of good reputation, 3 John 3–4.
Source of happiness, Jude 24–25.
See Attitude, Emotion, Joy.

HARASS

Attack, harass, Numbers 25:17 (NKJV).
Harass, meddle, Deuteronomy 2:19 (NKJV).
See Mistreatment, Persecution.

HARBINGER

Prophecy of boiling pot, Jeremiah 1:13–15.

HARDHEADED

Ineptness of king's viewpoint, 1 Kings 12:1–15.
Motivated by hook, bit, 2 Kings 19:28.
Opinionated fool, Proverbs 18:2.
See Stubborn.

HARDNESS

Hardened prostitute, Jeremiah 3:3.
Metal hearts, Jeremiah 6:28.
Caring neither for God nor man, Luke 18:1–5.
Facing judgment with hardness, Revelation 9:20–21; 16:10–11.
See Resolute.

HARDSHIP

"Hardship after hardship," Job 10:17 (NASB).
Accepting hardship, Job 13:15.
Gentle flowing waters, mighty flood waters, Isaiah 8:6–7.
Hardship implements spread of Gospel, Acts 8:3–4.
Purpose of hardship, 2 Corinthians 1:2–11.

Hardship in ministry, 2 Corinthians 6:4–10.
The Lord disciplines those He loves, Hebrews 12:5–11.
See Persecution, Testing.

HARDWARE

Maker of tools, Genesis 4:22.
Murderous hammer, Judges 4:21.
Hardware variety, 2 Samuel 12:31.
Made without hammer, 1 Kings 6:7.
Nail manufacture, 1 Chronicles 22:3.
See Armament, Tool.

HARM

Harmful census, 2 Samuel 24:1 (LB).
See Danger.

HARMLESS

Sheep among wolves, Matthew 10:16.
Genuinely harmless, Romans 16:19; Philippians 1:10; 2:15.
Exemplary high priest, Hebrews 7:26.

HARMONY

Harmonious relationship, 1 Samuel 18:1; Mark 9:50.
Two in agreement, Amos 3:3.
Harmony in mind, thought, 1 Corinthians 1:10.
Diversity to produce unity, Ephesians 4:11–16.
Sow in peace, James 3:18.
See Cooperation, Rapport, Unanimity.

HARP

Original harpist, Genesis 4:21.
Musical therapy, 1 Samuel 16:23.
Manufacturing harps, 1 Kings 10:12.
Priests as harpists, Nehemiah 12:27.
Tambourine, flute, harp, Job 21:12.
Melodious instrument, Psalm 81:2 (See Berk.).
Hanging place for harps, Psalm 137:2.
Banquet music, Isaiah 5:12.
Each had a harp, Revelation 5:8.
Harpists playing loudly, Revelation 14:2.
Victorious harp music, Revelation 15:2.
See Music.

HARVEST

Perpetual seasons, Genesis 8:22.
Harvest abundance, Genesis 41:49; Ezekiel 36:30.
Feast of harvest, Exodus 23:16.
Harvest gleaning, Leviticus 19:9; Deuteronomy 24:19.
First fruit to the Lord, Deuteronomy 26:1–4.
Stolen harvest, Deuteronomy 28:33; 1 Samuel 23:1.
Big planting, small harvest, Deuteronomy 28:38.
Fiery destruction of crops, Judges 15:4–5.
Ruth threshing, Ruth 2:21.
Unwanted rain, 1 Samuel 12:17.
Looted harvest, 1 Samuel 23:1.
"Reaping troubled harvest," Job 4:8 (NASB).
From among thorns, Job 5:5.
Weeds replace grain, Job 31:40; Jeremiah 12:13.
Greater joy than good harvest, Psalm 4:7 (LB).
Bountiful crop, Psalm 65:9–11.
Abundant fields, flocks, Psalm 65:13.
Productive land, Psalm 67:6.
Rain on mown hay, Psalm 72:6.
Mountain-top abundance, Psalm 72:16 (Berk.).
"Grain of Heaven," Psalm 78:24 (NIV).
Grasshoppers infest crops, Psalm 78:46.
Asleep during harvest, Proverbs 10:5.
"Make hay while the sun shines," Proverbs 10:5 (LB).
Cold weather plowing, Proverbs 20:4 (LB).
Bad harvest weather, Proverbs 26:1.
Poor harvest, Isaiah 5:10 (See AV).
Muted joy of harvest, Isaiah 16:9–10.
Vineyard in God's care, Isaiah 27:2–3.
First harvest, then bread, Isaiah 28:27–28.
Harvest produces seed, bread, Isaiah 55:10.
Eating one's own harvest, Isaiah 62:8–9.
Refusing to glorify God for harvest, Jeremiah 5:24.
Harvest denied disobedient, Jeremiah 8:13.
Sow wheat, reap thorns, Jeremiah 12:13.
No harvest celebrations, Jeremiah 48:33 (CEV).

Leaving a few grapes on vine, Jeremiah 49:9.

Time for flailing, Jeremiah 51:33 (LB).

Dangerous harvest, Lamentations 5:9 (CEV).

Stalks without grain, Hosea 8:7.

Harvest failure, Hosea 9:2.

Locust swarms, Joel 1:4 (CEV).

Lost harvest, Joel 1:10–11.

Abundant rain, abundant harvest, Joel 2:23–24.

Restored harvest, Joel 2:25.

Overabundant harvest, Amos 9:13 (CEV).

Planting but not harvesting, Micah 6:15.

Rejoicing with failed harvest, Habakkuk 3:17–18 (GNB).

Good crops withheld, Haggai 1:10–11.

Promised blessing on harvest, Haggai 2:19.

Parable of sower, Matthew 13:3–23.

Manually separating chaff from grain, Luke 6:1.

Animal's share, 1 Corinthians 9:9.

Farmer receives first share of crop, 2 Timothy 2:6.

Good crops and weeds, Hebrews 6:7–8.

Harvest illustrates patience, James 5:7 (See GNB).

Human harvest, Revelation 7:9–10.

Earth's final harvest, Revelation 14:14–20.

Monthly harvest throughout year, Revelation 22:2.

See Agriculture, Famine, Farmer, Gleaners, Seed, Threshing.

HASTE

In short order, Genesis 18:7 (Berk.).

Urgent business, 1 Samuel 21:8.

Time for haste, 2 Kings 4:29.

Haste makes waste, Proverbs 25:8 (KJV).

Swift messengers, Ezekiel 30:9.

News on the run, Habakkuk 2:2.

Good news to tell, Matthew 28:7.

Making haste to reach Jesus, Mark 5:2–6.

Food is ready, Luke 14:15–23.

Prodigal's father, Luke 15:20.

See Hurry.

HATRED

Avoid hatred, Leviticus 19:17; Proverbs 15:17.

Mistaking love for hatred, Deuteronomy 1:27.

Hated prophet, 1 Kings 22:8.

Royal hatred, Esther 5:10–14.

Hatred without reason, Psalm 69:4.

"Perfect hatred," Psalm 139:22 (NKJV, NRSV).

Cure for hatred, Proverbs 10:12.

Love for enemies, Matthew 5:43–44.

Hating heavenly light, John 3:20 (LB).

Hatred's basic cause, John 15:18–24.

Darkness of hatred, 1 John 2:9–11.

Hatred same as murder, 1 John 3:15.

Cannot love God, hate brother, 1 John 4:20–21.

See Dislike, Envy, Murder, Resentment.

HAUGHTY

Haughty brought down, 2 Samuel 22:28.

Haughtiness repaid, Psalm 31:23 (NRSV).

Haughty women, Isaiah 3:16.

Great pride, Isaiah 16:6; Jeremiah 48:29.

Haughty put to shame, Zephaniah 3:11.

See Arrogance, Vanity.

HAUNTED

Haunting fear of death, Hebrews 2:15 (AB).

Haunted by demons, Revelation 18:2 (GNB).

HAVEN *See Nest, Safety, Shelter.*

HAVOC *See Anarchy, Confusion.*

HEADSTRONG

Fool airs own opinion, Proverbs 18:2.

See Prejudice, Stubborn.

HEALING

Depending on physicians, 2 Chronicles 16:12.

Healed of leprosy, Leviticus 14:1–57 (NKJV).

The Great Healer, Psalm 103:3.

Healing blind, deaf, dumb, lame, Isaiah 35:5–6.

No balm in Gilead, Jeremiah 8:22.

Decisive healing, Jeremiah 17:14.

Useless remedies, Jeremiah 46:11.

Isaiah's prophecy of healing, Matthew 8:16–17; Isaiah 53:4.

Relationship of illness to sin, Matthew 9:1–7.

Double healing, Matthew 9:18–25.

Authority over illness, Matthew 10:1; Acts 3:11–16.

Arms, legs replaced, Matthew 15:31 (LB).

Epilepsy caused by demon, Matthew 17:14–20.

Healing increased popularity of Jesus, Mark 3:7–10.

Faith lacked for healing, Mark 6:4–6.

Fever rebuked, Luke 4:38–39.

Healing power emerged from Jesus, Luke 6:19.

Emphasizing healing above Healer, Luke 7:21–23.

Illness caused by spirit, Luke 13:10–16.

Long wait for healing, John 5:1–8.

Purpose for sickness, John 11:4.

Misunderstood healing of lame man, Acts 14:8–18.

Miracles in Paul's ministry, Acts 19:11–12.

Church sleeper restored, Acts 20:9–10.

Healing omitted among gifts, Romans 12:4–6 (See Romans 15:17–19).

Priority of healing ministry, 1 Corinthians 12:28–31.

Prayer for healing, no answer, 2 Corinthians 12:7–10.

Praying for sick, James 5:13–15.

See Medicine, Rheumatism, Sickness, Therapy.

HEALTH

Disease, sin, Leviticus 26:14–16.

Lifelong virility, Deuteronomy 34:7.

Evil spirits, poor health, 1 Samuel 16:16.

Hearty, healthful greeting, 1 Samuel 25:6.

Satan challenged God for Job's health, Job 2:3–6.

Death of healthy person, Job 5:26.

Worthless physicians, Job 13:4.

Bad breath, Job 19:17.

Wicked live to old age, Job 21:7.

Health restored, feel young again, Job 33:25 (CEV); Psalm 23:3 (LB).

Long life in answer to prayer, Psalm 21:4.

In great pain, Psalm 38:1–22.

Bodies sound, sleek, Psalm 73:4 (NRSV).

Pessimism over ill health, Psalm 116:10–11 (LB).

Healthy children, Psalm 128:3 (LB).

Fearfully, wonderfully made, Psalm 139:14.

Good news, good health, Proverbs 15:30.

Good sight, hearing, Proverbs 20:12 (LB).

Illness likened to poverty, Proverbs 22:22–23 (LB).

Dying before one's time, Ecclesiastes 7:17.

Nation of healthy citizens, Isaiah 33:24.

Fifteen years added to life, Isaiah 38:1–6.

"Please make me healthy," Isaiah 38:16 (CEV).

Forgotten health, Lamentations 3:17 (GNB).

Healthy youth for royal service, Daniel 1:3–6.

Refusing unhealthful food, Daniel 1:8–20.

Years of medical expense, Mark 5:25–26.

Impaired physically, not spiritually, Mark 9:43–48.

Crippled body caused by demon, Luke 13:10–13.

Sin as cause of ill health, John 5:14.

Responsibility for health of child, John 9:1–12.

Illness prompts Gospel ministry, Galatians 4:13–14.

Possibly poor eyesight, Galatians 6:11.

Physical training and godliness, 1 Timothy 4:8–9 (See CEV).

Keeping soul in good health, 3 John 2 (See CEV).

Health, wealth, spiritual vitality, 3 John 2–4.

See Healing, Immunity, Medicine, Rheumatism, Sickness, Therapy.

HEARING

Ears that do not hear, Deuteronomy 29:4.

Stone that could hear, Joshua 24:27.

Causing ears to tingle, 1 Samuel 3:11.

Making sure someone is listening, 2 Samuel 20:17.

Wise ears, Proverbs 18:15.

Words worth hearing, Proverbs 25:12.

Hearing messenger, ignoring message, Ezekiel 33:32.

Hearing in vain, Matthew 7:26; James 1:23–24.

See Ear, Message, Voice.

HEARSAY *See Gossip, Rumor.*

HEART

Quickened pulse, Song of Songs 5:4.

Hardened hearts, Zechariah 7:12 (LB).

God knows inner heart, 1 Samuel 16:7;
1 Chronicles 28:9; Matthew 9:4.
Softened heart, Job 23:16.
Center of emotion, Psalm 26:2–3; Proverbs
4:23; Ezekiel 11:19; 36:26; Colossians
3:15–17.
Throbbing heart, Psalm 38:10 (NRSV).
Prayer for pure heart, Psalm 51:10.
Heart attitudes, Proverbs 15:13–15; Mat-
thew 15:18–20.
Eternity in the heart, Ecclesiastes 3:11.
Heart attack, Ecclesiastes 12:6.
Mobile heart, Philemon 12 (GNB).
See Motivation.

HEARTACHE *See Disappointment, Grief,
Sorrow, Trauma.*

HEARTBEAT

Brevity of life, Job 7:6; 9:25; Psalm 39:5;
James 4:14.
Pounding heartbeat, Jeremiah 4:19.

HEARTFELT

Heartfelt prayer, James 5:16 (AB).

HEARTLESS

Murderer's heartless response, Genesis 4:9.
Heartless passers by, Lamentations 1:12.
When God seems heartless, Ezekiel 7:4–9.
Heartless piety, Luke 10:31.
Heartless toward God, man, Luke 18:1–5.
Empty words of comfort, James 2:16.
See Calloused, Hardness, Hypocrisy, Vicious.

HEAT

Cold, heat, Genesis 8:22.
Heat of day, Genesis 18:1.
Search for shade, Job 7:2 (CEV).
"Scorching desert," Psalm 107:4 (CEV).
Shelter from heat, Isaiah 4:5–6.
Furnace of testing, Daniel 3:21–23.
Heat of south wind, Luke 12:55.
Scorching sun, James 1:11.
Lake of fire, Revelation 19:19–21.
See Fire.

HEATHEN

Restored heathenism, 2 Chronicles 33:1–7.
Moses as a god, Exodus 7:1 (NKJV).

Under God's control, Psalm 47:8.
God as judge of gods, Psalm 82:1.
"God of gods," Psalm 84:7 (NRSV).
Eternity in the heart, Ecclesiastes 3:11.
Message to heathen, Daniel 4:1–18; 5:24–
29.
Defiled, detestable, Leviticus 18:24–30.
Heathen nations, 2 Kings 16:3; 17:8; Psalms
2:1; 9:15; 135:15; Ezekiel 39:21.
Eternity in heathen hearts, Ecclesiastes
3:21.
Praising heathen gods, Daniel 5:4 (NKJV).
Seeking Magi, Matthew 2:1–12.
Centurion came to Jesus, Matthew 8:5–13;
Luke 7:2–9.
Heathen Gentiles, Romans 2:14–15.
God revealed to those who did not seek,
Romans 10:20.
Pagan idols are demons, 1 Corinthians
10:20.
Gathered from all tribes and nations, Reve-
lation 7:9–10.
See Gentile, Idolatry, Pagan.

HEAVEN

"Firmament," Genesis 1:6–7 (KJV).
Holy dwelling place, Deuteronomy 26:15;
1 Kings 8:30; John 14:2.
Joy in heaven and earth, 1 Chronicles
16:31.
God's dwelling place, 2 Chronicles 6:33, 39.
Confused about eternal future, Job 10:19–
22.
Alleged remoteness of God, Job 22:12–14
(LB).
Heaven's potential northern sky location,
Job 26:7 (NKJV); Psalm 48:2 (NKJV).
More desirable than earth, Psalm 73:25.
Homesick for heaven, Psalm 84:2 (AB,
Berk.).
"Holy height," Psalm 102:19 (NRSV).
Heaven as up, Ecclesiastes 3:21 (AB).
Seeing the King, Isaiah 33:17, 21.
Everlasting light, Isaiah 60:19–20.
Heaven throne, earth footstool, Isaiah 66:1.
Ministering in heaven, Zechariah 3:1–10.
Treasure site, Matthew 6:19–20.
"Highest heaven," Mark 11:10 (NRSV).
View at death, Acts 7:55–56.

Anticipating heaven, 1 Corinthians 2:9–10; 2 Corinthians 5:2 (CEV).

Heaven cleansing, Revelation 12:7–9 (AB).

See Eternity, Immortality.

HEDONISM

Wiles of wicked woman, Genesis 39:6–19.

Defiant sin, Numbers 15:30–31.

Lust toward young virgins, Deuteronomy 22:23–29.

Practice of masturbation, Deuteronomy 23:9–14.

Strong man, sex, Judges 15:1–2.

Attraction of prostitute, Judges 16:1.

Homosexual activity, Judges 19:22.

Plunder taken in battle, 1 Samuel 30:16.

Hedonistic Solomon, 1 Kings 11:1–6.

Momentary joy, Job 20:5 (NASB).

"Taste of sin," Job 20:12 (CEV).

Resisting God, Job 21:14 (NRSV).

Sinful ideas, Job 22:15 (CEV).

Covenant to avoid lust, Job 31:1.

Wicked boast about desires, Psalm 10:3 (NRSV).

Boasting about evil, Psalm 52:1.

"Stay out all night," Psalm 59:15 (Berk.).

Habitual sin, Psalm 92:9 (Berk.).

Wicked desire perishes, Psalm 112:10 (NASB, NKJV).

Moral seduction, Proverbs 7:6–23.

Loving pleasure, Proverbs 21:17.

Seeking proper pleasure, Proverbs 24:13–14.

Assumed satisfaction, Ecclesiastes 1:17 (AB).

Meaningless pleasure, Ecclesiastes 2:1–3, 10 (See CEV, NASB).

"Song of fools," Ecclesiastes 7:5.

Search for pleasure, Ecclesiastes 8:15.

Materialistic view of pleasure, Ecclesiastes 10:19.

Pleasure-seeking youth, Ecclesiastes 11:9 (See NRSV).

Distorted values, Isaiah 5:20.

Alcohol's heroes, Isaiah 5:22.

Revelry halted, Isaiah 24:8–9.

Unsatisfied dreams, Isaiah 29:7–8.

Burning with lust, Isaiah 57:5.

Feet rushing into sin, Isaiah 59:7 (See CEV).

Give lessons to prostitutes, Jeremiah 2:33 (CEV).

Lust without shame, Jeremiah 3:3 (See CEV).

"Making sinful plans," Jeremiah 4:14 (CEV).

Men like stallions, Jeremiah 5:8.

Refusal to go God's way, Jeremiah 11:7–8.

Detestable acts in public, Jeremiah 13:26–27.

Wandering feet, Jeremiah 14:10.

Evil feasting avoided, Jeremiah 16:8–9.

Stubbornness of evil hearts, Jeremiah 16:12.

Looking to flesh for strength, Jeremiah 17:5.

Lifetime of evil, Jeremiah 32:30.

Judgment upon arrogance, Jeremiah 50:31–32.

An end to luxury, Jeremiah 51:13.

Forgotten enjoyment, Lamentations 3:17 (LB).

Good life gone, Lamentations 4:1, 5.

Beauty misused, Ezekiel 16:15.

Hedonistic sisters, Ezekiel 23:1–49.

End to noisy songs, Ezekiel 26:13.

Carnal pursuits of priests, Hosea 4:7.

Relished wickedness, Hosea 4:8.

Those who love shameful ways, Hosea 4:18.

Morning after, Joel 1:5.

Women who command husbands, Amos 4:1.

Clergyman for pleasure seekers, Micah 2:11.

Depending upon physical strength, Habakkuk 1:11.

Alcohol, nudity, Habakkuk 2:15.

Self-made idols, Habakkuk 2:18–19.

Wealth plundered, houses demolished, wine unused, Zephaniah 1:13.

Fate of carefree city, Zephaniah 2:15.

Emptiness of hedonistic gratification, Haggai 1:6.

High cost for dance, Mark 6:21–29.

Desire for more than one has, Luke 3:14.

Like children in marketplace, Luke 7:31–32.

Desire for recognition, Luke 11:43.

All kinds of greed, Luke 12:15–21.

Disillusioned with wild life, Luke 15:13.

Friends purchased with worldly wealth, Luke 16:9.

Influencing others to sin, Luke 17:1.

As in days of Noah, Luke 17:26–27.

Relationships in heaven, Luke 20:27–39.

Preferring darkness to light, John 3:19–21.

Primary concern for physical gratification, John 6:26.

Body as instrument of sin, Romans 6:12–13.

Hedonistic life-style, Romans 8:5–8.

"Wild parties," Romans 13:13 (CEV).

Evil plans, Romans 13:14 (LB).

Temporal attainment, 1 Corinthians 4:8.

Overt immorality, 1 Corinthians 5:1 (GNB).

Hedonism within Body of Christ, 1 Corinthians 5:9–13.

"Do anything we want," 1 Corinthians 6:12 (CEV).

"Every kind of impurity," Ephesians 4:19 (NASB, NRSV).

Hedonistic stomachs, Philippians 3:19.

"Wanton pleasure," 1 Timothy 5:6 (NASB).

Lovers of self, pleasure, 2 Timothy 3:1–4.

Thoughtless immorality, 2 Timothy 3:3 (LB).

Earth's glories, James 1:11.

Desires for pleasure, James 4:1 (GNB).

No friends of God, James 4:4 (LB).

"Drinking parties," 1 Peter 4:3 (NASB, NKJV).

Living for fun, James 5:5 (LB).

"Senseless animals," 2 Peter 2:12–14 (CEV).

Overt lust, 2 Peter 2:14 (AB).

Love of world, 1 John 2:15–17.

Poking fun, Jude 18 (NRSV).

Natural instincts, Jude 19.

Merchandizing in evil city, Revelation 18:3.

See Carnality, Debauchery, Flesh, Lust, Immorality, Pleasure.

HEED

Take care, Matthew 6:1.

Giving heed to Scripture, Hebrews 2:1–3.

See Alert, Attention, Response.

HEIGHT

Tower of Babel, Genesis 11:1–9.

Height of King Saul, 1 Samuel 10:23–24.

Goliath the giant, 1 Samuel 17:4; 2 Samuel 21:19; 1 Chronicles 20:5.

Lofty stars, Job 22:12.

Where eagles fly, Job 39:27–28.

"Holy height," Psalm 102:19 (NRSV).

Temple mountain, Isaiah 2:2.

Towering tree, Ezekiel 31:3–18; Daniel 4:10–12.

See Size.

HEIR

Substitute heir, Genesis 15:3; 21:10.

Beneficiary receives all, Genesis 25:5.

Daughter as full heir, Numbers 27:8.

Rights of oldest son, Deuteronomy 21:15–17.

Resistant to leaving legacy, Ecclesiastes 2:18.

Spiritual heirs, Romans 8:17; Galatians 3:29; Titus 3:7; Hebrews 1:14.

Conditions for exercising will, Hebrews 9:16–17.

See Daughter, Family, Inheritance, Son.

HEIRLOOM

Royal treasures, 2 Chronicles 5:1.

Two of Moses' tables, 2 Chronicles 5:10.

See Artifacts.

HELL

Confused about eternal future, Job 10:19–22.

"Down to the pit," Job 33:24.

Depth of the earth, Psalm 63:9.

Enlarged capacity, Isaiah 5:14 (KJV).

Agreement with hell, Isaiah 28:18 (KJV).

Fires of Topheth, Isaiah 30:33.

"The world below," Ezekiel 32:19 (CEV).

Broad road to hell, Matthew 7:13 (See GNB).

Fiery furnace, Matthew 13:37–42, 49–50.

Excluded from God's presence, 2 Thessalonians 1:9.

Lake of fire, Revelation 19:19–21.

Those not in Book of Life, Revelation 20:7–15.

See Demons, Lost, Satan, Judgment, Punishment.

HELLION *See Juvenile Delinquent, Renegade.*

HELP

Divine helper, Deuteronomy 33:29; 2 Chronicles 25:8; Psalm 27:9.

Strength, shield, Psalm 28:7.

Deliverer, Psalm 40:17.

Vainly crying for help, Psalm 69:3.

Antidote to fear, Isaiah 41:10; Hebrews 13:6.

Vain cry for help, Habakkuk 1:2 (LB).

Holy Spirit as helper, John 14:16–17 (GNB).

Helping others, Romans 12:13 (LB).

See Assistance.

HERALD

Prophesied herald, Isaiah 40:3 (See Matthew 3:1–3).

Pagan proclamation, Daniel 3:1–6.

Herald angels, Luke 2:8–13.

Mark of evangelist, 1 Timothy 2:7; 2 Timothy 1:11 (See AB).

See Clergy, Evangelist, Messenger, Prophecy.

HERBAL

Tithed herbs, Luke 11:42.

Medicinal leaves, Ezekiel 47:12; Revelation 22:2.

See Medicine.

HERDSMAN See Shepherd.

HEREAFTER

"Surely there is a hereafter," Proverbs 23:18 (NKJV).

HEREDITY

Inherited sin, Psalms 51:5; 58:3.

Father sins, children suffer, Lamentations 5:7.

Heredity proverb, Ezekiel 18:1–4.

New heredity in Christ, Romans 5:13–15.

See Inheritance.

HERESY

Death to heretics, Deuteronomy 18:20.

Prophecy of imagination, Ezekiel 13:1–23.

Heretical worship, Matthew 15:9.

Ignorance of Scriptures, Matthew 22:29.

Jesus criticized for healing, Mark 2:6–12.

Light becomes darkness, Luke 11:35.

Wisdom of Gamaliel, Acts 5:33–39.

Troubling message, Acts 15:24.

Exorcists at work, Acts 19:13–16.

Inevitable difficulties, 1 Corinthians 11:19.

Preaching false doctrine, 2 Corinthians 11:4–15.

Heresy-prone Galatians, Galatians 1:6–9.

Heretical infiltration, Galatians 2:4–5.

Bewitched Galatians, Galatians 3:1.

Penalty for misleading others, Galatians 5:10.

Paul wanted followers to know truth, Colossians 2:2–4.

Dangerous deceptive philosophy, Colossians 2:8.

Preventing heretical teaching, 1 Timothy 1:3–5.

End time heresy, 1 Timothy 4:1.

Godless chatter and opposing ideas, 1 Timothy 6:20–21.

Resistant to heresy, Hebrews 13:9.

False teachers, destructive heresies, 2 Peter 2:1–3 (See AB).

Lawless error, 2 Peter 3:17.

Alert to heresy, 1 John 4:1–3.

Heresy, wrong conduct, Jude 3–4 (See AB).

Bad teaching among good people, Revelation 2:13–15.

See Cult, Syncretism.

HERITAGE

Musical heritage, Genesis 4:21.

Image of God, image of man, Genesis 5:1–3.

Bargain heritage, Genesis 25:27–34.

Heritage of obedience, Numbers 14:24.

Covenant heritage, Deuteronomy 5:2–3.

Parental heritage, 1 Kings 11:9–13.

Disobedient children, grandchildren, 2 Kings 17:41.

Confessing sins of ancestors, Nehemiah 9:2.

Ancestral property, Nehemiah 11:20.

Spiritual heritage generation to generation, Psalm 44:1–3.

Tell future generations, Psalm 48:14.

Like fathers, like sons, Psalm 106:6.

Heritage for children, Proverbs 20:7.

Ancient boundary stone, Proverbs 22:28; 23:10–11.

Ancestral rock, Isaiah 51:1.

Ruins rebuilt, Isaiah 58:12.

Ignoring God's prior blessings, Jeremiah 2:5–8.

Ark of Covenant forgotten, Jeremiah 3:16.

Ancient paths, good way, Jeremiah 6:16.

Teetotaler tradition, Jeremiah 35:1–16.

Telling message to children's children, Joel 1:3.

Honoring those who murdered prophets, Matthew 23:29–32.

Genealogy of Jesus, Luke 3:23–37.

Comparing old and new, Luke 5:36–39.

Satan as spiritual father, John 8:44.

Knowledge of Old Testament heritage, Acts 7:1–60.

Israel's heritage as means to witness, Acts 13:13–52.

Laying good foundation, 1 Corinthians 3:10.

Lessons from Israel's history, 1 Corinthians 10:1–13.

Endless genealogies, 1 Timothy 1:4; Titus 3:9.

Grandmother's faith transmitted, 2 Timothy 1:5.

Childhood scriptural heritage, 2 Timothy 3:14–15.

Responsibility to next generation, Titus 2:3–5.

See Background, Family, Grandparents, Inheritance, Parents.

HERMENEUTICS

Bible study, righteous lifestyle, Psalm 119:9–11.

Purpose of searching Scriptures, Proverbs 1:1–3.

Persistent study abundantly rewarded, Proverbs 2:1–6.

Proper student attitude, Proverbs 19:20.

Learn, apply, Proverbs 22:17.

Emotion in learning, Proverbs 23:12.

Beyond monetary value, Proverbs 23:23.

Analytical study, research, Ecclesiastes 7:25.

Function of wisdom in decision making, Ecclesiastes 8:5.

Divine pedagogy, Isaiah 28:26.

Supreme challenge for Bible student, 2 Timothy 3:16.

HEROES

No prophet like Moses, Deuteronomy 34:10–12.

How David became famous, 2 Samuel 8:13.

Anonymous heroes, Hebrews 11:35–39.

Heroic suffering, 1 Peter 2:19.

See Fame.

HESITATION

Hesitant at tomb of Jesus, John 20:5, 8.

Both timid, bold, 2 Corinthians 10:1.

"Those who shrink back," Hebrews 10:39 (NRSV).

See Reluctance.

HETERODOXY

Wrong interpretation of Scripture, Jeremiah 8:8.

Shepherds who lead sheep astray, Jeremiah 50:6.

Avoid error, Romans 16:17.

Error of Galatians, Galatians 4:1–5.

See Cult, Heresy, Syncretism.

HEX

Under spell, Galatians 3:1 (See also GNB).

See Curse.

HIATUS

Pause in condemnation, Job 21:1–3.

HIDDEN See Secrecy, Secret.

HIDING

Avoiding God, Genesis 3:9–10.

Baby Moses hidden, Exodus 2:2–3.

Hidden spies, Joshua 6:17, 25.

Hiding in thickets, pits, caves, cisterns, 1 Samuel 13:6.

Hiding in a well, 2 Samuel 17:18.

God hides Himself, Isaiah 45:15.

See Escape.

HIDING PLACE

Shadow of divine wings, Psalm 17:8.

Sheltering tabernacle, Psalms 27:5; 31:20.

Musical refuge, Psalm 32:7.

Refuge of Scripture, Psalm 119:114.

Shelter in time of storm, Isaiah 32:2.

No place to hide, Jeremiah 49:10; Obadiah 3–4.

See Protection, Refuge, Shelter.

HIGHWAY

Public thoroughfare, Numbers 20:19.
Need for highways, Deuteronomy 19:1–3.
Highways abandoned for paths, Judges 5:6.
Fortified highway, 2 Chronicles 16:1 (LB).
Intercontinental highway, Isaiah 19:23.
Holiness highway, Isaiah 35:8.
Way through desert, Isaiah 40:3–4; 43:19.
Signs, guideposts, Jeremiah 31:21.
Broad and narrow way, Matthew 7:13–14.
Dangerous highway, Luke 10:30–33.
See Journey, Road, Travel.

HIKING

Long hike, no blisters, Deuteronomy 8:4 (Berk.).
Too exhausted to continue, 1 Samuel 30:10, 21.
Held to your paths, Psalm 17:5.

HILLS

Ancient hills, Genesis 49:26.
Land of hills and valleys, Deuteronomy 11:11.
Hills sacred to heathen, 1 Kings 20:23.
Melting mountains, Psalm 97:5.
Joyful hills, Psalm 98:8.
Hills of hope, Psalm 121:1.
Ancient mountains, Habakkuk 3:6.
Level place in hilly area, Luke 6:17.
See Geology.

HINDRANCE

Cherished sin, unanswered prayer, Psalm 66:18–19.
Sins as roadblock, Isaiah 59:2 (CEV).
Temple progress hindered, Haggai 1:3–4.
Hindering others from entering Kingdom, Matthew 23:13–15.
Rich receive less blessing than poor, Luke 6:20, 24–25.
Rejecting truth, hindering others, Luke 11:52.
Mob incited to hinder Paul and Silas, Acts 17:5–7.
"No obstacle in anyone's way," 2 Corinthian 6:3 (NRSV).
Hindered from running good race, Galatians 5:7.

"Everything that slows us down," Hebrews 12:1 (CEV).
Hindering authority in congregation, 3 John 9–10.
See Obstacles, Opposition.

HINTERLAND

Earth's farthest parts, Psalm 65:8 (AB); Acts 1:8 (See AB).

HISTORY

Days of old, Deuteronomy 32:7.
Living participants in history, Joshua 24:31 (LB).
Extensive genealogy, 1 Chronicles 1:1–5— 5:38.
Learn from history, Job 8:8–13 (LB); Psalm 78:2–3 (LB).
"Prehistoric times," Psalm 93:2 (LB).
Joseph, the unknown, Exodus 1:8.
Recorded stages of journey, Numbers 33:1– 49.
Asking about former days, Deuteronomy 4:32–35.
Reading history book to induce sleep, Esther 6:1.
Future history in God's hands, Job 12:23; 34:29–30; Psalms 2:1–6; 113:4.
Apostasy of nations, Psalm 2:1–3.
Inevitable fate of world governments, Psalm 2:7–9.
God will have last word in history, Psalm 9:5.
Evil brings about its own retribution, Psalm 9:15.
Promise of God to Israel, Psalm 45:16.
Time when peace will cover earth, Psalm 46:8–10.
Learning from history, Psalm 77:5, 11–12.
History in song, Psalm 78:1–72; 106:1–48.
Ponder the Lord's hand in history, Psalm 111:2–4.
History repeats itself, Ecclesiastes 1:9; 3:15.
World history capsule, Ecclesiastes 9:14– 15.
Evil deeds recorded, Isaiah 30:8.
Divine evaluation of nations, Isaiah 40:15– 17.
God knows end from beginning, Isaiah 46:10–11.

Ruins rebuilt, Isaiah 58:12.

A nation takes time to develop, Isaiah 66:8.

Ark of Covenant forgotten, Jeremiah 3:16.

The Lord of history revealed, Ezekiel 20:42.

Date recorded for future, Ezekiel 24:2.

Image depicting world history, Daniel 2:29–45.

Divine goodness in Israel's history, Micah 6:3–5.

Words of Jesus concerning end times, Mark 13:1–37.

Old manuscript, Mark 16:20 (GNB).

Many recorded New Testament events, Luke 1:1–2.

Orderly account of happenings, Luke 1:3–4.

Jesus identified with history, John 8:57–58.

Purpose of sacred history, John 20:30–31.

Inexhaustible history of Jesus, John 21:25.

History cited as defense, Acts 7:1–60.

Resume of Old Testament, gospel proclamation, Acts 13:16–41.

God's plan through history, Romans 1:1–6.

History's ultimate purpose, Romans 8:18–23.

Certain future judgment, Romans 9:28.

Lessons from history, 1 Corinthians 10:1–12.

Fulfillment of history, Ephesians 1:9–10.

Succinct history of Christ, 1 Timothy 3:16.

Demonic influence in history, Revelation 16:13–14.

When evil serves God's purpose, Revelation 17:17.

See Memorabilia.

HOBBY

Victory memorabilia, 1 Samuel 17:54.

Musical hobby, 1 Samuel 18:10; 19:9.

Idol collection, Isaiah 57:13.

HOLIDAY

Three annual festivals, Exodus 23:14–17.

Sabbatical year, Exodus 23:10–11.

Instructions for sacred feasts, Numbers 28:16–31 (Also chapter 29).

Loss of summer house, Amos 3:15.

"Refreshing rest," Romans 15:32 (NASB).

See Rest.

HOLINESS

Blameless holiness, Genesis 6:9.

Call to perfection, Genesis 17:1.

Reflecting God's radiance, Exodus 34:29–35.

Prime impetus to holiness, Leviticus 11:44–45.

Separated unto holiness, Leviticus 20:26; Deuteronomy 14:2.

Occupational holiness, Leviticus 21:8.

Abounding with God's favor, Deuteronomy 33:23.

Blameless before the Lord, 2 Samuel 22:24.

Pure cannot come from impure, Job 14:4.

Questioned holiness, Job 22:3.

Characteristics of holy life, Psalm 15:1–5.

Qualification for worship, Psalm 24:3–5.

"Holy splendor," Psalm 29:2 (NRSV).

"A godly man," Psalm 86:2 (NASB).

Overrighteous, Ecclesiastes 7:16.

Holiness of God and personal sinfulness, Isaiah 6:1–5.

Yearning for the Lord, Isaiah 26:9.

Highway of holiness, Isaiah 35:8.

Pursuit of righteousness, Isaiah 51:1.

Coming to the Lord with clean vessel, Isaiah 66:20.

Absolute holiness of God, Daniel 9:14.

Walking in ways of the Lord, Hosea 14:9.

Hate evil, love good, Amos 5:15.

Lips must first be purified, Zephaniah 3:9.

Only God is good, Mark 10:17–18.

Realization of sin in presence of Jesus, Luke 5:8.

Sinless Jesus, John 8:46 (See LB).

Sanctifying truth, John 17:17.

Righteousness comes from God, Romans 1:17.

Inner holiness, Romans 2:28–29.

False claims to holiness, Romans 4:2–5.

Righteousness not obtained from sacraments, Romans 4:9–12.

New life in Christ, Romans 6:4.

Freedom from mastery of sin, Romans 6:14.

Key to holiness, Romans 12:1–2.

Hate evil, cling to good, Romans 12:9.

Christian life-style, Romans 13:12–14.

True measure of spirituality, Romans 14:17–18.

Wise about good, innocent about evil, Romans 16:19.

"Completely innocent," 1 Corinthians 1:8 (CEV).

Ultimate Holy of Holies, 1 Corinthians 3:16.

Holy Spirit's human temple, 1 Corinthians 3:16–17; 6:19–20.

Holy Spirit in committed life, 2 Corinthians 3:7–8.

Impetus to holiness, 2 Corinthians 7:1.

Fruit of the Spirit, Galatians 5:22.

Attitude of mind and life-style, Philippians 4:8–9.

Life centered in Christ, Colossians 3:1–17.

Life that pleases God, 1 Thessalonians 4:1–8.

Holy Spirit and impact of Scripture, 2 Thessalonians 2:13.

Resisting ungodliness, Titus 2:11–12.

Made perfect through suffering, Hebrews 2:10.

Law makes nothing perfect, Hebrews 7:18–19.

Discipline that produces holiness, Hebrews 12:11.

Life-style of true disciple, James 3:17–18.

Personal initiative in holiness, James 4:7–10; 1 Peter 2:1.

Sanctifying work of the Spirit, 1 Peter 1:1–2.

Call to holiness, 1 Peter 1:13–16 (See AB).

Not conforming to world, 1 Peter 1:14–16.

Made holy obeying truth, 1 Peter 1:22.

Holiness in action, 1 Peter 3:9.

Christ's return impetus for holiness, 1 Peter 4:7–8.

Spiritual, material welfare, 2 Peter 1:3.

"Moral excellence," 2 Peter 1:5 (NASB).

Attributes of mature Christian, 2 Peter 1:5–9 (See AB).

Sin and provision for cleansing, 1 John 1:7–10 (Note: Spanish Bible translates "if we walk" **desde cuando,** "since we walk").

Purifying privilege, 1 John 3:1–3.

Deliverance from continual sin, 1 John 3:4–6.

Devil's work destroyed, 1 John 3:8.

Seen in God's sight, 1 John 5:18.

Keeping soul in good health, 3 John 2.

Partial holiness insufficient, Revelation 2:1–6, 13–15, 18–20.

Continuity of evil, good, Revelation 22:11.

See Sanctification, Separation.

HOLISTIC

Total involvement in loving God, Deuteronomy 6:5.

Enslaved bodies, Nehemiah 9:37.

Fearfully, wonderfully made, Psalm 139:13–16.

Bodily protection in fiery furnace, Daniel 3:27.

Holistic love for God, Mark 12:30; Luke 10:27.

Fourfold life of Jesus, Luke 2:52.

Light for the whole body, Luke 11:36.

Doubter's need for holistic proof, John 20:24–28.

Instruments of sin, Romans 6:13; 8:13.

Living sacrifice, Romans 12:1–2.

All-out righteousness, Romans 13:14.

Holy Spirit's holistic temple, 1 Corinthians 6:14–15; 19–20.

Body control, 1 Corinthians 9:27; Galatians 5:16.

Related parts of body, 1 Corinthians 12:12–26.

Christ revealed in our bodies, 2 Corinthians 4:10.

Role of body in marriage, Ephesians 5:33.

HOLY SPIRIT

Holy Spirit in creation, Genesis 1:2.

Special gifts through Holy Spirit, Exodus 31:1–5.

Transformed by Holy Spirit, 1 Samuel 10:6–9.

Words given by Holy Spirit, 2 Samuel 23:2.

Temple plans given by Holy Spirit, 1 Chronicles 28:12.

Inner guidance, Job 32:8; 33:4.

Holy Spirit removed, Psalm 51:11.

Water on thirsty land, Isaiah 44:3 (CEV).

Standard against evil, Isaiah 59:19–21.

Anointing to preach, Isaiah 61:1.

Grieving the Holy Spirit, Isaiah 63:10.

Commission to minister, Ezekiel 2:1–5.

Clean hearts, changed lives, Ezekiel 36:25–27.

Autumn, spring rains, Joel 2:23.

Young prophesy, old dream dreams, Joel 2:28.

Filled with the Spirit, Micah 3:8.

Not by might nor by power, Zechariah 4:6.

Birth of Jesus, Matthew 1:18.

Descending dove, Mark 1:10–11.

Jesus experienced Holy Spirit's fullness, Luke 4:1, 14; 10:21.

Living water from within, John 7:37–39.

Promised Counselor, John 14:16–17.

Holy Spirit's promised power, Acts 1:8.

Holy Spirit as Helper, John 14:26 (NASB, NKJV, GNB).

"The Advocate," John 15:26 (NRSV).

Holy Spirit's ministry, John 16:5–14; Romans 8:6–11.

Resurrection power, Romans 8:11; 1 Corinthians 6:14; Ephesians 1:18–21; 1 Peter 3:18.

Prayer guided by Holy Spirit, Romans 8:26–27.

Hope, joy, peace, Romans 15:13.

Guidance in Bible study, 1 Corinthians 2:6–16.

Beyond mortal experience, 1 Corinthians 2:9–10.

Holy Spirit's human temple, 1 Corinthians 3:16–17; 6:19–20.

Holy Spirit's guidance in marriage, 1 Corinthians 7:40.

Satisfying drink, 1 Corinthians 12:13.

Seal of ownership, 2 Corinthians 1:21–22.

Letter kills, Spirit gives life, 2 Corinthians 3:6; Ephesians 1:13.

Holy Spirit in commitment, 2 Corinthians 3:7–8.

Holy Spirit's relationship to Christ, Galatians 4:6 (See AB).

Purifying Holy Spirit, Galatians 5:16.

Spirit of wisdom, revelation, Ephesians 1:17.

Access to God through Holy Spirit, Ephesians 2:18–22.

Holy Spirit's inner power, Ephesians 3:20–22.

Grieving the Holy Spirit, Ephesians 4:30; Micah 2:7.

Holy Spirit's convicting power, 1 Thessalonians 1:4–5.

Antichrist restrained, 2 Thessalonians 2:7–8.

Holy Spirit impact, 2 Thessalonians 2:13; 1 Peter 1:1–2.

Soundness of faith, 2 Timothy 1:13–14.

Function, distribution of gifts, Hebrews 2:4.

"Yearns over us," James 4:5 (AB).

Author of Scripture, 2 Peter 1:20–21.

Anointed with truth, 1 John 2:20–27.

Confident of salvation, 1 John 3:24.

Holy Spirit contrasted to false spirits, 1 John 4:1–3.

Spirit testifies of Christ, 1 John 5:6.

Praying in the Holy Spirit, Jude 20.

"Rapt in His power," Revelation 1:10 (AB).

Holy Spirit speaking to churches, Revelation 2:29.

Sevenfold Holy Spirit, Revelation 3:1 (AB); 5:6 (AB).

See Trinity.

HOMAGE

False homage, Mark 15:19 (NRSV).
See Reverence.

HOME

Cave home, Genesis 19:30.

Love for childhood home, Genesis 31:30; Psalm 137:1–6.

Dedicating home to the Lord, Leviticus 27:14.

Newlywed's army status, Deuteronomy 24:5.

Best drinking water, 2 Samuel 23:15.

Hospitality for prophet, 2 Kings 4:8–10.

Dark household, Job 18:6 (LB).

God blessed our home, Job 29:4.

Desiring death at home, Job 29:18.

Jerusalem stones, dust, Psalm 102:14.

Building in vain, Psalm 127:1.

No song in homesick hearts, Psalm 137:4.

Women as home builders, Proverbs 14:1 (See GNB).

Establishing good home, Proverbs 24:3–4.

Seaside home, Acts 10:6.

Family leadership, Ephesians 5:21–23.

Home schooling, Ephesians 6:1–4.

Guest room, Philemon 22.

Tent or cottage, Isaiah 38:12; Hebrews 11:9–10.
God's future home, Revelation 21:3 (GNB).
See Family, Hospitality, Residence.

HOMECOMING

Jewish return to Palestine, Isaiah 60:4.
Jesus' Nazareth return, Luke 4:16–24.
Prodigal's homecoming, Luke 15:11–32.
Faithful worker's homecoming, Philippians 2:25–30.

HOMELESS

Restless wanderer, Genesis 4:14.
Woman in desert, Genesis 21:14.
Israelites homeless forty years, Numbers 32:13; Acts 7:35–36; Hebrews 3:1–11.
Lack of shelter, Job 24:8.
Unable to find residence, Psalm 107:4.
Street people, Lamentations 4:5.
Wandering Jews, Hosea 9:17.
Homeless Savior, Luke 9:58.
"Festival of Shelters," John 7:2 (GNB).
Hungry, homeless, 1 Corinthians 4:11.
See Abandoned, Orphan.

HOMEMAKER *See Home, Mother, Women.*

HOMESICK

Homesick for Egypt, Numbers 11:1–6.
"I just want to go home," 1 Kings 11:21–22 (CEV).
Far from home, Psalms 61:2; 137:4.
Homesick for Heaven, Psalm 84:2 (Berk.).
Homesick delinquent, Luke 15:11–32.
Spiritually homesick, Philippians 2:26 (AB, LB).
See Loneliness.

HOMOSEXUAL

Sodom's angelic visitors, Genesis 19:5.
Forbidden relationship, Leviticus 18:22–23; 20:13.
Male prostitutes, Deuteronomy 23:17.
Example of homosexual conduct, Judges 19:22–24.
Approved masculine love, 1 Samuel 18:1–4; 20:17–41; 2 Samuel 1:26; 19:1–6.
Eradication of deviates, 1 Kings 15:12 (See 14:24).

Male prostitutes enshrined, Job 36:14.
Boy prostitutes, Joel 3:3.
Unnatural passion and desire, Romans 1:24–27.
Homosexual activity condemned, 1 Corinthians 6:9–10.
Sexual perversion, 1 Timothy 1:10 (See AB).
Mother of perversion, Revelation 17:5 (GNB).
See Deviate.

HONESTY

Leadership integrity, Numbers 16:15; 1 Samuel 12:1–5.
Bribe refused, 2 Samuel 18:12; 1 Kings 13:8.
Expense vouchers not needed, 2 Kings 12:15.
Honest workers, 2 Chronicles 34:12 (CEV).
Claim of honesty, Job 33:1–5.
Honesty before the Lord, Psalm 24:3–4.
Protected by integrity, Psalm 25:21.
No deceit in God's house, Psalm 101:7.
Defended by honesty, Proverbs 12:13 (LB).
Honest life-style, Proverbs 20:7.
Weights and measures, Proverbs 20:10; Ezekiel 45:9–10.
Honest answer like a kiss, Proverbs 24:26.
Honest rebuke, Proverbs 27:5.
Integrity despised, Proverbs 29:10; Amos 5:10.
Honest character desired, Proverbs 30:7–9.
Search for one honest person, Jeremiah 5:1.
"Refuse to tell lies," Zephaniah 3:13 (CEV).
Advice to tax collectors, Luke 3:12–13.
Utter honesty, 2 Corinthians 1:12 (LB).
Deceit, honesty, Ephesians 4:14–15.
Testimony of man, testimony of God, 1 John 5:9.
See Integrity, Truth.

HONEY

Sweet flavor of manna, Exodus 16:31.
Honey not used for sacrifices, Leviticus 2:11.
Avoid too much honey, Proverbs 25:16, 27.
Taste of bridal lips, Song of Songs 4:11.
See Sweetness.

HONEYMOON

Extended honeymoon, Deuteronomy 24:5.
Honeymoon retreat, Song of Songs 8:14.
Young love, Jeremiah 2:1–3 (See CEV).
See Marriage.

HONOR

Honoring former leader, Joshua 22:1–5.
Sister's disgrace avenged, 2 Samuel 13:23–29.
Divine gift of honor, 1 Kings 3:13; Ecclesiastes 6:2.
Honor, respect, Job 29:7–10.
Honoring God, Psalm 23:3 (LB).
Nature, people praise the Lord, Psalm 148:1–14.
Humility before honor, Proverbs 18:12.
Usurped honor, Proverbs 25:6–7.
Noble man, Isaiah 32:8.
Honor among thieves, Jeremiah 49:9.
Alien honored, Daniel 5:29 (LB).
Honored prophet, Zechariah 3:1–9.
Humility begets honor, Matthew 23:12.
Asking for unearned honor, Mark 10:35–45.
Place of honor, Luke 14:8–11.
Respect of Cornelius for Peter, Acts 10:25–26.
Success must glorify God, 1 Corinthians 3:7.
Double honor, 1 Timothy 5:17.
See Citation, Commendation, Prestige, Respect.

HONORARIUM

Honorarium for prophet's services, 1 Samuel 9:1–9.
Requesting payment for ministry, 2 Kings 5:20–27.
Gift for prophet, 2 Kings 8:7–8.
Money, food, drink for workers, Ezra 3:7.
Choir members remunerated, Nehemiah 12:47.
Prostitute's honorarium to clients, Ezekiel 16:32–34.
Refusing king's gratuities, Daniel 5:17.
Lethal honorarium, Matthew 14:1–12.
Ministry payment, Luke 9:1–6; 1 Corinthians 9:7–14; 1 Timothy 5:17–18.
Spiritual wages, John 4:36.

Self-supported evangelism, 1 Corinthians 9:6–7.
No profiteering of Gospel, 2 Corinthians 2:17.
Love offering, 2 Corinthians 8:24; 9:5.
No charge for preaching, 2 Corinthians 11:7 (GNB).
Honorarium as ministry, Philippians 4:10–19 (See NRSV).
Greed avoided, 1 Thessalonians 2:5.
Employment to support ministry, 1 Thessalonians 2:9; 2 Thessalonians 3:6–10.
Double pay, 1 Timothy 5:17 (GNB).
Godliness, financial gain, 1 Timothy 6:5.
Getting rich on religion, 1 Timothy 6:6–10 (GNB).
Danger of greed in ministry, 1 Peter 5:2–3.
See Remuneration.

HOPE

Hope likened to death, Job 11:20.
Keep hoping, Job 13:15 (Berk.).
Eloquent declaration of hope, Job 19:25–26.
Hope for poor, needy, Psalm 9:18.
Hope in the Lord, Psalm 31:24.
Antidote for despair, Psalm 42:5; Jeremiah 31:15–17.
Continuity of hope, Psalm 71:5.
Deferred hope, Proverbs 13:12.
Hope in death, Proverbs 14:32.
Light shining in darkness, Isaiah 60:1–2.
False promises, Jeremiah 28:1–11.
Safety in times of trouble, persecution, Jeremiah 42:1–22.
Optimism in time of pessimism, Jeremiah 48:47.
"One ray of hope," Lamentations 3:21 (LB).
Troubled Valley, Hopeful Valley, Hosea 2:15 (CEV).
Behind devastation, ahead anticipation, Joel 2:3.
Hope against all hope, Romans 4:18.
Eternal encouragement, 2 Thessalonians 2:16–17.
Blessed hope, Titus 2:11–14.
Steadfast anchor, Hebrews 6:19 (See AB).
Living hope, 1 Peter 1:3.
Resurrection hope, 2 Peter 1:13–14.
See Faith, Trust.

HOPELESS

Dying gasp, Job 11:20.
Food for vultures, Job 15:23.
"You are done for," Hosea 13:9 (CEV).
Hopeless grief, 1 Thessalonians 4:13.
See Abandoned, Despair.

HORIZON

Horizon boundaries, Job 26:10.
Unsearchable horizons, Jeremiah 33:3.
Spiritual horizons, Philippians 3:12–14.
See Anticipation, Future, Vision.

HOROSCOPE

"Signs in the sky," Jeremiah 10:2–3.
See Astrology.

HORROR

Battle aftermath, Psalm 79:3.
Day of horror, Isaiah 13:16.
Brothers, neighbors in conflict, Isaiah 19:2.
"Awful horror," Matthew 24:15 (GNB).
Wishing but unable to die, Revelation 9:4–6.
See Disaster, Terror, Trauma.

HORSE

War horses, Exodus 14:9; 15:19.
Egyptian horses forbidden, Deuteronomy 17:16; Isaiah 31:1.
Superior horse, Job 39:19–25 (See Berk.).
No safety in horses, Psalm 33:17; Proverbs 21:31.
Bit, bridle, Psalm 32:9.
Horses swifter than eagles, Jeremiah 4:13.
Frightening stallions, Jeremiah 8:16.
"Faster than leopards," Habakkuk 1:8 (CEV, NIV).
Beautiful horses, Zechariah 6:2; Revelation 6:2–8.
Bells on horses, Zechariah 14:20.
Heaven's white horse, Revelation 19:11.
See Animals.

HORSE SENSE *See Pragmatic.*

HORTICULTURE

Vegetation for animals, Genesis 1:30.
Earth's first garden, Genesis 2:8.
Forbidden fruit, Genesis 2:16–17; Leviticus 19:23.
Care of fruit trees, Deuteronomy 20:19–20.
Solomon's knowledge of botany, 1 Kings 4:33.
Vegetable garden, 1 Kings 21:2.
Palatial gardens, 2 Kings 21:18; Esther 7:7.
Good vineyard stock abandoned, Jeremiah 2:21.
Horticultural beauty, Luke 12:27–28.
Caring for fruitless tree, Luke 13:6–9.
Grafted branches, Romans 11:24.
Flowers of field, 1 Peter 1:24.
See Agriculture, Farmer, Garden, Trees.

HOSPITAL

Desiring death at home, Job 29:18.

HOSPITALITY

Egyptian hospitality, Genesis 12:10–20.
Hospitality to visitors, Genesis 18:1–8.
Courtesy to departing guests, Genesis 18:16 (See NKJV).
Offering hospitality to angels, Genesis 19:1–4.
Hospitality to servant, Genesis 24:12–33 (See CEV).
Kindness rewarded with hospitality, Exodus 2:16–20.
Hospitality to strangers, Exodus 23:9; Leviticus 24:22; Deuteronomy 10:19; Ruth 2:14 (LB).
Hospitality denied, Numbers 20:14–21.
Refusing to show hospitality, Judges 8:4–6.
Overnight hospitality, Judges 19:1–10.
Example of hospitality, Judges 19:12–21.
Royal hospitality, 1 Kings 10:11–13.
Food, gift, 1 Kings 13:7.
"Come home with me," 1 Kings 13:15.
Hospitality to enemies, 2 Kings 6:8–23.
Prophet's chamber, 2 Kings 4:8–10; Philemon 22.
Remodeled guest room, Nehemiah 13:5 (LB).
Accused of no hospitality, Job 22:7–8.
Hospitality to travelers, Job 31:32.
The Lord's guest, Psalm 39:12 (LB).
Desecrated hospitality, Psalm 41:9; Obadiah 7.
Unwelcome guest, Psalm 101:7.

When to refuse hospitality, Proverbs 23:6.

Mourning preferred to feasting, Ecclesiastes 7:2.

Gift for departing visitor, Jeremiah 40:5.

One thousand banquet guests, Daniel 5:1.

Parting gifts, Micah 1:14.

Alcoholic hospitality, Habakkuk 2:15.

Sacred cooking pots, Zechariah 14:20–21.

Sickbed to kitchen, Matthew 8:14–15 (CEV).

Hospitality to ministry, Matthew 10:9–10; Luke 10:5–8.

Christian hospitality, Matthew 10:40–42 (GNB).

Hospitality rudely refused, Matthew 22:2–10.

Divine reciprocation of hospitality, Matthew 25:34–45.

Concern for hungry guests, Mark 8:1–3.

Cup of water, Mark 9:41.

Ready at the Lord's command, Mark 14:13–15.

Three-month hospitality, Luke 1:56.

Reaction to inhospitable people, Luke 9:5.

Accepting hospitality, Luke 10:5–8.

Putting first things first, Luke 10:38–42.

Hospitality to those who cannot repay, Luke 14:12–14.

Hospitality to tax collectors, sinners, Luke 15:1–7.

Heartily welcomed, Luke 19:6 (Berk.).

Host for last supper, Luke 22:7–12.

Curious interest, Luke 23:8.

Enemy who took bread, John 13:18–27.

Ample rooms in Father's house, John 14:2.

Peter, a guest, felt free to invite others, Acts 10:21–23.

Hospitable jailer, Acts 16:34.

Persecuted for hospitality, Acts 17:5–7.

Hospitality in evangelism, Acts 18:26.

Seven-day visit, Acts 21:3–4.

Island hospitality, Acts 28:1–2.

Hospitable city official, Acts 28:7.

Practice hospitality, Romans 12:13 (See LB).

Come stay awhile, 1 Corinthians 16:5–6.

Hospitality to stranger, 1 Corinthians 16:10–11.

Anticipated hospitality, 2 Corinthians 1:16.

Avoiding painful visit, 2 Corinthians 2:1.

Peter, Paul in Jerusalem, Galatians 1:18.

Hospitable Galatians, Galatians 4:14.

Messengers given good reception, 1 Thessalonians 1:8–10.

Paying for hospitality, 2 Thessalonians 3:7–10 (LB).

Hospitality in church leadership, Titus 1:7–8.

Hospitality to angels, Hebrews 13:2 (See CEV).

Sincerely hospitable, 1 Peter 4:9.

Denying hospitality to false teacher, 2 John 10–11.

Strangers who are Christians, 3 John 5–8.

Fellowship with the Lord, Revelation 3:20.

See Guests.

HOSTAGE

Simulated procedure, Genesis 42:14–20.

Held hostage in sealed cave, Joshua 10:16–18.

Hostages taken from Jerusalem, 2 Kings 14:14; 2 Chronicles 25:24.

See Captive, Prison.

HOSTESS

Resourceful hostess, 1 Samuel 25:18.

Widow hostess to prophet, 1 Kings 17:7–16.

Sickbed to kitchen, Matthew 8:14–15 (CEV).

HOSTILITY

Unanimous complaint, Exodus 16:2.

Putting end to hostility, 2 Samuel 2:26–29.

Hostile burning of prophecy, Jeremiah 36:20–24.

Hostility toward evangelists, Acts 17:5–7.

"Hostile in mind," Colossians 1:21 (NASB, NRSV).

Enemy as brother, 2 Thessalonians 3:15.

See Jealousy, Resentment.

HOUSE

Brick house, Genesis 11:3.

Stolen house gods, Genesis 31:19, 34; Judges 17:4.

Stone house, Leviticus 14:40–45.

Lazy man's house, Ecclesiastes 10:18.

House of wood, stone, Isaiah 9:10.

House on city wall, Joshua 2:15.
Rented house, Acts 28:30.
Living in tent, Hebrews 11:9–10.
See Residence.

HOUSE ARREST
House made into prison, Jeremiah 37:15.
Paul under house arrest, Acts 28:16.

HOUSE CHURCH
Greeting to house church, Romans 16:5;
Philemon 2.
Church meeting in home, 1 Corinthians
16:19.

HOUSEKEEPER
Hospitable Sarah, Genesis 18:6.
Happy mother at home, Psalm 113:9.
Ideal woman, Proverbs 31:1–31.
Overly busy housekeeper, Luke 10:40–41.
See Wife.

HUMANITY
Male, female plurality, Genesis 1:26–27.
Distinction animals, humans, Leviticus
24:21; 1 Corinthians 15:39.
"Human years," Job 10:5 (NRSV).
Frail humanity, Job 6:11–13.
We are but flesh, Psalm 78:38–39.
Humanity's blessings, Psalm 107:8 (NRSV).
Human, not divine, Isaiah 31:3.
"Somewhat like humans," Ezekiel 1:5 (CEV).
"Son of dust," Ezekiel 2:1, 3, 6; 3:10, 17 (LB).
Humanity of Jesus, Matthew 21:18.
Human and divine provision, Mark 6:35–
44.
Humanity's dual nature, Romans 7:21–25.
Jesus shared mortal humanity, Hebrews
2:14–18.
High priests men of weakness, Hebrews
7:28.
Humanity and evil desire, James 1:13–15.
See Flesh, Life, Mortality, Weakness.

HUMAN RELATIONS
Handling people, Exodus 18:14–27.
Courtesy to foreigners, Exodus 23:9.
Neighborhood relationship, Leviticus 6:2.
Witness opportunities, Deuteronomy
6:4–7.

Debt canceled every seven years, Deuter-
onomy 15:1.
Attitude toward poor, Deuteronomy 15:7–
11.
Protection of escaped slave, Deuteronomy
23:15–16.
Manner of speech, Judges 12:5–6.
Art of negotiation, Ruth 4:1–8.
Praising subject above king, 1 Samuel
21:11.
Warm salutation, 1 Samuel 25:6.
Showing favor for personal interest, 1 Sam-
uel 27:12.
Commendation of king, 1 Samuel 29:6–7.
Share and share alike, 1 Samuel 30:24.
Misunderstood kindness, 2 Samuel 10:1–4.
Solomon's alliance with Egypt, 1 Kings 3:1.
Wisdom of Solomon, 1 Kings 4:29–34.
King's inept viewpoint, 1 Kings 12:1–15.
Winning enemy's favor, 2 Kings 6:8–23.
Exemplary human relations, 2 Kings 7:3–9.
Inequity among citizens, Nehemiah 5:1–5.
Wisdom in appealing to king, Esther 7:3–4.
Renegade pleads for his life, Esther 7:7.
Abandoned by friends, Job 6:14–17.
Caring for those in need, Proverbs 3:27–
28.
Equity toward poor, Proverbs 29:14.
Revelation in human relations, Proverbs
29:18.
Human inequity, Proverbs 30:21–23.
Government based on good human rela-
tions, Isaiah 16:5.
Beauty for ashes, Isaiah 61:1–3.
Daily administration of justice, Jeremiah
21:12.
Pity those experiencing misfortune, Oba-
diah 12.
Justice, mercy, compassion, Zechariah 7:8–
10.
Cords of human love, Hosea 11:4.
Complaining about another's generosity,
Matthew 20:1–16.
Prophet without honor, Mark 6:4–6.
Like teacher, like student, Luke 6:40.
Greatest in kingdom, Luke 9:46–48.
Relationship between strangers, Luke
10:5–12.
Frankness of Jesus to Pharisees, Luke
11:37–54.

Desire for recognition in congregation, Luke 11:43.

Sharing with others, Luke 12:48.

Settling disputes out of court, Luke 12:58–59.

Honor for some above another, Luke 14:7–11.

Reaching out for those in need, Luke 14:12–14.

Go to war or negotiate peace, Luke 14:31–32.

Hospitality toward unbelievers, Luke 15:1–2.

Attitude of father, resentful brother, Luke 15:11–31.

Wealth in human relations, Luke 16:9.

Wrongly influencing others, Luke 17:1.

Employment, human relations, Luke 17:7–10.

Ingratitude to foreigner, Luke 17:11–19.

Kindness to Paul, the prisoner, Acts 24:23.

Joy, gentleness, Philippians 4:4–5.

Interest in other people, Colossians 4:7.

Relating mother's gentleness, 1 Thessalonians 2:7–8.

Mind your own business, 1 Thessalonians 4:11.

Paying poor wages, James 5:4.

See Courtesy, Employment, Hospitality, Labor, Psychology.

HUMANS See Humanity.

HUMILIATION

Imposed guilt of Joseph's brothers, Genesis 44:1–34.

Locals humiliated by aliens, Deuteronomy 28:43–44.

Cutting off thumbs and big toes, Judges 1:7.

Humiliation over another's success, 1 Samuel 18:7 (See 21:11; 29:5).

Act of kindness misinterpreted, 2 Samuel 10:1–4.

Stripped of one's honor, Job 19:9.

"Scorn of fools," Psalm 39:8.

Fortified city humiliated, Isaiah 27:10.

Into silence, darkness, Isaiah 47:5.

Fall of Moab, Jeremiah 48:16–39.

Jerusalem humiliated, Lamentations 1:1.

Humiliation of Satan as king of Tyre, Ezekiel 28:11–19.

Added humility of the cross, Matthew 27:39–44.

Pilate's question to King of kings, Mark 15:2.

Pre-Crucifixion humiliation, John 19:1–3.

Gazingstock, Hebrews 10:33 (AB).

See Embarrassment, Ignominy, Insult.

HUMILITY

Humble beginning from dust, Genesis 2:7.

Prayer of humility, Genesis 32:9, 10.

Humbly unaware of God's radiance, Exodus 34:29–35.

Most humble of all, Numbers 12:1 (CEV).

World's humblest man, Numbers 12:3.

Saul's humility at anointing, 1 Samuel 10:13–22.

Humility in assurance, 2 Samuel 7:18–29 (Also see LB).

Humility in king's presence, 2 Samuel 19:24–28.

God's attitude toward humility, pride, 2 Samuel 22:28.

Solomon's humility, 1 Kings 3:7.

Pathway to honor, wealth, 1 Kings 3:11–14; Proverbs 22:4.

Things great, small, 2 Kings 5:13.

Self-evaluation, 1 Chronicles 17:16–19.

Ezra's prayer attitude, Ezra 9:6.

Sensing utter depravity, Job 9:20.

All men alike before God, Job 33:6–7.

Serve the Lord with fear, trembling, Psalm 2:11.

Humility gains guidance, Psalms 25:9; 51:15–17.

God alone exalts, Psalm 75:6–7.

Doorkeeper in God's house, Psalm 84:10.

Praise, glory belong to God, Psalm 115:1.

Humble understanding, Psalm 119:130.

Prayer of humility, Psalm 123:1–2.

Humble attitude, Psalm 131:1.

Pride, humility, Psalm 138:6.

Spurning conceit, Proverbs 3:7 (LB).

Those of simple ways, Proverbs 9:6.

Listening to good counsel, Proverbs 9:9.

Humble spirit, Proverbs 16:19.

Humility before honor, Proverbs 18:12.

Humility, faith key to success, Proverbs 22:4.

Praise as test of humility, Proverbs 27:2.

Humbly claiming ignorance, Proverbs 30:2–4.

Arrogant to be humbled, Isaiah 2:12–17.

Humility, meekness bring joy, Isaiah 29:19.

Humility caused by anguish, Isaiah 38:15.

Lowly in spirit, Isaiah 57:15.

Prophet's fear, reluctance, Jeremiah 1:6–10.

Boasting only in the Lord, Jeremiah 9:23–24.

Humility in worship, Jeremiah 41:4–5.

Do not seek personal greatness, Jeremiah 45:5.

Seek righteousness and humility, Zephaniah 2:3.

Blessing upon meek and humble, Zephaniah 3:12.

Blessed are the meek, Matthew 5:5 (See CEV).

Centurion's humility, Matthew 8:5–10.

Miracles preferred private, Matthew 9:29–31.

Submission to teachers and masters, Matthew 10:24.

Humility of Jesus, Matthew 12:15–21; John 5:30; 13:1–17.

As a little child, Matthew 18:2–4; Mark 10:13–16.

Greatness through humility, Matthew 20:20–28.

Donkey chosen to serve Jesus, Matthew 21:1–7.

Servant attitude, Matthew 23:8–12; Romans 1:1.

First must be last, Mark 9:35.

Forerunner's humility, Luke 3:16.

Prophet without honor, Luke 4:23–24.

Humility required to follow Jesus, Luke 9:23–26.

Greatest in Christ's kingdom, Luke 9:46–48.

Excited about wrong phenomena, Luke 10:17–20.

Choosing place of honor, Luke 14:7–11.

Prodigal's humility, Luke 15:17–21.

Vanity, humility at worship, Luke 18:9–14 (See CEV).

Humbled before the Lord, John 1:27.

Humility exalts Christ, John 3:30.

Avoiding limelight, John 7:4 (Berk.).

Jesus demonstrated humility, John 13:6–9.

Awesome basis for humility, Romans 7:14–25.

Humble self-evaluation, Romans 12:3 (GNB).

Honor first to others, Romans 12:10.

Associate with people of low position, Romans 12:16 (GNB).

Glory belongs to God alone, 1 Corinthians 3:7.

"Stop being proud," 1 Corinthians 5:6 (CEV).

Education as humbling experience, 1 Corinthians 8:1–2.

Adapting to culture of others, 1 Corinthians 9:19–23.

Body of Christ functioning, 1 Corinthians 12:14–20.

Illustration of human body, 1 Corinthians 12:21–25.

Gift of love, 1 Corinthians 13:4.

Least of apostles, 1 Corinthians 15:9 (CEV).

Servant attitude, 2 Corinthians 4:5.

Common clay pots, 2 Corinthians 4:7 (GNB).

Vanity antidote, 2 Corinthians 11:30 (See 12:7–10).

Paul's thorn in flesh, 2 Corinthians 12:7.

Recognized weakness, 2 Corinthians 13:9.

Humbling experience of salvation, Ephesians 2:8–10.

Less than least, Ephesians 3:8–9.

The way up is down, Ephesians 4:8–10 (See LB); 1 Peter 5:6.

Attitude humility, Philippians 2:3–4.

Worst of sinners, 1 Timothy 1:15.

Attitude toward deserters, 2 Timothy 4:16.

Humble attitude toward wealth, 1 Timothy 6:17–19.

Humility toward all, Titus 3:2.

Greatness, servitude, Hebrews 3:5–6.

Humble circumstances, high position, James 1:9.

Discipleship life-style, James 3:17–18.

Humble before the Lord, James 4:10.

See Abase, Attitude, Demean, Discipleship, Meekness, Servant.

HUMOR *(Light touches, Whimsy)*

Fisherman's paradise, Genesis 1:20–21.

A wife "at last," Genesis 2:23 (Berk.).

Trapped by tar pits, Genesis 14:10.

Angel's whimsical description of unborn, Genesis 16:11–12.

Fast-food experts, Genesis 18:6–7.

Sorrowful laughter, Genesis 18:10–15.

No laughing matter, Genesis 19:14.

Newborn named "laughter," Genesis 21:1–6 (LB).

What ails you? Genesis 21:17 (NKJV).

One-up-manship among magicians, Exodus 7:8–12.

Talking donkey, Numbers 22:21–34.

Not an inch of space, Deuteronomy 2:5.

"You must not eat bats," Deuteronomy 14:18 (CEV).

Clergy serves "in all earnestness," Deuteronomy 18:6–7.

Incompatible ox, donkey, Deuteronomy 22:10.

Damaged knees hinder prayer, Deuteronomy 28:35.

Whistling for sheep, Judges 5:16 (CEV).

Idol protected by those he protects, Judges 6:31.

Tent flattened by bread loaf, Judges 7:13.

Reckless adventurers, Judges 9:4.

Trees seek king, Judges 9:7–15.

Big mouths, Judges 9:38.

Thirty sons, thirty daughters, Judges 12:9 (See verse 14).

Earth-shaking cheer, 1 Samuel 4:5.

Shy candidate for royal anointing, 1 Samuel 10:21–22.

Well-dressed giant, 1 Samuel 17:4–7 (LB).

Brave boy meets blustering giant, 1 Samuel 17:42–47.

Hearty, healthful greeting, 1 Samuel 25:6.

Grasped by the beard, 2 Samuel 20:9.

Public relations approach, 1 Kings 1:42.

Imported apes, baboons, 1 Kings 10:22; 2 Chronicles 9:21.

Freak accident, 2 Kings 1:2.

Poor quality drinking water, 2 Kings 2:19–22.

Growing beards, 1 Chronicles 19:5.

Laughter and tears, Ezra 3:12–13.

Henpecked husbands illegal, Esther 1:22.

Demeaned villain, Esther 5:14; 7:5–10.

Can't sleep? Read history, Esther 6:1.

Witless men, donkey colts, Job 11:12.

Acute indigestion, Job 20:20 (NRSV).

Divine sarcasm, Job 38:35.

Short on smarts, Job 39:13–17.

Resourceful elephant, Job 40:15–24.

Bad-natured leviathan (crocodile), Job 41:5.

Causing God to laugh, Psalm 2:4 (LB).

God as pugilist, Psalm 3:7.

"Gobble him down," Psalm 35:25 (CEV).

Inattentive cobra, Psalm 58:4–5.

Humor demanded from captives, Psalm 137:3 (NRSV).

Bedside frogs, Psalm 105:30.

Grumbling in tents, Psalm 106:25.

"I hurl my shoe," Psalm 108:9 (NRSV).

Mouths filled with laughter, Psalm 126:2.

Beauty only skin deep, Proverbs 11:22.

Love makes food taste better, Proverbs 15:17.

Good news, cheerful looks, Proverbs 15:30.

Hunger makes man work harder, Proverbs 16:26.

Wisdom of silence elevates fool, Proverbs 17:28.

Answering before listening, Proverbs 18:13.

"Drip-drip-drip," Proverbs 19:13 (GNB).

Marriage made in Heaven, Proverbs 19:14 (LB).

Haggling for best price, Proverbs 20:14.

Mortgaged bed, Proverbs 22:27.

Throat-cutting diet plan, Proverbs 23:1–3.

Stingy man's hospitality, Proverbs 23:6–8.

Drunkard's confusion, Proverbs 23:30–35.

Honest answer is like kiss, Proverbs 24:26.

Too much sleep, Proverbs 24:33–34.

Silly answer to silly question, Proverbs 26:5 (GNB).

Honor does not fit fool, Proverbs 26:1.

Fool's wisdom, Proverbs 26:3–13.

Drunkard's dilemma, Proverbs 26:9 (GNB).

Lazy man like swinging door, Proverbs 26:14 (GNB).

Too lazy to eat, Proverbs 26:15.

Meddling in affairs of others, Proverbs 26:17.

Hunger sweetens bitterness, Proverbs 27:7.

Precarious piety, Proverbs 27:14.

Chasing fantasies, Proverbs 28:19.

Danger of excessive perks, Proverbs 29:21 (GNB).

Lizards in kings' palaces, Proverbs 30:28.

HUMOR

Stirring up anger, Proverbs 30:33.

Ignorance is bliss, Ecclesiastes 1:18.

Politicians keep eyes on each other, Ecclesiastes 5:8.

Profuse words confuse meaning, Ecclesiastes 6:11.

Good old days, Ecclesiastes 7:10.

Fool does not know way to town, Ecclesiastes 10:15.

Carpentry of lazy man, Ecclesiastes 10:18.

Money not answer for everything, Ecclesiastes 10:19.

Tattle tale birds, Ecclesiastes 10:20.

Sky-watching farmer, Ecclesiastes 11:4.

Cramming for exams, Ecclesiastes 12:12.

God whistles, Isaiah 5:26; 7:18.

Strange long name, Isaiah 8:1 (See AB, GNB, LB).

Bird-like nations, Isaiah 10:14.

Short bed, narrow blanket, Isaiah 28:20.

Led by hook in nose, Isaiah 37:29.

Top heavy idol, Isaiah 41:7 (CEV).

Dogs with big appetites, Isaiah 56:11.

As many gods as towns, Jeremiah 2:28.

Profligate playboys, Jeremiah 5:8.

Scarecrow in melon patch, Jeremiah 10:5.

Idols a joke, Jeremiah 10:15 (CEV).

Futile horse race, Jeremiah 12:5.

Stolen eggs like unjust riches, Jeremiah 17:11.

Relevant humor, tragedy, Jeremiah 25:9 (CEV).

Beautiful heifer, gadfly, Jeremiah 46:20.

Joker becomes joke, Ezekiel 16:56–57 (GNB).

Liver consultation, Ezekiel 21:21.

Knocking knees, Daniel 5:6.

Barley bartered for wife, Hosea 3:2.

Women who command husbands, Amos 4:1.

Frying pan to fire, Amos 5:19.

Seaweed around Jonah's head, Jonah 2:5.

Indigestion for fish that swallowed Jonah, Jonah 2:10.

Trust no one, Micah 7:5 (LB).

Sacred trash cans, Zechariah 14:20 (LB).

"Jump around like calves at play," Malachi 4:2 (CEV).

Tax collectors, other sinners, Matthew 5:6; Mark 2:15 (CEV).

Tomorrow's worry, Matthew 6:34.

Tax-paying fish, Matthew 17:27.

To swallow a camel, Matthew 23:24.

Delighted listeners, Mark 12:35–37 (NIV).

Egotistical teachers, Mark 12:38–40.

Speck in brother's eye, plank in your own, Luke 6:41–42.

Durable purses, Luke 12:33 (GNB).

Herod the fox, Luke 13:31–32.

Whimsy of man once blind, John 9:24–34 (See Berk.).

Fish count, John 21:11.

Embarrassing the oppressors, Acts 16:35–39.

High-spirited evil spirit, Acts 19:13–16.

Sleeping during sermon, Acts 20:7–12.

Bachelor's marriage counsel, 1 Corinthians 7:27–28.

Make sad, cheer up, 2 Corinthians 2:1–2 (GNB).

Enduring a little foolishness, 2 Corinthians 11:1.

Wise fool, 2 Corinthians 11:16–19.

Super-apostles in Corinth, 2 Corinthians 12:11.

Devouring each other, Galatians 5:15.

Foolish talk and coarse joking, Ephesians 5:4.

Getting rich on religion, 1 Timothy 6:5–10 (GNB).

Owed a favor, Philemon 17–19.

Trained wild animals, untrained tongue, James 3:7–8.

Sweet in mouth, sour to stomach, Revelation 10:9–10.

See Amusement.

HUNGER

Severe famine, Genesis 12:10.

Remembering past hunger, forgetting God, Exodus 16:2–3.

Craving meat, Deuteronomy 12:20.

Hungry soldiers, 1 Samuel 14:24–30.

Food among thorns, Job 5:5.

Stealing food, Proverbs 6:30–31.

Motivated by appetite, Proverbs 16:26.

Dreaming of food, awakening to reality, Isaiah 29:8.

Hard work causes hunger, Isaiah 44:12.

Free food, Isaiah 55:1–2.

Desperation hunger, Lamentations 1:11.

Hungry children, Lamentations 4:4.

Death from famine, Lamentations 4:9.

Feverish hunger, Lamentations 5:10.

Food, water denied, Ezekiel 4:16–17.

Rebellious hunger, Amos 4:6.

Spiritual hunger, Amos 8:11–12; Matthew 5:6; 1 Peter 2:2.

Picking corn on Sabbath, Matthew 12:1–8.

Hunger hinders worship, 1 Corinthians 11:34.

See Appetite, Hunger.

HUNTING

Domestic, wild animals, Genesis 1:24–25.

Mighty hunter, Genesis 10:8–9.

Boy archer, Genesis 21:20.

Skillful hunter, Genesis 25:27.

Dressing hunted game, Leviticus 17:13.

Sadistic hunting expedition, 1 Samuel 18:24–27.

Flea hunt, 1 Samuel 26:20.

Wintry lion hunt, 2 Samuel 23:20.

Stalk like lion, Job 10:16; 38:39–40.

Abundant hunting, Psalm 76:4.

Hunting with snares, Psalm 141:9–10; Proverbs 1:17; Ecclesiastes 9:12; Amos 3:5.

Lazy hunter, Proverbs 12:27.

Worship of fishing, Habakkuk 1:16.

See Sportsman.

HURRY

Asking God to hurry, Psalm 70:1.

See Haste, Impatience.

HURT

Partial blindness as disgrace, 1 Samuel 11:2–11.

"I am hurting," Psalm 31:9 (CEV).

Comfort when hurting, Psalm 119:50 (CEV).

Hurting others, Psalm 139:24 (NASB).

Deep wounds, Lamentations 2:13.
Response when hurt by others, Luke 17:3, 4.
See Injury.

HUSBAND

Wife from husband's rib, Genesis 2:21–24.
Supernatural husbands, Genesis 6:4 (CEV).
Husband's involvement in wife's contracts, Numbers 30:10–15.
Husband rules household, Esther 1:22; 1 Corinthians 11:3.
Young marrieds, Proverbs 5:15–19 (See CEV).
Fury of betrayed husband, Proverbs 6:27–35.
Husband enjoying life, Ecclesiastes 9:9.
Husband's duty, Ephesians 5:25; 1 Corinthians 7:3; 1 Peter 3:7.
Winning unsaved husband, 1 Peter 3:1–2.
See Father, Leadership, Marriage, Parents.

HYBRID

Animal genetics, Genesis 30:37–39.

HYGIENE

Divine food preservation, Exodus 16:19–24.
Clean, unclean meat, Leviticus 11:1–47.
Cleanliness after obstetrics, Leviticus 12:1–7.
Preventing community infection, Numbers 5:1–4; Leviticus 13:45–46.
Bad food made good, 2 Kings 4:38–41.
Bad breath, Job 19:17.
Danger of deadly disease, Jeremiah 16:1–9.
Excrement used as fuel, Ezekiel 4:15.
Desiring food of pigs, Luke 15:16.
See Health, Sanitation.

HYMN

Song of Moses, Exodus 15:1–18, 21.
Inspiration for hymn, Deuteronomy 31:19–22 (See 32:1–43).
Deborah's song, Judges 5:1–31.
Psalms preview, 2 Samuel 22:1–51.
Song of gratitude, 1 Chronicles 16:7–36.
Stanza of two lines, 2 Chronicles 5:13; Ezra 3:11.
Song of joy and anguish, Isaiah 65:14.
Unheeded lyrics, Ezekiel 33:32.

Hymns turn to wailing, Amos 8:3, 10.
Heaven's hymn, Revelation 15:3–4.
See Lyrics.

HYPERBOLE

Numerous as sand, stars, Genesis 13:16; 22:17; 28:14; 1 Kings 4:20; 2 Chronicles 1:9; 1 Samuel 13:5; Hebrews 11:12.
Hyperbole expresses rapport, Genesis 33:10.
Vast horde covers earth, Numbers 22:6 (LB, Berk.).
Exaggerated the enemy, Deuteronomy 1:28.
Walls to sky, Deuteronomy 9:1.
Numerous as locusts, camels beyond counting, Judges 7:12.
Daughter worth seven sons, Ruth 4:15.
Praising subject above king, 1 Samuel 21:11.
Angelic king, 2 Samuel 14:17.
Measureless wisdom, 1 Kings 4:29.
Big feet, 2 Kings 19:24.
Enormous weight of problems, Job 6:1–3.
Anticipating long life, Job 29:18.
Meat like rain, Psalm 78:27.
Vast judgment, Isaiah 34:3–7.
Many widows, Jeremiah 15:8.
Contrasting superlatives, Lamentations 4:7–8.
Wine dripping from mountains, Amos 9:13.
Greedy as grave, Habakkuk 2:5.
Divine "foolishness," "weakness," 1 Corinthians 1:25.
Valid hyperbole, 2 Corinthians 7:14.
Eyes torn out, Galatians 4:15.
Recommended emasculation, Galatians 5:12 (NIV, NEB, GNB).
Seeming exaggeration is basic reality, Ephesians 1:18–22.
Less than least, Ephesians 3:8.
See Exaggeration, Figure-of-Speech.

HYPNOSIS

Hypnotized Christians, Galatians 3:1–2 (LB).
See Hallucination, Mob Psychology.

HYPOCHONDRIA

Subdued illness, Philippians 2:26–27 (AB).

HYPOCRISY

Insincere repentance, Exodus 9:27.

Deceived hearts, Deuteronomy 11:16 (KJV).

Feigned rapport in time of need, Judges 11:1–10.

Doing right with limitations, 2 Chronicles 25:2.

Accused of hypocrisy, Job 4:1–3; 11:4–6.

Undependable friends, Job 6:15–17.

Unable to fool God, Job 13:9.

Condemned by one's own words, Job 15:6.

Boasting of giving while withholding, Job 25:14.

"Consort with hypocrites," Psalm 26:4 (NRSV).

Hypocritical cordiality, Psalm 28:3.

Motives different from speech, Psalms 55:21; 62:4.

Hypocritical prayers incite God's anger, Psalm 80:4.

Prayer counted as sin, Psalm 109:7 (NRSV).

Double-minded men, Psalm 119:113.

Hateful thoughts, smooth talk, Proverbs 26:23 (CEV).

Disguising true self by false speech, Proverbs 26:24–26.

Sincere, insincere rapport, Proverbs 27:6.

Early morning religiosity, Proverbs 27:14.

Detestable prayers of lawbreakers, Proverbs 28:9.

Surprised hypocrites, Isaiah 33:14 (KJV).

Meaningless oaths, Isaiah 48:1–2.

Hypocritical piety, Isaiah 58:1–2 (LB).

Mockery fasting, Isaiah 58:4–5.

Holier than thou, Isaiah 65:4–5 (LB).

Dishonest statement, Jeremiah 5:1–2 (See GNB).

Flagrant hypocrisy, Jeremiah 7:9–11.

Hypocritical rapport, Jeremiah 12:6.

Threat to hypocrisy, Ezekiel 14:4.

Scorned for hypocrisy, Ezekiel 16:56–57.

Listening, not practicing, Ezekiel 33:31.

Boasting hypocrite, Hosea 12:8.

God's blessing misused, Hosea 13:6.

Boasting of hypocrisy, Amos 4:4–5.

Witnessing hypocrite, Jonah 1:9.

Hypocrite leaders, priests, Micah 3:11.

Worshiping the Lord, Molech, Zephaniah 1:5.

Defiled offerings from defiled people, Haggai 2:13–14.

Hypocritical fasting, repentance, Zechariah 7:1–6.

Repenting hypocrites, Malachi 2:13.

King Herod and the Magi, Matthew 2:7–8, 13.

Satan's use of Scripture, Matthew 4:1–11.

Righteousness of the Pharisees, Matthew 5:20.

Performing righteousness in public, Matthew 6:1.

Hypocrisy paid in full, Matthew 6:5 (GNB).

Avoid hyper-piety, Matthew 6:16–18.

Hypocrite's plea, Matthew 7:21–23 (See LB).

Hypocrisy of Pharisees, Matthew 15:7–9; 21:31–32; 23:1–3; Luke 11:45–54.

Seeking mercy while mistreating another, Matthew 18:23–35.

Man without wedding clothes, Matthew 22:11–13.

Clean outside, filthy inside, Matthew 23:25–28.

Hypocrisy akin to murder, Matthew 23:29–32.

Faithful, unfaithful service, Matthew 24:45–51.

Lip service, Mark 7:6.

Hypocrite miracles, Mark 9:38–41.

Practice what you preach, Luke 3:7–8.

"Play actors," Luke 12:56 (AB).

Identification of hypocrite, Luke 13:23–27.

Hypocritical honesty, Luke 20:20.

Hypocrite's praise, John 5:41–42.

Hypocrisy syndrome, John 7:19 (LB).

Devious search for salvation, John 10:1.

Hypocrite's judging others, Romans 2:1.

Saying one thing, doing another, Romans 2:21–24.

Those who cause divisions, Romans 16:17–18.

Christians in name only, Galatians 2:4 (AB).

Social hypocrisy, Galatians 2:11–13.

Insincere attention, Galatians 4:17.

Hypocritical pretense, Galatians 6:12–15.

False humility, Colossians 2:18.

Hypocrite liars, 1 Timothy 4:2 (Berk., NRSV).

Hypocritical godliness, 2 Timothy 3:5.

Unbridled tongue, James 1:26.

"Without hypocrisy," James 3:17 (NKJV).

Profession versus possession, Titus 1:16; 1 John 2:4–6; Jude 12–13.
Walking in darkness, 1 John 1:5–7.
Disruptive hypocrite, 3 John 9–10.
Misuse of Christian liberty, Jude 4.
Feigning life when spiritually dead, Revelation 3:1.
See Deceit, Sanctimonious, Sham.

HYPOTHESIS

Grinding a fool, Proverbs 27:22.
Nest among stars, Obadiah 4.
Gain world, lose soul, Mark 8:36; Luke 9:25.

Ten thousand guardians, 1 Corinthians 4:15.
Resounding gong, clanging cymbal, 1 Corinthians 13:1–3.
Preaching angel, Galatians 1:8.
See Figure-of-Speech.

HYSSOP

Sprinkling blood, Exodus 12:22.
Grown from walls, 1 Kings 4:33.
Instrument of cleansing, Psalm 51:7.
Vinegar on the cross, John 19:28–29.

HYSTERICAL

Hysterical king, Daniel 5:9–12 (LB).

I

ICE See Cold, Freeze, Snow, Winter.

ICON See Idolatry.

ICONOCLASTIC

Iconoclasm by divine decree, Genesis 35:2; Exodus 23:24; 34:13; Deuteronomy 7:5.
Moses, golden calf, Exodus 32:19–20.
God's supremacy above idols, Leviticus 26:1.
National iconoclasm, Numbers 33:51–52.
Avoid detracting architecture, Deuteronomy 16:21–22.
Impotent gods exposed, Deuteronomy 32:37–38.
Pledge to forsake foreign gods, Joshua 24:19–27.
Destroying pagan altars, Judges 6:25–32.
Silver idol, Judges 17:4.
Ignominy for idol, 1 Samuel 5:1–5.
Abandoned idols, 2 Samuel 5:21.
Rid of idolatry items, 1 Kings 15:12; 2 Kings 11:18; 18:4; 23:14; 2 Chronicles 14:3; 33:15.
Totem pole burned, 1 Kings 15:13.
Destroyed prophets, ministers, priests, 2 Kings 10:18–29; 18:4; 23:24.
Altars removed, 2 Chronicles 14:3–5; 34:33.
Burning gods, 2 Kings 19:18.
Time for reformation, 2 Kings 23:12–25.
Discarded altars, 2 Chronicles 30:14; 31:1.
"Massive campaign," 2 Chronicles 31:1 (LB).

Good young king, 2 Chronicles 34:3, 33.
Idols crushed into powder, 2 Chronicles 34:7.
Punish idols, Jeremiah 51:47.
Altars demolished, Ezekiel 6:4.
Rid of gods forever, Hosea 14:3.
Destroyed of evil properties, places, practices, Micah 5:10–15.
Destroying sorcery items, Acts 19:18–20.
See Exorcism, Idolatry.

IDEA

Evil ideas, Proverbs 17:4 (GNB).
See Creativity.

IDENTITY

Concealed identity, Genesis 42:7.
Joseph the unknown, Exodus 1:8.
Desert named Sin, Exodus 17:1.
Ultimate identity, Exodus 33:12–16.
Dedicating identified house, Leviticus 27:14.
Identified by pedigree, Numbers 1:18 (KJV).
Staffs identified, Numbers 17:1–2.
Evil act identified, Numbers 25:14.
Identified as the Lord's treasure, Deuteronomy 26:18.
God identifies disaster individual, Deuteronomy 29:21.
Friend or enemy, Joshua 5:13.
Identity by speech accent, Judges 12:5–6.
Unrecognized angel, Judges 13:16.

Famous son identified, 1 Samuel 1:1–20.

Wisdom, spiritual identity, 1 Kings 10:1.

Secret identity, Esther 2:10.

Mistaken identity, Esther 6:1–13.

Each star identified, Psalm 146:4.

Fool's identity, Ecclesiastes 10:3.

Fragrant identity, Song of Songs 1:3.

Women in need of identity, Isaiah 4:1.

The Lord's name written on hand, Isaiah 44:5 (NRSV).

Named before birth, Isaiah 49:1.

Worthless idols, worthless people, Jeremiah 2:5.

God's relationship people, Jeremiah 32:38.

Smudged identity, Lamentations 4:7–8.

Mark of repentance, Ezekiel 9:3–6.

Defiled identity, Ezekiel 20:39 (LB).

Pagan name, faith identified, Daniel 4:8.

Israel's lost identity, Hosea 1:9 (LB).

Jonah revealed identity, Jonah 1:5–11.

Like the Lord's signet ring, Haggai 2:23.

Prophet denying true identity, Zechariah 13:4–5.

Creator's identity ignored, Matthew 8:23–27.

Jesus identified, Matthew 16:13–20.

Demons have names, Mark 5:8–9.

Mistaken identity of Jesus, Mark 6:14–16, 45–51; John 7:27; 19:10–18.

Stranger's identity, Mark 14:13–15.

Identity of Jesus affirmed, Mark 15:1–2.

Registered in town of initial identity, Luke 2:1–4.

Mistaken identity of John the Baptist, Luke 3:15.

Demon recognized identity of Jesus, Luke 4:33–34.

Confused identity of Jesus, Luke 9:18–20.

Jesus unrecognized on road to Emmaus, Luke 24:13–35.

Identity of John the Baptist, John 1:19–27.

Doubting Jesus' identity, John 6:41–42.

Confused identity, John 9:9.

Voice identification, John 10:1–6.

Love as Christian identity, John 13:34–35.

Jesus identified Himself, John 14:26.

Joined to the Lord, John 15:4 (CEV).

Pilate, "King of the Jews," John 19:19–22.

Disciples first called Christians, Acts 11:26.

Saul's name change, Acts 13:9.

Accused of being terrorist, Acts 21:38–39.

Personal identity discovered, Roman 7:17–25.

Holy Spirit identification, Romans 8:16; 2 Corinthians 1:21–22.

Identified by name, Romans 16:3–12.

Faulty memory, 1 Corinthians 1:16.

All things to all men, 1 Corinthians 9:22.

Mark of ownership, 2 Corinthians 1:22 (GNB).

Living identification, 2 Corinthians 3:1–3.

Apostle's identity, 2 Corinthians 12:12.

Crucified with Christ, Galatians 2:20.

Marks of Jesus, Galatians 6:17 (Japanese: "branded with red hot iron").

Identified in Christ, Ephesians 1:11–12.

Marked by the Holy Spirit, Ephesians 1:13 (Note "seal" is an official identification, as on a document).

Love identified early Christians, Ephesians 1:15.

Membership in God's household, Ephesians 2:19–20.

Like no one else, Philippians 2:20–21.

Recorded in Book of Life, Philippians 4:3.

Christ in you, Colossians 1:2.

Identified by handwriting, 2 Thessalonians 3:17.

Gold, silver, wood, and earth, 2 Timothy 2:19.

Jesus identified with mankind, Hebrews 2:16–18 (See LB).

Identity with God's people, Hebrews 11:24–25.

Great men, small mention, Hebrews 11:32.

Chosen people, royal priesthood, 1 Peter 2:9.

Identified as children of God, 1 John 3:1–3.

Mark of the Christian, 1 John 3:11–14.

Friends greeted by name, 3 John 14.

Believers as priests, Revelation 1:6.

Identified with name of God, Revelation 3:12.

Identification seal, Revelation 7:3; 9:4.

Lost and redeemed, Revelation 13:16–18; 14:1.

Mark of the beast, Revelation 13:16–18; 14:1, 9–10.

Covered with blasphemous names, Revelation 17:3.

Names not written in Book of Life, Revelation 17:8.

Unknown name, Revelation 19:12.

God's name on forehead, Revelation 22:4.

See *Name, Seal, Self-image.*

IDEOLOGY

Avoiding heathen ways, Deuteronomy 18:9.

Certain of erroneous ideology, Acts 19:35–36.

See *Believe, Opinion, Prejudice.*

IDIOT See *Fool.*

IDLENESS

Diligent ants, Proverbs 6:6–8.

Sleeping in harvest, Proverbs 10:5.

Too lazy to repair house, Ecclesiastes 10:18.

Unemployed idleness, Matthew 20:6–7.

Talking not working, Acts 17:21.

No work, no food, 2 Thessalonians 3:10.

See *Laziness.*

IDOLATRY

Make no idols, Exodus 20:4.

Speak no idol's name, Exodus 23:13.

Food for idols, Exodus 34:15; Acts 21:25; 1 Corinthians 8:1–6.

Death to idolaters, Numbers 25:5.

God never appears as image, Deuteronomy 4:15–16.

Secret idols, Deuteronomy 27:15.

Idol insulted, Judges 6:28–31 (LB).

Making idol to please the Lord, Judges 17:3.

Priests in idol worship, Judges 18:30–31.

Toppled idol, 1 Samuel 5:1–5.

"Gold rats," 1 Samuel 6:5, 8 (CEV).

Strange use of idol, 1 Samuel 19:13–16.

Abandoned idols, 2 Samuel 5:21.

Son sacrificed to idol, 2 Kings 16:2–3.

Worthless idols, followers, 2 Kings 17:15 (CEV).

Idolatrous king, 2 Chronicles 28:1–4.

Repentant idolater, 2 Chronicles 33:1–17.

Idol in temple, 2 Chronicles 33:7 (See LB).

Idolatry put away, 2 Chronicles 34:1–7.

Worthless idols, Psalm 31:6.

Creator versus idols, Psalm 96:5.

Graphic description of idols, Psalm 115:2–8.

Idols made by hands, Psalm 135:15–18; Jeremiah 16:20.

Israel's superstitions, Isaiah 2:6–8.

Idol kingdoms, Isaiah 10:10.

Seeking advice from idols, Isaiah 19:3 (CEV).

Idols challenged, Isaiah 41:22–24 (CEV).

Idolatry described, Isaiah 44:9–20.

Shamed idol makers, Isaiah 45:16.

Ignorance of idol worship, Isaiah 45:20.

Burdensome images, Isaiah 46:1.

Powerless idols, Isaiah 46:2 (AB).

Impotent idols, Isaiah 46:6–7.

Behind closed doors, Isaiah 57:7–8 (LB).

Fragile idols, Isaiah 57:13 (CEV).

Loyalty to idols, Jeremiah 2:11 (See CEV).

In love with the gods, Jeremiah 2:25 (CEV).

As many gods as towns, Jeremiah 2:28; 11:15.

Queen of Heaven, Jeremiah 7:18.

Temple defiled by idols, Jeremiah 7:30 (See GNB, NRSV).

Idol cannot harm or help, Jeremiah 10:5 (CEV).

IDLENESS

WORKER ANT

NON-WORKER ANT

Worthless, silly idols, Jeremiah 10:15 (LB); Jonah 2:8.

"Idols cannot send rain," Jeremiah 14:22 (CEV).

Man-made gods, Jeremiah 16:19–20 (See GNB).

Futility of idols, Ezekiel 6:13.

Idols in the heart, Ezekiel 14:1–11.

Children sacrificed to idols, Ezekiel 23:37.

Decorative images in temple, Ezekiel 41:17–20.

Image built by Nebuchadnezzar, Daniel 3:1–6.

Misuse of God's provisions, Hosea 2:8.

Disgusting idol, disgusting follower, Hosea 9:10 (CEV).

"Pride of the priests," Hosea 10:5 (CEV).

Kissing idols, Hosea 13:2 (CEV).

Worship of what hands have made, Hosea 14:3.

Idol worship center, Amos 4:4 (AB).

Beguiling city, Nahum 3:4 (LB).

False security of man-made idols, Habak-kuk 2:18–19.

Recognizing the Lord, Molech, Zephaniah 1:5.

Marriage to idol's daughter, Malachi 2:11.

Worship of men, Acts 14:8–18.

Athenian idolatry, Acts 17:16–34.

Gospel hindered idol makers, Acts 19:20–41.

Worshiping created, not Creator, Romans 1:25.

"No such thing as an idol," 1 Corinthians 8:4 (NASB).

Pagan idols actually demons, 1 Corinthians 10:20.

Led astray to dumb idols, 1 Corinthians 12:2.

Weak, pitiful powers, Galatians 4:9 (CEV).

Keep yourself from idols, 1 John 5:21.

Idols into lake of fire, Revelation 21:8; 22:15.

See Heathen, Iconoclastic, Pagan.

IGNOMINY

Kings reduced to beggars, Judges 1:6–7 (LB).

Idol's ignominy, 1 Samuel 5:1–5.

Desecration of King Saul's body, 1 Samuel 31:8–10.

How the mighty have fallen, 2 Samuel 1:27.

Delegation put to shame, 2 Samuel 10:4–5; 1 Chronicles 19:1–5.

Willingness to accept rebuke, 2 Samuel 16:5–12.

Royal crown confiscated, 1 Chronicles 20:2.

Unworthy of dogs, Job 30:1.

Job became byword, Job 30:9–10.

Sin-bearer as worm, Psalm 22:6.

Food for jackals, Psalm 63:10.

Satan's pomp and ignominy, Isaiah 14:12–15.

Fortified city made desolate, Isaiah 27:10.

"Kingdom of Nothing," Isaiah 34:12 (CEV, NRSV).

Trampled like mud, Isaiah 41:25 (CEV).

Once lovely princess, Isaiah 47:1–3 (LB).

Silence and darkness, Isaiah 47:5.

Messiah called "a nobody," Isaiah 53:3 (CEV).

No tears at funeral, Jeremiah 22:18–19 (CEV).

Israel in ignominy, Jeremiah 33:24–26.

Prophet lowered into mud, Jeremiah 38:6.

Burial in ignominy, Jeremiah 41:9.

Heap of ruins, Jeremiah 51:37.

Jerusalem's ignominy, Lamentations 1:8 (CEV).

Luxury to ignominy, Lamentations 4:5.

Rub faces in manure, Malachi 2:3 (CEV).

Joseph's concern for Mary's presumed sin, Matthew 1:19.

Mockery against Jesus, Mark 14:65; 15:16–20, 19–32.

Humiliation before crucifixion, John 19:1–5.

Refusal to permit face-saving, Acts 16:35–40.

See Demean, Disgrace, Embarrassment, Humilia-tion, Shame.

IGNORANCE

Sins of ignorance, Leviticus 22:14; Num-bers 15:22–26; Hosea 4:5–6; Luke 23:34; John 16:2; 1 Timothy 1:13.

Innate ignorance, Job 11:7–8; 28:12–13; Psalm 139:6.

Ignorance covered by lies, Job 13:4 (GNB).

Foolish ignorance, Psalm 73:22 (NKJV).

Ignorance of future, Proverbs 27:1; Jeremiah 10:23.
Illiteracy, Isaiah 29:11–12.
Closed eyes, Isaiah 44:18.
Senseless skill, Jeremiah 10:14.
Pretended ignorance, Luke 22:57–60.
Altar to unknown god, Acts 17:23.
Ignorance overlooked, Acts 17:30.
Inexcusable guilt, Romans 1:19–25.
Spiritual ignorance, 1 Corinthians 2:7–10.
Partial ignorance, 1 Corinthians 13:12.
Willful ignorance, 1 Corinthians 15:34 (AB).
Uninformed opinions, 1 Timothy 1:7.
Ignorant, misguided, Hebrews 5:2 (NASB).
Ignorance with confidence, Hebrews 11:8.
That which is not understood, Jude 10.
See Blindness, Indifference, Insensitive, Unaware.

IGNORE

Ignoring acts of God, Nehemiah 9:17 (LB).
Not a passing thought, Psalm 142:4 (LB).
Who cares? Jeremiah 15:5.
Ignoring divine directive, Jeremiah 37:2.
See Neglect.

ILLEGAL *See Forbidden, Restriction.*

ILLEGITIMACY

Born of forbidden marriage, Deuteronomy 23:2.
Bastard intruder, Zechariah 9:6 (KJV).
Spiritually illegitimate, Hebrews 12:8.
See Abortion.

ILLICIT

Motherhood by incest, Genesis 19:30–38.
Illicit relationship in spiritual service, 1 Samuel 2:22.
Utterly defiled, Jeremiah 3:1–3.
Illicit conduct of two sisters, Ezekiel 23:1–49.
See Degradation, Immorality, Lust.

ILLITERACY

Meaningless writing, Isaiah 29:11–12.
Willful illiteracy, Matthew 13:15.
See Reading.

ILLNESS

Illness caused by sin, Leviticus 26:14–16; Matthew 9:1–7; John 5:14.
Hezekiah's illness, recovery, 2 Chronicles 32:24–26.
Satanic illness, Job 2:6–7.
Instructive illness, Job 33:14, 19–21.
Afflicted since youth, Psalm 88:15.
Will to live, Proverbs 18:14 (GNB).
Extensive medical expense, Mark 5:25–26.
Illness rebuked, Luke 4:38–39.
Illness caused by spirit, Luke 13:10–16.
Invalid for thirty-eight years, John 5:1–9.
Present suffering, coming glory, Romans 8:18; 2 Corinthians 4:17–18.
Illness causes concern, Philippians 2:26–27.
Made perfect through suffering, Hebrews 2:10.
Value of testing, trials, problems, James 1:2–4, 12; 1 Peter 1:6–7; 4:1–2.
Praying for sick, James 5:13–15.
See Disease, Medicine, Hygiene, Infirmity, Sickness.

ILLUMINATION

Light created, Genesis 1:3, 14–19.
Abundance of light, Isaiah 30:26; 60:19.
Profuse use of lamps, Acts 20:8.
Light makes everything visible, Ephesians 5:14.
Earth illuminated by angelic splendor, Revelation 18:1.
See Light, Visibility.

ILLUSTRATION

Illustration with parables, Psalm 78:1–8.
Little city illustrates world, sin, redemption, Ecclesiastes 9:14–15.
Divine use of illustration, Jeremiah 13:1–11.
Clay jar object lesson, Jeremiah 19:1–12.
Good figs, bad figs, Jeremiah 24:1–10.
Immeasurable grace of God, Jeremiah 31:37.
Broken promises illustrated, Jeremiah 35:1–16.
Illustrative hair, Ezekiel 5:1–7 (CEV).
Vine branch illustration, Ezekiel 15:1–7.
Illustration of two eagles, vine, Ezekiel 17:1–24.

Israel as lioness, fruitful vine, Ezekiel 19:1–14.

Valley of dry bones, Ezekiel 37:1–14.

Basket of ripe fruit, Amos 8:1–2.

Likening to fisherman, Habakkuk 1:14–17.

Measuring basket, Zechariah 5:5–11.

Why Jesus used parables, Matthew 13:10–13.

Poets of Athens, Acts 17:28.

Belt illustrates point, Acts 21:10–11.

Spiritual truth illustrated in human terms, Romans 6:19.

Unmuzzled ox, 1 Corinthians 9:9–14.

Illustration from life, Galatians 3:15.

Two women illustrate teaching, Galatians 4:21–31.

Harvest illustration, James 5:7.

See Object Lesson, Parable, Visual.

IMAGE

Infamous image, Isaiah 23:16.

Lost self-esteem, Lamentations 4:2.

Known as the Lord's messenger, Haggai 1:13.

Joseph guarded Mary's image, Matthew 1:19.

Egotistical self-image, Mark 12:38–40.

Danger of false image, 2 Corinthians 10:12.

Willing to accept fool's image, 2 Corinthians 11:16–19.

Prisoner's image, Philippians 1:12–14.

Savior, King, Colossians 1:15–20.

Image superior to angels, Hebrews 1:3–4.

Great patriarchs, small mention, Hebrews 11:32.

See Fame, Self-esteem, Self-image, Reputation.

IMAGES See Idolatry, Statue.

IMAGINATION

Evil inclinations, Genesis 6:5 (KJV).

Power of human imagination, Genesis 11:6.

Induced imagination, 2 Kings 7:6–7.

Imagined problems, Nehemiah 6:8.

Devising evil, Psalm 38:12; Proverbs 6:18.

Mischievous imagination, Psalm 62:3 (KJV).

Visions imagined, Ezekiel 13:1–7.

Imagined idols, Ezekiel 14:1–11.

Sins of imagination, Matthew 5:28.

Foolish heart darkened, Romans 1:21.

Invented stories, 2 Peter 1:16; 2:3.

See Frame-of-Reference, Mind.

IMITATION

Imitating heathen, 1 Samuel 8:19–20; 2 Kings 17:15.

Faulty original cisterns, Jeremiah 2:13.

Conversion suspected as imitation, Acts 9:26–27.

Imitators invited, 1 Corinthians 4:16; Philippians 4:9.

Model to imitate, 2 Thessalonians 3:9.

See Counterfeit, False, Hypocrisy.

IMMATURITY

"Lay aside immaturity," Proverbs 9:6 (NRSV).

Easily deceived, Hosea 7:11.

Immaturity of new convert, Acts 8:13–24.

New convert's instruction, Acts 18:24–26.

Immature believers, Acts 19:1–7.

Milk, solid food, 1 Corinthians 3:1–2.

Worldly immaturity, 1 Corinthians 3:3.

Thinking like children, 1 Corinthians 14:20 (CEV).

No longer infants, Ephesians 4:14 (See CEV).

Immature prophecies, 2 Thessalonians 2:1–2.

Unable to teach, Hebrews 5:12–13 (LB).

Spiritual immaturity, Revelation 3:8.

See Growth, Weakness.

IMMENSITY

Promised immensity, Jeremiah 33:3.

Holy Spirit's immense power, Ephesians 3:20–21.

See Quantity, Superlative.

IMMIGRATION

Postdiluvian immigration, Genesis 10:32.

Immigration by divine decree, Genesis 12:10–20.

See Alien.

IMMINENT

Imminent fulfillment, Joel 2:1–2; Obadiah 15; Zephaniah 1:14.

Death more certain than wealth, Luke 12:16–21.

Our Lord's nearness, Philippians 4:5.

Imminent justice, James 5:9.
End of age, 1 Peter 4:7.
No more delay, Revelation 10:6; 22:10.

IMMOBILIZE

Land immobilized, 2 Kings 3:19.

IMMODEST

Pagan immodesty, Numbers 25:1–2.
Utterly defiled, Jeremiah 3:1–3.
Immodest, proper boasting, Jeremiah 9:23–24.
Immodesty of two sisters, Ezekiel 23:1–49.
Lifted skirts, Nahum 3:5.
Alcohol, nudity, Habakkuk 2:15.
See Discretion, Immorality, Shame.

IMMOLATION

Self-inflicted wounds, 1 Kings 18:28.
Sacrifice of son, 2 Kings 16:3.
See Suicide.

IMMORALITY

Divine gift of two sexes, Genesis 1:26–27.
Deliberate immorality, Genesis 16:1–16 (Note 15:1–6).
Father's immoral offer, Genesis 19:4–8, 30–38.
Male covetousness, Exodus 20:17; Proverbs 6:23–24.
Immorality combined with idolatry, Numbers 25:1–3.
Wild parties, defiant conduct, Numbers 25:6–9.
Wanton woman's immorality, Judges 19:1–3.
Immorality in sacred places, 1 Samuel 2:22.
Immorality in politics, 2 Samuel 3:6–11.
Leisure leads to immorality, 2 Samuel 11:1–5.
Immorality used for vengeance, 2 Samuel 16:20–23.
Evil in a man's heart, Job 31:9–12.
Immorality reduces personal value, Proverbs 6:25–26.
Playing with fire, Proverbs 6:27.
"Surely there is a hereafter," Proverbs 23:18 (NKJV).
Please God, escape immorality, Ecclesiastes 7:26.

Worst of women, Jeremiah 2:33.
Life of prostitute, Jeremiah 3:1–2; Micah 1:7.
Morality vital to spirituality, Jeremiah 3:1–5.
Ministration of evil prophets, Jeremiah 23:10–14.
Deeds done in the dark, Ezekiel 8:12.
Merchandising feminine beauty, Ezekiel 16:15.
Children of immoral mother, Hosea 1:2 (LB).
Immorality incited by alcohol, Hosea 4:18 (CEV).
Nation likened to prostitute, Nahum 3:3–4.
Immorality of heart and mind, Matthew 5:27–28.
Royal immorality, Luke 3:19–20.
Immoral Christians, 1 Corinthians 5:9–11 (CEV).
Immorality condemned, 1 Corinthians 6:9–10.
Conquest of immorality, 1 Corinthians 9:27.
Unrepentant immorality, 2 Corinthians 12:21.
Unwholesome talk, Ephesians 4:29.
Immorality "put to death," Colossians 3:5–10.
"Evil desires of youth," 2 Timothy 2:22.
Evil heart, James 1:13–15.
Sin in broad daylight, 2 Peter 2:13–23.
"Gross immorality," Jude 7 (NASB).
"Corrupted flesh," Jude 23.
Immorality in Body of Christ, Revelation 2:20.
Mother of prostitutes, Revelation 17:1–6.
Immorality into lake of fire, Revelation 21:8; 22:15.
See Degradation, Incest, Lust, Morality, Rape, Vice.

IMMORTALITY

Deliverance from sinful immortality, Genesis 3:22.
Enoch's walk with God, Genesis 5:24.
Angel refused temporal food, Judges 13:16.
Rejoining lost loved ones, 2 Samuel 12:23.
Chariot ascent to heaven, 2 Kings 2:11.
No desire to live forever, Job 7:16.
Confusion about immortality, Job 10:19–22; 14:7–14.

Classic statement of faith, Job 19:25–26.
Eternal inheritance, Psalm 37:18.
Confidence of immortality, Psalm 49:15.
Eternity in hearts of men, Ecclesiastes 3:11.
Spirits of mortals, beasts, Ecclesiastes 3:21.
Resurrection of all mankind, Daniel 12:2–3.
Eternal life, John 3:14–16.
True immortality, John 8:51.
Jesus could not die before God's time, John 19:11.
Death of martyr, Acts 7:54–56.
Spiritual body, earthly body, 1 Corinthians 15:42–55.
Mortality and immortality, 2 Corinthians 5:1.
One who never changes, Hebrews 1:10–12.
Melchizedek, the immortal, Hebrews 7:1–3.
Perpetual life, Hebrews 7:8 (AB).
Blessed after life, James 5:10–11 (LB).
Born of immortal seed, 1 Peter 1:23.
Mortal body put aside, 2 Peter 1:13–14.
Divine sperm, 1 John 3:9 (AB).
Mortals unable to die, Revelation 9:6.
Immunity to second death, Revelation 20:4–6.
See Death, Heaven.

IMMUNITY

Immune to plagues, Exodus 8:22, 23.
Cities of refuge, Numbers 35:6–15.
Immunity from every disease, Deuteronomy 7:15.
Immune to human ills, Psalm 73:5.
Foolish claim to immunity, Isaiah 28:15.
See Protection.

IMPACT

Ezekiel overwhelmed, Ezekiel 3:15.
Like teacher, like student, Luke 6:40.
Paul's witness to Agrippa, Acts 26:28–29.
Worldwide impact, Romans 1:8.
Ministry impact, 1 Thessalonians 1:8–10.

IMPARTIAL

Avoid partiality, 1 Timothy 5:21.

IMPATIENCE

Lacking patience, Genesis 16:1–4.
Impatient community, Exodus 16:2.

Divine impatience, Deuteronomy 3:26.
Too impatient, Job 6:2 (AB).
Giving vent to anger, Proverbs 29:11.
Impatience with God, Isaiah 5:18–19; 45:9.
Jonah's impatience, Jonah 4:8–9.
Impatience of Jesus, Mark 9:19; Luke 12:50.
Impatient disciples, Luke 9:51–56.
Impatient housekeeper, Luke 10:40.
Exhausted patience, Acts 18:4–6.
See Disgust, Exasperation.

IMPEACH

King impeached, hero anointed, 1 Samuel 16:1–13.

IMPENITENCE

Warning against disobedience, Leviticus 26:21.
Impenitent heart, Deuteronomy 29:19–21.
One sin great as another, 1 Samuel 15:23; James 2:10.
Rebelling against light, Job 24:13.
Proud of wrongdoing, Psalm 52:1.
Hardened hearts, Psalm 95:8; Mark 3:5; Hebrews 3:7–8.
Ignoring reproof, Proverbs 29:1.
Impenitent resistance, Isaiah 48:4.
Willful impenitence, Jeremiah 44:15–19.
Unwilling to be convinced, Luke 16:31.
Impenitent hearts, John 12:37–40.
Rebellion against truth, 1 Thessalonians 2:15–16.
See Carnality, Rebellion, Rejection, Stubborn.

IMPERATIVE

Imperative to witness, Ezekiel 3:18–19.
Entrusted with secrets, 1 Corinthians 4:1–2.
See Urgency.

IMPERCEPTIVE

Israel's imperception, Isaiah 1:3.
Peter's imperception, Matthew 16:21–23.
Seared consciences, 1 Timothy 4:2.
See Superficial.

IMPERFECTION

None can boast, Proverbs 20:9.
Cheating, polluting, Amos 8:5, 6.

Lost saltiness, Luke 14:34–35.
One blemish among twelve, John 6:70–71.
Need for new covenant, Hebrews 8:7.
See Blemish, Defective, Fault.

IMPERTINENCE

Rebellious people, Numbers 14:35.
Pride, arrogance, 1 Samuel 2:3.
Impertinent youth, 2 Kings 2:23–24.
Lack of respect, Esther 5:9, 10.
Wisdom of sluggard, Proverbs 26:16.
Impertinent pagan king, Isaiah 37:10.
Refusal to go God's way, Jeremiah 11:7–8.
Accusing the Lord, Jeremiah 20:7.
See Disrespect.

IMPETUOUS

Impetuous revenge, John 18:10–11.
Controlled reactions, responses, James 1:19–20.
See Eagerness, Haste.

IMPETUS

King's business urgent, 1 Samuel 21:8.
Motivated by hook, bit, 2 Kings 19:28.
Good things stored in heart, Luke 6:45.
See Incentive, Motivation.

IMPIETY

Scoffing at God, Exodus 5:2; 2 Chronicles 32:16, 17.
Seeking to ignore the Lord, Job 21:14; Romans 1:28.
Sin of challenging God, Isaiah 5:18–19.
Laughing at truth spoken by Jesus, Matthew 9:23–24.
Temple impiety, Matthew 21:12–13.
See Blasphemy, Irreverence, Sacrilege.

IMPOLITE See Discourtesy, Rudeness.

IMPORTANCE

Comparing sun, moon, stars, Genesis 1:16.
What is most important, Luke 11:27–28.
Desire for importance, Luke 11:43.
Making people important, Colossians 4:7–17.
See Identity, Priority, Value.

IMPOSTOR

Sin of only one person, Numbers 16:22.
Vindication by earthquake, Numbers 16:28–34.
Impostor's manner of speech, Judges 12:5–6.
Dishonest report for personal gain, 2 Samuel 1:2–16.
Deceitful, malicious man, Proverbs 26:24–26.
Impostor gods, Jeremiah 10:11–12.
Cheating, partridge, lecherous man, Jeremiah 17:11.
Impostor prophets, Jeremiah 23:16–18; Ezekiel 13:1–3.
Impostors among sheep, John 10:1, 7–10.
Suspected of being an impostor, Acts 9:26–27.
Method of false teachers, 2 Peter 2:1.
See Deceit, Traitors, Wolf.

IMPOTENCE

Advanced in years, 1 Kings 1:1–4.
Lost desire, Ecclesiastes 12:5.
Impotent city, Ezekiel 26:2 (CEV).
See Geriatrics, Old Age, Senility.

IMPRECATION

Calling down fire, 2 Kings 1:10.
Prayer against adversaries, Nehemiah 4:5; Psalms 10:15; 55:15; 58:6; 68:2; 69:22; 109:6–7; 137:7.
Self-judgment, Ruth 1:17.
Eli's warning to Samuel, 1 Samuel 3:17.
David's claim of innocence, 2 Samuel 3:28–29.
Impending imprecation, Acts 23:3.
Foreboding imprecation, Galatians 1:19.
See Curse.

IMPRESSIVE

Overwhelmed by royal grandeur, 1 Kings 10:5–9; 2 Chronicles 9:3.
Humorous challenge, Acts 16:37.
Widened sphere of influence, Philippians 1:12–14.
See Display.

IMPRISONMENT

Placed with king's prisoners, Genesis 39:20.
Rebuking seer imprisoned, 2 Chronicles 16:7–10.
Deterrent to crime, Ecclesiastes 8:11.
House prison, Jeremiah 37:15–16.
Set free by angels, Acts 5:17–19.
Prison escape, Acts 12:1–10.
Set free by earthquake, Acts 16:16–40.
Paul arrested in Jerusalem, Acts 21:30–33.
Imprisoned aboard ship, Acts 27:1–2.
Prison epistles, Ephesians 6:20; 2 Timothy 2:9; Philemon 1:10, 13; Philippians 1:7, 13–14, 16; Colossians 4:3, 18.
Satan imprisoned, Revelation 20:1–3, 7–8.
See Arrest, Jail, Prison.

IMPROMPTU

Words thought up, John 7:16 (CEV).
See Ad Lib, Improvisation.

IMPROPRIETY

Embarrassing impropriety, Nahum 3:5.
Engaged couples avoid impropriety, 1 Corinthians 7:36–38.
"Entirely out of place," Ephesians 5:4 (NRSV).
See Exhibitionism, Immodest.

IMPROVEMENT

Tear down old, build new, Judges 6:25–26.
See Construction, Renewal.

IMPROVISATION

Divine improvisation, Exodus 4:10–12.
Royal ceremony improvised, 2 Kings 9:11–13.
Improvised prophecies, Ezekiel 13:1–3.
Musical instrument improvisation, Amos 6:5.
See Ad Lib.

IMPULSIVE

Think before you speak, Proverbs 16:23 (GNB).
Impulsive thoughts, Ecclesiastes 5:2 (NASB).

IMPURE

Pure joined to impure, 1 Corinthians 6:15.

INACCURACY

Negative, positive viewpoints, Numbers 13:17–33.
Fortunate inaccuracy, 1 Samuel 19:9–10.
Speaking to inanimate object, 1 Kings 13:2.
Deliberate inaccuracy, Jeremiah 8:8–9.
Crooked arrow, Hosea 7:16 (CEV).
See Error.

INAUGURATION

Joshua's inauguration, Numbers 27:23 (NKJV); Deuteronomy 31:1–8.
Secret inauguration, 2 Kings 9:1–13.
See Politics.

INCARCERATION See Jail, Prison.

INCARNATION

Incarnation prophesied, Genesis 3:15; Deuteronomy 18:15–18; Psalm 2:7; Isaiah 11:1.
Virgin birth predicted, Isaiah 7:14; 9:6.
Incarnation geography, Micah 5:2–3.
Ignorance concerning incarnation, Matthew 22:41–46.
The Word incarnate, John 1:14 (See CEV).
God incarnate in Christ, John 6:46; 14:8–13; Colossians 1:15; Romans 8:3; Hebrews 2:5–9.
Jesus claimed incarnation, John 7:25–29.
He who was rich became poor, 2 Corinthians 8:9.
Incarnate body, Colossians 1:22; 2:9.
Description of incarnation, 1 Timothy 3:16.
Incarnation requirement, Hebrews 2:16–18 (AB).
Incarnation defined, Hebrews 10:5–7 (AB).
Predestined incarnation, 1 Peter 1:18–20.
Test of orthodoxy, 1 John 4:2.
Incarnation reviewed, Revelation 12:1–5.
See Nativity, Redemption.

INCENSE

Ingredients for making incense, Exodus 30:34–35; Song of Songs 3:6.
No incense with sin offering, Leviticus 5:11.
Incense, jealous husband, Numbers 5:11–15.
Incense, idol worship, Jeremiah 41:5; Ezekiel 8:11.

Intercessory incense, Psalm 141:2.
Fragrant cloud, Ezekiel 8:10–11.
Gift of incense, Matthew 2:11.
See Aesthetics, Fragrance, Perfume.

INCENTIVE

Rewarded effort, Psalm 62:12.
See Encouragement, Impetus, Motivation.

INCEST

Daughters' incest with father, Genesis 19:30–38 (See CEV).
Incestuous marriage, Genesis 20:12.
Incest forbidden, Leviticus 18:6–18; 20:11–12, 17–21; Deuteronomy 27:22–23.
Rape of half-sister, 2 Samuel 13:1–19.
Violation of family members, Ezekiel 22:11.
Man takes father's wife, 1 Corinthians 5:1–2.
See Intermarriage.

INCH

Nine-inch span, Isaiah 40:12 (AB).
See Measurement.

INCIDENTAL

Details made incidental, Hebrews 9:5.

INCLINATION

"Behaving according to human inclinations," 1 Corinthians 3:3 (NRSV).

INCOME

Income from prostitution unacceptable, Deuteronomy 23:18.
Protecting debtor's income, Deuteronomy 24:6.
Giving on first day of week, 1 Corinthians 16:2.
Providing income for personal ministry, 1 Thessalonians 2:9.
See Finances, Honorarium, Wages.

INCOMPARABLE

Incomparable God, Isaiah 46:5.

INCOMPETENCE

Jewish workers called incompetent, Nehemiah 4:1–10.
Incompetent student, Proverbs 5:12–13.

House left untended, Ecclesiastes 10:18.
Incompetent gods who perish, Jeremiah 10:11–12.
Incompetent prophets see nothing, Ezekiel 13:1–3.
Weakness of broken arms, Ezekiel 30:21, 22.
See Failure, Weakness.

INCONSISTENT

Inconsistent use of God's wealth, Judges 17:4.
Jehu's inconsistency, 2 Kings 10:16–31.
Inconsistent attitude toward faults, Matthew 7:3–5.
Practice what you preach, Matthew 23:2–4.
Pious, hypocritical attitudes toward Jesus, Luke 6:1–11.
Profession without performance, Luke 6:46; Titus 1:16.
Criticizing Jesus, John 7:21–24.
Judging others, Romans 2:1, 21–23.
Chiding inconsistency, 2 Corinthians 11:16–21.
Inconsistent Galatians, Galatians 1:6–9.
Not consistent, Galatians 2:14 (NRSV).
See Hypocrisy, Unstable.

INCONVENIENCE

"Put up with anything," 2 Timothy 2:10 (CEV).

INCORRIGIBLE

Punishment induces rebellion, Isaiah 1:5 (AB).
Those who do not know how to blush, Jeremiah 6:15.
Anger beyond measure, Lamentations 5:21–22.
For continued sinning, certain judgment, Amos 1:3, 6, 9, 11, 13; 2:1, 4, 6 (Note nature of sin in each of these judgments).
God's grace to worst of sinners, 1 Timothy 1:15–16.
Incorrigible's refusal to repent, Revelation 9:20–21.
See Carnality, Depravity, Unpardonable.

INCUMBENT

Put out of office, Isaiah 22:19.
See Politics.

INDECISION

Lot's indecision leaving Sodom, Genesis 19:15–16.
No divine indecision, Numbers 23:19.
Delayed departure, Judges 19:1–10.
Between two opinions, 1 Kings 18:21.
Worship God, serve idols, 2 Kings 17:41.
Easily deceived, Hosea 7:11.
Cannot serve two masters, Matthew 6:24.
Turning away from commitment, Luke 9:62.
Double-minded, James 1:8.
See Reluctance, Vacillate.

INDEPENDENCE

Defiant sin, Numbers 15:30–31.
Greatest independence, Psalm 119:45.
Independent of God's way, Jeremiah 11:7–8.
Truth sets free, John 8:31–32, 36.
Body as unit, 1 Corinthians 12:12–30.
See Freedom.

INDIA

Xerxes' kingdom included India, Esther 1:1; 8:9.

INDICTMENT

Indicted for blasphemy, 1 Kings 21:13.
Prophet indicted, Jeremiah 26:1–24.
Pagan indictment, Daniel 3:12–18.
Courage to indict, Daniel 5:18–26.
Indictments of Jesus, Matthew 26:61–65; Mark 15:2, 26; Luke 23:2–3, 38; John 18:30, 33; 19:12, 19–22.
Personal indictment, Matthew 27:3.
Search for cause to criticize, Mark 3:2.
Indictment of Pharisees, Luke 11:45–54.
Stephen's indictment, Acts 6:11, 13.
Unjust indictment, Acts 16:20–21.
Ministry indictment, Acts 17:7; 18:13; 24:5; 25:18–19, 26–27.
See Arrest.

INDIFFERENCE

Angels' warning taken as joke, Genesis 19:14.
Indifferent to wonders, Psalm 106:7, 13.
Indifferent women, Isaiah 32:9.
Who cares? Jeremiah 12:11.
Those who pass by, Lamentations 1:12.
Indifferent to future judgment, Ezekiel 12:25–28.
Slumbering indifference, Jonah 1:5–6.
Spiritual indifference, Zephaniah 1:6.
Fate of carefree city, Zephaniah 2:15.
Indifferent priests, Malachi 1:6–14.
Rejected wedding invitation, Matthew 22:1–14.
Indifferent disciples, Mark 14:32–41.
See Apathy, Calloused, Insensitive, Lethargy.

INDIGESTION

Fish indigestion, Jonah 2:10.
The sight of food, Job 3:24 (NASB).
Internal churning, Job 30:27 (See Berk.).
Love hinders indigestion, Proverbs 15:17.
Sweet in mouth, sour to stomach, Revelation 10:9–10.
See Mouth.

INDIGNATION

God's indignation, Psalm 90:7, 11 (Berk.); Revelation 15:1 (AB).
"Burning indignation," Psalm 119:53 (Berk.).
See Anger, Disgust.

INDISCRETION

Blatant indiscretion, 2 Samuel 16:21–22.
See Immodest.

INDIVIDUAL

God singles out individual, Deuteronomy 29:21.
Without precedent, Isaiah 64:4.
Individual salvation, Romans 10:13.
"I am what I am," 1 Corinthians 15:10 (GNB).
See Personal.

INDOLENCE

Indolent sluggard, Proverbs 6:9–10.
Sleep, success, Proverbs 20:13.

Characteristics of indolence, Proverbs 26:13–16.

"Reluctant dragon," Isaiah 30:6–7 (LB, also Berk.).

Indolent slumber, Matthew 26:36–45.

See Laziness, Lethargy.

INDULGENCE

Too much food and drink, Proverbs 23:20.

From one sin to another, Jeremiah 9:3.

Jesus accused of indulgence, Matthew 26:6–13.

Continual indulgence, Ephesians 4:19.

See Gluttony, Hedonism.

INDUSTRIOUS

Energy and efficiency, 1 Kings 11:28.

Making most of time, opportunity, Psalm 90:12; Ecclesiastes 12:1; 1 Corinthians 7:29; Ephesians 5:16; Colossians 4:5.

Industrious ant, Proverbs 6:6.

Hard work, fantasy, Proverbs 28:19.

Totally industrious, Ecclesiastes 9:10.

Industrious Creator, John 5:17.

Continually industrious, Romans 12:11.

Exploring every opportunity, Ephesians 5:15–16; Colossians 4:5.

Self-supported ministry, 2 Thessalonians 3:6–9.

No work, no eat, 2 Thessalonians 3:10.

See Initiative, Motivation.

INDUSTRY

Industrial land desecration, Nahum 3:16.

See Ecology.

INEBRIATED *See Drunkenness.*

INEPT

Wild donkey's colt, Job 11:12.

Inept fool, Proverbs 26:1–12.

See Weakness.

INEQUITY

Making bricks without straw, Exodus 5:6–18.

One man's guilt hinders all, Numbers 16:22.

Honest weights, measurements, Deuteronomy 25:13–16.

Share and share alike, 1 Samuel 30:24.

Inequity among citizens, Nehemiah 5:1–5.

Security for wicked, Job 12:6.

Inequity in joys of wicked, Job 21:6–16.

Wrong made right, Proverbs 28:8.

Human inequity, Proverbs 30:23–33.

Pessimistic view, Ecclesiastes 1:15.

Political inequity, Ecclesiastes 5:8–9.

Righteous perish, wicked thrive, Ecclesiastes 7:15 (NRSV).

Seeming inequity, Ecclesiastes 8:14 (LB).

Common destiny, Ecclesiastes 9:1–2.

Fools in high positions, Ecclesiastes 10:5–7.

Seeming inequity in death of righteous, Isaiah 57:1–2.

Grain and wine to enemy, Isaiah 62:8–9.

"Why is life easy for sinners?" Jeremiah 12:1 (CEV).

Seeming inequity of testing, Jeremiah 15:15–18.

Inequity in use of power, Jeremiah 23:10.

Denial of rights and justice, Lamentations 3:34–36.

Enemies without cause, Lamentations 3:52.

Inequity in life and death, Ezekiel 13:19.

Divine use of evil government, Habakkuk 1:1–4.

Well-built houses, temple ruins, Haggai 1:4 (GNB).

Equity in tax collection, Luke 3:12–13.

Equity in labor relations, Luke 17:7–10.

See Cheating, Unfairness.

INEVITABLE

Time for everything, Ecclesiastes 3:1–8.

Inevitable judgment, Jeremiah 44:15–28.

Divine decisions irrevocable, Romans 11:29.

See Predestination.

INEXPERIENCE

Foolish sins, Numbers 12:11.

Father assisting inexperienced son, 1 Chronicles 22:5; 29:1.

Fearfully inexperienced, Jeremiah 1:6 (LB).

See Novice.

INFALLIBLE

When God has not spoken, Deuteronomy 18:21–22.

Infallible promises, Joshua 23:4.
No lie comes from truth, 1 John 2:20–21.
See Inspiration, Scriptures, Truth.

INFAMY

Defiant sin, Numbers 15:30–31.
Infamy to King's daughter, 2 Kings 9:30–37.
Bodies lying unburied, Jeremiah 9:22.
Burial of donkey, Jeremiah 22:19.
Royal infamy, Lamentations 5:12.
Sacred treasures in pagan temple, Daniel 1:2.
Crucifixion of Jesus, Mark 15:25–32.
Demeaning the Son of God, John 19:1–3; Hebrews 13:12–13.
Infamous sinning, 2 Peter 2:13–23.
See Degradation, Iniquity, Sacrilege.

INFANT

Foretold births, Genesis 16:11; 18:10; Judges 13:3; 1 Kings 13:2; 2 Kings 4:16; Isaiah 9:6; Matthew 1:21; Luke 1:13.
Weaning celebration, Genesis 21:8.
Adopted twins, Genesis 48:5.
Baby Moses, Exodus 2:2 (GNB).
Learning to talk, Isaiah 8:4.
Rejected choice of name, Luke 1:59–63.
Infant Savior, Luke 2:6–7.
See Birth, Childbirth.

INFANTICIDE

Slaughtered infants, Genesis 1:16, Nahum 3:10.
Male infanticide, Exodus 1:16; Matthew 2:16; Acts 7:19.
Sacrificed son, 2 Kings 16:3; 21:6; Ezekiel 20:31.
Children sacrificed, 2 Chronicles 28:3.
Brutal infanticide, Psalm 137:9.
No mercy on infants, Isaiah 13:18.
Mothers as cannibals, Lamentations 2:20.
See Abortion.

INFANT MORTALITY

Termination of infant mortality, Isaiah 65:20.
Improper care of newborn, Ezekiel 16:4–5.
Lower infant mortality, Ezekiel 36:14 (LB).
See Abortion, Infanticide.

INFATUATION

Samson's infatuation for Delilah, Judges 14:1–3.
True love mistaken as infatuation, 1 Samuel 18:20–29.
David, Bathsheba, 2 Samuel 11:2–5.
Love like morning mist, Hosea 6:4.
See Courtship.

INFERIORITY COMPLEX

No need to feel inferior, Deuteronomy 20:1.
Denying inferiority, Job 12:3; 13:2.
See Self-esteem.

INFERTILITY

Infertility in God's timing, Genesis 16:1–4.
Closed wombs, Genesis 20:17.
Husband, wife tension, Genesis 30:1–2, 22.
Beloved but barren, 1 Samuel 1:2–7.
Infertile land made productive, 2 Kings 2:19–22.
Land that produces sparingly, Isaiah 5:10.
Plight of eunuch, Isaiah 56:3–5.
Scatter salt on condemned land, Jeremiah 48:9.
Wombs that miscarry, Hosea 9:14.
Place of saltpits, Zephaniah 2:9.
See Barren, Childless, Pregnancy.

INFIDELITY

Other men's wives, 1 Corinthians 10:8 (LB).
See Lust.

INFINITE

Concept of space/time, Job 26:7–14.
The age of God, Job 36:26 (Berk.).
Limits of outer space, Psalm 147:4.
Infinite exaltation of Christ, Ephesians 1:18–23; Revelation 1:5.
"Boundless riches," Ephesians 2:7 (NRSV); 3:8 (NRSV).
See Eternity, Omnipotence, Space/Time.

INFIRMITY

"Stricken in years," Joshua 13:1 (KJV); 23:2 (KJV).
See Disease, Fever, Illness, Old Age, Sickness.

INFLATION

Inflation caused by famine, 2 Kings 6:24–25.

Declining value, James 5:3 (LB).

See Government, Money.

INFLUENCE

Musical father's influence, Genesis 4:21.

Like father, like son, Genesis 5:1–3.

Following wrong crowd, Exodus 23:2.

Vengeance against bad influence, Numbers 31:1 (LB).

Righteous conduct, Deuteronomy 4:5–6.

Resist wrong influence, Deuteronomy 12:4, 29–32; 18:9–13.

Wrong family influence, Deuteronomy 13:6–10.

Influence of good women, Ruth 4:11.

Son's influence over father, 1 Samuel 19:1–6.

Solomon's great wisdom, 1 Kings 4:29–34.

Wisdom, spiritual identity, 1 Kings 10:1.

Marriage to unbelievers, 1 Kings 11:1–8.

Bad parental influence, 1 Kings 22:51–53.

Bad influence of children, grandchildren, 2 Kings 17:41.

Mothers' influence on young kings, 2 Kings 23:31, 36; 24:8, 18.

Victim of bad influence, 2 Chronicles 13:7.

Evil woman's influence, 2 Chronicles 21:6.

Influence of evil king, 2 Chronicles 33:9 (LB).

Refusal to obey king's command, Esther 1:10–18.

Challenged to use influence with king, Esther 4:12–14; 9:12–13.

Influence used for good of others, Esther 10:3.

Wicked advice, Psalm 1:1 (NRSV).

Like idol, like follower, Psalm 135:15–18.

Written upon tablet of heart, Proverbs 3:1–4.

Parental influence, Proverbs 6:20–23.

Terminal impact of death, Proverbs 11:7.

Good and bad influence, Proverbs 13:20.

Good news and cheerful looks, Proverbs 15:30.

Children proud of parents, Proverbs 17:6.

Seeking political favors, Proverbs 19:6; 29:26.

Properly training a child, Proverbs 22:6.

Precarious influence, Proverbs 22:24 (GNB).

Best influence of no avail, Jeremiah 15:1.

Father's evil influence, Jeremiah 16:10–12.

Prophets who aid evildoers, Jeremiah 23:14.

Like mother, like daughter, Ezekiel 16:44.

Desire to be like others, Ezekiel 20:32–38.

Clergy's wrong influence, Hosea 4:9.

Like father, like children, Hosea 4:14.

Heathen influence, Hosea 7:8 (LB).

Father's immoral influence over son, Amos 2:7.

Responsible for nation's sin, Micah 1:13.

Influencing neighbors to alcoholism, Habakkuk 2:15.

Salt of earth, Matthew 5:13.

Let your light shine, Matthew 5:14–16; Philippians 2:15.

Evil influence over good, Matthew 13:24–30.

Wrong influence over children, Matthew 18:6; Mark 9:42.

Mother's desire for favors for sons, Matthew 20:20–24.

Posthumous influence, Matthew 26:13; Hebrews 11:4; 2 Peter 1:15.

Like teacher, like student, Luke 6:40.

Spiritual light from within, Luke 11:33–36.

Influencing others to sin, Luke 17:1–3.

Plot to kill Lazarus because of influence, John 12:9–11.

Satanic influence, John 13:2.

Relatives, friends of Cornelius, Acts 10:24–27.

Influence used against Paul, Barnabas, Acts 13:50.

Poisoning minds, Acts 14:2.

Influential women follow Christ, Acts 17:4.

Influence of Roman Christians, Romans 1:8.

Yeast of malice, wickedness, 1 Corinthians 5:8.

Exercise of liberty, eating, drinking, 1 Corinthians 8:7–13.

Do not cause others to stumble, 1 Corinthians 10:32–33.

Bad company, 1 Corinthians 15:33 (See GNB).

Those who refresh the spirit, 1 Corinthians 16:18.

Differing influences of Christians, 2 Corinthians 2:15–16.

Convert's influence encouraged others, Galatians 1:23–24.

Abraham blessed, became a blessing, Galatians 3:9.

Persecution widened sphere of influence, Philippians 1:12–14.

Channel of much blessing, Philippians 1:25–26.

Be above criticism, Philippians 2:15–16 (See 1 Corinthians 8:10–13).

Model to other believers, 1 Thessalonians 1:7–8.

How father should deal with children, 1 Thessalonians 2:11–12.

Avoid idle brothers, 2 Thessalonians 3:6.

Desire to be influential, 1 Timothy 3:1.

Do not share sins of others, 1 Timothy 5:22.

Grandmother's faith passed on, 2 Timothy 1:5.

Influence of Scriptures since childhood, 2 Timothy 3:14–15.

Avoid favoritism, James 2:1.

Strategic control of speech, James 3:2–6.

Influence unto salvation, 1 Peter 3:1–2.

Surviving in evil surroundings, 2 Peter 2:4–9.

Children of good parents, 2 John 4.

Wrong kind of congregational authority, 3 John 9–10.

See Leadership, Reputation, Responsibility.

INFORMATION

The secret and known, Deuteronomy 29:29.

Misinformation to protect spies, Joshua 2:1–6.

Captive's information about enemy, Judges 8:13–14.

Failure to evaluate bad counsel, Ezra 4:11–22.

Speaking in language understood, Isaiah 36:11.

Misleading information, Isaiah 37:7.

Watchman's responsibility, Ezekiel 33:1–9.

Attention to important information, Ezekiel 40:4.

Knowledge increased, Daniel 12:4.

Word-of-mouth publicity, Matthew 4:24.

Communicating God's message, Hebrews 1:1–2.

Blessed information, Revelation 1:3.

See Instruction, Media, News, Research, Statistics, Study.

INGRATITUDE

Ingratitude for guidance, Genesis 40:9–23.

Not recognizing Divine favor, Numbers 16:9–10.

Material, spiritual blessing, Deuteronomy 8:12–14.

Ingratitude for Creator's goodness, Deuteronomy 32:5–7; Judges 10:11–14.

New generation's ingratitude, Judges 2:10–12.

National ingratitude, Judges 8:33–35.

King's short memory, 1 Samuel 15:17–19.

Useless concern for another's property, 1 Samuel 25:21.

Ingratitude for royal gifts, 1 Kings 9:10–13.

Murder replaces gratitude, 2 Chronicles 24:22.

Danger of success, 2 Chronicles 26:15–16; Hosea 4:7.

Blasphemy and assassination instead of praise, Nehemiah 9:26.

Divine provision ignored, Psalms 78:16–31; 106:7.

Forgotten deliverer of city, Ecclesiastes 9:14–15.

Ingratitude for mercy, love, Ezekiel 16:4–22.

Ingratitude for healing, Luke 17:11–19.

Ingratitude prophesied, 2 Timothy 3:2.

See Rudeness.

INHABIT

Earth created to be inhabited, Isaiah 45:18.

INHERITANCE

Slave's potential inheritance, Genesis 15:3–4.

Manipulated inheritance, Genesis 25:5–6 (CEV).

Bargain birthright, Genesis 25:27–34; Hebrews 12:16–17.

Women without inheritance, Genesis 31:15–16.

No male survivors, Numbers 27:1–11.

Intermarriage, inheritance, Numbers 36:1–4.

Spiritual inheritance, Deuteronomy 4:9–10.

First son's inheritance, Deuteronomy 21:15–17.

Proxy first son, Deuteronomy 25:5–6.

Prostitute's son denied inheritance, Judges 11:1–3.

Inheritance, purchase, Ruth 4:6; Jeremiah 32:8.

Inherited throne, 1 Kings 1:47–48.

Righteousness inherited from father, 1 Kings 11:9–13.

Asking double portion prophet's spirit, 2 Kings 2:9.

Family without inheritance, 2 Kings 4:1–7.

Ancestral property, Nehemiah 11:20.

Equal inheritance for sons and daughters, Job 42:15.

Doing good with ill-gained wealth, Proverbs 28:8.

Wisdom plus inheritance, Ecclesiastes 7:11.

Neither good nor evil inheritance, Ezekiel 18:3–20.

Children cheated on inheritance, Micah 2:9 (CEV).

Early request for inheritance, Luke 15:12.

Probate of will, Hebrews 9:16–17.

Imperishable inheritance, 1 Peter 1:4.

See Birthright, Legacy.

INIQUITY

Evil as water, Job 15:15–16.

Unbalance between good and bad, Job 21:7–26.

Blatant iniquity, Psalm 53:1–3.

Sin on leash, Isaiah 5:18.

Isaiah's conviction of sin, Isaiah 6:5.

Not knowing how to blush, Jeremiah 6:15.

Instability of iniquity, Jeremiah 30:12–14.

Injustice, bloodshed, Ezekiel 9:9.

Iniquity causes downfall, Hosea 14:1.

Continued sinning, certain judgment, Amos 1:3, 6, 9, 11, 13; 2:1, 4, 6.

Insomnia, iniquity, Micah 2:1.

Curse concludes Old Testament, Malachi 4:6.

Overt hypocrisy, Matthew 23:28.

Cause of backsliding, Matthew 24:12.

Instruments of unrighteousness, Romans 6:13 (Japanese: "container of wickedness").

Commitment to sin or righteousness, Romans 6:19.

Sins piled up to heaven, Revelation 18:4–5.

See Carnality, Depravity, Evil, Sin.

INITIATIVE

Man who built city, Genesis 10:11–12.

Don't just stand there, Genesis 42:1–2 (LB).

Heart initiative for God's work, Exodus 35:20–21, 25–26, 29; Nehemiah 4:6.

No rest until task accomplished, Numbers 23:24.

Urgent business, 1 Samuel 21:8.

Prompt gathering of food, 1 Samuel 25:18.

Spiritual initiative, 2 Chronicles 31:21.

Initiative against sin, Psalm 18:23.

Rewarded initiative, Proverbs 12:11; 22:29; 24:27.

Similarity of slackness to destruction, Proverbs 18:9.

Initiative, fantasy, Proverbs 28:19.

Learn from ants, Proverbs 30:25.

Initiative in action, Ecclesiastes 9:10.

Lazy hands, leaking roof, Ecclesiastes 10:18.

Parable of talents, Matthew 25:14–30.

Paralytic let down from roof, Luke 5:17–26.

Divine initiative in soul winning, Luke 19:10.

Prayer initiative against temptation, Luke 22:40.

Christ's initiative, John 5:30 (NASB).

Put knowledge into action, John 13:17.

Initiative in heart acceptance of others, 2 Corinthians 7:2.

"At the front in everything," 2 Corinthians 8:7 (AB).

Making most of opportunities, Ephesians 5:15–16; Colossians 4:5.

Do not become lazy, Hebrews 6:11–12.

Scriptural teaching put into action, James 1:22–25.

Personal initiative in holy living, James 4:7–10.

See Ambition, Diligence.

INJURY

Perilous activities, Ecclesiastes 10:9.
See Accident, Wounds.

INJUSTICE

Justice toward strangers, widows, Exodus 22:21–22.
Avoid injustice, Exodus 23:1–7.
Practice Golden Rule, Deuteronomy 24:17–18.
Rights of others, Job 24:2–3.
Making injustice legal, Psalm 94:20 (GNB).
Divine values, Proverbs 17:15.
Seeming injustice, Ecclesiastes 8:14 (LB).
Unjust laws and oppressive decrees, Isaiah 10:1–4.
Injustice rewarded, Amos 5:11–12.
Evil government to punish God's people, Habakkuk 1:1–4.
Shameless injustice, Zephaniah 3:5.
Injustice in depth, Luke 16:10; Revelation 22:11.
Hated without reason, John 15:25.
Imprisoned for conversion of fortune-teller, Acts 16:16–40.
Injustice avenged, 1 Thessalonians 4:7.
See Unfairness.

IN-LAWS

In-laws as source of grief, Genesis 26:34–35 (See NKJV).
Taking father-in-law's advice, Exodus 28:1–27.
Wealthy in-law, Ruth 2:1 (LB).
See Marriage.

INNOCENCE

Innocent accused, Genesis 39:11–20.
Apparent guilt, Genesis 44:1–34.
Innocents protected, Exodus 23:7.
Sacrifice with unsolved murder, Deuteronomy 21:1–9.
Accusation against innocence, 1 Samuel 22:11–15.
David's innocence in murder of Abner, 2 Samuel 3:22–37.
Claim of righteousness, innocence, 2 Samuel 22:21–25.
No one innocent in God's sight, Job 9:2 (CEV).
Total innocence, Job 11:15.

Desire for innocent life, Psalm 19:13.
Cleansed for worship, Psalm 26:6.
Suffering in innocence, Psalms 59:3–4; 119:86.
Condemning innocent, Proverbs 17:15.
Beauty with innocence, Song of Songs 4:7.
Innocent congregation, guilty priests, Hosea 4:4 (CEV).
Guilty Jonah seen as innocent, Jonah 1:14.
Dishonest innocence, Micah 6:11.
Innocent disciples, Matthew 12:7 (CEV).
Pilate's claim of innocence, Matthew 27:24.
Suffering, innocence of Jesus, Luke 23:15–16; John 19:1–6.
Redemptive cleansing, Ephesians 5:26–27; 1 Thessalonians 3:13.
From guilt to innocence, Philippians 2:15 (See GNB).
Legalistic innocence, Philippians 3:6.
Innocent of accusation, Colossians 1:22; Titus 1:6.
Life-style of innocence, 1 Timothy 3:2–4.
Unpolluted innocence, James 1:27.
Attained innocence, 2 Peter 3:14.
Blameless before the Lord, Revelation 14:5.
See Guilt, Holiness, Purity.

INNOVATION

Nothing new, Ecclesiastes 1:10.
New way to Jesus, Luke 5:17–20.
Innovative covenant, Hebrews 8:13.
See Invention, New.

INNUENDO

Trees and a coronation, Judges 9:7–20.
Cry to the gods, Judges 10:14.
Elder brother's innuendo, 1 Samuel 17:28.
Taunting giant, 1 Samuel 17:41–44.
Sleeping god, 1 Kings 18:27.
Thorny reasoning, 2 Kings 14:9.
Crumbled vision, Nehemiah 4:2.
Mocking salute, Matthew 27:28–29; John 19:3.
"Super apostles," 2 Corinthians 11:5.
See Sarcasm.

INQUEST

Inquest following murder, Deuteronomy 21:1–9.
See Court, Justice.

INQUIRY See Question.

INQUIRY ROOM
Tent for inquirers, Exodus 33:7.
See Conversion, Counseling.

INQUISITIVE
Mother-in-law's inquiry, Ruth 3:16, 17.
Inquisitive angels, 1 Peter 1:12 (See GNB, LB).
See Curiosity.

INSANITY
Driven to insanity, Deuteronomy 28:34 (See LB).
Pretended insanity, 1 Samuel 21:12–14.
Mentally ill understand, Isaiah 32:4.
Insane king, Daniel 4:31–34.
Insanity, demon possession, Matthew 4:24 (CEV, LB).
Jesus' family thought Him insane, Mark 3:20–21 (See LB).
Accused of demon possession, John 10:20.
See Deranged, Irrational, Mental Health.

INSECTS
Threat of flies, Exodus 8:21.
Besieged by locusts, Exodus 10:4; Judges 6:5.
Insects listed in Bible, Exodus 16:20; Leviticus 11:22; Deuteronomy 7:20; Judges 14:8; 1 Samuel 24:14; Psalms 78:46; 105:31; Proverbs 6:6; 30:15, 28 (NKJV); Ecclesiastes 10:1; Isaiah 50:9; Joel 1:4; Amos 4:9; Matthew 23:24.
Inedible, edible insects, Leviticus 11:21–25; Deuteronomy 14:9, 19–20.
Advance platoon of hornets, Exodus 23:28; Joshua 24:12.
Swallow camel, Matthew 23:24.
Enemy like swarm of bees, Deuteronomy 1:44.
Honey from lion's carcass, Judges 14:8–9.
Satirical flea, 1 Samuel 24:14.
Easily crushed moth, Job 4:19.
Moth-eaten garment, Job 13:28; Isaiah 50:9.
Carnivorous flies, Psalm 78:45.
Plague of flies, gnats, Psalm 105:31.
Ants as teachers, Proverbs 6:6.
Ants succeed little-by-little, Proverbs 30:25.
Dead flies pollute perfume, Ecclesiastes 10:1.
"Whistle for flies," Isaiah 7:18.
Usurping locusts, Isaiah 33:4.
Spinning spider's web, Isaiah 59:5.
Locusts who attack only people, Revelation 9:3–6.
See Honey, Maggots.

INSECURITY
Insecurity of wicked, Psalm 37:1–2, 10.
Lost security, Isaiah 1:19 (AB).
No place to hide, Jeremiah 49:10.

Insecure eagle's nest, Jeremiah 49:16.
Babylon's wall insecure, Jeremiah 51:58.
High places insecure, Obadiah 3–4.
Foolish trusting in oneself, Luke 12:16–21.
Wealth's insecurity, 1 Timothy 6:17.
See Weakness.

INSENSITIVE

People like animals in distress, Deuteronomy 28:53–57.
As one under anesthesia, Proverbs 23:34–35.
Burning truth not understood, Isaiah 42:25.
Wealth numbs conscience, Hosea 12:8.
Insensitive to miracles, Matthew 11:20.
Caring neither for God or man, Luke 18:1–5.
Insensitive hearts, closed ears, eyes, Acts 28:27.
Seared conscience, 1 Timothy 4:1–2.
See Calloused, Heartless.

INSIGHT

Donkey who saw angel, Numbers 22:23–28 (Note verse 31).
Unreliable insight Proverbs 3:5 (NRSV).
Wisdom, insight, Proverbs 4:7 (NRSV).
Wise eyes in head, Ecclesiastes 2:14.
Shrewd, innocent, Matthew 10:16.
Misunderstanding figure-of-speech, Matthew 16:5–12.
Unaware of divine purpose, presence, Luke 24:13–27.
Hard teaching, John 6:60.
Wisdom of Gamaliel, Acts 5:30–40.
Practical insight, Ephesians 1:8 (AB).
Heart insight, Ephesians 1:18–19.
Full insight, Philippians 1:9.
Reward of careful reflection, 2 Timothy 2:7.
See Perfection, Sensitivity.

INSIGNIFICANT

House of clay, Job 4:19.
Mortals as worms, Job 25:6.
"I am insignificant," Job 40:4 (NASB).
Minuteness of man, Psalm 8:3–4.
Insignificant town, great destiny, Micah 5:2.
Day of small things, Zechariah 4:10.

Tiny mustard seed, Matthew 13:31–32.
Illustration of human body, 1 Corinthians 12:21–25.
See Small, Trivia.

INSINCERITY

Insincere repentance, Exodus 9:27.
Worship, play, Exodus 32:6.
Doing right but not wholeheartedly, 2 Chronicles 25:2.
Foam on water, Job 24:18.
Insincere cordiality, Psalm 28:3.
Backslider's insincerity, Jeremiah 2:27.
Friends and brothers insincere, Jeremiah 9:4–8.
Jeopardy of insincere faith, Ezekiel 14:4.
Love like morning mist, Hosea 6:4.
Insincere fasting and repentance, Zechariah 7:1–6.
King Herod and Magi, Matthew 2:7–8, 13.
Insincerity of Pharisees, Matthew 15:7–9; Mark 12:15–17.
Praising, then condemning, Matthew 21:6–11; 27:20–23.
Egotistical insincerity, Mark 12:38–40.
See Fickle, Flattery, Hypocrisy.

INSIPID

Not cold or hot, Revelation 3:15–16.

INSOMNIA

Reading at night, Esther 6:1.
Restless night, Job 7:3–4 (See KJV).
"Night racks my bones," Job 30:17 (NRSV).
Companion of night creatures, Job 30:29.
Tossing, turning, Psalm 56:8 (LB).
Stressful insomnia, Psalm 77:2–6 (RSV).
Frogs in bedrooms, Psalm 105:30.
Purposeful insomnia, Psalm 119:148.
"Restless minds," Ecclesiastes 2:23 (NASB, NRSV).
Rich man's gluttony, Ecclesiastes 5:12 (NASB).
Pondering world problems (Ecclesiastes 8:16 (CEV).
Wandering streets at night, Song of Songs 3:1, 2.
Cardiac insomnia, Song of Songs 5:2.
Time remaining until morning, Isaiah 21:11–12.

Short bed, narrow blanket, Isaiah 28:20.

Troubled dreams, Daniel 2:1.

Conscience-agitated insomnia, Daniel 6:16–23.

"Many a sleepless night," 2 Corinthians 11:27 (NRSV).

See Conscience, Sleep.

INSPECTION See Examination, Scrutiny.

INSPIRATION

Divine inspiration for song, Deuteronomy 31:19–22.

Prophecy set to music, 2 Kings 3:15–16.

Inspired temple plans, 1 Chronicles 28:12.

Absolute dependability of God's word, Psalm 12:6.

Inspired to write, Psalm 45:1 (See LB).

Discovered proverbs, Proverbs 25:1 (LB).

Flawless inspiration, Proverbs 30:5.

Instructed to write, Isaiah 30:8 (CEV).

Self-induced inspiration, Ezekiel 13:3, 8 (GNB).

Verbal Inspiration, Jeremiah 30:2; Revelation 1:11.

All Scripture inspired, Jeremiah 36:2; Ezekiel 1:3; Acts 1:16; 2 Timothy 3:16–17; 2 Peter 1:20–21; 3:15.

Dictated message, Jeremiah 36:17.

Statement of old manuscript, Mark 16:9–11 (GNB).

Many attempts to record events, Luke 1:1–4.

Holy Spirit's marriage guidance, 1 Corinthians 7:40.

Recognition of inspired Scripture, 1 Corinthians 14:37–38.

Scripture authorship, 2 Corinthians 3:3 (GNB).

Inspiring others, 2 Corinthians 7:13–15.

Personal advice, 2 Corinthians 8:10 (See AB).

Speaking ad lib, 2 Corinthians 11:17 (GNB).

Speaking in human terms, Ephesians 3:2–3.

Encouraging believer, 1 Thessalonians 2:11–12.

Total Word of God, 2 Timothy 3:16 (CEV).

Verbal communication preferred to written, 3 John 13–14.

Message conveyed by angel, Revelation 1:1–3.

Example of verbal inspiration, Revelation 1:11.

See Creativity.

INSTABILITY

Sinful Israel, 1 Kings 14:15.

"Impossible schemes," Psalm 131:1 (CEV).

Too much food, drink, Proverbs 23:20.

Spiritual vagabonds, Jeremiah 2:31.

Love like morning mist, Hosea 6:4.

"Fluttering back and forth," Hosea 7:11 (CEV).

Unstable Galatians, Galatians 1:6–9.

Tossed by waves, Ephesians 4:14.

Carried away by strange teachings, Hebrews 13:9.

See Carnality, Unstable, Weakness.

INSTALLATION

Moses gave control to Joshua, Deuteronomy 31:1–8.

Improvised ceremony for new king, 2 Kings 9:11–13.

See Government.

INSTIGATE See Cause, Guilt.

INSTINCT

Birds avoid nets, Proverbs 1:17.

Preparing for cold weather, Proverbs 6:7–8; 30:25.

Bird migration, Jeremiah 8:7.

See Nature.

INSTRUCTION

Disobeying instructions, Numbers 20:1–12.

Assigned teachers, 2 Chronicles 17:7–9.

Specific instructions, Joshua 8:8.

Corrective instruction, Job 6:24.

Children's instruction, Psalm 78:2–8.

Instruction resisted, Proverbs 5:12–13.

Divine instruction, Jeremiah 16:21.

Specific instructions erecting temple, Ezekiel 43:10–12.

Young men instructed, Daniel 1:3–20.

Two-word command, Mark 2:14.

The law a schoolmaster, Galatians 4:1 (KJV).

See Children, Learning Objectives, Students, Study, Teacher, Teaching.

INSTRUMENT

Writing with ordinary pen, Isaiah 8:1.

Chosen instrument, Haggai 2:23.

Instruments of unrighteousness, Romans 6:13 (Japanese: "container of wickedness").

Evangelism instruments, 1 Corinthians 3:5–9.

See Commitment, Ministry, Servant, Tool.

INSUBORDINATION

Unwilling to do evil, 1 Samuel 22:16–17.

Insubordinate servants, 1 Samuel 25:10.

Wife's insubordination, Esther 1:10–18.

See Disobedience, Stubborn.

INSULT

Deviates' insult to angelic guests, Genesis 19:5.

Silent response to insult, 1 Samuel 10:27.

Wife's insult, 2 Samuel 6:20 (LB).

Bald head insulted, 2 Kings 2:23–24.

Upset by criticism, Job 20:2–3.

Heart-breaking insults, Psalm 69:20 (NRSV).

Hometown insulted, John 1:46.

Cheap wine offered to Jesus, John 19:29 (CEV, NRSV).

"Know-it-all," Acts 17:18 (CEV).

Cretians insulted, Titus 1:12.

Insulting language, 1 Peter 2:1 (GNB).

Insulted for Christ, 1 Peter 4:14.

See Criticism, Defamation, Demean, Scoff, Scorn.

INSURANCE

Built-in safety devices, Deuteronomy 22:8.

Husband's neglect of family, 2 Kings 4:1–7.

Eternal inheritance, 1 Peter 1:3–4.

See Protection.

INSURRECTION

Uprising against Moses, Aaron, Numbers 24:1–25.

Insurrection to be put down, 2 Kings 9:6–7.

Royal insurrections, 2 Kings 12:19–20.

Multiple insurrection, 2 Kings 21:23–24.

Father killed by sons, 2 Chronicles 32:21.

See Purge, Rebellion, Renegade, Traitors.

INTANGIBLE

Intangible made tangible, Colossians 1:15 (GNB).

INTEGRATION

Ways of the heathen, Deuteronomy 18:9.

Dark, lovely, Song of Songs 1:5–6.

Jews and centurion, Acts 10:22, 28, 34–35.

See Racism.

INTEGRITY

Men of integrity, Exodus 18:21.

God's integrity, Numbers 23:19.

Making vow, oath, pledge, Numbers 30:1–2.

Integrity example, 1 Samuel 12:4.

Bribes refused, 2 Samuel 18:12; 1 Kings 13:8.

No need for expense accounts, 2 Kings 12:15.

Limited national integrity, 2 Chronicles 12:12.

Persistent integrity, Job 2:3, 9.

Job's integrity, Job 27:4–6; 29:14; 31:1–40.

Total lack of integrity, Psalm 5:9.

The Lord judges integrity, Psalm 7:8.

In-depth character, Psalm 15:1–5; Philippians 4:8.

Integrity basics, Psalm 24:4 (CEV).

Without deceit, Psalm 32:2.

Practicing deceit, Psalm 101:7.

Generosity, justice, Psalm 112:5.

Mercy, truth, Proverbs 3:3–4.

Motivated by integrity, Proverbs 11:3; 20:7.

Integrity designed by the Lord, Proverbs 16:11.

Wealth of honesty, Proverbs 19:1.

Walk in integrity, Psalm 20:7 (NKJV, NRSV).

Honest answer like kiss, Proverbs 24:26.

Despised integrity, Proverbs 29:10; Amos 5:10.

Faithfulness, truth, Isaiah 25:1 (NKJV).

Integrity brings success, Isaiah 32:8.

Truth nowhere to be found, Isaiah 59:15.

Search for one honest person, Jeremiah 5:1.

Integrity in government affairs, Daniel 6:1–4.
Kings lie to each other, Daniel 11:27.
Dishonest scales, Hosea 12:7.
"Refused to tell lies," Zephaniah 3:13 (CEV).
Speak truth to each other, Zechariah 8:16–17.
Fullest integrity, Luke 16:10.
Discernment of Jesus, John 2:24–25.
Consistent integrity, Romans 12:17.
Importance of paying debts, Romans 13:8.
Living life worthy of calling, Ephesians 4:1.
Neighborhood integrity, Ephesians 4:25.
Dependable honesty, Colossians 3:9–10.
Tirelessly doing right, 2 Thessalonians 3:13.
Faith plus good conscience, 1 Timothy 1:19.
Divine integrity, Titus 1:2.
Integrity in Christian living, Titus 2:7.
Reputed integrity, Hebrews 1:9 (AB).
Truth and love united, 2 John 1:3, 5–6.
Integrity in Heaven, Revelation 14:5.
Liars cast into lake of fire, Revelation 21:8.
City of total integrity, Revelation 21:27.
See Character, Dependability, Honesty, Truth.

INTELLECTUAL

Intellectual humility, Psalm 131:1.
Religion without reality, Proverbs 14:12.
Intellectuals destroyed, Obadiah 8.
Grecian Jews, Acts 9:29.
Demeaned by intellectuals, Acts 17:18 (See Berk.).
Profuse discussion of ideas, Acts 17:21.
Intellectuals, message of Cross, 1 Corinthians 1:18–24.
Spiritual wisdom, 1 Corinthians 2:6.
World's wisdom, 1 Corinthians 3:18–23.
Eyes of heart, Ephesians 1:18–19.
So-called intellectualism, Colossians 2:8 (See AB, LB); 1 Timothy 6:20–21.
God cannot lie, Titus 1:2.
Lacking wisdom, ask God, James 1:5–6.
See Education, Knowledge, Philosophy, Wisdom.

INTELLECTUAL PRIDE

Sarcastic to intellectually proud, Job 12:2–3 (AB).
Warning against intellectual pride, Isaiah 5:21.

Only basis for boasting, Jeremiah 9:23–24.
Fate of intellectuals, Obadiah 8.
Intellectual pride in Athens, Acts 17:16–34.
Folly of intellectual pride, 1 Corinthians 3:18–20.
Intellectual ego, 1 Corinthians 8:1–3; 2 Timothy 3:7.
"Proud knowledge," 2 Corinthians 10:5 (NRSV).
See Intelligence, Pride, Vanity.

INTELLIGENCE

"Wisest ladies," Judges 5:29 (NKJV, NRSV).
Solomon's intelligence, 1 Kings 4:29–34; 10:1–3.
Wild donkey's colt, Job 11:12.
Defending personal intelligence, Job 12:3; 13:2.
Search for intelligence, Job 28:12, 20–28.
Limited intelligence, Psalm 94:11 (LB).
Fear of the Lord, Psalm 111:10.
Intelligence a gift from God, Psalm 119:73 (LB); Daniel 1:17.
Simplistic intelligence, Psalm 119:130.
Intelligence beyond comprehension, Psalm 145:3.
Knowledge, rarest of jewels, Proverbs 20:15.
Brain versus brawn, Proverbs 24:5–6 (RSV).
Those wise in their own eyes, Isaiah 5:21.
Superior to best of king's court, Daniel 1:3–20.
Looking to God for knowledge, Daniel 2:14–28.
"Wise as the gods themselves," Daniel 5:11 (CEV).
Enforced stupidity, Obadiah 8 (LB).
Worldwide spiritual knowledge, Habakkuk 2:14.
Adults like children, Matthew 11:16–17.
Greatest intelligence, Matthew 12:42.
Intelligence of child Jesus, Luke 2:33.
Intelligent boy Jesus, Luke 2:42 (AB).
Intelligence versus faith, 1 Corinthians 1:21 (GNB).
Folly of intellectual pride, 1 Corinthians 3:18–20; 8:1–2.
Faith the ultimate intelligence, 1 Corinthians 3:18–23.
Enlightened heart, Ephesians 1:18–19.

Gift of understanding, 1 John 5:20.
Mind with wisdom, Revelation 17:9.
See Frame-of-Reference, Intellectual Pride, Knowledge, Mind.

INTEMPERANCE

Wine a mocker, Proverbs 20:1.
Excessive food and drink, Proverbs 23:20.
Wine sampling, Proverbs 23:29–31.
Much wine, Ecclesiastes 2:3.
Overt intemperance, Isaiah 5:11.
Laid low by wine, Isaiah 28:1, 7.
Social drinking, Habbakuk 2:15.
Drinking to drown troubles, Luke 21:34.
Continual intemperance, Ephesians 4:19.
See Alcohol.

INTENSITY

Greater, lesser lights, Genesis 1:16.
Increased flood intensity, Genesis 7:18.
Commitment with intensity, Nehemiah 5:14–16.
Path of righteous, Proverbs 4:18.
Full force anger, rage, Ezekiel 5:13 (GNB).
Intensity of God's love, Ephesians 2:4.
See Concentration.

INTENTION

Consciously doing what is right, Leviticus 22:29.
Life's highest intent, Joshua 24:15.
Hiding true intentions, 1 Samuel 16:1–5.
Intent and action, Proverbs 24:8 (LB).
Act of violence, Matthew 26:51, 52; Mark 14:46; Luke 22:49–51; John 18:10, 11.
Priority motivation, Matthew 6:33; John 4:34; Acts 20:24.
God's kind intention, Ephesians 1:9 (NASB).
See Motivation, Objective, Plan, Purpose.

INTERCESSION

Abraham's intercession for Sodom, Genesis 18:20–33.
Reuben's intercession for Joseph, Genesis 37:21–22.
Nephew interceded for uncle, Acts 23:16–22.
Intercession for runaway slave, Philemon 10–11.
See Asking, Mediator, Prayer.

INTERCOURSE See Marriage.

INTEREST

Noninterest loans to poor, Exodus 22:25; Leviticus 25:36–37.
Loans to brothers, Deuteronomy 23:19–20.
Lending money without interest, Psalm 15:5.
Money sharks, Proverbs 28:8.
See Mortgage.

INTERIM

Pause in persecution, Job 21:3.

INTERIOR DECORATING

Jewelled walls, Isaiah 54:12.
Palatial decor, Jeremiah 22:14.

INTERMARRIAGE

Intermarriage with heathen people, Joshua 23:12–13.
Request to marry heathen, 1 Kings 2:13–25.
Pledge not to intermarry with heathen, Nehemiah 10:30.
Children denied native language, Nehemiah 13:23–26.
Intermarriage between Jew and Greek, Acts 16:1.
See Alien, Miscegenation.

INTERMEDIARY

Intermediary for people's welfare, Esther 10:3.
Helping the helpless, Proverbs 31:8–9.
See Adocate, Redeemer.

INTERNSHIP

National internship, Deuteronomy 8:2.
Internship for eagle fledglings, Deuteronomy 32:11.
Refining process, Job 23:10; Zechariah 13:9; James 1:2–3.
See Qualification, Testing.

INTERPRETATION

Speaking in language understood, Isaiah 36:11.
Failure of Nebuchadnezzar's wise men, Daniel 2:1–11.

Daniel interpreted Nebuchadnezzar's dream, Daniel 2:24–49.

Interpretation of tongues, 1 Corinthians 14:26–28.

See Prophecy.

INTIMACY

First human conception, Genesis 4:1.

Meet the Lord three times annually, Deuteronomy 16:16.

"Deep calls to deep," Psalm 42:7.

God as friend, Psalm 54:4 (LB).

Intimate love, Song of Songs 4:16.

God's favorite, Isaiah 44:2 (CEV).

Marital intimacy, Ephesians 5:31–32.

Reach most holy place, Hebrews 6:19 (CEV).

See Marriage, Touch.

INTIMIDATION

Intimidating presence, Numbers 22:3–4.

David intimidated Saul, 1 Samuel 18:29.

Fear tactics, Ezra 4:4.

Hired intimidator, Nehemiah 6:13.

Song of ruthless made silent, Isaiah 25:5.

Many intimidated, Jeremiah 22:1–3 (CEV).

Needlessness of worry, Matthew 6:25–27.

Attempt to intimidate apostles, Acts 4:16–20.

Saul's intimidation of the church, Acts 8:3.

Resisting intimidation, Philippians 1:28 (AB).

No need for intimidation, 1 Peter 3:14 (RSV).

See Menace, Opposition, Threat.

INTOXICATION

Hilarious drinking, Genesis 43:34 (Berk.).

"Good spirits," Ruth 3:7.

See Drunkenness.

INTRIGUE

Sibling intrigue, Genesis 37:18–20.

Intrigue between Tamar, Judah, Genesis 38:11–26.

Ears tingle, 1 Samuel 3:11.

Leave revenge to God's timing, 1 Samuel 26:11.

Gallows for his own neck, Esther 5:11–14; 9:25.

See Drama, Stealth.

INTRODUCTION

Prelude to history, Genesis 1:1, 2.

Public relations approach, 1 Kings 1:42.

Forthright introduction, Job 33:1–5.

Foreword to book of Proverbs, Proverbs 1:1–6.

Terse introduction to birth of Jesus, Matthew 1:18.

Jesus related parable as crowd gathered, Luke 8:4–15.

Jesus introduced Himself, John 1:35–39.

Credentials to visiting instructors, Acts 15:22–31.

Wise introduction of new convert, Colossians 4:9. (See Philemon vv. 10–11.)

Book of Mark, Mark 1:1–2 (LB).

Letters of introduction, Acts 18:27.

Letters of recommendation, 2 Corinthians 3:1–3.

INTROSPECTION

Heart searching, Judges 5:16.

Inviting inner analysis, Psalm 139:23–24.

Need for self-evaluation, Romans 2:17–28; 2 Corinthians 13:5 (See AB).

See Assessment, Renewal, Self-evaluation, Self-interest.

INTRUDER

Aliens succeed above local citizens, Deuteronomy 28:43–44.

Enemy king's intrusion, 2 Chronicles 32:1–3.

Meddling in affairs of others, Proverbs 26:17.

See Foreigner.

INUNDATED *See Swamped.*

INVASION

Earthen ramps, Habakkuk 1:10.

INVENTION

Inventor of harp, flute, Genesis 4:21.

Manufacture of tools, Genesis 4:22.

David's musical instruments, 2 Chronicles 7:6; 29:26.

New machinery, 2 Chronicles 26:15.

Nothing new, Ecclesiastes 1:10.

Schemes of men, Ecclesiastes 7:29.

Wonder upon wonder, Isaiah 29:14.

Prophecy of mere imagination, Ezekiel 13:1–3.

Beyond inventive genius, 1 Corinthians 2:9.

See Original, Skill.

INVENTORY

Tabernacle inventory, Exodus 38:21 (NKJV).

Negative, positive viewpoints, Numbers 13:17–33.

Seventh-year debt cancellation, Deuteronomy 15:1.

Making much of little, 2 Kings 4:1–7.

Finding complete inventory, Job 5:24.

Greedy for gain, Jeremiah 8:10.

Ministry inventory, Acts 20:17–38.

"Check up on yourselves," 2 Corinthians 13:5 (LB).

Test your worth, Galatians 6:4.

See Assessment, Possessions.

INVESTIGATION

Investigated situation at Sodom and Gomorrah, Genesis 18:20–21.

Purpose of research project, 1 Kings 10:6–7.

Glory of kings, Proverbs 25:2.

Investigate ancient paths, Jeremiah 6:16.

See Survey.

INVESTMENT

Owning share of king, 2 Samuel 19:43.

Giving as spiritual investment, Proverbs 19:17.

Risky investment, Ecclesiastes 5:13–14 (LB).

Foreign and diversified investments, Ecclesiastes 11:1–2 (GNB).

Treasures on earth, treasures in heaven, Matthew 6:19–21.

Purchase of sure investment, Matthew 13:44.

False economy of materialism, Mark 8:36.

Gain world, lose self, Luke 9:25.

Wise and unwise use of money, Luke 19:11–27.

Safe eternal investment, 1 Timothy 6:17–19 (LB).

See Finance, Possessions, Property.

INVIGORATE

Strength for weary, Isaiah 40:29–31.

INVISIBLE

Reality of the invisible, 1 Peter 1:8–9.

Kingdom of God within you, Luke 17:20–21.

Intangible made tangible, Hebrews 11:1–3, 6.

See Faith, Reality, Unseen.

INVITATION

Invitation to once-wayward Israel, 2 Chronicles 30:6–9.

Deceitful invitation, Nehemiah 6:1–3.

Call to reason, Isaiah 1:18.

Cost-free invitation, Isaiah 55:1; Revelation 22:17.

Great invitation, Isaiah 55:1–13.

Superlative invitation, Jeremiah 33:3.

"It isn't too late," Joel 2:12 (CEV).

Invitation to come and rest, Matthew 11:28.

Rejecting wedding invitation, Matthew 22:1–14.

Follow Jesus, Mark 1:17.

Take up the cross, Mark 10:21.

Invitation to banquet, Luke 14:17.

Declined invitation, Acts 18:19–21.

Urge, appeal, beg, Romans 12:1 (CEV, NASB, NRSV).

Invited to heaven's wedding supper, Revelation 19:9.

See Call, Opportunity.

INVOICE

Discounting the bill, Luke 16:1–8.

See Cost, Debt, Obligation.

INVOLVEMENT

Compassion to foreign child, Exodus 2:1–10.

Lacking wholehearted involvement, Numbers 32:11.

Helping others, Deuteronomy 22:1–4.

Foolish involvement with one's neighbor, Proverbs 6:1–5.

Involvement resulting in healing, Mark 2:1–5.

Reluctant involvement in need of others, Mark 6:35–43.

Good Samaritan, Luke 10:30–37.

Hired hand, John 10:12–13.

Poured out like drink offering, Philippians 2:17; 2 Timothy 4:6.

Concern for others' development, Colossians 2:1–5.

See Caring, Compassion, Empathy, Sharing.

IRAQ

Egypt, Israel alliance, Isaiah 19:23–25 (LB).

IRON

Primitive bronze, iron, Genesis 4:22.

Iron bed, Deuteronomy 3:11.

Floating axhead, 2 Kings 6:4–7.

Ore from the earth, Job 28:2.

Iron shackles, Psalm 105:18.

Smelting various metals, Ezekiel 22:20.

Iron gate, Acts 12:10.

See Natural Resources.

IRONY

A wife's biting tongue, 2 Samuel 6:20.

Elijah's irony concerning Baal, 1 Kings 18:27.

Job and his accusers, Job 12:2.

Ironical declaration of "freedom," Jeremiah 34:17.

Taunted by Roman soldiers, Matthew 27:27–29.

Ironical evaluation of weak Christians, 1 Corinthians 4:8–18.

See Satire.

IRRATIONAL

Accused of being irrational, Job 18:2.

Irrationally drunk, Isaiah 28:7.

Family of Jesus thought Him insane, Mark 3:20–21.

Beside ourselves, 2 Corinthians 5:13.

See Insanity.

IRRELIGIOUS

Breaking Sabbath, Exodus 31:12–17.

Irreligious generation, Judges 2:10.

Work of the Lord in decline, 1 Samuel 3:1.

Prophet's message defied, Jeremiah 43:1–3.

Pagan beyond redemption, Jeremiah 51:9.

Disrespect for sanctuary, Ezekiel 25:1–4.

Hindered from worship by evil deeds, Hosea 5:4.

Laughing at truth spoken by Jesus, Matthew 9:23, 24.

See Apostasy, Rebellion.

IRRESPONSIBLE

Oath taken irresponsibly, Leviticus 5:4.

Irresponsible house maintenance, Ecclesiastes 10:18.

Deliberately writing falsehoods, Jeremiah 8:8.

False prophets, Jeremiah 23:16–18.

Prophets who see nothing, Ezekiel 13:1–3.

Forgetting necessities, Mark 8:14.

See Careless, Lethargy.

IRREVERENT

Worship, play, Exodus 32:6.

Destroying blasphemer, Leviticus 24:14–16.

Immorality in sacred places, 1 Samuel 2:22.

Irreverent accident, 2 Samuel 6:6–7 (GNB).

Total irreverence, 2 Chronicles 15:3.

Insulting the Lord, 2 Chronicles 32:17.

Destroyed reverence, Job 15:4 (Berk.).

Putting God to the test, Psalm 78:18–20, 41, 56.

Challenging God, Isaiah 5:18–19.

Irreverent fasting, Isaiah 58:4–5.

Laughing at Jesus, Matthew 9:23–24.

Irreverent use of temple, Matthew 21:12–13.

Communion table gluttony, 1 Corinthians 11:20–21 (LB).

Temple court defiled, Revelation 11:1–2.

See Blasphemy, Carnality, Profanity.

IRRIGATION

Earth's pre-deluge irrigation, Genesis 2:4–6, 10.

Dispute over water rights, Genesis 26:19–22.

Irrigation unnecessary, Deuteronomy 11:10.

Good land, bad water, 2 Kings 2:19–22.

Altered water flow, 2 Chronicles 32:30.

Abundant water, Psalm 65:9.

JANITOR

Spring water into valleys, Psalm 104:10 (KJV).

Controlled watercourse, Proverbs 21:1.

Reservoirs for irrigation, Ecclesiastes 2:6 (See NASB).

Abundance of water, Isaiah 41:18–20.

Thirsty land, Isaiah 44:3; 58:11.

Well-watered garden, Jeremiah 31:12.

See Agriculture, Farming, Water.

IRRITATION

Thorns in side, Judges 2:3.

Vinegar to teeth, smoke to eyes, Proverbs 10:26.

Not irritated by instruction, Proverbs 16:20.

Irritating person, Proverbs 19:13.

Irritable, touchy, 1 Corinthians 13:5 (LB).

Divine irritation, Hebrews 3:17 (AB).

See Abrasion, Conflict, Opposition.

ISLAM

First Arab/Israel tension, Genesis 21:8–10. (Note verse 16, near destruction Arab race.)

Ishmael as Muslim's father, Genesis 21:13; 25:12–18.

First instance of Arab opposing Israel, Nehemiah 2:19–20.

Ridicule of Jews, Nehemiah 4:1–10.

Islamic awakening, Psalm 68:31 (GNB).

Islam versus Israel, Psalm 83:1–8.

Highway for Arab world, Isaiah 19:23.

Lebanon, Israel, Isaiah 35:1–2.

Fate of those who oppose Israel, Isaiah 60:12.

Libya, Arabia, Ezekiel 30:5.

Arabs at Pentecost, Acts 2:11.

See Arab, Jihad.

ISLAND

Maritime people, Genesis 10:5 (KJV).

ISRAEL

Covenant with Abram, Genesis 15:1–5 (See Jeremiah 33:22).

Israel scattered, regathered, Nehemiah 1:8–9.

First example Arab/Israel tension, Nehemiah 2:19–20.

Sanballat's ridicule of Jewish capability, Nehemiah 4:1–10.

Fear of Israel, Joshua 2:9 (LB).

Contemporary prosperity, Psalm 85:1 (GNB).

Pray for peace of Jerusalem, Psalm 122:6.

Middle East alliance, Isaiah 11:10–11.

Suggested air defense, Isaiah 31:5.

Prophecy of abundance, Isaiah 32:2.

Gathering of Jews to Israel, Isaiah 43:5–7; Jeremiah 31:10.

Desert becomes garden, Isaiah 51:3; Jeremiah 32:42–44.

Return to homeland, Isaiah 60:1–22 (LB).

Fate of those who oppose Israel, Isaiah 60:12.

Promised to dispersed Israelites, Jeremiah 16:14–15.

Restoration of Israel as a nation, Jeremiah 23:5–8; 30:8–17; 33:23–26.

Nation abandoned, Jeremiah 33:24–26 (LB).

The Lord identified in history, Ezekiel 20:42.

Nugget description of Israel's restoration, Ezekiel 28:25.

Friction with Egypt, Ezekiel 29:16.

God will bring Israel home, Ezekiel 36:12 (CEV).

Valley of dry bones, Ezekiel 37:1–14.

International involvement, Ezekiel 38:1–13.

Divine promise to Israel, Hosea 14:4–7.

Israel's certain future, Amos 9:15.

Danger of harming Israel, Obadiah 10–15.

Israel to refresh world, Micah 5:7 (LB).

Permanent home for Jews, Amos 9:15; Zephaniah 3:20.

"Apple of His eye," Zechariah 2:8.

Lesson of fig tree, Mark 13:28–31.

Paul changed outreach to Gentiles, Acts 18:4–6.

Salvation of Israel, Romans 11:25–27.

See Messiah, Prophecy.

ITINERARY

Travel by stages, Genesis 13:3 (Berk.).

Journey recorded by Moses, Numbers 33:1–49.

Journey with the Lord's approval, Judges 18:6.

Itinerary for Jesus, Matthew 9:35; Mark 1:38; Luke 4:42–44; 8:1; 9:6.

No need for expense money, Mark 6:8–11.

Places Paul needed to visit, Acts 19:21.

Itinerary changed to avoid conflict, Acts 20:2–3.

Detailed listing of itinerary, Acts 21:1–8.

Ports visited en route to Rome, Acts 27:1–8.

Anticipated stopover, Romans 15:23–24.

Hospitality to itinerant minister, 1 Corinthians 16:10–11.

See Journey, Map, Schedule, Travel.

IVORY

Palatial spendor, 1 Kings 10:18; 22:39.

Imported luxury, 1 Kings 10:22; Ezekiel 27:6, 15.

Luxurious sleep, Amos 6:4.

J

JAIL

House arrest, Jeremiah 37:15.
Adventure in Philippian jail, Acts 16:23–34.
Jail ministry, Philemon 9 (See AB, GNB).
See Prison.

JAMBOREE

Big celebration, 2 Samuel 6:5.

JANITOR

Priestly janitors, 2 Chronicles 29:16–18.
Doorkeeper in God's house, Psalm 84:10.

JEALOUSY

Negative attitude of Cain, Genesis 4:3–7.
Greed over scarcity of land, Genesis 13:5–7.
Attitude of Ishmael toward Isaac, Genesis 21:8–10.
Envy caused by wealth, Genesis 26:12–14.
Sibling jealousy, Genesis 37:3–4.
Divine jealousy, Exodus 20:5; Deuteronomy 32:16, 21; Psalm 78:58; Isaiah 30:1–2.
God's name is "Jealous," Exodus 34:14.
Legal specifications for jealous husband, Numbers 5:12–31.
Jealousy of Miriam, Aaron, Numbers 12:1–9.
Not sharing honors, Judges 12:1–3.
Facing competition, 1 Samuel 17:55–58.
King's jealousy of subject, 1 Samuel 18:8.
Jealous citizens, 2 Samuel 19:43.
Marital jealousy, 1 Chronicles 15:29.
Poison to soul, Job 5:2.
Envious hostility, Psalm 68:16 (Berk.).
Envy of prosperity, Psalm 73:3–12.
Jealous husband, Proverbs 6:34.
Cancerous jealousy, Proverbs 14:30 (GNB).
Do not envy sinners, Proverbs 23:17.
Jealousy more cruel than anger, Proverbs 27:4.
Neighborhood envy, Ecclesiastes 4:4.
Jealous love, Song of Songs 8:6.
Idol of jealousy, Ezekiel 8:5.
Divine jealousy subsided, Ezekiel 16:42.
No fault found, Daniel 6:4.
Burning with jealousy, Zechariah 8:2.
Parable of vineyard workers, Matthew 20:1–16.

Jealousy within family, Luke 15:11–32.
Dissension, jealousy in church, Acts 6:1.
Religious jealousy, Acts 13:45.
Opposition caused by jealousy, Acts 17:5.
Spiritual envy, Romans 10:19.
Do not compare yourself with others, Galatians 6:4–5.
Envy among those who preach Christ, Philippians 1:15.
Jealousy cause of murder, 1 John 3:12.
See Covet.

JESUS

Conceived by Holy Spirit, Matthew 1:20.
Led by Holy Spirit, Luke 4:1.
Bread of life, John 6:35.
Light of the world, John 8:12.
The Door, John 10:9.
Way, truth and life, John 14:6.
True vine, John 15:1–7.
Melchizedek, Jesus, Hebrews 7:3 (AB).
Jesus Christ Himself, the Word of life, 1 John 1:1–4 (See John 1:1–3).
Advocate with Heavenly Father, 1 John 2:1–2.
Unique name for Jesus, Revelation 3:14.
Rider on white horse, Revelation 19:11–16.
Totality of the Son of God, Revelation 22:13.
See Begotten, Christ, Creator, Messiah, Redeemer.

JEW

Jewish brothers, Romans 7:1 (LB).
See Israel.

JEWELRY

Nose ring, Genesis 24:47.
Betrothal gifts, Genesis 24:52–53.
Hindrance to righteousness, Genesis 35:2–4.
Rings on fingers, Genesis 41:42; Esther 8:8; Luke 15:22.
Items of plunder, Exodus 3:22; 11:2; 12:35; 33:4–6; Isaiah 3:18–23.
Jewelry removed during mourning, Exodus 33:4.

Given to the Lord, Exodus 35:22; Numbers 31:50–52.

Jewelry and cosmetics snatched away, Isaiah 3:18–24.

Maiden and bride, Jeremiah 2:32.

Dull gold, strewn jewels, Lamentations 4:1.

Silver, gold, jewelry lose value, Ezekiel 7:19, 20.

Adulterous charms, Hosea 2:2 (Berk.).

Becoming like the Lord's signet ring, Haggai 2:23.

Pearl of great value, Matthew 13:45, 46.

Hairstyles and jewelry, 1 Timothy 2:9–10.

Inner beauty, 1 Peter 3:3–4.

Jewels adorning evil woman, Revelations 17:4.

See Cosmetics, Ring.

JIHAD

Jihad principle, John 16:2.
See Islam.

JOGGING *See Athletics, Running.*

JOKE

Impractical joking, Proverbs 26:18–19.

Coarse joking, Ephesians 5:4.
See Humor.

JOURNALISM

Dishonest writing, Jeremiah 8:8.

Write message plainly, Habakkuk 2:2.

News of Jesus' miracles, Matthew 9:26.
See Literature, Writing.

JOURNEY

Discontented journey, Exodus 16:1–3; 17:1–2.

Divinely directed journey, Numbers 9:23.

Destiny set for rebellious people, Numbers 14:35.

Wilderness itinerary, Numbers 21:10–19.

Wicked men's journey, Job 22:15.

Mountains turned into roads, Isaiah 49:11.

Destination unknown, Hebrews 11:8.
See Caravan, Destiny, Itinerary, Migration, Tourist, Travel.

JOY

Trumpets of rejoicing, Numbers 10:10 (RSV).

Joy to the Lord, Deuteronomy 30:10 (LB).

Enjoyment of salvation, 1 Samuel 2:1; Ezra 6:22; Psalms 13:5; 16:5–11; 20:5; 64:10; Habakkuk 3:18.

Divine attribute, 1 Samuel 2:21.

Joy of the Lord your strength, Nehemiah 8:10.

Scriptural source of joy, Nehemiah 8:17–18.

"Oh, the joy," Psalm 2:12 (Berk.).

Spiritual joy, material blessing, Psalm 4:7.

Joy in pleasant places, Psalm 16:5–6.

Joy replaces sorrow, Psalm 30:11–12.

River of delight, Psalm 46:4.

Joy in evangelism, Psalm 51:12–13.

Sole source true joy, Psalm 84:11.

Joy of revival, Psalm 85:6.

All fountains in the Lord, Psalm 87:6–7.

Irrepressible joy, Psalm 97:11 (AB).

Serve the Lord with gladness, Psalm 100:1–2.

Sorrow of death brings joy to the Lord, Psalm 116:15.

Delight in Bible study, Psalm 119:24; Jeremiah 15:16.

Soulwinner's tears and joy, Psalm 126:5–6.

Joy of salvation, Isaiah 12:2.

Universal rejoicing, Isaiah 44:23.

Nature rejoicing, Isaiah 55:12.

Weeping for joy, Jeremiah 31:9.

False joy of drunkenness, Jeremiah 51:39.

Clapping hands at fate of Nineveh, Nahum 3:19.

Jump for joy, Malachi 4:2 (CEV).

Rewarded with happiness, Matthew 25:21.

Christmas joy, Luke 2:10.

Joy in heaven over a soul's salvation, Luke 15:6–10.

Oil of joy, Hebrews 1:9.

Joy in suffering, James 1:2–6; 1 Peter 4:13.
See Contentment, Happiness.

JUDGE

Righteous judgment, Genesis 18:25; Deuteronomy 1:12–17.

Spiritual quality of a judge, Exodus 18:21–22; Ezra 7:25.

Priests and judges work together, Deuteronomy 17:8–11.

Judge's sentencing of criminal, Deuteronomy 25:1–3.

Judging temporal and spiritual wrongs, 1 Samuel 2:25.

Dishonest courts, 1 Samuel 8:1–3.

Judges as servants of God, 2 Chronicles 19:5–10.

God as judge, Ecclesiastes 3:17; Jeremiah 11:20.

Judge others, judge yourself, Romans 2:1.
See Judgment, Justice, Litigation.

JUDGMENT

Judgment inflicted, Genesis 19:11.

Swallowed up by earth, Numbers 16:31–34.

Death by fire during worship, Numbers 16:35.

Old Testament justice, 2 Samuel 1:1–16.

Famine as judgment, 2 Samuel 21:1.

God's judgment, man's, 2 Samuel 24:13–14.

Sword of judgment, 1 Chronicles 21:27–30.

Judgment fairness, Nehemiah 9:33 (See LB).

Meeting God in court, Job 9:32 (Berk.).

Self-concern for error, Job 19:4.

Let God be judge, Job 32:13.

Reward for one's deeds, Psalm 62:12.

Time set for judgment, Psalm 75:2 (NRSV).

God withheld judgment, Psalm 78:38.

God judges with equity, Psalm 98:8–9.

All-seeing judge, Proverbs 15:3.

Guilty, innocent, Proverbs 17:15.

National judgment, Isaiah 1:7–9.

Coming day of judgment, Isaiah 2:12–21.

Babylon, as prophesied, Isaiah 13:19–22.

Judgment likened to storm, Isaiah 28:2.

Those who trust in their wickedness, Isaiah 47:10–11.

Cup of divine fury, Isaiah 51:17 (NKJV).

Wicked plight, righteous fulfillment, Isaiah 65:13–14.

Destruction of wealth, security, Jeremiah 5:17.

Harvest judgment, Jeremiah 8:13.

Mercy follows judgment, Jeremiah 12:14–17.

Varied judgment, Jeremiah 15:1–2.

Peril of forsaking the Lord, Jeremiah 17:13.

Breaking potter's jar, Jeremiah 19:1–13.

Absence of joy and productive activity, Jeremiah 25:10.

Cup of God's wrath, Jeremiah 25:15–29.

Ironical declaration of "freedom," Jeremiah 34:8–22.

Second judgment upon evil king, Jeremiah 36:27–32.

Certain judgment, Jeremiah 37:9–10.

Multiple judgment, Jeremiah 44:1–14.

Inevitable judgment, Jeremiah 44:15–28.

"Sword of the Lord," Jeremiah 47:6–7.

Tyre, city of luxury, brought down, Ezekiel 27:1–36; 28:1–19.

The Lord judges like enemy, Lamentations 2:2, 5.

"I will show no pity," Ezekiel 7:4 (CEV).

Judgment justified, Ezekiel 14:22 (LB).

Instrument of judgment, Ezekiel 21:9 (LB).

Full penalty, Ezekiel 22:31 (LB).

Books of judgment, Daniel 7:10.

Certain judgment, Hosea 9:7.

Coming day of the Lord, Joel 2:1–2.

Judgment Valley, Joel 3:2 (CEV).

"I won't change my mind," Amos 1:3 (CEV).

For continued sinning, certain judgment, Amos 1:3, 6, 9, 11, 13; 2:1, 4, 6 (Note nature of sin in each of these judgments).

Chosen people's severe judgment, Amos 3:2 (LB).

Judgment for all nations, Obadiah 15.

Divine response to those who repent, Jonah 3:10.

The Lord slow to anger, Nahum 1:3.

Time of great judgment, Zephaniah 1:15 (CEV).

Silver and gold valueless in judgment, Zephaniah 1:18.

God of judgment becomes God of mercy, Zechariah 8:14–15.

Judgment concludes Old Testament, Malachi 4:6.

The Savior who brought a sword, Matthew 10:34–35.

Parables concerning final judgment, Matthew 13:36–43, 47–50.

Separating sheep from goats, Matthew 25:31–35.

Jesus eager for judgment to come, Luke 12:49.

Rejoicing angels, Luke 15:10.

As in days of Noah, Luke 17:26–30.

Jesus came to save, not judge, John 3:17 (NASB).

Redeemer, Judge, John 5:22–27.

Graves give up both good and evil, John 5:28–29.

Right judgment, John 7:24.

Jesus came to save, not judge, John 12:47.

Wisdom of Gamaliel, Acts 5:30–40.

Guilty in judgment of others, Romans 2:1.

Judged according to personal record, Romans 2:5–11.

No condemnation in Christ, Romans 8:1–2.

Only God can judge, Romans 8:33.

Earth's certain judgment, Romans 9:28.

Congregational discipline, 1 Corinthians 5:1–13.

Importance of self-judgment, 1 Corinthians 11:28–32.

Importance of conduct on earth, 2 Corinthians 5:10.

No favoritism with God, Colossians 3:25.

Excluded from God's presence, 2 Thessalonians 1:9.

Causing difficulty among believers, Titus 3:10–11.

Penalty paid for everyone, Hebrews 2:9.

Forbidden God's rest, Hebrews 3:11.

Like double-edged sword, Hebrews 4:12.

Nothing kept secret from God, Hebrews 4:13.

Judgment for sin, Hebrews 10:28–31 (See AB).

Christ will return to reward faithful, Hebrews 10:35–38.

All must give account to God, 1 Peter 4:4–6.

Sure judgment upon false teaching, 2 Peter 2:1–10.

Facing our Lord unashamed, 1 John 2:28.

Bed of suffering, Revelation 2:20–22.

Like a thief, Revelation 3:3.

Redeemer qualified to judge, Revelation 5:1–9.

Four horsemen, Revelation 6:1–6.

Earth shaken by great earthquake, Revelation 6:10–17.

Sounding forth cry of doom, Revelation 8:13.

Those not having seal of God on foreheads, Revelation 9:4.

Judgment and rewards, Revelation 11:18.

Conclusion of God's wrath, Revelation 15:1.

Beverage of judgment, Revelation 16:5, 6.

Agony of those who refuse to repent, Revelation 16:10–11.

Binding of Satan, Revelation 20:1–3.

Satan, false prophet and the unredeemed, Revelation 20:7–15.

Cast into lake of fire, Revelation 21:8.

When the die is cast, Revelation 22:11.

Reward for what one has done, Revelation 22:12.

See Condemnation, Guilt, Punishment.

JURY

Protect the innocent, Exodus 23:7.

Priests assist judge, Deuteronomy 17:8–12.

Ten-man jury, Ruth 4:1–4.

Infamous "trial" of Jesus, Matthew 27:11–26; Mark 15:1–15; Luke 23:1–25; John 18:28–40.

See Court, Verdict.

JUSTICE

Mood of Old Testament justice, 2 Samuel 1:1–16.

David guilty, not followers, 2 Samuel 24:12–17.

Justice to murderer's sons, 2 Kings 14:5–6.

Justice to unjust Haman, Esther 7:1–10.

"Perfectly fair" judge, Psalm 7:11 (LB).

Unjust judges, Psalm 58:1–2.

Future divine justice, Psalm 98:8–9.

The Lord defends the poor, Proverbs 22:22–23.

Those who convict the guilty, Proverbs 24:24–25.

Justice, injustice, Proverbs 28:8 (LB).

Fate of good, evil, Isaiah 65:13–14.

Disputing God's justice, Ezekiel 33:10–20.

"Judges are wolves," Zephaniah 3:3 (CEV).

Savior, Judge, John 5:22–27.

Justice for Judas, Acts 1:18–20.
Case against Paul, Acts 23:23–30.
Impartial justice, 1 Peter 1:17.
God's justice, Revelation 16:5–7.
See Judge, Judgment, Jury, Litigation, Mercy, Verdict.

JUSTIFICATION

Judgment justified, Ezekiel 14:22 (LB).
Mortal righteousness before God, Job 25:4.
Job justified, Job 42:7–10.
No one righteous, Psalm 143:2.
One who made justification possible, Isaiah 53:4–6.
Mode of justification, John 5:24; Acts 13:39; Romans 1:16–17.
Faith as synonym for righteousness, Romans 4:5–25.

Justification by faith, Romans 5:1; Galatians 2:16; 3:24.
See Pardon, Forgiveness, Redemption.

JUVENILE DELINQUENT

Wild parties, Numbers 25:1 (LB).
Old Testament delinquency procedure, Deuteronomy 21:18–21.
Death of delinquent son, 2 Samuel 18:19–53.
Delinquent teenager became king, 2 Kings 24:8–9.
Hateful, deceitful, rebellious child, Psalm 7:14 (CEV).
Children not delinquent, Proverbs 22:6.
Peril to those who cause delinquency, Luke 17:1–2.
Evil desires of youth, 2 Timothy 2:22.
See Disobedience, Rebellion, Renegade.

K

KEY

Key with authority, Isaiah 22:22.
Kingdom keys, Matthew 16:19.
Keys of death and hades, Revelation 1:18.
David's key, Revelation 3:7.
Key to the abyss, Revelation 9:1; 20:1.
See Fetters, Prison.

KICK

Kick in the hinder parts, Psalm 78:66 (KJV).

KIDNAPPING

Kidnapping and rescue, Genesis 14:12–16.
Joseph's kidnapping, Genesis 37:25–28.
Death penalty for kidnapping, Exodus 21:16; Deuteronomy 24:7.
Kidnapped wives, Judges 21:15–23.
Kidnapped families, 1 Samuel 30:3–5.
"Fatherless orphan," Job 24:9 (Berk.).
See Captive.

KINDLING

Twigs gathered for fires, Isaiah 27:11.
Twigs set ablaze, Isaiah 64:1–2.
See Cooking, Fire.

KINDNESS

Enemy subdued by kindness, 2 Kings 6:18–23.
"Plumage of kindness," Job 39:13 (Berk.).
Returning good for evil, Genesis 50:15–21.
Kindness to man, daughters, Exodus 2:16–21.
Kindness to strangers, Leviticus 19:34.
Kindness rewarded, 1 Samuel 30:11–18.
Enemy shown kindness, 2 Kings 6:8–23.
Kindness of pagan king, 2 Kings 25:27–30.
Divine loving-kindness, Psalm 23:6 (NASB).
Outreach to others, Proverbs 14:21.
Mother's kindness, Proverbs 31:20.
Evil name, deeds of kindness, Jeremiah 52:31–34.
Joseph's kindness to Mary, Matthew 1:19.
Kindness as spiritual service, Matthew 25:34–36; Luke 6:34–35.
"Jesus was kind," Romans 1:5 (CEV). (Note use of *kind, kindness* throughout CEV translation.)
Kindness in action, Romans 12:10–15.
Love is kind, 1 Corinthians 13:4.
Christian life-style, Ephesians 4:32; Colossians 3:12.

Experienced kindness, 1 Peter 2:3.
Faith plus kindness, 2 Peter 1:5–7.
See Benevolence, Charity, Condolence, Consideration, Consolation, Patience, Philanthropy.

KING *See Royalty.*

KINGDOM

Reign from India to Nile, Esther 1:1.
Purpose of God's eternal reign, Psalm 9:7–8.
Coming Kingdom of God, Daniel 2:44; Revelation 17:14.
Not of this world, John 18:36.
Domain, kingdom, Colossians 1:13 (NASB).
See Government, Nations.

KISS

First recorded kiss involved deceit, Genesis 27:22–27.
Men kissing, Genesis 27:27; 33:4; 45:15; 48:10; Exodus 4:27; 18:7; 1 Samuel 20:41; Luke 15:20; Acts 20:37.
Emotional kiss, Genesis 29:11; 45:15.
Parting kiss, Ruth 1:14.

Kiss of death, 2 Samuel 20:9–10; Luke 22:47–48.
Throw a kiss, Job 31:27 (NASB).
Departure from parents, 1 Kings 19:20.
Taste of bridal lips, Song of Songs 4:11.
Kiss an idol, Hosea 13:2 (NASB).
Betraying kiss, Matthew 26:48; Luke 22:48.
Kiss of contrition, Luke 7:38.
Worshipful kiss, Acts 20:37–38.
Holy kiss, Romans 16:16.
See Affection.

KITCHEN

Bedroom, kitchen frogs, Exodus 8:3.
Meat cooked in sacred place, Exodus 29:31.
Ancient dish washing, 2 Kings 21:13.
Cooking pots in the Lord's house, Zechariah 14:20–21.
See Cooking, Food, Gourmet, Meals, Menu.

KNEELING

Royal humility, 1 Kings 8:54; 2 Chronicles 6:13.

Kneeling in contrition, Ezra 9:5.

Humility in the Lord's presence, Psalm 95:6.

Every knee will bow, Isaiah 45:23; Romans 14:11; Philippians 2:9–11.

Courageous prayer, Daniel 6:10.

Divine example, Luke 22:41.

Martyr's posture, Acts 7:59–60.

Kneeling together, Acts 20:36.

Prayer meeting on beach, Acts 21:5.

See Genuflect, Prayer, Reverence.

KNOWLEDGE

Inception of secular knowledge, Genesis 3:5–6, 22–23.

Solomon's knowledge, 1 Kings 4:29–34; 10:1–3.

Secret things belong to God, Deuteronomy 29:29.

Source of knowledge and wisdom, Proverbs 2:1–5.

Divine performance, Proverbs 3:19–20.

Prudent knowledge, Proverbs 14:8.

Quest for knowledge, Proverbs 15:14.

Knowledge brings sorrow, Ecclesiastes 1:18.

Seduced by knowledge, Isaiah 47:10.

Gift from God, Daniel 1:17.

Knowledge increased, Daniel 12:4.

Common knowledge, Luke 1:1 (AB).

Unable to comprehend, Luke 9:44–45.

Putting knowledge into action, John 13:17.

Coming fullness, 1 Corinthians 13:9–12.

Knowing the Lord, Philippians 3:8.

See Education, Frame-of-Reference, Teaching, Wisdom.

KOSHER

Restricted meat, Genesis 32:32.

Kosher food, Judges 13:4 (LB).

Non-kosher food, Ezekiel 44:6–7.

Demonic pork, Mark 5:11–13.

All foods kosher, Mark 7:19 (LB).

See Diet, Food.

L

LABOR

Task of producing food, Genesis 3:17–19.

Value of laborers, Genesis 14:21.

Female labor, Genesis 29:9.

Management and labor, Exodus 5:2–5.

Day of rest, Exodus 20:9–11.

Honest work, honest pay, Leviticus 19:13; Luke 10:7.

Unacceptable earnings from prostitution, Deuteronomy 23:18.

Wages paid when due, Deuteronomy 24:14–15.

Foreign laborers, Deuteronomy 29:11.

Prayer for laborer's skills, Deuteronomy 33:11.

Woodcutters, water carriers, Joshua 9:26–27.

Slave labor force, 2 Samuel 20:24 (CEV).

Forced labor, Exodus 6:5; 1 Kings 9:15.

Foreign labor, 1 Chronicles 22:2.

Honest workers, 2 Chronicles 34:12 (CEV).

Working from morning to night, Nehemiah 4:21.

Hired man, Job 7:1.

Servants ignore master, Job 19:15–16.

Labor, manager, Psalm 123:2.

Lazy employees, Proverbs 10:26 (NRSV).

Rewarding manual labor, Proverbs 12:14 (NRSV).

Blessing of hard labor, Proverbs 14:23.

Avoid excessive perks, Proverbs 29:21 (GNB).

Joy in working, Proverbs 31:13 (NASB).

Meaningless toil, Ecclesiastes 4:8.

Hard work induces sound sleep, Ecclesiastes 5:12.

Laboring with all your might, Ecclesiastes 9:10.

Coping with angry boss, Ecclesiastes 10:4 (CEV).

Exploited workers, Isaiah 58:3; Jeremiah 22:13.

Foreign laborers, Isaiah 60:10.

Unfair treatment, Jeremiah 22:14 (CEV).

Labor unrest incited, Ezra 4:1–6.

Defrauding laborers, Malachi 3:5.

Concern for servant, Matthew 8:5–13.

Labor shortage, Matthew 9:37–38.

Students, servants beneath teachers, masters, Matthew 10:24.

Only a carpenter's son, Matthew 13:55; Mark 6:1–3.

Labor relations, Matthew 20:9–16; 21:33–41.

Endeared servant, Luke 7:2 (NKJV).

Good service rewarded, Luke 12:35–40.

Unable to do hard work, Luke 16:3 (NRSV).

Continually working, John 5:17.

Labor, ministry, Acts 18:3; 2 Thessalonians 3:6–10.

Trade unions, Acts 19:23–27.

Wages an obligation, not gift, Romans 4:4.

Wearying labor, 1 Corinthians 4:12 (AB).

Payment for labor, 1 Corinthians 9:7.

Deceitful workers, 2 Corinthians 11:13.

Aim for perfection, 2 Corinthians 13:11 (NIV).

Manual labor, Ephesians 4:28.

Doing good work as unto the Lord, Ephesians 6:5–8.

Slave, masters, Ephesians 6:9; Colossians 3:22–25; 4:1; 1 Timothy 6:1–2; Titus 2:9–10.

Working overtime, 1 Thessalonians 2:9.

Troublesome metalworker, 2 Timothy 4:14.

Dignity of labor, Acts 20:34 (GNB); Titus 3:14.

Slave who became brother, Philemon 8–21.

Work before rest, Hebrews 4:11.

Failing to pay laborer's wages, James 5:4.

See Employment, Management, Servant, Wages, Work (Physical).

LAD

Boys, lads, 1 John 3:7 (AB).

LADY

"A lady forever," Isaiah 47:7 (KJV).
See Women.

LAITY

Only prophets offer sacrifices, 1 Samuel 13:8–15.

Those assigned as gatekeepers, 1 Chronicles 9:22–27.

Laymen worshiping, 2 Chronicles 11:16 (See LB).

Ruling elders, Ruth 4:1–2; Proverbs 31:23.

Amos, the shepherd, Amos 1:1.

Ministry of aged widow, Luke 2:36–38.

Lay synagogue leadership, Mark 5:22; Luke 4:20–21.

Laity teaching and preaching, Acts 15:35.

Outstanding worker, Romans 16:13 (GNB).

Director of public works, Romans 16:23.

Paul worked to support ministry, 2 Thessalonians 3:6–10.

Troublesome layman, 2 Timothy 4:14.

Priesthood for believers, 1 Peter 2:5.

See Administration, Leadership, Ministry, Servant, Service, Stewardship.

LAMB

Lamb of God, Isaiah 53:7; John 1:29; 1 Corinthians 5:7; 1 Peter 1:19; Revelation 5:6; 6:1; 15:3; 17:14; 19:9; 21:22.
See Sheep, Shepherd.

LAME

Limitations of lameness, Leviticus 21:18; 2 Samuel 5:8.

Child crippled by fall, 2 Samuel 4:4.

The lame walk, Matthew 15:31; 21:14; Luke 7:22.

Crippled from birth, Acts 3:2; 14:8.
See Handicap.

LAMPS

Miracle light, Genesis 15:17.

Night light, Exodus 27:20, 21; Leviticus 24:2–4.

The Lord our lamp, 2 Samuel 22:29.

Lamp of wicked put out, Job 18:6; 21:17.

Keep lamp burning, Psalm 18:28.

Lamp of the Lord, Proverbs 20:27.

Lamp not hidden, Matthew 5:15.

Profuse use of lamps, Acts 20:8.
See Illumination, Lantern, Light.

LAND

Original proprietor, Genesis 13:14–17.

Divine ownership of all land, Exodus 19:5; Leviticus 25:23; Psalm 24:1.

Widow's land sale, Ruth 4:3–9.

Profitable land, Ecclesiastes 5:9.

Mortgaging land to buy food, Nehemiah 5:3.

Rented land, Matthew 21:33–41; Mark 12:1–9; Luke 20:9–16.

Purchased land, Genesis 33:19; 47:20; Ruth 4:3; 2 Samuel 24:24; Proverbs 31:16; Jeremiah 32:9; Luke 14:18; Acts 1:18.

Potter's field, Matthew 27:7.

See Estate, Ownership, Possessions, Property, Real Estate.

LANDFILL

Jerusalem landfill, 1 Kings 9:24 (CEV); 11:27 (GNB).

LANDMARK

Desert boundary, Exodus 23:31.

Permanent landmarks, Deuteronomy 19:14; 27:17; Proverbs 22:28; 23:10.

Jawbone hill, Judges 15:16–17 (LB).

Landmarks moved, Job 24:2; Hosea 5:10.

LAND REFORM

Distribution of land, Numbers 26:53–56.

LANDSCAPE

Pleasant landscape, Numbers 24:6.

Landfill, 1 Kings 9:24 (CEV); 11:27 (CEV).

Look to the hills, Psalm 121:1.

Flower-decked landscape, Song of Songs 2:12; Matthew 6:28–29.

Desert landscape, Isaiah 35:1.

LANGUAGE

Universal language, Genesis 11:1 (See AB).

Language confounded, Genesis 11:5–9.

Language influenced by intermarriage, Nehemiah 13:23–26.

Teaching in foreign language, Isaiah 28:11.

Aramaic replaced Hebrew, Isaiah 36:11.

Enemy's foreign language, Jeremiah 5:15.

Literary device concerning freedom, Jeremiah 34:17.

Multiple languages, Daniel 4:1.

Divine linguistics, Acts 2:8.

Effect of speaking in people's language, Acts 22:2.

See Communications, Speech, Linguistics.

LANTERN

Miner's lantern, Job 28:3 (CEV).

LARCENY *See Robbery, Stealing, Thieves.*

LARGE

Army of locusts, Joel 2:1–9.

LASCIVIOUSNESS

Perils to consider, Proverbs 5:3–13.

Lure of evil, Proverbs 7:6–27.

Overt perversion, Romans 1:27; 1 Corinthians 5:1.

Clear warning of Scripture, 1 Corinthians 6:9–18.

Unrepentant impurity, 2 Corinthians 12:21.

Lost sensitivity, Ephesians 4:19.

Sodom and Gomorrah, Jude 7.

See Debauchery, Lust, Immorality.

LASHES

Forty lashes maximum, Deuteronomy 25:2–3.

See Whipping.

LAST DAYS

Migration to Lord's mountain, Isaiah 2:2; Micah 4:1.

Sealed until last days, Daniel 12:9.

Outpouring in last days, Acts 2:17.

Life-styles of last days, 2 Timothy 3:1–9; 2 Peter 3:3.

See Second Coming.

LAST SUPPER *See Communion, Passover.*

LAUD

Evaluation of John the Baptist, Matthew 11:11–14.

Complimenting those previously rebuked, 2 Corinthians 7:14.

See Commendation, Compliment, Praise.

LAUGHTER

Laughter out of place, Genesis 18:10–15.

Divine laughter, Psalm 2:4.

Laughter with aching heart, Proverbs 14:13.

Meaningless laughter, Ecclesiastes 2:2.

Sorrow better than laughter, Ecclesiastes 7:3.

Laughter of fools, Ecclesiastes 7:6.

Scornful laughter, Ezekiel 25:1–4.

Laughter today, tears tomorrow, Luke 6:25; James 4:9.

See Amusement, Joy, Humor.

LAUNDRY

Washerman's field, Isaiah 7:3.

Using bleach, Malachi 3:2 (LB).

Whiter than any bleach, Mark 9:3 (NIV).

LAW

Commands, decrees, laws, Deuteronomy 6:1.

Respect to church, court, Deuteronomy 17:12.

Sorrowful reaction to law, Nehemiah 8:9–12.

Good, just laws, Nehemiah 9:13 (LB).

Priests as judges, Ezekiel 44:24.

Valid only during lifetime, Romans 7:1 (GNB).

Law points to Christ, Galatians 3:23–25; Hebrews 10:1 (See GNB).

Guarded by the law, Galatians 3:23 (Berk.).

Use the law lawfully, 1 Timothy 1:8 (NASB, NKJV).

Law is for lawbreakers, 1 Timothy 1:9.

See Court, Judgment, Justice, Lawyer, Verdict.

LAWLESS

Lawless sin, 1 John 3:4 (AB).

LAWYER

Legal cases decided, Exodus 18:13 (CEV).

Cheating in court, Job 31:21 (GNB).

Avoid hasty litigation, Proverbs 25:8.

"Lord, you are my lawyer," Lamentations 3:58 (LB).

Settle out of court, Matthew 5:25.

Lawyer pharisee, Matthew 22:35 (NKJV).

Mosaic lawyer, Luke 7:30 (AB).

Carnal lawyers, Luke 10:25; 11:46.

Defending oneself, Acts 26:1.

Christian versus Christian, 1 Corinthians 6:1.

Zenas, the lawyer, Titus 3:13.

See Jury, Law, Litigation.

LAZY

Too much sleep, Proverbs 6:10–11; 20:13; 24:33.

Blessing of hard work, Proverbs 14:23.

Similarity of slackness, destruction, Proverbs 18:9.

Lazy man like swinging door, Proverbs 26:14 (GNB).

Too lazy to eat, Proverbs 26:15.

Those who do nothing, Isaiah 30:7.

Dozing, daydreaming, Isaiah 56:10 (CEV).

Lax in the Lord's work, Jeremiah 48:10.

Disciples sleeping while Jesus prayed, Mark 14:32–41.

"Do not be lazy," Romans 12:11 (GNB).

"Loaf around," 2 Thessalonians 3:6–7, 10 (CEV).

Living lazy lives, 2 Thessalonians 3:11 (GNB).

Busybodies, 2 Thessalonians 3:11–12.

"Never be lazy," Hebrews 6:12 (CEV).

See Lethargy.

LEADERSHIP

Man's authority over creation, Genesis 1:26.

Chosen for greatness, Genesis 18:16–19.

Resentment toward youth in leadership, Genesis 37:5–11.

Youth in government service, Genesis 41:46.

Joseph's fairness to Egyptians, Genesis 47:13–26.

Humbly facing leadership responsibility, Exodus 3:11.

Lacking fluent speech, Exodus 4:10.

Dissatisfaction with leaders, Exodus 5:15–21; 15:22–24; 16:2–3; Numbers 14:1–4.

Decline caused by absence of good leader, Exodus 32:1–6.

Respect for leader, Exodus 33:8.

Leading disgruntled congregation, Numbers 11:4–15.

Humble Moses, Numbers 12:3 (See Berk.).

Revolt against leaders, Numbers 14:1–30; 20:1–5.

Vindication by earthquake, Numbers 16:28–34.

Debilitating guilt of leadership, Numbers 20:12.

Future accomplishment assured, Numbers 21:34.

Training for future leadership, Numbers 27:18–23.

Delegated leadership, Deuteronomy 1:12–13.

Impartial leadership, Deuteronomy 1:17.

God-given leadership, Deuteronomy 2:25.

Encouragement to leader, Deuteronomy 3:28.

Faithful leadership, Deuteronomy 8:2, 15.

Choosing right leader, Deuteronomy 17:14–15.

Time for leader to retire, Deuteronomy 31:2.

Mighty Joseph, Deuteronomy 33:17 (GNB).

Transfer of leadership, Deuteronomy 34:9.

Strong and courageous, Joshua 1:6 (See LB).

Courage under fire, Joshua 1:18.

Giving specific orders, Joshua 8:8.

Honoring former leader, Joshua 22:1–5.

Joshua's farewell, Joshua 23:1–8.

Good leader's influence, Joshua 24:31.

Rapport between leaders and people, Judges 5:2.

Leader's assessment of constituency, Judges 6:15; 1 Samuel 9:21.

Example for leadership success, Judges 7:17–18.

Reward of accomplishment, Judges 8:22–23.

Evil conduct following death of good leader, Judges 8:33–34.

Trees seek king, Judges 9:7–15.

Too talented to lead only one family, Judges 18:19.

From divine leadership to mortal, 1 Samuel 8:1–9.

God's preference, man's, 1 Samuel 10:17–19.

King Saul rejected by some, 1 Samuel 10:26–27.

King Saul's long reign over Israel, 1 Samuel 13:1.

Compromising leadership, 1 Samuel 15:24.

Confrontation between two kings, 1 Samuel 17:32–37.

Respect for disliked leader, 1 Samuel 24:1–11; 26:9–10.

David's respect for King Saul, 1 Samuel 24:1–7; 26:7–11.

Leader blamed for disaster, 1 Samuel 30:1–6.

David replaced Saul, 2 Samuel 2:1–7.

First words of new leader, 2 Samuel 2:5–7.

Struggle between houses of David, Saul, 2 Samuel 2:8–32.

Leadership struggle, 2 Samuel 3:1.

Long reign of King David, 2 Samuel 5:4.

Chosen to be king, 2 Samuel 7:8.

Humble leadership, 2 Samuel 7:18–24 (LB).

Success brought fame to David, 2 Samuel 8:13.

Justice to all, 2 Samuel 8:15.

Son conspired to supplant father, 2 Samuel 15:1–37; 16:5–8.

Grief put aside to continue leading people, 2 Samuel 19:1–8.

David's rapport with men of Judah, 2 Samuel 19:14.

Owning share of king, 2 Samuel 19:43.

Success through divine guidance, 2 Samuel 22:44–45.

Duty of good leadership, 2 Samuel 23:3–4.

David refused water which cost lives of his men, 2 Samuel 23:15–17.

David made Solomon king, 1 Kings 1:28–53.

Solomon's mercy to Adonijah, 1 Kings 1:43–53.

Joyful transfer of leadership, 1 Kings 1:47–48.

Prayer for wisdom, discernment, 1 Kings 3:5–15.

Childlike attitude, 1 Kings 3:7; Jeremiah 1:6.

Solomon's wisdom with disputing mothers, 1 Kings 3:16–28.

Delegating responsibility, 1 Kings 4:7.

Organization for building temple, 1 Kings 5:12–18.

King Solomon's admonition to people, 1 Kings 8:55–61.

Rehoboam succeeded father, Solomon, 1 Kings 11:41–42.

Advice of elders rejected, 1 Kings 12:1–11.

Servant leadership, 1 Kings 12:7; Matthew 20:28; Mark 10:43–44; John 13:5, 14, 22; Acts 20:18–19 (GNB); 1 Corinthians

16:15–16; 2 Corinthians 4:5 (See AB); Colossians 1:24–26; Titus 2:7; Hebrews 3:5; 1 Peter 1:12.

Transfer of leadership, 2 Kings 2:1–18.

Young kings of Judah, 2 Kings 23:31, 36; 24:8, 18.

David's openness to advice, 1 Chronicles 13:1.

Good leadership, 1 Chronicles 18:14.

Exemplary stewardship by leaders, 1 Chronicles 29:9.

"Undisputed ruler," 2 Chronicles 1:1 (CEV, LB).

First things first, 2 Chronicles 1:7–12.

Good advice spurned, 2 Chronicles 10:1–15.

Influence of backslidden leader, 2 Chronicles 12:1 (LB).

King's righteous example ignored, 2 Chronicles 27:2.

Delegated responsibility, Nehemiah 3:1–32.

Disgruntled people distress leader, Nehemiah 5:1–12.

No perks for leader, Nehemiah 5:14–18.

Looking out for people's welfare, Esther 10:3.

Leader consults others, Esther 1:13.

Lost reason, Job 12:24.

Scorned leader, Job 19:15.

Job remembered when he was treated with courtesy, Job 29:7–13.

Great men not always wise, Job 32:9–13.

Farmer unable to manage wild ox, Job 39:9–12.

Leader to strangers, Psalm 18:43–45.

Spiritual leader, Psalm 21:7.

Anointed above others, Psalm 45:7 (Berk.).

Leadership by small tribe, Psalm 68:27.

Divine use of human leaders, Psalm 77:20.

Integrity and skill, Psalm 78:72.

God's sure choice, Psalm 89:19–29.

Blessing upon those who do what is right, Psalm 106:3.

Leaders come and go, Psalm 109:8.

Death terminates leadership, Psalm 146:3–4.

National leadership lacking, Proverbs 11:14.

Blessing of righteousness in nation, Proverbs 14:34.

Kings search out concealed matters, Proverbs 25:2.

Corrupt leader, Proverbs 29:4 (LB).

King and teacher, Ecclesiastes 1:12.

Respect for king, Ecclesiastes 8:4.

Distorted leadership, Ecclesiastes 8:9.

Prejudiced leaders, Ecclesiastes 10:5–7.

Inexperienced leadership, Ecclesiastes 10:16 (See CEV, GNB); Isaiah 3:4.

Carnal leaders, Isaiah 1:23.

Qualified by cloak, Isaiah 3:6.

Nation no stronger than leader, Isaiah 7:7–9 (GNB).

Guiding people astray, Isaiah 9:16.

Fools, deceived leaders, Isaiah 19:13.

Leaders captured without fight, Isaiah 22:3.

Put out of office, Isaiah 22:19.

Firmly in position, Isaiah 22:23.

"Leaders are like babies," Isaiah 28:9 (CEV).

Drunkenness impairs decisions, Isaiah 28:7.

Example of faithful leadership, Isaiah 37:1–38.

Dangerous king called "bird of prey," Isaiah 46:11 (LB).

Strength to declare God's message, Jeremiah 1:6–10, 17–19.

Shepherds after God's own heart, Jeremiah 3:15.

Leaders, priests, prophets lose heart, Jeremiah 4:9.

Leaders, people turn against the Lord, Jeremiah 5:3–5.

Potential poison of wealth, power, Jeremiah 5:27–29.

Lax leaders delight people, Jeremiah 5:31.

Shepherds who do not seek the Lord, Jeremiah 10:21.

King, queen brought to judgment, Jeremiah 13:18.

Leaders rendered powerless, Jeremiah 15:1.

Judgment upon rebellious shepherds, Jeremiah 25:34–38.

Leader from within ranks of those to be led, Jeremiah 30:21.

Both king and priest forsaken, Lamentations 2:6.

Burden of Jeremiah for people, Lamentations 3:40–51.

Leaders confer in home, Ezekiel 8:1 (CEV).

Misguided by evil government, Ezekiel 11:1–4.

Wicked officials in city, Ezekiel 22:27 (See CEV).

"World's most powerful king," Ezekiel 26:7 (CEV).

Kings come and go, Daniel 2:21.

Leader's recognition of sovereign God, Daniel 4:34–37.

King at age of sixty-two, Daniel 5:30–31.

President Daniel, Daniel 6:2 (KJV).

"Leaders like crooks," Hosea 5:10 (CEV).

Ignoring God's guidance in choice of leadership, Hosea 8:4.

King of little value to wayward people, Hosea 10:3.

Prophet and leader, Hosea 12:13.

Respect for leaders, Hosea 13:1 (CEV).

Prophet given revelation of the Lord, Amos 3:7.

Complacency among national leaders, Amos 6:1.

Ineffective leadership, Habakkuk 1:4.

Leaderless people, Habakkuk 1:14.

National leaders punished, Zephaniah 1:8.

"Rulers cheat in court," Micah 7:3 (CEV).

"These goats," Zechariah 10:3 (LB).

Broken staff called Favor, Zechariah 11:10.

Murderous leadership of King Herod, Matthew 2:13–18.

Jesus taught with authority, Matthew 7:28–29.

Centurion unworthy to have Jesus in his home, Matthew 8:5–10.

Instructions to twelve apostles, Matthew 10:5–42 (See 11:1).

Laity in synagogue, Mark 5:22; Luke 4:20–21.

Enjoying control of people, Mark 10:42 (CEV).

"Everyone's slave," Mark 10:44–45 (CEV).

Night of prayer before important decision, Luke 6:12–16.

Guidelines for purposeful ministries, Luke 6:12–49.

Respect without obedience, Luke 6:46.

Management evaluated, Luke 16:2.

"Crooked judge," Luke 18:6 (CEV).

Jesus demonstrated servant leadership, John 13:3–9.

Jesus instructed apostles, Acts 1:1–2.

Delegating distribution of welfare to widows, Acts 6:1–4.

False leadership of Herod, Acts 12:21–23.

Conflict between Paul, Barnabas, Acts 15:36–40.

Giving encouragement, Acts 20:1.

Unbelievers serve God's purposes, Romans 9:17.

Diligent leadership, Romans 12:8.

"Accept humble duties," Romans 12:16 (GNB).

Respect, honor to all, Romans 13:7–8.

Those who follow personalities, 1 Corinthians 1:12.

Food offered to idols, 1 Corinthians 8:5–13 (LB).

Humility in leadership, 2 Corinthians 1:24.

Rapport with those being led, 2 Corinthians 7:2–4.

Rules avoided, 2 Corinthians 8:8–9 (GNB).

Sharing concerns of leader, 2 Corinthians 8:16.

Paul's admitted trickery, 2 Corinthians 12:16.

Avoiding harsh use of authority, 2 Corinthians 13:10.

Paul's rank in Judaism, Galatians 1:13–14.

Leaders meeting privately, Galatians 2:2 (NRSV).

Assumed importance, Galatians 2:6 (See CEV).

Leaders as pillars, Galatians 2:9.

Legalist's plight, Galatians 5:3 (LB).

Penalty for misleading others, Galatians 5:10.

"Gently lead," Galatians 6:1–2 (CEV).

For the good of all, Ephesians 4:11–13.

Submissive leadership, Ephesians 5:21.

Leadership in the home, Ephesians 5:22–33.

Paul's great love for followers, Philippians 1:3–11.

Leader's imprisonment caused others to witness, Philippians 1:12–14.

Leadership in absentia, Philippians 2:12, 14.

Exemplary leadership, Philippians 4:9.

Qualifications of Christ, Colossians 1:15–20.

Relentless effort on behalf of followers, Colossians 1:28–29.

Christ head over all, Colossians 2:9–10.

Paul's use of names, Colossians 4:7–17.

Leadership model, 1 Thessalonians 2:1–16.

Concern for constituents, 1 Thessalonians 3:1–3 (LB).

Desire to be overseer, 1 Timothy 3:1.

Recent convert unqualified, 1 Timothy 3:6.

Communication in person, by writing, 1 Timothy 3:14–15.

Servant, apostle, Titus 1:1.

Second level leadership, Titus 1:5.

Elder's credentials, Titus 1:5–9.

"Bullies," Titus 1:7 (CEV).

Leadership with authority, Titus 2:15.

Request instead of command, Philemon 8–10.

High priest selected from among people, Hebrews 5:1.

Admitted weakness, Hebrews 5:1–4 (GNB).

Gentle mark of good leadership, Hebrews 5:2–3.

Leaders who are examples, Hebrews 13:7.

Respect for leaders, Hebrews 13:17.

If you lack wisdom, ask God, James 1:5–6.

Exercising Heaven's wisdom, James 3:17–18.

Exemplary leadership, 1 Peter 5:2–5 (AB).

Joy of good report about followers, 3 John 3–4.

Wrong kind of authority in congregation, 3 John 9, 10.

Delegation of satanic authority, Revelation 13:2.

Temporary authority of beast, Revelation 13:5.

Demons influence leaders, Revelation 16:13–14.

One-hour reign of ten kings, Revelation 17:12.

See Administration, Laity.

LEARNING

Put words into mouths, Deuteronomy 31:19 (KJV).

Eagle training young to fly, Deuteronomy 32:11.

Hard questions, correct answers, 1 Kings 10:1–3.

God-given ability to understand Scripture, Psalm 119:125.

Continued learning sustains memory, Proverbs 19:27 (CEV).

Eye and ear never satisfied, Ecclesiastes 1:8.

Learning through guidance and correction, Jeremiah 10:23–24.

God-given intelligence, Daniel 1:17.

Progressive learning, Luke 8:10 (AB).

Fluent and intelligent, Acts 7:22.

Sharing insights into Scriptures, Acts 18:24–26.

Learning under famous teacher, Acts 22:3.

Learn what pleases the Lord, Ephesians 5:10.

Pointless quarreling over words, 2 Timothy 2:14.

Advanced learning, Hebrews 6:1.

Continual review, 2 Peter 1:12–15.

See Intelligence, Intellectual, Student, Teaching.

LEARNING OBJECTIVES

Reachable learning objectives, Deuteronomy 30:11.

Purpose of research project, 1 Kings 10:6–7.

Stated learning objectives, Proverbs 1:1–6.

Divine objective understood, Isaiah 2:3; 54:13.

Deliberately writing falsehoods, Jeremiah 8:8.

Daughters taught how to wail, Jeremiah 9:20.

School of hard knocks, Lamentations 3:30 (CEV).

Training for Daniel, friends, Daniel 1:3–4.

Communicating God's message to children, Joel 1:1–3.

Like teacher, like student, Luke 6:40.

Good teaching put into action, John 13:17.

Teaching the most excellent way, 1 Corinthians 12:31.

Making joy complete, 1 John 1:1–3.

See Counsel, Education.

LEATHER

Rejected hide, Exodus 29:14.
Leather retained by priest, Leviticus 7:8.
Leather girdles, 2 Kings 1:8.
Leather belt, Mark 1:6.
Simon the tanner, Acts 10:6.

LEAVEN

Procedure for making bread, Exodus 12:34.
Unleavened bread of necessity, Exodus 12:39.
Suitable for offering to the Lord, Leviticus 7:13.
No yeast with meat, Leviticus 10:12.
Boasting about bread, Amos 4:5.
Leaven as type of sin, 1 Corinthians 5:6–8.
See Bread, Fermentation.

LECHEROUS

Lecherous justice, 1 Samuel 8:3.
Premeditated lechery, Proverbs 1:10–13.
Unrequited appetites, Isaiah 56:11.
Greedy for gain, Jeremiah 8:10.
Hatching unlaid eggs, Jeremiah 17:11.
Rich at others' expense, Habakkuk 2:9 (CEV).
Trampling upon others, Amos 2:7.
Lecherous piety, Micah 3:11.
Greedy, lecherous Judas, Matthew 26:15–16.
Misused slave girl, Acts 16:19.
Cheating, polluting, Amos 8:5–6.
"Taken advantage of no one," 2 Corinthians 7:2 (NRSV).
See Greed, Selfishness.

LEFTOVERS

Loaves, fishes, John 6:12 (Berk.).

LEGACY

Inheritance of a spirit, 2 Kings 2:9–10.
No concern for survivors, Job 21:21.
Legacy of wisdom, skill, Ecclesiastes 2:21 (NASB).
Ask for ancient paths, Jeremiah 6:16.
Communicating God's message to children, Joel 1:1–3.
Probate of a will, Hebrews 9:16–17.
See Inheritance.

LEGAL

Loss of family records, Nehemiah 7:64.
See Court, Justice, Verdict.

LEGALISM

Circumcision at advanced age, Genesis 17:10–27.
Abstaining from fruit of grape, Numbers 6:2–4.
Gathering wood on Sabbath, Numbers 15:32–36.
Ultimate demands for obeying law, Joshua 1:18.
Good laws and regulations, Nehemiah 9:13.
Preventing merchandising on Sabbath, Nehemiah 13:15–19.
Taking the Bible as legalistic, Isaiah 28:13.
Worship based on rules, Isaiah 29:13.
Religious works involved in idolatry, Isaiah 46:1.
True meaning of circumcision, Jeremiah 4:4.
Picking corn on Sabbath, Matthew 12:1–8; Luke 6:1–5.
Traditions ignored, Matthew 15:1–9.
What enters mouth, what leaves, Matthew 15:10–20; Mark 7:15–23.
Fullest measure of the law, Matthew 23:23.
Some fast, others feast, Mark 2:18–20; Luke 5:33 (LB).
Sabbath legalism, Mark 2:23–27.
Good called evil, Mark 3:1–4.
"Petty rules," Mark 7:7 (LB).
Nullifying God's word, Mark 7:13 (See NKJV).
Rich young man's legalism, Mark 10:17–27.
Fulfilling requirements, Luke 2:39.
Legalism versus Christian virtue, Luke 10:25–37.
Burden of legality, Luke 11:45–46.
Spiritual growth hindered, Luke 11:52.
Jesus carefully watched by Pharisees, Luke 14:1.
Arguing over ceremonial washing, John 3:25.
Overt legalism, John 5:10.
Serving God seven days a week, John 5:16–17.
Moses as accuser, John 5:45.

Those who professed to keep the law, John 7:19.

Peter's vision of clean and unclean, Acts 10:9–16; 11:4–10.

Deliverance from legalism, Acts 10:24–28.

Old Testament doctrine, New Testament experience, Acts 15:1–11.

Synagogue ruler's conversion, Acts 18:8.

Paul's preaching contrary to law, Acts 18:13.

Appeasing legalists, Acts 21:17–26.

Case against Paul, Acts 23:23–30.

Respect for Old Testament, Acts 24:14–15.

Circumcised but not legalistic, Romans 2:25–27.

Faith upholds the law, Romans 3:31.

Faith of Abraham, Romans 4:1–3.

"Law came stealing in," Romans 5:20 (Berk.).

Purpose of the law, Romans 5:20–21.

Dead to legalism, Romans 7:4.

Passions aroused by legalism, Romans 7:5.

Purpose of the law in revealing sin, Romans 7:7–12, 14.

Conflict between faith, works, Romans 9:30–33; Galatians 3:2–5.

Establishing one's own righteousness, Romans 10:3.

Avoid controversy, Romans 14:1 (GNB).

No food unclean, Romans 14:14.

Liberty without license, 1 Corinthians 6:12.

Restricted freedom, 1 Corinthians 8:9 (CEV).

Legalism versus courtesy, 1 Corinthians 10:27–30.

Letter kills, Spirit gives life, 2 Corinthians 3:6.

Legalism dispute, Galatians 2:3, 11–21.

Elementary principles, Galatians 2:20–21 (NASB).

Legalism's death knell, Galatians 3:10–14; Philippians 3:8–9 (See AB).

Law points to Christ, Galatians 3:23–25 (See NRSV).

Legalism to fullest extent, Galatians 5:3.

Folly of legalism, Galatians 5:12.

Basic intent of law, Galatians 5:13–15.

Salvation by faith, not works, Ephesians 2:8–9.

Legalism annulled, Ephesians 2:15 (AB).

Paul's confidence in flesh, Philippians 3:2–11.

Let not others judge, Colossians 2:16.

Self-abasement, Colossians 2:18 (NRSV).

Dead to legalism, Colossians 2:20.

Understanding the law, 1 Timothy 1:8–11.

Theology of demons, 1 Timothy 4:1–4.

Talkers, deceivers, Titus 1:10–14.

Avoid legalistic arguments, Titus 3:9.

Salvation not possible through law, Hebrews 7:11.

Law makes nothing perfect, Hebrews 7:18–19.

Need for new covenant, Hebrews 8:7.

Regulations for worship, Hebrews 9:1.

Law pointed to perfection in Christ, Hebrews 10:1.

Physical act cannot bring spiritual result, Hebrews 10:2–4.

Old legalism, new liberty, Hebrews 12:18–24.

Grace versus ceremony, Hebrews 13:9.

Not redeemed with silver, gold, 1 Peter 1:18–19.

See Work (Spiritual).

LEGENDS

Harmful legends, 1 Timothy 1:4 (GNB).

LEGIBILITY *See Handwriting.*

LEGS

Legs too long, Leviticus 21:18 (Berk.).

LEISURE

Leisure leads to lust, 2 Samuel 11:1–5.

Take time for leisure, Mark 6:31.

See Holiday, Recreation, Relaxation, Rest.

LENT

Going without dessert, Daniel 10:3 (LB).

LEPROSY

Enforced isolation, Leviticus 13:4; Numbers 5:1–3.

Healed and cleansed, Leviticus 14:1–57 (KJV).

Suddenly leprous, Numbers 12:10.

Experience and healing of Naaman, 2 Kings 5:1–14.

Priest suddenly afflicted, 2 Chronicles 26:19.

Lifelong ailment of king, 2 Chronicles 26:21.

Therapy for leprosy, Deuteronomy 24:8; Matthew 8:2.

Ten healed, one expressed gratitude, Luke 17:12–19.

See AIDS, Disease.

LESBIANS

Women lusting for each other, Romans 1:26.

See Deviate, Homosexual.

LETHARGY

Lag behind, Deuteronomy 25:17–19.

Doing nothing, Isaiah 30:7.

Lethargic women, Isaiah 32:9.

Slumbering Jonah, Jonah 1:5–6.

Gethsemane lethargy, Matthew 26:40–45; Haggai 1:3–4.

Asleep in church, Acts 20:9.

Wake up from slumber, Romans 13:11.

See Complacency, Laziness.

LETTER WRITING

Letter with murderous motive, 2 Samuel 11:14–15.

Wrong address, 2 Kings 5:1–8.

Placing disturbing letter before the Lord, 2 Kings 19:14–19.

Letters for safe conduct, Nehemiah 2:7–9.

Unsealed open letter, Nehemiah 6:1–13.

Letter of defense, Acts 23:23–34.

Our lives communicate Christ's message, 2 Corinthians 3:1–3.

Beautiful letter, Philemon 1–25.

See Communication, Correspondence.

LEVITY

A little foolishness, 2 Corinthians 11:1.

See Humor.

LEWDNESS *See Depravity, Immorality, Nudity.*

LIAR

Bloodthirsty and deceitful liars, Psalm 5:6.

Deceit forbidden in God's house, Psalm 101:7.

"All men are liars," Psalm 116:11.

The Lord detests lying, Proverbs 12:22.

Wealth derived by lying, Proverbs 21:6.

Tongues taught to lie, Jeremiah 9:5.

Deceitful heart, Jeremiah 17:9.

"Hypocrisy of liars," 1 Timothy 4:2 (NRSV).

See Deceit, Dishonesty.

LIBATION

"Poured out as a libation," 2 Timothy 4:6 (NRSV).

LIBERALISM

Wayward community, Deuteronomy 13:12–18.

Words detect false prophet, Deuteronomy 18:21–22.

Law book lost in temple, 2 Chronicles 34:14–15.

Man's way, wrong way, Proverbs 14:12; 16:25.

Pleasant sermons requested, Isaiah 30:10.

People love dishonest prophets, priests, Jeremiah 5:31; 6:13.

Deceptive words, Jeremiah 7:4–8.

False Scripture interpretation, Jeremiah 8:8.

Preaching erroneous promises, Jeremiah 14:11–16.

Priests persecuted prophet, Jeremiah 20:1–2.

Evil prophets' ministry, Jeremiah 23:10–14.

"Preached in the name of Baal," Jeremiah 23:13 (CEV).

Man's words, God's words, Jeremiah 23:16–18.

Prophets proclaimed lies, Jeremiah 27:14–15; Ezekiel 22:28.

Lost sheep, false shepherds, Jeremiah 50:6; Micah 3:5–7.

Imagined prophecies, Ezekiel 13:2–16.

Recognizing the Lord, Molech, Zephaniah 1:5.

Arrogant prophets, profane priests, Zephaniah 3:4 (See GNB).

Priests give false teaching, Malachi 2:7–9.

Teaching untruth, Matthew 5:19.

Public acts of vain charity, Matthew 6:1–4.

False teaching discerned, Matthew 7:15–20.

Those who simply say "Lord, Lord," Matthew 7:21–23.

Blind leaders of blind, Luke 6:39.

Missing purpose of worship, Matthew 23:23–24.

Attempt to deny resurrection of Jesus, Matthew 27:62–66; 28:11–15.

Mere lip service, Mark 7:6–7.

Persecuted for proclaiming resurrection, Acts 4:1–4.

Modified use of Jesus' name, Acts 19:13.

"Twist God's message," 2 Corinthians 4:2 (CEV).

God's lavished grace, Ephesians 1:7–8.

Do not lie, Colossians 3:9.

Role of pride in false teaching, 1 Timothy 6:3–5.

Godless chatter, opposing ideas, 1 Timothy 6:20–21.

False teaching like gangrene, 2 Timothy 2:17 (NRSV).

Only a form of godliness, 2 Timothy 3:5.

Deceivers are themselves deceived, 2 Timothy 3:13.

Rejecting sound doctrine, 2 Timothy 4:3–4.

See Apostasy, Cult, Heresy, Modernism, Syncretism.

LIBERALITY

Giving and gaining, Proverbs 11:24–25 (KJV).

See Giving.

LIBERATION THEOLOGY

Injustice to the poor, Exodus 23:6; Leviticus 19:15; Psalm 12:5; Ecclesiastes 5:8; Amos 5:11–12.

Corrupt law courts, Deuteronomy 16:18–20; Psalm 82:2–4; Ecclesiastes 3:16; 5:8; Mark 14:53–65.

Concern for widows, Deuteronomy 24:17.

Honest government, Psalm 72:1–2; Proverbs 29:26; Jeremiah 22:1–4.

Fiscal dishonesty, Proverbs 28:8.

Discredited government leaders, Proverbs 31:4–5.

Oppressed peoples, Ecclesiastes 4:12; Amos 2:7.

Unjust laws, Isaiah 10:1–2.

Human rights, Lamentations 3:34–36; Isaiah 1:17.

See Human Relations, Inequity, Unfairness.

LIBERTY

King imprisoned and set free, 2 Kings 24:15; 25:27–29.

Greatest freedom, Psalm 119:45.

Proclaim freedom, Isaiah 61:1.

Conditional freedom, Jeremiah 34:8–11.

Feasting not fasting, Luke 5:33 (LB).

Truth sets us free, John 8:31, 32, 36.

Peter's vision of clean and unclean, Acts 10:9–16; 11:4–10.

Deeper meaning of deliverance from legalism, Acts 10:24–28.

Visitation privilege for prisoner, Acts 27:3.

Liberty no excuse for sin, Romans 6:1, 2.

Freedom from mastery of sin, Romans 6:14.

Once slaves to sin, now slaves to righteousness, Romans 6:18.

Atonement assures freedom free from legality, Romans 7:1–6.

Restricted liberty, 1 Corinthians 6:12 (GNB).

Liberty without license, 1 Corinthians 6:12 (See CEV).

Exercise of liberty eating, drinking, 1 Corinthians 8:7–13.

Restricted freedom, 1 Corinthians 8:9 (CEV).

Unmuzzled ox, 1 Corinthians 9:9–14.

Freedom in believer's conduct, 1 Corinthians 10:23–33.

Freedom in the Spirit, 2 Corinthians 3:17.

Human standards, 2 Corinthians 10:2 (NRSV).

From law to grace, Galatians 4:1–7 (Also previous chapter).

Called to be free, Galatians 5:13.

Filled with knowledge of God's will, Colossians 1:9–12.

Rescued from dominion of darkness, Colossians 1:13–14.

Word of God not chained, 2 Timothy 2:8–9 (See CEV).

Legalism of old, liberty of new, Hebrews 12:18–24.

Timothy released from prison, Hebrews 13:23.

The law that gives freedom, James 2:12–13.

Liberty misused, 1 Peter 2:16; Jude 4.

See Freedom.

LIBRARY

Many books, Ecclesiastes 12:12.
World of books, John 21:25.
See Literature, Writing.

LICE

Lice infestation, Exodus 8:16 (NKJV).
Picking lice from clothing, Jeremiah 43:13 (CEV, NRSV).

LICENSE

Carrying rules too far, Mark 2:23–27.
No license to sin, Romans 6:1; 1 Peter 2:16.
Liberty without license, 1 Corinthians 6:12.

LICENTIOUS

Wiles, treachery, Genesis 39:6–18.
Playing with fire, Proverbs 6:27–29.
Haughty women, Isaiah 3:16.
Adultery committed in profusion, Jeremiah 3:6.
Lust, promiscuity of two sisters, Ezekiel 23:1–49.
Continual lust for more, Ephesians 4:19.
See Adultery, Immorality, Lasciviousness.

LIE

Purge lying, Deuteronomy 19:16–19.
Lying to protect life, 1 Samuel 20:5–7.
Divinely approved discrepancy, 2 Chronicles 18:18–22.
Condemned by one's own words, Job 15:6.
"God's breath," Job 27:3–4 (Berk.).
Totally untrue, Psalm 5:9 (LB).
Punishment for false witness, Proverbs 19:5.
Prophets proclaimed lies, Jeremiah 27:14–15.
Initially positive response to false prophecy, Jeremiah 28:1–17 (Note verses 5–9).
Prophet commanded by king to lie, Jeremiah 38:24–27.
Believing lie, Jeremiah 43:1–7.
Two kings lie to each other, Daniel 11:27.
Tongues that speak deceitfully, Micah 6:12.
Contradictory reports, Matthew 26:60–61 (LB).
Jesus called a liar, Matthew 27:63 (CEV).
False witness against Jesus, Mark 14:53–59.
Worst kind of lie, James 3:14 (LB).
See Counterfeit, Deceit, False, Falsehood.

LIFE

From earth, to earth, Genesis 3:19.
"Life giving one," Genesis 3:20 (LB).
Shortened lifespan, Genesis 6:3.
"Satisfied with life," Genesis 35:29 (Berk.).
Life as pilgrimage, Genesis 47:9.
Value established by age, Leviticus 27:1–8.
Value of one compared to many, 2 Samuel 18:3.
Life like a hopeless shadow, 1 Chronicles 29:15.
Long and hard life, Job 7:1 (LB).
Rapid passage, Job 7:6; 9:25–26 (Berk.), Psalms 39:4–6; 89:47; 90:1–6, 10, 12.
"Human years," Job 10:5 (NRSV).
Dust to dust, Job 10:9 (LB).
Few days, Job 10:20.
Negative view of life's meaning, Job 14:1–2 (See CEV).
Length of life determined, Job 14:5.
"Prime of life," Job 29:4 (Berk.).
Life's measurement, Psalm 39:4–5.
Divine wonders before death, Psalm 88:10–12.
Brevity of life, Job 16:22; Psalm 89:47–48.
"As a tale that is told," Psalm 90:9 (KJV).
Seventy, eighty years, Psalm 90:10 (Berk.).
Like shadow, Psalm 102:11.
Satisfied life, Psalm 103:5 (NASB, NRSV).
Living, not dead, praise the Lord, Psalm 115:17.
Short life, Psalm 119:19 (GNB, LB).
Praising God throughout life, Psalms 119:175; 150:6.
Fragility of existence, Psalm 144:3–4.
Chasing wind, Ecclesiastes 1:17–18.
Time for everything, Ecclesiastes 3:1–8.
Cultish view of humans, animals, Ecclesiastes 3:19–21.
Life's quality, quantity, Ecclesiastes 5:20.
Meaningless days, Ecclesiastes 6:12.
Dying before one's time, Ecclesiastes 7:17.
Mystery of life, Ecclesiastes 7:24 (NRSV).

Sweetness of life, Ecclesiastes 9:4.

Enjoy life but with reservation, Ecclesiastes 11:8.

Death in early years of life, Isaiah 38:10.

Grave cannot praise God, Isaiah 38:18.

"Source of life," Isaiah 42:5 (CEV).

Earth, other planets, Isaiah 45:18.

Lamenting one's birth, Jeremiah 15:10.

Still alive, shouldn't complain, Lamentations 3:39 (CEV).

Those who should live die, should die live, Ezekiel 13:19.

Life belongs to God, Ezekiel 18:4 (GNB).

Prophecy to breath, Ezekiel 37:9.

Life, death, Jonah 2:6 (LB).

True immortality, John 8:51.

Death that gives life, Romans 6:4–5, 11.

Building good foundation, 1 Corinthians 3:10–15.

Rapid deterioration of human body, 2 Corinthians 4:16–18.

Our body a tent, 2 Corinthians 5:4.

His death, our life, 1 Thessalonians 5:10.

Flowers, grass wither, 1 Peter 1:24–25.

Body but a tent, 2 Peter 1:13.

See Longevity, Mortality, Old Age, Time.

LIFESTYLE

Domestic lifestyle, Deuteronomy 6:7–9.

What God asks of us, Deuteronomy 10:12–13.

"Life will be different," Deuteronomy 12:5 (CEV).

"Manner of life," Judges 18:7 (LB).

Citizens of darkness, Job 24:13–17.

Lifestyles of believers, unbelievers, Psalm 1:1–6.

Not the way of righteous, Psalm 15:1–3.

Blameless lifestyle, Psalms 84:11; 101:2.

Consistent goodness, Psalm 106:3 (LB).

Adopting heathen customs, Psalm 106:35.

Kindness ignored, Psalm 109:16.

Exemplary lifestyle, Psalm 119:1–5; Micah 6:8.

Divinely taught lifestyle, Psalm 143:8.

Virtuous traits, Proverbs 3:3 (LB).

Good, evil lifestyles, Proverbs 4:18–19 (See CEV).

Lifestyle procedure, Proverbs 4:25–27.

Recommended lifestyle, Ecclesiastes 8:15.

Fool's lifestyle, Ecclesiastes 10:3.

Learn to do good, Isaiah 1:17.

Garments of salvation, Isaiah 61:10.

Testing lifestyles, Jeremiah 6:27.

Lifestyle of righteous man, Ezekiel 18:5–9.

Practice what is preached, Ezekiel 33:31.

Price paid for evil lifestyle, Hosea 4:10 (CEV).

Walking in ways of the Lord, Hosea 14:9.

Shining light of witness, Matthew 5:16.

Truth put into practice, Matthew 7:24.

Spiritual, temporal life, Mark 8:35 (AB).

Deathly lifestyle, Romans 6:21.

Altered lifestyle, Romans 8:3–4.

Contrasting lifestyles, Romans 8:5.

Christian lifestyle, Romans 12:3–21; 13:12–14; Ephesians 4:1–3; 1 Thessalonians 4:9–12.

Harmonious lifestyle, Romans 12:16 (Berk.).

Responsibility to others, 1 Corinthians 8:9–13.

Loving lifestyle, 1 Corinthians 13:1–13.

Faith and love, 1 Corinthians 16:13–14.

Pleasing God and people, 2 Corinthians 8:21.

Christians with worldly lifestyle, 2 Corinthians 10:2.

Peter and Paul face to face, Galatians 2:11–21.

Fruit of the Spirit, Galatians 5:22 (Spanish Bible translates "gentleness" *manseumbree*, "tameness" as with tamed animal).

First priority in conduct, Galatians 6:15.

Our way of life, Ephesians 2:10 (CEV).

Lifestyle worthy of calling, Ephesians 4:1–2.

Forsake the past, Ephesians 4:17.

New lifestyle in Christ, Ephesians 4:22–24.

Imitators of God expressing love, Ephesians 5:1–2.

Ultimate career, life of love, Ephesians 5:1–2.

Sensible, intelligent, Ephesians 5:15 (AB).

Worthy of the gospel, Philippians 1:27 (See AB).

Enemies of the cross, Philippians 3:18–21.

Joy and gentleness, Philippians 4:4–5.

Attitude of mind dictates lifestyle, Philippians 4:8–9.

Filled with knowledge of God's will, Colossians 1:9–12.

Those who died with Christ, Colossians 2:20–23.

Resurrection lifestyle, Colossians 3:1–17.

Prepared for return of Christ, 1 Thessalonians 3:13.

Motivated to Christian lifestyle, 1 Thessalonians 4:11–12.

Dependent personality, 2 Thessalonians 1:11 (AB).

Faith plus good conscience, 1 Timothy 1:19.

Bishop's lifestyle, 1 Timothy 3:2–7 (AB).

Young Christians' lifestyle, 1 Timothy 4:12.

"Rich in good deeds," 1 Timothy 6:18.

Promised life, 2 Timothy 1:1 (AB).

Lifestyles in last days, 2 Timothy 3:1–5.

"Adorn the doctrine," Titus 2:10 (NASB, NKJV).

Marks of Christian lifestyle, Titus 3:1–2.

Enoch pleased God, Hebrews 11:5.

Instructions for Christian life-style, Hebrews 13:1–9.

Living by Scriptures, James 2:8–10.

True faith demonstrated, James 3:13.

Effective witnessing lifestyle, 1 Peter 2:12–15 (AB).

Mature Christian life, 2 Peter 1:5–9.

Live for the eternal, 2 Peter 3:11–14.

Lifestyle producing spiritual growth, 2 Peter 3:18.

Living by truth, 1 John 1:9, 10.

Doing what is right, 1 John 2:29.

Love results from obedience to Scripture, 2 John 6.

Evil conduct as negative witness, Jude 7.
See Conduct, Discipleship, Frame-of-Reference.

LIFETIME

Lifetime God, Isaiah 46:4 (LB).

LIGHT

Creation's greater, lesser lights, Genesis 1:16.

Roles of darkness, light, Exodus 20:21.

Olive oil for eternal flame, Leviticus 24:1–3 (LB).

Strength of rising sun, Judges 5:31.

Lamp of the wicked, Job 21:17.

Rebellion against light, Job 24:13, 16.

Light conveys audible sound, Job 38:7; Psalm 19:2–4.

Light, darkness, Job 38:19–20.

Divine light for mortals, Psalm 27:1; John 8:12.

Light reveals light, Psalm 36:9.

Glory-light, Psalm 50:2 (Berk.).

"Light sown like seed," Psalm 97:11 (NASB).

Light of Scriptures, Psalm 119:105.

Darkness as light, Psalm 139:12.

Dancing light, Proverbs 13:9 (Berk.).

One who lights deepest darkness, Isaiah 9:2.

Abundance of light, Isaiah 30:26.

Creator of light, darkness, Isaiah 45:7.

No need for sun, moon, Isaiah 60:19–20.

No one to light lamps, Jeremiah 25:10 (CEV).

Searching dark corners, Zephaniah 1:12 (LB).

Believers as light, Matthew 5:14; Philippians 2:15.

Lamps of ten virgins, Matthew 25:1–13.

Light to be displayed, not hidden, Mark 4:21–22.

"Light of all people," John 1:4 (NRSV).

Drawing, repelling light, John 3:20–21.

Shining, burning, John 5:35 (Berk.).

Follow light, avoid darkness, John 8:12.

Spiritual light, John 11:9–10.

Profuse use of lamps, Acts 20:8.

Light makes everything visible, Ephesians 5:14.

Rescued from darkness, Colossians 1:13–14.

Son shines like sun, Hebrews 1:3 (LB).

Seeing light, walking in darkness, 2 Peter 2:21.

Walk in the light, 1 John 1:7 (Note: Spanish Bible translates "if we walk" **desde cuando,** "Since we walk.")

Darkness to light, 1 John 2:7–8.

Earth illuminated by angelic splendor, Revelation 18:1.
See Candles, Illumination, Lamps, Window.

LIGHTNING

Sinai lightning, Exodus 19:16; 20:18.

Fire from heaven, Job 1:16 (AB).

Lightning strikes, Job 36:32 (Berk.).

Lightning unleashed, Job 37:3; 38:24, 35.

Enemy dispersed, 2 Samuel 22:15; Psalm 18:14.

Livestock struck by lightning, Psalm 78:48.
Luminous stabs, Psalm 97:4.
Lightning as weapon of war, Psalm 144:6.
Beyond mortal authority, Job 38:35.
"Rip the heavens apart," Isaiah 64:1 (CEV).
Speed of light, Ezekiel 1:13–14.
Trouble never strikes twice, Nahum 1:9.
Likened to Second Coming, Matthew 24:27.
See Lightning, Storm, Weather.

LIKE-MINDED

Like idol, like follower, Psalm 135:15–18.
Two in agreement, Amos 3:3.
Like teacher, like student, Luke 6:40.
Thinking as Jesus thought, Philippians 2:5–8.
See Agreement, Fellowship, Rapport.

LIKENESS See Profile, Similarities.

LIMELIGHT

Avoiding limelight, John 7:4 (Berk.).

LIMITATION

Testing divine patience, Numbers 14:18.
Naaman's conditional greatness, 2 Kings 5:1.
Evaluating military logistics, Luke 14:31–32.

LINEAGE

Preserving family lineage, Numbers 27:1–11; Deuteronomy 25:5–10.
Lineage of David, Ruth 4:15–17.
No son to sustain lineage, 2 Samuel 18:18.
Protection for future king, 2 Kings 11:1–3.
Prophet's lineage, Ezra 7:1–6.
Lineage of faith, Psalms 78:5–8; 145:4.
Terminated lineage, Psalm 109:13.
Desire for lineage, Isaiah 4:1.
Recorded lineage, Zephaniah 1:1.
See Family, Heritage, Inheritance.

LINEN

Royal cloth, Genesis 41:42.
Ten varieties of linen, Exodus 26:1 (GNB).
Synthetics forbidden, Leviticus 19:19; Deuteronomy 22:11.
Bed sheets, Proverbs 7:16.

Egyptian product, Ezekiel 27:16.
Burial cloth for Jesus, Mark 15:46; John 20:5.
See Clothing, Wardrobe.

LINGUISTICS

One common speech, Genesis 11:1 (See AB).
Confused languages, Genesis 11:7.
Pretending language not known, Genesis 42:23.
Bilingual, 2 Kings 18:26.
Strange sounds, Isaiah 28:11 (CEV).
Aramaic instead of Hebrew, Isaiah 36:11.
Strange language, Jeremiah 5:15.
Willing and unwilling to listen, Ezekiel 3:4–6.
Language and literature of Babylon, Daniel 1:3–4.
Calvary cry misunderstood, Matthew 27:46–47.
Day of Pentecost, Acts 2:1–12.
Specific dialect, Acts 2:6, 8 (AB).
Linguistic expertise, Acts 21:37–40 (See NASB, NRSV).
Message spoken in one's own language, Acts 22:1–2.
Speech of humans and angels, 1 Corinthians 13:1.
See Communications, Language.

LION

Hand-to-lion combat, Judges 14:5–6.
David and lion, 1 Samuel 17:36–37.
Killed by lions, 2 Kings 20:36–38.
Lions' den, Daniel 6:12–23.
See Animals.

LIQUOR

Drink stronger than wine, Leviticus 10:9.
Other fermented drink, Deuteronomy 29:6.
Alcohol and pregnancy, Judges 13:4–5.
Wine and beer, Proverbs 20:1; 31:4–6.
Beer with bad taste, Isaiah 24:9.
Drunken priests and prophets, Isaiah 28:7.
No strong drink for John the Baptist, Luke 1:15.
See Alcohol, Beer, Drunkenness, Wine.

LISTEN

Stone that listened, Joshua 24:27.
"Be quiet," 1 Samuel 15:16 (NKJV).
Attentive ear, Nehemiah 1:11; Psalm 28:1.
Pay close attention, Proverbs 5:1 (LB).
See Attention, Communication, Ear, Hearing, Heed.

LITERATURE

What poets say, Numbers 21:27–30.
A place for words, Deuteronomy 27:2–3.
Setting murder to verse, Judges 5:24–27.
Chapter transition, Judges 18:7 (LB).
Missing book discovered, 2 Chronicles 34:14–21.
Proverbs as ashes, Job 13:12.
Written record of agony, Job 19:23–24.
Descriptive use of words, Psalm 7:14.
Pen of skillful writer, Psalm 45:1.
Literature with musical accompaniment, Psalm 49:4.
Foreword to book of Proverbs, Proverbs 1:1–6.
Verbosity confuses meaning, Ecclesiastes 6:11.
Shortest short story, Ecclesiastes 9:14–15.
No end making books, Ecclesiastes 12:12 (See AB).
Unique figure-of-speech, Isaiah 14:23.
Figure-of-speech birth, death, Isaiah 26:19.
Description of judgment, Isaiah 30:14.
Dishonest pen, Jeremiah 8:8.
Instructions for writing book, Jeremiah 30:2.
Use of literary device concerning freedom, Jeremiah 34:17.
Book of sadness, Ezekiel 2:9–10.
Edible literature, Ezekiel 3:1–3.
Language, literature of Babylon, Daniel 1:3–4.
Message written with clarity, Habakkuk 2:2.
Gigantic flying scroll, Zechariah 5:1–2.
Flashback technique, Mark 6:14–29 (CEV).
Jesus' use of figures-of-speech, Mark 8:14–21.
Books of world could not contain full story, John 21:25.
Writing sequel, Acts 1:1.
Author of life itself, Acts 3:15.
Paul quoted poets of Athens, Acts 17:28.
"Words as weapons," 1 Timothy 1:18 (GNB).
Preferring not to write, 2 John 12 (See 3 John 13–14).
Happy reading, Revelation 1:3 (GNB).
Awesome power of small book, Revelation 10:2.
Book which cannot be revised, Revelation 22:18.
See Author, Fiction, Grammar, Poetry, Publication, Writing.

LITIGATION

Moses seated as judge, Exodus 18:13.
Demand and decree, Exodus 21:22.
Ruthless witnesses in court, Psalm 35:11.
Avoid hasty litigation against neighbors, Proverbs 25:8.
"Meet me in court," Isaiah 43:26 (CEV).
Priests served as judges, Ezekiel 44:24.
Grounds for litigation, Hosea 4:1 (LB).
Legal conflicts resulting from false oaths, Hosea 10:4.
Sound judgment in courtroom, Zechariah 8:16.
Settle matters out of court, Matthew 5:25.
Give more than amount sued, Matthew 5:40.
Conflict between adversaries going to magistrate, Luke 12:58.
Bringing theological dispute into secular courtroom, Acts 18:12–17.
Paul appealed to higher court, Acts 25:9–12.
Lawsuits among believers, 1 Corinthians 6:1–8.
See Judge, Justice, Lawyer.

LITURGY

Woman's purification, Numbers 5:11–31.
Prayer for protection, Numbers 10:35.
Lifeless worship, Isaiah 29:13.
Covering head in worship, 1 Corinthians 11:5–10.
Regulations for worship, Hebrews 9:1 (See GNB).
Debilitating rules, Hebrews 13:9.
See Worship.

LIVELIHOOD

Working too hard to earn livelihood, Psalm 127:2 (GNB).

LIVESTOCK

Large herds, Job 1:3.
Consistent breeding, Job 21:10.
See Cattle.

LOAN *See Borrowing, Credit, Finances, Mortgage.*

LOAN SHARK

Judgment of loan sharks, Zephaniah 1:11 (LB).

LOATHE

Loathe divine reproof, Proverbs 3:11 (NASB).
See Despise.

LOCAL

Those native born, Numbers 15:13.
Acceptance of hometown person, Matthew 13:57; Mark 6:4; John 4:44.

LOCK *See Key.*

LOFTY *See Highest.*

LOGIC

People who refuse to listen to reason, 1 Samuel 8:4–21.
Logic of repentance, Jeremiah 8:4–5 (CEV).
Strategy of Jesus in facing accusers, Matthew 21:25–27.
Pharisees unable to answer logical question, Matthew 22:41–46.
Logic of Jesus confounded critics, Mark 11:29–33.
Jesus and Pharisees, Luke 14:1–6.
Wisdom of Gamaliel, Acts 5:30–40.
Secular logic, 1 Corinthians 1:20 (AB).
Logic defends the gospel, Galatians 2:14–17.
See Argument, Wisdom.

LOGISTICS

Logistics for building temple, 1 Chronicles 22:14–16.

LONELINESS

Deep sense of loneliness, Job 19:13–14.
Companion of night creatures, Job 30:29.
Joyfully alone, Psalm 4:8 (LB).
Fair-weather friends, Psalms 31:11; 38:11; 2 Timothy 4:16.
Loss of closest friends, Psalm 88:8.
Insomnia induced by loneliness, Psalm 102:7.
No one cares, Psalm 142:4.
Neither son nor brother, Ecclesiastes 4:8.
Silently alone, Lamentations 3:28 (CEV).
Utter loneliness of Calvary, Mark 15:34.
Prodigal's loneliness, Luke 15:14–17.
Alone in time of need, John 5:7.
"Yearning to see you," Romans 1:11 (Berk.).
Spiritual loneliness, Philippians 2:25–30; 1 Thessalonians 2:17–20; 3:1–5.
Tears of loneliness, 2 Timothy 1:4.
Lonely for face-to-face fellowship, 3 John 14.
See Abandoned, Forsaken, Homesick, Testing.

LONGEVITY

Oldest man, Genesis 5:27.
Longevity shortened, Genesis 6:3; Psalm 90:10.
Assured longevity, Genesis 15:15.
Short life compared to ancestral longevity, Genesis 47:9.
No graves in Egypt, Exodus 14:11 (Note 13:19).
Commandment promise, Exodus 20:12; Ephesians 6:2–3.
Honesty, longevity, Deuteronomy 25:15.
Evil woman's blessing, 1 Kings 1:31.
Way of all earth, 1 Kings 2:2.
Obedience rewarded with longevity, 1 Kings 3:14; Proverbs 10:27.
Fifteen years added to Hezekiah's life, 2 Kings 20:5–6; Isaiah 38:5.
Death in full vigor, Job 5:26.
Our days in God's mind, Job 14:5 (Berk.).
Long evil life, Job 21:7.
Longevity in answer to prayer, Psalm 21:4.
Desire for long life, Psalm 34:11–13; 1 Peter 3:10–11.
Life but a breath, Psalm 39:5 (CEV).
Age seventy to eighty, Psalm 90:10.

Satisfying long life, Psalm 91:16.
Purposeful longevity, Psalm 119:17 (LB).
Long life for sinners, Ecclesiastes 8:12.
Enjoying life, Ecclesiastes 11:8.
Longevity desired in prime of life, Isaiah 38:9–22.
People live to age of trees, Isaiah 65:20–22.
Forefathers gone, Zechariah 1:5.
Cane in hand, Zechariah 8:4.
Enriched years, 1 Peter 3:10.
Our body but a tent, 2 Peter 1:13.
See Geriatrics, Old Age.

LONG-WINDED

Arrogant speech, 1 Samuel 2:3.
Words like blustering wind, Job 8:2.
Long-winded speeches, Job 16:3.
Apt speech, Proverbs 25:11.
Wise speech, Ecclesiastes 12:11.
Instructed tongue, Isaiah 50:4.
Paul's long sermon, Acts 20:7.
Need for disciplined tongue, James 1:26.
See Brevity, Loquacious, Speech, Speechless, Tact.

LOOTING

Victor's loot, Genesis 14:21 (GNB).
Enemy spoils, Numbers 31:1–54.
Girls as loot, Judges 5:30 (LB).
Crops, animals looted by enemy, Judges 6:3–6.
Robbing dead after battle, 2 Samuel 23:10.
Making frolic of looting, Jeremiah 50:11–12.
See Plunder, Robbery, Spoils, Stealing.

LOQUACIOUS

Big talk, Judges 9:38.
Words like blustering wind, Job 8:2.
Full of talk, Job 11:2 (NKJV).
Wisdom of silence, Job 13:5.
"Windbag," Job 15:2 (LB); Jeremiah 5:13 (LB).
Long-winded speeches, Job 16:3.
Full of words, Job 32:18.
Loquacious fool, Proverbs 10:8.
"Foot in your mouth," Proverbs 10:19 (LB).
Think before speaking, Proverbs 16:23 (GNB).
Too much talk, Proverbs 18:21 (CEV).

"Never tire of talking," Ecclesiastes 10:14 (CEV).
Pharaoh only loud noise, Jeremiah 46:17.
Paul's long sermon, Acts 20:7.
See Long-Winded.

LORD

Functioning Lordship, Psalm 16:5 (LB).
"Lord" translated "Sir," Luke 19:8 (GNB).
Jesus as Lord, Matthew 22:41–46; Acts 2:36; 1 Corinthians 8:6; 12:3.

LORD'S DAY

Setting aside day for rest, Genesis 2:2–3; Jeremiah 17:21–27.
No business on Sabbath, Nehemiah 10:31.
Merchandising on Sabbath, Nehemiah 13:15–18.
Avoid Sabbath desecration, Isaiah 56:2.
Sabbath fun, Isaiah 58:13 (LB).
The Lord's Sabbaths, Ezekiel 20:12.
Jesus criticized for Sabbath conduct, Mark 2:23–27; Luke 6:1–5.
See Lord's Day, Sunday.

LORD'S TABLE See Communion, Passover.

LOSS

Fall asleep rich, awaken poor, Job 27:19 (CEV).
Loss of material possessions, Hebrews 10:34 (GNB).

LOST

Depravity prior to flood, Genesis 6:5.
"Give up as lost," Ecclesiastes 3:6 (NASB).
Those far from the Lord, Ezekiel 11:15.
Divine attitude toward lost, Ezekiel 18:23–32.
Lost souls grieve the Lord, Ezekiel 33:11.
"Flock of lost sheep," Matthew 10:6 (CEV).
Without hope, without God, Ephesians 2:12.
Domain of darkness, Colossians 1:13 (NASB).
Life prior to regeneration, Titus 3:3.
Failure to combine hearing with believing, Hebrews 4:1–3.
God's grace to worst of sinners, 1 Timothy 1:15–16.

God wants all to be saved, 1 Timothy 2:3–4.

Names not in Book of Life, Revelation 17:8; 20:7–15.

See Rejection, Depravity, Unbelief.

LOTS

The Lord involved in casting lots, Leviticus 16:8.

Inheritance by lot, Numbers 26:55.

Maps made by casting lots, Joshua 18:8–10.

Prayer and chance, 1 Samuel 14:41–42.

Death by measurement, 2 Samuel 8:2.

Casting lots to schedule giving, Nehemiah 10:34.

Day of doom, Esther 3:2–7.

Divine control over chance, Proverbs 16:33.

Disputes settled by casting lots, Proverbs 18:18.

Lot determines priesthood, Luke 1:8–9.

See Chance, Coin Toss, Luck.

LOUD

"Loud songs of joy," Psalm 47:1 (NRSV).

See Boisterous.

LOVE

Mistaking love for hatred, Deuteronomy 1:27 (LB).

Love between two men, 2 Samuel 1:26.

Determining identity of true mother, 1 Kings 3:16–28.

Steadfast love, Job 10:12 (NRSV); Psalm 90:14 (NRSV).

Unfailing love, Psalm 23:6 (Berk.).

"Steady love," Psalm 33:18 (LB).

God's love better than life, Psalm 63:3 (KJV).

Loving those who hate, Psalm 109:4 (LB).

Our Lord's enduring love, Psalm 136:1–26.

Love, faithfulness, Proverbs 16:6.

Lovesick, Song of Songs 2:5 (Berk.).

True love cannot be quenched, Song of Songs 8:7.

"Kingdom of love," Isaiah 16:5 (CEV).

God's love never lessens, Isaiah 54:10.

Sex spoken of as "love," Ezekiel 16:8.

Lust called love, Ezekiel 23:17.

How God loves, Malachi 1:2.

Marriage on earth, relationship in heaven, Mark 12:18–27.

Greatest act of love, John 3:16.

Love's highest degree, John 13:1 (AB).

Implanted love, John 17:26.

Forgiving spirit of martyr, Acts 7:60.

Love fulfills law, Romans 13:8–10.

Others' good above self, 1 Corinthians 10:24.

Guided by love, 1 Corithians 13:1 (CEV).

Apt definition, 1 Corinthians 13:4–7 (GNB).

"Pursue love," 1 Corinthians 14:1 (NASB, NKJV, NRSV).

Loving heartcry, 2 Corinthians 6:11–12 (LB).

Covered with His love, Ephesians 1:4 (LB).

Imitators of God expressing love, Ephesians 5:1–2.

Christians keeping in touch, Ephesians 6:21–22.

Undying love, Ephesians 6:24.

Affection Jesus gives, Philippians 1:8.

Ministry of love, Colossians 3:12–14. (Japanese: "Love binds everything together in perfect harmony.")

Increasing love, 1 Thessalonians 3:12; 4:9–10.

Realizing, sharing, 2 Thessalonians 3:5 (AB).

Spiritual love's basis, 1 Timothy 1:5.

"Mutual love," Hebrews 13:1 (NRSV); 1 Peter 1:22 (NRSV).

Love's forgiving power, 1 Peter 4:8 (See NASB).

"Affection with love," 2 Peter 1:7 (NRSV).

God's perfect love, 1 John 2:5 (NRSV).

God's great love, 1 John 3:1–3 (See AB).

Mark of Christian, 1 John 3:11–14.

Actions speak louder than words, 1 John 3:18 (See AB).

Truth, love united, 2 John 3, 5–6.

Love in the truth, 3 John 1.

Love dearly, tenderly, Revelation 3:19 (AB).

See Affection, Camaraderie, Courtship, Marriage, Rapport, Romance.

LOWLINESS

Unworthy of king's presence, 2 Samuel 19:24–28.

Centurion's lowly attitude, Matthew 8:5–10.

Supreme example of lowliness, Matthew 8:20.

See Humility.

LOYALTY

Tested love to God, son, Genesis 22:1–14.

Lacking wholehearted loyalty, Numbers 32:11.

Turning from wrong family influence, Deuteronomy 13:6–10.

Continuing loyalty, Joshua 1:16–17.

Turning to rejected brother in time of need, Judges 11:1–10.

Loyal assistant, 1 Samuel 14:7.

Transferred loyalty, 1 Samuel 14:21–23.

Loyalty torn between father, close friend, 1 Samuel 19:1–2.

Friendship, loyalty at cutting edge, 1 Samuel 20:1–4.

Pagan feared David's loyalty, 1 Samuel 29:1–11.

Angelic loyalty, 1 Samuel 29:9 (GNB).

Loyalty of servant to king, 2 Samuel 15:19–21.

King David's loyalty doubted, 2 Samuel 19:1–8.

Neglecting personal appearance until sure of king's safety, 2 Samuel 19:24.

Protection for future king, 2 Kings 11:1–3.

Dubious loyalty, 1 Chronicles 12:19.

Loyalty to government, Ezra 7:26; Ecclesiastes 8:2; Romans 13:1; Titus 3:1; 1 Peter 2:13.

Divided loyalty, Psalm 119:113 (CEV).

Talk is cheap, Proverbs 20:6 (GNB).

Loyalty to gods, Jeremiah 2:11.

Changed loyalty in battle, Jeremiah 41:11–14.

Loving God above all, Matthew 10:37–39.

You cannot serve two masters, Luke 16:13.

Loyal to Christ's commands, John 14:21–24.

Hypocritical loyalty to Caesar, John 19:15.

Tested loyalty, John 21:15–17.

Daily death of true loyalty, 1 Corinthians 15:30–31.

See Dependability, Discipleship, Faithfulness, Love.

LUCID

Message spoken and written, Exodus 31:18; 32:16; Deuteronomy 10:4.

Writing guided by divine hand, 1 Chronicles 28:19; 2 Chronicles 36:22.

Message written with clarity, Habakkuk 2:2.

Divided loyalties, 1 Corinthians 7:32–34.

See Communication, Eloquence.

LUCIFER *See Satan.*

LUCK

Death by measurement, 2 Samuel 8:2.

Death by random arrow, 1 Kings 22:34–37; 2 Chronicles 18:33–34.

"Lucky to be here," 2 Chronicles 9:7 (CEV).

Date setting, Esther 3:7.

Divine control of chance events, Proverbs 16:33.

Settling disputes, Proverbs 18:18.

Good luck god, Isaiah 65:11 (CEV).

Use of magic charms, Ezekiel 13:18.

From frying pan to fire, Amos 5:19.

Guilt by casting lot, Jonah 1:7.

Casting lots for Jesus' garments, Matthew 27:35.

"Lucky fellow," Mark 10:49 (LB).

"Lucky man," Luke 12:19 (GNB).

Choice of replacement for Judas, Acts 1:18–26.

See Chance, Lots.

LUGGAGE

Recovered goods, Genesis 14:14–16.

Smuggled baggage, Genesis 44.1–12.

Queen's luggage, 1 Kings 10:2.

"Pack your bags," Jeremiah 10:17 (LB).

Belongings packed for exile, Ezekiel 12:1–7.

Traveling light, Luke 10:4.

Cumbersome spiritual luggage, Hebrews 12:1.

See Journey, Travel.

LUMBER

Chest of acacia wood, Exodus 25:10.

Protection for trees, Deuteronomy 20:19.

Leader among trees, Judges 9:7–15.

Wood for building temple, 1 Kings 5:3–11.

Selecting choice timber, 2 Kings 19:23.

Lumber from royal forest, Nehemiah 2:8.

Forestation procedure, Isaiah 6:13.

See Carpentry, Forestry, Trees.

LURE *See Tantalize, Temptation.*

LUST

Lot's offer of virgin daughters, Genesis 19:4–8.

Mixing immorality with worship, Numbers 25:1–2.

David and Bathsheba, 2 Samuel 11:1–27.

Immorality used for vengeance, 2 Samuel 16:20–23.

Weakness of King Solomon, 1 Kings 11:1–13.

Avoiding lust requires discipline, Job 31:1.

"Ogle at a girl," Job 31:1 (Berk.).

Lust as a crime, Job 31:11 (LB).

Take away lust, Psalm 141:4 (LB).

Lost value through lust, Proverbs 6:25–26.

Playing with fire, Proverbs 6:27.

Preventive wisdom, Proverbs 7:4–17 (LB).

Thinking only of sex, Isaiah 57:5 (CEV).

Searching for sex, Jeremiah 2:24 (LB).

Shameless lust, Jeremiah 3:3 (See CEV).

Adultery with stone and wood, Jeremiah 3:9.

Description of profligate men, Jeremiah 5:8.

Adultery, lust in heart, mind, Ezekiel 6:9.

Merchandising feminine beauty, Ezekiel 16:15.

Visual abomination, Ezekiel 20:7 (KJV).

Violation of family members, Ezekiel 22:11.

Two adulterous sisters, Ezekiel 23:1–49.

Lustful caressing, Ezekiel 23:2–3.

Lust induced by pornography, Ezekiel 23:14–17 (LB).

Lust called love, Ezekiel 23:17.

Father, son to same prostitute, Amos 2:7.

Adultery in heart, mind, Matthew 5:27–28.

Sexual impurity, Romans 1:24–26.

Slaves to lust, Romans 7:5.

Overcoming lust, Romans 13:14; Galatians 5:16, 24.

Engaged couples, 1 Corinthians 7:36–38.

Inward burning, 2 Cornithians 11:29.

Continual lust for more, Ephesians 4:19.

"Lusts of deceit," Ephesians 4:22 (NASB).

Death to lust, Colossians 3:5.

Heathen lust, 1 Thessalonians 4:5.

Evil desires of youth, 2 Timothy 2:22.

Expanding lust, James 1:15.

Sensual pleasures, James 4:3 (AB).

Abstain from lust, 1 Peter 2:11.

"Depraved lust," 2 Peter 2:10 (NRSV).

Overt lust, 2 Peter 2:14 (AB, GNB).

"Lust of the eye," 1 John 2:16.

Those who keep themselves pure, Revelation 14:4.

See Adultery, Depravity, Immorality, Pornography, Promiscuity.

LUXURY

Palace diet, 1 Kings 4:22–23.

Solid gold table setting, 1 Kings 10:21–22.

A tent or a palace, 1 Chronicles 15:1 (LB).

Week-long banquet, Esther 1:5–6.

Going without dessert, Daniel 10:3 (LB).

Sumptuous bed and board, Amos 6:3–4.

People in fine homes, temple in ruins, Haggai 1:1–4.

Jesus accused of luxury, Matthew 26:6–13.

Expensive perfume prepared Jesus for Cross, Mark 14:3–9.

Hairstyles and jewelry, 1 Timothy 2:9–10.

See Affluence, Hedonism.

LYE

Cleansing hands, Job 9:30 (Berk.).

LYNCHING

Hanging of king, Joshua 8:29.

Infamy to daughter of king, 2 Kings 9:30–37.

Jews had no right to crucify, John 18:28–32.

See Murder.

LYRICS

Songs of joy, Psalm 126:2.

Isaiah's ballad, Isaiah 5:1–8.

Meaningless lyrics sung by beautiful voice, Ezekiel 33:32.

See Hymn.

M

MACHINERY

Machinery not to be mortgaged, Deuteronomy 24:6.

New inventions, 2 Chronicles 26:15.

MACHO

Goliath's macho, 1 Samuel 17:42–44.

See Conceit, Hedonism.

MAGGOTS

Worms in dead bodies, Isaiah 66:24.

See Decay, Putrid.

MAGI

Suggested prophecy of Magi, Psalm 72:10, 15.

See Christmas.

MAGIC

Seeking God's will by divination, Genesis 30:27.

Unwise men of Egypt, Genesis 41:1–24.

Pretending to believe in divination, Genesis 44:5.

Professional magicians, Exodus 7:8–12; 8:1–19.

Israel superstitions, Isaiah 2:6–8.

False oracles, prophets, Jeremiah 23:33–40.

Baffled magicians, Daniel 1:20; 2:1–13; 4:4–7.

Sorcerer's vanity, Acts 8:9–11.

Satan's evil tricks, Ephesians 6:11 (GNB).

Counterfeit miracles, 2 Thessalonians 2:9–10.

Magicians into lake of fire, Revelation 21:8; 22:15.

See Divination, Fortune-telling, Mystical, Sorcery.

MAGISTRATE See Authority, Bureaucracy, Government, Leadership, Politics.

MAGNITUDE

Scope of God's presence, 1 Kings 8:27.

Eternal viewpoint, Jeremiah 33:3.

Army of locusts, Joel 2:1–9.

Magnitude of God's greatness, Romans 11:33–36.

Contemplating Christ's resurrection, Ephesians 1:18–23.

Geometric magnitude of Christ's love, Ephesians 3:17–18.

Right foot on sea, left foot on land, Revelation 10:2.

See Dimensions, Large, Quantity.

MAIM

Cutting off thumbs and big toes, Judges 1:7.

Crippled from childhood fall, 2 Samuel 4:4.

Wounds, welts from beating, Isaiah 1:5–6.

Symbolic broken arm, Ezekiel 30:21.

See Handicap, Injury.

MAINTENANCE

Temple maintenance, 2 Kings 12:4–5.

Lazy man's house, Ecclesiastes 10:18.

Oil protection against rust, Isaiah 21:5 (NIV, NRSV).

See Repair.

MAJESTY

Divine glory, majesty, splendor, 1 Chronicles 29:11.

Likened to majesty of sun, Job 37:21–24.

God's abundant majesty, Psalm 8:1 (LB).

Majestic voice of the Lord, Psalm 29:3–9.

Fiery majesty, Psalm 50:3.

Garments of eternal majesty, Psalm 93:1–2.

High, exalted, Isaiah 6:1.

See Royalty, Splendor.

MAJORITY

Following wrong crowd, Exodus 23:2.

Few become majority, Leviticus 26:8.

Confidence in numerical strength, Judges 7:2, 12.

One plus God equals majority, 1 Samuel 14:6–14.

Human strength of little value, Psalm 33:16.

Majority and minority, Matthew 7:13–14.

See Superiority, Supremacy.

MALCONTENT

Malcontent community, Exodus 16:2.

Testing God, Exodus 17:1–4.

Chasing wind, Ecclesiastes 1:17–18.

Money never satisfies, Ecclesiastes 5:10.

Help for the malcontent, Isaiah 29:24.

Blaming the Lord for problems, Habakkuk 1:1–4.

Prodigal son's malcontented brother, Luke 15:25–32.

Peril of grumbling, 1 Corinthians 10:10.

Admonition for good attitude, Philippians 2:14; 1 Timothy 6:6–8.

Content with what you have, Hebrews 13:5.

See Attitude, Complain, Discontent, Murmuring.

MALICE

Malice toward none, Leviticus 19:18.

Blighted personalities, Deuteronomy 32:32–33; Psalm 10:7–14; Proverbs 6:14–19; Romans 1:29–32.

Compassion versus malice, 2 Kings 6:21–22.

Wealth, prestige, malice, Esther 5:10–14.

Discipline against malice, Job 31:29–30.

Hidden malice, Psalm 28:3.

Lurking enemies, Psalms 56:5–6; 57:4–6; 59:3–7.

Malicious speech, Psalm 140:3; Proverbs 30:14.

Evil insomnia, Proverbs 4:16; Micah 2:1.

Folly of malice, Ezekiel 25:15–17.

Malice in practice, Matthew 5:38–41; Acts 23:12–14.

Divine condemnation, 1 John 2:9–11; 3:14, 15.

See Envy, Hatred, Resentment.

MALIGNANCY *See Cancer.*

MAMMOTH *See Immensity.*

MAN

Measure of a man, 1 Kings 2:2.

Low estimation of man's worth, Job 25:5–6.

Clay in Potter's hands, Isaiah 29:16; 45:9; 64:8; Jeremiah 18:6.

Setting traps for men, Jeremiah 5:26.

No man to be found, Ezekiel 22:30.

See Humanity, Mortality.

MANAGEMENT

Slave drivers, Exodus 1:11 (GNB).

Relative assisted management, Exodus 4:18.

Government attitude toward management, Exodus 5:2–5.

Young kings of Israel, 2 Kings 23:31, 36; 24:8, 18.

Delegated responsibility, Nehemiah 3:1–32.

Job assignments, Nehemiah 13:30.

Lazy employee, Proverbs 10:26 (NRSV).

Management by objective, Proverbs 6:6-8 (LB).

Unjust management, Jeremiah 22:13; Malachi 3:5; Luke 12:42-46; James 5:4.

Labor relations, Matthew 20:6-16; 21:33-41.

Faithful, prudent manager, Luke 12:42 (NRSV).

Trade unions, Acts 19:23-27.

Payment to laborers, Romans 4:4.

"Guardians and managers," Galatians 4:2 (NRSV).

Concern for servant, Matthew 8:5-13; Luke 7:3.

Avoiding harsh management, 2 Corinthians 13:10.

See Authority, Labor, Leadership, Organization.

MANDATE

Specific orders, Joshua 8:8.

Mandate for blessing, warning against disobedience, 1 Kings 9:1-9.

Pagan king persuaded to alter mandate, Ezra 4—8.

Clear mandate to Jeremiah, Jeremiah 11:6.

Mandate to witness, Ezekiel 3:18-19.

Two-word mandate, Mark 2:14.

Entrusted with secret things, 1 Corinthians 4:1-2.

Ministry mandate, 2 Timothy 4:1-5.

See Decree, Ultimatum.

MANIPULATE

Manipulated wealth, Proverbs 21:6.

Political manipulation, Ecclesiastes 5:8-9.

Inequity between friends, Jeremiah 9:5.

Manipulated wealth, Jeremiah 17:11.

Exploiting poor, Amos 5:11.

Cheating and polluting, Amos 8:5, 6.

Doing good without reciprocation, Luke 6:27-36.

Relationship to neighbors, Ephesians 4:25.

See Devious, Misuse.

MANNA

Appearance of manna, Exodus 16:14 (GNB, AB, LB).

Definition of manna, Exodus 16:31 (LB).

Size and color, Numbers 11:7 (GNB, RSV).

Spiritual lesson from manna, Deuteronomy 8:3.

Manna discontinued, Joshua 5:12.

Bread from heaven, Nehemiah 9:15.

MANNERS

Courtesy to visitors, Genesis 18:1-8.

Visiting angels, Genesis 19:1-2.

Biological expediency, Genesis 31:35.

Bad manners toward Great Provider, Exodus 16:1-18.

Courtesy to senior citizens, Leviticus 19:32; Job 29:7-8.

Bad manners, Judges 8:35; 1 Samuel 25:21; 2 Kings 2:23-24.

Wisdom of silence, Job 13:5.

Uncouth beauty, Proverbs 11:22.

Legalism versus courtesy, 1 Corinthians 10:27-30.

Love's exemplary manners, 1 Corinthians 13:5.

Good manners toward strangers, Colossians 4:5-6.

Avoid misuse of another's manners, 2 Thessalonians 3:7-10.

See Courtesy, Guests, Hospitality.

MANPOWER

Taking care of business, Deuteronomy 20:5-9.

Adequate manpower, Micah 5:5.

See Labor, Volunteers, Work.

MANUFACTURE

Tool manufacturing, Genesis 4:22.

Shortage of materials, Exodus 5:6-9.

Musical instruments, 2 Chronicles 7:6.

Commercial centers in Ezekiel's time, Ezekiel 27:12-23.

See Machinery, Tools.

MAP

Real estate map, Joshua 18:8-10 (LB).

Road signs, guideposts, Jeremiah 31:21.

Improvised map, Ezekiel 4:1.

See Itinerary.

MARANATHA

Come, Lord Jesus, 1 Corinthians 16:22 (GNB, AB).

MARATHON

Long race, Jeremiah 12:5.
See Athletics, Running.

MARCHING

Marching to the sea, Exodus 13:17–22; 14:1–31.
Encircling Jericho, Joshua 6:2–20.
Stormy marching, Judges 5:4.
Marching atop Jerusalem's wall, Nehemiah 12:27–39.
Trembling earth, Psalm 68:7.
Soldiers like serpents, Jeremiah 46:22.
Precision marching, Joel 2:8, 11.
See Parade.

MARITIME

Maritime people, Genesis 10:5.
Ships coming, Numbers 24:24.
Solomon's fleet, 1 Kings 9:26–27.
Fleet of trading ships, 1 Kings 22:48–49; 2 Chronicles 9:21; 20:36.
Lumber transported by sea, 2 Chronicles 2:16.
Seasoned sailors, 2 Chronicles 8:18 (Note use of rafts).
Reed skiffs, Job 9:26 (NRSV).
Sailing high seas, Psalm 107:23–30.
Weeping ships, Isaiah 23:1 (LB).
Down to the sea, Isaiah 42:10.
Woe to ships of Tarshish, Ezekiel 27:25–36.
Travel by air, sea, Isaiah 60:8–9.
Linen sails, Ezekiel 27:7.
Oar-driven ships, Ezekiel 27:8 (KJV).
Apostolic voyages, Acts 20:13; 27:2.
Shipwreck, Acts 27:27–44.
Winter harbor, Acts 28:11.
See Navigation, Seaworthy, Voyage.

MARKET

Temple market, John 2:13–16.
See Business, Salesmen, Trade.

MARKETING

Commerical centers, Ezekiel 27:2–23.
Many merchants, Nahum 3:16.

Idle in marketplace, Matthew 20:3.
Temple as marketplace, Luke 19:45–48.
Dealing in human merchandise, Acts 16:16–23.
See Barter, Commerce, Merchandise, Salesman.

MARKS

Needless bruises, Proverbs 23:29.
Wounds and welts, Isaiah 1:6.
Marks of sin on countenance, Isaiah 3:9.
Incurable wound, Jeremiah 30:12; Micah 1:9.
Mark of repentence, Ezekiel 9:4–6.
Colored and dappled horses, Zechariah 6:2–3.
Mark of the beast, Revelation 19:20.

MARRIAGE

First arranged marriage, Genesis 2:18–24.
Demons married to humans, Genesis 6:1–4 (LB).
Supernatural husbands, Genesis 6:4 (CEV).
Deceitful marital status, Genesis 12:10–20; 20:1–18; 26:7–11.
Search for Isaac's bride, Genesis 24:1–58; 25:19–20.
Marriage after wife's death, Genesis 25:1–2.
Bride's consent to marriage, Genesis 24:58; 1 Samuel 25:19–43.
Disappointed in-laws, Genesis 26:34–35.
Marriage between relatives, Genesis 29:23–30; 2 Chronicles 11:18 (See LB).
Premarital sex, Genesis 34:1–31.
Responsibility after illicit relationship, Exodus 22:16.
Incest, impropriety, Leviticus 20:14–21.
Special rules for clergy, Leviticus 21:1–15.
Husband's involvement in wife's business, Numbers 30:10–15.
Limited choice for women, Numbers 36:6.
"Wife of your bosom," Deuteronomy 13:6 (NKJV).
Divorce, remarriage, Deuteronomy 24:1–5.
Daughter given as reward, Joshua 15:16.
Father's intervention, Judges 15:1–2.
Wife shortage, Judges 21:14.
Kidnapped wives, Judges 21:20–23.
Blessing on second marriage, Ruth 1:9 (LB).

Age variable between Boaz, Ruth, Ruth 3:10–13 (See LB).

Property included wife, Ruth 4:5.

Wife-stealing, 2 Samuel 3:12–16.

David's many wives, 2 Samuel 5:13.

Marital strife, hatred, 2 Samuel 6:16–23.

Famous child of bad marriage, 2 Samuel 12:24–25.

Terminated relationships, 2 Samuel 20:3.

Disparity in ages, 1 Kings 1:1–4.

Ill-fated request for wife, 1 Kings 2:13–25.

Marriage alliance, 1 Kings 3:1.

Marriage to unbelievers, 1 Kings 11:1–8.

Abundant wives, 2 Chronicles 11:23.

Political marriage, 2 Chronicles 18:1; Daniel 11:6 (See CEV).

Holy and unholy marriages, Ezra 9:2 (See Berk.).

Roster of foreign wives, Ezra 10:16–44.

King and queen, Nehemiah 2:6.

Beautiful queen refused display, Esther 1:9–21.

Marital conflict, Job 2:9–10.

Strategic verse for marriage, Psalm 34:3.

No wedding songs, Psalm 78:63 (See KJV).

Estranged prostitutes, Proverbs 2:16–17 (LB).

Key to happy marriage, Proverbs 5:18–20.

Fury of betrayed husband, Proverbs 6:27–35.

Blessing of good wife, Proverbs 12:4.

Love forgets mistakes, Proverbs 17:9 (LB).

Favor of the Lord, Proverbs 18:22.

Good marriages made in heaven, Proverbs 19:14 (Also see LB).

Quarrelsome wife, Proverbs 21:9, 19; 25:24.

Two better than one, Ecclesiastes 4:9–12.

Enjoy life together, Ecclesiastes 9:9.

Sister, bride, Song of Songs 4:9 (Also see 8:1).

Taste of bridal lips, Song of Songs 4:11.

Marital intimacy, Song of Songs 4:16.

Mother's counsel, Song of Songs 8:2 (KJV).

True love cannot be quenched, Song of Songs 8:7.

Young wife rejected, Isaiah 54:6.

"Happily married," Isaiah 62:4 (CEV).

Israel as God's bride, Jeremiah 2:1–3.

Culminated joy, Jeremiah 7:34.

Forbidden in time of judgment, Jeremiah 16:1–4.

"No place to raise a family," Jeremiah 16:2 (CEV).

Marriage in distressing times, Jeremiah 33:10–11.

Husbands, wives rebel against God, Jeremiah 44:16–19.

Wife preferred strangers to husband, Ezekiel 16:32.

Restrictions on marriage for priests, Ezekiel 44:22.

Marriage of convenience, Daniel 11:6 (LB).

Hosea commanded to marry evil woman, Hosea 1:2–3.

Prostitute wife returns, Hosea 2:7 (See CEV).

Restored marriage, Hosea 2:16–20.

Love for adulterous wife, Hosea 3:1.

Unable to have children, Hosea 9:11.

Youthful marriage terminated, Joel 1:8.

Agreement necessary for walking together, Amos 3:3.

Women who command their husbands, Amos 4:1.

Marriage to daughter of god, Malachi 2:11.

Vows of youth, Malachi 2:15.

"Cheat in marriage," Malachi 3:5 (CEV).

Cause for divorce, Matthew 5:31–32.

Jesus and divorce, Matthew 19:3–9.

Advice of Pilate's wife, Matthew 27:19.

Heaven, marriage and remarriage, Mark 12:18–25; 1 Corinthians 7:39–40.

Brief marriage of prophetess, Luke 2:36–37.

One woman, many husbands, John 4:17–18.

Relationship of husband and wife, 1 Corinthians 7:1–7.

Bachelor's advice on marriage, 1 Corinthians 7:1–7.

Continence for prayer, 1 Corinthians 7:5 (CEV).

Marriage between unbelievers and believers, 1 Corinthians 7:10–16.

Troubled married life, 1 Corinthians 7:25–28 (See LB).

Wife traveling with husband, 1 Corinthians 9:5.

Paul described role of women, 1 Corinthians 11:2–16.

Role of husband and wife, Ephesians 5:21–33.

Rapport between wives and husbands, Colossians 3:18, 19; 1 Peter 3:1–2, 7.

Absence of love, 2 Timothy 3:3.

Elder permitted one wife, Titus 1:6.

Domestic responsibility of young wives, Titus 2:3–5.

Honorable, pure, Hebrews 13:4.

Wife loves husband's enemies, James 4:4 (LB).

Avoiding problems in marriage, 1 Peter 3:1–7.

No fear in love, 1 John 4:18.

Influence of Jezebel at Thyatira, Revelation 2:20.

No bride, bridegroom in Babylon, Revelation 18:23.

Garments of bride, Revelation 19:7–8; 21:2.
See Bride, Divorce, Husband, Intermarriage, Remarriage, Romance, Wedding.

MARTIAL LAW

City under martial law, Joshua 6:1.

MARTYR

Martyred priests, 1 Samuel 22:17–18.

Predicted martyrs, Matthew 10:21.

Death of John the Baptist, Matthew 14:1–12.

Those who only destroy body, Luke 12:4–5.

Stoning of Stephen, Acts 6:8–15; 7:1–60.

James slain with sword, Acts 12:2.

Prepared for martyrdom, Acts 21:13.

Living martyrdom, Romans 8:36.

Measure of love, 1 Corinthians 13:3.

Willing to lay down one's life for others, 1 John 3:16.

Faithful in persecution, Revelation 2:13.

Put to death for witness, Revelation 6:9.

Drunk with blood of saints, Revelation 17:6.

Beheaded for faithfulness and testimony, Revelation 20:4.
See Persecution.

MASCULINE

Doing a man's job, Judges 8:21 (GNB).

Strong in the battle, 2 Samuel 10:12.

Be seen as a man, 1 Kings 2:2.

Unmanly grief, Job 6:2 (AB).

Listen like a man, Job 40:7.

Handsome, eloquent, Psalm 45:2 (See GNB).

Elaborate masculine description, Song of Songs 5:9–16 (CEV).

A man to stand in the gap, Ezekiel 22:30.
See Athletics, Sportsman, Strength, Virility.

MASON

Use of specific materials, Genesis 11:3.

Large stones covered with plaster, Deuteronomy 27:2.

Palace construction, 2 Samuel 5:11.

Salaried workmen, 2 Kings 12:12.

Temple builders, 1 Chronicles 22:2; 2 Chronicles 24:12.

Faulty mortar, Ezekiel 13:10–11, 14.

Mortar and brickwork, Nahum 3:14.
See Construction.

MASQUERADE

False prophets, Jeremiah 23:16–18.

Ego displayed by teachers of law, Mark 12:38–40.

Satan as angel of light, 2 Corinthians 11:14.

Method of false teachers, 2 Peter 2:1.
See Camouflage, Pretense.

MASSACRE

Evil prophets destroyed, 1 Kings 18:40.

Royal family massacred, 2 Chronicles 22:10.

MASTERPIECES

Skilled in one's work, Proverbs 22:29.

Artist's mortality, Isaiah 44:11.
See Skill, Talent.

MASTURBATION

Father's bed defiled, Genesis 49:4.

Uncleanness in the camp, Deuteronomy 23:9–14.

MATERIALISM

Exchanging small possessions for greater, Genesis 45:20.

Odor of disobedience, Exodus 16:19–24.

Monetary value of human being, Leviticus 27:1–8.

Material security versus God's will, Numbers 32:14–27.

Any kind of idol, Deuteronomy 4:25 (See NKJV).

Gold, silver destroyed, Deuteronomy 7:25.

Plunder permitted, Joshua 8:1–2.

Gold a snare to good man, Judges 8:24–27.

Making idol to please the Lord, Judges 17:3.

Prayer for wisdom above material gain, 1 Kings 3:5–15 (See 4:29–34).

Less time to build temple than palace, 1 Kings 6:37–38; 7:1.

Materialism versus obedience, 1 Kings 13:7–10.

Depending on number of fighting men, 1 Chronicles 21:17.

Loss of material possessions, Job 1:13–21.

Nauseating affluence, Job 20:15.

Wicked often prosper, Job 21:7.

Folly of trusting wealth, Job 31:24–28; Psalm 49:5–12.

Riches, bribes, Job 36:18–19.

Greater joy than material gain, Psalm 4:7.

Everything belongs to God, Job 41:11; Psalms 24:1–2; 50:9–12.

Wealth can numb thoughts of God, Psalm 10:3–6.

Trusting solely in the Lord, Psalm 20:7.

Righteous poor, wicked wealthy, Psalm 37:16–17.

Short-lived prosperity, Psalm 37:35–36.

Stones, dust of Jerusalem, Psalm 102:14.

Eternal God and temporal creation, Psalm 102:25–27.

Creditors seize all, Psalm 109:11.

Greatest values in life, Psalm 119:36–37.

Value found only in Scripture, Psalm 119:72.

Treasure in God's promises, Psalm 119:162.

Heathen gods made by the hands of men, Psalm 135:15–18.

Total end of all for wicked man, Proverbs 11:7.

Riches not to be trusted, Proverbs 11:28.

Little with faith, much with turmoil, Proverbs 15:16.

Purchase of prestige, Proverbs 18:16.

Value of good name, Proverbs 22:1.

Vapor of vapors, Ecclesiastes 1:2 (AB).

Money alone never satisfies, Ecclesiastes 5:10.

Man born naked and so departs, Ecclesiastes 5:15.

Dangers of national wealth, Isaiah 2:7–8.

Lost security, Isaiah 2:19 (AB).

Man with cloak, Isaiah 3:6.

Ruins of rich, Isaiah 5:17.

Trust the Lord, not horses and chariots, Isaiah 31:1–3.

Rejecting idols of silver and gold, Isaiah 31:7.

Wood for making gods and cooking fires, Isaiah 44:14–20.

Impotence of man-made gods, Isaiah 46:6–7.

That which money cannot buy, Isaiah 55:1–2.

Destruction of wealth and security, Jeremiah 5:17.

Wealth given away in judgment, Jeremiah 17:3.

Stunted spiritual growth, Jeremiah 17:5–6 (LB).

Slaves set free, then enslaved, Jeremiah 34:8–22.

Gold dull, jewels strewn, Lamentations 4:1.

Priests owned no property, Ezekiel 44:28.

The god of fortresses, Daniel 11:38–39.

Wealth numbs conscience, Hosea 12:8; Amos 3:10.

Worship of what hands have made, Hosea 14:3.

Food, possessions do not satisfy, Micah 6:14.

Too many merchants desecrated land, Nahum 3:16.

Silver, gold valueless in judgment, Zephaniah 1:18.

Well-built houses, temple ruins, Haggai 1:4 (GNB).

Those never satisfied, Haggai 1:5–6.

Silver, gold like dust, dirt, Zechariah 9:3.

Reward of good stewardship, Malachi 3:8–10.

Kingdoms of the world, Matthew 4:8–9.

Treasures on earth, treasures in heaven, Matthew 6:19–21.

God provides for nature, cares for His children, Matthew 6:25–34.

Jesus had no place of residence, Matthew 8:20.

Clothes describe man, Matthew 11:7–9.

Gain world, forfeit soul, Matthew 16:25–26; Mark 8:36.

Money changers in temple, Matthew 21:12–13.

Temple gold, Matthew 23:16.

Deceitfulness of wealth, Mark 4:19.

Eternal value of soul, temporal values of life, Mark 8:35–37.

Rich young man failed spiritual test, Mark 10:17–27.

Sharing with others, Luke 3:11.

Earth's transient happiness, Luke 6:24 (LB).

Materialistic greed, Luke 12:13–21.

Those who must see signs and wonders, John 4:48.

Purchasing power of wages, John 6:7.

Disciples wanted restored earthly kingdom, Acts 1:4–8.

All things in common, Acts 4:32.

Scrolls of value destroyed by converted sorcerers, Acts 19:19.

Wood, hay and straw or gold, silver, costly stones, 1 Corinthians 3:12–13.

Enemies and attitudes in last days, 2 Timothy 3:1–5.

Love of money, Hebrews 13:5.

Poor can be rich in faith, James 2:5.

Danger of greed in ministry, 1 Peter 5:2–3.

Fragile realities of earth and sky, 2 Peter 3:5–13.

Living for what is eternal, 2 Peter 3:11–14.

Sharing material possessions with others, 1 John 3:17.

Release from nakedness and blindness, Revelation 3:18.

Merchants lament destruction of Babylon, Revelation 18:11–19.

Earth and sky flee from the eternal, Revelation 20:11.

Description of new Jerusalem, Revelation 21:15–27.

See Affluence, Covet, Greed, Secular, Wealth.

MATHEMATICS

Quantity beyond numbering, Genesis 15:5; 32:12.

Exact numerals, Ezra 2:64–67.

Mathematical balance in generations, Matthew 1:17.

Groups of fifty for five miracle loaves, Luke 9:14–15.

Human equations and power of God, John 6:1–13 (Note verse 7).

Geometric dimensions of Christ's love, Ephesians 3:14–19.

Spiritual growth mathematics, 2 Peter 1:5–8.

Dimensions of temple, Revelation 11:1–2.

Measurement of new Jerusalem, Revelation 21:16–17.

See Geometry, Multiplication.

MATURITY

Maturing of Samuel, 1 Samuel 3:19–21.

Gentleness, 2 Samuel 22:36 (LB).

Mature advice spurned, 2 Chronicles 10:1–15.

Stones, bronze, Job 6:12 (AB).

Ways of wisdom, Proverbs 2:12–20.

Sure road to maturity, Proverbs 9:1–6.

Depths of spiritual truth, John 6:60–69.

Purpose of suffering, Romans 5:3.

Freedom from mastery of sin, Romans 6:14.

Filled with hope, joy, peace, Romans 15:13.

Milk, solid food, 1 Corinthians 3:1–2; Hebrews 5:11, 14; 6:1–3; 1 Peter 2:2–3.

No longer a child, 1 Corinthians 13:11, 13; 14:20; Ephesians 4:14.

Willing to be accepted as fool, 2 Corinthians 11:16–19.

Spirit of wisdom, revelation, Ephesians 1:17.

Geometric spiritual dimensions, Ephesians 3:17–18 (See NRSV).

Becoming mature Christians, Ephesians 4:13.

Learn what pleases the Lord, Ephesians 5:10.

Standing at end of struggle, Ephesians 6:13.

Good work begun will be completed, Philippians 1:6.

Standing firm whatever circumstances, Philippians 1:27–30.

Forget past, press toward goal, Philippians 3:12–16.

Content in all situations, Philippians 4:12.

Marks of Christian maturity, Colossians 1:3–8.

Filled with knowledge of God's will, Colossians 1:9–12.

Spiritual need fulfilled in Christ, Colossians 1:15–23.

Conversion, growth, Colossians 2:6–7.

Mature in Christ, Colossians 4:12.

Motivated Christians, 1 Thessalonians 1:3.

Strong, blameless, 1 Thessalonians 3:13.

Motivated to Christian life-style, 1 Thessalonians 4:11–12.

Growing in faith, love, 2 Thessalonians 1:3.

Mature teaching on Christ's return, 2 Thessalonians 2:1–2.

Leadership not for immature convert, 1 Timothy 3:6.

Diligent quest for spiritual maturity, 1 Timothy 4:13.

Calm in all situations, 2 Timothy 4:5.

Christ made perfect through suffering, Hebrews 2:10.

Scriptural guidance discerning good from evil, Hebrews 5:11–14.

"Grow up," Hebrews 6:3 (CEV).

Discipline of testing, Hebrews 12:7; James 1:2–4.

Listen before speaking, James 1:19.

Strategic control of speech, James 3:2.

Sharing weakness with each other, James 5:16.

Strong, firm, and steadfast, 1 Peter 5:10.

Live godly life, 2 Peter 1:2, 3 (See AB).

Distinct element of spiritual maturity, 2 Peter 1:5–9.

Growing in grace, 2 Peter 3:18.

Deliverance from practicing sin, 1 John 3:8–10.

Health and wealth plus spiritual vitality, 3 John 2–4.

Temporal wealth and spiritual wealth, Revelation 3:15–18.

See Discipleship, Frame-of-Reference, Growth.

MAXIM

Deeds reveal person, 1 Samuel 24:13.

MAYOR

Five mayors, 1 Samuel 6:16 (LB).

Mayors of ten cities, Ecclesiastes 7:19 (LB).

MEALS

Dinner, Genesis 24:33; Luke 24:29, 30.

Lunch, Genesis 43:16; John 4:6, 31.

Breakfast, Judges 19:5; John 21:9.

Large table setting, Nehemiah 5:17.

Table grace, Mark 8:6–7; 14:22; Luke 24:30; Romans 14:6; 1 Timothy 4:4.

See Banquet, Delicacy, Diet, Feast, Food, Gourmet, Nutrition, Vegetable.

MEASUREMENT

Honest scales, Job 31:6.

Handful measurement, Isaiah 40:12.

Measuring device, Jeremiah 31:39; Ezekiel 40:3; 42:16; Zechariah 2:1.

Measuring new temple area, Ezekiel 40:5–49.

Astute measurement, Acts 7:5 (NRSV).

Measurement of new Jerusalem, Revelation 21:15–21.

See Dimensions, Inch, Mathematics, Standard.

MEAT

Man, animals originally vegetarian, Genesis 1:29–30; 2:9.

Beginning of meat as food, Genesis 9:3.

Broiled, not cooked, Exodus 12:8–9.

Utensil for meat, Exodus 27:3; 38:3; Numbers 4:14.

Craving for meat, Numbers 11:4–5, 18–20, 31–34.

Meat not to be eaten, Leviticus 11:1–47; Isaiah 66:17.

All you can eat, Deuteronomy 12:15.

Food containing blood, 1 Samuel 14:31–33.

Choice quality, Isaiah 25:6 (KJV).

Spiritual food, 1 Corinthians 3:1–3; Hebrews 5:11–14.

Meat market, 1 Corinthians 10:25 (NASB, NKJV, NRSV).

See Food.

MEDDLE

False reports and malicious witness, Exodus 23:1.

Meddling in affairs of others, Proverbs 26:17.

Busybodies, 2 Thessalonians 3:11.

From house to house, 1 Timothy 5:13.
Suffering as meddler, 1 Peter 4:15.
See Busybody, Gossip.

MEDIA

Voice transmitted worldwide, Psalm 19:4.
Let others praise you, Proverbs 27:2.
Secret thoughts conveyed to others, Ecclesiastes 10:20.
Engraved with iron tool, Jeremiah 17:1.
Scrolls for public reading, Jeremiah 36:6, 14–16.
Man with writing kit, Ezekiel 9:11.
Publishing message plainly, Habakkuk 2:2.
Flying scroll, Zechariah 5:1–4.
Word of mouth, Mark 1:28.
Decision to communicate by writing, Luke 1:1–4.
Angelic announcement of good news, Luke 2:10.
See Communication, Writing.

MEDIATOR

People in need of mediator, Exodus 20:19; Deuteronomy 5:27.
Burdened leadership, Deuteronomy 9:18.
Standing between living and dead, Numbers 16:48.

Job's cry for mediator between him and God, Job 9:33–35.
Ineffective mediators, Jeremiah 15:1.
People's dependence upon mediator, Jeremiah 42:1–4.
Message came through prophet, Haggai 1:1.
Faith of friends caused man's healing, Mark 2:1–5.
God only known through Christ, Luke 10:22; 1 Timothy 2:5; Hebrews 8:6; 9:15, 24; 12:24; 1 John 2:1.
Go between, Galatians 3:20 (AB).
Jesus between, 1 Timothy 2:4–5 (LB).
Jesus our guarantee, Hebrews 7:22.
See Redeemer, Redemption.

MEDICARE

Medical bills, Mark 5:25–34.

MEDICINE

Embalming in Egypt, Genesis 50:2–3.
Music therapy, 1 Samuel 16:14–23; 17:10.
"Quack doctors," Job 13:4 (See Berk.).
Attitude, health, Proverbs 17:22.
Alcohol as medicine, Proverbs 31:6–7.
Beyond medical help, Isaiah 1:6 (See AB).
Practical perscription, Isaiah 38:21.

MEAT

Careless attention to wound, Jeremiah 8:11 (Also see LB).

No balm in Gilead, Jeremiah 8:22.

Medicinal leaves, Ezekial 47:12; Revelation 22:2.

Jesus recognized medical doctors, Matthew 9:12.

Painkiller, Mark 15:23 (LB).

Good Samaritan, Luke 10:33–34.

Earth and saliva, John 9:6–7.

"Dear doctor Luke," Colossians 4:14 (LB).

Eye salve, Revelation 3:18.

See Health, Physician, Remedies, Surgery, Therapy.

MEDITATION

Daily meditation, Joshua 1:8.

Constant meditation, Psalm 1:2 (See Berk.).

"Silently search your heart," Psalm 4:4 (CEV, NKJV).

Time for reflection, Psalm 16:7.

Heart meditation, Psalm 19:14.

Thirst for living God, Psalm 42:1–2.

Deep calling unto deep, Psalm 42:7–8.

Meditation in temple, Psalm 48:9.

Silently seeking God, Psalm 62:1 (NKJV, NRSV).

Nightlong meditation, Psalm 63:6.

Grateful reflections, Psalms 77:10–12; 143:5.

Bible insight, Psalm 119:18 (Berk.).

Daylong experience, Psalm 119:97.

Wisdom from Scriptures, Psalm 119:98–100.

Prayer for inner peace, righteousness, Psalm 139:23–24.

Glory of kings, Proverbs 25:2.

"Think what God has done," Ecclesiastes 7:13 (CEV).

Spiritual delicacy, Jeremiah 15:16.

Communing outdoors, Ezekiel 3:22–23.

Silent before the Lord, Zephaniah 1:7; Zechariah 2:13.

Prayer closet, Matthew 6:5–6.

Pondering profound event, Luke 2:19 (See AB).

Daybreak solitude, Luke 4:42.

Jesus withdrew to pray, Luke 5:16.

Ultimate "Holy of Holies," 1 Corinthians 3:16.

Alone in Athens, 1 Thessalonians 3:1.

Reward of careful reflection, 2 Timothy 2:7.

Fix thoughts on Jesus, Hebrews 3:1.

Meditate about message, 1 John 2:24 (CEV).

Those who take Scriptures to heart, Revelation 1:3.

See Prayer, Quiet Time.

MEDIUMS *See Fortune-Telling, Witchcraft.*

MEEKNESS

Quality of life, Psalm 22:26; 37:11; 2 Timothy 2:24.

Soft response to anger, Proverbs 15:1; 16:32.

Quiet joy of contentment, Proverbs 30:7–8.

Humbly seeking the Lord, Zephaniah 2:3.

Day of small things, Zechariah 4:10.

Blessed are the meek, Matthew 5:5.

Divine example, Matthew 11:29; 27:13–14.

Right spirit in victory over evil, Luke 10:17–20.

Response to mistreatment, Romans 12:14.

Dimensions of love, 1 Corinthians 13:4–7; Ephesians 4:1–2.

Paul's timidity, 2 Corinthians 10:1.

Fruit of Spirit, Galatians 5:22–23.

Relating with gentleness, 1 Thessalonians 2:7–8.

See Gentleness, Humility.

MELANCHOLY

Saddened with life, Job 10:1 (Berk.).

Restless mind, Ecclesiastes 2:23.

Daughter taught to wail, Jeremiah 9:20.

Joy and gladness gone, Jeremiah 48:33.

Pouting Jonah, Jonah 4:5.

Heavy hearts, Luke 21:34.

See Mood, Pessimism, Sorrow.

MEMBERSHIP

Membership in God's household, Ephesians 2:19, 20.

Recorded in Book of Life, Philippians 4:3.

See Congregation.

MEMENTO *See Memorabilia.*

MEMORABILIA

Preserved manna, Exodus 16:33.

Sanctuary items taken to battle, Numbers 31:6.

Goliath's weapons, 1 Samuel 17:54.

Bronze serpent destroyed, 2 Kings 18:4.

Old Testament memorabilia, Hebrews 9:2–4 (See GNB).

See Memento.

MEMORIAL

Memorial to site of dream, Genesis 28:18–19.

Covenant memorial, Genesis 31:44–45.

Experience at Bethel, Genesis 35:9–15.

Passover memorial, Exodus 12:14.

Living memorial, Exodus 13:12–16.

Harvest festival, Leviticus 23:39–44.

Captured city named after captor, Numbers 32:42.

Ebenezer stone, 1 Samuel 7:12.

Absalom's memorial to himself, 2 Samuel 18:18.

Lord's Supper, 1 Corinthians 11:24–26.

See Honor, Landmark, Tombstone.

MEMORIZATION

Memorization commanded, Deuteronomy 6:6–9.

Solomon's songs, proverbs, 1 Kings 4:32.

Memorized promises, Joshua 23:14.

Treasured memorization, Psalm 119:11 (NRSV).

Deliverance, guidance, Deuteronomy 30:14; Psalm 119:11, 105, 129–130.

Treasured Scripture, Psalm 119:11 (NRSV).

Knowing, obeying the Lord's commands, Isaiah 48:17–18.

God's law in the heart, Proverbs 3:3; 7:2–3; Isaiah 51:7; Jeremiah 31:33; Romans 10:8; Hebrews 10:16.

Certain function of God's word, Isaiah 55:10–11.

Delectable Word of God, Jeremiah 15:16.

Childhood memorization, Joel 1:1–3.

Coming need for memorized Scripture, Amos 8:11–12.

Value of memorization, Micah 2:7.

Function of memorized Scripture, John 17:14–17; Colossians 3:16.

See Bible, Frame-of-Reference, Guidance, Scripture.

MEMORY

Sacred Memories, Genesis 46:1 (AB).

Remembering and implementing, Deuteronomy 4:9.

Things known in the heart, 1 Kings 2:44.

Memories of old temple as new temple begun, Ezra 3:10–13.

Wishing remembered day not to exist, Job 3:6.

Remembered happiness of younger years, Job 29:4–6.

Gratitude for God's goodness, Psalm 143:5.

Good old days, Ecclesiastes 7:10.

"Don't think about the past," Isaiah 43:18 (CEV).

God never forgets, Isaiah 49:15.

Discontinued memory, Isaiah 65:17.

Greater blessing, lesser blessing, Jeremiah 16:14–15.

Old days bitterly remembered, Lamentations 1:7.

Daniel made notes, did not trust memory, Daniel 7:1.

Remembering glory of better days, Haggai 2:3.

Rooster jars memory, Mark 14:66–72.

Not remembering those baptized, 1 Corinthians 1:16.

Memory lapse, 1 Corinthians 15:1 (AB).

Sins forgotten, Hebrews 10:17.

Refresh memory, 2 Peter 1:13.

See Memorization, Recollect, Reminiscence.

MENACE

Wicked bend their bows, Psalm 11:2.

Song of ruthless made silent, Isaiah 25:5.

Pharaoh only loud noise, Jeremiah 46:17.

See Danger, Threat.

MENOPAUSE

Beyond years of childbearing, Genesis 18:11.

MENSTRUATION

"Custom of women," Genesis 18:11 (Berk.).
Modified Levitical requirements, Leviticus 15:19–30; 20:18.
Defilement of idols, Isaiah 30:22.
Ezekiel's description of puberty, Ezekiel 16:5–9.
Intimacy forbidden, Ezekiel 18:6.
Women violated, Ezekiel 22:10.
Type of uncleanness, Ezekiel 36:17.
See Menopause.

MENTAL HEALTH

Pretended madness, 1 Samuel 21:12–14.
Mental therapy, Psalm 119:93.
Outer, inner feelings, Proverbs 14:13.
Cheerful heart, Proverbs 17:22; 18:14.
Daughters taught to wail, Jeremiah 9:20.
Becoming like animal, Daniel 4:31–34.
Members of Jesus' family suspected insanity, Mark 3:20–21.
Mental agony, Luke 22:44 (AB).
See Depression, Insanity.

MENTALITY

Witless man, Job 11:12.
Bible-centered mentality, Psalm 1:2.
Simple understanding, Psalm 119:130.
Parables to a fool, Proverbs 26:1–12.
Easily deceived, Hosea 7:11.
Adults like children, Matthew 11:16–17.
Intellectual pride, 1 Corinthians 3:18–20; 8:1–3.
Spirit of wisdom, revelation, Ephesians 1:17.
Mental enmity against God, Colossians 1:21.
Fix thoughts on Jesus, Hebrews 3:1.
Mentality of success, 1 Peter 1:13–15.
Mind clear of negative thoughts, 1 Peter 2:1.
Stimulated to wholesome thought, 2 Peter 3:1.
See Comprehension, Intelligence.

MENTAL TELEPATHY *See Mind Reading.*

MENU

Forty-year menu, Exodus 16:35.
Wickedness, violence, Proverbs 4:17.

Cheap food causes illness, Proverbs 23:6–8.
See Cooking.

MERCENARIES

Hiring foot soldiers, 2 Samuel 10:6; Ezekiel 30:5 (CEV).
Reckless adventures, Judges 9:4.
Hired chariots, 1 Chronicles 19:7.
Israeli soldiers for hire, 2 Chronicles 25:6–7.
Hired to intimidate, Nehemiah 6:13.
Cowardly mercenaries, Jeremiah 46:21.
See Army.

MERCHANDISE

Prostitute who paid, Ezekiel 16:33–34.
Accurate scales, Ezekiel 45:9–10.
Merchandise aborted in storm, Jonah 1:5.
No merchandise sales, Revelation 18:11.
See Barter, Commerce, Travel.

MERCIFUL *See Mercy.*

MERCILESS

Partial blindness inflicted, 1 Samuel 11:2–11.
Merciless genocide, 1 Samuel 15:3.
See Brutality, Sadistic, Torture.

MERCY

Divine willingness to extend mercy, Genesis 18:16–33.
Mercy in action, Genesis 39:21–23.
Pleading for God's mercy, Numbers 14:13–25.
David, Saul, 1 Samuel 24:10–17.
Solomon's mercy to Adonijah, 1 Kings 1:43–53.
Imprisoned, set free, 2 Kings 24:15; 25:27–29.
"Mercy" rendered as "love," Psalm 23:6 (See CEV).
Contrast between God's anger and love, Psalm 30:5.
Recollections of long life, Psalm 37:25–26.
Requesting God's mercy, Psalm 41:4.
Punishment with mercy, Psalm 89:30–34.
God's forgiveness, punishment, Psalm 99:8.
Undeserved mercy, Psalm 103:9–10.

God's innate mercy, Psalms 109:21; 145:8–9.

Spared by God's mercy, Psalm 130:3.

Kind man's benefits, Proverbs 11:17.

Benevolent of heart, Proverbs 14:21–22, 31.

Mercy to coward, Isaiah 30:17–18.

God's mercy to faithless Israel, Jeremiah 3:12–13; Hosea 14:4.

Mercy follows judgment, Jeremiah 12:14–17.

God's immeasurable mercy, Jeremiah 31:37.

Mercy to suffering Jeremiah, Jeremiah 38:6–13.

Babylonian mercy to poor, Jeremiah 39:10.

Mercy in time of judgment, Lamentations 3:31–33.

Divine patience with rebellious Israel, Ezekiel 20:1–44.

Plea to be merciful, Daniel 4:27.

Pardon for nation's bloodguilt, Joel 3:21.

Mercy-prone pagan sailors, Jonah 1:11–15.

"Let mercy be your first concern," Micah 6:8 (CEV).

God's forgiving grace, mercy, Micah 7:18.

The Lord slow to anger, Nahum 1:3.

God of judgment, of mercy, Zechariah 8:14–15.

"Blessed are the merciful," Matthew 5:7.

Forgive as God forgives, Matthew 6:14.

Human mercy of Jesus, Luke 5:12–13.

Admonition of Jesus, Luke 6:36.

God's love for sinners, Ephesians 2:1–5.

Mercy and grace unto salvation, Ephesians 2:6–10.

Christ-centered conduct, Colossians 3:12–13.

Mercy to unsaved, 2 Peter 3:9.

See Forgiveness, Grace, Pardon.

MERCY KILLING *See Euthanasia.*

MERRYMAKING

Tragedy at Job's home, Job 1:13–15.

Deep inner feelings, Proverbs 14:13.

Wanton merrymaking, Isaiah 5:12.

Terminated merrymaking, Lamentations 5:15.

High price for dance, Mark 6:21–29.

See Frivolous.

MESSAGE

Refusing to hear God's message, Judges 6:10.

Words given by Holy Spirit, 2 Samuel 23:2.

King's edict for sparing Jews, Esther 8:14.

Message universality, Psalm 49:1.

Those who avoid truth, Isaiah 30:10–11.

Speaking in understood language, Isaiah 36:11.

Messengers with no message, Lamentations 2:9.

Message written on wall, Daniel 5:5.

Mourning over message, Daniel 10:1–3.

Prophet given message, Obadiah 1 (CEV).

Spectacular message from heaven, Luke 2:8–14.

Sufficiently conveyed message, John 20:30–31.

Theme of post-resurrection apostles, Acts 4:2.

Resume of Old Testament, proclamation of Gospel, Acts 13:16–41.

Gospel known as "the Way," Acts 19:9, 23; 22:4; 24:22.

Gospel message in brief, 1 Corinthians 15:1–5.

Cheap merchandise, 2 Corinthians 2:17 (GNB).

Power of gospel message, Philippians 1:15–18; 1 Thessalonians 1:4–5.

Word of God in its fullness, Colossians 1:25–26.

Message Paul was called to proclaim, 1 Timothy 2:5–7.

Treasured message, 2 Timothy 1:14 (CEV).

Various ways of communicating God's message, Hebrews 1:1–2.

Faith as credibility to message, Hebrews 4:2.

Relevant message for all ages, 1 John 2:12–14.

Message conveyed by angel, Revelation 1:1–3.

See Communication, Preaching.

MESSENGER

Angelic messenger, Judges 13:6; Luke 1:19; Revelation 1:1.

Unheeded messengers, Jeremiah 25:4; Matthew 22:3.

Bearer of bad news, Ezekiel 33:21.

Messenger rooster, Mark 14:29–31, 66–72.

By divine appointment, John 1:6.

Young man who defended Paul, Acts 23:16–22.

See Message, Ministry, Missionary, Preaching.

MESSIAH

Messianic lineage, Ruth 4:13–17.

Length of David's reign, 2 Samuel 5:5.

Messianic line preserved, 2 Kings 8:16–19; 14:27.

King of earth, Psalm 47:7.

Messianic lineage, Psalm 89:3–4.

Solomon's messianic concepts, Proverbs 30:4.

Virgin birth prophecy, Isaiah 7:14.

Coming Messiah, Isaiah 9:1–7; 11:1–10.

Messianic day, Isaiah 28:5 (AB).

Tested stone in Zion, Isaiah 28:16.

Prophecy of John the Baptist, Christ, Isaiah 40:1–5.

Prophetic description of Jesus, Isaiah 53:1–12.

Coming of Christ, proclamation of Gospel, Isaiah 61:1–3.

Redeemer, King, Isaiah 63:1.

Birth in Bethlehem, Micah 5:2.

Desire of all nations, Haggai 2:7.

Triumphal entry into Jerusalem, Zechariah 9:9.

Prophecy of Judas, thirty pieces of silver, Zechariah 11:12–13.

Prophecy of the cross, Zechariah 12:10–11.

Conquering Lord of lords, Zechariah 14:3–4.

Authentic Messiah, Matthew 11:1–5.

Demons recognized Messiah, Luke 4:41.

Messiah discovered, John 1:45, 51 (LB).

Questioned messianic identity, John 7:25–27 (See LB).

Messiah affirmed, John 20:30–31 (NRSV).

Death of David, of Christ, messianic implications, Acts 2:29–35.

Anticipated salvation of Jew and Gentile, Galatians 3:6–9.

Sovereignty of Jesus, Revelation 1:5.

Unique name for Jesus, Revelation 3:14.

Rider on white horse, Revelation 19:11–16.

Totality of the Son of God, Revelation 22:13.

See Jesus, Second Coming.

METAL

Metal workers, Exodus 31:1–5; 1 Chronicles 22:15, 16; Isaiah 40:19.

Silver not precious metal, 1 Kings 10:21, 27.

Gold, silver, bronze, iron, 2 Chronicles 2:7.

Molten images, 2 Chronicles 28:2 (KJV).

Strength of iron, Jeremiah 15:12.

Gold and silver belong to God, Haggai 2:8.

See Alloy, Gold, Iron, Money, Ore.

METAPHOR

Rising like the sun, Judges 5:31.

Lord and shepherd, Psalm 23:1.

Sun and shield, Psalm 84:11.

Shield and rampart, Psalms 84:11; 91:4.

Sow and reap, Hosea 10:12.

Wickedness in the flesh, Zechariah 5:7, 8.

Salt of earth, Matthew 5:13.

Seed and soil, Matthew 13:19–23, 37–43.

Bread and body, Matthew 26:26.

Lamp of witness, John 5:35.

Bread of life, John 6:35.

Light of world, John 8:12.

Jesus as the gate, John 10:9.

True vine, John 15:5.

Sorrow turned to joy, John 16:20.

Speaking plainly, John 16:25.

Lampstands and stars, Revelation 1:20.

Incense and prayers, Revelation 5:8.

See Figure of Speech.

METEOROLOGY

Weather control, Job 28:24–27; 36:27–33; 37:6–21; Psalm 135:7.

Ancient concept of weather cycles, Ecclesiastes 1:7.

Divine meteorologist, Jeremiah 14:22.

Rain in spotted areas, Amos 4:7, 8.

Formation of clouds and rainfall, Amos 9:6.

Weather on request, Zechariah 10:1.

Forecasting weather, Matthew 16:2; Luke 12:54–56.

See Weather.

METEORS

Stars falling to earth, Revelation 6:13.
Meteor-like hailstones, Revelation 16:21.
See Astronomy.

METHODOLOGY *See Teaching.*

MIDDLE AGE

Prime of life, Job 29:4.
Death at middle age, Psalm 102:24.
"Noontide of my days," Isaiah 38:10 (Berk.).

MIDNIGHT

Midnight peril, Exodus 11:4.
Midnight prayer, Psalm 119:62.
Ten virgins, Matthew 25:6.
Midnight song, prayer, Acts 16:25.
Preaching until midnight, Acts 20:7.
See Darkness, Night, Nightmare, Sleep.

MIGRATION

Mankind moving eastward, Genesis 11:1–2.
Aliens succeed above nationals, Deuteronomy 28:43–44.
Building population by statistics, Nehemiah 11:1.
Hawk flies south, Job 39:26.
Birds know when to migrate, Jeremiah 8:7.
See Aliens, Birds, Flight, Immigration, Journey, Travel, Wandering.

MILDEW

Cleaning a house of mildew, Leviticus 14:33–48.
Terminal disorder, Deuteronomy 28:22.
Blight, mildew, Amos 4:9; Haggai 2:17.

MILITANT *See Antagonism.*

MILITARY

Clergy exemption, Numbers 1:47–49 (GNB).
Threat of iron chariots, Judges 1:19.
God as militarist, Judges 3:1–2.
Seeking divine strategy, 1 Samuel 14:8–15.
Sexual restraint before combat, 1 Samuel 21:4–5.
Military concern above promises, 2 Samuel 24:10.
Complete devastation, 2 Kings 3:19.
Men trained for service, 1 Chronicles 5:18.
Battle lines, 1 Chronicles 19:17.
Strength of God's army, Psalm 68:17.
"King among his troops," Job 29:25 (NRSV).
Fallible military, Isaiah 31:1–3.
Angel in military, Isaiah 37:36.
Call to arms for Israel invasion, Ezekiel 38:8.
Women in military, Nahum 3:13.
Nonmilitant resistance, John 18:36.
Centurion's devout family, Acts 10:1–2, 22.
Good Christian soldiers, 2 Timothy 2:1–4.
Fellow soldier, Philemon 2.
War in heaven, Revelation 12:7.
See Armament, Army, Mercenaries, Soldier.

MILK

Curds and milk for visitors, Genesis 18:8.
Milk camels, Genesis 32:15.
Curds and honey, Isaiah 7:22.
Water requested, milk served, Judges 4:19.
Dairy product in desert, 2 Samuel 17:29.
Lavish use of butter, Job 29:6 (KJV).
Milk to butter, Proverbs 30:33.
Spiritual food, 1 Corinthians 3:1–3; Hebrews 5:11–14.
See Food, Thirst.

MILLENNIUM *See Second Coming.*

MILLIONAIRE

More value than millions, Psalm 119:71–72 (LB).

MIND

The Lord knows our thoughts, Psalms 94:11; 139:1–4.
Anxiety control, Ecclesiastes 11:10.
Evil thoughts, Jeremiah 4:14.
Revealing thoughts of heart, Luke 2:34–35; 6:8.
Depraved minds, Romans 1:28.
Conflict between mind, body, Romans 7:21–25.
Natural mind, Spirit-controlled mind, Romans 8:6–9.
Futility thinking, Ephesians 4:17.
Attitude of mind dictates conduct, Philippians 4:8–9.
Egotistical mind, Colossians 2:18.
Corrupt mind, conscience, Titus 1:15.

Thoughts fixed on Jesus, Hebrews 3:1.
Minds prepared for action, 1 Peter 1:13.
See Attitude, Brain, Disposition, Frame-of-Reference, Thinking, Thought.

MIND READING
Jesus knew men's thoughts, Matthew 9:4; Luke 5:22; 6:8; 11:17.

MINERALS
Gold deposits, Genesis 2:11–12.
Bib!e minerals, Genesis 11:3; Numbers 21:9; 31:22; Deuteronomy 8:9; 29:23; Job 19:24; 28:18.
Degraded value of silver, 1 Kings 10:21, 27.
Mining deep into earth, Job 28:1–4.
Earth's depths, mountain peaks, Psalm 95:4.
Gold and silver belong to God, Haggai 2:8.
See Geology, Natural Resources.

MINING
Mining procedure, Job 28:1–11.
See Minerals.

MINISTRY
Happenstance ministry, Judges 17:7–13.
Strengthening others, Job 4:3.
Disobedience impairs ministry, Jeremiah 11:17.
Ministry in troubled times, Daniel 11:33 (LB).
Teaching, preaching, healing, Matthew 4:23; 9:18–25.
Relentless ministry, Mark 6:30–34.
Aged widow's ministry, Luke 2:36–38.
Ministry styles, Luke 9.
Rejecting those who minister, Luke 10:16.
Joy of ministry, Luke 10:17.
Misunderstanding Jesus' ministry, Luke 12:13–14.
Not personal power, piety, Acts 3:12 (NRSV).
Ministry unction, grace, Acts 4:33.
Partners in ministry, Acts 11:25–26.
Laity in ministry, Acts 15:35.
Holy Spirit restrained preaching, Acts 16:6–7.
Those who reject ministry, Acts 18:5–6.
Convert instructed to minister, Acts 18:24–26.

Self-evaluation of ministry, Acts 20:17–38.
Reporting arrest, Acts 28:17–28.
First servant, then ministry, Romans 1:1.
Ministry with mutual benefit, Romans 1:11.
Pride in ministry, Romans 11:13 (Berk.).
Prayer for ministry, Romans 15:31–32.
Varied tasks in ministry, 1 Corinthians 3:5–9.
Entrusted with secret things, 1 Corinthians 4:1–2.
Role of women, 1 Corinthians 9:5 (See LB).
In race, one wins; serving God, all win, 1 Corinthians 9:24–27.
Husband, wife need each other, 1 Corinthians 11:11 (See LB).
Ministry by God's mercy, 2 Corinthians 4:1 (NRSV).
Hardships in ministry, 2 Corinthians 6:4–10; 7:5–7.
Proof of validity, 2 Corinthians 13:2–3.
Approved by men or by God? Galatians 1:10.
Fear of failure, Galatians 2:1–2.
"Gently lead," Galatians 6:1–2 (CEV).
Ministry of prayer, Ephesians 6:18.
A channel of much blessing, Philippians 1:25–26.
"Upward call," Philippians 3:14 (NASB, NKJV).
Church's ministry outreach, Colossians 1:24–29.
Energized for ministry, Colossians 1:29.
Praying for those who minister, Colossians 4:3.
Faith, love, and hope, 1 Thessalonians 1:3.
Ministry endued with power, 1 Thessalonians 1:4–5.
Motivated ministry, 1 Thessalonians 2:1–6.
Faithful until Christ returns, 1 Timothy 6:11–16.
Disciplined ministry, 2 Timothy 1:7.
Ministry mandate, 2 Timothy 4:1–5.
Reward for faithful ministry, 2 Timothy 4:6–8.
Tools through whom God ministers, Titus 1:1–3.
Called to ministry of holiness, 1 Peter 1:15–16.
Holy priesthood of believers, 1 Peter 2:5.
"Not for sordid gain," 1 Peter 5:2 (NRSV).

"Herald of righteousness," 2 Peter 2:5 (NRSV).

Continuing zeal of aging worker, 2 Peter 1:13–14.

Fellowship based on ministry, 1 John 1:1–3.

Ministering in the Lord's name, 3 John 7.

Helping those who doubt, Jude 22–23.

Laborious, toil, trouble, Revelation 2:2 (AB).

Poor ministry performance, Revelation 3:2.

See Clergy, Missionary, Preaching, Service.

MINORITY

Righteous minority, Genesis 6:6–8.

Minority plus God, Leviticus 26:8, 1 Samuel 14:9–14; Jeremiah 42:2–22 (See 43:1–6).

Minority need not fear majority, Deuteronomy 20:1.

One routs one thousand, Joshua 23:10.

Smallest and weakest, Judges 6:14–16.

Gleaning exceeds harvest, Judges 8:2.

King chosen from minority tribe, 1 Samuel 9:21.

Few as effective as many, 1 Samuel 14:6.

Minority prophet, 1 Kings 18:22.

"Only a few of us," 1 Chronicles 16:19 (CEV).

Human strength of little value, Psalm 33:16.

Minority tribe led all others, Psalm 68:27.

Majority and minority in God's sight, Psalm 115:13.

Small, despised, faithful, Psalm 119:141.

Victory not always to swift and strong, Ecclesiastes 9:11.

Minority power, Isaiah 1:9 (AB).

Concern for being small, Isaiah 51:1–2 (LB).

Minority becomes majority, Isaiah 60:22.

Tiny grains of sand hold back ocean, Jeremiah 5:22.

Babylonian mercy to poor, Jeremiah 39:10.

Not one upright man remaining, Micah 7:2.

God's blessing upon meek and humble, Zephaniah 3:12.

Day of small things, Zechariah 4:10.

Wide and narrow ways, Matthew 7:13–14.

Mustard seed faith, Matthew 13:31–32; 17:20; Mark 4:30–32.

First last, last first, Matthew 19:30; Mark 10:31.

Many invited, few chosen, Matthew 22:1–14.

Facing adversary with limited troops, Luke 14:31–32.

Israel remnant, Romans 11:1–5 (See AB).

Humble backgrounds, abilities, 1 Corinthians 1:26.

Illustration of human body, 1 Corinthians 12:21–25.

See Racism, Small, Weakness.

MIRACLES

False prophet's miracles, Deuteronomy 13:1–5.

Purity prior to miracles, Joshua 3:5 (GNB).

Many, many miracles, Psalm 40:5 (LB).

Dearth of miracles, Psalm 74:9.

Selfish prayer rewarded, Psalm 106:14–15.

Not testing God, Isaiah 7:11–12.

Blind see, deaf hear, Isaiah 35:5.

Hezekiah's miracle, Isaiah 38:1–6.

Sun's shadow reversed, Isaiah 38:7–8.

Fiery furnace, Daniel 3:22–27.

Tell no one, Matthew 8:4.

Miracles could have saved Sodom, Matthew 11:23.

Loaves, fishes feed thousands, Matthew 16:7–10; Mark 8:1–21.

Attempt to prevent miracle, Matthew 27:62–66 (See 28:11–15).

Emphasizing healing above Healer, Luke 7:21–23.

Appointed time for miracles, John 2:4 (LB).

Purpose of miracles, John 2:11 (See AB).

Those who must see miracles to believe, John 4:48.

Miracles as publicity, John 7:1–5.

Messianic miracles, John 7:31.

Purpose of miracles, John 10:22–39; 20:30–31.

Sorcerer confounded by miracle, Acts 13:6–12.

Miracles in Paul's ministry, Acts 19:11–12.

Holy Spirit's miraculous resurrection power, Romans 8:11; Ephesians 1:18–21.

Pretended miracles, 2 Thessalonians 2:9 (CEV).

Functioning gifts of Spirit, Hebrews 2:4.

MIRROR

Women's contribution of mirrors for temple, Exodus 38:1–8.

Mirror-like skies, Job 37:17–18.
Water mirror, Proverbs 27:19.
Poor reflection, 1 Corinthians 13:12.
Our faces as mirrors, 2 Corinthians 3:18.
Reflected glory, Hebrews 1:3 (GNB).
Mirrors never lie, James 1:22–25.
See Cosmetics, Vanity.

MISANTHROPE See Deceit, Mistrust.

MISCARRIAGE
Miscarriage caused by poor water, 2 Kings
2:19–21 (GNB).
See Abortion, Birth.

MISCEGENATION
Distinction of each species, Genesis 1:24–
25.
Avoiding marriage to foreigner, Genesis
24:1–4.
Danger of marriage to pagans, Exodus
34:12–16; Deuteronomy 7:1–4.
Spiritual miscegenation, Ezra 9:4 (See
Berk.).
See Racism, Xenophobia.

MISCHIEF
Scheming to cause harm, Nehemiah 6:1–2.
Preventive care for children, Job 1:1–5.
In-depth mischief, Job 15:35.
Secret mischief, Psalm 10:7.
Lying awake to scheme, Psalm 36:4; Prov-
erbs 4:16.
Satanic view of man's motivations, Job 2:1–
10.
Minds busy with evil mischief, Isaiah 32:6.
See Devious.

MISER
Poverty from hoarding, Proverbs 11:24; Ec-
clesiastes 5:13.
Cold heart today, needy heart tomorrow,
Proverbs 21:13.
Miser's food, Proverbs 23:6–8.
Greed a form of idolatry, Colossians 3:5.
See Frugality, Stingy.

MISERY
"David was miserable," 1 Chronicles 21:13
(CEV).
See Agony, Anguish, Pain, Suffering, Torture.

MISFORTUNE
Unfortunate share others' good fortune,
2 Kings 7:3–9.
Satanic view of physical misfortune, Job
2:1–10.
Righteous suffer what wicked deserve, Ec-
clesiastes 8:14; 9:3.
Judgment brings righteousness, Isaiah
26:9.
From frying pan to fire, Amos 5:19.
Misfortune will not happen twice, Nahum
1:9.
See Accident.

MISINFORMATION See Deceit, Information,
Lie, Situation Ethics.

MISREPRESENTATION
Deceiving one's neighbor, Leviticus 6:1–2.
Negative and positive viewpoints, Numbers
13:17–33.
Discerning the prophets, Deuteronomy
18:21–22; Jeremiah 23:16–18.
Twisting words, Psalm 56:5.
Misrepresentation of God's law, Jeremiah
8:8.
Riches gained unjustly, Jeremiah 17:11.
Cheating and polluting, Amos 8:5, 6.
See Deceit, Falsehood, Lie.

MISSING See Absence.

MISSION
Sent on a mission, 1 Samuel 15:18.

MISSIONARY
Love for foreigners, Deuteronomy 10:19.
Journey with divine approval, Judges 18:6.
Solomon's attitude toward foreigners,
1 Kings 8:41–43.
Missionary assignment, 2 Kings 17:27–28.
Outreach to heathen, 1 Chronicles 16:23–
24; Psalm 96:3–10.
"Foreigners will hear," 2 Chronicles 6:32
(CEV).
Heathen as inheritance, Psalm 2:8.
"Tell the world," Psalm 9:11 (LB).
Ends of the earth, Psalm 22:27.
Worldwide outreach, Psalm 65:5.

"Tell every nation on earth," Psalm 96:3 (CEV).

Sent to other nations, Isaiah 66:19.

Benediction for missions, Psalm 67:1–2 (See LB).

Those who proclaim God's word, Psalms 68:11.

Declare God's glory among nations, Psalms 96:3, 10; 105:1.

Sow in tears, reap with joy, Psalm 126:5–6.

Alert during harvest, Proverbs 10:5.

Eternity in the heart, Ecclesiastes 3:11.

God reaches out to heathen, Isaiah 5:25–26.

Isaiah's missionary call, Isaiah 6:8–10; 12:4–5; 45:22.

Evangelize during night, with morning coming, Isaiah 21:11–12.

Light for Gentiles, Isaiah 49:6; 60:3.

Beautiful feet of those who bring good news, Isaiah 52:7; Nahum 1:15.

Those who did not ask for God's message, Isaiah 65:1–5.

"Earth's farthest bounds," Psalm 65:8 (NRSV).

Harvest past, summer ended, no salvation, Jeremiah 8:20.

Responsibility for failure to witness, Ezekiel 3:18–19.

Someone to stand in gap, Ezekiel 22:30.

Responsibility of watchman to warn wicked, Ezekiel 33:7–9.

Those who witness shine like stars, Daniel 12:3.

Ripe harvest, Joel 3:13–14.

Famine for words of the Lord, Amos 8:11–12.

Jonah's second call, Jonah 3:1–9.

God's name great among nations, Malachi 1:11.

Teaching, preaching, healing, Matthew 4:23.

Plentiful harvest, few workers, Matthew 9:37–38.

Gospel preached across world, Matthew 24:14.

Village evangelism, Mark 1:38; Luke 8:1; 9:6.

Great commission, Matthew 28:16–20; Mark 13:10; 16:15.

Biblical models, Luke 19:10; Acts 8:4–5; 15:7; 2 Peter 2:5.

Greatest model for mission, John 3:16.

Harvest time, John 4:35–38.

Missionary Jesus, John 7:35 (LB).

Lifting up Jesus draws lost to salvation, John 12:32.

Spiritual conquest, not earthly possession, Acts 1:6–8.

Message to entire world, Acts 10:9–20.

Missionary commissioning, Acts 13:2–4.

Macedonian vision, Acts 16:9–10.

"Chosen to be a missionary," Romans 1:1 (LB).

Faith reported world-wide, Romans 1:8.

Outreach to unevangelized, Romans 10:14–15; 15:21 (See LB).

Benediction upon world missions, Romans 16:25–27.

Payment for spiritual service, 1 Corinthians 9:9–14; 1 Timothy 5:17–18.

Adapting to another culture, 1 Corinthians 9:19–23.

Faithful outreach facing difficulties, 1 Corinthians 15:57–58.

Open door opportunity, 1 Corinthians 16:9.

Ambassadors in the world, 2 Corinthians 5:18–21.

Marks of serving disciple, 2 Corinthians 6:3–13.

Supported by others, 2 Corinthians 11:8.

Mission agency, Galatians 1:2 (LB).

Anticipated salvation of Jew and Gentile, Galatians 3:6–9.

Less than least, Ephesians 3:8–9.

Medical furlough, Philippians 2:25–30.

Rapid spread of Gospel message, Colossians 1:6.

Church and its outreach, Colossians 1:24–27.

Praying for a missionary, Ephesians 6:19–20; Colossians 4:3–4.

Thankful Lord for privilege of ministry, 1 Timothy 1:12–14.

Missionary message, 1 Timothy 2:5–7.

Called to be a full-fledged missionary, 2 Timothy 1:11.

Divine plan for perpetuation of Gospel, 2 Timothy 2:1–4.

Paul's ministry mandate to Timothy, 2 Timothy 4:1–5.

Missionary credentials, Titus 1:1–3.

Called to ministry of holiness, 1 Peter 1:15–16.

Willing to lay down one's life for others, 1 John 3:16.

Proclaiming angel, Revelation 14:6, 7.

See Contextualization, Evangelism.

MISTAKE

Divine regret, Genesis 6:5–8.

Blundering, Psalm 69:5 (Berk.).

Angry at God for personal mistake, Proverbs 19:3 (See GNB).

Learning from failure, mistakes, Proverbs 24:15–16.

Discovered mistake, Matthew 27:3.

See Error, Guilt, Wrong.

MISTAKEN IDENTITY

Identification by manner of speech, Judges 12:5–6.

Case of mistaken identity, Esther 6:1–13.

Jesus a stranger to His own followers, Mark 4:35–41.

Jesus mistaken for Elijah and John the Baptist, Mark 6:14–16; John 8:27–29.

See Identity, Stranger.

MISTREATMENT

Complaining of mistreatment, Exodus 17:1–3.

Partial blindness inflicted as disgrace, 1 Samuel 11:2–11.

"Trampled upon," Psalm 56:1 (NASB, NRSV).

House left untended, Ecclesiastes 10:18.

Making, breaking promise to slaves, Jeremiah 34:8–22.

Exploiting poor for personal gain, Amos 5:11.

"Treated badly," Matthew 5:10 (CEV).

Outrageous mistreatment, 1 Thessalonians 2:2 (AB).

See Abuse, Oppression, Persecution.

MISTRUST

Act of kindness misinterpreted, 2 Samuel 10:1–4.

Mistrusting friends, brothers, Jeremiah 9:4–8.

Assurance of prophet mistrusted, Jeremiah 43:1–3.

Untrustworthy neighbors, friends, Micah 7:5.

See Deceit, Fraud, Doubt.

MISUNDERSTANDING

Making wrong right, Numbers 5:6–7.

When others speak evil of you, Psalm 109:20.

Twisting of words, Psalm 56:5.

Better spoken than written, 2 John 12; 3 John 13–14.

See Communication.

MISUSE

Sacrifice misused, 1 Samuel 2:12–17.

David refused water which risked lives of his men, 2 Samuel 23:15–17.

Misusing others, James 5:4–5.

See Manipulate.

MOB

Demon named Mob, Mark 5:9 (GNB).

MOB PSYCHOLOGY

Complaining community, Exodus 16:2.

Following wrong crowd, Exodus 23:2 (See NKJV).

People prone to idolatry, Exodus 32:19–28.

Wrong kind of unanimity, Numbers 11:4–10.

Community-wide discontent, Numbers 14:1–4.

Lack of discernment, Deuteronomy 32:28.

Trampled by hungry mob, 2 Kings 7:17–20.

Jesus rejected city-wide, Matthew 8:34.

Triumphal entry, Matthew 21:8–13.

Mob psychology at Jesus' trial, Matthew 27:15–26; Mark 15:11.

Crowd curiosity, Mark 9:25 (GNB).

Potential mob violence during Passover, Mark 14:1–2.

People of synagogue versus Jesus, Luke 4:28–30.

People trampling each other, Luke 12:1.

Persuasive power of mob, Luke 23:13–25.

Following Jesus out of curiosity, John 12:9–11, 17–18.

Poisoning minds of others, Acts 14:2.

Worshiping Paul, Barnabas' spiritual power, Acts 14:8–18.

Bad characters incited, Acts 17:5–7.

United opposition, Acts 18:12 (Berk.).

People confused in riotous crowd, Acts 19:32.

Crowd incensed against Paul, Acts 22:22; 23:10.

See Anarchy, Public Opinion.

MOCKERY

"Mocked, slandered," Ezekiel 36:3–4 (LB).

Folly of mocking God, Numbers 15:30–31.

Youths mocked prophet, 2 Kings 2:23.

Town to town mockery, 2 Chronicles 30:10.

Messengers mocked, 2 Chronicles 36:16.

Wall builders mocked, Nehemiah 4:1.

Crucifixion prophecy, Psalm 22:7.

Mockery for acts of humility, Psalm 69:10–11.

Child mocks parents, Proverbs 30:17.

Whom are you mocking?, Isaiah 57:4.

Making mockery of fasting, Isaiah 58:4–5.

Disrespect for sanctuary, Ezekiel 25:1–4.

Mocking at truth spoken by Jesus, Matthew 9:23–24.

Soldiers mocking at cross, Matthew 27:27–31.

Making mockery of sacrifices, Luke 13:1.

Pentecost mocked, Acts 2:13.

Sneering about resurrection, Acts 17:32.

Jeers, flogging, Hebrews 11:36.

"Last days mockers," 2 Peter 3:3 (NASB).

Last days scoffers, Jude 18.

See Disdain, Scoff.

MODEL

Blameless model, Genesis 6:9.

Model of integrity, Genesis 21:22.

Backsliders laughable models, Exodus 32:25.

Royal model sublimated personal grief, 2 Samuel 19:1–8.

Model leader, people, Nehemiah 5:14–18.

Man who truly walked with God, Job 1:1.

Practice what you preach, Psalm 51:10–13.

Example of persecuted prophets, Matthew 5:11–12.

Pharisees poor models, Matthew 23:2.

Like teacher, like student, Luke 6:40.

Supreme model love, outreach, John 3:16–17.

Converts follow Paul's example, 1 Corinthians 4:15–16; 11:1; Galatians 4:12; 2 Thessalonians 3:6–10.

Poor Old Testament models, 1 Corinthians 10:1–10.

Ideal example, 1 Corinthians 11:1.

Deserving right to be heard, 2 Corinthians 4:1–2.

Lifestyle communicated by example, 2 Corinthians 6:4–10.

Model of Christian conduct, 2 Corinthians 7:2; 8:21; 9:13–14; 1 Thessalonians 1:7; 2 Thessalonians 3:9.

Supreme model of unselfishness, 2 Corinthians 8:7–9.

Ultimate career, life of love, Ephesians 5:1–2.

Model for courage, witness, Philippians 1:14.

Standing firm whatever circumstances, Philippians 1:27–30.

Supreme model, Ephesians 6:9; Philippians 2:6–11.

Paul's commendation of Timothy, Philippians 2:19–23.

Setting example, Philippians 3:17.

God's grace to worst sinner, 1 Timothy 1:15–16.

Model good teaching, 2 Timothy 1:13–14.

Paul's example to Timothy, 2 Timothy 3:10–11.

Elder's model family, Titus 1:6.

Good teacher's example, Titus 2:6–7.

Model High Priest, Hebrews 4:14–16.

Showing initiative, Hebrews 6:11–12.

Ultimate High Priest, Hebrews 8:1–6.

Faint resemblance, Hebrews 10:1 (GNB).

Christ's example provides model, Hebrews 10:24 (LB).

Models of faith, Hebrews 12:1–3.

"In His steps," 1 Peter 2:21.

Christ's model of love, 1 John 4:7–11.

See Example, Exemplary, Leadership.

MODERATION

Casting off restraint, Proverbs 29:18.

Balanced wisdom, piety, Ecclesiastes 7:16.

Relationship of husband, wife, 1 Corinthians 7:1–7.

Continual lust for more, Ephesians 4:19.

Wives not heavy drinkers, 1 Timothy 3:11 (LB).

See Discipline, Restraint, Temperance.

MODERNISM

Those who turn away, Judges 2:17; 1 John 2:19.

Pharisees and religion of Sham, Matthew 23:5–7.

Shipwrecked faith, 1 Timothy 1:18–19.

Turning to myths, 2 Timothy 4:4.

See Apostasy, Liberalism, Syncretism.

MODESTY

Innocent nudity, Genesis 2:25.

First awareness of nudity, Genesis 3:7 (See 2:25).

Noah's nakedness, Genesis 9:20–27.

Modest maiden, Genesis 24:61–65.

Touching private parts, Deuteronomy 25:11.

Secret parts, Isaiah 3:17 (NKJV).

Immodest threat, Jeremiah 13:26.

Shocking conduct, Ezekiel 16:27.

Lessons from lewdness, Ezekiel 23:48 (NKJV).

Miracles to be kept private, Matthew 9:29–31.

Modest thinking, Romans 12:3 (GNB).

Special modesty for body organs, 1 Corinthians 12:22–25.

Modest dress, 1 Timothy 2:9–10.

See Discretion.

MOLD See Mildew.

MOLDING

Clay molds for artifacts, 2 Chronicles 4:17.

Potter, clay, Isaiah 46:8; Jeremiah 18:1–4.

Molded, molder, Romans 9:20 (NASB).

MOLEST

Jesus molested, Mark 14:65.

See Demean, Persecution.

MONARCHY See Royalty.

MONEY

Currency by weight, Genesis 23:16; Ezra 8:24–27; Jeremiah 32:9.

Animals, land, people replace money, Genesis 47:16–21.

Monetary value of human being, Leviticus 27:1–8.

Value of silver in stewardship, Numbers 7:13–85; 10:2.

Services paid in cash, Deuteronomy 2:6.

Money carefully used, Ezra 7:17 (CEV).

Lending money without interest, Psalm 15:5.

Easy money, Proverbs 20:21 (GNB).

Money never satisfies, Ecclesiastes 5:10.

Distorted view of money, Ecclesiastes 10:19.

"Cheat and shortchange," Isaiah 59:6 (LB).

Valueless money, Ezekiel 7:19 (LB).

Prostitute giving rather than receiving fee, Ezekiel 16:32–34.

Currency value, designation, Ezekiel 45:12.

Silver, gold belong to God, Haggai 2:8.

Reward of good stewardship, Malachi 3:8–10.

Cannot serve God, money, Matthew 6:24.

Tainted money for betraying Jesus, Matthew 27:3–10; Luke 22:3–6.

No need for expense money, Mark 6:8–11.

Fraction of cent, Luke 12:59 (AB).

Estimating cost before construction, Luke 14:28–30.

Two coppers, Luke 21:2 (Berk.).

Human equations, Divine power, John 6:1–13.

Spiritual economics, Acts 3:6.

Power of God not for sale, Acts 8:18–24.

Angered by loss of income, Acts 16:16–24.

Profit limited by new life of converts, Acts 19:23–28.

Evangelist seeking employment, 1 Corinthians 9:6–7.

Unmuzzled ox, 1 Corinthians 9:9–14.

Root of evil, 1 Timothy 6:10.

"Not for sordid gain," 1 Peter 5:2 (NRSV).

See Currency, Gold, Payment, Stipend, Value.

MONOLOGUE

Reciting proverbs to musical accompaniment, Psalm 49:4.
See Eloquence.

MONOTHEISM

Silver idol for true God, Judges 17:4.
Only one God, Isaiah 43:10–13 (LB).
One true God versus many gods, Daniel 3:28–30; 4:18.
No God but the Lord, Hosea 13:4.
See God, Christ, Iconoclastic, Idolatry, Trinity.

MONOTONY

Same food for forty years, Exodus 16:35.
Dripping water, Proverbs 27:15.
See Boredom.

MONUMENT See Memorial.

MOOD

Striving for good mood, Psalm 43:5 (Also see LB).
Having bad day, Psalm 102:2.
"Always be cheerful," 2 Corinthians 5:6 (CEV).
See Attitude, Disposition, Frame-of-reference.

MOON

Not to be worshipped, Deuteronomy 4:19.
Abundant blessings of nature, Deuteronomy 33:13–16.
Inert sun, moon, Joshua 10:12–14.
Moon gazing, Job 31:26.
Herald the New Moon, Psalm 81:3.
Night witness, Psalm 89:37.
Marking seasons by moon, Psalm 104:19.
Romantic likeness, Song of Songs 6:10.
Humiliated moon, Isaiah 24:23.
Queen of heaven, Jeremiah 7:18 (AB).
Moon turned to blood, Joel 2:31.
See Astronomy, Moonlight.

MOONLIGHT

Night survey, Nehemiah 2:11–15.

MORALE

Taking care of business, Deuteronomy 20:5–9.

Leadership for those in trouble, 1 Samuel 22:2.
Ineptness of king's viewpoint, 1 Kings 12:1–15.
People working diligently together, Nehemiah 4:6.
Inequity among citizens, Nehemiah 5:1–5.
Security in the Lord, Psalm 127:1, 2.
Persecuted for destroying morale of soldiers, Jeremiah 38:1–6.
Joy, gladness gone, Jeremiah 48:33.
Demoralizing influence of hunger, Luke 15:13–20.
Morale, firm faith, Colossians 2:5 (NRSV).
See Optimism, Pessimism.

MORALITY

Abram, Sarai, Egyptians, Genesis 12:10–20.
Divine guidance in moral conduct, Genesis 20:1–18.
Remarriage of divorced persons, Deuteronomy 24:1–4.
Moral conduct of Boaz, Ruth 3:1–14.
Military morality, 1 Samuel 21:1–5.
Parable rebuking David, 2 Samuel 12:1–4.
David's respect for concubines, 2 Samuel 20:3.
Senile morality, 1 Kings 1:1–4.
Eunuchs looked after queen, Esther 1:10–11; 2:3.
Avoiding lust requires discipline, Job 31:1.
Morality vital part of spirituality, Jeremiah 3:1–5.
Dramatic puberty, Ezekiel 16:5–9.
Stern principle, Matthew 1:19 (LB).
Morality does not bring salvation, Matthew 19:16–26.
Those who need Great Physician, Mark 2:17; 10:17–20.
As in the days of Noah, Luke 17:26–30.
Loose marriage standards, John 4:16–18.
Frightening Felix, Acts 24:24–25 (Berk.).
Function of conscience, Romans 2:14–15.
Morality stems from youth training, Romans 2:17–18 (LB).
Overcoming immoral conduct, Romans 13:14.
Result of new birth, 2 Corinthians 5:17.
Special modesty toward body organs, 1 Corinthians 12:22–25.

"Bad company corrupts good morals," 1 Corinthians 15:33 (NASB).

Prompted by Holy Spirit, Galatians 5:22–23.

"Troublesome moral faults," Galatians 6:2 (AB).

Fruit of the heart, Hebrews 8:10.

"Moral excellence," 2 Peter 1:5 (NASB).

Those who keep themselves pure, Revelation 14:4.

See Chastity, Immorality, Purity, Virgin.

MORBID See Vulgar.

MORNING

"Cool of the day," Genesis 3:8.

Meet the Lord early, Genesis 19:27; Exodus 34:4–5.

Rising early, Genesis 22:3; Exodus 34:4; Job 1:5; Mark 1:35; Luke 21:38.

Early morning bath, Exodus 8:20.

Daybreak action around Jericho, Joshua 6:12–20.

Strength of rising sun, Judges 5:31.

Morning dew on fleece, Judges 6:38.

Doors opened by morning, 1 Samuel 3:15.

Early morning spectacle, 1 Samuel 5:4.

"Spring of the day," 1 Samuel 9:26 (KJV).

Early morning admonition, 2 Chronicles 20:20.

"See the breaking dawn," Job 3:9 (NASB).

Help at daybreak, Psalm 46:5.

Dawn greeted with music, Psalms 57:8; 108:2.

Morning blessing, Psalms 90:14; 92:2.

"Arouse the dawn," Psalm 108:2 (Berk.).

Pre-dawn prayer, Psalm 119:147.

Morning prayer, Psalms 5:3; 139:23–24.

Love of sleep, Proverbs 20:13.

Mistaken morning greeting, Proverbs 27:14.

Mother's work never finished, Proverbs 31:15.

Morning feast, Ecclesiastes 10:16–17.

"Until the day breathes," Song of Songs 4:6 (NRSV).

Dawn aesthetics, Song of Songs 6:10.

Night precedes morning, Isaiah 21:11–12.

Morning devotions, Isaiah 26:9.

'rength for the day, Isaiah 33:2 (See CEV).

Morning compasssions, Lamentations 3:23 (See LB).

End of sleepless night, Daniel 6:18–23.

Dawn to darkness, Amos 4:13.

Morning of all mornings, Matthew 28:1–10; Mark 16:1–8; Luke 24:1–12; John 20:1–9.

Crowing rooster and Peter, Mark 14:29–31, 66–72.

Crucifixion time, Mark 15:25 (LB).

Jesus at daybreak, Luke 4:42.

Dawn ministry, John 8:2.

Given the morning star, Revelation 2:28.

See Day, Devotions, Sun, Sunrise.

MORNING STAR

Dawn in your heart, 2 Peter 1:19.

Divine property, Revelation 2:28.

Bright morning star, Revelation 22:16.

See Astronomy, Second Coming.

MORTALITY

Death marks deliverance from sinful nature, Genesis 3:22.

Desire for immortality, 1 Kings 1:31.

Way of all earth, 1 Kings 2:2.

"Fragile as moths," Job 4:19 (CEV).

Lacking strength of stone, Job 6:12.

Life, breath in God's hands, Job 12:10.

Length of life determined, Job 14:5.

Pessimistic view of mortality, Job 14:7–11.

We are but men, Psalm 9:20.

Mortality in useless time of trouble, Psalm 60:11–12 (NKJV).

Life's mere breath, Psalms 62:9; 144:3–4.

Experiencing divine wonders before death, Psalm 88:10–12.

Created as mortals, Psalm 89:47 (GNB).

Imperfection for mortals, perfection for God, Psalm 119:96.

Wise man and fool soon forgotten, Ecclesiastes 2:16.

No power over day of death, Ecclesiastes 8:8.

Weak, frail, dying, Isaiah 2:22 (AB).

Egyptians mere mortals, Isaiah 31:3.

People drained of power, Isaiah 37:27 (NIV).

Death in early years, Isaiah 38:10.

Wide contrast between temporal, spiritual, Isaiah 40:7–8.

People age of trees, Isaiah 65:20–22.

Foolish depending on mortal flesh, Jeremiah 17:5.

Those who should live die, should die live, Ezekiel 13:19.

"Son of dust," Ezekiel 40:4 (LB).

Dual nature of man, Romans 7:21–25.

Constant threat of death, Romans 8:36 (see also GNB).

God's preparation exceeds human perception, 1 Corinthians 2:9–10.

Mortal body "perishable container," 2 Corinthians 4:7 (LB).

Human body's rapid deterioration, 2 Corinthians 4:16–18.

Human body as a tent, 2 Corinthians 5:4.

Paul experienced anxiety, Philippians 2:28.

Our body but a tent, 2 Peter 1:13.

Mortality of Jesus, 1 John 5:6.

Limited authority of the beast, Revelation 13:1–18.

Blood of dead man, Revelation 16:3.

See Death, Humanity, Life, Longevity.

MORTGAGE

Machinery not to be mortgaged, Deuteronomy 24:6.

Mortgaging property to buy food, Nehemiah 5:3.

Borrower, lender, Proverbs 22:7.

See Credit, Debt.

MOTHER

"Life-giving one," Genesis 3:20 (LB, note tense RSV).

Motherhood by incest, Genesis 19:30–38.

Love of mother for son, Genesis 21:14–16.

Mother of millions, Genesis 24:60 (GNB).

Desire for motherhood, Genesis 30:1.

Death in childbirth, Genesis 35:16–20.

Wisdom of Moses' mother, Exodus 2:1–10.

Mother honored, Exodus 20:12.

Mother's morality, Leviticus 18:7.

Mothers strengthen Israel, Ruth 4:11.

Praying woman's child dedicated, 1 Samuel 1:25–28.

Joyful motherhood, 1 Samuel 2:1–2.

Michal without children, 2 Samuel 6:23.

Mother of slain sons, 2 Samuel 21:10 (See LB).

Bathsheba's intercession for son, 1 Kings 1:11–21.

Ill-fated request for wife, 1 Kings 2:13–25.

Queen mother's influence, 1 Kings 2:19.

Solomon's identity of true mother, 1 Kings 3:16–28.

Mothers of young kings, 2 Kings 23:31, 36; 24:8, 18; 2 Chronicles 20:31; 27:1.

Animals of nature born in secret, Job 39:1.

Ostrich's poor motherhood, Job 39:13–17.

Descriptive evil example from motherhood, Psalm 7:14.

Following mother's example, Psalm 86:16 (GNB).

Barren woman becomes happy mother, Psalm 113:9.

Mother's faith, Psalm 116:16 (CEV).

Mother's teaching, Proverbs 1:8; 6:20.

Wise home builder, Proverbs 14:1 (GNB).

Respecting aged parents, Proverbs 23:22–25.

Mother's shame, Proverbs 29:15.

Instructive mother, Proverbs 31:1.

Woman of noble character, Proverbs 31:10–31.

Mother's kindness, Proverbs 31:20.

Respect for mother, Proverbs 31:31 (GNB).

Marriage counsel for daughter, Song of Songs 8:2 (KJV).

Sons of sorceress, Isaiah 57:3.

Children dead, Jeremiah 15:9 (LB).

Surrogate mother among birds, Jeremiah 17:11.

Like mother, like daughter, Ezekiel 16:44.

Desecrated mother, Ezekiel 19:10–14.

Bear mother robbed of cubs, Hosea 13:8.

Mother of Jesus at cross, Mark 15:40.

Reactions of Mary compared to shepherds, Luke 2:19–20.

Mother's reprimand, Luke 2:41–50.

Mother of Jesus unable to penetrate crowd, Luke 8:19–21.

Unmentioned mother, Luke 15:11–32.

Pain of childbirth brings joy, John 16:21.

Woman who was like mother to Paul, Romans 16:13.

Kept safe in childbirth, 1 Timothy 2:15.

Those who bring up children, 1 Timothy 5:10.

Women in heaven who gave birth, Revelation 12:1–6.

See Childbirth, Childless, Pregnancy.

MOTHER-IN-LAW

Exemplary relationship, Ruth 1:8–18.

Faith brings family conflict, Matthew 10:34–36.

Mother-in-law's illness, Mark 1:30.

See Son-in-Law.

MOTIVATION

Doing what is right, Genesis 4:7.

Evil sibling motivations, Genesis 37:19–27.

Motivated to serve God, Exodus 35:20–21, 25–26, 29 (See AB).

Consciously sacrifice, Leviticus 22:29.

Questionable sincerity, 1 Samuel 15:13–35.

Mistaken motives, 2 Samuel 10:1–4.

Respect for prophet motivated by fear, 2 Kings 1:1–15.

"A mind to work," Nehemiah 4:6 (NKJV).

Motive for worship, Job 1:9–11.

Thoughts motivate, Job 20:2 (NRSV).

Motivations received from the Lord, Psalm 20:4; 37:3–5.

Divine test of motive, thought, Psalm 26:2.

Highest motive life can know, Psalm 27:4.

Desire for scriptural motivation, Psalm 40:8.

Letting God fulfill His purpose, Psalm 57:2.

The Lord knows our thoughts, Psalm 94:11.

No place for deceit in God's house, Psalm 101:7.

Whole-hearted motivation, Psalm 119:10.

Choosing to follow way of truth, Psalm 119:30.

Finding life's greatest values, Psalm 119:36–37.

Seeking, considering, hastening to obey, Psalm 119:57–64.

Build in vain unless the Lord builds, Psalm 127:1.

Determination to fulfill destiny, Psalm 132:1–5.

Thoughts and motives, Psalm 139:1–4.

Guard your heart, Proverbs 4:23.

The lazy, the diligent, Proverbs 10:4.

Man's motives and God's decree, Proverbs 16:2.

Motivated by good appetite, Proverbs 16:26.

Love of pleasure, Proverbs 21:17.

Motivated to become rich, Proverbs 23:4–5; 28:20.

Keeping up with the Joneses, Ecclesiastes 4:4.

Working with diligence, Ecclesiastes 9:10.

Nothing hidden from God, Isaiah 29:15–16.

Noble man makes noble plans, Isaiah 32:8.

Knowing what is right, Isaiah 51:7.

"Making sinful plans," Jeremiah 4:14 (CEV).

God tests heart and mind, Jeremiah 11:20; 17:10.

Sincere search for God, Jeremiah 29:10–14.

God's law in mind and heart, Jeremiah 31:33.

All-seeing God rewards good, Jeremiah 32:19.

Singleness of heart and action, Jeremiah 32:38–39.

Divine motivation, Jeremiah 32:39.

Examine ways, return to Lord, Lamentations 3:40.

Undivided heart, Ezekiel 11:19.

God never acts without cause, Ezekiel 14:23.

Plundering with glee, Ezekiel 36:5.

Seek good, not evil, Amos 5:14.

Righteous live by faith, Habakkuk 2:4.

Challenge to work for divine cause, Haggai 2:4.

King Herod and Magi, Matthew 2:7–8, 13.

Motivated by call to discipleship, Matthew 4:20–22.

Anger a form of murder, Matthew 5:21–22.

Mortal motivations and divine motivations, Matthew 8:1–3.

Conduct cause, Matthew 12:35; Mark 7:20–23; Luke 2:34–35.

Mouth speaks what heart contains, Luke 6:43–45.

Good an evil stored in heart, Luke 6:45.

Jesus motivated to the cross, Luke 23:35–39.

Satanic motivation, John 13:2.

Love of the Lord motivates outreach to others, John 21:15–18.

Persistence in witnessing, Acts 5:42.

David's motivation, Acts 13:22.

Venturing with confidence into difficult places, Acts 20:22–24.

Inner motivation, Romans 2:28–29.

Lacking true motive, Romans 3:11 (LB).

Motivated by Spirit, not the law, Romans 7:6.

Struggle between flesh, spirit, Romans 7:15–18.

Wood, hay, straw or gold, silver, costly stones, 1 Corinthians 3:12–13.

Hidden motives brought to light, 1 Corinthians 4:5.

Motives for preaching, 1 Corinthians 9:16–18.

Doing all for God's glory, 1 Corinthians 10:31.

Motivated by message, 1 Corinthians 15:10.

Faithful whatever difficulties, 1 Corinthians 15:57–58.

Do everything in love, 1 Corinthians 16:13–14.

Motivated by love of Christ, 2 Corinthians 5:14.

Exploiting no one, 2 Corinthians 7:2.

"Come to the front," 2 Corinthians 8:7 (AB).

Giving from continuity of desire, 2 Corinthians 9:10.

"Kind intention," Ephesians 1:5 (NASB).

Life of love, Ephesians 5:1–2.

Doing good work unto the Lord, Ephesians 6:5–8.

Motivated preaching, Philippians 1:15–18 (See LB).

Truth proclaimed with false motives, Philippians 1:18.

"Make it my own," Philippians 3:12–13 (NRSV).

Forgetting past, pressing forward, Philippians 3:12–16.

Whatever you say or do, Colossians 3:17.

Do not serve God to please men, Colossians 3:23–24.

Properly motivated, 1 Thessalonians 1:3 (See AB).

Love and fellowship in ministry, 1 Thessalonians 2:7–9.

Motivated to Christian lifestyle, 1 Thessalonians 4:11–12.

Good purpose fulfilled, 2 Thessalonians 1:11 (See Psalm 37:4).

Desire to be overseer, 1 Timothy 3:1.

Money motivated, 1 Timothy 6:5 (AB).

Motivation toward wealth, 1 Timothy 6:9–10.

Evil desires of youth, 2 Timothy 2:22.

"Aim in life," 2 Timothy 3:10 (NRSV).

Preach, teach for dishonest gain, Titus 1:10–16.

Pure motives, Titus 2:8 (AB).

Favors extended with proper motivation, Philemon 14.

Fear as motivating factor, Hebrews 11:7.

Motivated, urged by faith, Hebrews 11:8, 27 (AB).

Faithfully running race, Hebrews 12:1–2.

Love of money, Hebrews 13:5.

"Eager to do right," Hebrews 13:21 (CEV).

Wrong motives, James 4:3.

Minds prepared for action, 1 Peter 1:13.

Role of evil desire in causing one to sin, James 1:13–15.

Scriptural teaching in action, James 1:22–25.

Actions speak louder than words, 1 John 3:18.

Ministering in name of the Lord, 3 John 7.

God searches mind and heart, Revelation 2:23.

Role of demons in world politics, Revelation 16:14.

When evil serves God's purpose, Revelation 17:17.

See Frame-of-Reference, Initiative, Objective, Plan, Purpose.

MOTIVE

Saul's selfish motive offering daughter to David, 1 Samuel 18:20–23.

Moving straight ahead, Proverbs 4:25–27.

God sees all man's ways, Proverbs 5:21.

The Lord blamed for our misdeeds, Isaiah 63:17.

Seek good, not evil, Amos 5:14.

Sin committed in heart, Matthew 5:27–28.

Decision to communicate by writing, Luke 1:1–4.

Emphasizing healing above Healer, Luke 7:21–23.

Motivated by hunger, Luke 15:13–20.
See Motivation, Objective.

MOUNTAINS

Ark rested on Ararat, Genesis 8:4.

Abraham offered Isaac on Moriah, Genesis 22:2.

Law given on Sinai, Exodus 19:20.

Moving mountains, Job 9:5; Ezekiel 38:20.

Many mountain peaks, Psalm 68:15 (GNB).

Pre-historic landscape, Psalm 90:1–2.

God's mountains, Psalm 95:4.

Melting mountains, Psalm 97:5.

Temple mountain, Isaiah 2:2.

Astonishment mountain, Ezekiel 35:7 (AB).

Object of divine affection, Ezekiel 36:1–12.

Oceanic mountains, Jonah 2:6 (AB, LB).

Renowned Mount Zion, Micah 4:1 (LB).

Ascension from Olivet, Acts 1:9–11.
See Geology, Geography, Obstacles, Travel.

MOUNTAIN TOP

Meeting with God, Exodus 19:20.

Place to die, Numbers 33:38–39.

Transfiguration, Matthew 17:1–2; Mark 9:2.

Ascension, Acts 1:9–11.
See Mountain, Prayer, Quiet time, Worship.

MOURNING

Widow's clothes, Genesis 38:14, 19.

Mourning Moses' death, Deuteronomy 34:8.

Mode of mourning, 2 Samuel 1:11–12.

Joy turned to sadness, 2 Samuel 19:2.

Widows who do not mourn, Job 27:15.

Polluted food for mourners, Hosea 9:4 (LB).

Strange rite at time of death, Deuteronomy 14:1–2; Micah 1:16.

Nation assembled to mourn, 1 Samuel 25:1.

Personal grief set aside, 2 Samuel 19:1–8.

Professional mourners, Jeremiah 9:17.

Weeping, wailing, Micah 1:8.

Flute as mourning instrument, Matthew 9:23, 24.

Mourning death of Dorcas, Acts 9:39.
See Death, Grief, Sorrow.

MOUSTACHE

Trimmed moustache, 2 Samuel 19:24.
See Whiskers.

MOUTH *See Food, Teeth.*

MUGGING

Afraid to walk in public places, Jeremiah 6:25.

MULES

Mules in the Bible, 2 Samuel 18:9; 1 Kings 1:33, 38, 44; Psalm 32:9; Isaiah 66:20.

MULTILINGUAL

Tower of Babel, Genesis 11:1–9.
Language confused by intermarriage, Nehemiah 13:23–27.
Language best understood, Isaiah 36:11.
Learning new language, Daniel 1:3–4.
Multilingual information, John 19:20.
Day of Pentecost, Acts 2:6.
See Communication, Language.

MULTIPLICATION See Mathematics.

MULTITUDE

Community in rebellion, Exodus 16:2.
Power in numbers, Numbers 22:2–4.
Multitudes followed Jesus, Matthew 4:25; 13:2; 15:30; 19:2; Mark 1:33; 2:13; 3:20; Luke 12:1.
Multitude of demons, Luke 8:26–31.
See Crowd, Mob Psychology.

MUMBLING See Murmuring.

MUMMY See Embalming.

MUNDANE

Great things, small things, 2 Kings 5:13.
Mundane activity leads to miraculous event, 2 Kings 6:1–7.
Writing with ordinary pen, Isaiah 8:1.
Day of small things, Zechariah 4:10.
See Boredom.

MURDER

First murder, Genesis 4:1–16.
Institution of capital punishment, Genesis 9:6.
Premeditated murder, Genesis 27:41–45; 2 Samuel 13:28–29.

Murder averted, Genesis 37:21–24.
Murder forbidden, Exodus 20:13; Matthew 19:18; Romans 13:9; 1 Peter 4:15; 1 John 3:15.
Hired murderer, Deuteronomy 27:25.
Sisera's plight, Judges 4:14–21; 5:24–31.
Thwarted murder, 1 Samuel 19:9–17.
Accused of aiding suicide, 2 Samuel 1:1–16.
Killing in self-defense, 2 Samuel 2:22–23.
David's plot against Uriah, 2 Samuel 11:14–17.
Smothered king, 2 Kings 18:14–15.
Murderer digs own grave, Proverbs 28:17 (GNB).
Unsuspecting victim, Jeremiah 11:18–19.
Total depravity throughout land, Micah 7:2.
Herod's slaughter of male babies, Matthew 2:13–18.
Death of John the Baptist, Matthew 14:1–12.
Judas murderers' accomplice, Matthew 26:14–16.
Seeking to murder, Mark 14:1.
Murder thwarted by Jesus, Luke 4:28–30.
Plan to murder Paul, Acts 23:12–22.
Jealousy the cause of murder, 1 John 3:12.
Incited to kill, Revelation 6:4.
See Crime, Hatred, Lynching.

MURMURING

Complaining against leadership, Exodus 5:15–21; 15:22–24; 16:2–3; Numbers 16:1–41; 20:1–4.
Leadership complaining to the Lord, Exodus 5:22, 23.
Testing Divine patience, Numbers 14:26–37.
Reprimanded for murmuring, Job 15:11–13; 34:34–37.
Counsel not to complain, Psalm 37:1.
David's lament, Psalm 44:1–26.
Temper flare against the Lord, Proverbs 19:3.
Lamenting one's birth, Jeremiah 15:10.
Doubting God's goodness, Malachi 3:14.

Martha's questioning, Luke 10:40.

Danger of faulting the Lord, Romans 9:19–20.

Avoid murmuring, Philippians 2:14 (KJV).

See Attitude, Complain, Criticism, Discontent.

MUSEUM

Giant king's bed, Deuteronomy 3:11 (LB).

Ruins rebuilt, Isaiah 58:12.

Historical items in tabernacle, Hebrews 9:3–4.

See Artifacts.

MUSIC

First musical instruments, Genesis 4:21.

Musical send-off, Genesis 31:27.

Song of Moses, Exodus 15:1–18, 21.

Hand-wrought trumpets, Numbers 10:2.

Trumpet fanfare, Numbers 10:10.

Singing at watering places, Numbers 21:17–18; Judges 5:11.

Jawbone lyrics, Judges 15:15–16 (GNB).

Wide area trumpet sound, 1 Samuel 13:3.

Music therapy, 1 Samuel 16:14–23.

Forboding harp, 1 Samuel 18:10; 19:9.

Prophecy set to music, 2 Kings 3:15–16.

Music ministry, 1 Chronicles 6:32.

Music with all their might, 1 Chronicles 13:8.

Music master, 1 Chronicles 15:27 (NKJV).

Praise with harp accompaniment, 1 Chronicles 25:3.

Payment to choir members, Nehemiah 12:47.

Unpaid musicians, Nehemiah 13:10–11.

Mournful music, Job 30:31; Matthew 9:23–24.

"Songs in the night," Job 35:10.

Moved to sing, Job 36:24 (Berk.).

"Shiggaion," Psalm 7:1 (NIV).

Harp an instrument of praise, Psalms 33:2–3; 43:4.

"Loud songs of joy," Psalm 47:1 (NRSV).

Riddle set to music, Psalm 49:4.

Singing with steadfast heart, Psalm 57:7.

Cobra and tune, Psalm 58:4–5.

Drunkard's song, Psalm 69:12.

Pleasant music, Psalm 81:2.

Marching music, Psalm 68:24–25; Isaiah 23:16.

Musical resume of history, Psalms 78:1–72; 106:1–48.

Strike up the band, Psalm 81:2.

Fountains in the Lord, Psalm 87:6–7.

Music and world evangelism, Psalm 96:1 (LB).

Praising with voice and instrument, Psalm 98:4–6.

Dawn music, Psalm 108:2.

Making Scripture the theme of song, Psalm 119:54.

Laughter and music go together, Psalm 126:2.

Silent instruments, Psalm 137:2–4 (LB).

Dire music, Proverbs 25:20.

Choirs and orchestras, Ecclesiastes 2:7–8 (LB).

"Song of fools," Ecclesiastes 7:5.

Romantic garden song, Song of Songs 5:2–8.

Evil woman's music, Isaiah 23:16.

Ruthless song silenced, Isaiah 25:5.

A new song, Isaiah 42:10.

No youth music, Lamentations 5:14 (CEV).

Meaningless lyrics, beautiful voice, Ezekiel 33:32.

Variety of instruments, Daniel 3:5.

Divine deaf ear to praise, Amos 5:23.

"Foolish songs," Amos 6:5 (CEV).

Songs turn to wailing, Amos 8:3, 10.

Brief song, Micah 2:4.

Wild music, Habakkuk 3:1 (AB).

Instrument instructions, Habakkuk 3:19.

"Sing and celebrate," Zechariah 2:10 (CEV).

Funeral song, Matthew 11:17 (CEV); Luke 7:31–32.

Angels praising God, Luke 2:13–14 (Notice, however, that the Bible uses "saying" and not "singing." Some believe angels will not sing until the work of redemption has been completed. Also, Mary's "song" is recorded in Scripture as "Mary said," Luke 1:46).

Potential singing stones, Luke 19:37–40.

Prison hymns, Acts 16:25.

Payment for spiritual service, 1 Corinthians 9:1–14.

Distinct rendition, 1 Corinthians 14:7.

Army bugler, 1 Corinthians 14:8 (See LB).

Hymns, spiritual songs, Colossians 3:16.
Congregational singing, Hebrews 2:12.
Angel choir, Revelation 5:11–12.
Song for exclusive congregation, Revelation 14:1–3.
Harps in heaven, Revelation 15:2–4.
Music forever silenced, Revelation 18:22.
See Choir, Harp, Hymn, Orchestra, Solo.

MUSLIM *See Islam.*

MUTE

Loss of speech, Ezekiel 3:26.
Mute before the Lord, Ezekiel 16:63.
Father of John the Baptist stricken mute, Luke 1:11–22.
Muteness caused by skepticism, Luke 1:19–20, 62–64.
Mute demon, Luke 11:14.
Silence in heaven, Revelation 8:1.
See Signing.

MUTINY

Threat of mutiny, Numbers 14:1–4.
Guards unwilling to follow evil command, 1 Samuel 22:16–17.
Divine command to destroy, 2 Kings 10:6–7.
King destroyed by associates, 2 Kings 12:19–20.
Mutinous slaves, Zechariah 2:9.
See Anarchy

MYRRH

Commercial commodity, Genesis 37:25.
Gift to long-lost son, Genesis 43:11.
Anointing oil, Exodus 30:23.
Royal cosmetic, Esther 2:12.
"Fragrant with myrrh," Psalm 45:8.
"Perfumed with myrrh," Song of Songs 3:6.
"Lips dripping with myrrh," Song of Songs 5:13.

MYRRH

Nativity gift, Matthew 2:11.
Embalming ingredient, John 19:39.
See Fragrance, Perfume.

MYSTERY

Exceedingly mysterious past, Ecclesiastes 7:24 (NASB).
Mysterious sight, Revelation 12:1, 3 (GNB).

MYSTICAL

Avoid mystical practices, Deuteronomy 18:9-13.

Prophet of God called seer, 1 Samuel 9:9.
Strange movement of shadow, 2 Kings 20:8-11.
Putting end to mediums and spiritists, 2 Kings 23:24.
Faith's mystic secret, 1 Timothy 3:9, 16 (AB).
See Magic, Séance, Sorcery.

MYTH

Myths, old wives' tales, 1 Timothy 1:3-4; 4:7.
See Fables.

N

NAGGING

"Drip-drip-drip," Proverbs 19:13 (GNB).
Fathers should not nag children, Ephesians 6:4.

NAIVE

"Prudence to the naive," Proverbs 1:4 (NASB).
Easily deceived, Hosea 7:11.
Validity of young faith, 1 Timothy 4:12.
See Amateur, Novice.

NAKEDNESS

Initial awareness of nudity, Genesis 3:7 (See 2:25).
Noah's nakedness, Genesis 9:20-25.
Act of shame, Jeremiah 13:26.
Gethsemane nude, Mark 14:51-52.
See Nudity.

NAME

Named by Adam, Genesis 2:19-20.
Giving meaning to name, Genesis 3:20.
Abram's famous name, Genesis 12:2 (LB).
Strange names of kings, Genesis 14:1-9.
Abram changed to Abraham, Genesis 17:5 (Note Abram means "exalted father," Abraham means "father of many").
New names, Genesis 17:15; 32:28; 41:45; Judges 6:32; Ruth 1:20; 2 Samuel 12:25; Acts 13:9.
Embarrassing name, Genesis 32:27-28 (AB).

Meaning of name, Exodus 2:10; Judges 13:17-18; 1 Samuel 25:25; Isaiah 62:4; Matthew 1:21; Hebrews 7:1-2.
Identified by family, Exodus 33:11; Numbers 11:28; 13:4-16; 14:6, 30; Joshua 1:1; 2:1; Judges 2:8; 1 Kings 16:34.
Preserving family name, Numbers 27:1-11.
"Josephites," Joshua 16:4 (NRSV).
Meaningful name change, Judges 6:32; 7:1; 8:28-30 (Gideon during his prowess, Jerub-Baal when speaking of his polygamy).
Name of angel, Judges 13:17-18.
Foreboding Ichabod, 1 Samuel 4:21-22.
Name preserved without son, 2 Samuel 18:18.
Name with two letters, 2 Kings 17:4.
Forgetting God's name, Psalm 44:20.
Awesome name, Psalm 99:3.
Value of good name, Proverbs 22:1.
Fragrant name, Song of Songs 1:3.
"Quick loot, fast plunder," Isaiah 8:1-4 (GNB).
Name above all names, Isaiah 9:6.
Power in God's name, Jeremiah 10:6 (LB).
Gods Bel, Marduk, Jeremiah 50:2.
Everlasting name, Isaiah 56:5.
Daniel's Babylonian name, Daniel 10:1.
Accurate name, Jeremiah 20:3 (AB).
Similar names of father, son, Jeremiah 22:24.
Evil name, good deeds, Jeremiah 52:31-34.
Girl named "unloved," boy named, "Not-my-people," Hosea 1:6-9 (GNB).

Troubled Valley, Hopeful Valley, Hosea 2:15 (CEV).

Defiled name, Hosea 4:15 (AB).

Name meaning "lots," Mark 5:9 (CEV).

Angel names newborn son, Luke 1:13.

By-passed family tradition, Luke 1:57–65.

Incidental name preserved, John 18:10.

Saul's name changed to Paul, Acts 13:9.

Paul's wise use of names, Colossians 4:7–17.

Name superiority, Hebrews 1:4.

Eternal name of God, Hebrews 1:8.

Christ called "the Name," 3 John 7.

Friends greeted by name, 3 John 14.

Unique name for Jesus, Revelation 3:14.

Name of temple in heaven, Revelation 15:5.

Covered with blasphemous names, Revelation 17:3.

Unknown name, Revelation 19:12.

See Identity.

NAP

Noonday nap, 2 Samuel 4:5 (See LB).

NARCISSISM

Personal needs ahead of divine guidance, Exodus 16:1–18.

Using sacred offering for personal gain, 1 Samuel 2:29.

Skilled at art of seduction, Jeremiah 2:33.

Greedy for gain, Jeremiah 8:10.

Good life gone, Lamentations 4:1, 5.

Women of Sodom, Ezekiel 16:49.

Personal desire above need of others, Amos 6:6.

Fate of carefree city, Zephaniah 2:15.

Fruit of selfishness, Haggai 1:2–5.

Concern for one's self more than for the Lord, Zachariah 7:4–6.

Value of serving God, Malachi 3:14–15.

Golden Rule reversed, Matthew 18:21–25.

Love for others grows cold, Matthew 24:12.

Doing good without expecting recriprocation, Luke 6:27–36.

Greatest in kingdom, Luke 9:46–48.

Desire for recognition in congregation, Luke 11:43.

All kinds of greed, Luke 12:15–21.

Desiring place of honor, Luke 14:7–11.

Backlash of selfishness, Luke 15:11–32.

Attitude between owners and workers, Luke 17:7–10.

Pharisees desired visible kingdom, Luke 17:20–21.

Hindrance of selfishness, Luke 18:18–25.

Temple as market place, Luke 19:45–48.

Christian attitude toward others, Romans 12:10.

Valid functioning of self-interest, 2 Corinthians 9:6–11.

Those whose god is their stomach, Philippians 3:19.

See Hedonism, Self-interest, Selfishness.

NATION *See Nations.*

NATIONALISM

Establishment of clans, Genesis 10:32.

Nation's originator, Genesis 19:37, 38.

Hagar's choice of wife for Ishmael, Genesis 21:21 (See v. 9 and 16:1–2).

Abraham's concern for wife for Isaac, Genesis 24:1–4.

Prenatal struggle, Genesis 25:22–23.

Commanded not to marry foreigner, Genesis 28:1 (See 26:34).

Earth divided into nations, Deuteronomy 32:8.

Nation great, terrible, 1 Chronicles 1:1–54.

Right to purchase slaves, Leviticus 25:44.

Love for foreigners, Deuteronomy 10:19.

Samson desired Philistine wife, Judges 14:1–2.

Keeping bloodline pure, Nehemiah 10:30.

Peaceful borders, Psalm 147:14.

None pleases the Lord, Isaiah 34:2.

Country born in a day, Isaiah 66:8.

Gospel to all nations, Matthew 24:14.

Jews and the centurion, Acts 10:22, 28, 34–35.

Intermarriage between Jew and Greek, Acts 16:1.

Respect for citizen of country, Acts 22:25–29.

See Alien, Foreigner, Miscegenation, Patriotism, Xenophobia.

NATIONS

Nations destroyed, Genesis 7:21.

Native-born, Numbers 15:13.

Earth divided into nations, Deuteronomy 32:8.

Powerful government at God's mercy, 1 Samuel 12:25.

Nations rise and fall, Job 12:23.

Wealth and idolatry, Isaiah 2:7–8.

Divine list of judged nations, Jeremiah 25:15–29.

Land of luxury brought down, Ezekiel 27:1–36 (See 28:1–19).

For continued sinning, certain judgment, Amos 1:3, 6, 9, 11, 13; 2:1, 4, 6 (Note the nature of sins).

All nations important to God, Amos 9:7 (CEV).

See Citizenship, Government.

NATIVITY

Star of Bethlehem prophesied, Numbers 24:17.

Birth of Jesus prophesied, Isaiah 7:10–14.

Bethlehem prophecy, Micah 5:2.

The Christmas story, Matthew 1:18–25; Luke 2:1–20.

Birth of Christ reviewed, Revelation 12:1–5.

See Christmas.

NATURAL RESOURCES

Vast resources, Genesis 1:28 (AB).

Metals mined on earth, Numbers 31:22.

Oil from rock, Deuteronomy 32:13.

Purifying bad water, 2 Kings 2:19–22.

Excrement used as fuel, Ezekiel 4:9–15.

Commercial centers in Ezekiel's time, Ezekiel 27:12–23.

Gold, silver belong to God, Haggai 2:8.

Salt loses saltiness, Luke 14:34–35.

See Agriculture, Ecology, Forestry, Gold, Iron, Metal, Nature, Silver.

NATURE

Plants "burst forth," Genesis 1:11 (LB).

"Swarms of living creatures, Genesis 1:20 (NASB).

Domestic and wild animals, Genesis 1:24–25.

Pleasing to the eye, Genesis 2:9.

Intelligence of serpent, Genesis 3:1.

Human supremacy over beasts, birds, Genesis 9:1–3.

Worship among trees, Genesis 13:18 (See 14:13; 18:1).

Landmark tree, Genesis 21:33.

Divine use of nature, Exodus 19:9.

Do not worship nature, Deuteronomy 4:15–20.

Protection of birds, Deuteronomy 22:6.

Lyric about the sun, Judges 5:31.

Parable about choice of king, Judges 9:7–15.

Solomon's knowledge of nature, 1 Kings 4:29–34.

All nature praises Creator, 1 Chronicles 16:31–33.

Power, authority of Creator, Job 9:1–10.

Nature as teacher, Job 12:7–8; Psalm 8:3–4; Matthew 6:28; Mark 4:28; 13:28.

Path for wind, storm, Job 28:25–27.

Homage to sun, moon, Job 31:26–28.

Procedure of rainfall, Job 36:27–30.

God spoke to Job of creation, Job 38:1–14, 31–33.

Revelation through nature, Psalm 19:1–14; Romans 1:18–20.

Nature illustrates Creator's greatness, Psalm 36:5–6.

River in city of God, Psalm 46:4.

Divine ownership, Psalm 50:9–12.

Awesome works of God, Psalm 66:5.

All nature praises God, Psalms 69:34; 96:11–12.

Nature's awe, Psalm 77:16–18; Ezekiel 38:20.

Bird nest near altar, Psalm 84:3.

Divine law governing nature, Psalm 89:8–13.

Joyful trees, Psalm 96:12.

Poem to God of nature, Psalm 104:1–26.

Holy Spirit's role, Psalm 104:30 (LB).

Cooperative Red Sea and Jordan, Psalm 114:3–5 (LB).

Earth entrusted to man, Psalm 115:16.

God of nature, Psalm 147:4–18.

Nature, people praise the Lord, Psalm 148:1–14.

Earth, sky show wisdom of God, Proverbs 3:19–20.

Danger of angry bear, Proverbs 17:12.

Power of God at work, Proverbs 30:4.

Fragrant terrain, Song of Songs 4:6.

Future harmony in nature, Isaiah 11:6–9.

People defile earth, Isaiah 24:5.

Divine glory revealed, Isaiah 35:1–2 (See Psalm 19:1–6).

Eating wild fruit, Isaiah 37:30.

Dying earth, Isaiah 51:6.

People live to age of trees, Isaiah 65:20–22.

Birds know God's way, Jeremiah 8:7.

Desolate birds, animals, Jeremiah 9:10.

Earth, sky reflect God's wisdom, Jeremiah 10:12–13.

Parched land, wildlife, Jeremiah 12:4.

God of all nature, Jeremiah 31:35.

Divine judgment against mountains and hills, Ezekiel 6:1–5.

Worship of sun, Ezekiel 8:16.

Creative functions, Amos 4:13.

Wild animals fear, Joel 2:22.

Lord of earth, Amos 9:5–6.

Advent majesty, Micah 1:3–4.

Symbol of divine provision, Matthew 6:28–30.

Value of one sparrow, Luke 12:6.

Wild flowers, Luke 12:27 (CEV).

Signs, disturbance in last days, Luke 21:25.

God revealed in nature, Romans 1:18–20.

Animals, plants await great event, Romans 8:22 (LB).

Men, animals of different flesh, 1 Corinthians 15:39.

God preserves nature, 1 Timothy 6:13 (AB).

Christ the Creator, Colossians 1:15–17.

See Animals, Animism, Birds, Natural Resources.

NAVIGATION

Ships built by King Solomon, 1 Kings 9:26–28.

Fleet of ships that never set sail, 1 Kings 22:48.

Paths of the seas, Psalms 8:8; 77:19; Isaiah 43:16.

Commercial navigation, Psalm 107:23–24.

Tyre, sea power, Ezekiel 26:15–18.

Oar-driven ships, Ezekiel 27:26; Jonah 1:13.

Shipwreck, Ezekiel 27:34; Acts 27:14–32.

Soundings determine position, Acts 27:27–29.

See Commerce, Maritime, Ocean, Shipping, Voyage.

NAVY

Solomon's ships, 1 Kings 9:26.

Jehoshaphat's fleet, 1 Kings 22:48.

NAVY

Vanquished sea power, Ezekiel 26:17 (See LB).
See Ocean.

NEAR See Imminent.

NECTAR See Fruit.

NEED
Exact need provided, Exodus 16:17–20.
Help from God alone, 2 Kings 6:26–27.
Turning to rejected brother, Judges 11:1–10.
Wealth numbs sense of need, Hosea 12:8.
Ignoring need, Amos 4:6.
Meeting need for cold water, Matthew 10:42.
Involvement in need of others, Mark 6:35–43.
Touch of need, Luke 8:43–48.
Reaching out to help others, Acts 11:27–30.
Macedonian call, Acts 16:9.
Christ met our greatest need, Romans 5:6–8.
Diversity in prayer, Ephesians 6:18.
Need fully supplied, Philippians 4:19 (AB).
Family members in need, 1 Timothy 5:3–8.
Minimum needs, 1 Timothy 6:8.
See Weakness.

NEGATIVE
Negative report of spies, Numbers 13:26–33.
Old Testament concludes with curse, Malachi 4:6.
Negative designation, John 1:19–23.
Letter kills but Spirit gives life, 2 Corinthians 3:6.
List of "don'ts," Colossians 2:21–22 (GNB).
See Positive.

NEGLECT
No evidence of neglect, Exodus 21:28.
Responsibility for negligence, Exodus 21:36.
Livestock in another man's pasture, Exodus 22:5.
Word of the Lord rare, 1 Samuel 3:1.

Neglect of duty, Nehemiah 9:35; Luke 12:47.
Lazy man's house, Ecclesiastes 10:18.
Neglected salvation, Jeremiah 8:20.
Foolish response to Divine message, Matthew 7:26.
Do not toss message aside, 2 Corinthians 6:1 (LB).
Neglecting good works, James 2:14; 4:17.
See Careless.

NEGOTIATION
Bargaining with God, Genesis 18:20–33.
Offering peace before battle, Deuteronomy 20:10.
Life for life, Joshua 2:14.
Land negotiation, Judges 11:12–24.
Egyptian alliance, 1 Kings 3:1.
Subversive negotiations, Nehemiah 6:1–12.
"Talk it over," Isaiah 1:18 (CEV).
Strategy facing superior enemy, Luke 14:31–32.
See Arbitration.

NEIGHBOR
Responsibility toward neighbor, Genesis 9:5.
Meeting neighbors, Genesis 34:1 (Berk.).
Integrity between neighbors, Exodus 20:16; Leviticus 19:13–18.
Liability for treacherous animal, Exodus 21:28–32.
Animal injury to neighbor's property, Exodus 22:5.
Criminal hatred to neighbor, Deuteronomy 19:11–13 (See Proverbs 14:12).
Demonstrated neighborliness, Deuteronomy 22:1–4.
Loving neighbor as yourself, 1 Samuel 18:1.
Help of good neighbors, Ezra 1:6.
Equity toward neighbor, Psalm 15:3.
Insincere neighbors, Psalm 28:3.
Insulted by neighbors, Psalm 31:11 (CEV).
A reproach to neighbors, Psalm 44:13.
Doing good to others, Proverbs 3:27–28.
Settle disputes privately, Proverbs 25:9–10.
Seldom visit neighbor, Proverbs 25:17.
Neighborhood integrity, Proverbs 26:18–19

Nearby neighbor better than distant relative, Proverbs 27:10.

Loudly blessing neighbor, Proverbs 27:14.

Keeping ahead of Joneses, Ecclesiastes 4:4.

Lust among neighbors, Jeremiah 5:8.

Speaking cordially with deceitful heart, Jeremiah 9:8.

Sharing shade, Zechariah 3:10.

Neighbors unaware of Christ's greatness, Matthew 13:53–58; Luke 4:22–24.

Love your neighbor, Matthew 22:34–40; Luke 4:22–24; Romans 13:9–10; James 2:8.

Familiarity breeds contempt, Mark 6:1–6.

Good news shared among neighbors, Luke 1:57–58.

Effective witness to neighbor, John 4:39.

Speak truthfully to neighbors, Ephesians 4:25.

Conduct toward unbelievers, Colossians 4:5.

Royal law of Scripture, James 2:8.

See Rapport, Relationship.

NEIGHBORHOOD

Choice of place to live, Genesis 13:10–13.

Dislike of wealthy neighbors, Genesis 26:12–17.

Making social calls, Genesis 34:1.

Desolate cities, Job 15:28 (NKJV).

Neighborhood dishonesty, Psalm 12:2.

Neighborhood watch, Psalm 104:20–23 (LB).

Avoid quarrel, Proverbs 11:12.

Keeping up with the Joneses, Ecclesiastes 4:4.

Congested areas, Isaiah 5:8.

When God establishes a community, Jeremiah 30:20.

Fountain flowing from the Lord's house, Joel 3:18.

Judgment upon evil community, Zephaniah 3:1.

Neighbors living in peace, Zechariah 8:16–17.

Salt and light in the world, Matthew 5:13–16.

Division in communities and families, Matthew 12:25.

Neighborhood relationships, Romans 12:16, 18.

Neighborhood peace, Ephesians 6:23 (NRSV).

House to house gossip, 1 Timothy 5:13.

Being example to unbelievers, 1 Peter 2:12.

City of total integrity, Revelation 21:27.

See Community.

NEOPHYTE

Father assists inexperienced son, 1 Chronicles 22:5; 29:1.

See Naive.

NEPHEW

Apostle Paul's nephew, Acts 23:16.

NEPOTISM

Rights of oldest son, Deuteronomy 21:15–17.

Special favor to daughter, Judges 1:12–15.

Sons succeed father, 1 Samuel 8:1–3.

Sons overlooked, 1 Samuel 12:1–2 (LB).

Army appointment for king's cousin, 1 Samuel 14:50.

Saul negated son's position, 1 Samuel 20:30–31.

Share and share alike, 1 Samuel 30:24.

Government jobs for sons, 2 Samuel 8:16.

Mother's wiles, 1 Kings 1:11–31.

David's son, 1 Chronicles 18:17.

Chosen to build temple, 1 Chronicles 28:10.

Son fulfills father's dream, 2 Chronicles 6:3–11.

Brother appointed mayor, Nehemiah 7:2.

Fools in high places, Ecclesiastes 10:5–7.

Family of David always on throne, Jeremiah 33:17.

Avoid partiality, 1 Timothy 5:21; James 2:1.

See Family, Favoritism, Politics.

NEST

Nest in rock, Numbers 24:21.

Eagle stirs nest, Deuteronomy 32:11.

Lofty nest of eagle, Job 39:27; Jeremiah 49:16.

Sparrows, swallows nesting at temple, Psalm 84:3.

Wandering from nest, Proverbs 27:8.

Nest for owls, Isaiah 34:15.

Security for doves, Jeremiah 48:28.
More comfort for birds than for Creator, Luke 9:58.
See Birds, Shelter.

NET *See Snare, Trap.*

NETWORKING
Putting in a good word, Genesis 40:14.
Using a mother's influence, 1 Kings 2:13.
Influence of others, Nehemiah 6:1–19.
Cultivating materialistic friendships, Proverbs 19:6.
Improper networking, Proverbs 25:6–7.
Primary rule for successful networking, Matthew 7:12; Luke 6:31.
Misused relationship, Matthew 26:47–52; Mark 14:43–46; Luke 22:47; John 18:1–4.
Saul recommended by Barnabas, Acts 9:27.
It's whom you know, Acts 12:20.
Neworking in the Body of Christ, Romans 14:19.
Developing rapport, 1 Corinthians 9:20–23.
Blessing conveyed believer to believer, 2 Corinthians 7:5–7.
Providing inspiration for others, 2 Corinthians 9:2; 1 Thessalonians 1:8.
Benefit of knowing Christ, Ephesians 3:12.
Making most of every opportunity, Ephesians 5:15–16.
See Influence, Rapport.

NEUTRALITY
Angel of the Lord, Joshua 5:13–15.
Cannot be spiritually neutral, Matthew 12:30; Mark 9:39–40; Luke 11:23; 16:13.

NEW
Nothing new, Ecclesiastes 1:10.
New song, Psalms 33:3; 40:3; 149:1; Isaiah 42:10; Revelation 14:3.
Given new name, Isaiah 56:4–5; 62:2; Acts 11:26; Revelation 3:12.
New things, Isaiah 42:9; 43:19; 48:6; Revelation 21:5.
Made new by faith, Ezekiel 11:19; 36:26; John 3:3; 2 Corinthians 5:17; Galatians 6:15; Ephesians 2:14–15; 1 Peter 1:23.
See Creation, Innovation.

NEW AGE
Becoming like God, Genesis 3:5.
Human exaltation, Genesis 11:4 (LB).
Condemnation of occult, Deuteronomy 18:19–22.
Men as gods, Isaiah 41:23; Ezekiel 28:2–3 (See LB).
Fallible new age creed, Isaiah 47:10.
Distorted truth, Jeremiah 8:8–9.
Thinking to be God, Ezekiel 28:2–3 (LB).
"Wise as the gods themselves," Daniel 5:11 (CEV).
Prospering deceit, Daniel 8:25.
"Worship their own strength," Habakkuk 1:11 (CEV).
Those who mishandle truth, Matthew 7:21–23.
Cause of error, Matthew 22:29.
Sorcerer's claim of divinity, Acts 8:10.
Unknown god, Acts 17:23.
Warning against error, Acts 20:28–31.
Human incapacity to generate truth, Romans 3:10–20 (Note 3:4).
Limitless source of truth, Romans 11:33–36.
Contrary teaching, Romans 16:17–18.
Holistic knowledge of truth, Romans 12:1–2 (See LB).
Earth's wisdom, 1 Corinthians 1:18–21; 3:19; Colossians 2:8–9.
Primary truth, 1 Corinthians 15:3–4.
Austere warning, 1 Corinthians 15:33–34; Colossians 2:8–15.
Mortal limitations, 1 Corinthians 15:50.
Truth obscurred, 2 Corinthians 4:1–6.
Source of power, 2 Corinthians 4:7.
Contaminated body, spirit, 2 Corinthians 7:1.
Satan's masquerade, 2 Corinthians 11:13–14.
Careful self-evaluation, 2 Corinthians 13:5.
Perverted truth, Galatians 1:6–9.
Inner reality, Galatians 2:20.
Misguided believers, Galatians 5:7.
Prayer for insight, Ephesians 1:18–23; 3:14–21.
Darkness, light, Ephesians 5:8–14.
Prepared for inner assault, Ephesians 6:10–18.

Universal declaration of truth, Philippians 2:9–11.

Valid inner diety, Colossians 1:27.

Lifestyle correction, Colossians 3:1–5.

Modern apostasy, 2 Thessalonians 2:3 (KJV).

Key to truth, 1 Timothy 3:16–17.

Last days conduct, 1 Timothy 4:1; 2 Timothy 3:1–7; 4:1–5.

Pseudo-knowledge, 1 Timothy 6:20 (GNB).

Lovers of self, 2 Timothy 3:2.

Resistance to truth, 2 Timothy 4:3.

Error rebuked, Titus 1:2–16.

Reincarnation refuted, Hebrews 9:27.

Eye witness to truth, 2 Peter 1:16.

Love of the world, 1 John 2:15–17.

Denying Christ's divinity, 1 John 2:22; 4:1–3.

Discerning spirits, 1 John 4:1–3.

666 the mark of man, Revelation 13:18.

See Animism, Cult, Spiritism.

NEWS

Good for some, bad for others, Joshua 5:1 (LB).

Causing ears to tingle, 1 Samuel 3:11.

Death of king, 2 Samuel 1:1–12.

Good news from distant land, Proverbs 25:25.

Concurrent messages, Jeremiah 51:31–32.

"Only bad news," Ezekiel 7:26 (CEV).

Bearer of bad news, Ezekiel 33:21.

News of ministry, Colossians 4:7.

Good news of faith, love, 1 Thessalonians 3:6.

See Media.

NIGHT

Camping at night, Genesis 28:11.

Night watches, 1 Samuel 11:11; Psalm 119:148; Lamentations 2:19; Matthew 14:25; Luke 12:38.

Temple light burns out, 1 Samuel 3:3.

Canopy for the Lord, 2 Samuel 22:12.

Night inspection, Nehemiah 2:11–16.

"Endless darkness," Job 3:9 (Berk.).

Deep sleep, Job 4:13.

"Songs in the night," Job 35:10.

Time for heart searching, Psalm 4:4; 16:7.

Plotting evil while falling asleep, Psalm 36:4.

Night meditation, Psalm 63:6.

Night songs, Psalm 77:6.

Calling to the Lord day, night, Psalm 88:1–2.

Moon designates seasons, Psalm 104:19.

Nocturnal animals, Psalm 104:22–23 (LB).

Giving thanks at midnight, Psalm 119:62, 148.

Seek the Lord morning, night, Isaiah 26:9.

No one to light lamps, Jeremiah 25:10 (CEV).

Dawn to darkness, Amos 4:13.

Cry of owl, Zephaniah 2:14.

No night in heaven, Zechariah 14:7.

Night divided into time zones, Mark 13:35.

Fear in the night, Luke 2:8–14.

Nativity night's brightness, Luke 2:9 (LB).

Night of prayer, Luke 6:12.

Nicodemus came to Jesus at night, John 3:1–2; 19:39.

Walking at night, John 11:9–10.

Night hours, Acts 23:23.

Wild parties, conduct, Romans 13:13 (LB).

See Darkness.

NIGHTMARE

Thick, dreadful darkness, Genesis 15:12 (See NKJV).

Troubled dream of future, Genesis 41:1–8.

Foreboding bread loaf, Judges 7:13–14.

Disturbing dreams, Job 4:13 (CEV).

Frightening dreams, Job 7:13–15; Daniel 2:1; 4:5.

Many cares cause dreams, Ecclesiastes 5:3.

Horrible nightmares, Daniel 2:1 (CEV).

See Night.

NOBILITY

True nobility, Psalm 16:3 (LB).

NOCTURNAL *See Darkness, Insomnia, Night.*

NOISE

Rebellious revelry, Exodus 32:17–20.

Temple construction noise reduction, 1 Kings 6:7.

Laughter and joy, Psalm 126:2.

End to noisy songs, Ezekiel 26:13.

See Shouting.

NOMAD

Cain, first wanderer, Genesis 4:13–14.
Those who love to wander, Jeremiah 14:10.
See Vagabond.

NOMINAL

Partial obedience, 2 Chronicles 27:2.
Nominal piety of King Zedekiah, Jeremiah 37:1–3.
Neither cold nor hot, Revelation 3:16.
See Carnality.

NON-PROFIT

Priests tax free, Ezra 7:24.
Paying taxes to government, Matthew 22:15–22.

NONSENSE

Talking nonsense, Job 6:25 (GNB).
Wisdom nonsense, 1 Corinthians 3:19 (GNB).
"Bombastic nonsense," 2 Peter 2:18 (NRSV).

NONVERBAL COMMUNICATION

Dove's communication, Genesis 8:10–11.
Removed sandal, Ruth 4:8 (See Joshua 5:15).
"Shook out my lap," Nehemiah 5:13 (KJV).
Putting foot to neck, Joshua 10:24.
Shake hands, Proverbs 6:1 (NKJV).
"I hurl my shoe," Psalm 108:9 (NRSV).
Wink, shuffle, point, Proverbs 6:13.
Visible evidence of sorrow, Isaiah 15:2–3.
Shake dust off feet, Luke 9:5.
Gesture for silence, Acts 21:40.
See Body language, Gesture.

NONVIOLENCE

Trusting God for deliverance, 2 Chronicles 32:1–21.
Evaluating military logistics, Luke 14:31–32.
Jesus nonviolent, John 18:36.

NOON

High day, Genesis 29:7 (NKJV).
Time for lunch, Genesis 43:16, 25.
Groping at midday, Deuteronomy 28:29.
Midday rest, 2 Samuel 4:5.

Noontime drinking spree, 1 Kings 20:16.
Death at noon, 2 Kings 4:20.
Noonday brightness, Job 11:17.
Prayer at noon, Psalm 55:17.
Midday plague, Psalm 91:6.
Noonday at night, Isaiah 58:10.
High noon adventure, Acts 22:6.
See Day, Time.

NORTH

Conjectured Heaven location, Psalm 48:2 (NKJV).
Omitted direction, Psalm 75:6 (NKJV).
Northern disaster, Jeremiah 6:1, 22; 13:20; 25:9.
Northern wind storm, Ezekiel 1:4–6.
Royal conflict, north, south, Daniel 11:6, 8–15, 40.
See Compass.

NORTH AMERICA

Prophecy some conjecture as referring to North America, Isaiah 18:1–2, 7.

NORTHERN LIGHTS *See Aurora borealis.*

NOSE

Bloody nose, Proverbs 30:33.

NOSTALGIA

Looking back on better days, Exodus 16:2–3.
Those who remembered glory of temple, Haggai 2:3.
Prodigal son, Luke 15:17.
Rich man in torment, Luke 16:25–27.
See Memory.

NOTES

Eating scroll, Ezekiel 3:1–4.
Daniel did not trust memory, Daniel 7:1.

NOTORIETY

How David became famous, 2 Samuel 8:13.
Role of humility in greatness, Matthew 23:12.
Respect of Cornelius for Peter, Acts 10:25–26.
See Fame.

NOURISHMENT *See Food, Gourmet, Nutrition, Provision.*

NOVELTY

Bible riddles, Judges 14:12–14; Ezekiel 17:2–10.

Ill-fated pet lamb, 2 Samuel 12:1–6.

Strange verse, 1 Chronicles 26:18.

World's shortest short story, Ecclesiastes 9:14–15.

Shortest verse in Bible, John 11:35.

See Humor.

NOVICE

Novice eaglet, Deuteronomy 32:11.

Twelve-year-old king, 2 Kings 21:1.

Father, inexperienced son, 1 Chronicles 22:5; 29:1.

Training for Daniel and friends, Daniel 1:3–4.

A king's favor, Daniel 2:49.

Validity of young faith, 1 Timothy 4:12.

See Amateur, Naive.

NOW

Psalm 118:24.

Living for today in God's favor, Ecclesiastes 9:7.

Delay ended, Ezekiel 12:28 (LB).

Best time for salvation, 2 Corinthians 6:2.

See Today.

NUCLEAR

Sky, earth destroyed by fire, 2 Peter 3:7, 10–12.

NUDITY

First awareness of nudity, Genesis 3:7. (See Genesis 2:25.)

NOSTALGIA

Shem's attitude toward father's privacy, Genesis 9:20–27.

Shame of exposed nakedness, Isaiah 47:2–3.

Act of shame, Jeremiah 13:26, 27.

Promiscuous nudity, Ezekiel 16:35–38.

Nudity as judgment, Hosea 2:2–3.

Brave warriors flee naked, Amos 2:16.

Drunken neighbor, Habakkuk 2:15.

Demon-possessed nude, Luke 8:27.

Sinful exposure, Revelation 16:15.

See Immodest, Nakedness.

NUISANCE

Thorns in side, Judges 2:3.

Disturbing privacy of others, Proverbs 25:17.

NUMBERS

Strength in numbers, Ecclesiastes 4:12.

Moabites intimidated by Israelites coming out of Egypt, Numbers 22:4–6.

Evaluating military logistics, Luke 14:31–32.

See Majority, Minority, Statistics.

NUMEROLOGY *See Forty.*

NURSES

Nurse named Deborah, Genesis 35:8.

Nurse for baby Moses, Exodus 2:7.

Mother-in-law nurse, Ruth 4:16.

Nurse, child flee for safety, 2 Samuel 4:4.

Hidden nurse, child, 2 Kings 11:2.

NUTRITION

Food in wilderness, Exodus 16:2–35.

Egyptian delicacies, Numbers 11:5.

Abagail's balanced diet, 1 Samuel 25:18.

Bread, fruit, 2 Samuel 16:1, 2.

Wine, oil, bread, Psalm 104:15.

Nutritious honey, Proverbs 24:13.

Nutritious raisins, Song of Songs 2:5.

Mother's milk, Isaiah 66:11.

Polluting wheat, Amos 8:6.

Salt that loses saltiness, Luke 14:34–35.

Desiring food of pigs, Luke 15:13–16.

See Diet, Food, Health.

O

OATH

Solemn covenant, Genesis 14:22–23; 26:26–29.

Avoid oaths with wicked people, Exodus 23:1.

Fake oaths, Leviticus 6:2–5; Jeremiah 7:8, 9.

Oath of doom, Joshua 6:26.

Nation under oath, 1 Samuel 14:24.

Nothing but the truth, 1 Kings 22:16.

Good men and sinners taking oaths, Ecclesiastes 9:2.

Taking false oath, Jeremiah 5:2.

The Lord almighty has sworn by Himself, Jeremiah 51:14.

Do not swear falsely, Zechariah 8:17.

Simply "yes" or "no," Matthew 5:33–37; James 5:12.

Idle oath, Matthew 26:63, 69–75.

Jesus challenged by demon, Mark 5:7.

Profane, murderous oath, Acts 23:12–14.

Swear not by heaven or earth, James 5:12.

Oath of an angel, Revelation 10:5–7.

See Covenant, Pledge, Promise, Vow.

OBEDIENCE

"A pleasure to the Lord," Genesis 6:8 (LB), 22.

Abraham's obedience of Abram, Genesis 12:1–4.

Circumcision at advanced age, Genesis 17:10–27.

Predicted result of obedience, Genesis 18:19.

Obedience brings blessing, Genesis 22:15–18.

Exercising complete obedience, Exodus 7:6.

Promised reward for obedience, Exodus 19:5.

Pledge of congregation, Exodus 24:1–7.

Promise of answered prayer, Exodus 33:17.

Journey by divine directive, Numbers 9:23.

Reward for father's obedience, Numbers 14:24.

Obedience rewarded, Deuteronomy 28:1–14; Job 36:11; Isaiah 48:17–18; Jeremiah 7:22–23; Revelation 3:10.

Obey to the letter, Joshua 1:7 (LB).

Complete reading of the law, Joshua 8:35.

Rationalized obedience, 1 Samuel 15:7–31.

Reward of long life, 1 Kings 3:14.

Materialism versus obedience, 1 Kings 13:7–10.

Great things, small things, 2 Kings 5:13.

Obedience brings security, 2 Kings 21:8.

Stay with God, He with you, 2 Chronicles 15:2 (LB).

No hurry to obey, 2 Chronicles 24:5 (CEV).

Scripture meaningful by obedience, Psalm 25:10; 103:17–21.

Made willing to obey, Psalm 51:10 (See LB).

"Make me want to obey," Psalm 51:12 (CEV).

Prayer for undivided heart, Psalm 86:11.

Glad obedience, Psalm 100:2 (LB).

Obedient angels, Psalm 103:20.

Fulfilling vows to the Lord, Psalm 116:14, 18–19.

Desire for full obedience, Psalm 119:1–5.

Following guidance of Scripture, Psalm 119:1–16, 57–64.

Obedient by choice, Psalm 119:30 (See GNB).

Pledge of obedience, Psalm 119:33–34 (LB).

Obedience preferred to making money, Psalm 119:36 (LB).

Once astray, now obedient, Psalm 119:67.

Guidance of Scripture for all of life, Psalm 119:111–112.

Obedience by Divine instruction, Psalm 143:10.

Thorough obedience, Proverbs 7:2.

Man's plans, God's will, Isaiah 30:1.

Nothing more important, Isaiah 33:6 (CEV).

Don't argue with Creator, Isaiah 45:9 (CEV).

Obedience under threat of death, Jeremiah 26:1–16.

Obedience to parents and grandparents, Jeremiah 35:1–16.

"You will want to obey," Ezekiel 11:19 (CEV).

Mighty are those who obey the Lord, Joel 2:11.

Jonah learned to obey, Jonah 3:3.

Do what God wants, Matthew 3:15 (CEV).

Desire to obey, Matthew 5:6, 10 (CEV, GNB).

Cannot obey two masters, Matthew 6:24.

Cost of following Jesus, Matthew 9:9.

Divine kinship, Mark 3:35.

Fulfilling requirements of the law, Luke 2:39.

Obedient child Jesus, Luke 2:41–52 (Note John 2:4 CEV).

Wisdom from doing God's will, John 7:17.

Obedience of Jesus, John 12:50; Romans 5:19; Hebrews 5:8–9.

Doing what Christ commands, John 14:15.

Obeying God rather than men, Acts 4:18–20; 5:29.

Obedience resulting from faith, Romans 1:5.

Obedience brings righteousness, Romans 2:13.

Fear and conviction, Romans 13:5.

Reputation for obedience, Romans 16:19.

Obedience in absentia, Philippians 2:12–13.

Athletes compete according to rules, 2 Timothy 2:5.

Turn away from wickedness, 2 Timothy 2:19.

Slaves' obedience, Titus 2:9–10.

Christ's example, Hebrews 10:10 (GNB).

By faith Noah and Abraham obeyed God, Hebrews 11:7–12.

Make sure to obey, Hebrews 12:25 (CEV).

"Obey your leaders," Hebrews 13:17 (NRSV).

"Obey God's message," James 1:22 (CEV).

Profession without obedience, 1 John 2:4–6.

Watchful obedience, 1 John 3:22 (AB).

Obedience to God's commands, 1 John 5:1–3 (See CEV).

See Discipleship, Disobedience, Submission, Surrender.

OBEISANCE *See Genuflect.*

OBELISK

Obelisk knocked down, Ezekiel 26:11 (AB).

OBESITY

Eating of fat prohibited, Leviticus 3:17; 7:24.

Very fat man, Judges 3:17.

Old, obese, 1 Samuel 4:18.

Fat, strong, 2 Samuel 1:22 (NKJV).

"Fat and rich," Job 15:27–28 (LB).

Enclosed in fat, Psalm 17:10 (Berk.).

Knife to throat, Proverbs 23:1–3.

Overeating, Proverbs 23:20.

Fat wasted away, Isaiah 17:4.

"Fat cows," Amos 4:1 (cev).
Physical responsibility, 1 Corinthians 6:19–20.
See Discipline, Gluttony, Health.

OBITUARY

Praise for evil dead, Ecclesiastes 8:10 (gnb).
See Death.

OBJECTIVE

Eyes on the Lord, Psalm 25:15.
Desire for full obedience, Psalm 119:1–5.
Look straight ahead, Proverbs 4:25–27.
Description of noble person, Isaiah 32:8.
Worldly objectives, spiritual objectives, Luke 12:29–31.
Aim for perfection, 2 Corinthians 13:11.
See Goal, Motivation, Target, Vision.

OBJECT LESSON

Old Testament object lessons, Jeremiah 1:13–17; 13:1–11.
Potter and clay, Jeremiah 18:1–8.
Tangible teaching, Ezekiel 4:1–13 (gnb).
Message of a coin, Matthew 22:17–22; Mark 12:13–17; Luke 20:20–26.
Belt object lesson, Acts 21:10–11.
See Illustration, Teaching, Visual.

OBLIGATION

Blessings bring obligation, Deuteronomy 4:32–40.
Refusing to be obligated, Genesis 14:22–24.
Recognized obligation, Psalm 116:12–17.
Reminder obligations owed, Philemon 17–19.
Responsibility to do good, James 4:17.
See Assignment, Debt, Duty, Responsibility.

OBLITERATION See Destruction, Genocide.

OBLIVION

Name blotted out, Deuteronomy 9:14; 29:20; Psalm 109:13; Isaiah 14:22.
Memory erased from earth, Deuteronomy 32:26; Job 18:17.
"Chased out of the world," Job 18:18 (nkjv).
Sins removed, Psalm 103:2–3; Acts 3:19.
Fortified city made desolate, Isaiah 27:10.
Silent, dark oblivion, Isaiah 47:5.

"End of the Philistines," Amos 1:8 (cev).
Judgment across face of earth, Zephaniah 1:2–3.
See Destruction.

OBSCENITY

Obscenity committed in anger, Deuteronomy 25:11–12.
Covenant to avoid lust, Job 31:1.
Obscenity avoided, Psalm 101:3 (lb).
Obscenity of two sisters, Ezekiel 23:1–49.
"Vulgar signs," Zephaniah 2:15 (cev).
Language purified, Zephaniah 3:9.
Avoid obscenity, Ephesians 5:4 (lb).
See Degradation, Depravity, Immorality.

OBSCURE

Writing difficult to understand, 2 Peter 3:15–16.

OBSEQUIOUS

Ruth's attitude to Boaz, Ruth 2:8–13.
Overt obsequiousness, 1 Samuel 25:23–41; 2 Samuel 9:6; 14:4–20.
Poor man, rich man, Proverbs 18:23.
Folly of flattery, Proverbs 28:23.
King paid honor to slave, Daniel 2:46–49.
Properly obsequious, Mark 1:7.
Loyalty exaggerated, Mark 14:31.
See Flattery, Obeisance.

OBSTACLE COURSE

Pathway becomes obstacle course, Jeremiah 6:21 (lb).

OBSTACLES

Facing obstacles, Deuteronomy 9:1–3.
The God who levels mountains, Isaiah 45:1–3.
Face set like flint, Isaiah 50:7.
Men on foot cannot compete with horses, Jeremiah 12:5.
Mustard seed faith moves mountain, Matthew 17:20; 21:21–22.
Stone rolled away, Mark 16:3–4.
Obstacle to running good race, Galatians 5:7.
See Hindrance.

OBSTINATE

Obstinate unanimity, Numbers 11:4–10.
No success outside God's will, Numbers 14:41–45.
Advice rejected, 1 Kings 12:12–15.
Persistent sins, 2 Chronicles 28:22–23.
Declared obstinate, Isaiah 48:4 (KJV).
Ignoring the word of the Lord, Jeremiah 7:13; 25:3.
Obstinate theology, Jeremiah 8:8.
Daring to burn prophecy, Jeremiah 36:20–24.
Sinful obstinacy, Jeremiah 44:15–27.
Obstructing rebuilding of temple, Haggai 1:3–4.
Obstinate demon, Mark 1:21–26.
See Rebellion, Resistant, Stubborn, Unwilling.

OBSTRUCTION

Obstructing rebuilding of temple, Haggai 1:3–4.
Separated by great chasm, Luke 16:26.
See Barrier.

OCCULT See Astrology, Cult, New Age, Séance, Sorcery, Spiritism.

OCCUPATION

Holiness by virtue of occupation, Leviticus 21:8.
Role of priest, Deuteronomy 18:1–2.
Occupation forces in place, Isaiah 22:7.
"What business are you in?" Jonah 1:8 (CEV).
Tentmakers, Acts 18:1–3.
Zenas, the lawyer, Titus 3:13.
See Employment.

OCEAN

Valley of sea, 2 Samuel 22:16.
Wisdom in the sea, Job 12:8.
Sea bottom, Job 36:30.
Ocean currents, Psalm 8:8.
Formation of continents, Psalm 24:2 (LB).
Oceanic mountains, Psalm 46:2 (NRSV); Jonah 2:6 (CEV).
Ocean capacity, Psalm 98:7 (AB).
Waters assigned to boundaries, Psalm 104:6–9.
Wonders of deep waters, Psalm 107:23–24.

Great sea creatures, Psalm 148:7.
Sleeping on the high seas, Proverbs 23:34.
Paths in the sea, Isaiah 43:16.
Tiny grains of sand hold back ocean, Jeremiah 5:22.
The God of all nature, Jeremiah 31:35.
Relentless waves, Ezekiel 26:3.
Cannot plow ocean, Amos 6:12 (AB).
Disturbance in last days, Luke 21:25.
No longer any sea, Revelation 21:1 (Also see GNB).
See Nature, Navigation, Sailing, Seaworthy.

OCTOGENARIAN See Old Age.

ODDS

Reduced odds, Genesis 18:24–32.
Gideon's fleece, Judges 6:37–39.
Overwhelming odds, Psalm 27:3.

ODOR

Internment of spices, perfumes, 2 Chronicles 16:14.
Fragrant wardrobe, Psalm 45:8.
Bridal fragrance, Song of Songs 4:10.
Royal incense, Daniel 2:46.
Stench replaces fragrance, Isaiah 3:24.
Fragrant house, John 12:3.
Odor of death, 2 Corinthians 2:16.
Golden bowls of incense, Revelation 5:8.
See Fragrance, Putrid, Stench.

OFFEND

By nothing offended, Psalm 119:165 (KJV, NRSV).
Offended by criticism, Job 20:2–3.
Offended brother, Proverbs 18:19 (NASB, NKJV).
Offensive Christian personality, 2 Corinthians 2:15–16.
See Reaction.

OFFERING

Door offering, Leviticus 1:3.
Salt-seasoned offering, Leviticus 2:13.
Offering box, 2 Kings 12:9–14.
One-third of a shekel, Nehemiah 10:32.
Sweet fragrance rejected, Jeremiah 6:20 (LB).

Persistent sacrifices offered in temple, Ezekiel 43:18–27.

Priests who defiled altar, Malachi 1:6–14.

Refined gold and silver, Malachi 3:2–4.

Giving on first day of week, 1 Corinthians 16:2.

See Contribution, Fund-raising, Giving, Stewardship, Tithe.

OFFICE

Removed from office, Psalm 109:8 (KJV).

OFFICIAL *See Leadership.*

OFF LIMITS *See Restrictions.*

OFFSPRING

Poor substitute for offspring, 2 Samuel 18:18.

No survivors, Job 18:19.

"God's offspring," Acts 17:29 (NRSV).

See Barren, Children, Pregnancy.

OFF-THE-RECORD

Nothing off-the-record, John 18:20.

OIL

Primitive oil exploration, Deuteronomy 32:13.

Rich oil, Judges 9:9 (NRSV).

See Natural Resources.

OLD AGE

Promised old age, Genesis 15:15; 1 Kings 3:14.

Ninety-nine, Genesis 17:1, 24.

Prospective centenarian father, Genesis 17:17.

Sex at old age, Genesis 18:12 (Berk.).

Old age prosperity, Genesis 24:1.

"Ripe old age," Genesis 25:7–8 (CEV).

Failing eyesight, Genesis 27:1; 48:10; 1 Samuel 3:2; 4:15.

Old man's revived spirit, Genesis 45:27.

Jacob, Pharaoh, Genesis 47:7–9, 28.

Swift, difficult passage of time, Genesis 47:9.

Stand up when old person appears, Leviticus 19:32.

Facing the future, Deuteronomy 31:1–2.

Near death, Deuteronomy 31:14 (See NKJV).

Vigorous old age, Deuteronomy 34:7; Joshua 14:11; Job 5:26; Luke 2:36, 37.

Old with work to be done, Joshua 13:1.

Going strong at eighty-five, Joshua 14:10–11 (See 23:1–3; 24:29).

"Stricken in years," Joshua 13:1 (KJV); 23:2 (KJV).

Death soon, Joshua 23:14 (CEV).

Restored vitality, Ruth 4:15 (LB).

Wealthy octogenarian, 2 Samuel 19:32–35.

OLD AGE

METHUSELAH'S BIRTHDAY.

Loss of physical sensitivities, 2 Samuel 19:35.

No body warmth, 1 Kings 1:1–4.

Time to die, 1 Kings 2:1.

Denied peaceful death, 1 Kings 2:6–9.

Old age consultants, 1 Kings 12:6.

"Full of days," 1 Chronicles 23:1 (NKJV).

David's death, 1 Chronicles 29:28.

Rapid passage of years, Job 9:25 (LB).

Wisdom of age, Job 12:12.

Limited years, Job 14:5.

Cause of wrinkles, Job 16:8 (Berk.).

Longevity of wicked, Job 21:7 (NRSV).

Death in full vigor, Job 5:26; 21:23–24.

Too old to help others, Job 30:2.

Conclude life in prosperity, pleasantness, Job 36:11 (NRSV).

Age of God, Job 36:26 (Berk.).

Recollections of long life, Psalm 37:25–26.

Brief life, Psalm 39:5.

Added years, Psalm 61:6.

Dread of old age, Psalm 71:9; Ecclesiastes 12:1.

Strength for weakness, Psalm 73:26.

Productive years, Psalm 92:12–15.

"Full of sap," Psalm 92:14 (NASB).

Value of many children, Psalm 127:3–4 (CEV).

Youth awareness of old age, Ecclesiastes 12:1.

"Your body will grow feeble," Ecclesiastes 12:3 (CEV).

Splendor of gray hair, Proverbs 16:31; 20:29.

Respect for older parents, Proverbs 23:22 (See 30:17).

"Worn out utensil," Psalm 31:12 (Berk.).

Guidance to the end, Psalm 48:14.

Bitter attitude, Ecclesiastes 6:3–6.

Living two thousand years, Ecclesiastes 6:6.

Good old days, Ecclesiastes 7:10 (See Lamentations 1:7).

Geriatric disabilities, Ecclesiastes 12:3–5.

God's consistent care, Isaiah 46:3–4 (See GNB).

Young at one hundred, Isaiah 65:20.

No security in old age, Jeremiah 6:11–12.

Aging process, Lamentations 3:4.

Shown no respect, Lamentations 5:12.

Summons to aged men, Joel 1:2 (LB).

Over ninety, Daniel 12:13 (AB).

Using a cane, Zechariah 8:4 (LB).

Full life, Malachi 2:5 (CEV).

"Getting on in years," Luke 1:7 (NRSV).

Octogenarian widow, Luke 2:36–37.

Sin causes old age, Romans 5:12 (LB).

Avoiding discouragement, 2 Corinthians 4:16–18; 5:1–10.

Needed a little longer, Philippians 1:25–26 (LB).

Do not mistreat old people, 1 Timothy 5:1–2.

Conduct in old age, Titus 2:2–3.

As good as dead, Hebrews 11:12 (AB).

See Geriatrics, Life, Longevity, Senility.

OMEN

Prophecy of boiling pot, Jeremiah 1:13–15.

Seeking omen at fork in road, Ezekiel 21:18–23.

See Foreboding, Prediction.

OMINOUS See Danger, Fear, Storm, Threat.

OMNIPOTENCE

All-powerful Lord, 1 Samuel 1:3 (CEV); Isaiah 5:16 (CEV).

No dwelling large enough for God, 1 Kings 8:27.

Mover of mountains, Job 9:5.

Beyond highest stars, Job 22:12.

In awe of God, Job 25:1–2; 26:14.

Sure of God's plan, purpose, Job 42:2.

Exalting God above heavens, Psalm 57:5.

Divine versatility, Psalm 115:3; Isaiah 43:13; Matthew 19:26.

Unlimited omnipotence, Psalm 135:6.

Source of everlasting strength, Isaiah 26:4.

Heavens and hand of God, Isaiah 40:12.

One who never wearies, Isaiah 40:28.

God nearby, Jeremiah 23:23–24.

Immeasurable grace of God, Jeremiah 31:37.

Nothing too hard for the Lord, Jeremiah 32:17, 27.

All things possible with God, Matthew 19:26.

Resurrection power innate with God, Acts 26:8.

All power, Romans 4:17–24.

Unsearchable riches, Romans 11:33–36.

None greater than God, Hebrews 6:13 (CEV).

Scope of God's greatness in Christ, Jude 24–25.

Sovereignty of Jesus over earth, Revelation 1:5.

Reign of omnipotent God, Revelation 19:6.
See Sovereignty.

OMNIPRESENCE

Undetected presence of the Lord, Genesis 28:16.

Omnipresent in Heaven, on earth, Deuteronomy 4:39; Isaiah 66:1.

Scope of God's presence, 1 Kings 8:27.

Omnipresent Lord, Psalm 139:5–12; Jeremiah 23:23, 24.

Divine periphery of vision, Proverbs 15:3.

One always nearby, Acts 17:27.

The One who fills the universe, Ephesians 4:10.
See Holy Spirit, Trinity.

OMNISCIENCE

Sodom survey, Genesis 18:20–21.

God sees every action, Job 31:4; 34:21.

God sees all, Psalm 33:13.

Unlimited understanding, Psalm 147:5.

Omniscience of God, Isaiah 40:13, 14.

Sparrows known, hair numbered, Matthew 10:28–30.

Greater wisdom than Solomon's, Matthew 12:42.

Earthly knowledge of Jesus, Matthew 14:13.

Time of Christ's coming held secret, Matthew 24:36.

Knowledge of all mankind, John 2:24.

Validity of Christ's diety, John 16:30.

Limiting wisdom of God, 1 Corinthians 1:25.

The Lord's mind, 1 Corinthians 2:16.
See Predestination.

ONE-ON-ONE

Personalized ministry, Acts 28:30.

OPENNESS *See Receptive.*

OPINION

Rebekah permitted her own decision, Genesis 24:54–58.

Negative, positive viewpoints, Numbers 13:17–33.

Influenced by popular opinion, 1 Samuel 14:45; 15:24; 2 Chronicles 20:21; Jeremiah 38:19.

Veteran soldier underrates abilities of boy, 1 Samuel 17:42.

Divided into factions, 1 Kings 16:21–22.

Wisdom has many sides, Job 11:6 (CEV, NASB).

Fool rejects advice, Proverbs 12:15 (NRSV).

Opinions of fool, Proverbs 18:2.

Answers before listening, Proverbs 18:13.

Wise in his own eyes, Proverbs 26:16.

Wrong and right boasting, Jeremiah 9:23–24.

Pilate's reticence, Matthew 27:23–27; Luke 23:13–25; John 19:4–16.

Demons refused permission to speak, Mark 1:33–34.

Ego of Pharisees, Luke 11:45–46.

Opinion of Pharisees toward Sabbath, Luke 13:10–17.

Different opinions concerning Jesus, John 7:12–13.

Reluctant Pharisees, John 12:42–43.

Opinion, inspiration, 1 Corinthians 7:12 (LB).

Widely varied opinions, 2 Corinthians 6:8–10 (GNB).

Paul, Peter face-to-face, Galatians 2:11–14.

Scripture not matter of personal opinion, 2 Peter 1:20–21.

"Destructive opinions," 2 Peter 2:1 (NRSV).
See Viewpoint.

OPINIONATED *See Obstinate, Opinion, Prejudice, Stubborn.*

OPPONENT

Facing formidable opponent, Numbers 21:21–26.

Future accomplishment assured, Numbers 21:34.

Son sought to impress father, 1 Samuel 14:1–14.

Revenge left to God's timing, 1 Samuel 26:1–11.

Trying to intimidate, Ezra 4:4.

Stirring up trouble, Nehemiah 4:8.

Facing enemy eye-to-eye, Jeremiah 34:3.

Total conquest of enemy, Jeremiah 50:35–40.

Satan, foremost opponent, Zechariah 3:1–2.

"Correcting opponents with gentleness," 2 Timothy 2:15 (NRSV).

See Adversary, Opposition.

OPPORTUNIST

Rejecting sure opportunity, 1 Samuel 24:1–8.

Dishonest report for personal gain, 2 Samuel 1:2–16.

Mother's wiles, 1 Kings 1:11–31.

Time for everything, Ecclesiastes 3:1–8.

Seeking right time, Isaiah 55:6.

Riches gained unjustly, Jeremiah 17:11.

Ministry for personal advantage, Romans 16:17–18.

Getting rich on religion, 1 Timothy 6:5–10.

See Insincerity.

OPPORTUNITY

Challenge, opportunity, Deuteronomy 8:1–3 (See CEV).

Given second chance, Jonah 1:1–3; 3:1–3.

Opportunity withdrawn, Proverbs 1:24–33; Hosea 5:6.

Opened doors will not be shut, Isaiah 45:1.

Seek the Lord while He may be found, Isaiah 55:6, 7.

Give glory to God before darkness comes, Jeremiah 13:16; John 12:35, 36.

Privilege of hearing Christ's message, Matthew 13:17.

Closed door of opportunity for repentence, Luke 13:25–28.

Excuses for not attending a banquet, Luke 14:16–24.

Greatest opportunity of all time, John 3:16–17.

Seizing the opportunity, John 9:4; Acts 21:40.

Turning to light before darkness comes, John 12:35–36.

Those scattered by persecution, Acts 11:19–21.

Jewish rejection, Gentile choice, Acts 13:46.

Arrested, requested witness opportunity, Acts 21:37.

Open door for gospel, 1 Corinthians 16:8, 9.

"Don't give the devil a chance," Ephesians 4:27 (CEV, NASB).

Opportunity still stands, Hebrews 4:1.

Divinely opened door, 2 Corinthians 2:12; Revelation 3:8.

See Challenge, Fortuity.

OPPOSITION

Let God confuse opposition, Exodus 23:27–33.

Parental opposition, Numbers 30:3–5.

Underestimated enemy, Deuteronomy 1:41–44.

Mutual respect between enemies, Deuteronomy 2:4–5.

Victory assured, Deuteronomy 3:2.

The God who overcomes opposition, Deuteronomy 20:1.

Threat of iron chariots, Judges 1:19.

Fighting the Lord's battles, 1 Samuel 25:28.

David lamented King Saul's death, 2 Samuel 1:1–27.

Confrontation between David's men and Abner's men, 2 Samuel 2:12–17.

Murder of enemy's son, 2 Samuel 4:1–12.

Prayer for guidance in confronting enemy, 2 Samuel 5:17–19.

Overcoming obstacles with God's help, 2 Samuel 22:30.

Destroying opposition, 1 Kings 2:13–46.

Killing in political parties, 2 Kings 21:23–24.

Opposition to rebuilding Jerusalem, Ezra 4:5, 12–16.

Hindering scheme of opposition, Nehemiah 4:1–21; 6:1–9.

Enemy's loss of self-confidence, Nehemiah 6:16.

Only God knows how many foes, Psalm 3:1–2.

Facing opposition with confidence, Psalm 3:6.

Enemies turned back in disgrace, Psalm 6:10.

Divine presence in times of trouble, Psalm 14:4–5.

Confident against any opposition, Psalm 27:3.

"Ruthless men," Psalm 54:3 (LB).

"Enemy troops," Psalm 56:1 (LB).

Prayer causes enemy to retreat, Psalm 56:9 (NRSV).

"Well conceived plot," Psalm 64:6 (NASB).

Enemy "summit conference," Psalm 83:5 (LB).

Opposition to prophets, Isaiah 30:10; Jeremiah 11:21; Amos 2:12, 13; Micah 2:6.

No fear of opposition, Jeremiah 1:17–19.

Hatred without reason, Psalm 69:4.

Plans, desires of wicked, Psalm 140:6–8.

At peace with one's enemies, Proverbs 16:7.

Provocation by fool, Proverbs 27:3.

Angry man stirs up dissension, Proverbs 29:22.

Strength of opposition, Isaiah 5:26–30.

Protection against evil strategy, Isaiah 8:10.

Turning back enemy at gate, Isaiah 28:6.

Egyptians were but men, Isaiah 31:3.

Opposition to hope, Isaiah 36:13–21.

King's dependence upon God's promises, Isaiah 37:1–38.

The God who can level mountains, Isaiah 45:1–3.

Fate of those who oppose Israel, Isaiah 60:12.

Given strength to declare God's message, Jeremiah 1:6–10, 17–19.

Persecutors put to shame, Jeremiah 17:18.

The Lord like a mighty warrior, Jeremiah 20:11.

Giving up to opposition, Lamentations 1:5.

Courage to face adverse circumstances, Ezekiel 2:6–7.

Opponents told to "shut up," Amos 2:12 (LB).

God tolerates no rivals, Nahum 1:2 (GNB).

Oppose God only once, Nahum 1:9 (GNB).

Love your enemy, Matthew 5:43–48.

Parable of landowner, son, Matthew 21:33–44.

Opponents of the resurrection, Matthew 27:62–66 (See also 28:11–15).

You forgive, God forgives, Mark 11:25.

Jesus' ability to confound critics, Mark 11:29–33.

Trying to catch Jesus in His own words, Mark 12:13–17.

Jesus kept silent when criticized, spoke to declare Himself the Christ, Mark 14:53–62.

Multitude of demons, Luke 8:26–31.

Folly of unfounded criticism, Luke 8:49–56.

Rejecting opposition to truth about Christ, Luke 10:16.

Strategy for facing superior enemy, Luke 14:31–32.

Opponents applauded Jesus' logic, Luke 20:39.

Harassing Jesus, John 5:16 (LB).

Debate between Jesus and teachers of darkness, John 8:13–59.

Plot to kill Lazarus because of influence, John 12:9–11.

Prayer in time of stress, Acts 4:23–26.

Saul as enemy of church, Acts 8:1–3.

Opposition of sorcerer, Acts 13:6–8.

Jealous Jewish leaders, Acts 13:45–51.

Poisoning minds, Acts 14:2.

Imprisoned for conversion of fortune-teller, Acts 16:16–40.

Mob incited against Paul and Silas, Acts 17:5–7.

"Worthless bums," Acts 17:5 (CEV).

Persistent opposition from Thessalonica, Acts 17:13.

Those who sneered at resurrection message, Acts 17:32.

Abusive opposition, Acts 18:6.

Publicly refuting preaching and teaching, Acts 19:8–9.

Physical harm caused by demons, Acts 19:13–16.

Entire city in uproar, Acts 19:23–41.

Itinerary changed to avoid conflict, Acts 20:2–3.

Accusations could not be proved, Acts 25:7.

When God is for us, Romans 8:31.

Be good to enemy, Romans 12:20.

Overcome evil with good, Romans 12:21.

Conflict from unbelievers, Romans 15:31–32.

Those who cause divisions, Romans 16:17.

Opposition to ministry, 1 Corinthians 16:9; 2 Timothy 3:8.

Purpose of testing, 2 Corinthians 1:2–11.

Pleasing God rather than men, Galatians 1:10.

Standing at end of struggle, Ephesians 6:13.

Paul's attitude toward opposition, Philippians 1:15–18.

Privilege of suffering, Philippians 1:29–30.

Enemies of the cross, Philippians 3:18–21.

Rising above opposition, 1 Thessalonians 2:1–2.

Hindered by Satan, 1 Thessalonians 2:18; 1 Peter 5:8–9.

Anticipating persecution in advance, 1 Thessalonians 3:4.

Leave revenge in God's hands, 2 Thessalonians 1:6–7.

Persecution inevitable for committed Christian, 2 Timothy 3:12.

Those who oppose message, 2 Timothy 4:14–15.

Not to point of shedding blood, Hebrews 12:4.

Fear not what man may do, Hebrews 13:6.

Witnessing in face of judgment, Revelation 11:3–12.

See Adversary, Enemy, Hindrance.

OPPRESSION

Oppressed laborers in Egypt, Exodus 5:6–18.

Successfully facing formidable opponent, Numbers 21:21–26.

Oppression of poor people, Deuteronomy 24:14–15; Proverbs 14:31; Ezekiel 22:29; Amos 5:11–12; 8:4–6.

Son more oppressive than father, 1 Kings 12:1–11.

Divine refuge, Psalms 9:9; 19:5.

Desperate times, Psalm 60:3.

Exemplary alternative, Isaiah 33:15–16.

"Fire of oppression," Isaiah 43:2 (LB).

No resistance, Isaiah 50:6–7.

"Trampled upon," Psalm 56:1 (NASB, NRSV).

Palace built by unrighteousness, Jeremiah 22:13–15.

Assurance to Israel in Egypt, Jeremiah 46:27.

No chance for escape, Jeremiah 48:44.

Enemies without cause, Lamentations 3:52.

Not practicing what they preach, Matthew 23:2–4.

See Persecution.

OPTIMISM

Determined, confident, Joshua 1:6, 9, 18 (GNB).

Optimism brings defeat, Joshua 7:3–4.

Boy brings hope to army of Israel, 1 Samuel 17:32.

Good news expected from good man, 2 Samuel 18:27.

Laughter, joy can return, Job 8:21.

Darkness like morning, Job 11:17.

"Cheer up!" Psalm 31:24 (LB).

Certainty of deliverance, Psalm 34:19.

"Happy ending," Psalm 37:37 (LB).

Hope in time of despair, Psalm 42:5.

Pessimism turns to optimism, Psalm 73:12–28.

Light dawns in darkness, Psalm 112:4.

No fear of bad news, Psalm 112:7–8.

The day the Lord has made, Psalm 118:24.

Lifting one's eyes to hills, Psalm 121:1.

Cheerful heart like medicine, Proverbs 17:22.

Light shining in darkness, Isaiah 60:1–2 (See CEV).

God's plans for you, Jeremiah 29:10–11.

False optimism, Ezekiel 13:10 (GNB).

Behind devastation, ahead anticipation, Joel 2:3.

"Things will be better," Haggai 2:15 (CEV).

Old age optimism, Romans 4:18–22.

Always cheerful, 2 Corinthians 5:6 (CEV).

Optimistic prayer, Philippians 1:3–6.

Motivated by joy, 1 Thessalonians 1:6.

Always joyful, 1 Thessalonians 5:16.

Eternal encouragement, 2 Thessalonians 2:16–17.

See Encouragement, Positive.

OPTION

Three choices of punishment, 1 Chronicles 21:8–13.

Delightful option, Psalm 1:1 (LB).

Better option than scarlet sins, Isaiah 1:18.

Boldness of speech, Jeremiah 1:6–10.

Valley of decision, Joel 3:14.

Choice of Jesus or Barabbas, Matthew 27:15–26.

Only one spiritual option, John 6:66–69.

Choice of two extremes, Acts 3:14.

Second option, Gentiles, Acts 13:46–48.

See Choice, Paradigm.

OPULENCE See Materialism, Wealth.

ORATOR See Eloquence.

ORCHARD

Fig tree for everyone, 1 Kings 4:25.

Cultivation produces fruit, Proverbs 27:18.

Almond trees, Numbers 17:8; Ecclesiastes 12:5; Jeremiah 1:11.

Shade of apple tree, Song of Songs 8:5.

Procedure for fertilizing tree, Luke 13:8.

See Fruit, Horticulture, Trees.

ORCHESTRA

Musical instruments a family tradition, Genesis 4:21.

Instrumental ensemble, 2 Samuel 6:5.

Four thousand piece orchestra, 1 Chronicles 23:5.

Exact number of musicians, 1 Chronicles 25:7.

Instruments celebrating rebuilt wall, Nehemiah 12:27–43.

Voice, instruments praising the Lord, Psalms 98:4–6; 150:3–6.

Choir, orchestra, Ecclesiastes 2:7–8 (LB).

Accompanying music, Habakkuk 3:19 (LB).

See Music.

ORDER

Confusion caused by disobedience, Deuteronomy 28:20.

Avoiding confusion in worship, 1 Corinthians 14:29–33, 40.

See Discipline, Propriety.

ORDINANCE

Everlasting ordinance, Exodus 12:14.

Same ordinance for alien, native, Numbers 9:14.

Undesired Sabbath merchandising, Nehemiah 13:15–19.

Ordinances broken, Isaiah 24:5.

Decrees to be remembered, Malachi 4:4.

Ordinances insufficient for salvation, Ephesians 2:15; Colossians 2:14–23; Hebrews 9:1–10.

See Legalism.

ORDINARY

Mundane activity, miraculous event, 2 Kings 6:1–7.

Leave ordinary ways, find understanding, Proverbs 9:6.

Jesus considered ordinary, Mark 6:3.

See Commonplace.

ORDINATION

Consecrated for service, Numbers 8:10; 27:18; Deuteronomy 34:9.

Commission with encouragement, Deuteronomy 3:28.

Laying on of hands, Acts 6:6; 13:1–3.

Paul's credentials as apostle, Galatians 1:1.

Avoid haste laying on hands, 1 Timothy 5:22 (See NRSV).

Called to be herald, apostle, teacher, 2 Timothy 1:11.

Christ Himself ordained by His Father, Hebrews 5:4–6.

Called to ministry of holiness, 1 Peter 1:15, 16.

See Call.

ORE

Mining operation, Job 28:3–4.

Gold and silver belong to God, Haggai 2:8.

See Gold, Natural Resources.

ORGANIZATION

Army of chosen men, 2 Samuel 6:1; 23:8–39.

Organization for building temple, 1 Kings 5:12–18.

Foremen, laborers, 2 Chronicles 2:2.

Well organized, Proverbs 15:22.

Organized priests, Ezekiel 40:44–46.

Appointing twelve apostles, Mark 3:13–19.

Organizing for miracle, Luke 9:14–15.

Welfare to widows organized, Acts 6:1–4.

Need for proper credentials, Acts 15:22–31.

Serving the Lord in unity, Romans 15:5–6; 1 Corinthians 1:10.

Church organization, 1 Corinthians 12:28–31.

Good organization, 1 Corinthians 14:33–40.

Building fitted together, Ephesians 2:21.

Diversity to produce unity, Ephesians 4:11–13.

Orderliness commended, Colossians 2:5.
Appointing elders, organizing details, Titus 1:1–5.
Operating through proper channels, Philemon 12–14.
Regulated universe, Hebrews 1:3 (LB).
Submit to authority, Hebrews 13:17.
See Congregation, Leadership, Plan.

ORGY

Overt lust of prostitute sisters, Ezekiel 23:1–31.
From one sin to another, Jeremiah 9:3.
Continual lust for more, Ephesians 4:19.
Sin in broad daylight, 2 Peter 2:13–23.
See Lust.

ORIGIN

"Quarry from which you were mined," Isaiah 51:1 (LB).

ORIGINALITY

The God without precedent, Isaiah 64:4.
Making up new laws, Matthew 23:2 (LB).
See Art, Author, Creativity.

ORNAMENTS See Jewelry.

ORNITHOLOGIST

Birds unclean for food, Leviticus 11:13–18.
Protection of birds, Deuteronomy 22:6.
Creator and ornithologist, Psalm 50:11.
Birds know seasons of migration, Jeremiah 8:7.
See Birds.

ORPHAN

Divine love for orphans, Exodus 22:22–24.
Tithe given to fatherless, Deuteronomy 26:12.
Background of Queen Esther, Esther 2:7.
Mistreated orphan, Job 24:9.
God looks after fatherless, Psalm 10:14; 68:5.
Orphaned by judgment, Psalm 109:9.
Protect orphan property, Proverbs 23:10; Isaiah 1:17.
Unwanted child, Ezekiel 16:2–5.
Spiritual orphan, John 14:18.
See Abortion, Children, Homeless, Refugee.

ORTHODOXY

Unbeliever not to be followed in worship, Deuteronomy 12:29–32.
Orthodox dispute, Acts 15:1–11.
Persevere in life, doctrine, 1 Timothy 4:16.
Holy Spirit promotes orthodoxy, 2 Timothy 1:13–14 (See NRSV).
No lie comes from truth, 1 John 2:20–21.
See Doctrine, Heterodoxy, Theology, Truth.

OSTENTATIOUS

Boasting of pious zeal, 2 Kings 10:16.
Solomon's overwhelming grandeur, 2 Chronicles 9:3.
Six month display of wealth, Esther 1:4.
Early morning religiosity, Proverbs 27:14.
Boast only about the Lord, Jeremiah 9:23–24.
Do not make acts of charity public, Matthew 6:1–4.
Non-verbal piety, Matthew 23:5.
Jesus accused of luxury, Matthew 26:6–13.
See Boasting, Display, Exhibitionism, Hedonism, Vanity.

OUTCAST See Leprosy, Poverty.

OUTER SPACE

Immeasurable scope of divine greatness, 2 Chronicles 6:12–19.
Wheels of Ezekiel's vision, Ezekiel 1:15–21.
See Astronomy, Space/Time.

OUTREACH

Solomon's attitude toward foreigners, 1 Kings 8:41–43.
Fountain flowing from sanctuary, Joel 3:18.
Rescue too late at lion's mouth, Amos 3:12.
Inviting others to seek the Lord, Zechariah 8:20–22.
Giving cup of cold water, Matthew 10:42.
Looking after needs of others, Matthew 25:34–40.
Faith reported all over world, Romans 1:8.
Care in one's conduct toward unbelievers, Colossians 4:5.
Remember those in prison, Hebrews 13:3.
See Charity, Evangelism, Missionary.

OUTWARD APPEARANCE

No need to fear giant, 1 Samuel 16:7.
Laughter with an aching heart, Proverbs 14:13.
Need for proper appraisal, John 7:24.
See Display, Wardrobe.

OVERBEARING

Disturbing privacy of others, Proverbs 25:17
See Abrasion.

OVERCOMERS

Evil one overcome, 1 John 2:13; 4:4.
Overcome the world, 1 John 5:5.
Overcomer eats at tree of life, Revelation 2:7.
See Victory.

OVERCONFIDENCE

Thinking it easy to face an enemy, Deuteronomy 1:41, 42.
Overconfidence causes defeat, Joshua 7:3–4.
Putting confidence in numerical strength, Judges 7:2, 12.
See Confidence, Presumption.

OVERTIME

Double duty, Nehemiah 4:22.
See Labor, Management.

OVERWEIGHT *See Corpulence.*

OWL

Unclean bird, Leviticus 11:13–17.
Desert creature, Psalm 102:6.
Screech owl, Isaiah 34:11 (See Leviticus 11:16 NIV).
See Birds.

OWNERSHIP

Mistreated slaves, Exodus 21:20–21.
Delayed of ownership, Leviticus 25:29.
Name on each staff, Numbers 17:1–2.
Inherited property, Numbers 36:1–9.
Respect neighbor's boundary, Deuteronomy 19:14.
Ancestral property, Nehemiah 11:20.
Property of angry man, Esther 8:1 (See 5:9 through chapters 6 and 7).
God owner of all, Psalms 24:1; 89:11.
Eating one's own harvest, Isaiah 62:8–9.
Jeremiah's field, Jeremiah 32:6–15.
Priests to own no property, Ezekiel 44:28.
Silver, gold belong to God, Haggai 2:8.
Plot to murder, steal, Mark 12:7.
Heir to the world, Romans 4:13 (GNB, LB).
Not fearful slaves, Romans 8:15 (LB).
Mark of ownership, 2 Corinthians 1:22 (GNB).
Deposit on final redemption, Ephesians 1:14 (Berk.).
See Possessions, Property.

P

PACIFISM

Unworthy to build house of God, 1 Chronicles 28:2–3.
Seek for peace, Psalm 34:14.
Warmongers, man of peace, Psalm 120:6–7.
Wisdom versus weapons, Ecclesiastes 9:18.
Coming world peace, Isaiah 2:4; Hosea 2:18.
See Peace, War.

PACK ANIMALS

Loaded camels, Genesis 37:25; 1 Kings 10:2.
Forty camels laden with fine merchandise, 2 Kings 8:9.
Beasts of burden, 1 Chronicles 12:40.
Pack animals carrying water, Isaiah 21:13.
See Transportation.

PAGAN

Impudent gods, Exodus 18:11 (Berk.).
Strange "reverence" of pagan idol, 1 Samuel 5:1–5.
Sacrifice of son, 2 Kings 16:3.
Pagan king speaks of Israel's "god," Isaiah 37:10.
One true God, many gods, Daniel 3:28–30; 4:18.
Pagans certain of erroneous belief, Acts 19:35–36.
Instinctive truth, Romans 1:19–20 (LB).
Gathered from all tribes, nations, Revelation 7:9–10.
See Gods and Goddesses, Heathen, Idolatry.

PAIN

"Unrelenting pain," Job 6:10 (NRSV).
Personal pain, Job 14:22.
Incessant pain, Job 30:17; 33:19; Isaiah 21:3; Jeremiah 15:18.
Painful laughter, Proverbs 14:13 (NASB).
Men suffering childbirth pains, Jeremiah 30:6.
Wounds wide as sea, Lamentations 2:13.
Response of Jesus to intense pain, Matthew 8:5–7.
Jesus faced terrible suffering, Matthew 16:21 (CEV).
Sedative at crucifixion, Mark 15:23–24, 36.
Flogging Jesus, John 19:1 (See LB).
All creation in pain, Romans 8:22.
Bite the tongue, Revelation 16:10 (GNB).
No more pain, Revelation 21:4.
See Suffering, Medicine, Rheumatism, Therapy.

PALACE

Embarrassed by palatial affluence, 2 Samuel 7:2.
Building palace higher priority than temple, 1 Kings 6:37–38; 7:1.
Assassination site, 2 Kings 15:25.
Archives kept in palace, Ezra 6:2.
Affluent display, Esther 1:2–8.
Palace garden, Esther 7:7.
See Royalty.

PANIC

Egyptian army in panic, Exodus 14:24 (CEV, NRSV).
Faith as antidote for fear, Exodus 14:25–27.
Enemy panic, Exodus 23:27–30 (See CEV); Joshua 10:10 (CEV).
Flight from imaginary enemy, Leviticus 26:17.
Enemies flee in seven directions, Deuteronomy 28:7.
One person frightens one thousand, Deuteronomy 32:30; Joshua 23:10.
Loss of thirty thousand foot soldiers, 1 Samuel 4:10.
Melting in all directions, 1 Samuel 14:16.
Death of hero routs army, 1 Samuel 17:51.
Hearts melt with fear, 2 Samuel 17:10.
Abandon camp, 2 Kings 7:7.

Chaff in the wind, Psalm 35:5.
People in panic, Isaiah 22:1–3 (LB).
Warriors in utter panic, Jeremiah 46:12.
Peril outside, plague inside, Ezekiel 7:15–17.
Knocking knees of panicked king, Daniel 5:6.
Restored calm, Daniel 5:9–12.
Nations in panic, Joel 2:6.
Bravest warriors panic, Amos 2:16.
From one fear to another, Amos 5:18, 19.
Terrified by glory of the Lord, Luke 2:9.
Fear of drowning, Luke 8:22–25.
See Fear.

PARABLE

Parable of trees, Judges 9:8–15.
Pet lamb, 2 Samuel 12:1–10.
Parable used to cause forgiveness, 2 Samuel 14:1–21.
Vine of Egypt, Psalm 80:8–16.
Old Testament object lesson, Jeremiah 13:1–11.
Potter, clay, Jeremiah 18:1–4.
Two baskets of figs, Jeremiah 24:1–10.
Parable of vine branch, Ezekiel 15:1–7.
Two eagles, vine, Ezekiel 17:1–24.
Valley of dry bones, Ezekiel 37:1–14.
See Illustration.

PARADE

Migration of family with possessions, Genesis 46:5–7.
Jericho march, Joshua 6:2–16.
Procession around wall, Nehemiah 12:31–43.
Marching in line, Joel 2:7–8.
See Marching.

PARADIGM SHIFT

Moses to Joshua 1:1–7.
Divine paradigm shift, Jonah 3:10.
From Saul to Paul, Acts 22:1–21.
Bragging coward, bold apostle, John 13:31–38; Acts 2:14–41.
See Conversion, Repentance.

PARADISE

Visit to Paradise, 2 Corinthians 12:3–4.
See Heaven.

PARADOX

Wealth is poverty, Proverbs 13:7.

Noonday darkness, Isaiah 58:10 (See Matthew 6:23).

Saving and losing, losing and saving, Matthew 10:39; Luke 9:23–25.

Divine foolishness, mortal wisdom, 1 Corinthians 1:25.

Contrasting circumstances, realities, 2 Corinthians 6:4–10.

Strength from weakness, 2 Corinthians 12:10–11.

Law that gives freedom, James 2:12–13.

See Contrast.

PARAGON *See Excellence, Exemplary, Model, Perfection.*

PARAMOUR

Adulterous paramour, Hosea 3:1 (AB, Berk.).

PARASITE

In pursuit of a flea, 1 Samuel 24:14.

Garden snail, Psalm 58:8.

See Insect, Lecherous.

PARDON

Total forgiveness, Jeremiah 50:20.

Utter rejection, Lamentations 5:21–22.

Forgiven enemy, Romans 5:10.

See Forgiveness.

PARENTS

Relationship between Adam, Eve, Genesis 4:1–2.

Like father, like son, Genesis 5:1–3.

Age of Old Testament fathers, Genesis 11:10–26.

Bearing children at advanced age, Genesis 16:16; 17:1–21; 21:1–5 (See Romans 4:18–21).

Father head of house, Genesis 18:19.

Favorite children, Genesis 25:28 (KJV).

Witness to offspring, Exodus 10:2.

Teaching children, Exodus 12:26–27; Deuteronomy 6:20–24.

Reward for honoring parents, Exodus 20:12.

Death for assaulting parents, Exodus 21:15, 17.

Observing the Lord's Day, Leviticus 23:3.

Testing divine patience, Numbers 14:18.

Father's negative influence, Numbers 30:3–5.

Remembering and following divine teaching, Deuteronomy 4:9.

Consistent influence, Deuteronomy 6:6–9.

Spiritual duty of parents to children, Deuteronomy 11:1–7.

Father prays for guidance, Judges 13:8.

Loyalty torn between father, friend, 1 Samuel 19:1–2.

Son's concern for parents, 1 Samuel 22:3.

Father, son together in death, 2 Samuel 1:23.

Rivalry between father, son, 2 Samuel 15:1–37.

Bad influence, 1 Kings 22:51–53.

Son less evil than parents, 2 Kings 3:1–3.

Model of praise, confession, Nehemiah 9:6–37.

Confessing ancestors' sins, Nehemiah 9:2.

When forsaken by parents, God may be trusted, Psalm 27:10.

Blessing from generation to generation, Psalms 44:1–3; 78:1–7.

Spiritual confidence since birth, Psalm 71:5–6, 17–18.

Children special blessing from the Lord, Psalm 127:3–5.

Advice of King Solomon to son, Proverbs 1:8–19.

Discipline of good father, Proverbs 3:11–12; 4:1–10.

Parental influence, Proverbs 6:20–23.

Wise, foolish sons, Proverbs 10:1.

Proper discipline of children, Proverbs 13:24; Hebrews 12:5–11.

Children should be proud of parents, Proverbs 16:6; 17:6 (NIV, NRSV).

Grief caused by foolish son, Proverbs 17:25.

Children who rob parents, Proverbs 19:26; 28:24.

Properly training child, Proverbs 22:6.

Child's heart yields to discipline, Proverbs 22:15.

Children a joy to parents, Proverbs 23:25 (See GNB).

Stealing from parents, Proverbs 28:24 (See GNB).

Ridicule of parents, Proverbs 30:17 (GNB).

"Daddy" and "Mommy," Isaiah 8:4 (LB).

Father conveying God's truth to children, Isaiah 38:18–19.

Abraham and Sarah, Isaiah 51:2.

Evil influence of fathers, Jeremiah 16:10–12.

When it is better not to have had children, Jeremiah 22:30.

Obedience to parents and grandparents, Jeremiah 35:1–16.

Fathers unable to help children, Jeremiah 47:3.

Children sacrificed to idols, Ezekiel 16:20.

Message conveyed to children's children, Joel 1:3.

Joseph and Mary into and out of Egypt, Matthew 2:13–21.

Gospel can turn children against parents, Matthew 10:32–36.

Causing child to go astray, Mark 9:42.

Parents given son in declining years, Luke 1:5–25.

Parents thoughtful of children, Luke 1:17 (CEV).

Mary and Joseph did not realize Son's significance, Luke 2:25–35.

Unaware of child's potential, Luke 2:41–52.

Parents surprised by answer to their prayers, Luke 8:56.

Concern for only child, Luke 9:38.

Parents support children, not children parents, 2 Corinthians 12:14.

Loved child imitates parent, Ephesians 5:1 (LB).

How father should deal with children, 1 Thessalonians 2:11–12.

Influence of Scriptures since childhood, 2 Timothy 3:14–15.

Family of elder must be exemplary, Titus 1:6.

King without father or mother, Hebrews 7:1–3.

Message for all ages, 1 John 2:12–14.

Children of good parents, 2 John 4.

Joy of believer's children, 3 John 4.

See Family, Father, Mother.

PARIAH See Leprosy, Poverty.

PARITY

God's ways and man's, Isaiah 55:8; Ezekiel 18:29.

Questioning why evil prospers, Jeremiah 12:1.

See Fairness.

PAROLE

King imprisoned and set free, 2 Kings 24:15; 25:27–29.

Satan released from prison, Revelation 20:1–3, 7–10.

See Justice.

PAROUSIA See Rapture.

PARSIMONIOUS

Stingy man causes illness, Proverbs 23:6–8.

Attitude of disciples, Matthew 26:8–9; John 12:4–5.

See Stingy.

PARSONAGE

House next door to synagogue, Acts 18:7.

PARTIALITY

Avoid partiality, Deuteronomy 1:17.

Parental preference, Genesis 25:28; 27:6–17; 33:2; 37:3; 42:4.

Partiality to no one, Job 32:21–22.

Questioning why evil prospers, Jeremiah 12:1.

Accusing God of partiality, Ezekiel 33:20.

Hatred between Samaritans, Jews, Luke 9:51–56.

Favoring one man against another, 1 Corinthians 4:6.

Partiality forbidden among believers, 1 Timothy 5:21.

See Favoritism.

PARTICIPATION

Ox, donkey cannot plow together, Deuteronomy 22:10.

Iron sharpens iron, Proverbs 27:17.

Two in agreement, Amos 3:3.

Participation resulted in healing, Mark 2:1–5.

All participating in worship, 1 Corinthians 14:26.

Carrying one's own load, Galatians 6:5.

Some participated, some did not, Philippians 4:15–19.

See Cooperation, Teamwork, Unity.

PARTING

Purposeful separation from loved ones, John 14:28.

Jesus went away so Holy Spirit could come, John 16:5–7.

Paul's emotional parting at Ephesus, Acts 20:17–38.

See Separation.

PARTNERSHIP

As iron sharpens iron, Proverbs 27:17.

Two better than one, Ecclesiastes 4:9–12.

Two in agreement, Amos 3:3.

Partners with Jesus, Mark 3:13.

Disciples sent out two-by-two, Mark 6:7.

Barnabas and Saul, Acts 11:22–26.

Ministry partnership, 2 Corinthians 8:23.

Gospel partnership, Philippians 1:5 (NIV, NKJV).

See Camaraderie, Cooperation, Teamwork, Unity.

PARTY

Wild parties, Numbers 25:1 (LB); Romans 13:13 (LB).

Week long party, Judges 14:12 (CEV).

Royal drinking party, 1 Kings 20:16.

Secular entertainment, Isaiah 5:12.

Noise of carefree crowd, Ezekiel 23:42.

Evil parties, Hosea 2:11 (LB).

See Hedonism, Revelry.

PASSENGERS

Many passengers aboard ship, Acts 27:37.

PASSION

Quiet romance Boaz, Ruth, Ruth 3:7–18.

Pounding heartbeat, Song of Songs 5:4 (NIV).

Unrequited sexual desire, Ezekiel 16:23–30.

Intense passion, Hosea 7:6.

Marriage relationship in heaven, Mark 12:18–27.

Continual lust for more, Ephesians 4:19 (NIV).

"Passions of youth," 2 Timothy 2:22 (GNB).

See Emotion, Love, Lust, Romance.

PASSOVER

Establishment of Passover, Exodus 12:3–49.

Passover month, Deuteronomy 16:1 (LB).

Special Passover sites, Deuteronomy 16:5–7.

Observed by Jesus, Matthew 26:17–20.

"Feast of Thin Bread," Luke 22:1 (CEV).

Adapted to Body of Christ, 1 Corinthians 5:7; 11:23–26.

See Communion.

PASSPORT

Authorization for travel, Nehemiah 2:1–8.

See Credentials.

PAST

Sense of past, future, Ecclesiastes 2:11 (NRSV).

Good old days, Job 17:11 (LB); Ecclesiastes 7:10 (LB).

Mysterious past, Ecclesiastes 7:24 (NASB).

Past not remembered, Isaiah 65:17.

See Conscience, Memory, Nostalgia, Recollect, Reminiscence, Remorse.

PASTOR

Uniting behind new leader, Joshua 1:16–18.

People without spiritual guidance, Judges 2:18–19.

Shepherd and ruler, 1 Chronicles 11:1–2.

After God's own heart, Jeremiah 3:15.

Two functions of priest, Ezekiel 40:44–46.

Shepherd's responsibility, Amos 1:1 (LB).

Keep eye on troublemakers, Romans 16:17 (NASB, NRSV).

Ideal pastor, 2 Corinthians 1:24—2:1–5 (AB).

Using sharp discipline, 2 Corinthians 13:10.

Faithful without pastoral supervision, Philippians 2:12–13.

Marks of successful pastor, 1 Thessalonians 2:7–12.

Pastoral function, 1 Thessalonians 5:12; 2 Timothy 2:2–6; 4:1–5.

How to criticize pastor, 1 Timothy 5:19 (LB).

See Clergy, Prophet.

PASTURE See Grass.

PATIENCE

Testing divine patience, Numbers 14:18.
Be patient, don't worry, Ruth 3:18 (CEV).
Patiently see what God will do, 1 Samuel 12:16; Psalm 37:7.
Patience when angry, Psalm 4:4.
Accepting discipline, Proverbs 3:11.
Patiently wait, Psalm 37:34 (LB).
Patience rewarded, Psalm 40:1; Isaiah 25:9; James 5:11.
Divine patience, Psalm 86:15.
Waiting patiently for the Lord, Psalm 130:5–6.
Agony of waiting, joy of fulfillment, Proverbs 13:12.
Those who speak in haste, Proverbs 29:20.
Conclusion worth waiting for, Ecclesiastes 7:8.
Proper time for every procedure, Ecclesiastes 8:6.
Trying God's patience, Isaiah 7:13 (GNB).
Delay in answered prayer, Isaiah 49:8.
Patience of suffering Savior, Isaiah 53:7.
Certain God will fulfill revelation, Habakkuk 2:3.
"You have worn out the Lord," Malachi 2:17 (CEV).
Growth takes time, Mark 4:28.
Patient wait for healing, John 5:1–8.
Impatience with those who reject message, Acts 18:5–6.
Accepting affliction patiently, Romans 12:12.
Patient contentment in all situations, Philippians 4:11–13.
"Endure everything with patience," Colossians 1:11 (NRSV).
Compassion, patience, Colossians 3:13.
Good soldiers, 2 Timothy 2:3–5.
"Put up with anything," 2 Timothy 2:10 (CEV).
Kind to everyone, 2 Timothy 2:24 (See NRSV).
Old age patience, Titus 2:2.
Patient awaiting promise, Hebrews 6:12 (CEV).
"Having patiently waited," Hebrews 6:15 (NASB).

Eternal perspective, Hebrews 10:34.
Finding God's will, Hebrews 10:36 (AB, GNB).
Learning patience through trials, testing, James 1:2–4.
Patience "in full bloom," James 1:4 (LB).
Submission to Divine wisdom, James 4:7.
Farmer's patience awaiting harvest, James 5:7.
Patience of the Lord toward the lost, 2 Peter 3:9.
See Composure, Maturity, Perseverance, Self-control, Tolerance.

PATRIARCH

Influence of living patriarchs, Joshua 24:31.
See Prophet.

PATRIOTISM

Those who sit at home, Numbers 32:6.
Duty of citizens to new leadership, Joshua 1:16–17.
Defense of one's country, 1 Samuel 17:26–51.
Loyalty to national leaders, 2 Samuel 1:18–27; 2:10.
Brave fighters, 2 Samuel 10:12.
Love of country, 1 Kings 11:21.
Concern for national survival, Esther 4:13–17.
Spiritual burden, Nehemiah 1:2–11.
Prayer for community, Psalm 122:6.
Weeping for their country, Psalm 137:1.
National rejoicing, Isaiah 66:10.
Personal, national repentance, Daniel 9:1–19.
Good words for centurion, Luke 7:4–5.
Submission to authorities, Romans 13:1–7.
See Citizenship, Nationalism.

PATROL

Satan's earth patrol, Job 1:7 (LB).

PATRONAGE

Across racial lines, 1 Samuel 13:19–20.

PATTERN See Model.

PAWN

Clothing not to be held overnight, Exodus 22:26–27.

Rules for operating pawn service, Deuteronomy 24:10–17.

Inhumane conduct, Job 22:6.

"Widow's cow," Job 24:3 (Berk.).

Conduct of money lender, Ezekiel 18:7–16.

See Barter, Borrowing.

PAYMENT

Royal payment refused, Genesis 14:22–24.

Requesting payment for spiritual ministry, 2 Kings 5:20–27.

Money, food, drink for temple workers, Ezra 3:7.

Prostitute giving rather than receiving, Ezekiel 16:32–34.

Wages an obligation, not gift, Romans 4:4.

Divine deposit on our final redemption, Ephesians 1:14.

See Barter, Honorarium, Stipend, Wages.

PEACE

Nation at peace, Joshua 14:15; 23:1.

Three-year peace, 1 Kings 22:1–5.

Desire for peace, security, 2 Kings 20:19.

Divine ability to bring peace, Psalm 46:9.

Oceans and nations, Psalm 65:7.

Living under shadow of the Almighty, Psalm 91:1–2.

An honor to avoid strife, Proverbs 20:3.

The Peacemaker, Isaiah 53:5.

Proclaiming peace when there is no peace, Jeremiah 6:14.

Break the bow, Jeremiah 49:35.

Israel, land of unwalled villages, Ezekiel 38:10–12.

Swords beaten into plowshares, Micah 4:3.

Blessed are the peacemakers, Matthew 5:9.

World peace impossible without Christ, Matthew 24:6–8.

Jesus predicted no peace on earth, Mark 13:6–8.

Peace Jesus gives, Luke 24:36 (AB).

Heart peace, 1 Corinthians 1:3 (AB); 1 Thessalonians 1:1 (AB); 2 Thessalonians 1:2 (AB).

Soul peace, Galatians 1:3 (AB).

Peace defined, Philippians 4:7 (AB).

See Pacificism.

PEACEMAKERS

Those who promote peace, Proverbs 12:20.

"Blessed are the peacemakers," Matthew 5:9.

Pursuit of peace, Romans 14:19.

See Pacifism.

PEASANTS

Prosperous peasants, Judges 5:7 (NRSV).

PEDIGREE

Classified by pedigrees, Numbers 1:18 (NKJV).

PENALTY

Destiny set for rebellious people, Numbers 14:35.

Paying penalty for subversion, Esther 7:1–10.

Penalty for doubting angel, Luke 1:18–20.

See Judgment.

PENANCE See Penitence.

PENETRATE

Function of yeast, Galatians 5:9.

PENITENCE

Disaster delayed, 1 Kings 21:29.

Tears of contrition, confession, Ezra 10:1.

Acknowledgment of sin, Psalm 32:5–6.

God does not ask penance, Psalm 51:16–17 (LB).

Penance for Israel, Ezekiel 4:4–6.

Sackcloth on man, animals, Jonah 3:8.

Penitence guilt of Judas, Matthew 27:3.

Role of grief in repentance, 1 Corinthians 5:1, 2.

See Repentance.

PENMANSHIP

Writing with clarity, Deuteronomy 27:8; Habakkuk 2:2.

Using large letters, Galatians 6:11.

See Graphology.

PENTECOST

Day of Pentecost, Acts 2:1–41.
Second touch, Acts 11:15.
See Holy Spirit.

PEOPLE

Don't fear people, Matthew 10:28.
See Humanity.

PERCEPTION

Unaware of the Lord's presence, Genesis 28:16.
Donkey who saw an angel, Numbers 22:23–31.
Seeing, hearing, understanding, Numbers 24:15–16 (GNB).
Eyes that see, ears that hear, Deuteronomy 29:2–4.
Opening eyes to see God's provision, 2 Kings 6:16–17.
Slowly perceived message, Job 4:12 (See GNB).
Fear tests words, Job 12:11.
Work of the spirit within, Job 32:8.
Perception in study of Scriptures, Psalm 119:18.
"Wise of heart," Proverbs 16:21 (NRSV).
Evil good, good evil, Isaiah 5:20.
Perception in visions, dreams, Daniel 1:17.
Perceptive queen, Daniel 5:10–11.
Shrewd, innocent, Matthew 10:16.
Perception of adults compared to children, Matthew 11:25.
Hearing but not understanding, Matthew 13:14–15.
Savior's dual mission comprehended, Luke 2:28–32.
Jesus knew when He had been touched, Luke 8:43–48.
Herod's lack of perception, Luke 9:7–9.
Followers of Jesus unable to understand, Luke 9:44–45.
Jesus' perception of man, John 2:25.
Samaritan woman perceived who Jesus was, John 4:27–30.
Lack of spiritual perception, John 8:47.
Spiritual blindness, spiritual sight, John 9:39–41.
Some heard thunder, others angel's voice, John 12:28–29.
Misunderstanding words of Jesus, John 16:17–18.
Wisdom of Gamaliel, Acts 5:30–40.
Inner perception, Romans 12:1–3 (GNB).
Beyond human perception, experience, 1 Corinthians 2:9–10.
Spirit of wisdom, revelation, Ephesians 1:17.
Eyes of heart, Ephesians 1:18–19.
Depth of insight, Philippians 1:9.
Proper understanding of the law, 1 Timothy 1:8–11.
Reward of careful reflection, 2 Timothy 2:7.
Pointless quarreling over words, 2 Timothy 2:14.
From "milk" to "solid food," Hebrews 5:11–14; 6:1–3.
Wisdom of the mind, Revelation 17:9.
See Comprehension, Understanding.

PERFECTION

Blameless conduct, Genesis 17:1.
Divine perfection, faithfulness, Deuteronomy 32:4.
Made pure through testing, Job 23:10.
Perfect in God's eyes, Psalm 4:1 (LB).
A perfect way, Psalm 18:32.
Limited perfection, Psalm 119:96.
Impossibility of perfection, Ecclesiastes 7:20.
High cost of perfection, Matthew 19:21.
Evaluation of Nathanael by Jesus, John 1:47.
Aim for perfection, 2 Corinthians 13:11.
Progress toward perfection, Philippians 3:12 (LB).
Perfect, perfection, maturity, Philippians 3:15 (Compare NASB, NIV, NRSV).
Perfect High Priest, Hebrews 4:15; 7:26.
Suffering perfected Jesus, Hebrews 5:9 (CEV).
Those who claim perfection, 1 John 1:8–10.
Sinless Savior, 1 Peter 1:18–19; 2:22.
See Excellence, Exemplary, Model.

PERFUME

Fragrant incense, Exodus 30:7.
Temple fragrance not for personal enjoyment, Exodus 30:34–38.
Purposeful use of perfume, Ruth 3:3.
Fragrant clothing, Psalm 45:8.
Many fragrances, Song of Songs 4:10–14.
Anointing of Jesus, Matthew 26:6–13.
Aromatics, Mark 16:1 (Berk.).
See Aesthetics, Cosmetics, Fragrance, Myrrh.

PERIL

Facing formidable opponent, Numbers 21:21–26.
David's lack of confidence, 1 Samuel 27:1.
Go to neighbor for help, Proverbs 27:10.
Facing grim destiny, Jeremiah 15:2–3.
Peril outside, plague inside, Ezekiel 7:15–17.
Responsibility of watchman, Ezekiel 33:1–9.
See Catastrophe, Danger.

PERJURY

Thoughtlessly taking an oath, Leviticus 5:4.
Giving false testimony, Leviticus 6:3; Deuteronomy 19:16–21.
Lying in court, Proverbs 19:5, 9 (GNB).
Falsehood concerning law of the Lord, Jeremiah 8:8.
False prophets, Jeremiah 23:16–18.
Perjurers, 1 Timothy 1:10.
See Court, Deceit, Dishonesty, Lawyer, Verdict.

PERKS

No perks, Nehemiah 5:14–18.
Danger of excessive perks, Proverbs 29:21 (GNB).
Without advantages, Acts 4:13 (AB).
See Incentive.

PERMANENT

Temporary, permanent, Psalm 15:1 (AB).
God's work endures, Ecclesiastes 3:14.
See Absolute.

PERMISSION

Entering God's presence, Psalm 24:3–4 (See Ephesians 2:18).
Gates open, Isaiah 26:2. (See John 10:9.)
Opportunity for anyone, Isaiah 55:1–3.

Come, Matthew 11:28, 29.
Bold admittance, Hebrews 4:14–16.
Full right to enter, 2 Peter 1:11 (GNB).
See Approval, Credentials.

PERPETUAL

Unending faithfulness, Joshua 24:18.
One who never changes, Hebrews 1:10–12.
See Eternity.

PERPLEXITY

Sacrifice of daughter, Judges 11:30–40.
Lamp of the Lord, 2 Samuel 22:29.
Waters up to neck, Psalm 69:1.
"They scratched their heads," Mark 12:17 (LB).
Those who confuse others, Galatians 1:6–9.
Some writing difficult to understand, 2 Peter 3:15–16.
See Confusion.

PERSECUTION

Self-inflicted persecution, Judges 10:6–16; Galatians 5:12 (GNB).
Satanic challenge, Job 2:4–5.
Unchallenged persecution, Psalm 7:2 (LB).
Lurking enemies, Psalm 11:2; 56:5; Proverbs 29:10.
Friend persecutes, Psalm 55:12–13.
Trampled upon, Psalm 56:1 (NASB, NRSV).
Desperate times, Psalm 60:3 (NIV).
Shame endured for God's glory, Psalm 69:7.
Wishing for persecutor to be persecuted, Psalm 119:84–88.
Let the Lord vindicate, Psalm 135:14 (NIV).
Musical persecution, Psalm 137:1–4.
Sword of the Lord bathed in blood, Isaiah 34:6.
Prayer for deliverance from persecutors, Jeremiah 15:15.
Let persecutors be put to shame, Jeremiah 17:18.
Beaten for proclaiming truth, Jeremiah 20:1–2.
Swift pursuit of enemy, Lamentations 4:19.
Saved from trouble, Daniel 3:16–18.
Opportunity to witness, Matthew 10:16–20.
Fear not those who only kill body, Matthew 10:28.

Peter wanted easy way to discipleship, Mark 8:31–38.

Son of proprietor killed by tenants, Mark 12:1–12.

Scoffing at Jesus on the Cross, Mark 15:29–32.

Rejoice when criticized for faith, Luke 6:22–23.

Secret believers, John 12:42–43.

World first hated our Lord, John 15:18–19.

Advance warning of persecution, John 16:1–4.

Flogging of Jesus, John 19:1.

Persecuted for proclaiming resurrection, Acts 4:1–4.

Rejoicing in persecution, Acts 5:41.

Martyr's death, Acts 6:8–15; 7:1–60.

Persecution implements spread of Gospel, Acts 8:3–4.

Early church in time of peace, Acts 9:31.

Persecution enhanced witness, Acts 11:19–21.

Jealous Jewish leaders, Acts 13:45–51.

Persecution enabled encouragement, Acts 14:19–22; Hebrews 11:35.

Imprisoned for conversion of fortune-teller, Acts 16:16–40.

Persistent opposition, Acts 17:13.

Inevitable persecution, Acts 20:17–24; 21:10–14; 2 Timothy 3:12.

Paul's former role persecuting Christians, Acts 22:19–20.

Imprisonment opened door to Rome, Romans 1:13.

Rejoice in suffering, Romans 5:3–4.

Present suffering, coming glory, Romans 8:18.

When God is for us, Romans 8:31.

Be joyful, patient, Romans 12:12.

Bless those who persecute, Romans 12:14.

Strengthened by faithful Lord, 1 Corinthians 1:8–9.

Aspects of persecution, 2 Corinthians 6:4–10.

Persecution implemented joy, generosity, 2 Corinthians 8:1–5.

"Violently persecuted," Galatians 1:13–14 (NRSV).

Bearing marks of Jesus, Galatians 6:17.

"Flaming arrows," Ephesians 6:16 (NIV, NRSV).

Work of church enhanced, Philippians 1:14; 2 Thessalonians 1:3–4.

Privilege of suffering, Philippians 1:29–30.

Sharing sufferings of Christ, Philippians 3:10–11.

Paul asked friends to remember his bondage, Colossians 4:18.

Joy given by Holy Spirit, 1 Thessalonians 1:6.

Similarity in suffering, 1 Thessalonians 2:14.

Anticipating persecution, 1 Thessalonians 3:3–4.

Leave revenge with God, 2 Thessalonians 1:6–10.

"Endure your share," 2 Timothy 2:3 (CEV).

Chained like criminal, 2 Timothy 2:9 (NIV).

Safety in the Lord, 2 Timothy 4:18.

Perfected through suffering, Hebrews 2:10.

Persecution of new converts, Hebrews 10:32–34.

Persecution rather than pleasures of sin, Hebrews 11:25.

Insult and injury, Hebrews 11:36.

Intense persecution, Hebrews 11:37 (AB).

Fear not what man may do, Hebrews 13:6.

Willingness to suffer, Hebrews 13:11–14.

Maturing value of testing, James 1:2–4, 12.

Purpose of trials and grief, 1 Peter 1:6, 7.

Bearing pain of unjust suffering, 1 Peter 2:19–21.

Suffering for what is right, 1 Peter 3:13, 17.

Suffering in the name of Christ, 1 Peter 4:12–16 (See LB).

Sure rescue in the Lord, 2 Peter 2:7–9.

Brothers, companions at all times, Revelation 1:9.

Do not fear suffering, Revelation 2:10.

Faithful in face of persecution, Revelation 2:13.

The Lord disciplines those He loves, Revelation 3:19.

Put to death for faithful witness, Revelation 6:9.

Witnessing in face of judgment, Revelation 11:3–12.

Satan given temporary power to persecute, Revelation 13:5–7.

Test of endurance, faithfulness, Revelation 13:10; 14:12.

Drunk with blood of saints, Revelation 17:6.

All tears wiped away, Revelation 21:4.

See Oppression, Suffering, Testing.

PERSISTENT

Unending faithfulness, Joshua 24:14.

Persistently idolatrous, Judges 6:1 (LB); 13:1 (LB).

Constant prayer, Nehemiah 1:4 (AB).

Persistence toward doing evil, Nehemiah 9:28.

Faithful in daily prayer, Psalm 5:3.

Persistent prayer, Psalm 55:17.

Searching for wisdom and insight, Proverbs 2:1–6.

Activity with full energy, Ecclesiastes 9:10.

For continued sinning, certain judgment, Amos 1:3, 6, 9, 11, 13; 2:1, 4, 6 (Note nature of sin in each of these judgments).

Enduring to the end, Mark 13:13.

New way to get to Jesus, Luke 5:17–20.

Persistent widow, reluctant judge, Luke 18:1–5.

Climbing tree to see Jesus, Luke 19:1–9.

Invalid who waited thirty-eight years, John 5:1–8.

Persistence in witnessing, Acts 5:42.

Persistent opposition, Acts 17:13.

"Never give up," 2 Corinthians 4:16 (CEV).

Example of those who lived by faith, Hebrews 12:1–3.

Reward for Job's patience, James 5:11.

See Courage, Relentless, Tireless.

PERSONAL

Responsible for personal guilt only, Deuteronomy 24:16; Job 19:4; Jeremiah 31:29, 30.

Salvation, sin personal, Ezekiel 18:20.

Personal touch of Jesus, Matthew 9:25; Mark 9:27.

Whosoever, John 3:16; Romans 10:13.

See Individual.

PERSONALITY

Personality of unborn child, Genesis 16:11–12.

Twins' contrasting personalities, Genesis 25:27.

Blighted personality, Deuteronomy 32:32–33.

Quarrelsome personality, Proverbs 27:15–16.

Faces reflect hearts, Proverbs 27:19.

Clash of apostolic personalities, Acts 15:36–41; Galatians 2:11.

Struggle between flesh, spirit, Romans 7:15–18, 21–25.

Reactions to Christian personality, 2 Corinthians 2:15–16.

Fruit of Spirit, Galatians 5:22.

Joy, gentleness, Philippians 4:4–5.

Personality given by Holy Spirit, 1 Thessalonians 1:6.

Inner beauty, 1 Peter 3:3–4.

Additions to faith, 2 Peter 1:5–9.

See Attitude, Character, Frame-of-Reference, Identity.

PERSONNEL

People more valuable than material things, Genesis 14:21.

Limited personnel, Judges 6:5.

Seven men plus one additional, Micah 5:5.

See Discipleship, Followers, Leadership.

PERSPECTIVE

God's point of view and man's, Job 10:3–7; Isaiah 55:8, 9.

Learning what cannot be seen, Job 34:32.

Short duration of life, Psalm 39:4.

Wicked lack eternal perspective, Psalm 92:6, 7.

Lifted up between earth and heaven, Ezekiel 8:3.

Wide and narrow, Matthew 7;13–14.

Knowing Old, New Testaments, Matthew 13:52 (LB).

Looking only on surface, 2 Corinthians 10:7.

Filled with knowledge of God's will, Colossians 1:9–12.

Word of God in its fullness, Colossians 1:25–26.

A day like a thousand years, 2 Peter 3:8.

See Viewpoint.

PERSUASION

Moses' plea for guide through desert, Numbers 10:29–33.

Vindication by earthquake, Numbers 16:28–34.

Asking for special favor, Judges 1:13–15.

Wiles of Samson's wife in solving his riddle, Judges 14:11–19.

Hearts won through clever manipulation, 2 Samuel 15:1–6.

Motivated by hook and bit, 2 Kings 19:28.

Pagan king persuaded to permit temple rebuilding, Ezra 4–8.

Let the Lord make your cause valid, Psalm 37:6.

Speaking with gentle tongue, Proverbs 25:15.

Deceitful, malicious man, Proverbs 26:24–26.

Believe Good News, Mark 1:14–15 (GNB).

Like teacher, like student, Luke 6:40.

Influencing others to sin, Luke 17:1.

Basis for persuasion, teaching, Acts 17:2–4.

Paul's preaching, teaching, Acts 19:8.

King would not be persuaded, Acts 26:28.

Paul's admitted trickery, 2 Corinthians 12:16 (NIV).

Coaxing to persuade, Galatians 4:20 (AB).

Persuasive words, Colossians 2:4 (NKJV).

Ultimate in being properly motivated, 1 Thessalonians 1:3.

Gospel communicated with words, power, 1 Thessalonians 1:4–5.

See Convincing, Eloquence.

PERUSAL

Perusal of teaching, Ephesians 3:4 (Berk.).

PERVERSION

Mixing religion with immorality, Numbers 25:1–2.

Silver to dross, wine to water, Isaiah 1:22.

Deliberately falsifying, Jeremiah 8:8.

Suggestion of social disease, Jude 7–8.

Mother of prostitutes, perverts, Revelation 17:5 (GNB).

Fate of perverts, Revelation 21:8; 22:15 (GNB).

See Immorality.

PESSIMISM

Speak neither good nor bad, Genesis 31:24, 29 (NKJV).

Dreaded future, Exodus 16:3.

Pessimistic spies, Numbers 13:25–31; 14:36–38.

Seeing nothing good, Job 9:25 (KJV).

"Pining away," Psalm 6:2 (NASB).

"From bad to worse," Psalm 25:17 (LB).

Fate of pessimistic spies to Canaan, Numbers 14:36–38.

Wishing to die, 1 Kings 19:4.

Persistent prophetic pessimism, 1 Kings 22:8.

Pessimism of unbelief, 2 Kings 18:29–35.

Negative view toward meaning of life, Job 1–2.

Pessimism realized, Job 3:25.

Persistent calamity, Job 18:12.

Pessimism turns to optimism, Psalm 73:12–28.

Pessimistic about ill health, Psalm 116:10–11 (LB).

All seems meaningless, Ecclesiastes 1:2.

Negative view of existence, Ecclesiastes 4:1–3.

From one trouble to another, Amos 5:19.

Old Testament ends with curse, Malachi 4:6.

Hope when no basis for hope, Romans 4:18–22.

"As good as dead," Hebrews 11:11–12.

Darkness, gloom, Hebrews 12:18 (NASB).

See Attitude, Despair, Frame-of-reference.

PESTILENCE

Blood sucking flies, Exodus 8:24 (AB).

Price of disobedience, Deuteronomy 28:15–24; Psalm 78:50.

Haunt of jackals, Jeremiah 9:11.

Promise of better times, Joel 2:25–26.

Locusts who attack people, Revelation 9:3–6.

See Disease, Epidemic.

P

PETITION

Document opposing temple rebuilding, Ezra 4:12–16.
See Documentation.

PETROLEUM

Source of oil, Deuteronomy 32:13.
See Natural Resources.

PETS

Noah and dove, Genesis 8:9.
One little lamb, 2 Samuel 12:1–6.
Monkeys, peacocks, 1 Kings 10:22 (CEV).
Pet bird for girls, Job 41:5.
See Animals.

PETTING

Lustful caressing, Ezekiel 23;2–3.

PHARISEE

Mockery of fasting, Isaiah 58:4–5.
Beware of false praise, Jeremiah 12:6.
Pharisaic hypocrisy, Matthew 15:9.
Religion of Sham, Matthew 23:5–7.
View of the resurrection, Acts 23:6–8.
Methods of disruptive hypocrite, 2 John 9–10.
See Hypocrisy.

PHARMACY

Herbal prescription, Exodus 30:25.
Anointing oil, Exodus 37:29.
See Medicine.

PHILANTHROPY

God, who sees all, rewards, Jeremiah 32:19.
Do not make acts of charity public, Matthew 6:1–4.
Woman who helped poor, Acts 9:36–42.
Sharing with those in need, 1 John 3:17.
See Benevolence, Sharing, Stewardship, Welfare.

PHILOSOPHY

Human viewpoint, Ecclesiastes 1:2.
Fragile human wisdom, Isaiah 29:14.
Philosophers belittled Christian message, Acts 17:18.
Not wise but fools, Romans 1:22.
Human wisdom versus God's, 1 Corinthians 1:19–20; 2:6; 3:19–20.
Deceptive philosophy, Colossians 2:8.
See Intelligence, Wisdom.

PHONY

"Fake surprise," Malachi 2:17 (LB).
Hyper-piety, Matthew 6:16–18.

PETS

LET ME GUESS. YOUR PARENTS NEVER LET YOU HAVE A PET AS A CHILD?

Phony exhibitionists, Matthew 23:5–7.

Clean outside, phony inside, Matthew 23:25–28.

Ego displayed by teachers of law, Mark 12:38–40.

Conversion believed to be phony, Acts 9:26–27.

False humility, Colossians 2:18.

See Artificial, False, Hypocrisy, Sham.

PHYSICAL

Mere arm of flesh, 2 Chronicles 32:8.

Prayer for physical strength, Nehemiah 6:9.

Fearfully, wonderfully made, Psalm 139:14.

Not to swift or strong, Ecclesiastes 9:11.

Beautiful body, Song of Songs 7:1–9 (LB).

Examining liver for guidance, Ezekiel 21:21.

Healing increased popularity of Jesus, Mark 3:7–10.

Better to be limited physically than lost, Mark 9:43–48.

Man of short stature, Luke 19:1–6.

Body the Holy Spirit's temple, 1 Corinthians 6:19–20.

Rapid deterioration of human body, 2 Corinthians 4:16–18.

See Mortality.

PHYSICIAN

Physician morticians, Genesis 50:2.

Seeking only medical help, 2 Chronicles 16:12.

Ignorant, "quack" doctors, Job 13:4 (LB, Berk.).

Careless attention to wound, Jeremiah 8:11.

Doctor needed in Gilead, Jeremiah 8:22.

Only sick people need doctor, Matthew 9:12; Luke 5:31.

Ineffective physicians, Mark 5:25–26.

Greetings from Doctor Luke, Colossians 4:14.

See Health, Medicine, Therapy.

PHYSIQUE

Well built, handsome, Genesis 39:6.

Blemished physique, Leviticus 21:17–20.

Bearing of prince, Judges 8:18 (NIV).

Angel came to Samson's mother, Judges 13:6–7.

Tall King Saul, 1 Samuel 10:23–24.

Appearance of boy David, 1 Samuel 16:12.

Handsome Absalom, 2 Samuel 14:25.

Bodies sound, sleek, Psalm 73:4 (NRSV).

Brain over brawn, Proverbs 24:5–6 (NRSV).

Feminine physique, Song of Songs 7:1–6.

Zacchaeus' short stature, Luke 19:1–10.

See Athletics, Giant, Handsome, Tall.

PIETY

Piety caused by fear, 2 Chronicles 20:29.

Scorn for acts of humility, Psalm 69:10–11.

Early morning religiosity, Proverbs 27:14.

Real pious camouflage, Isaiah 58:1–2 (LB).

Meaning of fasting, Isaiah 58:3–7.

Pious speech from wayward hearts, Jeremiah 5:1, 2.

Those who offer false praise, Jeremiah 12:6.

Scorning those who have done wrong, Ezekiel 16:56, 57.

Satan's use of Scripture, Matthew 4:1–11.

Those truly pious, Matthew 5:1–12.

Performing righteousness, Matthew 6:1.

Sabbath observance, Matthew 12:1–13.

Gross sinners compared to Pharisees, Matthew 21:31–32.

Ultimate test, Matthew 22:36–40.

Missing real purpose of worship, Matthew 23:23–24.

Morality and materialism, Mark 10:17–25.

Hypocritical attitudes toward Jesus, Luke 6:1–11.

Mistaken personal piety, Acts 3:12 (NRSV).

Face of angel, Acts 6:15.

Righteousness not obtained observing sacraments, Romans 4:9–12.

Victory over carnal nature, Romans 8:1–17.

Love chapter, 1 Corinthians 13:1–13.

Showing love to those who cause grief, 2 Corinthians 2:5–11.

Spirit's presence in life of commitment, 2 Corinthians 3:7–8.

Seeking righteousness by human effort, Galatians 3:3.

Fruit of the Spirit, Galatians 5:22–25.

Jesus piety, Hebrews 5:7 (CEV).

True religion, James 1:27.
Lifestyle of true disciple, James 3:17–18.
Call to holiness, 1 Peter 1:13–16.
Spiritual growth, 2 Peter 1:5–9.
See Commitment, Spirituality.

PILFER See Loot, Plunder.

PILGRIM

Life seen as pilgrimage, Genesis 47:9.
Aliens, pilgrims, 1 Chronicles 29:15 (NKJV);
    Psalm 39:12; Hebrews 11:13; 13:14.
The Lord's guest, Psalm 39:12 (LB).
Strangers in the world, Psalm 119:19; He-
    brews 11:8–10; 1 Peter 1:1–2, 17.
Wanderers because of disobedience, Hosea
    9:17.
No enduring city, Hebrews 13:14.
Aliens, exiles, 1 Peter 2:11 (NRSV).

PILLAR

Lot's wife, Genesis 19:26; Luke 17:32.
Anointing object, Genesis 28:18–22.
Historic markers, Exodus 24:1–4.
Boundary marker, Joshua 15:6.
Death of Samson, Judges 16:25–30.
Temple adornment, 1 Kings 7:13–22.
See Architecture.

PITFALL

Tar pits of Siddim, Genesis 14:10.
Danger of pride in conquest of demons,
    Luke 10:16–20.
See Pride, Snare, Trap.

PITY

Pharaoh's daughter and baby Moses, Exo-
    dus 2:5–6.
Destruction without pity, Deuteronomy
    7:16.
No pity in judgment, Lamentations 2:2.
"I will show no pity," Ezekiel 7:4 (CEV).
Joseph's unfounded pity for Mary, Mat-
    thew 1:19.
Jesus refused pity, Luke 23:27–28.
See Compassion.

PKs

Evil sons, 1 Samuel 2:12–17, 22–25; 3:10–
    14.
See Clergy.

PLAGUE

Plague as judgment, Genesis 12:17; Exodus
    11:1; Psalm 106:29–30 (All KJV).
Promised protection, Psalm 91:10 (KJV).
Stalking peril, Jeremiah 9:21.
See Epidemic.

PLAN

Journey with the Lord's approval, Judges
    18:6.
Hiding true intentions, 1 Samuel 16:1–5.
"Impossible scheme," Psalm 131:1 (CEV).
Planning ahead, Proverbs 13:16 (LB).
Man's plans, God's purpose, Proverbs
    19:21.
Patience needed to persuade, Proverbs
    25:15.
Do not hide plans from God, Isaiah 29:15
    (CEV).
Drawing plan for battle, Ezekiel 4:1–3.
Design, measurement and arrangements,
    Ezekiel 43:10–12.
Estimate cost before construction, Luke
    14:28–30.
Master planner at work, Romans 12:12 (LB).
Planning journey, 2 Corinthians 1:15–17.
No certainty of tomorrow, James 4:13–16.
Redemption planned before creation, 1 Pe-
    ter 1:18–20.
See Design, Map.

PLATFORM

Ezra high on speaker's platform, Nehemiah
    8:5 (CEV).

PLATITUDES

Making promises to curry loyalty, 1 Samuel
    22:6–8.
Flattering lips speak with deception, Psalm
    12:1–2.
Those who do not want to hear truth, Isa-
    iah 30:10–11.
Fine-sounding arguments, Colossians 2:4.
See Hyperbole.

PLAY

Carnality in action, Exodus 32:6.
Playing rough, 2 Samuel 2:14.
National celebration, 2 Samuel 6:5.
Frolicking animals, Job 40:20.
Child and cobra, Isaiah 11:8.
See Games, Recreation.

PLAYBOY

Immorality in foreign country, Numbers 25:1.
Carousing soldiers, 1 Samuel 30:8.
Wise man's moral weakness, 1 Kings 11:1–4.
Playing with fire, Proverbs 6:27–28.
Lack of discretion, Proverbs 7:6–23.
He who loves pleasure, Proverbs 21:17.
Pandering pleasure and desire, Ecclesiastes 2:10.
Preferring play to work, Ecclesiastes 4:7–8.
End to noisy songs, Ezekiel 26:13.
Influencing others to sin, Luke 17:1.
Those who carouse, 2 Peter 2:13–16.
See Hedonism, Narcissism.

PLAY-ON-WORDS

Use of a literary device, Jeremiah 34:17.
See Figure-of-speech.

PLEASURE

Time to rejoice, not weep, Nehemiah 8:9–10.
Nauseating pleasure, Job 20:12–16; Proverbs 21:17.
Giving God pleasure, Job 22:2–3.
Joy beyond levity of wine, Psalm 4:7.
True joy only from the Lord, Psalm 84:11.
Whale at play, Psalm 104:26 (LB).
Covert pleasures, Proverbs 9:17.
Love of pleasure, Proverbs 21:17.
Meaningless activity, Ecclesiastes 2:1–11.
"I commend enjoyment," Ecclesiastes 8:15 (NRSV).
Alcoholism, Isaiah 5:11–12.
Wages of sin, Lamentations 1:14; Romans 6:23.
Unable to remember enjoyment, Lamentations 3:17 (LB).
Peril of ease, Amos 6:1.

Fisherman burns incense to net, Habakkuk 1:16.
Deathly conduct, 1 Timothy 5:6.
Lovers of pleasure, 2 Timothy 3:4.
Refusing pleasures of Egypt, Hebrews 11:24–25.
Joy of problems, testing, James 1:2–4.
Sensual pleasures, James 4:3 (AB).
Those who carouse, 2 Peter 2:13–16.
Joy of good reputation, 3 John 3–4.
See Comfort, Hedonism, Narcissism, Play.

PLEBISCITE

Uncalled but unanimous vote, Exodus 16:2.
Agreement with will of God, 1 Chronicles 13:2–4.
Choice of Jesus or Barabbas, Matthew 27:15–26.
See Mob Psychology, Vote.

PLEDGE

Pledge of unified congregation, Exodus 24:1–7.
Making, paying pledge, Deuteronomy 23:21.
Keeping vow to God, Psalm 65:1.
Rash promises to God, Ecclesiastes 5:2.
Better no vow than not fulfill, Ecclesiastes 5:5.
Taking false oath, Jeremiah 5:2.
See Covenant, Promise, Vow.

PLENTY

Promised abundance, Leviticus 26:5; Deuteronomy 30:9; Psalm 132:15; Isaiah 30:23; Amos 9:13.
Eat until satisfied, Joel 2:26.
Abundant life in Christ, John 10:10.
Abounding in God's grace, 2 Corinthians 9:8.
God's rich grace, Ephesians 1:7–8.
Good land, unproductive land, Hebrews 6:7–8.
Ample provision for life of godliness, 1 Peter 1:3.
See Abundance.

PLETHORA

Abounding love, compassion, Psalm 86:15.
God's everlasting love, Jeremiah 31:3.

Limitless redemption, John 3:16.
Abounding grace, 2 Corinthians 9:8.
Rich in mercy, Ephesians 2:4–5.
Christ's multi-dimensional love, power, Ephesians 3:17–21.
Limitless provision, Philippians 4:19.
Lavished love, 1 John 3:1.
See Abundance.

PLUNDER

"Fat on plunder," Judges 5:7 (NRSV).
Crops and animals plundered, Judges 6:3–6.
Plunder of dead soldiers, 1 Samuel 31:8–10.
Plundering passersby, Psalm 89:41.
Making frolic of plunder, Jeremiah 50:11–12; Ezekiel 36:4–6.
See Looting, Spoils.

POETRY

Song of Moses, Exodus 15:1–9.
Lyrics about deliverance, Numbers 21:27–30.
Poetic prayer, Joshua 10:12–13 (CEV).
Setting murder to verse, Judges 5:24–27.
Rhyming riddle, Judges 14:14 (NRSV).
Hannah's song, 1 Samuel 2:1–10.
Elegy, 2 Samuel 1:19–27; 3:33–34.
Rhyming couplet, Nehemiah 4:10 (CEV).
Psalms poetic examples, 1:3–4; 8:3–4; 12:6; 16:6; 23:1–6; 28:6–7; 34:3; 28:5–6; 40:1–3; 42:7; 51:7; 68:2; 84:1–12; 85:10–13; 90:1–17; 91:1–16; 100:1–5; 102:9; 103:2–5; 104:2–4; 107:1–9; 121:1–8; 139:23–24; 150:1–6.
Poetic taunt, Isaiah 14:4–21 (CEV).
Elizabeth's song, Luke 1:42–45.
Love chapter as poetry, 1 Corinthians 13:1–13 (CEV).
See Literature, Lyrics.

POINT-OF-VIEW See Viewpoint.

POISE

Poise in every circumstance, Proverbs 1:2 (LB).
Cool spirit, Proverbs 17:27 (NASB, NRSV).
"Quiet words," Ecclesiastes 9:17 (NRSV).
"Calmness will undo great offenses," Ecclesiastes 10:4 (NASB).
Silent poise, Mark 15:3–5.
Happy, unruffled, Acts 2:46–47 (Berk.).
Keep cool, 2 Timothy 4:4–5 (AB).
Inadequate poise, 2 Peter 3:17 (NASB, NKJV).
See Assurance. Confidence.

POISON

Deliverance from snakebite, Numbers 21:4–9.
Venom of vipers, Deuteronomy 32:24.
Fangs of an adder, Job 20:16.
Deaf cobra, Psalm 58:4.
Broken fangs, Psalm 58:4–6 (LB).
Poisonous speech, Psalm 140:3; James 3:8.
Pestilence of locusts, Revelation 9:7–11.
See Venom.

POLAR REGIONS See Compass.

POLICE

Security at Eden entrance, Genesis 3:24.
Security for Sabbath duty, 2 Kings 11:4–12.
Day and night protection, Nehemiah 4:9.
Guard at our Lord's tomb, Matthew 27:65–66.
Temple police refused to arrest Jesus, John 7:45 (LB, NASB).
Jewish police, John 18:12 (LB).
Satan under arrest, Revelation 20:1–3.
See Angels, Guardian, Protection.

POLITENESS See Courtesy, Guests, Hospitality, Manners.

POLITICS

Building first city, Genesis 4:17.
Prenatal struggle, Genesis 25:22–23.
Marriage to please father, Genesis 28:6–8.
Drastic change in government, Exodus 1:8–14.
Choosing right leader, Deuteronomy 17:14–15.
Short, concise speech, Judges 9:1–2.
David and Saul, 1 Samuel 17:32–37; 2 Samuel 2:8–32.
Strong and weak parties 2 Samuel 3:1.
Immorality in politics, 2 Samuel 3:6–11.

Campaigning for office, 2 Samuel 15:1–6.

Share of king, 2 Samuel 19:43.

Seeking to take over throne, 1 Kings 1:1–27.

Political marriage, 1 Kings 3:1; 2 Chronicles 18:1.

Secret anointing of king, 2 Kings 9:1–13.

The priest and the king, 2 Kings 11:15–18.

Ages of young kings, 2 Kings 21:1, 19; 23:36; 24:18; 2 Chronicles 33:1, 21; 34:1; 36:2, 5, 9, 11.

Political killings, 2 Kings 21:23–24.

Teen-age king, 2 Kings 24:8, 9.

Inevitable fate of world governments, Psalm 2:7–9.

Politicians and justice, Psalm 58:1 (LB).

Out of office, Psalm 109:8 (NKJV).

Death terminates secular leadership, Psalm 146:3–4.

Favor of a ruler, Proverbs 19:6.

Good, bad leadership, Proverbs 28:12.

Politics needs good mothers, Proverbs 31:31 (LB).

Political preacher, Ecclesiastes 1:12 (KJV).

Politicians check on each other, Ecclesiastes 5:8–9.

Right and left, Ecclesiastes 10:2.

Fools in high positions, Ecclesiastes 10:5–6.

Governed by children, Isaiah 3:4.

Refusal to participate, Isaiah 3:6–7.

Put out of office, Isaiah 22:19.

Man who refused bribes, Isaiah 33:15–16.

Reward of evil politics, Jeremiah 22:13.

Political assassination, Jeremiah 41:2.

King in respectable exile, Jeremiah 52:31–34.

Wicked officials in city, Ezekiel 22:27.

Foreign youth given high positions, Daniel 2:48–49.

King at age sixty-two, Daniel 5:30–31.

Integrity in government affairs, Daniel 6:1–4.

Daniel as president, Daniel 6:2 (KJV).

Political pressure, Daniel 6:12–16.

Political marriage, Daniel 11:6 (LB).

Ignoring divine guidance in choice of leaders, Hosea 8:4.

Future of world political systems, Micah 7:16–17.

Politics of prostitution, Nahum 3:4.

Evil politics, Habakkuk 2:12.

Church and state, Haggai 1:1 (CEV).

Religion, politics, Zechariah 7:2 (LB).

Wife's advice to Pilate, Matthew 27:19.

Effort to draft Jesus, John 6:15.

Pharisees feared political reaction, John 11:48.

Killing to gain political favor, Acts 12:1–4.

Political motivation for imprisonment, Acts 24:27.

Deceitful scheming, Ephesians 4:14.

"Party of the circumcision," Galatians 2:12 (NASB).

Praying for those in authority, 1 Timothy 2:1–4.

Do not show favoritism, James 2:1 (NIV).

Role of demons in world politics, Revelation 16:14.

One hour reign of ten kings, Revelation 17:12.

See Bureaucracy, Government.

POLLUTION

River pollution, Exodus 7:20.

Air pollution, Exodus 9:8–10 (LB).

Silver to dross, wine to water, Isaiah 1:22.

Foul-smelling canals, Isaiah 19:6.

Bodies unburied, Jeremiah 9:22.

Defiled with blood, Lamentations 4:14.

Polluted food for mourners, Hosea 9:4 (LB).

Polluting wheat, Amos 8:6.

Polluted Jerusalem, Zephaniah 3:1 (AB).

Salt loses saltiness, Luke 14:34–35.

See Defile, Ecology, Putrid, Stench.

POLYANDRY

Two husbands by deceit, Genesis 12:18–19; 20:1–13.

POLYGAMY

First examples of bigamy, Genesis 4:19; 16:3; 26:34–35.

First record of polygamy, Genesis 28:9.

Second wife after monogamy, Genesis 29:16–30.

Consideration for first wife, Exodus 21:10.

Polygamy forbidden, Deuteronomy 17:17; Leviticus 18:18.

Spoils of war, Deuteronomy 20:10–15.

Royal polygamy, 1 Samuel 25:39–44; 1 Kings 11:1–3.

One man, seven women, Isaiah 4:1.

Elder must have but one wife, Titus 1:6.

See Marriage.

POMPOUS *See Vanity.*

PONDER

Pondering scripture, Psalm 1:2 (Berk.).

POOR

Harvest gleaning for poor, Leviticus 19:9–10.

Poor, rich, 1 Samuel 2:7.

Benevolent spirit, Job 29:11–15; 30:25; 31:15–22.

Sense of true value, Psalm 37:16; Proverbs 13:7; 28:6.

Call to altruism, Psalm 82:3–4.

Divine opportunity, Proverbs 19:17; Matthew 25:42–45.

Penalty for selfishness, Proverbs 21:13.

See Benevolence, Poverty, Philanthropy, Welfare.

POPULARITY

King's lack of popularity, 1 Samuel 10:26–27.

Pleased subjects, 2 Samuel 3:36.

Winning favor of people, 2 Samuel 15:1–6.

David's fear of Absalom's popularity, 2 Samuel 15:13–14.

Many sought Job's favor, Job 11:19.

The wide, the narrow, Matthew 7:13–14.

Pharisees fear of crowd, Matthew 21:45–46.

Seeking praise of men, John 12:42–43.

Healing increased Jesus' popularity, Mark 3:7–10.

Cornelius respect for Peter, Acts 10:25–26.

Royal murder to gain popularity, Acts 12:1–4.

Unknown yet well-known, 2 Corinthians 6:9.

Popularity and effective service, Galatians 1:10 (GNB).

Favor resulting from dependability, Colossians 3:22.

See Approval, Celebrity, Esteem, Fame, Respect.

POPULATION

"Population explosion," Genesis 6:1 (LB); Exodus 1:7 (LB).

God's plan for increase, Genesis 9:1.

Rapid population growth after flood, Genesis 10:1–32.

Census involved men twenty years or older, Numbers 26:2.

Increasing strain on government, Deuteronomy 1:9–13.

Population growth, Deuteronomy 10:22; 2 Samuel 24:3 (LB).

Threat of population reduction, Deuteronomy 28:62.

Population of Israel reduced, 2 Kings 10:32.

Satanic census, 1 Chronicles 21:1–2.

Large city, small population, Nehemiah 7:4.

Building population by statistics, Nehemiah 11:1.

Few in number, Psalm 105:12–13.

Scarcity of people, Isaiah 13:12.

Population growth encouraged, Jeremiah 29:4–6.

People taken into exile, Jeremiah 52:28–30.

Population decimated by divine judgment, Ezekiel 5:12.

Increased birth rate, lowered infant mortality, Ezekiel 36:14 (LB).

Israel's future population, Hosea 1:10.

Nineveh considered large city, Jonah 3:3.

Census of entire Roman world, Luke 2:1–3.

"Increased and multiplied," Acts 7:17 (NRSV).

See Census, Citizenship, Community.

PORK

Abstain from pork, Leviticus 11:7; Isaiah 65:4; 66:17.

Jewelry not for pigs, Matthew 7:6.

Habitat for demons, Matthew 8:30–32.

Mud dwellers, 2 Peter 2:22.

See Kosher, Meat.

PORNOGRAPHY

Lust instilled by pictures, Ezekiel 23:14–17 (See LB).

See Lust.

POSITION

Doorkeeper in God's house, Psalm 84:10.
Asking for prestige rather than earning it, Mark 10:33–40.
Paul's rank in Judaism, Galatians 1:13–14.
Blessed in heavenly realms, Ephesians 1:3.
Those who demand first place, 3 John 9.
See Prestige.

POSITIVE

God's attitude toward creation, Genesis 1:4, 10, 12, 18, 21, 25, 31.
Good news, good health, Proverbs 15:30.
Message not yes or no, 2 Corinthians 1:18–20.
Letter kills, Spirit gives life, 2 Corinthians 3:6.
Positive view of problems, 2 Corinthians 4:17–18.
See Attitude, Negative, Optimism.

POSSESSIONS

Exchanging what you have for what is better, Genesis 45:20.
Permanent ownership of Israel, Deuteronomy 4:40.
Earth is God's property, Psalm 95:4–5.
Stones and dust of Jerusalem, Psalm 102:14.
Eating one's own harvest, Isaiah 62:8–9.
Kingdoms of the world, Matthew 4:8–9.
Ananias and Sapphira, Acts 5:1–11.
Faith title deed, Hebrews 11:1 (AB).
See Affluence, Property.

POSSESSIVE

Owning share of king, 2 Samuel 19:43.
Misuse of sacrifice to the Lord, 1 Samuel 2:12–17.
Requesting payment for spiritual ministry, 2 Kings 5:20–27.
Greedy for gain, Jeremiah 8:10.
See Greed.

POSTERITY

Witness to future generations, Exodus 16:32–34.
Father's preventive care for children, Job 1:1–5.
Life of Jesus for continuing generations, Luke 1:1–4.
See History.

POSTHUMOUS

Memories of kindness perpetuated, Matthew 26:6–13.
Dead yet continuing to speak, Hebrews 11:4.
Good deeds follow good people, Revelation 14:13.
See Legacy.

POSTPONE

Postponed temple rebuilding, Haggai 1:3–4.
See Delay.

POSTURE

Princely bearing, Judges 8:18.
Posture correction, Luke 13:10–13 (See AB).
Reclining at meal time, Luke 22:14.
See Physique.

POTENTIAL

Potential childhood capability, Jeremiah 1:6–8.
Potential blessing lost to idols, Hosea 9:10.
Evaluating military potential, Luke 14:31–32.
Unlimited spiritual potential, 1 John 3:1–3.
See Capability, Future.

POVERTY

Inexcusable mistreatment, Exodus 23:6.
Abolish poverty, Deuteronomy 15:4, 7–8, 11.
Pet lamb of poor family, 2 Samuel 12:1–6.
Poor people spared captivity, 2 Kings 24:14.
Born without possessions, Job 1:21 (AB).
Function of evil, Psalm 14:6.
Better righteous poverty than wicked wealth, Psalm 37:16–17.
Bandit's prey, Proverbs 6:11 (Berk.).
Little with faith, much with turmoil, Proverbs 15:16.
Simple food with peace and quiet, Proverbs 17:1.
Painful poverty, Proverbs 19:7.
Poverty better than dishonesty, Proverbs 19:22.

Rich and poor have common origin, Proverbs 22:2.

The Lord defends the poor, Proverbs 22:22–23.

Justice, injustice toward poor, Proverbs 28:8 (LB).

Help those who are helpless, Proverbs 31:8–9.

Government subsidy to poor, Jeremiah 39:10; 40:7–9.

Poor people taken captive, Jeremiah 52:15.

Prosperity forgotten, Lamentations 3:17.

Valued as a pair of shoes, Amos 2:6; 8:6.

Exploiting poor for personal gain, Amos 5:11.

Poverty's deepest dimensions, Haggai 2:16–17.

Judah's poverty, Zechariah 8:13 (LB).

Poor in spirit, Matthew 5:3.

Jesus and earthly possessions, Matthew 8:19, 20.

Humble disciples, humble equipment, Mark 6:8–11.

Poor can inherit kingdom, Luke 6:20.

Good news for poor people, Luke 7:22 (NRSV).

Poverty of Jesus, Luke 9:58.

Christ's love surmounts poverty, Romans 8:35 (GNB).

Productive poverty, 2 Corinthians 6:10.

Poverty generates generosity, 2 Corinthians 8:2 (NRSV).

Concern for poor, Galatians 2:9–10.

Living in tent en route to city of God, Hebrews 11:9–10.

Enduring poverty, Hebrews 11:37–38.

Poor can be rich in faith, James 2:5.

Poor exploited by rich, James 2:6.

True wealth, Revelation 2:9.

See Poor, Welfare.

POWER

Flaunting power, 1 Kings 12:1–11.

Power from wealth, Ruth 2:1 (KJV).

Raw spiritual power, Isaiah 19:1.

Power in God's name, Jeremiah 10:6 (LB).

Nothing too hard for God, Jeremiah 32:27.

No longer powerful, Ezekiel 26:2 (CEV).

Power of Divine message, Luke 4:32.

Divine power relinquished, Luke 14:41 (GNB).

"Royal power," Luke 19:12 (NRSV).

Witnessing power, Acts 1:8.

Resurrection power, Romans 8:11; Ephesians 1:18–20.

Strength from weakness, 2 Corinthians 12:9.

Divine breath will overthrow man of sin, 2 Thessalonians 2:8.

Scripture's power, Hebrews 4:12 (See AB).

Protected by God's power, 1 Peter 1:5 (NRSV).

See Omnipotence.

POWERLESS

Powerless to face enemy, Leviticus 26:37; Deuteronomy 28:32; Joshua 7:12.

Unable to drive out invader, Judges 1:21.

Admitting lack of strength, 2 Chronicles 20:12.

Men become like women, Isaiah 19:16; Jeremiah 50:37; 51:30; Nahum 3:13.

See Frailty, Weakness.

PRACTICAL *See Feasible, Pragmatic.*

PRACTICE

Seeming to fail in practice, Job 4:1–5.

Practice what you preach, Psalm 51:10–13; Ezekiel 33:31.

PRAGMATIC

Evil men recognize God's power, Exodus 8:1–19.

Medical proof of virginity, Deuteronomy 22:13–19.

Afraid of ark of the Lord, 2 Samuel 6:9–11.

Death by measurement, 2 Samuel 8:2.

Three choices for punishment, 1 Chronicles 21:8–13.

Father's preventive care for children, Job 1:1–5.

Contentment with daily bread, Proverbs 30:8.

Stark evaluation of life, Ecclesiastes 5:15; 7:1–5.

Looking frankly at emptiness of life, Isaiah 55:2.

Presumed proof of goddess' power, Jeremiah 44:11–19.

Test and compare, Daniel 1:12–15.

Proving the Lord by tithing, Malachi 3:10.

Wisdom of serving God, Malachi 3:14–15.

View of Jesus toward Sabbath, Matthew 12:1–13.

Pragmatic way to meet Jesus, Luke 5:17–20.

Receiving good for doing good, Luke 6:37–38.

Good things from good heart, evil from evil, Luke 6:45.

Centurion's view of Jesus, Luke 7:1–10.

Looking at circumstances instead of Jesus, Luke 9:10–17.

Letter of law made practical in spirit, Luke 10:35–37.

Pharisees desired visible kingdom, Luke 17:20, 21.

Believing visible evidence, John 4:39–42.

Seeing is believing, John 9:35–38.

Believing key to seeing, John 11:40.

Doubting Thomas, John 20:24–29.

Sufficient evidence to make decision, John 20:30–31.

Realizing God's work cannot be stopped, Acts 5:38, 39.

Those who demand pragmatic evidence, 1 Corinthians 1:22–25.

Put truth to test, 1 Thessalonians 5:21.

Pragmatic aspects of faith, Hebrews 11:1–3.

Eye witness to reality, 1 John 1:1–4.
See Reality, Tangible.

PRAISE

Song of Moses, Exodus 15:1, 2.

Woman lauded for murder, Judges 5:24–27.

Self praise, Nehemiah 5:19.

"Stand up and praise the Lord," Nehemiah 9:5.

Praise for past blessings, Nehemiah 9:7–38.

Avoiding partiality and flattery, Job 31:21, 22.

Harp as instrument of praise, Psalm 43:4.

Sing praise with understanding, Psalm 47:7 (KJV).

Giving praise to God's Word, Psalm 56:10.

Singing with steadfast heart, Psalm 57:7.

"Silent praise," Psalm 65:1 (LB).

"Let God be magnified," Psalm 70:4 (NASB, NKJV).

Man's wrath praises God, Psalm 76:10 (KJV).

Cry of praise to the Lord, Psalm 89:8.

Giving the Lord glory due Him, Psalm 96:8.

David's song of praise, Psalm 103:1–22.

Motivation for praise, Psalm 107:8, 15, 21, 31.

"God of my praise," Psalm 109:1 (NKJV, NRSV).

Praise, glory belong only to God, Psalm 115:1; Acts 12:21–23; 1 Corinthians 3:7.

Nature, people praise the Lord, Psalm 148:1–14.

Last verse of Psalms, Psalm 150:6.

Let another praise you, Proverbs 27:2.

Praise, test of humility, Proverbs 27:21.

Folly of flattery, Proverbs 28:23.

Talented people encouraging each other, Isaiah 41:7.

Joy, gladness, Jeremiah 33:11.

Daniel's gratitude to God for needed wisdom, Daniel 2:19–23.

Praise from pagan lips, Daniel 4:37.

When God turns deaf ear to praise, Amos 5:22; 8:3, 10.

Jesus' evaluation of John the Baptist, Matthew 11:11–14.

Crowd praised Jesus prior to crying out, "Crucify Him!" Matthew 21:6–11 (Note 27:20–23).

Children's praise, Matthew 21:15–16.

Danger of praise, Luke 6:26.

Receive praise from God, 1 Corinthians 4:5.

Giving compliments, 2 Corinthians 7:14.

Let the Lord commend, 2 Corinthians 10:17–18.

Trying to please others, Galatians 1:10.

Motivation preaching, teaching, 1 Thessalonians 2:1–6.

No search for praise, 1 Thessalonians 2:6.

Praise God for ministry success, 1 Thessalonians 3:8–10.

Good deeds made known, 1 Timothy 5:25.

Praise to Redeemer and Creator, Revelation 5:13–14.

Outcry of praise to God, Revelation 7:11–12.

Fear causes people to give glory to God, Revelation 11:13.

Concluding proclamation of faith in God, Revelation 15:3–4.

See Worship.

PRANK *See Mischief.*

PRAYER

Prayer answered before completion, Genesis 24:15.

Pregnancy in answer to prayer, Genesis 25:21.

Prayer of humility, Genesis 32:9–10.

God's answer to grumbling community, Exodus 16:3–5; Mark 11:24.

Prayer for protection, Numbers 10:35.

Damage to knees hinders prayer, Deuteronomy 28:35.

Persistent prayer in time of need, 1 Samuel 7:8.

Praying for rain, 1 Samuel 12:18.

Sin of failing to pray, 1 Samuel 14:19 (GNB).

Personal decision, seeking divine guidance, 1 Samuel 14:36–41.

Prayer through night, 1 Samuel 15:10.

Unanswered prayer, spiritism, 1 Samuel 28:5–20.

David's prayer for guidance, 2 Samuel 5:17–19.

Receiving assurance of divine guidance, 2 Samuel 7:18–29.

Prayer for end of famine, 2 Samuel 21:1.

Solomon's prayer for wisdom, discernment, 1 Kings 3:1–15; 4:29–34.

God listens when people pray, 1 Kings 8:52; Psalm 6:9.

Talking personally with God, 2 Chronicles 6:4 (LB).

Prayer of national repentance, 2 Chronicles 7:14.

Constant prayer, Nehemiah 1:4 (AB).

For favors rendered, Nehemiah 5:19; 6:14.

Prayer for physical strength, Nehemiah 6:9.

Prayer model, Nehemiah 9:6–31.

Cry of anguish in time of suffering, Job 6:8–10.

Job knew his advocate was in heaven, Job 16:19.

Presuming a God removed from man's affairs, Job 22:12–14.

Unanswered prayers, Job 30:20.

God's varied answers, Job 33:14–17.

Vitality of answered prayer, Job 33:26; Psalm 34:17.

Persistent daily prayer, Psalms 5:3; 55:17 (LB).

Confident God will answer, Psalms 17:6; 138:1–3; Ephesians 3:12.

Importance of praise with prayer, Psalm 18:3.

Prayer in time of trouble, Psalm 18:6.

High motive, Psalm 27:4.

Seek God's face, Psalm 27:8.

Pleading prayer, Psalm 28:6 (NRSV).

Divinely implanted desire for prayer, Psalm 37:3–5 (See 20:4–5).

Secret petitions, Psalm 37:4 (AB).

Patiently wait, Psalm 37:34 (LB).

Thirst for the living God, Psalm 42:1–2.

Deep calling unto deep, Psalm 42:7–8.

Immediate results, Psalms 56:9 (LB); 70:5.

Seeking high rock, Psalm 61:1–2.

God answers prayer, Psalm 65:2 (NRSV).

Sin hinders answer to prayer, Psalm 66:18–19.

Desperation prayer, Psalm 69:1–3.

Eager for answer, Psalm 77:2–4 (LB).

Danger of testing God, Psalm 78:18–22.

Prayers which incite God's anger, Psalm 80:4.

Prayer for revival, Psalm 85:1–7.

Prayer for undivided heart, Psalm 86:11.

Calling to the Lord day, night, Psalm 88:1–2.

Qualification for answered prayer, Psalm 91:14–16.

Talking to God who answers, Psalm 99:6.

God never too busy to hear, Psalm 102:17 (LB).

Reasons to praise God, Psalm 103:1–22.

Reward of selfish prayer, Psalm 106:14–15.

Man of prayer, Psalm 109:4.

Condemning prayer, Psalm 109:7 (See GNB, NRSV).

Prayer in time of deep depression, Psalm 116:1–4.

Release from anguish, Psalm 118:5.

Giving thanks at midnight, Psalm 119:62.

Bible-centered prayer, Psalm 119:65.

"Do something, Lord," Psalm 119:126 (CEV).

Prayer of humility, Psalm 123:1–2.

Prayer for inner peace, righteousness, Psalm 139:23–24.

Altar of prayer, Psalm 141:2.

Desires of righteous fulfilled, Psalm 145:17–19; Proverbs 10:24; 37:4.

Prayer unanswered, Proverbs 1:29–31; Jeremiah 7:16.

Ultimate request for guidance, Proverbs 3:5–6.

Agony of waiting, joy of fulfillment, Proverbs 13:12.

Detestable prayers of lawbreakers, Proverbs 28:9.

Cautious words in God's presence, Ecclesiastes 5:2.

Meaningless offerings, Isaiah 1:11–17 (NIV).

Not testing the Lord, Isaiah 7:12.

Whispered prayer, Isaiah 26:16 (LB).

The Lord quick to answer, Isaiah 30:19.

God's glory first in time of trouble, Isaiah 37:14–20.

Relentless prayer until answer comes, Isaiah 62:6–7.

Answer before request, Isaiah 65:24.

Backslider's prayer in time of trouble, Jeremiah 2:27.

Pointless prayer, Jeremiah 11:14 (LB); Lamentations 3:8; Micah 3:4.

Painfully honest prayers, Jeremiah 11:18–23; 12:1–6; 15:10–21; 17:12–18; 18:18–23; 20:7–18.

Clouds block out prayer, Lamentations 3:44 (CEV).

Prayer unanswered though seekers shout, Ezekiel 8:18.

Idols hinder prayers, Ezekiel 14:4 (LB).

Answered prayer of wayward people, Ezekiel 36:37–38.

Prayer support, Daniel 2:17–19.

Answered or unanswered, Daniel 3:16–18.

Faith ahead of loyalty to king, Daniel 6:5–11.

Timing of answered prayer, Daniel 10:12 (LB).

Awe of talking to God, Daniel 10:15–21.

Prayer to various gods, Jonah 1:5.

Praying inside fish, Jonah 2:1.

Unqualified to pray, Micah 3:1–4.

Prayer set to music, Habakkuk 3:1 (AB).

Lips must first be purified, Zephaniah 3:9.

Lord hears those who listen, Zechariah 7:13.

Praying for rain, Zechariah 10:1.

Privacy of prayer, Matthew 6:5–13; Luke 5:16.

Long public prayers, Matthew 6:7 (CEV).

Result of hypocrite's prayer, Matthew 6:16 (Berk.).

Asking, seeking, knocking, Matthew 7:7–8.

Faith touches God's willingness to respond, Matthew 8:2–4.

Prayer for harvest, Matthew 9:37–38.

Faith to remove mountains, Matthew 21:21–22.

Example of Jesus in early morning, Mark 1:35.

Power of prayer in times of crisis, Mark 9:14–29.

Blind man's simple request, Mark 10:46–52.

Mealtime prayer, Mark 14:22 (AB, LB).

Ministry of aged widow, Luke 2:36–38.

Willingness of Jesus to answer, Luke 5:12–13.

Jesus spent night in prayer, Luke 6:12.

Asking for help, surprised at answer, Luke 8:56.

Praying for harvesters rather than harvest, Luke 10:1–2.

Request for prayer teaching, Luke 11:1.

God's goodness in answer to prayer, Luke 11:5–13.

Persistent prayer, Luke 18:1–8 (CEV).

Proud Pharisee, humble tax collector, Luke 18:9–14.

Performance prayers, Luke 20:47.

Promised answer to prayer, John 14:13–14; 16:23–24.

Chosen for guidance, blessing, John 15:16.

Joyful answers to prayer, John 16:24.

Prayer of Jesus before going to cross, John 17:1–26.

Desire for earthly blessing, promise of opportunity, Acts 1:6–7.

Group prayer, Acts 1:14 (Berk., CEV).

Prayer for guidance, conduct of earthly procedure, Acts 1:24–26.

Prayer in time of stress, Acts 4:23–26.

Prayer for personal advantage, Acts 8:24.

Power of prayer in time of need, Acts 12:5.

Kneeling to pray, Psalm 95:6; Daniel 6:10; Acts 9:40; 20:36; 21:5.

Outdoor prayer time, Acts 21:5.

Consistent prayer for other Christians, Romans 1:8–10; 1 Corinthians 1:4–9; Ephesians 1:11–23; Philippians 1:3–6; Colossians 1:3–14.

Words beyond normal vocabulary, Romans 8:15–16.

Blissful prayer, Romans 8:15 (AB).

Prayer guided by Holy Spirit, Romans 8:26–27.

"Wrestling in prayer," Romans 15:30 (AB, CEV).

Prayer for one's own personal ministry, Romans 15:31–32.

Head covered, uncovered, 1 Corinthians 11:4–5.

Fervent prayer, 2 Corinthians 9:14 (LB).

Rejoicing when prayer not answered, 2 Corinthians 12:7–10.

Access to God through the Holy Spirit, Ephesians 2:18.

Dimensional prayer, Ephesians 3:14–21.

Prayer as abundant resource, Ephesians 3:20–21; Philippians 1:9.

Praying for those who minister, Ephesians 6:19–20; Colossians 4:3–4; 1 Thessalonians 1:2–3; 3:10.

Prayers filled with praise, Philippians 1:3 (LB).

Joyful prayer, Philippians 1:4.

Persistent prayer, Philippians 4:6–7 (Note: Swedish Bible translates "supplication" as "agonizing expectation").

Thanking God for others, Colossians 1:3–6; 2 Thessalonians 1:3.

"Devote yourselves to prayer," Colossians 4:2 (AB, NASB, NRSV).

Prayer warrior, Colossians 4:12.

"Never stop praying," 1 Thessalonians 5:17 (CEV).

Coming to our High Priest, Hebrews 4:14–16 (AB).

Cries of Jesus to His Heavenly Father, Hebrews 5:7.

Abraham waited patiently for God's promise, Hebrews 6:13–14.

Our High Priest in heaven, Hebrews 8:1–2.

Coming to God in full assurance, Hebrews 10:19–23.

Asking God for wisdom, James 1:5–7 (AB).

Praying with wrong motives, James 4:3.

Prayer's powerful potential, James 5:16 (AB, NRSV).

Power of Elijah's prayer, James 5:17–18.

Prayers hindered in bad marriage, 1 Peter 3:7.

The Lord attentive to prayer, 1 Peter 3:12.

Disciplined prayer, 1 Peter 4:7 (NRSV).

Cast all cares upon the Lord, 1 Peter 5:7.

Confidence, conditions, 1 John 5:14–15 (NRSV).

Assurance of answered prayer, 1 John 3:21–22.

Pray in the Holy Spirit, Jude 20.

Incense, and the prayers of saints, Revelation 8:3–4.

Concluding proclamation of faith, Revelation 15:3–4.

Not to pray to or worship angels, Revelation 22:8–9.

See Amen, Grace Before Meals, Intercession, Mountain Top, Quiet Time, Worship.

PRAYER LIST

Praying for people by name, 1 Thessalonians 1:2.

PRAYER MEETING

Appointed time for temple prayer, Acts 3:1.

Prayer meeting on beach, Acts 21:5.

PREACHER *See Clergy.*

PREACHING

Poor speaker, Exodus 4:2 (GNB).

Speaking from personal experience, Exodus 20:12 (Berk.).

Given words to speak, Numbers 22:38.

Troublemaker preaching, 1 Kings 18:17 (GNB).

Preaching vocabulary, Ecclesiastes 12:10.

"Don't preach the truth," Isaiah 30:10 (CEV).

"Encourage my people," Isaiah 40:1 (CEV).

Street preaching, Jeremiah 2:2 (LB).

Preaching at temple gate, Jeremiah 7:1–15.

City gate ministry, Jeremiah 17:19–27.

Strong preaching ridiculed, Jeremiah 17:15 (LB).

Strong preaching resisted, Jeremiah 18:18 (See GNB).

Inner compulsion to preach, Jeremiah 20:7–11 (LB).

"In the name of Baal," Jeremiah 23:13 (CEV).

Imagined message, Jeremiah 23:16 (CEV).

"Sad news," Jeremiah 23:33–40 (LB).

Falling on deaf ears, Jeremiah 25:3–4.

False messages, Lamentations 2:14 (LB).

Ineffective preaching, Ezekiel 33:30–32.

Good care of sheep, Ezekiel 34:14.

Given a message, Obadiah 1 (CEV).

Strong preaching resisted, Micah 2:6 (GNB).

False preaching, Matthew 7:2–22 (See CEV).

Amazing sermons, Matthew 7:28 (LB).

Jesus' synagogue sermons, Luke 4:14–15 (LB).

Effective preaching, Luke 7:29 (LB).

Jesus' sermons attracted sinners, Luke 15:1–2 (LB).

Shouting message, John 1:15 (CEV).

Speak plainly, Acts 2:29 (Berk.).

Using variety, Acts 2:40 (Berk.).

Dire threats, bold preaching, Acts 4:29.

Powerful preaching, Acts 9:22 (GNB).

Preaching alleged as amateur, Acts 17:18 (Berk.).

Bold and persuasive preaching, Acts 19:8.

Women proclaiming the message, Acts 21:9 (GNB).

Preaching impact, Romans 10:17 (GNB).

Using simple vocabulary, 1 Corinthians 2:1 (GNB).

Compulsion to preach, 1 Corinthians 9:16 (CEV).

"Tremendous opportunities," 2 Corinthians 2:12 (LB).

Preaching with conviction, 2 Corinthians 4:13.

Motivation for preaching, 2 Corinthians 5:11.

"Never heard worse preacher," 2 Corinthians 10:10 (LB).

Wasted effort, Galatians 4:11.

"Listening to the message," Ephesians 1:13 (NASB).

Imprisoned for preaching, Ephesians 3:1 (See AB).

Fearless preaching, Ephesians 6:19–20.

Motive for preaching, Philippians 1:15–17.

Wise preaching, Colossians 1:28.

"As clear as possible," Colossians 4:4 (CEV).

Be pleasant, hold interest, Colossians 4:6 (CEV).

Preaching with conviction, 1 Thessalonians 1:5.

Double honor for preaching, 1 Timothy 5:17.

Called to preach, 2 Timothy 1:11 (CEV).

Resisting resistance, 2 Timothy 4:2 (AB, See CEV, NRSV).

Wanted: Ear-pleasing teaching, 2 Timothy 4:3 (LB).

Preach, encourage, exhort, refute, Titus 1:9.

Not giving desired message, Jude 3 (CEV).

See Clergy, Congregation, Sermon.

PRECARIOUS *See Danger.*

PRECAUTION *See Prevention.*

PREDATOR *See Wolf.*

PREDESTINATION

Chosen for greatness, Genesis 18:16–19.

Birth of nation, Genesis 21:12–13.

Sovereign purpose, Genesis 45:4–7.

Destined purpose, Exodus 9:16.

Future accomplishment assured, Numbers 21:34.

Predestined city, 2 Chronicles 6:6.

Predestined lifespan, Job 14:5 (See GNB).

Chosen people, Psalm 33:12.

Chosen person, Psalm 65:4; Jeremiah 1:4–5.

All things ordained, Psalm 139:15–16.

Time for everything, Ecclesiastes 3:1–8.

Things planned long ago, Isaiah 25:1.

God chooses year and day, Isaiah 34:8 (CEV).

Planned, performed, Isaiah 37:26.

Predetermined course of history, Isaiah 41:4 (GNB).

The Lord will do what He has said, Isaiah 46:11.

God's perfect timing, Isaiah 49:8.

Appointed prophet before birth, Jeremiah 1:5.

Destined for peril and death, Jeremiah 15:2.

Jesus knew what He would do, John 6:6, 37–45.

Those given to Jesus by the Father, John 17:1–12.

Destined to be lost, John 17:12 (See AB).

History predestined, Acts 17:26.

Predestined goodness, Romans 8:28–33.

God's choice, Romans 9:10–21 (CEV).

Irrevocable Divine decisions, Romans 11:29.

Set apart from birth, Galatians 1:15–17.

Foreseen by Scriptures, Galatians 4:8.

Chosen before creation, Ephesians 1:4–6, 11–12.

God's plan, Ephesians 1:11 (CEV).

Filled with knowledge of God's will, Colossians 1:9–12.

Destined for persecution, trials, 1 Thessalonians 3:1–5.

Rejecting destiny planned by God, 1 Peter 2:8.

Determined number of martyrs, Revelation 6:9–11.

Names in Book of Life, Revelation 17:8.

See Destiny, Fate, Foreknowledge.

PREDICTION

Predicted deliverance, Genesis 50:24–25.

As the Lord promised, 2 Chronicles 6:10.

People quick to disobey God, Judges 2:10–13, 19; 3:7, 12; 4:1.

Future left safely in God's hands, Isaiah 46:8–11.

Good news, bad news, Jeremiah 34:1–7.

Prophecy of imagination, Ezekiel 13:1–23.

Book of the future, Daniel 10:20 (LB).

Predicted ministry, Luke 1:11–17.

Forecasting weather, Luke 12:54–56.

Untimely prediction request, Acts 1:7.

See Estimation, Prophecy.

PREEMINENCE

God as first priority, Genesis 1:1.

The God greater than numbers, Deuteronomy 20:1.

Preeminent Lord, Isaiah 46:9.

Knowing who is the Lord, Ezekiel 6:10, 14; 7:4, 9, 27; 12:16, 20; 13:9, 23; 14:11.

Earth filled with the Lord's glory, Habakkuk 2:14.

Danger of pride in conquest of demons, Luke 10:16–20.

Qualifications of preeminent Christ, Colossians 1:15–20.

Preeminent to angels, Hebrews 1:3–4.

See Supremacy.

PREEXISTENCE

Messiah pre-dates Christmas, Micah 5:2.

Preexistence before Abraham, John 8:58.

Co-existence with God, John 17:5, 24; Colossians 1:17; Hebrews 7:3.

Alpha and Omega, Revelation 22:13.

See Christ, Creator, Messiah.

PREFABRICATED

Temple stones, 1 Kings 6:7 (LB).

See Construction.

PREFERENCE

Same rules for all, Numbers 15:15.

Gifts expected from those who gave most, Numbers 31:27–31.

Right of first son, Deuteronomy 21:15–17.

Volunteer assignment, Nehemiah 11:1–2.

One day, one thousand, Psalm 84:10.

Better option than sins as scarlet, Isaiah 1:18.

Jerusalem, apple of God's eye, Zechariah 2:8.

See Favoritism.

PREGNANCY

"Pregnancy-troubles," Genesis 3:16 (Berk.).

Pregnant with divine help, Genesis 4:1.

Season for conception, Genesis 18:10 (NKJV, AB, Berk.).

Household infertility, Genesis 20:17–18.

Children born in old age, Genesis 21:1–7.

Rebekah's pregnancy answered prayer, Genesis 25:21.

Struggling fetuses, Genesis 22; 25:22.

Onan's procedure toward command of Judah, Genesis 38:8–10.

Rights of pregnant woman, Exodus 21:22.

Sterile woman conceived Samson, Judges 13:1–8.

Avoiding alcohol during pregnancy, Judges 13:2–4.

Beyond age of childbearing, Ruth 1:11.

Miscarriage from bad water, 2 Kings 2:19–21 (GNB).

Embryo development, Psalm 139:13–15.

Wonder of body being formed, Ecclesiastes 11:5 (See CEV).

Time of birth, Isaiah 26:17; 66:9.

Fetus in God's care, Isaiah 44:2 (CEV).

God's prenatal plan for Jeremiah, Jeremiah 1:4–5.

No role for men, Jeremiah 30:6.

Nursing, pregnancy, Hosea 1:8.

Pregnant virgin, Matthew 1:25 (LB).

Given son in declining years, Luke 1:5–25.

Five month seclusion, Luke 1:24.

Baby leaped in mother's womb, Luke 1:39–44.

Passion, plan, John 1:13 (LB).

Pain, joy in pregnancy, John 16:21.

Rejoicing although barren, Galatians 4:27.

Natural, miraculous pregnancies, Galatians 4:28 (AB).

Needed physical delivery power, Hebrews 11:11 (AB).

See Abortion, Childbirth, Childless, Conception, Fertility, Gestation, Infertility, Procreation.

PREHISTORIC

"Prehistoric times," Psalm 93:2 (LB).

PREJUDICE

Hagar's choice of wife for Ishmael, Genesis 21:21.

Abraham's concern for wife for Isaac, Genesis 24:1–4.

Wealth, prestige could not numb resentment, Esther 5:10–14.

Prejudice without reason, Psalm 69:4.

Eyes closed to facts, Proverbs 1:29 (LB).

Opinionated person, Proverbs 18:1 (GNB).

Fool's prejudice, Proverbs 18:2.

Prejudice, bribery, Proverbs 28:21 (LB).

One upright man, no upright woman, Ecclesiastes 7:27–28.

Prejudiced listeners, Matthew 13:14–15.

Racist tradition overlooked, Matthew 15:21–28.

Mutual prejudice Samaritans, Jews, Luke 9:51–56.

Family prejudice, Luke 12:49–53.

Refusing to believe revealed truth, John 9:39–41.

Prejudiced toward truth, John 18:37.

Prejudice against new convert, Acts 9:26.

Deliverance from legalism, Acts 10:24–28.

No racial prejudice in God's heart, Acts 10:34–35; 15:5–9.

Poisoning the mind, Acts 14:2.

Acceptance of others, 2 Corinthians 7:2.

Class prejudice in church, James 2:1–8, 16 (See AB).

Darkness of hatred, 1 John 2:9–11.

Viewpoint of world, 1 John 4:5.

See Favoritism, Opinion, Partiality, Racism.

PRELIMINARY

Events preliminary to Parousia, Matthew 24:36–42.

Preliminary parable, Luke 8:4–15.

See Second Coming.

PRELUDE *See Introduction.*

PREMEDITATED

Premeditated betrayal of Jesus, Matthew 26:14–16.

PRENATAL

Son committed before birth, 1 Samuel 1:11–12.

Destiny of unborn, Psalm 139:15, 16.

Called in the womb, Isaiah 49:1–6 (LB).

Prenatal plan for prophet, Jeremiah 1:4–5.

See Predestination.

PREPARATION

Spiritual preparation for future victory, Joshua 3:5.

Dig ditches to receive water, 2 Kings 3:15–17.

Extra containers needed, 2 Kings 4:3–4.

Fetus development, Ecclesiastes 11:5.

Divine preparation far in advance, Isaiah 25:1.

Preparing way of the Lord, Isaiah 40:3.

Instrument of judgment, Ezekiel 21:9 (LB).

Break up unplowed ground, Hosea 10:12.

Preparatory preaching, Matthew 3:1–3; Mark 1:2–8; Luke 3:1–20.

Unprepared among ten virgins, Matthew 25:1–13.

Advance preparation, Mark 11:1–2.

Prayer before important decision, Luke 6:12–16.

Prepared for persecution, Luke 21:12–15.

Prepared to meet evil, Ephesians 6:13.

Prepared mind, spirit, 1 Peter 1:13–15.

See Anticipation, Prayer.

PRESENT See Now.

PRESIDENT

Daniel as president, Daniel 6:2 (KJV, LB).

PRESSURE

Delegating work to others, Exodus 18:17–27.

Waters up to neck, Psalm 69:1.

King Herod yielded to pressure, Matthew 14:6–11.

Divine pressure to fulfill destiny, Luke 12:50.

Night coming, work to do, John 9:4.

Paul's pressure to reach Jerusalem, Acts 20:16.

Compelled to work for living, 1 Corinthians 9:6.

Keep your head in all situations, 2 Timothy 4:5.

See Anxiety, Duress, Stress.

PRESTIGE

Heroes of old, Genesis 6:4.

Dislike of neighbor's wealth, Genesis 26:12–17.

Garments with dignity, honor, Exodus 28:2.

Need for prestige as leader, Numbers 27:20–23.

Captured city named after captor, Numbers 32:42.

God-given prestige, Deuteronomy 2:25; 4:5–6.

Prestige ordained by God, Deuteronomy 26:19; Joshua 6:27; 2 Samuel 7:9; 1 Kings 3:13; Proverbs 8:18.

Prestige from the Lord, Joshua 4:14.

"Ride on white donkeys," Judges 5:10.

Reward of accomplishment, Judges 8:22–23.

Humility over prestigious anointing, 1 Samuel 10:13–22.

Little known sons, daughters, 1 Samuel 14:49.

Mighty have fallen, 2 Samuel 1:27.

Death of great man, 2 Samuel 3:38.

David's name made great, 2 Samuel 7:9; 8:13.

Prestigious Solomon, 1 Kings 4:29–34.

Fame throughout big family, 1 Chronicles 12:30.

David a giant among nations, 1 Chronicles 14:17.

Shepherd boy to king, 1 Chronicles 17:7.

Prestigious exploits, 2 Chronicles 26:15.

Those who seek favors, Job 11:19.

Prestigious treatment remembered, Job 29:7–13.

None prestigious in God's sight, Job 33:6.

Doorkeeper job preferred, Psalm 84:10.

Righteous man remembered, Psalm 112:6.

God blesses small, great alike, Psalm 115:13.

Terminal impact of death, Proverbs 11:7.

A nobody, a somebody, Proverbs 12:9.

Humility before honor, Proverbs 18:12.

Purchase of prestige, Proverbs 18:16; 22:7.

Conduct, conversation linked together, Proverbs 22:11.

Wait for invitation of great men, Proverbs 25:6–7.

Seeking one's own honor, Proverbs 25:27.

Let another praise you, not yourself, Proverbs 27:2.

Prestigious lizards, Proverbs 30:28.

Unrewarding prestige, Ecclesiastes 6:2.

Our prestigious Lord, Isaiah 26:8.

Genuine mark of prestige, Isaiah 32:8.

Wealth does not insure prestige, Jeremiah 22:14–15.

Poor people prominent under Babylonian rule, Jeremiah 39:10; 40:11–12.

Lost national prestige, Jeremiah 51:7–8.

Humiliation supplants prestige, Lamentations 4:12.

Prestige offered dream interpretation, Daniel 2:6.

Jewish youth prestigious in Babylon, Daniel 2:48–49.

Hedonistic motivation, Hosea 4:7.

Complacency among national leaders, Amos 6:1.

Special prestige for great prophet, Zechariah 3:1–9.

Honor to whom due, Malachi 1:6.

Name above all names, Matthew 4:23–25 (See Isaiah 9:6).

Prestigious teaching, Matthew 7:28–29.

Greatest, least, Matthew 11:11; 18:1–5.

Jesus without prestige in His home town, Matthew 13:55–58.

Desire for prestige in spiritual service, Matthew 18:1.

First last, last first, Matthew 19:30; Mark 10:31.

New Testament measure for greatness, Matthew 20:25–28.

Attitude of Jesus toward earthly titles, Matthew 23:1–11.

Role of humility in greatness, Matthew 23:12.

Jesus called those He wanted, Mark 3:13.

Asking for prestige rather than earning it, Mark 10:11–40.

Jesus' commendation of John the Baptist, Luke 7:24–28.

Desire to be greatest in kingdom, Luke 9:46–48.

Exibitionism for prestige, Luke 11:43.

Prestigious clerical robes, Luke 20:46–47.

Prophet in his own country, John 4:44.

Jesus pressured to gain prestige, John 7:1–5.

Friends instead of servants, John 15:14–15.

Prince, Savior, Acts 5:31.

Prestigious sorcerer, Acts 8:9–11.

Respect of Cornelius for Peter, Acts 10:25–26.

Prominent women chose to follow Christ, Acts 17:4.

Insulting someone of high rank, Acts 23:4, 5.

Humble backgrounds, abilities, 1 Corinthians 1:26–29 (See LB).

Paul's Judaism rank, Galatians 1:13–14.

Those who only seem important, Galatians 2:6 (See CEV).

Blessed in Heavenly realms, Ephesians 1:3.

Small man given big position, Ephesians 3:8–9.

Life's highest prestige, Ephesians 3:12.

Social ranking, Ephesians 6:5–9.

Paul could have boasted of former status, Philippians 3:2–11.

Qualifications of Christ as Savior, King, Colossians 1:15–20.

Purpose, means of spiritual success, 2 Thessalonians 1:11–12.

Infamous prestige, 1 Timothy 1:15.

Desire to be overseer, 1 Timothy 3:1.

Credentials in ministry, Titus 1:1–3.

Prestige subordinate to following God's will, Titus 2:9–10.

God's Son superior to angels, Hebrews 1:3–4.

Greatest of all high priests, Hebrew 7:26.

David, Samuel given small mention, Hebrews 11:32.

Pride in humble circumstances, James 1:9 (See LB).

Clothes do not make the man, James 2:1–5.

Identified as children of God, 1 John 3:1–3.

Those who usurp prestige, 3 John 9–10.

Believers as priests, Revelation 1:6.

Seated with the Lord on His throne, Revelation 3:21.

Illumination of angel's presence, Revelation 18:1.

The ultimate prestige, Revelation 21:27.

See Acclaim, Eminent, Fame, Honor.

PRESUMPTION

Motivation for Towel of Babel, Genesis 11:4.

Disobeying the Lord's command, Numbers 14:41–44.

Attitude toward Divine specifications, Numbers 20:8–12.

Questioning Divine promises, Numbers 21:5.

Acting presumptuously, Deuteronomy 1:43 (NKJV).

Speaking other than the Lord's message, Deuteronomy 18:20.

Entering forbidden area, 2 Chronicles 26:16.

Presumptuous sins, Psalm 19:13.

Presumption about future, Proverbs 27:1; Isaiah 56:12; James 4:13–14.

Taking prosperity, life for granted, Luke 12:19.

Presuming God's grace available at man's convenience, Acts 24:25.

See Overconfidence.

PRETENSE

Pretended insanity, 1 Samuel 21:13.

Pretended rapport, 2 Samuel 3:27.

Some pretend wealth, others poverty, Proverbs 13:7.

Bold front, Proverbs 21:29.

Boast of giving but do not give, Proverbs 25:14.

Early morning religiosity, Proverbs 27:14.

Strutting rooster, Proverbs 30:31.

Boast about the Lord, Jeremiah 9:23–24.

Pharaoh only loud noise, Jeremiah 46:17.

King Herod, Magi, Matthew 2:7, 8.

Do not make acts of charity public, Matthew 6:1–4.

Children pretending, Matthew 11:16–17 (LB).

Empty sincerity of Pharisees, Mark 12:15–17.

Those who perform only for pretense, Mark 12:38–40.

"Claiming to be somebody," Acts 5:36.

Pretending to be brothers, Galatians 2:4 (GNB).

Pretending to be what one is not, Galatians 6:12–15.

False humility, Colossians 2:18.

Pretended miracles, 2 Thessalonians 2:9 (CEV).

Making false claim of holy life, 1 John 1:8–10.

Feigning life when spiritually dead, Revelations 3:1.

See Counterfeit, Sham.

PREVARICATE

God cannot lie, Numbers 23:19.

Honest weights, measurements, Deuteronomy 25:13–16.

Prevarication for personal gain, 2 Samuel 1:2–16.

Deliberately writing falsehoods, Jeremiah 8:8.

Friends, brothers untrustworthy, Jeremiah 9:4–8.

Believing a lie, Jeremiah 43:1–7.

See Deceit, Dishonesty, False, Lie.

PREVENTION

Approval of parents, Numbers 30:3–5.

Preventing injury, Deuteronomy 22:8.

Elimination of blacksmiths, 1 Samuel 13:19.

The Lord on our side, Psalm 124:1–5.

Ounce of prevention, Luke 12:39.

Touch nothing unclean, 2 Corinthians 6:17.

See Admonition, Warning.

PREVIEW

Preview only of promised land, Numbers 27:12–14.

Transfiguration preview of glory, Luke 9:28–36.

PRICE

Practice of barter, Ezekiel 27:12–23.

Cheating on weight and cost, Amos 8:5–6.

High price for dance, Mark 6:21–29.

Price of discipleship, John 16:1–4.

See Cost, Discipleship.

PRIDE

Danger of material possessions, Deuteronomy 8:11–20; Psalm 52:7; Proverbs 18:11–12; Jeremiah 48:7.

Small leader demanded humility from strong, Judges 9:14–15.

Improper time for boasting, 1 Samuel 2:1–3.

Divine attitude toward humility, pride, 2 Samuel 22:28; Psalm 138:6.

Boastful attitude to King, 1 Kings 12:10–11.

Sarcasm to proud accusers, Job 12:2–3.

Accused of self-righteousness, Job 34:1–9; 36:4.

Pride numbs spirituality, goodness, Psalm 10:2–11.

Flattering lips, boastful tongue, Psalm 12:4.

Boast in the Lord, Psalm 34:2.

Vanity lessens realization of sin, Psalm 36:2.

Boast in the Lord, Psalm 44:8.

Possessive pride, Psalm 49:11.

Pomp without insight, Psalm 49:20 (Berk.).

Boasting of evil, Psalm 52:1–2.

The Lord hates pride, Proverbs 8:13.

Pride brings destruction, Proverbs 16:18.

"Arrogant pride," Proverbs 21:24 (NKJV).

Patience preferred to pride, Ecclesiastes 7:8.

Proud, conceited, humbled, Isaiah 2:12 (CEV).

Selfish pride, Isaiah 5:21.

Example of humble tools, Isaiah 10:15.

Satanic origination of pride, Isaiah 14:13–15.

Crown of pride, Isaiah 28:1, 3, 5.

God does not yield glory to another, Isaiah 42:8; 48:11.

Spiritual pride, Isaiah 65:5.

No basis for pride, Jeremiah 9:23–24.

Pride, arrogance, Jeremiah 48:29.

Ego offended by faith, Daniel 3:8–20.

Shattered pride, Daniel 4:37 (CEV).

Vain ambition, Daniel 5:20–23.

Proud of wealth, self-righteousness, Hosea 12:8.

Spiritual pride of disobedient people, Amos 4:5.

"We did it on our own," Amos 6:13 (CEV).

Wages of pride, Zephaniah 2:10 (LB).

Fate of carefree people, Zephaniah 2:15.

Blowing your own horn, Matthew 6:2 (CEV).

Desiring kingdom greatness, Matthew 18:1–10.

Vanity denounced by Jesus, Matthew 23:6–12; Mark 12:38–39.

Fruit of the heart, Mark 7:21–23.

Parental pride of Joseph, Mary, Luke 2:33.

Desire to be greatest in kingdom, Luke 9:46–48.

Pride concerning wrong things, Luke 10:17–20.

Vain man, humble man at worship, Luke 18:9–14.

Proud sorcerer, Acts 8:9–10.

Price paid for Herod's pride, Acts 12:19–23.

Intellectual pride in Athens, Acts 17:16–34.

No place for Christian pride, Romans 3:27; 4:2.

Spiritual pride, Romans 4:2–5.

People of low position, Romans 12:16.

Proper Christian pride, Romans 15:17 (LB).

Simple people brought to Christ, 1 Corinthians 1:26–31.

Arrogance regarding spiritual success, 1 Corinthians 4:1–21.

Proud of immorality, 1 Corinthians 5:1–2.

Boasting about local church, 1 Corinthians 5:6 (See AB, CEV).

Intellectual pride, 1 Corinthians 8:1–3; 2 Timothy 3:7.

Proper function, 2 Corinthians 5:12.

Pride about authority from the Lord, 2 Corinthians 9:15; 10:8.

Falsely evaluating one's self, 2 Corinthians 10:12.

Recognize weakness, subdue pride, 2 Corinthians 11:30.

Humbling thorn in flesh, 2 Corinthians 12:7–10.

Danger of conceit, Galatians 5:26.

False estimation of greatness, Galatians 6:3.

Do nothing in vanity, Philippians 2:3.

Boasting about others, 2 Thessalonians 1:4.

Conceit in false doctrine, 1 Timothy 6:3–5 (See GNB).

Take pride in humble circumstances, James 1:9.

God resists proud people, James 4:6.

God gives grace to the humble, 1 Peter 5:5–6.

Empty, boastful words, 2 Peter 2:18.

"Foolish pride," 1 John 2:16 (CEV).

Those who demand first place, 3 John 9.

Blind materialism, Revelation 3:17–18.

Refusing to admit sin, Revelation 18:7–8.

See Arrogance, Conceit, Vanity.

PRIEST

First recorded priesthood, Genesis 14:18 (See Hebrews 5:6–11).

Father of Moses, Exodus 18:1.

Pre-dated giving of law, Exodus 19:22–24.

Neophyte priests, Exodus 24:5.

Priestly lineage, Exodus 27:21; 28:43; 29:9.

Marriage, other rules of priests, Leviticus 21:7–15.

Without blemish, Leviticus 21:17–23.

Priests as leaders, Joshua 3:5; 2 Chronicles 11:13.

Non-taxed priests, Ezra 7:24.

Celibacy evaluated by Jesus, Matthew 19:12.

Jesus not a Levite, Hebrews 7:14.

Royal priesthood, 1 Peter 2:9.

See Clergy.

PRIORITY

God as first priority, Genesis 1:1.

Comparing sun, moon with stars, Genesis 1:16.

God supreme above idols, Leviticus 26:1.

The Lord's portion first priority, Numbers 18:29.

Material security versus God's will, Numbers 32:14–27.

Grief for ark greater than death of sons, 1 Samuel 4:16–18.

Palace 13 years, temple 7 years, 1 Kings 6:37–38; 7:1.

First things first, 2 Chronicles 1:7–12; Proverbs 24:27; Haggai 1:3–4; Matthew 6:33; Luke 9:59–62; 10:38–42.

Priority investing of time, Psalm 84:10.

Time for everything, Ecclesiastes 3:1–8.

Priorities change with progress, Isaiah 28:28.

Missionary, evangelistic priority, Isaiah 52:7.

Witness priority, Ezekiel 3:18–19.

Treasures on earth or in heaven, Matthew 6:19–21.

Purchasing pearl of great value, Matthew 13:45–46.

Forsaking all, Matthew 19:28–30.

First last, last first, Matthew 19:30; 20:16; Mark 10:31.

Last act of Jesus before crucifixion, Matthew 20:29–34.

Morality, materialism, Mark 10:17–25.

Priority commandments, Mark 12:28–34.

Post-resurrection priority, Mark 16:15.

Sinful woman's worship, Luke 7:36–38.

Excited about wrong phenomena, Luke 10:17–20.

Temporal and spiritual, Luke 11:27–28.

Greed over possessions, Luke 12:14–15.

Greatest priority, Luke 12:29–31.

Most highly valued, Luke 16:14–15.

Rich young ruler's priorities, Luke 18:18–23.

Earthly priority, spiritual opportunity, Acts 1:6–7.

Priority in obedience, Acts 5:29.

"Of first importance," 1 Corinthians 15:3 (NASB, NRSV).

Giving priority to stewardship, 2 Corinthians 8:10.

Faith expressed through love, Galatians 5:6.

What matters most, Galatians 6:15.

Most important priorities, 1 Timothy 6:21 (LB); 2 Timothy 1:3 (LB).

Danger of putting money first, 1 Timothy 6:10.

Priority delivery of God's message, Hebrews 1:1–2.

Disgrace for Christ preferred to earthly treasures, Hebrews 11:26.

See Ambition, Goal, Motivation, Values.

PRISON

Egyptian prison, Genesis 40:2–3.

Held in custody for breaking Sabbath, Numbers 15:34.

Prison labor, Judges 16:21.

King imprisoned, released, 2 Kings 24:15; 25:27–29.

Kindness to prisoners, Jeremiah 38:7–28; Acts 16:33; 24:23; 27:1–3.

Life imprisonment, Jeremiah 52:11.

Visiting hours, Matthew 11:2; 25:35–46; Acts 24:23.

Prison evangelism, Acts 16:22–34.

Visitation permitted, Acts 27:3.

Under house arrest, Acts 28:16.

Witness to officials, Philippians 1:13.

Prison fellowship, Colossians 4:10.

Prison convert, Philemon 10.

Empathy for prisoners, Hebrews 13:3.

Released from prison, Hebrews 13:23.

Satan incarcerated, Revelation 20:1–3.

See Arrest, Jail.

PRISONER See Captive, Prison.

PRIVACY

Moment's privacy, Job 10:20.

Disturbing privacy of others, Proverbs 25:17.

Private thoughts of gravity, Daniel 7:28.

Keep stewardship private, Matthew 6:2–4.

Private prayer, Matthew 6:5–6.

Fasting in secret, Matthew 6:16–18.

Futile attempt for privacy, Luke 9:10–11.

Private meeting of leaders, Galatians 2:2 (GNB).

Deeds of darkness, Ephesians 5:8–14.

Urban privacy, 1 Thessalonians 3:1.

See Meditation, Seclusion.

PRIVILEGE

Royal privacy, Judges 3:17–20 (LB).

Use of privilege to glorify God, Daniel 1:9–10.

Privilege brings responsibility, Amos 3:2.

Knowing Divine secrets, Matthew 13:11.

Privileged information, Matthew 13:17; Romans 5:12; 1 Corinthians 2:9–10; Colossians 1:25–27; 1 John 2:20.

Privileged threesome, Mark 5:37.

Much given, much required, Luke 12:48.

Greatest of all privileges, 1 John 3:1–2.

Seated in place of privilege, Revelation 3:21.

Privileged guests, Revelation 19:9.

First resurrection, Revelation 20:6.

See Opportunity, Perks, Right.

PROBATE

Probated will, Hebrews 9:16–17.

See Legacy.

PROBING

Probing deep into the earth, Job 28:1–4.

Glory of kings, Proverbs 25:2.

See Exploration, Search.

PROBLEMS

Giant gives boy no problem, 1 Samuel 17:48.

Overcoming problems with Divine help, 2 Samuel 22:30.

Not blaming God for problems, Job 1:22.

Problems inherent to mortality, Job 5:7.

"From bad to worse," Psalm 25:17 (LB).

Troubles more numerous than hairs of head, Psalm 40:11–12.

The Lord does as He pleases, Psalm 135:6.

Problems test friendship, Proverbs 17:9.

Secret to true relaxation, Proverbs 19:23.

Certainty of answered prayer, Isaiah 49:8.

Thanking God in adverse circumstances, Jeremiah 33:10–11.

More blessings than problems, Zechariah 9:12 (LB).

Disciples feared storm while Jesus slept, Matthew 8:23–27.

Worries of life, Mark 4:19.

Predicted marriage problems, 1 Corinthians 7:28.

The God of all comfort, 2 Corinthians 1:3–4.

Clear marks of disciple, 2 Corinthians 6:3–13.

Blessings surmount problems, Ephesians 1:11–12.

Standing at end of struggle, Ephesians 6:13.

Problems enhance progress, Philippians 1:12.

Sharing problems, Philippians 4:14.

Maturing value of trials and problems, James 1:2–4, 12.

See Difficulty, Enemy, Obstacles, Hindrance.

PROCEDURE

Prayer for protection, Numbers 10:35.

Proper marking of boundaries, Numbers 34:1–12.

Avoid ways of heathen, Deuteronomy 18:9.

Estimate cost, then build, Luke 14:28–30.

See Plan.

PROCESSION

Migration of Joseph's family, Genesis 46:5–7.

Encircling Jericho, Joshua 6:1–20.

Triumphal entry of Jesus, Matthew 21:1–11.

See Marching, Parade.

PROCLAMATION

Nationwide communication, 2 Chronicles 30:1–10; Esther 1:22.

False prophets, Jeremiah 23:16–18; Ezekiel 13:1–3.

Heralding command, Daniel 3:4–7.

Message written with clarity, Habakkuk 2:2.

Angelic proclamation, Luke 2:9–12.

See Announcement, Decree.

PROCRASTINATION

Do not delay offering, Exodus 22:29.
Delayed departure, Judges 19:1–10.
Regal procrastination, Esther 5:8.
Do not wait another day, Proverbs 27:1.
Putting family first, 1 Kings 19:20–21.
No hurry to obey, 2 Chronicles 24:5 (CEV).
Ignoring Word of the Lord, Jeremiah 7:13.
Days not prolonged, Ezekiel 12:22–28.
No delay in the Lord's timing, Habakkuk 2:3; Matthew 24:48–51.
Procrastinators and temple rebuilding, Haggai 1:3–4.
Attempting to delay God's call, Matthew 8:21–22; Luke 9:59–62.
Five procrastinating virgins, Matthew 25:2–13.
Making excuses, Luke 14:16–21.
Rich man, Lazarus, Luke 16:19–31.
No time like present, Acts 24:25.
Now is the day of salvation, 2 Corinthians 6:2.
No more delay, Revelation 10:6.
See Delay, Excuses.

PROCREATION

God's command to His creation, Genesis 1:22, 27–28.
Dominant husband, John 1:13.
See Pregnancy.

PRODUCT

Shortage of manufacturing materials, Exodus 5:6–9.
See Manufacture.

PRODUCTIVITY

Productive in old age, Psalm 92:12–15.
Land that produces sparingly, Isaiah 5:10.
Time to enlarge, Isaiah 54:2.
Good land, unproductive land, Hebrews 6:7–8.
See Agriculture, Horticulture, Prolific.

PROFANITY

Misusing God's name, Exodus 20:7 (AB, GNB); Deuteronomy 5:11 (GNB).
"Damned woman," 2 Kings 9:34 (GNB).

Speaking against the Lord, 2 Chronicles 32:16.
Love to curse, Psalm 109:17 (See Berk.).
Challenging God, Isaiah 5:18–19.
Speech of vile person, Isaiah 32:6 (KJV).
Profaned name sanctified, Ezekiel 36:23 (See KJV).
Purified language, Zephaniah 3:9.
Satan as instructor, 1 Timothy 1:20.
Slandering the Lord's name, James 2:7.
Do not swear by heaven or earth, James 5:12.
See Blasphemy.

PROFESSIONAL

Professional opposition to building temple, Ezra 4:5.
Women skilled in wailing, Jeremiah 9:17–20.
See Skill.

PROFIT

Wisdom's income, Proverbs 3:13–14 (NRSV).
Worthy elders, 1 Timothy 5:17.
Religious profiteering, 1 Timothy 6:5 (AB).

PROFLIGATE

Male donkeys pursuit, Jeremiah 2:24.
Wicked women, Jeremiah 2:33.
Unable to blush, Jeremiah 6:15.
Sow the wind, Hosea 8:7.
See Depravity, Immorality, Lust, Renegade, Vice.

PROFOUND

"Too deep for words," Romans 8:26 (NASB, NRSV).
Complicated wisdom, Ephesians 3:10 (AB).
Difficult to understand, Hebrews 5:11 (See CEV).
Profound name, Revelation 19:12 (AB).
See Intellectual, Simplicity.

PROGNOSIS See Predestination, Prophecy.

PROGRESS

Staying too long in one place, Deuteronomy 1:6–8.
Shepherd boy to king, 1 Chronicles 17:7.
Humble beginning, great future, Job 8:7.
"From strength to strength," Psalm 84:7.

Priorities change with progress, Isaiah 28:28.

Challenge to progress, Isaiah 54:2.

Country born in a day, Isaiah 66:8.

The Lord guides and corrects, Jeremiah 10:23–24.

Growth takes time, Mark 4:28.

Comparing old and new, Luke 5:36–39.

Abounding spiritual progress, Ephesians 3:17–19.

Buying up opportunities, Ephesians 5:15–16.

Difficulties enhance progress, Philippians 1:12.

Progress toward perfection, Philippians 3:12 (LB).

Slow spiritual progress, Hebrews 5:13 (LB).

"Steady goodness," James 3:13 (LB).

Progress in Christian living, 2 Peter 1:5–9.

Making progress, Revelation 2:19 (GNB).

See Accomplishment.

PROJECT

Creator's creation project, Genesis 1:10, 12, 18, 21, 25.

When God terminates project, Genesis 11:1–9.

Delayed temple project, 2 Samuel 7:1–17.

Foundations laid for temple, Ezra 3:10–13.

Commitment to rebuilding wall, Nehemiah 5:14–16.

Project in vain without the Lord, Psalm 127:1.

Determination to fulfill destiny, Psalm 132:1–5.

The Lord's advance planning, Isaiah 25:1.

Ark built by faith, Hebrews 11:7.

See Construction, Development.

PROLIFIC

Thirty sons, thirty daughters, Judges 12:9.

Prolific wisdom, talent, 1 Kings 4:29–34.

PROMINENCE

Death of great man, 2 Samuel 3:38.

City on hill, Matthew 5:14.

First last, last first, Matthew 19:30.

See Fame, Prestige.

PROMISCUITY

Discretion in relationships, Leviticus 18:30.

Defiant sin, Numbers 15:30–31.

Blatant immorality, Numbers 25:6–9.

Illicit relationships among clergy, 1 Samuel 2:22.

Promiscuous judgment, 2 Samuel 12:1–12.

Royal promiscuity, 1 Kings 11:1–3.

Apparent promiscuity, Isaiah 8:3.

Unrequited sexual desire, Ezekiel 16:23–30.

Sibling promiscuity, Ezekiel 23:1–49.

Sexual looseness, 1 Corinthians 6:18 (AB).

See Hedonism, Immorality, Lust, Shame.

PROMISE

God's promise to Noah, Genesis 9:8–16.

God's promise to Abram, Genesis 12:2–3; 13:14–17; 15:2–5.

Childbirth at advanced age, Genesis 16:16; 17:1–21; 21:1–5.

Testing covenant of promise, Genesis 22:1–18 (See 13:16; 15:5).

Making vows, Numbers 30:2–5.

Divine promise to David, 2 Samuel 7:1–16.

Promise fulfilled, 2 Samuel 9:1–13.

Fate of only child, Judges 11:29–39.

Promise keepers, Psalm 76:11 (NKJV); 2 Corinthians 7:1.

Sacred promises, Psalm 108:7 (LB).

Covenant remembered forever, Psalm 111:5; Jeremiah 29:10–11.

Certainty of national restoration, Jeremiah 33:23–26.

"All kinds of promises," Jonah 1:16 (CEV).

Powerful promise, Luke 1:37 (AB).

God keeps His promises, Romans 4:18–25.

God never breaks promise, Romans 9:6 (CEV).

Abraham waited patiently for God's promise, Hebrews 6:13–14.

Jesus, our guarantee, Hebrews 7:22.

See Contract, Covenant, Oath, Pledge, Vow.

PROMISE KEEPERS See Pledge, Promise, Vow.

PROMOTION

Promoted from tending sheep pens, Psalm 78:70.

Let others praise you, Proverbs 27:2.

Babylonian promotions, Daniel 2:48–49.

Disciples promoted to apostles, Luke 6:12–15.

Promote faith, Titus 1:1 (AB).

See Advance, Citation, Publicity.

PROMPT

Prompt results, 2 Chronicles 29:36.

PRONOUN

Capitalized deity pronoun, Matthew 1:18 (AB).

PROOF

Seeing is believing, 1 Kings 10:7; 2 Chronicles 9:6; John 20:8.

"Saw with my own eyes," 1 Kings 10:7 (CEV).

Living proof, 2 Kings 8:5.

Tested promises, Psalm 119:140 (LB).

Evidence turns against accuser, Proverbs 25:8.

Do not betray another's confidence, Proverbs 25:9.

Failure of wise men, Daniel 2:1–11.

Proof of repentance, Matthew 3:8 (CEV).

No need for external evidence, Mark 8:11–12.

Doubter's proof, Luke 1:18–20.

Testimony of man born blind, John 9:25.

Jesus challenged to prove divinity, John 10:22–39.

Crucifixion wounds provide identity, John 20:20–29.

"Proven character," Romans 5:4 (NASB).

Love demonstrated, Romans 5:8.

"Prove yourselves," James 1:22 (NASB).

See Apologetics, Pragmatic, Validity.

PROPERTY

Wealthy Abram, Genesis 13:2.

Greed over scarcity of land, Genesis 13:5–11.

Dispute over property rights, Genesis 21:22–31.

"God's territory," Genesis 32:1–2 (LB).

Old items replaced by new, Genesis 45:20.

Mistreatment of slaves, Exodus 21:20–21.

Animals damage neighbor's property, Exodus 22:5.

Land belong to God, Leviticus 25:23 (GNB).

Delayed of ownership, Leviticus 25:29.

Name on each staff, Numbers 17:1–2.

Priests owned no property, Numbers 18:20.

Distribution of land, Numbers 26:53–56.

Material security versus God's will, Numbers 32:14–27.

Marked boundaries, Numbers 34:1–12.

Inheritance property, Numbers 36:1–9.

Divine warning against greed, Deuteronomy 2:5.

Permanent ownership, Deuteronomy 4:40.

Respecting neighbor's boundary, Deuteronomy 19:14.

Return lost property, Deuteronomy 22:1–3.

Town, country, Deuteronomy 28:3.

Clear forest area, Joshua 17:15–18.

Enjoying benefits developed by others, Joshua 24:13.

Property included wife, Ruth 4:5.

Gift of property, 1 Samuel 27:5–6.

Threshing floor altar site, 2 Samuel 24:18–25.

Well-situated city with poor water, 2 Kings 2:19–22.

Repairing temple, 2 Kings 12:4–5.

Ancestral property, Nehemiah 11:20.

Property of angry man, Esther 8:1 (See 5:9—7:10).

Cheating on boundary stones, Job 24:2.

God's total ownership, Psalm 24:1–2.

Stones, dust of Jerusalem, Psalm 102:14.

Widow's boundaries, Proverbs 15:25.

Ancient boundary stone, Proverbs 22:28; 23:10–11.

Greed for property, Isaiah 5:8–9.

Jeremiah's purchase of field, Jeremiah 32:6–15.

Barren Israel to become fruitful, Jeremiah 32:42–44.

Boasting and trusting in wealth, Jeremiah 49:4.

Land not to be sold, Ezekiel 48:13–14.

Property as prostitution payment, Hosea 2:12 (CEV).

Kingdoms of the world, Matthew 4:8–9.

Jesus owned no property, Matthew 8:20 (See CEV).

Rich man's tomb for Jesus, Matthew 27:57–61.

Plot to murder, steal property, Mark 12:7.

Will probate, Hebrews 9:16–17.

Confiscated property, Hebrews 10:34.

See Ownership, Real Estate, Residence.

PROPHECY

Women prophets, Exodus 15:20; Judges 4:4; 2 Kings 22:14; Nehemiah 6:14; Isaiah 8:3; Luke 2:36–38; Acts 21:9; Revelation 2:20.

Prophetic visions and dreams, Numbers 12:6.

Qualification as a prophet, 1 Samuel 10:12.

Time when peace will cover earth, Psalm 46:8–10.

Pray for peace of Jerusalem, Psalm 122:6.

Mournful, inspired predictions, Isaiah 17:1 (AB).

God fulfills prophet's message, Isaiah 44:26.

End known from beginning, Isaiah 46:10–11.

Prophecy of boiling pot, Jeremiah 1:13–15.

Certainty of God's word, Ezekiel 12:26–28.

False prophecy, Ezekiel 13:1–23.

Prophesy to breath, Ezekiel 37:9.

Futile effort to understand, Daniel 12:4 (GNB).

Meaning of personal prophecy withheld, Daniel 12:8–9, 13.

"It will happen," Habakkuk 2:3 (CEV).

Prophesied name, Matthew 2:23 (CEV).

Pharisees asked for prophetic sign, Matthew 12:38–40.

Forecast weather but not discern signs, Matthew 16:1–4.

"Time comes to an end," Luke 21:24 (CEV).

Isaiah's revelation of Jesus, John 12:37–41.

Prime purpose of prophecy, John 13:19.

Predicting severe famine, Acts 11:28–30.

Resurrection as fulfillment of prophecy, Acts 13:32–39.

Prophecy gift defined, 1 Corinthians 14:22 (LB).

Message of salvation through Abraham, Galatians 3:6–9.

Folly of date setting, 2 Thessalonians 2:1–3 (See LB).

Prophetic intimations, 1 Timothy 1:18 (AB).

Scoffers in last days, 2 Peter 3:3–4.

Needed wisdom, understanding, Revelation 17:9 (GNB).

Do not seal prophecy, Revelation 22:10.

See Dispensations, Divination, Foreknowledge, Fortune-Telling, Last Days, Predestination, Prediction, Sorcery.

PROPHET

Invalid prophet, Deuteronomy 13:1–5.

Anonymous prophets 1 Samuel 2:27; 1 Kings 13:11; Acts 11:27; 13:1; 1 Corinthians 12:28; 14:29.

Prophet's accuracy, 1 Samuel 9:6 (See CEV).

Musical prophets, 1 Samuel 10:5.

Suspected of being a prophet, 1 Samuel 10:11.

Assassination of prophets, 1 Kings 18:4; Matthew 23:37.

Trustworthy prophets, 2 Chronicles 20:20.

Rejected prophets, 2 Chronicles 36:15–16.

No more prophets, Psalm 74:9.

Do not harm prophets, Psalm 105:15.

Professional prophet, Isaiah 3:2 (AB).

Sources of information, Amos 3:7.

Deceitful prophets, Micah 3:5 (CEV).

Prophet without honor, Matthew 13:57.

See Clergy, Prophecy.

PROPHETESS

Musical prophetess, Exodus 15:20–21.

Israel's prophetess leader, Judges 4:4–10.

Intimidating prophetess, Nehemiah 6:14.

Devout widowed prophetess, Luke 2:32–36.

See Prophet.

PROPITIOUS

Seeking at right time, Isaiah 55:6.

New every morning, Lamentations 3:22–24.

PROPOSAL

Fear of refusal, Genesis 24:5.

See Engagement, Marriage.

PROPRIETY

Act of shame, Jeremiah 13:26.

Always right time to do good, Mark 3:1–6.

See Tact.

PROSELYTE

Alien celebrating Passover, Exodus 12:48.
Illustration of stolen harvest, Deuteronomy 28:33.
Converts from Judaism, Acts 6:5; 13:43; 17:4.
See Conversion.

PROSPERITY

Joseph prospered in Egypt, Genesis 39:2.
God's provision, blessing, Deuteronomy 8:7–20.
Fortunes restored, Deuteronomy 30:1–3 (NIV).
Wicked often prosper, Job 21:7.
Prosperity terminated, Job 24:24 (See GNB).
Reward for obeying God, Job 36:11.
Prosperity of Job's remaining years, Job 42:12.
Foolish evaluations, Psalm 30:6–7 (LB).
"Pastures clothed with flocks," Psalm 65:13 (NKJV).
Prisoners find prosperity, Psalm 68:6 (NRSV).
Prosperous hands, Psalm 90:17 (NRSV).
Stealing from poor, giving to rich, Proverbs 22:16.
Prosperous idolaters, Isaiah 2:7–8.
Land "flowing with milk and honey," Jeremiah 11:5.
Prosperous wicked, Jeremiah 12:1–3.
National prosperity, Ezekiel 16:13–14.
Tree of prosperity, Ezekiel 17:22–24.
Rural prosperity, Ezekiel 36:11 (See KJV).
Prosperity linked to conduct, Daniel 4:27.
Fragile prosperity, Hosea 13:15 (CEV).
Lost prosperity returned, Joel 3:1 (CEV).
Spiritual prosperity, 2 Peter 1:2 (AB).
Health, wealth, spiritual vitality, 3 John 2–4.
Stewardship based on personal income, 1 Corinthians 16:2.
See Affluence, Wealth.

PROSTITUTE

Deceived by daughter-in-law, Genesis 38:13–19.
Do not degrade daughter, Leviticus 19:29.
Prostitute's lifestyle, Proverbs 5:1–10; 7:6–27; 9:14–17; Isaiah 23:15–16; Hosea 2:3.
Forgotten prostitute, Isaiah 23:16.
Roadside solicitation, Jeremiah 3:2 (See LB).
Merchandising feminine beauty, Ezekiel 16:15.
Youthful prostitutes, Ezekiel 23:2–3 (LB).
Sexual services as barter, Hosea 2:5.
Property as prostitution payment, Hosea 2:12 (CEV).
Men blamed for prostitution, Hosea 4:13–14 (See CEV).
Wanton lust, Nahum 3:3–4.
Idolatry as prostitution, Revelation 17:2 (AB).
See Adultery, Debauchery, Degradation, Wiles.

PROSTRATE

Prostrate in prayer, Ezra 10:1 (LB, NRSV).

PROTECTION

God's blessing and protection for Ishmael, Genesis 21:9–21.
Prayer for protection, Numbers 10:35.
No curse on those who have been blessed, Numbers 22:12.
City walls to sky, Deuteronomy 9:1.
Threat of iron chariots, Judges 1:19.
Strong tower in besieged city, Judges 9:51.
Safety in fields of Boaz, Ruth 2:4–22.
Unsure of God's protection, 1 Samuel 27:1–2.
Killing in self-defense, 2 Samuel 2:22–23.
Building city around fortress, 1 Chronicles 11:7–9.
Divine protection, Psalm 5:11 (NRSV).
Only sure protection, Psalm 11:1 (LB).
"Walls of a fort," Psalm 31:21 (LB).
"Every storm of life," Psalm 32:7 (LB).
God our refuge, strength, Psalm 46:1–3.
"Sheltered olive tree," Psalm 52:8 (LB).
The Lord as protector, Psalm 121:3 (CEV).
"Powerful arm," Psalm 138:7 (CEV).
Unprotected vineyard, Isaiah 5:5.
Protection against evil strategy, Isaiah 8:10.
Depending on military protection, Isaiah 31:1.
Undependable resource, Isaiah 36:6.
Angel of the Lord destroys enemy soldiers, Isaiah 37:36.
Those called by His name need fear no danger, Isaiah 43:1–2.

No protective charm, Jeremiah 7:4 (LB).

Message of boldness, conduct of coward, Jeremiah 26:13–15, 20–24.

Protection in trouble and persecution, Jeremiah 42:1–22.

Wise dove, Jeremiah 48:28.

Safety in midst of peril, Ezekiel 34:25.

Protection in fiery furnace, Daniel 3:22–27.

Daniel in lion's den, Daniel 6:13–24.

Gates wide open to enemy, Nahum 3:13.

Jerusalem, city without walls, Zechariah 2:3–5.

Personal care, Zechariah 10:12 (LB).

Escape to Egypt, Matthew 2:12–15.

Value of sparrow, value of soul, Matthew 10:28–30.

Jesus requested protection, Mark 3:9 (LB).

Jesus not die before His time, Luke 4:28–30; John 7:30.

Trusting the Lord, trusting in weapons, Luke 22:35–38.

Protection from evil one, John 17:15.

Protection of night, Acts 17:10.

Assured divine protection, Acts 18:9–11.

Protected against murder threat, Acts 23:12–24.

Shield of faith, Ephesians 6:16.

Ministering spirits to those who believe, Hebrews 1:14.

"Run to God for safety," Hebrews 6:18 (CEV).

Shielded by God's power, 1 Peter 1:5.

Kept safe from evil one, 1 John 5:18–19.

Crying out for protection, Revelation 6:15–17.

See Refuge, Safety, Shelter.

PROTEST

Attacking God, Job 15:13 (CEV).

Stripped, barefoot, Isaiah 20:2–4.

Entire city in protest, Acts 19:23–41.

"Argue with God," Romans 9:20 (NRSV).

See Mob Psychology, Rebellion.

PROTOCOL

Nocturnal conduct of Boaz and Ruth, Ruth 3:7–15.

Lack of respect, Esther 5:9–10.

Passover protocol, Mark 14:1–2.

Going through proper channels, Philemon 12–14.

See Courtesy, Propriety.

PROTOTYPE

Example of persecuted prophets, Matthew 5:11–12.

Prototype prayer, Matthew 6:9–13.

Deserving right to be heard, 2 Corinthians 4:1–2.

Unselfishness prototype, 2 Corinthians 8:7–9.

See Example, Model, Original.

PROVERBS

Three thousand proverbs, 1 Kings 4:32.

Origin of saying, 1 Samuel 10:11–12.

Deeds reveal person, 1 Samuel 24:13.

Purpose of proverbs, Proverbs 1:1–6.

Research into proverbs, Ecclesiastes 12:9.

Example outside Book of Proverbs, Ezekiel 16:44.

Censored proverb, Ezekiel 18:2–4.

See Literature, Poetry, Wisdom.

PROVISION

Holy Spirit's provision in creation, Genesis 1:2.

God speaks, events occur, Genesis 1:9, 11, 14.

Provision for loyal Abraham, Genesis 22:1–14.

Carts provided for Joseph's brothers, Genesis 45:16–20.

Springs, palm trees, Exodus 15:27.

Provision needed, nothing more, Exodus 16:16–18.

God's presence, ultimate provision, Exodus 33:15.

Ebenezer, the Lord's help, 1 Samuel 7:12.

No help from king, 2 Kings 6:26–27.

Bread from heaven, Nehemiah 9:15.

Strength comes from God, Psalm 18:32.

Provision in bad times, Psalm 37:18–19 (See GNB).

Divine provision recalled in old age, Psalm 37:25.

Wealth of earth belongs to God, Psalm 50:9–15.

God's love, strength, Psalm 62:11–12.

Rain provided for crops, pastures, Psalm 65:9–13.

God's blessing on those who praise Him, Psalm 67:5–6.

Help from the Lord's hand, Psalm 109:26–27.

Eternal faithfulness, Psalms 117:2; 118:29.

Barns filled, flocks abundant, Psalm 144:13.

Food for righteous, Proverbs 10:3.

Happiness from honesty, God's provision, Proverbs 30:7–9.

Strength provided each morning, Isaiah 33:2; Lamentations 3:23; Zephaniah 3:5.

Certain supply of need, guidance, Isaiah 49:10.

Dying earth, Isaiah 51:6.

God's righteousness lasts forever, Isaiah 51:8.

The Lord will guide, Isaiah 58:11.

Fate of good, evil, Isaiah 65:13–14.

Turning away from provision, Jeremiah 2:13–18.

Nothing too hard for the Lord, Jeremiah 32:17, 27.

Protection in fiery furnace, Daniel 3:22–27.

Daniel in lion's den, Daniel 6:13–24.

Jonah and great fish, Jonah 1:17.

Not by might nor by power, Zechariah 4:6.

Provision for nature and believers, Matthew 6:25–34; Luke 12:22–31.

Income provided for twelve apostles, Matthew 10:9–10.

Feeding five thousand, Matthew 14:13–21; Mark 6:35–44.

Coin in fish's mouth, Matthew 17:24–27.

God's goodness in answer to prayer, Luke 11:5–13.

Given words to speak, Luke 21:15.

Special provision sustained Jesus, John 4:31–34.

Promised answer to prayer, John 14:13–14.

Provision for our greatest need, Romans 5:6–8.

Increased need, increased provision, Romans 5:20.

Right of apostle to receive provision, 1 Corinthians 9:7–14.

Made competent for ministry, 2 Corinthians 3:6 (NIV).

Total provision, 2 Corinthians 9:10–11.

God knows our needs, Ephesians 1:8 (LB).

Promised resurrection power, Ephesians 1:18–21; 3:20–21.

Concern for pastor, Philippians 4:10–19.

Provision for everything, Philippians 4:13.

Promise as prayer, Philippians 4:19 (CEV).

Spiritual need provided in Christ, Colossians 1:15–23.

Mighty strength provided, Colossians 1:29 (See GNB).

Given strength, 1 Timothy 1:12.

Payment for those in Christian work, 1 Timothy 5:17–18.

Nothing into the world, nothing out, 1 Timothy 6:6–8.

Confidence in the One whom we believe, 2 Timothy 1:12.

Provision when friends desert, 2 Timothy 4:16–18.

Equipped by the God of peace, Hebrews 13:20–21.

Every good gift from above, James 1:16–27.

Cast all cares upon the Lord, 1 Peter 5:7.

Provision for spiritual and material welfare, 2 Peter 1:3.

God's best in abundance, Jude 2.

Never again hunger or thirst, Revelation 7:16.

See Abundance, Assistance, Need, Supplies, Support.

PROVOCATION

Trouble caused by carelessness, Exodus 21:35–36.

Prayer for protection, Numbers 10:35.

Foolish sins, Numbers 12:11.

Successfully facing formidable opponent, Numbers 21:21–26.

Upset by criticism, Job 20:2–3.

Giving heed to instruction, Proverbs 16:20.

Daring to scoff at the Lord's name, Isaiah 36:18–21; 37:6.

At odds with one's Maker, Isaiah 45:9.

Ignoring the word of the Lord, Jeremiah 7:13.

Mixing human blood with sacrifices, Luke 13:1.

Attitude of prodigal son's brother, Luke 15:25–32.
See Aggressive, Dispute, Trouble.

PRUDENCE

Joseph in Potiphar's house, Genesis 39:4–10.
Disciplined conduct, Psalms 39:1; 112:1.
"Learn prudence," Proverbs 8:5 (NRSV).
Circumspective, Proverbs 14:8–18.
Open to counsel, Proverbs 24:6.
Prudent response, Daniel 2:14 (AB).
Faithful, prudent, Luke 12:42 (NRSV).
See Discernment, Discretion, Tact.

PRURIENT *See Hedonism, Immorality, Lust.*

PSALMS

Preview of David's songs, 2 Samuel 22:1–51.
Singer of psalms, 2 Samuel 23:1.
David quoted, Luke 20:42; Acts 13:33, 35.
Communicating with Psalms, Ephesians 5:19; Colossians 3:16.
Sing Psalms, James 5:13 (NKJV).
See Hymn, Music, Poetry, Singing.

PSALTRIES

Prophet's music, 1 Samuel 10:5.
Psaltries resounding, 2 Samuel 6:5.
Praising God, 1 Chronicles 13:8.
Levite musicians, 2 Chronicles 5:12.
Prelude to heathen worship, Daniel 3:5.
See Music.

PSYCHIATRY

Renewed by Scripture, Psalm 119:93.
Mental renewing, Romans 12:1–2.
See Mental Health.

PSYCHOLOGY

Careful speech, Genesis 31:24, 29.
Public relations approach, 1 Kings 1:42.
Appealing to ego in protesting, Ezra 4:14.
Mob psychology at trial of Jesus, Matthew 27:15–26; Mark 15:11–15 (See Matthew 21:1–11; Mark 11:8–10).
Crowd psychology, John 6:1, 2.
See Mob Psychology.

PUBERTY

Description of puberty, Ezekiel 16:5–9.
See Adolescence.

PUBLICANS

Reputation of tax collectors, Matthew 5:46; 9:11; 11:19; 18:15–17.
Calling of Matthew, Matthew 9:9–13.
Conversion examples, Matthew 21:32.
Calling of Levi, Mark 2:14; Luke 5:27.
Change of values, Luke 3:12–14.
Two kinds of sinners, Luke 18:9–14.
Jesus and Zacchaeus, Luke 19:1–10.
See Laity, Secular.

PUBLICATION

Published word, Psalm 68:11 (NKJV).
Endless supply of books, Ecclesiastes 12:12.
See Books.

PUBLICITY

Let others praise you, Proverbs 27:2.
Word-of-mouth publicity, Matthew 4:24; 9:26; Luke 5:12–15.
Jesus urged to seek publicity, John 7:1–5 (See Berk.).
Not looking for praise, 1 Thessalonians 2:6.
See Media.

PUBLIC OPINION

Life spared by public opinion, 1 Samuel 14:45.
Majority procedure, Matthew 7:13–14.
Danger of public reaction, Matthew 14:5.
Jesus before Pilate, Matthew 27:19–26; Mark 15:1–15.
Minority fears, John 7:13.
Innocent man made political ploy, Acts 12:3.
See Consensus, Mob Psychology, Plebiscite.

PUBLIC RELATIONS

Public relations approach, 1 Kings 1:42.
Affairs of people, Nehemiah 11:24.
See Politics.

PYRAMID

PUBLISH

"Publish the name of the Lord," Deuteronomy 32:3 (KJV).

"Published peace," Nahum 1:15 (KJV).

PUGILIST *See Boxing.*

PULPIT

Ezra standing above people, Nehemiah 8:5.

PULSE *See Heart, Heartbeat.*

PUNGENT *See Fragrance.*

PUNISHMENT

Death penalty, Genesis 9:5–6; Numbers 35:16–21.

Punishment by fire, Numbers 11:1.

Swallowed by earth, Numbers 16:31–33.

Whipping with thorns and briers, Judges 8:16.

Punishment for disgracing sister, 2 Samuel 13:23–29.

Better God's punishment than men's, 2 Samuel 24:13–14.

Israel uprooted, 2 Chronicles 7:20.

Less punishment than deserved, Ezra 9:13.

Fair punishment, Nehemiah 9:33 (CEV).

God has right to judge, Psalm 51:4.

Merciful punishment, Psalm 89:30–34.

Divine forgiveness and punishment, Psalm 99:8.

Punishment short of death, Psalm 118:18.

God's arm coming down in punishment, Isaiah 30:30.

Sins paid back, Isaiah 65:6.

God uses dictators, brings them into judgment, Jeremiah 25:11–14.

Sword that cannot rest, Jeremiah 47:6–7.

Cost for doubting an angel, Luke 1:18–20.

Ananias and Sapphira, Acts 5:1–11.

Guards who failed to hold Peter in prison, Acts 12:18–19.

See Discipline, Judgment, Lashes, Prison, Torture.

PURCHASE

Conditional terms, Ruth 4:1–10.

Barter purchase, Ezekiel 27:12–23.

Deposit on final redemption, Ephesians 1:14.

See Barter, Marketing.

PURGE

Recruited to turn against king, 2 Kings 9:14–24.

Reformation in Israel, 2 Kings 9—10.

PURITY

Circumcision at advanced age, Genesis 17:10–27.

Guided by the Lord in moral conduct, Genesis 20:1–18.

Clear oil used in tabernacle, Exodus 27:20.

Pure cannot come from impure, Job 14:4.

Personal purity brings God's blessing, Psalm 18:20–21.

Whiter than snow, Psalm 51:7.

Purity of heart, a gift from God, Psalm 51:10.
Adolescence depicted, Ezekiel 16:5–13.
Women violated, Ezekiel 22:10.
Dead Sea purified, Ezekiel 47:8 (LB).
The Lord has first right to the body, 1 Corinthians 6:13–16.
Purity through Holy Spirit, Galatians 5:16.
Mark of true Christian, Ephesians 5:1–3.
"Love incorruptible," Ephesians 6:24 (NASB).
"Without stain or reproach," 1 Timothy 6:14 (NASB).
Purified by blessed hope, Titus 2:11–14.
Call to holiness, 1 Peter 1:13–16.
Purified by obeying truth, 1 Peter 1:22.
Angels' pure attire, Revelation 15:6.
Garments of bride in heaven, Revelation 19:7–8.
See Chastity, Holiness, Transformation, Virtue.

PURPOSE

Hiding purpose of actions, 1 Samuel 16:1–5.
Nehemiah's avowed purpose to rebuild wall, Nehemiah 5:14–16.
Eloquent description of purpose, Isaiah 32:8.
Divine purpose in creating, Isaiah 45:18.
God never acts without cause, Ezekiel 14:23.
Salt, light in world, Matthew 5:13–16.
"Kind intention," Ephesians 1:5 (NASB).
Filled with knowledge of God's will, Colossians 1:9–12.
Properly motivated, 1 Thessalonians 1:3.
See Determination, Motivation.

PURSE

Sharing common purse, Proverbs 1:14.
Expense money for long journey, Proverbs 7:19–20.
Bags of gold, Isaiah 46:6.
Journey by faith, Matthew 10:9–10; Luke 10:4; 22:35.
Sly fingers steal, John 12:6.
See Money.

PURSUIT

Pursue peace, Psalm 34:14.
Pursue righteousness, Proverbs 15:9 (NIV).
"Pursue love," 1 Corinthians 14:1 (NASB, NKJV, NRSV).
See Search.

PUTRID

Divine preservation of food, Exodus 16:19–24.
Ultimate end of man, Job 13:28.
Flies, perfume, Ecclesiastes 10:1.
Stench instead of fragrance, Isaiah 3:24.
Worms in dead bodies, Isaiah 66:24.
Drunken nausea, Jeremiah 23:27; 48:26.
Place for vultures, Luke 17:37.
See Decay, Filth.

PYRAMID

Monument in Egypt, Isaiah 19:19–20. (Note: Some think these verses refer to the Great Pyramid.)

Q

QUACK

Worthless physicians, Job 13:4.

QUALIFICATION

Witnessing about personal experience, Psalm 51:10–13.
Qualification for answered prayer, Psalm 91:14–16.
Worthy things to say, Proverbs 8:6.
Qualifications for following Jesus, Luke 9:23–26.
Savior, King qualifications, Colossians 1:15–20.
Leadership qualification, 1 Timothy 3:1–13.
Widow's registry qualification, 1 Timothy 5:9–10.
Qualified to succeed, Hebrews 13:20–21.
Redeemer qualified to judge, Revelation 5:1–9.
See Ability.

QUALITY

High quality gold, Genesis 2:12 (Berk.).
Clear oil used in tabernacle, Exodus 27:20.
Durable clothing, Deuteronomy 8:4.

Vineyard's gleaning exceeds another's harvest, Judges 8:2.

Quality talent, Psalm 45:1.

Purposeful activity, Ecclesiastes 4:6.

Tested for quality, Jeremiah 6:27; 1 Corinthians 3:13 (NASB).

New every day, Lamentations 3:22–24.

Salt loses saltiness, Luke 14:34–35.

Needed qualities, 2 Peter 1:5–8.

Divine love's incredible quality, 1 John 3:1 (AB).

See Exemplary, Model, Value.

QUALMS

Needless worry, Matthew 6:25–27.

Timid and bold, 2 Corinthians 10:1.

See Anxiety, Apprehension, Timidity, Worry.

QUANTITY

"Tale of the bricks," Exodus 58 (KJV).

Little is much, Deuteronomy 7:7; Psalm 37:16 (GNB).

Honest weights and measures, Deuteronomy 25:13–16.

Putting confidence in numerical strength, Judges 7:2, 12.

Thirty sons, thirty daughters, Judges 12:9.

Weight of misery, Job 6:2–3.

"Heaps" brought to temple, 2 Chronicles 31:5–8.

Size of one's gift, 2 Corinthians 8:12.

Sins piled up to heaven, Revelation 18:4–5 (NIV).

See Dimensions, Immensity, Weight.

QUARANTINE

Preventing infection from spreading, Leviticus 13:45–46.

Afflicted with leprosy, 2 Kings 15:5.

See Disease, Health.

QUARREL

First recorded quarrel, Genesis 4:8 (Berk.).

Many quarrels, Exodus 18:13.

Evidence turns against accuser, Proverbs 25:8.

Settle misunderstandings quickly, Matthew 5:25.

How to solve disagreement between brothers, Matthew 18:15–17.

Contest enemy or seek peace, Luke 14:31–32.

Forgiveness for enemy, Romans 5:10.

Women's quarrel, Philippians 4:2 (See LB).

Teachings cause quarrels, 1 Timothy 1:3–4.

"Fight over words," 2 Timothy 2:14 (GNB).

See Argument, Dispute, Controversy, Strife.

QUEEN OF HEAVEN

Pagan worship, Jeremiah 44:17, 19, 25.

QUESTION

Satan's tantalizing questions, Genesis 3:1 (LB).

Question mark food, Exodus 16:31 (LB).

Questions for spies to Canaan, Numbers 13:18–20.

God asks questions, Numbers 14:11.

Questions for subversion, Judges 16:6–18.

Mother-in-law's inquiry, Ruth 3:16–17.

All questions answered, 1 Kings 10:1–3.

Divine actions questioned, 2 Kings 6:33.

Most ignorant of men, Proverbs 30:2–4.

Answers to unasked questions, Isaiah 65:1 (CEV).

Wise put to shame, Jeremiah 8:9.

Jeremiah questioned God's way, Jeremiah 12:1.

Search for answer, Jonah 1:7–8.

Inquiring about Divine love, Malachi 1:2.

Unable to understand angels, Luke 1:18, 34.

Paul accused of being terrorist, Acts 21:38.

See Cross-Examination, Doubt.

QUICKSAND

Sinking in mire, Psalm 69:2.

QUIET See Silence.

QUIET TIME

Pre-dawn prayer in time of trouble, Psalm 119:147.

Strength every morning, Isaiah 33:2.

Outdoor retreat, Ezekiel 3:22–23.

Closet prayer, Matthew 6:5–6.

QUICKSAND

WELL, ACCORDING TO THE MAP WE'RE ALMOST THERE.

Jesus retired to hills, Matthew 14:23; 15:29.
Example of Jesus in early morning, Mark 1:35.
Finding quiet place, Mark 6:31; 7:24.
Jesus sought solitude, Luke 4:42; 5:16.
Spending night in prayer, Luke 6:12.
Gethsemane prayer, Luke 22:41.
Roof prayer, Acts 10:9 (CEV).
See Devotions, Intercession, Prayer.

QUINTESSENTIAL

God's quintessential love, John 3:16.
Exalted Savior, Ephesians 1:21.
Name above all names, Philippians 2:9–10.
Unprecedented promise, provision, 1 Corinthians 2:9.

QUOTA

Daily quota, Exodus 5:13 (NKJV).

R

RACE

Choice of wife for Ishmael, Genesis 21:21
A wife for Isaac, Genesis 24:1–4.
Black is beautiful, Song of Songs 1:5 (NRSV).
All nations important to God, Amos 9:7 (CEV).

RACISM

Tension between Arabs, Israel, Genesis 21:8–10.
Racial intermarriage forbidden, Genesis 28:1.
Egyptians and Hebrews, Genesis 43:32.
Moses' foreign wife, Numbers 12:1.
Request to marry heathen, 1 Kings 2:13–25.
Pledge to avoid intermarriage, Nehemiah 10:30.

Those not assisting Israelites, Nehemiah 13:1–3.
Queen's secret identity, Esther 2:10.
Anti-Semitic bribery, Esther 3:8–9.
Continual racial resentment, Esther 5:10–14.
Hated without reason, Psalm 69:4.
Dark and lovely, Song of Songs 1:6 (See LB).
Noise of aliens, Isaiah 25:5.
Skin color by Creator's choice, Jeremiah 13:23.
Jesus overlooked racist tradition, Matthew 15:21–28.
Treatment given gentiles, Matthew 20:25.
Despised Gentile, Mark 7:26 (LB).
Black man helped Jesus carry cross, Mark 15:21; 15:21. (Note: Cyrene a city in North Africa).

Prophet from Galilee, John 7:41–52.
Deliverance from racism, Acts 10:24–28.
No racial prejudice with the Lord, Acts 10:34–35; 15:5–8.
Avoid preferences, prejudices, 1 Corinthians 4:6 (GNB); James 2:1–4.
All one in Christ, Galatians 3:28.
See Discrimination, Prejudice.

RAIN

First rainfall, Genesis 7:11–12 (See 2:4–6).
Plague of hail, Exodus 9:22–34.
Rainless sky, parched earth, Leviticus 26:19–20.
Rain denied, Deuteronomy 11:17; 28:24.
Nature's abundant blessings, Deuteronomy 33:13–16.
Thunder and rain, 1 Samuel 12:18.
Heavy rain, 1 Kings 18:41.
Hindered by rain, Ezra 10:9.
Outdoor conference in downpour, Ezra 10:10–15 (CEV).
Rainy season, Ezra 10:13.
Evaporation, rain, Job 36:27–28; 37:11.
"Waterskins of the heavens," Job 38:37 (NRSV).
"Thick clouds dark with water," Psalm 18:11 (NRSV).
Gift of north wind, Proverbs 25:23.
Heavy rain no value, Proverbs 28:3.
Storage for rain, Ecclesiastes 1:7.
Accurate meterological information, Ecclesiastes 11:3.
Rain like Scripture, Isaiah 55:10–11.
"Idols can't send rain," Jeremiah 14:22 (CEV).
Autumn and spring rains, Joel 2:23; Acts 14:17.
Ocean evaporation, rain, Amos 5:8.
Formation of clouds and rainfall, Amos 9:6.
Dew from heavens, Zechariah 8:12.
Prayer for rain, Zechariah 10:1 (LB).
Rain withheld as judgment, Zechariah 14:17.
Rain no respecter of persons, Matthew 5:45.
Predicting rain, Luke 12:54.
Patient farmer awaiting rain, James 5:7.
See Meteorology, Weather.

RAINBOW

Bow in sky, Genesis 9:13, 16 (KJV).

RALLY

Sacred day, Numbers 29:1.
Vast assembly, 1 Kings 8:65.
See Congregation.

RANK

Least and greatest, Jeremiah 42:1–3.
Social ranking, Ephesians 6:5–9.
Those who demand first place, 3 John 9.
See Position.

RANSOM

Christ our ransom, Matthew 20:28; 1 Timothy 2:6.

RAPE

Men raping men, Genesis 19:5 (LB).
Infatuation, adultery, Genesis 34:1–19.
Girl's scream unheard, Deuteronomy 22:25–27.
Rape of half-sister, 2 Samuel 13:1–19.
Accusation of rape, Esther 7:8.
Mistreated captives, Isaiah 13:16; Zechariah 14:2.
Plight of Jerusalem women, Lamentations 5:11.
See Incest.

RAPPORT

Rapport between God's people, Leviticus 26:1–13.
Friend or enemy, Joshua 5:13.
Samson and Philistine woman, Judges 14:7.
Rapport between old man, boy, 1 Samuel 3:1–18.
Heart and soul agreement, 1 Samuel 14:7 (NIV).
Rapport between, David, Jonathan, 1 Samuel 18:1–4.
Deceitful rapport, 2 Samuel 3:27.
Rapport rejected, 2 Samuel 10:1–4 (LB).
Absalom won hearts of people, 2 Samuel 15:1–6.
David's rapport with men of Judah, 2 Samuel 19:14.
World-wide rapport, 1 Kings 10:23–24.

Strange rapport donkey, lion, 1 Kings 13:23–28.

King's rapport with people, 2 Chronicles 1:1.

Rapport between man, God, Psalm 85:10–11.

Filial rapport, Proverbs 4:3–4.

No rapport between righteous and wicked, Proverbs 29:27.

Marital rapport, Proverbs 31:11.

Friends and brothers not trusted, Jeremiah 9:4–5.

Divinely-given rapport, Daniel 1:9 (See NKJV).

Jesus criticized for rapport with sinners, Matthew 9:10–12.

"Side with My party," Matthew 19:21 (AB).

Rapport as avenue of witness, John 13:34–35.

Friends instead of servants, John 15:14–15.

Early Christian community, Acts 2:46–47.

Rapport in synagogue, Acts 13:13–15.

Mutual occupation, Acts 18:1–3.

Grief at time of separation, Acts 20:36–38.

Speaking in people's language, Acts 22:2.

Paul's reputation as former Pharisee, Acts 23:6.

Friends in far away place, Acts 28:15.

Prayer for acceptable service, Romans 15:31–32.

Rapport among believers, 1 Corinthians 1:10–17.

Put visitor at ease, 1 Corinthians 16:10–11 (AB).

Differing reactions to Christian personality, 2 Corinthians 2:15–16.

Hearts opening to each other, 2 Corinthians 6:11–13 (See GNB).

Rapport between leader, followers, 2 Corinthians 7:2–4.

Rapport between ministers of Gospel, 2 Corinthians 8:16–18.

Men pleasers, Galatians 1:10 (Berk.).

Paul's visit with Peter in Jerusalem, Galatians 1:18.

Given right hand of fellowship, Galatians 2:9–10.

Share burdens, Galatians 6:2.

Rapport given by the Spirit, Ephesians 4:3 (GNB).

Like father and son, Philippians 2:22.

Concern for followers' development, Colossians 2:1–5.

Family rapport, Colossians 3:18–21.

Actions toward others, Colossians 4:5.

Wise use of names, Colossians 4:7–17.

Gentle like mother, 1 Thessalonians 2:7.

Overflowing rapport among believers, 1 Thessalonians 3:12.

Enriching fellowship, 2 Thessalonians 1:3–4.

No place for arguments and quarrels, 2 Timothy 2:23–24.

Compliments precede request, Philemon 1–7.

Confident of rapport, Philemon 21.

How Jesus identified with mankind, Hebrews 2:17–18.

Empirical rapport, Hebrews 5:1–2 (See AB).

Loving as believers, Hebrews 13:1.

Known as God's friend, James 2:21–23.

Confessing sins one to another, James 5:16.

Loving deeply from heart, 1 Peter 1:22.

Keys to rapport, 1 Peter 3:8–9; 4:8–10.

Fellowship in difficult times, Revelation 1:9.

See Familiarity, Fellowship, Unanimity.

RAPTURE

Time of Christ's return kept secret, Mark 13:32.

Watching for the Lord to come, Luke 12:35–40.

Those dead, those alive, John 11:25.

Promise of Christ's return, John 14:3.

Mistaken information about rapture, John 21:20–23.

Resurrection at rapture, 1 Corinthians 15:51–55.

"May the Lord come soon," 1 Corinthians 16:22 (CEV).

Waiting for Christ's return, 1 Thessalonians 1:10.

Those prepared for rapture, 1 Thessalonians 3:13.

Folly of date setting, 2 Thessalonians 2:1–3.

Purified by blessed hope, Titus 2:11–14.

Coming Lord and King, Hebrews 9:24–28.

Living hope, 1 Peter 1:3–5.

Scoffers in last days, 2 Peter 3:3–4.

See Second Coming.

RATIONAL

Prodigal came to his senses, Luke 15:17.
Wisdom of Gamaliel, Acts 5:30–40.
Keep your head in all situations, 2 Timothy 4:5 (NIV).
See Reason.

RATIONALIZE

Questioning misfortune, Judges 6:13.
Rationalized obedience, 1 Samuel 15:7–31.
Misunderstood goodwill gesture, 2 Samuel 10:1–4.
Putting blame on God, 2 Kings 6:33.
Disputing mercy, justice of God's ways, Ezekiel 33:10–20.
See Pragmatic.

RATS

Golden rats, 1 Samuel 6:15, 18.

RAW MATERIAL

Wealth in the earth, Genesis 2:11–12.
Abundant exotic material, 2 Chronicles 1:15.
Wood for making gods, cooking fires, Isaiah 44:14–20.
Wood fit for a king, Ezekiel 19:11.
Cheating on weight, cost, Amos 8:5–6.
See Natural Resources.

REACTION

Negative reaction of Cain, Genesis 4:3–7.
Insulted—be happy, excited, Matthew 5:11–12 (CEV).
"Very upset," Matthew 26:22 (GNB).
Nativity reactions, Luke 2:19–20.
Traumatic congregational reaction, Acts 5:11 (AB).
Differing reactions to converts, 2 Corinthians 2:15–16.
Disciplined reactions, James 1:19–20.
See Answer, Attitude, Response.

READING

Message to read, Deuteronomy 6:9.
Literacy program, Deuteronomy 11:19–21.
Reading with clarity, Nehemiah 8:8.
Many books cause weariness, Ecclesiastes 12:12.

Consumed scroll sweet as honey, Ezekiel 3:1–3.
Posted sign, John 19:19–20.
Purposeful reading, John 20:31–32.
Reading without understanding, Acts 8:26–39.
Important reading, Colossians 4:16.
Public reading of Scripture, 1 Timothy 4:13.
Scrolls, parchments, 2 Timothy 4:13.
See Literacy.

READY

Ready to travel, Exodus 12:11.
Getting ready for death, 1 Kings 20:1.
Ready for rapture, Matthew 24:44.
Ready to learn, Luke 11:1.
Ready for salvation, Acts 16:30.
Eagerly ready to serve, 2 Corinthians 8:19; 9:2; 1 Peter 5:2.
Prepared for good work, 2 Timothy 2:21; Titus 3:1.
Ready to witness, 1 Peter 3:15.
See Awareness, Alert, Preparation.

REAL ESTATE

Desirable land, Genesis 11:2; 13:10 (LB).
Purchase of tent site, Genesis 33:19.
Government purchasing agent, Genesis 47:20.
Delay of ownership, Leviticus 25:29.
Israel's permanent deed, Deuteronomy 4:40.
Waterfront property, Deuteronomy 8:7.
Boundary line, Deuteronomy 27:17.
Clearing forest, Joshua 17:14–18.
Selecting property, Joshua 18:8–10 (LB).
Marriage complication, Ruth 4:1–6 (See LB).
Widow's land for sale, Ruth 4:3.
Purchase of land for altar, 2 Samuel 24:24.
Handfuls of dust, 1 Kings 20:10.
Not for sale, 1 Kings 21:1–16.
Satisfactory terrain, bad water, 2 Kings 2:19.
Too busy to buy real estate, Nehemiah 5:16.
No new houses, Nehemiah 7:4 (CED).
Evil acquisition, Job 20:19 (Berk.).
Pleasant boundaries, Psalm 16:6.
All property belongs to God, Psalm 24:1.

Widow's real estate protected, Proverbs 15:25.

Woman involved in land purchase, Proverbs 31:16.

Greed for property, Isaiah 5:8.

Purchase of field, Jeremiah 32:6-15.

Land sales resume, Jeremiah 32:43-44.

Seller unable to recover land, Ezekiel 7:13.

Jesus owned no property, Matthew 8:20.

Leased land, Matthew 21:33-41; Mark 12:1-9.

Living in rented house, Acts 28:30.

See Ownership, Parsonage, Possessions, Property, Residence.

REALISM

Negative and positive viewpoints, Numbers 13:17-33.

The Lord's demands within reach, Deuteronomy 30:11.

REALITY

Scripture blessings and curses, Joshua 8:34.

Witnessing to personal experience, Psalm 51:10-13.

Like a dream, Psalm 126:1 (NRSV).

Awakening to find dream untrue, Isaiah 29:8.

Reality precludes fasting, Mark 2:18-20.

Experiencing kingdom reality, Luke 17:20-21.

Reality of life in Christ, 2 Timothy 1:1.

Faith without works, James 2:14-18.

Reality of unseen, 1 Peter 1:8, 9.

Experiencing reality of Christ, 1 John 1:1-4.

See Doubt, Truth.

REAP

Joy at harvest time, 1 Samuel 6:13.

Reap what is sown, Job 4:8; Hosea 10:13-14; Obadiah 1:15; Galatians 6:7.

Sow in tears, reap with joy, Psalm 126:5.

Lazy at harvest time, Proverbs 10:5.

Size of harvest, 2 Corinthians 9:6.

See Harvest.

REASON

Satanic reasoning, Genesis 3:1-5.

Reasoning with God, Exodus 32:11-14.

Refusing to listen to reason, 1 Samuel 8:4-21.

Lost reason, Job 12:24.

Questioning why wicked prosper, Jeremiah 12:1-3.

Disputing mercy and justice, Ezekiel 33:10-20.

Wisdom of Gamaliel, Acts 5:30-40.

Use of reasoning in teaching, Acts 17:1-3.

Reason versus revelation, 1 Corinthians 1:20-31.

Powerful delusion distorts reason, 2 Thessalonians 2:11-12.

See Argument, Dispute.

REBELLION

No success outside God's will, Numbers 14:41-45.

Those who refuse to hear, Judges 6:10.

Prosperous wicked rebel, Job 21:7-16.

Rebellion against light, Job 24:13, 16.

When God gives up, Psalm 81:12 (KJV).

Police intervention, Proverbs 17:11.

Trying patience of God, Isaiah 7:13.

Rebelling against prophet's message, Jeremiah 42:2-22.

Vow to Queen of Heaven, Jeremiah 44:24-30.

"Don't plot against the Lord," Nahum 1:9 (CEV).

Hearts hard as flint, Zechariah 7:11-12.

Argument with God, Romans 9:20.

Enmity in mind against God, Colossians 1:21.

Attitude toward spiritual rebellion, 2 Thessalonians 3:14-15.

Remembered rebellion, Hebrews 3:15 (NRSV).

Agony of rebellious, Revelation 16:10-11.

See Discontent, Disobedience, Insurrection, Mob Psychology.

REBUKE

Willing to accept rebuke, 2 Samuel 16:5-12.

Youth points out mistake of age, Job 32:6-12.

Wise rebuke accepted, Proverbs 25:12.
Rebuking a fool, Proverbs 26:5.
Value of open rebuke, Proverbs 27:5.
Wounds of friend, Proverbs 27:6.
Peter rebuked Jesus; Jesus rebuked Peter, Mark 8:32–33.
Rebuked demon, Mark 9:25; Luke 4:33–36.
Jesus rebuked mother, John 2:4 (See CEV).
Unable to accept rebuke, Acts 7:51–58.
Rebuked, struck by high priest's command, Acts 23:1–5.
Unregretted sorrow for causing hurt, 2 Corinthians 7:8–9.
Recognized weakness, 2 Corinthians 13:9.
Rebuked Christians, Galatians 3:1 (AB).
Christian method of rebuke, 2 Thessalonians 3:14–15.
Rebuking older person, 1 Timothy 5:1 (See NRSV).
Rebuked publicly, 1 Timothy 5:20.
See Reprimand, Scolding.

RECEIPT

Gift receipted, Philippians 4:18 (GNB).

RECEPTIVE

Defying message of prophet, Jeremiah 43:1–3.
Those who ought to be receptive, Ezekiel 3:4–9.
Open-minded Lydia, Acts 16:14 (GNB).
Eagerly receptive, Acts 17:11–12.
See Rapport, Response.

RECIPE

Bread recipe, Ezekiel 4:9.

RECIPROCATION

Blessing and injury reciprocated, Genesis 12:3.
Reciprocated kindness, Joshua 2:12–14.
Evil repays evil, Judges 1:6–7.
Exchange of gifts between royalty, 2 Chronicles 9:12.
Golden rule upheld, Proverbs 24:29.
Divine response to personal idolatry, Ezekiel 14:4.
Golden Rule, Matthew 7:12.
Divine reciprocation, Zechariah 1:3; Matthew 25:34–45.

Doing good without reciprocations, Luke 6:27–36.
Hospitality without reciprocation, Luke 14:12–14.
Glory to glory, John 17:1 (LB).
Boomerang effect of immorality, 1 Corinthians 6:18–20.
Repaying past generosity, 2 Corinthians 8:14.
Blessed and a blessing, Galatians 3:9.
See Golden Rule, Recompense, Retaliation, Retribution, Revenge.

RECITATION

Reciting to musical accompaniment, Psalm 49:4.
See Eloquence.

RECKLESS

Driving like madman, 2 Kings 9:20.
Careless about danger, Proverbs 22:3.
See Reckless, Undisciplined.

RECOGNITION

Honor not fitting for fool, Proverbs 26:1.
Recognizing people by name, Romans 16:3–15.
Wise use of names, Colossians 4:7–17.
Small mention to prominent characters, Hebrews 11:32.
Song of Moses sung in heaven, Revelation 15:2–4.
See Fame, Identity.

RECOLLECT

Former things not recollected, Isaiah 65:17.
Remembering better days, Haggai 2:3.
See Memory.

RECOMMENDATION

God's commendation of Job, Job 1:8.
Jesus' evaluation of John the Baptist, Matthew 11:11–14.
No need for human credentials, John 5:31–40.
Recommended by friend, Acts 9:26–27.
Letters of introduction, 1 Corinthians 16:3; 2 Corinthians 3:1–3 (NIV).

Those of whom one can speak well, 3 John 12.
See Citation, Commendation.

RECOMPENSE

Priest's income, Deuteronomy 18:1–2.
Rewards of obedience, Deuteronomy 28:1–14.
Good, bad deeds rewarded, Isaiah 3:10–11.
God accepts no price or reward, Isaiah 45:13.
Reward for pride, Zephaniah 2:9–10.
Content with one's income, Luke 3:14.
Doing good without expecting reward, Luke 6:27–36.
Recompense for kindness to poor, Luke 14:14.
Assured recompense, Hebrews 10:35.
See Honorarium, Payment, Salary.

RECONCILIATION

Brothers reconciled, Genesis 33:1–20.
The Lord rewards, Ruth 2:12; 2 Samuel 22:25.
Reconcilation of David and Abner, 2 Samuel 3:6–21.
Disputing friends reconciled, Job 42:7–11.
Righteous and sinner receive their due, Proverbs 11:31.
Reconcilation precedes worship, Matthew 5:23–24.
Reconciled to God, Romans 5:10; 2 Corinthians 5:18–21 (See GNB).
Unity with Redeemer, Ephesians 2:14–18.
Reconciliation of all things, Colossians 1:20.
High Priest of reconciliation, Hebrews 2:17.
See Forgiveness, Restoration.

RECONNAISSANCE

Canaan reconnaissance, Numbers 13:1–2.
Reconnaissance report, Joshua 2:1–24.
Danite spies, Judges 18:2–10.
Satanic reconnaissance of earth, Job 1:7.
Thieves' reconnaissance, Isaiah 39:1–6.
See Evaluation, Survey.

RECONSTRUCTION

Ruined towns rebuilt, Isaiah 44:26; Ezekiel 36:33 (CEV).
Jerusalem rebuilt, Isaiah 58:12.

RECORDING

Voices recorded on stone, Joshua 24:27.

RECREATION

Mighty hunter, Genesis 10:9.
Enjoying bow, arrow, Genesis 21:20.
Early morning play, Exodus 32:6.
Eating with rejoicing, Deuteronomy 27:7.
No place to rest, Deuteronomy 28:65.
Telling riddles, Judges 14:12–18.
Sadistic recreation, Judges 16:25.
Gross indecency, Judges 19:22–26.
Boxing, wrestling, 2 Samuel 2:14.
Camping out on rooftop, Nehemiah 8:13–17.
Dancing children, Job 21:11.
Whales at play, Psalm 104:26 (LB).
Meaningless pleasures, Ecclesiastes 2:1–3; 2:1–3.
Renewal of strength, Isaiah 40:30–31.
Sabbath fun, Isaiah 58:3–14 (LB).
Instrumental jam session, Amos 6:5.
Children play in streets, Zechariah 8:5.
Adults in childish recreation, Matthew 11:16–17.
Relaxed eating, Mark 14:3.
Gossip as recreation, 1 Timothy 5:13.
See Amusement, Athletics, Play.

RECRUITMENT

Taking care of business, Deuteronomy 20:5–9.
Recruiting mighty and brave, 1 Samuel 14:52.
Leadership for those in trouble, 1 Samuel 22:2.
Recruited for disloyalty, 2 Kings 9:14–24.
Finest young men recruited, Daniel 1:3–4.
United to follow Jesus, Luke 8:1–3.
See Soldier, Volunteer.

RECTITUDE

Religious, moral rectitude, Isaiah 26:7 (AB).

RECUPERATION

Mental attitude, Proverbs 4:20–22.
Restored to health, Isaiah 38:16; Jeremiah 30:17.
See Health, Therapy.

REDEEMER

Heartcry for mediator, Job 9:33–35.
Predicted Redeemer, Isaiah 53:1–12.
Strength of great Redeemer, Jeremiah 50:34.
Prophet bearing sin of people, Ezekiel 4:4–6.
Redeemer's assurance, Revelation 1:17–18.
Worthy to open scroll, Revelation 5:1–10.
See Salvation.

REDEMPTION

Search for salvation, Job 9:2.
Advocate at God's throne, Job 16:19–21.
Depth of mercy, forgiveness, Psalm 51:1–2.
Sins gone from God's memory, Psalm 103:11–12.
Many sins, much forgiveness, Psalm 130:3–4.
Unique parable of redemption, Ecclesiastes 9:14–15.
Come let us reason, Isaiah 1:18.
Guilt atoned by fire, Isaiah 6:6–7.
Joy of salvation, Isaiah 12:2; 35:1–2.
Sins paid for, Isaiah 40:1, 2.
Creator cares for Creation, Isaiah 42:5–7.
Declaring one and only Savior, Isaiah 43:10–13.
Sold, redeemed, Isaiah 52:3.
Global redemption, Isaiah 52:10.
Prophetic description of Jesus, Isaiah 53:1–12.
Coming of Christ and proclamation of Gospel, Isaiah 61:1–3.
Healing and salvation, Jeremiah 17:14.
Great Redeemer's Strength, Jeremiah 50:34.
Beyond redemption, Hosea 7:13.
Seeking atonement for sin, Micah 6:7.
Healing sun of righteousness, Malachi 4:2.
Parable of landowner, son, Matthew 21:33–44; Mark 12:1–12.
Disciples could not understand, Mark 9:30–32.
Jesus foretold death, resurrection, Mark 10:32–34.
Sin, not pain, took life of Jesus, Mark 15:33–37.
Redeemer, judge, John 5:22–23.

Willing Redeemer, John 10:17–18.
Perfect timing in Christ, Romans 5:6.
Function of Redeemer, Romans 8:1–4.
He who was rich became poor, 2 Corinthians 8:9.
Christ accursed on Cross, Galatians 3:13–14.
From law to grace, Galatians 4:1–7.
Result of promise, Galatians 4:21–31.
God's love for unlovely, Ephesians 2:1–5.
Rescued from dominion of darkness, Colossians 1:13–14.
Sins of ignorance, 1 Timothy 1:12–14.
Redemption for worst of sinners, 1 Timothy 1:15–16.
God wants all to be saved, 1 Timothy 2:3–4.
Divine plan from beginning of time, 2 Timothy 1:8–10.
Salvation not possible through the law, Hebrews 7:11.
Without blood no covenant, Hebrews 9:18–22.
Supreme sacrifice, Hebrews 9:24–28; 1 John 4:9–10.
Redemption planned before creation, 1 Peter 1:18–20.
All must give account, 1 Peter 4:4–6.
Only Redeemer qualified to judge, Revelation 5:1–14.
Redeemed from all nations, Revelation 7:9–17.
Inevitable defeat of Satan, Revelation 12:1–9.
See Salvation.

REFEREE

God blows whistle, Isaiah 7:18.

REFINE

Metal refiners, 1 Chronicles 28:18; Malachi 3:2–3.
Disciplinary refining, Job 5:17; 23:10.
Silver refined, Proverbs 25:4.
Illustration of judgment, Ezekiel 22:22.
Refined through stumbling, Daniel 11:35.
Refining brings eternal glory, 2 Corinthians 4:17; Hebrews 12:11.
See Discipline, Testing.

REFORM See Rehabilitate.

REFRESHING
"Like fresh air," 2 Timothy 1:16 (AB).

REFRIGERATION
Summer snow, Proverbs 25:13.

REFUGE
No refuge for wanderer, Genesis 4:13–14.

Cities of refuge, Exodus 21:13; Numbers 35:6; Deuteronomy 4:41–43; 19:3; Joshua 20:2, 9; 1 Chronicles 6:67.

Covered by God's hand, Exodus 33:22.

Everlasting arms, Deuteronomy 33:27.

Founder of Luz, Judges 1:22–26.

Strong tower in besieged city, Judges 9:51.

Escape from famine, Ruth 1:1–3.

Hiding in thickets, caves, pits, cisterns, 1 Samuel 13:6.

Fortress, deliverer, 2 Samuel 22:1–4; Psalm 18:2.

Protection for future king, 2 Kings 11:1–3.

Shadow of divine wings, Psalm 17:8–9.

Shelter from angry tongues, Psalm 31:20.

Hiding place, Psalm 32:7.

Refuge, strength, Psalm 46:1–3.

Seeking housetops, Isaiah 22:1.

Shelter, shade, Isaiah 25:4; 32:2.

Egypt, place of refuge, Jeremiah 41:16–18.

Refuge for those who trust, Nahum 1:7.

Joseph, Mary, Jesus, Matthew 2:13–18.

Pilgrims on earth, 1 Peter 2:11.

See Protection, Shelter.

REFUGEE
"Hide our refugees," Isaiah 16:3 (CEV).

Refugees denied entry, Lamentations 4:15 (CEV).

REFUTE
Satan questioned divine truth, Genesis 3:2–5.

Approval of parents, Numbers 30:3–5.

Elihu challenged Job to refute, Job 33:31–33.

Youth chides wisdom of age, Job 32:6–9.

Refraining from response to one who affronted name of the Lord, Isaiah 36:18–22 (See 37:1–7).

False prophets foiled, Isaiah 44:25.

See Disagreement.

REGENERATION
New heart, spirit, Jeremiah 24:7; Ezekiel 11:19–20; 36:26–29.

REFEREE

Born again, John 3:3; Titus 3:5; 1 Peter 1:23.

Depth of redemption, Romans 6:3–23.

Those who have died with Christ, Colossians 2:20–23.

See Conversion, Salvation.

REGRESSION

Silver to dross, wine to water, Isaiah 1:22.

REGRET

Creator's regret, Genesis 6:6.

Foolish sins, Numbers 12:11.

Sacrifice of daughter, Judges 11:30–40.

Poor student's regret, Proverbs 5:12–13.

Chasing wind, Ecclesiastes 1:17–18.

Ashamed, silent before the Lord, Ezekiel 16:63.

Royal regret, Daniel 6:13–18.

Remembering glory of better days, Haggai 2:3.

Judas' regret, Matthew 27:3.

Second coming will cause regret, Revelation 1:7.

See Disappointment, Discouragement, Remorse.

REGULATIONS

Ultimate demands for obeying law, Joshua 1:18.

Pagan king persuaded to permit temple rebuilding, Ezra 4–8.

Carrying regulations too far, Mark 2:23–27.

See Restrictions, Rules.

REHABILITATE

Defilement in sanctuary, 2 Chronicles 29:1–11.

Beauty for ashes, Isaiah 61:1–3.

Restoring backslider, James 5:19–20.

See Transformation.

REIGN *See Kingdom, Royalty.*

REINCARNATION

Erroneous reincarnation, Matthew 11:13–14; 14:1; 17:13.

Only one life, Hebrews 9:27.

REINFORCEMENT

Oral message put into writing, Deuteronomy 31:9.

Reinforced instructions, Joshua 1:8; 23:6.

Parables as reinforcement, Matthew 13:34; Mark 4:34.

Compare John 1:1–9 with 1 John 1:1–7.

Giving emphasis to former command, 1 John 2:7–8.

Importance of repetition, 2 Peter 1:12–15.

Word of prophets validated, 2 Peter 1:19.

See Instruction, Teaching.

REINSTATE

Making wrong right, Numbers 5:6–7.

Debt cancelled every seven years, Deuteronomy 15:1.

Brother spared, 1 Kings 1:49–53.

Job reinstated, Job 42:7–10.

Making, breaking promise to slaves, Jeremiah 34:8–22.

The Lord returns to those who return to Him, Zechariah 1:3.

See Restoration.

REJECTION

Rejecting God's message, Judges 6:10; Isaiah 30:10.

Turning to rejected brother in time of need, Judges 11:1–10.

Multiple rejection, Job 19:19.

Prophecy of cry from cross, Psalm 22:1.

Rejected by friends, Psalm 31:11–13 (See LB).

Old age fearing rejection, Psalm 71:9, 18.

"No one paid attention," Proverbs 1:24 (NASB).

Rejected Savior, Isaiah 53:3.

God revealed to those not asking, Isaiah 65:1.

Rejecting God's grace, Isaiah 65:12.

Backs turned to God, Jeremiah 2:27; 32:33.

God turns His back, Jeremiah 18:17.

Prophet's message brings threat of death, Jeremiah 26:1–16.

Burned scroll, Jeremiah 36:1–26.

Rejected message, Jeremiah 43:1–7; 44:4–5, 15–19.

Garbage dump, Lamentations 3:45 (GNB).

God's deaf ear to praise, Amos 5:22; 8:3, 10.

City-wide rejection, Matthew 8:34.

Gospel divides world and households, Matthew 10:32–36.

Witnessing miracles with hard hearts, Matthew 11:20.

Parable of landowner and son, Matthew 21:33–44.

Rejecting banquet invitation, Matthew 22:1–14.

Prayer of Jesus over rebellious Jerusalem, Matthew 23:37.

Supreme example of rejection, Matthew 27:46.

Sowing seed on various kinds of soil, Mark 4:3–20.

Rejecting those who witness, Luke 10:16.

Rejecting, hindering, Luke 11:52.

Christ rejected by His own people, John 1:11.

Accepting and rejecting the Messiah, John 7:25–31.

Doubt augmented by hearing truth, John 8:45–47.

Unbelief in face of proof, John 12:37–40.

Paul, Barnabas turn to Gentiles, Acts 13:46–48; 18:6.

Entire city in uproar, Acts 19:23–41.

Stumble over provision for redemption, Romans 9:33.

Divine compassion to disobedient, Romans 10:21.

Differing reactions to truly Christian personality, 2 Corinthians 2:15–16.

Witnessing to those blinded by Satan, 2 Corinthians 4:1–6.

Some accept, others reject, 1 Thessalonians 2:1–2.

Followers of anti-Christ, 2 Thessalonians 2:4–12.

Those who could not hold true to faith, 1 Timothy 1:18–19.

Turning from God, Hebrews 3:12.

Failure to combine hearing with believing, Hebrews 4:1–2.

Rejection caused by disobedience, 1 Peter 2:8.

Those who do not obey Gospel, 1 Peter 4:17.

See Blindness, Denial.

REJOICE *See Happiness, Praise, Singing.*

RELATIONSHIP

Three forefathers of mankind, Genesis 9:18–19.

Marriage to stepsister, Genesis 20:12–16.

Forbidding marriage to foreigners, Genesis 24:2–3.

Bond between relatives, Genesis 29:1–14.

Change in relationship, Genesis 31:2.

Clan relationships, Numbers 26:1–51.

Brother born of evil woman, Judges 11:1–10.

Broken circle among twelve tribes, Judges 21:1–6.

Hatred of wife for husband, 2 Samuel 6:16–23.

Marriage confirms alliance, 1 Kings 3:1.

Love for mother-in-law, Ruth 1:8–18.

No offspring, descendants, Job 18:19 (NKJV).

Apple of God's eye, Psalm 17:8.

Recognized relationship, Psalm 119:74.

Sister, bride, Song of Songs 4:9.

Golden Rule, Matthew 7:12.

Jesus' evaluation of His mother, Matthew 12:46–50.

Attitude of Jesus toward relationships, Mark 3:31–35.

Answered prayer and good relationships, Mark 11:25.

Marriage on earth, relationship in heaven, Mark 12:18–27.

Relationship to God, neighbors, Mark 12:28–34.

Presumed relationship to the Lord, Luke 13:22–30.

Christ first above family, Luke 14:26.

Love the supreme relationship, John 13:34.

True meaning of a friend, John 15:12–17.

New relationships in Christ, John 19:26–27.

Reactions to truly Christian personality, 2 Corinthians 2:15–16.

Identified in Christ, Ephesians 1:11–12.

Relationship through Holy Spirit, Ephesians 2:22.

Husband, wife, Ephesians 5:21–33.

Slave, owner, same Master, Ephesians 6:9.

Concern for followers' development, Colossians 2:1–5.

Spiritual son, 1 Timothy 1:2, 18; 2 Timothy 1:2; 2:1.

Relationship with Christ, 2 Timothy 2:11–13; Hebrews 2:11–16.

God's friend, James 2:21–23.

Confessing sins one to another, James 5:16.

Children of God, 1 John 3:1–3.

Sanctified, preserved, Jude 1 (NKJV).

See Body of Christ, Brotherhood, Family.

RELATIVE

Relatives fail to help, Job 19:14 (NRSV).

Peaceful relatives, Psalm 133:1 (CEV).

See Brother, Family, Father, Mother, Parents, Sister.

RELATIVITY

Millennia compressed into days, 2 Peter 3:8.

RELAXATION

Sure rest, divine protection, Deuteronomy 33:12.

David frequently played harp, 1 Samuel 18:10.

Steadfast heart, Psalm 57:7.

Quietness, rejoicing, Zephaniah 3:17.

Importance of relaxation, Mark 6:31.

Perilous relaxation, Luke 12:19 (NRSV).

See Recreation.

RELEASE

King imprisoned, set free, 2 Kings 24:15; 25:27–29.

Broken promise to slaves, Jeremiah 34:8–22.

Rescued from darkness, dominion, Colossians 1:13, 14.

See Freedom.

RELENTLESS

Relentless searching, Psalm 105:4 (LB).

Never satisfied, Proverbs 30:15–16.

Relentless effort, Ecclesiastes 9:10.

Never give up, Ephesians 6:18 (GNB).

See Determination.

RELIABLE

Standing at end of struggle, Ephesians 6:13.

Steadfast whatever circumstances, Philippians 1:27–30.

No lie comes from truth, 1 John 2:20–21.

See Dependability.

RELICS *See Memento.*

RELIEF

God ever present in trouble, Psalm 14:4–5.

Padding for prophet's comfort, Jeremiah 38:11–13.

See Comfort, Deliverance.

RELIGION

Personal piety insufficient, Job 4:6.

Natural perception, Job 12:7–16.

Religion without reality, Proverbs 14:12; 16:25.

Man-made religion, Isaiah 29:13.

Digging their own cisterns, Jeremiah 2:13.

Idols in heart, Ezekiel 14:1–11.

Those who say, "Lord, Lord," Matthew 7:21–23.

Picking grain on Sabbath, Matthew 12:1–8.

Gross sinners compared to Pharisees, Matthew 21:31–32.

Clean outside, filthy inside, Matthew 23:25–28.

Lip service, Mark 7:6–7.

Morality, materialism, Mark 10:17–25.

Practice what you preach, Luke 3:7–8.

Attitude of Pharisees toward helping others, Luke 13:10–17.

Pharisees, tax collector, Luke 18:9–14.

Reading Bible in vain, John 5:39–40.

Erroneously thinking to serve God, John 16:1–4.

Deity-minded, demon-motivated Athenians, Acts 17:22–23 (AB, Berk.).

Pagans certain of false religion, Acts 19:35–36.

Religious knowledge insufficient, Romans 8:3 (LB).

Religion without enlightenment, Romans 10:2 (AB).

Proficient in religion, Galatians 1:14 (GNB).

Emptiness of mere religion, Galatians 3:10–14.

"Mystery of our religion," 1 Timothy 3:16 (NRSV).

Gist of Christianity, Titus 1:1–3 (GNB).

Cheap religion, James 1:26 (LB).

See Formality, Legalism, Modernism, Syncretism.

RELUCTANCE

Reluctance of Lot to leave Sodom, Genesis 19:15–16.

Negative and positive viewpoints, Numbers 13:17–33.

Ignoring word of the Lord, Jeremiah 7:13.

Reluctance of demon to leave one possessed, Mark 1:21–26.

Fearful Jesus might be reluctant to heal, Luke 5:12–14.

See Hesitation, Resistant.

REMARRIAGE

Second wife, Genesis 25:1.

Remarriage of divorced persons, Deuteronomy 24:1–4.

Ruth and Boaz, Ruth 3:1; 4:10.

Return to first husband, Hosea 2:7 (GNB).

Remarriage instruction, Romans 7:1–3.

Remarriage for widows, 1 Corinthians 7:8–9; 1 Timothy 5:11.

See Divorce, Marriage.

REMEDIES

Poultice of figs, 2 Kings 20:7.

Soothing oil, Isaiah 1:6; Luke 10:34.

No balm in Gilead, Jeremiah 8:22.

Wine for stomach, 1 Timothy 5:23.

Anointing oil, James 5:14.

See Medicine, Therapy.

REMEMBRANCE *See Memorial.*

REMINISCENCE

Asking about former days, Deuteronomy 4:32–35.

Divine goodness remembered, Nehemiah 9:6–37; Job 29:2–6.

"Good old days," Psalm 77:5 (LB); Ecclesiastes 7:10.

Divine reminiscence, Isaiah 43:16–28 (LB).

Past not brought to mind, Isaiah 65:17.

Bitter reminiscence, Lamentations 1:7 (See LB).

Glory of better days, Haggai 2:3.

Prodigal's reminiscence, Luke 15:17.

See Memory, Retrospect.

REMNANT

Righteous remnant upon earth, Genesis 6:5–14.

"Save what's left of Israel," Jeremiah 31:7 (CEV).

Not one upright, Micah 7:2.

Remnant believers in Israel, Romans 11:1–5.

See Minority, Israel.

REMODEL

Tent remodelling, Isaiah 54:2.

Remodeled guest room, Nehemiah 13:5 (LB).

REMORSE

National remorse, Numbers 14:39.

Divine grief, 1 Chronicles 21:14–17.

Tears of remorse, Ezra 10:1.

Lamenting personal sin, Psalms 38:2–6; 51:1–17.

Psalm of remorse, Psalm 51:1–19.

Isaiah's self-analysis, Isaiah 6:5.

Cutting off hair to show remorse, Jeremiah 7:29.

Remorse as judgment comes, Jeremiah 25:34.

Eyes dry from weeping, Lamentations 2:11.

Remorse of king, Daniel 6:13–18.

Remembering glory of better days, Haggai 2:3; Luke 15:17.

Backslider's remorse, Matthew 26:75.

Guilt of Judas, Matthew 27:3–5.

Remorse of lost souls, Luke 13:28.

Ashamed for past conduct, Romans 6:21.

Role of remorse in repentance, 1 Corinthians 5:1–2.

Lost blessing sought with tears, Hebrews 12:16–17.

Remorse when unprepared for Second coming, Revelation 1:7.

Agony of those who refuse to repent, Revelation 16:10–11.

See Anguish, Conviction, Regret, Sorrow.

REMOTE

Distant and deep, Ecclesiastes 7:24 (KJV).

REMUNERATION

Requesting payment for spiritual ministry, 2 Kings 5:20–27.
Gift for prophet's services, 2 Kings 8:7–8.
Unpaid choir singers, Nehemiah 13:10 (LB).
God accepts no remuneration, Isaiah 45:13.
No remuneration for hard work, Ezekiel 29:16–20 (LB).
Refusing bribes, rewards, Daniel 5:17.
Worker deserves wages, Luke 10:7.
"At his own expense," Acts 28:30 (NRSV).
Wages of sin, Romans 6:23; 2 Peter 2:15.
Material payment for spiritual service, 1 Corinthians 9:9–14.
See Honorarium, Stipend, Wages.

RENEGADE

Infamy to daughter of king, 2 Kings 9:30–37.
Mistaken praise, Esther 6:1–12. (See chapters 5:9–14; 6:10.)
Lamp of wicked, Job 18:5–6.
Worthless idols, worthless people, Jeremiah 2:5.
Refusal to go God's way, Jeremiah 11:7, 8.
Renegade repentance, Luke 15:13–21.
See Insurrection, Rebellion.

RENEWAL

Tear down old, build new, Judges 6:25–26.
Renewed by Scripture, Psalm 119:93.
Streams on dry ground, Isaiah 44:3.
Ask for ancient paths, Jeremiah 6:16.
Introspection and renewal, Lamentations 3:40.
New heart, new spirit, Ezekiel 36:26.
"Renew you in His love," Zephaniah 3:17 (NRSV).
Flame of renewal, 2 Timothy 1:6.
See Revival, Repentance, Transformation.

RENTAL

Difference between borrowing and renting, Exodus 22:14–15.
Apostle's rented house, Acts 28:30.

RENUNCIATION

Divine renunciation, Matthew 27:46.
Peter's denial of Christ, Mark 14:66–72.
Leaving all to follow Jesus, Luke 5:27–28; 18:29, 30.
Dead to sin, Romans 6:2, 11; Colossians 3:3.
Old nature crucified, Galatians 5:24; 1 Peter 2:24.
All things as loss, Philippians 3:8.
See Repentance, Revival.

REPAIR

"Good as new," 2 Chronicles 24:13 (CEV).
Temple doors repaired, 2 Chronicles 29:3.
Lazy man's house, Ecclesiastes 10:18.
Proper repair of garment, Matthew 9:16.

REPARATION See Forgiveness, Repentance, Restoration.

REPENTANCE

Insincere repentance, Exodus 9:27.
Rewards for repentance, Leviticus 26:40–42; Deuteronomy 30:1–10; Judges 3:9–15; Nehemiah 1:9; Jeremiah 7:3.
Merciful God, Deuteronomy 4:29–31.
Prosperity following repentance, Deuteronomy 30:1–10.
National repentance, Joshua 24:16–27; 1 Samuel 7:3; 2 Chronicles 7:14.
Serious about repenting, 1 Samuel 7:3 (LB).
Royal repentance, 1 Samuel 15:13–35.
God's word caused royal repentance, 2 Kings 22:11.
Evil king's repentance, 2 Chronicles 33:12.
Tears of repentance, Ezra 10:1.
Limited repentance, Job 34:31–33.
Submission and repentance, Job 42:1–9.
Sure forgiveness, Psalm 32:5, 6.
Repentant prayer, Psalm 41:4; Lamentations 5:21–22.
Source of new joy, Psalm 51:12–13.
Death bed repentance, Psalm 66:13–14.
Merriment instead of repentance, Isaiah 22:12–13.
Do not miss opportunity, Isaiah 55:6–7.
Need for repentance, Isaiah 64:5.
God's great love to faithless Israel, Jeremiah 3:11–17.

Come home unfaithful children, Jeremiah 3:14 (CEV).

Repentance in shame, Jeremiah 3:24–25.

A witness to others, Jeremiah 4:1–2 (See LB).

Break up unplowed ground, Jeremiah 4:3 (NIV).

Asking for old paths, Jeremiah 6:16.

Sackcloth, ashes, Jeremiah 6:26.

Call to repentance, Jeremiah 7:1–15.

Refusal to turn back, Jeremiah 8:4–7; Zechariah 1:4.

Refusing to repent, Jeremiah 8:6; Revelation 9:20–21; 16:10–11.

Pride hinders repentance, Jeremiah 13:15.

Prayer of truly repentant, Jeremiah 14:20–22.

Insincere repentance, Jeremiah 21:1–10.

"Change your ways," Jeremiah 25:5 (CEV).

Tears of repentance, Jeremiah 31:9; 50:4–5.

Repentant youth, Jeremiah 31:19.

Mark of repentance, Ezekiel 9:3–6.

Turning from wicked past, Ezekiel 16:59–63.

Contrast between backsliding, repentance, Ezekiel 18:24–31.

The Lord wants all to live, Ezekiel 18:32.

Conscious need for repentance, Ezekiel 20:43.

The Lord prefers repentance to judgment, Ezekiel 33:10–12.

Daniel's prayer of repentance, Daniel 9:1–19.

Break up ground, sow righteousness, Hosea 10:12.

Key to God's guidance, Hosea 12:6.

Sins cause stumble, Hosea 14:1–2.

Congregational response, Joel 1:14; 2:12–17 (See LB).

"It isn't too late," Joel 2:12 (CEV).

Testing, trials fail to cause repentance, Amos 4:6–11.

Ninevites heeded Jonah's warning, Jonah 3:3–6.

Sackcloth on people, animals, Jonah 3:8.

God's response to those who repent, Jonah 3:10.

Those who fall may rise, Micah 7:8–9.

Insincere fasting, repentance, Zechariah 7:1–6; Malachi 2:13.

"Return to me," Malachi 3:7 (CEV).

Repentance preaching, Matthew 3:1–3 (See CEV).

Repentant guilt, Matthew 27:3.

Definitions of repentance, Mark 1:4 (AB); Luke 3:3 (AB); 13:5 (AB).

Sinful woman's visualized repentance, Luke 7:36–50.

Confessing evil deeds, Acts 19:18–19.

Ashamed of past sins, Romans 6:21.

Role of grief in repentance, 1 Corinthians 5:1–2.

Godly sorrow brings repentance, 2 Corinthians 7:9–10 (See GNB).

Turning to God from idols, 1 Thessalonians 1:9 (See GNB, NEB).

Tears for doing wrong, James 4:9 (LB).

Repentance undesired, Revelation 2:21 (AB).

Unrepentant evil queen, Revelation 18:7–8.

See Remorse, Renunciation, Revival.

REPETITION

Repeated instructions, Joshua 1:8; 23:6.

Repetition of miracle at Red Sea, river Jordan, Joshua 4:23.

History repeats itself, Ecclesiastes 3:15.

Farmer does not plow continuously, Isaiah 28:24.

Message repetition, Jeremiah 25:3–4.

Repetitious bad news, Jeremiah 51:31–32.

Identical trouble does not happen twice, Nahum 1:9.

Repetitous prayer, Matthew 6:7.

Repetition for emphasis, Philippians 3:1 (See AB).

Importance of repetition, 2 Peter 1:12–15.

See Emphasis.

REPLY *See Answer, Response.*

REPORT

Report to father-in-law, Exodus 18:5–12.

Deceitful report, 1 Samuel 27:10–11.

Good report anticipated, 2 Samuel 18:27.

Numerous bad reports, Jeremiah 51:31–32.

Eyewitness report, John 19:35 (Berk.).

Paul's summary of ministry, Acts 21:19.

Speaking only of what Christ has done, Romans 15:18–19.

Circular letter, Colossians 4:16.
Believers' progress report, 1 Thessalonians 3:6–10.

REPOSE

Place of certainty, Deuteronomy 33:27.
Steadfast heart, Psalm 57:7.
See Rest.

REPRESENTATIVE

Representatives for people, Exodus 18:14–27.
Looking out for welfare of people, Esther 10:3.
Christ's ambassadors, 2 Corinthians 5:20.
See Government.

REPRESSION

Futile effort to suppress truth, Jeremiah 38:1–13.

REPRIEVE

Slow to anger, Numbers 14:18.
Disaster delayed, 1 Kings 21:29.
Need for quick punishment, Ecclesiastes 8:11.
Restrained wrath of God, Isaiah 48:9.
Partial reprieve, Jeremiah 37:21.
Judgment against tree, Luke 13:7–9.
Divine power restrained, Romans 9:22.
Divine patience in days of Noah, 1 Peter 3:20.
See Forgiveness, Mercy, Pardon.

REPRIMAND

Abrasive friends reprimanded, Job 42:7–9.
Wounds of friend, Proverbs 27:6.
Sincere reprimand, Proverbs 28:23.
Evil spirit reprimanded, Mark 1:23–26.
Mother's reprimand, Luke 2:41–50.
See Rebuke, Reproof, Scolding.

REPRISAL

Reprisal invited, 1 Kings 19:2.
Stark visualization of reprisal, Psalms 58:10; 68:23.
Golden Rule reversed, Proverbs 24:29.

Returning love for grief, 2 Corinthians 2:5–11.
Leave revenge with the Lord, 1 Thessalonians 5:15.
See Revenge.

REPROACH

Silence toward those who reproach, 1 Samuel 10:27.
Causing reproach, Nehemiah 5:9 (NIV).
Daring to reproach the Lord's name, Isaiah 36:18–21 (See 37:6).
Den of jackals, Jeremiah 9:11.
Facing grim destiny, Jeremiah 15:2–3.
Disrespect for the sanctuary, Ezekiel 25:1–4.
Dishonoring the Lord's name, Ezekiel 36:20; Romans 2:23, 24.
Public insult, Hebrews 10:33.
Suffering reproach, Hebrews 11:24–26.
See Disobedient, Sacrilege.

REPROBATE

Worldwide iniquity, Genesis 6:5–7.
Divine warning, Deuteronomy 28:15–67.
Contemptible sons, 1 Samuel 3:13.
The Lord provoked to anger, 1 Kings 21:22.
When God gives up on people, Psalm 18:11–12.
Deaf ears to Divine warning, Isaiah 65:12.
Those who do not know how to blush, Jeremiah 6:15.
Beyond help of prayer, Jeremiah 7:16.
When who you know does not help, Jeremiah 15:1.
Anger beyond measure, Lamentations 5:21–22.
Reprobate priests, Hosea 4:17.
For continued sinning, certain judgment, Amos 1:3, 6, 9, 11, 13; 2:1, 4, 6.
Once the door is closed, Luke 13:25–28.
"You don't belong to God," John 8:47 (CEV).
Total depravity, Romans 1:28.
Sin in broad daylight, 2 Peter 2:13–22.
See Backsliding, Dissipation, Profligate.

REPRODUCTION

God's command to creation, Genesis 1:22, 27–28.
See Abortion, Birth Control, Fruit, Propagation.

REPROOF

Rebuking neighbor, Leviticus 19:17.
"Smart aleck," 1 Samuel 17:28 (GNB).
Slap on face, 1 Kings 22:24.
Job helped others, can't help himself, Job 4:3–5.
Willing to be reproved, Job 6:24; Proverbs 17:10.
Dubious friends reproved, Job 42:7.
Rejecting reproof, Proverbs 1:29–31.
Reproof rebutted, Proverbs 9:7 (NASB).
Parental reproof, Proverbs 15:5.
Reproof like fine gold, Proverbs 25:12.
Wounds of friend, Proverbs 27:6.
Worth of honest rebuke, Proverbs 28:23.
Song of fools, Ecclesiastes 7:5.
Discipline with justice, Jeremiah 30:11.
Bold reproof, Daniel 5:22–23 (CEV).
Scolding evil spirit, Mark 1:23–26.
Rebuke sinful brother, Luke 17:3.
Productive hurt, 2 Corinthians 7:8–12.
Written rather than spoken, 2 Corinthians 13:10.
"I am surprised at you!" Galatians 1:6 (GNB).
Expose darkness, Ephesians 5:11.
Public reproof, 1 Timothy 5:20.
Preaching and teaching, 2 Timothy 4:1–2; Titus 2:15.
Commendation before reproof, Revelation 2:2–6,13–16,19–20.
See Reprimand.

REPTILE See Crocodile, Snakes.

REPUTATION

Righteous man blameless, Genesis 6:9.
Abraham's reputation, Genesis 21:22.
A desert named Sin, Exodus 17:1.
Holiness by virtue of occupation, Leviticus 21:8.
Holy community, Numbers 16:3.
Impeccable reputation, 1 Samuel 2:1–5.
Name well known, 1 Samuel 18:30.
Found faultless, 1 Samuel 29:3.
High compliments, 1 Samuel 29:6–9.
Reputation as troublemaker, 2 Samuel 20:1 (NIV).
"A godly man," Psalm 86:2 (NASB).
Glorious reputation, Psalm 87:3.
Reputation as man of prayer, Psalm 109:4.

Value of good name, Proverbs 22:1; Ecclesiastes 7:1.
Bad reputation, Proverbs 24:8 (GNB).
Building one's own reputation, Proverbs 25:27.
Let others assess, Proverbs 27:2 (LB).
Parent's reputation, Proverbs 27:11.
Fragrant name, Song of Songs 1:3.
Looking for one honest person, Jeremiah 5:1.
Least, greatest, Jeremiah 42:1–3.
Daniel's reputation known to queen, Daniel 5:10–12.
Integrity in government affairs, Daniel 6:1–3.
Jealousy incited, Daniel 6:4–8.
"God thinks highly of you," Daniel 10:11 (CEV).
Reputation as the Lord's messenger, Haggai 1:13.
People seek for those who know the Lord, Zechariah 8:23.
Reputation of Virgin Mary protected, Matthew 1:19.
False prophets, Matthew 7:15–20.
Worthy person, Matthew 10:11.
John the Baptist's greatness, Matthew 11:11.
Role of humility in greatness, Matthew 23:12.
Neighbors did not expect divinity in Jesus, Luke 4:22–24.
Sinful woman washed Jesus' feet, Luke 7:37–39.
Lasting reputation for wrong doing, Luke 17:32.
Nazareth's low reputation, John 1:46.
Jesus' conflicting reputation, John 7:12.
Loving reputation, John 13:35.
Early Christians' reputation, Acts 4:12–13 (See AB).
Spiritual reputations, Acts 6:3–6.
Mistrust by co-workers, Acts 9:26.
Righteous, God-fearing man, Acts 10:22.
Respect of Cornelius for Peter, Acts 10:25–26.
Good motivation of David, Acts 13:22.
Marred reputation, Acts 15:37–38.
Spoken well of, Acts 16:2.
Noble character of Bereans, Acts 17:11.

Highly respected, Acts 22:12.

I am a Pharisee, Acts 23:6.

World-famous faith, Romans 1:8 (See CEV).

Always doing what is right, Romans 12:17.

Reputation for obedience, Romans 16:19.

Mark of integrity, 2 Corinthians 8:18–24.

Uncertain reputations, 2 Corinthians 12:20 (See AB).

Convert's reputation encouraged others, Galatians 1:23–24.

Living life worthy of calling, Ephesians 4:1.

Exemplary reputation, Philippians 2:20–21.

Reputation as Christians, Colossians 1:3–6.

Conduct toward unbelievers, Colossians 4:5.

Reputation prerequisite to witness, 1 Thessalonians 4:11–12.

Mentioned with pride, 2 Thessalonians 1:4 (AB).

"High standing," 1 Timothy 3:13 (NASB).

Conduct, doctrine, 1 Timothy 4:16.

"Well attested," 1 Timothy 5:10 (NRSV).

Good, bad reputations plainly seen, 1 Timothy 5:24–25 (GNB).

Prostitute's faith and obedience, Hebrews 11:31.

Joy of good reputation, 3 John 3–6.

Good reputation, 3 John 12.

Positive and negative reputation, Revelation 2:1–6.

See Conduct, Esteem, Leadership, Lifestyle.

REQUEST

Requesting special favor, Judges 1:13–15.

Request to live in small town, 1 Samuel 27:5.

Fatal request, 1 Kings 2:13–25.

Desiring double portion of prophet's spirit, 2 Kings 2:9.

Blind man's simple request, Mark 10:46–52.

Compliments precede request, Philemon 1–7.

Request, not command, Philemon 8–9.

See Desire, Prayer, Wish.

RESENTMENT

Danger of resentment, Job 5:2.

RESIDENCE

Mobile homes, Genesis 13:3.

Cave residence, Genesis 19:30 (NRSV).

Dedicating home to the Lord, Leviticus 27:14.

Towns established, Numbers 35:1–8.

Dedicated home, Deuteronomy 20:5.

Property bearing God's name, Deuteronomy 12:21.

Residence search opens ministry, Judges 17:7–13.

Ivory palace, 1 Kings 22:39.

Divine residence in transit, 1 Chronicles 17:5.

"Dwelling of light," Job 38:19 (NKJV).

Tomb residence, Psalm 49:11; Mark 5:1–3.

Tent more durable than house, Proverbs 14:11.

Lazy man's house, Ecclesiastes 10:18.

Jesus had no residence, Matthew 8:20; Luke 9:58.

"Home owners," Matthew 24:43 (CEV).

Seaside residence, Acts 10:6.

See Home, Property, Real Estate.

RESPECT

Respect parents, Exodus 20:12; Leviticus 19:3; Proverbs 1:8; 6:20; Ephesians 6:1–2; Colossians 3:20.

Show respect for elderly, Leviticus 19:32; 1 Timothy 5:1–2.

Scripture respected, Nehemiah 8:5.

Respect for government leaders, Acts 23:5; Romans 13:1.

Spiritual leaders given respect, 1 Thessalonians 5:13.

Respect for clergy, 1 Timothy 5:17.

Mutual respect, 1 Peter 2:17.

See Honor.

REQUIREMENT

Abstaining from fruit of grape, Numbers 6:2–4.

What the Lord requires, Deuteronomy 10:12–13; Micah 6:8.

Avoid heathen ways, Deuteronomy 18:9.

Requirements for leadership, Joshua 1:18.

What God requires, He provides, Isaiah 2:3.
Building a good society, Zechariah 7:9; 8:16.
See Responsibility.

RESCUE

Kidnapping and rescue of Lot, Genesis 14:12–16.
Queen advocate for her people, Esther 8:3–11.
Mercy to suffering prophet, Jeremiah 38:6–13.
Jonah and great fish, Jonah 1:17.
See Deliverance.

RESEARCH

Research at Sodom, Gomorrah, Genesis 18:20–21.
Searching royal archives, Ezra 5:17.
Good, bad advice sources, Proverbs 12:5–6.
Royal research, Proverbs 25:2–3.
Frustrated research, Ecclesiastes 1:12–14.
Desiring more prophetic truth, Daniel 7:19.
Careful investigation, Luke 1:3.
Prophetic research, 1 Peter 1:10–11.
See Comparison, Evaluation, Study.

RESENTMENT

Revenge left to Divine timing, 1 Samuel 26:1–11.
Resentful citizens, 1 Samuel 30:3–6.
Wife detested emotion display, 2 Samuel 6:14–16.
Misunderstanding gesture of goodwill, 2 Samuel 10:1–4.
Inequity among citizens, Nehemiah 5:1–5.
Wealth, prestige couldn't numb resentment, Esther 5:10–14.
At odds with one's Maker, Isaiah 45:9.
Resentment toward helping others on Sabbath, Luke 13:10–17.
Pharisees' resentment toward Jesus, Luke 15:1–7.
Prodigal son's brother, Luke 15:11–32.
See Attitude, Hatred, Jealousy.

RESIDENCE

Residing in cave, Genesis 19:30 (NIV, NRSV).
Priority to residence over palace, 1 Kings 6:37–38; 7:1.
Divine residence, 2 Chronicles 6:39.

"Tent-dwelling women," Judges 5:24 (NRSV).
Residence determined by casting lots, Nehemiah 11:1–2.
Tent or cottage, Isaiah 38:12.
Self-built houses, Isaiah 65:21.
Palace does not make better king, Jeremiah 22:15 (CEV).
Summer and winter homes, Amos 3:15.
Desert dwellers, Obadiah 19.
Fine residences, temple ruins, Haggai 1:2–5.
No residence for Jesus, Matthew 8:20; John 1:37–39.
"Hometown," Luke 2:3 (CEV).
Residence of demons, Luke 8:30.
Timothy's home town, Acts 16:1.
House convenient to Synagogue, Acts 18:7.
Paul's rented house, Acts 28:30.
Earthly body like tent, 2 Corinthians 5:1.
Eager for heavenly home, 2 Corinthians 5:2 (CEV).
Living in tent en route to city of God, Hebrews 11:9–10.
See Home, House, Palace, Parsonage.

RESIDUE

Ashes from altar ceremonially clean, Numbers 19:9.
Juice left in grapes, Isaiah 65:8.
See Remnant.

RESILIENT

Race not to swift or strong, Ecclesiastes 9:11.
See Courage, Discipline.

RESISTANCE

Only Levites responded, Exodus 32:25–26.
Choice between life or death, Deuteronomy 30:19.
Hindered from choosing, 1 Kings 18:21.
Resist sinful enticement, Proverbs 1:10; 4:14.
Giving no resistance, Isaiah 50:6–7; Luke 6:29.
Made strong by God's power, Jeremiah 1:17–19.
No resistance to enemy, Lamentations 1:5.
Message resistance, Hosea 11:2.
Hearts like flint, Zechariah 7:12 (NIV).

Resistant city, Matthew 23:37.

Resistance of demon to leave one possessed, Mark 1:21–26.

Hindrance of wealth, Luke 18:18–25.

Resisting temptation through prayer, Luke 22:40.

Jesus offered no resistance, Luke 22:47–53.

Mob incited against Paul, Silas, Acts 17:5–7.

Resist impurity, Romans 6:13.

Stability to resist Satan, Ephesians 6:13.

Resisting ungodliness, evil passions, Titus 2:11–12.

Do not harden your heart, Hebrews 3:7–8, 15.

Alert to spiritual error, 2 Peter 3:17.

See Discipline, Holiness, Unwilling.

RESOLUTE

Resolute faithfulness, Joshua 24:14.

Brace yourself, Job 38:3 (NIV).

Progress in spite of circumstances, Psalm 44:18.

Resolute obdience, Psalm 57:7.

Don't faint, Proverbs 24:10 (NKJV).

See Determination.

RESOURCE *(Material)*

People more valuable than material, Genesis 14:21.

Sharing earth resources, Ecclesiastes 5:9 (NKJV).

Wood for making gods, cooking fires, Isaiah 44:14–20.

Dying earth, Isaiah 51:6.

Creation demonstrates available resources, Jeremiah 32:17–21.

Gold, silver belong to God, Haggai 2:8.

See Natural Resources.

RESOURCE *(Spiritual)*

Seeking inner strength, Job 6:13.

When man's help worthless, Psalm 108:12.

Resource hidden in heart, Psalm 119:11.

Dependability of divine strength, Isaiah 40:28–31.

Nothing too hard for God, Jeremiah 32:27.

Strength from the Lord, Habakkuk 3:19.

Inner resource, Ephesians 6:10 (LB).

RESPECT

Harm to parents forbidden, Exodus 21:15.

Stand when older person appears, Leviticus 19:32.

Mutual respect between enemies, Deuteronomy 2:4–5.

Show respect to church and court, Deuteronomy 17:12.

Do not respect prophet who proclaims error, Deuteronomy 18:21–22.

Honoring former leader, Joshua 22:1–5.

Unwasted words, 1 Samuel 3:19.

Stone god's respect for ark of God, 1 Samuel 5:1–5.

Respect for position, 1 Samuel 24:1–7; 26:7–11.

Success through blessing, guidance, 2 Samuel 22:44–45.

Children show no respect, Job 19:18.

Respect at city gate, Job 29:7–10.

Earned respect, Job 29:21.

Respect for those older, Job 32:4–6; 1 Timothy 5:1–2.

Attitude toward aged parents, Proverbs 23:22.

Respect for mother, Proverbs 31:31 (See GNB).

Promise of peaceful and honorable death, Jeremiah 34:4–5.

Honor to whom due, Malachi 1:6.

Respecting the Lord's name, Malachi 2:4–5.

Respect, obedience, Luke 6:46.

Jesus accused of disrespect, John 18:19–24.

Respect of Cornelius for Peter, Acts 10:25–26.

Recognition of apostle, 1 Corinthians 9:1–6.

Respect toward seniors, 1 Timothy 5:1–2.

Accused yet admired, 1 Peter 2:12.

Consideration for everyone, 1 Peter 2:17.

Respect for those older, 1 Peter 5:5.

Take Scriptures to heart, Revelation 1:3.

See Courtesy, Disrespect, Genuflect.

RESPITE *See Comfort, Relief.*

RESPONSE

Agreement voiced by congregation, Deuteronomy 27:14–26.

Response of poor student, Proverbs 5:12–13.

Refraining from response to one who affronted the Lord's name, Isaiah 36:18–22 (See 37:1–7).

Ignoring Word of the Lord, Jeremiah 7:13.

Those who ought to respond eagerly, Ezekiel 3:4–9.

Nineveh more responsive than Jerusalem, Matthew 12:41–42.

Do not harden heart, Hebrews 3:7–8, 15.

Opening to Him who knocks, Revelation 3:20.

See Answer.

RESPONSIBILITY

Attempt to shift responsibility, Genesis 3:13.

Accusation, responsibility, Genesis 16:5.

Seeking substitute for responsibility, Exodus 4:10–13 (See 6:30).

The Lord delegates responsibility, Deuteronomy 1:9–18.

Responsibility delegated to father-in-law, Exodus 18:13–26.

Conditions for experiencing God's blessing, Exodus 15:26.

Remembering, following, perpetuating, divine teaching, Deuteronomy 4:9.

Experience brings responsibility, Deuteronomy 11:26–28.

Taking care of business, Deuteronomy 20:5–9.

Responsibility for individual guilt, Deuteronomy 24:16; Job 19:4; Jeremiah 31:30; Ezekiel 18:20.

Delegated responsibility, 1 Kings 4:7.

Assigned gatekeepers, 1 Chronicles 9:22–27.

Willingly assuming responsibility, Nehemiah 10:32, 35.

Personal grief put aside to lead people, 2 Samuel 19:1–8.

Responsibility for warning wicked, Ezekiel 3:17–19.

Family responsibility for sin, Ezekiel 18:4–20.

Responsibility of watchman, Ezekiel 33:1–9.

Privilege brings responsibility, Amos 3:2.

Refusal to accept responsibility, Jonah 1:3.

Responsible for nation's sin, Micah 1:13.

Burden of responsibility lightened, Matthew 11:28–30.

Wrong influence over children, Matthew 18:6.

Use of talents, Matthew 25:14–30.

Washing hands of crucifixion responsibility, Matthew 27:24.

Forgetting to bring necessities, Mark 8:14.

Care of unproductive fig tree, Luke 13:6–9.

Influencing others to sin, Luke 17:1.

Doing one's duty, Luke 17:10.

Responsible stewardship, Luke 21:1–4.

Personal responsibility to hearing truth, John 3:18–19.

Those who truly care for the sheep, John 10:11–14.

Delegating distribution of welfare, Acts 6:1–4.

Responsibility to all cultures, Romans 1:14–17.

Result of Adam's disobedience, Romans 5:12.

Responsibility for those who are weak, Romans 15:1.

Teamwork in reaching others, 1 Corinthians 3:6–9.

Entrusted with secret things of God, 1 Corinthians 4:1–2.

Leadership regarding gifts of Spirit, 1 Corinthians 12:27–30.

Aim for perfection, 2 Corinthians 13:11.

Carrying one's own load, Galatians 6:5.

Responsible for joy of others, Philippians 1:26.

Do not neglect your gift, 1 Timothy 4:14.

Families should take care of those in need, 1 Timothy 5:3–8.

Responsibility of obtaining wealth, 1 Timothy 6:17–19.

Responsibility to proclaim message, Titus 1:1–3.

Given responsibility for one's own affairs, Titus 1:5.

Providing for personal needs, Titus 3:14.

Human responsibility for evil, James 1:13–15.

Responsibility for teaching content, James 3:1.

R

Responsibility ignored, James 4:17.

All must give account of themselves, 1 Peter 4:4–6.

Seeing light, walking in darkness, 2 Peter 2:21.

See Leadership.

REST

Creative rest, Genesis 2:2.

Time set aside for rest, Exodus 23:12; 34:21.

Comforting bed, Job 7:13.

Lie down without fear, Job 11:19.

Assurance in rest, Psalm 3:5.

Sweet sleep, Proverbs 3:24.

Uncomfortable accommodations, Isaiah 28:20.

Avoiding work on Sabbath, Jeremiah 17:21–27.

Pleasant sleep, Jeremiah 31:26.

No rest for weary, Lamentations 5:5.

Soul rest, Matthew 11:28–30.

Quiet place for rest, Mark 6:31–32.

Travel weary, John 4:6.

Sabbath rest, Hebrews 4:9 (NASB, NIV, NRSV).

Repose of death, Revelation 14:13.

See Night, Sleep, Weariness.

RESTAURANT

Abraham as table waiter, Genesis 18:7–8.

Public eating places, Exodus 32:6; Psalm 23:5.

RESTITUTION

Good returned for evil, Genesis 47:1–11.

Responsibility for injury, Exodus 21:33–36.

Five-fold restitution, Exodus 22:1–15.

Setting things right with neighbor, Leviticus 6:1–6.

Prolonged retribution, Deuteronomy 23:2–6.

Making wrong right, Numbers 5:6–7; Nehemiah 5:1–13.

Guilt offering for desecrating ark of God, 1 Samuel 6:17.

Conflict between David and Saul, 1 Samuel 26:1–25.

Putting end to jealous conflict, 2 Samuel 2:26–29.

Showing kindness to enemy kin, 2 Samuel 9:1–13.

Restitution between nations, 1 Kings 20:34.

Return of property and income, 2 Kings 8:5–6.

Defilement in sanctuary, 2 Chronicles 29:1–11.

Money lenders brought to justice, Nehemiah 5:9–12.

Forced to restore what was not stolen, Psalm 69:4.

Seven-fold restitution, Proverbs 6:31.

Our Lord's reward for giving us salvation, Isaiah 53:10–12.

Crown of beauty, Isaiah 61:1–3.

Mercy for nation that repents, Jeremiah 18:1–12.

Setting things right, Lamentations 3:40.

Reprieve from death, Ezekiel 33:15.

Restitution begins in the heart, Joel 2:13.

Stone rejected by builders, Matthew 21:42.

Example of Zaccheus, Luke 19:8.

Peter restored to full fellowship, John 21:15–18.

Adam's guilt and grace of God, Romans 5:12–19 (See 8:1–4).

See Forgiveness, Pardon.

RESTLESS

Restless wanderer, Genesis 4:8–12.

Instability caused by disobedience, Deuteronomy 28:64–67.

Social and political unrest, 2 Chronicles 15:3–7.

Insomnia, Job 7:2–3.

Restless thoughts at night, Ecclesiastes 2:23.

Unrequited love, Song of Songs 3:1–2.

No peace for wicked, Isaiah 48:22; 57:20–21; 59:8.

Restless pursuit, Lamentations 5:5.

Unrewarded search for peace, Ezekiel 7:25.

Therapy for restlessness, Philippians 4:4–7; 1 Peter 5:7.

No rest day or night, Revelation 14:11.

See Anxiety, Anguish, Insomnia, Turmoil, Unrest.

RESTORATION

Broken tablets restored, Deuteronomy 10:2–4.

Backslider's restoration, 1 Samuel 15:24–25.

Parable used to bring restoration, 2 Samuel 14:1–21.

Partial restoration of captive king, 2 Kings 24:15; 25:27–30.

Doubly restored, Job 42:10.

Confession and restoration, Psalm 50:1–23.

Transgressors restored, Psalm 51:12.

Restoration, guidance, Isaiah 57:18.

Rebuilt ruins, Isaiah 58:12.

Divine offer of restoration, Jeremiah 3:22; Hosea 14:4.

Certainty of national restoration, Jeremiah 33:23–26.

Magnitude of divine restoration, Micah 7:19.

Stone rejected by builders, Matthew 21:42.

Christ's glory restored, John 17:5.

Son received back as from dead, Hebrews 11:19.

Restoring backslider to fellowship, James 5:19–20.

See Redemption.

RESTRAINT

Forbidden to taste food, 1 Samuel 14:24–28.

Imbibing without restraint, Esther 1:7, 8.

Nations resisting God's law, Psalm 2:3.

Keeping self-control, Proverbs 29:11.

Keeping silent, Ecclesiastes 3:7.

Restraint toward one who affronted the Lord, Isaiah 36:18–22; 37:1–7.

Unrestrained anger, Isaiah 64:9.

Demons refused permission to speak,, Mark 1:33–34.

See Discipline, Patience.

RESTRICTION

Restriction in garden of Eden, Genesis 2:16–17.

Cherubim guarding garden of Eden, Genesis 3:24.

Conditional greatness, 2 Kings 5:1.

Laws, regulations, Nehemiah 9:13.

Restriction on Sabbath merchandising, Nehemiah 13:15–19.

Effort to restrict truth, Jeremiah 38:1–6.

Demons refused permission to speak, Mark 1:33–34.

Carrying rules too far, Mark 2:23–27.

Athletes compete according to rules, 2 Timothy 2:5.

Restricted sacred mountain, Hebrews 12:18–21.

See Forbidden, Limitation, Regulations.

RESULTS

Results in personal witness, Psalm 126:6.

God's Word always brings results, Isaiah 55:10–11.

Results from prayer, Jeremiah 33:3; Luke 11:9; John 15:7.

Result of shining light, Matthew 5:16.

To whom much given, much expected, Luke 12:41–48; 19:11–26.

Cut down tree bearing no fruit, Luke 13:6–8.

Results from outreach, Luke 13:13–23.

Chosen to produce results, John 15:8, 16.

Jesus anticipated results, John 17:20.

See Accomplishment, Harvest.

RESUME

Resume of Israel's history, Psalms 78:1–72; 105:1–45; 106:1–48.

Wise man's summation, Ecclesiastes 12:13–14.

Stephen's resume of strategic history, Acts 7:1–53.

Paul's resume of Old Testament, Acts 13:16–41.

Resume of God's plan through the ages, Romans 1:1–6.

Resume of Christ's earth tenure, 1 Timothy 3:16 (See Luke 24:27).

See Conclusion, Finale.

RESURRECTION

Unsure of resurrection, Job 14:7–14.

Classic statement of faith, Job 19:25–26.

Prophecy of Christ's resurrection, Psalm 16:9–10.

Confidence in resurrection, Psalm 49:15.

Earth gives birth to the dead, Isaiah 26:19.

Valley of dry bones, Ezekiel 37:1–14.

Human resurrections, Daniel 12:2.

Post-resurrection promise, Daniel 12:13.

R

Jonah, type of Christ's resurrection, Matthew 12:38–40.

Pharisees guard against deceitful claim, Matthew 27:11–15; 62–66.

Attempt to cover up resurrection of Jesus, Matthew 28:11–15.

Prelude to resurrection, Mark 9:1–13.

Jesus foretold death, resurrection, Mark 10:32–34; Luke 18:31–39.

Predicted resurrection, Mark 14:28.

Rejecting resurrection message, Luke 16:27–31.

Refusing to believe, Luke 24:11–12.

Resurrection body of Jesus, Luke 24:37–39.

Temple, bodily resurrection, John 2:19–21.

Graves give up good, evil, John 5:29.

One raised from the dead, John 12:1–10 (See 11:1–44).

Convincing proofs, Acts 1:3.

Death of David, of Christ, Messianic implications, Acts 2:29–35.

Rejecting resurrection message, Acts 4:2.

Brought back from death, Acts 9:36–41.

Good news, Acts 13:32–33.

Resurrection central to Christian teaching, Acts 17:1–4.

Opposition to idolatry, Acts 17:16–18.

Varying response to resurrection message, Acts 17:32.

Paul's plea before Felix, Acts 24:1–21.

Doubts, questions about resurrection, Acts 25:19.

Jews should have known God could raise the dead, Acts 26:8.

Resurrection confirms Lordship of Christ, Romans 1:1–4.

New life in Christ, Romans 6:4.

Only one death for Christ, Romans 6:9–10.

Resurrection assures freedom from legality, Romans 7:1–6.

The Holy Spirit brought Christ back from the dead, Romans 8:11; 1 Peter 1:21; Ephesians 1:18–21.

Act of God's power, 1 Corinthians 6:14.

Impact of resurrection message, 1 Corinthians 15:12–58.

Resurrection strength, 2 Corinthians 1:9.

"Heavenly dwelling," 2 Corinthians 5:2 (NRSV).

Weakness relates to the Cross, 2 Corinthians 13:4.

Citizenship in Heaven, Philippians 3:20–21.

God's power put to work, Ephesians 1:20 (NRSV).

Impact of resurrection upon Christian's life, 1 Peter 1:21.

Vision of resurrected Christ, Revelation 1:17–18.

Resurrection of two witnesses, Revelation 11:3–12.

Fatal wound healed, Revelation 13:3.

Martyrs restored to life, Revelation 20:4–6.

See Gospel, Immortality.

RETALIATION

Eye for an eye, Exodus 21:23–25; Deuteronomy 19:19; Matthew 5:38–44.

Do not retaliate, Leviticus 19:18.

Reversal of fortunes, Esther 5:9; 7:10.

Jews liquidated their enemies, Esther 9:1–17.

Stark picture of vengeance, Psalms 58:10; 68:23.

Do not pay back wrong, Proverbs 20:22; 24:29.

Leave works of enemy in God's hands, Lamentations 3:55–66.

Turn other cheek, go extra mile, Matthew 5:38–41.

Basics of Golden Rule, Luke 6:27–36.

Exemplary response to evil, Romans 12:17; 1 Peter 2:12–17; 3:9.

Love those who cause grief, 2 Corinthians 2:5–11.

Leave revenge in God's hands, 2 Thessalonians 1:6–7; 2 Timothy 3:14.

See Retribution, Revenge.

RETARDED

Those with no wisdom, Job 26:3.

Limited sense, Psalm 92:6; Jeremiah 10:8; 51:17.

Understanding to the simple, Psalm 119:130 (LB).

Weak-minded youth, Proverbs 7:7; 9:14–18.

Animal mentality, Daniel 4:16; 2 Peter 2:12; Jude 10.

See Mental Health, Mentality.

RETICENT

Negative, positive viewpoints, Numbers 13:17–33.

Testing divine patience, Numbers 14:18.

Taking care of business, Deuteronomy 20:5–9.

Reluctance in expressing spiritual concern, Romans 9:1–2.

Apostle's reticence, 2 Corinthians 10:1.

See Shy, Timidity.

RETIREMENT

Aaron's retirement, Numbers 20:26 (See Berk.).

Virility retained until death, Deuteronomy 34:7.

Work unfinished, Joshua 13:1.

Going strong at eighty-five, Joshua 14:10–11.

Joshua's farewell, Joshua 23:1–8.

Looking back across exemplary life, 1 Samuel 12:3.

Denied fruit of life's labor, Ecclesiastes 6:1, 2.

King at age sixty-two, Daniel 5:30–31.

Old age sitting in streets, Zechariah 8:4.

Consistent worship during advanced age, Luke 2:36–38.

Families should care for those in need, 1 Timothy 5:3–8.

See Geriatrics, Old Age.

RETREAT (Rest)

Rock of refuge, Psalm 71:3.

Get away from it all, Jeremiah 9:2.

Quiet place for rest, Mark 6:31.

Jesus withdrew from crowd to pray, Luke 5:16.

Praying through the night, Luke 6:12.

Futile attempt to hold retreat, Luke 9:10–11.

Countryside retreat, John 3:22; John 11:54.

Athens suitable place to be left alone, 1 Thessalonians 3:1.

See Holiday, Rest.

RETREAT (Submission)

Cowardly retreat, Psalm 78:9.

One warrior stumbling over another, Jeremiah 46:12, 16.

Hiss of fleeing serpent, Jeremiah 46:22.

Brave warriors flee naked, Amos 2:16.

See Defeat.

RETRIBUTION

Servant's attitude toward unfair employer, Genesis 16:1–10.

Forgiveness instead of retribution, Genesis 50:15–21.

Prolonged retribution, Deuteronomy 23:2–6.

"Settle accounts," 1 Samuel 15:2 (LB).

Reaction to rejection, 2 Samuel 10:1–19.

Folly of relationship with evil woman, 2 Samuel 12:1–13.

Negotiated retribution, 2 Samuel 21:1–9.

Executing unfaithful fathers, sparing sons, 2 Kings 14:5–6.

Gallows for his own neck, Esther 5:14; 9:25.

Enemy falls into pit he designed, Psalm 57:6.

Stark picture of vengeance, Psalms 58:10; 68:23.

When not to do as others have done, Proverbs 24:29.

Kindness to enemy, Proverbs 25:21–22.

Evil begets evil, Ecclesiastes 10:8.

Destroyer destroyed, Isaiah 33:1.

Sins paid back, Isaiah 65:6.

Strike back against enemies, Jeremiah 49:2.

Reaping harvest of oppression, Lamentations 1:3 (LB).

Folly of retribution, Ezekiel 25:15–17.

Reciprocal retribution, Daniel 6:24.

Punishment for mockers, Zephaniah 2:8–10.

Never seek retribution, Luke 6:27–28; 1 Corinthians 13:5 (RSV).

Leave revenge in God's hands, 2 Thessalonians 1:6.

Harm received for harm done, 2 Peter 2:13.

Golden rule stated negatively, Revelation 18:6.

See Retaliation, Revenge, Vengeance.

RETROGRESS

Journey one should never make again, Deuteronomy 28:68.

Go forward but fall backward, Isaiah 28:13.

No longer habitable, Jeremiah 9:11.

See Failure, Retreat.

RETROSPECT

Remembering happier days, Lamentations 1:7 (LB).

Long years of Divine goodness and faithfulness, Psalm 37:25.

Remembering glory of better days, Haggai 2:3.

Looking back upon history, Acts 7:1–53.

See Memory, Reminiscence.

REUNION

Reunion between Jacob, Esau, Genesis 33:1–20.

Reunion between Joseph, brothers, Genesis 45:1–15.

Eagerness to meet father, Genesis 46:29.

Absalom's return to King David, 2 Samuel 14:1–35.

Prodigal son, Luke 15:11–31.

Long absence, Romans 15:22 (GNB).

Paul fearful of reunion with Corinthians, 2 Corinthians 12:20–21.

Reunion of all believers, 1 Thessalonians 4:13–18.

Friends reunited, 2 Timothy 1:17.

See Restoration.

REVEAL See Discovery, Display.

REVELATION

God's message in deep sleep, Genesis 15:12–16.

Heavenly visitors, Genesis 18:1–10.

Sibling identity revealed, Genesis 45:1–15.

God's revelation to Moses, Exodus 3:1–10, 12, 14–15; 6:1–11.

Do not worship God in nature, Deuteronomy 4:15–20.

Divine silence, 1 Samuel 3:1.

Leave revenge to God, 1 Samuel 25:39.

Plea for revenge, 1 Kings 2:5–6.

God speaks in different ways, Job 33:14.

Skies proclaim glory of God, Psalm 19:1–6.

God-given ability to understand Scripture, Psalm 119:125.

Eternity in men's hearts, Ecclesiastes 3:11.

New and hidden things, Isaiah 48:6.

Ezekiel's vision, Ezekiel 1:1.

God reveals Himself through judgment, Ezekiel 5:13; 6:7, 10, 13–14; 7:4, 9, 27.

Revelation received in vision, Daniel 2:19.

Prophets informed of divine plans, Amos 3:7.

Creator reveals thoughts to man, Amos 4:13.

Those who could not accept identity of Jesus, John 10:24–30.

Mistaking voice of God for thunder, John 12:28–29.

Reason versus revelation, 1 Corinthians 1:20–31.

No specific command, 1 Corinthians 7:25.

God's message revealed in creation, Romans 1:18–20.

Revelation to those who did not seek it, Romans 10:20.

Caught up into third heaven, 2 Corinthians 12:1–4.

Guided by revelation, Galatians 2:2.

First prophets, then Christ, Hebrews 1:1–2.

See Prophecy, Scripture.

REVELRY

Spiritual festival turns to wantonness, Exodus 32:5–6.

Celebration of harvest, Judges 9:27.

Evil mob in high spirits, Judges 16:23–25.

Celebrating plunder, 1 Samuel 30:16.

Entertainment with no thought of spiritual need, Isaiah 5:12.

Revelry of Tyre, Sidon, Isaiah 23:6–12.

Halted revelry, Isaiah 24:8–9.

Noise of carefree crowd, Ezekiel 23:42.

Wild parties, Romans 13:13 (CEV, LB).

See Carousing, Hedonism, Orgy.

REVENGE

First murder, Genesis 4:1–16.

Servant attitude to unfair employer, Genesis 16:1–10.

Revenge forbidden, Leviticus 19:18.

Injury for injury, Leviticus 24:19–20.

Harass and attack, Numbers 25:17 (NKJV).

Revenge for bad influence, Numbers 31:1 (LB).

Tit for tat, Joshua 10:1.

Evil repays evil, Judges 1:6–7 (LB).

Threatened revenge, Judges 8:4–9.

Sharing honors in military victory, Judges 12:1–3.

Philistine fields aflame, Judges 15:4–5.

Evil for evil, Judges 15:10–11.

Massive act of revenge, Judges 20:1–48.

Not taking revenge, 1 Samuel 24:1–13.

Gratitude for no revenge, 1 Samuel 25:32–34.

Murder in revenge, 2 Samuel 3:22–34.

David's attitude toward murder of Saul's son, 2 Samuel 4:1–12.

Murder to avenge sister's disgrace, 2 Samuel 13:23–29.

Alleged man of blood, 2 Samuel 16:5–8.

Reward of evil, 1 Kings 2:5–6.

Overt revenge, 2 Kings 11:1.

Revenge against those who did not assist, Nehemiah 13:1–3.

Proper revenge, Psalm 6:10.

Evil brings its own revenge, Psalm 9:15.

Self-induced revenge, Psalm 37:14–15.

Enemy falls into pit he designed, Psalm 57:6.

Stark picture of vengeance, Psalms 58:10; 68:22–23.

Revenge against gossip, Psalm 64:8.

Let the Lord vindicate, Psalm 135:14; Ezekiel 25:12–17; 2 Thessalonians 1:6–7; 5:15.

Evil for evil, Proverbs 20:22 (LB).

Avoid revenge, Proverbs 24:29.

Inevitable revenge, Jeremiah 51:49.

Counsel against revenge, Proverbs 24:29.

Traitor suffers what he imposed, Isaiah 33:1.

Time for Divine vengeance, Jeremiah 51:6, 56.

Leave works of enemy in God's hands, Lamentations 3:55–66.

Revenge first in the heart, Ezekiel 25:15–17.

Vengeful spirit punished, Amos 1:11–12.

Those who mock God's people, Zephaniah 2:9–10.

Turn opposite cheek, go extra mile, Matthew 5:38–42.

Basics of Golden Rule, Luke 6:27–38.

Calling down fire from Heaven, Luke 9:54–55.

Forgiving spirit of martyr, Acts 7:60.

Do not return evil for evil, Romans 12:17.

Never take revenge, 1 Corinthians 13:5 (RSV).

Showing love to those who cause grief, 2 Corinthians 2:5–11.

No need to avenge wrong, Galatians 5:10.

Kindness in place of vengeance, 1 Thessalonians 5:15.

Leave revenge in God's hands, 2 Thessalonians 1:6.

Leave revenge to God, 2 Timothy 4:14 (AB).

Do not retaliate against those who do wrong, 1 Peter 2:12–17, 23.

Walking in steps of Christ, 1 Peter 2:21–25.

Do not repay evil with evil, insult with insult, 1 Peter 3:9.

Harm received for harm done, 2 Peter 2:13.

Those who crucified witness Christ's return, Revelation 1:7.

Martyrs call out for revenge, Revelation 6:9–11.

Judgment of God upon evil, Revelation 16:5–7.

Golden Rule stated negatively, Revelation 18:6.

See Avenge, Retaliation, Retribution, Sadistic, Vengeance.

REVERENCE

Reverence for God, Genesis 17:3; Exodus 3:5.

Reverence for place of worship, Leviticus 19:30; 26:2.

Worship only at place designated by God, Deuteronomy 12:13–14.

Prophet who speaks in error, Deuteronomy 18:21–22.

Those who honor God, those who do not, 1 Samuel 2:30.

A god of stone shows reverence for ark of God, 1 Samuel 5:1–5.

Death from looking into ark of God, 1 Samuel 6:19–20.

Touching ark of God, 2 Samuel 6:6–11.

David's reverence, 1 Chronicles 13:12.

Nehemiah's prayer, Nehemiah 1:4–7.

Recognizing God's majesty, Job 37:23–24.

R

True reverence in worship, Malachi 2:4–5.

Observance of Sabbath, Matthew 12:1–13.

Call no one on earth "father," Matthew 23:8–10.

Head covering in worship, 1 Corinthians 11:3–10.

Ark built with reverence, Hebrews 11:7 (NASB).

Take Scriptures to heart, Revelation 1:3.

Living creatures, elders, Revelation 4:8–11.

Heaven's worship drama, Revelation 7:11–12.

See Worship.

REVIEW

Memory refreshed, 2 Peter 1:12–15.
See Resume.

REVISION

Book that cannot be revised, Revelation 22:18.

REVIVAL

Tear down old, build new, Judges 6:25, 26.

Disobedience of faithful, 1 Samuel 12:20.

Backslider returning to the Lord, 1 Samuel 15:24–25.

Revival promise, 2 Chronicles 7:14.

Evil revival, 2 Chronicles 33:1–7.

Restored joy of salvation, Psalms 51:12; 80:7.

"Make us strong again," Psalm 80:3 (CEV).

Prayer for revival, Psalms 80:18; 85:1–7.

Poured out Spirit, Isaiah 32:15.

Streams on dry ground, Isaiah 35:6; 44:3.

Self-examination, Lamentations 3:40–42.

"Give us a fresh start," Lamentations 5:21 (CEV).

Heart of flesh or stone, Ezekiel 11:19.

Coming spiritual revival in Israel, Ezekiel 39:28–29.

Acknowledge the Lord, Hosea 6:2–3.

Break up unplowed ground, sow righteousness, Hosea 10:12.

True repentance, Hosea 14:2.

Response to those who repent, Joel 2:12–13.

Stop wrong, begin right, Amos 5:14 (CEV).

Prayer for past blessings, Habakkuk 3:2.

Desert revivalist, Matthew 3:1–12; Mark 1:5

Fan into flame the gift of God, 2 Timothy 1:6.

Time to awaken, Revelation 3:2.
See Renewal, Renunciation, Repentance.

REVOLT *See Anarchy, Mutiny.*

REVOLUTION *See Civil War.*

REWARD

Obedience rewarded, Genesis 22:15–18; Leviticus 25:18–19; Deuteronomy 4:40; 6:3.

Reward for honoring parents, Exodus 20:12; Ephesians 6:1–3.

Good weather, security, Leviticus 26:3–45; Deuteronomy 11:13–29.

Honesty, longevity, Deuteronomy 25:15.

Reward of accomplishment, Judges 8:22–23.

Delilah bribed to deliver Samson, Judges 16:1–5.

Rewarded for faithfulness to mother-in-law, Ruth 2:7–12.

Mother's reward for giving son, 1 Samuel 2:18–21.

Reward for act of kindness, 1 Samuel 30:11–18.

Anticipating reward, Nehemiah 5:19.

Ironical reward, Esther 5:14; 6:13.

Worthlessness rewarded, Job 15:31 (See GNB).

Reward for good mother, Proverbs 31:31.

Bread cast upon waters, Ecclesiastes 11:1.

Good, bad deeds rewarded, Isaiah 3:10–11.

All in God's hands, Isaiah 49:4.

Fate of good, evil, Isaiah 65:13–14.

God sees all, rewards good, Jeremiah 32:19.

Rewarded for kindness to prophet, Jeremiah 38:7–13.

Refusing bribes, rewards, Daniel 5:17.

Heavenly reward following resurrection, Daniel 12:13.

Receiving what one deserves, Zechariah 1:6.

Reward for self-denial, Matthew 16:24–28.

Good works rewarded, Matthew 25:34–46; Romans 2:7, 10.

Leaving all to follow Jesus, Mark 10:28–31.

Persecution rewarded, Luke 6:22–23.

Runner trains to win crown, 1 Corinthians 9:24–27.

Followers are ministry reward, 1 Thessalonians 2:17–19.

Prayer that friend would be rewarded, 2 Timothy 1:16–18.

Farmer receives first share of crop, 2 Timothy 2:6.

Sure reward for obedience, disobedience, 2 Timothy 2:11–13.

Crown rewards faithful ministry, 2 Timothy 4:6–8.

Those who forfeited reward, Hebrews 3:16–19.

God does not forget good works, Hebrews 6:10.

Confidence will be rewarded, Hebrews 10:35.

Crown of life for those who persevere, James 1:12.

Danger of losing one's full reward, 2 John 8.

Seated one day on the throne, Revelation 3:21.

Reward for what one has done, Revelation 22:12.

See Recompense.

RHEUMATISM

Bodily pain, Job 14:22.

Bone pains, Job 30:17; 33:19.

Searing pain, Psalm 38:7.

Body raked with pain, Isaiah 21:3.

No more pain, Revelation 21:4.

RIDDANCE

Infamy to daughter of king, 2 Kings 9:30–37.

Egypt's dread of Israel, Psalm 105:38.

Quandry for ignorant man, Proverbs 30:2–4.

False concern for safety of Jesus, Luke 13:31.

RIDDLE

Abraham laughed at God, Genesis 17:17; 18:10–15.

Riddles learned from dreams, Genesis 37:5–11; 40:9–22; 41:15–31; Daniel 2:29–45; 4:4–33.

Rhyming riddle, Judges 14:14 (NRSV).

"Dark saying," Psalm 49:4 (See NIV and KJV).

Two eagles and vine, Ezekiel 17:1–21.

Jesus accused of obscure speech, John 16:29 (GNB).

RIDICULE

"Feeble Jews," Nehemiah 4:1–2

Ridiculed by friends, Job 12:4.

Scorn for acts of humility, Psalm 69:10–11.

Youth ridiculed for faith, Psalm 129:1–2.

Parents ridiculed, Proverbs 30:17 (GNB).

Do not fear reproach of men, Isaiah 51:7.

Despised, rejected, Isaiah 53:3.

God's people ridiculed, Micah 2:4.

Laughingstock, Job 12:4; Lamentations 3:14.

"They make sport of me," Job 30:1 (NRSV).

"Making fun of nations," Psalm 2:4 (CEV).

Strong preaching ridiculed, Jeremiah 17:15 (LB).

"Sad news," Jeremiah 23:33–40 (LB).

Object of ridicule, Jeremiah 48:39.

Once exalted city scoffed, Lamentations 2:15.

Disrespect for temple, Ezekiel 25:3 (See LB).

Ridiculed prophet, Ezekiel 33:30–33 (LB).

Those who dared to ridicule Jesus, Matthew 9:23, 24; Luke 4:33–35; 8:50–53.

Crucifixion of Jesus, Mark 15:21–32.

Day of Pentecost, Acts 2:13.

See Demean, Humiliation, Taunt.

RIGAMAROLE

Insincere prayer, Matthew 6:7 (See LB).

RIGHT

Led the right way, Job 23:10–12; Psalm 119:35.

The right path, Psalm 16:11.

Following Good Shepherd, Psalm 23:1–2; Luke 1:79.

Trust, commitment rewarded, Proverbs 3:5–6.

Tutored in right way, Isaiah 2:3.

Level path, Isaiah 26:7.

Source of right guidance, Jeremiah 42:3.

The narrow way, Matthew 7:13–14.

See Holiness, Righteousness.

RIGHT BRAIN *See Aesthetics.*

RIGHTEOUSNESS

Made righteous by God's presence, Exodus 33:16.

Cause for assurance, Joshua 22:31.

Some good in Judah, 2 Chronicles 12:12.

Man who truly walked with God, Job 1:1.

Bildad's correct assessment, Job 8:5–6.

"No human is innocent," Job 9:2, 20 (CEV).

Personal righteousness, Job 34:1–4; Psalm 18:20–21.

Definition of righteous man, Psalm 1:1–3.

Marks of righteous person, Psalm 15:1–5; Proverbs 13:5.

Blameless before the Lord, Psalm 26:1, 11.

Purity of heart, gift from God, Psalm 51:10.

Right prevails, Psalm 58:11.

Righteous person and good life, Psalm 112:1–10; Ezekiel 18:5–9.

Those who walk according to Scripture, Psalm 119:1–16.

Insufficient righteousness, Psalm 130:3.

Growth in perception, Proverbs 4:18.

Man's ways may seem right, Proverbs 21:2.

Measured by plumbline, Isaiah 28:17.

National righteousness, Jeremiah 31:12–34.

God's total forgiveness, Jeremiah 50:20.

Neither good nor evil shared from father to son, Ezekiel 18:3–20.

Righteousness of God, Daniel 9:14.

Mark of man who pleases the Lord, Micah 5:8.

Beatitudes, Matthew 5:3–16.

Test of righteousness in time of wickedness, Matthew 24:12–13.

Righteousness comes by faith, Romans 1:17.

Hate evil, cling to good, Romans 12:9.

Seeking righteousness by human effort, Galatians 3:3.

Legalism false criteria for judgment, Colossians 2:16.

Lifestyle of those risen with Christ, Colossians 3:1–17.

The law makes nothing perfect, Hebrews 7:18, 19.

See Consecration, Discipline, Discipleship.

RIGHTS

First son's rights, Deuteronomy 21:15–17.

Rights of Roman citizen, Acts 22:25–29.

See Citizenship, Privilege.

RIGHTWING *See Conservative.*

RING

Nose ring, Genesis 24:47.

Signet ring of government status, Genesis 41:42; Esther 3:10.

Rings for temple use, Exodus 35:22.

Signet ring for document seal, Esther 8:8.

Item of finery, Isaiah 3:18–23.

Relationship symbol, Luke 15:22.

See Jewelry.

RISK

Put in jeopardy, Job 13:14.

Risking life to serve, Philippians 2:30.

RITUAL

Circumcision at advanced age, Genesis 17:10–27.

Envious brothers, Genesis 37:4.

Prayer for protection, Numbers 10:35.

Misuse of sacrifice, 1 Samuel 2:12–17.

Religious works involved in idolatry, Isaiah 46:1.

Barrier of law broken in Christ, Ephesians 2:14–16; Colossians 2:13–15; Hebrews 7:18; 8:13; 10:1.

See Formality, Liturgy.

RIVAL

Jealous wife, 1 Samuel 1:2–7.

Frustrated Saul, 1 Samuel 18:8.

David's opportunity to kill Saul, 1 Samuel 26:1–25.

Brother spared, 1 Kings 1:49–53.
At peace with enemies, Proverbs 16:7.
Labor, skill, rivalry, Ecclesiastes 4:4 (NASB).
"God tolerates no rivals," Nahum 1:2 (GNB).
Bickering among laborers, Matthew 20:12.
Evaluating military logistics, Luke 14:31–32.
Prodigal, brother, Luke 15:25–32.
See Competition, Jealousy.

RIVER

Rivers of the Bible, Genesis 2:11, 14; Exodus 1:22; Deuteronomy 2:36; Joshua 16:5; Judges 5:21; 2 Kings 5:12; 17:6; Ezekiel 1:1; Daniel 8:16.
River responds to Elijah's cloak, 2 Kings 2:13–14.
River of Salvation, Psalms 36:8; 46:4; Isaiah 32:2.
Jordan flowing backward, Psalm 114:3 (Berk.).
Flowing tears, Lamentations 2:18.
Dry river bed, Isaiah 11:15.
God's wrath against Pharaoh's claim to Nile, Ezekiel 29:3–5.
River of life, Revelation 22:1–2.
See Geography.

ROAD

Main road through country, Deuteronomy 2:27.
Military route, Joshua 10:9–11; Judges 20:31.
Only one right road, Proverbs 16:17.
Highway for Israel's remnant, Isaiah 11:16.
Way of holiness, Isaiah 35:8–10.
Prepared way for the Lord, Isaiah 40:3–4; Matthew 3:1–3.
Glorious highway for God's people, Isaiah 57:14 (LB).
Road signs, Jeremiah 31:21; Ezekiel 21:19.
Broad road and narrow roads, Matthew 7:13–14.
Adventure on the Jericho road, Luke 10:30–37.
Desert road, Acts 8:26 (GNB).
See Highway, Journey, Transportation, Travel.

ROAR

When God roars, Isaiah 33:3 (CEV).

ROBBERY

Responsibility for killing thief, Exodus 22:2–3.
Forbidden by law, Leviticus 19:13; Isaiah 61:8.
Need for two or three witnesses, Deuteronomy 19:15.
Lurking in ambush, Judges 9:25.
Protection against enemies of the road, Ezra 8:21–23.
Breaking and entering, Job 24:16.
Career robbers, Proverbs 1:11–16.
Bandit's prey, Proverbs 6:11 (Berk.).
Treasures surveyed for subsequent thievery, Isaiah 39:1–6.
Robbers den, Jeremiah 7:11.
Death penalty, Ezekiel 18:10–13.
Robbery and extortion, Ezekiel 22:29.
Robber bands, Hosea 6:9; 7:1.
Thievery of tax collectors and soldiers, Luke 3:12–14.
Danger on Jericho road, Luke 10:25–37.
Christian reaction to plundering, Hebrews 10:34 (AB).
See Stealing, Thieves.

ROBE

Robe of righteousness, 2 Chronicles 6:41; Isaiah 61:10; Revelation 6:11; 7:9–13.
Purple robe, Esther 8:15; Daniel 5:7; Luke 16:19.
Threads of gold, Psalm 45:13.
Priests' garments considered holy, Ezekiel 42:14; 44:19.
Royal robes, Acts 12:21.
See Wardrobe.

ROCK

Rock struck by Moses, Deuteronomy 8:15; Psalm 78:18–22.
The Lord our Rock, 2 Samuel 22:32, 47; 23:3; Psalms 18:2; 31:2; Isaiah 17:10.
Source of oil, Deuteronomy 32:13; Job 29:6.
"Mighty rock," Psalm 28:1 (CEV).
Sure footing, Psalm 40:2.
Rock eternal, Isaiah 26:4 (NIV).

R

God's followers as rocks in a thirsty land, Isaiah 32:2.

Christ living stone, believers lesser stones, 1 Peter 2:4–5.

See Geology.

ROCK AND ROLL

"Song of fools," Ecclesiastes 7:5 (NIV).

End to noisy songs, Ezekiel 26:13.

Earth's music silenced, Revelation 18:22.

RODENTS

Eating rats, Isaiah 66:17.

ROLE

Roles reversed, Luke 16:25.

ROMAN CATHOLICS

Prayer to saints, Job 5:1; 15:15.

"Queen of Heaven," Jeremiah 44:17, 19, 25.

Celibacy advocated by Jesus, Matthew 19:11–12.

Jesus and His mother, Mark 3:31–35.

Apostle Paul and celibacy, 1 Corinthians 7:8, 27.

"Mortal sin," 1 John 5:16 (NRSV).

ROMANCE

A mate "at last," Genesis 2:23 (Berk.).

Bride for Isaac, Genesis 24:1–58; 25:19–20.

Captive women, Deuteronomy 21:10–14.

Men outnumbered women, Judges 21:1–23.

Woman proposed to man, Ruth 3:9.

Love, infatuation, 1 Samuel 18:20–29.

Demanding another man's wife, 2 Samuel 3:12–16.

Lovesick, 2 Samuel 13:1–4.

Man and maid, Proverbs 30:18–19.

Time of restraint, Ecclesiastes 3:5.

Expressing affection, Song of Songs 1:15; 2:14; 4:1–16; 6:4–12; 7:1–8.

Romantic garden song, Song of Songs 5:1–8.

See Courtship, Infatuation.

ROOF

Grass roof, 2 Kings 19:26; Psalm 129:6; Isaiah 37:27.

Leaking roof, Proverbs 19:13; 27:15.

Roof prayer, Acts 10:9.

ROOM *See Accommodations, Hospitality.*

ROOTS *See Ancestors, Background, Family, Heritage.*

ROPE

Pegs and ropes for tabernacle, Exodus 35:18; 39:40.

Rope of deliverance in Jericho, Joshua 2:15.

Ropes dropped from hands, Judges 15:13–14.

See Fetters.

ROTATION

Seventh year rest for fields, Exodus 23:10, 11.

ROTATION

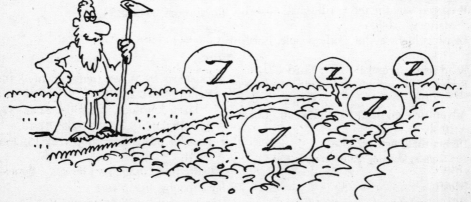

ROTTEN *See Decay, Putrid, Stench.*

ROUNDELAY

History repeats itself, Ecclesiastes 3:15.

ROYALTY

Choosing king from among trees, Judges 9:7–20.

Predicted oppression by king, 1 Samuel 8:10–19 (LB).

Preferring civil to spiritual leadership, 1 Samuel 10:17–19.

Thirty-two kings, 1 Kings 20:1, 16.

"God save the king," 2 Kings 11:12 (NKJV); Psalm 20:6 (LB).

Several palaces, 1 Chronicles 15:1 (LB).

Confiscated crown, 1 Chronicles 20:2.

Friend of king, 1 Chronicles 27:33.

Denied royal grave, 2 Chronicles 28:27.

Three month reign, 2 Chronicles 36:1–2.

Exemplary king, Psalm 21:7.

Demeaned royalty, Jeremiah 13:18 (LB).

King, queen brought to judgment, Jeremiah 13:18.

Respectable exile, Jeremiah 52:31–34.

Pilate's question to Jesus, Mark 15:2.

Queen of the South, Luke 11:29–31.

King of the Jews, John 19:19–22.

See Palace.

RUBBISH

Silver thrown into streets, Ezekiel 7:19.

Earth's content compared to God's best, Philippians 3:7–10.

RUBBLE *See Devastation, Ruins.*

RUDENESS

Forgetting God's goodness, Psalm 106:7–8, 13.

Staring at those God uses, Acts 3:12.

"Entirely out of place," Ephesians 5:4 (NRSV).

See Discourtesy.

RUIN

"Jerusalem in ruins," Psalm 79:1 (NRSV).

Reduced to ruins, Psalm 89:40.

Impressive construction, impending ruins, Mark 13:1–2.

Complete destruction, Luke 6:49.

See Destruction.

RULES

Regulation of music used in worship, 1 Chronicles 6:31–32.

God makes rules, Job 34:33 (CEV).

Carrying rules too far, Mark 2:23–27.

Need for proper credentials, Acts 15:22–31.

Rules to obey, Acts 16:4 (GNB).

Playing according to rules, 2 Timothy 2:5.

Regulations for worship, Hebrews 9:1.

See Regulations.

RUMOR

Fear of rumor to enemy, Numbers 14:13–16.

Evil rumor discerned, Nehemiah 6:10–13.

Wisdom a rumor, Job 28:20–22 (GNB, NRSV).

Spread no rumors, Psalm 15:1–3 (GNB).

Disbelieving threat of murder, Jeremiah 40:13–16; 41:1–2.

First one rumor, then another, Jeremiah 51:46.

Rumor from the Lord, Obadiah 1 (KJV).

Misunderstood statement, John 21:22–23 (NIV).

See Gossip.

RUNNER-UP

Coming in second, Acts 1:23–26.

RUNNING

Renewal of strength, Isaiah 40:30–31.

Running long race, Jeremiah 12:5.

See Athletics.

RURAL

Rural choices of Abram, Lot, Genesis 13:12.

Town, country, Deuteronomy 28:3.

RUSE

Circumstantial evidence against Joseph, Genesis 39:6–20.

Fake body, 1 Samuel 19:12–17.

Deceitful plan to destroy Paul, Acts 23:12–22.

RUSH

Paul's hurry to reach Jerusalem, Acts 20:16.

RUSSIA

Israel and northern Europe, Ezekiel 38:15–19.

RUST

Oil as protection against rust, Isaiah 21:5.

Gold and silver corroded, James 5:3.

See Corrosion.

S

SABBATH

Origin of Sabbath, Genesis 2:3.

Historic observance, Exodus 16:23–30.

Sabbath Day mandate, Exodus 20:8.

Animal's day of rest, Exodus 23:12.

Sabbath business, Nehemiah 13:16–21.

Joyful Sabbath worship, Isaiah 58:13 (CEV).

Sabbath gate, Ezekiel 46:1.

Full meaning of Sabbath, Hebrews 4:8–10.

See Sunday, Lord's Day.

SACRAMENT

Sacrifice of a son, 2 Kings 16:3.

Religious works involved in idolatry, Isaiah 46:1.

Meaning of circumcision, Jeremiah 4:4.

The Lords supper, Matthew 26:17–30; Mark 14:12–26; 1 Corinthians 11:17–30.

Those circumcised who do not keep the law, Romans 2:25–27.

Circumcision did not bring salvation, Romans 4:1–13.

Personal righteousness not through sacraments, Hebrews 9:8–10.

Physical act cannot bring spiritual result, Hebrews 10:1–4.

See Baptism, Communion.

SACRED

Sacred location for altar, Deuteronomy 12:5–6.

Sacred courtroom, Deuteronomy 17:8.

Grave of Moses, Deuteronomy 34:6.

Purpose of temple, 2 Chronicles 2:5–6.

Articles from Jerusalem put into pagan temple, Daniel 1:1–2.

Truly sacred, Matthew 23:16–17.

Sacred mountain not to be touched, Hebrews 12:18–21.

See Consecration, Holy.

SACRIFICE

Aroma of good sacrifice, Genesis 8:20–21; Leviticus 23:18; 2 Corinthians 2:15; Ephesians 5:1–2.

Test of father's love to God, son, Genesis 22:1–14.

Infanticide forbidden, Leviticus 18:21; Deuteronomy 12:31.

Continuing sacrifice, Numbers 28:1–6.

Sacrifice of only child, Judges 11:29–39.

Honoring sacrifice, 2 Samuel 23:15–17.

Cheap stewardship refused, 2 Samuel 24:21–24.

Pagan practice of infanticide, 2 Kings 3:26–27; 16:1–3; 2 Chronicles 28:3; Isaiah 57:5; Jeremiah 19:5; Ezekiel 16:20; 23:37.

Death to give life, Isaiah 43:4 (LB).

Human sacrifice, Jeremiah 7:31–32.

Finest youth killed in battle, Jeremiah 48:15.

Death of Ezekiel's wife a lesson for wicked Israel, Ezekiel 24:15–24.

Persistent sacrifices in temple, Ezekiel 43:18–27.

Abundant sacrifices, Micah 6:7.

Living sacrifice, Mark 10:28–31; Luke 18:28–30.

Mixing human blood with sacrificial blood, Luke 13:1.

Death of wheat kernel, John 12:24–26.

Willingness of Jesus to be sacrificed, John 18:1–11.

Diminished sacrifice, Acts 19:19.

Poured out offering, 2 Timothy 4:6.

Power, meaning of Christ's blood, Hebrews 9:8–15.

Willing to lay down one's life, 1 John 3:16.

See Altar, Consecration, Surrender.

SACRILEGE

Sacrilegious Pharaoh, Exodus 5:2.

Tempting the Lord, Exodus 17:7.

Profane fire, Leviticus 10:1 (NKJV).

Punishment of expulsion, Leviticus 19:8.

Sabbath labor, Numbers 15:32–36.

Mixing immorality with worship, Numbers 25:1–2.

Sacrilegious idol, Judges 17:3.

Illicit relationship in spiritual service, 1 Samuel 2:22.

Using sacred offering for personal gain, 1 Samuel 2:29.

Desecrated Ark of God, 1 Samuel 5:1–2.

Death from looking into Ark of God, 1 Samuel 6:19–20.

Touching Ark of God, 2 Samuel 6:6–11.

Breaking, entering temple, 2 Chronicles 24:7.

Insulting the Lord, 2 Chronicles 32:17.

Mocking God's messengers, 2 Chronicles 36:16.

Destroyed reverence, Job 15:4 (Berk.).

"Sneering at God," Psalm 1:1 (CEV).

"Impious people," Psalm 74:18, 22 (NRSV).

Disturbed at prayer, Psalm 109:4 (Berk.).

Sin of challenging God, Isaiah 5:18–19.

Pagan temple profaned by murder, Isaiah 37:38.

Sabbath breaking, Isaiah 58:13.

Wrong kind of offering, Isaiah 66:3.

Disrespect for sanctuary, Ezekiel 25:1–4.

Misuse of temple furnishings, Daniel 5:2.

Laughing at Jesus, Matthew 9:23–24; Luke 4:33–35; 8:50–53.

Attributing work of God to demons, Matthew 9:34.

Using temple for business, Matthew 21:12–13; Mark 11:15–17.

Empty sincerity of Pharisees, Mark 12:15–17.

Scoffing at Crucifixion, Mark 15:29–32.

Mixing human blood with sacrifices, Luke 13:1.

Striking Jesus in the face, John 18:22.

Destroying temple, 1 Corinthians 3:17.

Gluttony at Lord's table, 1 Corinthians 11:20–21 (LB).

See Abomination, Blasphemy, Impiety, Infamy, Irreligious, Irreverent.

SADISTIC

Cutting off thumbs and big toes, Judges 1:7.

Violent murder, Judges 4:21; 5:24–27.

Dismembered concubine, Judges 19:27–30.

Gouging out eyes, 1 Samuel 11:1–2.

Entire population destroyed, 1 Samuel 15:3.

Vulgar dowry request, 1 Samuel 18:25.

Suicide prevented sadism, 1 Samuel 31:4.

Sadistic amusement, 2 Samuel 2:12–16.

Father sees children slaughtered, Jeremiah 39:6.

Enjoying other's misfortune, Lamentations 2:15.

Sadistic applause, Ezekiel 25:6 (LB).

Plundering with glee, Ezekiel 36:5.

Spiked logs dragged over people, Amos 1:3 (CEV).

See Torture.

SADNESS

Temporary sadness, 1 Peter 1:6–7.

See Mourning, Regret, Sorrow.

SAFETY

No safe place to dock ark, Genesis 8:8–9 (See verse 12).

Safe towns, Deuteronomy 19:1–4 (CEV).

Built-in safety device, Deuteronomy 22:8.

Safety for woman in fields, Ruth 2:4–22.

Safe travel, Isaiah 35:8–9.

Crossing deep rivers, Isaiah 43:2 (CEV).

City gates open, Isaiah 60:11.

Enemies lurk along roads, fields, Jeremiah 6:25.

Wise dove, Jeremiah 48:28.

Safety in lions' den, Daniel 6:13–24; Nahum 2:11.

No safety after battle, Micah 2:8 (GNB).

Children playing in streets, Zechariah 8:5.

Safety of darkness, Acts 17:10.

Protected in storm and shipwreck, Acts 27:13–44.

Kept safe, 1 Timothy 2:15 (NIV).

"Run to God for safety," Hebrews 6:18 (CEV).

Shielded by God's power, 1 Peter 1:5 (NIV).
See Protection, Security, Shelter.

SAGACITY

Wisdom of Gamaliel, Acts 5:30–40.

Eyes of heart, Ephesians 1:18–19.
See Discernment, Intelligence, Wisdom.

SAILING See Maritime, Navigation, Voyage.

SAINTS

Prayer to saint, Job 5:1.

No trust in saints, Job 15:15 (See KJV).

Word definition, Colossians 1:2 (AB).

SALARY

Priests eat food offerings, Numbers 18:11–13.

Prostitute's unacceptable stewardship, Deuteronomy 23:18; Ezekiel 16:32–34.

Salary paid with food, 2 Chronicles 2:10.

Some money, some provisions, Ezra 3:7.

Priests, singers support themselves, Nehemiah 13:10–11.

Income for twelve apostles, Matthew 10:9–10.

Parable of workers in vineyard, Matthew 20:1–16.

Content with earnings, Luke 3:14.

Sending out of Twelve, Luke 9:1–6.

Spiritual wages, John 4:36.

Tents during week, ministry on Sabbath, Acts 18:1–5; 20:33–35; 1 Thessalonians 2:9; 2 Thessalonians 3:6–10.

Volunteer ministry, Acts 28:30 (AB).

Inequity in self-support, 1 Corinthians 9:6–14.

Concern for pastor, Philippians 4:10–19.

"Paid in full," Philippians 4:18 (NRSV).

Payment for those in ministry, 1 Timothy 5:17–18.

Dignity of labor, Titus 3:14.

Withholding payment from those who labor, James 5:4.

Danger of greed in ministry, 1 Peter 5:2–3.

Grain for a day's wages, Revelation 6:6.
See Honorarium, Stipend, Wages.

SALES See Barter, Commerce, Merchandise.

SALESMEN

Sale of burial plot, Genesis 23:12–16.

Young brother for sale, Genesis 37:19–36.

Varied merchandise for sale, Nehemiah 13:20.

Selling to sailors, Isaiah 23:2.

Barter system, Ezekiel 27:12–25.

Dishonest sales technique, Hosea 12:7.

Lady cloth sales person, Acts 16:13–15.
See Commerce, Market.

SALT

Lot's wife, Genesis 19:26.

Salt as condiment, Leviticus 2:13; Job 6:6.

Covenant of salt, Numbers 18:19.

Land made sterile, Judges 9:42–45.

Valley of salt, 2 Samuel 8:13.

Water softener and conditioning, 2 Kings 2:19–22.

Covenant of salt, 2 Chronicles 13:5.

Salt valley, 2 Chronicles 25:11.

Salt amply supplied, Ezra 7:22 (CEV).

Absence of salt, Job 6:6–7.

Wasteland forever, Zephaniah 2:9.

Believers called salt of earth, Matthew 5:13; Mark 9:50.

Salt not salty, Matthew 5:13 (CEV).
See Flavor, Food, Gourmet.

SALUTATION

Greeting to angels, Genesis 19:1–2.

Invoking God's blessing, Genesis 43:29; Ruth 2:4.

Wishing good health and long life, 1 Samuel 25:6.

"Hail" as a greeting, Matthew 26:49; 28:9.

Salutation with "Peace," Luke 10:5; John 20:21.
See Greeting.

SALVATION

Well paid, Job 1:9 (LB).

Strong tower in besieged city, Judges 9:51.

Forgiving, gracious, compassionate God, Nehemiah 9:17.

Loss of salvation, Psalm 69:28.

Undeserved salvation, Psalm 103:9–10.

Act of divine mercy, Psalm 130:3–4.

Walking in the Way, Isaiah 35:8.

Salvation's price illustrated, Isaiah 53:1–12.

Come, buy without money, Isaiah 55:1.

Seek the Lord while He may be found, Isaiah 55:6–7.

Sin causes God not to hear, Isaiah 59:1–3.

God revealed Himself to those who did not ask, Isaiah 65:1.

The God who saves, heals, Jeremiah 17:14.

Those found written in the book, Daniel 12:1.

Saving power like rain, Hosea 10:12 (CEV).

No God but the Lord, Hosea 13:4.

All who call will be saved, Joel 2:32; Romans 10:13.

Burning stick snatched from fire, Zechariah 3:2.

Healing sun of righteousness, Malachi 4:2.

Those who truly believe, Matthew 21:50–54.

Jesus chose the only way, Matthew 26:50–54.

Those who need the Great Physician, Mark 2:17.

Rich young man kept the law, Mark 10:17–27.

Salvation effort, Luke 13:24 (AB).

Those who will receive, believe, John 1:12.

Imperative New Birth, John 3:1–8.

Message of salvation, John 5:24.

Drawn to Christ, John 6:44.

Salvation only through Holy Spirit, John 6:63–65 (LB).

Only one gate, John 10:1–9.

Turn to the light, escape darkness, John 12:35–36.

Jesus came to save, not judge, John 12:47.

Salvation in no other name but Christ, Acts 4:12.

Salvation through faith apart from legalism, Acts 15:1–11; Romans 3:22–24.

Salvation described, Acts 16:31 (AB).

Unearned gift of salvation, Romans 4:4–8.

God's all-encompassing goodness, Romans 4:16.

Justification by faith alone, Romans 5:1–2.

God's love demonstrated toward sinners, Romans 5:8.

God's friends, Romans 5:11 (LB).

Death through Adam, life in Christ, Romans 5:12–19.

The gift of God, Romans 6:23.

Deliverance from sin through Christ alone, Romans 7:24–25.

No condemnation in Christ, Romans 8:1–2.

Ignorant of Gospel, Romans 10:3.

Salvation within easy reach, Romans 10:8 (LB).

Role of witness in salvation, Romans 10:9–10.

Message of salvation came through Abraham, Galatians 3:6–9.

Mercy, grace of God, Ephesians 2:1–10.

Rescued from darkness, Colossians 1:13–14.

Christ Jesus came to save sinners, 1 Timothy 1:15.

Mediator between God, men, 1 Timothy 2:5.

Unmerited grace, Titus 3:4–8.

Message to be carefully heeded, Hebrews 2:1–3.

True rest for people of God, Hebrews 4:9–11.

Total salvation for those who trust, Hebrews 7:25.

Power, meaning of blood of Christ, Hebrews 9:8–15.

First covenant put into effect with blood, Hebrews 9:18–22.

Supreme sacrifice, Hebrews 9:24–28.

Perfect Savior, perfect salvation, Hebrews 10:11–14.

Not silver, gold but blood of Christ, 1 Peter 1:18–19.

Born again of imperishable seed, 1 Peter 1:23.

Fearful option, 1 Peter 4:17–18.

Fact of sin, provision for cleansing, 1 John 1:8–10.

Supreme gift of love, 1 John 4:9–10.

Gift of eternal life, 1 John 5:11–12.

Opening door to Him who knocks, Revelation 3:20.

See Conversion, Convert, New Birth, Redemption.

SAMPLE

Seeing but not experiencing, Numbers 27:12–14.

Samples of fruit, Deuteronomy 1:24–25.

Sampled words, food, Job 34:3.

Sermon exerpt, Mark 1:7 (LB).

Tasting that the Lord is good, 1 Peter 2:3.

See Taste.

SANCTIFICATION

Sanctified seventh day, Genesis 2:2–3 (KJV).

Firstborn, Exodus 13:2.

Those truly holy, Numbers 16:3–7.

Call to sanctification, Joshua 3:5 (NKJV).

Made pure through testing, Job 23:10.

Covenant to avoid lust, Job 31:1.

Sanctified before birth, Jeremiah 1:5.

Sanctified Savior, John 10:36 (NRSV).

Sanctifying work of Holy Spirit, impact of Scripture, 2 Thessalonians 2:13.

Basics of sanctification, Romans 8:1–2; 12:1–2; 1 Corinthians 6:19–20; Ephesians 4:17–24; 5:17; Philippians 3:7–11; Colossians 3:1–3.

See Consecration, Discipleship, Holiness.

SANCTIMONIOUS

Claiming perfection, Job 33:9.

Pretended piety, Isaiah 58:2.

Holier-than-thou, Isaiah 65:5.

Pious hypocrites, Matthew 6:5; Mark 12:38–40; Luke 18:11.

Pharisees' resentment to Jesus, Luke 15:1–7.

Wretched and blind, Revelation 3:17.

See Hypocrisy, Sham.

SANCTUARY

Worship among trees, Genesis 13:18 (See 14:13; 18:1).

Committing all of sanctuary to the Lord, Numbers 7:1.

Frightened of place of worship, Numbers 17:12–13.

Place chosen by God, Deuteronomy 12:11.

No temple available, 1 Kings 3:2.

Quiet temple construction, 1 Kings 6:7.

Temple dedication, 1 Kings 8:62–65.

Six-year hiding place, 2 Kings 11:1–3.

Repairing temple, 2 Kings 12:4–5.

Murder in pagan temple, 2 Kings 19:37.

Setting fire to temple, 2 Kings 25:8–9.

Temple cannot contain God's greatness, 2 Chronicles 2:6.

Closed sanctuary reopened, 2 Chronicles 29:3, 7.

Forsaken temple, Nehemiah 13:11 (NKJV).

Love for house of God, Psalm 26:8.

Temple mediation, Psalm 48:9.

Beauty of sanctuary, longing for worship, Psalm 84:1–2; Isaiah 60:13.

Entering sanctuary, Psalm 100:4.

Fire destroyed sanctuary, Isaiah 64:11.

Filled with glory of the Lord, Ezekiel 10:4.

God's glory seen but not God Himself, Ezekiel 43:1–5.

Gate closed during working days, Ezekiel 46:1.

The Lord is in His Holy Temple, Habakkuk 2:20.

People in fine houses, temple in ruins, Haggai 1:1–4.

Disgraced temple, Malachi 2:11 (CEV).

Bring tithes to storehouse, Malachi 3:10.

Money changers driven out of temple, Matthew 21:12–13; Mark 11:15–17; Luke 19:45–46; John 2:13–21.

Truly sacred, Matthew 23:16–17.

Lack of permanence in temple, Mark 13:1–2.

"Place where robbers hide," Luke 19:46 (CEV).

Ultimate "Holy of Holies," 1 Corinthians 3:16.

Resurrected Christ, Hebrews 9:24.

Measure temple, count worshippers, Revelation 11:1.

Temple court defiled, Revelation 11:1–2.

Tabernacle of Testimony, Revelation 15:5.

Filled with the glory of God, Revelation 15:8.

No need for temple of worship, Revelation 21:22.

See Synagogue, Temple.

SAND

Oceans subdued, Job 38:8–11.

SANGUINE
Sanguine words, Deuteronomy 33:1–29.

SANHEDRIN
Heavenly Sanhedrin, Revelation 7:13 (AB).

SANITATION
Provision of pure food, Exodus 16:19–24.
Skin infection, Leviticus 13:6.
Care of venereal disease, Leviticus 15:2–7.
Procedure with those suffering disease, Numbers 5:1–3.
Care in touching dead body, Numbers 19:14–21.
Disposal of excrement, Deuteronomy 23:12–13.
Bad water purified, 2 Kings 2:19–22.
Purifying rooms of temple, Nehemiah 13:9.
Bodies lying unburied, Jeremiah 9:22.
Place of disease and death, Jeremiah 16:1–9.
Improper care of newborn, Ezekiel 16:4–5.
Washing hands before eating, Matthew 15:1–9; Mark 7:2–7.
See Cleanliness, Disease, Ecology, Health, Purity.

SANITY
Given understanding, Isaiah 32:4.
Restored to sanity, Daniel 4:29–37; Mark 5:2–20.
See Insanity, Mental Health.

SARCASM
Stimulant to action, Joshua 17:14–18.
Parable of trees, Judges 9:7–15.
Challenging pagan gods, Judges 10:14.
What ails you? Judges 18:23 (NKJV).
Neglected duty, 1 Samuel 26:15.
Wife's rebuke, 2 Samuel 6:20.
Sarcastic prophet, 1 Kings 18:27 (See GNB).
Taunting pride, 1 Kings 20:10–11.
Botanical communication, 2 Kings 14:9.
Military sarcasm, 2 Kings 18:23–24.
Quip from Job, Job 12:2; 26:2 (LB).
Job's "friend," Job 18:5 (LB).
Mocking builders of wall, Nehemiah 4:1–3.
Sarcasm against intellectual pride, Job 12:2–3 (AB).
Sarcastic rebuttal, Job 38:19–21.

Scarecrow in melon patch, Jeremiah 10:5 (NIV).
Speaking truth in sarcasm, Matthew 27:28–29; Luke 23:35–39; John 19:19.
Disciples sarcastic to Jesus, Mark 8:4 (LB).
Jesus mocked on cross, John 19:1–3.
"Super apostles," 2 Corinthians 11:5.
Deft use of words, 2 Corinthians 11:16–19.
Instructive example, 2 Corinthians 12:13 (LB).
Cut off those who cut off, Galatians 5:12 (LB).
See Criticism, Taunt, Innuendo, Insult, Irony.

SATAN
Brief history of fall from heaven, Isaiah 14:12–15.
Typology in king of Tyre, Ezekiel 28:11–19.
Satan's role as accuser, Job 1:12 (AB); Zechariah 3:1–2.
Satanic adversary, Job 16:9 (AB).
Holy Spirit led Jesus to confrontation, Matthew 4:1 (See CEV).
Satan confronted with Scripture, Matthew 4:1–11; Luke 4:1–13.
Jesus accused of satanic power, Matthew 9:32–34.
Satan's destiny, Romans 16:20.
Satanic schemes, 2 Corinthians 2:1–11 (See LB).
Deny Satan opportunity, Ephesians 4:27 (GNB).
The tempter, 1 Thessalonians 3:5.
Lawless one's ignominious defeat, 2 Thessalonians 2:8.
Satan as teacher, 1 Timothy 1:18–20.
Satan rendered powerless, Hebrews 2:14 (CEV).
Battleground in which Satan attacks, 1 John 2:15–17.
Work of the devil, 1 John 3:7–8.
Unharmed by Satan, 1 John 5:18.
Only authority over evil, Jude 9.
Star fallen from sky, Revelation 9:1–2 (See Isaiah 14:12).
Birth of Christ reviewed, Revelation 12:1–5.
Conquered and yet conqueror, Revelation 12:7–10.

Angel overpowering, binding Satan, Revelation 20:1–3.
See Demons, Evil, Hell.

SATIATE

"Satiated with their own devices," Proverbs 1:31 (NASB).

SATIRE

Joseph called a dreamer by his brothers, Genesis 37:19.
Satirical parable, Judges 9:8–15.
Divine satire against Egyptians, Judges 10:11–14.
Goliath's disdain of David, 1 Samuel 17:41–44.
Acrid speech from wife to husband, 2 Samuel 6:16–20.
Elijah chided prophets of Baal, 1 Kings 18:27–28.
Taunts of Job's three "friends," Job 4:1–6; 8:2; 11:1–12; 15:1–3; 22:1–4.
Pessimistic assessment of life, Ecclesiastes 2:1–11.
Scoffing at futility of military might, Isaiah 8:9–10.
Use of literary device concerning freedom, Jeremiah 34:17.
Medicine for one who will not be healed, Jeremiah 46:11.
Ironical message concerning idols, Ezekiel 20:39–42.
Folly of rebellious people, Hosea 8:7–9.
Satire used by Jesus, Matthew 23:1–33.
Jesus chided Nicodemus, John 3:10.
See Sarcasm.

SATISFACTION

"Satisfied with life," Genesis 35:29 (Berk.); Psalm 103:5 (NASB, NRSV).
Pleased populace, 2 Samuel 3:36.
Satisfied to see the Lord's likeness, Psalm 17:15.
Desires satisfied, strength renewed, Psalm 103:5.
Righteous desires, Proverbs 10:24.
Voicing simple need, Proverbs 30:7–8.
Money never satisfies, Ecclesiastes 5:10.
Reward for obedience, Isaiah 48:17–18.

Needs satisfied, Isaiah 58:11; Philippians 4:19.
Wrong search for satisfaction, James 4:1–3.
Joy of good reputation, 3 John 3–4.
See Contentment, Fulfillment.

SATURATION

Worldwide evangelization, Mark 16:15.
Message saturation, Acts 5:28.
Widespread acceptance in Samaria, Acts 8:14.
All Jews and Greeks heard message, Acts 19:10.

SAVAGE

People like animals, Deuteronomy 28:53–57.
Gross recreation, Judges 19:22–26.
Womens' hair and lions' teeth, Revelation 9:8.

SAVINGS

Careful frugality, Proverbs 13:11.
Treasures on earth or in heaven, Matthew 6:19–21.
See Investment.

SAVIOR *See Mediator, Redeemer.*

SCALES *See Weight.*

SCANDAL

Joseph falsely accused, Genesis 39:11–20.
Giving false testimony, Deuteronomy 19:16, 21.
Hatred without reason, Psalm 69:4.
Lying lips and deceitful tongues, Psalm 120:2.
Choice morsels to those who wish to hear, Proverbs 26:22.
Do not fear reproach of men, Isaiah 51:7.
Impeccable witness, Daniel 6:3–5.
Rejoice when people speak falsely of you, Matthew 5:11–12.
Avoiding scandal, Matthew 18:15–17.
See Gossip.

SCAPEGOAT

Old Testament scapegoat, Leviticus 16:8–22.

SCARCITY *See Shortage.*

SCARECROW

Idols like scarecrows, Jeremiah 10:5 (LB).

SCARS

Marks of a slave, Galatians 6:17 (See also GNB).

SCAVENGER

Scavenger eagle, Job 39:29–30.
Food for jackals, Psalm 63:10.
Flesh of people food for birds, Jeremiah 7:33.
Feast for animals after battle, Ezekiel 39:14–20.
Vultures, Luke 17:37.
See Gleaners.

SCHEDULE

Scheduled offerings, Deuteronomy 16:16–17.
Schedule for sacrifices, 1 Kings 9:25.
All day schedule, Nehemiah 4:21.
Waters up to neck, Psalm 69:1.
Time for everything, Ecclesiastes 3:1–8.
The Lord plans far in advance, Isaiah 25:1.
Perfect timing, Isaiah 49:8.
Noon schedule delayed until night, Jeremiah 6:4–5.
Temple activity concluded, Mark 11:11.
Itinerary of Jesus, Luke 4:42–44.
Request denied to reschedule Ephesus, Acts 18:19–21.
Ministry, travel schedule, Acts 20:1–6, 13–16; 21:1–8.
God always on schedule, Romans 5:6.
Satan's awareness of shortage of time, Revelation 12:12.
See Itinerary.

SCHEME

Scheme for first murder, Genesis 4:8.
Counselors hired to frustrate temple building, Ezra 4:5.
Sanballat's scheme to hinder Nehemiah, Nehemiah 6:1–9.

Strategy of Judas, Mark 14:10–11, 43–46.
"Schemes of the devil," Ephesians 6:11 (NASB).
See Deceit, Strategy.

SCHISM

Rebellious congregation, Numbers 14:1–4.
Create schism, Isaiah 7:6 (Berk.).
Deliberately writing falsehoods, Jeremiah 8:8.
Argument over ceremonial washing, John 3:25.
Pagans certain of erroneous belief, Acts 19:35–36.
Accused of mishandling truth, Acts 21:19–24.
Division among believers, 1 Corinthians 1:12; 3:1–9.
Promoting controversies, 1 Timothy 1:4.
Schism about words, 2 Timothy 2:14.
Preaching, teaching for dishonest gain, Titus 1:10–16.
See Abrasion, Argument, Dispute. Disruption.

SCHOLARSHIP

Passing royal exam, Daniel 1:18–20.
Folly of intellectual pride, 1 Corinthians 3:18–20.
See Academic, Intellectual.

SCHOOL

Home school, Deuteronomy 4:9–10; 6:7–9; 11:19–21; Psalm 78:5–6.
Specialized Bible training, Deuteronomy 31:10–13.
Small classroom, 2 Kings 6:1.
Scholarly prophet, Ezra 7:6–11 (GNB).
Babylonian training, Daniel 1:3–21.
Tutor, teacher, Acts 22:3.
See Education, Teaching.

SCIENCE

Science of astronomy, Job 9:9; 38:31; Amos 5:8.
Oceanography, Psalm 8:8.
Definitive statement, John 8:32
False science, 1 Timothy 6:20 (KJV).
See Space/Time.

S

SCOFF

Do not curse those the Lord has not cursed, Numbers 23:8.

Scoffing at pagans with unanswered prayers, 1 Kings 18:22–38.

Mocking God's messengers, 2 Chronicles 36:16.

Daring to evaluate Divinity, Job 21:14–15.

Scorn for acts of humility, Psalm 69:10–11.

Questioning Divine wisdom, Psalm 73:6–11.

Put out the scornful, Proverbs 22:10.

Daring to scoff at the Lord's name, Isaiah 36:18–21; 37:6.

Idols likened to scarecrows, Jeremiah 10:5.

Disrespect for sanctuary, Ezekiel 25:1–4.

Scoffing at alleged unfairness, Ezekiel 33:20.

Those who mock, Isaiah 57:3–4; Zephaniah 2:10.

Mocking Jesus, Mark 15:16–20.

Demon who laughed at Jesus, Luke 4:33–35.

Demeaning Jesus, Luke 22:63–65.

Scoffing incited by envy, Acts 13:45.

Some rejected, others asked to hear more, Acts 17:32.

Scoffers in last days, 2 Peter 3:3–4.

See Criticism, Demean, Rudeness, Scorn.

SCOLDING

Levites had gone too far, Numbers 16:7.

Wounds of a friend, Proverbs 27:6.

Scolding insufficient discipline, Proverbs 29:19.

Jesus scolded an evil spirit, Mark 1:23–26.

See Criticism.

SCOPE

Small, insignificant greatness, Proverbs 30:24–28.

Given eternal viewpoint, Jeremiah 33:3.

See Dimensions.

SCORCHED EARTH

Towns destroyed by Israelite army, Numbers 31:10.

Devastated Jericho, Joshua 6:20–21.

SCOFF

Laying land completely waste, 2 Kings 3:19.

Eden-like area becomes scorched earth, Joel 2:3.

See Destruction, Genocide.

SCORN

Scorned brother, Genesis 37:19 (CEV).

Scornful kick, 1 Samuel 12:29 (NKJV).

Veteran soldier's scorn toward boy, 1 Samuel 17:41–44.

Wife scorned husband, 2 Samuel 6:16–22.

Contempt for unfortunate, Job 12:5.

Scorned by friends, Psalm 31:11 (LB).

Scroll burned in scorn, Jeremiah 36:1–26.

Ridiculed territory, Jeremiah 48:39.

Object of horror, Jeremiah 49:17.

Ridicule of once exalted city, Lamentations 2:15.

Supreme example of rejection, Matthew 27:46.

Those who laughed at Jesus, Mark 5:39–40.

Message of Cross foolishness to lost, 1 Corinthians 1:18.

Enduring scorn, Hebrews 11:24–26 (GNB).

See Ridicule, Scoff, Taunt.

SCORPION

Desert scorpions, Deuteronomy 8:15.

Living among scorpions, Ezekiel 2:6.

Scorpion for egg, Luke 11:12.

SCRIPTURE

Not to be altered, Deuteronomy 4:2.

Truth learned, lived, Deuteronomy 6:6–9; 10:18–21.

Scripture contains both blessings and curses, Joshua 8:34.

Relaying instructions, Joshua 1:8; 23:6.

Complete reading of the law, Joshua 8:35.

Blessing, warning as death approaches, Joshua 23:14–16.

Small emphasis given to word of the Lord, 1 Samuel 3:1.

God reveals Himself through His Word, 1 Samuel 3:21.

Trustworthy words, 2 Samuel 7:28; Nehemiah 9:8; Psalm 12:6.

The Lord our lamp, 2 Samuel 22:29.

Not one word of God's promise can fail, 1 Kings 8:56.

Reading of Scripture long neglected, 2 Kings 22:10–20.

The Lord does what He promises, 2 Chronicles 6:4, 14–15.

Scripture abandoned, 2 Chronicles 12:1.

No God, no priest, no law in Israel, 2 Chronicles 15:3.

Book of law lost in temple, 2 Chronicles 34:14–15.

Respect for scriptures, Nehemiah 8:5.

Lifetime study, Ezra 7:10 (CEV).

Day after day Scripture reading, Nehemiah 8:17–18.

Bread from heaven, Nehemiah 9:15.

Delight in law of the Lord, Psalm 1:2; Jeremiah 15:16.

Obeying teachings of God's Word, Psalm 18:22.

Flawless Word of God, Psalms 18:30; 19:7–8; Proverbs 30:5; Ezekiel 12:26–28.

Sweeter than honey, Psalms 19:10; 119:103.

Seeing light in God's light, Psalm 36:9.

God's Word gives credence to words of believers, Psalm 37:30–31.

Knowledge of God's Word leads to desire for His will, Psalm 40:8.

Giving praise to God's Word, Psalm 56:10.

God's covenant never changes, Psalms 105:8–9; 111:5.

Delight in the Lord's commands, Psalm 112:1.

Blessing for obeying Scripture, Psalm 119:1–16.

God's word in heart, Psalm 119:11; Isaiah 51:7.

Prayer for perception in study of Scripture, Psalm 119:18.

Seeking, considering, hastening to obey, Psalm 119:57–64.

Affliction turns us to Scripture, Psalm 119:71.

Eternal Word of the Lord, Psalm 119:89.

Lamp, light, Psalm 119:105.

God-given ability to understand, Psalm 119:125.

"Bag of seed," Psalm 126:6 (NASB).

Trusting confidently in God's promises, Psalms 130:5–6; 145:13.

Lamp, light, discipline, Proverbs 6:20–23.

Attitudes toward Scripture, Proverbs 13:13 (AB).

Discovered proverbs, Proverbs 25:1 (LB).

Honor of kings, Proverbs 25:2.

Message in depth, Isaiah 28:13 (KJV).

Sword of Lord bathed in blood, Isaiah 34:6.

Searching scripture, Isaiah 34:16 (KJV).

Dependence upon God's promises, Isaiah 37:1–38.

Word of God stands forever, Isaiah 40:8.

God's Word will not return empty, Isaiah 55:10–11.

Challenging fulfillment of Scripture, Jeremiah 17:15.

Persecuted for proclaiming God's Word, Jeremiah 20:7–8; 37:20–21.

Substituting dreams for the Word of God, Jeremiah 23:25–32.

Fire, hammer, Jeremeiah 23:29.

Verbal inspiration of Scripture, Jeremiah 30:2; Revelation 1:11.

Those who would silence God's Word, Jeremiah 47:6–7.

Promise of judgment fulfilled, Lamentations 2:17.

Scroll eaten, sweet as honey, Ezekiel 3:1–3.

Adept scriptural understanding, Daniel 9:2.

Famine for words of the Lord, Amos 8:11–12.

Certain God's revelation will come to pass, Habakkuk 2:3.

Satan's misuse of Scripture, response of Jesus, Matthew 4:1–11; Luke 4:1–13.

Not by bread alone, Matthew 4:4 (See Deuteronomy 8:3).

All truth will be fulfilled, Matthew 5:17–18 (CEV).

Sower parable, Matthew 13:1–23.

Believe good news, Mark 1:14–15.

Wealth, worry numb understanding of Scripture, Mark 4:19.

Revelation without external evidence, Mark 8:11–12.

Many attempted to record New Testament events, Luke 1:1–4.

Living Word pierces soul, Luke 2:34–35.

Jewish synagogue reading custom, Luke 4:16.

Parable of sower, Luke 8:4–15.

Taking Jesus at His word, John 4:50.

Message of salvation, John 5:24.

Those who read in vain, John 5:39–40.

Living Scripture, John 6:63 (See CEV).

Sanctifying truth, John 17:17.

Conversion of Ethiopian eunuch, Acts 8:26–39.

Use of Scripture in bold witness, Acts 13:13–52.

Example of reasoning, Acts 17:2–4.

Eager to examine Scriptures, Acts 17:11.

Thorough knowledge of Scriptures, Acts 18:24–26.

Scriptures as authority concerning Jesus, Acts 18:28.

Those who do not have scriptural guidance, Romans 2:14–15.

God's Word does not fail, Romans 9:6–7.

Faith comes through the Word, Romans 10:17.

Holy Spirit's guidance in Bible study, 1 Corinthians 2:6–16.

Milk and solid food, 1 Corinthians 3:1–2; Hebrews 5:11–14; 1 Peter 2:2.

Bread of truth, 1 Corinthians 5:8.

Recognition of writings as authentic, 1 Corinthians 14:37–38.

Received by revelation, Galatians 1:12.

Cleansing water, Ephesians 5:26.

Helmet, sword, Ephesians 6:17.

Power of Gospel however proclaimed, Philippians 1:15–18.

Richness of the Word in one's life, Colossians 3:16.

Scripture impact, 2 Thessalonians 2:13.

Public reading of Scripture, 1 Timothy 4:13.

Word of God not chained, 2 Timothy 2:8.

Correctly handling Word of truth, 2 Timothy 2:15.

Foundation stands firm, 2 Timothy 2:19.

Influence of Scriptures since childhood, 2 Timothy 3:14–15.

Use of Scripture in teaching and training, 2 Timothy 3:16.

All Scripture God-breathed, 2 Timothy 3:16–17.

Paying attention to Scripture, Hebrews 2:1–3 (See NASB).

Double-edged sword, Hebrews 4:12.

Scriptures discern good from evil, Hebrews 5:11–14.

Birth through the Word of truth, James 1:18.

Cleansing work of Scripture, James 1:21.

"Obey God's message," James 1:22 (CEV).

Divine mirror, James 1:23–26.

Royal law of Scripture, James 2:8.

Purified by obeying truth, 1 Peter 1:22.

"Living and enduring Word of God," 1 Peter 1:23 (NRSV).

Men like grass but the Word stands forever, 1 Peter 1:24–25.

Divine purpose in giving Scriptures, 2 Peter 1:15.

Inspired by Holy Spirit, 2 Peter 1:20–21.

Bringing Scripture to mind, 2 Peter 3:2.

Distorted scripture, 2 Peter 3:16.

God's Word fulfilled in those who obey, 1 John 2:5.

Love results from obedience to Scripture, 2 John 6.

Book of Revelation given by angel, Revelation 1:1.

Promised blessing for those who take to heart, Revelation 1:3.

Word of God incarnate, Revelation 19:13.

All Scripture must be fulfilled, Revelation 22:10.

Finality of Scripture record, Revelation 22:18–19.

See Bible, Guidance, Inspiration, Revelation.

SCRUTINY

Identification by manner of speech, Judges 12:5–6.

Veteran soldier's errant scrutiny a boy, 1 Samuel 17:42.

Seeing is believing, 1 Kings 10:6–9.

Evil scrutiny of earth, Job 1:6–7.

Mankind scrutinized from heavenly throne, Psalm 11:4.

God sees all, Psalm 33:13.

Divine scrutiny, Psalm 139:23–24 (LB).

Jesus carefully watched by critics, Luke 14:1.

See Examination, Surveillance.

SCULPTURE

Chisel at work, Deuteronomy 10:1.

Idol maker burns wood for carving, Isaiah 44:15–17.

Decorative images in temple, Ezekiel 41:17–20.

See Artist, Talent.

SEA *See Ocean.*

SEAL

Signet ring, Genesis 41:42.

Marked by seal, Nehemiah 10:1–27.

Business transaction, Jeremiah 32:11–14.

Prophesy verified, Daniel 9:24.

Seal of promise, Ephesians 1:13.

See Identity.

SEA MONSTER

"Escaping sea monster," Job 26:13 (CEV).

SEAMSTRESS

Edenic garments, Genesis 3:7.

Time to mend, Ecclesiastes 3:7.

Sewing magic charms, Ezekiel 13:17–18.

Repairing old garment, Matthew 9:16; Mark 2:21.

Woman who helped poor, Acts 9:36–42.

See Clothing, Wardrobe.

SÉANCE

Sorcery forbidden, Exodus 22:18.

Sorcery abandoned, Numbers 24:1.

Prophet of God called seer, 1 Samuel 9:8–9.

Endor séance, 1 Samuel 28:5–25.

Dead cannot return, 2 Samuel 12:22–23.

Putting end to mediums, spiritists, 2 Kings 23:24.

Inquire of God rather than spiritists, Isaiah 8:19.

Spirits of the departed, Isaiah 14:9–10.

Making fools of diviners, Isaiah 44:25.

Fortune, destiny, Isaiah 65:11.

Deceitful diviners, mediums, Jeremiah 27:9–15.

See Fortune-telling, Magic, Sorcery, Spiritism.

SEARCH

Truly holy, Numbers 16:3–7.

Search for God, Job 11:7 (KJV).

Mining deep into earth, Job 28:1–4.

Glory of kings, Proverbs 25:2.

Search for one righteous man, Psalm 53:2 (LB).

Relentless searching, Psalm 105:4 (LB).

Chasing wind, Ecclesiastes 1:17–18.

"Give up as lost," Ecclesiastes 3:6 (NASB).

No one to give answers, Isaiah 41:28.

Ask for ancient paths, Jeremiah 6:16.

See Exploration.

SEASONS

Stars mark seasons, Genesis 1:14.

Establishment of seasons after flood, Genesis 8:22.

Season when kings go to war, 2 Samuel 11:1.

Summer, winter, Psalm 74:17.

Lunar designation, Psalm 104:19.

Honor, seasons, Proverbs 26:1 (LB).

Autumn crocus, Isaiah 35:1 (AB).

Birds know when to migrate, Jeremiah 8:7.

Creator determines climate, Daniel 2:20–21.

Confusion in planting and harvest, Amos 9:13.

Summer, autumn, winter, Zechariah 8:19 (LB).

See Autumn, Spring, Summer, Winter.

SEAWORTHY

Seaworthy ships, Ezekiel 27:4–9.

See Maritime.

SECLUSION

No place to hide, Leviticus 26:25.

Cities of refuge, Numbers 35:6–15.

Suitable seclusion in Athens, 1 Thessalonians 3:1.

See Privacy.

SECOND COMING

Need to evangelize, Isaiah 21:11–12.

Time of judgment, Isaiah 26:21; 66:15–16.

Yearning for Messiah, Isaiah 64:1.

Vision of Christ's coming, Daniel 7:9–14.

"Go about your business," Daniel 12:9 (CEV).

Misguided desire for day of the Lord, Amos 5:18.

Advent majesty, Micah 1:3–4.

Silence before the Lord, Zephaniah 1:7.

Desired of all nations will come, Haggai 2:7.

"The Lord will have His day," Zechariah 14:1 (CEV).

Day of His coming, Malachi 3:2.

World-wide spectacle, Matthew 24:30.

Watching for the Lord to come, Luke 12:35–40.

Predicted time, Luke 21:32 (AB).

Those dead, those alive when Christ returns, John 11:25.

Promise of Christ's return, John 14:3; Acts 1:10–11.

Mistaken information as to return, John 21:20–23.

Certain judgment coming, Romans 9:28.

Resurrection Christ's coming, 1 Corinthians 15:51–55.

Climax of the ages, Ephesian 1:10 (AB).

Faithful church, Philippians 1:6 (See AB).

Alertly watching, 1 Thessalonians 1:3 (LB).

Waiting for Christ's return, 1 Thessalonians 1:10; James 5:7–8.

Prepared for second coming, 1 Thessalonians 3:13.

Confusing rumor, 2 Thessalonians 2:1–2 (LB).

Man of sin overthrown, 2 Thessalonians 2:8.

Faithful until Christ returns, 1 Timothy 6:11–16.

Last days' conduct, attitudes, 2 Timothy 3:1–5.

Purified by blessed hope, Titus 2:11–14.

Christ's return as Lord, King, Hebrews 9:24–28.

Reward for faithful, Hebrews 10:35–38.

"Very little while," Hebrews 10:37 (AB).

Birth of a living hope, 1 Peter 1:3–5.

A lifestyle conditioned by second coming, 1 Peter 4:7–8.

Scoffers in last days, 2 Peter 3:3–4.

Coming like a thief, 2 Peter 3:10.

Unashamed at His coming, 1 John 2:28.

Scoffers, divisive influences, Jude 17–18.

Coming in clouds, Revelation 1:7.

Coming soon, Revelation 3:11.

Promised return of Christ, Revelation 22:7, 12, 20.

See Messiah, Rapture.

SECRECY

Secret inspection, Nehemiah 2:11–16.

Sweetness of stolen things, Proverbs 9:17.

Idolatry behind closed doors, Isaiah 57:7–8 (LB).

Adulterous sites, Jeremiah 3:6.

Daniel's secrecy, Daniel 7:28.

Whispers to be proclaimed, Matthew 10:27.

Jesus requested secrecy, Matthew 16:20; Mark 3:11–12; 8:30; 9:30.

Jesus could not keep His presence secret, Mark 7:24.

Revealing thoughts of the heart, Luke 2:34–35.

Secret betrayal by Judas, Luke 22:3–6.

Jesus withdrew from public activity, John 11:54.

Secret motives brought to light, 1 Corinthians 4:5.

Deeds of darkness, Ephesians 5:8–14.

Judgment message kept secret, Revelation 10:4 (CEV).

See Confidential, Darkness, Secret.

SECRET

God knows deepest secret, Deuteronomy 29:29; Job 12:22; 34:21–22; Ecclesiastes 12:14; Isaiah 29:15–16; Hebrews 4:13.

Animals born in secret, Job 39:1.

"My secret heart," Psalm 51:6 (NRSV).

The Lord knows our thoughts, Psalm 94:11.

Secret slander, Psalm 101:5.

Thoughts and motives, Psalm 139:1–4.

Keeping or telling secrets, Proverbs 11:13.

Birds tell secrets, Ecclesiastes 10:20.

Deeds of darkness, Ezekiel 8:12–13.

Secrets made known, Matthew 13:35.

Time of Christ's coming a secret, Matthew 24:36; Mark 13:32.

Nothing hidden that will not be known, Luke 8:17; 12:2–3.

God's secret made known, Ephesians 1:9–10.

Not to be kept secret, Revelation 22:10 (GNB).

See Secrecy, Hiding, Hiding Place.

SECRETARY

In charge of money, 2 Kings 12:10–12.

Leadership position, 2 Kings 25:19.

Man of insight—a scribe, 1 Chronicles 27:32.

Dispatching orders, Esther 3:12; 8:9.

Jeremiah dictated to Baruch, Jeremiah 36:4, 15–16.

Paul's secretary, Romans 16:22.

See Dictation.

SECRET BELIEVERS

Secret believer in king's palace, Esther 4:12–16.

Secret believers, John 12:42–43; 19:38.

See Convert.

SECTARIAN

Rules taught by men, Isaiah 29:13.

False interpretation of Scripture, Jeremiah 8:8.

Pagans certain of erroneous belief, Acts 19:35–36.

Proclaiming dreams instead of Word, Jeremiah 23:25–32.

See Cults, Denomination, Syncretism.

SECULAR

Need for building roads, Deuteronomy 19:1–3.

No time to pray, 1 Samuel 14:19 (GNB).

Seeing, hearing, not understanding, Mark 4:11–12.

Secularizing the temple, John 2:13–16.

Theological dispute in secular courtroom, Acts 18:12–17.

City director of public works, Romans 16:23.

"People of this world," 1 Corinthians 3:3 (CEV).

Earth minded, 1 Corinthians 15:47–48 (Berk.).

Praying for those in authority, 1 Timothy 2:1–4.

Christian's secular reputation, 1 Timothy 3:7 (AB).

Secular viewpoint, 1 John 4:5.

See Carnal, Labor, Materialism, Worldliness.

SECURITY

Security at entrance to Garden of Eden, Genesis 3:24.

Dove's security, Genesis 8:6–12.

Security facing danger, Numbers 24:21.

Gates tightly shut, Joshua 6:1 (LB).

Strong tower in besieged city, Judges 9:51.

"Special bodyguards," 1 Kings 1:38 (CEV).

Security force, 2 Kings 11:4–8.

Desire for peace, security, 2 Kings 20:19.

City built around fortress, 1 Chronicles 11:7–9.

Sinfully depending on number of fighting men, 1 Chronicles 21:17.

God stays with those who stay with Him, 2 Chronicles 15:2 (LB).

Secure tent, Job 5:24 (NASB).

Lie down without fear, Job 11:19.

Eagle finds security in height, Job 39:27–28.

The Lord is my rock, Psalm 18:1–2.

Trusting solely in the Lord, Psalm 20:7.

Kept safe, Psalm 27:5; 32:7.

God our refuge, strength, Psalm 46:1–3.

Blotted out of book of life, Psalm 69:28.

Living under shadow of the Almighty, Psalm 91:1–2.

God's faithfulness our shield, Psalm 91:4 (NRSV).

Secure trust in the Lord, Psalm 125:1.

Name of the Lord a strong tower, Proverbs 18:10.

Labor and good food, Ecclesiastes 5:18–20.

In clefts of the rock, Song of Songs 2:14.

Firmly in place, Isaiah 22:23.

Tested stone in Zion, Isaiah 28:16.

Looking to earthly, Isaiah 30:1–3.

Gates always open, Isaiah 60:11.

Security of walls, Jeremiah 4:6 (CEV).

"Abundant peace, security," Jeremiah 33:6.

False trust in deeds, riches, Jeremiah 48:7; Mark 4:19.

Wise dove, Jeremiah 48:28.

Promised security for Israel, Isaiah 62:8 (LB).

False security, Jeremiah 49:16.

Complacent Bedouins, Jeremiah 49:31.

Safety in midst of peril, Ezekiel 34:25.

Imagined security, Ezekiel 39:6 (CEV).

No safety in high place, Obadiah 1:3–4.

No security after battle, Micah 2:8 (GNB).

Security in lions' habitat, Nahum 2:11.

False security of dishonest gain, Habakkuk 2:9.

Man-made idols, Habakkuk 2:18–19.

Money bags never wear out, Luke 12:33 (CEV).

Inadequate self-security, Luke 17:33 (NRSV).

Jesus avoided those who would take His life, John 7:1.

Function of good shepherd, John 10:1–15.

Jesus avoided public places, John 11:54.

Standing at end of struggle, Ephesians 6:13.

Absolute confidence in Christ, 2 Timothy 1:12.

Jesus our guarantee, Hebrews 7:22.

Kingdom that cannot be shaken, Hebrews 12:28–29.

Eternal inheritance, 1 Peter 1:3–4.

Keeping power, Jude 1.

Gates never shut, Revelation 21:25.

See Anchor, Protection, Shelter.

SEDAN CHAIR

Royal palanquin, Song of Songs 3:9 (NRSV).

SEDATIVE

Wine at Crucifixion, Mark 15:23–24, 36.

See Medicine.

SEDENTARY

Physical sensitivities at age eighty, 2 Samuel 19:35.

See Geriatrics, Old Age, Senility.

SEDUCTION

Seduction refused, Genesis 39:6–20.

Wickedness of Amnon toward Tamar, 2 Samuel 13:1–20.

Seductive ways of prostitute, Proverbs 7:6–27; Jeremiah 3:1–2.

National seduction, 2 Kings 21:9; Ezekiel 13:10–11.

Haughty women of Zion, Isaiah 3:16–17.

Worst of women, Jeremiah 2:33.

Merchandising feminine beauty, Ezekiel 16:15.

Adulterous look, Hosea 2:2.

False Christs, prophets, Mark 13:22.

Young distorters of truth, Acts 20:30.

False spirits, 1 Timothy 4:1.

Taking advantage of weak-willed women, 2 Timothy 3:6.

Deceiving, being deceived, 2 Timothy 3:13.

Warning sounded, 1 John 2:26.

See Deceit, Wiles.

SEED

Cycle of seasons, Genesis 8:22.

Light sown like seed, Psalm 97:11 (NASB).

Planting seed, celebrating harvest, Psalm 126:6 (CEV).

Seeds do not germinate, Joel 1:17.

Parable of sower, Matthew 13:3–30.

Seed dies to live, 1 Corinthians 15:36–38, 42 (AB).

Christ as Abraham's "seed," Galatians 3:16.

Good crops and weeds, Hebrews 6:7–8.

See Farmer, Harvest.

SEEKERS

Tent for inquirers, Exodus 33:7.

Intently seeking the Lord, 2 Chronicles 31:21.

Thirsting for God, Psalms 42:1–4; 63:1–8; 143:6.

Those who wanted to see Jesus, John 12:20–22.

See Evangelism.

SEER See Prophet.

SEGREGATION

Same rules for all, Numbers 15:15.

Segregation of foreigners, Nehemiah 13:1–3.

Mutual hatred of Samaritans and Jews, Luke 9:51–56; John 4:9.

Prophet from Galilee, John 7:41–52.

See Alien, Prejudice, Racism, Xenophobia.

SELECTION

Improving species of animals, Genesis 30:41–42.

Choice of Jesus or Barabbas, Matthew 27:15–26.

See Choice.

SELF-ACCEPTANCE

Loss of personal worth, Deuteronomy 28:68.

Self-acceptance prompts bold prayer, Nehemiah 5:19.

Admitting wrong, Zechariah 1:6.

Paul accepted himself for what he was, 1 Corinthians 15:10.

See Confidence, Ego.

SELF-CENTERED See Pride, Vanity.

SELF-CONFIDENCE

Erroneous self-confidence, 2 Chronicles 12:1.

Lost self-confidence, Nehemiah 6:16 (NIV).

In time of weakness, Job 6:13.

Lack of self-confidence, Job 9:20.

Righteous in one's own eyes, Job 32:1.

Boast only about the Lord, Jeremiah 9:23–24 (NKJV).

Paul could be timid and bold, 2 Corinthians 10:1.

See Assurance, Confidence.

SELF-CONTROL

Tongue control, Psalm 39:1–2.

Controlling one's temper, Proverbs 16:32 (GNB).

Keeping oneself under control, Proverbs 29:11.

Refusal to drink wine, Jeremiah 35:6.

Act in times of duress, James 1:19–20.

No one is perfect, James 3:2 (NKJV).

Mature, gracious Christianity, 2 Peter 1:6.

See Discipline, Self-denial, Temperment.

SELF-DEFENSE

Vindication by earthquake, Numbers 16:28–34.

Cities of refuge, Numbers 35:6–15.

Lack of confidence, 1 Samuel 27:1.

Killing in self-defense, 2 Samuel 2:22–23.

Fearful of personal safety, Acts 5:13–14.

See Protection.

SELF-DENIAL

Self-denial demonstrated, Genesis 22:1–12.

Sexual restraint, 1 Samuel 21:4–5.

Avoid over-eating, Proverbs 23:1–2, 20.

Taking up the cross, Matthew 10:38; 16:24; Luke 14:27.

Self-denying discipleship, Mark 10:28; Luke 14:33; 18:29–30.

Bodily subjection, 1 Corinthians 9:27.

Flesh crucified, Galatians 5:24.

Put off old self, Ephesians 4:22–24 (NIV).

Impelled to self-denial, Philippians 3:8.

Earthly nature put to death, Colossians 3:5.

Practicing "won't" power, Titus 2:12.

Abstain from lust, 1 Peter 2:11; 4:2.

See Discipline, Discipleship, Unselfishness.

SELF-DESTRUCTION

Self-destructing enemies, Psalm 55:9–10 (LB).

See Suicide.

SELF-ESTEEM

Low self-esteem, Job 9:21 (See Berk.).

Man's estimation and God's, Proverbs 16:2; 21:2.

Proud of alleged ability, Isaiah 5:21.

Lost self-esteem, Lamentations 4:2.

Proper love of self, Mark 12:31.

Honest self-esteem, Romans 12:3 (GNB).

Considered least worthy, 1 Corinthians 15:9 (LB).

Falsely evaluating oneself, 2 Corinthians 10:12.

Avoid self-delusion, Galatians 6:1.

See Pride, Self-image, Vanity.

SELF-EXAMINATION

Standing before God, 2 Chronicles 6:12–19.

Difficult procedure, Psalm 19:12.

Examine, test our ways, Lamentations 3:40.

Heart repentence, Joel 2:13.

Hypocrite's need for self-examination, Matthew 7:5.

Need for personal evaluation, Romans 2:17–29.

Self-examination at Lord's table, 1 Corinthians 11:28–29.

Examination of faith, 2 Corinthians 13:5.

Refusing to see oneself with reality, James 1:23–25.

See Introspection.

SELF-IMAGE

Pride, arrogance, 1 Samuel 2:3.

Rebuttal against oppressors, Job 12:1–3.

Low evaluation of man, Job 25:6.

Youth chides wisdom of age, Job 32:6–9.

Wrong, right boasting, Jeremiah 9:23–24.

More than wealth makes a king, Jeremiah 22:14–15.

Religious performance, Matthew 6:1–4.

Drawing attention to alleged piety, Matthew 6:16–18.

Self-image of Jesus, Matthew 12:41.

Determining who is greatest, Mark 9:33–37.

Love of neighbor, oneself, Mark 12:31.

Loyalty exaggerated, Mark 14:31.

Prodigal's opinion of himself, Luke 15:21.

Justified in eyes of men, Luke 16:15 (NIV).

Folly distorted self-image, Acts 12:21–23.

Paul's estimation of himself, 1 Corinthians 15:9.

Danger of false self-image, 2 Corinthians 10:12.

Self-image in ministry, 2 Corinthians 11:5–6; 12:11.

Productively aware of weakness, 2 Corinthians 11:30.

Mirror of truth, James 1:23–25.

See Ego, Self-esteem.

SELF-INTEREST

Morose selfishness, Exodus 16:2–3.

Selfish marital relationship, Deuteronomy 22:13–19.

Personal motivations as key to status and well-being, Deuteronomy 28:1–68. (Note: Rewards for obedience, verses 1–14; warning against disobedience, verses 15–68.)

Fortunes restored, Deuteronomy 30:1–3.

Art of careful negotiation, Ruth 4:1–8.

Leadership for those in trouble, 1 Samuel 22:2.

David's lack of confidence, 1 Samuel 27:1.

Showing favor for personal interest, 1 Samuel 27:12.

Share, share alike, 1 Samuel 30:24.

Dishonest report for personal gain, 2 Samuel 1:2–16.

Looking from two perspectives, 2 Samuel 12:1–13.

Requesting payment for spiritual ministry, 2 Kings 5:20–27.

Self-interest at expense of others, 2 Kings 6:24–31.

Evaluating personal options, 2 Kings 7:3–4.

Trampled by hungry mob, 2 Kings 7:17–20.

Concern of one man, action of another, 2 Kings 8:7–15.

Overcome by personal pride, 2 Chronicles 26:16.

God's provision, sick man's pride, 2 Chronicles 32:24–26.

Pleasing the king, Esther 2:1–4.

Man who built gallows for his own neck, Esther 5:11–14; 9:25.

Mistaken praise, Esther 6:1–12.

Satanic view of human motivations, Job 2:1–10.

The Lord on our side, Psalm 124:1–5.

Looking back on academic folly, Proverbs 5:13.

Treasures of no value, Proverbs 10:2.

Dread and desire, Proverbs 10:24.

Self-interest principle functioning, Proverbs 11:24–25.

God's will versus self-interest, Proverbs 19:21; Zechariah 7:4–6.

Improper self-interest, Proverbs 25:6–7, 27.

Refusal to go God's way, Jeremiah 11:7–8.

Choice for national well-being, Jeremiah 27:12–15.

Shepherds care more for themselves than for flocks, Ezekiel 34:2.

Personal desire above need of others, Amos 6:6.

Fate of secure city, Zephaniah 2:15.

Reward for tithing, Malachi 3:10.

Self-interest enhanced by serving God, Malachi 3:14–17.

Self-interest in its highest function, Matthew 6:33.

Golden Rule reversed, Matthew 18:21–25.

"What will we get?" Matthew 19:27 (CEV).

Complaining about another's generosity, Matthew 20:1–16.

Self-interest wrongly pursued, Mark 8:36.

Selfish request for honor, Mark 10:35–45.

Slumbering disciples, Matthew 26:36–46; Mark 14:32–42; Luke 22:39–46.

Jesus deserted by followers, Mark 14:50–54.

Thievery of tax collectors, soldiers, Luke 3:12–14.

Stewardship, self-interest, Luke 6:38.

Desiring healing of valuable servant, Luke 7:1–3.

Denial of self for best interest of self, Luke 9:23–25.

Greatest among apostles, Luke 9:46–48; 22:24–27.

Right spirit victory over evil, Luke 10:17–20.

Martha's distraction, Luke 10:38–42.

Evil of vanity, Luke 11:43.

Greedy self-interest, Luke 12:15–21.

Desiring place of honor, Luke 14:7–11.

Reaching out to those in need, Luke 14:12–15.

Go to war or negotiate peace, Luke 14:31–32.

Prodigal son, resenting brother, Luke 15:11–32.

Attitude of employer toward labor, Luke 17:7–10.

Pharisees desired visible kingdom, Luke 17:20–21.

Rich man's self-interest and spiritual need, Luke 18:18–25.

Disciples desired earthly status, Acts 1:6.

Fearful of personal safety, Acts 5:13–14.

Desiring spiritual power for personal gain, Acts 8:18–24.

Loss of revenue from manufacturing idols, Acts 19:23–26.

Judging others and ignoring personal guilt, Romans 2:1–16.

Christian attitude toward others, Romans 12:10.

Spiritual self-interest, 2 Corinthians 8:10 (Berk.).

Reaping what one sows, 2 Corinthians 9:6–8.

Wisdom of self-examination, 2 Corinthians 13:5.

Serving the Lord with wrong motives, Philippians 1:15–19.

Distorted self-interest, Philippians 2:21.

S

SELFISHNESS

Syndrome of Last Days, 2 Timothy 3:2–5.

Unsatisfied inner desires, James 4:1–2.

See Hedonism, Narcissism, Selfishness.

SELFISHNESS

Attitude of management toward labor, Exodus 5:2–5.

Conflict between David, Saul, 1 Samuel 26:1–25.

Cursed for hoarding, Proverbs 11:26.

Selfish stupidity, Proverbs 18:1 (CEV).

Selfish possessiveness, Isaiah 5:8.

Denying food and drink, Isaiah 32:6.

Selfish shepherds, Ezekiel 34:2, 18.

Religiosity, selfishness, Hosea 10:1.

Cheap value on human beings, Amos 2:6.

Dishonestly selfish, Habakkuk 2:6.

Selfish feasting, Zechariah 7:6.

People in fine homes, temple in ruins, Haggai 1:1–4.

Give to those who ask, Matthew 5:42.

Ignoring need of others, Matthew 25:43–44.

Seeking best for themselves, Mark 10:37.

Greed over one's possessions, Luke 12:14–15.

Choosing place of honor, Luke 14:7–11.

Preaching hindered business, Acts 19:20–41.

Ruled by personal desire, Romans 8:5–8 (CEV).

Self-seeking, Philippians 2:21.

Unwilling to share ministry financing, Philippians 4:15–19.

Good deeds made known, 1 Timothy 5:25.

Love of self, 2 Timothy 3:2.

Unsatisfied inner desires, James 4:1–2.

See Greed, Self-interest.

SELF-PITY

Self-pity of disgruntled followers, Numbers 16:12–14.

Royal self-pity, 1 Samuel 22:6–8.

Rebuffed by subordinate, Esther 5:9–10.

Weight of misery, Job 6:2–3.

Yearning for death, Job 7:13–16.

Job's plight, Job 19:13–21 (NKJV).

Living righteously for no seeming purpose, Psalm 73:12–13.

Daughters taught how to wail, Jeremiah 9:20.

Seeming inequity of testing, Jeremiah 15:15–18.

Blaming the Lord for trouble, Jeremiah 20:7–8; Habakkuk 1:1–4.

Lamented day of birth, Jeremiah 20:14–15.

Self-pitying domestic, Luke 10:38–42.

Refusal of Jesus to accept pity, Luke 23:27–28.

Avoid self-pity in all circumstances, Philippians 2:14–16.

See Complain, Discontent, Persecution, Pessimism.

SELF-RIGHTEOUS

Self-righteousness affronted, Deuteronomy 3:3–11.

Job's attitude, Job 9:20.

Accused of being self-righteous, Job 33:8–13; 34:1–9; 36:4.

Those pure in their own eyes, Proverbs 30:12.

No need for God, Isaiah 50:11 (LB).

Righteousness as filthy rags, Isaiah 64:6.

Scorning those who have done wrong, Ezekiel 16:56–57.

Vain self-righteousness, Hosea 12:8.

Claiming piety superior to ancestors, Matthew 23:30.

Seeking self justification, Luke 10:29; 16:15.

Holier than thou, Luke 18:9.

Self-righteous accusers, John 8:3–11.

Boasting before men not valid before God, Romans 4:2.

Those who commend themselves, 2 Corinthians 10:12.

Self-delusion, Galatians 6:3.

Personal example, Philippians 3:3–11.

See Hypocrisy, Piety.

SELF-SATISFACTION

Satisfied with one's work, Ecclesiastes 2:24 (NASB).

SELF-WILL *See Obstinate, Stubborn.*

SELLING *See Marketing, Purchase.*

SEMINARY

No formal training, John 7:13–15.
See Theology.

SENILITY

Childless old woman, Genesis 18:10–12.
Work for old man to do, Joshua 13:1; 14:10–11.
Loss of sensitivities, 2 Samuel 19:35.
David's senility, 1 Kings 1:1–4.
See Geriatrics, Impotence, Old Age, Sedentary,

SENIORS *See Elders, Geriatrics, Old Age, Respect.*

SENSATIONALISM

Attitude toward father's nudity, Genesis 9:20–27.
Jesus asked miracles be kept private, Matthew 9:29–31.
Sensational Lazarus, John 12:9.
"All this foolishness," Acts 14:15 (CEV).
Spectacular prophecies, 2 Thessalonians 2:1–2.
Wanting ears tickled, 2 Timothy 4:3 (NASB).
See Exhibitionism, Spectacular.

SENSES

Darkness that could be felt, Exodus 10:21.
Temple fragrance not for personal enjoyment, Exodus 30:34–38.
Perfume for lady, Ruth 3:3.
Eyes that see, ears that hear, Deuteronomy 29:2–4.
Partial blindness inflicted as disgrace, 1 Samuel 11:2–11.
Numbed senses of octogenarian, 2 Samuel 19:35.
Motivated by hook and bit, 2 Kings 19:28.
Satanic view of man's motivations, Job 2:1–10.
Sight, hearing, Proverbs 20:12 (LB).
Eyes, ears that do not function, Jeremiah 5:21; Ezekiel 12:2.
Birds know seasons of migration, Jeremiah 8:7.
Demon possessed, blind and mute, Matthew 12:22–30.
Calvary taste, Matthew 27:34, 48.
Trance induced by hunger, Acts 10:10.

Lust of eyes, 2 Peter 2:14; 1 John 2:16.
Seen, touched, 1 John 1:1.
See Hearing, Perception, Sight, Taste, Touch.

SENSELESS

Nation without sense, Deuteronomy 32:28.
See Insensitive.

SENSITIVITY

Yearning for the Lord, Isaiah 26:9.
Shocked by lewd conduct, Ezekiel 16:27.
Jesus knew when He had been touched, Luke 8:43–48.
Physical illustration of spiritual truth, John 6:53–64.
Lack of spiritual perception, John 8:47.
Neither thunder nor angel's voice, John 12:29.
Not over sensitive, 1 Corinthians 13:5 (LB).
Trouble prepares us to help others, 2 Corinthians 1:3–4.
Sensitivity produced by Godly sorrow, 2 Corinthians 7:10–13.
Enlightened sensitivity, Ephesians 1:18–21.
Degrees of spiritual sensitivity, Hebrews 5:11–14.
See Insight, Perception.

SENSUAL

Lust seemingly turned to love, Genesis 34:1–4.
Mixing pagan religion with immorality, Numbers 25:1–3.
Evil earnings forbidden as offering, Deuteronomy 23:18.
Immoral use of place of worship, 1 Samuel 2:22–25.
Imbibing without restraint, Esther 1:7–8.
Replacing queen, Esther 2:1–4.
Covenant to avoid lust, Job 31:1.
Captivated by sensual beauty, Proverbs 6:25.
Proud women, Isaiah 3:16 (CEV).
From one sin to another, Jeremiah 9:3.
Continual lust for more, Ephesians 4:19.
See Immorality, Lust.

SENTENCE

Capital punishment, Exodus 21:12–14.
Just sentence, Psalm 51:4 (NRSV).

S

Facing grim destiny, Jeremiah 15:2–3.
Sentenced to death, Daniel 6:16.
See Prison.

SENTIMENTAL

Meat not eaten, Genesis 32:32.
See Emotion.

SEPARATION

Separation in Garden of Eden, Genesis 2:16–17.
Old Testament command to separation, Exodus 34:11–16.
Discerning clean, unclean, Leviticus 10:10.
Early joys of marriage, Deuteronomy 24:5.
Separated from heathen, Joshua 23:7.
Samson desired Philistine wife, Judges 14:1–2.
Separation Hill, 1 Samuel 23:28 (GNB).
Solomon's partial commitment 1 Kings 3:3.
Pledge to avoid intermarriage, Nehemiah 10:30.
Solomon's problem, Nehemiah 13:26.
Separated from evil by choice, Psalm 1:1.
Godly set apart, Psalm 4:3.
Do not envy sinners, Proverbs 23:17.
Touch no unclean thing, Isaiah 52:11.
Separated from revelers, Jeremiah 15:16–17 (See CEV).
Temple, idols, Ezekiel 43:8.
Separation by decision, Daniel 1:8–20; 3:8–12.
Teetotalers forced to drink wine, Amos 2:12.
Two in agreement, Amos 3:3.
Jesus criticized for fellowship with sinners, Matthew 9:10–12; Mark 2:15–17; Luke 5:27–31.
Ultra-separationist Pharisees, Matthew 9:11–13.
Test of righteousness in time of wickedness, Matthew 24:12–13.
What enters into a person, what comes out, Mark 7:15–23.
You cannot serve two masters, Luke 16:13.
Refusing to separate from praise of men, John 12:42–43.
Spiritual misfits, John 17:14 (LB).
Is not of the world, John 17:15–16.
Peter and Gentiles, Acts 11:1–3.

Christian lifestyle, Romans 13:12–14.
True measure of spirituality, Romans 14:17–18.
Do not cause another to stumble, Romans 14:20–23.
Christians married to non-Christians, 1 Corinthians 7:10–16.
Food sacrificed to idols, 1 Corinthians 8:1.
Liberty in eating, drinking, 1 Corinthians 8:7–13; 10:23–33.
Believers not to join unbelievers, 2 Corinthians 6:14–18.
Sever yourself, 2 Corinthians 6:17 (AB).
Living by world standards, 2 Corinthians 10:2.
Crucified with Christ, Galatians 2:20.
Improper association, Ephesians 5:7.
Separation versus legalism, Colossians 2:16.
Reject iniquity, 2 Timothy 2:19.
To the pure, always pure, Titus 1:15.
Resisting ungodliness, lusts, Titus 2:11–12.
Separation of Moses from Pharaoh's daughter, Hebrews 11:23–24.
Faithfully running race, Hebrews 12:1–2.
Submit to God, resist devil, James 4:7.
Strangers in the world, 1 Peter 1:1–2 (NIV).
Call to holiness, 1 Peter 1:13–16.
Astonishing separation, 1 Peter 4:3–4 (AB).
Flesh, eyes, pride, 1 John 2:15–17.
Come out from iniquity, Revelation 18:4–5.
See Legalism, Worldliness.

SEPULCHER

Graves hewn out of rock, Isaiah 22:16.
Choicest tombs, Genesis 23:6.
Festive sepulcher, 2 Chronicles 16:14.
See Burial, Tomb.

SEQUEL

Report continued, Acts 1:1.

SERENDIPITY

Altered events, Genesis 22:6–18.
Unexpected family joy, Genesis 29:9–14.
Red Sea rescue, Exodus 14:21–28.
Surprise for Boaz, blessing for Ruth, Ruth 3:1–15.
"Wine of astonishment," Psalm 60:3 (KJV).
Unexpected wonders, Isaiah 64:3.

Astonishing, resolate, mountain, Ezekiel 35:7 (AB).

Fourth figure in fiery furnace, Daniel 3:19–28.

King's experience of joy, Daniel 6:16–27.

Startling angel appearance, Luke 1:11–12 (NRSV).

Serendipity for shepherds, Luke 2:8–18.

Discovering water of life, John 4:4–15.

Linguistics spectacle, Acts 2:1–8.

Ethiopian eunuch, Acts 8:26–39.

Serendipity conversion, Acts 9:1–8.

Deliverance by earthquake, Acts 16:23–34.

See Blessing, Surprise.

SERIOUS

Value of sorrow over laughter, Ecclesiastes 3:4.

Pondering mother, Luke 2:19.

Serious assessment, Philippians 4:8.

See Industrious.

SERMON

Angel's short sermon, Judges 2:1–5.

Good things from God's house, Psalm 65:4.

Historical sermon, Psalm 78:1–72.

Disliked sermon, Jeremiah 26:7–9 (CEV).

"Amen" of agreement to message, Jeremiah 28:5–6.

Confusing messages, Ezekiel 20:49 (CEV).

Sermon exerpt, Mark 1:7 (LB).

Surprising sermon, Mark 1:22 (LB).

Sermons of Jesus, Luke 4:14–15 (LB).

Hard content, John 6:60.

Mistaking God's voice for thunder, John 12:28–29.

Resume of Old Testament, proclamation of Gospel, Acts 13:16–41.

Long sermons, Acts 2:40 (LB); 20:7.

Congregation, Preaching, Worship.

SERPENT See Snakes.

SERVANT

Servant's attitude toward unfair employer, Genesis 16:1–10.

Declining freedom, Exodus 21:5.

Forced into servitude, Joshua 9:22–27.

Servants who break away from masters, 1 Samuel 25:10.

Loyalty of servant to king, 2 Samuel 15:19–21.

Spiritual training of servants, 2 Chronicles 9:7 (KJV).

Servant earns role of brother, Proverbs 17:2.

Honored servant, Proverbs 27:18.

Servant attitude, Matthew 10:24.

Status through humility, servitude, Matthew 20:20–28.

Faithful, unfaithful service, Matthew 24:45–51.

Wanting to be first the easy way, Mark 10:35–45.

Black man helped Jesus carry cross, Mark 15:21 (Note: Cyrene a country in North Africa).

Servant leadership, Matthew 20:28; Mark 10:43–44; John 13:5, 14, 22–23; Acts 20:18–19; 1 Corinthians 16:15–16; 2 Corinthians 4:5 (AB); Galatians 6:2; Titus 2:7.

John the Baptist, forerunner, Luke 3:1–20.

First servant, then ministry, Romans 1:1.

Paul considered himself least of apostles, 1 Corinthians 15:9; Ephesians 3:8–9.

Submission to each other, 1 Corinthians 16:15–16.

God's assistants, 2 Corinthians 6:4 (Berk., LB).

Loving service, Galatians 5:13.

God's workmanship, Ephesians 2:10.

Slaves, masters, Ephesians 6:5–9; Colossians 3:22; 1 Timothy 6:1; Titus 2:9; 1 Peter 2:18.

Christ a bond-servant, Philippians 2:7 (NASB, NKJV).

Ministering servant, Titus 1:1–3.

Servant mode of incarnation, Hebrews 10:5–7.

Humble circumstances high position, James 1:9 (NIV).

See Commitment, Discipleship, Service.

SERVICE

Tabernacle items anointed for service, Exodus 40:9–11.

Material security versus Lord's will, Numbers 32:14–27.

Prenatal commitment, 1 Samuel 1:11–12.

Eagerly volunteering, 1 Kings 19:20.

S

Requesting payment for spiritual service, 2 Kings 5:20–27.

Those assigned as gatekeepers, 1 Chronicles 9:22–27.

Serving God, Job 22:2 (Berk.).

Motivated by fear, Psalm 2:11.

Serve the Lord with gladness, Psalm 100:1–2.

Blameless ministers, Psalm 101:6.

Conditional freedom, Jeremiah 34:8–11.

Women who command husbands, Amos 4:1.

Total loyalty, Matthew 6:24.

First priority—service, Matthew 6:33 (CEV).

Service follows blessing, Matthew 8:14–15.

Authority of teachers and masters, Matthew 10:24.

Last act of Jesus prior to crucifixion, Matthew 20:28–34.

Donkey chosen to serve Jesus, Matthew 21:1–7.

Parable of two sons, Matthew 21:28–31.

Attitude of servant in spiritual service, Matthew 23:8–12.

Faithful, unfaithful service, Matthew 24:45–51.

Wanting to be first the easy way, Mark 10:35–45.

Joy of serving Christ, Luke 10:17.

Putting first things first, Luke 10:38–42.

Expected service, Luke 17:7–10.

Serving God seven days a week, John 5:16–17.

Jesus washed disciples' feet, John 13:1–17.

Misguided service, John 16:2 (LB).

Outreach to others, John 21:15–17.

John as helper, Acts 13:5.

Service with humility, Acts 20:19.

Set free to serve, Romans 7:6.

Talent and call to service, Romans 11:29.

Strong looking after weak, Romans 15:1.

Hard worker, Romans 16:12 (NASB).

Serving without remuneration, 1 Corinthians 9:7–12.

Servant attitude in preaching, 1 Corinthians 9:19–23.

In serving God, all may win, 1 Corinthians 9:24–27.

Different kinds of gifts and service, 1 Corinthians 12:4–11.

Total function of Body of Christ, 1 Corinthians 12:14–20.

Validated discipleship, 2 Corinthians 9:13–14.

Labor of love, Galatians 5:13.

God's workmanship, Ephesians 2:10.

The way up is down, Ephesians 4:8–10.

SERVICE

FILL'ER UP AND CHECK THE TIRES.

Varied talents in Body of Christ, Ephesians 4:11–13.

"I do my share," Colossians 1:24 (NASB).

Working long hours, 1 Thessalonians 2:9 (CEV).

Need for full time Christian service, 2 Timothy 2:1–4.

Active duty, 2 Timothy 2:4 (GNB).

Service as building materials, 1 Peter 2:4–5.

"Hard work," Revelation 2:2 (CEV).

See Ministry, Servant, Vocation.

SEWING

First tailor and seamstress, Genesis 3:7.

Skilled tailors, Exodus 28:3.

Time to mend garments, Ecclesiastes 3:7.

Sewing on magic charms, Ezekiel 13:18.

How not to patch old garment, Matthew 9:16.

See Clothing, Wardrobe.

SEXUAL

Relationship between Adam, Eve, Genesis 4:1–2, 25.

Connubial enjoyment, Genesis 18:12 (Berk.).

Rape, Genesis 34:1–31.

Masculine sex appeal, Genesis 39:6–7.

Abstinence before worship, Exodus 19:14–15.

Code for sexual relations, Leviticus 18:6–23.

Sexually damaged animals unfit, Leviticus 22:24–25.

Abstinence and vows, Numbers 30:3–12 (Berk.).

Injury to sexual organs, Deuteronomy 23:1.

Chastity in conduct, Deuteronomy 25:11–12.

Restraint of soldiers, 1 Samuel 21:4–5 (GNB).

Pounding heart, Song of Songs 5:4 (NIV).

Thinking only of sex, Isaiah 57:5 (CEV).

"Making love," Jeremiah 2:33 (Berk.).

Morality vital to spirituality, Jeremiah 3:1–5.

"Age for love," Ezekiel 16:8.

Earth marriage, Heaven's relationship, Mark 12:18–27.

Sexual restraint in marriage, 1 Corinthians 7:5.

Modesty concerning body organs, 1 Corinthians 12:22–25.

Young widows' desires, 1 Timothy 5:11.

Marriage bed, Hebrews 13:4.

See Chastity, Immorality, Lust, Marriage, Passion.

SHADING

Separation of light from darkness, Genesis 1:4.

SHADOW

Strange movement of shadow, 2 Kings 20:8–11.

Valley of death's shadow, Psalm 23:4; Matthew 4:16.

Shadow of divine wings, Psalm 57:1.

Shadow of God's hand, Isaiah 51:16.

See Darkness, Light.

SHALLOWNESS

People quick to complain, Numbers 11:4–11.

Pride, arrogance, 1 Samuel 2:3.

Beautiful but dumb, Proverbs 11:22.

Fool's likeness, Proverbs 26:1–11.

Forever unsatisfied, Proverbs 30:15–16.

Avoid meaningless offerings, Isaiah 1:13 (NIV).

Proud women, Isaiah 3:16.

Skilled at art of seduction, Jeremiah 2:33.

"Talks-Big-Does-Nothing," Jeremiah 46:17 (CEV).

An end to noisy songs, Ezekiel 26:13 (NIV).

Merely lip service, Ezekiel 33:31–32.

Shallow roots, Mark 4:16–17.

No foundation, Luke 6:49.

Shallow Pharisees, Luke 15:1–7.

Marginal commitment, John 6:66.

Shallow doctrinal opinions, Galatians 1:6–9.

Children tossed by wind, Ephesians 4:14.

See Immaturity.

SHAM

Put up bold front, Proverbs 21:29 (NIV).

Herod's sham, Magi's astuteness, Matthew 2:7–8, 12.

Religion of sham, Matthew 23:5–7.

Sham humility, Colossians 2:18.

Hypocritical claim of holy life, 1 John 1:8–10.

S

Sham conduct in church, 3 John 9–10.
Feigning life when spiritually dead, Revelation 3:1.
See Deception, Falsehood, Hypocrisy, Immaturity, Sanctimonious.

SHAME

First display of shame, Genesis 3:10.
Creator's regret, Genesis 6:6.
Attitude toward father's privacy, Genesis 9:20–27.
Shame for immoral sons, 1 Samuel 2:22–25; 8:1–3.
Shameful royal death, 1 Samuel 31:8–10.
Inundated by guilt, shame, Ezra 9:5–9.
Those put to shame, those not, Psalm 25:2–3.
Deep sense of disgrace, Psalm 44:15.
Put to shame, Psalm 119:78.
Asleep during harvest, Proverbs 10:5 (NKJV).
Mother's shame, Proverbs 29:15.
Moon disgraced, sun ashamed, Isaiah 24:23.
Shamed by others, Isaiah 26:11.
Mountain wilts with shame, Isaiah 33:9 (CEV).
Idol makers ashamed, Isaiah 45:16.
Shame of getting caught, Jeremiah 2:26.
Refusing to be ashamed, Jeremiah 3:3 (NKJV).
Unable to blush, Jeremiah 6:15.
Too ashamed to talk, Ezekiel 16:63.
Fallen princes, Ezekiel 32:30.
Preferring shame to honor, Hosea 4:18 (LB).
Shameless evil, Zephaniah 3:5 (See CEV).
Shamed by nudity, Revelation 16:15.
See Disgrace, Embarrassment, Humiliation, Wantonness.

SHARING

Sharing earth's wealth, Ecclesiastes 5:9 (KJV).
Two in agreement, Amos 3:3.
Faith of friends resulted in healing, Mark 2:1–5.
Sharing with others, Luke 3:11.
Christian kind of sharing, Acts 2:44.
"Glad and generous hearts," Acts 2:46 (NRSV).

Early Christians shared all things, Acts 4:32.
Sharing scriptural insights, Acts 18:24–26; Romans 15:14.
Share with needy Christians, Romans 12:13 (GNB).
Sharing both good, bad, 2 Corinthians 1:7.
Sharing equally in stewardship, 2 Corinthians 8:11–15.
Some pay, others receive, 2 Corinthians 11:7–8.
Blessed and a blessing, Galatians 3:9.
Burdens shared, Galatians 6:2.
Student sharing with teacher, Galatians 6:6.
"Sharing in the Gospel," Philippians 1:5 (NRSV).
Shared report, Colossians 4:16 (LB).
Empathy with prisoners, Hebrews 13:3.
See Caring, Discipleship, Fellowship.

SHARP

Iron sharpens iron, Proverbs 27:17.
Blunt iron edge, Ecclesiastes 10:10 (NRSV).
Diamond point, Jeremiah 17:1 (GNB).

SHAVING

Shave and clean clothes, Genesis 41:14.
Head shaved, Numbers 6:9; Job 1:20.
Body hair removed, Numbers 8:7.
Losing half of beard, 2 Samuel 10:4.
Sharp sword used for shaving, Ezekiel 5:1.
Mark of distinction, Acts 21:24.
See Barber, Moustache, Whiskers.

SHEEP

Initial object of sacrifice, Genesis 4:4–8.
Divine provision for sacrifice, Genesis 22:3–14.
Wool for cloth, Genesis 31:19; 38:12–17.
Wool for clergy, Deuteronomy 18:3–5.
Milk, mutton, Deuteronomy 32:13–14.
Tribute from king to king, 2 Kings 3:4.
Lamb of God, John 1:29.
Lost sheep, Matthew 18:11–13; Luke 15:4–7.
See Pastor, Shepherd.

SHEKINAH

Shenikah cloud, Ezekiel 9:3 (AB).

Bodies full of eyes, Ezekiel 10:12.

Abominations before his eyes, Ezekiel 20:7 (KJV).

Visible desires removed, Ezekiel 24:16 (See KJV, LB).

Using eyes for good or evil, Matthew 6:22–23.

Partial, then full vision, Mark 8:22–25 (See LB).

Joyful gift of sight, Luke 7:21 (AB).

Eyes of heart, Ephesians 1:18–19 (NIV).

See Blindness, Eyes, Vision.

SIGHTSEEING

Unpleasant sights, Deuteronomy 28:34.

Tour of Zion, Psalm 48:12–13.

See Tourist.

SIGN

Wife-search guidance sign, Genesis 24:12–14 (See AB).

Wet and dry fleece, Judges 6:36–40.

Decimated altar, 1 Kings 13:3.

Sign of the shadow, 2 Kings 20:9.

Refusing to put God to test, Isaiah 7:11–14.

See Guidance, Token.

SIGNAL

Pointing spear, Joshua 8:18, 26 (LB).

Trumpet signal, Numbers 10:1–7.

SIGNATURE

Signing document, Nehemiah 10:1–28 (LB).

"Here is my signature," Job 31:35 (NASB, NRSV).

See Handwriting.

SIGNING

Hands held high, Exodus 17:8–13.

Speaking with signing, Luke 1:62–62.

See Deafness, Non-verbal.

SIGNS OF THE TIMES

Characteristics of last days, 2 Timothy 3:1–7.

SILENCE

Speaking neither good nor evil, Genesis 31:24.

Silent toward those who insulted, 1 Samuel 10:27.

Stand still, see what God will do, 1 Samuel 12:16.

"Be quiet," 1 Samuel 15:16 (NKJV).

Nothing to say, Nehemiah 5:8.

Painful silence, Job 2:13.

Wisdom of silence, Job 13:5.

Let others speak, Job 13:13.

Respect for those older, Job 32:4.

Silent meditation, Psalm 4:4 (LB).

Eloquent silence, Psalm 19:3 (LB).

Mute God, Psalm 83:1 (Berk.).

Wise man holds tongue, Proverbs 10:14 (LB).

Wisdom of silence, Proverbs 10:19; 17:28.

Avoid quarrel, Proverbs 11:12 (LB).

Guardian of the soul, Proverbs 13:3.

Silence prevents quarrel, Proverbs 17:14.

Guarding tongue, Proverbs 21:23.

Those who speak in haste, Proverbs 29:20.

Too much talk, Ecclesiastes 5:3.

Dramatic use of silence, Isaiah 36:13–21.

Silence of the Savior, Isaiah 53:7; Matthew 26:57–67; Mark 14:53–62; John 19:8–9.

Futile effort to suppress truth, Jeremiah 38:1–6.

Divine silence, Hosea 3:4 (CEV).

Prudent man's silence, Amos 5:13.

Silent about the Lord's name, Amos 6:10.

Prophetic silence, Zechariah 13:1–5.

Demons kept silent, Mark 1:33–34.

Pondering in heart, Luke 2:19.

Cynical tongues silenced, Luke 20:20–26.

Silent witness, 1 Peter 3:1–2.

Musicians put to silence, Revelation 18:22.

See Tact.

SILVER

Spanish silver, Jeremiah 10:9 (GNB).

See Gold, Money.

SIMILARITY

Common destiny, Ecclesiastes 9:1–2.

Similar names of father and son, Jeremiah 22:24.

Like teacher, like student, Luke 6:40.

Compare John 1:1–9 with 1 John 1:1–7.

See Like-Minded.

S

SIMILE

Like tree, like chaff, Psalm 1:3–4 (NIV).
As with shield, Psalm 5:12.
Apple of eye, Psalm 17:8 (NIV).
Compacted city, Psalm 122:3 (NIV).
Like weaned child, Psalm 131:2 (NIV).
Like Sodom and Gomorrah, Isaiah 1:9.
"Freedom" in quotation marks, Jeremiah 34:17 (NIV).
Those who move landmarks, Hosea 5:10 (NKJV).
Like unmarked graves, Luke 11:44.
See Figure of Speech.

SIMPLICITY

Great things, small things, 2 King 5:13.
Plain path, Psalm 27:11 (KJV).
Special protection for simple folk, Psalm 116:6.
Understanding to the simple, Psalm 119:130.
The simple life, Psalm 131:1–2.
Writing with ordinary pen, Isaiah 8:1 (See Berk.).
Comprehension of children, Matthew 11:25; Luke 18:17.
Attitude of Jesus to children, Matthew 18:1–6; Mark 10:13–16.
Confused by simple truth, Mark 4:10–13 (See LB).
Travel with humble equipment, Mark 6:8–11.
Blind man's request, Mark 10:46–52.
Simple, profound, Luke 10:21 (AB).
"Speaking plainly," John 16:29 (NRSV).
"Simplicity of heart," Acts 2:46 (NKJV).
Simple men confounded scholars, Acts 4:13.
Spiritual truth in human terms, Romans 6:19.
Confounded by simple message, 1 Corinthians 1:18–21.
Humble backgrounds, abilities, 1 Corinthians 1:26.
Using simple words, 1 Corinthians 2:1 (GNB).
Faith ultimate intelligence, 1 Corinthians 3:18–23.
Simple yes, no, James 5:12 (AB).
See Clarity, Naive.

SIN

Image of God, image of man, Genesis 5:1–3.
Accidental sin, Genesis 9:22–27.
Sin against man, sin against God, 1 Samuel 2:25.
Disobedience of faithful, 1 Samuel 12:20.
One sin as great as another, 1 Samuel 15:23; James 2:10.
Sin considered trivial, 1 Kings 16:31.
Son less evil than parents, 2 Kings 3:1–3.
Lesser degree of sin, 2 Kings 17:1–2.
Purpose for avoiding evil, Job 2:3 (AB).
Sins forgiven, discarded, Job 14:16–17 (CEV).
Cherished becomes like venom, Job 20:12–14.
Nothing hidden from God, Job 34:21–22.
Unconscious faults, Psalm 19:12 (AB).
Forgiven sins honor God, Psalm 25:11.
Strength sapped by sin, Psalm 31:10 (LB).
Lost conscience, Psalms 36:1–2.
Healing for sin, Psalm 41:4.
Sinful nature inherited at birth, Psalm 51:5; 58:3–5.
Corrupted by sin, Psalm 53:1.
Prayer unanswered when sin is cherished, Psalm 66:18–19.
Key to victory over sin, Psalm 119:11, 128.
Ravages of wickedness, Isaiah 9:18.
Forgiveness of sin like cloud removed, Isaiah 44:22–23.
Need for repentance, Isaiah 64:5.
Leopard cannot change spots, Jeremiah 13:23.
Utterly sinful heart, Jeremiah 17:9 (See AB).
Wages of sin, Lamentations 1:14; Romans 6:23.
Increasing magnitude, Ezekiel 8:12–17.
Each individual's sins, Ezekiel 18:14 (LB).
Degrees of sin in God's sight, Ezekiel 16:48–52.
Death penalty, Ezekiel 18:4; Romans 6:21; Ephesians 2:1.
Certain wages of sin, Ezekiel 33:13.
Sins written down, stored, Hosea 13:12 (CEV).
Three sins, even four, Amos 1:3, 6, 9, 11, 13; 2:1, 4, 6.
Cleansing fountain, Zechariah 13:1 (CEV).

Old Testament ends with curse, Malachi 4:6.

Sin, not Cross, took life of Jesus, Mark 15:33–37, 44.

Much guilt, less guilt, Luke 7:36–50.

Nothing hidden but will be made known, Luke 12:2–3.

Darkness preferred to light, John 3:19–21.

Savior, judge, John 5:22–24.

Sin done in ignorance, Acts 3:17; 1 Timothy 1:12–14.

Claiming sins serve good purpose, Romans 3:5 (LB).

No one righteous, Romans 3:10–18.

Sin not accounted by God, Romans 4:8 (GNB).

Sin's relentless spread, Romans 5:12 (AB).

Alluring sin, Romans 6:7 (LB).

Purpose of law in revealing sin, Romans 7:7–12, 14.

"Sin, devilish stuff," Romans 7:13 (LB).

"Trespass," Galatians 6:1 (NASB).

"Forgiveness of our trespasses," Ephesians 1:7 (NASB, NRSV).

Leader's sin, 1 Timothy 5:20 (CEV).

Life prior to regeneration, Titus 3:3.

Unintentional sin, Hebrews 9:7.

Sins forgotten in mercy of salvation, Hebrews 10:17.

Sin clings closely, Hebrews 12:1 (NRSV).

Role of evil desire in causing sin, James 1:13–15.

Big sin, small sin, all sin, James 2:10.

Sin of neglect, James 4:17.

Love of world, 1 John 2:15–17.

"Sin is lawlessness," 1 John 3:4.

"Mortal sin," 1 John 5:16 (NRSV).

Definition of sin, 1 John 5:17.

Whole world controlled by evil one, 1 John 5:19.

When evil serves God's purpose, Revelation 17:17.

See Besetting Sin, Depravity, Evil, Iniquity, Temptation, Wrong.

SINAI

Sinai similarity, Psalm 97:2 (AB).

SINCERITY

Earnestness of new clergy, Deuteronomy 18:6–7.

Avoiding flattery, Job 32:21.

Sackcloth, ashes, Jeremiah 6:26.

Sincerely seeking God, Jeremiah 29:13.

Hyper-piety, Matthew 6:16–18.

Faith tested, Matthew 15:21–28.

Fullest measure of the law, Matthew 23:23.

Questioning Angel's cordial greeting, Luke 1:28–31.

Produce sincere fruit, Luke 3:7–8.

Insincerity of spiritual expression, Romans 9:1–2.

Bread of sincerity, truth, 1 Corinthians 5:8.

Boldness, sincerity, 2 Corinthians 1:12; 2:17.

Sincere Christian service, Colossians 3:23–24.

Love that comes from the heart, 1 Peter 1:22; 4:8.

Actions speak louder than words, 1 John 3:18.

Those who take Scriptures to heart, Revelation 1:3.

See Motivation.

SINGING

Perks for singers, Nehemiah 13:5.

Sing praise with understanding, Psalm 47:7 (KJV).

Songs to the Lord, Psalms 81:1; 95:1.

Bed time songs, Psalms 149:5.

Mountain songs, Isaiah 30:29.

Potential singing stones, Luke 19:37–40.

Inner music, 1 Corinthians 14:15.

Communicative singing, Ephesians 5:19.

Sing praise, James 5:13.

See Hymns, Music.

SINGLE

Self-indulgent single, Proverbs 18:1 (NRSV).

Fear of disgrace, Isaiah 4:1.

"Gift of staying single," Matthew 19:11 (CEV).

Accepting married or unmarried state, 1 Corinthians 7:32–35.

See Continence, Discipline, Marriage.

SINNER

Endless anguished conscience, Deuteronomy 28:67; Job 15:20; Ecclesiastes 2:23; Romans 2:9.

Shallow joy, Proverbs 14:13.

S

Good man's sense of sin, Isaiah 6:5.

Notorious, wicked, Luke 15:2 (AB).

Friend of sinners, Luke 7:39; 19:7; John 8:11; Romans 5:8.

See Evil, Wickedness.

SISTER

Wife was also sister, Genesis 20:12.

Paul's sister, Acts 23:16.

See Daughter.

SITUATION ETHICS

Satan's reasoning, Genesis 3:1–5.

Wife said to be sister, Genesis 12:10–13; 20:1–18; 26:7–11.

Daughters offered in immorality, Genesis 19:4–8.

Crafty midwives, Exodus 1:12–22 (See LB).

Becoming purposely unclean, Leviticus 21:1–4.

Deceit protected spies, Joshua 2:1–6.

Lauding woman for murder, Judges 5:24–27.

Trying to make wrong right, 1 Samuel 15:9–15.

Protective falsehood, 1 Samuel 16:1–5; 19:11–17; 20:1–8.

Protected fugitives, 2 Samuel 17:17–20.

Prophet's pretense, 1 Kings 20:35–43.

Giving false information, 2 Kings 6:18–20.

Pagan prophets, priests destroyed, 2 Kings 10:15–29.

Divinely approved lie, 2 Chronicles 18:18–22.

Stealing to satisfy hunger, Proverbs 6:30.

Doing wrong for piece of bread, Proverbs 28:21.

King commanded Jeremiah to lie, Jeremiah 38:24–27.

See Compromise.

SIZE

Gideon's army, Judges 7:2–3.

Big family, Judges 12:9.

Day of small things, Zechariah 4:10.

See Dimensions, Measurement.

SKELETON *See Bones.*

SKEPTICISM

Skepticism of Abraham, Sarah, Genesis 17:17.

Crisis thought to be joke, Genesis 19:14.

Disbelief in divine provision, Numbers 11:20.

Penalty for skepticism, Numbers 20:12; Luke 1:20.

Questioning God, Job 21:14–15.

Doubting Christ's power, Matthew 13:58; John 12:37.

Rejected resurrection report, Luke 24:11.

Come, see, John 1:46.

Eyewitness rejected, John 3:11.

Jesus' skeptical brother, John 7:5.

See Doubt, Unbelief.

SKILL

Lost skill for farming, Genesis 4:9–12.

Tool maker, Genesis 4:22.

Building tower of Babel, Genesis 11:1–9.

Divine gift of skill, Genesis 31:1–5; Exodus 31:1–5; 35:35; Isaiah 54:16.

Wise-hearted tailors, Exodus 28:3 (KJV).

God-given skills, Exodus 36:1.

Ability to design, produce, Exodus 38:23 (See KJV).

Elimination of blacksmiths, 1 Samuel 13:19.

Highly skilled craftsman, 1 Kings 7:14 (See KJV).

Transported skill, 2 Kings 25:11–12.

Various skills, 1 Chronicles 5:18; 2 Chronicles 34:12; Daniel 1:4, 17; 9:22.

Variety of skilled workmen, 1 Chronicles 22:15.

Master craftsman, 2 Chronicles 2:13 (LB).

Skilled machinists, 2 Chronicles 26:15.

Victory not necessarily to swift and strong, Ecclesiastes 9:11.

Success requires more than skill, Isaiah 25:11.

Artist is mortal, Isaiah 44:11.

Faulty skill, Jeremiah 18:4 (See AB).

Disaster to swift, strong, Jeremiah 46:6.

Skilled ship crews, Ezekiel 27:8–9.

Trying to purchase spiritual skill, Acts 8:18–23.

Complimented for skill, Hebrews 3:3 (LB).

Those expert in iniquity, 2 Peter 2:14.

See Ability, Athletics, Talent.

SKY

Sky dome, Genesis 1:6 (NRSV).

"Open expanse of the heavens," Genesis 1:20 (NASB).

Rider in the sky, Deuteronomy 33:26.

Rain clouds become God's canopy, 2 Samuel 22:12; Psalm 18:11.

He who spreads out the skies, Job 37:18.

Resounding skies during heavy rainfall, Psalm 77:17.

Raining righteousness, Isaiah 45:8.

Judgment reaches to the skies, Jeremiah 51:9.

Weather forecasting, Matthew 16:2–3; Luke 12:54–56.

Stars of the sky, Hebrews 11:12.

See Astronomy, Meteorology.

SLANDER

False report, Exodus 23:1.

Criticism of king, 2 Samuel 6:17–23.

Mistrust of good motive, 2 Samuel 10:3.

Scourge of tongue, Job 5:21.

Concerned with error of others, Job 19:4.

Slander of many, Psalm 31:13.

"Speak insolent things," Psalm 94:4 (NKJV).

Secret slander, Psalm 101:5.

Verbal attack, Psalm 109:1–3.

Smear campaign, Psalm 119:69 (NASB).

Let the Lord vindicate, Psalm 135:14.

Hatred and slander, Proverbs 10:18.

Destructive mouths, Proverbs 11:9.

Power of words, Isaiah 29:20–21.

Those who attack with tongues, Jeremiah 18:18; Micah 2:4.

Undercutting prophet's message, Amos 7:10.

Jesus criticized on cross, Matthew 27:39–44.

Pharisees looked for fault in Jesus, Mark 3:1–6.

False accusation of demon-possession, Luke 7:33.

Poisoning the mind, Acts 14:2.

Slandering type, Romans 1:29.

Slander no one, Titus 3:2; James 4:11–12.

See Gossip, Scoff, Scorn.

SLAUGHTER

Reasoning for mass slaughter, 1 Samuel 27:8–11.

Trampled to death by mob, 2 Kings 7:17–20.

Innocent blood, 2 Kings 21:16.

Battlefield slaughter, Isaiah 37:36; Amos 5:3.

Facing grim destiny, Jeremiah 15:2–3.

Too little, too late, Amos 3:12.

Third of mankind destroyed, Revelation 9:18.

See Carnage, Genocide, Scorched Earth, War.

SLAVERY

Slaves circumcised, Genesis 17:27.

Prestigious slave purchase, Genesis 39:1.

Slave drivers, Exodus 1:11 (GNB).

Limited slavery, Exodus 21:2.

Slaves set free, Deuteronomy 15:12–18; Job 3:19.

Plight of conquered, Deuteronomy 20:10–11.

Sold into slavery, Judges 4:1.

Remembered years after slavery, 1 Kings 6:1 (LB).

Use of forced labor, 1 Kings 9:15.

Jewish exemptions, 2 Chronicles 8:9.

Homeborn slaves, Ecclesiastes 2:7 (NASB)

Humans trapped, made slaves, Jeremiah 5:26 (CEV).

Valley of slaughter, Jeremiah 7:32.

Slaves set free, then again enslaved, Jeremiah 34:8–22.

Special purpose for selling slaves, Joel 3:6.

Highly prized slave, Luke 7:2 (LB).

Enslaved by sin, John 8:34; Acts 8:23; Romans 6:16; 7:23; 2 Timothy 2:26.

No longer called slaves, John 15:15 (NASB).

Jewish slaves, Acts 6:9 (AB).

Onesimus introduced, Colossians 4:9 (See Philemon 10–11).

Slave to whatever masters, 2 Peter 2:19.

Bodies, souls of men, Revelation 18:13.

See Bondage, Servant.

S

SLEEP

Deep sleep, Genesis 15:12; Job 4:13; Daniel 8:18; Jonah 1:5.

Angels retired in Lot's home, Genesis 19:1–4.

Frogs disturb sleep, Exodus 8:3.

Potentially perilous sleep, 1 Samuel 26:12.

Little time for sleep, Nehemiah 4:21–23.

No blankets, Job 24:7.

Go to bed rich, awaken poor, Job 27:19 (CEV).

Companion of night creatures, Job 30:29.

Time for heart searching, Psalm 4:4.

Peaceful sleep, Psalm 4:8.

Plotting evil falling asleep, Psalm 36:4.

Presuming God sleeps, Psalm 44:23.

Songs in the night, Psalm 77:6.

As if God sleeps, Psalm 78:65.

Frogs invade rooms, Psalm 105:30.

Giving thanks at midnight, Psalm 119:62, 148.

Gift of sleep, Psalm 127:2.

Sweet sleep, Proverbs 3:24.

Lazy slumber, Proverbs 6:9–11.

Early morning religiosity, Proverbs 27:14.

Poor man sleeps better, Ecclesiastes 5:12.

Do not disturb, Song of Songs 3:5.

Short bed, narrow blankets, Isaiah 28:20.

Ivory bed, Amos 6:4.

Historic sleep, awakening, Matthew 1:24; Luke 9:32.

Sound sleep, Matthew 8:23–25 (CEV).

Gethsemane slumber, Matthew 26:36–45.

Asleep during sermon, Acts 20:7–12.

See Dream, Morning, Nightmare, Rest.

SLEUTH *See Spy.*

SLING SHOT

Southpaw expertise, Judges 20:16.

David and Goliath, 1 Samuel 17:40–50.

Sling shots in battle, 2 Kings 3:25; 2 Chronicles 26:14.

SLING SHOT

Stones must lie loose in sling shot, Proverbs 26:8.

SLOGAN

Trustworthy saying, 1 Timothy 4:9–10.
See Slogan.

SLOW

Danger to those who lag behind, Deuteronomy 25:17–19.

SLUGGISH

"Sluggish spirit," Romans 11:8 (NRSV).

SMALL

Divine love for small nation, Deuteronomy 7:7.

Branch of tree, Jeremiah 1:11–12.

One chapter books, Obadiah 1–21; Philemon 1–25; 2 John 1–13; 3 John 1–14; Jude 1–25.

"Day of small beginnings," Zechariah 4:10 (CEV).

Small as mustard seed, Mark 4:31; Luke 13:19.

Power of a small faith, Luke 17:5–6.

Man short of stature, Luke 19:1–10.

Widow's mite, Luke 21:1–4.

Remnant of Israel, Romans 11:1–5.

Small objects, large capabilities, James 3:3–4.

Small tongue, big talk, James 3:5.
See Insignificant, Trivia.

SMEAR

Smear campaign, Psalm 119:69 (NRSV).

SMELL *See Fragrance, Odor.*

SMILE

"Something to smile about," Job 8:21 (CEV).

Smile replaces complaint, Job 9:27.

Smile on wicked schemes, Job 10:3.

Surprising smile, Job 29:24.

"That I may smile again," Psalm 39:13 (NASB, NRSV).

See Congenial.

SMOKE SIGNAL

Warning message, Jeremiah 6:1 (LB).
See Communication.

SMUGGLE

False Christians smuggled in, Galatians 2:4 (AB).

SNACK

Roasted grain, 1 Samuel 17:17.

Grain kernels, Luke 6:1.

SNAKE CHARMER

Cobra refuses to listen, Psalm 58:4.

Cobra and tune, Psalm 58:5.

Snake bites before charmed, Ecclesiastes 10:11.

Snakes that cannot be charmed, Jeremiah 8:17.

SNAKES

Curse upon serpent, Genesis 3:14.

Staff turned into snake, Exodus 4:1–5; 7:8–12.

Royal symbol, Exodus 4:3 (AB).

Perilous snakebite, Numbers 21:6; Deuteronomy 8:15.

Bronze serpent, Numbers 21:9; 2 Kings 18:4; John 3:14.

Deaf cobra, Psalm 58:4–5.

Broken fangs, Psalm 58:4–6 (LB).

Wine like venom, Proverbs 23:32.

Snake on rock, Proverbs 30:19.

Beware of breaking into wall, Ecclesiastes 10:8 (See KJV).

Child safe near cobra, Isaiah 11:8.

Adders, darting snakes, Isaiah 30:6 (See Berk.).

Serpents eating dust, Isaiah 65:25.

Poisonous snake attack, Jeremiah 8:17 (CEV).

Bitten by surprise, Amos 5:19.

Fish or snake, Matthew 7:10.

Wise as serpents, Matthew 10:16.

No fear of serpents, Mark 16:17–18; Luke 10:19.

Survived snake bite, Acts 28:1–6.

SNARE

Evil nations become snares and traps, Joshua 23:12–13.

Danger along path, Job 18:10; Psalm 142:3; Jeremiah 18:22.

Wicked ensnared by their own hands, Psalm 9:16.

Hidden net, Psalm 35:7.

Deliverance from fowlers, snare, Psalm 91:3.

Arrogant dig pitfalls, Psalm 119:85.

Snare of wicked avoided, Psalms 119:110; 141:9.

Traps to catch men, Jeremiah 5:26.

Nets, snares, Hosea 5:1.

Brother setting nets for brother, Micah 7:2.

See Trap.

SNEER

Sneering enemies, Ezekiel 36:2 (LB).

See Cold, Freeze, Winter.

SNEEZE

Seven sneezes, 2 Kings 4:35.

SNOW

Hunting in snowfall, 2 Samuel 23:20.

Streams flow with melting snow, Job 6:16.

Snow to wash hands, Job 9:30 (NKJV).

Divine command, Job 37:6.

Inexhaustible design in snowflake, Job 38:22.

Summer snow, Proverbs 26:1.

Whiter than snow, Isaiah 1:18.

Mountain peaks, Jeremiah 18:14.

See Cold, Freeze, Winter.

SOAP

Dirty beyond use of soap, Jeremiah 2:22 (See LB).

Laundry soap, Malachi 3:2.

Unable to rid stain of guilt, Matthew 27:24.

See Cleansing, Detergent.

SOBER

Silence before the Lord, Zephaniah 1:7.

Alert and self-controlled, 1 Thessalonians 5:6; 1 Timothy 3:2.

Sober disposition, Titus 2:2, 12.

See Serious.

SOBRIETY

Alcohol not for those in leadership, Proverbs 31:4–5.

Refusal to drink wine, Jeremiah 35:1–6.

Lifetime sobriety, Luke 7:33 (LB).

Temperate use of wine, Titus 1:7.

See Alcohol, Drunkenness.

SOCIAL

Making social calls, Genesis 34:1.

See Hospitality.

SOCIALISM

Common ownership, Acts 4:32–35.

See Communism, Politics.

SOCIALIZING

Avoid socializing, Jeremiah 16:8 (See LB).

Conversation with friends, Ephesians 5:19 (LB).

See Rapport.

SOCIAL JUSTICE

Rich exploit poor, James 2:6.

See Inequity, Women's Rights.

SOCIETY

One common language, Genesis 11:1.

Dislike of wealthy neighbors, Genesis 26:12–17.

Separated from evil by choice, Psalm 1:1.

Contemporary society, Proverbs 4:17.

Seldom visit your neighbor, Proverbs 25:17.

Salt of earth, Matthew 5:13.

Tit for tat, Luke 14:12–14.

As in days of Noah, Luke 17:26–30.

Avoid social evils, Acts 2:40 (LB).

Global society, Acts 17:26.

Wild parties, Romans 13:13 (LB).

High, low rank, Ephesians 6:5–9.

Simple people brought to Christ, 1 Corinthians 1:26–31.

See Community, Neighborhood.

SODOM

Miracles could have saved Sodom, Matthew 11:23.

SODOMY

Origin of sodomy, Genesis 19:5.
See Deviate.

SOIL

Love for soil, 2 Chronicles 26:10.
Ancient mountains, everlasting hills, Deuteronomy 33:15.
Top soil, 2 Kings 5:17.
Good soil, poor soil, Ezekiel 19:10–14.
Types of soil quality, Luke 8:1–15.
See Agriculture.

SOLDIER

The Lord a soldier, Exodus 15:3.
Clergy exemption, Numbers 1:45–50.
Conscription age, Numbers 1:45; 26:2.
Large army, Joshua 4:13; 2 Chronicles 14:8; 17:14–18; 26:13.
Reckless adventurers, Judges 9:4; 11:3.
No weapon in Israel, 1 Samuel 13:19–22.
Choosing the mighty and brave, 1 Samuel 14:52.
Sexual restraint of soldiers, 1 Samuel 21:4–5.
Fighting the Lord's battles, 1 Samuel 25:28.
Military family, 1 Chronicles 8:40.
Defecting soldiers, 1 Chronicles 12:1–2, 19–20.
Abundant young recruits, 2 Chronicles 25:5.
Angel in the military, Isaiah 37:36.
No one will go into battle, Ezekiel 7:14.
"Troops of Heaven," Luke 2:13 (AB).
Devout centurion, Acts 10:1–2, 7, 22.
See Disarmed, Draft Dodger, Mercenaries, Military.

SOLICITATION

Solicitation for immorality, Numbers 25:1–2.
Asking for much, 2 Kings 4:3.

SOLICITUDE

Great solicitude, Colossians 2:1 (AB).

SOLITUDE

Invasion of solitude, Genesis 32:24.
Alone with God, Exodus 34:1–3.
Desire for the desert, Psalm 55:7; Jeremiah 9:2.
Jesus alone in the hills, Matthew 14:23; 15:29.
Small group solitude, Matthew 17:1; Mark 6:31.
Solitude disturbed, Mark 7:24.
Frequent solitude for Jesus, Luke 5:16; Luke 22:41.
Solitude in urban setting, 1 Thessalonians 3:1.
See Meditation, Quiet Time.

SOLO

Song of praise, Exodus 15:21.
Unvoiced solo, 1 Corinthians 14:15.
Singing for others, 1 Corinthians 14:26 (CEV).
Sing by yourself, James 5:13.
See Hymn, Music, Singing.

SOLUTION

Alternative solution, John 5:2–9.
See Answer.

SON

Father's willingness to sacrifice son, Genesis 22:1–18.
Bless these lads, Genesis 48:16.
Favored by brothers, Deuteronomy 33:24–25.
Threat to children if commands disobeyed, Joshua 6:26.
Many sons, Judges 8:30–31.
Father's shame for immoral sons, 1 Samuel 2:22–23.
Son's influence over father, 1 Samuel 19:1–6.
Father, son together in death, 2 Samuel 1:23.
Rivalry between father, son, 2 Samuel 15:1–37.
Attitude of David toward rebellious son, 2 Samuel 18:5.
No son to carry father's name, 2 Samuel 18:18.
Father would have died in place of son, 2 Samuel 18:32–33.
Son's fame exceeds father's, 1 Kings 1:47–48.

S

Father's joy seeing his son become king, 1 Kings 1:47–48.

Aged father's counsel to son, 1 Kings 2:1–9.

King Solomon succeeded by son, 1 Kings 11:41–42.

Son's evil less than parents, 2 Kings 3:1–3.

Sacrifice of son, 2 Kings 16:3.

Father's righteousness refuted, 2 Kings 21:1–6.

Fate of father becomes fate of sons, Esther 9:12–14.

Neither good nor evil from father to son, Ezekiel 18:3–20.

Joy, delight to parents, Luke 1:14–15.

Obedience of child Jesus, Luke 2:41–52.

Son yet in body of ancestor, Hebrews 7:9–10.

Son received back as from dead, Hebrews 11:19.

See Children, Family.

SONG *See Hymn, Music, Singing.*

SONG WRITER *See Composer.*

SOON *See Imminent.*

SOPHISTRY

Sophistic temptation, Genesis 3:1–7; 2 Corinthians 11:3.

Absurd temptation of Jesus, Matthew 4:1–11; Luke 4:1–13.

Preventive warning, 2 Corinthians 2:11.

Counterfeit display, 2 Thessalonians 2:9.

World led astray, Revelation 12:9.

See Wiles.

SORCERY

Confronting magicians of Egypt, Exodus 7:6–12; 4:1–5.

Sorcery abandoned, Numbers 24:1.

Substitute for prayer, 1 Samuel 28:5–20.

False prophets foiled, Isaiah 44:25.

Fortune and destiny, Isaiah 65:11.

Those who prophesy lies, Jeremiah 27:9–15.

Use of magic charms, Ezekiel 13:20.

So-called men of wisdom, Daniel 2:1–4.

Failure of sorcerers, astrologers, Daniel 5:7–8.

Simon in Samaria, Acts 8:9–11.

See Fortune Telling, Magic.

SORDID

Sordid episode, Judges 9:15–30.

Human blood mixed with sacrifice, Luke 13:1.

Bloody grapes, Revelation 14:20.

See Debase, Devile, Vulgar.

SORROW

Embraced corpse, Genesis 50:1.

Time to conclude mourning, Genesis 50:4.

Shaving head of mourner, Deuteronomy 14:1–2.

All Israel assembled to mourn Samuel, 1 Samuel 25:1.

Weeping until exhausted, 1 Samuel 30:4.

Song of lament, 2 Samuel 1:17–27.

Reaction to son's death, 2 Samuel 12:16–23.

Grief over death of son, 2 Samuel 18:19–53.

Joy in sober time, Nehemiah 8:9–12 (LB).

Dirt on head, Nehemiah 9:1 (CEV).

Night obliterated by sorrow, Job 3:6.

Sorrow will pass as waters gone by, Job 11:16.

Bodily pain, Job 14:22 (KJV).

Widows do not weep, Job 27:15.

Exhausting sorrow, Psalm 6:6

Daily sorrow, Psalm 13:2 (NKJV).

Night weeping, morning joy, Psalm 30:5.

Deepest sorrow, Psalm 31:9–10 (Berk.).

The Lord's presence, Psalm 34:18 (Berk.).

Divine comfort, Psalm 34:19.

Sorrow numbs appetite, Psalm 42:3.

Tears in God's bottle, Psalm 56:8 (Berk.).

Weary of crying, Psalm 69:3 (NKJV).

"Bread of tears," Psalm 80:5.

Tears become blessings, Psalm 84:6 (AB).

Heart smitten, Psalm 102:4 (KJV).

Sorrow of death, joy to the Lord, Psalm 116:15.

Laughter with aching heart, Proverbs 14:13.

Song for heavy heart, Proverbs 25:20.

Set free from sorrow, Isaiah 14:3 (CEV, NKJV).

Joys of life gone, Isaiah 24:7 (LB).

Tears wiped away, Isaiah 25:8.

Judgment brings righteousness, Isaiah 26:9.

Sorrowful soil, Isaiah 33:9.

Gladness, joy overcome sorrow, sighing, Isaiah 35:10.

Sorrow banished, Isaiah 65:19.

Sorrow of disobedience, Jeremiah 3:21.

Comfort in sorrow, Jeremiah 8:18.

No balm in Gilead, Jeremiah 8:22.

"Fountain of tears," Jeremiah 9:11.

Mourning forbidden in time of judgment, Jeremiah 16:5–7.

Joy, gladness gone, Jeremiah 48:33.

Sorrowing city, Lamentations 1:1–2.

Weeping with no one to comfort, Lamentations 1:16.

Eyes dry from weeping, Lamentations 2:11.

"Rivers of tears," Lamentations 3:48 (NRSV).

Joy turns to sorrow, Lamentations 5:15.

Sorrowful song, Ezekiel 19:1–14 (CEV).

Songs turn to wailing, Amos 8:3.

Tears of false repentance, Malachi 2:13.

Comfort for those who mourn, Matthew 5:4.

Grief of disciples, Matthew 17:22–23.

Crushing sorrow, Matthew 26:38 (GNB).

Laughter can follow tears, Luke 6:21 (NIV).

Death of Lazarus, John 11:1–44.

Grief turns to joy, John 16:20.

Grief at burial of Stephen, Acts 8:2.

Counselor shares from experience, 2 Corinthians 1:3–4.

Depth of sharing, 2 Corinthians 2:1–4.

Sorrow according to God's will, 2 Corinthians 7:9 (NASB).

Disappearing sorrow, Philippians 2:27–28.

Sorrow at time of death, 1 Thessalonians 4:13–18.

Tears, foundation for joy, 2 Timothy 1:3–4.

Tears of repentence, James 4:9 (LB).

Second coming will bring sorrow, Revelation 1:7.

Tears wiped away, Revelation 7:17; 21:4 (See Isaiah 25:8).

Agony caused by refusal to repent, Revelation 16:10–11.

See Anguish, Grief, Tears.

SOUL

Eternity in human hearts, Ecclesiastes 3:11.

Spirit returns to God, Ecclesiastes 12:6–7.

Body destroyed, not soul, Matthew 10:28; 1 Corinthians 15:54.

Worth of one lost soul, Matthew 18:12–14; Luke 15:1–32.

Eternal value of soul, temporal values of life, Mark 8:35–37.

Assured immortality, John 8:51; John 11:25–26; 1 Corinthians 15:53.

Soul peace, Galatians 1:3 (AB).

Where soul and spirit meet, Hebrews 4:12 (GNB).

Assembled martyrs, Revelation 20:4.

See Immortality.

SOUL-WINNING

Seeking soul, 1 Kings 18:1; Matthew 12:42.

Outreach to lost, Psalm 51:13.

Tell someone every day, Psalm 96:2 (LB).

Compassion for soul-winning, Psalm 126:5–6.

The wise who win souls, Proverbs 11:30.

Harvest past, summer ended, no salvation, Jeremiah 8:20.

Day coming when soul-winning not necessary, Jeremiah 31:34.

Penalty for failing to witness, Ezekiel 3:18–19.

Identification on forehead of those who repent, Ezekiel 9:3–11.

Shepherds refuse to look for lost sheep, Ezekiel 34:1–31.

Those who witness shine like stars, Daniel 12:3.

Rescue too late at lion's mouth, Amos 3:12.

Inviting others to seek the Lord, Zechariah 8:20–22.

Fishers of men, Matthew 4:19; Luke 5:10.

Plentiful harvest, few workers, Matthew 9:37–38.

Worth of one lost sheep, Matthew 18:12–14.

Some refuse, others accept, Matthew 22:1–14.

S

Winning converts to error, Matthew 23:15.

Praying for harvesters rather than harvest, Luke 10:1–2.

Parables of lost sheep, lost coin, lost son, Luke 15:1–32.

Expediency of witness, John 4:35.

Lifting up Jesus to draw men, John 12:32.

Jesus anticipated results, John 17:20.

Last words of Jesus, Acts 1:6–7.

Simultaneous conversion, baptism, Acts 8:35–36.

Exciting harvest news, Acts 15:3.

Imprisoned for conversion of fortune teller, Acts 16:16–40.

Relentless effort, Acts 20:31.

Desired harvest, Romans 1:13.

Paul would himself be lost to bring salvation to Israel, Romans 9:1–4; 10:1.

Instruments in bringing people to Christ, 1 Corinthians 3:5–9.

Becoming as slave for others, 1 Corinthians 9:20.

Spiritual persuasion, 2 Corinthians 5:11 (See Berk., LB).

Tears of compassion, Philippians 3:18.

Soul-winner's glory, joy, 1 Thessalonians 2:19–20.

Coming day when soul-winning not needed, Hebrews 8:10–11.

Turning sinner from error of his way, James 5:20.

Snatch from fire, Jude 23.

Combined ministry of Holy Spirit, church, Revelation 22:17.

See Evangelism, Witness.

SOUND

Voices recorded on stone, Joshua 24:27.

Imagined sounds of danger, 2 Kings 7:6–7.

Audible star light, Job 38:7.

Vocal vibrations, Psalm 29:5.

See Media.

SOURCE

Revitalization of strength, Isaiah 40:30–31.

Divine source of provision, Exodus 16:1–18.

Armed with Divine strength, 2 Samuel 22:40.

Pure from impure, Job 14:4.

Wings like eagles, Isaiah 40:30–31.

Serving with external strength, Isaiah 41:10; Micah 3:8; Zechariah 4:6; Philippians 4:13; 1 Timothy 1:12.

Looking to flesh for strength, Jeremiah 17:5.

Source new everyday, Lamentations 3:22–24.

Source of wisdom, power, Daniel 2:20.

Power from above, Acts 1:8; 4:33.

Heavenly source, John 3:27.

In all grace abounding, 2 Corinthians 9:8.

Source of spiritual power, Ephesians 6:10–18.

See Provision.

SOUR GRAPES

Sour grapes for Jonah, Jonah 4:1.

SOUTH *See Compass.*

SOUTHPAW

Left-handed, Judges 3:15.

Seven hundred left-handed soldiers, Judges 20:16.

Secrets between hands, Matthew 6:3.

SOUVENIR

Souvenir manna, Exodus 16:32 (CEV).

David's souvenirs from battle with Goliath, 1 Samuel 17:54.

Tears in a bottle, Psalm 56:8 (KJV).

Time to throw away, Ecclesiastes 3:6.

See Artifacts.

SOVEREIGNTY

None other in Heaven or earth, Deuteronomy 4:39.

God uses evil to carry out plans, Judges 14:1–4.

Absolute sovereignty of God in every situation, 1 Samuel 14:6.

Everything under control, 1 Chronicles 29:12.

God over government, 2 Chronicles 20:6; Proverbs 21:1; Psalm 47:1–3.

Actions beyond questioning, Job 9:12.

Beyond highest stars, Job 22:12.

Everything belongs to God, Job 41:11.

"O Lord, our sovereign," Psalm 8:1 (NRSV).

Purpose of God's eternal reign, Psalm 9:7–8.

One on throne, Psalm 29:10.

Most high above all earth, Psalm 83:18.

Sovereign acts of God, Psalm 135:6.

The Lord is everywhere, Psalm 139:5–12.

Man's plans, God's determinations, Proverbs 16:9.

Man's steps directed by the Lord, Proverbs 20:24.

What God does will endure, Ecclesiastes 3:14.

Divine decree, Isaiah 14:24.

As God plans, so it will be, Isaiah 16:14.

Perfect faithfulness of God, Isaiah 25:1.

Victory ordained long before coming of enemy, Isaiah 37:26.

Impossible to reverse acts of God, Isaiah 43:13.

Divine acts, authority, Isaiah 44:24–25.

None other but the Lord, Isaiah 45:5–6.

Nebuchadnezzar's recognition of sovereign God, Daniel 4:34–37.

Jesus could not die before God's time, John 19:11.

Sovereignty in redemption, Romans 9:14–18.

Qualifications of Christ as Savior and King, Colossians 1:15–20.

Eternal, immortal, invisible, 1 Timothy 1:17.

Sovereignty over all earth, Revelation 1:5.

Things shut and things opened, Revelation 3:7.

Lord of Lords, King of Kings, Revelation 17:14; 19:16.

Totality of Son of God, Revelation 22:13.
See Determinism, Predestination.

SPACE

Expanse of sky, Genesis 1:17 (NIV).

Ancient space flight, 2 Kings 2:11.

Space turns thinking inward, Psalm 8:3–8.

Creation proclaims God's righteousness, Psalm 50:6.

All space cannot contain God's love, Psalm 108:4–5.

Material universe vanishes, salvation endures, Isaiah 51:6.

Nest among stars, Obadiah 4.

"High above the sky," Romans 8:39 (LB).
See Astronomy, UFO.

SPACE/TIME

Vastness of creation, Genesis 2:1.

Earth in space, Job 26:7.

Job's concept of space/time, Job 26:7–14.

In hollow of God's hand, Isaiah 40:12.

Creator of earth, heavens, Isaiah 45:18.

Role of heaven, earth, Isaiah 66:22–23.

Creator continuing work, John 5:17.

Revelation of God in nature, Romans 1:18–20.

Purpose of creation, human life, Romans 8:18–23.

One who fills whole universe, Ephesians 4:10.

Regulated universe, Hebrews 1:3 (LB).

Universe formed at God's command, Hebrews 11:3.

Earth, sky flee from the eternal, Revelation 20:11.
See Space, Universe.

SPAIN

Silver from Spain, Jeremiah 10:9 (GNB).

Jonah's flight to Spain, Jonah 1:2 (CEV).

SPANKING

Spanking children, Proverbs 22:15 (GNB); 23:13–14 (GNB); 29:15 (LB).

SPARROW

Sparrow finds nest, Psalm 84:3.

Lonely as sparrow, Psalm 102:7.

Monetary value of sparrow, Matthew 10:29; Luke 12:6.
See Birds.

SPECIES

Distinct species, Genesis 1:25; 1 Corinthians 15:39.

SPECIFIC

Not plural, singular, Galatians 3:16.

"To be specific," Ephesians 3:6 (NASB).

SPECTACLE

First rainbow, Genesis 9:12–17.

Migration of family with all their possessions, Genesis 46:5–7.

Vindication by earthquake, Numbers 16:28–34.

Angel who ascended in flame of fire, Judges 13:20.

Chariot of fire, whirlwind, 2 Kings 2:11–12.

Stripped, barefoot, Isaiah 20:2–4.

Proclaiming dreams instead of the Word, Jeremiah 23:25–32.

God's glory seen, not God Himself, Ezekiel 43:1–5.

Nothing like this has happened before, Joel 1:2–3.

Army of locusts, Joel 2:1–9.

Something beyond belief, Habakkuk 1:5.

Flying scroll, Zechariah 5:1–2.

Mount of transfiguration, prelude to resurrection, Matthew 17:1–8; Mark 9:1–13.

Events at time of crucifixion, Matthew 27:15–54; Mark 15:21–32.

Pharisees wanted sign from heaven, Mark 8:11–12.

Frightened at sight of angel, Luke 1:11–12.

Spectacular communication from heaven, Luke 2:8–14.

Excited about wrong phenomena, Luke 10:17–20.

People curious to see miracles performed, John 6:1–2, 26–27.

Day of Pentecost, Acts 2:1–21.

Staring at those God uses, Acts 3:12.

Spectacular conversion, Acts 9:1–5.

Tongues a sign for unbelievers, 1 Corinthians 14:22–25.

Paul caught up into third heaven, 2 Corinthians 12:1–4.

Contemplating resurrection, exaltation of Christ, Ephesians 1:18–23.

Coming to Mount Zion, Hebrews 12:22–24.

Christ coming in clouds, Revelation 1:7.

Vision of Christ among golden lamp stands, Revelation 1:12–16.

All creation singing praises to the Lamb, Revelation 5:13–14.

Destruction on earth, sky, Revelation 6:12–14; 8:4–5.

Censer hurled to earth, Revelation 8:5–7.

Cloud for robe, rainbow for hat, Revelation 10:1.

Earth illuminated by angelic splendor, Revelation 18:1.

SPECTACULAR

Proclaiming dreams instead of the Word, Jeremiah 23:25–32.

Uprecedented happening, Joel 1:2–3.

Army of locusts, Joel 2:1–9.

Advent majesty, Micah 1:3–4.

Flying scroll, Zechariah 5:1–2.

Mount of transfiguration, Matthew 17:1–8.

World-wide spectacle, Matthew 24:30.

Events at time of crucifixion, Matthew 27:15–54.

Pharisees wanted sign from heaven, Mark 8:11–12.

Frightened at sight of an angel, Luke 1:11–12.

Spectacular communication from heaven, Luke 2:8–14.

Excited about the wrong phenomena, Luke 10:17–20.

People curious to see miracles performed, John 6:1–2, 26–27.

Caught up into third heaven, 2 Corinthians 12:1–4.

Censer hurled to earth, Revelation 8:5–7.
See Awe.

SPEECH

Authority of Creator's speech, Genesis 1:3, 6, 9, 14, 20, 24, 26.

Unable to speak peaceably, Genesis 37:4 (NKJV).

Speech impediment, Exodus 4:10.

Gift of speech, Exodus 4:11–12 (NRSV).

Unwasted words, 1 Samuel 3:19.

Rallying citizens in time of crisis, 2 Chronicles 32:6–7.

Speechless, Nehemiah 5:8.

Talk, say nothing, Job 8:2 (CEV).

Condemned by personal speech, Job 15:6.

Speech after speech, Job 18:2.

Crushed with words, Job 19:1.

Maintaining pure speech, Job 27:3–4.

Forthright introduction, Job 33:1–5.

Talk much, say little, Job 38:2 (CEV).

Enemy speech not to be trusted, Psalm 5:9.

"No truth in their mouths," Psalm 5:9 (NRSV).

Speaking lies and flattery, Psalm 12:2.

Power of speech, Psalm 12:4.

Resolving not to sin with one's mouth, Psalm 17:3.

Words pleasing to God, Psalm 19:14.

God's voice, powerful, majestic, Psalm 29:4.

Blessing of honest speech, Psalm 34:12–13.

God's word credence to righteous speech, Psalm 37:30.

Keeping tongue from speaking wrong, Psalm 39:1.

Speech smooth as butter, Psalm 50:19.

Slander against relative, Psalm 50:20.

Words known in advance, Psalm 139:4.

Speech of righteous, wicked, Proverbs 10:11, 19–20.

Fruit of one's lips, Proverbs 12:14.

Just a kind word, Proverbs 15:4 (GNB).

Think before speaking, Proverbs 16:23 (GNB).

Restrained speech, Proverbs 17:27.

Speech with knowledge, rarest of jewels, Proverbs 20:15.

Right words at right time, Proverbs 25:11.

Speaking with gentle tongue, Proverbs 25:15.

Con man, Proverbs 26:24.

Healing blind, deaf and dumb, Isaiah 35:5–6.

Cordial speech, deceitful heart, Jeremiah 9:8.

Importance of worthy speech, Jeremiah 15:19.

Speaking with wisdom, tact, Daniel 2:14–15 (GNB).

Quiet in times of evil, Amos 5:13.

Kind, comforting words, Zechariah 1:13.

Lips that preserve knowledge, Malachi 2:7.

Words from the heart, Matthew 15:18 (CEV).

Attempting to trap Jesus, Matthew 22:15; Mark 12:13–17.

Two-word command, Mark 2:14.

Expectant father striken with muteness, Luke 1:11–22.

Use of gracious words, Luke 4:22.

Mute demon, Luke 11:14.

Speech provided for difficult time, Luke 12:11.

No one ever spoke like Jesus, John 7:46.

Speaking without figures of speech, John 16:29–30.

Distinct voice, John 20:14–16.

"Not to say too much," 2 Corinthians 2:5 (NASB).

Writing more effectively than speaking, 2 Corinthians 10:10–11.

Foolish talk, Ephesians 5:6 (CEV).

Whatever you say or do, Colossians 3:17.

Conversation full of grace, Colossians 4:6.

Quick to listen, slow to speak, James 1:19–20.

Bridle tongue, James 1:26.

Offensive speech, James 3:2 (AB).

Guard your tongue, James 3:3–6.

Words that cut like sword, Revelation 1:16.

See Answer, Communication, Conversation, Eloquence.

SPEECHLESS

Speechless in prayer, 1 Samuel 1:9–15.

Nothing to say, Nehemiah 5:8.

Tongues stick to roof of mouth, Job 29:10.

Ashamed, silent before the Lord, Ezekiel 16:63.

Embarrased disciples, Mark 14:40.

Muteness caused by skepticism, Luke 1:19–20, 62–64.

Cynical tongues made silent, Luke 20:20–26.

Silence in Heaven, Revelation 8:1.

See Mute.

SPEED

Fast-food, Genesis 18:6–7.

Reckless driving, 2 Kings 9:20.

Swift ostrich, Job 39:18.

Speedy writer, Psalm 45:1 (LB).

Speedy goat, Daniel 8:5.

Supposed prophecy of modern traffic, Nahum 2:4.

"Wind in their wings," Zechariah 5:9.

Speed of angels, Hebrews 1:7 (LB).

See Haste.

SPELL

Placed under spell, Galatians 3:1 (GNB).
See Trance.

SPELLBOUND

Seeing is believing, 1 Kings 10:6–7.
Astonished, Ezekiel 3:15 (NKJV, NRSV).
Ashamed, silent before the Lord, Ezekiel 16:63.
Reaction of Jesus' parents to attestation, Luke 2:28–33.
See Awe, Serendipity.

SPENDING

Pleasure brings poverty, Proverbs 21:17.
Never enough money, Ecclesiastes 5:10.
Purses with holes, Haggai 1:6.

SPERM

Divine sperm, 1 John 3:9 (AB).

SPICES

Flavors of love, Song of Songs 4:13–14.
See Fragrance.

SPIDER

Fragile as spider's web, Job 8:14.
Cobwebs for clothing, Isaiah 59:5–6.
See Insects.

SPINSTER

Unwed maidens, Psalm 78:63 (KJV).
Remaining unmarried, 1 Corinthians 7:27–28.
See Celibacy.

SPIRITISM

Seeking God's will by divination, Genesis 30:27.
Divination cup, Genesis 44:5.
Mediums, wizards, Leviticus 20:27 (LB).
Dead cannot return, 2 Samuel 12:22–23.
Consulting dead concerning living, Isaiah 8:19.
Seeking omen at fork in road, Ezekiel 21:18–23.
Spiritists in Babylon, Daniel 2:1–4.
Failure of sorcerers, astrologers, Daniel 5:7–8.

Diviners lose skill, Micah 3:7.
Witchcraft terminated, Micah 5:12.
"Mistress of sorceries," Nahum 3:3–4.
False visions of diviners, Zechariah 10:2.
Simon in Samaria, Acts 8:9–11.
Those cast into lake of fire, Revelation 21:8.
See Seance, Sorcery.

SPIRITUAL HUNGER

Seeking eagerly, 2 Chronicles 15:15.
Longing heart, Psalms 38:9; 73:25; Isaiah 26:9.
Famine for words of the Lord, Amos 8:11–12.
Earth filled with the Lord's glory, Habakkuk 2:14.
Blessed are those who hunger, Matthew 5:6; Luke 6:21.
Newborn hunger, 1 Peter 2:2.
See Students, Study.

SPIRITUALITY

Being truly holy, Numbers 16:3–7.
Yearning for the Lord, Isaiah 26:9.
Spiritual, temporal, John 8:23.
Righteousness in Christ, 1 Corinthians 1:4–9.
Status of idols, 1 Corinthians 8:4.
Fullest measure of the law, Matthew 23:23.
Experiencing God's kingdom within, Luke 17:20–21.
Keeping soul in good health, 3 John 2.
Temporal wealth, spiritual wealth, Revelation 3:15–18.
See Commitment, Holiness, Piety.

SPIRITUAL PRIDE

Being truly holy, Numbers 16:3–7.
Righteous in one's own eyes, Job 32:1.
Holier than thou, Ecclesiastes 7:16.
Wise put to shame, Jeremiah 8:9.
Spiritual pride of disobedient people, Amos 4:5.
See Hypocrisy, Vanity.

SPIT

Vulgar request to God, Job 7:19 (RSV).
Someone spit upon, Job 17:6 (KJV).
Healing technique, Mark 8:23–24.

SPLENDOR

Splendor of God, Psalm 8:1–9.
The Lord's splendor in temple, Isaiah 6:1–4.
No more need for sun and moon, Isaiah 60:19–20.
Palace built by unrighteousness, Jeremiah 22:13–15.
Mount of transfiguration, Mark 9:2–13.
Description of new Jerusalem, Revelation 21:15–27.
See Spectacular.

SPOILS

"Keep the loot," Genesis 14:21 (GNB).
Plunder permitted at Ai, Joshua 8:1–2; 22:8.
Crops, animals taken by enemy, Judges 6:3–6.
Plunder aftermath of battle, 1 Samuel 30:16.
Robbing dead after battle, 2 Samuel 23:10.
Grain, wine to enemy, Isaiah 62:8–9.
Do not take from those experiencing disaster, Obadiah 13.
Soldier's temptation to extort, Luke 3:14.
See Looting, Plunder.

SPONSORSHIP

Not sponsored by people, Galatians 1:1 (AB).

SPORTSMAN

Old Testament hunters, Genesis 10:8–9, 25:27.
Ishmael, the archer, Genesis 21:20.
Blessing upon outdoorsmen, Deuteronomy 33:18 (LB).
Setting traps for men, Jeremiah 5:26.
Men cannot outrun horses, Jeremiah 12:5.
Ready with bow, arrow, Lamentations 2:4.
Swift riding horses, Habakkuk 1:8.
Growing up in desert, Luke 1:80.
Invitation to go fishing, Luke 5:1–11.
Peter the fisherman, John 21:3–11.
Running race with endurance, Hebrews 12:1.
See Fisherman, Hunting.

SPRAIN

Ankle sprain, 2 Samuel 22:37 (NIV).

SPRING

Nature "burst forth," Genesis 1:11 (LB).
Seedtime, harvest, Genesis 8:22.
Time for kings to go to war, 2 Samuel 11:1.
A day in April, Nehemiah 2:1 (LB).
God at work, Psalm 65:9–13 (LB).
New growth appears, Proverbs 27:25.
Winter past, flowers appearing, Song of Songs 2:11–12.
Spring's spiritual illustration, Isaiah 61:11.
Time for birds to migrate, Jeremiah 8:7.
"Early in April," Ezekiel 40:1 (LB).
Seeds do not germinate, Joel 1:17.
See Seasons.

SPRINGS

Coming from under temple, Joel 3:18.
Springs of the spirit, John 7:38.
"Springs of living water," Revelation 7:17.
See Water, Wells.

SPRINKLE

Sprinkle before eating, Mark 7:4 (LB).
See Ceremony, Cleansing.

SPRINTER

Fleet-footed, 2 Samuel 2:18.

SPY

A spy against his brothers, Genesis 37:2.
"Spy" accuses brothers, Genesis 42:8–9.
Condolence misunderstood as spying, 2 Samuel 10:1–4.
Spies explore Canaan, Numbers 13:1–16.
Elisha a "spy," 2 Kings 6:9–13.
Watching from window, Proverbs 7:6–13.
Spying for Pharisees, Luke 20:20.
Spy infiltration, Galatians 2:4 (GNB).
See Surveillance.

STABILITY

God greater than numbers, Deuteronomy 20:1–4.
Lack of discernment, Deuteronomy 32:28 (NIV).
Stable, fixed, Psalm 91:1 (AB).
The Lord on our side, Psalm 124:1–5.
Looking to flesh for stability, Jeremiah 17:5.
Stability in congregation, Galatians 1:6–9.

Standing at end of struggle, Ephesians 6:13.
That which was from beginning, 1 John 1:1.
See Dependabilty.

STAFF

Choosing mighty and brave for service,
1 Samuel 14:52.
King Solomon's fortunate officials, 1 Kings
10:8.
See Organization.

STAMINA

Virility retained until death, Deuteronomy
34:7.
Work for old man, Joshua 13:1.
Not giving up to weariness, Judges 8:4.
Limited stamina, 1 Samuel 30:9–10.
Satan challenged Job's stamina, Job 2:1–10.
Faltering stength, Proverbs 24:10.
Race not to swift or strong, Ecclesiastes
9:11.
Renewal of strength, Isaiah 40:30–31.
Men cannot outrun horses, Jeremiah 12:5.
Stand firm in faith, 1 Corinthians 16:13;
1 Thessalonians 3:8.
See Strength, Virility.

STAND

Standing until mission accomplished,
1 Samuel 16:11.
Stand against evil, Ephesians 6:11.

STANDARD

Honest weights, measures, Deuteronomy
25:13–16.
Working by high standards, Proverbs
22:29.
Weights, measures, Ezekiel 45:10–15.
Humility standard greatness, Matthew
20:25–28.
Do not cause another to stumble, Romans
14:20–23.
"Hold to the standard," 2 Timothy 1:13
(NRSV).
See Measurement.

STARS

Impure stars, Job 25:5 (AB).
Lighting up sky, Philippians 2:15 (GNB).
See Astronomy.

STARVATION *See Famine, Hunger.*

STATISTICS

Innumerable dust, stars, Genesis 13:16;
15:5.
Specific enumeration of trained men, Genesis 14:14.
Greater than numbers, Deuteronomy
20:1–4.
Thirty sons, thirty daughters, Judges 12:9,
13–14.
Thousands, tens of thousands, 1 Samuel
18:7 (See 21:11; 29:5).
Death by measurement, 2 Samuel 8:2.
Depending on military statistics, 1 Chronicles 21:17.
Exact number of musicians, 1 Chronicles
25:7.
Census of aliens, 2 Chronicles 2:17–18.
Temple inventory, Ezra 1:9–11.
People taken into exile, Jeremiah 52:28–30.
Measuring Jerusalem's width, length, Zechariah 2:1–2.
Measurement of flying scroll, Zechariah
5:2.
Genealogy of Jesus, Matthew 1:1–17.
Each sparrow known, hairs numbered,
Matthew 10:28–30; Luke 12:7.
Roman world census, Luke 2:1–3.
Number of fish caught, John 21:11.
Growing New Testament church, Acts 16:5.
Number of people saved in ark, 1 Peter
3:20.
Those sealed against judgment, Revelation
7:3–8.
Measure temple, count worshippers, Revelation 11:1.
Measurements of new Jerusalem, Revelation 21:15–21.
See Population.

STATUE

Temple images, 1 Kings 6:23–28.

STATURE *See Physical.*

STATUS

Neighbors who become wealthy, Genesis
26:12–17.
The Lord determines status, 1 Samuel 2:7.

Least, greatest in society, 2 Kings 23:2.
Low, high, rich, poor, Psalm 49:2.
First last, last first, Matthew 19:30; 20:16.
God unimpressed by status, Galatians 2:6 (AB).
Blessed in heavenly realms, Ephesians 1:3.
Masters and slaves, Ephesians 6:5–8.
Paul could boast of former status, Philippians 3:2–11.
See Fame, Prestige.

STATUTE OF LIMITATIONS

Seven-year debt cancellation, Deuteronomy 15:1–6.

STEADFAST

"Steadfast love of God," Psalm 52:8 (NRSV).
Standing at end of struggle, Ephesians 6:13.
Remaining steadfast through faith, Hebrews 12:1–3.
Learning perseverance through trials and testing, James 1:2–4.
Reward for Job's patience, James 5:11.
See Courage, Perseverance, Stand.

STEALING

Enemy spoils, Numbers 31:1–54.
Need for two or three witnesses, Deuteronomy 19:15.
Riches gained unjustly, Jeremiah 17:11.
Temple robbery, Romans 2:22.
Petty thievery, Titus 2:10 (AB).
See Robbery, Thief.

STEALTH

Mode for murder, Judges 4:21; Judges 5:24–27.
King Herod, Magi, Matthew 2:7–8, 13.
See Ambush, Crafty, Ruse.

STENCH

Dead frogs, Exodus 7:18; 8:13–14.
Stench of disobedience, Exodus 16:19–24.
Sick drunk, Isaiah 28:7.
Worms in dead bodies, Isaiah 66:24.
Blood of dead man, Revelation 16:3.
See Filth, Putrid.

STERILE

Women's barrenness, Genesis 11:30; 15:2; 1 Samuel 1:2; 2 Samuel 6:23; 2 Kings 4:11–17; Luke 1:7; 20:27–29.
Unable to have children, Hosea 9:11.
See Barren, Childless.

STEWARDSHIP

Pleasing aroma, Genesis 8:20–21 (Note Amos 5:21–22 KJV, margin).
Abram's tithe to Melchizedek, Genesis 14:18–20; Hebrews 7:1–2.
Coming before the Lord empty-handed, Exodus 23:15 (NIV).
Stewardship from willing heart, Exodus 25:2; Exodus 35:29 (AB).
Abundant giving, Exodus 36:2–7.
Offering from those of limited means, Leviticus 5:7–11.
Thanksgiving offering, Leviticus 7:12.
Giving less than best, Leviticus 22:17–22; Numbers 18:29.
Stewardship, Numbers 7:13–85; 10:2.
Gifts from those who fought in battle, Numbers 31:27–31.
Items consecrated before offering, Deuteronomy 12:26.
Giving ratio to receiving, Deuteronomy 16:16–17.
Prostitution earnings unacceptable, Deuteronomy 23:18.
Cherished child given to the Lord, 1 Samuel 1:25–28.
Bizarre offering, 1 Samuel 6:2–5.
Offering required to obtain divine guidance, 1 Samuel 9:1–9.
Reward dedicated to God, 2 Samuel 8:9–12.
David refused cheap stewardship, 2 Samuel 24:21–24.
Three sources of funds for temple, 2 Kings 12:4–5.
Personal treasures given to temple, 1 Chronicles 29:3–4.
Proper stewardship attitude, 1 Chronicles 29:13–14; Psalm 24:1.
Offeratory music, 2 Chronicles 29:28–29.
Abundant offerings, 2 Chronicles 29:35; 31:5–8.

Money, food, drink for temple workers, Ezra 3:7.

Value of sacrifice, offering, Psalm 50:23.

The kind of sacrifice God blesses, Psalm 51:15–17.

Giving out of gratitude, Psalm 54:6–7.

Blessing upon generous sharing, Psalm 112:5–9.

Honor the Lord with personal wealth, Proverbs 3:9–10 (See LB).

Stewardship to others, Proverbs 3:27–28.

"Good man's earnings," Proverbs 10:16 (LB).

Generosity prospers, Proverbs 11:24–25 (See LB, NRSV).

Blessing for generous man, Proverbs 22:9.

Unearned status, Proverbs 25:6–7, 27.

False boast of giving, Proverbs 25:14.

Fulfil pledge, Ecclesiastes 5:4–5.

Bread cast upon waters, Ecclesiastes 11:1.

Meaningless offerings brought by Israel, Isaiah 1:11–17.

Vanity giving, Isaiah 1:13 (AB).

Prophecy concerning Tyre, Isaiah 23:15–18.

Relating fasting to care of others, Isaiah 58:3–7.

Wrong kind of offering, Isaiah 66:3.

Bringing offerings unsuitable to the Lord, Jeremiah 6:20.

People in fine homes, temple in ruins, Haggai 1:1–4.

Defiled offerings from defiled people, Haggai 2:13–14.

Priests who defiled altar, Malachi 1:6–14.

Eager but erroneous giving, Malachi 2:12 (CEV).

Refined gold, silver, Malachi 3:2–4.

Stealing from God, Malachi 3:8–10.

Reconciliation precedes stewardship, Matthew 5:23–24.

Private stewardship, Matthew 6:2–4.

Treasures on earth, treasures in heaven, Matthew 6:19–21.

Paying taxes to government, Matthew 22:15–22; Mark 12:17.

Fullest measure of giving, Matthew 23:23.

Anointing of Jesus, Matthew 26:6–13; Mark 14:3–9.

Judas' tainted money, Matthew 27:3–8.

Rich man donated tomb for Jesus, Matthew 27:57–61.

Those given much, those given little, Mark 4:24–25; Luke 12:48.

Widow's small offering, Mark 12:41–44; Luke 21:1–4.

Sharing with others, Luke 3:11.

Abundance rewarded those who give, Luke 6:38.

Gentile built synagogue, Luke 7:1–5.

Women helped support ministry, Luke 8:1–3.

Stewardship, heart purity, Luke 11:41 (LB).

Tithe, neglect justice, Luke 11:42.

Give possessions to the poor, Luke 12:33–34.

Casual giving, Luke 21:1–2 (LB).

Dishonest stewardship, Acts 5:1–11.

Woman who helped the poor, Acts 9:36–42.

Devout centurion, Acts 10:2.

Reaching out to help others, Acts 11:27–30.

Self-supported ministry, Acts 20:33–35.

Contribute to needs of fellow Christians, Romans 12:13 (NRSV).

Sharing spiritual, material blessings, Romans 15:26–27.

Found faithful, 1 Corinthians 4:2.

Clergy support, 1 Corinthians 9:7–14; Philippians 4:10–19.

Greater gift than money, 1 Corinthians 13:3.

Sunday giving, 1 Corinthians 16:2.

Ministry profiteering, 2 Corinthians 2:17.

Persecution, poverty brought generosity, 2 Corinthians 8:1–5.

Size of gift, 2 Corinthians 8:12.

Shared responsibility, 2 Corinthians 8:13–15, 19 (See AB).

"Bountiful gift," 2 Corinthians 9:5 (NASB, NRSV).

Sowing, reaping, 2 Corinthians 9:6–7.

Giving from desire, 2 Corinthians 9:10.

Some pay, others receive, 2 Corinthians 11:7–8.

Concern for poor, Galatians 2:9–10.

Generosity fruit of Spirit, Galatians 5:22 (NRSV).

Stewardship of God's grace, Ephesians 3:2 (AB).

Stingy stewardship, Philippians 4:15.

Gift receipted, Philippians 4:18 (GNB).

Greed avoided, 1 Thessalonians 2:5.

Wrongly cultivating donors, 1 Thessalonians 2:5 (LB).

Monetary wealth, good deeds, 1 Timothy 6:11–19 (See LB).

Gifts, sacrifices, Hebrews 8:3.

Abel's good offerings, Hebrews 11:4.

Share with others, Hebrews 13:16.

Using one's gift for good of others, 1 Peter 4:10.

See Benevolence, Donation, Generosity, Giving, Offering, Commitment, Philanthropy, Tithe, Welfare.

STILLBORN *See Fetus.*

STINGY

"Tightfisted," Deuteronomy 15:7 (NIV).

Result of stinginess, Proverbs 11:24; 21:13; 28:27.

Stingy man's food, Proverbs 23:6–8.

Folly of hoarding, Ecclesiastes 5:13.

Stingy stewardship, Philippians 4:15–19.

See Frugality, Miser.

STIPEND

Income for priests, Deuteronomy 18:1–2.

Evil earnings forbidden in temple, Deuteronomy 23:17–18.

Requesting payment for ministry, 2 Kings 5:20–27.

High cost of dance, Mark 6:21–29.

See Honorarium, Payment, Salary, Wages.

STOCK MARKET

Such as playing the market, Proverbs 28:20.

"Bad investment," Ecclesiastes 5:14 (NASB).

STOMACH

Knife to throat, Proverbs 23:2.

To swallow camel, Matthew 23:24.

Making stomach god, Philippians 3:19.

See Diet, Digestion, Food, Gluttony, Indigestion, Obesity.

STONE

Stone as witness, Joshua 24:27.

Living stones church construction, 1 Peter 2:5.

STONE'S THROW

Somber measurement, Luke 22:41 (AB, GNB, LB).

STONING

Death for touching sacred mountain, Exodus 19:10–23.

Punishment for Sabbath breaking, Numbers 15:36.

Death to idolotry or animism, Deuteronomy 17:2–7.

Detected adultery, Deuteronomy 22:21.

Death to Achan, Joshua 7:19–26.

Martyrdom of Stephen, Acts 7:59.

Near death of Paul, Acts 14:19–20.

Heroes of faith, Hebrews 11:36–39.

See Martyr, Persecution.

STORM

Symbol of divine anger, 2 Samuel 22:7–16.

Tempest surrounding God, Psalm 50:3.

Refuge from storm, Isaiah 4:5–6.

Army of storm clouds, Joel 2:2 (LB).

Water surging from sky, earth, Genesis 7:11–12.

Brimstone storm, Genesis 19:24.

Storm on command, Exodus 9:23.

Giant hailstones, Joshua 10:11.

Fear of thunder, 1 Samuel 7:10.

Mighty wind, Job 1:19.

Majestic thunder, Job 37:4 (GNB).

Thick, dark clouds, Psalm 18:11 (NRSV).

Storm at sea, Psalm 107:25–30 (LB).

Judgment likened to storm, Isaiah 28:2.

Storm calmed when Jonah thrown overboard, Jonah 1:10–15.

Whirlwind invokes judgment, Nahum 1:3.

Obedient wind, waves, Matthew 8:23–27; Mark 6:45–52; Psalm 89:9.

Prelude to hurricane, Acts 27:13–14 (NIV).

See Weather, Wind.

STORY TELLING

Parable with music, Psalm 49:4.

STRAGGLER

Danger to those who lag behind, Deuteronomy 25:17–19.
See Delay, Procrastination.

STRANGER

Golden Rule toward aliens, Exodus 22:21; Leviticus 19:34.
Courtesy to foreigners, Exodus 23:9.
Fear of strangers, Numbers 13:17–33.
Stranger's ministry, Deuteronomy 18:6–8.
Misunderstood stranger's gesture, 2 Samuel 10:1–4.
Special courtesy to stranger, Ruth 2:14–18.
Identity of stranger, Mark 14:13–15.
Entering communities and homes of strangers, Luke 10:5–12.
Hospitality to recommended stranger, 1 Corinthians 16:10–11.
"Friendly to strangers," Titus 1:8 (CEV).
"Welcome strangers into your home," Hebrews 13:2 (CEV).
Fellowship with all who come to worship, James 2:1–4.
Love strangers, 1 Peter 4:9 (AB).
See Alien, Xenophobia.

STRATEGY

Kidnapping and rescue, Genesis 14:12–16.
People divided for protection, Genesis 32:6–8.
Israelites appeared to be wandering, Exodus 14:1–4.
Military maneuver and ambush, Joshua 8:3–23.
God uses evil to carry out His plans, Judges 14:1–4.
Elimination of blacksmiths, 1 Samuel 13:19.
God-given strategy, 1 Samuel 14:9–15.
Divine guidance in defeating enemy, 2 Samuel 5:22–25.
Enemy "summit conference," Psalm 83:5 (LB).
Best strategy fails against the Lord, Proverbs 21:30.
Visualized battle strategy, Ezekiel 4:1–3.
Plight of Babylonian wise men, Daniel 2:8.
Jesus' strategy facing accusers, Matthew 21:24–27.

Strategy to destroy Jesus, Mark 15:1 (See LB).
Deliberating military strategy, Luke 14:31–32.
See Scheme.

STREET

Danger on street, Joshua 2:19; Hosea 7:1; Lamentations 4:18.
No street message, 2 Samuel 1:20.
Muddy street, 2 Samuel 22:43.
Shelter for street people, Job 31:32.
Wisdom in the street, Proverbs 1:20–21 (NIV).
Crying in the streets, Isaiah 24:11.
Deserted streets, Jeremiah 33:10.
Corpses in streets, Ezekiel 11:6.
Busy traffic, Nahum 2:4.
Banquet for street people, Luke 14:15–24.
Residence on Straight Street, Acts 9:10–11.
See City, Highway, Urban.

STREET EVANGELISM

Shout in the streets, Jeremiah 2:2 (LB).
Sermon at temple gate, Jeremiah 7:1–15.
Invitation extended to streets, Matthew 22:8–9.
See Evangelism, Witness.

STREET PEOPLE

Hospitality for stranger on street, Job 31:32.
Living on the streets, Lamentations 4:5.

STRENGTH

Dove found security in ark, Genesis 8:6–12.
Smallest, weakest, Judges 6:14–16.
Prelude to birth of strongest man, Judges 13:2–16.
Stronger, weaker, 2 Samuel 3:1.
Exhausted in battle, 2 Samuel 21:15.
Human strength versus lion, 2 Samuel 23:20.
Building city around fortress, 1 Chronicles 11:7–9.
Depending on strength of fighting men, 1 Chronicles 21:17.
Prayer for physical strength, Nehemiah 6:9.

Strength of elephant, Job 40:15–24 (NIV footnote).

God-given strength, Psalm 18:32.

Strength sapped by sin, Psalm 31:10 (LB).

Strong as an ox, Psalm 92:10 (GNB).

Soul strength, Psalm 138:3 (NRSV).

Wisdom's greater strength, Proverbs 24:5 (LB).

Strength in numbers, Ecclesiastes 4:12.

Working with dull axe, Ecclesiastes 10:10.

Trust in the Lord, not horses and chariots, Isaiah 31:1–3.

Daily strength, Isaiah 33:2 (CEV).

Strength, repose from the Lord, Isaiah 35:3–4.

Wings like eagles, Isaiah 40:29–31.

Sufficiency of our God, Isaiah 41:10.

Least becomes great, Isaiah 60:22.

Made strong by God's power, Jeremiah 1:17–19.

Boasting only in the Lord, Jeremiah 9:23–24.

Lord like mighty warrior, Jeremiah 20:11.

Nothing too hard for God, Jeremiah 32:27.

Strength of great Redeemer, Jeremiah 50:34.

Mighty are those who obey the Lord, Joel 2:11.

Filled with power, Micah 3:8.

Feet like feet of deer, Habakkuk 3:19.

Not by might nor by power, Zechariah 4:6.

Greatest strength is faith in God, Zechariah 12:5.

Shattered chains, Mark 5:3–4 (RSV).

Strength-giving faith, Romans 4:20 (GNB).

Strong looking after weak, Romans 15:1.

Weakness, strength illustrated, 2 Corinthians 13:4.

Standing firm in faith, 1 Corinthians 16:13–14.

Promised resurrection power, Ephesians 1:18–21.

Holy Spirit's power, Ephesians 3:20–21.

Spiritual union with the Lord, Ephesians 6:10 (GNB).

One angel overpowering, binding Satan, Revelation 20:1–3.

See Power, Vigorous, Vitality.

STRESS

Delegating work to others, Exodus 18:17–27.

God greater than fiercest battle, Deuteronomy 20:1–4.

Jealous wife, 1 Samuel 1:2–11.

King's business urgent, 1 Samuel 21:8 (NIV).

Leadership for those in stress, 1 Samuel 22:2.

Stressing circumstances, Job 1:6–22.

Refining finest gold, Job 23:10; Isaiah 48:10.

Aging caused by stress, Psalm 6:7.

New attitude, Psalm 40:1–3.

Refuge, strength for every stress, Psalm 46:1–3.

One who helps, sustains, Psalm 54:4.

For times of stress, a God who hears, Psalm 55:1–17.

No need for fear, Psalm 56:3–4.

Steadfast, singing heart, Psalm 57:7–8.

Rest in God alone, Psalm 62:1–2.

Promises made under stress, Psalm 66:13–14.

Waters up to neck, Psalm 69:1.

Insomnia induced by stress, Psalm 77:2–6 (RSV).

Dwelling place for yearning soul, Psalm 84:1–12.

Sheep of His pasture, Psalm 100:1–5.

Steadfast heart, Psalm 108:1–5.

Distress, anguish, Psalm 116:3 (NRSV).

Refuge in times of anguish, Psalm 118:1–9.

Answer to those who taunt, Psalm 119:41–48.

The Lord on our side, Psalm 124:1–5.

Sleep a gift from the Lord, Psalm 127:2.

Out of depths, Psalm 130:1–6.

Bold and stout-hearted, Psalm 138:3.

When no one else cares, Psalm 142:1–7.

Pleasant ways and paths of peace, Proverbs 3:13–18.

Cheerful heart, Proverbs 17:22; 18:14.

Gift of contentment, Proverbs 30:7–8.

Prayer for strength in time of distress, Isaiah 33:2.

Renewal of strength, Isaiah 40:30–31; Isaiah 41:10.

Peace through obedience, Isaiah 48:17–18.

S

The Lord will guide, satisfy, strengthen, Isaiah 58:11.

Flowers in place of sorrow, Isaiah 61:1–3.

The Lord shared their distress, Isaiah 63:9.

Where to find rest for the soul, Jeremiah 6:16.

The Lord understands, gives counsel, Jeremiah 15:15–16.

Sure resource in time of trouble, Lamentations 3:19–33.

Sleepless king, relaxed prisoner, Daniel 6:16–23.

Witness in time of stress, Jonah 1:4–9.

Strength from the Lord, Habakkuk 3:19.

Quietness, gladness, Zephaniah 3:17.

Reacting to those who persecute, Matthew 5:11–12.

Rest for your soul, Matthew 11:28–30.

Jesus' mastery over fear, Luke 8:22–25.

Small faith in great God, Luke 11:20.

No need for stress, Luke 12:22–34.

Jesus gives light, John 8:12.

Confidence in future, stability to present, John 14:1–6.

Trusting One who gives peace, John 16:33.

Fasting because of stress, Acts 27:33–36.

Suffering strengthens faith, Romans 5:1–11.

More than conquerers, Romans 8:12–39 (Note fear, verse 15).

Strength, confidence in sufficient Lord, 1 Corinthians 1:8–9.

Victoriously facing problems, 2 Corinthians 4:7–18.

Facing life with dimensions of faith, Ephesians 3:14–21.

Generating inner peace, Philippians 4:4–7 (See Nehemiah 8:10b).

Antidote for stress, 1 Thessalonians 5:16–18.

The Lord knows what He is doing, 2 Thessalonians 1:3–5.

Anchor for soul, Hebrews 6:19–20.

Restoration for those who suffer, 1 Peter 5:10.

Abundant grace and peace, 2 Peter 1:2.

Testing as an act of divine love, Revelation 3:19.

Absence of stress, Revelation 21:1–5.

See Anxiety, Duress, Tension.

STRIFE

Effort to avoid strife, Genesis 13:8.

Prenatal prediction, Genesis 25:23.

Settling disputes, Exodus 18:13–16 (GNB).

The God greater than numbers, Deuteronomy 20:1–4.

Jealous wife, 1 Samuel 1:2–7.

Conflict between David and Saul, 1 Samuel 26:1–25.

Marital strife, 2 Samuel 6:16–22

Reputation as troublemaker, 2 Samuel 20:1.

The Lord on our side, Psalm 124:1–5.

Stop strife before it starts, Proverbs 17:14; 20:3.

Neighborhood strife, Proverbs 25:8.

Wise in his own eyes, Proverbs 26:16.

Avoid quarrels of others, Proverbs 26:17.

Blessed peacemakers, Matthew 5:9.

Division in communities and families, Matthew 12:25.

Strife among Christians, Acts 15:36–40; 2 Corinthians 12:20.

Devouring each other, Galatians 5:15.

"Competing against one another," Galatians 5:26 (NRSV).

Mark of good disciple, 2 Timothy 2:24.

See Abrasion, Conflict, Dissension, Jealousy, Quarrel.

STRIPES *See Whipping.*

STRIVING

"Striving after wind," Ecclesiastes 2:17 (NASB).

STRUGGLE

Becoming master over sin, Genesis 4:7.

Fighting the Lord's battles, 1 Samuel 25:28.

Turning battle back at gate, Isaiah 28:6.

Struggle against wickedness, Matthew 24:12–13.

Struggling against wind, Mark 6:48 (CEV).

Fight good fight of faith, 1 Timothy 6:11–12.

No easy way, 2 Timothy 3:1 (LB).

See Anxiety, Conflict, Duress.

STUBBORN

Stiff-necked people, Exodus 32:9; 33:5; Deuteronomy 9:6.

"Stop being so stubborn," Deuteronomy 10:16 (CEV).

Presumptuously stubborn, Deuteronomy 17:12 (KJV).

Stubborn as a mule, Psalm 32:9

Rebellious cobra, Psalm 58:3–5.

Fool's opinion, Proverbs 18:2.

Refusing counsel, Proverbs 29:1.

Iron neck stubbornness, Isaiah 48:4.

Break up unplowed ground, Jeremiah 4:3.

Proud, stubborn, Jeremiah 11:8 (LB).

Stubborn hearts, Zechariah 7:11–12.

"Don't be stubborn," Hebrews 4:7 (CEV).

See Obstinate, Resistance.

STUDENTS

Asking good questions, 1 Kings 10:1–3.

King Solomon's fortunate officials, 1 Kings 10:8.

Lifetime study of Scriptures, Ezra 7:10 (CEV).

Habitual study, Psalm 1:2 (AB).

True wisdom comes from Scriptures, Psalm 119:97–100.

Giving heed to instruction, Proverbs 16:20.

Discernment provides knowledge, Proverbs 18:15.

Pay attention to teacher, Proverbs 23:11 (GNB).

Wisdom-loving son delights father, Proverbs 29:3.

Weary from studying, Ecclesiastes 12:12.

Rebellious students, Jeremiah 32:33.

God-given knowledge, Daniel 1:17.

Students rank beneath teachers, Matthew 10:24.

Hearing, not understanding, Mark 4:11–12.

In-depth learning, Mark 4:34.

Willingness to learn, Luke 11:1.

Listening with eagerness, Acts 17:11–12.

Thorough knowledge of Scriptures, Acts 18:24–26.

Holy Spirit's guidance in Bible study, 1 Corinthians 2:6–16.

Folly of intellectual pride, 1 Corinthians 3:18–20.

Faith the ultimate intelligence, 1 Corinthians 3:21–23.

Supreme examination, 2 Corinthians 13:5.

Student sharing with teacher, Galatians 6:6 (CEV).

Properly receiving the Word of God, 1 Thessalonians 2:13.

Correctly handling Scripture, 2 Timothy 2:15.

Slow learners, Hebrews 5:11–14.

Faith as sure antidote for doubt, Hebrews 11:1–3.

Take Scriptures to heart, Revelation 1:3.

See Academic, Learning, Study.

STUDY

Can't sleep? Read history, Esther 6:1.

Opened eyes, Psalm 119:18.

"Nuggets of truth," Proverbs 1:6 (LB).

Do not neglect God's Word, Psalm 119:16.

Prayer for perception in Bible study, Psalms 119:18; 119:33–38.

Royal research study, Proverbs 25:2.

Excessive study, Ecclesiastes 12:12.

Motivation for study, Daniel 7:19.

Lack of study, Matthew 22:29.

Wealth, worry impair study, Mark 4:19.

Missing the point, John 5:39–40 (NRSV).

Good teaching into action, John 13:17.

Eager to study Scriptures, Acts 17:11.

Bible-centered fellowship, Acts 18:24–26.

Holy Spirit's guidance, 1 Corinthians 2:6–16 (AB).

Search for spiritual maturity, 1 Timothy 4:13.

Searching intently, 1 Peter 1:10–12.

See Education, Students.

STUMBLE

Inevitable stumbling, Luke 17:1 (NIV, NRSV).

Kept from stumbling, Jude 24 (NASB, NKJV).

STUPIDITY

Stupid actions, 2 Samuel 24:10 (CEV).

"How stupid I am," Psalm 69:5 (LB).

Stupid as an animal, Psalm 73:22 (GNB).

Assumed stupidity, Proverbs 30:2 (NRSV, NASB).

Wise made stupid, Obadiah 8 (LB).

See Folly, Ignorance.

S

STYLE

Well-dressed giant, 1 Samuel 17:4–7 (LB).
"Praise is becoming," Psalm 147:1 (NASB).
Spiritual style in any season, Isaiah 11:5.
Royal style, prophet's desert garb, Matthew 11:7–9.
Clean robes, Revelation 22:14.
See Garment, Clothing, Fashion, Wardrobe.

SUBCONSCIOUS

Corrupt subconscious thoughts, Genesis 6:5; Jeremiah 4:14; Matthew 15:19; Romans 1:28.
Fortified mind, Deuteronomy 6:5–6.
Heart and spirit, Psalm 51:10.
Motivational resources, Psalm 119:11.
Fountain in the heart, Proverbs 4:23.
Deceitfulness of heart, Jeremiah 17:9.
Vitality for subconscious, Ephesians 4:22.
Cultivating subconscious, Philippians 4:8; 1 Thessalonians 4:11–12.
Mental purity and corruption, Titus 1:15.
Inner mind perceived, Hebrews 4:12.
Written in the mind, Hebrews 10:16.
See Frame-of-Reference, Motivation, Thought.

SUBJECTION

Partial blindness inflicted as disgrace, 1 Samuel 11:2–11.
Forced to slavery, Nehemiah 5:1–5.
"If I perish, I perish," Esther 4:16.
Subjected to the Lord's commands, Isaiah 48:17–18.
Conditional freedom, Jeremiah 34:8–11.
No chance for escape, Jeremiah 48:44.
Knowing who is the Lord, Ezekiel 6:10, 14; 7:4, 9, 27; 12:16, 20; 13:9, 23; 14:11.
Silent subjection, Ezekiel 16:63.
Demons subjected to silence, Mark 1:33–34.
See Submission, Yielding.

SUBJECT MATTER

Clear communication, Numbers 12:4–8.
Wisdom of Solomon, 1 Kings 4:29–34.
Worthy subject matter, Proverbs 8:6.
See Conversation, Frame-of-Reference, Rapport.

SUBMISSION

Beaten into submission, Exodus 21:20–21.
Forbidden to taste food, 1 Samuel 14:24–28.
Submission to royal authority, 1 Samuel 26:7–11.
Total submission, 1 King 20:1–6.
Woman's willing submission, Esther 4:12–16.
Satanic view of submission, Job 2:1–10.
Made pure through testing, Job 23:10.
One does not contend with God, Job 40:2.
Delayed submission, Job 42:1–9.
Like idol, like follower, Psalm 135:15–18.
Revelation inspires submission, Proverbs 29:18.
Clay submitted to potter, Isaiah 45:9; 64:8.
One who suffered for us, Isaiah 53:1–7.
Submitting to worthless idols, Jeremiah 2:5.
Pressured submission, Jeremiah 49:35.
Knowing who is the Lord, Ezekiel 6:10, 14; 7:4, 9, 27; 12:16, 20; 13:9, 23; 14:11.
Refusing submission to pagan gods, Daniel 3:8–30.
Gethsemane submission, Mark 14:36.
Jesus washed disciples' feet, John 13:1–17.
Willingness of Jesus to be sacrificed, John 18:1–11.
"Yielding in faith," Romans 1:5 (Berk.).
Position in life submissive to will of God, Titus 2:9–10.
The way up is down, Hebrews 2:9.
Jesus' reverent submission, Hebrews 5:7 (NRSV).
Submit to God, resist Satan, James 4:7.
See Obedience, Surrender.

SUBSTITUTE

Substitute sacrifice, Genesis 22:1–13.
No substitute for guilt, Deuteronomy 24:16.
Requesting substitute for responsibility, Exodus 4:10–13; 6:30.
Bronze substituted for gold, 1 Kings 14:25–28.
Substitute to divine plan, Jeremiah 2:13.
Christ substituted for us, 2 Corinthians 5:21.
See Alternative, Mediator.

SUBURB

Suburbs comprise city, Genesis 10:11–12 (AB).

Suburbs of Sodom, Gomorrah, Jude 7.

SUBVERSION

Subversion detected by manner of speech, Judges 12:5–6.

Questions for subversion, Judges 16:6–18.

Subversive plot to assassinate king, Esther 2:21.

Penalty for subversion, Esther 7:1–10.

Deliberately writing falsehoods, Jeremiah 8:8.

Riches gained unjustly, Jeremiah 17:11.

False prophets, Jeremiah 23:16–18.

Poisoning minds of others, Acts 14:2.

Subverting Bible teaching, Galatians 1:6–9.

Fine-sounding arguments, Colossians 2:4.

See Fifth Column, Trickery.

SUCCESS

Successful creation, Genesis 1:10, 12, 18, 21, 25.

Joseph prospered in Egypt, Genesis 39:2.

Promised success, Exodus 34:10; Deuteronomy 26:19.

God-given ability to produce wealth, Deuteronomy 8:18.

The Lord gives success, Deuteronomy 28:6 (CEV).

Abounding with God's favor, Deuteronomy 33:23.

"A tremendous day," Joshua 4:14 (LB).

Gideon's example for success, Judges 7:17–18.

Shepherd boy to king, 2 Samuel 7:1–16.

Strength from God, 2 Samuel 22:33.

Success formula, 2 Chronicles 26:5.

Succeeding with God's help, Nehemiah 6:16.

Assured true success, Psalm 1:3.

Success delights guide, Psalm 37:23–24.

Success in Divine purpose, Psalm 57:2.

Giving God glory for success, Psalms 115:1; 118:23.

In-depth success, Proverbs 3:1–4.

Key to success, Proverbs 16:3; 21:30.

Seeking first the kingdom of God, Proverbs 21:21; Matthew 6:33.

Humility, faith, Proverbs 22:4.

Result of hard work, Proverbs 22:29 (LB).

Righteous man falls, gets up, Proverbs 24:15–16.

Emptiness of mere success, Ecclesiastes 2:4–11.

Success inequity, Ecclesiastes 8:14.

Victory not always to swift, strong, Ecclesiastes 9:11.

Noble man makes noble plans, Isaiah 32:8 (NIV).

Man who refuses bribes, Isaiah 33:15–16.

Those whom the Lord commissions achieve success, Isaiah 48:15.

Success assured whatever circumstances, Jeremiah 17:7–8.

Prosperity linked to conduct, Daniel 4:27.

Pagan gods honored for success, Hosea 10:1 (CEV).

Not by might nor by power, Zechariah 4:6.

Measure for greatness, Matthew 20:25–28.

Fishermen's failure turned to success, Luke 5:1–11.

Excited about wrong phenomena, Luke 10:17–20.

Vine, fruit, John 15:1–8.

Chosen for guidance, blessing, John 15:16.

Speaking only of what Christ has done in us, Romans 15:18–19.

Success comes from God, 1 Corinthians 3:6–8.

In race, one wins; serving God, all win, 1 Corinthians 9:24–27.

Spreading fragrance of Christ, 2 Corinthians 2:14.

Let the Lord commend, 2 Corinthians 10:17–18.

Paul's commendation of Timothy, Philippians 2:19–23.

"Make it my own," Philippians 3:12–13 (NRSV).

Widely reported success, 1 Thessalonians 1:8–10.

Joy and glory, 1 Thessalonians 2:17–19.

Praise to God for success in ministry, 1 Thessalonians 3:8–10.

Purpose, means of spiritual success, 2 Thessalonians 1:11–12.

S

Prepared by God to succeed, Hebrews 13:20–21.

Business success, certainty of death, James 1:10.

Mentality of success, 1 Peter 1:15.

Attributes of mature Christian life, 2 Peter 1:5–9.

Certainty of success in Christian life, Jude 24–25.

See Accomplishment, Achievement, Victory.

SUCCESSOR

Successor to Moses, Deuteronomy 31:1–8; Deuteronomy 34:9.

Sons replaced father, 1 Samuel 8:1.

David, Saul's successor, 2 Samuel 2:7.

Mother's role in son's advancement, 1 Kings 1:11–31.

Dual successors, 1 Kings 16:21–22.

Secret anointing of king, 2 Kings 9:1–13.

Chosen to build temple, 1 Chronicles 28:2–10.

Son fulfills father's dream, 2 Chronicles 6:3–11.

Candidates to succeed queen, Esther 2:1–4.

See Heir.

SUCCINCT *See Clarity.*

SUDAN

Sudanese prayers, Psalm 68:31 (GNB).

SUFFERING

Purpose of testing, Deuteronomy 8:1–5; Psalm 119:71; John 11:4; Romans 5:3–4 (NRSV).

Suffering without blaming God, Job 1:22.

Moaning, groaning, Job 3:24 (CEV).

Weight of suffering, Job 6:2–3.

Tested to come forth as gold, Job 23:10.

God speaks through suffering, Job 33:14; 19–21; 36:15.

"Songs in the night," Job 35:10.

"Pain is ever with me," Psalm 38:17 (NRSV).

Desperate times, Psalm 60:3.

Refined like silver, Psalm 66:10.

Constant suffering, Psalm 73:14 (GNB).

Discipline brings blessing, Psalm 94:12.

The Lord does as He pleases, Psalm 135:6.

Going through crucible, Proverbs 17:3; Isaiah 48:10.

Physical beating, Isaiah 1:5–6.

The Lord takes our infirmities, sorrows, Isaiah 53:4.

God's thoughts higher than yours, Isaiah 55:9.

Purposeful suffering, Jeremiah 15:11–15.

Righteous, unrighteous suffer equally, Ezekiel 21:4 (LB).

Suffering a means of learning, Matthew 11:28–30.

Blind to purpose of crucifixion, Matthew 16:21–23.

Suffering of innocent Savior, Luke 23:15–16.

Marks of suffering, Luke 24:40.

Persecution implements spread of Gospel, Acts 8:3–4.

Present suffering, coming glory, Romans 8:18.

Patience suffering, Romans 12:12.

Kept strong in Christ, 1 Corinthians 1:8–9.

Purpose of trouble, 2 Corinthians 4:17–18 (AB).

Bearing marks of Jesus, Galatians 6:17.

Privilege of suffering, Philippians 1:29–30 (AB).

Anticipating persecution in advance, 1 Thessalonians 3:4.

Suffering perfected Savior, Hebrews 2:10; 5:9 (CEV, LB).

Undeserved suffering, 1 Peter 2:19.

Attitude toward suffering, 1 Peter 4:1–2.

Suffering for Christ, 1 Peter 4:12–16.

All tears wiped away, Revelation 21:4.

See Commitment, Persecution.

SUFFICIENT

All-sufficient Lord, Isaiah 44:24.

God's righteousness lasts forever, Isaiah 51:8.

Nothing too hard for God, Jeremiah 32:27.

Needs supplied, Philippians 4:13–19.

Sufficient provision for godliness, 2 Peter 1:3.

See Provision.

SUFFOCATE

Death by suffocation, 2 Kings 8:15.
Soul suffocation, Job 7:15 (NASB).

SUFFRAGE

God's plan for women and their rights, Genesis 3:16.
Business woman, Acts 16:13–15.
Woman's role in marriage, 1 Corinthians 7:4.
See Equal Rights, Women's Rights.

SUGGESTION

Power of suggestion, Genesis 3:17 (Berk.).
Satanic suggestion, John 13:2 (LB).

SUICIDE

Better off dead, Genesis 27:46.
Royal suicide on battlefield, 1 Samuel 31:1–6.
Accused of murder for abetting suicide, 2 Samuel 1:1–16.
Disgruntled suicide, 2 Samuel 17:23.
Death by arson, 1 Kings 16:18.
Dying before one's time, Ecclesiastes 7:17.
Covenant with death, Isaiah 28:15–18.
Death of Judas, Matthew 27:3–5.
Demon suicide, Luke 8:26–34.
Man who almost killed himself, Acts 16:25–28.
Assisted suicide, Jonah 1:12 (Note 1 Samuel 31:4).
See Coup de Grace, Self-Destruction.

SUITOR See Courtship, Romance.

SUMMATION

Wise man's summation, Ecclesiastes 12:13–14.
See Resume.

SUMMER

Summer assured, Genesis 8:22.
Summer fruit, 2 Samuel 16:2 (NKJV).
Intense heat, Psalm 32:4.
Creator's design, Psalm 74:17.
Learn from the ants, Proverbs 6:6–8; 30:25.
Summer snow, Proverbs 26:1.
Tragic summer, Jeremiah 8:20.
Ripened fruit, Jeremiah 40:10–12.

Late June, Ezekiel 1:1 (LB).
Late August, Ezekiel 8:1 (LB).
Mid-May, Ezekiel 31:1 (LB).
Chaff on threshing floor, Daniel 2:35.
Summer house, Amos 3:15.
Approaching summer, Matthew 24:32; Mark 13:28; Luke 21:30.
See Seasons.

SUMMONS See Decree, Mandate.

SUN

Sun stood still, Joshua 10:12–13.
Reversal of sun's shadow, 2 Kings 20:9–11; Isaiah 38:7–8.
Tent for sun, Psalm 19:4 (See KJV).
Immune to sunstroke, sunburn, Psalm 121:6.
Sun up, sun down, Ecclesiastes 1:5.
Intensity of sun increased, Isaiah 30:26.
Sun turned to darkness, Joel 2:31.
Far from sight of sun, Micah 3:6 (CEV).
"Sun's light failed," Luke 23:45 (NRSV).
Brighter than sunshine, Acts 26:13.
See Astronomy, Morning, Sunset.

SUNDAY

No Sunday sales, Nehemiah 10:31; 13:16–17.
Sabbath observance, Isaiah 58:13–14; Matthew 12:1–13.
Day of resurrection, Matthew 28:1 (GNB); Luke 24:1; John 20:1.
Sabbath preparation, Mark 15:42.
Serving God seven days a week, John 5:16–17.
Regularly attending Sabbath worship, Acts 14:1; 17:2.
One day more sacred than another, Romans 14:5.
See Legalism, Sabbath.

SUN DIAL

Instructive shadow, Isaiah 38:8.

SUNRISE

"Cloudless sunrise," 2 Samuel 23:4 (LB).
See Morning, Quiet Time, Sun.

S

SUNSET

Accuracy of sunset, Psalm 104:19.
Frightening twilight, Isaiah 21:4.
Sunset healing, Luke 4:40.
See Night, Sun.

SUPERFICIAL

Pride, arrogance, 1 Samuel 2:3.
Laughter with aching heart, Proverbs 14:13.
Deceitful, malicious man, Proverbs 26:24–26.
Avoid superficial offerings, Isaiah 1:13.
Doing good beyond superficiality, Luke 6:27–36.
Superficial adults like children, Luke 7:31–32.
Lacking spiritual depth, John 6:66.
Superficial service, 1 Corinthians 3:10–15.
Judging by appearances, 2 Corinthians 10:7 (CEV).
See Hypocrisy, Phony, Pretense, Shallowness, Sham.

SUPERIORITY

God as first priority, Genesis 1:1.
Protected from superior enemy, Exodus 14:15–31.
Measure of holiness, Numbers 16:3–7.
The God greater than numbers, Deuteronomy 20:1–4.
Superior human wisdom, 1 Kings 4:29–34.
Claiming superiority, Psalm 35:26 (GNB).
Race not to swift or strong, Ecclesiastes 9:11.
Wrong, right boasting, Jeremiah 9:23–24.
God the creator, gods who perish, Jeremiah 10:11–12.
Knowing who is the Lord, Ezekiel 6:10, 14; 7:4, 9, 27; 12:16, 20; 13:9, 23; 14:11.
All one in Christ, Galatians 3:28.
Christ superior to angels, Hebrews 1:3–4.
See Majority.

SUPERLATIVE

Tens of thousands, 1 Samuel 18:7.
Great father, greater son, 1 Kings 1:47–48.
Great, mighty, awesome God, Nehemiah 9:32.
Love better than life, Psalm 63:3.

Measureless salvation, Psalm 71:15.
Immeasurable anticipations, Jeremiah 33:3.
Superlative thousands, Daniel 7:10; Revelation 5:11.
Superlative faith, Luke 7:9.
Beyond human conception, perception, 1 Corinthians 2:9.
Lavished with blessing, Ephesians 1:7–8.
Superlative riches, Ephesians 2:7.
Holy Spirit's superlative power within us, Ephesians 3:20–21.
Highest position, Philippians 2:9.
Surpassing greatness, Philippians 4:7–8.
Christ above all, Colossians 1:15–20.
Joy of problems, testing, James 1:2–4.
See Hyperbole.

SUPERNATURAL See Miracles.

SUPERSTITION

Ark of Covenant for good omen, 1 Samuel 4:3.
Dangerous gods of hills, 1 Kings 20:23.
Use of incense, Jeremiah 44:18.
Use of magic charms, Ezekiel 13:18.
Disciples thought to be gods, Acts 14:11–15.
Sign of the serpent, Acts 28:3–6.
See Magic, Séance, Sorcery, Spiritism.

SUPERVISION

Rebelling against supervision, Numbers 14:1–4.
Approval of parents, Numbers 30:3–5.
Faithful service without supervision, Philippians 2:12–13.
See Discipline, Guidance.

SUPPLICATION

Persistent prayer, 1 Samuel 1:20; 7:8; Philippians 4:6.
Looking persistently unto the Lord, Psalm 123:2.
Friend in need, Luke 11:5–8.
Supplication, Philippians 4:6 ("Supplication" translate "agonizing anticipation" in Swedish Bible, "begging" in German. Note Hebrews 5:7 NRSV).
See Intercession, Prayer.

SUPPLY

Unhappy with God's provision, Numbers 11:4–6.
Wife shortage, Judges 21:14.
Dying earth, Isaiah 51:6.
No wine at wedding, John 2:1–5.
Fully supplied, Philippians 4:19 (AB).
See Provision, Resource.

SUPPORT

Commission with encouragement, Deuteronomy 3:28.
Weak as spider's web, Job 8:14.
Divine support in troubled times, Psalm 14:4–5.
Two better than one, Ecclesiastes 4:9–12.
Overt financial support, 2 Corinthians 8:1–5.
Some pay, others receive, 2 Corinthians 11:7–8.
See Assistance.

SUPPRESSION

Futile effort to suppress truth, Jeremiah 38:1–6.
Suppression of miracle reports, Matthew 8:4.
Attempts to suppress resurrection of Jesus, Matthew 27:62–66; 28:11–15.
Suppressed demons, Mark 1:33–34.
Holy Spirit's suppression, 2 Thessalonians 2:7.
See Censure.

SUPREMACY

Prenatal superiority, Genesis 25:23.
Subservient sheaves, Genesis 37:5–7.
Hand on neck, Genesis 49:8.
Power in numbers, Numbers 22:2–4.
God who overcomes great enemies, Deuteronomy 20:1.
Apparent supremacy of enemy invalidated, Joshua 11:1–6.
Praising subject above king, 1 Samuel 21:11.
Immeasurable greatness of God, 2 Chronicles 6:12–19.
The God who speaks and acts, Isaiah 44:24–28.
No other God like the Lord, Isaiah 46:9.
Wrong, right boasting, Jeremiah 9:23–24.
God the Creator, gods who perish, Jeremiah 10:11–12.
Christ's supremacy over angels, Hebrews 1:4.
Sovereignty of Jesus over all earth, Revelation 1:5.
See Conquest.

SUPREME COURT

Jerusalem Supreme Court, Mark 15:1 (LB).

SURETY

Son's guarantee to father, Genesis 42:37.
Words of caution, Proverbs 6:1–5; 11:15; 22:26.
See Assurance, Confidence.

SURGERY

Circumcision at advanced age, Genesis 17:10–27.
Spiritual, physical circumcision, Colossians 2:11 (LB).
See Medicine, Therapy.

SURPRISE

Harvesters see ark of God, 1 Samuel 6:13.
Surprise arrow, Psalm 64:7 (AB).
"Wine of astonishment," Psalm 60:3 (KJV).
Awesome, unexpected acts of God, Isaiah 64:3.
Grapes in desert, Hosea 9:10.
Return of Christ at unexpected hour, Matthew 24:44.
Surprising sermon, Mark 1:22 (LB).
Frightened at sight of angel, Luke 1:11–12.
Surprised Pharisees, John 18:6.
Message heard by those who did not seek, Romans 10:20.
Like a thief, 2 Peter 3:10.
See Amazement, Awe, Serendipity, Speechless.

SURRENDER

Fortunes restored, Deuteronomy 30:1–3.
Partial blindness inflicted as disgrace, 1 Samuel 11:2–11.
Surrender to power of God, 1 Samuel 14:1–14.

S

Ammonites surrendered to David, 2 Samuel 10:1–19.

Total surrender, 1 Kings 20:1–6.

Surrender followed severe testing, Job 42:1–9.

Potter, clay, Isaiah 45:9; 64:8.

Reward for obedience, Isaiah 48:17–18.

Visible act of surrender, Jeremiah 2:37.

Listening in desperation, Jeremiah 38:14–28.

Spiritual surrender, Mark 8:33–35; Romans 12:1–2.

See Commitment, Defeat.

SURROGATE

Bearing child for another, Genesis 16:1–5; 21:9–11; 30:1–6.

Actual mother as surrogate, Exodus 2:1–9.

Surrogate mother among birds, Jeremiah 17:11.

SURVEILLANCE

"Eyes of the Lord," 2 Chronicles 16:9.

Satan's continual earth surveillance, Job 1:7.

Mankind observed from heavenly throne, Psalm 11:4.

Enemy surveillance, Psalm 56:6.

Window surveillance of street activity, Proverbs 7:6–13.

Temple surveillance, Mark 11:11.

Faithfulness without pastoral supervision, Philippians 2:12–13.

See Scrutiny.

SURVEY

Situation survey of doomed cities, Genesis 18:20–21.

Questions for spies on Canaan survey, Numbers 13:18–20.

Maddening survey, Deuteronomy 28:34.

Survey prior to plunder of royal treasures, Isaiah 39:1–6.

Thessalonian survey, 1 Thessalonians 3:1–11.

See Appraisal, Evaluation.

SURVEYOR

Measured for judgment, Lamentations 2:8.

SURVIVAL

People divided for protection, Genesis 32:6–8.

No graves in Egypt, Exodus 14:11.

Chance survival, 2 Samuel 8:2.

Protection against enemies of road, Ezra 8:21–23.

Survival of felled tree, Job 14:7–9.

The Lord on our side, Psalm 124:1–5.

Ask for ancient paths, Jeremiah 6:16.

Birds know seasons of migration, Jeremiah 8:7.

Empty cisterns, parched fields, Jeremiah 14:1–6.

Ten percent survival, Amos 5:3.

Contest enemy, seek peace terms, Luke 14:31–32.

Desiring food of pigs, Luke 15:16.

See Endurance, Tenacity.

SUSPICION

Negative, positive viewpoints, Numbers 13:17–33.

Proof of virginity, Deuteronomy 22:13–19.

Identification by manner of speech, Judges 12:5–6.

Wrongly suspecting woman of drunkenness, 1 Samuel 1:9–16.

Mistrusted men came to show condolence, 2 Samuel 10:1–4.

See Mistrust.

SUSTENANCE

Need for food, water, Job 22:7–8.

Wickedness, violence, Proverbs 4:17.

See Food, Provision.

SWAMPED

In over one's head, Psalm 40:12 (LB).

SWEAR See Cursing.

SWEETHEART

Wisdom a sweetheart, Proverbs 7:4 (LB).

See Engagement.

SWEETNESS

Tempting to taste, 1 Samuel 14:24–28.

Honey from rock, Psalm 81:16.

Eating too much honey, Proverbs 25:16.

See Ambrosia, Gourmet, Honey, Taste.

SWIFTNESS

Disciple who outran Peter, John 20:4.
See Athletics, Running.

SWIMMING

Spreading hands to swim, Isaiah 25:11.
Plunge into sea, Jonah 2:1–10.
Swim to freedom, safety, Acts 27:42–44.

SWINE

Bean pods for food, Luke 15:16 (Berk.).
See Pork.

SYMBOLISM

Symbolic rainbow, Genesis 9:12–17.
Hand under thigh, Genesis 24:2, 9.
Avoid symbols which hinder worship, Deuteronomy 16:21–22.
Symbol of judgment, forgiveness, 1 Chronicles 21:27–30.
Prophecy of boiling pot, Jeremiah 1:13–15.
Smashing jar from potter, Jeremiah 19:1–13.
Good figs, bad figs, Jeremiah 24:1–10.
Act of rebellious idolatry, Ezekiel 8:17.
Symbol of Holy Spirit's power, Zechariah 4:1–6.
Jesus washed feet of disciples, John 13:2–17.
Symbolic name for city, Revelation 11:8.
See Nonverbal, Visual.

SYMPATHY

Historic sympathy, Exodus 2:5–6.
Delegation sent to express condolence, 2 Samuel 10:1–2.
Suspicious condolence, 2 Samuel 10:1–4.
Those at ease have contempt for others, Job 12:5.
Vain search for sympathy, Psalm 69:20.
Divine sympathy, Psalm 78:39; 103:13; Isaiah 63:9.
Sympathy put into action, Isaiah 58:7.
Help in time of need, Luke 10:33–35; Acts 20:35.
Shared sorrow, John 11:19–33.
Tears of Jesus, John 11:35.
Bearing burdens of others, Galatians 6:2; Hebrews 13:3.

Remembering another's tears, 2 Timothy 1:4.
Divine empathy, Hebrews 4:15 (See GNB).
Truest form of sympathy, Hebrews 13:3.
Sympathy from a distance, Revelation 18:10.
See Caring, Compassion, Empathy, Involvement.

SYNAGOGUE

Danger in synagogue, Matthew 10:17; Luke 12:11.
Jesus ministered in synagogues, Matthew 12:9; Mark 1:21; John 6:59; 18:20.
Jesus' synagogue sermons, Luke 4:14–15 (LB).
Synagogue membership, John 9:22; 16:2.
Apostles witnessed in synagogues, Acts 13:5; 14:1; 18:19.
Former synagogue fanatic, Acts 26:11.
See Temple.

SYNCRETISM

No additional gods, Exodus 20:3, 23 (AB).
Jealous God forbids rivals, Exodus 34:14.
Confused mother, son, Judges 17:1–6.
No relationship between ark, god, 1 Samuel 5:1–5.
Using idol to provide deliverance, 1 Samuel 19:11–17.
Involvement with other gods, 1 Kings 11:4–6.
Heathen worship provided, 1 Kings 11:8.
Procedure to dilute faith of Israel, 1 Kings 12:25–33.
Appointing those unqualified to office of priest, 1 Kings 13:33.
Mixing paganism with worship of true God, 1 Kings 14:1–18.
Worthless idols, 1 Kings 16:25–26.
No God in Israel, 2 Kings 1:1–4.
Pagans, ministers, priests destroyed, 2 Kings 10:18–29.
Partial obedience, 2 Kings 15:1–4.
Worshiping the Lord, other gods, 2 Kings 17:33.
Defilement in sanctuary, 2 Chronicles 29:1–11.
Idol in temple, 2 Chronicles 33:7 (See LB).
True God seen as one of many gods, Isaiah 37:10.

S

Clearly stated divine rule, Isaiah 42:8.

No place for fallen gods, Isaiah 43:12–13.

Blending teaching of law with idolatry, Jeremiah 2:8.

None handle truth honestly, Jeremiah 5:1–2.

Defiling house of the Lord, Jeremiah 7:9–11.

Harm to those who dilute worship, Jeremiah 7:16–19.

Attempt to mix monotheism, idolatry, Ezekiel 14:3–5.

Do not involve idols in worship, Ezekiel 20:7–8.

Swear by the Lord and Molech, Zephaniah 1:4–6.

Marriage to daughter of foreign god, Malachi 2:11.

Worshiping created things, not Creator, Romans 1:21–25.

Cannot blend holiness with evil, 1 Corinthians 10:21.

Believers, unbelievers, 2 Corinthians 6:14–17.

Diluting Gospel message, Galatians 1:6–9.

Attempting to please legalists, Galatians 6:12.

Deceptive philosophy and human tradition, Colossians 2:8, 23.

Avoid those who dilute gospel message, 2 Thessalonians 3:6.

Confusion at church in Ephesus, 1 Timothy 1:3–7.

Blending secular with spiritual, 1 Timothy 6:3–10.

Turning from truth to myths, 2 Timothy 4:5.

Worldly adaption to life of believer, 1 John 2:15–17.

See Heresy.

SYNERGY

Walking in agreement, Amos 3:3.

SYNTHETIC

Synthetic procedures banned, Leviticus 19:19.

Blending wool and linen, Deuteronomy 22:11.

SYPHILIS

Epidemic stopped, Numbers 25:6–9 (See GNB).

T

TABLE

Furniture makers' specifications, Exodus 25:23; 37:10.

Bread set before the Lord, Exodus 40:22.

Responsible for care of table, Numbers 3:31.

Scraps under table, Judges 1:7.

Always welcome to table, 2 Samuel 9:7.

Table set for visiting queen, 1 Kings 10:4–5.

Large amount of table guests, 1 Kings 18:19; Nehemiah 5:17.

See Furniture.

TACT

Using tact in diplomacy, Genesis 41:33–46.

Tactful comparison of accomplishments, Judges 8:2.

Tense tact, 2 Samuel 2:4–5.

Waiting for proper time to speak, Job 32:4–6.

Anger turned away by gentle words, Proverbs 15:1.

"Word spoken at right circumstances," Proverbs 25:11 (NASB).

When to speak, Ecclesiastes 3:7.

Proper time, procedure, Ecclesiastes 8:5–6.

Taught tact, Isaiah 28:26.

"A word in season," Isaiah 50:4 (KJV).

Tactful response to false prophecy, Jeremiah 28:1–17.

Speaking with wisdom, tact, Daniel 2:14 (NIV).

Wise as snakes, innocent as doves, Matthew 10:16 (CEV).

Response of Jesus to critics, Matthew 21:23–27; Mark 12:34.

Gracious words of Jesus, Luke 4:22.

Tact of Jesus with Samaritan woman, John 4:4–26.
Timely validation of ministry, Acts 23:6.
Relating to unbelievers, 2 Corinthians 2:15–16.
Avoidance of stumbling blocks, 2 Corinthians 6:3–13.
Speaking truth in love, Ephesians 4:15.
Tactful in conversation with others, Colossians 4:6.
Tact concerning debt, Philemon 18–19.
Dealing gently with those who need guidance, Hebrews 5:2.
Tact in times of duress, James 1:19–20.
Wisdom from heaven, James 3:17–18.
See Courtesy.

TACTICS

Military maneuver and ambush, Joshua 8:3–23.
Perfume for lady, Ruth 3:3.
Setting traps for men, Jeremiah 5:26.
See Military.

TAILOR

First garment makers, Genesis 3:7.
Clothing for high priest, Exodus 28:3.
Apparel not to be worn by opposite sex, Deuteronomy 22:5.
Mixing wool and linen, Deuteronomy 22:11.
Proper repair of garment, Matthew 9:16; Mark 2:21.
Matching patches on garment, Luke 5:36.
See Sewing, Wardrobe.

TALENT

Lost skill for farming, Genesis 4:9–12.
Musical talent a family tradition, Genesis 4:21.
Assumed lack of talent, Exodus 4:10–12 (See 6:30).
Talented minds, hands, Exodus 28:3; 31:3; 38:23; 1 Kings 7:14; 1 Chronicles 22:15–16; 2 Chronicles 2:13–14; 26:15.
Special gifts through Spirit of God, Exodus 31:1–5; 35:30–35.
God-given ability to produce wealth, Deuteronomy 8:18.
Elimination of blacksmiths, 1 Samuel 13:19.

Solomon multi-talented, songs, 1 Kings 4:32.
Cunning men, 1 Chronicles 22:15 (KJV).
Farmer cannot manage wild ox, Job 39:9–12.
Pen of skillful writer, Psalm 45:1.
God's blessing upon work of hands, Psalm 90:17.
Race not to swift or strong, Ecclesiastes 9:11.
Those wise in their own eyes, Isaiah 5:21.
Farmer's God-given skills, Isaiah 28:24–29.
Artist is mortal, Isaiah 44:11 (NRSV).
Skilled in doing evil, Jeremiah 4:22.
Men have talent but God is sovereign, Jeremiah 10:8–10.
Finest of young men chosen for service, Daniel 1:3–4.
Parable of talents, Matthew 25:14–30.
Those given much, those given little, Mark 4:24–25; Luke 12:48.
Neighbors did not expect divinity in Jesus, Luke 4:22–24.
Relationship between talent, God's call, Romans 11:29.
Function of body members, Romans 12:4–8; 1 Corinthians 12:14–20.
Gifts from God, 1 Corinthians 4:7.
Special talents, special tasks, Ephesians 4:7, 11–13 (LB).
Do not neglect your gift, 1 Timothy 4:14.
Fan gift of God into flame, 2 Timothy 1:6.
Holy Spirit designates gifts, Hebrews 2:4.
Prepared to succeed as believer, Hebrews 13:20–21.
Using one's gift for others' good, 1 Peter 4:10 (See AB).
See Ability, Capability, Skill.

TALKATIVE

Slow of speech, Exodus 4:10.
Windy words, Job 8:2.
Deceitful, malicious man, Proverbs 26:24–26.
Quick mouth, Ecclesiastes 5:2.
Words unwisely spoken, Ecclesiastes 5:6.
Only loud noise, Jeremiah 46:17.
Accused of babbling, Acts 17:18.
"Talking like a fool," 2 Corinthians 11:1 (LB).
See Loquacious.

T

TALL

Legs too long, Leviticus 21:18 (Berk.).
Towering enemies, Numbers 13:33; Deuteronomy 2:21.
King-sized bed, Deuteronomy 3:11.
Bearing of prince, Judges 8:18.
Stature of King Saul, 1 Samuel 10:23–24.
Nine feet tall, 1 Samuel 17:4.
Short bed, narrow blanket, Isaiah 28:20.
See Giant, Physique.

TAME

Noah and dove, Genesis 8:8–9.
Future harmony of nature, Isaiah 11:6–9.
Training wild animals, James 3:7.
See Animals, Domesticate.

TAN

"Sun has gazed on me," Song of Songs 1:6 (NRSV).

TANGIBLE

Clear communication, Numbers 12:4–8.
The Lord's demands within reach, Deuteronomy 30:11.
Faith more important than things tangible, 2 Corinthians 5:7.
Intangible made tangible, Hebrews 11:3 (See GNB).
Seen and touched, 1 John 1:1.
See Clarity, Comprehension.

TANTALIZE

Tantalizing questions, Genesis 3:1 (LB).
Wiles of evil woman, Judges 16:4–20.
Perfume for lady, Ruth 3:3.
Haughty women of Zion, Isaiah 3:16–17.
Guilt of influencing others to sin, Luke 17:1.
See Seduction.

TARGET

The Lord's demands within reach, Deuteronomy 30:11.
Used for target practice, Job 16:12 (GNB).
Human target, Lamentations 3:12.
Using faulty bow, Hosea 7:16.
See Objective.

TASK *See Assignment, Duty, Responsibility.*

TAN

TASTE

Sampling food offered for sacrifice, 1 Samuel 2:13–14.

Unpalatable food, 2 Kings 4:40.

Special Bethlehem water, 1 Chronicles 9:15–19.

Salt enhances taste, Job 6:6.

Gall of bitterness, Lamentations 3:15.

Calvary taste, Matthew 27:34, 48.

"Wonderful stuff," John 2:10 (LB).

See Food, Gourmet, Sweetness.

TATTOO

Tattooed hand, Isaiah 44:5 (AB).

TAUNT

Challenge to fight, 1 Samuel 14:12 (See LB).

Sleeping security, 2 Samuel 26:14–16 (LB).

Taunts like wounds, Psalm 42:10 (LB).

Poetic taunt, Isaiah 14:4–21 (CEV).

See Irony, Ridicule, Scoff.

TAXES

Percentage to government, Genesis 47:13–26; 1 Samuel 8:15; 2 Kings 23:35; Esther 10:1.

Twenty-five annual tons of gold, 1 Kings 10:14 (CEV).

Arrested for tax evasion, 2 Kings 17:4.

Clergy tax-free, Ezra 7:24.

Borrowing money to pay taxes, Nehemiah 5:4.

Tax revenue misused, Ecclesiastes 10:19 (AB).

Tax coin in fish mouth, Matthew 17:24–27 (Note: Jesus paid tax, v. 27).

Pagan, tax collector, Matthew 18:17.

Calling of tax collector, Mark 2:13–17; Luke 5:27–31.

"Tax collectors and other sinners," Mark 2:15 (CEV).

Correct procedure paying taxes, Mark 12:17.

Taxation, census, Luke 2:1–5 (See KJV).

Advice to tax collectors, Luke 3:12–13.

Give to government what is due, Luke 20:25.

Citizen's obligation, Romans 13:6–7.

See Government.

TEACHER

Divine instructor, Exodus 4:15; Deuteronomy 4:36; Psalms 25:12; 32:8; Isaiah 28:26; 48:17.

Commissioned to teach, Leviticus 10:11.

Need for teacher, 2 Chronicles 15:3.

Itinerant teachers, 2 Chronicles 17:7–9.

Teacher knows subject, Psalm 94:10.

Worthy things to say, Proverbs 8:6.

Good teaching vocabulary, Ecclesiastes 12:9–10.

Teacher disciplines, Jeremiah 32:33.

Teaching truth, Malachi 2:6.

Amazed at Jesus' teaching, Mark 1:22 (CEV).

Promised Counselor, John 14:16–17, 26; 16:5–14.

Need for a teacher to explain truth, Acts 8:30–31.

Teachers of first Christians, Acts 11:26.

Abundance of teachers, Acts 15:35.

Teachings faithfully followed, 1 Corinthians 11:2.

Divine calling, Ephesians 4:11.

Master teacher, Ephesians 4:20 (LB).

Taught by God Himself, 1 Thessalonians 4:9.

Misinformed teachers, 1 Timothy 1:7.

Teachers needing teaching, Hebrews 5:12.

Teachers should be select group, James 3:1.

See Education, Learning, School.

TEACHING

Home school, Exodus 10:2; Deuteronomy 6:6–9; Isaiah 38:19; Ephesians 6:4.

Children taught to worship, Exodus 12:26–27.

Remembering, following divine teaching, Deuteronomy 4:9.

Duty of parents to children, Deuteronomy 11:1–7.

Words put into the mouth, Deuteronomy 31:19 (KJV).

Teaching Divine instructions, Joshua 23:6; 1:8.

God reveals Himself through His Word, 1 Samuel 3:21.

Clarity in teaching, Nehemiah 8:8 (NIV).

"My teaching is pure," Job 11:4 (NASB).

Divine instruction despised, Psalm 50:17.

Historical resume, Psalm 78:1–72.

Purity taught to youth, Psalm 119:9.

Enlightening pedagogy, Psalm 119:130.

Learning objectives for book of Proverbs, Proverbs 1:1–6.

Advice of King Solomon to son, Proverbs 1:8–19.

Knowledge made acceptable, Proverbs 15:2 (NASB).

Pleasant words enhance teaching, Proverbs 16:21.

Repetition for emphasis, Isaiah 28:13.

Understanding brings terror, Isaiah 28:19.

Technique illustrated by farmer, Isaiah 28:23–28.

Instructed tongue, Isaiah 50:4 (NIV).

God's word will not return empty, Isaiah 55:10–11.

Boldness of speech, a gift from God, Jeremiah 1:6–10.

Proclaiming dreams, not God's Word, Jeremiah 23:25–32.

Spiritual teaching discontinued, Lamentations 2:9 (GNB).

Moral teaching by immoral example, Ezekiel 23:48 (KJV).

Lips that preserve knowledge, Malachi 2:7.

Teaching untruth, Matthew 5:19.

Teacher-student rapport, Matthew 10:24–25.

Teaching with authority, Mark 1:22, 27.

Hearing, not understanding, Mark 4:11–12.

Thorough teaching, Mark 4:34.

Causing child to go astray, Mark 9:42.

Living Word pierces heart, Luke 2:34–45.

Commission to preach, teach, Luke 4:14–21.

Spiritual dropouts, John 6:60–69.

Theme of post-resurrection apostles, Acts 4:2.

Need for teacher, Acts 8:26–39.

Teaching duo, Acts 11:22–26.

Teaching from experience, Acts 14:19–22.

Use of reasoning, Acts 17:1–3.

Teaching honor students, Acts 17:11–12.

Eighteen-month curriculum, Acts 18:11.

"Wonderful Bible teacher," Acts 18:24 (LB).

Teaching with accuracy, Acts 18:25.

Sad parting with students, Acts 20:25–38.

Compassionate teaching, Acts 20:31 (GNB).

Bold teaching, Acts 28:31 (NIV).

Uphold teaching standard, Romans 6:17 (AB).

Spiritual truth in human terms, Romans 6:19.

Cooperative learning, Romans 15:14.

Teacher's request for prayer, Romans 15:31–32.

Eloquence unnecessary, 1 Corinthians 2:1.

Faithful students, 1 Corinthians 11:2.

Understandable teaching, 2 Corinthians 1:13–14.

Teaching with conviction, 2 Corinthians 4:13.

Teaching without eloquence, 2 Corinthians 11:6.

Student shares with teacher, Galatians 6:6.

Vital teaching, Ephesians 4:22–24.

Praying for those who teach, Ephesians 6:19–20.

Repetition for emphasis, Philippians 3:1; 2 Peter 1:12–15.

God's Word in its fullness, Colossians 1:25–26.

Pupils' spiritual development, Colossians 2:1–5.

Reinforced teaching, 1 Thessalonians 1:4–5.

Letting message ring out, 1 Thessalonians 1:8.

Teacher's joy, crown, 1 Thessalonians 2:17–19.

Praise to God for success in ministry, 1 Thessalonians 3:8–10.

Teaching by speech, writing, 2 Thessalonians 2:15.

Teaching those who adhere to law, 1 Timothy 1:3–11.

Teaching objective, 1 Timothy 1:5 (NASB, NRSV).

Purpose of becoming teacher, 1 Timothy 2:1–7.

Quality of a leader, 1 Timothy 3:2.

Teaching by correspondence, 1 Timothy 3:14–15.

Caution concerning false teaching, 1 Timothy 4:1–6.

Devoted to gift of teaching, 1 Timothy 4:13–14.

Teacher's salaries, 1 Timothy 5:17 (CEV).

Pride in false doctrine, 1 Timothy 6:3–5.

Teachers teaching teachers, 2 Timothy 2:1–4.

Cancerous teaching, 2 Timothy 2:17 (AB).

Classroom dispute, 2 Timothy 2:23–26.

Effective pre-school, 2 Timothy 3:15.

Proper teaching for all ages, Titus 2:1–10.

No grounds for criticizing teacher, Titus 2:7–8 (CEV).

Teaching with authority, Titus 2:15.

Difficult explanation, Hebrews 5:11 (AB, CEV).

Slow learners, Hebrews 5:11–14.

Depth perception in teaching, learning, Hebrews 6:1–3.

Taught with clarity, Hebrews 9:8 (GNB).

Teachers should be select group, James 3:1 (CEV).

When oral teaching exceeds writing, 2 John 12; 3 John 13–14.

See Children, Education, Learning Objectives, Reinforcement.

TEAMWORK

Taking care of business, Deuteronomy 20:5–9.

Leadership for those in trouble, 1 Samuel 22:2.

Working diligently together, Nehemiah 4:6.

Iron sharpens iron, Proverbs 27:17.

Two better than one, Ecclesiastes 4:9–10.

Skilled crews on ships, Ezekiel 27:8–9.

Disciples sent out two-by-two, Mark 6:7.

Healing of paralytic man, Luke 5:17–26.

Set apart, laying on of hands, Acts 13:1–3.

Teamwork in reaching others, 1 Corinthians 3:6–9.

Body as unit, 1 Corinthians 12:12–30.

See Cooperation, Partnership, Unity.

TEARS

Cry for help, Judges 10:14 (CEV).

Phony tears, Judges 14:11–19.

Tears of gratitude, 1 Samuel 20:41.

Fear of confessing wrong to another, 1 Samuel 24:16–17.

Weeping until exhausted, 1 Samuel 30:4; Psalm 6:6.

Altered countenance, Job 16:16.

Red-eyed from weeping, Psalm 31:9 (LB).

Weeping as part of prayer, Psalm 39:12.

Loss of appetite, Psalm 42:3.

"Bread of tears," Psalm 80:5.

Burdened soul-winning, Psalm 126:6.

"Fountain of tears," Jeremiah 9:1 (See LB).

Unable to shed tears, Lamentations 2:11 (LB).

Rivers of tears, Lamentations 3:48 (NRSV).

Peter cried hard, Matthew 26:75 (CEV).

Redeemer's tears, Luke 19:41.

Weeping en route to crucifixion, Luke 23:27 (CEV).

Tears of compassion, Philippians 3:18 (CEV).

See Anguish, Emotion, Grief, Sorrow.

TECHNIQUE

Formula for success, Joshua 1:8.

Purifying bad water, 2 Kings 2:19–22.

Wailing technique, Jeremiah 9:20.

Satan's technique, Luke 4:13.

See Skill.

TEEN AGE *See Youth.*

TEETH

Making lions harmless, Psalm 58:6.

Gnashing teeth, Psalm 112:10; Matthew 8:12; 13:42, 50; 22:13; Mark 9:18; Luke 13:28.

Sour taste, Proverbs 10:26.

Teeth like swords, Proverbs 30:14.

Lost inability for chewing, Ecclesiastes 12:3 ("Grinders" may refer to teeth of old man.)

Gnashing teeth, Lamentations 2:16.

"Ground their teeth," Acts 7:54 (NRSV).

See Dentistry.

TELEVISION

Suggested guidance in use of television, Proverbs 14:7 (GNB); Matthew 6:22, 23; Romans 12:2; Ephesians 5:15–6; Philippians 4:8; 1 Thessalonians 5:21–2.

TEMPER

Angry revenge, Deuteronomy 19:6.

"Bad tempered boor," 1 Samuel 25:25 (LB).

"Hot head," 2 Samuel 20:1 (LB).

Very angry, Nehemiah 5:6.

Divine anger, Psalm 6:1 (LB).

The Lord's momentary temper, Psalm 30:5.

The Lord slow to anger, Psalm 86:15; Nahum 1:3.

Quick temper, Proverbs 14:29.

Temper control, Proverbs 16:32.

Violent temper penalized, Proverbs 19:19 (NRSV).

Avoid angry man, Proverbs 22:24.

Furious anger, Daniel 3:19 (LB).

God's temper, Hosea 11:9 (CEV).

"Angry tempers," 2 Corinthians 12:20 (NASB).

Be slow to anger, James 1:19–20.

See Attitude, Anger, Emotion, Hostility, Resentment.

TEMPERAMENT

Ox, donkey cannot plow together, Deuteronomy 22:10.

Hot-headed fool, Proverbs 14:16–17; Ecclesiastes 7:9.

Controlling temper major conquest, Proverbs 16:32.

Beware the hot-tempered man, Proverbs 22:24–25.

Lacking self-control, Proverbs 25:28.

Fool, wise man, Proverbs 29:11.

Anger condemned by Jesus, Matthew 5:22.

Even temperament, James 1:19–20.

See Conduct, Frame-of-Reference, Lifestyle, Personality.

TEMPERANCE

Sexual restraint, 1 Samuel 21:4–5.

Led astray by alcohol, Proverbs 20:1.

Excess food, drink cause laziness, Proverbs 23:20–21.

Lingering over wine, Proverbs 23:30–33.

Best of meats, finest wine, Isaiah 25:6.

Laid low by wine, Isaiah 28:1–7.

Refusal to drink wine, Jeremiah 35:1–14.

Nazirites forced to drink wine, Amos 2:12.

Not heavy drinkers, 1 Timothy 3:3, 11 (CEV).

Drinking wine, 1 Timothy 5:23.

See Abstinence.

TEMPEST *See Storm, Wind.*

TEMPLE

Realization, vision, 2 Samuel 7:1–7; 1 Chronicles 22:1–19.

Temple construction, 1 Kings 6:1–37.

Jerusalem captured, temple razed, 2 Kings 24:10–13; 25:9–17.

Temple restoration, Ezra chapters 1–3.

Temple porches, Luke 20:1 (AB).

The curtain, Christ's body, Hebrews 10:20.

See Synagogue.

TEMPORAL

Abundant blessings, Genesis 24:35; Isaiah 30:23; Amos 9:13.

Putting physical needs spiritual, Exodus 16:1–30.

Promise of good health, Exodus 23:25.

Too much emphasis on temporal, Numbers 11:4–11.

Promised temporal blessings, 1 Kings 3:13.

Immeasurable greatness of God, 2 Chronicles 6:12–19.

Bread and honey, Psalm 81:16.

Evaluation of life, Ecclesiastes 5:15.

Spiritual blessing key to temporal, Matthew 6:33.

Earth marriage, Heaven relationships, Mark 12:18–27.

Limited temporal happiness, Luke 6:24 (LB).

Earth, sky flee from eternal, Revelation 20:11.

See Materialism, Physical.

TEMPORARY

Death always imminent, 1 Samuel 20:3; Isaiah 2:22.

All leave possessions to others, Psalm 49:10, 16–20.

Built-in obsolescence, Psalm 49:12.

Passing breeze, Psalm 78:39.

We are dust, Psalm 103:14.

Life like morning mist, James 4:14 (NIV).

Temporary grief, trials, 1 Peter 1:6.

Human body as a tent, 2 Peter 1:13.

See Death, Transient.

TEMPTATION

Tantalizing questions, Genesis 3:1 (LB).

Satanic persuasion, Genesis 3:1–6; Matthew 4:3–11; 2 Corinthians 2:11.

Handling temptation, Genesis 4:7.

Resisting temptation, Genesis 39:6–10.

Personal responsibility in temptation, Deuteronomy 11:16.

Visual temptation, Joshua 7:21.

Hedonistic inclinations, 1 Kings 11:1, 4.

Resolute response to wife's urging, Job 2:9–10.

Temptation refuge, Psalm 46:1 (AB).

Overtly resisting temptation, Proverbs 1:10–17.

Facility for resisting temptation, Proverbs 2:10–12, 16.

Playing with fire, Proverbs 6:27–29.

Man who pleases God escapes immorality, Ecclesiastes 7:26.

Made strong by God's power, Jeremiah 1:17–19.

Divine illustration to rebellious Israel, Jeremiah 35:1–16.

Prior resolution to resist temptation, Daniel 1:8.

Temptation of Jesus, Matthew 4:1–11 (Note Holy Spirit, v. 1).

Ministering angels, Matthew 4:11.

Temptation, tempter, Matthew 18:7 (LB).

Using Scripture to confront devil, Luke 4:1–13.

One-time-only temptation, Luke 4:7 (AB).

Satanic technique, Luke 4:13.

Temptation defined, Luke 17:1 (AB).

"Puny body" resistance, Romans 6:12 (LB).

Physical restraint, Romans 6:13.

Sin's allure, Romans 6:7 (LB).

Deliverance by faithful God, 1 Corinthians 10:13.

"Outwitted by Satan," 2 Corinthians 2:11 (NRSV).

Deny the devil, Ephesians 4:27 (GNB).

"Schemes of the devil," Ephesians 6:11 (NASB).

Standing at end of struggle, Ephesians 6:13.

Shield of faith, Ephesians 6:16.

Supporting and surveying one another, 1 Thessalonians 3:5.

Resisting ungodliness and passions, Titus 2:11–12.

Jesus tempted to help those tempted, Hebrews 2:18; 4:15.

Anchor for soul, Hebrews 6:18–20.

Promised deliverance, Hebrews 7:23–28.

God tempts no one, James 1:13–14.

Evil desires, 2 Peter 1:4.

Sure rescue in the Lord, 2 Peter 2:7–9.

Battleground in which Satan attacks, 1 John 2:15–17.

Work of the devil, 1 John 3:7–8.

Keep yourself from idols, 1 John 5:21.

Immorality in Body of Christ, Revelation 2:20.

See Lust, Seduction.

TEMPTRESS

Eve's influence over Adam, Genesis 3:6.

Wife, daughter, Deuteronomy 13:6.

Samson, Delilah, Judges 16:1–31.

David, Bathsheba, 2 Samuel 11:2–5.

Wanton weakness of world's wisest man, 1 Kings 11:1–4.

Wife's urging to evil, 1 Kings 21:25; Job 2:9–10.

Folly of temptress, Proverbs 5:3–5; Ezekiel 13:18–19; Mark 6:22.

Flirtation, Isaiah 3:16.

See Flirtation, Seduction.

TEN COMMANDMENTS

Cited, repeated, Exodus 20:3–17; Deuteronomy 5:7–21.

Ten Commandments rewritten, Exodus 34:1.

Contemporized version, Deuteronomy 5:6–22 (CEV).

Moses evaluated Sinai, Deuteronomy 33:1–2.

TENACITY

Unending faithfulness, Joshua 24:14.

Resisting exhaustion, Judges 8:4.

Satanic view of man's motivations, Job 2:1–10.

Survival of felled tree, Job 14:7–9.

The Lord on our side, Psalm 124:1–5.

Small but tenacious, Proverbs 30:24–28.

Race not to swift or strong, Ecclesiastes 9:11.

Tenacity of those who live by faith, Hebrews 12:1–3.

Reward for Job's patience, James 5:11.

See Perseverance, Persistence, Strength, Survival.

TENDER-HEARTED

Testing divine patience, Numbers 14:18.

Gentleness of strong man, Ruth 3:5–15.

Demonstrated concern, 2 Chronicles 28:15; Luke 10:25–37; Acts 28:2.

Father's tender heart, Psalm 103:13.

Food for the hungry, Isaiah 58:7.

Concern for others, Isaiah 63:9.

Joseph's tenderness to Mary, Matthew 1:19.

Tenderness of Jesus, John 11:35–36; Hebrews 4:15.

Living example, Acts 20:35.

Concern for the weak, Romans 15:1.

Shared burdens, Galatians 6:2.

Prison outreach, Hebrews 13:3.

Orphans, widows, James 1:27.

Caring, Compassion.

TENDERNESS

Tender son, Proverbs 4:3 (NASB).

TENSION

Constant anxiety, Deuteronomy 28:66–67.

Rest in the Lord's protection, Deuteronomy 33:12.

Desire for peace, security, 2 Kings 20:19.

"Inward agitation," Job 20:2 (NASB, NRSV).

Endless churning inside, Job 30:27 (CEV).

Trusting the Lord whatever circumstances, Psalm 3:1–8.

Rest without tension, Psalm 4:8.

Wrestling one's thoughts, Psalm 13:2, 5 (NIV).

Relaxation in the Lord, Psalm 37:7; Proverbs 19:23.

Be still and know, Psalm 46:10.

Fear of death, Psalms 55:4–5; 116:1–4.

Casting cares upon the Lord, Psalm 55:22.

Steadfast heart, Psalm 57:7; Proverbs 3:13–18.

Daily burden bearer, Psalm 68:19.

Danger coveting wicked's good fortune, Psalm 73:2–5.

Cry of distress, Psalm 77:2.

Consolation from anxiety, Psalm 94:19.

Deliverance from distress, Psalm 107:6.

Storm becomes as whisper, Psalm 107:29.

Release from anguish, Psalm 118:5.

Renewal through Scripture, Psalm 119:93.

Trust cannot be shaken, Psalm 125:1.

Prayer for instruction, confidence, Psalm 143:10.

Going through crucible, Proverbs 17:3.

Poor man sleeps better than rich man, Ecclesiastes 5:12.

Learn to banish anxiety, Ecclesiastes 11:10 (NIV).

Kept in perfect peace, Isaiah 26:3.

Seek quietness, trust, Isaiah 30:15.

Quietness and confidence, Isaiah 32:17; 35:3–4.

Wings like eagles, Isaiah 40:29–31.

Stomach in knots, Lamentations 1:20 (CEV).

Spirits lifted in time of tension, Lamentations 3:22–26.

Quiet rejoicing in the Lord, Zephaniah 3:17.

Rest for weary and burdened, Matthew 11:28–30.

Stress between evil and good, Romans 7:14–20.

Peaceful, Spirit-controlled mind, Romans 8:6.

Abundant joy and peace, Romans 15:13.

Divine deliverance, 1 Corinthians 10:13.

Turning to God of all comfort, 2 Corinthians 1:3–4.

Peace-filled mind, 2 Thessalonians 1:2 (LB).

God's peace available at all times, 2 Thessalonians 3:16.

Rest for people of God, Hebrews 4:9–11.

Promised help in time of trouble, Hebrews 4:14–16.

Frustrated desires, James 4:2.

Be self-controlled, 1 Peter 1:13.

Cast all cares upon the Lord, 1 Peter 5:7.

Abundant grace, peace, 2 Peter 1:2.

See Anxiety, Stress.

TENT

Tent community, Genesis 4:20.

Place of residence, Genesis 9:21; 12:8; 13:5; Exodus 18:7.

Objects of beauty, Numbers 24:5.

"Tent-dwelling women," Judges 5:24 (NRSV).

Commanded to live in tents, Nehemiah 8:14 (LB).

Protected tent, Psalm 91:10 (AB).

Shelter for shepherds, Isaiah 38:12; Jeremiah 6:3.

Famous tent maker, Acts 18:1–3.
See Residence.

TENURE

King Saul's long reign over Israel, 1 Samuel 13:1.
Long reign of King David, 2 Samuel 5:4.
Birds know seasons of migration, Jeremiah 8:7.
No permanent place, Jeremiah 16:1–13.
See Time.

TERMINAL *(Illness)*

Visiting one terminally ill, 2 Kings 13:14.
Sick and dying, Job 17:1 (LB).
Desiring death at home, Job 29:18.
Guidance when dying, Psalm 23:4 (LB).

Hoping for someone's death, Psalm 41:7–9 (LB).
Terminal illness, Isaiah 38:1.
Seeming inequity of death of righteous, Isaiah 57:1–2.
See Death.

TERMINATION

Debt cancelled every seven years, Deuteronomy 15:1.
Lamp of wicked, Job 18:5–6.
God pronounces "the end," Ezekiel 7:2.
"End of the Philistines," Amos 1:8 (CEV).
Conclusion of wrath of God, Revelation 15:1.
See Conclusion, Ending.

TERMINOLOGY

Quarreling over words, 2 Timothy 2:14.

TERMINOLOGY

TERRAIN

Rainless sky, parched earth, Leviticus 26:19–20.

Marking boundaries, Numbers 34:1–12.

Blessing in city, country, Deuteronomy 28:3.

Boasting of land possessed, Jeremiah 49:4.

Exceptionally large city, Jonah 3:3.

Level place in hilly area, Luke 6:17.

See Desert, Geography, Mountains, Territory, Valley.

TERRITORY

Entry refused into promised land, Numbers 14:35.

Footstep ownership, Joshua 1:2–4.

Lands of other nations, Psalm 111:6.

Small, insignificant greatness, Proverbs 30:24–28.

Those who live by sea, Zephaniah 2:5–6.

See Property.

TERROR

"Shaking with terror," Psalm 6:2 (NRSV).

Impending terror, Isaiah 7:17 (LB).

"Shake and shudder," Isaiah 32:11 (CEV).

"Carnival of terror," Lamentations 2:22 (GNB).

See Fear.

TERRORISM

Bodily mutilation, Judges 1:7; 1 Samuel 11:2–11.

Dangerous roads, Judges 5:6–7 (CEV); Jeremiah 6:25.

David as terrorist, 1 Samuel 27:6–12.

Intimidation of city, 2 Chronicles 32:18.

No fear of terror at night, Psalm 91:5; Song of Songs 3:8.

Security against attack, Psalm 124:1–5.

Travel mercies, Ezra 8:21–23.

Impending terror, Isaiah 24:17.

Surrounded by terror, Jeremiah 49:29.

Fearful events on earth, Luke 21:11–13.

Mob of bad characters, Acts 17:5–7.

Accused of being terrorist, Acts 21:38.

See Anarchy, Genocide, Mob Psychology, Plunder.

TESTIMONY

Backsliders a laughingstock, Exodus 32:25.

Invitation to hear, Psalm 66:16.

Testimony summation, Ecclesiastes 12:13–14.

We are the Lord's witnesses, Isaiah 43:10.

Tell what the Lord has done, Mark 5:18–19; Acts 5:20–21; 22:15.

Commission to witness, Acts 1:8.

Christ-centered testimony, Romans 15:18–19.

Worst of sinners a testimony to others, 1 Timothy 1:15–16.

Unashamed witness, 2 Timothy 1:8.

Constantly prepared to witness, 1 Peter 3:15.

See Evangelism, Soul-winning, Witness.

TESTING

Test of father's love to God, son, Genesis 22:1–14.

Evaluated through testing, Deuteronomy 8:2.

God permits testing to prove worth, Deuteronomy 13:1–4.

Divinely appointed testing, Job 1:7–8.

Helping others, failing himself, Job 4:1–5.

Tested to come forth as gold, Job 23:10.

Dual function of clouds, Job 37:13–14.

"Every storm of life," Psalm 32:7 (LB).

No immunity for righteous, Psalm 34:17.

Facing disaster with confidence, Psalm 57:1.

Desperate times, Psalm 60:3.

Refined like silver, Psalm 66:10.

"Bread of tears," Psalm 80:5.

Blessing of divine discipline, Psalm 94:12–13.

Going through crucible, Psalm 66:10; Proverbs 17:3.

Light dawns in darkness, Psalm 112:4.

Chastening but deliverance, Psalm 118:18.

Affliction turns us to Scripture, Psalm 119:71.

Do not falter in times of trouble, Proverbs 24:10; Ezekiel 21:13.

Dross from silver, Proverbs 25:4.

Gentle flowing waters or mighty flood, Isaiah 8:6–7.

Humility caused by anguish, Isaiah 38:15.

"For my own good," Isaiah 38:17 (CEV).

No need to fear danger, Isaiah 43:1–2.

Confidence in dark, Isaiah 50:10.

Testing people's ways, Jeremiah 6:27.

"Why is life easy for sinners?" Jeremiah 12:1 (CEV).

Spirits lifted, Lamentations 3:22–32.

Deliverance from fiery furnace, Daniel 3:16–17, 22–27.

Daniel in lions' den, Daniel 6:13–24.

Refuge for those who trust, Nahum 1:7.

Satanic testing, Matthew 4:1 (CEV).

Building upon rock or sand, Matthew 7:24–27.

Jesus makes burden light, Matthew 11:28–30.

"Life gets hard," Matthew 13:21 (CEV).

Faith of Canaanite woman tested, Matthew 15:21–28.

Teacher experiences what he teaches, Acts 14:19–22.

Purpose of suffering, Romans 5:3.

Everything in God's will, Romans 8:28; Ephesians 1:11–12.

Faithful God will deliver, 1 Corinthians 10:13.

Certain victory in Christ, 1 Corinthians 15:57–58.

Purpose of testing, 2 Corinthians 1:2–11.

Generosity in difficult times, 2 Corinthians 8:1–5.

"Do not fail the test," 2 Corinthians 13:6 (NASB).

Standing at end of struggle, Ephesians 6:13.

Shield of faith, Ephesians 6:16.

Adverse circumstances special blessing, Philippians 1:12.

Do everything with patience, Colossians 1:11 (NRSV).

Destined for persecution, trials, 1 Thessalonians 3:1–5.

Faith survives testing, 2 Thessalonians 1:4–5.

Made perfect through suffering, Hebrews 2:10.

Jesus tempted as we are, Hebrews 4:15.

Promised deliverance in Christ, Hebrews 7:23–28.

Confident now of fulfillment in future, Hebrews 11:13.

Faith survives, Hebrews 11:17. (LB)

Persecution as avenue of blessing, Hebrews 11:35.

Testing resisted short of shedding blood, Hebrews 12:4.

Disciplining trials, Hebrews 12:7 (NRSV).

Maturing value of testing, James 1:2–4, 12.

Positive result of testing, James 5:11.

Purpose of trials, grief, 1 Peter 1:6–7.

Do not fear suffering, Revelation 2:10.

The Lord disciplines those He loves, Revelation 3:19.

Satan given temporary power to persecute, Revelation 13:5–7.

See Affliction, Deliverance, Persecution, Suffering.

TEXTILES

Blue, purple, scarlet yarn, fine linen, Exodus 35:35.

Apparel worn by opposite sex, Deuteronomy 22:5.

Mixing wool, linen, Deuteronomy 22:11.

Combing flax for linen, Isaiah 19:9.

Extensive merchandising, Ezekiel 27:12–23.

See Clothing, Wardrobe.

THANKSGIVING

Harvest token, Leviticus 19:24; Deuteronomy 26:10; Proverbs 3:9–10.

Prayer after meal, Deuteronomy 8:10.

Prayer of gratitude, 2 Samuel 7:18–29.

Song of praise, 2 Samuel 22:1–51; Psalm 98:1.

Gratitude for Divine faithfulness and goodness, 1 Kings 8:14–21.

Songs of gratitude, Psalms 9:11; 33:2.

Perpetual gratitude, Psalm 35:28.

Value of sacrifice, offering, Psalm 50:23.

Thanking God for enduring love, Psalm 106:1.

Thanksgiving leads to witnessing, Psalm 107:1–3.

Refusing to glorify God for harvest, Jeremiah 5:24.

Gratitude to God for wisdom, Daniel 2:19–23.

Thankful for food, Joel 2:26.

Prayer of thanks before eating, John 6:11.

Key to answered prayer, Philippians 4:6.

Overflow with thankfulness, Colossians 2:6–7.

Thankful for everything, 1 Thessalonians 5:18.

See Gratitude, Praise.

THEATER

Rally cancelled in theater, Acts 19:29–31.

Christians on display, 1 Corinthians 4:9.

See Audiovisual, Drama.

THEOCRACY

The Divine plan, Exodus 24:1–7.

Lord over all, Deuteronomy 4:39; 5:25–29; 33:2–5; 1 Chronicles 29:12; Psalms 47:2; 135:6.

Taking credit for God's blessing, Judges 7:2–3.

Preferred theocracy, Judges 8:22–23.

Change from divine leadership to mortal, 1 Samuel 8:1–9.

Bridge between theocratic, temporal rule, 1 Samuel 15:1.

Monarch turning against the Lord's servants, 1 Samuel 22:17.

Leadership by hook, bit, 2 Kings 19:28.

Surest mode for guidance and success, Nehemiah 1:1–11.

Divine superiority over earthly monarchy, Proverbs 21:1.

Creator, Ruler of universe, Isaiah 40:11–17.

Earth filled with Divine glory, Habakkuk 2:14.

Coming theocracy, Revelation 19:6.

See Sovereignty.

THEOLOGY

Full gamut of theology, Genesis 1:1; Revelation 22:20–21.

Doctrine falls like rain, Deueronomy 32:2 (KJV).

Saying God is dead, Psalm 115:2 (LB).

God spoken of as "god" by pagan king, Isaiah 37:10.

Deceitful theology, Jeremiah 8:8.

Reading Bible in vain, John 5:39–40.

Wisdom of Jesus, John 7:14–15.

Concise purpose of divine revelation, John 20:30–31; 2 Timothy 3:16; 2 Peter 1:21.

Lacking theological training, Acts 4:13.

Theological dispute in secular courtroom, Acts 18:12–17.

Respect for Old Testament teaching, Acts 24:14–15.

Simplicity of message, 1 Corinthians 2:1–5.

Message of wisdom to mature Christians, 1 Corinthians 2:6.

Error of Galatian Christians, Galatians 3:1–5.

Succinct theology, Ephesians 4:5.

Egotistical theologians, 1 Timothy 1:3–7 (LB).

See Contextualization, Cult, Error, Heresy, Heterodoxy, Orthodoxy, Seminary, Syncretism, Trinity.

THEORETICAL

Theoretical love, 1 John 3:18 (AB).

THERAPY

Deliverance from snakebite, Numbers 21:4–9.

Music therapy, 1 Samuel 16:14–23.

Body-to-body resuscitation, 2 Kings 4:32–37.

Ceremonial procedures, 2 Kings 5:8–14; John 5:7.

Scraping boils, Job 2:7–8.

Healing attitude, Proverbs 17:22.

Soothing oil, Isaiah 1:6; Luke 10:34.

Poultice of figs, Isaiah 38:21.

Soul therapy, Jeremiah 6:16.

No balm in Gilead, Jeremiah 8:22.

Incurable ailment, Jeremiah 30:12–13.

Many remedies, no healing, Jeremiah 46:11.

Therapeutic leaves, Ezekiel 47:12; Revelation 22:2.

Healing on Sabbath opposed by Pharisees, Luke 13:10–17.

Use of wine, 1 Timothy 5:23.

Efficacy of prayer, James 5:14.

See Medicine.

THESIS

Unfailing promises, Joshua 23:4.

Concise thesis of Gospel, 1 Timothy 4:9–10.

See Opinion, Viewpoint.

THIEF

Eat but do not take away, Deuteronomy 23:24.

Honest weights and measurements, Deuteronomy 25:13–16.

Bandit's poverty, Proverbs 6:11 (Berk.).

Disgrace of being caught, Jeremiah 2:26.

Riches gained unjustly, Jeremiah 17:11.

Honor among thieves, Jeremiah 49:9.

Preferred thieves, Obadiah 1:5–6 (LB).

Thieves dig through, Matthew 6:19–20 (Berk.).

Temptation of tax collectors and soldiers, Luke 3:12–14.

Mark of conversion, Ephesians 4:28.

See Plunder, Stealing.

THINKING

Personal evaluation, Psalm 119:59.

Danger of evil thoughts, Jeremiah 4:14 (LB).

God's law in mind, heart, Jeremiah 31:33.

Thinking known to God, Ezekiel 11:5 (LB).

God's thoughts, Amos 4:13 (CEV).

"Collect your thoughts," Zephaniah 2:1 (AB).

Polluted thoughts, Mark 7:20 (LB).

"Long thoughts," Luke 1:66 (LB).

Revealing thoughts of heart, Luke 2:34–35; Hebrews 4:12.

Poisoning minds, Acts 14:2.

Natural, Spirit-controlled thinking, Romans 8:6–8.

Thought renewal, Romans 12:2–3 (CEV).

Thinking clarified, Philippians 3:15 (CEV).

Mental attitude dictates behavior, Philippians 4:8–9.

Peril of evil thoughts, Colossians 1:21 (CEV).

Fix thoughts on Jesus, Hebrews 3:1 (NIV).

Prepare minds for action, 1 Peter 1:13.

God searches mind, heart, Revelation 2:23.

See Attitude, Brain, Frame-of-Reference, Thought.

THIN-SKINNED

Homicidal jealousy, Genesis 4:3–16.

Thin-skinned brothers, Genesis 37:3–4.

Thin-skinned racist, Esther 5:9–13.

Disease of envy, Proverbs 14:30.

Busy homemaker upset, Luke 10:38–42.

Thin-skinned Pharisee, Luke 13:13–17.

Prodigal son's jealous brother, Luke 15:25–32.

Unable to hear rebuke, Acts 7:51–58.

Leadership clash between Barnabas, Saul, Acts 15:36–40.

See Attitude, Covet, Envy, Jealousy.

THIRST

Water for thirsty child, Genesis 21:14–19.

Importance of well in dry country, Genesis 21:25–31; 26:12–17.

Singing at watering places, Judges 5:11.

Strong man's need for liquid, Judges 15:17–19.

Thirst for good water, 2 Samuel 23:15–17 (LB).

God offers joyful river, Psalm 36:8.

Spiritual thirst, Psalm 42:1–4.

Awakening to thirsty reality, Isaiah 29:8.

Burning sand becomes pool, Isaiah 35:7.

Parched tongues, Isaiah 41:17

Israel turned away from living water, Jeremiah 2:13–18.

Poisoned water, Jeremiah 8:14; 23:15.

Empty jars return from cisterns, Jeremiah 14:3.

Springs that fail, Jeremiah 15:18.

Children without food and drink, Lamentations 4:4.

Water for sale, Lamentations 5:4.

Scant rainfall, Amos 4:7–8.

Cup of cold water, Matthew 10:42.

Rivers of living water, John 7:38.

Holy Spirit as satisfying drink, 1 Corinthians 12:13.

Springs of living water, Revelation 7:16–17.

See Milk, Water.

THORNS

Thorns, sin's curse, Genesis 3:18; Hebrews 6:8.

Thistle, tree, 2 Kings 14:9.

Judgment upon harvest, Job 31:40.

Fuel for cooking, Psalm 58:9; Ecclesiastes 7:6.

Flash fire, Psalm 118:12.

Blemished altars, Hosea 10:8.

Thorn hedge, Micah 7:4.

Fruit not found on thornbush, Matthew 7:16.

Choking thorns, Matthew 13:7.

Crown of thorns, Matthew 27:28–29 (Genesis 3:17–18).

THOROUGH

Taking care of business, Deuteronomy 20:5–9.

Thorough reading of the law, Joshua 8:34–35.

Nehemiah's skill in rebuilding wall, Nehemiah 6:1.

Thoroughly keeping divine commands, Proverbs 7:2.

Making most of every opportunity, Ephesians 5:15–16.

See Dependability.

THOUGHT

Wicked thought, Deuteronomy 15:9; Proverbs 15:26; Jeremiah 4:14; Matthew 9:4; 15:19.

Thoughts pleasing to God, Psalm 19:14.

Divine introspection, Psalm 26:2; Jeremiah 17:10.

Futile thoughts, Psalm 94:11.

Thought determines action, Proverbs 4:23 (GNB).

Warped minds, Proverbs 12:8.

Cost conscious thinking, Proverbs 23:7.

Thought control, Ecclesiastes 11:10.

Wicked thoughts, Jeremiah 4:14.

Self-evaluation, Haggai 1:5–6.

Relationship of thought and action, Romans 2:1–11.

Humility thinking, Romans 12:3.

How to have pure thoughts, Romans 13:14.

Out of one's mind, 2 Corinthians 5:13.

Things worth thinking about, Philippians 4:8.

Practice thought control, Colossians 3:1–12.

See Frame-of-Reference, Mind, Motivation, Thinking.

THOUGHTFUL

Providing for another's need, Ruth 2:15–16.

Thoughtful rescue, Jeremiah 38:7–13.

See Consideration.

THREAT

Threatened by deviates, Genesis 19:9.

Do not threaten, Genesis 31:24, 29 (GNB); Ephesians 6:9.

Wicked bend bows, Psalm 11:2.

Drawn sword, bent bow, Psalm 37:14.

Song of threat diminished, Isaiah 25:5.

Thousand flee from enemy, Isaiah 30:17.

Hezekiah intimidated, Isaiah 36:4–10.

Death threat to prophet, Jeremiah 26:1–16.

Threat of murder, Jeremiah 40:13–16; 41:1–2.

Only loud noise, Jeremiah 46:17.

Threat of death to friends, Daniel 3:8–15.

Dire threats, bold preaching, Acts 4:29.

Murderous threats, Acts 9:1.

Christ's example, 1 Peter 2:23.

See Intimidation, Menace, Warning.

THRIFT *See Frugality, Stingy.*

THUNDER

Thunderous judgment, Exodus 9:23.

Frightening thunder, 1 Samuel 7:10.

Special manifestation, 1 Samuel 12:16–18.

Heaven's thunder, Revelation 4:5; 16:18.

Articulate thunder, Revelation 10:3.

See Lightning.

TIDINGS

Destiny set for rebellious people, Numbers 14:35.

False prophets, Jeremiah 23:16–18.

Prophet's certainty of voice of the Lord, Jeremiah 32:1–12.

One message after another of bad news, Jeremiah 51:31–32.

Bearer of bad news, Ezekiel 33:21.

See Media, Tidings.

TIME

"Daytime, night time," Genesis 1:5 (LB).

"It came to pass," Genesis 4:3, 8 (NKJV).

Love makes time pass quickly, Genesis 29:14–20.

Small time segment, Genesis 47:9.

Night-long wind opened Red Sea, Exodus 14:21–22.

Wishing time to pass, Deuteronomy 28:67.

Time as mere shadow, 1 Chronicles 29:15.

Blotting out one night, Job 3:6.

How time flies, Job 7:6.

Rapid time passage, Job 9:26 (LB).

"Human years," Job 10:5 (NRSV).

Life passes quickly, Job 7:25; 9:25–26; 16:22; Psalm 89:47.

Life but a breath, Psalm 39:5.

No time in eternity, Job 24:1 (NRSV).

Our times in God's hands, Psalm 31:15.

Ancient skies, Psalm 68:32–33.

"Good old days," Psalm 77:5 (LB); Ecclesiastes 7:10.

Fleeting time, Psalm 89:47.

Thousand years as one day, Psalm 90:4 (LB); 2 Peter 3:8.

Life's time span, Psalm 90:10.

Calculated time, Psalm 90:12; Ephesians 5:15–16; Colossians 4:5.

Time to act, 119:126.

Generations pass, earth remains, Ecclesiastes 1:4.

Seek the Lord morning, night, Isaiah 26:9.

Day passes quickly, Jeremiah 6:4–5.

Covenant with day, night, Jeremiah 33:20–21.

"Day at a time," Matthew 6:34 (LB).

Time zones, Luke 17:30–35 (See Mark 13:35).

Beyond all time, John 1:1 (AB).

Coordinated time of miracle, John 4:46–53.

Man who waited thirty-eight years, John 5:1–9.

Eternal time, temporal time, John 7:6.

Brief moments, John 13:33 (LB).

"A little while," John 16:17–18.

Seven weeks pass, Acts 2:1 (LB).

Time is short, 1 Corinthians 7:29.

Rapid deterioration of human body, 2 Corinthians 4:16–18.

Fulfillment of times, Ephesians 1:9–10.

Making most of time, Ephesians 5:16 (NRSV).

Time, epochs, 1 Thessalonians 5:1 (NASB).

Beginning of time, 2 Timothy 1:9.

Years never end, Hebrews 1:12 (AB).

Meaning of "today" in God's reckoning, Hebrews 4:7.

Mist in time, James 4:14.

"The last hour," 1 John 2:18.

Timeless existence of God, Revelation 1:8.

No more delay, Revelation 10:6.

Satan's awareness of shortage of time, Revelation 12:12.

The beginning, end, Revelation 22:13.

See Eternity, Life, Mortality, Tenure.

TIMIDITY

Timidity of guilty people, Numbers 17:12–13.

Samuel reluctant to inform Eli of his vision, 1 Samuel 3:15–16.

Tongues stick to roof of mouth, Job 29:10.

The Lord on our side, Psalms 124:1–5; 139:1–18.

Timid to profess faith, John 12:42–43; Acts 5:13.

Fearful of personal safety, Acts 5:13–14.

Both timid and bold, 1 Corinthians 2:3; 2 Corinthians 10:1.

Encourage the timid, 1 Thessalonians 5:14 (See CEV).

Spirit of timidity, 2 Timothy 1:7.

No timidity because of Paul's chains, 2 Timothy 1:16–18.

See Apprehension, Fear, Qualms.

TIMING

Leave revenge to God's timing, 1 Samuel 26:1–11.

The Lord's timing, Psalm 119:126; Isaiah 49:8; 60:22.

Time for everything, Ecclesiastes 3:1–8.

Proper time, procedure, Ecclesiastes 8:5–6.

Time to prepare, time to plant, Isaiah 28:24–25.

Seeking at right time, Isaiah 55:6.

Mistake in timing, Haggai 1:2–5 (CEV).

Jesus could not die before His time, Luke 4:28–30.

Jesus offered no resistance to oppressors, Luke 22:47–53.

Time speeds by, Acts 25:13 (Berk.).

Perfect timing in Christ, Romans 5:6.

See Destiny, Fortuity.

TIRELESS

Tireless Heavenly Father, John 5:17.

See Creator, Energy.

TITHE

Tithe to Melchizedek, Genesis 14:18–20; Hebrews 7:1–2.

Pledge to give tithe, Genesis 28:22.

One-fifth to Pharaoh, Genesis 47:24–26.

Value of silver, Numbers 7:13–19; 10:2.

Tithing tithe, Numbers 18:26.

Tenth for personal consumption, Deuteronomy 14:22–23.

Welfare funds, Deuteronomy 14:28 (LB); 26:12.

Evil earnings forbidden, Deuteronomy 23:18.

Dependability when making pledge, Deuteronomy 23:23.

Tithe of tithes, Nehemiah 10:38 (KJV).

Meaningless offerings, Isaiah 1:13; Matthew 23:23.

Challenge to tithe, Malachi 3:6–10.

Tithing without good spiritual conduct, Luke 11:42.

"Pick of the heap," Hebrews 7:4 (AB).

See Giving, Offering, Stewardship.

TITLE

Leaders called dukes, Genesis 36:15–18 (KJV).

"King of the Jews," John 19:19–22.

See Identity, Name.

TODAY

Living for today in God's favor, Ecclesiastes 9:7.

The "now" of Salvation, 2 Corinthians 6:2.

"Today" in God's reckoning, Hebrews 4:7.

See Now.

TOGETHERNESS

Wrong kind of togetherness, Exodus 23:2; Numbers 11:4–10.

Avoid togetherness with heathen, Deuteronomy 18:9.

People working diligently together, Nehemiah 4:6.

Glorify the Lord together, Psalm 34:3.

Iron sharpens iron, Proverbs 27:17.

Like teacher, like student, Luke 6:40.

See Cooperation, Rapport, Teamwork.

TOILET

Primitive toilet, Deuteronomy 23:12–13 (CEV).

See Hygiene, Sanitation.

TOKEN

Promise in sky, Genesis 9:12–13.

Circumcision, Genesis 17:11.

Token of love between brothers, Genesis 33:1–11.

Sign of blood, Exodus 12:13.

Token of divine provision, Exodus 16:32–34.

Harvest token, Leviticus 23:9–13.

Removal of sandal, Ruth 4:7–8.

King's token piety, Jeremiah 37:1–3.

Break bow, Jeremiah 49:35.

One who dipped his hand, Matthew 26:23–25.

See Nonverbal Communication, Visual.

TOLERANCE

Tolerant of foreigners, Exodus 23:9 (CEV).

Unwilling to tolerate food, Numbers 11:4–6.

Tolerating ridicule, Psalm 123:3–4.

Slow to anger, great in power, Nahum 1:3.

Attitude toward lost, Matthew 9:10.

"Tolerance of Jesus for sleeping disciples," Matthew 26:37–46.

Those of differing views, Mark 9:38–39; Luke 9:49–50; Philippians 1:17–18.

Tolerating opinions of others, Romans 14:1–8.

"Put up with anything," 2 Timothy 2:10 (CEV).

See Patience, Understanding.

TOMB

Choicest tombs, Genesis 23:6.

Unknown tomb of Moses, Deuteronomy 34:6.

Self-made tomb, 2 Chronicles 16:14.

Garden burial, 2 Kings 21:26.

Graves hewn out of rock, Isaiah 22:16.

Desecrated tombs, Amos 2:1 (LB).

The empty tomb, Matthew 28:1–10; Mark 16:1–7; Luke 24:1–8; John 20:1–9.

See Burial, Grave.

TOMBSTONE

Rachel's pillar, Genesis 35:20.
Absalom's memorial to himself, 2 Samuel 18:18.
Prophet's resting place, 2 Kings 23:16–18.
See Memorial.

TOMORROW

Destiny set for rebellious people, Numbers 14:35.
Tomorrow coming, Proverbs 4:18.
Over-confidence about tomorrow, Proverbs 27:1; James 4:14.
Future tomorrow established, Acts 17:31; Romans 2:16.
See Future.

TONGUE

Spreading false reports, Exodus 23:1.
Rabble of complaint, Numbers 11:4–6.
Criticizing those the Lord has not denounced, Numbers 23:8.
Talk about spiritual matters, Deuteronomy 6:4–7.
Stewardship of speech, Deuteronomy 23:23.
Pride, arrogance, 1 Samuel 2:3.
Crushed with words, Job 19:2.
Disciplined tongue, Psalm 34:13; Proverbs 13:3 (See LB); 21:23.
Purity of speech, Proverbs 4:24.
Silver-tongued, Proverbs 10:20.
Words like rare jewel, Proverbs 20:15.
Word aptly spoken, Proverbs 25:11.
Deceitful, malicious man, Proverbs 26:24–26.
Vileness from every mouth, Isaiah 9:17.
Sticking out tongue, Isaiah 57:4.
Like deadly arrow, Jeremiah 9:8.
Wrong, right boasting, Jeremiah 9:23–24.
Critical tongues made silent, Luke 20:20–26.
Glossolalia caution, 1 Corinthians 14:23 (AB).
Whatever you say or do, Colossians 3:17.
Double-tongued, 1 Timothy 3:8 (NASB, NRSV).
Do not talk back, Titus 2:9.

Control tongue, control body, James 3:2 (CEV).
Guard tongue well, James 3:3–6.
Insuring good relationships, 1 Peter 3:10.
See Conversation, Gossip, Slander, Speech.

TONGUES

One common language, Genesis 11:1.
Strange tongues, Isaiah 28:11 (KJV).
Speaking in language understood, Isaiah 36:11.
Gift of tongues, Acts 19:1–7.
Paul, glossolalia, Acts 19:1–7; 1 Corinthians 14:18 (LB).
Words beyond normal vocabulary, Romans 8:16, 26–27.
No mention gift of tongues in Romans, Romans 12:4–8; 15:17–19.
Role of tongues in Body of Christ, 1 Corinthians 12:27–31.
See Gift, Glossolalia.

TOOL

Maker of tools, Genesis 4:22.
Tool use avoided, Exodus 20:25.
Subservient tools, Isaiah 10:15.
Tools through whom God ministers, Titus 1:1–3.
See Servant.

TORMENT

Desperate times, Psalm 60:3.
Torment in hell, Luke 16:22–23.
Merciless locusts, Revelation 9:3–5.
Wish to die, cannot, Revelation 9:6.
Aftermath of beast mark, Revelation 14:9–11.
Agony for refusing repentance, Revelation 16:10–11.
Lake of fire, Revelation 20:10.
See Punishment, Suffering, Torture.

TORNADO

Riding the wind, Job 30:22 (NRSV).
Whirlwind origin, Job 37:9 (Berk.).

TORTURE

Cutting off thumbs, big toes, Judges 1:7.
Tortured with thorns, briars, Judges 8:16.

Partial blindness inflicted as disgrace, 1 Samuel 11:2–11.

Fear of torture, 1 Samuel 31:4.

Satanic view of man's motivations, Job 2:1–10.

Sadistic killing of children, Psalm 137:9.

Intoxicated by torture, Isaiah 51:21–23.

Wicked find no rest, Isaiah 57:20–21.

Facing grim destiny, Jeremiah 15:2–3.

Jeremiah's torture, Jeremiah 38:6–13.

No chance for escape, Jeremiah 48:44.

Leaders, common people tortured, Lamentations 5:11–13.

Fear of sword, Ezekiel 11:8.

Spiked logs dragged over people, Amos 1:3 (CEV).

Torture chamber, Matthew 18:34 (CEV, LB).

Merciless locusts, Revelation 9:3–5.

See Sadistic, Torment.

TOTAL

"Every whit," Deuteronomy 13:16 (KJV).

TOTALITARIAN

Oppressive totalitarian ruler, 1 Kings 12:1–11.

Oppressed with no comforter, Ecclesiastes 4:1.

Life under godless government, Isaiah 25:3; 26:13; Romans 13:1; 1 Peter 2:13–14.

Tyranny abolished, Isaiah 54:14.

Temporary authority of the Beast, Revelation 13:5.

See Communism, Despot, Dictator.

TOTEM POLE

Repulsive pole, 1 Kings 15:13.

TOUCH

Forbidden fruit, Genesis 3:3.

Defiling touch, Leviticus 5:2; 15:11; Isaiah 52:11; 2 Corinthians 6:17; Colossians 2:21.

Dead body touched, Numbers 19:13.

Touching Great Physician, Matthew 9:20–22 (CEV); 14:36; Mark 3:10; Luke 6:19.

Cleansing touch, Mathew 8:3.

Healing touch, Matthew 8:15; 9:29–30; Mark 7:33–35; Luke 22:51.

Touch of sight, Matthew 20:34.

Children touched by Jesus, Mark 10:13–16.

See Communication, Intimacy.

TOUGH

"Hard like a diamond," Ezekiel 3:9 (CEV).

TOURIST

Seeing unpleasant sights, Deuteronomy 28:34.

Protection against enemies of road, Ezra 8:21–23.

Provision for safe travel, Nehemiah 2:7.

Travel reports, Job 21:29 (GNB).

Touring Zion, Psalm 48:12–13.

Foreigners' uproar, Isaiah 25:5.

Desert tourist retreat, Jeremiah 9:2.

Road signs and guideposts, Jeremiah 31:21.

Silent highways, Lamentations 1:4 (LB).

Things packed for exile, Ezekiel 12:7.

Errant tourist, Jonah 1:3.

Jerusalem tourism, Zechariah 8:20 (LB).

Jesus refused tourism, Matthew 24:1–2 (LB).

Travelling with light baggage, Mark 6:8.

See Sightseeing, Travel.

TOWER

Towers of the Bible, Genesis 11:4, 9; Judges 8:17; 9:40, 47, 49; Song of Songs 4:4; 7:4; Luke 13:4.

TOWN

Small town spared disaster of large city, Genesis 19:15–22.

Country town residence requested, 1 Samuel 27:5.

"Establish a town," Psalm 107:3 (NRSV).

TRADE

International trading, Genesis 24:10; Isaiah 61:6.

Import, export in Solomon's time, 1 Kings 9:26–27; 10:14–15, 28–29.

Deceitful buyer, Proverbs 20:14.

Barter for merchandise, Ezekiel 27:12.

Balance of trade, Ezekiel 27:12–24.

See Barter, Commerce, Merchandise.

TRADEMARK

"Marks of Jesus," Galatians 6:17 (Japanese implies "with a red hot iron").

TRADITION

Meat left uneaten, Genesis 32:32.
Reject heathen traditions, Deuteronomy 18:9.
Putting foot to neck, Joshua 10:24.
Traditional wearing of jewelry, Judges 8:24.
Sacrifice of daughter, Judges 11:30–40.
Removal of sandal, Ruth 4:7–8.
Old way best way, Jeremiah 6:16.
Communicating God's message to children, Joel 1:1–3.
Washing hands before eating, Matthew 15:1–9.
Myths and tales, 1 Timothy 4:7.
See Culture.

TRAFFIC

No traffic during Sabbath, Nehemiah 13:15–22.
Wild animals laugh at man's commotion, Job 39:5–7.
Some think prophecy of modern traffic, Nahum 2:4.
Children playing in streets, Zechariah 8:5.
See Journey, Travel, Transportation.

TRAGEDY

More powerful in death than in life, Judges 16:30.
Death caused by bad news, 1 Samuel 4:12–18.
End of Jezebel, 2 Kings 9:30–37.
Tragedy predicted, Jeremiah 34:1–7.
Jerusalem's tragic fall, Lamentations 1:9 (CEV).
Youthful marriage terminated, Joel 1:8.
Jesus desired judgment to come, Luke 12:49.
Fallen tower, Luke 13:4–5.
See Catastrophy, Disaster, Trauma.

TRAINING

Trained men in Abram's household, Genesis 14:14.
Training for future leadership, Numbers 27:18–23.
Eagle training young to fly, Deuteronomy 32:11.
Learning to wage war, Judges 3:1–2.
Men trained for service, 1 Chronicles 5:18.
Wild ox trained, Job 39:9–12.
Instructions to twelve apostles, Matthew 10:5–32; 11:1.
Well-trained family, Titus 1:6.
See Apprentice, Instruction, Follow-up.

TRAITOR

Complaining among leaders, Numbers 12:1–11.
Disloyalty to leadership, Numbers 16:1–33.
Traitor to evil city, Joshua 2:1–24.
Plot to overthrow government, 2 Samuel 15:10.
Amnesty to traitors, 2 Samuel 19:16–23.
Recruited to turn against king, 2 Kings 9:14–24.
Frustrated traitor, 2 Kings 11:13–14.
King destroyed by associates, 2 Kings 12:19–20.
Death penalty for treason, Esther 2:23.
Jesus betrayed by Judas, Matthew 26:14–16; Mark 14:42–45; Luke 22:3–6, 47–48; John 13:21–30; 18:1–3.
Pretense of righteousness, Luke 20:20.
Ultimate end for traitor, Acts 1:18–20.
Those who turn their backs, 2 Peter 2:20–22.
Deception among believers, Jude 3–4.
See Disloyalty.

TRAITS See Character, Habits, Lifestyle, Weakness.

TRANCE

Vision of the Lord, Numbers 24:2–4.
Peter's vision, Acts 10:9–16; 11:1–10.
Direction by vision, Acts 22:12–21.
Unsure of mode of experience, 2 Corinthians 12:1–4.
See Dream, Vision.

TRANQUILITY

Place of tranquility, Deuteronomy 33:27.
Love, faithfulness, peace, Psalm 85:10.

Tranquility from self control, Proverbs 29:11.

Voicing simple need, Proverbs 30:7–8.

Tranquil sleep, Ecclesiastes 5:12.

Obedience brings tranquility, Isaiah 48:17–18.

Tranquility renewed daily, Lamentations 3:22–24.

Living in peace and contentment, Micah 4:4.

Quietly rejoicing in the Lord, Zephaniah 3:17.

See Peace, Relaxation, Repose.

TRANSFORMATION

Tear down the old, build new, Judges 6:25–26.

Endowed by Holy Spirit, 1 Samuel 10:6–9.

Poor and needy lifted, Psalm 113:7–8.

Sins once scarlet become like snow, Isaiah 1:18.

Potter and clay, Jeremiah 18:1–4.

Heart of stone to heart of flesh, Ezekiel 11:19.

Clean hearts, changed lives, Ezekiel 36:25–27.

Satan witnessed transformation, Zechariah 3:1–7.

Being born again, John 3:1–8.

Conversion of sorcerer, Acts 8:9–13.

Saul's transformation, Acts 9:1–18.

Repentance in action, Acts 19:18–19.

Dead to sin, alive to God, Romans 6:11.

Not conformed, transformed, Romans 12:2; 1 Peter 1:14.

Inner transformation, Romans 12:2 (GNB).

New creation in Christ, 2 Corinthians 5:17; Ephesians 4:22–24.

From darkness to light, Ephesians 5:8–10.

Positive conduct of those transformed, Colossians 2:20–23.

Blasphemer transformed, 1 Timothy 1:12–16

Surprising transformation, 1 Peter 4:4 (NRSV).

Doing what is right, 1 John 2:29.

See Regeneration, Renewal, Salvation.

TRANSIENT

Destiny set for rebellious transients, Numbers 14:35.

All die and leave possessions to others, Psalm 49:10, 16–20.

Royalty is transient, Proverbs 27:24.

Transient human body but a tent, 2 Peter 1:13.

See Pilgrim, Tourist.

TRANSITION

God's command to Abraham, Genesis 12:1–9.

From chapter to chapter, Exodus 7:25 (LB).

Decisive transition after death of Moses, Joshua 1:1–2.

Duty of citizens to leadership change, Joshua 1:16–17.

Temporal transition, eternal absolutes, Isaiah 40:7–8.

Foolish dependance upon mortal flesh, Jeremiah 17:5.

Darkness to light, 1 John 2:8.

See Change, Progress.

TRANSLATION

Speaking in language understood, Isaiah 36:11.

No translation necessary, Acts 2:6.

See Communications, Linguistics.

TRANSMUTATION

Stewardship rewarded, Proverbs 19:17.

Earthly obedience evokes Heaven's blessing, Malachi 3:8–12.

Transmuting earthly wealth to eternal wealth, Matthew 6:19–20.

Divine principle for stewardship, 2 Corinthians 9:6.

Treasure in heaven, 1 Timothy 6:18–19 (LB).

See Reward.

TRANSPORTATION

Transportation provided as act of love, Genesis 45:16–20.

Transportation for forty sons, thirty grandsons, Judges 12:14.

Chariot of fire, whirlwind, 2 Kings 2:11–12.

TRANSPORTATION

"Chariots of God," Psalm 68:17.
Royal palanquin, Song of Songs 3:9 (NRSV).
Intercontinental highway, Isaiah 19:23.
Mountains turned into roads, Isaiah 49:11.
Wealth to those who lived by many waters, Jeremiah 51:13.
Donkey chosen to serve Jesus, Matthew 21:1–7; Mark 11:1–7.
See Caravan, Chariot, Commerce, Journey, Maritime, Pack Animals, Travel.

TRAP

Tar pits of Siddim, Genesis 14:10.
"Caught in a trap," Joshua 8:22 (LB).
Net, pit, Psalms 35:7; 119:85, 110; 140:5; 141:9.
Men like trapped birds, Jeremiah 5:26.
Attempts to trap Jesus, Matthew 16:1; 22:15; Mark 12:13; Luke 11:53–54; John 8:6.
See Snare.

TRAUMA

Traumatic joy, sorrow, Genesis 45:1–5.
Father given traumatic information about son, Genesis 45:25–28.
"In shock," Ezra 9:3 (CEV).
Shocked, stunned, Isaiah 29:9 (CEV).
Hurting another brings greater hurt to self, Jeremiah 7:18–19.
Haunt of jackals, Jeremiah 9:11.
Numerous widows, Jeremiah 15:8.
Men as in pains of childbirth, Jeremiah 30:6.

Peril outside, plague inside, Ezekiel 7:15–17.
Nations in anguish, Joel 2:6.
From one fear to another, Amos 5:18–19.
Singing turns to wailing, Amos 8:3.
Avoid those experiencing disaster, Obadiah 13.
Traumatic glory of the Lord, Luke 2:9.
Fear of drowning, Luke 8:22–25.
Congregational trauma, Acts 5:11 (AB).
Spiritual trauma, 2 Corinthians 1:3–7.
Hard pressed from every side, 2 Corinthians 4:8.
Traumatized children, Colossians 3:21 (AB).
See Catastrophe, Distress, Shock.

TRAVEL

Washing feet after journey, Genesis 18:4; 19:2.
Not traveling after sunset, Genesis 28:11.
Three days journey, Exodus 3:18.
Taking care of family welfare, Exodus 4:18.
Travelling by divine instructions, Numbers 9:23.
Prayer for protection, Numbers 10:35.
Passage denied, Numbers 20:14–21.
Listing journeys, Numbers 33:1–48.
Travel directions, Deuteronomy 1:2.
Roads to refuge cities, Deuteronomy 19:1–3.
Ship transportation, Deuteronomy 28:68.
Entire nation's journey, Joshua 4:1.
Dangerous roads, Judges 5:6–7 (CEV).
"Ride on white donkeys," Judges 5:10.
Exhausted, famished, Judges 8:4 (NRSV).

T

Travel for forty sons, thirty grandsons, Judges 12:14.

Journey with divine approval, Judges 18:6.

Early morning departure, 1 Samuel 17:20.

Day's journey, 1 Kings 19:4.

Travel energy, 1 Kings 19:7.

Unsafe to travel, 2 Chronicles 15:5.

Restricted travel, 2 Chronicles 16:1 (LB).

Shared travel expenses, Ezra 1:4 (LB).

Arrive, three day rest, Ezra 8:32 (CEV).

Fatal detour, Job 6:18.

Speed boats, Job 9:26.

Avoiding lighted pathway, Job 24:13.

Travel expands knowledge, Job 36:3.

Sent around the world, Psalm 67:2 (LB).

Eye on the road, Proverbs 16:17 (GNB).

Sleeping on high seas, Proverbs 23:34.

Dangerous routes, Isaiah 30:6; 33:8.

Safe travel, Isaiah 35:8–9.

Desert roads, Isaiah 43:19 (CEV).

Mountains turned into roads, Isaiah 49:11.

Importance of roads, Isaiah 57:14 (LB).

Crooked roads, Isaiah 59:8.

Travel by air and sea, Isaiah 60:8–9 (LB).

Treacherous desert, Jeremiah 2:6 (CEV).

Find the good way, Jeremiah 6:16.

Road signs and guideposts, Jeremiah 31:21.

Silent highways, Lamentations 1:4 (LB).

Divine obstruction, Hosea 2:6.

Altered travel plans, Matthew 2:12.

Nativity journey, Luke 2:1–5.

Missing traveller, Luke 2:44.

Wearisome travel, John 4:6.

Jesus avoided dangerous travel, John 7:1.

"High above the sky," Romans 8:39 (LB).

Stop over en route, Romans 15:24.

Wife traveling with husband, 1 Corinthians 9:5 (GNB).

Letters of introduction, 1 Corinthians 16:3.

Care planning journey, 2 Corinthians 1:15–17.

See Itinerary, Journey, Migration, Road Sign, Transportation.

TREACHERY

Stolen birthright, Genesis 27:1–40.

False affection, Judges 16:18–19.

Refusal to use treachery, 1 Samuel 26:1–25.

Treacherous conversation, 2 Samuel 3:27.

Pretense of securing food, 2 Samuel 4:5–7.

Misunderstanding gesture of goodwill, 2 Samuel 10:1–4.

Strategy for legal murder, 2 Samuel 11:15.

Avoiding evil scheme, Nehemiah 6:2–4.

Trumped-up charges, Esther 3:8.

"Wantonly treacherous," Psalm 25:3 (NRSV).

Security against attack, Psalm 124:1–5.

Deceitful, malicious man, Proverbs 26:24–26.

Untrustworthy friends, brothers, Jeremiah 9:4–8.

King Herod, Magi, Matthew 2:7–8, 13.

Guilt of influencing others to sin, Luke 17:1.

Cynical tongues made silent, Luke 20:20–26.

See Deception.

TREASON *See Disloyalty, Traitors.*

TREASURE

God's "special treasure," Exodus 19:5 (NKJV).

Treasured like jewels, Deuteronomy 32:34 (LB).

Searching for treasure, Job 28:1–4, 9–11.

Scripture treasured, Psalm 119:11 (NASB, NRSV).

Silver thrown into streets, Ezekiel 7:19.

Treasure taken away, Obadiah 6 (CEV).

Gold, silver belong to God, Haggai 2:8.

The Lord's treasured possessions, Malachi 3:17.

Spiritual treasure, 2 Timothy 1:14 (CEV).

Precious faith, 2 Peter 1:1.

See Value.

TREATY

Broken treaties, Isaiah 33:8 (CEV).

TREES

Fruit trees spared, Deuteronomy 20:19–29.

Soothsayer's tree, Judges 9:37 (Berk.).

Shaded idols, 2 Kings 17:10.

Survival of felled tree, Job 14:7–9.

Grafted branches, Romans 11:24.

Varieties of trees, Genesis 35:4; Exodus 15:27; 36:20; Numbers 17:8; Judges 9:10; 1 Samuel 14:2; 2 Samuel 5:23; 1 Kings

19:4; Nehemiah 8:15; Song of Songs 2:3; Isaiah 6:13; 14:8; 41:19; 44:14.

Three years of purification, Leviticus 19:23.

Trees and tithe, Leviticus 27:30.

Neutrality of timber, Deuteronomy 20:19–20.

Broom tree, Psalm 120:4.

Widespread tree planting, Isaiah 41:19.

Agency of punishment, Jeremiah 6:6.

Tree branches destroyed, Jeremiah 11:16.

Good, bad, Matthew 12:33.

See Forestry, Horticulture.

TRESPASSING

Promise not to trespass, Numbers 20:17 (Berk.).

TRIALS *See Persecution, Suffering, Testing, Trouble.*

TRIBULATION

Daughters taught to wail, Jeremiah 9:20.

Facing grim destiny, Jeremiah 15:2–3.

No chance for escape, Jeremiah 48:44.

Words of Jesus concerning end times, Mark 13:1–37.

See Millenium, Second Coming.

TRIBUTE

Posthumous tribute, 2 Samuel 3:33–39.

Jesus' evaluation of John the Baptist, Matthew 11:11–14.

Commending great faith, Matthew 15:28; Luke 7:9.

Empty sincerity of Pharisees, Mark 12:15–17.

Fragrant tribute, Mark 14:3–9.

Greatness, subservience, Luke 7:28.

Widow's mite, Luke 21:1–4.

See Citation, Praise.

TRICKERY

Attempted trick, Mark 12:15 (LB).

See Subversion.

TRINITY

Plural Godhead, Genesis 1:26 (AB); 3:22 (AB).

Threefold benediction, Numbers 6:24–26.

Father, Son in Old Testament, Proverbs 30:2–4.

Holy, holy, holy is the Lord, Isaiah 6:3.

God, Holy Spirit, Isaiah 48:16.

Trinity in one verse, Matthew 28:19.

Oneness of Jesus and God, John 12:44–45; 15:26–27.

Christ's trinitarian teaching, John 14:25–31; 15:26–27.

Trinitarian benediction, 2 Corinthians 13:14.

Christ, God and Holy Spirit, Ephesians 2:22.

Fullness of Deity, Colossians 2:9–10.

Spiritual function of Father and Son, 2 Thessalonians 3:5.

Three who bear record, 1 John 5:6–8.

See Theology.

TRITE *See Insignificant, Trivia.*

TRIUMPH *See Conquest, Victory.*

TRIUMPHAL ENTRY

Prophesied triumphal entry, Zechariah 9:9.

TRIVIA

Regarding something lightly, Deuteronomy 1:41.

Sins considered trivial, 1 Kings 16:31.

Trivial to the Lord, 2 Kings 3:18.

Accused of saying nothing, Job 8:2 (CEV).

Foam on water, Job 24:18.

No trivia with God, Job 36:5 (Berk.).

Trivial people, Psalm 62:9.

"Empty breath," Psalm 94:11 (NRSV).

"Trivial matter," Ezekiel 8:17.

Message heard as trivia, Ezekiel 33:32.

"A thing of naught," Amos 6:13 (KJV).

Trivia prayer, Matthew 6:7 (GNB).

Many distractions, Luke 10:38–42.

"So small a thing," Luke 12:26 (NRSV).

No worry about incidentals, Matthew 6:25–33 (LB).

A little foolishness, 2 Corinthians 11:1.

"Silly talk," Ephesians 5:4 (NASB).

Empty words, Ephesians 5:6.

Eternal trivia, Philippians 3:7–9.

Meaningless talk, 1 Timothy 1:6.

"Every day affairs," 2 Timothy 2:4 (NRSV).

T

Avoid trivial conversation, 2 Timothy 2:16, 23 (AB).

Itching ears, 2 Timothy 4:3–4 (CEV).

"Bombastic nonsense," 2 Peter 2:18 (NRSV).

See Insignificant, Small.

TROPHY See Memorabilia.

TROUBADOUR

Walking through city with harp and sad song, Isaiah 23:16.

End to noisy songs, Ezekiel 26:13.

See Music.

TROUBLE

Do not cause trouble, Deuteronomy 2:9, 19.

Asking for trouble, 2 Chronicles 25:19.

Born to trouble, Job 5:7; 14:1.

Delivered from seven troubles, Job 5:19.

Weighty troubles, Job 6:2.

"Parents of trouble," Job 15:35 (CEV).

Hungry trouble, Job 18:12.

Ever present God, Psalms 14:4–5; 18:6.

Sure deliverance, Psalm 34:19.

"More troubles than I can count," Psalm 40:12 (CEV).

Ever present help, Psalm 46:1.

Facing disaster with confidence, Psalm 57:1.

Promises made in time of trouble, Psalm 66:13–14.

Waters up to neck, Psalm 69:1.

Distress call, Psalm 120:1.

Surrounded by trouble, Psalm 138:7.

Some delivered, others in trouble, Proverbs 11:8 (NRSV).

Friend in need, Proverbs 17:17.

God's glory first, Isaiah 37:14–20.

Self-inflicted trouble, Jeremiah 4:18; Ezekiel 22:1–5.

Faithfulness causing imprisonment, Jeremiah 37:1–21.

Rod of testing, Ezekiel 21:13.

Trouble Valley, Hopeful Valley, Hosea 2:15 (CEV).

Negative response to trouble, Amos 4:6.

Escape lion, meet bear, Amos 5:19.

Sit in darkness, Micah 7:8.

Refuge for those who trust the Lord, Nahum 1:7.

"Ocean of troubles," Zechaiah 10:11 (CEV).

Those who are persecuted, Matthew 5:10.

"You are in for trouble," Matthew 23:16 (CEV).

Persecution implements spread of Gospel, Acts 8:3–4.

Experience in storm and shipwreck, Acts 27:13–44.

Means of God's blessing, Romans 5:3.

Those who purposely cause trouble, Romans 16:17.

God of all comfort, 2 Corinthians 1:3–4.

Progress from dire circumstances, Philippians 1:12 (NASB).

Multiple troubles, James 1:12 (AB).

Purpose of trials and grief, 1 Peter 1:6–7.

See Hardship, Testing.

TROUBLE-MAKER

Community of trouble-makers, Exodus 16:2.

Negligent care dangerous animal, Exodus 21:35–36.

Augmenting gossip, trouble, Exodus 23:1.

One person's sin, Numbers 16:22.

Facing formidable opponent, Numbers 21:21–26.

Prophet called trouble maker, 1 Kings 18:16–18.

Trouble-maker built gallows for his own neck, Esther 5:11–14; 9:25.

Marks of evil character, Proverbs 6:16–19.

One who affronted the Lord's name, Isaiah 36:18–22; 37:1–7.

Boomerang principle of harming others, Jeremiah 7:18–19.

Fine-sounding arguments, Colossians 2:4.

Troublesome metal worker, 2 Timothy 4:14–15.

What to do with trouble-maker, Titus 3:10.

Self-imposed suffering, 1 Peter 4:15.

See Abrasion, Meddle.

TRUST

Remembering Egypt instead of trusting God, Exodus 16:2–3.

Exemplary leadership, 2 Kings 18:5.

Confidence against all circumstances, Job 13:15.

"I trust you completely," Psalm 28:7 (CEV).

Our times in God's hands, Psalm 31:15.

Child-like trust, Psalm 131:1–2.

Betraying confidence, Proverbs 11:13.

Kept in perfect peace, Isaiah 26:3.

Trust in the Lord rather than men, Isaiah 36:4–10.

Trust God, Isaiah 43:10 (CEV).

Confidence in the potter, Isaiah 45:9.

Trust in man, Jeremiah 17:5.

Safer to trust God than run away, Jeremiah 42:1–22.

Cannot trust best friend, Micah 7:5 (CEV).

Trust in midst of trouble, Habakkuk 3:17–18.

"Depend only on Him," Matthew 5:3 (CEV).

Needless fear in time of storm, Mark 4:35–41.

Assurance to those who trust the Lord, John 6:37.

Do not test the Lord, 1 Corinthians 10:9–10.

Trust, assurance, confidence, Hebrews 2:13 (AB).

Invisible reality, Hebrews 11:1.

Cast all cares upon the Lord, 1 Peter 5:7.

See Confidence, Faith.

TRUSTEE

"Guardians and trustees," Galatians 4:2 (NRSV).

Personal talent trustee, 1 Peter 4:10 (AB).

TRUSTWORTHY

Our trustworthy Lord, 2 Chronicles 6:4, 14–15.

Looking for one trustworthy person, Jeremiah 5:1.

Always doing what is right, Romans 12:17.

Our trustworthy God, 1 Corinthians 1:9 (LB).

Faithful service without supervision, Philippians 2:12–13.

Proved trustworthy, 1 Timothy 1:12 (CEV).

Trustworthy employees, Titus 2:9–10.

See Dependability.

TRUTH

Scripture contains blessings and curses, Joshua 8:34.

Speak the truth, Job 6:25 (LB).

Let God judge, Job 32:13.

Ears hear, eyes see, Job 42:5.

"Lips free of deceit," Psalm 17:1 (NRSV).

God's covenant never changes, Psalms 105:8–9; 111:5.

"Nuggets of truth," Proverbs 1:6 (LB).

Truth its own defense, Proverbs 12:13 (LB).

"Eternity in the heart," Ecclesiastes 3:11.

Twisting truth, Jeremiah 8:8 (LB).

Sincere search for God, Jeremiah 29:10–14.

Faithfulness rewarded with imprisonment, Jeremiah 37:1–21.

Futile effort to suppress truth, Jeremiah 38:1–6.

Listening out of desperation, Jeremiah 38:14–28.

Truth proclaimed with boldness, Ezekiel 33:21–33.

Positive, negative result, Hosea 14:9.

Witnessing miracles with hard hearts, Matthew 11:20.

Purpose of parables, Matthew 13:10–13.

Believe good news, Mark 1:14–15.

Mother of Jesus too frightened to comprehend, Mark 16:1–8.

Truth gives life, destruction, Luke 20:17–18.

"Fountain of truth," John 3:33 (LB).

Deceived by truth, John 7:45–47.

Knowing truth gives freedom, John 8:32.

Doubt augmented by truth, John 8:45–47.

Spiritual blindness, spiritual sight, John 9:39–41.

Walking in light, John 12:35–36.

Prejudiced against truth, John 15:37.

Pilate's immortal question, John 18:38.

Response to resurrection message, Acts 17:32.

"Sober truth," Acts 26:25 (NRSV).

Truth declared with power, Romans 1:4.

Truth known instinctively, Romans 1:18 (LB).

Those who stumble over redemption, truth, Romans 9:33; 1 Corinthians 15:12–19.

T

Reason versus revelation, 1 Corinthians 1:20–25.

"Truthful speech," 2 Corinthians 6:7 (NIV, NRSV).

From God, not man, Galatians 1:11–12.

Truth proclaimed with false motives, Philippians 1:18.

Strong grip on truth, 2 Thessalonians 2:15 (LB).

Teachings which cause controversy, 1 Timothy 1:3–4.

Pillar, bulwark, 1 Timothy 3:15 (NRSV).

God cannot lie, Titus 1:2; Hebrews 6:18.

"Practice the truth," 1 John 1:6 (NASB, NKJV).

Certain of truth, 1 John 2:21.

Truth, love united, 2 John 1:3, 5–6.

Love in truth, 3 John 1.

See Absolute, Honesty, Integrity, Orthodoxy.

TUNNEL

Drilling rocks, Job 28:9–10 (Berk.).

TURMOIL

Unable to tolerate food, Numbers 11:4–6.

Uproar in town, 1 Samuel 4:12–17.

Army shaken by panic sent by God, 1 Samuel 14:15.

Warriors stumbling over each other, Jeremiah 46:12.

Bedlam in doomed city, Nahum 3:1–2.

See Confusion, Unrest.

TWILIGHT See Sunset.

TWINS

Jacob and Esau, Genesis 25:21–26.

Obstetrical trickery, Genesis 38:27–30.

Strife before birth, Hosea 12:3.

Disciple twin, John 20:24 (Berk., CEV, LB, NRSV).

TYPOLOGY

Struck rock, Numbers 20:7–11; 1 Corinthians 10:1–4

Bronze snake, Numbers 21:6–9; John 3:14–15

Cities of refuge, Numbers 35:6–34; Hebrews 6:18.

Time for rest, Joshua 11:23; Hebrews 4:8–11.

Angel Lucifer, Ezekiel 28:11–19.

Earthly type, Hebrews 8:5.

Law as shadow of future, Hebrews 10:1.

Old Testament type reviewed, 1 Corinthians 10:1–11.

See Example, Prototype.

TYRANT

Life under tyranny, Exodus 1:14; 5:8; Ecclesiastes 4:1–5.

Son more oppressive than Solomon, 1 Kings 12:1–11.

Oppressive ruler, Proverbs 28:3.

Song to defeated tyrant, Isaiah 14:4–21 (CEV).

See Despot, Dictator, Totalitarian.

U

UFO

Unusual sights in sky, Jeremiah 10:2 (GNB).

Wheels of Ezekiel's vision, Ezekiel 1:15–21.

See Space, Space/Time.

UGLINESS

Sick drunk, Isaiah 28:7.

Divine countenance blemished by vicarious guilt, Isaiah 53:1–3.

ULTIMATUM

Optional ultimatum, Jeremiah 38:14–28.

Ultimatum for failure to witness, Ezekiel 3:18–19.

Threat of death to Daniel's friends, Daniel 3:8–15.

Ultimatum to Belshazzar, Daniel 5:25–30.

Choice of Jesus or Barabbas, Matthew 27:15–26.

Ultimatum for divisive person, Titus 3:10.

See Decree, Warning.

UNANIMITY

Wrong kind of unanimity, Exodus 16:2; Numbers 11:4–10.

Responding in acclamation, Exodus 24:3.

Choosing individuals to represent the whole, Numbers 4:1–4.

People united behind new leadership, Joshua 1:16–18.

Unanimity in discontent, Joshua 9:18–19.

Nation united, Joshua 10:29–42.

Love between friends, 1 Samuel 20:17.

Pleased populace, 2 Samuel 3:36.

Divided into factions, 1 Kings 16:21–22.

Disagreeing with consensus, 1 Kings 22:13–14.

United enemy, 2 Kings 3:21.

Diligent unanimity, Nehemiah 4:6.

Bowing before the Lord, Nehemiah 8:3–6.

Language confused by intermarriage, Nehemiah 13:23–27.

Glorify the Lord together, Psalm 34:3.

Brothers' good rapport, Psalm 133:1–3.

Strength in numbers, Proverbs 30:25.

Two better than one, Ecclesiastes 4:8–12.

Unanimity in lament, Jeremiah 9:20.

Rejection of prophet by arrogant men, Jeremiah 43:1–3.

People united against prophet, Jeremiah 44:11–19.

Young, old united in death, Lamentations 2:21.

People of synagogue versus Jesus, Luke 4:28–30.

Like teacher, like student, Luke 6:40.

United to follow Jesus, Luke 8:1–3.

Demons in unanimity, Luke 8:26–33.

United behind common goal, Luke 10:1–2.

Union of believers, John 17:11, 22.

All together in one place, Acts 2:1.

One in heart, mind, Acts 4:52.

Unanimity with others, Romans 12:18.

Unanimity of mind and thought, 1 Corinthians 1:10.

Hindrances to unity among Christians, 1 Corinthians 3:1–9.

Body as unit, 1 Corinthians 12:12–30.

Unanimity of minister, ministry, 2 Corinthians 8:16–24.

Keys to Christian unity, Philippians 2:1–11.
See Fellowship, Rapport.

UNAPPRECIATED *See Disdain, Dislike.*

UNAPPRECIATIVE

Failure to show gratitude, Judges 8:35.

Misunderstanding gesture of goodwill, 2 Samuel 10:1–4.

Ungrateful for deliverance, Ecclesiastes 9:14–15; Jeremiah 2:5–8.

Ingratitude to foreigner, Luke 17:11–19.

No gratitude shown to servant, Luke 17:7–10.

Only one in ten expressed appreciation, Luke 17:11–19.

UNAWARE

Generation in spiritual ignorance, Judges 2:10.

Unaware of God's plan for man, 1 Samuel 27:12.

Wealth numbs conscience, Hosea 12:8.
See Ignorance.

UNBELIEF

Making joke of truth, Genesis 17:17; 19:14.

Moses discredited, Exodus 4:1.

Blatant unbelief, Exodus 5:2.

Taunting the Lord's presence, Exodus 17:7.

Israel's failure to obey promises, Deuteronomy 1:28–33.

Sure victory or sure defeat, Joshua 23:6–13.

Faith to unbelief in one generation, Judges 2:10.

Pessimism of unbelief, 2 Kings 18:29–35.

No God, no priest, no law, 2 Chronicles 15:3.

Death to unbelievers, 2 Chronicles 15:13.

Rebellion of prosperous wicked, Job 21:7–16.

Rejecting light, Job 24:13.

Contrasting belief, unbelief, Psalm 1:1–6.

Sin abounded in spite of mercy, judgment, Psalm 78:32.

So few believe, Isaiah 53:1 (LB).

God made known through judgment, Ezekiel 11:7–12.

Idols in heart, Ezekiel 14:1–11.

Laughing at truth spoken by Jesus, Matthew 9:23–24.

Attributing work of God to demons, Matthew 9:34.

Hindrance to miracles, Matthew 13:58.

Requesting increased faith, John 9:24 (LB).

Unbelief faces proof, John 12:37–40.

Acting in ignorance, Acts 3:17.

Unable to believe answered prayer, Acts 12:13–15.

Intellectual idolatry, Acts 17:16–34.

Certain of unbelief, Acts 19:35–36.

Empty minds, darkness, Romans 1:21 (GNB).

Faith becomes nonsense, 1 Corinthians 1:18 (GNB).

Message like death smell, 2 Corinthians 2:16.

Blinded by Satan, 2 Corinthians 4:1–6.

Danger of intellectual pride, 2 Timothy 3:7.

Deceiving others, deceived themselves, 2 Timothy 3:13.

Failure to combine hearing, believing, Hebrews 4:1–3.

Abandoned faith, Hebrews 6:6 (GNB).

Scoffers in last days, 2 Peter 3:3–4.

Denying that Jesus is the Christ, 1 John 2:22–23.

Those cast into lake of fire, Revelation 21:8; 22:15.

See Doubt, Skepticism.

UNBORN

People yet unborn, Psalm 22:31.

UNCERTAINTY

Boasting about tomorrow, Proverbs 27:1.

Going with confidence into difficult places, Acts 20:22–24.

Obedience toward unknown objectives, Hebrews 11:8.

"Shifting shadow," James 1:17 (NASB).

See Hesitation.

UNCHANGEABLE

Unfailing promises, Joshua 23:4.

Unending faithfulness, Joshua 24:14.

Certainty of day, night, Jeremiah 33:19–22.

One who never changes, Hebrews 1:10–12.

See Dependability.

UNCLE

Quarrelling cousins, wise uncle, Genesis 13:7–9.

Loving uncle, Genesis 29:13–14.

Neither uncle nor father, Leviticus 20:21.

Uncle becomes father, Deuteronomy 25:5–6.

Uncle Paul, courageous nephew, Acts 23:12–22.

UNCLEAN

Edible, inedible insects, Leviticus 11:20–23.

Bathed but unclean, Numbers 19:7.

King afflicted with leprosy, 2 Kings 15:5.

Purifying bad water, 2 Kings 2:19–22.

Men of bad circumstances share good fortune, 2 Kings 7:3–9.

Washing prostitutes, chariots, 1 Kings 22:38.

Soap that does not wash away guilt, Jeremiah 2:22.

Place of disease, death, Jeremiah 16:1–9.

Uncleanness in God's sight, Ezekiel 36:17.

Clothing of those engaged in immorality, Jude 23.

See Contamination, Filthy.

UNCOMPLICATED

Great things, small things, 2 Kings 5:13.

Simple can understand, Psalm 119:130.

Content with simple things, Psalm 131:1–2.

Understood by children, Matthew 11:25; Luke 18:17.

See Simplicity.

UNCONCERNED

Ignoring Word of the Lord, Jeremiah 25:3.

Those who pass by, Lamentations 1:12.

Unconcerned Jerusalem, Luke 13:34.

Pharisees unconcerned for sinners, Luke 15:1–7.

Caring neither for God or man, Luke 18:1–5.

See Complacency.

UNCOOPERATIVE *See Resistant, Stubborn.*

UNCOUTH *See Vulgar.*

UNCTION

Being truly holy, Numbers 16:3–7.

Speaking words given by the Lord, Numbers 23:12.

Discerning the prophets, Deuteronomy 18:21–22.

Touched by spirit of the Lord, 1 Samuel 10:6.

Given words to speak, 2 Samuel 23:2; Numbers 24:1–2; Matthew 10:19–20.

Touched by the Lord's hand, Ezra 7:6.

Instructed tongue, Isaiah 50:4.

Divine touch, Jeremiah 1:9.

Living creatures led by the Spirit, Ezekiel 1:12.

Spirit empowered, Micah 3:8.

Strength from the Lord, Habakkuk 3:19.

Holy Spirit's influence over unborn child, Luke 1:41.

Power of Holy Spirit, Luke 4:14–15.

Danger of pride in conquest of demons, Luke 10:16–20.

Asking for unction, Luke 11:9–13.

Shining, burning, John 5:35 (Berk., LB, RSV).

Witnessing boldly with unction, Acts 4:5–13.

Ministry with power, grace, Acts 4:33.

Evidence of unction, Acts 6:8–13.

Rebuking Satan, Acts 13:6–12.

Fervor, burning enthusiasm, Acts 13:25 (RSV).

No racial distinction, Acts 15:8–9.

Weapons of world, divine weapons, 2 Corinthians 10:3–5.

"Sense of urgency," 2 Timothy 4:2 (AB).

Scripture unctionized by Holy Spirit, 2 Peter 1:21.

See Commitment, Holiness, Holy Spirit.

UNDEPENDABLE

Those who broke faith with God, Deuteronomy 32:51.

Weak as spider's web, Job 8:14.

Froth on water, Job 24:18.

Undependable drunkards, gluttons, Proverbs 23:20.

Friends, brothers untrustworthy, Jeremiah 9:4–8.

Slaves set free, again enslaved, Jeremiah 34:8–22.

"Shifting shadow," James 1:17 (NASB).

See Unstable.

UNDERESTIMATE

Positive, negative viewpoints, Numbers 13:17–33.

Underestimating enemy, Deuteronomy 1:41–44.

Small, insignificant greatness, Proverbs 30:24–28.

Contrasting temporal, eternal values, Matthew 6:19–21.

Underestimating Son of God, Matthew 13:57; John 1:46.

Underestimating individual worth, 1 Corinthians 6:20; 1 Peter 1:18–19.

See Assessment, Demean, Value.

UNDERHANDED See Deceit, Deception, Connivance.

UNDERMINE See Betray.

UNDERPRIVILEGED

Providing for underprivileged, Leviticus 23:22.

Inequity among citizens, Nehemiah 5:1–5.

Sons of sorceress, Isaiah 57:3.

Status of servant, Luke 17:7–10.

See Orphan, Poverty.

UNDERSCORE See Emphasis, Reinforcement.

U

UNDERSTANDING

Eyes see, ears hear, Deuteronomy 29:2–4.

Purposeful comprehension, 1 Chronicles 22:12.

Seeing light in God's light, Psalm 36:9.

God-given ability to understand Scripture, Psalm 119:125.

Persistent search for understanding, Proverbs 2:1–6.

Refusal, inability to read, Isaiah 29:11–12.

Those with insight understand, Daniel 12:10 (NASB).

Effect of attitudes on understanding, Matthew 13:14–15.

Childhood understanding, Luke 10:21.

Sharing Scriptural insights, Acts 18:24–26.

Seeing light, not understanding voice, Acts 22:9.

Taught by the Holy Spirit, 1 Corinthians 2:6–16.

Milk, solid food, 1 Corinthians 3:1–2.

Tolerant understanding, 1 Corinthians 11:18–19.

"Power to comprehend," Ephesians 3:18 (NRSV).

Thinking clarified, Philippians 3:15 (CEV).

Filled with knowledge of God's will, Colossians 1:9–12.

Lacking understanding, 1 Timothy 1:7 (AB).

See Discernment, Tolerance, Wisdom.

UNDESIRABLE

Rejected Israel, Ezekiel 16:2–5 (CEV).

See Unworthy.

UNDISCIPLINED

Lack of discernment, Deuteronomy 32:28.

Undisciplined son, 1 Kings 1:5–6 (LB).

Destructive duplicity, Proverbs 11:3.

Warped minds, Proverbs 12:8.

Too much food, drink, Proverbs 23:20.

Undisciplined attitude, Isaiah 30:15.

Spiritual vagabonds, Jeremiah 2:31.

Undisciplined nation, Ezekiel 9:9.

See Delinquency, Irresponsibility.

UNEMPLOYMENT

No jobs, Zechariah 8:10 (LB).

UNETHICAL *See Unscrupulous.*

UNEXPECTED

Burning bush, Exodus 3:1–3.

Awesome, unexpected acts of God, Isaiah 64:3.

Disrupted banquet, Daniel 5:5–28.

Grapes in desert, Hosea 9:10.

Anticipating the unexpected, Zechariah 8:6 (LB).

Confronted by dazzling light, Acts 9:3–4.

Message heard by those who did not ask, Romans 10:20.

See Serendipity, Surprise.

UNFAIRNESS

Rights of oldest son, Deuteronomy 21:15–17.

Righteous suffer as do wicked, Ecclesiastes 8:14.

Making, breaking promise to slaves, Jeremiah 34:8–22.

Cheating on weight, cost, Amos 8:5–6.

See Inequity, Injustice.

UNFAITHFUL

Destiny set for rebellious people, Numbers 14:35.

Turning quickly to heathen gods, Judges 8:33–34.

Woman unfaithful to husband, Judges 19:1–3.

"We have broken faith," Ezra 10:2 (NRSV).

Divine disappointment, Isaiah 5:7.

Eyes, ears that do not function, Ezekiel 12:2.

Peter's unfaithfulness, Matthew 26:31–35, 69–75.

Test of faithfulness, Luke 16:12.

Unfaithful wife, James 4:4 (LB).

See Disloyalty.

UNFIT

Sold for nothing, Isaiah 52:3.

High cost of spiritual fitness, Matthew 10:37–38.

Unfit banquet guests, Matthew 22:8.

Self-condemnation, Acts 13:46.

See Backsliding.

UNFORGIVABLE SIN See Unpardonable Sin.

UNFORGIVING

Prolonged retribution, Deuteronomy 23:2–6.

Stark picture of vengeance, Psalms 58:10; 68:23.

See Resentment, Retaliation.

UNFULFILLED

Destiny set for rebellious people, Numbers 14:35.

Partial fulfillment, Deuteronomy 32:48–52.

Unfulfilled life, Job 7:1–2.

Three things never satisfied, Proverbs 30:15–16.

Emptiness of success, affluence, Ecclesiastes 2:4–11.

Life's emptiness, Isaiah 55:2.

No rest for wicked, Isaiah 57:20–21.

Empty cisterns, parched fields, Jeremiah 14:1–6.

Empty jars return from cisterns, Jeremiah 14:3.

Visions come to nothing, Ezekiel 12:21–25.

Wealth plundered, houses demolished, wine unused, Zephaniah 1:13.

Those never satisfied, Haggai 1:5–6.

Continual lust for more, Ephesians 4:19.

See Emptiness.

UNHAPPINESS

Leadership for those in trouble, 1 Samuel 22:2.

Inequity among citizens, Nehemiah 5:1–5.

Never satisfied, Proverbs 30:15–16.

Unhappiness from forsaking the Lord, Jeremiah 2:19.

Judgment bringing absence of joy, Jeremiah 25:10.

See Grief, Sorrow.

UNINTELLIGENT

Willful ignorance, 2 Chronicles 30:10; 36:16; Job 21:13–15; Zechariah 7:11–12; Matthew 13:15; Romans 1:28; 2 Peter 3:5.

Wild donkey's colt, Job 11:12.

Boastful of ignorance, Proverbs 1:7.

Likenesses of fool, Proverbs 26:1–11.

See Ignorance.

UNIQUE

"One of a thousand," Job 33:23 (NRSV).

Unique Savior, John 3:16 (AB).

UNISEX

Men, women not to wear other's clothing, Deuteronomy 22:5.

UNISON

Unison affirmation, Joshua 24:22.

Voice of city, 1 Samuel 4:13 (KJV).

Singers, dancers in unison, Psalm 87:7 (NRSV).

U

UNITED STATES

Scripture some think refers to United States, Isaiah 18:1–2, 7.

UNITY

People welded together, Genesis 11:3–4 (LB).
Family unity, Genesis 13:8 (LB).
Wrong kind of unity, Numbers 11:4–10.
King, people united, 1 Samuel 12:14.
Heart, soul in unity, 1 Samuel 14:7.
Two becoming one in spirit, 1 Samuel 18:1–4.
Mutual love between friends, 1 Samuel 20:17.
Effort to reunite nation, 2 Chronicles 11:1 (LB).
Multitude as one, Nehemiah 8:1.
At peace with one's enemies, Proverbs 16:7.
Grains of sand hold back ocean, Jeremiah 5:22.
Two sticks become as one, Ezekiel 37:17–23.
Two in agreement, Amos 3:3.
Serving shoulder-to-shoulder, Zephaniah 3:9.
People at peace with each other, Mark 9:50.
Mark of true discipleship, John 13:34–35.
"Perfected in unity," John 17:23 (NRSV).
Unity in group prayer, Acts 1:14 (Berk.).
Devotion to one another, Romans 12:10.
Divine call to unity, 1 Corinthians 1:10–17; 2 Corinthians 13:11; Ephesians 4:3; 1 Peter 3:8.
Joined by Holy Spirit, 2 Corinthians 13:13 (CEV).
Unity in Christ, Galatians 3:28 (LB); Ephesians 2:14.
"Built together spiritually," Ephesians 2:22 (NRSV).
Unity provided by Holy Spirit, Ephesians 4:3 (GNB).
Diversity producing unity, Ephesians 4:11–13.
"Side by side," Philippians 1:27 (AB).
"In the fight together," Philippians 1:30 (LB).
Instructions on unity, Philippians 4:1–9.
United in love, Colossians 2:2.
Orderly array, solid front, Colossians 2:5 (AB).

"Put up with each other," Colossians 3:13 (CEV).
"Try to get along," 1 Thessalonians 5:13 (CEV).
Faith held in common, Titus 1:4.
See Camaraderie, Cooperation, Cybernetics, Rapport, Unanimity.

UNIVERSALISM

One Lord over all earth, Zechariah 14:9.
Works insufficient for salvation, Matthew 7:22–23; Romans 3:20; Ephesians 2:8–9; Titus 3:5.
No universal salvation, Luke 13:22–30.
Righteousness available to all who believe, Romans 10:4.
Potential of universal salvation, 1 Thessalonians 4:10.
God wants all to be saved, 1 Timothy 2:3–4.
All must give account of themselves, 1 Peter 4:4–6.
See Cult, Heresy, Heterodoxy, New Age.

UNIVERSE

Greatness of heavens, smallness of man, Psalm 8:3–4.
Cosmic powers, Ephesians 6:12 (GNB).
Universe formed at God's command, Hebrews 11:3.
See Astronomy, Cosmic, Creation, Space/Time.

UNKIND

Purposeful oppression, Exodus 1:8–14; 5:6–18.
Taking advantage of employees, Deuteronomy 24:14.
Illustration of unkindness, 2 Samuel 12:1–6.
Attribute of arrogance, Psalm 10:2.
"Show him how it feels," Psalm 109:6 (LB).
No thought of unkindness, Psalm 109:16.
Unkindness affronts God, Proverbs 14:31.
Unkind to relatives, Isaiah 58:7.
Purposeful practice of unkindness, Ezekiel 22:27–29.
Example to others, Acts 20:35.
Unpaid wages, James 5:4.
See Cruelty, Heartless.

UNKNOWN

Parable of forgotten Deliverer, Ecclesiastes 9:13–15.
Athenian god, Acts 17:23.
See Anonymity, Secrecy, Stranger.

UNMARRIED *See Single.*

UNPALATABLE

Polluted wheat, Amos 8:6.
Salt loses saltiness, Luke 14:34–35.
Neither cold nor hot, Revelation 3:15–16.
See Appetite.

UNPARDONABLE

Anger beyond measure, Lamentations 5:21–22.
Beyond redemption, Hosea 7:13.
Attributing work of God to demons, Matthew 9:34.
See Reprobate, Unpardonable Sin.

UNPARDONABLE SIN

Holy Spirit grieved, Isaiah 63:10; Ephesians 4:30; 1 Thessalonians 5:19.
Unpardonable sin defined, Matthew 12:31–32; Mark 3:20–30; Luke 12:10.
Ananias and Sapphira, Acts 5:1–10.
Given over to Satan, 1 Timothy 1:20.
Those who turned away, Hebrews 6:4–6.
Sin unto death, 1 John 5:16.

UNPRECEDENTED

Unprecedented man of wisdom, 1 Kings 4:29–34.
The God without precedent, Isaiah 64:4.
Unprecedented promise, Jeremiah 33:3.
"Unheard of disaster," Ezekiel 7:5.
Unprecedented information, Joel 1:2–3 (LB).
Army of locusts, Joel 2:1–9.
See Original, Unique.

UNPREPARED

Guilty people unprepared for worship, Numbers 17:10–13.
Unexpected evil times, Ecclesiastes 9:12.
Sudden appearance, Malachi 3:1.
Conduct before flood, Matthew 24:38–39.

Prepared for second coming, Matthew 24:44; Luke 21:34.
Unworthy servant, Matthew 24:45–51.
Parable of ten virgins, Matthew 25:1–13.
Startled jailer, Acts 16:25–32.
See Lost.

UNPRODUCTIVE

Land that produces sparingly, Isaiah 5:10.
Visions come to nothing, Ezekiel 12:22–25.
See Agriculture, Harvest.

UNPROTECTED

Protection removed, Isaiah 5:5.

UNQUALIFED

Unworthy to build house of God, 1 Chronicles 28:2–3.
Totally unqualified, Titus 1:16 (AB).
See Skill, Talent, Unreliable, Unstable.

UNRELIABLE

Lack of discernment, Deuteronomy 32:28.
Need to learn from ant, Proverbs 6:6.
Unfit for job, Proverbs 18:9; 24:30–31.
Unreliable workman, Ecclesiastes 10:18.
Using dishonest scales, Hosea 12:7.
See Deceit, Unstable.

UNREPENTANT

Judgment upon the persistently unrepentant, Leviticus 26:18–20.
Defiant sin, Numbers 15:30–31.
Divine patience with unrepentant, 2 Kings 8:16–19.
Lamp of wicked, Job 18:5–6.
Playing with fire, Proverbs 6:27–29.
Proclaiming innocence, obviously guilty, Jeremiah 2:34–35.
Hard as stones, Jeremiah 5:3.
Unrepentant, shameless, Jeremiah 8:8–12.
Burning prophecy of Jeremiah, Jeremiah 36:20–24.
Nonfunctioning eyes, ears, Ezekiel 12:2.
See Depravity, Wickedness.

UNRESPONSIVE

Failure to respond, Leviticus 5:1.
Refraining from response, Isaiah 36:18–22 (See 37:1–7).

U

Unresponsive to discipline, Jeremiah 2:30.
Ignoring Word of the Lord, Jeremiah 25:3–4, 7.
Refusing to see, hear, Ezekiel 12:1–2.
See Calloused.

UNREST

Complaining community, Exodus 16:2.
Daily instability, Deuteronomy 28:67.
Unrest caused by troublemaker, 2 Samuel 20:1–2.
Inequity among citizens, Nehemiah 5:1–5.
Chasing wind, Ecclesiastes 2:1.
Unrest day, night, Ecclesiastes 2:23.
Wicked find no rest, Isaiah 57:20–21.
Torment for false worship, Revelation 14:11.
See Restless.

UNRIGHTEOUSNESS

Overt unrighteousness, Romans 1:18–25.
Instruments of unrighteousness, Romans 6:13.
Refusal to believe truth, 2 Thessalonians 2:9–10.
Blatant conduct, 2 Thessalonians 2:10–15.
God's wrath on unrighteousness, Ephesians 5:6; Colossians 3:6.
See Evil.

UNSATISFIED

Prayer for protection, Numbers 10:35.
Unable to tolerate food, Numbers 11:4–6.
All things wearisome, Ecclesiastes 1:2.
Appetite never satisfied, Ecclesiastes 6:7.
Futility of thought, Ephesians 4:17.
Unsatisfied lust, Ephesians 4:19.
See Discontent.

UNSAVED *See Lost.*

UNSCRUPULOUS

Blatant display of immorality, Numbers 25:6–9.
Discerning the prophets, Deuteronomy 18:21–22.
Selfish marital relationship, Deuteronomy 22:13–19.

Palace built by unrighteousness, Jeremiah 22:13–15.
Unscrupulous treatment of slaves, Jeremiah 34:8–22.
Daring to burn prophecy of Jeremiah, Jeremiah 36:21–22.
Prophets who see nothing, Ezekiel 13:1–3.
Despising those who speak truth, Amos 5:10.
Unscrupulous business ethics, Amos 8:5–6.
Mixing human blood with sacrifices, Luke 13:1.
Taking unscrupulous advantage of others, James 5:4–5.
See Deceit, Dishonesty, Scheme.

UNSEEN

Cannot see God and live, Exodus 33:20.
Unseen God, John 1:18; 5:37; Colossians 1:15; 1 Timothy 1:17; 6:16.
God's best beyond visibility, 1 Corinthians 2:9–10.
Visible from invisible, Hebrews 11:3.
Reality of unseen, 1 Peter 1:8–9.
See Invisible.

UNSELFISHNESS

Abraham's example, Genesis 13:6–9.
Unselfishness between brothers, Genesis 33:1–11.
Unselfish option for younger husband, Ruth 4:1–6.
Expression of comradeship, 1 Samuel 18:4.
Share, share alike, 1 Samuel 30:24.
Unselfish gratitude, 2 Samuel 19:29–30 (LB).
Prophet's chamber, 2 Kings 4:8–10.
Unselfish sharing of good fortune, 2 Kings 7:3–9.
Wise king's unselfish prayer, 2 Chronicles 1:7–12.
Unselfish leader, Nehemiah 5:14–15.
Woman's willingness to do her duty, Esther 4:12–16.
Pleasing others, Romans 15:1–3.
Concern for others, 1 Corinthians 10:33.
Supreme model of unselfishness, 2 Corinthians 8:7–9.
Paul's attitude to Corinthians, 2 Corinthians 13:9.

Student sharing with teacher, Galatians 6:6.

Enduring to help others, 2 Timothy 2:10.

See Philanthropy, Generosity, Sharing.

UNSKILLED *See Amateur, Novice.*

UNSTABLE

Unstable appetites, Numbers 11:4–6.

Lack of discernment, Deuteronomy 32:28.

Giving vent to anger, Proverbs 29:11.

Spiritual vagabonds, Jeremiah 2:31.

Easily deceived, Hosea 7:11.

Doctrinal instability, Galatians 1:6–7; Ephesians 4:14.

See Insecurity, Instability.

UNTHANKFUL *See Ingratitude.*

UNTRUTH

False promises, Jeremiah 28:1–11.

See Deceit, Fabrication, Lie.

UNWILLING

First example of unwillingness, Genesis 2:16–17; 3:6.

Daughter-in-law's unwillingness, Ruth 1:14–18.

Unwilling to hear, 2 Chronicles 30:10; 36:16; Proverbs 5:12; Isaiah 30:12; Jeremiah 6:10; Zechariah 7:12.

Refusal to obey, Psalm 81:11; Isaiah 65:12; Jeremiah 7:13.

Example of unwillingness, Jonah 1:1–3.

Banquet invitation refused, Matthew 22:3.

Unwilling to accept Divine blessing, Matthew 23:37; Luke 13:34.

Divine reluctance to invoke judgment, 2 Peter 3:9.

See Disobedience, Resistance, Rebellion, Obstinate.

UNWISE *See Foolish.*

UNWORTHY

Destiny set for rebellious people, Numbers 14:35.

Evil earnings forbidden in house of Lord, Deuteronomy 23:18.

Unworthy to build house of God, 1 Chronicles 28:2–3.

Parables to fool, Proverbs 26:1–12.

Unworthy appeal for God's great mercy, Daniel 9:18.

Unworthy of following Christ, Matthew 10:37–39.

Unworthy banquet guests, Matthew 22:8.

Sense of unworthiness, Acts 13:46.

See Abandoned, Rejection, Value.

UPROAR

Uproar against God, Psalm 74:23 (NASB, NRSV).

UPSTART

Usurping the throne, 1 Kings 1:5–53; 2:13–17.

See Fledgling, Novice.

UPWARD

Elijah to heaven in whirlwind, 2 Kings 2:11.

Christ's ascension, Acts 1:9.

High journey, Deuteronomy 33:26–27; 2 Samuel 22:10–14.

Creator of skies, Job 37:16–18.

Upward look, Psalm 121:1.

See Flight, Height.

U

URBAN

Building first city, Genesis 4:17.

Urban development, Genesis 10:11–12.

Country man, city man, Genesis 13:12.

Cities totally given to debauchery, Genesis 18:16–33.

Dynamic communities, Numbers 13:27–28; Deuteronomy 6:10–12.

Fortified cities, Deuteronomy 9:1 (AB).

Town, country, Deuteronomy 28:3.

Five mayors, 1 Samuel 6:16 (LB).

Struggle for ownership, 2 Kings 13:25.

Urban water works, 2 Chronicles 32:30.

Preferred city, 2 Chronicles 33:7 (CEV).

City planning, Nehemiah 11:1.

USED

Desolate cities, Job 15:28 (KJV).

Daybreak for city in need, Psalm 46:5.

Urban violence, Psalm 55:9–11.

Neighborhood watch, Psalm 101:8 (LB).

Compact Jerusalem, Psalm 122:3.

City government, Proverbs 31:23.

Congested cities, Isaiah 5:8.

Ruined city, Isaiah 17:1.

Beautiful city, Isaiah 60:15 (CEV).

Restored city, Jeremiah 30:17–18 (LB).

Vanquished city, Lamentations 2:15.

Unsafe streets, Hosea 7:1.

Vast city, Jonah 3:3 (RSV, LB).

Plunder victims, Nahum 3:1.

Nineveh's charms, Nahum 3:4 (LB).

City built on crime, violence, Habakkuk 2:12 (CEV).

Once proud city, Zephaniah 2:14 (LB).

City measurement, Zechariah 2:1–2.

Violence, crime, Zephaniah 3:1 (LB).

Children playing in the streets, Zechariah 8:5.

City without boundaries, Zechariah 2:4 (CEV).

Total urban rejection, Matthew 8:34.

Heart cry for urban population, Matthew 23:37; Luke 13:34.

Message-saturated city, Acts 5:28.

"Dangers in the city," 2 Corinthians 11:26 (NASB, NRSV).

New Jerusalem, Revelation 21:2, 15–27.

See City, Street, Utilities.

URGENCY

Hasty meal, Exodus 12:11.

King's business urgent, 1 Samuel 21:8.

Urgent retreat, 2 Samuel 15:14.

Urgent call for help, Psalm 70:5 (GNB).

Making most of time, Psalm 90:12; Ecclesiastes 9:10; Ephesians 5:15–16.

Dial 9–1–1, Psalms 91:1; 120:1.

Urgent proclamation, Isaiah 62:1.

Urgent report to bring, Matthew 28:5–10.

Extend invitations urgently, Luke 14:21.

Shortness of time, 1 Corinthians 7:29–31.

No wasted opportunities, Colossians 4:5.

See Evangelism, Expedient, Haste, Missionary, Soul-winning.

USED

Used gods traded in, Jeremiah 2:10–11 (LB).

USELESS

More useless than crooked arrow, Hosea 7:16

See Value, Valueless, Worthless.

USURP

Usurping throne, 1 Kings 1:5–53 (2:13–17).

UTILITIES

Water brought into city, 2 Kings 20:20.
Urban water works, 2 Chronicles 32:30.

V

VACATION *See Holiday.*

VACILLATE

God does not change His mind, Numbers 23:19.
Wavering between two opinions, 1 Kings 18:21.
Vacillating between pessimism, optimism, Psalm 73:1–28.
Spiritual indecision, Psalm 119:113 (LB).
Easily deceived, Hosea 7:11.
Vacillating Galatians, Galatians 1:6–9.
See Indecision.

VAGABOND

"A tramp upon the earth," Genesis 4:12 (LB).
Self-imposed wandering, Numbers 14:35.
Satan the vagabond, Job 1:7.
Straying like lost sheep, Psalm 119:176; 1 Peter 2:25; 2 Peter 2:15.
Leaving home, Proverbs 27:8.
Spiritual vagabonds, Jeremiah 2:31.
See Nomad, Wandering.

VAGUE

Inept watchman, Isaiah 56:10.
Uncertain prophets, Micah 3:11.
Write message plainly, Habakkuk 2:2.
Trumpeting uncertain sound, 1 Corinthians 14:8–9.
Epistles vague to some, 2 Peter 3:15–16.
Wandering stars, Jude 13.
See Ambiguous, Uncertainty.

VALIDITY

Documentation of ministry, Matthew 11:4–5.
Attempt to distort resurrection reality, Matthew 27:62–66; 28:11–15.
Believe good news, Mark 1:14–15.
Scripture does not require external evidence, Mark 8:11–12.
Living by truth, John 3:21.
Jesus had no need for human credentials, John 5:31–40.
Two witnesses make testimony valid, John 8:17.
Truth gives freedom, John 8:32.
New convert's validity, Acts 9:26–27.
Scripture authority concerning Jesus, Acts 18:28.
Scripture valid in law court, Romans 3:4 (CEV).
Radiant validity, 2 Corinthians 3:7–8.
Love validated, 2 Corinthians 8:24.
Apostolic validity, 2 Corinthians 12:12.
Ministry validated, 2 Corinthians 13:2–3.
Love validates faith, Galatians 5:5.
Validated by Holy Spirit, Ephesians 1:13.
Validity of faith made known, 1 Thessalonians 1:8–10.
Approved by God rather than men, 1 Thessalonians 2:4–6.
All Scripture God-breathed, 2 Timothy 3:16–17.
Faith gives validity to message, Hebrews 4:2.
Sureness, certainty of faith, Hebrews 11:1.
See Authenticity, Genuine.

VALLEY

Valley filled with praise, 2 Chronicles 20:26.
Death valley, Psalm 23:4.
Valleys raised, mountains lowered, Isaiah 40:4.

Valley of dry bones, Ezekiel 37:1.

Troubled Valley, Hopeful Valley, Hosea 2:15 (CEV).

Valley of decision, Joel 3:14.

See Terrain.

VALUE

People more valuable than materials, Genesis 14:21.

Value country well, Genesis 21:25–31; 26:12–17.

"Special treasure," Exodus 19:5 (NKJV).

Human being's monetary value, Leviticus 27:1–8.

Loss of personal worth, Deuteronomy 28:68.

Spoils for conqueror, Judges 5:30.

"Useless as a dead dog," 2 Samuel 16:9 (CEV).

Value of one, ten thousand, 2 Samuel 18:3.

Silver not precious metal, 1 Kings 10:21, 27.

Value distorted by famine, 2 Kings 6:25.

Worthless idols, worthless followers, 2 Kings 17:15 (CEV).

Millions spent on temple, 1 Chronicles 29:6–7 (LB).

Silver of little value, 2 Chronicles 9:20.

Low estimation human worth, Job 25:5–6; Amos 2:6.

People sold for pittance, Psalm 44:12.

God's love more valuable than life, Psalm 63:3.

Life's greatest values, Psalm 119:36–37.

Value lost through lust, Proverbs 6:25–26.

Wisdom greater value than money, Proverbs 16:16.

Better simple food with peace, quiet, Proverbs 17:1.

Pain of being poor, Proverbs 19:7.

Stealing from poor, giving to rich, Proverbs 22:16.

Devoting energy to becoming rich, Proverbs 23:4–5.

Born naked, depart naked, Ecclesiastes 5:15.

Confused values, good, evil, Isaiah 5:20.

Greatest value, Isaiah 33:6.

Sold without value, redeemed, Isaiah 52:3.

That which money cannot buy, Isaiah 55:1–2.

Some juice left in grapes, Isaiah 65:8.

Losing in bad exchange, Jeremiah 2:11.

Gold, gems with lost value, Lamentations 4:1; Ezekiel 7:19–20.

Silver thrown into streets, Ezekiel 7:19.

Useless, worthless, Ezekiel 15:5 (CEV).

Prostitute giving rather than receiving, Ezekiel 16:32–34.

Cheap price for adulterous woman, Hosea 3:2 (LB).

Lost value of children, Joel 3:3.

Stolen treasure, Obadiah 6 (CEV).

Silver, gold like dust, dirt, Zechariah 9:3.

Value of sparrow, value of soul, Matthew 10:28–30.

Losing life to find it again, Matthew 10:39.

Purchase of sure investment, Matthew 13:44.

Value of one lost sheep, Matthew 18:12–14.

Temple gold, Matthew 23:16.

Eternal value of soul, Mark 8:35–37.

First last, last first, Mark 10:31.

Widow's two small coins, Mark 12:41–44; Luke 21:1–4.

Putting first things first, Luke 10:38–42.

One Christian's value, Luke 12:6–7.

Value of what is lost, Luke 15:1–32.

Price indicates value, John 3:16; 1 Corinthians 6:20; 1 Peter 1:18–19; Revelation 1:5.

Spiritual economics, Acts 3:6.

Scrolls of value destroyed, Acts 19:19.

Wood, hay, straw—gold, silver, costly stones, 1 Corinthians 3:12–13.

Greater value than money, 2 Corinthians 12:14 (LB).

"Proven worth," Philippians 2:22 (NASB).

"Surpassing value," Philippians 3:8 (NASB, NRSV).

Proper understanding of law, 1 Timothy 1:8–11.

Instruments of gold, silver, wood, clay, 2 Timothy 2:20–21.

Good land, unproductive land, Hebrews 6:7–8.

Loss of material possessions, Hebrews 10:34 (GNB).

Disgrace greater value than treasures, Hebrews 11:26.

Sold birthright, Hebrews 12:16–17.

Eternal inheritance, 1 Peter 1:4.

Greatest value, 1 Peter 1:7.

Not redeemed with silver and gold, 1 Peter 1:18–19.

Men reject, God choses, 1 Peter 2:4.

Least important, most important, 1 Peter 2:7.

Precious faith, 2 Peter 3:11–14.

See Cost, Treasure, Worth.

VALUELESS

Foam on water, Job 24:18.

Valueless money, Ezekiel 7:19 (LB).

See Worthless.

VALUES

Life, death, 2 Samuel 19:6.

Distorted values, Psalm 52:7 (KJV); Isaiah 5:20.

Evil as good, good as evil, Isaiah 5:20.

Ruined temple, luxurious homes, Haggai 1:2–3.

VANITY

Success caused pride, downfall, 2 Chronicles 26:16.

Victim of vanity, 2 Chronicles 32:24–26.

Six-month display of king's wealth, Esther 1:1–5.

Affronted ego, Esther 3:5; 5:9.

Accused of hypocrisy, Job 11:4–6.

"Think you are so great," Job 12:2 (CEV).

Vanity numbs realization of sin, Psalm 36:2.

Obtaining divine attention, Psalm 138:6.

Pretending to be what one is not, Proverbs 12:9; 13:7.

Vanity on display, Proverbs 21:24.

Strutting rooster, Proverbs 30:31.

Haughty women become bald, Isaiah 3:16–17.

Those wise in their own eyes, Isaiah 5:21.

Pride of conqueror brought down, Jeremiah 50:11–12.

Deification of self, Ezekiel 16:23–24.

Skill in business brings vanity of heart, Ezekiel 28:4–5.

Egypt's claim of possessing the Nile, Ezekiel 29:3–5.

Vanity over wealth, self-righteousness, Hosea 12:8.

Destruction of wise men, Obadiah 8.

Proud, arrogant, strut around, Zephaniah 3:11 (CEV).

Seeking notice, acclaim, Luke 11:43.

Choosing place of honor, Luke 14:7–11.

Vain sorcerer, Acts 8:9.

High cost of flagrant vanity, Acts 12:19–23.

Boast only in the Lord, 1 Corinthians 1:31.

Physique, talent come from God, 1 Corinthians 4:7.

Pride over immorality, 1 Corinthians 5:1–2.

Danger of intellectual pride, 1 Corinthians 8:1–3.

"Know it all," 1 Corinthians 9:22–23 (LB).

Comparing oneself with oneself, 2 Corinthians 10:12.

Those who only seem to be important, Galatians 2:6.

Vain self-appraisal, Galatians 6:3 (See AB).

Making impression on others, Philippians 2:3 (LB).

Role of conceit in false doctrine, 1 Timothy 6:3–5.

Monetary wealth, wealth of good deeds, 1 Timothy 6:11–19.

Empty, boastful words, 2 Peter 2:18.

False claim of holy life, 1 John 1:8–10.

Vanity causing disruption in congregation, 3 John 9–10.

Pride, blasphemy, Revelation 13:5.

See Arrogance. Conceit, Pride.

VANQUISHED

Refusing treachery against enemy, 1 Samuel 26:1–25.

Enjoying plunder taken in battle, 1 Samuel 30:16.

Death by measurement, 2 Samuel 8:2.

Haunt of jackals, Jeremiah 9:11.

Break bow, Jeremiah 49:35.

Enemy put to silence, Jeremiah 51:55.

Deserted city, Lamentations 1:1.

Ashamed, silent before the Lord, Ezekiel 16:63.

See Defeat.

VANTAGE

View of Canaan, Deuteronomy 3:27; 32:48–52; 34:1–5.

Immeasurable greatness of God, 2 Chronicles 6:12–19.

Window vantage onto street, Proverbs 7:6–13.

Vantage between earth, heaven, Ezekiel 8:3.

Lofty vantage of New Jerusalem, Revelation 21:10.

See Viewpoint, Reconnaissance.

VARIANCE *See Argument, Conflict, Disagreement, Dispute.*

VARIETY

Variety in species, Genesis 1:24–25.

Same food for forty years, Exodus 16:35.

Inexhaustible snowflake design, Job 38:22.

Gold cup designs, Esther 1:7.

New every day, Lamentations 3:22–24.

Wide variety of merchandise, Ezekiel 27:12–23.

Variety of gifts among Christians, 1 Corinthians 12:4–11.

"Rich variety," Ephesians 3:10 (NRSV).

See Diversity.

VASTNESS

Army of locusts, Joel 2:1–9.

Comtemplating resurrection, exaltation, Ephesians 1:18–23.

Holy Spirit's power within, Ephesians 3:20–21.

See Immensity, Infinite, Space/Time.

VEGETABLES

Remembered vegetables of Egypt, Numbers 11:4–6.

Field of peas, 2 Samuel 23:11 (GNB).

Vegetables for king, 1 Kings 21:2.

Garden slug, Psalm 58:8.

Bean pods, Luke 15:16 (Berk.).

See Garden, Horticulture.

VEGETARIAN

Man, animals originally vegetarian, Genesis 1:29–30.

Using meat as food, Genesis 9:3.

Caution regarding eating of meat, Genesis 9:4.

Discontent over meatless diet, Numbers 11:4–6.

Greedy for meat, Numbers 11:31–34 (CEV).

Vegetable meal preferred, Proverbs 15:17.

Vegetable diet, Daniel 1:8–16.

Vegetable diet, Romans 14:2.

See Diet.

VEGETATION

Vegetables, meat, Genesis 9:3.

Abundant vegetation, Psalm 104:13–15.

See Agriculture.

VELOCITY *See Speed.*

VENDETTA *See Enemy, Revenge.*

VENEREAL DISEASE

Object of curse, 2 Samuel 3:29 (GNB).

VENGEANCE

No refuge in cities of refuge, Deuteronomy 19:11–13; Joshua 20:1–3.

Dramatic reversal of fortunes, Esther 5:9—7:10.

Golden rule reversed, Proverbs 24:29.

Folly of revenge, Ezekiel 25:15–17.

Leave revenge in God's hands, 2 Thessalonians 1:6–7.

Those who crucified Jesus shall see Him coming again, Revelation 1:7.

See Retribution, Revenge.

VENOM

Venom of judgment, Numbers 21:6–9.

Snakes' venom, Deuteronomy 32:24; Job 20:16; Psalm 58:4–5.

Lips like venom, Psalm 140:3; James 3:7–8.

Locusts like scorpions, Revelation 9:7–11.

See Poison, Snakes.

VENTILATION

Ventilation space in ark, Genesis 6:16 (CEV).

See Air Conditioning.

VENTRILOQUIST

Voice coming from earth, Isaiah 29:4.

VERBAL

Verbal commitment, Exodus 24:7.

VERBOSE

Words like blustering wind, Job 8:2.
Wrong, right boasting, Jeremiah 9:23–24.
Cynical tongues made silent, Luke 20:20–26.
Long-winded, Loquacious, Talkative.

VERDICT

Jury by plebiscite, Joshua 24:14–21; Matthew 27:15–23.
Wisdom of Solomon, 1 Kings 3:16–28.
Pilate said, "Not guilty," John 19:6 (AB).
See Judge, Jury.

VERSATILITY

All kinds of work, Exodus 1:14.
Wood for making gods, cooking fires, Isaiah 44:14–20.
All-sufficiency of our Lord, Isaiah 44:24–28.
From one sin to another, Jeremiah 9:3.
New everyday, Lamentations 3:22–24.
Training for Daniel, friends, Daniel 1:3–4.
Scripture's versatility, 2 Timothy 3:16–17.
See Ability, Ambidextrous, Talent.

VETERINARY

Animal miscarriage, Job 21:10.

VEXATION

Testing Moses' patience, Exodus 17:1–2.
Making wrong a right, Numbers 5:6–7.
Rebuffed by subordinate, Esther 5:9–10.
Giving heed to instruction, Proverbs 16:20.
See Anger, Disgust, Hatred, Trouble Maker.

VIBES

Good vibes lead to friendship, 1 Samuel 18:1–2 (LB).

VIBRATION

Divine vibrations, Psalm 29:5.

VICARIOUS

Sin's penalty taken for us, Isaiah 53:1–7; John 15:13; Galatians 3:13; Hebrews 2:9; 1 Peter 3:18.
In love with pictures, Ezekiel 23:14–17.
Experiencing in thought what others perform, Romans 2:1–11.
Willing to be cursed for other's salvation, Romans 9:3–4.
Concern for spiritual development of followers, Colossians 2:1–5.
See Empathy, Substitute.

VICE

Evil earnings forbidden, Deuteronomy 23:18.
Covenant to avoid lust, Job 31:1.
Playing with fire, Proverbs 6:27–28.
Haughty women, Isaiah 3:16.
Unable to blush, Jeremiah 6:15.
Vice of two sisters, Ezekiel 23:1–49.
For continued sinning, certain judgment, Amos 1:3, 6, 9, 11, 13; 2:1, 4, 6.
Vice in broad daylight, 2 Peter 2:13–22.
See Debauchery, Depravity, Immorality, Lust.

VICIOUS

Appeasment of jealousy, Genesis 37:23–24.
Weapons of violence, Genesis 49:5.
Destruction of children, Exodus 1:22.
Mutilation of hands, feet, Judges 1:6.
Violent murder, Judges 4:21; 5:24–27.
People burned to death, Judges 9:49.
Violent treaty, 1 Samuel 11:1–2.
Death of Absalom, 2 Samuel 18:9–15.
Sadistic killing, 2 Kings 25:7.
Prophet lowered into mud, Jeremiah 38:6.
See Ferocity, Heartless.

VICTIM

"Persecuted without cause," Psalm 119:86 (NRSV).
See Martyr, Persecution.

VICTORY

Master over sin, Genesis 4:7.
Victory song, Exodus 15:1–18.
Assured victory, Deuteronomy 3:2.
Yours to conquer, Joshua 8:1 (LB).
Victorious in death more than life, Judges 16:30.
"We won!" 2 Samuel 18:28 (CEV).
Resource in time of weakness, 2 Chronicles 14:11.

Certainty of God's promises, 2 Chronicles 20:17.

Victory, defeat in God's hands, 2 Chronicles 25:8.

Trusting God for deliverance, 2 Chronicles 32:1–21.

Power of God's name in time of trouble, Psalms 54:1; 118:8–12.

God, not man, best help in time of trouble, Psalm 60:11–12.

Key to victory over sin, Psalm 119:133.

Strength to declare God's message, Jeremiah 1:6–10, 17–19.

Jesus responded to Satan with Scripture, Matthew 4:1–11.

Freedom from mastery of sin, Romans 6:14.

Nothing separates from God's love, Romans 8:37–39 (LB).

In serving God, all may win, 1 Corinthians 9:24–27.

Armor of God, Ephesians 6:10–18.

Encouraging report, 1 Thessalonians 3:6–8.

Ultimate victory over man of sin, 2 Thessalonians 2:8.

Mature Christian life, 2 Peter 1:5–9.

Deliverance from continual sin, 1 John 3:4–6.

Satan's work destroyed, 1 John 3:8.

Overcoming world through faith, 1 John 5:4.

Certainty of success in Christian life, Jude 24–25.

Satan's inevitable defeat, Revelation 12:1–9.

VAGUE

Rejoicing in victory over Babylon, Revelation 19:6–8.
See Conquest.

VIEWPOINT

Negative, positive viewpoints, Numbers 13:17–33.
God's viewpoint, and man's, Job 10:3–7; Isaiah 55:8–9.
Two sides of wisdom, Job 10:5–6.
Bible-centered viewpoint, Psalm 1:2.
Ask for eternal viewpoint, Jeremiah 33:3.
Conflicting viewpoints, Galatians 2:11.
"Adopt no other view," Galatians 5:10 (NASB).
Positive, negative viewpoints, Titus 1:15 (LB).
See Opinion, Prejudice, Vantage.

VIGIL

Lamps burning continually, Leviticus 24:1–4.

VIGILANCE

Remembering, following divine teaching, Deuteronomy 4:9.
King's business urgent, 1 Samuel 21:8.
Working, protecting, Nehemiah 4:16.
Total vigilance against attack, Nahum 2:1.
Making most of opportunities, Ephesians 5:15–16.
Ready to serve, witness, Ephesians 6:15.
Beware fine-sounding arguments, Colossians 2:4.
See Alert.

VIGOROUS

Not giving in to weariness, Judges 8:4.
Vigor of strong man, Judges 15:16.
Strength in numbers, Proverbs 30:25.
Full of vigor, Ecclesiastes 9:10.
Race not to swift or strong, Ecclesiastes 9:11.
Strength for weary, Isaiah 40:29–31.
Longevity like days of tree, Isaiah 65:22.
See Health, Strength, Virility, Vitality.

VILLAGE

Village evangelism, Mark 1:38; Luke 8:1; 9:6.

VINDICATION

Vindication by earthquake, Numbers 16:28–34.
Cities of refuge, Numbers 35:6–15.
Act of mercy rewarded, 1 Samuel 24:1–22.
Elijah versus Baal, 1 Kings 18:22–38.
Beleagured Job vindicated, Job 42:7–10.
Vindicated by divine might, Psalm 54:1 (NRSV).
Self-vindication, Acts 24:10–27.
See Innocence.

VINDICTIVE

Confrontation between two forces, 2 Samuel 2:12–17.
Vindictive conduct, 2 Samuel 4:1–12.
Variance of attitudes, 2 Kings 6:20–23.
Revenge of bad conscience, 2 Chronicles 16:7–10; 18:23–27.
Contemplated genocide, Esther 3:6.
Stark picture of vengeance, Psalms 58:10; 68:23.
Evil to those who do evil, Psalm 137:8–9.
When not to do as others have done, Proverbs 24:29.
Divine vindictiveness, Habakkuk 1:1–4.
Conflict between husband, wife, Mark 6:17–29.
Potential mob violence during Passover, Mark 14:1–2.
Call for divine vengeance, Luke 9:51–56.
Violence in believer's momentary anger, John 18:10–11.
Evil characters incited against evangelists, Acts 17:5–7.
Vindictive strife, Acts 23:9–12.
See Revenge.

VINEYARD

Grazing law, Exodus 22:5.
Vineyards at rest, Exodus 23:11; Leviticus 25:4.
Benevolent use of vineyard, Leviticus 19:10; Deuteronomy 24:21.
Enjoying the vineyard, Deuteronomy 20:6; 23:24.
Crop management, Deuteronomy 22:9.
"Notable vine," Ezekiel 34:29 (LB).
See Horticulture.

V

VIOLENCE

Incessant violence, Genesis 6:13; Isaiah 59:6; Jeremiah 6:7; Ezekiel 8:17.

Violent thieves, Job 24:2–4; Amos 3:10.

Urban violence, Psalm 55:9; Micah 6:12.

Violence avoided, Psalm 17:4 (NIV).

Garments of violence, Psalm 73:6.

"Wine of violence," Proverbs 4:17.

"Violence is everywhere," Hosea 4:2 (CEV).

"Violently persecuted," Galatians 1:13 (NRSV).

See Bloodshed, Carnage.

VIP

God's big man, Ephesians 3:8–9.

VIRGIN

Father's evil offer of virgin daughters, Genesis 19:4–8.

Defiled virgin, Genesis 34:1–4.

Virgin spared in time of war, Numbers 31:17–18.

Plundered virgins, Deuteronomy 21:10–14.

Medical proof of virginity, Deuteronomy 22:13–19.

Sacrifice of daughter, Judges 11:30–40.

Incarnation prophesied, Isaiah 7:14; Matthew 1:22–23.

Matrimonial happiness, Isaiah 62:5.

Pregnant virgin, Matthew 1:25 (LB).

Ten virgins, Matthew 25:1–13.

No specific command, 1 Corinthians 7:25–26.

Presented to husband, 2 Corinthians 11:2–3.

See Chastity.

VIRGIN BIRTH

Prophesied virgin birth, Isaiah 7:14 (NRSV).

Virgin birth, Matthew 1:18–25; Luke 2:1–7.

Essence of virgin birth, John 1:14; 1 John 4:9.

See Nativity.

VIRGIN MARY

Relationship of Jesus to His mother, Mark 3:31–35.

See Roman Catholics.

VIRILITY

Geriatric virility, Genesis 17:17; 18:11–14; Deuteronomy 34:7; Psalm 92:14–15.

Joseph's virility, Genesis 39:6.

Animals offered in sacrifice, Leviticus 22:24–25.

Worship requirement, Deuteronomy 23:1.

Virile soldiers, 2 Samuel 10:12.

Old age, youth, 1 Kings 2:1–4.

Virile soldiers, 1 Chronicles 12:8–14.

Freedom from human illness, Psalm 73:5.

Race not to swift or strong, Ecclesiastes 9:11.

"Die during my best years," Isaiah 38:10 (CEV).

Strength for weary, Isaiah 40:29–31.

Spiritual virility, Jeremiah 17:7–8.

Looking in vain for man among men, Ezekiel 22:30.

Virile men, prostitute, Ezekiel 23:20.

Pagan virility, Habakkuk 1:11.

"Mature man," Ephesians 4:13 (NASB).

"Power of procreation," Hebrews 11:11 (NRSV).

See Athletics, Soldier.

VIRTUE

Nakedness of Noah, Genesis 9:20–27.

Father's offer of virgin daughters, Genesis 19:4–8.

Modest Rebekah, Genesis 24:61–65.

Dependable employees, 2 Chronicles 34:12; Nehemiah 13:13.

Loyalty, kindness, Proverbs 3:3 (LB).

Looking for one honest person, Jeremiah 5:1.

Act of shame, Jeremiah 13:26.

Daniel's impeccable virtues, Daniel 6:4.

Cheap price for lost virtue, Hosea 3:2 (LB).

Incapable of virtue, Hosea 8:5.

Unable to do right, Amos 3:10.

Stern principle, Matthew 1:19 (LB).

Always doing what is right, Romans 12:17.

Virtue as means of witness, 1 Peter 3:1–2.

See Chastity, Purity.

VISA

Travel across national boundaries, Nehemiah 2:1–10.

VISAGE

Radiant visage, Exodus 34:29–32; 2 Corinthians 3:7–8.

Wisdom brightens visage, Ecclesiastes 8:1.

Visage betrays conscience, Isaiah 3:9.

Transfigured visage, Matthew 17:1–3.

Angel at empty tomb, Matthew 28:1–4.

Countenance of Stephen, Acts 6:15.

See Countenance, Face.

VISIBILITY

Not putting the Lord to the test, Isaiah 7:10–12.

Certainty of day, night, Jeremiah 33:19–22.

Ezekiel's vision, Ezekiel 1:25–28.

Blind man's ears caused eyes to open, Luke 18:35–43.

Seeing not necessarily believing, John 7:3–5.

Faith more important than things tangible, 2 Corinthians 5:7.

Light makes everything visible, Ephesians 5:14.

Invisible made visible, Colossians 1:15 (GNB).

Jesus clearly seen, Hebrews 2:9.

Reality of unseen, 1 Peter 1:8–9.

See Clarity, Tangible.

VISION

Appearance of the Lord, Genesis 18:1.

Visions rare, 1 Samuel 3:1, 15.

Opening eyes to see God's provision, 2 Kings 6:16–17.

Divine message through dreams, visions, Job 33:14–17.

Lacking vision of future, Ecclesiastes 3:22.

Cause of dreams, Ecclesiastes 5:3.

Perceptive vision, Isaiah 1:1 (AB).

Noble person eloquently described, Isaiah 32:8.

Lofty view, Isaiah 33:16.

God makes a new thing, Isaiah 43:19.

Time for vision, Isaiah 54:2–3; Micah 7:11.

Ezekiel's vision, Ezekiel 1:1.

Vision comes to nothing, Ezekiel 12:22–25.

Prophecy of imagination, Ezekiel 13:1–23.

Visions recorded, Daniel 7:1.

Only one saw vision, Daniel 10:7 (NRSV).

Young prophesy, old dream dreams, Joel 2:28.

Something beyond belief, Habakkuk 1:5.

"So-called visions," Zechariah 13:4 (CEV).

Partial, then full vision, Mark 8:22–25.

Fisherman's vision, Luke 5:1–11.

Trance or dream, Acts 10:9–16 (CEV).

Surface vision, 2 Corinthians 10:7.

Caught up into third heaven, 2 Corinthians 12:1–4 (GNB).

Eyes of heart, Ephesians 1:18–19.

See Dream, Eyes, Horizon, Sight.

VISITATION

Sick call, Isaiah 39:1–2.

Attitude toward outsiders, Colossians 4:5.

VISITOR

Public relations approach, 1 Kings 1:42.

Visiting one terminally ill, 2 Kings 13:14.

Intended encouragement, Job 2:11–13.

Gift for departing visitor, Jeremiah 40:4–5.

Wise men, Jesus, Matthew 2:1–2.

Ministry to sick, Matthew 25:36; James 5:14.

Short visit, John 2:12.

Visitor brings blessing, Romans 15:29.

Coming to stay awhile, 1 Corinthians 16:5–6.

Refreshing visitors, 1 Corinthians 16:18.

Planning double visit, 2 Corinthians 1:16.

Paul's visit with Peter, Galatians 1:18.

Eagerness to visit, 1 Thessalonians 3:11.

Guest room, Philemon 22.

See Guests, Hospitality.

VISUAL

Avoid detracting architecture, Deuteronomy 16:21–22.

Memorial stone, Joshua 24:26–27 (LB).

God's visible arm, Isaiah 30:30.

Prophecy of boiling pot, Jeremiah 1:13–15.

Old Testament object lessons, Jeremiah 13:1–11; 19:1–12.

Good figs, bad figs, Jeremiah 24:1–10.

Siege of Jerusalem illustrated, Ezekiel 4:1–3.

Basket of ripe fruit, Amos 8:1–2.

Measuring basket, Zechariah 5:5–11.

V

Visual marks of cross as identity, John 20:20–29.

Using object to illustrate point, Acts 21:10–11.

Christ as visualization of deity, Colossians 1:15; 2:9.

See Audiovisual.

VITALITY

Vitality of bread loaf, Judges 7:13–15.

Race not to swift or strong, Ecclesiastes 9:11.

Strength for weary, Isaiah 40:29–31.

Vitality to arid land, Ezekiel 47:6–12.

Daniel's vitality, Daniel 10:15–19.

Filled with power, Micah 3:8.

Vitality from the Lord, Habakkuk 3:19.

Spiritual union with the Lord, Ephesians 6:10 (GNB).

Resurrection vitality, Philippians 3:10.

Promise of life in Christ, 2 Timothy 1:1.

See Health, Strength, Virility.

VOCABULARY

Common language, Genesis 11:1 (ASB, RSV).

Wrong use of words, Leviticus 24:13–16.

"Hunt for words," Job 18:2 (NASB).

Resolving not to sin with words, Psalm 17:3.

Simple words, profound meaning, Psalm 23:1–6.

Finding right word, Proverbs 15:23 (GNB).

Buying truth, not selling, Proverbs 23:23.

Apt choice of vocabulary, Proverbs 25:11.

Charming but malicious speech, Proverbs 26:24–26.

Instructed tongue, Isaiah 50:4.

Learning new vocabulary, Daniel 1:3–4.

Lips purified, Zephaniah 3:9.

Use of pleasant words, Luke 4:22.

Words beyond normal vocabulary, Romans 8:16, 26–27; 1 Corinthians 2:1 (GNB).

Avoiding persuasive words, 1 Corinthians 2:4.

Spiritual thoughts, spiritual words, 1 Corinthians 2:13 (NASB).

See Communication, Eloquence, Speech.

VOCALIST *See Choir, Solo.*

VOCATION

Different vocations, Genesis 4:2–3.

Unique role of priest, Deuteronomy 18:1–2.

Protecting debtor's earning power, Deuteronomy 24:6.

Evaluation of life, Ecclesiastes 5:15.

Fellow tent makers, Acts 18:1–4.

See Employment, Labor, Skill.

VOICE

Vocal vibrations, Psalm 29:5.

Throaty outcry, Luke 23:18 (AB).

Voice identification, John 10:4–5.

See Singing, Speech, Ventriloquist.

VOLCANO

Smoking mountains, Psalm 144:5.

Stream of burning sulphur, Isaiah 30:33.

Volcano caused by falling star, Revelation 9:1–2.

VOLITION

Heart volition to do God's work, Exodus 35:20–29.

Sin of only one person, Numbers 16:22.

Not giving in to weariness, Judges 8:4.

King's business urgent, 1 Samuel 21:8.

Leadership under divine guidance, 2 Chronicles 31:20–21.

Earth formed for a purpose, Isaiah 45:18.

Great peace to those who obey, Isaiah 48:17–18.

Evil actions, choices, Isaiah 65:11–12.

Birds know seasons of migration, Jeremiah 8:7.

Valley of decision, Joel 3:14.

Influencing others to sin, Luke 17:1.

Filled with knowledge of God's will, Colossians 1:9–12.

See Initiative, Motivation.

VOLUNTEER

Distress, debt, discontent, 1 Samuel 22:2.

Volunteering personally, 2 Chronicles 17:16.

People volunteer freely, Psalm 110:3 (NASB).

"At his own expense," Acts 28:30 (NRSV).

Not volunteering, 1 Corinthians 9:17 (LB).

See Call, Choice, Commitment.

VOTE

Appointment of leader, Numbers 27:16.
Choosing right leader, Deuteronomy 17:14–15.
Trees seek king, Judges 9:7–15.
Choice of Jesus or Barabbas, Matthew 27:15–26.
Casting lots to determine God's will, Acts 1:23–26.
Agreeing in united mind and thought, 1 Corinthians 1:10.
See Politics.

VOW

Conditional vow, Genesis 28:20–21.
"Explicit vow," Leviticus 27:2 (NRSV).
Keeping your word, Numbers 21:2; Deuteronomy 23:21; Ecclesiastes 5:4.
Making, keeping vows, Numbers 30:2–5.
Daughter sacrificed for vow, Judges 11:30–35.
"Sacred promise," Judges 21:1 (CEV).
Mother's promise for a son, 1 Samuel 1:11.
Keeping one's vow to God, Psalm 65:1; Ecclesiastes 5:4–5.
Think, then promise, Ecclesiastes 5:2 (CEV).
Vow to Queen of Heaven, Jeremiah 44:24–30.
Forced to break vow, Amos 2:12; Numbers 6:1–3.
Keep promises, Matthew 5:33 (CEV).
Peter vowed not to betray, Mark 14:29–31, 66–72.
Haircut in response to vow, Acts 18:18.
See Pledge, Promise.

VOYAGE

Voyage for gold, 1 Kings 22:48.
Experienced sailors, 2 Chronicles 8:18.
Widely divergent cargo, 2 Chronicles 9:21.
Speed boats, Job 9:26.
Paths in sea, Isaiah 43:16.

Dependable sea transportation, Isaiah 60:9.

Rebel voyager, Jonah 1:1–3.

Perilous voyage, Acts 27:1–44.

See Maritime, Navigation.

VULGAR

People like animals in times of distress, Deuteronomy 28:53–57.

Vulgar request for dowry, 1 Samuel 18:25.

Affronting God with vulgarity, Job 7:19 (GNB).

Sick drunk, Isaiah 28:7.

Vulgar eating, drinking, Isaiah 36:12.

Vulgar demeaning of Jesus, John 9:34 (LB).

See Debase.

VULNERABILITY

Foolish sins, Numbers 12:11.

Negative, positive viewpoints, Numbers 13:17–33.

No success outside God's will, Numbers 14:41–45.

Do not take on ways of heathen, Deuteronomy 18:9.

Perfume for lady, Ruth 3:3.

Surrender to power of God, 1 Samuel 14:1–14.

Refusal to take advantage of vulnerability, 1 Samuel 26:1–25.

Lack of confidence, 1 Samuel 27:1.

Misunderstanding gesture of goodwill, 2 Samuel 10:1–4.

Weariness lures enemy to strike, 2 Samuel 21:15–17.

Protection against enemies along road, Ezra 8:21–23.

Times of trouble, Proverbs 24:10.

Those who trust in material security, Isaiah 31:1–3.

Haunt of jackals, Jeremiah 9:11.

Looking to flesh for strength, Jeremiah 17:5.

No chance for escape, Jeremiah 48:44.

Guilt of influencing others to sin, Luke 17:1.

See Weakness.

VULTURES *See Scavengers.*

W

WAGES

Wages due daily, Leviticus 19:13; Deuteronomy 24:15.

Evil earnings forbidden, Deuteronomy 23:18.

Room, board, spending money, Judges 17:10.

Dissatisfied workers, Matthew 20:1–14.

Proper care of servants, Job 31:13–14; Colossians 4:1.

Expecting free service without pay, Jeremiah 22:13.

No wages, no business opportunities, Zechariah 8:10.

Rejected wages, Zechariah 11:13 (CEV).

Insufficient wages, Haggai 1:6 (GNB).

Serving without pay, 1 Corinthians 9:7, 12.

Unfair laborers, Malachi 3:5; James 5:4.

Wages an obligation, not a gift, Romans 4:4.

See Honorarium, Remuneration, Salary, Stipend.

WAITER

Headwaiter, John 2:9 (NASB).

WAITING

Long years, short time, Genesis 29:20.

"Havingly patiently waited," Hebrews 6:15 (CEV).

See Delay, Procrastination.

WALK

Righteous path, wicked way, Proverbs 4:18–19, 25, 27.

Stately strides, Proverbs 30:29–31 (NIV).

Ask for ancient paths, Jeremiah 6:16.

One who brings good news, Isaiah 52:7; Nahum 1:15; Romans 10:15.

Jesus took lengthy walk, John 7:1 (KJV).

New spiritual walk, Romans 6:4; Galatians 5:16; Ephesians 4:1–32.

Believer's walk, Colossians 2:6 (KJV).

See Feet, Hiking, Journey.

WALL

Thick walls insecure, Jeremiah 5:17 (CEV).

City walls burned, Jeremiah 49:27 (CEV).

VULTURES/SCAVENGERS

Seeking walled security, Jeremiah 4:6 (CEV).
Earthen ramps, Habakkuk 1:10.

WANDERING

Wandering murderer, Genesis 4:12.
Groping in the streets, Lamentations 4:14.
Uprooted nation, Numbers 32:10–15; Hosea 9:17.
Straying sheep, 1 Peter 2:25.
Eternal disorientation, Jude 11–13.
See Vagabond.

WANTONNESS

No evil earnings in house of the Lord, Deuteronomy 23:18.
People like animals in times of distress, Deuteronomy 28:53–57.
Imbibing without restraint, Esther 1:7–8.
Playing with fire, Proverbs 6:27–28.
Delinquent son, Proverbs 29:3; Luke 15:13.
Adultery in profusion, Jeremiah 3:6.
Deceit with no shame, Jeremiah 8:8–12.
Continual lust for more, Ephesians 4:19.
Flagrant worldliness, James 5:5; 2 Peter 2:18.
See Debauchery, Depravity, Immorality, Lust.

WAR

Victory assured in advance, Numbers 21:34.
Power in numbers, Numbers 22:2–4.
God greater than numbers, Deuteronomy 20:1.
Civilian and military, Deuteronomy 20:5–9.

Price of possession, Joshua 1:12–15.
Use of ambush, Joshua 8:14–29.
Apparent supremacy of enemy, Joshua 11:1–6.
Learning to wage war, Judges 3:1–2.
Those excluded from battle, Judges 12:1–3.
Surrender to power of God, 1 Samuel 14:1–14.
Futility of war, 2 Samuel 1:27.
Fortunes of war, 2 Samuel 11:25 (CEV).
Trained for battle, 2 Samuel 22:35.
Brother against brother, 2 Chronicles 11:4.
Children destined for war, Job 27:14.
God trained David for war, Psalm 18:34.
Courage in time of war, Psalm 27:3.
Those who hate peace, Psalm 120:6–7.
Time for war, Ecclesiastes 3:8.
Millennial peace among nations, Isaiah 2:4.
Awesome defeat, Isaiah 13:11–18.
Devastating statement of God's judgment, Isaiah 34:1–7.
Daring to scoff at name of the Lord, Isaiah 36:18–21.
Break bow, Jeremiah 49:35.
Coming great war against Israel, Ezekiel 38 and 39.
Plowshares to swords, Joel 3:10.
No world peace without Christ, Matthew 24:6–8; Mark 13:6–8.
Four horsemen, Revelation 6:1–6.
One fourth of earth's population destroyed, Revelation 6:8.
War in heaven, Revelation 12:7.
See Army, Military, Scorched Earth, Soldier.

WARDROBE

Tunic of many colors, Genesis 37:3 (NKJV).

Widow's clothes, Genesis 38:14.

Clothes make the man, Exodus 28:2; James 2:2–3 (AB).

Goliath's weighty armor, 1 Samuel 17:4–7 (LB).

Prison clothes, 2 Kings 25:29.

Royal wardrobe, Esther 6:8, 15; Psalm 45:13; Acts 12:21.

Wardrobe items, Isaiah 20:2; Jeremiah 13:2.

Warm weather, warm clothes, Job 37:17.

Dressed for church, Psalm 29:2 (Berk.).

Fragrant wardrobe, Psalm 45:8.

Gold interwoven gown, Psalm 45:13.

Winter wear, Proverbs 31:21.

Wearing white, Ecclesiastes 9:8.

Extreme weather concern, Ecclesiastes 11:4.

Fragrant garments, Song of Songs 4:11.

Leadership to man with cloak, Isaiah 3:6.

Luxurious wardrobe denied, Isaiah 3:18–24.

Elaborate robe, Isaiah 6:1.

Garments of righteousness, Isaiah 11:5.

Cloud shadow, Isaiah 25:5 (AB).

Useless fabric, Isaiah 59:5–6.

Clothing for idols, Jeremiah 10:8–9 (LB).

Wardrobe market, Ezekiel 27:24.

Everyone in sackcloth, Jonah 3:5 (CEV).

Foreign wardrobe, Zephaniah 1:8.

Joshua's filthy clothes, Zechariah 3:3.

Camouflaged piety, Matthew 6:17–18 (LB).

Palace wardrobe, Matthew 11:8.

Camel's hair clothing, Mark 1:6.

Wardrobe instructions, Mark 6:9.

"Swaddling clothes," Luke 2:7–12.

Repairing old garment, Luke 5:36.

"Dressed for action," Luke 12:35 (GNB).

Best robe, Luke 15:22.

Well-dressed rich man, Luke 16:19.

"Shiver in the cold," 1 Corinthians 4:11 (AB).

Clothed for Christian service, Ephesians 6:15 (NRSV).

"Only rags to wear," 1 Corinthians 4:11 (CEV).

Clothing wears out, Hebrews 1:11.

Corrupt wardrobe, Jude 23.

Clothing dirtied by sin, Revelation 3:4 (CEV).

Sun as a garment, Revelation 12:1.

See Clothing, Seamstress, Wedding.

WARDROBE (Spiritual)

Garments of righteousness, Job 29:14.

Priests clothed with salvation, Psalm 132:16.

Rich garments replace filthy clothes, Zechariah 3:4.

Wedding clothes, Matthew 22:11.

Dressed as bride, Revelation 21:2.

WARNING

Warning of angels taken as joke, Genesis 19:14.

Disobeying God's commands, Deuteronomy 4:2–4.

Joshua's blessing and warning, Joshua 23:14–16.

Warning to friends, 1 Samuel 15:6.

Letter of warning, 2 Chronicles 21:12–15.

False warning, Proverbs 26:13.

Shout like trumpet, Isaiah 58:1.

Prophecy of boiling pot, Jeremiah 1:13–15.

Trumpet sound, Jeremiah 6:17 (LB).

Warning rejected, Jeremiah 26:2–9.

Cry of terror, Jeremiah 49:29.

Warning lost souls, Ezekiel 3:18–19.

Watchman's responsibility, Ezekiel 33:1–9.

Prosperity linked to conduct, Daniel 4:27.

"Sound a warning," Hosea 8:1 (CEV).

Ninevites heeded warning, Jonah 3:3–6.

Warned in a dream, Matthew 2:13.

Information ahead of time, Matthew 24:22–25.

"Watch out," Matthew 24:42 (GNB).

Example of Lot's wife, Luke 17:32.

Advance warning, John 16:14.

Paul warned not to go to Jerusalem, Acts 21:3–4.

Warning concerning false teaching, 1 Timothy 4:1–6.

Warning divisive person, Titus 3:10.

Heavenly warning, Hebrews 12:25.

False teaching and wrong conduct, Jude 3–4.

Sounding forth cry of doom, Revelation 8:13.

No more delay, Revelation 10:6.

See Admonition, Caution.

WASHING

Washing for sanitary purpose, Leviticus 13:53–54.

Symbol of innocence, Deuteronomy 21:6–7; Psalm 26:6; Matthew 27:24.

Bathing in salt water, 2 Chronicles 4:6.

Stain soda and soap will not cleanse, Jeremiah 2:22.

See Bath.

WASTE

Careful storage of food, Genesis 41:35–36; Proverbs 21:20.

Nothing wasted, Exodus 16:4–18.

Purifying bad water, 2 Kings 2:19–22.

Learn lesson from ant, Proverbs 6:6–8.

Careful stocking of supplies, Proverbs 21:20.

Purses with holes in them, Haggai 1:6.

Squandered wealth, Luke 15:13.

Attitude of Jesus to waste, John 6:12.

See Conservation, Discard.

WATER

Wells in dry country, Genesis 21:25–31; 26:12–17.

Living by well, Genesis 25:11 (KJV).

Dispute over water rights, Genesis 26:19–22.

Water discovered, Genesis 26:32.

Importance of being near water, Exodus 2:15–17.

Bitter water made sweet, Exodus 15:25.

Idolatrous drinking water, Exodus 32:19–20 (CEV).

No water for crops, Leviticus 26:18–20.

Drinking water for sale, Numbers 20:19.

Song to desert well, Numbers 21:17–18.

Irrigation versus abundant rainfall, Deuteronomy 11:10–11.

Revitalizing water, Judges 15:19.

Municipal waterworks, 2 Kings 20:20.

David's thirst but refusal to drink, 1 Chronicles 11:15–19.

Many cisterns, 2 Chronicles 26:10.

Supply cut off, 2 Chronicles 32:4.

Distilled water, Job 36:27 (Berk.).

Drought, abundance, Psalm 107:33–35.

Drinking from brook, Psalm 110:7.

Gift of the Creator, Psalm 148:4–5.

Polluted water, Proverbs 25:26.

Dripping water, Proverbs 27:15.

Reservoirs for irrigation, Ecclesiastes 2:6.

Jerusalem water supply, Isaiah 36:2.

Uninterrupted supply, Isaiah 58:11.

Living water rejected, Jeremiah 2:13 (LB).

Poisoned water, Jeremiah 8:14.

Springs that fail, Jeremiah 15:18.

Daily allotment, Ezekiel 4:11.

Dead Sea water purified, Ezekiel 47:8 (LB).

Praying for rain in springtime, Zechariah 10:1.

Living water, John 4:4–14.

No longer any sea, Revelation 21:1.

Water given as gift, Revelation 21:6 (NRSV).

See Irrigation, Rain, Thirst, Wells.

WATERFALL

Roaring waterfalls, Psalm 42:7.

See Nature.

WAYWARD

Wayward group members, 1 John 2:19 (CEV).

See Backsliding, Carnality, Juvenile Delinquent.

WEAK-MINDED

Senseless thinking, Psalm 92:6; Jeremiah 10:8.

Given animal's mind, Daniel 4:16; 2 Peter 2:12.

Likenesses of fool, Proverbs 26:1–11.

Easily deceived, Hosea 7:11.

Futility thinking, Ephesians 4:17.

See Retarded.

WEAKNESS

Fear of rumor, Numbers 14:13–16.

Weakness over strength, Deuteronomy 7:1; 2 Samuel 3:1.

Smallest nation, Deuteronomy 7:7.

Quick to disobey, Judges 2:10–13, 19; 3:7, 12; 4:1.

Struggle between strong, weak, 2 Samuel 3:1.

W

Divine resource in time of weakness, 2 Chronicles 14:11.

Unable to face enemy, 2 Chronicles 20:12.

"This feeble bunch," Nehemiah 4:2 (CEV).

Faltering trust, Job 8:14.

Omnipotent God touches weak, Job 36:5.

"Turtle dove and hawks," Psalm 74:19 (LB).

Weakness from fasting, Psalm 109:24.

Futility of human effort, Psalm 127:1.

Faith exceeds physical strength, Psalm 147:10–11.

Too much food, drink, Proverbs 23:20.

People drained of power, Isaiah 37:27.

Mount up on wings like eagles, Isaiah 40:29–31.

Weak idols, Isaiah 57:13.

Least becomes great, Isaiah 60:22.

Sand holds back ocean, Jeremiah 5:22.

Frailty of foot, Jeremiah 12:5.

Warrior with hands tied, Jeremiah 14:9 (CEV).

Taking advantage of weak people, Jeremiah 22:1–3.

Challenge of weakness, Jeremiah 42:2–22; 43:1–6.

Weaker sex, Jeremiah 51:30.

Easily deceived, Hosea 7:11.

Strong made weak, Amos 2:14.

God's blessing upon meek, humble, Zephaniah 3:12.

Day of small things, Zechariah 4:10.

Too weak to do right, Mark 14:38 (CEV).

Dependence upon divine strength, John 15:5.

"Puny body," Romans 6:12 (LB).

Flesh's weakness, Romans 8:3 (AB).

Man's sin mars righteous law, Romans 8:3–4.

Strength for spiritual weakness, Romans 8:13–24.

Accepting one's weak faith, Romans 14:1 (NRSV).

Simple, unsuspecting, Romans 16:18.

Strength in weakness, 1 Corinthians 1:27; 2 Corinthians 12:9–10; Hebrews 11:33–34.

Responsibility of strong to weak, 1 Corinthians 8:9–13.

Human incompetence, 2 Corinthians 3:5.

Jars of clay, 2 Corinthians 4:7.

"He is a weakling," 2 Corinthians 10:10 (CEV).

Antidote for vanity, 2 Corinthians 11:30; 12:7–10.

Dynamic of the Cross, 2 Corinthians 13:4.

"Weaklings such as we," Hebrews 2:6 (CEV).

High priests men of human weakness, Hebrews 7:28.

See Immaturity, Vulnerability.

WEALTH

Earth's wealth, Genesis 2:11–12.

Promise, warning, Deuteronomy 6:10–12.

Tainted gold, silver, Deuteronomy 7:25.

Wealth an impetus to backsliding, Deuteronomy 8:13–14; 31:20; 32:15; Psalm 62:10.

Ability to produce wealth, Deuteronomy 8:18; Ecclesiastes 5:19.

Mighty man of wealth, Ruth 2:1 (KJV).

The Lord gives, takes away, 1 Samuel 2:7.

Plunder dedicated to God, 2 Samuel 8:9–12.

Tons of gold, 2 Chronicles 9:13–16 (GNB).

Solomon's great wealth, 2 Chronicles 9:22.

Great wealth, Job 1:3.

Avoid trusting wealth, Job 31:24–28; Psalm 49:5–12.

Producing wealth for others, Psalm 39:6.

Transient wealth, Psalm 49:16–20.

Growing rich by harming others, Psalm 52:7.

Greatest of all wealth, Psalm 119:14.

Barns filled, flocks abundant, Psalm 144:13.

Honor the Lord with one's wealth, Proverbs 3:9–10.

Wealth stolen by strangers, Proverbs 5:8–10.

Wisdom the truest wealth, Proverbs 8:17–19; 16:16.

Ill-gotten wealth, Proverbs 10:2.

Pretrense of wealth, Proverbs 13:7.

Greatest value, Proverbs 16:8.

Greater than gold or silver, Proverbs 16:16.

Purchase of prestige, Proverbs 18:16.

Priceless value of good name, Proverbs 22:1.

Power of money, Proverbs 22:7.

Stealing from poor, giving to rich, Proverbs 22:16.

Exhausted becoming rich, Proverbs 23:4–5.

Do not envy wicked, Proverbs 24:19–20.

Getting rich quick, Proverbs 28:22 (LB).

Prayer of true wisdom, Proverbs 30:8–9.

Wealth of wisdom, knowledge, Ecclesiastes 1:16 (NASB).

Meaningless accumulation of wealth, Ecclesiastes 2:4–11.

Money alone never satisfies, Ecclesiastes 5:10.

Wealth plus happiness, Ecclesiastes 5:19–20.

Money as shelter, Ecclesiastes 7:12.

Money's presumed function, Ecclesiastes 10:19.

Mid-life loss of unjust wealth, Jeremiah 17:11; 5:27.

City of luxury brought down, Ezekiel 27:1–36; 28:1–19.

Exploiting poor for personal gain, Amos 5:11.

Gold and silver belong to God, Haggai 2:8.

Eternal wealth, Matthew 6:19–21.

Wealth a spiritual liability, 1 Timothy 6:9.

Rich man provided tomb for Jesus, Matthew 27:57–61.

Poor can inherit kingdom, Luke 6:20.

"Money bags that never wear out," Luke 12:33 (CEV).

Much given, much required, Luke 12:48.

Surprised beggar, Acts 3:1–8.

Sharing spiritual and material blessings, Romans 15:26–27.

Spiritually rich, 2 Corinthians 6:10 (GNB).

Assured wealth, 2 Corinthians 9:11.

God's grace lavished on us, Ephesians 1:7–8.

Jesus the source, Philippians 4:19.

Abiding wealth, 1 Timothy 6:5–6 (CEV).

Bring nothing into world, take nothing out, 1 Timothy 6:6–8.

Dangerous wealth, 1 Timothy 6:9–10.

Functioning wealth, 1 Timothy 6:17–19.

High position is, instead, low, James 1:10.

Eternal inheritance, 1 Peter 1:3–4.

Gold perishes, 1 Peter 1:7.

Not redeemed with silver, gold, 1 Peter 1:18–19.

True wealth, Revelation 2:9.

Temporal wealth, spiritual wealth, Revelation 3:15–18.

See Affluence, Materialism, Ownership.

WEANING

Weaning celebration, Genesis 21:8.

See Infant.

WEAPONS

No weapons in Israel, 1 Samuel 13:19–22.

Spiritual weapons, 1 Samuel 17:45; 2 Corinthians 10:4; Ephesians 6:17; Hebrews 4:12.

Bronze bow, 2 Samuel 22:35.

Primitive weapons, 2 Chronicles 26:10–14.

Spear, battle-axe, Psalm 35:3 (NASB).

The Lord on our side, Psalm 124:1–5.

Satisfied sword, Jeremiah 46:10.

Break bow, Jeremiah 49:35.

Arsenal of the Lord, Jeremiah 50:25.

Trusting the Lord, trusting in weapons, Luke 22:35–38.

See Army, Military, War.

WEARINESS

Creator's time for rest, Genesis 2:2.

Weary of life, Genesis 27:46; Ecclesiastes 4:1–2.

Exhausted men, Judges 8:4.

Bread for exhausted men, Judges 8:15.

Vulnerable to enemy attack, 2 Samuel 17:1–2.

Exhausted in battle, 2 Samuel 21:15.

"Completely exhausted," Psalm 6:2–3 (GNB).

Worn out worker, Ecclesiastes 3:9 (Berk.).

Refusing opportunity for rest, Isaiah 28:11–12.

Strength for the weary, Isaiah 40:29–31.

Weariness induced by sin, Jeremiah 9:3–5.

Ill, impaired by weariness, Daniel 8:27; 10:17.

Wearied by prophetic vision, Daniel 10:16.

"You have worn out the Lord," Malachi 2:17 (CEV).

Respite for weariness, Matthew 11:28–30; Romans 8:31–39.

No chance for rest in busy ministry, Mark 6:30–34.

Travel weary, John 4:6.

Weary man at worship, Acts 20:7–12.

Exhausting ministry, 2 Corinthians 7:5–7.

Not weary of doing good, Galatians 6:9.

"God got tired of them," Hebrews 3:9–10 (CEV).

See Exhaustion, Rest, Tireless.

WEATHER

Sky water, earth water, Genesis 1:6–8.

Earth before rainfall, Genesis 2:4–6.

Cool time of day, Genesis 3:8.

First rainfall, Genesis 7:11–12; 2:4–6.

Seasons established after flood, Genesis 8:22.

Clouds collected, Genesis 9:14 (Berk.).

Hot summer's day, Genesis 18:1 (LB).

Creator controls weather, Exodus 9:29 (LB).

Rainless sky, parched earth, Leviticus 26:19, 20.

Reward for obedience, Deuteronomy 11:13–29.

"Rain at the right season," Deuteronomy 11:14–15 (CEV).

Blessings of nature, Deuteronomy 33:13–16.

Praying for rain, 1 Samuel 12:18; 1 Kings 18:16–46; James 5:17–18.

Cause of drought, 2 Samuel 21:1 (KJV).

Good weather blessing from God, 1 Kings 8:35–36.

Rainy season affected worship and confession, Ezra 10:13.

Cloud cover, Job 26:8–9 (KJV).

Path for wind, storm, Job 28:25–27.

Accurate description of rainfall, Job 36:27–30; 37:6, 15–16.

Cattle as forecasters, Job 36:33.

Warm weather, warm clothes, Job 37:17.

Storehouses for snow, hail, Job 38:22.

Sky seen revealing reality of God, Psalm 18:9–14.

Rain for crops and pastures, Psalm 65:9–13; Joel 2:23–24.

Rain likened to blessing, Psalm 72:6.

Skies at God's command, Psalm 77:16–19.

Tumbleweed like a wheel, Psalm 83:13 (KJV).

Cloud chariots, Psalm 104:3.

Lord of all weather, Psalm 135:6–7; Jeremiah 10:13.

Work avoided in cold weather, Proverbs 20:4 (KJV).

North wind brings rain, Proverbs 25:23 (Note contradictory KJV).

WEATHER

Snow, rain out of season, Proverbs 26:1.

Driving rain of little value, Proverbs 28:3.

Too concerned about weather, Ecclesiastes 11:4.

Winter past, flowers appearing, Song of Songs 2:11–12.

Wind, rain, hail, Isaiah 28:2.

"Flood in a mighty windstorm," Isaiah 59:19 (CEV).

Clouds from evaporation, Jeremiah 10:13.

God who made and sustains universe, Jeremiah 51:15–16.

Storm from the north, Ezekiel 1:4.

Cloudy day, Ezekiel 30:3 (KJV).

Dry weather from the east, Hosea 13:15.

Rain given, withheld, Amos 4:7.

Violent storm at sea, Jonah 1:4, 10–15.

Whirlwind invokes judgment, Nahum 1:3.

Dew from heavens, Zechariah 8:12.

Prayer for springtime rain, Zechariah 10:1.

Weather forecasting, Matthew 16:1–3.

Wind obedient to Creator's command, Mark 4:35–41; Luke 8:22–25.

Predicting rain, Luke 12:54–56.

Mistaking voice of God for thunder, John 12:28–29.

Sailing delayed, Acts 27:6–9.

Gentle wind, hurricane, Acts 27:13–14.

"Shiver in the cold," 1 Corinthians 4:11 (AB).

Wind forbidden to blow, Revelation 7:1.

Hailstones from sky, Revelation 16:21.

See Meteorology, Rain, Seasons, Snow, Storm.

WEDDING

Long delayed wedding, Genesis 29:28.

Dowry payment, Genesis 34:12; Exodus 22:16–17.

Wedding riddle, Judges 14:12–13.

Esther's great banquet, Esther 2:18.

Bridal attire, Jeremiah 2:32 (Berk.).

Bride stands at right side, Psalm 45:9 (CEV).

Arrival of bridegroom, Song of Songs 3:9–11.

Dressed like bridegroom, Isaiah 61:10.

Newlyweds disturbed, Joel 2:16.

Parable of virgins, Matthew 25:1–13.

Invited guests, John 2:1.

Site of Christ's first miracle, John 2:1–11.

No more weddings, Revelation 18:23; 19:7.

Garments of bride, Revelation 19:7–8; 21:2.

Bride of Christ, Revelation 21:9.

See Marriage, Romance.

WEEDS

Eating voluntary growth, 2 Kings 19:29; Isaiah 37:30.

Make enemy like tumbleweed, Psalm 83:13 (KJV).

Nettles, brambles, Isaiah 34:13.

Good crops, weeds, Hebrews 6:7–8.

Thorns spoil harvest, Matthew 13:3–8, 18–23.

Weeds planted by enemy, Matthew 13:24–29, 36–42.

See Thorns.

WEIGHT

Money by weight, Genesis 23:16; Ezra 8:24–27; Jeremiah 32:9.

Accurate scales, Leviticus 19:36; Deuteronomy 25:13; Ezekiel 45:10.

Divine delight in accuracy, Proverbs 11:1; 16:11.

Divine dislike of inaccuracy, Proverbs 20:10; Micah 6:11.

Fat wastes away, Isaiah 17:4.

Weights, measures, Ezekiel 45:10–15 (GNB).

See Measurement, Standard.

WELCOME

Welcomed prophet, 2 Kings 4:8–10.

Familiarity breeds contempt, Proverbs 25:17.

Welcome to all, Isaiah 55:1–2.

Welcome as spiritual act, Matthew 10:40–42 (GNB).

How not to take advantage of host, Luke 14:8–11.

Tax collectors, "sinners" welcomed, Luke 15:1–7.

Awaited welcome, 2 Corinthians 6:2 (AB).

Receiving less than desired guest, Galatians 4:14.

Welcome to strangers, Hebrew 13:2.

Divine welcome, Revelation 22:17.

See Guests, Hospitality, Hostess.

WELFARE

Mutual responsibility, Genesis 9:5.

Food stored for welfare, Deuteronomy 14:28–29; 26:12.

Concern for those in need, Deuteronomy 15:7–11; Job 29:16.

Harvest gleaners, Deuteronomy 24:19–21.

Welfare supplies, Deuteronomy 26:12.

Heartless attitude, Job 12:5; 22:7–9.

Eyes to blind, feet to lame, Job 29:15.

Needy cry for help, Job 30:24 (NRSV).

Sharing with others, Job 31:16–22.

Poor, homeless not forgotten, Psalm 9:18 (CEV).

Welfare rewarded, Psalm 41:1–3 (LB); Matthew 25:34–40; Hebrews 6:10.

Kindness to needy, Proverbs 14:21.

God loves poor people, Proverbs 14:31.

Demean poor, demean God, Proverbs 17:5.

Welfare a spiritual investment, Proverbs 19:17.

Ignoring need, Proverbs 21:13 (LB).

Blessing for generous man, Proverbs 22:9.

Outreach to enemy, Proverbs 25:21.

Leader oppresses poor, Proverbs 28:3.

Concern for poor rewarded, Proverbs 28:27; 31:20.

Those who cannot help themselves, Proverbs 31:8–9.

Welfare as spiritual service, Isaiah 58:6–10.

Babylonian mercy to poor, Jeremiah 39:10; 40:7–9.

Welfare for orphans and widows, Jeremiah 49:11; Zechariah 7:8–10.

Cheap value on human beings, Amos 2:6.

Responding to request for aid, Matthew 5:42.

Private welfare, Matthew 6:2–4.

Cup of cold water, Matthew 10:42.

Expensive perfume prepared Jesus for Cross, Mark 14:3–9.

Practical welfare for paralytic man, Luke 5:17–26.

Good Samaritan, Luke 10:30–37.

Altruistic welfare, Luke 14:12–14.

Surprised beggar, Acts 3:1–8.

Early Christian welfare, Acts 4:32–35.

Woman who helped the poor, Acts 9:36–42.

Generous centurion, Acts 10:1–2.

Welfare recognized by the Lord, Acts 10:4.

Reaching out to help others, Acts 11:27–30.

Share with those in need, Romans 12:13.

Church-centered welfare, Romans 15:26–27.

Seeking good of others above self, 1 Corinthians 10:24.

Greater gift than money, 1 Corinthians 13:3.

Concern of early Christians, Galatians 2:9–10.

Proper care for widows, relatives, 1 Timothy 5:3–8.

Widows on welfare, 1 Timothy 5:9–11.

Women helping women, 1 Timothy 5:16.

Share with others, Hebrews 13:16; 1 John 3:17.

Looking after those in need, James 1:27.

Proper attitude toward poor, James 2:1–8.

Faith without works, James 2:14–18.

See Benevolence, Philanthropy.

WELL-DRESSED *See Style, Wardrobe.*

WELL-BEING

Full report, Ephesians 6:21.

WELLS

Wells in arid areas, Genesis 21:25–31.

Wells destroyed, restored, Genesis 26:12–18.

Abundant cisterns, 2 Chronicles 26:10.

Irrigation reservoirs, Ecclesiastes 2:6.

Wells of salvation, Isaiah 12:3.

Jacob's well, John 4:4–10.

See Cistern, Springs, Water.

WETLANDS

Rushes, mire, Job 8:11 (KJV).

Wetland animals, Psalms 68:30.

See Ecology.

WHALE

"Great whales," Genesis 1:21 (KJV).

Whales at play, Psalm 104:26 (LB).

See Animals.

WHEEL

Roll like tumbleweed, Psalm 83:13 (KJV).
Wheel in a wheel, Ezekiel 1:15–20.
The Lord removed Egyptian wheels, Exodus 14:25.
High speed wheels, Isaiah 5:28.
Clattering wheels, Nahum 3:2.

WHIPPING

Whip of thorns, Judges 8:7 (CEV).
Whips, scorpions, 1 Kings 12:11.
Fool's mouth invites flogging, Proverbs 18:6 (NRSV).
Child's discipline, Proverbs 22:6, 15.
Rod for fools, Proverbs 26:3 (AB).
Horse whips, Nahum 3:2.
Flogging of Jesus, Matthew 27:26; Mark 15:15; John 19:1.
Apostle Paul flogged, Acts 22:22–29.
See Punishment.

WHISKERS

Whiskers shaved ignominiously, 1 Chronicles 19:1–5.
Hygienic shave, Leviticus 14:9.
Stylized beard, Leviticus 19:27; 21:5.
Feigned madness, 1 Samuel 21:13.
Half-shaved beards, 2 Samuel 10:4.
Untended mustache, 2 Samuel 19:24.
Grasping man by beard, 2 Samuel 20:9.
Oil down Aaron's beard, Psalm 133:1–2.
See Beard, Moustache, Shaving.

WHISPER

Whispered gossip, Proverbs 26:22 (AB, Berk.).

WHISTLE

When the Lord whistles, Isaiah 7:18 (LB).

WHITEWASH

Whitewashed lies, Job 13:4 (NRSV).

WICKEDNESS

Wickedness diverted, Genesis 11:8; Job 5:12.
Defiant sin, Numbers 15:30–31; Exodus 23:2.
Sin of only one person, Numbers 16:22.
Divine patience with unrepentent, 2 Kings 8:16–19.
Infamy to king's daughter, 2 Kings 9:30–37.
Devious speech, Psalm 5:9.
Plotting against righteous, Psalm 37:12.
Wickedness preferred, Psalm 52:3.
Wicked insomnia, Proverbs 4:16.
Loaded with guilt, Isaiah 1:4.
Power of wickedness taken away, Isaiah 37:27.
False prophets, diviners, Isaiah 44:25.
Wicked like restless sea, Isaiah 57:20.
Wicked prosperity, Jeremiah 12:1–3 (LB).
Palace built by unrighteousness, Jeremiah 22:13–15.
Repentence of heart, Joel 2:13.
For continued sinning, certain judgment, Amos 1:3, 6, 9, 11, 13; 2:1, 4, 6.
Hands skilled in wickedness, Micah 7:3.
Sin in broad daylight, 2 Peter 2:13–22.
See Carnality, Debauchery, Evil.

WIDOW

Widows not to be exploited, Exodus 22:22.
Tithe benefits widows, Deuteronomy 26:12.
Three widows in one family, Ruth 1:1–5.
Concubine widows, 2 Samuel 20:3.
Widow threatened by creditor, 2 Kings 4:1.
Widows who do not mourn, Job 27:15.
Father to fatherless, Psalm 68:5.
Numerous widows, Jeremiah 15:8.
Priests' widows, Ezekiel 44:22.
Sorrow of young virgin, Joel 1:8.
Widow's mite, Mark 12:42–44; Luke 21:1–4.
Long years of widowhood, Luke 2:36–37.
Ministry of aged widow, Luke 2:36–38.
Caring for widows, 1 Timothy 5:3–16.
Congregational concern, James 1:27.

WIDOWER

Abraham, death of Sarah, Genesis 23:1–20.
Boaz and Ruth, Ruth 3:7–18.

WIFE

Creator's design, Genesis 2:18, 24.
Wife search, Genesis 24:14.
Husband's involvement in wife's contracts, Numbers 30:10–15.

Wiles of new bride, Judges 14:11–19.
Wife's insult, 2 Samuel 6:20 (LB).
Bossy wife, 1 Kings 21:1–16.
Favorite among many wives, 2 Chronicles 11:21.
Influence of evil wife, 2 Chronicles 21:6.
Wife's refusal to be put on display, Esther 1:9–21.
Complaining wife, Job 2:9–10.
Fruitful vine, Psalm 128:3.
Husband's crown, Proverbs 12:4.
Favor of the Lord, Proverbs 18:22 (CEV).
Woman of noble character, Proverbs 31:10–31.
Death of Ezekiel's wife, Ezekiel 24:15–27.
Joseph's enigma concerning Mary, Matthew 1:18, 19.
Pilate's wife, Matthew 27:19.
Loving husband's enemies, James 4:4 (LB).
See Bride, Marriage, Wedding.

WILDERNESS See Desert.

WILD OATS

Sins of youth, Psalm 25:6–7.
Reaping what is sown, Galatians 6:7–8.

WILES

"Wiliest of all," Genesis 3:1 (Berk.).
Clever wiles of wives, Judges 14:11–19; 1 Kings 1:11–31.
Perfume for lady, Ruth 3:3.
False prophets, Jeremiah 14:13–15.
Influencing others to sin, Luke 17:1.
Schemes of Satan, 2 Corinthians 2:11; 11:3; Ephesians 6:11.
See Flirtation, Seduction.

WILL (Volitional)

Freedom of choice, Genesis 13:10–13.
No success outside God's will, Numbers 14:41–45.
Questioning God's will, Joshua 24:15.
Desires God places in our hearts, Psalms 20:4–5; 37:3–5.
Let God plan, Psalm 40:5.
Divine purposes fulfilled, Psalm 138:8.
Man's plans, God's will, Isaiah 30:1.
Valley of decision, Joel 3:14.
Human, divine motivation, Matthew 8:1–3.

Wisdom from doing God's will, John 7:17.
Relationship between talent, God's will, Romans 11:29.
Folly of missing God's will, Ephesians 5:17.
Promise concerning knowing God's will, Colossians 1:9–14.
Good purpose fulfilled, 2 Thessalonians 1:11.
Captive to devil's will, 2 Timothy 2:26.
Position subordinate to witness, God's will, Titus 2:9–10.
Deliberate sin, Hebrews 10:26.
Perseverance in finding, doing God's will, Hebrews 10:36 (GNB).
Hindered from will of God, 1 John 2:15–17.
See Guidance, Obedience.

WILL (Legal) See Legacy.

WILLING

Willing to sacrifice son, Genesis 22:1–18.
Spontaneous commitment, Judges 5:2.
Volunteers for Jerusalem, Nehemiah 11:2.
Motivating desire, Psalm 40:8.
Prerequisite to blessing, Isaiah 1:19.
Willing followers, Mark 1:16–18.
Willing candidate for faith, Mark 9:17–25.
See Obedient.

WIND

Wind over water, Genesis 8:1; Exodus 15:10.
Wind in four directions, Exodus 10:19; Job 27:21; Job 37:17; Song of Songs 4:16.
Provision of food, Numbers 11:31.
Riding the wind, Job 30:22 (NRSV).
Handful of wind, Proverbs 30:4 (GNB).
No one restrains the wind, Ecclesiastes 8:8 (NRSV).
Conveying life, Ezekiel 37:9.
Poisonous east wind, Amos 4:9 (AB).
Intense wind, Jonah 1:4.
Contrary wind, Matthew 14:24 (NKJV).
Wind storm, Mark 4:37; Acts 27:14.
Angel wind, Hebrews 1:7 (NIV).
Wind forbidden to blow, Revelation 7:1.
See Storm.

WINDBAG

Making promises to curry loyalty, 1 Samuel 22:6–8.

Words like blustering wind, Job 8:2.

Bragging about wealth, Psalm 49:6.

Boasting of imagined gifts, Proverbs 25:14.

Empty words, Isaiah 36:4–7.

Prophets called windbags, Jeremiah 5:13 (LB).

Sin to brag, James 4:16.

See Loquacious.

WINDOW

Many windows, 1 Kings 7:3–4 (LB).

Narrow windows, Ezekiel 41:26.

WINE

Wine used in spiritual offering, Exodus 29:40.

Abstinent priests, Leviticus 10:9.

Nazarite vow, Numbers 6:3–4.

Purchase of wine, Deuteronomy 14:26.

Wine from snake venom, Deuteronomy 32:33 (GNB).

Antidote for weariness, 2 Samuel 16:2.

Beverage of soldiers, 2 Chronicles 11:11.

Wine steward, Nehemiah 2:1.

Social consumption, Esther 1:7–8; 5:6.

Vented wineskin, Job 32:19 (Berk.).

Illustrative wine, Psalm 60:3 (GNB, LB).

Gladdened heart, Psalm 104:15.

Love of wine, fattening food, Proverbs 21:17; 23:1–2.

Wine, leadership, Proverbs 31:4.

False cheer, Ecclesiastes 2:3.

Love better than wine, Song of Songs 4:10 (KJV).

Vintage years, Isaiah 25:6.

Cup of Divine fury, Jeremiah 25:15.

"Wine flowed freely," Daniel 5:1 (LB).

Teetotalers forced to drink wine, Amos 2:12; Numbers 6:3–4.

Treacherous wine, Habakkuk 2:5 (CEV).

Fermentation of wine, Mark 2:22.

"Cheap wine," John 19:29 (CEV, NRSV).

"Juice of grapes," Mark 14:23 (AB).

Setting good example, Romans 14:21.

Digestive function, 1 Timothy 5:23.

Wine of lust, Revelation 18:3 (GNB).

See Abstinence, Alcohol, Drunkenness, Liquor, Intemperance.

WINK

Malicious wink, Psalm 35:19.

Gesture of scoundrel, Proverbs 6:12–14; 10:10.

Haughty women of Zion, Isaiah 3:16–17.

Divine wink, Acts 17:30.

See Flirtation, Seduction.

WINTER

February twenty-eighth, Esther 9:1 (LB).

Divine breath produces ice and cold, Job 37:10.

Storehouses of snow, Job 38:22 (KJV).

Winter clothing, Proverbs 31:21.

Joy of winter's end, Song of Songs 2:11.

"December," Jeremiah 28:1 (LB); Ezekiel 33:21 (LB); Haggai 2:10 (LB).

"January," Jeremiah 39:1 (LB).

"Mid-February," Ezekiel 32:1 (LB).

Cold journey, Matthew 24:20; 2 Timothy 4:21.

Time of potential peril, Mark 13:18–19.

Choice for spending winter months, Titus 3:12.

See Cold, Seasons, Snow, Weather.

WISDOM

Wise hearted, Exodus 28:3 (KJV); 35:10 (AB).

Wise behavior, 1 Samuel 18:14 (KJV).

Priority prayer for wisdom, 1 Kings 3:9–15; 4:29–34.

Reputation for wisdom, 2 Chronicles 9:23.

Need to obtain advice more than give, 2 Chronicles 10:1–8.

Wisdom's many sides, Job 11:6 (CEV).

Wisdom not inherited, Job 11:12 (LB).

Wisdom of youth, age, Job 32:4–9.

Words without knowledge, Job 38:2.

Divine supply of light, Psalm 36:9.

Wealth without wisdom, Psalm 49:20.

Pomp without insight, Psalm 49:20 (Berk.)

"How to use wisdom," Psalm 105:22 (CEV).

Fear of the Lord, Psalm 111:10.

Wisdom for study of Scriptures, Psalm 119:33–38; 97–100.

Asking God for discernment, Psalm 119:125.

Wisdom like "sweetheart," Proverbs 7:4 (LB).

Folly of lacking wisdom, Proverbs 8:32–36.

Always for the best, Proverbs 19:8 (LB).

Wisdom brightens countenance, Ecclesiastes 8:1.

Divine omniscience, Isaiah 40:13–14.

Learning of wise overthrown, Isaiah 44:25.

God's thoughts higher than ours, Isaiah 55:9.

Wisdom banished, Jeremiah 49:7 (CEV).

"Wiser than Daniel," Ezekiel 28:3.

Wisdom of trusting the Lord, Hosea 14:9.

Wise as snakes, innocent as doves, Matthew 10:16.

Greater wisdom than Solomon's, Matthew 12:42.

Truth understood by children, Luke 10:21.

Articulate wisdom, Luke 11:49 (AB).

Given wisdom in difficult time, Luke 12:11–12; 21:15.

Knowledge beyond classroom, John 7:15.

Understanding divine thoughts, 1 Corinthians 2:16 (CEV).

Wise fools, 1 Corinthians 4:10.

Eyes of heart, Ephesians 1:18–19.

Complicated wisdom, Ephesians 3:10 (AB).

"Power to comprehend," Ephesians 3:18 (NRSV).

Knowledge, insight, Philippians 1:9.

Reward of careful reflection, 2 Timothy 2:7.

We are given understanding, 1 John 5:20.
See Intellectual, Intelligence.

WISH

Three choices for punishment, 1 Chronicles 21:8–13.

The God who grants desires, Psalm 20:4; 21:2; 37:4.

"With our best wishes," Acts 15:29 (GNB).
See Desire, Request.

WITCHCRAFT

Witchcraft destroyed, Exodus 22:18; 2 Kings 23:24; Micah 5:12.

Abstinence from witchcraft, Leviticus 19:31; 20:6; Isaiah 8:19.

Sin of divination, 1 Samuel 15:23.

King who consulted witch, 1 Samuel 28:5–20.

Mediums consulted, Isaiah 19:3.
See Sorcery.

WITNESS

Convincing example, Genesis 39:3–4.

Witness in pagan Egypt, Genesis 42:18.

Moses became like God to Pharaoh, Exodus 7:1–2.

Backslidden believers a laughingstock, Exodus 32:25.

Presence of God the ultimate identity, Exodus 33:15–16.

Witness through good conduct, Deuteronomy 4:6.

"Tell of it," Judges 5:10 (AB).

Unwasted words, 1 Samuel 3:19.

Witness test, 2 Chronicles 32:31.

Enemies recognized God-given success, Nehemiah 6:15–16.

Refusal to bow down, honor man, Esther 3:1–5.

Hiding from witness, Job 31:34 (Berk.).

Role of prayer in effective witness, Job 33:26–28.

Public witness, Psalm 31:19 (LB).

David's song of transformation, Psalm 40:1–4.

Telling everyone, Psalm 40:9 (LB).

Witnessing about personal experience, Psalm 51:10–13.

Women's witness, Psalm 68:11 (GNB).

"Let God be magnified," Psalm 70:4 (NASB, NKJV).

Witnessing the incomprehensible, Psalm 71:15 (RSV).

Day long witnessing, Psalm 71:24.

Daily witness, Psalm 96:2 (LB).

Let the redeemed of the Lord speak, Psalm 107:1–3.

Things worth talking about, Psalm 119:27 (KJV).

Witness to those in authority, Psalm 119:46.

Sow in tears, reap with joy, Psalm 126:5–6.

Speaking in praise of the Lord, Psalm 145:21.

Tongues of silver, Proverbs 10:20.

Lack of tact, Proverbs 27:14.

Called to convey message, Isaiah 6:8–10.

Private experience publicly proclaimed, Isaiah 12:1–6.

Convey God's message to others, Isaiah 38:18–19.

Shout the news, Isaiah 40:9; 41:27.

Declaring one Savior, Isaiah 43:10–13.

Words the Lord puts into your mouth, Isaiah 51:16.

Beautiful feet of those who witness, Isaiah 52:7; Micah 3:8.

God's word will not return to Him empty, Isaiah 55:10–11.

Telling what the Lord has done, Isaiah 62:7.

Tell of the Lord's kindness, Isaiah 63:7.

Those who witness dishonestly, Jeremiah 5:1–2.

Day coming when witnessing not necessary, Jeremiah 31:34.

Responsibility for failing to witness, Ezekiel 3:18–19.

Wearing mark of repentance, Ezekiel 9:3–6.

Looking in vain for someone to stand in gap, Ezekiel 22:30.

Responsibility of watchman to warn, Ezekiel 33:7–9.

Witness in court of king, Daniel 3:8–18.

King's acknowledgement of Daniel's faith, Daniel 4:8.

Impeccable witness, Daniel 6:3–5.

Faith ahead of loyalty to king, Daniel 6:5–11.

Those who witness shine like stars, Daniel 12:3.

Generation to generation, Joel 1:3.

Ashamed to mention the Lord's name, Amos 6:10.

Witness in time of stress, Jonah 1:4–9.

Prophet an exception to those whom he warned, Micah 3:8.

Haggai called the Lord's messenger, Haggai 1:13.

Like the Lord's signet ring, Haggai 2:21.

People seek those who know the Lord, Zechariah 8:23.

Like jewels in crown, Zechariah 9:16.

"Speak for me, Lord," Malachi 2:7 (CEV).

Becoming fishers of men, Matthew 4:19.

Let your light shine, Matthew 5:14–16.

Witness to family, Mark 5:18–20.

Giving to those unprepared to receive, Matthew 7:6.

Association with sinners, Matthew 9:10–12.

Brought before men of high standing, Matthew 10:16–20.

God acknowledges those who acknowledge Him, Matthew 10:32–33.

Failure to witness, Matthew 26:31–35, 69–75; Mark 14:27–31; 66–72.

Centurion compelled to witness, Matthew 27:54.

Shouting the message, Mark 1:3 (Berk.).

Reaching the "scum," Mark 2:16 (LB).

Sowing seed on various soil, Mark 4:3–20.

Lamp to be displayed, not hidden, Mark 4:21, 22.

Ashamed to witness, Mark 8:38.

Shepherds "spread the word," Luke 2:16–18.

Baptism as witness, Luke 3:3 (LB).

Witness of demons, Luke 4:33–41.

Fishers of men, Luke 5:1–11.

Reaching out to lost, Luke 5:27–32.

Parable of sower, Luke 8:4–15.

Declaring Lordship of Christ, Luke 9:18–20.

Rejecting those who witness, Luke 10:16.

Spiritual light from within, Luke 11:33–36.

Those who acknowledge Christ, those who deny, Luke 12:8–9.

Given words to speak, Luke 21:15.

Those who display true light, John 1:8–9.

Friend of bridegroom, John 3:26–30.

Tact in witness, John 4:4–26.

Harvest time now, John 4:35–38.

Effective woman's witness, John 4:39–42.

Fearing opposition, John 7:12–13.

Miracle caused many to believe, John 12:9–11.

Those who testify, John 15:26–27.

Secret loyalty, John 19:38.

Spiritual conquest should motivate, Acts 1:6–8.

Simple men confounded scholars, Acts 4:13.

Courage in face of opposition, Acts 4:18–20.

Requisite for bold witness, Acts 4:31.

Persistence in witnessing, Acts 5:42.

Angelic guidance, Acts 8:26.

Ananias guided to Saul, Acts 9:10–17.

Convert's witness questioned, Acts 9:19–22, 26.

Scattered by persecution, witnessing faithfully, Acts 11:19–21.

Fruit of effective witness, Acts 11:20, 21.

Use of Scripture in bold witness, Acts 13:13–52.

Basis for persuasion, teaching, Acts 17:2–4.

Tactful witness, Acts 17:21–28 (CEV).

Power of personal testimony, Acts 21:37–40; 22:1–21; 26:1–18, 28–29.

Prisoner's request to witness, Acts 21:37 to 22:39; 26:1–32.

Detailed personal conversion, Acts 22:1–21.

Reluctant prospective convert, Acts 26:28 (NASB).

Bondage became means for witnessing, Acts 28:17–28.

Unashamed of Gospel, Romans 1:16.

Role of witness in salvation, Romans 10:9–10.

Bringing message to those who have not heard, Romans 10:14–15.

One plants, one waters, God gives growth, 1 Corinthians 3:5–9.

Holy Spirit enhances witnessing, 1 Corinthians 12:3.

Importance of being understood, 1 Corinthians 14:13–19.

Sign for unbelievers, 1 Corinthians 14:22–25.

Gospel message in brief, 1 Corinthians 15:1–5.

Spreading fragrance of Christ, 2 Corinthians 2:14.

Convert confirms message, 2 Corinthians 3:1–3.

Radiance of face, 2 Corinthians 3:18.

Deserving right to be heard, 2 Corinthians 4:1–2.

Witnessing to those blinded by Satan, 2 Corinthians 4:3–6.

Compelled by love of Christ, 2 Corinthians 5:14.

Christ's ambassadors in world, 2 Corinthians 5:18–21.

Clarity of Gospel message, Galatians 1:8.

Speaking truth in love, Ephesians 4:15.

Ready to serve, witness, Ephesians 6:15 (GNB).

Imprisonment widened witness, Philippians 1:12–14.

Witness in whatever circumstances, Philippians 1:27–30.

Witness by example, Philippians 1:28–29 (CEV).

Paul struggled over converts, Colossians 2:1.

Make most of every opportunity, Colossians 4:5 (GNB).

Importance of lifestyle in witness, 1 Thessalonians 4:11–12.

Those who have believed, 2 Thessalonians 2:13–15.

Blasphemer became minister of Gospel, 1 Timothy 1:12–16.

Persevere in life, doctrine, 1 Timothy 4:16.

Good deeds made known, 1 Timothy 5:25.

Not ashamed to testify, 2 Timothy 1:8–9 (AB).

Need for actively sharing faith, Philemon 6.

Witness of living in good relationships, Hebrews 12:14–15.

Good life validates witness, 1 Peter 2:12–15.

Silent witness, 1 Peter 3:1–2.

Prepared to give answer, 1 Peter 3:15.

Speaking, serving to glory of God, 1 Peter 4:11.

Sharing experience, 2 Peter 1:16–21.

Experiencing reality of Christ, 1 John 1:1–4.

Evil conduct as negative witness, Jude 7.

Helping those who doubt, Jude 22–23.

Faithful to point of death, Revelation 2:13.

Put to death for witness, Revelation 6:9.

Witnessing in face of judgment, Revelation 11:3–12.

Proclaiming angel, Revelation 14:6–7.

Tabernacle of testimony in heaven, Revelation 15:5.

Beheaded for faithfulness, testimony, Revelation 20:4.

Reporting what is seen and heard, Revelation 22:8.

Holy Spirit, church in evangelism, Revelation 22:17.

See Evangelism, Missionary, One-on-One, Soul Winning, Testimony.

WOLF

Wolf attacking people, Jeremiah 5:6.

Disguised in sheep's clothing, Matthew 7:15.

Sheep among wolves, Matthew 10:16; John 10:11–13; Acts 20:29.

See Animals.

WOMEN

Man's helper, Genesis 2:18.

"Life giving one," Genesis 3:20 (LB).

Good-looking women, Genesis 6:1–2 (Berk.).

Husband's deceitfulness, Genesis 20:1–18; 12:10–20.

Shepherdess, Genesis 29:9.

Women without inheritance, Genesis 31:15–16.

Miriam's song of praise, Exodus 15:21.

Sold as slave but granted rights, Exodus 21:7–11.

Daughters who had no brother, Numbers 27:1–11.

Husband's involvement in wife's contracts, Numbers 30:10–15.

Death to enemy women, children, Numbers 31:7–18.

Asking special favor, Judges 1:13–15.

"Wisest ladies," Judges 5:29 (NKJV, NRSV).

Spoils for conqueror, Judges 5:30 (LB).

Demeaned by woman, Judges 9:50–55.

Woman's value degraded, Judges 19:1–30.

Kidnapping wife, Judges 21:20–21.

Change of mind, Ruth 1:8 (LB).

Short work break, Ruth 2:7.

Women strengthening Israel, Ruth 4:11.

Daughter-in-law worth seven sons, Ruth 4:13–15.

Prompt gathering of food, 1 Samuel 25:18.

David's respect for concubines, 2 Samuel 20:3.

Language of woman's heart, 1 Kings 10:2 (NKJV).

Evil woman, 1 Kings 19:1–2.

Well-to-do woman, 2 Kings 4:8 (KJV).

Mothers listed, not fathers, 2 Kings 23:31, 36; 24:8, 18.

Prophetess counseled king, 2 Chronicles 34:22–28.

Daughters assisted rebuilding wall, Nehemiah 3:12.

WOLF

DAISY... LISTEN.... UM.... I HAVEN'T BEEN COMPLETELY HONEST WITH YOU.

Beautiful queen refused to be put on display, Esther 1:9–21.

Beauty treatments, Esther 2:3, 9, 12.

Queen's influence over king, Esther 9:12.

Women's witness, Psalm 68:11 (GNB).

Boisterous woman, Proverbs 9:13 (NASB).

Blessing of good wife, Proverbs 12:4.

One upright man, no women, Ecclesiastes 7:28.

Weaker sex, Isaiah 19:16; Jeremiah 50:37; 51:30; Nahum 3:13; 1 Peter 3:7.

Consistent lady, Isaiah 47:7 (KJV).

Beautiful, delicate, Jeremiah 6:2.

Queen of Heaven, Jeremiah 7:18; 44:18–19.

King, queen brought to judgment, Jeremiah 13:18.

Woman made superior to man, Jeremiah 31:22.

Fate of young women, Lamentations 3:51 (RSV).

Women prophets, Ezekiel 13:17 (CEV).

Queen's wisdom, Daniel 5:10–11.

Women command husbands, Amos 4:1.

Mary compared to shepherds, Luke 2:19–20.

Ministry of aged widow, Luke 2:36–38.

Women who traveled with Jesus, Luke 8:1–3.

Separating men, women, John 4:27.

Effectiveness of woman's testimony, John 4:39–42.

Ministry to women, Acts 16:13.

Business woman, Acts 16:13–15.

Prominent women at Thessalonica, Acts 17:4, 12.

Daughters with gift of prophecy, Acts 21:9.

Assistance to co-worker, Romans 16:2 (NASB).

Woman like mother to Paul, Romans 16:13.

Advice to unmarried women, 1 Corinthians 7:25–26.

Wife traveling with husband, 1 Corinthians 9:5.

Role of women, 1 Corinthians 11:2–16.

Women in worship, 1 Corinthians 14:33–36; 1 Timothy 2:9–15.

Wives likened to Church, Ephesians 5:25.

Sexual desire, 1 Timothy 5:11.

Responsibility of young wives, Titus 2:3–5.

Epistle dedicated to chosen lady, 2 John 1–5.

See Birth, Lady, Mother, Pregnancy, Wife.

WOMEN'S RIGHTS

Creator's plan, Genesis 3:16.

Freedom to decide marriage, Genesis 24:54–58; Numbers 36:6.

Daughter sold as servant, Exodus 21:7–11.

Rights of pregnant woman, Exodus 21:22.

Father's authority over daughter, Numbers 30:3–5.

Husband's superiority over wife, Numbers 30:10–16.

Apparel worn by opposite sex, Deuteronomy 22:5.

Selfish marital relationship, Deuteronomy 22:13–19.

Women divided among spoils, Judges 5:30.

Sacrifice of daughter, Judges 11:30–40.

Substituting heterosexual for homosexual, Judges 19:22–25.

Stolen wives, Judges 21:15–23.

Woman of character, Ruth 3:1–13.

Value of woman, Ruth 4:9–12.

Beloved but barren, 1 Samuel 1:2–7.

Solomon's counsel with two mothers, 1 Kings 3:16–28.

Daughters working with fathers, Nehemiah 3:12.

Male chauvinism, Esther 1:10–22.

Daughters' inheritance, Job 42:15.

Women as home builders, Proverbs 14:1 (GNB).

Good wife's description, Proverbs 31:10.

Haughty women, Isaiah 3:16.

Self-sufficient women in need of name, Isaiah 4:1.

Women who command husbands, Amos 4:1.

Women unfit soldiers, Nahum 3:13 (See LB, RSV).

Mother chose name of son, Luke 1:59–66.

Responsibility of servant returned from fields, Luke 17:7–10.

Marriage or career, 1 Corinthians 7:34 (LB).

Relationship of woman, man, 1 Corinthians 11:3–12 (GNB, LB).

Women's questions in early church, 1 Corinthians 14:34–35.

Two quarrelling women, Philippians 4:2
(LB).

Women not to teach, 1 Timothy 2:11–12.

Relationship between husband, wife, 1 Peter 3:1–7.

See Discrimination, Feminist.

WONDER

"Wonders without number," Job 5:9 (CEV).

A wonder to many, Psalm 71:7 (NKJV).

Unsearchable horizons, Jeremiah 33:3.

Ezekiel overwhelmed, Ezekiel 3:15.

Staring at those God uses, Acts 3:12.

See Awe, Serendipity, Surprise.

WOOD *See Forestry, Lumber, Trees.*

WOODWORKING *See Carpentry.*

WOOL *See Sheep, Shepherd.*

WORD

God does what He says, Numbers 23:19.

Discerning the prophets, Deuteronomy
18:21, 22.

Keeping one's word, Deuteronomy 23:23;
Joshua 9:18–20.

Unfailing promises, Joshua 23:4.

Word of the Lord rare, 1 Samuel 3:1.

Word not trustworthy, 1 Samuel 19:6, 10.

Potential power of a prophet's words, Jeremiah 1:10.

Play on words, Jeremiah 34:17.

Inclusive word, Hebrews 4:12 (AB).

See Scripture.

WORK *(Physical)*

Forced to serve with rigor, Exodus 1:13–14
(KJV).

Unfairness to workers, Exodus 5:6–18.

Priest different from laity, Deuteronomy
18:1–2.

Taking care of business, Deuteronomy
20:5–9.

Concentrated work, Nehemiah 5:16.

Divine blessing upon work, Psalm 90:17.

Profitability of work, Proverbs 14:23.

Work avoided in cold weather, Proverbs
20:4 (KJV).

Strength in numbers, Proverbs 30:25.

Satisfying work, Ecclesiastes 3:13.

Working with diligence, Ecclesiastes 9:10.

Digging cistern, Jeremiah 2:13.

Avoiding Sabbath work, Jeremiah 17:21–
27.

See Labor.

WORK *(Spiritual)*

Battle to believe, 1 Chronicles 19:13.

Good, bad deeds rewarded, Isaiah 3:10–11.

Deeds like straw burning, Isaiah 33:11
(CEV).

Religious works involved in idolatry, Isaiah
46:1.

Trusting in your own deeds, Jeremiah 48:7.

Good people evil, evil people good, Ezekiel
18:24–27 (CEV).

Good deeds forgotten, Ezekiel 33:13 (CEV).

Rich young man who kept law, Mark
10:17–27.

Mixing human blood with sacrificial, Luke
13:1.

Salvation effort, Luke 13:24 (AB).

Kindness to poor, Acts 10:4.

Legalism at Jerusalem, Acts 15:1–11.

Reward for good works, Romans 2:5–11.

Obedience brings righteousness, Romans
2:13.

Deeds good as doctrine, 2 Corinthians 9:13
(LB).

Difference between faith, works, Galatians
3:2–5.

Death knell to legalism, Galatians 3:10–14.

"Fruitful labor," Philippians 1:22 (NASB,
NRSV).

Working out your own salvation, Philippians 2:12–13.

Misguided works, Philippians 3:4–6.

Depending on Christ alone, Philippians 3:7
(LB).

Self-abasement, Colossians 2:18 (NRSB).

Widow known for good works, 1 Timothy
5:9–10 (CEV).

Rich in good works, 1 Timothy 6:11–19.

Good, useful deeds, Titus 3:8 (GNB).

The law makes nothing perfect, Hebrews
7:18–19.

Law pointing to perfection in Christ, Hebrews 10:1.

Sacrificial good works, Hebrews 13:15–16.

Faith without works, James 2:14–18.

Reward for one's works, Revelation 22:12.

See Legalism.

WORLD

Creation, status of earth, Nehemiah 9:6; Job 26:7; Psalm 102:25; Hebrews 11:3.

Divine proprietor, Psalm 24:1; Romans 4:13 (GNB, LB, NEB).

World census, Luke 2:1–3.

Earth's termination, 2 Peter 3:10.

See Earth.

WORLDLINESS

Reluctance to leave worldly community, Genesis 19:15–16.

Forbidden land preferred, Numbers 32:1–12.

Making idol to please the Lord, Judges 17:3.

Desire to be like unbelievers, 1 Samuel 8:1–22.

Partial commitment, 1 Kings 3:3.

No help from wrong friends, Jeremiah 2:37.

Sons, daughters sacrificed to idols, Ezekiel 16:20.

Daniel resolved not to defile himself, Daniel 1:8–20.

Potential blessing lost to idols, Hosea 9:10.

Salt loses flavor, lights hidden, Matthew 5:13–16.

Cannot serve two masters, Matthew 6:24; Luke 16:13.

Witnessing miracles with hard hearts, Matthew 11:20.

Worldliness prior to return of Christ, Matthew 24:37–38.

Jesus ate with "sinners," Mark 2:15–17.

Definitions of worldliness, John 17:25; Romans 1:21.

Worldly minded, Romans 8:5–8.

Not conforming to world, Romans 12:1–2; 1 Peter 1:14.

Food sacrificed to idols, 1 Corinthians 8:1.

Eating, drinking, 1 Corinthians 15:32.

Standards of the world, 2 Corinthians 2:2.

Believers not to join unbelievers, 2 Corinthians 6:14–18.

Crucified with Christ, Galatians 2:20.

Purity through Holy Spirit, Galatians 5:16.

Way of death, Ephesians 2:1.

Do not grieve Holy Spirit, Ephesians 4:30.

Dead to world, Colossians 3:3 (LB).

Love for world, love of ministry, 2 Timothy 4:9.

Loving the world, 2 Timothy 4:10 (GNB).

Resisting ungodliness, passions of world, Titus 2:11–12.

Choice to identify with God's people, Hebrews 11:24–25.

Friendship with world, James 4:4 (LB).

Strangers in world, 1 Peter 1:1–2, 17.

Suffering removes worldly desires, 1 Peter 4:1–2.

"What Gentiles like to do," 1 Peter 4:3.

Evil desires, 2 Peter 1:4.

Those who carouse, 2 Peter 2:13–16.

Kept from will of God, 1 John 2:15–17.

World control by evil one, 1 John 5:19.

Keep yourself from idols, 1 John 5:21.

Influence of Jezebel in church at Thyatira, Revelation 2:18.

Lamenting destruction of Babylon, Revelation 18:11–19.

See Carnality.

WORM

Worm food, Exodus 16:20; Job 24:20.

Man a worm, Job 25:6.

Judgment worms, Acts 12:23.

See Ignominy.

WORRY

Donkeys, people, 1 Samuel 9:3–5; 10:2.

Unnecessary fear, 1 Kings 1:50–53.

Desire for peace, security, 2 Kings 20:19.

Wrestling one's thoughts, Psalm 13:2.

Songs in night, Psalm 42:8.

No fear of bad news, Psalm 111:6.

Heavy heart needs encouragement, Proverbs 12:25 (KJV).

Do not dwell on the past, Isaiah 43:18.

Non-productive worry, Matthew 6:27, 28.

Worry blinds eyes to truth, Matthew 13:22.

Life's worries, Mark 4:19.

Circumstances need not cause worry, Luke 8:22–25.

"Do not keep striving," Luke 2:29 (NRSV).

Dangerous worry, Luke 21:34 (NRSV).

Worry about wine at wedding, John 2:1–5.

The Lord always at hand, Acts 2:25–28.

Hope when no basis for hope, Romans 4:18–22.

Paul's anxiety, Philippians 2:28.

Antidote to worry, Philippians 4:6–7.

God's best in abundance, Jude 2.

See Anxiety.

WORSHIP

Personal worship altars, Genesis 12:8; 13:18; 33:18–20; 35:3.

Abram's place of worship, Genesis 13:3–4.

Worship among trees, Genesis 13:18; 14:13; 18:1.

Unaware of the Lord's presence, Genesis 28:16.

Earnest Sabbath remembrance, Exodus 20:8 (AB).

Temple fragrance not for personal enjoyment, Exodus 30:34–38.

Insincere worship, Exodus 32:6.

Sober worship, Leviticus 10:8–10.

Consciously doing what is right, Leviticus 22:29.

Death by fire during worship, Numbers 16:35.

Mixing immorality with worship, Numbers 25:1–2.

God and His works, Deuteronomy 3:24.

God never appears as an image, Deuteronomy 4:15–16.

Do not worship God in nature, Deuteronomy 4:17–20.

Worship in depth, Deuteronomy 6:4–9.

Meeting the Lord three times annually, Deuteronomy 16:16.

Agreement voiced by congregation, Deuteronomy 27:14–26.

Sacrifice to demons, Deuteronomy 32:17.

"Make yourselves acceptable," Joshua 7:13 (CEV).

Priests engaged in idol worship, Judges 18:30–31.

Outdoor worship, 1 Kings 3:2.

Worshipping the Lord, other gods, 2 Kings 17:33.

Regulation of music used in worship, 1 Chronicles 6:31–32.

Self-evaluation, 1 Chronicles 17:16–19.

Morning, evening worship, 1 Chronicles 23:30.

Temple for people more than for God, 2 Chronicles 2:6.

Freedom of worship, 2 Chronicles 11:16 (LB).

All in spirit of worship, 2 Chronicles 29:28.

Lengthy reading of Scripture, Nehemiah 8:1–6.

Conversing, arguing with God, Job 13:3 (LB).

Critics see a God far removed from man's affairs, Job 22:12–14.

Recognizing God's majesty, Job 37:23–24.

Fervent, devoted worship, Psalm 18:1–2 (AB).

Love for God's house, Psalm 26:8.

Giving glory to the Lord, Psalm 29:1–2.

Thirst for living God, Psalm 42:1–2.

Harp as instrument of praise, Psalm 43:4.

Meditation in temple, Psalm 48:9.

Sacrifice God blesses, Psalm 51:15–17.

Exalting God above heavens, Psalm 57:5.

Rich spiritual feast, Psalm 63:5 (NRSV).

Good things from God's house, Psalm 65:4.

Musical procession, Psalm 68:24–25.

"Good to be near God," Psalm 73:28 (NRSV).

Beauty of sanctuary impells worship, Psalm 84:1–2.

Cry of praise, Psalm 89:8.

Day long worship, Psalm 89:16.

Splendor of holiness, Psalm 96:9.

Praising God seven times daily, Psalm 119:164.

Joy of going to God's house, Psalm 122:1.

God who answers prayer, Psalm 138:1–3.

Recognizing God's greatness beyond comprehension, Psalm 145:3.

Nature, people praise the Lord, Psalm 148:1–14.

Cautious words in God's presence, Ecclesiastes 5:2.

Meaningless offerings, Isaiah 1:11–17.

Lifeless worship, Isaiah 29:13.

God's glory only for Him, Isaiah 42:8.

Listeners who hear nothing, Isaiah 42:20.

None other but the Lord, Isaiah 45:5–6.

Proper Sabbath observance, Isaiah 58:13–14.

True worship forsaken, Jeremiah 2:5.

Unsuitable offerings, Jeremiah 6:20.

Beware deceptive words, Jeremiah 7:4–8.

Fraudulent idols, Jeremiah 10:4.

Reverence for the Lord, Jeremiah 10:6–7.

Sun worship, Ezekiel 8:16.

Lacking true faith, Ezekiel 14:4.

Hero worship, Daniel 2:46.

Worship of human image, Daniel 3:1–6.

Praising heathen gods, Daniel 5:4.

Awe of talking to God, Daniel 10:15–21.

Deeper meaning of worship, Hosea 6:6.

Those who feed on the wind, Hosea 12:1.

Profane worship, Amos 2:7–8 (LB).

When God turns deaf ear to praise, Amos 5:22; 8:3, 10.

What the Lord expects, Micah 5:6–8.

Fisherman worshipping net, Habakkuk 1:16.

Futile worship of idols, Habakkuk 2:18–19.

The Lord is in His Holy Temple, Habakkuk 2:20.

Be still before the Lord, Zechariah 2:13.

Unaware of blemished sacrifices, Malachi 1:6–14.

Useless altar fires, Malachi 1:10 (CEV).

True worship, Malachi 2:4–5.

Pretense of worship, Matthew 2:8.

Worshipping the Christ child, Matthew 2:11.

Jesus attended place of worship, Matthew 12:9; Mark 1:21.

Phony worship, Matthew 15:8–9.

Long public prayers, Matthew 6:7 (CEV).

Children praise the Lord, Matthew 21:16.

Missing purpose of worship, Matthew 23:23–24.

Lip service, Mark 7:6–7.

Constant temple worship, Luke 2:36–37.

Worship in home of Mary, Martha, Luke 10:38–42.

Vain man, humble man, Luke 18:9–14.

Worship mode, Acts 2:42–47.

Regular attendance at worship, Acts 14:1; 17:2.

Long sermon, Acts 20:7.

True worship, Romans 12:1 (GNB).

Ultimate "Holy of Holies," 1 Corinthians 3:16.

Undistracted devotion, 1 Corinthians 7:35 (NASB, NKJV).

Use of head covering in worship, 1 Corinthians 11:3–7.

Wrong attitudes in worship, 1 Corinthians 11:17–32.

Led astray to dumb idols, 1 Corinthians 12:2.

Good order in worship, 1 Corinthians 14:1–40.

Participation of all in worship, 1 Corinthians 14:26.

Avoiding confusion in worship, 1 Corinthians 14:29–33, 40.

Conduct, activity in worship, Ephesians 5:19–21.

Rules concerning women in worship, 1 Timothy 2:9–15.

High Priest in heaven, Hebrews 8:1–2.

Regulations for worship, Hebrews 9:1.

Physical act cannot bring spiritual result, Hebrews 10:1–4.

Sincerity, assurance, Hebrews 10:19–22.

Impetus for worship, Hebrews 12:28–29.

Come near to God, He will come near to you, James 4:8.

Reverent fear of God, 1 Peter 1:17.

Living creatures, elders around throne, Revelation 4:8–11.

Worship in music, song, Revelation 5:11–14.

Drama of worship in Heaven, Revelation 7:11–12.

Incense, prayers of saints, Revelation 8:3–4.

Concluding proclamation of faith, Revelation 15:3–4.

Rejoicing in Heaven, Revelation 19:6–8.

Do not worship angels, Revelation 19:10.

No churches in heaven, Revelation 21:22.

Not to pray to or worship angels, Revelation 22:8–9.

See Congregation, Sanctuary, Synagogue, Temple.

WORTH

Monetary value of human being, Leviticus 27:1–8.

Truly holy, Numbers 16:3–7.

Debt cancelled every seven years, Deuteronomy 15:1.

People as the Lord's treasure, Deuteronomy 26:18.

Total loss of personal worth, Deuteronomy 28:68.

Daughter-in-law better than seven sons, Ruth 4:15.

Silver of little value, 1 Kings 10:21.

Solomon's net worth, 2 Chronicles 9:13–14.

Precious metal replaces ordinary, Isaiah 60:17.

Change in people's value, Lamentations 4:2.

Likened to the Lord's signet ring, Haggai 2:23.

Day of small things, Zechariah 4:10.

Salt loses its saltiness, Luke 14:34–35.

Dependability in God's sight, Luke 16:10–12.

Value of servant, Luke 17:7–10.

"Proven worth," Philippians 2:22 (NASB).

"Like precious faith," 2 Peter 1:1 (NKJV).

Stone precious to some, rejected by others, 1 Peter 2:7–8.

See Value.

WORTHLESS

Worthless idols, worthless followers, 2 Kings 17:15 (CEV).

Trusting what is worthless, Job 15:31.

Sold for nothing, Isaiah 52:3.

Silver thrown into streets, Ezekiel 7:19.

Worthless vines, Ezekiel 15:2–6 (LB).

Worthless personal attainment, Philippians 3:7–11.

See Rejection.

WOUNDS

Value of injury, Proverbs 20:30.

Covered with wounds, sores, Isaiah 1:6.

Wounds as mere scratches, Jeremiah 8:11 (GNB).

Good Samaritan, Luke 10:30–35.

Jesus' flogging wound, John 19:1 (LB).

Fatal wound healed, Revelation 13:3.

See Injury.

WRESTLING

Jacob's Divine encounter, Genesis 32:22–32.

Face rubbed into ground, Lamentations 3:16 (GNB).

Satan as opponent, Ephesians 6:22.

See Athletics.

WRETCHED *See Demean, Ignominy, Leprosy, Poverty.*

WRITING

Writing on front, back, Exodus 32:15–16.

Memorial book, Exodus 17:14 (KJV).

Handwriting of God, Exodus 31:18; 32:16; Deuteronomy 10:4.

Second draft, Exodus 34:1.

Ten famous words, Deuteronomy 4:13 (Berk.).

Writing on stones, Deuteronomy 27:8.

Moses as author, Deuteronomy 31:24.

Written plan, 1 Chronicles 28:19.

Early correspondence, 2 Chronicles 2:11.

Personal experiences, Job 19:23–24.

"Filled with beautiful words," Psalm 45:1 (CEV).

Written record, Proverbs 7:3 (LB).

Just the right word, Proverbs 15:23 (GNB).

Shortest short story, Ecclesiastes 9:14–15.

Large tablet, common script, Isaiah 8:1 (Berk., AB).

Deceitful theology, Jeremiah 8:8.

Writing tools, Jeremiah 17:1 (KJV).

Book writing instructions, Jeremiah 30:2.

Danger of writing truth, Jeremiah 36:4–32.

Taking dictation, Jeremiah 36:6, 16–18.

Edible scrolls, Ezekiel 3:1–3.

Writing kit, Ezekiel 9:2, 11; Jeremiah 36:2.

Parables, allegories, Ezekiel 20:49 (AB).

Put it in writing, Daniel 6:6–9.

Message written down, Nahum 1:1 (CEV).

Plain writing all can read, Habakkuk 2:2.

Gigantic scroll, Zechariah 5:1–2.

Addressing reader, Mark 13:14; John 11:1 (LB).

Attempts to record New Testament events, Luke 1:1–4.

Inexhaustible subject, John 21:25.

"Cannot be put into words," Romans 8:26 (CEV).

Simplistic vocabulary, 1 Corinthians 2:1 (GNB).

Writing superior to speaking, 2 Corinthians 10:10.

Handicapped by chains, Colossians 4:18 (AB).

Play on words, 2 Thessalonians 3:11.

Purpose for writing, 1 John 1:4 (NRSV).

Commanded to write, Revelation 1:10–11; 21:5.

See Author, Literature.

WRONG

Unintentional sin, Leviticus 4:1–5.

Testing divine patience, Numbers 14:18.

Defiant sin, Numbers 15:30–31.

Guilt for one person's sin, Numbers 16:22.

Wrongly suspecting woman of drunkenness, 1 Samuel 1:9–16.

Limited admission of wrong, Job 34:31–33.

Wrongdoing categorized, Proverbs 6:16–19 (LB).

Pardon for nation's bloodguilt, Joel 3:12.

Accused yet admired, 1 Peter 2:12.

See Error.

X

XENOPHOBIA

Sarah, Hagar, Genesis 21:8–10, 21.

Abraham's concern to find wife for Isaac, Genesis 24:1–4.

Courtesy to foreigners, Exodus 23:9.

Providing for strangers, Leviticus 23:22.

Report of spies who explored Canaan, Numbers 13:17–33.

Loaning money to foreigner, Deuteronomy 23:19–20.

Showing kindness to foreigner, Ruth 2:10.

Misunderstanding goodwill gesture, 2 Samuel 10:1–4.

No marriage to foreigners, Nehemiah 10:30.

Language confused by intermarriage, Nehemiah 13:23–27.

Hatred of Jews, Esther 3:8–15.

Do good to foreigners, Jeremiah 22:3.

Falling into foreign hands, Ezekiel 11:9.

Delivered from malicious neighbors, Ezekiel 28:24.

Ingratitude to foreigner, Luke 17:11–19.

See Alien, Foreigner, Gentile.

X-RAY

Divine penetration, Hebrews 4:12.

YIELDING TO TEMPTATION

Hayes

Y

YEAR

Designed by Creator, Genesis 1:14.

Measurement of life span, Genesis 11:10–32.

First month of year, Exodus 12:2.

Lunar determination of time, Numbers 10:10.

Divine reckoning of time, Psalm 90:4.

See Calendar.

YIELDING

Yielding to temptation, Genesis 3:6; Joshua 7:21; 1 Kings 11:4.

Foolish sins, Numbers 12:11.

Potter and clay, Isaiah 45:9; 64:8.

See Submission, Surrender, Weakness.

YOM KIPPUR

Day of atonement, Leviticus 16:1–34.

YOUTH

Resentment toward youth in leadership, Genesis 37:5–11.

Youthful, prestigious Joseph, Genesis 41:41–46 (LB).

Census of men twenty or older, Numbers 26:2; 1 Chronicles 27:23.

Young woman's vow, Numbers 30:3–5.

Early joys of marriage, Deuteronomy 24:5.

Sacrifice only child, Judges 11:28–40.

Age variable between Boaz and Ruth, Ruth 3:10–13.

Growth in spirit, character, 1 Samuel 2:26.

Impressive young man, 1 Samuel 9:2.

Age of Saul when he became king, 1 Samuel 13:1.

Boldness of Jonathan against Philistines, 1 Samuel 14:1–14.

David chosen over older brothers, 1 Samuel 16:4–12.

Confrontation between David, Saul, 1 Samuel 17:32–37.

Veteran soldier underrated boy, 1 Samuel 17:42.

Saul went home, David prepared for action, 1 Samuel 24:22.

Father would have died in place of son, 2 Samuel 18:32–33.

Younger men, not elders, advise, 1 Kings 12:1–15.

Youths ridiculed Elisha's baldness, 2 Kings 2:23–24.

Sixteen-year-old king, 2 Kings 14:21–22; 2 Chronicles 26:1.

Ages of young kings, 2 Kings 21:1, 19; 23:36; 24:18; 2 Chronicles 33:1, 21; 34:1; 36:2, 5, 9, 11.

Father, inexperienced son, 1 Chronicles 22:5; 29:1.

Resisting counsel, 2 Chronicles 10:6–11.

Victim of bad influence, 2 Chronicles 13:7.

The Lord honored in early reign of young king, 2 Chronicles 17:1–4.

Good young king, 2 Chronicles 34:1–5 (LB).

Longing for younger years, Job 29:4–6.

Respect for elders, Job 32:4.

Wisdom of old, young, Job 32:4–9.

Sins of youth, Psalm 25:7.

Youthful faith, Psalm 71:5.

Afflicted from youth, Psalm 88:15.

Days of youth shortened, Psalm 89:45.

Youth's purity, Psalm 119:9.

More understanding than those older, Psalm 119:100.

Youth, old age, Proverbs 20:29.

Cautious happiness, Ecclesiastes 11:9.

Counsel to young, Ecclesiastes 12:1–7.

All have become ungodly, Isaiah 9:17.

Youth's fear of death, Isaiah 38:10–20.

Sins of youth forgotten, Isaiah 54:4 (CEV).

Why some die young, Isaiah 57:1–2 (LB).

Young at one hundred, Isaiah 65:20.

Youthful limitations, capabilities, Jeremiah 1:6–10 (LB).

Finest youth killed in battle, Jeremiah 48:15.

Youth facing problems, Lamentations 3:27 (LB).

Plight of young girls, Lamentations 3:51 (LB).

"Worth weight in gold," Lamentations 4:2 (NIV).

No youth music, Lamentations 5:14.

Young prostitutes, Ezekiel 23:2–3 (LB).

Chosen for royal service, Daniel 1:3–6.

Daniel resolved not to defile himself, Daniel 1:8–20.

Young prophesy, old dream dreams, Joel 2:28.

Attractive young men, young women, Zechariah 9:17.

Role of recent convert, 1 Timothy 3:6.

Young not to be looked down upon, 1 Timothy 4:12.

Evil desires of youth, 2 Timothy 2:22 (GNB).

Respect for those who are older, 1 Peter 5:5.

Youth overcomes evil, 1 John 2:13.

See Athletics, Children.

Z

ZEAL

Keep fire burning, Leviticus 6:13.

Zeal for spiritual vitality, Deuteronomy 6:4–7.

Earnestness of new priest, Deuteronomy 18:6–7.

The Lord's demands within reach, Deuteronomy 30:11.

Burning zeal, Psalm 69:9 (LB).

Do not envy sinners, Proverbs 23:17.

Zeal of the Lord, Isaiah 9:7.

Zealous for new gods, Isaiah 57:7–10 (LB).

Press on to acknowledge the Lord, Hosea 6:3.

Zealous fanatics, Matthew 23:15.

Burning, shining, John 5:35 (ASB, RSV).

Eagerness to be baptized, Acts 8:36–37.

Zealous ministry, Acts 18:24–28.

Zeal without knowledge, Romans 10:1–2.

Never lacking zeal, Romans 12:11.

Paul's former fanaticism, Galatians 1:13–14 (NRSV).

Former zeal lost, Galatians 4:15 (AB).

Ready to serve, witness, Ephesians 2:10; 6:10–20.

Never lazy, Hebrews 6:12 (CEV).

Losing first love, Revelation 2:4.

See Vision, Unction.

ZODIAC

Term used in astronomy, Job 9:9 (LB).

God's message in the stars, Psalm 19:1–6 (Note words "speech," "language," "voice" in the text. Then compare verses 7–13.).

ZOOLOGY

Distinction of species, Genesis 1:25; 1 Corinthians 15:39.

Naming of birds, animals, Genesis 2:20.

Solomon's expertise, 1 Kings 4:33–34.

Apes, baboons, 1 Kings 10:22.

Creature book, Isaiah 34:16 (GNB).

See Animals.

AFTERWORD

The compiling of this book has provided me many hours of diversion while engaged in the development of InterComm, our global outreach for equipping national Christian leaders with effective media for evangelism and training across the Two Thirds' world. In hotel rooms, airport lobbies, overland journeys and elsewhere in as many as forty countries, the manuscript for *Where to Find It in the Bible* slowly took shape.

If you wish, I will send you exciting information about InterComm without obligation.

Ken Anderson
InterComm
1520 East Winona Avenue
Warsaw, IN 46580–4639

In Memoriam
Ken Anderson
December 23, 1917—March 12, 2006

Ken Anderson will be remembered as one of the world's most significant communicators.

Ken was a pastor.

As a public speaker, he spoke to audiences in more than 100 countries.

As an author and editor, he created Youth for Christ's first magazine and seventy-seven books, including the volume that you're holding. God has used *Where to Find It in the Bible* to help millions interact quickly and successfully with God's Word, the Bible.

Ken made his greatest contributions to the kingdom of God as a filmmaker. He began in film ministry at Baptista Films, then later founded Gospel Films, Ken Anderson Films, and InterComm. He produced more than 200 films that have been seen around the world.

Countless others—now serving in ministries worldwide—depended on Ken as a mentor and an encourager.

Please join Thomas Nelson in giving thanks to God for a life well spent serving Him.